Baseball america®
2012 PROSPECT
HANDBOOK

BASEBALL AMERICA INC. · DURHAM, N.C.

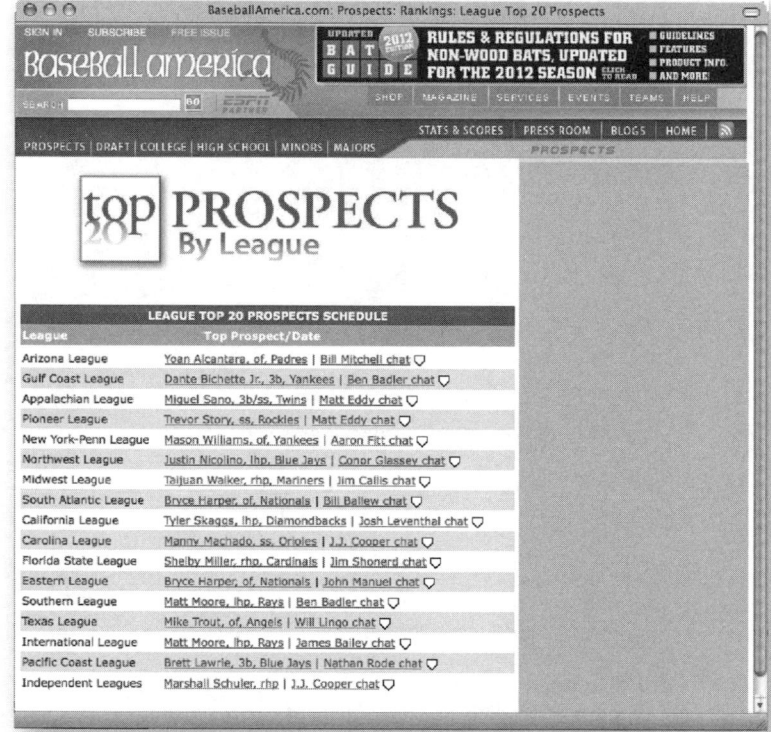

Baseball america
2012 PROSPECT
HANDBOOK

Editors
Jim Callis, Will Lingo, John Manuel

Assistant Editors
Ben Badler, J.J. Cooper, Matt Eddy, Aaron Fitt,
Conor Glassey, Josh Leventhal, Nathan Rode, Jim Shonerd

Database and Application Development
Tim Collins, Brent Lewis

Contributing Writers
Andy Baggarly, James Bailey, Bill Ballew,
Jack Etkin, Matthew Forman, Derrick Goold,
Tom Haudricourt, Bill Mitchell, John Perrotto, Phil Rogers

Photo Editor
Nathan Rode

Editorial Assistant
Tim Ednoff

Design & Production
Sara Hiatt McDaniel, Linwood Webb

Cover Photo
Mike Trout by John Williamson

Baseball america

A division of GrindMedia, a Source Interlink Media Division

SENIOR VICE PRESIDENT, GRINDMEDIA: Norb Garrett

PRESIDENT/PUBLISHER: Lee Folger
EDITORS IN CHIEF: Will Lingo, John Manuel
EXECUTIVE EDITOR: Jim Callis
DESIGN & PRODUCTION DIRECTOR: Sara Hiatt McDaniel
TECHNOLOGY MANAGER: Brent Lewis

Distributed by Simon & Schuster
ISBN-13: 978-1-932391-40-4
Statistics compiled and provided by Major League Baseball Advanced Media.

BaseballAmerica.com

EDITOR'S NOTE: Transactions for this book go through Dec. 12, so the last significant player transactions included here came out of the Rule 5 draft and the Jarrod Parker/Trevor Cahill trade between the Diamondbacks and Athletics. As always, you can find players even if they have changed organizations by using the handy index in the back. We also have an Appendix of notable international free agents on Page 494. >> For the purposes of this book, a prospect is any player who has no more than 50 innings pitched, 30 relief appearances or 130 at-bats in the major leagues, regardless of service time. Finally, the grades you'll find for each team's drafts are based solely on the quality of the players signed, with no consideration for whom players were traded for or how many picks a team might have lost.

TABLE OF CONTENTS

430

CARL KLINE

In the first half of 2010, Matt Moore was a struggling A-ball pitcher; in 2011, he was the minors' top pitcher and a playoff ace, shackling the Rangers in the American League Division Series

FOREWORD

When the final out of the 2011 World Series was recorded, I remember looking out onto the field and noticing that seven of the nine players were scouted and developed by the Cardinals. Not only was this an exciting moment here in St. Louis, but it showed how important it is to have a strong scouting and player-development staff.

Understanding the value of prospects and talent has become one of the most important aspects of our business. Baseball America was ahead of the curve when it introduced the Prospect Handbook. It allows for club management to get a comprehensive look at each organization's prospects. From the trade deadline to the Winter Meetings, this Handbook is a valuable resource.

Information drives all of our decisions today and the Prospect Handbook has so much to offer. We use this book to complement our scouts' information. In the event we miss a player, we can use it as a resource to supplement information we may be lacking. Baseball America does a great job in breaking down a player's strengths and weaknesses as well as providing a rundown on each individual player's expectations.

The organizational summary is very helpful in comprehending the depth of each team and clearly gives a timeline of when these players may make it to the big leagues. Baseball America's extensive coverage of the minor leagues gives instant credibility to this book.

As the industry continues to place more value on prospects and as teams continue to invest more in Latin America and the draft, the Prospect Handbook will keep finding its way onto every baseball executive's desk. It's a great tool and one we'll always maintain in our toolbox.

JOHN MOZELIAK
SENIOR VICE PRESIDENT/GENERAL MANAGER
ST. LOUIS CARDINALS

INTRODUCTION

The most amazing thing about sending the Prospect Handbook to press is not how happy we are about it—though to be sure we are very happy—it's how we always wish that we had more time.

Thanks to the constraints of printing and distribution, the Prospect Handbook must go to the printer right before Christmas, so that it can work its way to you before pitchers and catchers report, and even more important, before your fantasy draft. Were that not so, I have no doubt that we would take another few days, or even weeks with the book. There is always a report to improve, a ranking to tweak—and this year a Baseball America Grade to argue about.

Baseball America Grades are one of the most significant changes to the book since it debuted in 2001. We make changes to the book every year, from the modest, such as changing the statistical categories we list, to the more significant, such as adding minor league depth charts.

We have long discussed adding a thumbnail view of each prospect in the book, so you could see at a glance how we view a player and so it's easier to compare players across organizations. We decided to take the plunge this year, going through several iterations of exactly how to do it before settling on the BA Grade.

You can read more about the ins and outs of the system on the facing page, but in simplest terms we are projecting a prospect's realistic ceiling on the 20-80 scouting scale, balanced with the degree of risk that he'll reach that ceiling. We found it useful in assembling the book, so we think you'll find it useful in reading it.

Beyond that, you'll find the same prospect goodness that you have come to expect, with 900 scouting reports plus a few more in the back for international free agents who had not signed by our transaction deadline.

The Prospect Handbook has become our signature publication, and in many ways it is both the culmination of all the work we have done in 2011, and the foundation for all the work we will do in 2012. The book requires an amazing amount of work, in the reporting, editing and production of all this information. I would conservatively estimate that this book features 200,000 words on the state of player development in baseball today, and for those words to both read so well and look so good is a tribute to all of the names that you'll find on Page 3.

In particular, thanks are due to Jim Callis, who makes the Prospect Handbook the focus of his professional life (and maybe his entire life) beginning in mid-October. He, or more accurately his family, also make the supreme sacrifice of having him coming from his home in suburban Chicago to BA Towers in Durham, N.C., for days at a time right before Thanksgiving and again before Christmas, all to make sure the book is the best it can be.

And while you probably don't think about how clean and attractive this book's design is, but it is a beautifully designed book, and that's thanks to design and production director Sara Hiatt McDaniel. I have enough things spinning around in my head every morning as the Prospect Handbook deadline approaches. It's comforting to know that I don't have to worry about anything related to the design.

I could go on and on about all of the people who worked long hours to bring you the best baseball information in the business, but you're ready to read about prospects. So enjoy the bounty, and thank you for continuing to make this the industry standard.

WILL LINGO
EDITOR IN CHIEF
BASEBALL AMERICA

For the first time, Baseball America has assigned Grades and Risk Factors for each and every one of the 900 prospects in the Prospect Handbook. For the BA Grade, we used a 20-to-80 scale, similar to the scale scouts use, to keep it familiar. However, most major league clubs put an overall numerical grade on players, called the Overall Future Potential or OFP. Often the OFP is merely an average of the player's tools.

The BA Grade is NOT an OFP. It's a measure of a prospect's value and attempts to gauge the player's realistic ceiling. Because we're writing about prospects, there are no 20s or 30s in this book. The lowest grade given for a realistic ceiling is a 40. But there is an 80 in the book—Nationals outfielder Bryce Harper. Thanks to his prodigious power, Harper has the highest ceiling of any prospect in the game. He's not a perfect prospect, but he's at the top of the scale with his athleticism, 40-homer potential and Larry Walker-like right field tools.

However, the realistic ceiling grade doesn't tell a prospect's entire story. How close that player is to reaching his ceiling matters just as much. The less we believe we have to project on the prospect, the less risky he is. That's why we also have assigned every player a Risk Factor to go with their BA Grade. That scale is fairly self-explanatory, ranging from Safe (least risk) to Extreme (riskiest). The closer a player is to reaching his realistic ceiling, the safer he rates.

Harper is an 80, but there is some chance he won't reach his realistic 40-homer ceiling. We gauged his risk as Low. In comparison, the two players who rival Harper the most for the title of Best Prospect in the minors already have made some impact in the major leagues while retaining their prospect eligibility. So Rays lefthander Matt Moore and Angels outfielder Mike Trout both earn the Safe designation.

The ideal combination is for prospects to have high ceilings thanks to prodigious, top-of-the-scale tools; success in the minor leagues; and a small gap between the player's potential and the player's 'now' skills.

The goal of the Grade/Risk system is to allow readers to take a quick look at how strong their team's farm system is, and also how much immediate help the big league club can expect from its prospects. It should also help with our Organization Rankings, but those will not simply flow, in formulaic fashion, from the Grades/Risk Factor results. Some staff members favor star power in a farm system while others favor depth; that cannot be easily summed up in a spreadsheet.

Like any first-time endeavor, the BA Grade/Risk will have its blind spots. That happened with the first

BA Grade Scale

75-80: Franchise players and No. 1 starters, such as Albert Pujols, Alex Rodriguez, Derek Jeter and Roy Halladay.

65-70: No. 2 starters and perennial all-stars in the mold of Chase Utley, Matt Cain, Matt Kemp and Adrian Beltre.

55-60: First-division regulars and No. 3 starters and elite closers, such as Jonathan Papelbon, James Shields and Torii Hunter would earn these grades.

45-50: Most players reside here. The high end (50s with lower risk) are second-division regulars with higher peaks, eighth-inning relievers and fourth starters on playoff teams. The lower end are platoon/utility players, back-end starters and relievers. Think of Jamey Carroll, Joe Blanton and Angel Pagan.

35-40: Players with fifth-starter or utility/backup catcher upside, or relief specialists. It will be rare for a 35 to make the book. This category includes the likes of Doug Slaten, Matt Treanor and Alfredo Simon.

Risk Factors

SAFE: Has shown realistic ceiling in big leagues; ready to contribute in 2012.

LOW: Likely to reach realistic ceiling, certain big league careeer barring injury.

MEDIUM: Still some work to do to turn tools into major league-caliber skills.

HIGH: Most draft picks in their first seasons, players with plenty of projection left.

EXTREME: Teenagers in Rookie ball or players with significant injury histories.

Handbook too, and we have tried—and we think succeeded—in making the book better year by year. We hope the addition of the BA Grade/Risk system is the next step in making the Prospect Handbook more indispensable than ever to the game's fans and fantasy players.

AN OVERVIEW

Another feature of the Prospect Handbook is a depth chart of every organization's minor league talent. This shows you at a glance what kind of talent a system has and provides even more prospects beyond the Top 30.

Players are usually listed on the depth charts where we think they'll ultimately end up. To help you better understand why players are slotted at particular positions, we show you here what scouts look for in the ideal candidate at each spot, with individual tools ranked in descending order.

LF	CF	RF
Power	Fielding	Power
Hitting	Hitting	Hitting
Fielding	Speed	Arm Strength
Arm Strength	Power	Fielding
Speed	Arm Strength	Speed

3B	SS	2B	1B
Power	Fielding	Hitting	Power
Hitting	Arm Strength	Fielding	Hitting
Fielding	Hitting	Power	Fielding
Arm Strength	Speed	Speed	Arm Strength
Speed	Power	Arm Strength	Speed

C
Fielding
Hitting
Arm Strength
Power
Speed

STARTING PITCHERS

No. 1 starter	No. 2 starter	No. 3 starter	No. 4-5 starters
• Two plus pitches	• Two plus pitches	• One plus pitch	• Command of two major league pitches
• Average third pitch	• Average third pitch	• Two average pitches	• Average velocity
• Plus-plus command	• Average command	• Average command	• Consistent breaking ball
• Plus makeup	• Average makeup	• Average makeup	• Decent changeup

CLOSER

- One dominant pitch
- Second plus pitch
- Plus command
- Plus-plus makeup

TOP 50 PROSPECTS

When Baseball America ranks prospects, there's almost always a byline attributing who finally put the players in order, who decided, "OK, this guy's 6 and this guy's 7." But all our rankings are more than one person's opinion. They are most often a reflection of the consensus of sources on the subject—managers, coaches, scouts, front-office personnel, the whole spectrum.

Except here, really. In this section of the Handbook, we get personal. Sifting through all the information we've gathered to this point, four of our editors give their own personal takes on the game's top 50 prospects. This helps form the basis of the arguments that shape Baseball America's Top 100 Prospects. That list comes out during spring training, and we consider it the definitive guide to the best talent in the minor leagues.

The rules for these lists are the same for any prospect who appears in the Handbook: no more than 130 at-bats, 50 innings or 30 relief appearances in the major leagues. We do not consider service time in our eligibility requirements.

As with any prospect list, these rankings represent how each person regarded the top minor league talent in the game at a moment in time. Ask us again in a few months—or even tomorrow—how these prospects stack up, and you'll get a different answer.

JIM CALLIS

1. Mike Trout, of, Angels	26. Travis d'Arnaud, c, Blue Jays
2. Matt Moore, lhp, Rays	27. Jarrod Parker, rhp, Athletics
3. Bryce Harper, of, Nationals	28. Brett Jackson, of, Cubs
4. Julio Teheran, rhp, Braves	29. Gary Brown, of, Giants
5. Jurickson Profar, ss, Rangers	30. Francisco Lindor, ss, Indians
6. Jesus Montero, c, Yankees	31. Javier Baez, ss, Cubs
7. Manny Machado, ss, Orioles	32. Jonathan Singleton, 1b/of, Astros
8. Anthony Rendon, 3b/2b, Nationals	33. Christian Yelich, of, Marlins
9. Dylan Bundy, rhp, Orioles	34. Nolan Arenado, 3b, Rockies
10. Trevor Bauer, rhp, Diamondbacks	35. Billy Hamilton, ss, Reds
11. Gerrit Cole, rhp, Pirates	36. James Paxton, lhp, Mariners
12. Shelby Miller, rhp, Cardinals	37. Mike Montgomery, lhp, Royals
13. Jameson Taillon, rhp, Pirates	38. Manny Banuelos, lhp, Yankees
14. Devin Mesoraco, c, Reds	39. Hak-Ju Lee, ss, Rays
15. Tyler Skaggs, lhp, Diamondbacks	40. Arodys Vizcaino, rhp, Braves
16. Taijuan Walker, rhp, Mariners	41. Yonder Alonso, 1b, Reds
17. Danny Hultzen, lhp, Mariners	42. Anthony Rizzo, 1b, Padres
18. Miguel Sano, 3b/ss, Twins	43. Jake Marisnick, of, Blue Jays
19. Bubba Starling, of, Royals	44. Nick Castellanos, 3b, Tigers
20. Carlos Martinez, rhp, Cardinals	45. Zack Wheeler, rhp, Mets
21. Martin Perez, lhp, Rangers	46. Yasmani Grandal, c, Reds
22. Drew Pomeranz, lhp, Rockies	47. Brad Peacock, rhp, Nationals
23. Jacob Turner, rhp, Tigers	48. Anthony Gose, of, Blue Jays
24. Archie Bradley, rhp, Diamondbacks	49. Rymer Liriano, of, Padres
25. Wil Myers, of, Royals	50. Matt Harvey, rhp, Mets

J. J. COOPER

1. Bryce Harper, of, Nationals
2. Matt Moore, lhp, Rays
3. Mike Trout, of, Angels
4. Julio Teheran, rhp, Braves
5. Trevor Bauer, rhp, Diamondbacks
6. Devin Mesoraco, c, Reds
7. Jurickson Profar, ss, Rangers
8. Manny Machado, ss, Orioles
9. Jesus Montero, c, Yankees
10. Gerrit Cole, rhp, Pirates
11. Dylan Bundy, rhp, Orioles
12. Shelby Miller, rhp, Cardinals
13. Jameson Taillon, rhp, Pirates
14. Miguel Sano, 3b/ss, Twins
15. Tyler Skaggs, lhp, Diamondbacks
16. Mike Montgomery, lhp, Royals
17. Bubba Starling, of, Royals
18. Taijuan Walker, rhp, Mariners
19. Danny Hultzen, lhp, Mariners
20. Archie Bradley, rhp, Diamondbacks
21. Travis d'Arnaud, c, Blue Jays
22. Manny Banuelos, lhp, Yankees
23. Wil Myers, of, Royals
24. Martin Perez, lhp, Rangers
25. Carlos Martinez, rhp, Cardinals
26. Drew Pomeranz, lhp, Indians
27. Jarrod Parker, rhp, Athletics
28. Jacob Turner, rhp, Tigers
29. Xander Bogaerts, ss, Red Sox
30. Randall Delgado, rhp, Braves
31. Mike Olt, 3b, Rangers
32. Nolan Arenado, 3b, Rockies
33. Hak-Ju Lee, ss, Rays
34. Billy Hamilton, ss, Reds
35. Yonder Alonso, 1b, Reds
36. Brad Peacock, rhp, Nationals
37. Rymer Liriano, of, Padres
38. Wily Peralta, rhp, Brewers
39. Gary Brown, of, Giants
40. Brett Jackson, of, Cubs
41. Zack Wheeler, rhp, Mets
42. Arodys Vizcaino, rhp, Braves
43. Jarred Cosart, rhp, Astros
44. Yasmani Grandal, c, Reds
45. Taylor Jungmann, rhp, Brewers
46. Dellin Betances, rhp, Yankees
47. Francisco Lindor, ss, Indians
48. Anthony Rendon, 3b, Nationals
49. Oscar Taveras, of, Cardinals
50. Addison Reed, rhp, White Sox

WILL LINGO

1. Bryce Harper, of, Nationals
2. Matt Moore, lhp, Rays
3. Mike Trout, of, Angels
4. Julio Teheran, rhp, Braves
5. Jesus Montero, c, Yankees
6. Jurickson Profar, ss, Rangers
7. Shelby Miller, rhp, Cardinals
8. Gerrit Cole, rhp, Pirates
9. Trevor Bauer, rhp, Diamondbacks
10. Dylan Bundy, rhp, Orioles
11. Manny Machado, ss, Orioles
12. Devin Mesoraco, c, Reds
13. Travis d'Arnaud, c, Blue Jays
14. Jameson Taillon, rhp, Pirates
15. Jarrod Parker, rhp, Athletics
16. Tyler Skaggs, lhp, Diamondbacks
17. Jacob Turner, rhp, Tigers
18. Mike Montgomery, lhp, Royals
19. Bubba Starling, of, Royals
20. Miguel Sano, 3b/ss, Twins
21. Zack Wheeler, rhp, Mets
22. Manny Banuelos, lhp, Yankees
23. Taijuan Walker, rhp, Mariners
24. Drew Pomeranz, lhp, Rockies
25. Danny Hultzen, lhp, Mariners
26. Gary Brown, of, Giants
27. Carlos Martinez, rhp, Cardinals
28. Brad Peacock, rhp, Nationals
29. Kelvin Herrera, rhp, Royals
30. Arodys Vizcaino, rhp, Braves
31. Will Middlebrooks, 3b, Red Sox
32. Addison Reed, rhp, White Sox
33. Brett Jackson, of, Cubs
34. Archie Bradley, rhp, Diamondbacks
35. Zach Lee, rhp, Dodgers
36. Yonder Alonso, 1b, Reds
37. Christian Yelich, of, Marlins
38. Matt Harvey, rhp, Mets
39. Nick Castellanos, 3b, Tigers
40. Anthony Rizzo, 1b, Padres
41. Wil Myers, of, Royals
42. Jarred Cosart, rhp, Astros
43. George Springer, of, Astros
44. Anthony Gose, of, Blue Jays
45. Rymer Liriano, of, Padres
46. Randall Delgado, rhp, Braves
47. Wily Peralta, rhp, Brewers
48. Jonathan Singleton, 1b/of, Astros
49. Jean Segura, ss, Angels
50. Hak-Ju Lee, ss, Rays

The Diamondbacks' Tyler Skaggs emerged as one of the minors' best lefthanders in 2011

The third overall pick in 2010, Baltimore's Manny Machado has reached high Class A

JOHN MANUEL

1. Bryce Harper, of, Nationals
2. Matt Moore, lhp, Rays
3. Mike Trout, of, Angels
4. Jurickson Profar, ss, Rangers
5. Jesus Montero, c, Yankees
6. Julio Teheran, rhp, Braves
7. Shelby Miller, rhp, Cardinals
8. Dylan Bundy, rhp, Orioles
9. Miguel Sano, 3b/ss, Twins
10. Trevor Bauer, rhp, Diamondbacks
11. Manny Machado, ss, Orioles
12. Gerrit Cole, rhp, Pirates
13. Jameson Taillon, rhp, Pirates
14. Tyler Skaggs, lhp, Diamondbacks
15. Danny Hultzen, lhp, Mariners
16. Archie Bradley, rhp, Diamondbacks
17. Devin Mesoraco, c, Reds
18. Taijuan Walker, rhp, Mariners
19. Carlos Martinez, rhp, Cardinals
20. Anthony Rendon, 3b/2b, Nationals
21. Francisco Lindor, ss, Indians
22. Travis d'Arnaud, c, Blue Jays
23. Manny Banuelos, lhp, Yankees
24. Bubba Starling, of, Royals
25. Gary Brown, of, Giants
26. Martin Perez, lhp, Rangers
27. Wil Myers, of, Royals
28. Billy Hamilton, ss, Reds
29. Mike Montgomery, lhp, Royals
30. Brad Peacock, rhp, Nationals
31. Yonder Alonso, 1b, Reds
32. Jonathan Singleton, 1b/of, Astros
33. Drew Pomeranz, lhp, Rockies
34. Jarrod Parker, rhp, Athletics
35. Jacob Turner, rhp, Tigers
36. Anthony Gose, of, Blue Jays
37. Arodys Vizcaino, rhp, Braves
38. Brett Jackson, of, Cubs
39. James Paxton, lhp, Mariners
40. Zack Wheeler, rhp, Mets
41. Mike Olt, 3b, Rangers
42. Randall Delgado, rhp, Braves
43. Dellin Betances, rhp, Yankees
44. Matt Harvey, rhp, Mets
45. Rymer Liriano, of, Padres
46. Nick Castellanos, 3b, Tigers
47. A.J. Cole, rhp, Nationals
48. Nolan Arenado, 3b, Rockies
49. Matt Szczur, of, Cubs
50. Jarred Cosart, rhp, Astros

01 WASHINGTON NATIONALS: Bryce Harper leads a strong group of upper-level talent. Washington's 2011 draft class has as much upside as any in recent memory but depends on the health of Anthony Rendon and Matt Purke.

02 TEXAS RANGERS: The Rangers' aggressiveness in Latin America—which landed top prospects Jurickson Profar (Curacao) and Martin Perez (Venezuela)—and emphasis on athletes with upside impresses scouts outside the organization.

03 KANSAS CITY ROYALS: Even after graduating some of their record nine players in the 2011 Top 100, the Royals still have plenty of talent left on the farm. Kansas City hopes its pitchers step forward like Eric Hosmer did in 2011.

04 ARIZONA DIAMONDBACKS: Unprecedented draft bounty with Nos. 3 and 7 picks in 2011 landed RHPs Trevor Bauer and Archie Bradley to to with LHP Tyler Skaggs, giving Arizona an unmatched trio of strikeout artists.

05 TORONTO BLUE JAYS: GM Alex Anthopoulos has refocused organization with emphasis on scouting, and it's paying off with serious pitching depth. Toronto also has strong talent up the middle, starting with C Travis d'Arnaud.

06 NEW YORK YANKEES: Latin American talent dominates the Yankees Top 10 (Jesus Montero, Manny Banuelos), but recent drafts contribute as well, from 2006 (RHP Dellin Betances) to 2011 (3B Dante Bichette Jr.).

07 CINCINNATI REDS: Like the Yankees, Reds Top 10 starts with an offensive catcher in Devin Mesoraco. The depth of talent at upper levels gives Cincinnati reinforcements for 2012 and plenty of trade fodder.

08 SAN DIEGO PADRES: The system lacks a surefire future star, but former GM Jed Hoyer left the organization in better shape than he found it, due in part to a productive 2011 draft class.

09 SEATTLE MARINERS: Looking for a pitching trio to rival that of the Diamondbacks? In 2012, it may be Seattle's as LHPs Danny Hultzen and James Paxton and RHP Taijuan Walker move along.

10 BOSTON RED SOX: Former GM Theo Epstein leaves behind a deep system that lacks a true No. 1 prospect but has enviable depth. The Red Sox's biggest need remains 2011's issue of upper-level starting pitching.

11 TAMPA BAY RAYS: LHP Matt Moore gives Tampa an elite prospect in the mold of current Rays star David Price. The system's depth got a jolt from 12 picks in the first two rounds of the 2011 draft.

12 ST. LOUIS CARDINALS: Recent graduates contributed to the World Series championship, and star power is on the way with live-armed RHPs Shelby Miller and Carlos Martinez.

13 PITTSBURGH PIRATES: After nearly 20 years of losing records, the Pirates still have work to do. Their $13 million investment in their first two 2011 draft picks (RHP Gerrit Cole, OF Josh Bell) buoys the system significantly.

14 CHICAGO CUBS: One of Jim Hendry's last acts as GM was to spend $12 million on their 2011 draft class. The system is more notable for solid depth than top-tier talent.

15 ATLANTA BRAVES: In contrast to the Cubs, Braves are top-heavy with pitching and shortstops. Two years of frugal, college-heavy drafts have filled holes but left the system thin on impact athletes.

16 **COLORADO ROCKIES:** The Rockies continue to have more success with Latin American pitching development than the draft. They could use bouncebacks from LHPs Tyler Matzek and Christian Friedrich and RHP Peter Tago.

17 **HOUSTON ASTROS:** Former GM Ed Wade finally pointed the organization in the right direction by dealing Hunter Pence and Michael Bourn for prospects. New GM Jeff Luhnow brings a strong scouting/development track record from St. Louis.

18 **LOS ANGELES ANGELS:** Minor League Player of the Year Mike Trout would be the class of most any organization. Angels' inconsistent drafts, waning presence in Latin America have thinned the rest of the system.

19 **MINNESOTA TWINS:** Not only was 2011 tough in the big leagues, but Minnesota's last four first-round picks either struggled or didn't play. The system's emerging Latin American talent remains far from the majors.

20 **BALTIMORE ORIOLES:** No system is as top-heavy as Baltimore's, headed by its last two first-rounders in RHP Dylan Bundy and SS Manny Machado. Their big spending on the 2009 draft class has yet to pay dividends.

21 **SAN FRANCISCO GIANTS:** It's unusual to see the Giants with so few power arms. Recent graduations such as Madison Bumgarner, Buster Posey and Brandon Belt have left the system thin, but with good reason.

22 **DETROIT TIGERS:** No club is as aggressive using prospects in deals as the Tigers have for big leaguers such as Miguel Cabrera and Doug Fister. Their Latin American efforts are starting to bear fruit.

23 **LOS ANGELES DODGERS:** The McCourt ownership mess has wreaked havoc on a previously prosperous farm system, particularly in international signings, where Dodgers must bottom-feed rather than leading the way.

24 **NEW YORK METS:** The dynamic pitching duo of RHPs Zack Wheeler and Matt Harvey gives the Mets some hope. Tommy Tanous becomes the franchise's third scouting director in three years.

25 **MILWAUKEE BREWERS:** The NL Central title in 2011 came at the cost of the system's depth, but Brewers have solid upper-level role players. The franchise is counting on 2011 first-round duo RHP Taylor Jungmann and LHP Jed Bradley.

26 **OAKLAND ATHLETICS:** GM Billy Beane has embarked on yet another rebuilding cycle in Oakland, but the A's haven't had much luck with the draft, international signings or prospect trades of late.

27 **PHILADELPHIA PHILLIES:** During the best run of big league success in franchise history, GM Ruben Amaro consistently has traded prospects for big leaguers. The system still has talent but it's almost all of high-risk variety.

28 **MIAMI MARLINS:** Failures with pitching development prompted a new farm director (Marty Scott). Will the new stadium that goosed big league spending also lead to more aggressiveness in the draft and Latin America?

29 **CLEVELAND INDIANS:** The Tribe emptied out its system with graduations (Lonnie Chisenhall, Jason Kipnis) and the Ubaldo Jimenez trade. What's left are spare parts and relief pitchers.

30 **CHICAGO WHITE SOX:** Combine win-now deals with an unwillingness to spend in the draft and corruption-fueled turnover and ineffectiveness in Latin America, and you get baseball's worst farm system.

Arizona Diamondbacks

BY BILL MITCHELL

After the worst back-to-back seasons in franchise history, the Diamondbacks reversed course and won 94 games in 2011, overtaking the defending World Series champion Giants to capture the National League West crown and earn their first postseason berth since 2007. Arizona took the Brewers into extra innings in the Division Series before losing Game Five 3-2 in the 10th.

The Diamondbacks started their turnaround in July 2010, when general manager Josh Byrnes and manager A.J. Hinch were fired. Interim general manager Jerry Dipoto quickly pulled off trades that sent Dan Haren to the Angels and Edwin Jackson to the White Sox. The moves relieved the club of $39 million in financial commitments and added big leaguers Dan Hudson and Joe Saunders (who combined for 29 wins in 2011) and pitching prospects Tyler Skaggs, David Holmberg and Patrick Corbin.

When former Padres GM Kevin Towers took the same job in Arizona last September, he retained Dipoto as senior vice president of scouting and player development. He also kept interim manager Kirk Gibson, who proved to be a natural and won the NL manager of the year award in his first full season. Towers did reshuffle the front office, hiring former Brewers assistant scouting director Ray Montgomery as scouting director and shifting field coordinator Mike Bell to farm director.

The key to the 2011 season was Towers' fortification of a bullpen that had posted an MLB-worst 5.74 ERA the year before. The biggest additions were free agent J.J. Putz, who saved 45 games, and David Hernandez, who took to a set-up role after coming from the Orioles in a deal for Mark Reynolds that saved another $13 million. Offensively, Justin Upton stayed healthy all season and emerged as a legitimate MVP candidate at age 23.

The farm system provided unlikely contributors in Josh Collmenter, who continued to defy skeptics by wining 10 games after joining the rotation in May, and Paul Goldschmidt, who came up in August to put an end to a revolving door at first base. Rule 5 acquisition Joe Paterson served as a capable lefty reliever.

The Diamondbacks' talent level also improved significantly on the minor league level in 2011, and they now boast a deep pool of pitching talent. Skaggs is one of the best lefty pitching prospects in the game, and Holmberg and Corbin give Arizona two more promising southpaws. Jarrod Parker returned after Tommy John surgery cost him all of 2010 and earned a spot on the postseason roster. Arizona was then able to deal from a position of strength in December, sending Parker, outfielder Collin Cowgill and reliever Ryan

Kevin Towers made all the right adjustments to engineer a quick turnaround in Arizona

TOP 30 PROSPECTS

1. Trevor Bauer, rhp	**16.** Marc Krauss, of
2. Archie Bradley, rhp	**17.** Kyle Winkler, rhp
3. Tyler Skaggs, lhp	**18.** Ryan Wheeler, 3b/1b
4. Matt Davidson, 3b/1b	**19.** Kevin Munson, rhp
5. A.J. Pollock, of	**20.** Yonata Ortega, rhp
6. David Holmberg, lhp	**21.** Charles Brewer, rhp
7. Chris Owings, ss	**22.** Ty Linton, of
8. Wade Miley, lhp	**23.** David Nick, 2b
9. Patrick Corbin, lhp	**24.** Michael Perez, c
10. Bobby Borchering, of/1b/3b	**25.** Tyler Green, rhp
11. Anthony Meo, rhp	**26.** Jesse Darrah, rhp
12. Adam Eaton, of	**27.** J.R. Bradley, rhp
13. Andrew Chafin, lhp	**28.** Brett Lorin, rhp
14. Keon Broxton, of	**29.** John Pedrotty, lhp
15. Evan Marshall, rhp	**30.** Socrates Brito, of

Cook to the Athletics for Trevor Cahill.

Dipoto and Montgomery oversaw a draft that added even more mound talent, as the Diamondbacks had two of the top seven picks and landed Trevor Bauer and Archie Bradley. The Angels took note of Dipoto's role, hiring him as GM in October.

Arizona also has position prospects on the way, most of them products of a 2009 draft in which they had seven picks in the first two rounds. Goldschmidt came out of that crop, as did third baseman Matt Davidson and outfielder A.J. Pollock. Those two teamed with Skaggs and Parker to help Double-A Mobile win the Southern League championship.

General Manager: Kevin Towers. **Farm Director:** Mike Bell. **Scouting Director:** Ray Montgomery.

Class	Team	League	W	L	Pct	Finish*	Manager(s)
Majors	Arizona Diamondbacks	National	94	68	.580	3rd (16)	Kirk Gibson
Triple-A	Reno Aces	Pacific Coast	77	67	.535	5th (16)	Brett Butler
Double-A	Mobile BayBears	Southern	84	54	.609	1st (10)†	Turner Ward
High A	Visalia Rawhide	California	63	77	.450	8th (10)	Jason Hardtke
Low A	South Bend Silver Hawks	Midwest	67	72	.482	10th (16)	Mark Haley
Short-season	Yakima Bears	Northwest	33	43	.434	8th (8)	Audo Vicente
Rookie	Missoula Osprey	Pioneer	41	35	.539	t-4th (8)	Hector de la Cruz
Rookie	AZL Diamondbacks	Arizona	20	36	.357	12th (13)	Andy Green

| **Overall 2011 Minor League Record** | | | 385 | 384 | .501 | 17th (30) | |

*Finish in overall standings (No. of teams in league). †League champion.

LAST YEAR'S TOP 30

Player, Pos.		Status
1.	Jarrod Parker, rhp	(Athletics)
2.	Tyler Skaggs, lhp	No. 3
3.	Matt Davidson, 3b	No. 4
4.	Chris Owings, ss	No. 7
5.	Marc Krauss, of	No. 16
6.	A.J. Pollock, of	No. 5
7.	Bobby Borchering, 3b	No. 10
8.	Wade Miley, lhp	No. 8
9.	Patrick Corbin, lhp	No. 9
10.	Keon Broxton, of	No. 14
11.	Paul Goldschmidt, 1b	Majors
12.	Ty Linton, of	No. 22
13.	Kevin Munson, rhp	No. 19
14.	Eric Smith, rhp	Dropped out
15.	Mike Belfiore, lhp	Dropped out
16.	Ryan Wheeler, 3b	No. 18
17.	Karn Mickolio, rhp	(Hiroshima/Japan)
18.	Collin Cowgill, of	(Athletics)
19.	Wagner Mateo, of	Dropped out
20.	Tyler Green, rhp	No. 25
21.	Robby Rowland, rhp	Dropped out
22.	David Holmberg, lhp	No. 6
23.	J.R. Bradley, rhp	No. 23
24.	Charles Brewer, rhp	No. 21
25.	Raul Navarro, ss	Dropped out
26.	Chase Anderson, rhp	Dropped out
27.	Bryan Shaw, rhp	Majors
28.	Ronny Mejias, ss	Dropped out
29.	Zach Walters, ss	(Nationals)
30.	Adam Eaton, of	No. 12

BEST TOOLS

Best Hitter for Average	A.J. Pollock
Best Power Hitter	Bobby Borchering
Best Strike-Zone Discipline	Adam Eaton
Fastest Baserunner	Westley Moss
Best Athlete	Keon Broxton
Best Fastball	Archie Bradley
Best Curveball	Trevor Bauer
Best Slider	Andrew Chafin
Best Changeup	Chase Anderson
Best Control	David Holmberg
Best Defensive Catcher	Fidel Pena
Best Defensive Infielder	Chris Owings
Best Infield Arm	Chris Owings
Best Defensive Outfielder	A.J. Pollock
Best Outfield Arm	Adam Eaton

PROJECTED 2015 LINEUP

Catcher	Miguel Montero
First Base	Paul Goldschmidt
Second Base	Aaron Hill
Third Base	Matt Davidson
Shortstop	Stephen Drew
Left Field	A.J. Pollock
Center Field	Chris Young
Right Field	Justin Upton
No. 1 Starter	Trevor Bauer
No. 2 Starter	Archie Bradley
No. 3 Starter	Ian Kennedy
No. 4 Starter	Tyler Skaggs
No. 5 Starter	Daniel Hudson
Closer	David Hernandez

TOP PROSPECTS OF THE DECADE

Year	Player, Pos.	2011 Org.
2002	Luis Terrero, of	Mexico City (Mexican)
2003	Scott Hairston, 2b	Mets
2004	Scott Hairston, 2b	Mets
2005	Carlos Quentin, of	White Sox
2006	Stephen Drew, ss	Diamondbacks
2007	Justin Upton, of	Diamondbacks
2008	Carlos Gonzalez, of	Rockies
2009	Jarrod Parker, rhp	Diamondbacks
2010	Jarrod Parker, rhp	Diamondbacks
2011	Jarrod Parker, rhp	Diamondbacks

TOP DRAFT PICKS OF THE DECADE

Year	Player, Pos.	2011 Org.
2002	Sergio Santos, ss	White Sox
2003	Conor Jackson, of	Red Sox
2004	Stephen Drew, ss	Diamondbacks
2005	Justin Upton, of	Diamondbacks
2006	Max Scherzer, rhp	Tigers
2007	Jarrod Parker, rhp	Diamondbacks
2008	Daniel Schlereth, lhp	Tigers
2009	Bobby Borchering, 3b	Diamondbacks
2010	*Barret Loux, rhp	Rangers
2011	Trevor Bauer	Diamondbacks

*Did not sign.

LARGEST BONUSES IN CLUB HISTORY

Travis Lee, 1996	$10,000,000
Justin Upton, 2005	$6,100,000
John Patterson, 1996	$6,075,000
Archie Bradley, 2011	$5,000,000
Stephen Drew, 2004	$4,000,000

ARIZONA DIAMONDBACKS

TOP 2012 ROOKIE: Trevor Bauer, rhp. The No. 3 overall pick in the 2011 draft drew consideration for Arizona's postseason roster and could crack the Opening Day roster.

BREAKOUT PROSPECT: Evan Marshall, rhp. His stuff and mindset give him a chance to make it to Arizona in his first full pro season.

SLEEPER: Fidel Pena, 2b/c. He can catch or play the middle infield, and he's a solid gap-to-gap hitter from both sides of the plate.

SOURCE OF TOP 30 TALENT

Homegrown	26	Acquired	4
College	14	Trades	3
Junior college	1	Rule 5 draft	1
High school	9	Independent leagues	0
Draft-and-follow	0	Free agents/waivers	0
Nondrafted free agents	0		
International	2		

LF
Bobby Borchering (10)
Marc Krauss (16)
Ty Linton (22)
David Winfree

CF
A.J. Pollock (5)
Adam Eaton (12)
Keon Broxton (14)
Socrates Brito (30)
Justin Bianco
Yorman Garcia
Ender Inciarte

RF
Cole Gillespie
Alfredo Marte

3B
Matt Davidson (4)
Matt Helm

SS
Chris Owings (7)
Josh Parr
John Leonard
Raul Navarro
Pedro Ruiz

2B
David Nick (23)
Mark Hallberg
Ronny Mejias
Fidel Pena

1B
Ryan Wheeler (18)
Wagner Mateo
Yazy Arbelo
Jon Griffin

C
Michael Perez (24)
Konrad Schmidt
Roidany Aguila
Rossmel Perez

LHP

LHSP	LHRP
Tyler Skaggs (3)	Zach Kroenke
David Holmberg (6)	Eury de la Rosa
Wade Miley (8)	Will Locante
Patrick Corbin (9)	Michael Blake
Andrew Chafin (13)	Patrick Schuster
John Pedrotty (29)	Mike Belfiore
Taylor Siemens	Daniel Taylor

RHP

RHSP	RHRP
Trevor Bauer (1)	Evan Marshall (15)
Archie Bradley (2)	Kevin Munson (19)
Anthony Meo (11)	Yonata Ortega (20)
Kyle Winkler (17)	Chris Odegaard
Charles Brewer (21)	Mike Bolsinger
Tyler Green (25)	D.J. Johnson
Jesse Darrah (26)	Willy Paredes
J.R. Bradley (27)	Cody Geyer
Brett Lorin (28)	
Eric Smith	
Jeff Shields	
Bradin Hagens	
Chase Anderson	

2011 — BONUSES: $11.9 MILLION

BEST PURE HITTER: C Michael Perez (5) could provide uncommon offense for his position, thanks to a quick lefthanded stroke and average power potential.

BEST POWER HITTER: 1B Jon Griffin (21) led the Rookie-level Pioneer League with 18 homers, tying Paul Goldschmidt's franchise record at Missoula. The 6-foot-7, 250-pound Griffin hit 69 homers in four years between junior college and Central Florida.

FASTEST RUNNER: OF Chris Ellison (39) used his plus speed to steal 15 bases at Missoula, though he was caught nine times.

BEST DEFENSIVE PLAYER: SS Josh Parr (12) is a reliable defender whose pro debut was cut short by a fastball to the face, fracturing his cheekbone.

BEST FASTBALL: Arizona loaded up on power arms in the draft, starting with two of the first seven overall picks, RHPs Trevor Bauer (1) and Archie Bradley (1). The Diamondbacks have clocked them both as high as 98 mph, and Bradley reportedly hit 101 mph in the Oklahoma 6-A championship game. He usually works at 92-95 mph and has the best pure arm in this crop.

BEST SECONDARY PITCH: Bauer has a number of intriguing secondary pitches, with the best being a sharp curveball that rates as a plus-plus pitch at times. Chafin throws a wipeout slider, and Marshall's curveball also can be a weapon.

BEST PRO DEBUT: Griffin and LHP Taylor Siemens (18), who topped the Pioneer League in ERA (2.23) and opponent average (.226). He succeeds with an 88-90 mph sinker and deception. Bauer pitched his way to Double-A two weeks into his pro career and fanned 43 in 26 overall innings.

BEST ATHLETE: Bradley would have played quarterback at Oklahoma if he hadn't turn pro. OF Justin Bianco (3) has solid tools across the board.

MOST INTRIGUING BACKGROUND: 3B/1B Tyler Bream's (42) father Sid played 12 seasons in the big leagues.

CLOSEST TO THE MAJORS: Bauer was considered for Arizona's postseason roster and should be the first 2011 draftee to reach the big leagues. Marshall closed out the Double-A Southern League championship game and could join the Diamondbacks bullpen in the near future.

BEST LATE-ROUND PICK: Winkler would have been a supplemental first-round pick if not for a stress fracture in his elbow that required surgery. LHP John Pedrotty (13) throws three pitches for strikes.

THE ONE WHO GOT AWAY: The Diamondbacks were close but couldn't corral RHP Matt Price (6) or OF Ben Roberts (7). Price took his plus fastball back to South Carolina, where he was the closer on the last two College World Series championship teams. Roberts, a stunning athlete for a Montana high school product, will play at Washington State.

ASSESSMENT: No team ever before had two of the first seven picks, and Arizona took full advantage with Bauer and Bradley. The Diamondbacks also picked up more arms and may have the game's best group of pitching prospects.

2010 — BONUSES: $4.4 MILLION

The Diamondbacks didn't sign RHP Barret Loux (1), which wound up getting them the 2011 first-rounder that became Archie Bradley. The best picks so far are INF Zach Walters (9), who was traded to the Nationals for Jason Marquis last summer, and OF Adam Eaton (19), a career .340 hitter in pro ball.

GRADE: C

2009 — BONUSES: $9.3 MILLION

Arizona had seven picks before the third round, but 1B Paul Goldschmidt (8) beat them all to the majors. The top four choices—OF/1B/3B Bobby Borchering (1), OF A.J. Pollock (1), 3B/1B Matt Davidson (1s), SS Chris Owings (1s)—are the system's top four position prospects.

GRADE: B

2008 — BONUSES: $4.5 MILLION

The Diamondbacks signed five major leaguers, but none of LHPs Daniel Schlereth (1, traded to Tigers) and Wade Miley (1s), RHPs Bryan Shaw (2) and Ryan Cook (27) and OF Collin Cowgill (5, traded to Athletics) looks like an impact player. Arizona failed to sign another big leaguer, LHP Josh Spence (25), and the eventual No. 2 overall pick in 2011, LHP Danny Hultzen (10).

GRADE: C+

2007 — BONUSES: $5.1 MILLION

RHP Jarrod Parker (1) came back from Tommy John surgery in 2011, then was the key part of the trade that brought Trevor Cahill from the A's. RHP Josh Collmenter (15) won 10 games as a rookie. RHPs Barry Enright (2), Bryan Augenstein (7, since traded) and Evan Scribner (28) and LHP Scott Maine (6, since dealt) also have reached the big time.

GRADE: B+

Draft analysis by Jim Callis. Numbers in parentheses indicate draft rounds.

1 TREVOR BAUER, RHP

Born: Jan. 17, 1991. **Bats:** R. **Throws:** R. **Height:** 6-1. **Weight:** 175. **Drafted:** UCLA, 2011 (1st round). **Signed by:** Hal Kurtzman.

BA GRADE
70
MEDIUM

TONY FARLOW

Bauer earned all-state honors as a junior at Hart High (Newhall, Calif.) before deciding to tackle a bigger challenge, graduating in December of his senior year and enrolling early at UCLA. He immediately became the Bruins' best pitcher, going 34-8, 2.36 in three seasons and setting school records for career wins, strikeouts (460) and innings (373). He led NCAA Division I in strikeouts in both 2010 and 2011, breaking Mark Prior's Pacific-10 Conference record with 203 last spring. Bauer won both Baseball America's College Player of the Year award and USA Baseball's Golden Spikes Award in 2011. He and Gerrit Cole became the second pair of teammates ever to go in the first three picks in a draft, with the Pirates selecting Cole No. 1 overall and the Diamondbacks taking Bauer at No. 3. Bauer became the first of the 2011's draft elite prospects to sign, agreeing to a four-year major league contract in July. The deal includes a $3.4 million bonus and $4.45 million in guarantees, and he could earn as much as $7 million if he quickly reaches the majors to stay. He's expected to do just that, needing just three starts at high Class A Visalia to earn a promotion to Double-A Mobile. He looked a little tired at times with the BayBears, but he tossed five innings of one-run ball to clinch the Southern League championship.

Bauer takes an unconventional approach to pitching, studying advanced concepts like biomechanics, effective velocity and pitch tunneling. He has a tremendous work ethic and a drive to succeed. He adheres to an extreme long-toss regimen, throwing at distances up to 400 feet, and works out with rubber tubes before and during his starts. Bauer has drawn a lot of attention for his unorthodox style, sometimes overshadowing the quality of his stuff. He generates 92-98 mph fastballs with extreme torque, not unlike Tim Lincecum, and usually sits at 94-95. His best pitch is his plus-plus curveball, a 12-to-6 downer that plays off the plane of his fastball. He has an extremely deep repertoire that features a plus slider, an above-average changeup and a solid splitter. He's also working on a

SCOUTING GRADES

Fastball: 70.	**Command/**
Curveball: 70.	**Control:** 55.
Changeup: 60.	**Delivery:** 60.

Based on 20-80 scouting scale, where 50 represents major league average, and future projection rather than present tools.

pitch that he calls "The Bird," a zone-crossing slurve that he's making up as he goes along. Though he's not physically imposing, Bauer has conditioned himself to handle heavy workloads and completed his last nine starts for UCLA. He generally throws strikes but can be more efficient with his pitch counts, something that should happen once he become less conscious about piling up strikeouts. He puts considerable effort into each pitch, though he has a loose arm and a very efficient delivery that adds deception.

Arizona signed Bauer before the Aug. 15 deadline with the thought he could contribute in September or the playoffs, but decided to shut him down after the Southern League postseason. He'll report to big league camp with a legitimate chance to earn a spot in the big league rotation, if not on Opening Day then quite likely by the second half of the season. He not only has top-of-the-rotation potential, but his approach is so revolutionary that his success in the majors could cause teams to rethink how they condition and develop young pitchers.

Year	Club (League)	Class	W	L	ERA	G	GS	CG	SV	IP	H	HR	BB	SO	K/9	WHIP	AVG
2011	Visalia (CAL)	HiA	0	1	3.00	3	3	0	0	9	7	1	4	17	17.0	1.22	.200
	Mobile (SL)	AA	1	1	7.56	4	4	0	0	17	20	2	8	26	14.0	1.68	.286
Minor League Totals			1	2	5.96	7	7	0	0	26	27	3	12	43	15.1	1.52	.257

2 ARCHIE BRADLEY, RHP

Born: Aug. 10, 1992. **B-T:** R-R. **Ht.:** 6-4. **Wt.:** 225. **Drafted:** HS—Broken Arrow, Okla., 2011 (1st round). **Signed by:** Kyle Denney.

The Diamondbacks received the No. 7 overall choice in the 2011 draft for failing to sign 2010 first-rounder Barret Loux. Instead of going conservative with an unprotected pick, they went for Bradley, who had extra leverage as an Oklahoma quarterback recruit. He beat Owasso, then the nation's top-ranked team, in the Oklahoma state 6-A championship game with a 14-strikeout, two-hit shutout while hitting 101 mph on the scoreboard radar gun. He signed at the Aug. 15 deadline for $5 million, a franchise record for a drafted pitcher. Bradley was the talk of Arizona's instructional league camp, with scouts from other organizations using terms such as "spectacular" and "the real deal." Bradley usually throws his fastball at 92-98 mph, operating on an excellent downhill plane and with heavy life. His power curveball, which arrives at 82-85 mph, can be just as overpowering. He's still developing a changeup after not needing one in high school, but it projects to be at least an average pitch. He's athletic and repeats his clean delivery well. Like fellow 2011 first-rounder Trevor Bauer, Bradley has No. 1-starter potential and should move quickly through the minors. After making two brief appearances last September, he'll get his first real taste of pro ball at low Class A South Bend to start 2012.

BA GRADE
70
HIGH

Year	Club (League)	Class	W	L	ERA	G	GS	CG	SV	IP	H	HR	BB	SO	K/9	WHIP	AVG
2011	Missoula (PIO)	R	0	0	0.00	2	1	0	0	2	1	0	0	4	18.0	0.50	.143
Minor League Totals			0	0	0.00	2	1	0	0	2	1	0	0	4	18.0	0.50	.143

3 TYLER SKAGGS, LHP

Born: July 13, 1991. **B-T:** L-L. **Ht.:** 6-4. **Wt.:** 195. **Drafted:** HS—Santa Monica, Calif., 2009 (1st round supplemental). **Signed by:** Bobby DeJardin (Angels).

The Diamondbacks wanted Skaggs with the 41st overall choice in the 2009 draft, but the Angels took him one pick earlier and signed him for $1 million. Arizona finally got its man in July 2010, when he was the key piece in a four-player package Los Angeles gave up for Dan Haren. In his first full year in the system, Skaggs rated as the No. 1 prospect in the high Class A California League and was named Diamondbacks minor league pitcher of the year. Skaggs' money pitch is his 12-to-6 curveball with late, sharp break that's a true swing-and-miss pitch. He sets it up by moving his lively 88-93 mph fastball around the strike zone. His fastball velocity increased in 2011, sitting in the low 90s more consistently, and he may add more as he fills out his projectable frame. His changeup is at least an average pitch, a 78-82 mph offering that sinks below the zone with a side-to-side curl. Skaggs repeats his delivery well and throws strikes. He has great poise on the mound and is a fierce competitor. Originally projected as a No. 3 starter, Skaggs has revised that outlook and now looks like he can pitch at the front of a rotation. He handled Double-A so easily that he'll probably open 2012 at Triple-A Reno as a 20-year-old.

BA GRADE
65
LOW

Year	Club (League)	Class	W	L	ERA	G	GS	CG	SV	IP	H	HR	BB	SO	K/9	WHIP	AVG
2009	Angels (AZL)	R	0	0	0.00	3	2	0	0	6	4	0	1	7	10.5	0.83	.182
	Orem (PIO)	R	0	0	4.50	2	0	0	0	4	5	0	1	6	13.5	1.50	.278
2010	Cedar Rapids (MWL)	LoA	8	4	3.61	19	14	0	0	82	78	6	21	82	9.0	1.20	.252
	South Bend (MWL)	LoA	1	1	1.69	4	4	0	0	16	13	1	4	20	11.3	1.06	.224
2011	Visalia (CAL)	HiA	5	5	3.22	17	17	0	0	101	81	6	34	125	11.2	1.14	.219
	Mobile (SL)	AA	4	1	2.50	10	10	0	0	58	45	4	15	73	11.4	1.04	.216
Minor League Totals			18	11	3.04	55	47	0	0	267	226	17	76	313	10.6	1.13	.229

4 MATT DAVIDSON, 3B/1B

Born: March 26, 1991. **B-T:** R-R. **Ht.:** 6-3. **Wt.:** 225. **Drafted:** HS—Yucaipa, Calif., 2009 (1st round supplemental). **Signed by:** Jeff Mousser.

For the second straight season, Davidson had to share third base with fellow 2009 premium pick Bobby Borchering. The recipient of a $900,000 bonus, Davidson struggled in high Class A at the end of 2010 but drove in 106 runs and improved his defense when he returned to Visalia in 2011. He moved up to Double-A for the Southern League championship series and homered in the clincher. Davidson has strong, quick hands that give him power to all fields. He's a very consistent hitter with a good approach at the plate, so his strikeout totals should come down as he matures. He handles secondary pitches well but can get beat by good fastballs on the inner half. While Davidson never will be known for his defense, he should be able to handle third base. He doesn't have much range and needs to improve his consistency, but he has soft hands and a strong arm. He's a below-average runner. The system's top position prospect, Davidson will head back to Mobile in 2012 and should reach the majors the following season. He won't have to spend any more time at first base or DH now that Borchering is moving to the outfield. He projects as a No. 4 or 5 hitter in a big league lineup.

BA GRADE **55** MEDIUM

Year	Club (League)	Class	AVG	G	AB	R	H	2B	3B	HR	RBI	BB	SO	SB	CS	OBP	SLG
2009	Yakima (NWL)	SS	.241	72	270	29	65	15	0	2	28	21	75	0	2	.312	.319
2010	South Bend (MWL)	LoA	.289	113	415	58	120	35	3	16	79	43	109	0	2	.371	.504
	Visalia (CAL)	HiA	.169	21	71	6	12	1	0	2	11	12	25	0	0	.298	.268
2011	Visalia (CAL)	HiA	.277	135	535	93	148	39	1	20	106	52	147	0	1	.348	.465
Minor League Totals			.267	341	1291	186	345	90	4	40	224	128	356	0	5	.345	.436

5 A.J. POLLOCK, OF

Born: Dec. 5, 1987. **B-T:** R-R. **Ht.:** 6-1. **Wt.:** 205. **Drafted:** Notre Dame, 2009 (1st round). **Signed by:** Mike Daughtry.

The No. 17 overall pick in the 2009 draft, Pollock signed for $1.4 million and missed all of his first full pro season after fracturing a growth plate in his throwing elbow during a spring-training drill. He looked as good as ever when he returned in 2011, leading the Southern League in runs (103) and hits (169) while helping Mobile to the championship. Pollock's total package is greater than the sum of its parts. First and foremost, he's a blue-collar player with great makeup and excellent instincts in all phases of the game. He's a line-drive, gap-to-gap hitter who squares balls up consistently and produces lots of doubles. He could develop 15-homer power once he gets stronger. He makes contact so easily that it hampers his ability to draw walks. Though he has just average speed, Pollock is the system's best baserunner and stole 36 bases in 43 tries in 2011. He's solid defensively at all three outfield positions, making good reads in center field and displaying an average arm. Pollock is ready for a move to Triple-A in 2012 and could fill a need at the big league level at some point in the season. Though some scouts see him as a fourth outfielder because he isn't loaded with plus tools, the Diamondbacks envision him becoming a solid regular.

BA GRADE **55** MEDIUM

Year	Club (League)	Class	AVG	G	AB	R	H	2B	3B	HR	RBI	BB	SO	SB	CS	OBP	SLG
2009	South Bend (MWL)	LoA	.271	63	255	36	69	12	3	3	22	16	36	10	4	.319	.376
2010	Did Not Played—Injured																
2011	Mobile (SL)	AA	.307	133	550	103	169	41	5	8	73	44	86	36	7	.357	.444
Minor League Totals			.296	196	805	139	238	53	8	11	95	60	122	46	11	.345	.422

6 DAVID HOLMBERG, LHP

Born: July 19, 1991. **B-T:** R-L. **Ht.:** 6-4. **Wt.:** 219. **Drafted:** HS—Port Charlotte, Fla., 2009 (2nd round). **Signed by:** Joe Siers (White Sox).

The Diamondbacks would have been more than satisfied with their July 2010 trade of Edwin Jackson to the White Sox if they had acquired only Daniel Hudson in return. But they got another potential future starter in Holmberg, who made a smashing full-season debut in 2011. He improved his velocity while maintaining his command, which managers rated as the best in the low Class A Midwest League. Holmberg stands out for his poise and pitchability. After his fastball topped out around 90 mph in his first two pro seasons, he worked at 88-93 mph in 2011. He can locate his fastball to either side of the plate with good sink. He also firmed up his cutter/slider, though his solid-to-plus changeup remains his plus pitch. Holmberg also has a curveball that has the potential to become an average pitch. He repeats his delivery well, giving him plus command that helps his pitches play up. He had a doughy body in the past, but now he's in better shape

BA GRADE **55** MEDIUM

and built for durability. Holmberg struggled when he got to the hitter-friendly California League last July, so he'll repeat high Class A to open 2012. He's still on course to reach Double-A before he turns 21 and to eventually become a No. 3 starter.

Year	Club (League)	Class	W	L	ERA	G	GS	CG	SV	IP	H	HR	BB	SO	K/9	WHIP	AVG
2009	Bristol (APP)	R	2	2	4.73	14	7	0	0	40	40	5	18	37	8.3	1.45	.256
2010	Great Falls (PIO)	R	1	1	4.46	8	8	0	0	40	52	2	9	29	6.5	1.51	.315
	Missoula (PIO)	R	1	4	3.86	7	7	0	0	37	47	2	7	47	11.3	1.45	.294
2011	South Bend (MWL)	LoA	8	3	2.39	14	14	1	0	83	65	3	13	81	8.8	0.94	.212
	Visalia (CAL)	HiA	4	6	4.67	13	13	0	0	71	73	5	35	76	9.6	1.51	.263
Minor League Totals			16	16	3.84	56	49	1	0	272	277	17	82	270	8.9	1.32	.260

7 CHRIS OWINGS, SS

Born: Aug. 12, 1991. **B-T:** R-R. **Ht.:** 5-9. **Wt.:** 175. **Drafted:** HS—Gllbert, S.C., 2009 (1st round supplemental). **Signed by:** George Swain.

Most of the Diamondbacks' best position prospects are products of the 2009 draft, in which Owings went 41st overall and signed for $950,000. He missed the second half of 2010 after coming down with plantar fasciitis, inflammation on the bottom of both his feet. He struggled in 2011 as a 19-year-old in high Class A, ending the season in a 12-for-73 (.164) slump that included 19 strikeouts. Owings has the quickest bat for his system and is strong for his size, giving him surprising power that could produce 15 homers per season. His difficulties come at the plate because he lacks patience and doesn't recognize pitches well. He tends to look for fastballs and often chases breaking balls out of the zone. He has slightly above-average speed and runs the bases well. Owings has the tools to be an above-average defender at shortstop. He has solid range and a plus arm, though he needs to improve his focus after committing 32 errors in 117 games at Visalia. Owings will need at least two more years in the minors, but he's still just 20 and projects as a future middle-infield starter in Arizona. Though he might benefit from repeating high Class A, the Diamondbacks plan to send him to Double-A with other members of his draft class.

BA GRADE
55
HIGH

KEN WEISENBERGER

Year	Club (League)	Class	AVG	G	AB	R	H	2B	3B	HR	RBI	BB	SO	SB	CS	OBP	SLG
2009	Missoula (PIO)	R	.306	24	108	20	33	5	1	2	10	3	25	3	0	.324	.426
2010	South Bend (MWL)	LoA	.298	62	255	39	76	19	2	5	28	9	50	1	3	.323	.447
2011	Visalia (CAL)	HiA	.246	121	521	67	128	29	6	11	50	15	130	10	4	.274	.388
Minor League Totals			.268	207	884	126	237	53	9	18	88	27	205	14	7	.294	.410

8 WADE MILEY, LHP

Born: Nov. 13, 1986. **B-T:** L-L. **Ht.:** 6-1. **Wt.:** 220. **Drafted:** Southeastern Louisiana, 2008 (1st round supplemental). **Signed by:** Trip Couch.

A supplemental first-round pick who signed for $887,000 in 2008, Miley struggled in his first 1½ pro seasons. After improving his conditioning, he was the system's most improved player in 2010 and continued on that path in 2011. He jumped from Double-A to the majors, going 4-2 in seven starts as the Diamondbacks overtook the Giants for the National League West title in September. Miley throws his fastball, which ranges from 88-94 mph and sits at 91-92, at an angle that makes it tough on hitters. His fastball command can be an issue at times but has improved. He has three effective secondary pitches, though they sometimes lack consistency. His changeup is a plus pitch at times but he doesn't always use it enough. He throws two breaking pitches, with his slider better than his curveball, and both can get slurvy. He does the little things well, such as handling the bat, fielding his position and holding runners on base. Miley profiles as a back-of-the-rotation starter with his four-pitch mix, and he'll contend for a starting job in spring training. Arizona has more talented arms coming up behind him, so he'll likely get pushed to a swingman or middle-relief role in the future.

BA GRADE
50
LOW

Year	Club (League)	Class	W	L	ERA	G	GS	CG	SV	IP	H	HR	BB	SO	K/9	WHIP	AVG
2008	Yakima (NWL)	SS	1	1	4.91	7	0	0	0	11	11	0	5	11	9.0	1.45	.250
2009	South Bend (MWL)	LoA	5	9	4.12	21	21	0	0	114	127	8	29	91	7.2	1.37	.287
	Visalia (CAL)	HiA	1	1	4.80	3	3	0	0	15	18	0	4	11	6.6	1.47	.295
2010	Visalia (CAL)	HiA	4	5	3.25	14	14	0	0	80	81	1	37	50	5.6	1.47	.266
	Mobile (SL)	AA	5	2	1.98	13	13	1	0	73	60	5	28	63	7.8	1.21	.232
2011	Mobile (SL)	AA	4	2	4.78	14	14	0	0	75	74	6	28	46	5.5	1.35	.257
	Reno (PCL)	AAA	4	1	3.64	8	8	1	0	54	53	4	16	56	9.3	1.27	.255
	Arizona (NL)	MAJ	4	2	4.50	8	7	0	0	40	48	6	18	25	5.6	1.65	.304
Major League Totals			4	2	4.50	8	7	0	0	40	48	6	18	25	5.6	1.65	.304
Minor League Totals			24	21	3.69	80	73	2	0	422	424	24	147	328	7.0	1.35	.264

9 PATRICK CORBIN, LHP

Born: July 19, 1989. **B-T:** L-L. **Ht.:** 6-3. **Wt.:** 165. **Drafted:** Chipola (Fla.) JC, 2009 (2nd round). **Signed by:** Tom Kotchman (Angels).

One of the better athletes in the system, Corbin played both baseball and basketball at Mohawk Valley (N.Y.) CC before transferring to Chipola (Fla.) JC in 2009. The Angels drafted him in the second round that June, then sent him to the Diamondbacks in the Dan Haren trade 13 months later. Part of Mobile's 2011 championship club, he led the Southern League in innings (160) and strikeouts (142). Like fellow lefties Tyler Skaggs and David Holmberg, Corbin experienced a bump in fastball velocity in 2011. His heater now ranges from 89-94 mph and usually operates at 90-92. He's still very lanky and could gain more speed as he gets stronger. He throws with terrific angle to the plate and his three-quarters delivery also creates nice downward plane. Both of Corbin's secondary pitches have the potential to become plus offerings, with his changeup more consistent than his late-breaking slider. The biggest quibbles scouts have are with his arm action and slight build, but he has been durable and fills the strike zone. His athleticism helps him field his position well and control the running game. Corbin will move to Triple-A in 2012 and be in line for a promotion if there's an opening at the major league level. He projects as a No. 4 starter.

BA GRADE
50
MEDIUM

Year	Club (League)	Class	W	L	ERA	G	GS	CG	SV	IP	H	HR	BB	SO	K/9	WHIP	AVG
2009	Orem (PIO)	R	4	2	5.05	13	12	0	0	46	59	6	11	46	8.9	1.51	.291
2010	Cedar Rapids (MWL)	LoA	8	0	3.86	9	9	0	0	58	52	2	10	42	6.5	1.06	.245
	R. Cucamonga (CAL)	HiA	5	3	3.88	11	11	0	0	60	57	7	18	64	9.5	1.24	.247
	Visalia (CAL)	HiA	0	1	1.38	8	8	0	0	26	17	1	9	30	10.4	1.00	.189
2011	Mobile (SL)	AA	9	8	4.21	26	26	1	0	160	172	15	40	142	8.0	1.32	.275
Minor League Totals			26	14	4.00	67	66	1	0	351	357	31	88	324	8.3	1.27	.262

10 BOBBY BORCHERING, OF/1B/3B

Born: Oct. 25, 1990. **B-T:** B-R. **Ht.:** 6-3. **Wt.:** 200. **Drafted:** HS—Fort Myers, Fla., 2009 (1st round). **Signed by:** Ray Blanco.

Borchering was the 16th overall pick in the 2009 draft, one of five players selected by the Diamondbacks before the second round. Signed for $1.8 million, he has as much raw power as anyone in the system and showed it by hitting 24 homers in high Class A at age 20 last season. He swung at a lot of pitches out of the zone early in the year but started to make adjustments and lay off offspeed pitches in the dirt. A switch-hitter, Borchering is equally effective from both sides of the plate. His propensity for striking out likely will preclude him from hitting for a high average, and he has batted just .266 in three pro seasons. Borchering entered pro ball as a third baseman, as did 2009 sandwich pick Matt Davidson, and they had to share time at both infield corners in the last two seasons. Borchering never showed much progress in the infield—one scout declared him "allergic to leather"—and Arizona finally moved him to left field during instructional league. He's a below-average runner with fringy arm strength, but he has enough athleticism to get the job done in the outfield. How he fares in Double-A against more challenging pitching this year will be telling.

KEN WEISENBERGER

BA GRADE
55
HIGH

Year	Club (League)	Class	AVG	G	AB	R	H	2B	3B	HR	RBI	BB	SO	SB	CS	OBP	SLG
2009	Missoula (PIO)	R	.241	22	87	10	21	8	1	2	11	5	27	0	0	.290	.425
2010	South Bend (MWL)	LoA	.270	135	523	74	141	31	2	15	74	54	128	1	1	.341	.423
2011	Visalia (CAL)	HiA	.267	135	531	80	142	29	3	24	92	49	162	4	1	.332	.469
Minor League Totals			.266	292	1141	164	304	68	6	41	177	108	317	5	2	.333	.444

11 ANTHONY MEO, RHP

BA GRADE
55
HIGH

Born: Feb. 19, 1990. **B-T:** R-R. **Ht.:** 6-2. **Wt.:** 185. **Drafted:** Coastal Carolina, 2011 (2nd round). **Signed by:** George Swain.

The highest-drafted pitcher in Coastal Carolina history—and third-highest draftee ever, behind big leaguers Kirt Manwaring and Mickey Brantley—Meo enhanced his already-strong stock with the final two outings of his college career. He threw the first no-hitter in Big South Conference tournament history, striking out nine in as many innings against Radford, then beat Connecticut and eventual Red Sox first-rounder Matt Barnes in the NCAA regionals. The Diamondbacks stocked up on power arms in the 2011 draft and were delighted to get Meo in the second round, where they signed him at the Aug. 15 deadline for a slightly above-slot $625,000. His best pitch is a 91-98 mph fastball. He also has a solid changeup and a slider that lacks consistency but plays nicely off his fastball. Meo employs a unique, deceptive delivery that makes it hard for righthanders to pick up the ball. He throws with a lot of effort, but his pitches get on the batter quickly and he has no problem throwing strikes. Some scouts believe his mechanics will fit better in a relief role. The

Diamondbacks will develop Meo as a starter with No. 3 upside, but he also has the potential to be a closer. If they want to challenge him, he could see high Class A at some point during his first full pro season.

Year	Club (League)	Class	W	L	ERA	G	GS	CG	SV	IP	H	HR	BB	SO	K/9	WHIP	AVG
2011	Diamondbacks (AZL)	R	0	0	0.00	1	1	0	0	1	0	0	0	2	18.0	0.00	.000
	Missoula (PIO)	R	0	0	0.00	1	0	0	0	2	0	0	0	1	4.5	0.00	.000
Minor League Totals			0	0	0.00	2	1	0	0	3	0	0	0	3	9.0	0.00	.000

12 ADAM EATON, OF

BA GRADE 55 MEDIUM

Born: Dec. 6, 1988. **B-T:** L-L. **Ht.:** 5-9. **Wt.:** 180. **Drafted:** Miami (Ohio), 2010 (19th round). **Signed by:** Frankie Thon Jr.

Eaton has made a career of exceeding expectations and he hasn't stopped since signing for $35,000 as a 19th-round college senior in 2010. He won the Rookie-level Pioneer League batting title (.385) in his pro debut and reached Double-A midway through his first full pro season. The undersized gamer has a career .340 average in the minors and kept hitting in the Arizona Fall League after the season, batting .344/.410/.475. Eaton is a line-drive hitter with enough power to hit 10-15 homers per year. He has a somewhat unorthodox style, with one scout likening it to a Japanese approach in which he gets an early jump out of the batters box. He makes consistent contact, drawing nearly as many walks as strikeouts. His biggest drawback at the plate is his struggles against lefthanders, who held him to .263/.386/.331 numbers last season and eventually may relegate him to a platoon role. Eaton has plus speed and knows how to use it to create havoc on the bases. He can play all three outfield positions, with solid range in center and above-average range on the corners, and he has the strongest outfield arm in the system. Some scouts still see Eaton as a fourth outfielder, but his doubters are diminishing. He may start 2012 in Triple-A and could finish the season in Arizona.

Year	Club (League)	Class	AVG	G	AB	R	H	2B	3B	HR	RBI	BB	SO	SB	CS	OBP	SLG
2010	Missoula (PIO)	R	.385	68	226	48	87	14	4	7	37	35	44	20	8	.500	.575
2011	Visalia (CAL)	HiA	.332	65	244	54	81	15	3	6	39	42	41	24	8	.455	.492
	Mobile (SL)	AA	.302	56	212	31	64	7	4	4	28	30	35	10	6	.409	.429
Minor League Totals			.340	189	682	133	232	36	11	17	104	107	120	54	22	.456	.500

13 ANDREW CHAFIN, LHP

BA GRADE 55 HIGH

Born: June 17, 1990. **B-T:** R-L. **Ht.:** 6-2. **Wt.:** 205. **Drafted:** Kent State, 2011 (1st round supplemental). **Signed by:** Nate Birtwell.

Chafin bounced back from missing all of 2010 following Tommy John surgery to become the fourth Kent State pitcher (after big leaguers Dustin Hermanson, Travis Miller and John Van Benschoten) to go in the first or sandwich round of the draft. After handing Brewers first-rounder Taylor Jungmann his first loss of the season in an NCAA regional playoff, Chafin went 43rd overall in June and signed at the deadline for $875,000. His pro debut consisted of one scoreless inning in the Rookie-level Arizona League, where he struck out two batters but yielded a double off the left-field fence to Cubs first-rounder Javier Baez. Chafin's fastball ranged from 90-95 mph during the college season, though he tired late and worked 88-92 mph during instructional league. He commands his fastball well to both sides of the plate, but his best pitch is a slider that can be unhittable at times. He also has an average changeup that he honed when he was unable to throw a breaking ball during his rehab. Chafin gets nice angle on his pitches, though some scouts worry about his choppy mechanics with a funky finish. He has been described as having a starter's repertoire with a reliever's delivery. The Diamondbacks will develop him as a starter but could be tempted to expedite him to the majors as a late-inning reliever. They'll send him to one of their Class A affiliates to begin 2012.

Year	Club (League)	Class	W	L	ERA	G	GS	CG	SV	IP	H	HR	BB	SO	K/9	WHIP	AVG
2011	Diamondbacks (AZL)	R	0	0	0.00	1	1	0	0	1	1	0	0	2	18.0	1.00	.250
Minor League Totals			0	0	0.00	1	1	0	0	1	1	0	0	2	18.0	1.00	.250

14 KEON BROXTON, OF

BA GRADE 55 EXTREME

Born: May 7, 1990. **B-T:** R-R. **Ht.:** 6-3. **Wt.:** 195. **Drafted:** Santa Fe (Fla.) CC, 2009 (3rd round). **Signed by:** Luke Wrenn.

Broxton turned down a football scholarship to play wide receiver at Florida Atlantic in order to play baseball at Santa Fe (Fla.) CC before the Diamondbacks picked him in the third round in 2009. He's extremely athletic and possesses the best set of tools in the system. He's still a long way from proving that he'll be able to hit quality pitching, though he did show improvement in the second half last year, when he batted .272/.373/.407 in high Class A. Broxton has above-average raw power and speed, but he doesn't make enough consistent contact to get the most out of them. He gets beat by offspeed pitches and struggles to control the strike zone. Broxton excels more on defense and could play center field in the big leagues right now. His speed allows him to chase down balls deep in the gaps, and he also gets good jumps and takes sound routes. His arm gives him yet another plus tool. Though the jury is still out on whether Broxton can turn his physical gifts into production at the plate, the sky's the limit if he eventually figures things out. He'll get his first taste of Double-A this year.

Year	Club (League)	Class	AVG	G	AB	R	H	2B	3B	HR	RBI	BB	SO	SB	CS	OBP	SLG
2009	Missoula (PIO)	R	.246	72	272	38	67	11	9	11	37	19	93	6	1	.302	.474
2010	South Bend (MWL)	LoA	.228	133	531	74	121	17	19	5	32	65	172	21	13	.316	.360
2011	South Bend (MWL)	LoA	.231	20	78	8	18	0	2	0	1	7	30	6	4	.294	.282
	Visalia (CAL)	HiA	.251	110	406	69	102	14	5	7	44	62	142	27	8	.349	.362
Minor League Totals			.239	335	1287	189	308	42	35	23	114	153	437	60	26	.323	.380

15 EVAN MARSHALL, RHP

BA GRADE
55
MEDIUM

Born: April 18, 1990. **B-T:** R-R. **Ht.:** 6-2. **Wt.:** 208. **Drafted:** Kansas State, 2011 (4th round). **Signed by:** Joe Robinson.

Marshall started 2010 in Kansas State's rotation before finding his niche as the Wildcats' set-up man. Placing an increased emphasis on their bullpen, the Diamondbacks popped Marshall in the fourth round last June and signed him for $232,500. He concluded a spectacular pro debut by saving the championship clincher in Southern League playoffs, striking out three of the five batters he faced. Marshall pitches with a maximum-effort delivery, throwing hitters off because he flies open so quickly. As one scout said, "He does a lot of things wrong but it works for him." Marshall attacks opponents with a 91-96 mph fastball and an 82-86 mph curveball. His curve has so much quick bite that it resembles a slider. His 82-84 mph changeup has late dive and mimics his fastball. His changeup wasn't very reliable in college but looked better in his pro debut. Marshall is wired to be a late-inning reliever and will move quickly, perhaps even reaching the big leagues at some point in 2012.

Year	Club (League)	Class	W	L	ERA	G	GS	CG	SV	IP	H	HR	BB	SO	K/9	WHIP	AVG
2011	Yakima (NWL)	SS	0	0	0.75	11	0	0	2	12	10	0	2	13	9.8	1.00	.213
	Visalia (CAL)	HiA	0	1	1.59	15	0	0	4	17	14	2	5	18	9.5	1.12	.212
	Mobile (SL)	AA	0	0	0.00	1	0	0	0	2	2	0	0	0	0.0	1.00	.286
Minor League Totals			0	1	1.16	27	0	0	6	31	26	2	7	31	9.0	1.06	.217

16 MARC KRAUSS, OF

BA GRADE
45
MEDIUM

Born: Oct. 5, 1987. **B-T:** L-R. **Ht.:** 6-2. **Wt.:** 235. **Drafted:** Ohio, 2009 (2nd round). **Signed by:** Frankie Thon Jr.

Krauss hit .302/.372/.504 in his first two pro seasons, propelling him to a No. 5 ranking on this list a year ago. But a subpar year in Double-A, along with concerns about his bat speed and athleticism, have dropped his stock. He hit just .242 at Mobile and looked stiff in the batter's box. He has above-average on-base skills and raw power, but scouts worry that he won't hit consistently enough or catch up to good fastballs. After handling lefthanders well in the past, he hit just .219/.308/.344 against them in 2011. Krauss has gone from looking like a potential No. 5 hitter a year earlier to perhaps no more than a platoon player now. That's a worry for a thick-bodied guy with below-average speed who has to rely on his bat to carry him. Though he's a little better with the glove than he usually gets credit for, he's limited to left field. He also has seen time in right, where he's passable despite a fringy arm. Krauss will get a chance to get back on track in 2012 when he moves to the more hitter-friendly Pacific Coast League.

Year	Club (League)	Class	AVG	G	AB	R	H	2B	3B	HR	RBI	BB	SO	SB	CS	OBP	SLG
2009	South Bend (MWL)	LoA	.304	32	115	14	35	12	1	2	17	14	21	0	1	.377	.478
2010	Visalia (CAL)	HiA	.302	138	530	107	160	27	4	25	87	57	141	1	3	.371	.509
2011	Mobile (SL)	AA	.242	125	433	69	105	25	6	16	65	64	123	3	3	.340	.439
Minor League Totals			.278	295	1078	190	300	64	11	43	169	135	285	4	7	.359	.478

17 KYLE WINKLER, RHP

BA GRADE
55
EXTREME

Born: June 18, 1990. **B-T:** R-R. **Ht.:** 5-11. **Wt.:** 205. **Drafted:** Texas Christian, 2011 (10th round). **Signed by:** Kyle Denney.

When Matt Purke had shoulder problems, Winkler replaced him as Texas Christian's ace last year and went 8-2, 1.39 for the Horned Frogs. Though he's a sub-6-foot righthander, he showed enough stuff to warrant discussion as a late first-round pick. That ended when he came down with arm problems right before the draft, causing him to drop all the way to the 10th round. He was diagnosed with a stress fracture in his elbow and had surgery in July before signing for $240,000 a month later. When healthy, Winkler has frontline-starter stuff. He can get hitters out with a 91-96 mph fastball with heavy life down in the zone or with his slider. He can run his slider up to 87 mph but it has better break in the low 80s, and some scouts preferred the hard curveball he threw in high school. He also throws a changeup, but it's too firm in the mid-80s and not as effective as his other offerings. Winkler's delivery offers some deception and he throws without too much effort. He's extremely competitive, and his size and medical history may lead to a future in the bullpen. He was still rehabbing his elbow in the fall and wasn't ready to pitch during instructional league.

Year	Club (League)	Class	W	L	ERA	G	GS	CG	SV	IP	H	HR	BB	SO	K/9	WHIP	AVG
2011	Did Not Play—Injured																

18 RYAN WHEELER, 3B/1B

BA GRADE

45

MEDIUM

Born: July 10, 1988. **B-T:** L-R. **Ht.:** 6-4. **Wt.:** 220. **Drafted:** Loyola Marymount, 2009 (5th round). **Signed by:** Hal Kurtzman.

Wheeler was a college first baseman when the Diamondbacks drafted him in the fifth round in 2009, and he won their minor league player of the year award in his pro debut. Afterward, he moved across the diamond to third base and didn't make the same offensive impact in 2010. He got his bat going again in Double-A last year, using his strong wrists and the leverage in his swing to serve as Mobile's second-most dangerous hitter, after Paul Goldschmidt. Wheeler was the BayBears' top hitter in the playoffs as they won the Southern League championship. His bat looked quicker in 2011 and he did a better job of catching up with good fastballs. He projects as a solid hitter with average power. That would be enough to become a major league regular at third base, but the question is whether Wheeler can stay there. Though he has enough arm strength for the hot corner, his range is below average and he's erratic. He probably won't dislodge Goldschmidt at first base, so his value may come as a corner utility player. A well below-average runner, he has played briefly in left field as a pro. Following a strong performance in the Arizona Fall League, Wheeler will head to Triple-A.

Year	Club (League)	Class	AVG	G	AB	R	H	2B	3B	HR	RBI	BB	SO	SB	CS	OBP	SLG
2009	Yakima (NWL)	SS	.363	64	234	44	85	20	3	5	36	37	28	7	4	.461	.538
	South Bend (MWL)	LoA	.345	8	29	4	10	1	1	1	5	5	4	0	1	.472	.552
2010	Visalia (CAL)	HiA	.284	113	465	62	132	25	2	9	57	35	98	3	1	.340	.404
	Mobile (SL)	AA	.254	19	67	8	17	3	0	3	10	5	16	0	0	.315	.433
2011	Mobile (SL)	AA	.294	131	480	69	141	30	2	16	89	45	102	3	4	.358	.465
Minor League Totals			.302	335	1275	187	385	79	8	34	197	127	248	13	10	.372	.456

19 KEVIN MUNSON, RHP

BA GRADE

45

MEDIUM

Born: Jan. 13, 1989. **B-T:** R-R. **Ht.:** 6-2. **Wt.:** 200. **Drafted:** James Madison, 2010 (4th round). **Signed by:** Shawn Barton.

Munson posted a 1.59 ERA in his 2010 pro debut, handling the transition so easily that the Diamondbacks thought he had a chance to be a big league contributor as early as 2012. That ETA seemed optimistic after he struggled with his command and control for most of last year in high Class A, though he finished with a strong final month after learning to trust his fastball. James Madison recruited Munson as a catcher and righthander, but quickly realized his arm strength would serve him best on the mound. He works mainly off his fastball, which operates at 91-95 mph and has good sink. His other pitch is a 79-83 mph slider that some scouts say looks more like a cutter. Munson walked nearly a batter per inning in the first four months of last season, and he doesn't have a history of filling the strike zone. His delivery is partly to blame, as he has a short arm action and lands on a stiff front leg, though it also provides deception. He threw strikes in August and in the Arizona Fall League, so he might have turned a corner. Munson likely will return to Double-A after finishing 2011 there. If he can continue to harness his fastball, he still could be in line for a callup at some point this year.

Year	Club (League)	Class	W	L	ERA	G	GS	CG	SV	IP	H	HR	BB	SO	K/9	WHIP	AVG
2010	South Bend (MWL)	LoA	2	0	1.10	12	0	0	3	16	8	1	5	17	9.4	0.80	.143
	Visalia (CAL)	HiA	0	0	13.50	1	0	0	0	1	1	0	2	0	0.0	4.50	.333
2011	Visalia (CAL)	HiA	4	3	4.02	42	0	0	0	54	44	4	41	76	12.7	1.58	.221
	Mobile (SL)	AA	0	0	0.00	2	0	0	0	3	3	0	1	2	6.0	1.33	.273
Minor League Totals			6	3	3.30	57	0	0	3	74	56	5	49	95	11.6	1.43	.208

20 YONATA ORTEGA, RHP

BA GRADE

50

HIGH

Born: Nov. 11, 1986. **B-T:** R-R. **Ht.:** 6-1. **Wt.:** 220. **Signed:** Dominican Republic, 2004. **Signed by:** Junior Noboa.

Since signing Ortega at the age of 17 in 2004, the Diamondbacks have been waiting patiently for the hard-throwing Dominican Republic native to harness an arm that ranks among the livest in the system. In his first two seasons in the United States, he put up 6.40 and 6.87 ERAs. He led Arizona farmhands with 33 saves in 2010, earning a spot on the 40-man roster, and while he wasn't as consistent last season, he averaged a career-high 12.0 strikeouts per nine innings. Ortega can blow hitters away with a 94-98 mph fastball. He also shows the makings of a plus splitter and can get swings and misses with his low-80s slider. He still has trouble commanding his pitches, however, and doesn't have much feel for his slider. There's a quality late-inning reliever in there, waiting to come out, if Ortega can build on the strides he made late in 2011. He limited Double-A hitters to a .115 average following a late-July promotion, though he had trouble finding the strike zone. Ortega will return to Mobile this season and he'll move quickly if he can start putting his pitches where he wants.

Year	Club (League)	Class	W	L	ERA	G	GS	CG	SV	IP	H	HR	BB	SO	K/9	WHIP	AVG
2005	Diamondbacks (DSL)	R	0	1	3.77	8	2	0	0	14	17	0	8	11	6.9	1.74	.304
2006	Diamondbacks (DSL)	R	2	7	3.43	14	11	0	0	63	56	2	25	56	8.0	1.29	.235
2007	Missoula (PIO)	R	0	2	6.40	19	0	0	1	32	38	6	18	26	7.2	1.73	.275
2008	Did Not Play—Injured																
2009	South Bend (MWL)	LoA	0	2	6.87	30	0	0	1	38	49	2	24	38	9.0	1.92	.308
2010	South Bend (MWL)	LoA	3	3	4.10	35	0	0	22	42	42	1	15	41	8.9	1.37	.259
	Visalia (CAL)	HiA	1	1	1.42	13	0	0	11	13	7	1	3	15	10.7	0.79	.156
2011	Visalia (CAL)	HiA	3	1	4.81	34	0	0	9	39	37	3	21	58	13.3	1.47	.247
	Mobile (SL)	AA	1	0	2.55	14	0	0	1	18	7	2	11	18	9.2	1.02	.115
Minor League Totals			10	17	4.48	167	13	0	45	259	253	17	125	263	9.1	1.46	.251

21 CHARLES BREWER, RHP

BA GRADE

45

MEDIUM

Born: April 7, 1988. **B-T:** R-R. **Ht.:** 6-4. **Wt.:** 205. **Drafted:** UCLA, 2009 (12th round). **Signed by:** Hal Kurtzman.

Brewer won three Arizona state 4-A championships at Chaparral High in the Phoenix suburbs before heading to UCLA, where he pitched with Trevor Bauer in 2009. The Diamondbacks brought Brewer back home that June, drafting him in the 12th round and signing him for $50,000. He has had little difficulty in pro ball, going 23-11, 2.45 overall and pitching well in Double-A last year. A line drive broke his pitching hand in June, but he returned at the end of the regular season and won the clinching game of the Southern League semifinals. Brewer has a prototypical pitcher's body and good arm action. He locates his 88-93 mph fastball well and backs it up with a 74-78 curveball that features nice depth. He also throws an effective changeup and flashes a slider with good tilt that he didn't use much in 2011. Brewer doesn't blow batters away, instead keeping them off balance by commanding and mixing his pitches. He doesn't have a true out pitch, which ultimately may lead him to the bullpen. So far, he's done nothing to suggest that he can't be a good No. 4 starter. After getting roughed up in the Arizona Fall League, Brewer probably will open 2012 back in Mobile.

Year	Club (League)	Class	W	L	ERA	G	GS	CG	SV	IP	H	HR	BB	SO	K/9	WHIP	AVG
2009	Missoula (PIO)	R	7	2	2.47	17	7	0	0	55	43	4	15	61	10.0	1.06	.216
2010	South Bend (MWL)	LoA	4	5	1.83	13	13	0	0	69	55	3	20	78	10.2	1.09	.216
	Visalia (CAL)	HiA	7	3	2.98	14	14	0	0	82	74	5	15	75	8.3	1.09	.239
2011	Diamondbacks (AZL)	R	0	0	0.00	1	1	0	0	3	3	0	0	4	12.0	1.00	.250
	Mobile (SL)	AA	5	1	2.58	11	11	2	0	52	48	2	19	48	8.3	1.28	.257
Minor League Totals			23	11	2.45	56	46	2	0	261	223	14	69	266	9.2	1.12	.232

22 TY LINTON, OF

BA GRADE

50

EXTREME

Born: Jan. 17, 1991 . **B-T:** R-R. **Ht.:** 6-3. **Wt.:** 195. **Drafted:** HS—Charlotte, 2010 (14th round). **Signed by:** George Swain.

The Diamondbacks swayed Linton from a North Carolina football scholarship to play safety just before the 2010 signing deadline with a $1.25 million bonus, knowing he was an extremely raw if talented athlete. He got just one plate appearance at Rookie-level Missoula that summer, then returned there in 2011 after beginning the year in extended spring training. He missed nearly half of the schedule with a variety of minor injuries, making it a frustrating season and difficult to evaluate his progress. Linton had a reputation for hitting off his front foot in high school, but he did a better job of staying back and driving the ball with author-ity in his first real taste of pro ball. However, he swung and missed too frequently, striking out in 36 percent of his plate appearances. His bat speed, raw power and foot speed all rate as above average, though it remains to be seen if he can maximize them. Linton may lack the arm strength to play anywhere but left field, so he'll have to hit. One scout commented that he still looks like a football player learning to play baseball. At this point, his main concern is to get at-bats against higher-tier pitching. Linton still isn't ready for full-season ball, so he'll open 2012 in extended spring training and report to short-season Yakima in June.

Year	Club (League)	Class	AVG	G	AB	R	H	2B	3B	HR	RBI	BB	SO	SB	CS	OBP	SLG
2010	Missoula (PIO)	R	—	1	0	0	0	0	0	0	0	1	0	0	0	1.000	—
2011	Missoula (PIO)	R	.257	39	136	18	35	7	4	3	17	10	53	3	6	.322	.434
Minor League Totals			.257	40	136	18	35	7	4	3	17	11	53	3	6	.327	.434

23 DAVID NICK, 2B

BA GRADE

45

HIGH

Born: Feb. 3, 1990. **B-T:** R-R. **Ht.:** 6-2. **Wt.:** 180. **Drafted:** HS—Cypress, Calif., 2009 (4th round). **Signed by:** Jeff Mousser.

Another product of Arizona's deep 2009 draft, Nick switched from shortstop to second base after coming out of the Cypress (Calif.) High program that has produced four big leaguers and recent top-10 picks Scott Moore (Tigers, 2002) and Josh Vitters (Cubs, 2007). Nick has been overshadowed by the six position players the Diamondbacks selected ahead of him, but he put himself on the prospect map with a strong season in high Class A last year. He's a hard-nosed kid who wants to be good. He's an aggressive hitter who puts the ball in play, drilling line drives and providing good pop for a middle infielder. His on-base skills and his speed are both fringy. Nick is a steady defender who makes the routine play and turns the double play well. He has cleaned up his arm stroke, but his arm strength limits him to second base and prevents him from playing on the left side of the infield in a utility role. Nick's best attribute is his makeup, which is off the chart. Ticketed for Double-A in 2012, he'll have to continue to overachieve to make it to the big leagues.

Year	Club (League)	Class	AVG	G	AB	R	H	2B	3B	HR	RBI	BB	SO	SB	CS	OBP	SLG
2009	Missoula (PIO)	R	.286	66	273	46	78	18	3	6	35	22	49	16	8	.351	.440
2010	South Bend (MWL)	LoA	.251	128	495	66	124	22	7	7	49	41	97	12	7	.318	.366
2011	Visalia (CAL)	HiA	.300	132	564	99	169	35	5	13	68	30	80	5	5	.342	.449
Minor League Totals			.279	326	1332	211	371	75	15	26	152	93	226	33	20	.335	.416

24 MICHAEL PEREZ, C

BA GRADE

50

EXTREME

Born: Aug. 7, 1992. **B-T:** L-R. **Ht.:** 5-11. **Wt.:** 180. **Drafted:** HS—San Juan, P.R., 2011 (5th round). **Signed by:** Frankie Thon Jr.

A 2011 fifth-round pick who signed for $235,000, Perez attracted the Diamondbacks because he's a lefthanded-hitting catcher with offensive potential. He signed in August and played in just seven pro games last summer, though he smashed a long home run to center field in his first at-bat. Perez has a short, fast stroke that gives him the chance to hit for average with at least average power. If his 10 strikeouts in 23 pro at-bats are any indication, he'll need some time to develop. That's true of his defense as well because Perez is relatively new to catching. He gave up 13 steals and two passed balls in five games behind the plate in the Arizona Fall League. He has solid arm strength but his receiving is still a work in progress. Perez isn't very big, so there are some concerns as to how well he'll be able to handle the workload of a catcher. He's not close to ready for full-season ball and probably will spend 2012 at Missoula.

Year	Club (League)	Class	AVG	G	AB	R	H	2B	3B	HR	RBI	BB	SO	SB	CS	OBP	SLG
2011	Diamondbacks (AZL)	R	.217	7	23	5	5	2	0	2	3	2	10	1	0	.280	.565
Minor League Totals			.217	7	23	5	5	2	0	2	3	2	10	1	0	.280	.565

25 TYLER GREEN, RHP

BA GRADE

45

HIGH

Born: Nov. 24, 1991. **B-T:** R-R. **Ht.:** 6-1. **Wt.:** 185. **Drafted:** HS—Clute, Texas, 2010 (8th round). **Signed by:** Trip Couch.

The Diamondbacks gave Green an above-slot $750,000 bonus just before the 2010 signing deadline, luring him away from a commitment to Texas Christian, where he would have been a two-way player. He didn't pitch in the minors that summer but showed enough in spring training to earn a full-season assignment to low Class A at age 19. He went 2-0, 2.95 in his first nine outings before tailing off, going 4-8, 6.17 in his final 17 starts. Green has a slick, quick arm that generates 87-95 mph fastballs, though he has a tough time throwing them for strikes. His second-best pitch is a fringy 12-to-6 curveball that generates swings and misses when it's on. He also has a slider and changeup, but both are below-average pitches at this point. Green has a deceptive delivery from a higher arm slot and pitches with some effort, costing him some control and command. He can stay in the rotation and possibly become a No. 3 or 4 starter if his secondary pitches develop, though his future may be brighter as a hard-throwing reliever. He'll remain in the rotation this year in high Class A.

Year	Club (League)	Class	W	L	ERA	G	GS	CG	SV	IP	H	HR	BB	SO	K/9	WHIP	AVG
2011	South Bend (MWL)	LoA	6	8	4.97	25	22	0	1	114	118	10	49	79	6.2	1.46	.270
Minor League Totals			6	8	4.97	25	22	0	1	114	118	10	49	79	6.2	1.46	.270

26 JESSE DARRAH, RHP

BA GRADE

45

HIGH

Born: March 28, 1990. **B-T:** L-R. **Ht.:** 6-2. **Wt.:** 190. **Drafted:** Fresno Pacific, 2011 (8th round). **Signed by:** John Bartsch.

After spending his first two college seasons at Sacramento State, Darrah set a Fresno Pacific record for strikeouts (101 in 89 innings) last spring. The Diamondbacks made him the first NAIA pitcher selected in the 2011 draft, grabbing him in the eighth round and signing him for $105,000. He continued to miss bats in his pro debut, averaging 10.3 whiffs per nine innings at Missoula. With a strong body and some effort in his delivery, Darrah throws a 90-94 mph fastball. His best secondary pitch is a changeup that he throws with the same release point and arm speed as his heater. His curveball is a plus pitch at times, and he also has a fringy slider that's really just a variation of his curve that he can throw for strikes more easily. Darrah pitches from a high three-quarters slot and repeats his mechanics well. Arizona believes he was a good value pick in a draft in which they loaded up on arms. He projects as a back-of-the-rotation starter and will make the jump to low Class A in 2012.

Year	Club (League)	Class	W	L	ERA	G	GS	CG	SV	IP	H	HR	BB	SO	K/9	WHIP	AVG
2011	Missoula (PIO)	R	5	2	4.55	14	11	0	0	59	57	5	25	68	10.3	1.38	.252
Minor League Totals			5	2	4.55	14	11	0	0	59	57	5	25	68	10.3	1.38	.252

27 J.R. BRADLEY, RHP

BA GRADE
45
HIGH

Born: June 9, 1992. **B-T:** R-R. **Ht.:** 6-3. **Wt.:** 185. **Drafted:** HS—Nitro, W.Va., 2010 (2nd round). **Signed by:** Shawn Barton.

One of just five West Virginia high school players ever selected in the first two rounds of the draft, Bradley has shown his inexperience and lack of pitchability since signing for $643,500 in 2010. Despite his uneven pro debut, the Diamondbacks assigned him to low Class A at age 18 last year, and he continued to lack consistency. Bradley projects to have an average fastball and currently pitches at 88-92 mph on a downhill plane with nice sink. He developed a changeup last year that could eventually become his best pitch. He throws both a curveball and slider, but neither is special and they often morph into an ineffective slurve. Bradley throws strikes but doesn't always command his stuff, getting into trouble when he elevates his fastball. He has an athletic frame that could put on more weight, which would give his fastball more velocity. Bradley looked like no more than a No. 4 starter last season, but he'll still be just 19 when the 2012 season begins. He may repeat low Class A in an attempt to find him some success.

Year	Club (League)	Class	W	L	ERA	G	GS	CG	SV	IP	H	HR	BB	SO	K/9	WHIP	AVG
2010	Missoula (PIO)	R	1	7	5.93	14	14	0	0	55	66	7	24	40	6.6	1.65	.301
2011	South Bend (MWL)	LoA	6	16	4.98	27	27	1	0	143	169	16	51	88	5.6	1.54	.291
Minor League Totals			7	23	5.24	41	41	1	0	197	235	23	75	128	5.8	1.57	.294

28 BRETT LORIN, RHP

BA GRADE
45
HIGH

Born: March 31, 1987. **B-T:** L-R. **Ht.:** 6-7. **Wt.:** 245. **Drafted:** Long Beach State, 2008 (5th round). **Signed by:** Tim Reynolds (Mariners).

Originally drafted by the Mariners in the fifth round in 2008 and traded a year later to the Pirates as part of a five-player package for Ian Snell and Jack Wilson, Lorin is on the move again after the Diamondbacks took him in the major league phase of the Rule 5 draft in December. After missing the first half of the 2010 season with a hip injury, he bounced back to rank third in ERA (2.84) and WHIP (1.04) in the high Class A Florida State League last year. At 6-foot-7 and 245 pounds, Lorin has the look of a power pitcher but instead is all about finesse. His best attribute is his command of his fastball, which ranges form 87-91 mph and touches 94. He pitches from a low slot and with a long arm action, drawing comparisons to Kameron Loe, but his arm slot keeps him from using his height to generate more velocity. Lorin has good feel for his average changeup, and his slider showed improvement last year. With the pitching depth in the Diamondbacks system, Lorin faces an uphill battle to make the roster out of spring training. If he doesn't, Arizona will have to expose him to waivers and offer him back to Pittsburgh. His best bet is to prove his worth as a long reliever and spot starter. He's effective against righthanders and keeps the ball on the ground, a trait that will help him at hitter-friendly Chase Field.

Year	Club (League)	Class	W	L	ERA	G	GS	CG	SV	IP	H	HR	BB	SO	K/9	WHIP	AVG
2008	Everett (NWL)	SS	1	0	2.82	5	5	0	0	22	17	1	9	29	11.7	1.16	.207
	Wisconsin (MWL)	LoA	0	2	4.80	8	6	0	0	30	30	1	16	32	9.6	1.53	.275
2009	Clinton (MWL)	LoA	5	4	2.44	16	16	0	0	89	61	9	25	87	8.8	0.97	.192
	West Virginia (SAL)	LoA	3	1	1.57	7	7	0	0	34	33	2	10	29	7.6	1.25	.264
2010	Pirates (GCL)	R	0	0	1.29	3	3	0	0	7	1	1	3	10	12.9	0.57	.043
	West Virginia (SAL)	LoA	2	3	5.18	12	9	0	0	42	50	5	9	32	6.9	1.42	.298
2011	Bradenton (FSL)	HiA	7	6	2.84	25	17	1	1	117	103	7	19	99	7.6	1.04	.230
Minor League Totals			18	16	3.03	76	63	1	1	341	295	26	91	318	8.4	1.13	.232

29 JOHN PEDROTTY, LHP

BA GRADE
45
HIGH

Born: Nov. 28, 1989. **B-T:** L-L. **Ht.:** 6-4. **Wt.:** 220. **Drafted:** Holy Cross, 2011 (13th round). **Signed by:** Todd Donovan.

Pedrotty didn't pitch much at Portsmouth (R.I.), where he was a teammate of former Red Sox No. 1 prospect Ryan Westmoreland. After pitching ineffectively in his first two years at Holy Cross, Pedrotty emerged as the top starter for the Crusaders in 2011. The Diamondbacks signed him for $70,000 as a 13th-round pick and were pleasantly surprised with what they saw in his pro debut. Pedrotty has a loose arm and a smooth delivery with some deception. He pounds the strike zone and gets some swings and misses with his sinking 88-92 mph fastball. He has a reliable changeup, and he can locate his fringy curveball and slider where he wants. Pedrotty has a chance to be a back-of-the-rotation starter if his breaking pitches develop. He'll spend his first full pro season in low Class A.

Year	Club (League)	Class	W	L	ERA	G	GS	CG	SV	IP	H	HR	BB	SO	K/9	WHIP	AVG
2011	Yakima (NWL)	SS	2	4	3.04	15	13	0	0	68	61	3	29	70	9.3	1.32	.236
Minor League Totals			2	4	3.04	15	13	0	0	68	61	3	29	70	9.3	1.32	.236

30 SOCRATES BRITO, OF

BA GRADE
50
EXTREME

Born: Sept. 6, 1992. **B-T:** L-L. **Ht.:** 6-2. **Wt.:** 197. **Drafted:** Dominican Republic, 2010. **Signed by:** Junior Noboa.

The Diamondbacks signed Brito out of the Dominican Republic for $190,000 in February 2010, then voided the deal and re-signed him for $90,000 when he failed a steroid test two months later. After serving a 50-game suspension, Brito saw his first pro action in the Rookie-level Dominican Summer League in 2010 before making his U.S. debut last year. His game mentality quickly made him a favorite of coaches and scouts in the Arizona League. Brito, who has drawn comparisons to Garret Anderson, has a rock-solid physique with room to get stronger. He shows a lot of power during batting practice and should have more pop in games once he gets his upper and lower halves working more in sync. Brito has slightly above-average speed and is still refining his basestealing skills. He has played all three outfield spots and probably fits best in right field. He has a strong arm that's still a touch inaccurate. He'll still be only 19 this year, which he'll begin in extended spring training before heading to Missoula or Yakima in June.

Year	Club (League)	Class	AVG	G	AB	R	H	2B	3B	HR	RBI	BB	SO	SB	CS	OBP	SLG
2010	Diamondbacks (DSL)	R	.293	22	82	11	24	4	1	0	8	9	15	0	4	.363	.366
2011	Diamondbacks (AZL)	R	.275	55	236	29	65	3	7	1	29	13	50	18	10	.315	.360
Minor League Totals			.280	77	318	40	89	7	8	1	37	22	65	18	14	.328	.362

Atlanta Braves

BY BILL BALLEW

The Braves have promoted an impressive group of prospects to Atlanta during the past two seasons, resulting in a subtle youth movement that came together earlier than expected. Jason Heyward and Jonny Venters made significant impacts while making their big league debuts in 2010—Heyward won Baseball America's Rookie of the Year Award—before Brandon Beachy, Freddie Freeman and Craig Kimbrel were integral parts of an 89-win season in 2011. Kimbrel and Freeman finished 1-2 in National League rookie of the year voting.

Despite a 9-18 freefall in September that turned what appeared to be a certain wild-card berth into a near miss, the Braves have enough young talent to remain optimistic about the future. Atlanta also received contributions from Randall Delgado and Mike Minor. Top prospects Julio Teheran and Arodys Vizcaino made cameos in the majors, and unheralded farmhands such as Jose Constanza, Cristhian Martinez and Anthony Varvaro also chipped in. Most of them will figure prominently in the club's plans for 2012.

Player development always has been a priority for the Braves and also helped bolster the big league club at the trading deadline. General manager Frank Wren acquired Michael Bourn, who filled holes in center field and atop the lineup, from the Astros in exchange for former top prospect Jordan Schafer and pitchers Juan Abreu, Paul Clemens and Brett Oberholtzer. Wren was adamant about not trading any of his six best prospects and emerged from the process with those pieces intact.

Down on the farm, the Braves provided an example of how development and winning don't go hand in hand at the minor league level. Atlanta's six farm clubs combined for a .469 winning percentage that ranked 27th among the 30 organizations. Rookie-level Danville was the only affiliate to make the playoffs.

In the meantime, individual accomplishments were plentiful. Teheran ranked second in the minors with 15 victories and was named the Triple-A International League's pitcher and rookie of the year. First baseman Joey Terdoslavich's 52 doubles broke a high Class A Carolina League record that had stood for 65 seasons. Shortstop Andrelton Simmons won the CL batting title at .311, while catcher Evan Gattis did the same in the low Class A South Atlantic League with a .322 mark.

In scouting director Tony DeMacio's two years on the job, Atlanta has shifted its draft philosophy. The

DAVID STONER

Brandon Beachy was part of a wave of young arms breaking into Atlanta's rotation

TOP 30 PROSPECTS

1. Julio Teheran, rhp	**16.** Todd Cunningham, of
2. Arodys Vizcaino, rhp	**17.** Kyle Kubitza, 3b
3. Randall Delgado, rhp	**18.** Dimasther Delgado, lhp
4. Andrelton Simmons, ss	**19.** Cody Martin, rhp
5. Sean Gilmartin, lhp	**20.** Navery Moore, rhp
6. Edward Salcedo, 3b/ss	**21.** David Hale, rhp
7. Tyler Pastornicky, ss	**22.** Adam Milligan, of
8. Christian Bethancourt, c	**23.** Mycal Jones, of
9. Zeke Spruill, rhp	**24.** Billy Bullock, rhp
10. Brandon Drury, 3b	**25.** Carlos Perez, lhp
11. Joey Terdoslavich, 1b	**26.** Erik Cordier, rhp
12. J.J. Hoover, rhp	**27.** Evan Gattis, c
13. J.R. Graham, rhp	**28.** Tommy La Stella, 2b
14. Matt Lipka, ss/2b/of	**29.** Cory Gearrin, rhp
15. Nick Ahmed, ss	**30.** Phil Gosselin, 2b

Braves used to focus on younger players and mined talent-rich Georgia as well as any club protected its borders. Now they concentrate primarily on college players who might have lower ceilings but cost less and will move faster through the minors.

Atlanta has spent just $7.6 million on DeMacio's two drafts, which ranks ahead of only the White Sox in bonus spending over the last two years.

Farm director Kurt Kemp resigned on Sept. 1, and Atlanta decided to replace him from within. Assistant GM Bruce Manno will oversee player development, and Kemp's former assistant Ronnie Richardson was promoted to director of minor league operations.

General Manager: Frank Wren. **Farm Director:** Bruce Manno. **Scouting Director:** Tony DeMacio.

Class	Team	League	W	L	Pct	Finish*	Manager(s)
Majors	Atlanta Braves	National	89	73	.549	5th (16)	Fredi Gonzalez
Triple-A	Gwinnett Braves	International	78	65	.545	5th (14)	Dave Brundage
Double-A	Mississippi Braves	Southern	61	79	.436	9th (10)	Rocket Wheeler
High A	Lynchburg Hillcats	Carolina	60	78	.435	8th (8)	R. Albert/L. Salazar
Low A	Rome Braves	South Atlantic	60	80	.429	11th (14)	M. Walbeck/R. Albert
Rookie	Danville Braves	Appalachian	39	29	.574	t-4th (10)	Randy Ingle
Rookie	GCL Braves	Gulf Coast	24	34	.414	12th (15)	Jonathan Schuerholz
Overall 2011 Minor League Record			322	365	.469	27th (30)	

*Finish in overall standings (No. of teams in league). †League champion.

LAST YEAR'S TOP 30

Player, Pos.		Status
1.	Julio Teheran, rhp	No. 1
2.	Freddie Freeman, 1b	Majors
3.	Randall Delgado, rhp	No. 3
4.	Mike Minor, lhp	Majors
5.	Craig Kimbrel, rhp	Majors
6.	Matt Lipka, ss	No. 14
7.	Arodys Vizcaino, rhp	No. 2
8.	Brandon Beachy, rhp	Majors
9.	Brett Oberholtzer, lhp	(Astros)
10.	J.J. Hoover, rhp	No. 12
11.	Carlos Perez, lhp	No. 25
12.	Christian Bethancourt, c	No. 8
13.	Erik Cordier, rhp	No. 26
14.	Tyler Pastornicky, ss	No. 7
15.	Andrelton Simmons, ss	No. 4
16.	Edward Salcedo, ss	No. 6
17.	David Hale, rhp	No. 21
18.	Dimasther Delgado, lhp	No. 18
19.	Mycal Jones, 2b/ss	No. 23
20.	Todd Cunningham, of	No. 16
21.	Elmer Reyes, 2b	Dropped out
22.	Adam Milligan, of	No. 22
23.	Joe Leonard, 3b	Dropped out
24.	David Filak, rhp	Dropped out
25.	Phil Gosselin, 2b	No. 30
26.	Paul Clemens, rhp	(Astros)
27.	Juan Abreu, rhp	(Astros)
28.	Brett Butts, rhp	Dropped out
29.	Cory Harrilchak, of	Dropped out
30.	Richard Sullivan, lhp	Dropped out

BEST TOOLS

Best Hitter for Average	Tyler Pastornicky
Best Power Hitter	Joey Terdoslavich
Best Strike-Zone Discipline	Todd Cunningham
Fastest Baserunner	Matt Lipka
Best Athlete	Matt Lipka
Best Fastball	Julio Teheran
Best Curveball	Arodys Vizcaino
Best Slider	J.J. Hoover
Best Changeup	Julio Teheran
Best Control	Zeke Spruill
Best Defensive Catcher	Christian Bethancourt
Best Defensive Infielder	Andrelton Simmons
Best Infield Arm	Andrelton Simmons
Best Defensive Outfielder	Todd Cunningham
Best Outfield Arm	Cory Harrilchak

PROJECTED 2015 LINEUP

Catcher	Brian McCann
First Base	Freddie Freeman
Second Base	Dan Uggla
Third Base	Edward Salcedo
Shortstop	Andrelton Simmons
Left Field	Joey Terdoslavich
Center Field	Michael Bourn
Right Field	Jason Heyward
No. 1 Starter	Julio Teheran
No. 2 Starter	Tommy Hanson
No. 3 Starter	Mike Minor
No. 4 Starter	Jair Jurrjens
No. 5 Starter	Randall Delgado
Closer	Craig Kimbrel

TOP PROSPECTS OF THE DECADE

Year	Player, Pos.	2011 Org.
2002	Wilson Betemit, ss	Tigers
2003	Adam Wainwright, rhp	Cardinals
2004	Andy Marte, 3b	Pirates
2005	Jeff Francoeur, of	Royals
2006	Jarrod Saltalamacchia, c	Red Sox
2007	Jarrod Saltalamacchia, c	Red Sox
2008	Jordan Schafer, of	Astros
2009	Tommy Hanson, rhp	Braves
2010	Jason Heyward, of	Braves
2011	Julio Teheran, rhp	Braves

TOP DRAFT PICKS OF THE DECADE

Year	Player, Pos.	2011 Org.
2002	Jeff Francoeur, of	Royals
2003	Luis Atilano, rhp (1st round supp.)	Nationals
2004	Eric Campbell, 3b (2nd round)	Reds
2005	Joey Devine, rhp	Athletics
2006	Cody Johnson, of	Yankees
2007	Jason Heyward, of	Braves
2008	Brett DeVall (1st round supp.)	Out of baseball
2009	Mike Minor, lhp	Braves
2010	Matt Lipka, ss	Braves
2011	Sean Gilmartin, lhp	Braves

LARGEST BONUSES IN CLUB HISTORY

Mike Minor, 2009	$2,420,000
Jeff Francoeur, 2002	$2,200,000
Matt Belisle, 1998	$1,750,000
Jason Heyward, 2007	$1,700,000
Edward Salcedo, 2010	$1,600,000

ATLANTA BRAVES

TOP 2012 ROOKIE: Tyler Pastornicky, ss. The lone highlight of the Yunel Escobar trade for the Braves could take over their starting shortstop job.

BREAKOUT PROSPECT: Kyle Kubitza, 3b. The 2011 third-round pick has all the tools scouts want to see in a prototypical third baseman.

SLEEPER: Andy Otero, lhp. After undergoing elbow surgery in 2010 and returning to action last year, the little lefty should be back at full strength in 2011. He flashed a low-90s fastball and plus curve before he got hurt.

SOURCE OF TOP 30 TALENT			
Homegrown	26	Acquired	4
College	13	Trades	4
Junior College	4	Rule 5 draft	0
High school	3	Independent leagues	0
Draft-and-follow	0	Free agents/waivers	0
Nondrafted free agents	0		
International	6		

LF
Adam Milligan (22)
Jose Constanza
Chase Larsson

CF
Matt Lipka (14)
Todd Cunningham (16)
Mycal Jones (23)
Kurt Fleming
Tony Mueller

RF
David Rohm
Cory Harrilchak
Felix Marte

3B
Edward Salcedo (6)
Brandon Drury (10)
Kyle Kubitza (17)
Joe Leonard
Carlos Franco

SS
Andrelton Simmons (4)
Tyler Pastornicky (7)
Nick Ahmed (15)
Brandon Hicks
Ronald Luna
Logan Robbins
Seth Moranda

2B
Tommy La Stella (28)
Phil Gosselin (30)
Elmer Reyes
Jordan Kreke

1B
Joey Terdoslavich (11)
Ernesto Mejia
Jakob Dalfonso
William Beckwith
Chris Garcia
Jackson Laumann

C
Christian Bethancourt (8)
Evan Gattis (27)
Matt Kennelly
Braeden Schlehuber
Nick DeSantiago

LHP

LHSP	LHRP
Sean Gilmartin (5)	Robert Fish
Dimasther Delgado (18)	Ryan Buchter
Carlos Perez (25)	Richard Sullivan
Andy Otero	Luis Avilan
Chris Masters	Chase Shreve
	Matt Chaffee

RHP

RHSP	RHRP
Julio Teheran (1)	J.J. Hoover (12)
Arodys Vizcaino (2)	J.R. Graham (13)
Randall Delgado (3)	Cody Martin (19)
Zeke Spruill (9)	Navery Moore (20)
David Hale (21)	Billy Bullock (24)
Caleb Brewer	Erik Cordier (26)
Todd Redmond	Cory Gearrin (29)
Aaron Northcraft	Jairo Asencio
David Filak	Anthony Varvaro
Lucas LaPoint	Brett Butts
Willie Kempf	Jaye Chapman
Cory Rasmus	Benino Pruneda
	Danilo Alvarez
	Mark Lamm
	Gus Schlosser
	Andrew Wilson
	Jarrett Miller
	John Cornely

2011   BONUSES: $3.7 MILLION

BEST PURE HITTER: After hitting .398 and nearly winning the Big South Conference triple crown in the spring, 2B Tommy La Stella (8) batted .328 in low Class A in his pro debut. If he can stay at second base and avoid a move to the outfield, he could be an everyday player.

BEST POWER HITTER: In terms of raw power, OF Chase Larsson (9), a 6-foot-4, 220-pounder who was the NCAA Division II player of the year and led that level in homers (29), RBIs (84), total bases (190) and slugging (1.000). 3B Kyle Kubitza (3) may have more usable power in the long run, though most of his pop currently goes to the alleys.

FASTEST RUNNER: SS Logan Robbins (10) has 65 speed on the 20-80 scouting scale.

BEST DEFENSIVE PLAYER: SS Nick Ahmed (2) has the range, arm and athleticism desired at his position. He wasn't 100 percent in his debut as he continued to recover from a collapsed lung sustained in a first-base collision in April.

BEST FASTBALL: RHP J.R. Graham (4) is just 6 feet and 175 pounds, but he has a fast arm that delivers fastballs that sit at 95-96 mph and top out at 98.

BEST SECONDARY PITCH: LHP Sean Gilmartin's (1) changeup or RHP Mark Lamm's (6) slider. Gilmartin's changeup helps his 88-91 mph fastball play up and helps him profile as a potential No. 3 starter.

BEST PRO DEBUT: La Stella, who added nine homers and a .944 OPS in low Class A. Graham led the Rookie-level Appalachian League with a 1.72 ERA. RHPs Cody Martin (7) and Gus Schlosser (17) had sub-2.00 ERAs and combined for 14 saves in low Class A.

BEST ATHLETE: OF Chris Bullard (34) played four seasons at linebacker for Western Kentucky's football team. He's raw but offers enticing power and speed.

MOST INTRIGUING BACKGROUND: Unsigned RHP Matt Kimbrel's (32) brother Craig is Atlanta's closer. C Troy Snitker's (19) dad Brian is the Braves' third-base coach, and unsigned 3B Jacoby Almaraz's (40) uncle Johnny is the team's director of international scouting and operations. 1B Jackson Laumann's (31) father Doug is White Sox scouting director.

CLOSEST TO THE MAJORS: As a lefty who can throw three average-or-better pitches for strikes, Gilmartin could move quickly. He excelled in five low Class A starts at the end of the season.

BEST LATE-ROUND PICK: A Tommy John surgery survivor like his former Vanderbilt teammate Lamm, RHP Navery Moore (14) has a lively 92-96 mph fastball. Signability concerns dropped Moore in the draft, and he signed for $400,000.

THE ONE WHO GOT AWAY: LHP Carlos Rodriguez (20), who has a projectable 6-foot-3 frame and an easy delivery, opted for Oregon State over pro ball.

ASSESSMENT: The Braves were one of the more conservative teams in the draft, ranking 24th in bonus spending in 2011. Most of their picks are safe bets to reach their ceilings but lack big upsides.

2010   BONUSES: $3.9 MILLION

SS Andrelton Simmons (2) won the high Class A Carolina League batting title in his first full pro season, and his glovework is more impressive than his bat. Many of the Braves' top position prospects come from this draft, including 2B/SS/OF Matt Lipka (1s), OF Todd Cunningham (2), 1B Joey Terdoslavich (6) and 3B Brandon Drury (13).

GRADE: C+

2009   BONUSES: $4.4 MILLION

LHP Mike Minor (1) reached Atlanta in his first full pro season and nailed down a rotation spot in his second. RHP David Hale (3) and OF Mycal Jones (4) are high-risk, high-reward types.

GRADE: B

2008   BONUSES: $5.1 MILLION

Even without a first-round pick and their top choice (LHP Brett DeVall, 1s) going bust, the Braves scored with RHP Craig Kimbrel (3). RHP Paul Clemens (7) and LHP Brett Oberholtzer (8) helped land Michael Bourn in a trade last July. RHPs Zeke Spruill (2) and J.J. Hoover (10) are two more promising arms from this crop. Signing 3B Anthony Rendon (27), who became the No. 6 overall pick in 2011, would have been a coup.

GRADE: B+

2007   BONUSES: $4.9 MILLION

Despite a horrible sophomore slump, OF Jason Heyward (1) still should be a star. 1B Freddie Freeman (2) should be another lineup mainstay, and SS/3B Brandon Hicks (3) and RHP Cory Gearrin (4) have also gotten big league time. So too has unsigned OF/1B Brandon Belt (11).

GRADE: A

Draft analysis by Jim Callis. Numbers in parentheses indicate draft rounds.

1 JULIO TEHERAN, RHP

Born: Jan. 27, 1991. **B-T:** R-R. **Ht.:** 6-2.
Wt.: 170. **Signed:** Colombia, 2007. **Signed by:**
Miguel Teheran/Carlos Garcia.

No teenage pitcher over the past two decades has sped through the Braves system faster than Teheran. He signed as a 16-year-old out of Colombia in 2007 for $850,000, the largest bonus for an international amateur pitcher that year. The Yankees actually offered him more money, but Atlanta had an edge in that his cousin Miguel was one of the scouts who signed him. Teheran battled shoulder tendinitis during his 2008 pro debut but hasn't slowed down since. He ranked as the No. 1 prospect in the Rookie-level Appalachian League in 2009 and again in the high Class A Carolina League the following year. That success notwithstanding, Teheran put together his best pro season in 2011. He made a pair of emergency starts in Atlanta in mid-May before returning for three appearances in September. In between, he led the Triple-A International League with 15 wins while ranking second in ERA (2.55) and opponent average (.232).

With an electric arm, excellent instincts and maturity beyond his years, Teheran makes pitching look easy. He mixes four pitches to keep hitters off balance and does a good job of getting ahead in the count. A lanky hurler who throws on an impressive downward plane, Teheran works low in the zone and also is capable of getting batters to chase high fastballs. His heater sits at 93-95 mph and touches 97. He commands the pitch to both sides of the plate and isn't afraid to pitch inside. His changeup is nearly as good as his fastball, featuring outstanding depth and fade. He seems to know to throw his changeup when the batter least expects it. Teheran throws two breaking balls—a curveball in the low 80s with late bite, and a slider he uses less frequently—and developing a consistently reliable one is his main need at this point. Otherwise, he just needs to refine a few things, such as his fastball command

BA GRADE
70
LOW

DAVID STONER

SCOUTING GRADES

Fastball: 70. **Command/**
Curveball: 55. **Control:** 60.
Changeup: 65. **Delivery:** 55.

Based on 20-80 scouting scale, where 50 represents major league average, and future projection rather than present tools.

and his pickoff move. The Braves have ironed out his delivery and will continue to monitor his mechanics in order to minimize the violence associated with generating such tremendous power. His pitching coaches rave about Teheran's work ethic, desire to improve and willingness to accept constructive criticism.

Teheran has the ability to become a No. 1 starter. He'll need to add some strength and become a little sharper with all of his pitches in order to attain that status—which is why he may start 2012 back in Triple-A—but the goal is well within reach.

Year	Club (League)	Class	W	L	ERA	G	GS	CG	SV	IP	H	HR	BB	SO	K/9	WHIP	AVG
2008	Danville (APP)	R	1	2	6.60	6	6	0	0	15	18	2	4	17	10.2	1.47	.305
2009	Danville (APP)	R	2	1	2.68	7	7	0	0	44	36	2	7	39	8.0	0.98	.229
	Rome (SAL)	LoA	1	3	4.78	7	7	0	0	38	42	2	11	28	6.7	1.41	.288
2010	Rome (SAL)	LoA	2	2	1.14	7	7	0	0	39	23	1	10	45	10.3	0.84	.168
	Myrtle Beach (CAR)	HiA	4	4	2.98	10	10	0	0	63	56	6	13	76	10.8	1.09	.233
	Mississippi (SL)	AA	3	2	3.38	7	7	0	0	40	29	2	17	38	8.6	1.15	.204
2011	Gwinnett (IL)	AAA	15	3	2.55	25	24	0	0	145	123	5	48	122	7.6	1.18	.232
	Atlanta (NL)	MAJ	1	1	5.03	5	3	0	0	20	21	4	8	10	4.6	1.47	.276
Major League Totals			1	1	5.03	5	3	0	0	20	21	4	8	10	4.6	1.47	.276
Minor League Totals			28	17	2.96	69	68	0	0	384	327	20	110	365	8.6	1.14	.232

2 ARODYS VIZCAINO, RHP

Born: Nov. 13, 1990. **B-T:** R-R. **Ht.:** 6-0. **Wt.:** 190. **Signed:** Dominican Republic, 2007. **Signed by:** Alfredo Dominguez (Yankees).

Acquired from the Yankees in the December 2009 deal that sent Javier Vazquez to New York, Vizcaino partially tore an elbow ligament in his first season in the Braves system but put that behind him in 2011. He appeared in the Futures Game while rising from high Class A Lynchburg to Atlanta, moving from the rotation to the bullpen when he got to Triple-A Gwinnett. Vizcaino's fastball sits at 93-95 mph and touches 97. He also has sharp-breaking curveball that's a plus pitch but he tends to fall in love with it too much. He made impressive strides with his changeup in 2011 to give him three solid offerings. He does an excellent job of challenging hitters when he's behind in the count but needs to improve his fastball command in order to stay ahead. Given the way he responded to relieving as well as the depth of starters in Atlanta, Vizcaino could remain in the bullpen. At the same time, a potential No. 2 or 3 starter is a prized commodity. One way or the other, he'll take a prominent role with the Braves as he gains experience.

BA GRADE

60

MEDIUM

Year	Club (League)	Class	W	L	ERA	G	GS	CG	SV	IP	H	HR	BB	SO	K/9	WHIP	AVG
2008	Yankees (GCL)	R	3	2	3.68	12	6	0	0	44	38	5	13	48	9.8	1.16	.222
2009	Staten Island (NYP)	SS	2	4	2.13	10	10	0	0	42	34	2	15	52	11.1	1.16	.211
2010	Myrtle Beach (CAR)	HiA	0	0	4.61	3	3	0	0	14	16	1	3	11	7.2	1.39	.296
	Rome (SAL)	LoA	9	4	2.39	14	14	0	0	72	63	1	9	68	8.5	1.00	.229
2011	Lynchburg (CAR)	HiA	2	2	2.45	9	9	0	0	40	31	3	10	37	8.3	1.02	.207
	Mississippi (SL)	AA	2	3	3.81	11	8	0	0	50	44	3	18	55	10.0	1.25	.234
	Gwinnett (IL)	AAA	1	0	1.29	6	0	0	0	7	7	1	0	8	10.3	1.00	.259
	Atlanta (NL)	MAJ	1	1	4.67	17	0	0	0	17	16	1	9	17	8.8	1.44	.239
Major League Totals			1	1	4.67	17	0	0	0	17	16	1	9	17	8.8	1.44	.239
Minor League Totals			19	15	2.91	65	50	0	0	269	233	16	68	279	9.3	1.12	.227

3 RANDALL DELGADO, RHP

Born: Feb. 9, 1990. **B-T:** R-R. **Ht.:** 6-3. **Wt.:** 200. **Signed:** Panama, 2006. **Signed by:** Luis Ortiz.

Delgado was an unsung hero in Atlanta's unsuccessful playoff drive. After making a pair of emergency starts early in the year, he allowed a total of seven earned runs in five September starts. Unheralded when he signed at age 16 out of Panama, he has progressed faster than expected because his maturity and coachability allow him to make quick adjustments. Delgado maintain a 92-94 mph fastball but struggles at times to command the pitch. His best offering is a plus curveball with sharp downward bite, and he also has a solid changeup. He has a smooth, quick delivery and does a good job of using the same arm speed with all of his pitches. Delgado tends to lose some deception when his arm action gets long. Despite his strong frame, he doesn't have an abundance of athleticism and doesn't handle the bat well, particularly in terms of bunting. The Braves believe Delgado is ready to join the back of their rotation to open the 2012 season, though spending some more time in Triple-A to hone his fastball command could be beneficial as well. He profiles as an eventual No. 3 starter with a ceiling of a No. 2.

BA GRADE

60

MEDIUM

Year	Club (League)	Class	W	L	ERA	G	GS	CG	SV	IP	H	HR	BB	SO	K/9	WHIP	AVG
2007	Braves (DSL)	R	1	2	2.00	11	10	0	0	45	34	2	12	50	10.0	1.02	.213
2008	Danville (APP)	R	3	8	3.13	14	14	0	0	69	63	5	30	81	10.6	1.35	.249
2009	Rome (SAL)	LoA	5	10	4.35	25	25	1	0	124	123	9	49	141	10.2	1.39	.256
2010	Myrtle Beach (CAR)	HiA	4	7	2.76	20	20	0	0	117	89	7	32	120	9.2	1.03	.210
	Mississippi (SL)	AA	3	5	4.74	8	8	0	0	44	36	2	20	42	8.7	1.28	.222
2011	Mississippi (SL)	AA	5	5	3.84	21	21	2	0	117	116	11	46	110	8.4	1.38	.258
	Gwinnett (IL)	AAA	2	2	4.15	4	4	0	0	22	19	4	11	25	10.4	1.38	.238
	Atlanta (NL)	MAJ	1	1	2.83	7	7	0	0	35	29	5	14	18	4.6	1.23	.220
Major League Totals			1	1	2.83	7	7	0	0	35	29	5	14	18	4.6	1.23	.220
Minor League Totals			23	39	3.56	103	102	3	0	538	480	40	200	569	9.5	1.26	.239

4 ANDRELTON SIMMONS, SS

Born: Sept. 4, 1989. **B-T:** R-R. **Ht.:** 6-2. **Wt.:** 170. **Drafted:** Western Oklahoma State JC, 2010 (2nd round). **Signed by:** Gerald Turner.

Western Oklahoma State JC head coach Kurt Russell discovered Simmons in Curacao, and several clubs were interested in him as a pitcher after seeing his fastball hit 98 mph in his lone juco season. Atlanta granted his wish to play shortstop, and he responded by winning the Carolina League batting title (.311) in 2011. Managers rated him as the circuit's top defensive shortstop, best infield arm and most exciting player. Simmons is a premier defender with a cannon for an arm and soft, quick hands. He covers lots of real estate with his quickness, ability to charge the ball and feel for the position. He committed careless errors by trying to make every play early in 2011 but improved in that regard. An aggressive hitter, Simmons knows the strike zone but doesn't walk much. He has bat speed and can turn on fastballs, but he won't have more than gap power. An average runner, he needs to improve his reads and jumps after getting thrown out 18 times in 44 steal attempts. Simmons will open 2012 in Double-A Mississippi, and more than few observers believe he already can play defense at a major league level. Tyler Pastornicky may get the first crack at the Braves' shortstop job, but Simmons is their shortstop of the future.

BA GRADE
55
MEDIUM

Year	Club (League)	Class	AVG	G	AB	R	H	2B	3B	HR	RBI	BB	SO	SB	CS	OBP	SLG
2010	Danville (APP)	R	.276	62	239	36	66	11	1	2	26	16	14	18	4	.340	.356
2011	Lynchburg (CAR)	HiA	.311	131	517	69	161	35	6	1	52	29	43	26	18	.351	.408
Minor League Totals			.300	193	756	105	227	46	7	3	78	45	57	44	22	.347	.392

5 SEAN GILMARTIN, LHP

Born: May 8, 1990. **B-T:** L-L. **Ht.:** 6-2. **Wt.:** 195. **Drafted:** Florida State, 2011 (1st round). **Signed by:** Hugh Buchanan.

The Braves took Gilmartin with the 28th overall pick in the 2011 draft, marking the second time in three years they went with an advanced college lefthander in the first round. He has drawn comparisons to Mike Minor, taken seventh overall by Atlanta in 2009. Signed for $1,134,000, Gilmartin had no problem handling low Class A hitters in his brief pro debut. Gilmartin has a clean arm action and above-average athleticism. A two-way player at Florida State, he throws an 88-91 mph fastball with good life and a solid slider. His best pitch is a plus changeup, and he knows how to set up hitters while mixing all of his offerings. While he won't get many swings and misses against advanced hitters, Gilmartin is an efficient hurler who records lots of groundouts. He fields his position well and can swing the bat. An eventual No. 3 starter, Gilmartin has the polish to move as quickly as the Braves need. They sent him to the Arizona Fall League and will ship him to Double-A Mississippi to begin his first full pro season. He may not need much more than a year in the minors.

BA GRADE
55
MEDIUM

BILL SETLIFF

Year	Club (League)	Class	W	L	ERA	G	GS	CG	SV	IP	H	HR	BB	SO	K/9	WHIP	AVG
2011	Braves (GCL)	R	0	1	9.00	1	1	0	0	2	3	0	0	1	4.5	1.50	.333
	Rome (SAL)	LoA	2	1	2.53	5	5	0	0	21	18	3	2	30	12.7	0.94	.217
Minor League Totals			2	2	3.09	6	6	0	0	23	21	3	2	31	12.0	0.99	.228

6 EDWARD SALCEDO, 3B/SS

Born: July 30, 1991. **B-T:** R-R. **Ht.:** 6-3. **Wt.:** 205. **Signed:** Dominican Republic, 2010. **Signed by:** Roberto Aquino.

Salcedo was a hot prospect on the international market in 2007, but he lost two years while MLB investigated his identity and birthdate. He finally signed for in February 2010 for $1.6 million, a franchise record for a foreign amateur. He has spent most of his career struggling at low Class A Rome, but he has shown improvement and his natural ability has begun to emerge. Salcedo has above-average power potential, thanks to his quick bat and smooth stroke. Tremendously raw when he signed, he showed a more advanced approach and greater knowledge of the strike zone in 2011. He's a below-average runner, so his move from shortstop to third base was inevitable. Salcedo has the arm strength and agility for the hot corner, but he makes too many errors (40 in 100 games at third) by trying to force plays. Scouts are mixed on whether he should remain on the dirt or move to an outfield corner. Salcedo could move faster now that he has started to build a solid foundation. He'll move up to high Class A in 2012 and could reach Double-A Mississippi in the second half, though he doesn't figure to be big league-ready before 2014.

BA GRADE
55
HIGH

Year	Club (League)	Class	AVG	G	AB	R	H	2B	3B	HR	RBI	BB	SO	SB	CS	OBP	SLG
2010	Braves (DSL)	R	.297	23	74	16	22	5	1	1	11	18	19	8	1	.453	.432
	Rome (SAL)	LoA	.197	54	193	23	38	5	4	2	16	11	56	6	5	.239	.295
2011	Rome (SAL)	LoA	.248	132	508	83	126	27	6	12	68	41	105	23	10	.315	.396
Minor League Totals			.240	209	775	122	186	37	11	15	95	70	180	37	16	.312	.374

7 TYLER PASTORNICKY, SS

BA GRADE

50

LOW

Born: Dec. 13, 1989. **B-T:** R-R. **Ht.:** 5-11. **Wt.:** 170. **Drafted:** HS—Bradenton, Fla., 2008 (5th round). **Signed by:** Joel Grampietro (Blue Jays).

Swapping Yunel Escobar for Alex Gonzalez hasn't worked out as the Braves hoped, but they did get Pastornicky as part of the July 2010 trade with the Blue Jays. The son of former big leaguer Cliff Pastornicky, he blossomed in all phases of the game in 2011 and would have made his major league debut if not for a high ankle sprain in mid-August. Pastornicky competes as well as anyone in the system and has excellent instincts. He has a good feel for hitting and makes consistent line-drive contact, though he could stand to draw a few more walks. He doesn't have a lot of strength, but he has a quick bat and could develop some gap power. Pastornicky has plus speed and the aptitude to steal bases. He has above-average range at shortstop, and he could get more out of his average arm with a more consistent arm slot. Pastornicky has proven to be better than Atlanta expected and now is knocking on the door to the big leagues. With Gonzalez gone after signing as a free agent with the Brewers, Pastornicky is clearly the best in-house option to replace him.

Year	Club (League)	Class	AVG	G	AB	R	H	2B	3B	HR	RBI	BB	SO	SB	CS	OBP	SLG
2008	Blue Jays (GCL)	R	.263	50	160	32	42	6	3	1	17	21	21	27	5	.349	.356
2009	Lansing (MWL)	LoA	.269	109	413	63	111	11	9	1	31	39	50	51	15	.336	.346
	Dunedin (FSL)	HiA	.270	15	63	9	17	3	0	0	3	3	7	6	3	.303	.317
2010	Dunedin (FSL)	HiA	.258	77	287	50	74	16	0	6	35	39	49	24	7	.348	.376
	Mississippi (SL)	AA	.254	38	134	22	34	5	2	2	15	16	22	11	2	.333	.366
2011	Mississippi (SL)	AA	.299	90	355	50	106	13	5	6	36	24	34	20	8	.345	.414
	Gwinnett (IL)	AAA	.365	27	104	15	38	2	0	1	9	8	11	7	3	.407	.413
Minor League Totals			.278	406	1516	241	422	56	19	17	146	150	194	146	43	.345	.374

8 CHRISTIAN BETHANCOURT, C

BA GRADE

55

HIGH

Born: Sept. 2, 1991. **B-T:** R-R. **Ht.:** 6-2. **Wt.:** 195. **Signed:** Panama, 2008. **Signed by:** Luis Ortiz.

Scouts have been enthralled with Bethancourt's potential since he played in the 2004 Little League World Series for Panama. Four years later, he signed with Atlanta for $600,000. His lack of maturity and consistency has been frustrating at times, but he's a rare catching prospect with all-around potential. No one questions Bethancourt's raw tools. He has soft hands, plus arm strength and a quick release that helped him throw out 38 percent of basestealers in 2011. He also possesses good hand-eye coordination, makes consistent contact and shows solid raw power. He also runs well for a catcher. However, several scouts question Bethancourt's approach at the plate and behind it. He's a free swinger who rarely walks and wastes too many at-bats. Defensively, he often picks at pitches in the dirt instead of shifting his body. His body language and lack of fire at times also leave a lot to be desired. Bethancourt is still just 20, so he has time to develop. The Braves challenged him to show improvement in 2011 and he responded impressively. If he continues to work hard and hone his skills, he can become a big league starter and perhaps an all-star. He should spend the majority of 2012 in Double-A.

Year	Club (League)	Class	AVG	G	AB	R	H	2B	3B	HR	RBI	BB	SO	SB	CS	OBP	SLG
2008	Braves (DSL)	R	.267	34	116	12	31	6	3	0	17	11	25	1	0	.328	.371
2009	Braves (GCL)	R	.284	32	116	22	33	9	1	2	19	11	22	7	0	.344	.431
	Danville (APP)	R	.260	14	50	10	13	5	0	2	8	6	16	1	1	.339	.480
2010	Rome (SAL)	LoA	.251	108	399	31	100	19	2	3	34	14	62	11	3	.276	.331
2011	Rome (SAL)	LoA	.303	54	221	25	67	10	3	4	33	8	27	6	3	.323	.430
	Lynchburg (CAR)	HiA	.271	45	166	11	45	6	0	1	20	3	35	3	2	.277	.325
Minor League Totals			.271	287	1068	111	289	55	9	12	131	53	187	29	9	.303	.373

9 ZEKE SPRUILL, RHP

Born: Sept. 11, 1989. **B-T:** B-R. **Ht.:** 6-4. **Wt.:** 185. **Drafted:** HS—Marietta, Ga., 2008 (2nd round). **Signed by:** Brian Bridges.

After missing time because of off-field issues in 2009 and a broken right hand (the result of punching a dugout wall) in 2010, Spruill finally put together the full season the Braves hoped for in 2011. He led the minors with six complete games and ranked third with 175 innings, and he also topped the Carolina League with a 1.01 WHIP. Spruill found success by pounding the bottom of the strike zone with his sinking 91-94 mph fastball, pitching to contact and not worrying about strikeouts. He uses his fastball command to get ahead in the count, then mixes in his secondary pitches to keep hitters off balance. Spruill's solid changeup also has good sink and he throws it with the same arm action he employs with his fastball. His slider has been inconsistent but shows impressive tilt and movement when he's throwing it well. He gets in trouble when he leaves his pitches up in the zone. In danger of becoming a forgotten prospect before his breakout season, Spruill will return to Double-A to open 2012. If he continues on this path, he can become a workhorse No. 3 or 4 starter in the big leagues.

BA GRADE
50
MEDIUM

Year	Club (League)	Class	W	L	ERA	G	GS	CG	SV	IP	H	HR	BB	SO	K/9	WHIP	AVG
2008	Braves (GCL)	R	7	0	2.93	10	3	0	0	40	42	1	8	32	7.2	1.25	.268
2009	Braves (GCL)	R	1	0	4.58	4	4	0	0	20	24	2	5	23	10.5	1.47	.289
	Rome (SAL)	LoA	8	6	3.03	20	19	0	1	116	120	9	24	95	7.4	1.24	.261
2010	Braves (GCL)	R	0	0	3.00	2	2	0	0	3	4	0	1	1	3.0	1.67	.333
	Myrtle Beach (CAR)	HiA	3	5	5.54	14	13	1	0	65	83	4	13	41	5.7	1.48	.310
2011	Lynchburg (CAR)	HiA	7	9	3.19	20	20	5	0	130	108	7	23	92	6.4	1.01	.227
	Mississippi (SL)	AA	3	2	3.20	7	7	1	0	45	45	3	17	16	3.2	1.38	.266
Minor League Totals			29	22	3.55	77	68	7	1	418	426	26	91	300	6.5	1.24	.262

10 BRANDON DRURY, 3B

Born: Aug. 21, 1992. **B-T:** R-R. **Ht.:** 6-2. **Wt.:** 190. **Drafted:** HS—Grants Pass, Ore., 2010 (13th round). **Signed by:** Brett Evert.

Oregon's top high school position player in the 2010 draft, Drury signed for $85,000 as a 13th-rounder but hit just .198/.248/.292 in his pro debut. He looked like a different hitter in 2011, leading the Appalachian League with 92 hits and falling .0003 shy of the batting title. Drury employs a compact stroke while keeping his hands back and generating above-average bat speed. He excels at making contact—almost to a fault because he walked just six times in 63 games in 2011—and does a nice job of using the entire field. He gets good carry on his hits because of the backspin he generates, and his doubles could turn into homers as he adds more strength and experience. A shortstop in high school, Drury has made a smooth adjustment to third base. He displays average range with solid arm strength and good instincts at the hot corner. The only thing he doesn't do well is run, as he possesses below-average speed. His work ethic and makeup are considered major assets. Edward Salcedo is his competition to be Atlanta's third baseman of the future, and Drury may eventually win out because he's the better defender. He'll get his first taste of full-season ball at Rome in 2012.

BA GRADE
55
HIGH

Year	Club (League)	Class	AVG	G	AB	R	H	2B	3B	HR	RBI	BB	SO	SB	CS	OBP	SLG
2010	Braves (GCL)	R	.198	52	192	20	38	7	1	3	17	9	50	2	2	.248	.292
2011	Danville (APP)	R	.347	63	265	40	92	23	0	8	54	6	35	3	0	.367	.525
Minor League Totals			.284	115	457	60	130	30	1	11	71	15	85	5	2	.316	.427

11 JOEY TERDOSLAVICH, 1B

BA GRADE
50
MEDIUM

Born: Sept. 9, 1988. **B-T:** B-R. **Ht.:** 6-1. **Wt.:** 200. **Drafted:** Long Beach State, 2010 (6th round). **Signed by:** Brian Hunter.

The nephew of former all-star Mike Greenwell, Terdoslavich was born to hit. In 2011, his first full pro season, he broke a 65-year-old Carolina League record with 52 doubles. He also paced the circuit in extra-base hits (74) while ranking second in total bases (254), third in batting (.286) and homers (20) and fourth in RBIs (82). The Braves named him their minor league player of the year. A switch-hitter, Terdoslavich is aggressive from both sides of the plate with an uppercut swing and a high finish that generates impressive backspin. He doesn't strike out excessively for a power hitter and could hit in the neighborhood of .270 with 20 or more homers per year. Terdoslavich has yet to find a defensive home after splitting time between first and third base in his pro debut and playing almost exclusively at first last year. He saw some time in left field during instructional league but has below-average speed and just average arm strength. Atlanta officials are intrigued with Terdoslavich's offensive potential and are interested to see how he fares in Double-A this year.

Year	Club (League)	Class	AVG	G	AB	R	H	2B	3B	HR	RBI	BB	SO	SB	CS	OBP	SLG
2010	Danville (APP)	R	.296	49	189	27	56	10	2	2	24	15	27	3	3	.351	.402
	Rome (SAL)	LoA	.316	21	79	7	25	9	0	0	10	5	18	0	0	.365	.430
2011	Lynchburg (CAR)	HiA	.286	131	483	72	138	52	2	20	82	41	107	2	0	.341	.526
Minor League Totals			.292	201	751	106	219	71	4	22	116	61	152	5	3	.346	.485

12 J.J. HOOVER, RHP

BA GRADE
50
MEDIUM

Born: Aug. 13, 1987. **B-T:** R-R. **Ht.:** 6-3. **Wt.:** 215. **Drafted:** Calhoun (Ala.) CC, 2008 (10th round). **Signed by:** Brian Bridges.

Hoover progressed nicely as a starter in his first three-plus seasons in the minors, and he posted a 2.84 ERA and 65 strikeouts in 67 innings in the Mississippi rotation at the outset of 2011. But he also got bombed in a pair of starts at Gwinnett in mid-May, and a month later the Braves moved him to the bullpen. He took to the switch, compiling a 0.77 ERA and 47 strikeouts in 35 relief innings between the two clubs. A burly hurler with a thick and strong lower body, Hoover has workhorse capability as a starter and an aggressive approach as a reliever. His fastball sits at 88-92 mph when he starts and picks up 2-3 mph when he relieves. His heater has decent movement, though it flattens out and becomes hittable when he doesn't stay on top of it. His low-80s slider has good deception and complements his fastball well. He improved the depth and fade of his changeup last season but rarely threw it when he worked out of the bullpen. Scouts consider Hoover a below-average athlete with a maxed-out body. He tried hard to force Atlanta's hand with his strong performance, hoping it would result in a September callup, but instead received a trip to the Arizona Fall League to continue making the transition to relieving. His likely ceiling is as a No. 4 starter or a seventh-inning reliever. After getting added to Atlanta's 40-man roster in November, he'll likely open 2012 in Triple-A and make his major league debut at some point during the campaign.

Year	Club (League)	Class	W	L	ERA	G	GS	CG	SV	IP	H	HR	BB	SO	K/9	WHIP	AVG
2008	Danville (APP)	R	1	0	0.00	2	0	0	0	5	4	0	1	6	11.6	1.07	.235
2009	Myrtle Beach (CAR)	HiA	0	0	9.00	1	1	0	0	3	3	1	5	2	6.0	2.67	.250
	Rome (SAL)	LoA	7	6	3.35	25	18	0	1	134	135	9	25	148	9.9	1.19	.259
2010	Myrtle Beach (CAR)	HiA	11	6	3.26	24	24	0	0	133	126	7	35	118	8.0	1.21	.245
	Mississippi (SL)	AA	3	1	3.48	4	4	0	0	21	15	1	15	34	14.8	1.45	.203
2011	Mississippi (SL)	AA	2	5	2.48	31	12	0	1	87	65	5	28	86	8.9	1.07	.206
	Gwinnett (IL)	AAA	1	1	3.38	12	2	0	1	19	12	0	12	31	14.9	1.29	.174
Minor League Totals			25	19	3.14	99	61	0	3	401	360	23	121	425	9.5	1.20	.236

13 J.R. GRAHAM, RHP

BA GRADE
50
HIGH

Born: Jan. 14, 1990. **B-T:** R-R. **Ht.:** 6-0. **Wt.:** 185. **Drafted:** Santa Clara, 2011 (4th round). **Signed by:** Tom Davis.

Graham made the most of his three-year stint at Santa Clara, going from being an Angels 46th-round pick out of high school to a Braves fourth-rounder in June. Initially a two-way player for the Broncos, he focused on pitching in the second half of his college career. He made his first college start midway through his final season, then moved seamlessly into that role in pro ball after signing for $174,600. He led the Appalachian League with a 1.72 ERA, ranked second with a 1.13 WHIP and didn't allow a homer in 58 innings. A bulldog on the mound who overcame being born three months premature as a two-pound baby, Graham doesn't have classic size for a righthander and concerns some scouts with the limited downward angle on his pitches. At the same time, his strong core and quick-twitch athleticism help generate a hard, moving fastball. He sits at 92-95 mph as a starter, working at 95-96 and topping out at 98 as a reliever. He overpowered Rookie-level hitters, getting them to chase his four-seam heat up in the zone. Graham throws a solid slider with good lateral movement at 82-85 mph. He needs more depth on his below-average changeup, which is too firm and unlikely to fool many hitters at higher levels. After putting together an impressive pro debut, Graham will open the 2012 season in Rome's rotation in order to get him some innings. The bullpen is likely his long-term destination, and he'll have closer stuff if he can improve his slider.

Year	Club (League)	Class	W	L	ERA	G	GS	CG	SV	IP	H	HR	BB	SO	K/9	WHIP	AVG
2011	Danville (APP)	R	5	2	1.72	13	8	0	0	58	52	0	13	52	8.1	1.13	.245
Minor League Totals			5	2	1.72	13	8	0	0	58	52	0	13	52	8.1	1.13	.245

14 MATT LIPKA, SS/2B/OF

BA GRADE
50
HIGH

Born: April 15, 1992. **B-T:** R-R. **Ht.:** 6-1. **Wt.:** 200. **Drafted:** HS—McKinney, Texas, 2010 (1st round supplemental). **Signed by:** Gerald Turner.

The Braves have gone heavy with college players during their first two drafts with scouting director Tony DeMacio. The lone early-round exception is Lipka, who was taken with the 35th overall pick in 2010 and signed for $800,000 after turning down a baseball scholarship to Alabama and numerous opportunities to play college football as a wide receiver. Despite possessing plus speed with tremendous work ethic and makeup, Lipka struggled in his first full pro season. After earning all-star honors in the Rookie-level Gulf Coast League in 2010, he showed a limited ability to drive the ball in low Class A. With a bottom hand-dominant swing, he didn't record an extra-base hit until the 37th game of the season and homered only once all year. Lipka has a defensive approach at the plate and needs to do a better job of employing his plus-plus speed by becoming more adept at small ball, such as dropping down bunts and working counts for walks. He also could do a better job of using the entire field. He's still learning to read pitchers after getting caught 14 times in 42 steal attempts last year. As a defender, Lipka offers good range and solid arm strength but awkward actions at shortstop and an unusual throwing motion. He also saw time at second base in 2011, and since drafting him Atlanta has suggested he could wind up in center field, where he spent most of his time in instructional league. A new defensive home could take some of the pressure off Lipka, who seemed to be constantly trying to prove he should stay at shortstop last year. He'll probably move up to high Class A in 2012.

Year	Club (League)	Class	AVG	G	AB	R	H	2B	3B	HR	RBI	BB	SO	SB	CS	OBP	SLG
2010	Braves (GCL)	R	.302	48	192	33	58	8	4	1	24	14	22	20	3	.357	.401
	Danville (APP)	R	.125	4	16	1	2	0	0	0	1	1	2	1	0	.176	.125
2011	Rome (SAL)	LoA	.247	127	530	78	131	21	3	1	37	42	83	28	14	.305	.304
Minor League Totals			.259	179	738	112	191	29	7	2	62	57	107	49	17	.316	.325

15 NICK AHMED, SS

BA GRADE
50
HIGH

Born: March 15, 1990. **B-T:** R-R. **Ht.:** 6-3. **Wt.:** 205. **Drafted:** Connecticut, 2011 (2nd round). **Signed by:** Kevin Barry.

The fifth college shortstop taken in the 2011 draft, Ahmed went 85th overall and signed for $417,600. He attracted attention thanks in part to Connecticut teammates George Springer and Matt Barnes, both first-round selections, but also added impressive size and strength last offseason thanks to physical maturation and dedication in the weight room. A high-energy player, Ahmed showed his toughness last spring by returning quickly from a collapsed lung he suffered during a collision at first base. He's a good athlete with plus arm strength and a quick release that generated 91-94 mph heat as a reliever during his sophomore season at UConn. A smart defender with solid range, he positions himself well with his quick feet and ability to read hops. While he makes most of the routine plays, he doesn't possess the smoothest infield actions and looks awkward on occasion. Offensively, he manages the strike zone well, generates walks and has solid speed. He doesn't drive the ball consistently and can struggle against quality fastballs. Ahmed has a chance to be a regular at shortstop but may profile better as a utility player. He'll open his first full pro season in low Class A.

Year	Club (League)	Class	AVG	G	AB	R	H	2B	3B	HR	RBI	BB	SO	SB	CS	OBP	SLG
2011	Danville (APP)	R	.262	59	248	46	65	13	2	4	24	30	46	18	6	.346	.379
Minor League Totals			.262	59	248	46	65	13	2	4	24	30	46	18	6	.346	.379

16 TODD CUNNINGHAM, OF

BA GRADE
45
MEDIUM

Born: March 20, 1989. **B-T:** B-R. **Ht.:** 6-0. **Wt.:** 200. **Drafted:** Jacksonville State, 2010 (2nd round). **Signed by:** Brian Bridges.

The Braves used the 53rd overall pick in the 2010 draft on Cunningham, more specifically his bat. He won batting titles in the summer Texas Collegiate (.310) and Cape Cod (.378) leagues before batting .359 as a Jacksonville State junior. He hasn't delivered as much offense in pro ball, though he did go straight to low Class A after signing and was bothered by a strained right elbow in 2011. Club officials were encouraged by his performance in the Arizona Fall League and still believe he can become an impact player. Cunningham has a smooth, compact stroke from both sides of the plate. He produces line drives and does an excellent job of using the middle of the field. He excels at making contact and has strong hands, but he doesn't have much power. He profiles as a leadoff hitter but will need to draw more walks to fit that role. He has the above-average speed desired at the top of a lineup, but he's still learning to read pitches and steal bases.

Cunningham has good instincts in center field, where he shows plus range and good first-step quickness. He has below-average arm strength, though the accuracy of his throws helps overcome their lack of carry. The Braves are likely to challenge Cunningham by putting him in Double-A to open this season, believing he could blossom provided he remains healthy throughout the campaign.

Year	Club (League)	Class	AVG	G	AB	R	H	2B	3B	HR	RBI	BB	SO	SB	CS	OBP	SLG
2010	Rome (SAL)	LoA	.260	65	231	32	60	9	3	1	20	14	30	7	4	.341	.338
2011	Braves (GCL)	R	.182	4	11	2	2	0	1	0	4	1	5	1	0	.286	.364
	Lynchburg (CAR)	HiA	.257	87	334	59	86	12	4	4	20	33	47	14	6	.348	.353
Minor League Totals			.257	156	576	93	148	21	8	5	44	48	82	22	10	.344	.347

17 KYLE KUBITZA, 3B

BA GRADE
50
HIGH

Born: July 15, 1990. **B-T:** L-R. **Ht.:** 6-3. **Wt.:** 190. **Drafted:** Texas State, 2011 (3rd round). **Signed by:** John Barron.

The highest-drafted position player and third-highest overall pick in Texas State history, Kubitza went in the third round last June and signed for $261,000. He left school as the Bobcats' career leader in walks (125) while ranking second all-time in homers (27), and his patience and power were evident in his pro debut. Kubitza understands the strike zone and uses that knowledge to get in hitter's counts. He possesses a line-drive stroke and drives balls to the alleys, and he could have average or better home run power once he adds some loft to his swing and turns on more pitches. He tends to tinker with his stance, but club officials believe he'll settle down as his comfort level increases. Kubitza runs well for his size and has good instincts on the bases. With soft hands, solid arm strength and good footwork, he has the tools to get the job done at third base but lacks consistency. He should start 2012 in low Class A and could finish the year in high Class A.

Year	Club (League)	Class	AVG	G	AB	R	H	2B	3B	HR	RBI	BB	SO	SB	CS	OBP	SLG
2011	Danville (APP)	R	.321	44	162	36	52	16	3	1	34	24	38	9	3	.407	.475
Minor League Totals			.321	44	162	36	52	16	3	1	34	24	38	9	3	.407	.475

18 DIMASTHER DELGADO, LHP

BA GRADE
50
HIGH

Born: March 9, 1989. **B-T:** L-L. **Ht.:** 6-2. **Wt.:** 180. **Signed:** Panama, 2007. **Signed by:** Luis Ortiz.

Delgado put together an impressive comeback that went underreported in 2011. He missed all of the previous season after he was involved in an automobile accident in his native Panama, resulting in a broken femur in his right leg, a torn ligament in his right knee and a broken left hand. He spent most of 2011 in the Lynchburg rotation and got stronger as the season progressed, going 5-2, 2.98 in the second half. Delgado's strength is his overall feel for pitching. He keeps hitters off balance by mixing a low-90s fastball, above-average changeup and a slow curveball. He employs a pronounced overhand delivery that gives him good leverage and movement on his pitches while creating good deception against left-handers, who batted just .204 against him last year. Delgado commands both sides of the plate with his fastball and isn't afraid to pitch inside. He has one of the better changeups in the organization, and his curveball is effective as long as he doesn't hang it. His control was unusually shaky in 2011, though it got better as the season progressed. A good all-around athlete who fields his position well, Delgado could become a middle-of-the-rotation starter. He'll move up to Double-A this year.

Year	Club (League)	Class	W	L	ERA	G	GS	CG	SV	IP	H	HR	BB	SO	K/9	WHIP	AVG
2007	Braves (DSL)	R	3	3	2.43	13	12	0	0	59	49	1	12	86	13.0	1.03	.217
2008	Braves (GCL)	R	5	1	4.31	11	3	0	0	40	51	2	9	39	8.8	1.51	.297
2009	Rome (SAL)	LoA	5	7	3.61	17	17	0	0	100	89	4	26	104	9.4	1.15	.237
2010	Did Not Play—Injured																
2011	Lynchburg (CAR)	HiA	9	6	3.94	23	17	0	0	96	86	8	48	77	7.2	1.40	.243
Minor League Totals			22	17	3.57	64	49	0	0	295	275	15	95	306	9.3	1.26	.244

19 CODY MARTIN, RHP

BA GRADE
50
HIGH

Born: Sept. 4, 1989. **B-T:** R-R. **Ht.:** 6-2. **Wt.:** 210. **Drafted:** Gonzaga, 2011 (7th round). **Signed by:** Brett Evert.

Martin saved 15 games in his first two seasons at Gonzaga before moving into the Zags rotation as a junior in 2010. Though he went 5-7, 6.55 in 14 starts, the Twins drafted him in the 20th round, yet he opted to return for his senior season. He returned to the bullpen and earned first-team All-America honors, leading NCAA Division I with a 0.86 ERA and setting a school record with 12 saves. He signed for $45,000 as a seventh-round pick. Martin, whose father Chuck pitched in the Braves system in the mid-1980s, had a stellar pro debut. He posted a 1.08 ERA and nine saves while striking out 13.2 batters per nine innings. Martin pounds the strike zone with four pitches and his impeccable command. His 90-94 mph fastball has plus movement, generating a lot of swings and misses. His best pitch may be his mid-80s slider, and he also has a solid curveball and changeup. Martin keeps hitters off balance with his repertoire, and some scouts suggest he should get another look as a starter. The current plan calls for him to open 2012 in the Lynchburg bullpen, and he could rise quickly and has set-up man potential if he remains a reliever.

Year	Club (League)	Class	W	L	ERA	G	GS	CG	SV	IP	H	HR	BB	SO	K/9	WHIP	AVG
2011	Danville (APP)	R	0	0	0.00	8	0	0	3	9	2	0	1	14	14.0	0.33	.069
	Rome (SAL)	LoA	1	0	1.48	14	0	0	6	24	18	2	4	35	12.9	0.90	.212
Minor League Totals			1	0	1.08	22	0	0	9	33	20	2	5	49	13.2	0.75	.175

20 NAVERY MOORE, RHP

BA GRADE
50
HIGH

Born: Aug. 10, 1990. **B-T:** R-R. **Ht.:** 6-2. **Wt.:** 212. **Drafted:** Vanderbilt, 2011 (14th round). **Signed by:** Hugh Buchanan.

The lone over-slot signing in the Braves' 2011 draft class, Moore received a $400,000 bonus in the 14th round. After having Tommy John surgery in high school, he pitched just 13 innings in his first two seasons at Vanderbilt before tying a school record with 11 saves last spring. Moore's calling card is his arm strength. His fastball resides in the 92-96 mph range and has above-average movement. He has struggled with the release point of his slider, which tends to sweep more than drop. His long arm action has caused some evaluators if it will prevent him from developing a plus breaking ball, which would limit his role in the bullpen. In addition to improving his slider, he also needs to tighten up his command. If everything comes together for Moore, he could develop into a set-up man or perhaps even a closer. He'll make his pro debut at one of Atlanta's Class A affiliates and could move quickly through the system.

Year	Club (League)	Class	W	L	ERA	G	GS	CG	SV	IP	H	HR	BB	SO	K/9	WHIP	AVG
2011	Did Not Play—Signed Late																

21 DAVID HALE, RHP

BA GRADE
50
HIGH

Born: Sept. 27, 1987. **B-T:** R-R. **Ht.:** 6-2. **Wt.:** 205. **Drafted:** Princeton, 2009 (3rd round). **Signed by:** Kevin Barry.

Hale has experienced Jekyll-and-Hyde seasons during his first two full years as a pro. In 2010, he began the year by going 0-4, 7.99 in six starts at Rome before changing roles and going 5-3, 2.16 with five saves as a reliever. Last year at Lynchburg, he posted a 5.91 ERA out of the Lynchburg bullpen before moving back to the rotation and going 3-4, 3.66 in 13 starts. A two-way player who spent most of his time at Princeton as a center fielder, Hale still is figuring out the cat-and-mouse game that is the duel between pitcher and batter. Scouts rave about his lightning-quick arm, which generates a 92-94 mph fastball that touches 96. He also throws a mid-80s slider that's one of the best in the system, but he's still trying to improve his feel for a changeup. He works behind hitters too often because an inconsistent release point hampers his command. Hale initially preferred working as a reliever because the routine was more similar to being an everyday player. The development of his changeup will determine what role he serves in the future. A promotion to Double-A is next on his agenda.

Year	Club (League)	Class	W	L	ERA	G	GS	CG	SV	IP	H	HR	BB	SO	K/9	WHIP	AVG
2009	Danville (APP)	R	2	1	1.13	7	1	0	1	16	7	0	5	12	6.8	0.75	.130
2010	Rome (SAL)	LoA	5	8	4.13	28	7	0	5	94	97	1	44	69	6.6	1.51	.268
2011	Lynchburg (CAR)	HiA	4	6	4.10	28	13	1	0	101	106	9	30	86	7.7	1.35	.275
Minor League Totals			11	15	3.89	63	21	1	6	211	210	10	79	167	7.1	1.37	.262

22 ADAM MILLIGAN, OF

BA GRADE
50
HIGH

Born: March 14, 1988. **B-T:** L-R. **Ht.:** 6-3. **Wt.:** 210. **Drafted:** Walters State (Tenn.) CC, 2008 (6th round). **Signed by:** Brian Bridges.

For the second time in as many seasons and the third time in four years as a pro, an injury sidelined Milligan for an extended period time. A right knee injury cost him his first pro summer after he signed in 2008, and a torn rotator cuff in his right shoulder knocked him out for all but 21 games in 2010. His 2011 season ended in mid-July when he reinjured his right knee. Yet the Braves, who drafted him three times before landing him, still remain high on his offensive upside after seeing him bat .301/.356/.546 as a pro. Originally ticketed to play football at Austin Peay State before spending two years with the Walters State (Tenn.) CC baseball program, Milligan has well above-average raw power can hit the ball out of the park to all fields. He's overly aggressive at the plate, however, and will have to prove he can make enough contact against more advanced pitching. Milligan has below-average speed, but he runs the bases well and covers enough ground on the outfield corners. He has fringy arm strength and lacks accuracy on his throws, so he fits better in left field. Atlanta hopes he finally will stay healthy when he moves up to Double-A in 2012.

Year	Club (League)	Class	AVG	G	AB	R	H	2B	3B	HR	RBI	BB	SO	SB	CS	OBP	SLG
2009	Danville (APP)	R	.439	9	41	9	18	5	1	2	10	3	7	0	0	.500	.756
	Rome (SAL)	LoA	.345	52	197	28	68	14	2	10	33	12	43	4	5	.393	.589
	Myrtle Beach (CAR)	HiA	.167	6	24	2	4	1	0	1	6	0	8	0	0	.200	.333
2010	Myrtle Beach (CAR)	HiA	.200	21	85	13	17	3	0	4	8	9	35	2	0	.277	.376
2011	Lynchburg (CAR)	HiA	.291	64	237	35	69	19	4	12	40	16	76	1	0	.345	.557
Minor League Totals			.301	152	584	87	176	42	7	29	97	40	169	7	5	.356	.546

23 MYCAL JONES, OF

BA GRADE
50
HIGH

Born: May 30, 1987. **B-T:** R-R. **Ht.:** 5-10. **Wt.:** 170. **Drafted:** Miami Dade JC, 2009 (4th round). **Signed by:** Buddy Hernandez.

Jones has experienced a roller-coaster ride since the end of the 2010 season. A shortstop in his first two years as a pro, he moved to second base in instructional league and then to center field in spring training. He missed the first month of the 2011 season with a foot injury and was arrested for driving under the influence a week after he returned to action, which led to a 10-day suspension. His batting average sank to .212 on July 11 before he rebounded to hit .289 the rest of the way. At his best, Jones gets on base by working the count and driving the ball from pole to pole. He possesses a quick swing with some pop, but he can try to do too much at times instead of employing his plus speed to his greatest advantage. He's raw as a basestealer, too. Jones has become a more disciplined hitter since he signed and has a better understanding of the strike zone, though he still swings and misses too much. He looked comfortable in center field by the end of the season, showing above-average range and arm strength. Jones has displayed considerable promise but has yet to put together an impressive showing from start to finish in any of his three pro seasons. He'll try to do so this year, when he could get his first taste of Triple-A.

Year	Club (League)	Class	AVG	G	AB	R	H	2B	3B	HR	RBI	BB	SO	SB	CS	OBP	SLG
2009	Danville (APP)	R	.258	64	244	50	63	18	6	4	27	26	55	19	4	.337	.430
2010	Rome (SAL)	LoA	.261	53	199	27	52	12	0	6	34	11	48	6	3	.301	.412
	Myrtle Beach (CAR)	HiA	.269	69	275	51	74	19	1	7	22	31	66	15	4	.354	.422
	Mississippi (SL)	AA	.200	7	30	5	6	0	1	2	5	1	9	1	0	.226	.467
2011	Mississippi (SL)	AA	.252	100	373	63	94	25	1	7	36	56	90	17	6	.359	.381
Minor League Totals			.258	293	1121	196	289	74	9	26	124	125	268	58	17	.340	.409

24 BILLY BULLOCK, RHP

BA GRADE
45
MEDIUM

Born: Feb. 27, 1988. **B-T:** R-R. **Ht.:** 6-6. **Wt.:** 225. **Drafted:** Florida, 2009 (2nd round). **Signed by:** Billy Corrigan (Twins).

After the Twins took Scott Diamond from the Braves in the 2010 major league Rule 5 draft but decided against keeping him on their big league roster, they traded Bullock to Atlanta for Diamond. Bullock overpowered Double-A hitters, limiting them to a .193 average while striking out 11.8 per nine innings, but he also struggled at times with his control. He uses his size to throw on a downhill plane, working mainly with a heavy 92-94 mph fastball with some armside run. His feel for his slider comes and goes. It resides in the low 80s with hard, late cut at its best but often becomes slurvy and hangs up in the zone. Bullock has tried to add a changeup during his first two full pro seasons but has yet to find any consistency with that offering as well. He has the makeup of a closer in that he's not afraid to challenge hitters and can put poor performances in the past, though he doesn't quite have the stuff. A probable set-up man, he'll open the 2012 season in Triple-A and could receive his first big league callup later in the year.

Year	Club (League)	Class	W	L	ERA	G	GS	CG	SV	IP	H	HR	BB	SO	K/9	WHIP	AVG
2009	Elizabethton (APP)	R	1	0	1.23	7	0	0	3	7	3	0	1	10	12.3	0.55	.125
	Beloit (MWL)	LoA	3	0	2.73	26	0	0	8	26	25	0	12	35	12.0	1.41	.253
2010	Fort Myers (FSL)	HiA	0	4	3.62	28	0	0	14	37	39	2	19	45	10.8	1.55	.281
	New Britain (EL)	AA	2	4	3.44	30	0	0	13	37	34	3	24	60	14.7	1.58	.239
2011	Mississippi (SL)	AA	3	1	4.53	50	0	0	11	50	35	2	34	65	11.8	1.39	.193
	Gwinnett (IL)	AAA	1	0	0.00	1	0	0	0	1	2	0	0	1	9.0	2.00	.400
Minor League Totals			10	9	3.58	142	0	0	49	158	138	7	90	216	12.3	1.44	.234

25 CARLOS PEREZ, LHP

BA GRADE
50
EXTREME

Born: Nov. 20, 1991. **B-T:** L-L. **Ht.:** 6-2. **Wt.:** 205. **Signed:** Dominican Republic, 2008. **Signed by:** Roberto Aquino.

After signing for $600,000 in 2008 and earning top-prospect honors in the Appalachian League in 2010, Perez looked liked the Braves' next international pitching phenom. But his stuff and poise regressed last year in low Class A, and he struggled with his control and command. Perez worked in the low 90s and touched 94 mph with his fastball in the Appy League, but mostly pitched at 86-89 in 2011. Scouts noted the sloppy front side in his delivery, which limited his arm speed. He didn't attack hitters like he had in the past, fell behind in the count and too often left the ball over the middle of the plate. Perez tightened the spin on his curveball in 2010 but it lacked consistency last year. The same was true of his changeup, which shows good fade at times. He's still just 20, so the Braves will send him back to Rome and hope he learns from his mistakes. He still has the upside of a No. 3 starter if he can figure everything out.

Year	Club (League)	Class	W	L	ERA	G	GS	CG	SV	IP	H	HR	BB	SO	K/9	WHIP	AVG
2009	Braves (GCL)	R	1	2	5.28	10	5	0	0	31	35	2	13	23	6.8	1.57	.292
2010	Danville (APP)	R	2	0	1.13	6	6	0	0	32	20	0	14	27	7.6	1.06	.185
	Rome (SAL)	LoA	0	1	3.86	2	2	0	0	7	8	1	3	4	5.1	1.57	.267
2011	Rome (SAL)	LoA	4	10	4.82	28	23	0	1	125	138	7	66	109	7.8	1.63	.278
Minor League Totals			7	13	4.25	46	36	0	1	195	201	10	96	163	7.5	1.53	.266

26 ERIK CORDIER, RHP

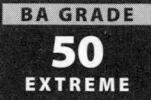

BA GRADE
50
EXTREME

Born: Feb. 25, 1986. **B-T:** R-R. **Ht.:** 6-4. **Wt.:** 230. **Drafted:** HS—Brussels, Wis., 2004 (2nd round). **Signed by:** Phil Huttmann (Royals).

Acquired from the Royals in a trade for shortstop T.J. Pena in the spring of 2007, Cordier has had difficulty staying healthy. He missed the entire 2005 (knee injury) and 2007 (Tommy John surgery) seasons, then had another elbow operation last January to remove a bone spur. He returned by late May but never got untracked. He also got struck by a couple of liners late in the year, resulting in abbreviated starts, yet he said at the end of the season that his arm felt as good as it had since the previous campaign. When he's 100 percent, Cordier is a true power pitcher with a mid-90s fastball that touches 97. At times, his slider gives him a second plus pitch. His changeup lacks consistency but looked better late in the year and in the Arizona Fall League. Because he has fringy command and has yet to prove durable, Cordier is a candidate to move to the bullpen in the near future. The Braves' depth of starting pitching at the upper levels of the organization also could contribute to a change in roles. He figures to return to Triple-A to start 2012.

Year	Club (League)	Class	W	L	ERA	G	GS	CG	SV	IP	H	HR	BB	SO	K/9	WHIP	AVG
2004	Royals (AZL)	R	2	4	5.19	11	11	0	0	35	38	1	21	22	5.7	1.70	.279
2005	Did Not Play—Injured																
2006	Idaho Falls (PIO)	R	1	0	3.38	3	3	0	0	16	11	0	3	19	10.7	0.88	.186
	Burlington (MWL)	LoA	3	1	2.70	7	7	0	0	37	27	3	14	23	5.6	1.12	.203
2007	Did Not Play—Injured																
2008	Braves (GCL)	R	0	0	0.00	3	2	0	0	5	4	0	1	5	9.0	1.00	.211
	Rome (SAL)	LoA	1	2	5.18	9	9	0	0	40	51	3	21	31	7.0	1.80	.317
2009	Myrtle Beach (CAR)	HiA	7	8	3.87	25	25	1	0	121	115	13	74	88	6.5	1.56	.257
2010	Mississippi (SL)	AA	11	7	3.71	25	21	0	0	136	116	3	69	113	7.5	1.36	.236
	Gwinnett (IL)	AAA	1	1	5.63	2	2	0	0	8	7	0	7	4	4.5	1.75	.233
2011	Mississippi (SL)	AA	0	1	5.40	1	1	0	0	5	6	1	0	4	7.2	1.20	.286
	Gwinnett (IL)	AAA	5	8	5.13	19	19	0	0	86	88	9	51	61	6.4	1.62	.267
Minor League Totals			31	32	4.15	105	100	1	0	488	463	33	261	370	6.8	1.48	.253

27 EVAN GATTIS, C

BA GRADE
50
EXTREME

Born: Aug. 18, 1986. **B-T:** R-R. **Ht.:** 6-4. **Wt.:** 230. **Drafted:** Texas-Permian Basin, 2010 (23rd round). **Signed by:** Gerald Turner.

A bargain for $1,000 in the 23rd round of the 2010 draft, Gattis seemed to emerge from nowhere during the second half of his first full pro season. He opened 2011 in extended spring training and played only part-time upon joining Rome in early May. The promotion of Christian Bethancourt in late June opened an opportunity behind the plate and Gattis made the most of it. He hit .382 in August and won the South Atlantic League batting title with a .322 average. He also tied for fifth with 22 homers despite playing in just 88 games. Gattis has a quick, compact swing that generates plus raw power. He gets excellent leverage from his tall frame and can hit lasers when he gets his arms extended. He lacks patience at the plate, something more advanced pitchers may be able to exploit. Though he's a below-average runner, he's not bad for his size or his position. Gattis does a good job of working with pitchers but looks rusty and mechanical at times behind the plate. That's understandable considering that Gattis didn't play baseball for four years. He originally committed to Texas A&M but never wound up in College Station, admittedly terrified of playing big-time college baseball. He spent a month in drug rehab because his parents worried that he smoked marijuana too often, then hurt his left knee at Seminole State (Okla.) JC and left. He spent three years driving around the country and living out of his pickup. Gattis has the arm strength and receiving skills to make it as a catcher, but he still has a lot of work to do behind the plate. He threw out just 23 percent of basestealers and committed 10 errors and 15 passed balls in 52 games last year. If he can't polish his catching, he'd have to make it as a first baseman, where he saw some action in 2011. Gattis is already 25 but he's intriguing and could jump on the fast track if he gets off to a hot start in high Class A this year.

Year	Club (League)	Class	AVG	G	AB	R	H	2B	3B	HR	RBI	BB	SO	SB	CS	OBP	SLG
2010	Danville (APP)	R	.288	60	222	33	64	10	0	4	29	6	44	0	0	.339	.387
2011	Rome (SAL)	LoA	.322	88	338	58	109	24	2	22	71	25	53	2	4	.386	.601
Minor League Totals			.309	148	560	91	173	34	2	26	100	31	97	2	4	.367	.516

28 TOMMY La STELLA, 2B

Born: Jan. 31, 1989. **B-T:** L-R. **Ht.:** 5-11. **Wt.:** 185. **Drafted:** Coastal Carolina, 2011 (8th round). **Signed by:** Billy Best.

La Stella began his college career at St. John's before transferring to Coastal Carolina, where he nearly won the Big South Conference triple crown as a redshirt junior in 2011. After signing for $105,000 as an eighth round pick, he shook off a 4-for-31 in pro ball to hit at a .358 clip in his final 55 games. La Stella's calling card is his bat. He hit second in the lineup at Rome and displayed the ability to make consistent hard contact and some surprising pop. He employs an unusual batting stance with his feet close together and his lead foot open before stepping in toward the plate. He has above-average bat speed as well as a discerning eye at the plate. La Stella runs the bases well but isn't blessed with a lot of quickness or athleticism. Because his arm and range are fringy, most scouts believe he'll be hard pressed to remain in the infield at higher levels. He could end up in left field, where he played in the Cape Cod League during the summer of 2010. Ticketed for high Class A in 2012, La Stella will go as far as his bat will take him.

Year	Club (League)	Class	AVG	G	AB	R	H	2B	3B	HR	RBI	BB	SO	SB	CS	OBP	SLG
2011	Rome (SAL)	LoA	.328	63	232	46	76	13	5	9	40	26	28	2	2	.401	.543
Minor League Totals			.328	63	232	46	76	13	5	9	40	26	28	2	2	.401	.543

29 CORY GEARRIN, RHP

Born: April 14, 1986. **B-T:** R-R. **Ht.:** 6-3. **Wt.:** 200. **Drafted:** Mercer, 2007 (4th round). **Signed by:** Al Goetz.

When Peter Moylan went on the disabled list last April, the Braves replaced the side-arming Australian with another sidewinder in Gearrin. He posted a 3.60 ERA in 13 appearances before returning to Triple-A in early June. When Atlanta recalled him a month later, he surrendered 10 runs in 3 1/3 innings over five outings and was demoted to Gwinnett for the rest of the year. Gearrin cuts his pitches across the plate with Frisbee-style life that helps produce groundballs. He works mainly with an 89-91 mph fastball with late movement and a sweeping 77-80 mph slider. He does a good job of adding and subtracting from his pitches, though his control tends to waver. Gearrin is tough on righthanders, who batted just .143/.260/.167 with 18 strikeouts in 50 plate appearances against him in the majors. Lefties see him a lot better, however, and pounded him to the tune of .393/.514/.643 in the big leagues. His splits were pronounced but not as extreme in the minors. With Moylan having offseason rotator-cuff surgery, Gearrin never will have a better opportunity to stick with the Braves than he'll get in spring training. He could claim a middle-relief role if he can figure lefthanders out.

Year	Club (League)	Class	W	L	ERA	G	GS	CG	SV	IP	H	HR	BB	SO	K/9	WHIP	AVG
2007	Danville (APP)	R	1	1	4.44	18	0	0	0	26	21	1	16	37	12.6	1.41	.214
2008	Rome (SAL)	LoA	3	2	2.82	19	0	0	1	22	19	1	15	36	14.5	1.52	.218
	Myrtle Beach (CAR)	HiA	3	1	5.32	17	0	0	0	24	19	2	21	36	13.7	1.69	.218
2009	Myrtle Beach (CAR)	HiA	0	2	1.84	27	0	0	17	29	22	2	3	32	9.8	0.85	.198
	Mississippi (SL)	AA	1	2	2.84	20	0	0	2	25	19	2	8	20	7.1	1.07	.213
2010	Gwinnett (IL)	AAA	3	5	3.36	52	0	0	0	80	72	6	32	66	7.4	1.29	.246
2011	Atlanta (NL)	MAJ	1	1	7.85	18	0	0	0	18	17	0	12	25	12.3	1.58	.243
	Gwinnett (IL)	AAA	4	1	1.80	35	0	0	4	50	42	0	20	60	10.8	1.24	.226
Major League Totals			1	1	7.85	18	0	0	0	18	17	0	12	25	12.3	1.58	.243
Minor League Totals			15	14	3.08	188	0	0	24	257	214	14	115	287	10.0	1.28	.225

30 PHIL GOSSELIN, 2B

Born: Oct. 3, 1988. **B-T:** R-R. **Ht.:** 6-1. **Wt.:** 190. **Drafted:** Virginia, 2010 (5th round). **Signed by:** Billy Best.

Gosselin creates mixed opinions among talent evaluators. The Braves think he was a steal in the fifth round of the 2010 draft, while scouts with other teams believe his grit stands out more than his physical ability. A hard-nosed player with keen instincts, he missed the last two weeks of the 2011 season and a planned trip to the Arizona Fall League when he injured his thumb sliding into a base. Gosselin has a quick bat and barrels the ball consistently, though he offers only modest gap power. He has fringy speed but has a knack for taking the extra base. After seeing action at several positions in college at Virginia, Gosselin has played exclusively at second base in pro ball. He has good footwork and does a solid job of turning the double play. His arm strength is no better than average, which limits his ability to play on the left side of the infield. Nevertheless, he still profiles more as a utilityman than as a regular. He'll play in Double-A this year.

Year	Club (League)	Class	AVG	G	AB	R	H	2B	3B	HR	RBI	BB	SO	SB	CS	OBP	SLG
2010	Rome (SAL)	LoA	.294	57	214	26	63	9	3	2	24	25	51	7	3	.374	.393
	Myrtle Beach (CAR)	HiA	.154	6	26	2	4	1	1	0	0	0	7	0	0	.154	.269
2011	Lynchburg (CAR)	HiA	.264	115	424	60	112	24	6	6	63	37	76	6	2	.324	.392
Minor League Totals			.270	178	664	88	179	34	10	8	87	62	134	13	5	.335	.387

Baltimore Orioles

BY WILL LINGO

A nd now, for something completely different. The Orioles have tried just about everything to reverse their run of losing seasons, which has reached 14 straight, finding occasional glimmers of hope but nothing close to sustained success. In fact, after the team at least stayed out of the cellar in the American League East for its first 10 losing seasons, it has been locked firmly in last place over the last four.

Those four seasons coincide with the tenure of Andy MacPhail, who joined the organization as president of baseball operations in the middle of the 2007 season after a distinguished tenure with the Twins and Cubs. Things never clicked in Baltimore, however, and he stepped aside after a 69-93 finish in 2011. For every positive step the Orioles seem to take—trading for Adam Jones or drafting Matt Wieters—they take several negative ones, such as drafting Matt Hobgood, their 2009 No. 5 overall pick who already looks like a wasted selection.

While Zach Britton stepped forward in his 2011 rookie season, two other young pitchers, Brian Matusz and Chris Tillman, had poor years. Matusz's 10.69 ERA was the worst in major league history for a pitcher with at least 10 starts. Down below, the farm system has premium prospects in Dylan Bundy and Manny Machado, but little behind them.

When MacPhail stepped down, the Orioles' first finalists to replace him were Diamondbacks senior vice president Jerry Dipoto and Blue Jays assistant GM Tony LaCava. Dipoto took the Angels' GM job and LaCava turned down a contract offer. LaCava reportedly balked at not receiving full hiring and firing control from owner Peter Angelos. Baltimore eventually hired Dan Duquette, the former Expos and Red Sox GM who hadn't worked in Organized Baseball since Boston fired him in 2002. He left the front office mostly intact, hiring Blue Jays crosschecker Gary Rajsich as scouting director to replace Joe Jordan, who became the Phillies' farm director.

Angelos is now on his eighth different GM since buying the Orioles 18 years ago. MacPhail lasted the longest, at four and a half years. Before him, Angelos ran off baseball icon Roland Hemond, who left after the 1995 season; Hall of Famer Pat Gillick, who fled after 1998 despite making the AL Championship Series twice in three years; Frank Wren, who lasted only one season and has found success as GM of the

DIAMOND IMAGES

Matt Wieters blossomed as a homegrown star in 2011, while other players regressed

TOP 30 PROSPECTS

1. Dylan Bundy, rhp	16. Matt Angle, of
2. Manny Machado, ss	17. Bobby Bundy, rhp
3. Jonathan Schoop, inf	18. Kyle Simon, rhp
4. Parker Bridwell, rhp	19. Glynn Davis, of
5. L.J. Hoes, of/2b	20. Tim Berry, lhp
6. Nicky Delmonico, 3b/1b	21. Gabriel Lino, c
7. Ryan Flaherty, inf/of	22. Roderick Bernadina, of
8. Jason Esposito, 3b	23. Ryan Adams, 2b
9. Xavier Avery, of	24. Tyler Townsend, 1b
10. Dan Klein, rhp	25. Brandon Waring, 3b/1b
11. Mike Wright, rhp	26. Oliver Drake, rhp
12. Clay Schrader, rhp	27. Trent Mummey, of
13. Joe Mahoney, 1b/of	28. Wynn Pelzer, rhp
14. Aaron Baker, 1b	29. Kyle Hudson, of
15. Ryan Berry, rhp	30. Eduardo Rodriguez, lhp

Braves; Syd Thrift, a recycling experiment similar to Duquette that lasted three years; and Jim Beattie and Mike Flanagan, who served together for three years before Flanagan did a year and a half on his own.

Angelos has done a poor job of creating a unified baseball operation pulling in the same direction toward a shared goal, instead fostering an atmosphere where departments seem to function as autonomous units. Duquette, of course, pledges to change that. Empty promises have remained one of the few constants with the Orioles during the last 14 years.

General Manager: Dan Duquette. **Farm Director:** John Stockstill. **Scouting Director:** Gary Rajsich.

Class	Team	League	W	L	Pct	Finish*	Manager(s)
Majors	Baltimore Orioles	American	69	93	.426	12th (14)	Buck Showalter
Triple-A	Norfolk Tides	International	56	87	.392	13th (14)	Gary Allenson
Double-A	Bowie Baysox	Eastern	75	66	.532	4th (12)	Gary Kendall
High A	Frederick Keys	Carolina	80	59	.576	1st (8)†	Orlando Gomez
Low A	Delmarva Shorebirds	South Atlantic	55	85	.393	t-13th (14)	Ryan Minor
Short-season	Aberdeen Ironbirds	New York-Penn	24	51	.320	14th (14)	Leo Gomez
Rookie	GCL Orioles	Gulf Coast	38	22	.633	2nd (15)	Ramon Sambo
Overall 2011 Minor League Record			328	370	.470	26th (30)	

*Finish in overall standings (No. of teams in league). †League champion.

LAST YEAR'S TOP 30

Player, Pos.		Status
1.	Manny Machado, ss	No. 2
2.	Zach Britton, lhp	Majors
3.	Xavier Avery, of	No. 9
4.	L.J. Hoes, 2b	No. 5
5.	Dan Klein, rhp	No. 10
6.	Wynn Pelzer, rhp	No. 28
7.	Mychal Givens, ss	Dropped out
8.	Ryan Adams, 2b/3b	No. 23
9.	Ryan Berry, rhp	No. 15
10.	Jonathan Schoop, ss	No. 3
11.	Joe Mahoney, 1b/of	No. 13
12.	Parker Bridwell, rhp	No. 4
13.	Matt Angle, of	No. 16
14.	Bobby Bundy, rhp	No. 17
15.	Matt Hobgood, rhp	Dropped out
16.	Trent Mummey, of	No. 27
17.	Connor Narron, ss/3b	Dropped out
18.	Tyler Townsend, 1b	No. 24
19.	Ronnie Welty, of	Dropped out
20.	Brandon Snyder, 1b	Dropped out
21.	Luis Lebron, rhp	Dropped out
22.	Tyler Henson, of	(Dodgers)
23.	Brandon Waring, 3b/1b	No. 25
24.	Chorye Spoone, rhp	(Red Sox)
25.	Eddie Gamboa, rhp	Dropped out
26.	Greg Miclat, ss	(Rangers)
27.	Brandon Erbe, rhp	Dropped out
28.	Caleb Joseph, c	Dropped out
29.	Pedro Florimon, ss	(Twins)
30.	Adrian Rosario, rhp	(Mets)

BEST TOOLS

Best Hitter for Average	Manny Machado
Best Power Hitter	Aaron Baker
Best Strike-Zone Discipline	Tyler Kelly
Fastest Baserunner	Glynn Davis
Best Athlete	Xavier Avery
Best Fastball	Dylan Bundy
Best Curveball	Dylan Bundy
Best Slider	Mike Wright
Best Changeup	Dan Klein
Best Control	Oliver Drake
Best Defensive Catcher	Caleb Joseph
Best Defensive Infielder	Manny Machado
Best Infield Arm	Billy Rowell
Best Defensive Outfielder	Matt Angle
Best Outfield Arm	Matt Angle

PROJECTED 2015 LINEUP

Catcher	Matt Wieters
First Base	Nicky Delmonico
Second Base	Jonathan Schoop
Third Base	J.J. Hardy
Shortstop	Manny Machado
Left Field	L.J. Hoes
Center Field	Adam Jones
Right Field	Nick Markakis
Designated Hitter	Ryan Flaherty
No. 1 Starter	Dylan Bundy
No. 2 Starter	Zach Britton
No. 3 Starter	Jake Arrieta
No. 4 Starter	Brian Matusz
No. 5 Starter	Jeremy Guthrie
Closer	Dan Klein

TOP PROSPECTS OF THE DECADE

Year	Player, Pos.	2011 Org.
2002	Richard Stahl, lhp	Out of baseball
2003	Erik Bedard, lhp	Red Sox
2004	Adam Loewen, lhp	Blue Jays
2005	Nick Markakis, of	Orioles
2006	Nick Markakis, of	Orioles
2007	Billy Rowell, 3b	Orioles
2008	Matt Wieters, c	Orioles
2009	Matt Wieters, c	Orioles
2010	Brian Matusz, lhp	Orioles
2011	Manny Machado, ss	Orioles

TOP DRAFT PICKS OF THE DECADE

Year	Player, Pos.	2011 Org.
2002	Adam Loewen, lhp	Blue Jays
2003	Nick Markakis, of	Orioles
2004	*Wade Townsend, rhp	Out of baseball
2005	Brandon Snyder, c	Orioles
2006	Billy Rowell, 3b	Orioles
2007	Matt Wieters, c	Orioles
2008	Brian Matusz, lhp	Orioles
2009	Matt Hobgood, rhp	Orioles
2010	Manny Machado, ss	Orioles
2011	Dylan Bundy, rhp	Orioles

*Did not sign.

LARGEST BONUSES IN CLUB HISTORY

Matt Wieters, 2007	$6,000,000
Manny Machado, 2010	$5,250,000
Dylan Bundy, 2011	$4,000,000
Adam Loewen, 2002	$3,200,000
Brian Matusz, 2008	$3,200,000

BALTIMORE ORIOLES

TOP 2012 ROOKIE: Ryan Flaherty, inf/of. The major league Rule 5 draft pick has the pop to win Baltimore's third-base job or serve as a versatile bat off the bench.

BREAKOUT PROSPECT: Tim Berry, lhp. He fell to the 50th round of the 2009 draft because he needed Tommy John surgery, but he's healthy now and has the three-pitch mix to succeed as a starter.

SLEEPER: Zach Davies, rhp. A 26th-round pick in June, he signed for $575,000 and earns Mike Leake comparisons.

SOURCE OF TOP 30 TALENT			
Homegrown	26	Acquired	4
College	11	Trades	3
Junior college	1	Rule 5 draft	1
High school	9	Independent leagues	0
Draft-and-follow	0	Free agents/waivers	0
Nondrafted free agents	1		
International	4		

LF
L.J. Hoes (5)
Trent Mummey (27)
Steve Bumbry

CF
Xavier Avery (9)
Matt Angle (16)
Glynn Davis (19)
Kyle Hudson (29)
John Ruettiger
Miguel Abreu

RF
Roderick Bernadina (22)
Ronnie Welty

3B
Nicky Delmonico (6)
Ryan Flaherty (7)
Jason Esposito (8)
Brandon Waring (25)
Matt Antonelli

SS
Manny Machado (2)
Mychal Givens
Steven Tolleson

2B
Jonathan Schoop (3)
Ryan Adams (23)
Connor Narron
Dudley Leonora

1B
Joe Mahoney (13)
Aaron Baker (14)
Tyler Townsend (24)
Brandon Snyder

C
Gabriel Lino (21)
Michael Ohlman
Wynston Sawyer
Brian Ward
Caleb Joseph
Adam Davis

LHP

LHSP	LHRP
Tim Berry (20)	Troy Patton
Eduardo Rodriguez (30)	Zach Phillips
Trent Howard	Cole McCurry
Cameron Coffey	Jason Gurka
Rick Zagone	Pedro Viola
Matt Taylor	Jorge Rivera
	Ashur Tolliver

RHP

RHSP	RHRP
Dylan Bundy (1)	Dan Klein (10)
Parker Bridwell (4)	Clay Schrader (12)
Mike Wright (11)	Wynn Pelzer (28)
Ryan Berry (15)	Miguel Socolovich
Bobby Bundy (17)	Eddie Gamboa
Kyle Simon (18)	Miguel Chalas
Oliver Drake (26)	Devin Jones
Zach Davies	Jose Nivar
David Baker	Luis Lebron
Tyler Wilson	Josh Dowdy
Steve Johnson	
Tim Bascom	
Matt Hobgood	
Mark Blackmar	

DRAFT ANALYSIS

2011

BEST PURE HITTER: The Orioles put $1.525 million behind their conviction that 3B/1B Nicky Delmonico (6) will hit enough to play a corner spot. He has a smooth lefthanded swing and advanced approach.

BEST POWER HITTER: In a crop with just seven signed position players, Delmonico stands out. He has shown plus raw power at his best.

FASTEST RUNNER: Baltimore didn't sign any true burners, but OF Jalen Simmons (24) has 70 speed on the 20-80 scouting scale. OF Johnny Ruettiger (8) is a step slower, but his speed plays better.

BEST DEFENSIVE PLAYER: 3B Jason Esposito (2) has excellent footwork, good hands and easy infield actions. He probably could handle shortstop or second base, and his play at third draws comparisons to Ryan Zimmerman and Matt Dominguez.

BEST FASTBALL: RHP Dylan Bundy (1) may have had the best pure stuff in the draft. He touches triple digits and sits in the 94-98 mph range with his fastball. He throws strikes with that pitch and his low-90s two-seamer. RHP Mike Wright (3) hit 96 mph while striking out No. 6 overall pick Anthony Rendon in the spring and sits at 92-94 as a starter.

BEST SECONDARY PITCH: Bundy has an advanced arsenal, with a power curveball in the upper 70s as well as an impressive changeup for his age. Wright's slider has plus potential.

BEST PRO DEBUT: LHP Trent Howard (7) went 3-2, 3.48 with 45 strikeouts in 41 innings at short-season Aberdeen. RHP Tyler Wilson (10) posted a 1.91 ERA over 33 innings at two levels. RHP Mark Blackmar (16) pitched 18 scoreless innings in the Rookie-level Gulf Coast League.

BEST ATHLETE: The 6-foot-4, 195-pound Simmons had a football scholarship to play wide receiver at Presbyterian (S.C.).

MOST INTRIGUING BACKGROUND: Bundy's older brother Bobby also pitches in the Orioles system. Delmonico's father Rod is the former coach at Tennessee and coached the Netherlands in the 2009 World Baseball Classic, while his older brother Tony plays in the Dodgers system. Ruettiger's uncle Dan "Rudy" Ruettiger was the Notre Dame football walk-on who inspired the movie "Rudy." Blackmar's father Phil won three events on the PGA golf tour.

CLOSEST TO THE MAJORS: Bundy is the rare high schooler who combines plus stuff and polish. RHP Kyle Simon (4) could move quickly if his velocity bounces back to the low 90s after a heavy college workload.

BEST LATE-ROUND PICK: Baltimore gave RHP Zach Davies (26) $575,000 to keep him from going to Arizona State. His athletic 6-foot, 165-pound frame and command of a four-pitch mix reminds scouts of former Sun Devils ace Mike Leake.

THE ONE WHO GOT AWAY: The O's made runs at several more bats, including OF Jason Coats (12), who returned to Texas Christian, and oft-injured OF Adam Matthews (23), who went back to South Carolina.

ASSESSMENT: Bundy could be the best player in the entire draft and Wright has a live arm, giving the Orioles a strong pitching class. Esposito and Delmonico must come through to bring Baltimore some bats.

2010

SS Manny Machado (1) is living up to his billing as the No. 3 overall pick. RHP Parker Bridwell (9) is developing nicely as a starter, while RHPs Dan Klein (3) and Clay Schrader (10) may bolster the big league bullpen in the near future.

GRADE: A

2009

The Orioles overdrafted RHP Matt Hobgood (1) at No. 5 and gave first- or sandwich-round money to SS/2B Mychal Givens (2), C Michael Ohlman (11) and LHP Cameron Coffey (22). None rank on our Top 30 two years later. This crop's best prospect is RHP Ryan Berry (9), who missed much of 2011 because of a cyst near his throwing shoulder.

GRADE: D

2008

After looking like he'd be Baltimore's ace, LHP Brian Matusz (1) had a historically bad 2011 season. OFs Xavier Avery (2), L.J. Hoes (3) and Kyle Hudson (4) all flash promise but have a long way to go to become big league regulars.

GRADE: C

2007

C Matt Wieters (1) earned the first of what could be many All-Star Game berths in 2011. RHP Jake Arrieta (5) is still finding his way in the major league rotation, and OF Matt Angle (7) debuted with the Orioles last year.

GRADE: A

Draft analysis by John Manuel (2011) and Jim Callis (2007-10).
Numbers in parentheses indicate draft rounds.

1 DYLAN BUNDY, RHP

Born: Nov. 15, 1992. **B-T:** B-R. **Ht.:** 6-1.
Wt.: 200. **Drafted:** HS—Owasso, Okla., 2011 (1st round). **Signed by:** Ernie Jacobs.

BA GRADE
70
MEDIUM

DAVID STONER

Bundy is the brother of Bobby Bundy, a 2008 eighth-round pick of the Orioles who reached Double-A last season. Dylan started out at Sperry (Okla.) High, playing with Bobby in 2008, but he transferred from the 3-A program to one of the state's 6-A powerhouses, Owasso High, in 2010. He found the going no tougher there, winning second-team All-America honors as a junior by going 11-1, 1.58 and hitting .442. He was Baseball America's High School Player of the Year in 2011, going 11-0, 0.20 and batting .467. In his two years at Owasso, he had 322 strikeouts in 151 innings. His only disappointment came when Owasso lost to Broken Arrow High, featuring friend and rival Archie Bradley, in the Oklahoma state championship game. Bundy, who didn't pitch in that contest after winning a quarter-final game two days earlier, one-upped Bradley by going fourth overall in the draft to the Orioles, while Bradley went seventh to the Diamondbacks. Bundy had floated a $30 million asking price before the draft, but he gave up a Texas scholarship to sign at the Aug. 15 deadline for a $6.225 major league contract that included a $4 million bonus. It was the richest deal for a drafted player in franchise history, beating the $6 million bonus Baltimore paid Matt Wieters in 2007. Bundy made his first Orioles appearance in instructional league and won high praise both for his arm and his makeup.

Tick off everything scouts want in an ace, and Bundy has it. Fastball? He pitches at 94-98 mph and touches 100 with his four-seamer, which features explosive life. He also uses a low-90s two-seamer to get groundballs and also has a cutter in the same range that essentially gives him a third plus fastball. Complementary pitches? In addition to his cutter, his upper-70s curveball already grades as a plus pitch, and he shows good feel for a solid changeup. Mechanics? Bundy is a great athlete with good body control, so his mechanics are clean and balanced and he repeats his delivery well. That should give him good command, and he also shows a great feel for his craft. About the only way he doesn't fit the ace prototype is with his listed 6-foot-1 size, but he's strong and athletic and still gets good downhill plane on his pitches. He earns high praise for his makeup, and the attribute that might set Bundy apart the most is his work ethic. His workouts are the stuff of Oklahoma legend, going beyond the basics of running, lifting weights and long-tossing to push himself to do such things as digging holes, doing lunges around the warning track and chopping down trees and carrying them around.

Bundy's humble goal when he started high school was to throw harder than Bobby, who has touched 97 mph. He accomplished that in short order and was elated to join his brother in the Orioles organization. He figures to begin his pro career at low Class A Delmarva in 2012, and he could quickly pass Bobby on his way to the big leagues. Bundy is so advanced that some scouts considered him the equal of the three college pitchers (Gerrit Cole, Danny Hultzen, Trevor Bauer) who went ahead of him in the draft, and he might not need more than two years in the minors.

SCOUTING GRADES

Fastball: 70.	**Command/**
Curveball: 65.	**Control:** 60.
Changeup: 55.	**Delivery:** 60.

Based on 20-80 scouting scale, where 50 represents major league average, and future projection rather than present tools.

Year	Club (League)	Class	W	L	ERA	G	GS	CG	SV	IP	H	HR	BB	SO	K/9	WHIP	AVG
2011	Did Not Play—Signed Late																

2 MANNY MACHADO, SS

Born: July 6, 1992. **B-T:** R-R. **Ht.:** 6-3. **Wt.:** 185. **Drafted:** HS—Hialeah, Fla., 2010 (1st round). **Signed by:** John Martin.

After Bryce Harper and Jameson Taillon went 1-2 in the 2010 draft, Machado was a clear choice with the third overall pick, so the Orioles grabbed him and signed him for $5.25 million. He ranked as the No. 1 prospect in the high Class A Carolina League and No. 2 in the low Class A South Atlantic League in his first full pro season, even with a dislocated left kneecap in May that sidelined him for a month. Machado has all the tools to be an all-star shortstop. He's an above-average hitter with a knack for making solid contact, and he has the bat speed and strength to generate average power. He's a rangy teenager who's still filling out and getting stronger. Machado has good hands and range and a plus arm, so he'll be a fine defensive shortstop as long as he doesn't outgrow the position. In instructional league, Baltimore emphasized putting together good at-bats and improving his two-strike approach, as well as using his legs more and getting his feet in better position on defense. He's an average runner. The Orioles see no deficiencies in Machado that experience and maturity won't clear up. The only real question is whether he eventually slides over to third base, but they'll try to keep him at shortstop. He could open 2012 at Double-A Bowie.

BA GRADE
70
MEDIUM

Year	Club (League)	Class	AVG	G	AB	R	H	2B	3B	HR	RBI	BB	SO	SB	CS	OBP	SLG
2010	Orioles (GCL)	R	.143	2	7	1	1	0	0	1	2	0	1	0	0	.143	.571
	Aberdeen (NYP)	SS	.345	7	29	2	10	1	1	0	3	3	2	0	0	.406	.448
2011	Delmarva (SAL)	LoA	.276	38	145	24	40	8	2	6	24	23	25	3	1	.376	.483
	Frederick (CAR)	HiA	.245	63	237	24	58	12	3	5	26	22	48	8	5	.308	.384
Minor League Totals			.261	110	418	51	109	21	6	12	55	48	76	11	6	.337	.426

3 JONATHAN SCHOOP, INF

Born: Oct. 6, 1991. **B-T:** R-R. **Ht.:** 6-1. **Wt.:** 187. **Signed:** Curacao, 2008. **Signed by:** Ernst Meyer.

Schoop emerged as a prospect in 2010, then enjoyed a true breakout season in 2011, playing alongside Manny Machado to give the Orioles a dynamic infield pairing. He hit .171 for the Netherlands at the World Cup in Panama in October but drove in the winning run with a single in the gold medal game against Cuba. Schoop started 2011 playing third base next to Machado in low Class A, then took over at shortstop when Machado got hurt. When both were at Frederick, Schoop played mostly second base. He has the arm and hands for any infield spot, and some club officials would argue he's a better shortstop than Machado. Schoop made great progress at second and turns the double play beautifully, though he may outgrow the middle infield. His bat should play anywhere, as he shows good bat speed and should have average power. He still has holes offensively, such as a tendency to swing at breaking balls out of the zone, but those are all correctable. He also shows great makeup. He's a slightly below-average runner. The Orioles like seeing Schoop and Machado together, but they may have both open the season playing shortstop if one of them shows his bat is ready for Double-A in spring training. In the long term, Schoop is most likely to end up at third base.

BA GRADE
60
HIGH

Year	Club (League)	Class	AVG	G	AB	R	H	2B	3B	HR	RBI	BB	SO	SB	CS	OBP	SLG
2009	Orioles (DSL)	R	.239	68	247	28	59	7	3	0	35	24	39	11	3	.320	.291
2010	Orioles (GCL)	R	.250	17	60	11	15	4	0	3	16	7	7	0	0	.329	.467
	Bluefield (APP)	R	.316	39	133	16	42	11	1	2	16	12	14	1	1	.372	.459
	Frederick (CAR)	HiA	.238	6	21	5	5	3	0	0	3	1	4	0	0	.273	.381
2011	Delmarva (SAL)	LoA	.316	51	212	45	67	12	3	8	34	20	32	6	4	.376	.514
	Frederick (CAR)	HiA	.271	77	299	37	81	12	2	5	37	22	44	6	3	.329	.375
Minor League Totals			.277	258	972	142	269	49	9	18	141	86	140	24	11	.342	.401

4 PARKER BRIDWELL, RHP

Born: Aug. 2, 1991. **B-T:** R-R. **Ht.:** 6-4. **Wt.:** 190. **Drafted:** HS—Hereford, Texas, 2010 (9th round). **Signed by:** Ernest Jacobs.

Bridwell was a legitimate prospect in both football and baseball coming out of high school, and he also played basketball. He passed up a baseball scholarship at Texas Tech to sign as a ninth-round pick out of the 2010 draft for an above-slot $625,000. He opened the 2011 season in extended spring and then struggled in low Class A, so he stepped back to short-season Aberdeen and fared better there. As a less-heralded Texas prep pitching prospect with a heavy fastball, Bridwell is a righthanded version of Zach Britton, though his sinker isn't as dynamic. Bridwell is athletic with a live arm, and the ball jumps out of his hand. He pitches at 89-92 mph and can touch 95 with his fastball. He throws both a good downer curveball and a second breaking ball with more power. He shows good feel for his changeup, which he rarely used in high school. Bridwell is working on his control and command, understandable given his level of experience. His delivery tends to get off balance as his pitch count rises. The Orioles still are working through some basics with Bridwell, such as smoothing out his mechanics and building his arm strength, but the raw material is there for at least a mid-rotation starter. He'll go back to Delmarva to begin 2012.

BA GRADE

55

HIGH

Year	Club (League)	Class	W	L	ERA	G	GS	CG	SV	IP	H	HR	BB	SO	K/9	WHIP	AVG
2010	Orioles (GCL)	R	0	0	5.40	2	2	0	0	2	1	0	3	4	21.6	2.40	.167
	Aberdeen (NYP)	SS	0	0	0.00	2	0	0	0	4	3	0	1	2	4.5	1.00	.214
2011	Aberdeen (NYP)	SS	2	5	4.53	12	11	0	0	54	56	2	22	57	9.6	1.45	.271
	Delmarva (SAL)	LoA	0	3	7.06	5	5	0	0	22	23	0	13	13	5.4	1.66	.271
Minor League Totals			2	8	5.00	21	18	0	0	81	83	2	39	76	8.4	1.51	.266

5 L.J. HOES, OF/2B

Born: March 5, 1990. **B-T:** R-R. **Ht.:** 6-1. **Wt.:** 190. **Drafted:** HS—Washington, D.C., 2008 (3rd round). **Signed by:** Dean Albany.

Frustrated at returning to high Class A Frederick, Hoes got off to a slow start in 2011, so the Orioles challenged him with a promotion. He made an adjustment with Bowie hitting coach Denny Hocking that allowed Hoes to tap into his power. In the final two months, he hit six homers—one shy of his total from his first three pro seasons. Hoes consistently has proven his ability to make contact and hit for average, so instructors were impressed he was willing to try mechanical changes to bring out more power. Baltimore has tried him at both second base and in left field, and he's clearly more comfortable in the outfield. There's split opinion on whether Hoes will have enough power to profile there, but some think his power outburst late in 2011 shows that he will. He also saw time at third base in Double-A, but he doesn't have a standout defensive tool as an infielder. He's an average runner and has an average arm. It's clear the Orioles have something in Hoes, but it's still not clear exactly what that is. The best case is that he's an everyday left fielder, and the worst case is probably a utility player. He'll move up to Triple-A Norfolk to see if his power continues to develop.

BA GRADE

50

MEDIUM

Year	Club (League)	Class	AVG	G	AB	R	H	2B	3B	HR	RBI	BB	SO	SB	CS	OBP	SLG
2008	Orioles (GCL)	R	.308	48	159	36	49	4	3	1	18	30	22	10	0	.416	.390
2009	Delmarva (SAL)	LoA	.260	119	431	42	112	19	0	2	47	23	80	20	5	.299	.318
2010	Aberdeen (NYP)	SS	.464	8	28	8	13	5	1	1	5	2	1	1	1	.531	.821
	Bowie (EL)	AA	.222	3	9	1	2	0	0	0	1	0	1	0	0	.222	.222
	Frederick (CAR)	HiA	.278	97	353	52	98	19	2	3	44	53	70	10	8	.375	.368
2011	Frederick (CAR)	HiA	.241	41	158	23	38	7	0	3	17	10	25	4	2	.297	.342
	Bowie (EL)	AA	.305	95	344	47	105	17	1	6	54	43	56	16	7	.379	.413
Minor League Totals			.281	411	1482	209	417	71	7	16	186	161	255	61	23	.354	.371

6 NICKY DELMONICO, 3B/1B

Born: July 12, 1992. **B-T:** L-R. **Ht.:** 6-3. **Wt.:** 210. **Drafted:** HS—Knoxville, Tenn., 2011 (6th round). **Signed by:** Adrian Dorsey.

Delmonico comes from a baseball family, with his father Rod coaching at Tennessee for 18 seasons until 2007 and his brother Tony playing in the Dodgers system. Nicky was viewed as a potential first-round pick heading into 2011, but his disappointing spring with the bat (in part because of a back injury) and his commitment to Georgia drove him down to the sixth round. The Orioles signed him at the deadline for $1.525 million. Delmonico went to instructional league and impressed Baltimore with his pure lefthanded swing. He doesn't have great bat speed but has such a good feel for hitting that he'll learn which pitches he can attack and should have better than average power. While some scouts think he has the tools to move behind the plate, as his brother did as a pro, Delmonico has no interest in catching and will play an infield corner. He has plenty of arm for third base, but the question will be his range. He's a below-average runner. The Orioles may challenge Delmonico with a low Class A assignment to open his pro career, though they believe he may struggle there at first. But they like his makeup and think he'll develop into an impact bat.

BA GRADE
55
HIGH

Year	Club (League)	Class	AVG	G	AB	R	H	2B	3B	HR	RBI	BB	SO	SB	CS	OBP	SLG
2011	Did Not Play—Signed Late																

7 RYAN FLAHERTY, INF/OF

Born: July 27, 1986. **B-T:** L-R. **Ht.:** 6-3. **Wt.:** 220. **Drafted:** Vanderbilt, 2008 (1st round supplemental). **Signed by:** Antonio Grissom (Cubs).

Flaherty batted cleanup behind Pedro Alvarez at Vanderbilt before going 39 picks after him in the 2008 draft, signing with the Cubs for $1.5 million. His father Ed has won two NCAA Division III College World Series as the head coach at Southern Maine. The Orioles plucked Flaherty in the major league Rule 5 draft in December. Flaherty's bat speed, strength and the loft in his swing all work in his favor. He does a nice job of working counts to get pitches he can hammer, and he has the ability to drive the ball to all fields. He will strike out, though not excessively for someone with his pop. Flaherty has wasted much of his pro career manning the middle infield, where he lacks the requisite range and athleticism, and is better suited for third base. He hasn't gotten enough time to work out his kinks there, with 25 errors in 102 pro games. He has enough arm for the position and could become an adequate defender. He also played left and right field last season, and he did OK despite well below-average speed. Flaherty will compete with Robert Andino and Chris Davis for the third-base job in Baltimore. Even if he loses out, he still should get at-bats as a corner reserve.

BA GRADE
50
MEDIUM

Year	Club (League)	Class	AVG	G	AB	R	H	2B	3B	HR	RBI	BB	SO	SB	CS	OBP	SLG
2008	Boise (NWL)	SS	.297	56	219	39	65	19	2	8	26	24	51	4	2	.369	.511
2009	Peoria (MWL)	LoA	.276	131	485	81	134	24	5	20	81	50	98	7	6	.344	.470
2010	Tennessee (SL)	AA	.183	23	71	10	13	2	0	1	9	10	12	1	0	.286	.254
	Daytona (FSL)	HiA	.286	108	420	65	120	34	3	9	63	41	74	6	3	.348	.445
2011	Tennessee (SL)	AA	.305	83	302	52	92	20	2	14	66	40	55	4	6	.384	.523
	Iowa (PCL)	AAA	.237	49	173	22	41	11	1	5	22	10	44	1	0	.277	.399
Minor League Totals			.278	450	1670	269	465	110	13	57	267	175	334	23	17	.346	.462

8 JASON ESPOSITO, 3B

Born: July 19, 1990. **B-T:** R-R. **Ht.:** 6-2. **Wt.:** 205. **Drafted:** Vanderbilt, 2011 (2nd round). **Signed by:** Adrian Dorsey.

A seventh-round pick of the Royals coming out of a Connecticut high school in 2008, Esposito turned down a reported seven-figure offer to attend Vanderbilt. He was the Commodores' third baseman from the day he set foot on campus, starting all 196 games of his college career. The Orioles took him with the 64th overall pick last June and signed him for $600,000. Esposito is a prototype third baseman defensively, with good actions and soft hands. He has the range to play shortstop at times, and he has plenty of arm for the hot corner, having worked as a pitcher in high school and touching 90 mph. Esposito's bat improved as his college career went along and he slugged .530 last year despite the less-lively metal bats, but there are questions about how he'll fare against pro pitching. He struggled against velocity at times in college and has more power to the gaps than over the fence. He stole 66 bases in three college seasons, though he's just an average runner who relies more on instincts than speed. Interestingly, Esposito was compared to fellow Northeast prep product and Vanderbilt star Ryan Flaherty coming out of high school. Baltimore hopes Esposito will hit enough to be an

BA GRADE
50
HIGH

everyday third baseman and may challenge him by sending him to high Class A for his pro debut.

Year	Club (League)	Class	AVG	G	AB	R	H	2B	3B	HR	RBI	BB	SO	SB	CS	OBP	SLG
2011	Did Not Play—Signed Late																

9 XAVIER AVERY, OF

RODGER WOOD

BA GRADE

55

EXTREME

Born: Jan. 1, 1990. **B-T:** L-L. **Ht.:** 6-0. **Wt.:** 188. **Drafted:** HS—Ellenwood, Ga., 2008 (2nd round). **Signed by:** Dave Jennings.

Baltimore signed Avery away from a Georgia football scholarship for $900,000 in 2008. He earned a promotion to Double-A at age 20 in 2010, but he didn't build on that success in his return to Bowie last season. He did play better in the Arizona Fall League, batting .288/.378/.414. Avery's tools stand out in an organization short on premium athletes. He shows bat speed and strong hands at the plate, and he's an above-average runner who has become a good defender in center field. He has improved his bunting to make better use of his speed and continues to work on hitting the ball on the ground. The key to Avery's success will be whether he can develop a better approach at the plate. His swing mechanics are sound, but he doesn't recognize pitches well. As a result, he's often slow to get his swing started, leading not only to strikeouts but also to fewer solid hits and more weak contact. For all his athleticism, he has below-average power and arm strength. Avery has a tremendous work ethic, making the Orioles think he can develop into a leadoff hitter. It will all come down to his approach, which he'll try to refine when he goes back to Bowie to begin 2012.

Year	Club (League)	Class	AVG	G	AB	R	H	2B	3B	HR	RBI	BB	SO	SB	CS	OBP	SLG
2008	Orioles (GCL)	R	.280	47	175	27	49	8	1	0	7	10	51	13	3	.333	.337
2009	Delmarva (SAL)	LoA	.262	129	473	55	124	15	8	2	36	27	111	30	10	.306	.340
2010	Frederick (CAR)	HiA	.280	109	447	73	125	25	6	4	48	42	96	28	14	.349	.389
	Bowie (EL)	AA	.234	27	107	10	25	6	0	3	18	7	34	10	0	.288	.374
2011	Bowie (EL)	AA	.259	138	557	72	144	31	2	4	26	49	156	36	14	.324	.343
Minor League Totals			.265	450	1759	237	467	85	17	13	135	135	448	117	41	.324	.355

10 DAN KLEIN, RHP

BA GRADE

50

HIGH

Born: July 27, 1988. **B-T:** R-R. **Ht.:** 6-3. **Wt.:** 190. **Drafted:** UCLA, 2010 (3rd round). **Signed by:** Mark Ralston.

A standout quarterback in high school who became the closer for UCLA's College World Series runner-up team in 2010, Klein was on the fast track and reached Double-A by the middle of his first full season, but he didn't pitch after May 1 and had shoulder surgery in August. Dr. Lewis Yocum repaired a small tear in his labrum, and loosened his shoulder capsule from a previous operation that knocked Klein out for the 2009 season. When healthy, Klein throws his fastball at 91-93 mph with good life. His solid changeup is the finest among Orioles farmhands, and his curveball ranks as one of the system's best as well. He also throws a slider. His easy delivery allows him to command his pitches and should lend itself to durability. Klein has enough stuff to start, but Baltimore already had shelved a plan to have him work as a starter before he had his second shoulder operation in three years. Klein is already 23, but the good news is that his recent surgery went well and the Orioles think he'll actually come back stronger because he'll have better range of motion in his arm. He's expected to return to the mound in June, and if he's healthy he won't spend much more time in the minors.

Year	Club (League)	Class	W	L	ERA	G	GS	CG	SV	IP	H	HR	BB	SO	K/9	WHIP	AVG
2010	Aberdeen (NYP)	SS	1	0	0.00	5	0	0	1	6	1	0	1	10	14.2	0.32	.048
2011	Frederick (CAR)	HiA	0	1	1.15	7	0	0	0	16	9	2	3	21	12.1	0.77	.161
	Bowie (EL)	AA	3	0	1.08	9	0	0	0	17	14	0	3	16	8.6	1.02	.230
Minor League Totals			4	1	0.93	21	0	0	1	39	24	2	7	47	10.9	0.80	.174

11 MIKE WRIGHT, RHP

BA GRADE

50

HIGH

Born: Jan. 3, 1990. **B-T:** R-R. **Ht.:** 6-5. **Wt.:** 195. **Drafted:** East Carolina, 2011 (3rd round). **Signed by:** Chris Gale.

When Wright heard his sister scream, he knew he was an Oriole. Both were following the 2011 draft at home on their computers, and her connection was faster so she saw first that Baltimore took him in the third round. He signed quickly for slot money, $363,300, and pitched 46 innings at three minor league stops. He also worked 100 innings during the spring at East Carolina, but injured his foot stepping on a bottle cap and didn't pitch in instructional league. Wright is a sinker/slider pitcher, usually working in the low 90s and touching 96 mph with his two-seam fastball, and he keeps the ball down and generates a lot of groundouts. His slider is a solid pitch and has more upside than his changeup, though his changeup is more consistent right now. He's a strike-thrower who will sharpen his command as he moves up, as he already has learned that pro hitters will punish mistakes in the zone. Wright has the look of a mid-rotation starter, as he's competitive on the mound and has a 6-foot-5 frame that could carry a few more pounds of muscle. After getting his feet wet last summer, he'll probably open his first full season in low Class A.

Year	Club (League)	Class	W	L	ERA	G	GS	CG	SV	IP	H	HR	BB	SO	K/9	WHIP	AVG
2011	Orioles (GCL)	R	0	0	0.00	1	0	0	0	1	0	0	0	1	9.0	0.00	.000
	Aberdeen (NYP)	SS	2	1	3.77	7	7	0	0	31	29	3	6	29	8.4	1.13	.248
	Delmarva (SAL)	LoA	1	1	10.54	4	1	0	0	14	21	3	4	12	7.9	1.83	.356
Minor League Totals			3	2	5.72	12	8	0	0	46	50	6	10	42	8.3	1.31	.279

12 CLAY SCHRADER, RHP

BA GRADE
50
HIGH

Born: April 28, 1990. **B-T:** L-R. **Ht.:** 6-0. **Wt.:** 200. **Drafted:** San Jacinto (Texas) JC, 2010 (10th round). **Signed by:** Rich Morales.

A Texas prep product, Schrader started his college career as a two-way player at Texas-San Antonio in 2009. He transferred to juco power San Jacinto (Texas) in 2010 and led the Gators to a runner-up finish in the Junior College World Series as a closer, posting 12 saves and a 2.61 ERA with 55 strikeouts in 31 innings. The Orioles signed him away from an Oklahoma commitment for $300,000. Schrader posted dominant numbers in two Class A stops in 2011, but he was shut down in August with tendinitis and tenderness in his forearm. He has an aggressive mentality and two potential plus pitches in his fastball, which ranges from 91-94 mph, and his curveball with good bite. He also throws a sinker and slider. Schrader has some effort in his delivery and throws across his body and lands on a stiff front leg, which creates deception but also raises injury concerns. He has a knack for missing bats, but club officials worry that his command issues will come back to bite him at higher levels. He also needs to develop an overall better feel for his pitches. Schrader will return to high Class A to being 2012 and could move quickly if he sharpens his command. He profiles best as a set-up man.

Year	Club (League)	Class	W	L	ERA	G	GS	CG	SV	IP	H	HR	BB	SO	K/9	WHIP	AVG
2010	Aberdeen (NYP)	SS	1	0	0.00	7	0	0	1	8	4	0	4	10	11.3	1.00	.148
	Delmarva (SAL)	LoA	0	1	6.75	3	0	0	0	4	4	0	2	6	13.5	1.50	.250
2011	Delmarva (SAL)	LoA	1	1	2.05	12	0	0	2	22	11	1	13	38	15.5	1.09	.145
	Frederick (CAR)	HiA	1	1	1.13	15	0	0	3	24	8	1	19	35	13.1	1.13	.101
Minor League Totals			3	3	1.71	37	0	0	6	58	27	2	38	89	13.8	1.12	.136

13 JOE MAHONEY, 1B

BA GRADE
50
HIGH

Born: Feb. 1, 1987. **B-T:** L-L. **Ht.:** 6-6. **Wt.:** 240. **Drafted:** Richmond, 2007 (6th round). **Signed by:** Dean Albany.

Mahoney put himself on the Orioles' radar in 2010, earning organization minor league player of the year honors and reaching Double-A after getting himself in better shape. He couldn't build on that success in 2011, in part because a strained quadriceps limited him to 323 at-bats. He did make up for some of that lost time in the Arizona Fall League, where he hit .325/.360/.542. Mahoney offers offensive upside, with the ability to make contact as well as drive the ball. He needs to be more consistent at the plate, as his swing can get long at times because of mechanical flaws that cause his back side to break down and get him off balance. He's an average defender at first base, but he needs to show more consistency there. He's an average runner when healthy, but leg problems have meant he hasn't gotten much of a look in left field. His arm would play fine there. Mahoney looks like a solid bat, though he'll need to be more than that to find an everyday role as a corner player. Baltimore wants to push him to Triple-A Norfolk to see if he's ready to take another step forward with his bat.

Year	Club (League)	Class	AVG	G	AB	R	H	2B	3B	HR	RBI	BB	SO	SB	CS	OBP	SLG
2007	Aberdeen (NYP)	SS	.269	65	242	31	65	10	2	9	44	19	57	1	1	.330	.438
2008	Delmarva (SAL)	LoA	.222	95	352	37	78	22	1	7	61	24	96	2	0	.275	.349
2009	Delmarva (SAL)	LoA	.278	108	395	61	110	16	7	7	53	30	93	29	1	.331	.408
	Frederick (CAR)	HiA	.267	7	30	2	8	4	0	1	5	0	10	0	1	.258	.500
2010	Frederick (CAR)	HiA	.299	72	271	37	81	18	0	9	49	22	56	5	3	.358	.465
	Bowie (EL)	AA	.319	52	191	30	61	12	2	9	29	17	39	8	1	.378	.545
2011	Frederick (CAR)	HiA	.500	3	8	0	4	2	0	0	2	4	1	0	0	.667	.750
	Bowie (EL)	AA	.289	85	315	43	91	24	5	11	67	25	84	7	2	.344	.502
Minor League Totals			.276	487	1804	241	498	108	17	53	310	141	436	52	9	.332	.443

14 AARON BAKER, 1B

BA GRADE
50
HIGH

Born: Sept. 10, 1987. **B-T:** L-R. **Ht.:** 6-2. **Wt.:** 240. **Drafted:** Oklahoma, 2009 (11th round). **Signed by:** Mike Leuzinger (Pirates).

Baker is the grandson of Jerry Mays, who played in two Super Bowls and was an all-American Football League player as an offensive and defensive lineman. He came to the Orioles in the deadline trade of Derrek Lee to the Pirates last July, bringing a tool the system is woefully short on: power. Scouts grade

Baker's power as at least plus, and some give it 70 grades on the 20-80 scale. His swing is about strength more than bat speed, but he has a good idea of the strike zone and is willing to take a walk. His strikeouts are certainly tolerable if he produces homers as expected. Baker was a catcher in high school and at times in college, but he has moved to first base as a pro and gotten bigger. He played at 240-245 pounds last summer and has said he wants to get back to 220-225 in 2012. He should be an adequate first baseman with a solid glove but little range. His arm is fine and he's a well below-average runner. Baker didn't perform well in his limited time at Double-A at the end of last season, so he'll probably return there to open 2012.

Year	Club (League)	Class	AVG	G	AB	R	H	2B	3B	HR	RBI	BB	SO	SB	CS	OBP	SLG
2009	State College (NYP)	SS	.247	62	227	38	56	15	7	3	32	32	54	2	0	.341	.414
2010	West Virginia (SAL)	LoA	.253	125	459	64	116	34	2	18	79	52	115	3	6	.340	.453
2011	Bradenton (FSL)	HiA	.282	103	386	53	109	21	3	15	73	44	92	1	2	.351	.469
	Frederick (CAR)	HiA	.386	12	44	8	17	3	0	2	9	6	9	0	0	.472	.591
	Bowie (EL)	AA	.196	15	46	2	9	2	0	0	3	0	19	0	0	.188	.239
Minor League Totals			.264	317	1162	165	307	75	12	38	196	134	289	6	8	.343	.448

15 RYAN BERRY, RHP

BA GRADE

50

HIGH

Born: Oct. 1, 1991. **B-T:** R-R. **Ht.:** 6-1. **Wt.:** 195. **Drafted:** Rice, 2009 (9th round). **Signed by:** Rich Morales.

Berry put himself on the fast track in his pro debut in 2010, jumping to high Class A and getting in 117 innings after shoulder problems had dented his draft stock at Rice in 2009. He fell from a possible first-round pick to the ninth round, where he signed for $417,600. His shoulder started bothering him again in spring training last year, and doctors discovered that he had a cyst in a muscle around his shoulder. Berry tried to pitch through the pain and developed tendinitis, so he had surgery to remove the cyst and then spent the first half of 2011 rehabbing. He made it back to Frederick by season's end and impressed the Orioles with the way he closed the year. Berry's fastball returned to its previous 88-92 mph levels and he was working on getting back the life and command that allows him to succeed despite average velocity. He was fine-tuning his mechanics to help him keep the ball down in the zone. He also throws an effective knuckle-curve, a slurvy breaking ball and an average changeup. Berry was fully healthy at the end of 2011 and Baltimore doesn't foresee any long-term problems after the removal of the cyst. He'll probably open 2012 in Double-A, with the chance for a major league look later in the year.

Year	Club (League)	Class	W	L	ERA	G	GS	CG	SV	IP	H	HR	BB	SO	K/9	WHIP	AVG
2010	Delmarva (SAL)	LoA	0	3	3.50	8	8	0	0	46	49	4	11	43	8.4	1.29	.268
	Frederick (CAR)	HiA	2	2	3.04	17	12	0	2	71	57	5	25	63	8.0	1.15	.218
2011	Orioles (GCL)	R	0	0	1.80	5	0	0	0	10	5	1	7	9	8.1	1.20	.147
	Aberdeen (NYP)	SS	1	1	4.84	10	2	0	0	22	27	2	8	19	7.7	1.57	.293
	Frederick (CAR)	HiA	0	0	0.00	1	1	0	0	4	3	0	0	4	9.0	0.75	.200
Minor League Totals			3	6	3.28	41	23	0	2	154	141	12	51	138	8.1	1.25	.241

16 MATT ANGLE, OF

BA GRADE

45

LOW

Born: Sept. 10, 1985. **B-T:** L-R. **Ht.:** 5-10. **Wt.:** 175. **Drafted:** Ohio State, 2007 (7th round). **Signed by:** Rich Morales.

Angle made his major league debut with two games last July, then returned to Baltimore at the end of August, making appearances at all three outfield positions and earning praise from manager Buck Showalter for his savvy and reliability. Angle's greatest value lies in his defensive versatility, as he's an above-average outfielder with a strong, accurate arm. He has the speed, arm and acumen to play all three outfield positions well. In that way he's similar to Trent Mummey, though Angle is probably more trustworthy with making the routine plays. At the plate, he puts the ball in play and makes use of his plus speed. He's a good basestealer thanks to his quickness and instincts. Angle offers no real power, and not enough overall impact in his bat to profile as an everyday player. But he has the perfect skill set to serve as an extra outfielder, and he'll try to win one of those jobs on the major league roster in spring training. If not, he'll play center field in Triple-A and wait for his opportunity.

Year	Club (League)	Class	AVG	G	AB	R	H	2B	3B	HR	RBI	BB	SO	SB	CS	OBP	SLG
2007	Aberdeen (NYP)	SS	.301	66	236	60	71	4	4	0	14	47	40	34	4	.421	.352
2008	Delmarva (SAL)	LoA	.287	126	478	82	137	22	5	4	35	71	86	37	11	.385	.379
2009	Frederick (CAR)	HiA	.289	123	478	78	138	17	4	1	32	59	72	40	12	.370	.347
	Bowie (EL)	AA	.357	8	28	6	10	1	0	0	1	4	5	2	0	.438	.393
2010	Bowie (EL)	AA	.383	14	60	11	23	2	0	1	9	6	5	5	2	.433	.467
	Norfolk (IL)	AAA	.260	87	350	55	91	4	4	1	24	41	54	24	4	.338	.303
2011	Norfolk (IL)	AAA	.271	108	424	67	115	13	3	4	33	47	88	27	3	.347	.344
	Baltimore (AL)	MAJ	.177	31	79	12	14	4	0	1	7	12	13	11	1	.293	.266
Major League Totals			.177	31	79	12	14	4	0	1	7	12	13	11	1	.293	.266
Minor League Totals			.285	532	2054	359	585	63	20	11	148	275	350	169	36	.372	.351

17 BOBBY BUNDY, RHP

BA GRADE
50
HIGH

Born: Jan. 13, 1990. **B-T:** R-R. **Ht.:** 6-2. **Wt.:** 218. **Drafted:** HS—Sperry, Okla., 2008 (8th round). **Signed by:** Jim Richardson.

Bundy may wind up being known as Dylan's brother, but he showed last season that he's a legitimate prospect in his own right. While his younger brother—the Orioles' 2011 first-round pick and already their top prospect—has the stuff to be a star, Bobby profiles as more of a middle-of-the-rotation starter. He was a high school star in his own right in Oklahoma but fell to the eighth round of the 2008 draft after injuring his knee playing basketball. He earned his first Double-A action late last season after the best extended run of his career in high Class A. Bundy has an 88-93 mph fastball with some sink and commands it well. He throws both a slider and curveball, though neither is even average at this point, which led to problems at Bowie. The slider has more potential, but he needs to stay on top of it and locate it better. The same goes for his changeup, which is too inconsistent to be effective. He'll need to develop a better feel for his complementary pitches to find success at higher levels. Bundy earns high marks for his makeup and competitiveness. Baltimore will send him back to Double-A in 2012, hoping he can put the lessons learned there last year to good use.

Year	Club (League)	Class	W	L	ERA	G	GS	CG	SV	IP	H	HR	BB	SO	K/9	WHIP	AVG
2008	Orioles (GCL)	R	0	0	9.00	2	0	0	0	2	5	1	0	4	18.0	2.50	.455
2009	Bluefield (APP)	R	2	7	5.10	12	12	1	0	55	47	6	19	38	6.3	1.21	.229
2010	Delmarva (SAL)	LoA	4	6	3.65	28	18	1	0	116	100	12	42	91	7.1	1.22	.238
2011	Frederick (CAR)	HiA	11	5	2.75	20	20	1	0	121	102	8	31	100	7.4	1.10	.230
	Bowie (EL)	AA	1	3	9.60	5	4	0	0	15	25	3	11	13	7.8	2.40	.357
Minor League Totals			18	21	3.88	67	54	3	0	309	279	30	103	246	7.2	1.24	.243

18 KYLE SIMON, RHP

BA GRADE
50
HIGH

Born: Aug. 18, 1990. **B-T:** R-R. **Ht.:** 6-5. **Wt.:** 219. **Drafted:** Arizona, 2011 (4th round). **Signed by:** John Gillette.

Simon was a starter for most of his three years at Arizona, and he earned all-Pacific-10 Conference honors in 2011 by going 11-3, 2.72. The Orioles took him in the fourth round and signed him quickly for a slot bonus of $231,300. That allowed him to start his pro career right away, though Baltimore used him very cautiously after he worked 129 innings in the spring. He pitched in relief at Aberdeen and Delmarva, usually working one-inning stints. Simon is big but not overpowering, succeeding more with heavy sink and a good feel for pitching. He has a low three-quarters delivery that gives him deception and good movement. His fastball operates in the high 80s and touches 93 mph. His slider moves but he needs to tighten its break and his command of it. Simon also has an 84-87 mph cut fastball as well as a changeup. He should be an innings-eating starter, and he'll go back to low Class A to begin his first full pro season.

Year	Club (League)	Class	W	L	ERA	G	GS	CG	SV	IP	H	HR	BB	SO	K/9	WHIP	AVG
2011	Aberdeen (NYP)	SS	1	0	0.00	6	0	0	1	8	3	0	3	2	2.3	0.75	.120
	Delmarva (SAL)	LoA	0	2	4.15	8	0	0	0	9	6	1	2	7	7.3	0.92	.194
Minor League Totals			1	2	2.16	14	0	0	1	17	9	1	5	9	4.9	0.84	.161

19 GLYNN DAVIS, OF

BA GRADE
50
EXTREME

Born: Dec. 7, 1991. **B-T:** R-R. **Ht.:** 6-3. **Wt.:** 170. **Signed:** CC of Baltimore County-Catonsville (Md.) CC, NDFA 2010. **Signed by:** Chris Gale.

While not exactly a hotbed, CC of Baltimore County-Catonsville has proven to be an interesting source of talent for the Orioles, with five players drafted and signed since 2002. The most notable is righthander Chorye Spoone, who reached Triple-A last season before signing with the Red Sox as a minor league free agent. Catonsville's best prospect in the long run may be one who wasn't drafted all. Orioles scouts followed Davis leading up to the 2010 draft but decided not to select him. They wanted to follow him all summer, not worry about the signing deadline and refrain from alerting other teams in case he returned to junior college. Baltimore signed Davis for $120,000 after he played well for the Youse's Orioles squad that serves as a scout team for the organization. Davis has a live body and wiry strength, and his top-of-the-scale speed makes him the fastest runner in the system. He also has a slightly above-average arm and should become a plus defender in center field as he learns the position after playing shortstop as an amateur. He has a good swing but is refining his approach at the plate. While he may develop some power as he matures, it never will be a focal point of his game. Optimists see him as a possible leadoff or No. 2 hitter, while others see him at the bottom of the order, though it's really too early to tell. Glynn focused on hitting, bunting and basestealing in instructional league, where he was one of the Orioles' top performers. He'll move up to low Class A in 2012.

Year	Club (League)	Class	AVG	G	AB	R	H	2B	3B	HR	RBI	BB	SO	SB	CS	OBP	SLG
2011	Orioles (GCL)	R	.435	6	23	4	10	2	0	1	2	4	3	1	1	.519	.652
	Aberdeen (NYP)	SS	.271	62	255	34	69	14	0	1	14	25	53	23	9	.337	.337
	Frederick (CAR)	HiA	.250	1	4	0	1	0	0	0	0	0	1	0	0	.250	.250
Minor League Totals			.284	69	282	38	80	16	0	2	16	29	57	24	10	.351	.362

20 TIM BERRY, LHP

BA GRADE

50

EXTREME

Born: March 18, 1991. **B-T:** L-L. **Ht.:** 6-1. **Wt.:** 168. **Drafted:** HS—San Marcos, Calif., 2009 (50th round). **Signed by:** Mark Ralston.

Berry established himself as a prep standout in the San Diego area, throwing a 17-strikeout no-hitter early in his senior season in 2009. He dropped off the scouting radar when he injured his elbow shortly thereafter, though, and most teams thought he was headed to college at Oregon. The Orioles took a flier in the 50th round and signed him for $125,000, even though they knew he would need Tommy John surgery. He didn't make his pro debut until 2010, when he threw just 20 innings, but got in a full 26 starts last year. Berry pitches at 88-92 mph with his fastball and has the potential to boost his velocity as he adds strength to his frame. His curveball could be a plus pitch with good bite, and he has nice deception on his changeup. He'll need to tighten his curve and improve the consistency and command of all his pitches. He mixed good starts with horrendous ones last season. That's why the Orioles focused on the process and not the results, recognizing his upside. He may go back to low Class A to get 2012 off to a positive start, but he'll move up pretty quickly and could make a big leap forward this season.

Year	Club (League)	Class	W	L	ERA	G	GS	CG	SV	IP	H	HR	BB	SO	K/9	WHIP	AVG
2010	Orioles (GCL)	R	0	1	1.35	14	0	0	0	20	13	0	14	23	10.4	1.35	.181
2011	Delmarva (SAL)	LoA	3	7	5.17	26	26	0	0	117	107	11	61	96	7.4	1.44	.251
Minor League Totals			3	8	4.61	40	26	0	0	137	120	11	75	119	7.8	1.43	.241

21 GABRIEL LINO, C

BA GRADE

50

EXTREME

Born: May 17, 1993. **B-T:** R-R. **Ht.:** 6-3. **Wt.:** 198. **Signed:** Venezuela, 2009. **Signed by:** Calvin Maduro.

Calvin Maduro, who was signed out of Aruba by the Orioles in 1991 and pitched in the big leagues with them and the Phillies, has gone from playing to scouting for the organization in the Caribbean. His first significant prospect could be Lino, who impressed observers with his skills behind the plate during his U.S. debut in 2011. He's solidly built for a teenager and has a well above-average arm. He also shows a promising ability to work with pitchers. He's still unrefined defensively, committing five errors and four passed balls in just 26 games last year while throwing out 28 percent of basestealers. But the raw material is there. As a hitter, Lino offers promising power potential and a nice approach for a teenager. He has the demonstrated the ability to make two-strike adjustments and to take the ball the other way, as well as laying off pitchers' pitches. Like most catchers he won't offer much in the way of speed, especially once he fills out his 6-foot-3 frame. Lino will get a chance to prove himself in full-season ball this year, advancing to low Class A.

Year	Club (League)	Class	AVG	G	AB	R	H	2B	3B	HR	RBI	BB	SO	SB	CS	OBP	SLG
2010	Orioles2 (DSL)	R	.200	54	140	15	28	10	0	0	19	28	21	4	0	.359	.271
2011	Orioles (GCL)	R	.282	28	78	10	22	6	1	2	11	8	13	1	0	.371	.462
Minor League Totals			.229	82	218	25	50	16	1	2	30	36	34	5	0	.363	.339

22 RODERICK BERNADINA, OF

BA GRADE

50

EXTREME

Born: Aug. 10, 1992. **B-T:** R-R. **Ht.:** 5-10. **Wt.:** 167. **Signed:** Curacao, 2009. **Signed by:** Ernst Meyer.

The Orioles scout Curacao as hard as any organization, with Jonathan Schoop as the most promising result of those efforts currently in the system. Bernadina, who signed for $35,000, soon could join him. He's the younger brother of Nationals outfielder Roger Bernadina, who has played parts of the last four seasons in the major leagues. Roger needed six years to get there after he first signed, and Roderick could require similar patience. He has right-field tools, starting with impressive bat speed and raw power. He can crush fastballs and covers the plate well, possessing decent strike-zone judgment. He's willing to use the opposite field or take a walk, though he just as often swings out of his shoes or has trouble making contact against offspeed stuff. He has average speed and arm strength, which should make him a solid defender in right. Baltimore still isn't quite sure what it has in Bernadina, who's learning the nuances of outfield defense and baserunning. If he refines his swing and his approach, he could become an everyday right fielder in the big leagues.

Year	Club (League)	Class	AVG	G	AB	R	H	2B	3B	HR	RBI	BB	SO	SB	CS	OBP	SLG
2010	Orioles1 (DSL)	R	.242	70	223	37	54	13	3	1	26	30	38	13	8	.347	.341
2011	Orioles (GCL)	R	.239	51	184	30	44	14	3	4	28	22	26	6	2	.341	.413
Minor League Totals			.241	121	407	67	98	27	6	5	54	52	64	19	10	.344	.373

23 RYAN ADAMS, 2B

BA GRADE

45

MEDIUM

Born: April 21, 1987. **B-T:** R-R. **Ht.:** 6-0. **Wt.:** 195. **Drafted:** HS—New Orleans, 2006 (2nd round). **Signed by:** Mike Tullier.

Adams didn't put together a great season in 2011, but he did make his major league debut and played through what he thought was a groin injury all year. Treatment didn't work and the pain got worse as the season went on until doctors discovered in September that he had a sports hernia. He had surgery to repair it and should be healthy for spring training. When healthy, Adams showed the Orioles what he always has shown them: a productive hitter who struggles to find a place to play defensively. He has a knack for making solid contact with some pop, though his swing can get long and he strikes out too much for his profile as an offensive second baseman. Despite his hard work, Adams still struggles to make the routine play at second, which managers simply won't tolerate and explains why he played sparingly in the big leagues. Adams doesn't have enough power for first base or left field, and he doesn't fit well as a utilityman because he can't play shortstop. He's passable at third base. His arm is average but he has below-average speed. Adams continues to work on his defense, and unless he wins a job out of spring training he'll go back to Triple-A and again try to hit enough for Baltimore to find a place for his bat.

Year	Club (League)	Class	AVG	G	AB	R	H	2B	3B	HR	RBI	BB	SO	SB	CS	OBP	SLG
2006	Bluefield (APP)	R	.256	34	133	24	34	8	1	2	7	19	32	2	2	.361	.376
	Aberdeen (NYP)	SS	.316	6	19	2	6	3	0	1	5	4	7	0	0	.458	.632
2007	Aberdeen (NYP)	SS	.236	67	246	29	58	10	2	3	22	18	63	8	3	.296	.329
2008	Delmarva (SAL)	LoA	.308	119	448	68	138	26	5	11	57	36	109	12	5	.367	.462
2009	Frederick (CAR)	HiA	.288	59	215	27	62	14	0	2	25	19	41	2	4	.349	.381
2010	Bowie (EL)	AA	.298	134	530	81	158	43	0	15	68	47	121	2	3	.365	.464
2011	Norfolk (IL)	AAA	.284	94	377	46	107	28	3	10	37	30	103	5	2	.341	.454
	Baltimore (AL)	MAJ	.281	29	89	9	25	4	0	0	7	6	25	0	0	.333	.326
Major League Totals			.281	29	89	9	25	4	0	0	7	6	25	0	0	.333	.326
Minor League Totals			.286	513	1968	277	563	132	11	44	221	173	476	31	19	.351	.431

24 TYLER TOWNSEND, 1B

BA GRADE
45
HIGH

Born: May 14, 1988. **B-T:** L-R. **Ht.:** 6-3. **Wt.:** 205. **Drafted:** Florida International, 2009 (3rd round). **Signed by:** John Martin.

Townsend continues to impress the Orioles with his performance, but at the same time he creates frustration because he has struggled to stay on the field. He has been bothered by hamstring problems in each of his two full pro seasons, and he missed more than a month in high Class A last year. He tried to return at the end of 2011 but went back on the disabled list before Frederick's run to the Carolina League title. Townsend has some of the system's best power, generating it with a smooth, lefthanded swing that allows him to hit for average as well as put the ball over the fence. He played mostly in the outfield in college, but works better at first base because he's a below-average runner with an average arm. He'll be average defensively, though he needs more repetitions to refine his skills. Baltimore worked with Townsend on his offseason conditioning to make sure his hamstring issues are resolved once and for all. He'll compete with Aaron Baker for the first-base job in Double-A, and the loser might head back to high Class A unless Townsend gives the outfield another try.

Year	Club (League)	Class	AVG	G	AB	R	H	2B	3B	HR	RBI	BB	SO	SB	CS	OBP	SLG
2009	Aberdeen (NYP)	SS	.143	31	119	11	17	7	0	4	16	10	39	1	1	.226	.303
2010	Orioles (GCL)	R	.385	3	13	3	5	4	0	0	5	1	2	0	0	.429	.692
	Delmarva (SAL)	LoA	.342	30	117	16	40	12	2	3	26	9	18	0	1	.398	.556
	Frederick (CAR)	HiA	.284	19	67	6	19	5	2	3	14	10	15	1	0	.385	.552
2011	Orioles (GCL)	R	.235	5	17	3	4	2	0	1	8	3	4	0	0	.333	.529
	Frederick (CAR)	HiA	.317	67	252	43	80	24	2	13	50	11	64	2	2	.358	.583
Minor League Totals			.282	155	585	82	165	54	6	24	119	44	142	4	4	.343	.518

25 BRANDON WARING, 3B/1B

BA GRADE
45
HIGH

Born: Jan. 2, 1986. **B-T:** R-R. **Ht.:** 6-3. **Wt.:** 215. **Drafted:** Wofford, 2007 (7th round). **Signed by:** Steve Kring (Reds).

The Orioles acquired Waring with Ryan Freel and Justin Turner in a December 2008 trade that sent Ramon Hernandez to the Reds. Waring has some of the best power in the system and has hit 70 homers in three seasons since the deal, yet never has been able to earn a long look for advancement. The Carolina League MVP in 2009, he ended that season and spent all of the next two in Double-A. Waring's bat has stagnated. He made an adjustment in his swing last season, moving his hands down to free them up more, and it helped for a while. He cut down on his strikeouts but he finished the year batting a career-low .222. He may never hit for average because he's too aggressive, but Waring is a confident hitter with a balanced approach and legitimate power to all fields. He has improved his defense to the point that some scouts now rate him as an average defender at third base. He has the hands and arm strength to make the routine plays. He also has played a good bit at first base and can handle left field in a pinch, though he's a below-average runner. He has been blocked by such players as Josh Bell and Brandon Snyder, but they've failed at the big league level, so maybe Waring will get a look in 2012.

Year	Club (League)	Class	AVG	G	AB	R	H	2B	3B	HR	RBI	BB	SO	SB	CS	OBP	SLG
2007	Billings (PIO)	R	.311	68	267	63	83	17	2	20	61	21	83	1	0	.369	.614
	Dayton (MWL)	LoA	1.000	1	1	0	1	0	0	0	2	0	0	0	0	1.000	1.000
2008	Dayton (MWL)	LoA	.270	119	441	63	119	23	2	20	71	43	156	1	0	.346	.467
2009	Frederick (CAR)	HiA	.273	128	473	70	129	35	2	26	90	51	121	5	3	.354	.520
	Bowie (EL)	AA	.292	8	24	4	7	3	0	1	6	3	9	0	0	.414	.542
2010	Bowie (EL)	AA	.242	129	472	70	114	32	2	22	70	59	179	0	1	.338	.458
2011	Bowie (EL)	AA	.222	115	406	60	90	21	3	21	59	33	127	0	0	.288	.443
Minor League Totals			.261	568	2084	330	543	131	11	110	359	210	675	7	4	.339	.492

26 OLIVER DRAKE, RHP

BA GRADE
45
HIGH

Born: Jan. 13, 1987. **B-T:** R-R. **Ht.:** 6-4. **Wt.:** 220. **Drafted:** Navy, 2008 (43rd round). **Signed by:** Dean Albany.

Teams are hesitant to draft players from the service academies because no matter their talent, their military commitments usually put them too far behind to succeed in pro baseball. Drake posted a 3.48 ERA at Navy in 2007-08, and most teams didn't realize he was a draft-eligible sophomore who wouldn't have to fulfill his military commitment if he didn't return for his junior year. The Orioles knew him from the Youse's Orioles squad in the Cal Ripken Collegiate League that serves as a scout team for the organization and took him in the 43rd round in 2008. After he compiled a 1.00 ERA that summer, they signed him for $100,000. He moved slowly through the farm system until last year, when he fashioned a 27-inning scoreless streak in high Class A to earn a promotion to Double-A (and an emergency appearance in Triple-A). Drake features a sinking fastball that ranges from 89-95 mph and usually sits in the low 90s. While he has an average changeup, he'll have to improve his curveball to succeed at higher levels. He does mix his pitches well and has good control, though he'll also need to sharpen his command. Drake was added to the 40-man roster in November, and he'll start 2012 back in Bowie. If he gets his breaking ball figured out, he'll profile as an innings-eating starter.

Year	Club (League)	Class	W	L	ERA	G	GS	CG	SV	IP	H	HR	BB	SO	K/9	WHIP	AVG
2008	Bluefield (APP)	R	1	0	0.77	7	0	0	0	12	7	1	2	11	8.5	0.77	.167
	Aberdeen (NYP)	SS	0	0	0.87	5	0	0	1	10	9	0	1	13	11.3	0.97	.214
2009	Delmarva (SAL)	LoA	8	9	4.34	25	24	0	0	131	138	6	42	104	7.2	1.38	.277
2010	Frederick (CAR)	HiA	6	6	4.36	24	21	0	0	128	135	19	30	100	7.0	1.34	.272
2011	Frederick (CAR)	HiA	8	3	2.14	14	13	2	0	97	78	1	18	80	7.4	0.99	.224
	Bowie (EL)	AA	3	5	5.20	12	12	2	0	64	77	8	24	47	6.6	1.58	.292
	Norfolk (IL)	AAA	0	0	0.00	1	0	0	0	2	1	0	1	2	9.0	1.00	.143
Minor League Totals			26	23	3.80	88	70	4	1	443	445	35	125	357	7.2	1.29	.262

27 TRENT MUMMEY, OF

BA GRADE
45
HIGH

Born: Jan. 5, 1989. **B-T:** L-L. **Ht.:** 5-10. **Wt.:** 185. **Drafted:** Auburn, 2010 (4th round). **Signed by:** Dave Jennings.

The Orioles were looking for Mummey to get on the fast track in his first full pro season in 2011, but an outfield wall slowed him down. Promoted to high Class A after he got off to a hot start, he slammed into the fence while diving for a ball and sustained a concussion on May 4. That kept him out for a month, and he had been back for just a week when he injured his right hamstring, which kept him out for the rest of the season. Mummey draws comparisons to Nate McLouth as an undersized guy who will squeeze every ounce out of his ability. As his outfield collision showed, he goes all out all the time. His best tool is his above-average speed, and he also has the instincts to steal bases. With his quickness and strong arm, he has the ability to play all three outfield positions. Mummey is quick to the ball and has a simple swing. He goes to the plate with a plan and has a good feel for the strike zone. He doesn't offer much power, so he'll have to maximize his speed and on-base ability to establish an everyday role. Otherwise he profiles as a useful fourth outfielder. After losing development time last year, Mummey probably will go back to Frederick to open 2012.

Year	Club (League)	Class	AVG	G	AB	R	H	2B	3B	HR	RBI	BB	SO	SB	CS	OBP	SLG
2010	Aberdeen (NYP)	SS	.266	49	207	30	55	16	2	3	24	23	28	6	2	.342	.406
	Delmarva (SAL)	LoA	.167	13	54	7	9	0	3	0	5	3	8	2	2	.224	.278
2011	Delmarva (SAL)	LoA	.291	14	55	9	16	2	2	2	12	10	11	12	2	.377	.509
	Frederick (CAR)	HiA	.293	15	58	13	17	2	2	1	10	6	8	7	1	.369	.448
Minor League Totals			.259	91	374	59	97	20	9	6	51	42	55	27	7	.336	.409

28 WYNN PELZER, RHP

BA GRADE
45
HIGH

Born: June 23, 1986. **B-T:** R-R. **Ht.:** 6-1. **Wt.:** 205. **Drafted:** South Carolina, 2007 (9th round). **Signed by:** Pete DeYoung (Padres).

The Orioles got Pelzer from the Padres in a July 2010 deadline trade for Miguel Tejada, a deal that has done little for either side. Pelzer has floundered as a starter and reliever the last two years, and Baltimore declined to protect him on its 40-man roster for the second straight offseason. Pelzer has a good sinker/slider combination, which theoretically would make him at least a useful reliever. His fastball ranges from 87-93 mph and has been clocked as high as 97 in the past. His slider has shown flashes of becoming a plus pitch, though both offerings have slipped a little since the trade. His control has regressed, too. Pelzer never has had a consistently reliable curveball or changeup, so his future probably will be as a reliever. He had a 2.81 ERA in that role last season, compared to 5.09 as a starter. Perhaps Baltimore's new leadership will give Pelzer a longer look, though he'll probably have to sustain some Triple-A success before earning a big league shot.

Year	Club (League)	Class	W	L	ERA	G	GS	CG	SV	IP	H	HR	BB	SO	K/9	WHIP	AVG
2008	Fort Wayne (MWL)	LoA	9	6	3.19	29	23	0	0	118	114	9	32	100	7.6	1.23	.248
	Lake Elsinore (CAL)	HiA	0	0	27.00	1	0	0	0	1	3	0	1	0	0.0	4.00	.500
2009	Lake Elsinore (CAL)	HiA	11	8	3.94	27	27	0	0	151	134	6	59	147	8.8	1.28	.244
2010	San Antonio (TL)	AA	6	9	4.20	22	18	0	0	94	102	9	56	83	7.9	1.67	.277
	Bowie (EL)	AA	1	0	4.50	10	1	0	0	20	24	2	7	20	9.0	1.55	.296
2011	Bowie (EL)	AA	5	7	4.14	29	10	0	1	76	76	6	45	65	7.7	1.59	.265
	Norfolk (IL)	AAA	0	1	3.09	8	0	0	0	12	9	0	9	7	5.4	1.54	.220
Minor League Totals			32	31	3.89	126	79	0	1	472	462	32	209	422	8.0	1.42	.258

29 KYLE HUDSON, OF

Born: Jan. 7, 1987. **B-T:** L-L. **Ht.:** 5-11. **Wt.:** 162. **Drafted:** Illinois, 2008 (4th round). **Signed by:** Troy Hoerner.

It has been a long, slow climb for Hudson—and by no means is his development complete—but he reached a significant milestone when he made his big league debut last September. Hudson opened 2011 with his third stint in high Class A but played well enough to earn three promotions. Most significant, he was added to the 40-man roster, a tangible signal that the Orioles see something in him. Hudson is a premium athlete, a four-sport standout as an Illinois high schooler who went on to play three years as a wide receiver on the University of Illinois football team. As his football playing time diminished, he turned his focus to the diamond, where he first drew notice with his blazing speed. Hudson still is refining his baseball skills, in particular his swing and his instincts on the basepaths and in the outfield. He made huge strides with the bat last season, hitting for average at all three of his stops, but questions remain about whether his stroke will play in the big leagues. He offers no power and realizes that his job is to get on base. He has improved his baserunning but still gets caught stealing more often than someone with his speed should. Despite his wheels, Hudson isn't quite as good defensively as Matt Angle and has seen more time in left field than in his center. He does cover a lot of ground but has a fringy arm. Hudson's bat probably limits him to a reserve outfield role in the majors.

Year	Club (League)	Class	AVG	G	AB	R	H	2B	3B	HR	RBI	BB	SO	SB	CS	OBP	SLG
2008	Aberdeen (NYP)	SS	.216	11	37	5	8	1	0	0	5	8	12	4	3	.356	.243
2009	Delmarva (SAL)	LoA	.284	117	398	61	113	8	2	0	21	49	85	31	16	.365	.314
	Frederick (CAR)	HiA	.250	6	20	4	5	0	0	0	0	4	6	3	0	.400	.250
2010	Frederick (CAR)	HiA	.260	136	516	83	134	17	3	0	28	62	129	40	15	.348	.304
2011	Frederick (CAR)	HiA	.279	23	86	12	24	3	0	0	2	10	16	8	6	.354	.314
	Bowie (EL)	AA	.308	28	91	9	28	3	1	0	10	10	24	7	2	.376	.363
	Norfolk (IL)	AAA	.297	68	246	39	73	7	1	0	11	33	55	26	8	.382	.333
	Baltimore (AL)	MAJ	.143	14	28	3	4	0	0	0	2	0	6	2	0	.143	.143
Major League Totals			.143	14	28	3	4	0	0	0	2	0	6	2	0	.143	.143
Minor League Totals			.276	389	1394	213	385	39	7	0	77	176	327	119	50	.362	.314

30 EDUARDO RODRIGUEZ, LHP

Born: April 1, 1993. **B-T:** L-L. **Ht.:** 6-2. **Wt.:** 174. **Signed:** Venezuela, 2010. **Signed by:** Calvin Maduro.

Former president of baseball operations Andy MacPhail wasn't able to turn around the major league club, but he did at least try to make Baltimore more active in the international market. The Orioles still remain among the game's lowest spenders internationally, unwilling to shell out big bonuses, so the signing of Rodriguez for $175,000 before the 2010 season qualified as a big splash for them. He pitched well in his pro debut in the Rookie-level Dominican Summer League, then built on that last year with a 1.81 ERA that would have ranked second in the Rookie-level Gulf Coast League had he not just missed qualifying. Rodriguez is a command-and-feel lefty, usually pitching in the high 80s and occasionally dialing his fastball up to 93 mph. His fastball has good life and sink. He has a slurvy breaking ball and an average changeup that needs to get more consistent. While Rodriguez has some polish, he's still working out the kinks in his complementary pitches and polishing his command, so his GCL stardom was a surprise to Baltimore. He earned a shot at the Delmarva rotation in 2012 and profiles as a No. 4 or 5 starter.

Year	Club (League)	Class	W	L	ERA	G	GS	CG	SV	IP	H	HR	BB	SO	K/9	WHIP	AVG
2010	Orioles1 (DSL)	R	3	4	2.33	12	12	1	0	66	49	0	28	62	8.5	1.17	.213
2011	Orioles (GCL)	R	1	1	1.81	11	10	0	1	45	28	0	17	46	9.3	1.01	.177
	Aberdeen (NYP)	SS	0	0	6.75	1	1	0	0	4	6	1	1	4	9.0	1.75	.333
Minor League Totals			4	5	2.28	24	23	1	1	114	83	1	46	112	8.8	1.13	.204

Boston Red Sox

BY JIM CALLIS

After trading for Adrian Gonzalez and signing free-agent Carl Crawford in a three-day span at the 2010 Winter Meetings, the Red Sox had the look of a legitimate championship contender. They shook off a 2-10 start in April to play as well as any team in baseball for most of the season, entering September with the American League's best record.

Boston exited with the humiliation of the biggest final-month collapse in major league history. Despite the third-highest payroll in baseball and the presence of 15 former all-stars on their roster, the Red Sox dropped 20 of their final 27 games to hand the AL East to the Yankees and blow a nine-game wild-card edge over the Rays.

Their disintegration on the field had repercussions off it as well. Two days after the season ended, Boston declined to pick up the option on the contract of Terry Francona, who won 744 games and two World Series titles in eight seasons as manager.

Following his dismissal, the Boston Globe ran a story in which a team source implied that Francona lost control of the team because he was distracted by marital issues and possible problems with painkillers, which he denied. The same story alleged that Josh Beckett, Jon Lester and John Lackey—who combined for two wins and a 6.55 ERA in September—often drank beer, ate fried chicken and played video games in the clubhouse on days they weren't starting.

While Francona's departure seemed inevitable in the season's final weeks, general manager Theo Epstein's came as a shock. Epstein, who built the Red Sox's first championship teams since 1918, accepted a five-year, $18.5 million deal to become the Cubs' president of baseball operations on Oct. 25.

That set off a series of promotions in Boston's front office. Senior vice president/assistant GM Ben Cherington took over as GM, just as he had (along with Jed Hoyer) when Epstein took a three-month sabbatical after the 2005 season. Well regarded in the industry, Cherington has been with the club since 1999, working his way up from area scout to farm director to vice president of player personnel.

Cherington elevated Mike Hazen and Brian O'Halloran to assistant GMs, Dave Finley to director of player personnel and Ben Crockett to farm director. He fired senior vice president Craig Shipley, whose duties included overseeing international scouting, and put Eddie Romero in charge of those efforts.

The Red Sox may have embarrassed themselves and missed the playoffs for a second straight season, but

BILL MITCHELL

Ben Cherington rose from area scout to become Red Sox general manager

TOP 30 PROSPECTS

1. Will Middlebrooks, 3b	16. Drake Britton, lhp
2. Xander Bogaerts, ss	17. Felix Doubront, lhp
3. Blake Swihart, c	18. Henry Owens, lhp
4. Anthony Ranaudo, rhp	19. Kolbrin Vitek, 3b
5. Bryce Brentz, of	20. Kyle Stroup, rhp
6. Brandon Jacobs, of	21. Jose Vinicio, ss
7. Garin Cecchini, 3b	22. Kyle Weiland, rhp
8. Matt Barnes, rhp	23. Stolmy Pimentel, rhp
9. Ryan Lavarnway, c	24. Oscar Tejeda, 2b
10. Jackie Bradley, of	25. Derrik Gibson, ss
11. Alex Wilson, rhp	26. Alex Hassan, of
12. Jose Iglesias, ss	27. Raul Alcantara, rhp
13. Miles Head, 1b	28. Lars Anderson, 1b
14. Sean Coyle, 2b	29. Christian Vazquez, c
15. Brandon Workman, rhp	30. Heiker Meneses, inf

they still won 90 games and will remain a contender in the near future. Likewise, Boston's farm system didn't cover itself in glory in 2011, yet still has plenty of talent. The system does lack an elite prospect, and many of its best players haven't advanced past Class A.

For the third time in four years, the Red Sox set a new franchise record for draft spending, upping the ante to $11 million in 2011. The draft changes that came out of baseball's new collective bargaining agreement may hit Boston more than any club, as it will have a relatively small signing bonus cap and fewer extra picks going forward.

General Manager: Ben Cherington. **Farm Director:** Ben Crockett. **Scouting Director:** Amiel Sawdaye.

Class	Team	League	W	L	Pct	Finish*	Manager(s)
Majors	Boston Red Sox	American	90	72	.556	5th (14)	Terry Francona
Triple-A	Pawtucket Red Sox	International	81	61	.570	2nd (14)	Arnie Beyeler
Double-A	Portland Sea Dogs	Eastern	59	83	.415	12th (12)	Kevin Boles
High A	Salem Red Sox	Carolina	64	75	.460	7th (8)	Bruce Crabbe
Low A	Greenville Drive	South Atlantic	78	62	.557	4th (14)	Billy McMillon
Short-season	Lowell Spinners	New York-Penn	29	45	.392	13th (14)	Carlos Febles
Rookie	GCL Red Sox	Gulf Coast	27	33	.450	11th (15)	George Lombard
Overall 2011 Minor League Record			338	359	.485	20th (30)	

*Finish in overall standings (No. of teams in league). †League champion.

LAST YEAR'S TOP 30

Player, Pos.		Status
1.	Jose Iglesias, ss	No. 12
2.	Anthony Ranaudo, rhp	No. 4
3.	Drake Britton, lhp	No. 16
4.	Josh Reddick, of	Majors
5.	Felix Doubront, lhp	No. 17
6.	Stolmy Pimentel, rhp	No. 23
7.	Garin Cecchini, 3b	No. 7
8.	Lars Anderson, 1b	No. 28
9.	Kolbrin Vitek, 3b	No. 19
10.	Oscar Tejeda, 2b	No. 24
11.	Will Middlebrooks, 3b	No. 1
12.	Yamaico Navarro, ss/3b	(Pirates)
13.	Sean Coyle, 2b	No. 14
14.	Xander Bogaerts, ss	No. 2
15.	Derrik Gibson, ss	No. 25
16.	Ryan Lavarnway, c	No. 9
17.	Bryce Brentz, of	No. 5
18.	Brandon Workman, rhp	No. 15
19.	Alex Wilson, rhp	No. 11
20.	Kyle Weiland, rhp	No. 22
21.	Tim Federowicz, c	(Dodgers)
22.	Jeremy Hazelbaker, of	Dropped out
23.	Junichi Tazawa, rhp	Dropped out
24.	Madison Younginer, rhp	Dropped out
25.	Che-Hsuan Lin, of	Dropped out
26.	Chris Balcom-Miller, rhp	Dropped out
27.	Brandon Jacobs, of	No. 6
28.	Juan Carlos Linares, of	Dropped out
29.	Miguel Celestino, rhp	Dropped out
30.	Ryan Westmoreland, of	Dropped out

BEST TOOLS

Best Hitter for Average	Garin Cecchini
Best Power Hitter	Bryce Brentz
Best Strike-Zone Discipline	Alex Hassan
Fastest Baserunner	Felix Sanchez
Best Athlete	Derrik Gibson
Best Fastball	Alex Wilson
Best Curveball	Anthony Ranaudo
Best Slider	Alex Wilson
Best Changeup	Noe Ramirez
Best Control	Keith Couch
Best Defensive Catcher	Christian Vazquez
Best Defensive Infielder	Jose Iglesias
Best Infield Arm	Will Middlebrooks
Best Defensive Outfielder	Jackie Bradley
Best Outfield Arm	Che-Hsuan Lin

PROJECTED 2015 LINEUP

Catcher	Blake Swihart
First Base	Adrian Gonzalez
Second Base	Dustin Pedroia
Third Base	Will Middlebrooks
Shortstop	Jose Iglesias
Left Field	Carl Crawford
Center Field	Jacoby Ellsbury
Right Field	Xander Bogaerts
Designated Hitter	Kevin Youkilis
No. 1 Starter	Jon Lester
No. 2 Starter	Clay Buchholz
No. 3 Starter	Josh Beckett
No. 4 Starter	Anthony Ranaudo
No. 5 Starter	Matt Barnes
Closer	Daniel Bard

TOP PROSPECTS OF THE DECADE

Year	Player, Pos.	2011 Org.
2002	Seung Song, rhp	Lotte (Korea)
2003	Hanley Ramirez, ss	Marlins
2004	Hanley Ramirez, ss	Marlins
2005	Hanley Ramirez, ss	Marlins
2006	Andy Marte, 3b	Pirates
2007	Daisuke Matsuzaka, rhp	Red Sox
2008	Clay Buchholz, rhp	Red Sox
2009	Lars Anderson, 1b	Red Sox
2010	Ryan Westmoreland, of	Red Sox
2011	Jose Iglesias, ss	Red Sox

TOP DRAFT PICKS OF THE DECADE

Year	Player, Pos.	2011 Org.
2002	Jon Lester, lhp (2nd round)	Red Sox
2003	David Murphy, of	Rangers
2004	Dustin Pedroia, ss (2nd round)	Red Sox
2005	Jacoby Ellsbury, of	Red Sox
2006	Jason Place, of	Yankees
2007	Nick Hagadone, lhp (1st round supp.)	Indians
2008	Casey Kelly, rhp/ss	Padres
2009	Reymond Fuentes, of	Padres
2010	Kolbrin Vitek, 3b	Red Sox
2011	Matt Barnes, rhp	Red Sox

LARGEST BONUSES IN CLUB HISTORY

Jose Iglesias, 2009	$6,250,000
Casey Kelly, 2008	$3,000,000
Anthony Ranaudo, 2010	$2,550,000
Blake Swihart, 2011	$2,500,000
Daisuke Matsuzaka, 2006	$2,000,000
Ryan Westmoreland, 2008	$2,000,000

BOSTON RED SOX

TOP 2012 ROOKIE: Ryan Lavarnway, c. He'll back up Jarrod Saltalamacchia behind the plate, and his power will earn him some at-bats at first base and DH.

BREAKOUT PROSPECT: Kyle Stroup, rhp. The 1,504th and final pick in the 2008 draft, he has a 91-97 mph fastball and promising secondary stuff.

SLEEPER: Cody Kukuk, lhp. An eighth-round draft choice last year, he's extremely projectable and already reaches 94 mph.

SOURCE OF TOP 30 TALENT			
Homegrown	30	Acquired	0
College	10	Trades	0
Junior college	0	Rule 5 draft	0
High school	12	Independent leagues	0
Draft-and-follow	0	Free agents/waivers	0
Nondrafted free agents	0		
International	8		

LF
Brandon Jacobs (6)
Alex Hassan (26)
Kendrick Perkins

CF
Jackie Bradley (10)
Kolbrin Vitek (19)
Jeremy Hazelbaker
Che-Hsuan Lin
Peter Hissey
Keury de la Cruz
Williams Jerez
Ryan Westmoreland
Felix Sanchez
Cody Koback
Manuel Marcos

RF
Bryce Brentz (5)
Juan Carlos Linares
Henry Ramos
Ynoel Aguero

3B
Will Middlebrooks (1)
Xander Bogaerts (2)
Garin Cecchini (7)
David Renfroe
Travis Shaw
Nick Moore

SS
Jose Iglesias (12)
Jose Vinicio (21)
Derrik Gibson (25)
Mookie Betts
Jose Garcia
Raimel Flores

2B
Sean Coyle (14)
Oscar Tejeda (24)
Heiker Meneses (30)

1B
Miles Head (13)
Lars Anderson (28)
Michael Almanzar
Boss Moanaroa

C
Blake Swihart (3)
Ryan Lavarnway (9)
Christian Vazquez (29)
Luis Exposito
Dan Butler
Oscar Perez
Jordan Weems

LHP

LHSP
Felix Doubront (17)
Henry Owens (18)
Cody Kukuk
Manuel Rivera
Pedro Reyes
Miguel Pena
Zach Good

LHRP
Drake Britton (16)
Chris Hernandez

RHP

RHSP
Anthony Ranaudo (4)
Matt Barnes (8)
Alex Wilson (11)
Brandon Workman (15)
Kyle Stroup (20)
Kyle Weiland (22)
Stolmy Pimentel (23)
Raul Alcantara (27)
Miguel Celestino
Chris Balcom-Miller
Noe Ramirez
Will Inman
Brock Huntzinger
Keith Couch
Luis Diaz
Jason Garcia
Dioscar Romero

RHRP
Junichi Tazawa
Madison Younginer
Josh Fields
Chris Martin
Luis Bastardo
Marco Duarte
Chorye Spoone
Caleb Clay
Matt Spalding
Andrew Jones
Braden Kapteyn

2011   BONUSES: $11.0 MILLION

BEST PURE HITTER: C Blake Swihart (1) has the bat to be an impact player even if he doesn't stay behind the plate, though the Red Sox think he will. He led the U.S. national 18-and-under team in hitting (.448) and homers (five in 17 games) in 2010.

BEST POWER HITTER: OF Williams Jerez (2) is a potential five-tool player with plenty of raw power. 3B/1B Travis Shaw (9) has the most present power, along with the lefthanded stroke to drive balls off and over Fenway Park's Green Monster.

FASTEST RUNNER: OF Cody Koback (10) is the fastest player to come out of Wisconsin in recent memory, with 70-75 speed on the 20-80 scouting scale. SS Mookie Betts (5) is a plus runner.

BEST DEFENSIVE PLAYER: Boston scouts say OF Jackie Bradley (1s) plays center field better than any amateur they've ever seen. He tracks balls effortlessly from gap to gap and has a strong arm.

BEST FASTBALL: RHP Matt Barnes (1) has a heater that sits in the mid-90s, tops out at 97 mph and features armside run. Projectable LHP Cody Kukuk (7), who's a slender 6-foot-4 and already touches 94 mph, could catch Barnes down the road.

BEST SECONDARY PITCH: RHP Noe Ramirez (4) makes his living pitching off his outstanding changeup. As for breaking balls, Barnes has a sharp curveball and Kukuk flashes a hard slider.

BEST PRO DEBUT: Shaw batted .262/.371/.446 with eight homers at short-season Lowell. RHP Andrew Jones (18) posted a 1.41 ERA and 21-2 K-BB ratio in 32 innings while reaching low Class A.

BEST ATHLETE: Betts, who received interest from NCAA Division I basketball programs as a point guard, was the Tennessee male high school bowler of the year in 2010. Jerez has all-around tools and originally attracted scouts as a lefthanded pitcher.

MOST INTRIGUING BACKGROUND: OF Matt Marquis (41) has overcome hemophilia, which he treats with medication, to make it to pro ball. 3B/2B Matt Gedman's (45) dad Rich made two all-star teams as a Red Sox catcher and is the hitting coach at Lowell. Shaw's father Jeff pitched in two All-Star Games and saved 203 games in 12 years in the big leagues. 3B Nick Moore (30) is the godson of Rob English, the part-time scout who signed him.

CLOSEST TO THE MAJORS: Ramirez, who's more polished than Barnes. Boston will develop him as a starter.

BEST LATE-ROUND PICK: Jones was a revelation with his low-90s sinker. LHP Zach Good (20) has a similar fastball. RHP Matt Spalding's (29) fastball can reach 95 mph.

THE ONE WHO GOT AWAY: The Red Sox went all out to sign OF Senquez Golson (8), one of the draft's best athletes and fastest players. They flew him and his family to Boston the day before the signing deadline and offered him a seven-figure deal, but he decided to attend Mississippi, where he's a cornerback on the football team.

ASSESSMENT: As usual, the Red Sox had extra picks and spent lavishly. Barnes, Swihart, LHP Henry Owens (1s) and Bradley cost a combined $6.65 million and will replenish a system thinned by promotions and trades.

2010   BONUSES: $10.7 MILLION

In a typical Red Sox draft, they had extra picks and spent extra money, bringing in several of the system's best hitting prospects in 3Bs Kolbrin Vitek (1) and Garin Cecchini (4), OF Bryce Brentz (1s) and 2B Sean Coyle (3). They paid $2.55 million for RHP Anthony Ranaudo (1s), their top pitching prospect.

GRADE: B

2009   BONUSES: $7.1 MILLION

Boston found a pitcher on the verge of the majors in RHP Alex Wilson (2) and a pair of potent Georgia high school bats in OF Brandon Jacobs (10) and 1B Miles Head (26). OF Reymond Fuentes was a key part of the Adrian Gonzalez trade with the Padres.

GRADE: C+

2008   BONUSES: $10.5 MILLION

This crop produced plenty of trade fodder, as RHP Casey Kelly (1) was the headliner in the Gonzalez deal, RHP Bryan Price (1s) helped bring Victor Martinez from the Indians and C Tim Federowicz (7) was part of a three-team Erik Bedard swap last July. RHP Kyle Weiland (3), C Ryan Lavarnway (6) and Federowicz all made their big league debuts in 2011.

GRADE: B

2007   BONUSES: $4.8 MILLION

Another part of the Gonzalez trade, 1B Anthony Rizzo (6) is his successor in San Diego. LHP Nick Hagadone (1s) also has played in the majors since going to Cleveland for Martinez. 3B Will Middlebrooks (5) is Boston's best prospect. That's a pretty solid crop considering the Red Sox didn't have a first-rounder.

GRADE: B

Draft analysis by Jim Callis. Numbers in parentheses indicate draft rounds.

1 WILL MIDDLEBROOKS, 3B

Born: Sept. 9, 1988. **B-T:** R-R. **Ht.:** 6-4. **Wt.:** 200.
Drafted: HS—Texarkana, Texas, 2007 (5th round).
Signed by: Jim Robinson.

BA GRADE
60
MEDIUM

MIKE JANES

Middlebrooks had multiple options when he came out of Liberty-Eylau High (Texarkana, Texas) in 2007. He threw low 90s fastballs and occasionally spun plus curveballs as a pitcher, and he drew interest from college football programs as both a quarterback and a punter. His future appeared even brighter at third base than on the mound or the gridiron, however, and that was the path he chose. Considered a supplemental first-round talent, Middlebrooks slid to the fifth round because of signability concerns and a commitment to Texas A&M, and he landed an above-slot $925,000 bonus. He has moved slowly but surely through the Red Sox system, improving his performance in each of his four pro seasons. He had his best year yet in 2011, when managers rated him as the best hitting prospect in the Double-A Eastern League. He went 1-for-2 in the Futures Game, earned EL all-star honors and reached Triple-A Pawtucket in August. He finished his year by smacking four homers in 13 Arizona Fall League games before straining a ligament in his left hand chasing a foul ball, an injury that didn't require surgery. Boston added him to its 40-man roster in November.

If scouts drew up a blueprint for a third baseman, it would look like Middlebrooks. He has the size, athleticism, power and arm strength coveted at the hot corner. He continues to learn more about his swing and increase his home run production each year, with more to come in the future. Right now, most of his homers come to the opposite field and are line drives that carry out of the park. With his bat speed and the strength in his 6-foot-4, 200-pound frame, he could hit 25 or more homers a season if he turns on more pitches and adds more loft to his stroke. Middlebrooks is an aggressive hitter who doesn't walk much and may not hit more than .275 or so in the majors, though that's an acceptable trade-off for

everything else he offers. He needs to manage at-bats better and make sure his load and timing don't get out of sync. While he remains streaky, his hot spells are lasting longer and his cold spells are ending more quickly. He's doing a better job of waiting for pitches he can hammer rather than getting himself out early in counts. He also understands that he's at his best when he lets his power come naturally, though he can get home run-conscious at times. Middlebrooks is a below-average runner but moves well for his size and isn't a liability on the bases. He's an asset at third base, where he's extremely agile and has a cannon for his arm. He competes well and has emerged as a leader in the system.

Middlebrooks could use a full 2012 season in Triple-A, after which Red Sox will face an interesting decision. They hold a $12 million option for 2013 on Kevin Youkilis, who has had injury problems the last two years and may not be able to take the pounding at the hot corner at age 34. Middlebrooks figures to push Youkilis to DH or out of town at that point, and he has the tools to blossom into an all-star.

SCOUTING GRADES

Batting: 50. **Defense:** 60.
Power: 65. **Arm:** 70.
Speed: 40.

Based on 20-80 scouting scale, where 50 represents major league average, and future projection rather than present tools.

Year	Club (League)	Class	AVG	G	AB	R	H	2B	3B	HR	RBI	BB	SO	SB	CS	OBP	SLG
2008	Lowell (NYP)	SS	.254	59	209	21	53	17	2	1	21	12	73	10	0	.298	.368
2009	Greenville (SAL)	LoA	.265	103	374	53	99	25	3	7	57	48	123	7	4	.349	.404
2010	Salem (CAR)	HiA	.276	114	435	69	120	31	2	12	70	35	121	5	3	.331	.439
2011	Lowell (NYP)	SS	.333	4	12	4	4	1	0	3	6	2	1	1	0	.400	1.167
	Portland (EL)	AA	.302	96	371	54	112	25	1	18	80	21	95	6	0	.345	.520
	Pawtucket (IL)	AAA	.161	16	56	4	9	0	0	2	8	3	18	3	1	.200	.268
Minor League Totals			.272	392	1457	205	397	99	8	43	242	121	431	32	8	.330	.440

2 XANDER BOGAERTS, SS

Born: Oct. 1, 1992. **B-T:** R-R. **Ht.:** 6-3. **Wt.:** 175. **Signed:** Aruba, 2009. **Signed by:** Mike Lord.

Signed for $410,000 out of Aruba, Bogaerts had a stellar pro debut that made him Boston's most highly anticipated international prospect since Hanley Ramirez. When he came to the United States and dominated in extended spring training, the Red Sox sent him to low Class A Greenville at age 18 last June, and he responded by smashing 16 homers in 72 games. His twin brother Jair is a first baseman in the system. Bogaerts doesn't look young when he's in the batter's box. He has an easy swing loaded with natural power, and he makes hard contact to all fields. While he still needs to learn the strike zone, he has shown the ability to make adjustments and handle breaking balls. He could be a .280 hitter with 30 homers in the majors, and that might be setting the bar low. Bogaerts has fluid actions at shortstop, but he lacks the quick feet for the position and will outgrow it once he fills out. With his plus athleticism, average speed and a strong arm, he'll be able to transition to third base or right field. Bogaerts has the highest ceiling among Red Sox prospects. He'll remain at shortstop in 2012, and Boston will have to send him to high Class A Salem at age 19 to challenge him. If he moves just one level a year, he'd still arrive in the majors at 22.

BA GRADE
65
HIGH

Year	Club (League)	Class	AVG	G	AB	R	H	2B	3B	HR	RBI	BB	SO	SB	CS	OBP	SLG
2010	Red Sox (DSL)	R	.314	63	239	39	75	7	5	3	42	30	37	4	5	.396	.423
2011	Greenville (SAL)	LoA	.260	72	265	38	69	14	2	16	45	25	71	1	3	.324	.509
Minor League Totals			.286	135	504	77	144	21	7	19	87	55	108	5	8	.359	.468

3 BLAKE SWIHART, C

Born: April 3, 1992. **B-T:** B-R. **Ht.:** 6-1. **Wt.:** 175. **Drafted:** HS—Rio Rancho, N.M., 2011 (1st round). **Signed by:** Matt Mahoney.

Swihart starred with the U.S. national 18-and-under team in 2010, batting .448/.492/.845. The Red Sox drafted him 26th overall last June, making him their highest-drafted catcher since No. 14 pick John Marzano in 1984. Swihart signed at the Aug. 15 deadline for $2.5 million, a franchise record for a position player. Swihart has uncommon offensive potential and athleticism for a catcher. A switch-hitter, he handles the bat better from his natural right side and has more pull power as a lefty. In instructional league, he doubled off the wall batting lefthanded against a rehabbing Clay Buchholz. Swihart projects as at least a plus hitter with a chance for average or better power. He has quick feet and moves well behind the plate, showing promising blocking and receiving skills despite catching for little more than a year. He also has plus arm strength and has made strides streamlining his release. He has average speed but will lose a step as he matures. He has a long way to go to reach his ceiling, but Swihart has the Buster Posey starter kit. There's no reason to think Swihart can't catch, but if Boston wants to expedite his bat, he's athletic enough to play on the infield and outfield corners, something he did up until his sophomore year of high school. After seeing time in the Florida and Dominican instructional leagues, he could jump to low Class A in his first full pro season.

BA GRADE
65
HIGH

Year	Club (League)	Class	AVG	G	AB	R	H	2B	3B	HR	RBI	BB	SO	SB	CS	OBP	SLG
2011	Red Sox (GCL)	R	.000	2	6	0	0	0	0	0	0	0	2	0	0	.000	.000
Minor League Totals			.000	2	6	0	0	0	0	0	0	0	2	0	0	.000	.000

4 ANTHONY RANAUDO, RHP

Born: Sept. 9, 1989. **B-T:** R-R. **Ht.:** 6-7. **Wt.:** 231. **Drafted:** Louisiana State, 2010 (1st round supplemental). **Signed by:** Matt Dorey.

Ranaudo had a roller-coaster 2010, beginning the year as the draft's top pitching prospect before coming down with a stress reaction in his elbow in his first start for Louisiana State. He recorded a 7.32 ERA that spring and slid to the 39th overall pick, then regained his luster by working 30 innings without an earned run in the Cape Cod League. After getting a $2.55 million bonus at the 2010 signing deadline, he made 26 starts and reached high Class A in his 2011 pro debut. Ranaudo gets swings and misses with a fastball that usually ranges from 91-96 mph, though his velocity faded a bit at the end of his first pro season. He uses his size to pitch down in the zone with his heater, which he can locate on both sides of the plate. Ranaudo also has the best curveball in the system and flashes a solid changeup, but he needs to improve the consistency of both pitches. Though he had elbow issues in two of this three seasons at LSU, he stayed healthy and worked 127 innings in 2011. After hitting the wall last July, Ranaudo recovered and posted a 2.35 ERA in his final five starts

BA GRADE
55
MEDIUM

RODGER WOOD

without his sharpest stuff. Ticketed for Double-A in 2012, he profiles as a steady No. 3 starter who could be big league-ready in 2013.

Year	Club (League)	Class	W	L	ERA	G	GS	CG	SV	IP	H	HR	BB	SO	K/9	WHIP	AVG
2011	Greenville (SAL)	LoA	4	1	3.33	10	10	0	0	46	35	4	16	50	9.8	1.11	.211
	Salem (CAR)	HiA	5	5	4.33	16	16	0	0	81	80	6	30	67	7.4	1.36	.262
Minor League Totals			9	6	3.97	26	26	0	0	127	115	10	46	117	8.3	1.27	.244

5 BRYCE BRENTZ, OF

Born: Dec. 30, 1988. **B-T:** R-R. **Ht.:** 6-1. **Wt.:** 180. **Drafted:** Middle Tennessee State, 2010 (1st round supplemental). **Signed by:** Danny Watkins.

An Indians 30th-round pick out of high school as a pitcher, Brentz made it clear his future was as a hitter when he led NCAA Division I in batting (.465), home runs (28) and slugging (.930) as a sophomore in 2009. The 36th overall pick the next June, he signed for $889,200. He scuffled in his pro debut but rebounded in 2011, hitting 30 homers and sharing Boston's minor league offensive player of the year award with catcher Ryan Lavarnway. In a system filled with intriguing sluggers, Brentz has the most usable power. He combines explosive bat speed with pure strength, and he turned a corner when he realized his homers would come naturally. He toned down an all-or-nothing approach and used the whole field more often in 2011, though his plate discipline still has room for improvement. With fringy speed and plus arm strength, Brentz has the tools for right field. He has 21 errors in 152 pro games in right, many coming on throws he shouldn't have made. The Red Sox were looking for a righthanded bat and a right fielder this offseason. Brentz isn't ready to fill those needs yet, but he could be in mid-2013. A potential .270 hitter with 30-homer power, he's headed to Double-A.

BA GRADE

55

MEDIUM

Year	Club (League)	Class	AVG	G	AB	R	H	2B	3B	HR	RBI	BB	SO	SB	CS	OBP	SLG
2010	Lowell (NYP)	SS	.198	69	262	28	52	14	4	5	39	21	76	5	4	.259	.340
2011	Greenville (SAL)	LoA	.359	40	170	43	61	10	3	11	36	14	35	2	2	.414	.647
	Salem (CAR)	HiA	.274	75	288	48	79	15	1	19	58	26	80	1	1	.336	.531
Minor League Totals			.267	184	720	119	192	39	8	35	133	61	191	8	7	.327	.489

6 BRANDON JACOBS, OF

Born: Dec. 8, 1990. **B-T:** R-R. **Ht.:** 6-1. **Wt.:** 225. **Drafted:** HS—Lilburn, Ga., 2009 (10th round). **Signed by:** Tim Hyers.

If the Red Sox hadn't stepped in with a $750,000 bonus in the 10th round of the 2009 draft, Jacobs would have played running back at Auburn. His .242/.310/.404 performance in his first two pro seasons belied his offensive potential, which prompts comparisons to former MVP Kevin Mitchell, but he finally broke through in 2011. Jacobs matured as a hitter in his first taste of full-season ball, shortening his swing, using the opposite field more often and refining his two-strike approach. He stays inside the ball well and has the strength and bat speed to hit it out to right-center. He may always pile up strikeouts, but he makes enough hard contact to hit for solid average with plenty of power. Though Jacobs stole 30 bases in 2011, he has fringy speed and won't run as much at higher levels. His arm is average at best, so he's relegated to left field, where he needs to improve his jumps. Jacobs could battle Bryce Brentz for a corner-outfield job in Boston down the road. Brentz has better bat speed and defensive skills, but Jacobs is no slouch in the former category and he's a better pure hitter. He's ready to tackle high Class A at age 21.

BA GRADE

55

MEDIUM

Year	Club (League)	Class	AVG	G	AB	R	H	2B	3B	HR	RBI	BB	SO	SB	CS	OBP	SLG
2009	Red Sox (GCL)	R	.250	8	24	1	6	2	0	0	0	2	8	0	0	.333	.333
2010	Lowell (NYP)	SS	.242	64	236	30	57	18	2	6	31	21	59	4	1	.308	.411
2011	Greenville (SAL)	LoA	.303	115	442	75	134	32	3	17	80	43	123	30	7	.376	.505
Minor League Totals			.281	187	702	106	197	52	5	23	111	66	190	34	8	.352	.467

7 GARIN CECCHINI, 3B

Born: April 20, 1991. **B-T:** L-R. **Ht.:** 6-2. **Wt.:** 200. **Drafted:** HS—Lake Charles, La.,
2010 (4th round). **Signed by:** Matt Dorey.

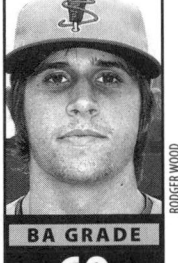

Cecchini might have been a first-round pick in 2010 had he not blown out the anterior
cruciate ligament in his right knee and required reconstructive surgery that March. His
rumored price tag made teams back off until the Red Sox drafted him in the fourth round,
and they signed him for $1.31 million at the deadline. He tore up older competition
in the short-season New York-Penn League last summer until an errant pitch broke his
right wrist in late July. His brother Gavin is a potential first-rounder in the 2012 draft.
Cecchini is the best pure hitter in the system. He has outstanding hand-eye coordination,
and he manages at-bats and controls the strike zone well for a youngster. He inside-outs a
lot of balls now, and he should have solid power once he gets stronger and turns on more
pitches. Cecchini worked diligently to get back in shape after his knee injury, regaining
his average speed. A high school shortstop, he moved to third base at Lowell and made
10 errors in 26 games. He has the hands, arm and agility to get the job done once he learns the position. Will
Middlebrooks and Xander Bogaerts, the system's top two prospects, profile best at the hot corner. So does
Cecchini, who will advance to low Class A and could start to move quickly if he stays healthy.

Year	Club (League)	Class	AVG	G	AB	R	H	2B	3B	HR	RBI	BB	SO	SB	CS	OBP	SLG
2011	Lowell (NYP)	SS	.298	32	114	21	34	12	1	3	23	17	19	12	2	.398	.500
Minor League Totals			.298	32	114	21	34	12	1	3	23	17	19	12	2	.398	.500

8 MATT BARNES, RHP

Born: June 17, 1990. **B-T:** R-R. **Ht.:** 6-4. **Wt.:** 205. **Drafted:** Connecticut, 2011 (1st
round). **Signed by:** Ray Fagnant.

The Red Sox fell in love with Barnes when they saw him duel Anthony Ranaudo in a
Cape Cod League matchup in 2010, and they were delighted to get him with the 19th
overall pick last June. He set a Connecticut school record with 247 career strikeouts and
led the Huskies to their first-ever NCAA super-regional in 2011. He signed minutes
before the Aug. 15 deadline for $1.5 million. Barnes can work in the mid-90s with his
fastball as a starter, holding his velocity deep into games and topping out at 97. His
effortless heat and explosive life are reminiscent of Daniel Bard's. Barnes had a quality
curveball in the past, though it regressed in 2011 when he started working on a slider that
Boston likely will have him scrap. He has made progress with his changeup but it lacks
consistency. Barnes throws strikes but sometimes misses up in the zone when he doesn't
stay on top of his pitches. He has an easy delivery but it lacks deception. Barnes has better
pure stuff than Ranaudo, but not as much polish and mound presence. He'll probably follow Ranaudo's path in
2012, making his pro debut in low Class A and pushing for a midseason promotion. Barnes may not need much
time in the minors, especially if he regains his curve.

Year	Club (League)	Class	AVG	G	AB	R	H	2B	3B	HR	RBI	BB	SO	SB	CS	OBP	SLG
2011	Did Not Play—Signed Late																

9 RYAN LAVARNWAY, C

Born: Aug. 7, 1987. **B-T:** R-R. **Ht.:** 6-4. **Wt.:** 225. **Drafted:** Yale, 2008 (6th round).
Signed by: Ray Fagnant.

Lavarnway won the NCAA Division I batting (.467) and slugging (.873) titles as a
sophomore and set an Ivy League record with 33 career homers. The Red Sox paid him
$325,000 as a 2008 sixth-round pick because they liked his bat, and even they were
skeptical he could make it to the majors as a catcher. He did just that in 2011, when he
earned his second straight Boston minor league co-offensive player of the year award. He
nearly saved the Red Sox's season in his first big league start behind the plate, providing a
much-needed victory in Game 161 by hitting two homers and throwing out a basestealer.
Lavarnway generates plus power with a combination of strength and discipline. He works
counts, lets pitches travel deep and pounds the ball to all fields. His swing is relatively
compact considering his long arms. Lavarnway's defensive improvement is a tribute to
his intelligence and work ethic. He lacks athleticism and agility, but he has transformed
himself from a dreadful receiver to an adequate one. While his arm strength is just fringy, his quick release and
throwing accuracy allowed him to erase 38 percent of basestealers in 2011. Because he has well below-average
speed, his only other option is first base. It's still uncertain if Lavarnway can be a big league regular behind the
plate, but the Red Sox won't put anything past him. In 2012, he'll serve as Jarrod Saltalamacchia's backup and

get 300 or so at-bats while also seeing time at first base and DH.

Year	Club (League)	Class	AVG	G	AB	R	H	2B	3B	HR	RBI	BB	SO	SB	CS	OBP	SLG
2008	Lowell (NYP)	SS	.211	22	71	10	15	5	0	2	9	8	18	0	0	.317	.366
2009	Greenville (SAL)	LoA	.285	106	404	60	115	36	2	21	87	50	113	1	2	.367	.540
2010	Salem (CAR)	HiA	.289	82	304	66	88	18	0	14	63	44	62	1	0	.392	.487
	Portland (EL)	AA	.285	44	158	25	45	9	0	8	39	26	42	0	0	.395	.494
2011	Portland (EL)	AA	.284	55	208	35	59	5	0	14	38	25	47	0	0	.360	.510
	Pawtucket (IL)	AAA	.295	61	227	40	67	18	0	18	55	32	60	1	1	.390	.612
	Boston (AL)	MAJ	.231	17	39	5	9	2	0	2	8	4	10	0	0	.302	.436
Major League Totals			.231	17	39	5	9	2	0	2	8	4	10	0	0	.302	.436
Minor League Totals			.284	370	1372	236	389	91	2	77	291	185	342	3	3	.376	.521

10 JACKIE BRADLEY, OF

BA GRADE
55
MEDIUM

Born: April 19, 1990. **B-T:** L-R. **Ht.:** 5-10. **Wt.:** 180. **Drafted:** South Carolina, 2011 (1st round supplemental). **Signed by:** Quincy Boyd.

Bradley looked like a surefire first-round pick after hitting .368 with 13 homers in 2010, when he was named Most Outstanding Player at the College World Series. He became too homer-conscious as college baseball toned down its metal bats last spring, and he missed two months after injuring a tendon in his left wrist. Though he batted just .247 with six homers in 2011, Bradley's center-field prowess was too much for the Red Sox to pass up with the 40th overall pick. He won a second straight CWS with South Carolina before signing for $1.1 million at the deadline. Few players cover center field as well as Bradley, who has average stopwatch speed but superb instincts. He has a strong arm for the position, too, and his stellar defense will take some pressure off his bat. Bradley is at his best offensively when he stays inside the ball and uses the opposite field. He's not physical, but he has a sound lefthanded stroke, a good grasp of the strike zone and average power. His speed plays up on the bases as it does in the outfield. If Bradley gets back to his old self at the plate, he could reach Boston by the end of 2013. He could open his first full pro season in high Class A and finish it in Double-A.

Year	Club (League)	Class	AVG	G	AB	R	H	2B	3B	HR	RBI	BB	SO	SB	CS	OBP	SLG
2011	Lowell (NYP)	SS	.190	6	21	5	4	0	0	0	4	5	5	0	2	.320	.190
	Greenville (SAL)	LoA	.333	4	15	2	5	1	0	1	3	0	3	0	0	.333	.600
Minor League Totals			.250	10	36	7	9	1	0	1	3	4	8	0	2	.325	.361

11 ALEX WILSON, RHP

BA GRADE
55
MEDIUM

Born: Nov. 3, 1986. **B-T:** R-R. **Ht.:** 6-0. **Wt.:** 215. **Drafted:** Texas A&M, 2009 (2nd round). **Signed by:** Jim Robinson.

Wilson has made a habit of bouncing back from adversity. He had Tommy John surgery while in college in 2007 but recovered to become a second-round pick two years later. He reached Double-A Portland in his first full pro season in 2010 and got hammered for a 6.66 ERA, then returned there last year and conquered the Eastern League. He finished 2011 with four strong starts in Triple-A and won the organization's minor league pitcher of the year award. Wilson has the best fastball and breaking ball in the system. He operates at 93-96 mph and can reach back for 98 with his fastball, which features some sink and run. His 82-85 mph slider has hard bite and be unhittable at times. His changeup is an average pitch, though he doesn't use it often. Because he has two overpowering pitches and had violence to his delivery, scouts have projected Wilson as a reliever since his college days. But he toned down his mechanics in 2011, improving his command and his ability to maintain his stuff deeper into games. He does have the mentality to work the late innings, and he'll probably break into the majors as a reliever in 2012. It's not out of the question that he could be a No. 3 starter, though.

Year	Club (League)	Class	W	L	ERA	G	GS	CG	SV	IP	H	HR	BB	SO	K/9	WHIP	AVG
2009	Lowell (NYP)	SS	0	1	0.50	13	13	0	0	36	10	0	7	33	8.3	0.47	.085
2010	Salem (CAR)	HiA	2	1	3.40	11	11	0	0	56	43	4	15	50	8.1	1.04	.212
	Portland (EL)	AA	4	5	6.66	16	16	0	0	78	95	15	34	56	6.4	1.65	.302
2011	Portland (EL)	AA	9	4	3.05	21	21	0	0	112	103	8	37	99	8.0	1.25	.246
	Pawtucket (IL)	AAA	1	0	3.43	4	4	0	0	21	19	2	7	24	10.3	1.24	.235
Minor League Totals			16	11	3.77	65	65	0	0	303	270	29	100	262	7.8	1.22	.238

12 JOSE IGLESIAS, SS

BA GRADE
55
HIGH

Born: Jan. 5, 1990. **B-T:** R-R. **Ht.:** 5-11. **Wt.:** 175. **Signed:** Cuba, 2009. **Signed by:** Craig Shipley/Johnny DiPuglia.

Iglesias began playing in Cuba's top league as a 17-year-old and defected a year later at the 2008 World Junior Championships in Edmonton. He signed with the Red Sox in September 2009, getting a four-year, $8.25 million big league contract that included a franchise-record $6.25 million bonus. Boston initially hoped that he'd be ready to take over at shortstop in 2012, but that won't transpire after he had a rough year with the bat in Triple-A last season. Iglesias is more than capable defensively. He has incredibly quick hands and feet, along with a strong arm, keen instincts and uncanny body control. Managers rated him the best defensive shortstop in the International League last year, and he led the circuit in both fielding percentage (.973) and total chances (441). He's a Gold Glove waiting to happen, though he'll have to show more offensively before getting regular playing time in the majors. Iglesias is too aggressive at the plate yet has a feel for putting the bat on the ball, a combination that yields a lot of weak contact. He has some bat speed but lacks strength and thus power. The Red Sox could live with his glove if he were an adequate hitter who could bat .250-.260 with some modest pop, but scouts from organizations question whether he'll be able to even do that. He's an average runner who can steal a few bases with his instincts. When Iglesias got a brief callup last May, he was 21 and became the youngest Boston position player since Rich Gedman in 1980. He came back up in September when rosters expanded, but Iglesias will have to show he can hold his own against Triple-A pitching before he returns to the majors.

Year	Club (League)	Class	AVG	G	AB	R	H	2B	3B	HR	RBI	BB	SO	SB	CS	OBP	SLG
2010	Lowell (NYP)	SS	.350	13	40	8	14	2	2	0	7	7	8	2	1	.458	.500
	Portland (EL)	AA	.285	57	221	29	63	10	3	0	13	8	49	5	2	.315	.357
2011	Pawtucket (IL)	AAA	.235	101	357	35	84	9	0	1	31	21	58	12	4	.285	.269
	Boston (AL)	MAJ	.333	10	6	3	2	0	0	0	0	0	2	0	0	.333	.333
Major League Totals			.333	10	6	3	2	0	0	0	0	0	2	0	0	.333	.333
Minor League Totals			.261	171	618	72	161	21	5	1	51	36	115	19	7	.308	.316

13 MILES HEAD, 1B

BA GRADE
55
HIGH

Born: May 2, 1991. **B-T:** R-R. **Ht.:** 6-0. **Wt.:** 215. **Drafted:** HS—Fayetteville, Ga., 2009 (26th round). **Signed by:** Tim Hyers.

Like Brandon Jacobs, Head is a Georgia high school product who signed for over-slot money in the 2009 draft and broke out in 2011. Signed for $335,000 as a 26th-round pick, he was leading the low Class A South Atlantic League in hitting (.338) and OPS (1.021) last June when he earned a promotion to high Class A. He didn't tear up the Carolina League, but he also wasn't overmatched at age 20. Head has one of the best bats in the system, the product of a loose swing, quick hands and a mature approach. He has above-average power potential but doesn't try to force the issue, instead focusing on driving the ball up the middle. He has a good sense of the strike zone and shortens his stroke with two strikes. Head doesn't provide much beyond offense. Managers rated him the SAL's best defensive first baseman and he does have soft hands, but he's a well below-average runner with substandard athleticism and range. Head will have to really produce at the plate to overcome the stigma of a short, righthanded-hitting first baseman—and he may just do that.

Year	Club (League)	Class	AVG	G	AB	R	H	2B	3B	HR	RBI	BB	SO	SB	CS	OBP	SLG
2009	Red Sox (GCL)	R	.103	10	29	1	3	0	0	0	0	3	8	0	0	.188	.103
2010	Lowell (NYP)	SS	.240	65	229	21	55	16	2	1	35	30	36	1	1	.328	.341
2011	Greenville (SAL)	LoA	.338	66	263	61	89	25	1	15	53	30	53	4	2	.409	.612
	Salem (CAR)	HiA	.254	63	232	27	59	12	1	7	29	20	56	0	2	.328	.405
Minor League Totals			.274	204	753	110	206	53	4	23	117	83	153	5	5	.351	.446

14 SEAN COYLE, 2B

BA GRADE
55
HIGH

Born: Jan. 17, 1992. **B-T:** R-R. **Ht.:** 5-8. **Wt.:** 175. **Drafted:** HS—Fort Washington, Pa., 2010 (3rd round). **Signed by:** Chris Calciano.

Coyle may stand just 5-foot-8, but Boston believed enough in his bat to invest a third-round pick and a $1.3 million in him in 2010. He justified that faith by posting an .826 OPS in low Class A as a 19-year-old, and his toughness was even more impressive. An errant pitch hit him the face and broke his jaw in June, yet he missed just 10 days and batted .268/.375/.460 in the second half. As a tiny second baseman in the Red Sox system, Coyle can't avoid some Dustin Pedroia comparisons. They only work to a point, because Coyle has more natural power but isn't the same hitter or defender. He produces solid pop with his bat speed, strong lower half and ability to barrel the ball. He has the patience to draw walks and wait for pitches to drive, though he'll have to make more contact at higher levels. Coyle has plus speed and good instincts on the bases, and he knows how to pick his spots to steal a few bases. He has all the ingredients to become a quality defender at second base, as his quickness, hands and arm are all assets. Boston doesn't need to rush him and will advance him one level at a time, with high Class A his next stop in 2012.

Year	Club (League)	Class	AVG	G	AB	R	H	2B	3B	HR	RBI	BB	SO	SB	CS	OBP	SLG
2010	Red Sox (GCL)	R	.200	3	10	5	2	1	0	0	0	1	1	0	0	.333	.300
2011	Greenville (SAL)	LoA	.247	106	384	77	95	27	7	14	64	60	110	20	6	.362	.464
Minor League Totals			.246	109	394	82	97	28	7	14	64	61	111	20	6	.361	.459

15 BRANDON WORKMAN, RHP

BA GRADE
55
HIGH

Born: Aug. 13, 1988. **B-T:** R-R. **Ht.:** 6-4. **Wt.:** 195. **Drafted:** Texas, 2010 (2nd round). **Signed by:** Jim Robinson.

For a player who signed for $800,000, Workman had a relatively anonymous pro debut last year. The Red Sox kept him on tight pitch counts during the first half of the season in low Class A, and he seemed to get stronger when they turned him loose in July and August. Workman likes to pitch off his 91-94 mph fastball, which can reach 96 and features tail, run and steep downhill plane. He can hold his velocity deep into starts. He has a solid curveball, though he eschewed it in favor of a cutter during his final season of college at Texas. The Red Sox took the cutter away from Workman early in 2011 to make him focus on his curve, then gave it back to him in the second half. His cutter runs up to 84 mph and gets swings and misses from lefthanders. He also has a changeup that has some sink and grades as average when he maintains his arm speed. He throws strikes but needs to improve his command of his fastball, which gets hittable when he leaves it up in the zone. Workman has the stuff, control and body to profile as a starter, though some scouts envision him as late-inning reliever and maybe even a closer. The Red Sox will keep him in the rotation for now, and he could reach Double-A at some point in 2012.

Year	Club (League)	Class	W	L	ERA	G	GS	CG	SV	IP	H	HR	BB	SO	K/9	WHIP	AVG
2011	Greenville (SAL)	LoA	6	7	3.71	26	26	0	0	131	128	10	33	115	7.9	1.23	.260
Minor League Totals			6	7	3.71	26	26	0	0	131	128	10	33	115	7.9	1.23	.260

16 DRAKE BRITTON, LHP

BA GRADE
55
EXTREME

Born: May 22, 1989. **B-T:** L-L. **Ht.:** 6-2. **Wt.:** 200. **Drafted:** HS—Tomball, Texas, 2007 (23rd round). **Signed by:** Jim Robinson.

Last season was supposed to be Britton's breakthrough. The Red Sox signed him away from Texas A&M with a $700,000 bonus in the 23rd round of the 2007 draft, then nursed him back to health after he blew out his elbow and needed Tommy John surgery the following year. He barely pitched in 2009 and was kept on tight pitch counts in 2010. Boston finally took the training wheels off last year, and it couldn't have been much more of a disaster. Britton led the Carolina League with 13 losses, didn't win a game after May 7, turned in just two quality starts in 26 outings and recorded a 6.91 ERA that would have ranked as the worst in all of Class A had he worked enough innings to qualify. The silver lining is that Britton still showed better stuff than most lefthanders, working with a 90-96 mph sinker and flashing a plus slider after switching from a big-breaking curveball. He even showed some feel for a changeup. Britton's biggest problem is that he lacks control and consistency with his pitches and emotions. Too often last year, he'd fall behind in the count, slow the game to a glacial pace and be unable to extract himself from jams. His secondary pitches would come and go. Scouts inside and outside of the organization think Britton's problems are more mental than physical, and many believe he's destined for the bullpen. Britton needs innings, so Boston has no plans to change his role yet, and hopes he can pick up the pieces after protecting him on the 40-man roster in November.

Year	Club (League)	Class	W	L	ERA	G	GS	CG	SV	IP	H	HR	BB	SO	K/9	WHIP	AVG
2008	Lowell (NYP)	SS	1	2	4.28	8	7	0	0	34	30	3	16	26	7.0	1.37	.234
2009	Red Sox (GCL)	R	0	0	0.00	4	4	0	0	7	2	0	4	11	14.1	0.86	.080
	Lowell (NYP)	SS	0	0	1.93	3	3	0	0	5	4	0	3	8	15.4	1.50	.235
2010	Greenville (SAL)	LoA	2	3	2.97	21	21	0	0	76	69	5	23	78	9.3	1.22	.240
2011	Salem (CAR)	HiA	1	13	6.91	26	26	0	0	98	111	12	55	89	8.2	1.70	.285
Minor League Totals			4	18	4.82	62	61	0	0	219	216	20	101	212	8.7	1.45	.255

17 FELIX DOUBRONT, LHP

BA GRADE
50
MEDIUM

Born: Oct. 23, 1987. **B-T:** L-L. **Ht.:** 6-2. **Wt.:** 190. **Signed:** Venezuela, 2004. **Signed by:** Miguel Garcia.

After Doubront pitched well as both a starter and reliever in short stints in Boston in 2010, the club figured he'd be able to reinforce the rotation or bullpen if needed last year. But he wasn't up to the task. Doubront didn't show up in spring training in the best of shape and experienced elbow stiffness that prevented him from building up his arm strength. He strained his groin in May and a hamstring in July, and lacked consistency with his stuff and command all year. While the Red Sox were collapsing in September and in need of arms, they didn't trust him with more than mop-up duty. When Doubront is fully healthy and at his best, he throws a sinker that operates at 88-92 mph when he starts and sits at 92-93 when he relieves. His curveball, cutter and changeup all can be solid pitches, though their reliability fluctuated throughout 2011. He repeats his high three-quarters delivery well, allowing him to throw strikes, but he also lapses into nibbling too much at times. Doubront's stock took a hit inside and outside the organization last year, and he'd help his cause by arriving in spring training in peak condition. He'll get the opportunity to make the Red Sox in spring training, though in which role remains unclear.

Year	Club (League)	Class	W	L	ERA	G	GS	CG	SV	IP	H	HR	BB	SO	K/9	WHIP	AVG
2005	Red Sox/Padres (VSL)	R	7	1	0.97	13	13	0	0	65	32	0	29	58	8.1	0.94	.152
2006	Red Sox (GCL)	R	2	3	2.52	11	11	0	0	54	41	6	13	36	6.0	1.01	.212
	Lowell (NYP)	SS	2	0	4.91	2	2	0	0	11	7	1	3	7	5.7	0.91	.179
2007	Greenville (SAL)	LoA	3	7	8.93	11	11	0	0	42	63	8	17	22	4.7	1.89	.337
	Lowell (NYP)	SS	1	3	5.66	8	8	0	0	35	41	2	11	25	6.4	1.49	.283
2008	Greenville (SAL)	LoA	12	8	3.67	23	23	0	0	115	115	9	24	118	9.2	1.21	.260
	Lancaster (CAL)	HiA	1	1	3.86	3	3	0	0	14	15	1	4	20	12.9	1.36	.278
2009	Portland (EL)	AA	8	6	3.35	26	26	1	0	121	119	8	52	101	7.5	1.41	.255
2010	Portland (EL)	AA	4	0	2.51	8	8	0	0	43	39	0	17	38	8.0	1.30	.250
	Pawtucket (IL)	AAA	4	3	3.16	9	8	0	0	37	36	1	16	34	8.3	1.41	.261
	Boston (AL)	MAJ	2	2	4.32	12	3	0	2	25	27	3	10	23	8.3	1.48	.270
2011	Portland (EL)	AA	1	0	1.80	1	1	0	0	5	4	0	0	9	16.2	0.80	.211
	Lowell (NYP)	SS	0	0	0.00	1	1	0	0	2	0	0	0	4	18.0	0.00	.000
	Pawtucket (IL)	AAA	2	5	4.22	18	16	0	0	70	65	10	26	61	7.8	1.29	.241
	Boston (AL)	MAJ	0	0	6.10	11	0	0	1	10	12	1	8	6	5.2	1.94	.316
Major League Totals			2	2	4.84	23	3	0	3	35	39	4	18	29	7.4	1.61	.283
Minor League Totals			47	37	3.65	134	131	1	0	614	577	46	212	533	7.8	1.28	.248

18 HENRY OWENS, LHP

BA GRADE
50
HIGH

Born: July 21, 1992. **B-T:** L-L. **Ht.:** 6-6. **Wt.:** 190. **Drafted:** HS—Huntington Beach, Calif., 2011 (1st round supplemental). **Signed by:** Tom Battista.

In an unusually down year for high school talent in Southern California, Owens was the lone prep pitcher who drew first-round consideration. The Red Sox got him near the top of the sandwich round with pick No. 36 and signed him at the deadline for $1.55 million. Owens has solid stuff for a lefty and the room to add plenty of strength to his skinny frame, but he stands out the most with his feel for pitching. He usually throws 88-91 mph on cruise control, showing the ability to get 92-93 mph whenever he needs it and maxing out at 94. Owens can spin a curveball, throwing a 75-76 mph breaker with depth and also flipping up a loopier high-60s bender to keep hitters off balance. He can throw the curve for strikes in any count. His changeup has some promise, and he also has messed around with a slider and cutter. Some area scouts were disappointed Owens didn't add more velocity in high school and questioned his projection, but Boston is thrilled to have him. Because he didn't pitch after signing late, he'll likely make his pro debut at Lowell in June. If everything comes together, he could develop into a No. 3 starter.

Year	Club (League)	Class	W	L	ERA	G	GS	CG	SV	IP	H	HR	BB	SO	K/9	WHIP	AVG
2011	Did Not Play—Signed Late																

19 KOLBRIN VITEK, 3B

BA GRADE
50
HIGH

Born: April 1, 1989. **B-T:** R-R. **Ht.:** 6-2. **Wt.:** 195. **Drafted:** Ball State, 2010 (1st round). **Signed by:** Sam Ray.

Boston's top pick in 2010, Vitek went 20th overall and signed for $1.359 million. A two-way star at Ball State, he rated as one of the best bats in the draft, but he has yet to hit with much authority in two years as a pro. The Red Sox are still confident he'll be productive at the plate, which may happen once he gets comfortable at third base or moves to the outfield. Vitek has a simple, quick swing and consistently keeps his hands inside the ball. That's conducive to hitting line drives and using the opposite field, though he won't tap into his average power potential unless he starts turning on more pitches. After making some adjustments to handle breaking pitches, he made more consistent contact in his first full pro season than he did in his debut. Vitek is a good athlete with plus speed once he gets going and above-average arm strength. He showed an 88-92 mph fastball and threw three pitches for strikes at Ball State. Vitek played third base as a sophomore before moving to second base as a junior to conserve his arm, and he has struggled moving back to the hot corner. Inconsistent footwork has contributed to his .886 fielding percentage there, and some scouts wonder if his hands are good enough to stay in the infield. He'll probably wind up in the outfield, and his tools give him a chance to handle center field. Boston will keep him at third base when it sends him to Double-A to open the 2012 season.

Year	Club (League)	Class	AVG	G	AB	R	H	2B	3B	HR	RBI	BB	SO	SB	CS	OBP	SLG
2010	Lowell (NYP)	SS	.270	56	204	30	55	13	3	4	30	26	61	13	2	.360	.422
	Greenville (SAL)	LoA	.275	12	40	7	11	3	1	0	3	7	13	4	1	.383	.400
2011	Salem (CAR)	HiA	.281	123	473	78	133	22	6	3	43	45	102	10	3	.350	.372
Minor League Totals			.278	191	717	115	199	38	10	7	76	78	176	27	6	.355	.388

20 KYLE STROUP, RHP

BA GRADE
50
HIGH

Born: March 13, 1990. **B-T:** R-R. **Ht.:** 6-6. **Wt.:** 235. **Drafted:** HS—Fox Lake, Ill., 2008 (50th round). **Signed by:** Chris Mears.

Since baseball instituted the draft in 1965, the last overall pick never has signed and gone on to reach the majors. Only two of the final choices, Don Wakamatsu (1984) and Desi Wilson (1989), played in the big leagues after re-entering a subsequent draft. Stroup has a chance to make history, as he has become a legitimate prospect since signing for $150,000 as the 1,504th selection in 2008. He barely pitched in pro ball before last year, signing late in 2008, working 24 innings in Rookie ball in 2009 and missing all of 2010 after blowing out his right knee covering first base. He didn't look like anything special at the beginning of last year either, going 1-5, 7.05 through mid-May before finishing on a 5-1, 1.85 roll. Big and physical, Stroup throws a steady 91-95 mph fastball that tops out at 97. He gets good extension out front in his delivery, making his heater seem quicker, and he can run it to either side of the plate. While his breaking ball varies between a curveball and slider, he does show some feel for spinning the ball. His changeup is further advanced than his breaker and features some sink. Stroup has some effort in his delivery, but he has a compact arm action that allows him to command his pitches. He missed a month last year with an oblique strain, and the Red Sox would love to see what the potential No. 3 starter could do with a fully healthy 2012 season in high Class A.

Year	Club (League)	Class	W	L	ERA	G	GS	CG	SV	IP	H	HR	BB	SO	K/9	WHIP	AVG
2009	Red Sox (GCL)	R	1	1	4.50	12	0	0	0	24	28	0	14	19	7.1	1.75	.301
2010	Did Not Play—Injured																
2011	Greenville (SAL)	LoA	6	6	3.67	21	21	1	0	96	101	6	26	75	7.1	1.33	.269
Minor League Totals			7	7	3.84	33	21	1	0	120	129	6	40	94	7.1	1.41	.276

21 JOSE VINICIO, SS

BA GRADE
55
EXTREME

Born: July 10, 1993. **B-T:** B-R. **Ht.:** 5-11. **Wt.:** 150. **Signed:** Dominican Republic, 2009. **Signed by:** Manny Nanita.

Vinicio celebrated his 16th birthday by signing with the Red Sox for $1.95 million, at the time a franchise record for a foreign amateur. Two months later, Jose Iglesias upped the mark to $6.25 million, part of his $8.25 million major league contract. They're similar players, defensive whizzes at shortstop who will have to get stronger to hit effectively. Boston sent Vinicio straight to Rookie-level Gulf Coast League for his 2010 pro debut, and he was still the GCL's third-youngest regular when he repeated the league last summer. His actions, range, hands and arm all rate as plus tools for a shortstop. His biggest need defensively is to settle down, as he gets too flashy at times and made 29 errors in 50 games in 2011. Vinicio has yet to put on much weight, still carrying 150 pounds on his 5-foot-11 frame. He does have quick hands and some life in his bat, and he has an all-fields approach, so he should be able to hit for average once he matures physically and tightens his strike zone. He's an above-average runner who's still learning to use his speed on the bases, and he led the GCL by getting caught 10 times in 29 steal attempts. Provided that he can add strength, Vinicio looks like a better bet to provide some offense than Iglesias. At the same time, he's five levels lower in the system. Still just 18, Vinicio will probably spend 2012 in extended spring training and Lowell.

Year	Club (League)	Class	AVG	G	AB	R	H	2B	3B	HR	RBI	BB	SO	SB	CS	OBP	SLG
2010	Red Sox (GCL)	R	.253	43	158	23	40	4	6	1	22	7	26	13	1	.290	.373
2011	Red Sox (GCL)	R	.291	50	179	22	52	7	5	2	18	7	33	19	10	.337	.419
Minor League Totals			.273	93	337	45	92	11	11	3	40	14	59	32	11	.315	.398

22 KYLE WEILAND, RHP

BA GRADE
45
MEDIUM

Born: Sept. 12, 1986. **B-T:** L-R. **Ht.:** 6-4. **Wt.:** 195. **Drafted:** Notre Dame, 2008 (3rd round). **Signed by:** Chris Mears.

The Red Sox thought they had plenty of pitching depth to carry them through the 2011 season, but when injuries ravaged their staff, they had to turn to Weiland to make three critical starts in September. He lost two and received no decision in the other, allowing 12 runs in 11⅔ innings. Club officials don't fault Weiland, saying he was put in a difficult situation and undermined by shoddy defense behind him. They still see him as a potential rotation contributor in the future. Weiland has a hard sinker that sits in the low 90s and touches 96. He has improved his curveball to the point where it gets swings and misses, and he has developed a cutter that makes him more effective against lefthanders than righthanders. He doesn't tip off his changeup like he used to, though it's still a fringy pitch. Weiland relishes pitching inside and does an excellent job of controlling the running game. When he keeps his pitches down, he's tough to beat, but he got caught up in the strike zone too often in the majors. Weiland set single-season (16) and career (25) save records at Notre Dame, and his stuff would play up if he moved to the bullpen. But Boston has no immediate plans to do so, and he'll open 2012 on call in Triple-A.

Year	Club (League)	Class	W	L	ERA	G	GS	CG	SV	IP	H	HR	BB	SO	K/9	WHIP	AVG
2008	Lowell (NYP)	SS	3	3	1.50	15	10	0	0	60	36	1	10	68	10.2	0.77	.166
2009	Salem (CAR)	HiA	7	9	3.46	26	26	0	0	133	119	4	57	112	7.6	1.33	.240
2010	Portland (EL)	AA	5	9	4.42	25	25	0	0	128	112	13	49	120	8.4	1.25	.236
2011	Pawtucket (IL)	AAA	8	10	3.58	24	24	0	0	128	108	10	55	126	8.8	1.27	.232
	Boston (AL)	MAJ	0	3	7.66	7	5	0	0	25	29	5	12	13	4.7	1.66	.287
Major League Totals			0	3	7.66	7	5	0	0	25	29	5	12	13	4.7	1.66	.287
Minor League Totals			23	31	3.51	90	85	0	0	449	375	28	171	426	8.5	1.22	.227

23 STOLMY PIMENTEL, RHP

BA GRADE
50
HIGH

Born: Feb. 1, 1990. **B-T:** R-R. **Ht.:** 6-4. **Wt.:** 230. **Signed:** Dominican Republic, 2006. **Signed by:** Luis Scheker.

Signed for $25,000 out of the Dominican Republic in 2006, Pimentel made steady progress in four pro seasons until he reached Double-A in 2011. He threw harder than ever, but every aspect of his game besides velocity regressed terribly. He went 0-9, 9.12 as opponents batted .352 against him in 15 Portland starts, including four outings in which he allowed more runs than he recorded outs. He improved following a July demotion to high Class A, but that couldn't take much of the tarnish off a disappointing year. In his quest to throw harder—and his fastball did reach 97 mph—Pimentel lost his mechanics, command and ultimately his confidence. Increased velocity meant less plane, angle and movement on his fastball, which is more effective and has more riding life when he throws in the low 90s. His changeup was a swing-and-miss pitch in the past, but merely average at best in 2011. The lone positive in Pimentel's development last year was that he may have found a breaking ball. After struggling to spin a curveball for years, he scrapped it in favor of a low-80s slider/cutter. The Red Sox hope he has gotten back on track to becoming a No. 3 starter, but won't know for sure until they see how he fares when he returns to Double-A.

Year	Club (League)	Class	W	L	ERA	G	GS	CG	SV	IP	H	HR	BB	SO	K/9	WHIP	AVG
2007	Red Sox (DSL)	R	3	1	2.90	14	13	0	0	62	44	2	22	60	8.7	1.06	.202
2008	Lowell (NYP)	SS	5	2	3.14	13	11	0	0	63	51	7	17	61	8.7	1.08	.224
2009	Greenville (SAL)	LoA	10	7	3.82	24	23	1	0	118	135	12	29	103	7.9	1.39	.290
2010	Salem (CAR)	HiA	9	11	4.06	26	26	0	0	129	120	11	42	102	7.1	1.26	.248
2011	Portland (EL)	AA	0	9	9.12	15	15	0	0	50	75	8	23	30	5.4	1.95	.352
	Salem (CAR)	HiA	6	4	4.53	11	10	0	0	52	50	8	16	35	6.1	1.28	.259
Minor League Totals			33	34	4.32	103	98	1	0	473	475	48	149	391	7.4	1.32	.264

24 OSCAR TEJEDA, 2B

BA GRADE
50
HIGH

Born: Dec. 26, 1989. **B-T:** R-R. **Ht.:** 6-1. **Wt.:** 177. **Signed:** Dominican Republic, 2006. **Signed by:** Luis Scheker.

Tejeda followed a breakthough year in 2010 with the worst full-season performance of his career in 2011. He was the fifth-youngest regular in the Eastern League at age 21, so there's reasonable hope for improvement, though scouts were troubled that he often failed to expend much effort. When he signed for $525,000 out of the Dominican Republic in 2006, one rival international scouting director compared him to Alfonso Soriano. Tejeda has a very quick bat and more power than most middle infielders, but his aggressive approach holds him back at the plate. He might be a .260 hitter with 15-20 homers per year, which would be enough to profile as a regular at second base but tougher if he has to move to an outfield corner. That's a possibility because Tejeda has below-average speed and fringy range at second, and he also could outgrow the position. His hands and arm work in the middle infield, but he doesn't show the instincts to make more than the routine plays. He led EL second basemen with 24 errors last season after topping Carolina League second sackers with the same number in 2010. He'll return to Double-A this season and needs to mature in all areas of the game.

Year	Club (League)	Class	AVG	G	AB	R	H	2B	3B	HR	RBI	BB	SO	SB	CS	OBP	SLG
2007	Red Sox (GCL)	R	.295	45	173	23	51	13	1	1	21	15	27	6	2	.344	.399
	Lowell (NYP)	SS	.298	22	94	14	28	5	2	0	12	6	26	4	1	.347	.394
2008	Greenville (SAL)	LoA	.261	97	372	44	97	18	1	4	38	20	76	11	5	.301	.347
2009	Greenville (SAL)	LoA	.257	99	370	50	95	13	3	3	50	30	89	3	5	.311	.332
2010	Salem (CAR)	HiA	.307	126	508	76	156	32	5	11	69	32	96	17	7	.344	.455
2011	Portland (EL)	AA	.249	123	457	50	114	24	1	5	41	29	101	13	4	.297	.339
Minor League Totals			.274	512	1974	257	541	105	13	24	231	132	415	54	24	.319	.377

25 DERRIK GIBSON, SS

BA GRADE
50
HIGH

Born: Dec. 5, 1989. **B-T:** R-R. **Ht.:** 6-1. **Wt.:** 170. **Drafted:** HS—Seaford, Del., 2008 (2nd round). **Signed by:** Chris Calciano.

Gibson remains the best athlete in the system, but he hasn't hit in two years of full-season ball, putting up .235/.321/.303 numbers in 2010-11. He still has the same quick bat, sound swing and disciplined approach that were part of the package the Red Sox paid $600,000 for after drafting him in the second round in 2008. While Gibson needs to get stronger and that would help him at the plate, his biggest problem is that he's too hard on himself and loses confidence when he's not going well. He may not ever hit for home run power, but he does have the tools to bat at the top of a lineup. He's has well above-average speed, though he could be more daring on the bases. To his credit, Gibson hasn't let his offensive struggles affect his defense. He has the quickness, range and arm strength for shortstop. Scouts aren't in love with his funky throwing motion, but he gets the job done. In his two full years at the position, he has led South Atlantic and Carolina league shortstops in fielding percentage. Gibson also has played second base and third base in pro ball, and he could have a future as a speedy, athletic utilityman if his bat doesn't come around. He'd probably be best served by returning to Salem to start 2012.

Year	Club (League)	Class	AVG	G	AB	R	H	2B	3B	HR	RBI	BB	SO	SB	CS	OBP	SLG
2008	Red Sox (GCL)	R	.309	27	94	15	29	6	1	0	9	14	18	14	0	.411	.394
	Lowell (NYP)	SS	.086	14	35	4	3	0	0	0	3	6	11	2	0	.233	.086
2009	Lowell (NYP)	SS	.290	67	255	54	74	15	4	0	25	39	42	28	5	.395	.380
2010	Greenville (SAL)	LoA	.230	122	487	77	112	22	3	2	40	61	101	39	7	.321	.300
2011	Salem (CAR)	HiA	.240	128	445	56	107	20	3	1	30	48	86	24	9	.321	.306
Minor League Totals			.247	358	1316	206	325	63	11	3	107	168	258	107	21	.340	.318

26 ALEX HASSAN, OF

BA GRADE 45 MEDIUM

Born: April 1, 1988. **B-T:** R-R. **Ht.:** 6-3. **Wt.:** 195. **Drafted:** Duke, 2009 (20th round). **Signed by:** Quincy Boyd.

Scouts weren't sure if Hassan offered more promise as a hitter or pitcher after watching him for three years at Duke. The Red Sox had divergent opinions even after taking him the 20th round of the 2009 draft, and decided to make him a full-time outfielder after he batted .289 while earning all-star honors in the Cape Cod League that summer. Since signing for $90,000, he has sprayed line drives all over the field and gotten on base. No one in the system controls the strike zone better than Hassan, who works deep counts and isn't afraid to hit with two strikes. He has a lot of moving parts to his swing, but he has good rhythm and makes consistent contact, so Boston hasn't tried to change it. His stroke is geared to the opposite field, but he's starting to get stronger and turn on more pitches. More power is critical for Hassan, who drives more doubles to the gaps than homers over the fence. He's sort of a tweener who doesn't have the pop to be an everyday player on an outfield corner and doesn't run well enough to man center field on a regular basis. With fringy speed and average arm strength, Hassan fits best in left field. He's a steady defender who recorded 11 assists and topped Eastern League outfielders with a .995 fielding percentage in 2011. He'll advance to Triple-A and could see his first big league action in 2012.

Year	Club (League)	Class	AVG	G	AB	R	H	2B	3B	HR	RBI	BB	SO	SB	CS	OBP	SLG
2009	Greenville (SAL)	LoA	.313	8	32	6	10	3	1	1	7	2	7	0	0	.353	.563
	Lowell (NYP)	SS	.333	26	93	14	31	5	1	1	11	8	11	1	1	.382	.441
2010	Pawtucket (IL)	AAA	.000	3	3	0	0	0	0	0	1	0	0	0	0	.000	.000
	Salem (CAR)	HiA	.287	104	342	46	98	28	3	8	48	57	69	6	1	.397	.456
2011	Portland (EL)	AA	.291	126	454	75	132	34	1	13	64	76	79	8	2	.404	.456
Minor League Totals			.293	267	924	141	271	70	6	23	131	143	166	15	4	.396	.457

27 RAUL ALCANTARA, RHP

BA GRADE 55 EXTREME

Born: Dec. 4, 1992. **B-T:** R-R. **Ht.:** 6-3. **Wt.:** 180. **Signed:** Dominican Republic, 2009. **Signed by:** Manny Nanita.

Alcantara has filled up his trophy case since signing out of the Dominican Republic for $500,000 in 2009. The Red Sox named him their minor league Latin program pitcher of the year in his pro debut, and the Gulf Coast League honored him as its pitcher of the year in his first year in the United States. Last summer, he led the GCL in ERA (0.75), WHIP (0.60) and opponent average (.147). Though he's far from a finished product, Alcantara is advanced for his age and has one of the highest ceilings among Boston's lower-level minor leaguers. Using an easy arm action and sound delivery, he pitches off a 90-95 mph fastball. His hard slider has the makings of a plus pitch, while he's still refining his changeup. He already throws strikes with ease, so the next step is improving his ability to locate his pitches where he wants. Alcantara earned a promotion to Lowell last August and could push for a low Class A assignment this spring.

Year	Club (League)	Class	W	L	ERA	G	GS	CG	SV	IP	H	HR	BB	SO	K/9	WHIP	AVG
2010	Red Sox (DSL)	R	5	3	3.28	13	13	1	0	60	61	1	8	34	5.1	1.14	.260
2011	Red Sox (GCL)	R	1	1	0.75	9	9	0	0	48	23	0	6	36	6.8	0.60	.147
	Lowell (NYP)	SS	0	3	6.23	4	4	0	0	17	25	0	6	14	7.3	1.79	.333
Minor League Totals			6	7	2.72	26	26	1	0	126	109	1	20	84	6.0	1.03	.234

28 LARS ANDERSON, 1B

BA GRADE 45 MEDIUM

Born: Sept. 25, 1987. **B-T:** L-L. **Ht.:** 6-4. **Wt.:** 215. **Drafted:** HS—Carmichael, Calif., 2006 (18th round). **Signed by:** Blair Henry.

Anderson ranked No. 1 on this list in the 2009 Prospect Handbook, when he was coming off a .317/.417/.517 season in which he reached Double-A at age 20. One scout who saw him that summer said Anderson was ready to hit major league pitching if needed. Three years later, he has only a couple of September callups and 40 big league at-bats on his résumé. Anderson still has impressive size, bat speed, strength and hand-eye coordination. He has maintained his patience at the plate and led the International League with 80 walks in 2011. But he's not going to get a chance as a major league regular until he hits for more power and proves he can hit lefthanders. Anderson lacks loft in his swing and doesn't turn on enough pitches. He now looks more like a platoon player than a middle-of-the-order cornerstone. Anderson has worked hard to improve his defense and does a nice job around the bag at first base. He's a below-average runner but doesn't clog the bases. With Adrian Gonzalez signed through 2018, Anderson has no shot at starting at first base for the Red Sox. They nearly sent him to the Athletics last July in a trade for Rich Harden, but balked at the last second after reviewing Harden's medical records. He won't be a star, but Anderson might be able to hit .280 with 15 homers and a lot of walks for a team looking for an inexpensive first baseman.

Year	Club (League)	Class	AVG	G	AB	R	H	2B	3B	HR	RBI	BB	SO	SB	CS	OBP	SLG
2007	Greenville (SAL)	LoA	.288	124	458	69	132	35	3	10	69	71	112	2	4	.385	.443
	Lancaster (CAL)	HiA	.343	10	35	13	12	2	0	1	9	11	9	0	0	.489	.486
2008	Lancaster (CAL)	HiA	.317	77	306	58	97	19	1	13	50	46	64	0	0	.408	.513
	Portland (EL)	AA	.316	41	133	27	42	13	0	5	30	29	43	1	0	.436	.526
2009	Portland (EL)	AA	.233	119	447	50	104	23	0	9	51	63	114	2	0	.328	.345
2010	Portland (EL)	AA	.355	17	62	13	22	5	0	5	16	7	16	1	1	.408	.677
	Pawtucket (IL)	AAA	.262	113	409	49	107	32	3	10	53	44	109	2	2	.340	.428
	Boston (AL)	MAJ	.200	18	35	4	7	1	0	0	4	7	8	0	0	.326	.229
2011	Pawtucket (IL)	AAA	.265	136	491	65	130	31	2	14	78	80	120	5	0	.369	.422
	Boston (AL)	MAJ	.000	6	5	2	0	0	0	0	0	0	3	0	0	.000	.000
Major League Totals			.175	24	40	6	7	1	0	0	4	7	11	0	0	.292	.200
Minor League Totals			.276	637	2341	344	646	160	9	67	356	351	587	13	7	.372	.438

29 CHRISTIAN VAZQUEZ, C

BA GRADE
50
HIGH

Born: Aug. 21, 1990. **B-T:** R-R. **Ht.:** 5-9. **Wt.:** 195. **Drafted:** HS—Gurabo, P.R., 2008 (9th round). **Signed by:** Edgar Perez.

Overmatched in his first exposure to full-season ball as a 19-year-old in 2010, Vazquez returned to Greenville last season and raised his OPS from .665 to .863 and his home run output from three to 18. And his bat isn't even the most impressive part of his game. The Red Sox named him their 2011 minor league defensive player of the year, quite an honor in a system that also includes standout glovemen such as Jose Iglesias and Che-Hsuan Lin. Vazquez has plus catch-and-throw skills, though he still needs to clean up his receiving a little more. His average arm strength plays up because he gets rid of the ball quickly and makes accurate throws, and he threw out 33 percent of basestealers last year. A strong leader with passion for the game, he's bilingual and communicates well with English- and Spanish-speaking pitchers alike. Vazquez is strong and has solid power potential. With his compact swing, willingness to use the opposite field and command of the strike zone, he has a chance to hit for a decent average as well. He's a below-average runner but not terrible for a catcher. Vazquez is ready to make the jump to high Class A.

Year	Club (League)	Class	AVG	G	AB	R	H	2B	3B	HR	RBI	BB	SO	SB	CS	OBP	SLG
2008	Red Sox (GCL)	R	.190	21	58	7	11	1	0	0	5	6	17	0	0	.266	.207
2009	Red Sox (GCL)	R	.278	10	36	5	10	5	0	0	7	4	7	0	0	.366	.417
	Lowell (NYP)	SS	.123	21	65	4	8	2	0	2	9	11	16	0	0	.250	.246
2010	Greenville (SAL)	LoA	.263	79	270	34	71	11	0	3	32	23	62	3	1	.328	.337
2011	Greenville (SAL)	LoA	.283	105	392	71	111	27	3	18	84	43	84	1	1	.358	.505
Minor League Totals			.257	236	821	121	211	46	3	23	137	87	186	4	2	.333	.404

30 HEIKER MENESES, INF

BA GRADE
45
MEDIUM

Born: July 1, 1991. **B-T:** R-R. **Ht.:** 5-9. **Wt.:** 160. **Signed:** Venezuela, 2007. **Signed by:** Angel Escobar.

After batting just .223/.337/.304 in three years of Rookie ball, Meneses hit his way from low Class A to Double-A at age 20 last season. He's not very physical at 5-foot-9 and 160 pounds, but he's surprisingly strong for his size and has a quick bat. He makes hard line-drive contact, though he's not going to be a home run threat and still needs to tone down his aggressive approach. He's a solid runner who looks to steal and take extra bases. Meneses saw action at shortstop, second base and third base in 2011, and he profiles best at second base. He has the hands and footwork for short, but his arm and range are better suited for second. He has quick hands and turns the double-play pivot exceptionally well. If he doesn't develop into a regular, Meneses has what it takes to become a valuable utilityman. He'll return to Portland to begin 2012.

Year	Club (League)	Class	AVG	G	AB	R	H	2B	3B	HR	RBI	BB	SO	SB	CS	OBP	SLG
2008	Red Sox (DSL)	R	.220	43	132	20	29	1	2	0	16	29	44	9	3	.376	.258
2009	Red Sox (DSL)	R	.199	65	216	48	43	2	6	1	17	34	68	25	5	.341	.278
2010	Red Sox (GCL)	R	.250	56	208	27	52	8	3	3	24	12	47	17	6	.304	.361
2011	Greenville (SAL)	LoA	.277	51	206	38	57	6	2	2	22	18	56	17	5	.358	.354
	Portland (EL)	AA	.265	24	83	13	22	3	0	0	6	3	25	2	0	.311	.301
	Salem (CAR)	HiA	.356	26	101	23	36	9	5	1	13	8	24	6	1	.416	.574
Minor League Totals			.253	265	946	169	239	29	18	7	98	104	264	76	20	.347	.344

Chicago Cubs

BY JIM CALLIS

As you might have heard, the Cubs haven't won a World Series since 1908 or appeared in one since 1945. Their win total just declined for the third year in the row, and they finished 2011 with the second-worst record and fourth-oldest roster in the National League. Their farm system can't offer many immediate solutions.

Yet optimism runs rampant among Chicago fans, thanks to a front-office makeover that began with the firing of Jim Hendry in mid-August. Hendry was the most accomplished GM in the franchise's modern history, building five winning teams and three playoff clubs in nine full seasons. But his increasing focus on the short term eventually left the Cubs with an aging roster, a bloated payroll and no obvious way to escape.

Owner Tom Ricketts actually fired him four weeks before the move was announced, but Hendry stayed on to conclude negotiations with the most expensive draft class in franchise history. Chicago handed out seven-figure bonuses to shortstop Javier Baez (first round), first baseman Dan Vogelbach (second), outfielder Shawon Dunston Jr. (11th) and righthander Dillon Maples (14th) while spending a total of $12 million. By comparison, it paid $8.7 million in bonuses in the previous two drafts combined.

The Cubs also have been aggressive seeking talent in Latin America and Asia, and Ricketts' commitment to player development attracted interest throughout the industry. Theo Epstein mentioned it as a major factor in why he decided to leave the Red Sox, where he won two World Series in nine years as GM, to become Chicago's president of baseball operations in October. He received a five-year, $18.5 million contract.

Padres GM Jed Hoyer and vice president of scouting and player development Jason McLeod also took notice. Hoyer and McLeod, who helped build those championship teams in Boston before revitalizing the farm system in two years in San Diego, assumed the same roles in Chicago a week after Epstein came aboard. The Cubs continued to bolster what had been one of baseball's smallest front offices by hiring well-regarded Diamondbacks pro scout Joe Bohringer as director of pro scouting.

The team also retained most members of the previous administration, with the notable exception of legendary scout Gary Hughes, a special assistant who resigned out of loyalty to Hendry. Vice president of player personnel Oneri Fleita, who has overseen

MORRIS FOSTOFF

Theo Epstein took notice of the Cubs' new commitment to player development

TOP 30 PROSPECTS

1. Brett Jackson, of	**16.** Marco Hernandez, ss/2b
2. Javier Baez, ss	**17.** Reggie Golden, of
3. Matt Szczur, of	**18.** Jae-Hoon Ha, of
4. Trey McNutt, rhp	**19.** Robert Whitenack, rhp
5. Dillon Maples, rhp	**20.** Jeimer Candelario, 3b
6. Welington Castillo, c	**21.** Steve Clevenger, c
7. Rafael Dolis, rhp	**22.** Jose Rosario, rhp
8. Junior Lake, ss	**23.** Logan Watkins, 2b/ss/of
9. Josh Vitters, 3b/1b	**24.** Jeff Beliveau, lhp
10. Dan Vogelbach, 1b	**25.** Ben Wells, rhp
11. Dae-Eun Rhee, rhp	**26.** Marcus Hatley, rhp
12. Dallas Beeler, rhp	**27.** Casey Weathers, rhp
13. Chris Carpenter, rhp	**28.** Taiwan Easterling, of
14. Zeke DeVoss, 2b	**29.** Hayden Simpson, rhp
15. Tony Zych, rhp	**30.** Shawon Dunston Jr., of

the farm system and international scouting operations, received a four-year contract extension prior to Epstein's arrival. Tim Wilken, who had been director of amateur and pro scouting, now will focus on the draft.

Epstein and Co. have their work cut out for them. The big league club has more bad contracts than under-30 cornerstones and will need at least a year to rebuild, even with the Cubs' vast resources. Outfielder Brett Jackson is ready to play in the majors, but the system's other blue-chip prospects, Baez and outfielder Matt Szczur, are at least a couple of years away.

General Manager: Jed Hoyer. **Farm Director:** Oneri Fleita. **Scouting Director:** Tim Wilken.

Class	Team	League	W	L	Pct	Finish*	Manager(s)
Majors	Chicago Cubs	National	71	91	.438	t-14th (16)	Mike Quade
Triple-A	Iowa Cubs	Pacific Coast	66	77	.462	12th (16)	Bill Dancy
Double-A	Tennessee Smokies	Southern	83	57	.593	2nd (10)	Brian Harper
High A	Daytona Cubs	Florida State	76	61	.555	2nd (12)†	Buddy Bailey
Low A	Peoria Chiefs	Midwest	60	79	.432	15th (16)	Casey Kopitzke
Short-season	Boise Hawks	Northwest	36	40	.474	5th (8)	Mark Johnson
Rookie	AZL Cubs	Arizona	28	28	.500	t-6th (13)	Juan Cabreja
Overall 2011 Minor League Record			349	342	.505	14th (30)	

*Finish in overall standings (No. of teams in league). †League champion.

LAST YEAR'S TOP 30

Player, Pos.		Status
1.	Chris Archer, rhp	(Rays)
2.	Brett Jackson, of	No. 1
3.	Trey McNutt, rhp	No. 4
4.	Hak-Ju Lee, ss	(Rays)
5.	Josh Vitters, 3b	No. 9
6.	Chris Carpenter, rhp	No. 13
7.	Matt Szczur, of	No. 3
8.	Hayden Simpson, rhp	No. 29
9.	Rafael Dolis, rhp	No. 7
10.	Brandon Guyer, of	(Rays)
11.	Alberto Cabrera, rhp	Dropped out
12.	Darwin Barney, ss/2b	Majors
13.	D.J. LeMahieu, inf	(Rockies)
14.	Scott Maine, lhp	Dropped out
15.	Jay Jackson, rhp	Dropped out
16.	Robinson Chirinos, c	(Rays)
17.	Welington Castillo, c	No. 6
18.	Marcus Mateo, rhp	Majors
19.	Robinson Lopez, rhp	Dropped out
20.	Kyle Smit, rhp	Dropped out
21.	Logan Watkins, 2b/of/ss	No. 23
22.	Ryan Flaherty, 2b/3b	(Orioles)
23.	Reggie Golden, of	No. 17
24.	Ben Wells, rhp	No. 25
25.	Aaron Kurcz, rhp	Dropped out
26.	Brooks Raley, lhp	Dropped out
27.	Junior Lake, ss/3b	No. 8
28.	Jae-Hoon Ha, of	No. 18
29.	Esmailin Caridad, rhp	Dropped out
30.	Dae-Eun Rhee, rhp	No. 11

BEST TOOLS

Best Hitter for Average	Javier Baez
Best Power Hitter	Dan Vogelbach
Best Strike-Zone Discipline	Matt Cerda
Fastest Baserunner	Matt Szczur
Best Athlete	Matt Szczur
Best Fastball	Rafael Dolis
Best Curveball	Trey McNutt
Best Slider	Kevin Rhoderick
Best Changeup	Dae-Eun Rhee
Best Control	Dallas Beeler
Best Defensive Catcher	Welington Castillo
Best Defensive Infielder	Elliot Soto
Best Infield Arm	Junior Lake
Best Defensive Outfielder	Jae-Hoon Ha
Best Outfield Arm	Anthony Giansanti

PROJECTED 2015 LINEUP

Catcher	Geovany Soto
First Base	Dan Vogelbach
Second Base	Zeke DeVoss
Third Base	Javier Baez
Shortstop	Starlin Castro
Left Field	Josh Vitters
Center Field	Matt Szczur
Right Field	Brett Jackson
No. 1 Starter	Matt Garza
No. 2 Starter	Andrew Cashner
No. 3 Starter	Trey McNutt
No. 4 Starter	Dillon Maples
No. 5 Starter	Dae-Eun Rhee
Closer	Carlos Marmol

TOP PROSPECTS OF THE DECADE

Year	Player, Pos.	2011 Org.
2002	Mark Prior, rhp	Yankees
2003	Hee Seop Choi, 1b	Kia (Korea)
2004	Angel Guzman, rhp	Cubs
2005	Brian Dopirak, 1b	Astros
2006	Felix Pie, of	Orioles
2007	Felix Pie, of	Orioles
2008	Josh Vitters, 3b	Cubs
2009	Josh Vitters, 3b	Cubs
2010	Starlin Castro, ss	Cubs
2011	Chris Archer, rhp	Rays

TOP DRAFT PICKS OF THE DECADE

Year	Player, Pos.	2011 Org.
2002	Bobby Brownlie, rhp	Out of baseball
2003	Ryan Harvey, of	Red Sox
2004	Grant Johnson, rhp (2nd round)	Out of baseball
2005	Mark Pawelek, lhp	Out of baseball
2006	Tyler Colvin, of	Cubs
2007	Josh Vitters, 3b	Cubs
2008	Andrew Cashner, rhp	Cubs
2009	Brett Jackson, of	Cubs
2010	Hayden Simpson, rhp	Cubs
2011	Javier Baez, ss	Cubs

LARGEST BONUSES IN CLUB HISTORY

Mark Prior, 2001	$4,000,000
Kosuke Fukudome, 2007	$4,000,000
Corey Patterson, 1998	$3,700,000
Josh Vitters, 2007	$3,200,000
Luis Montanez, 2000	$2,750,000

CHICAGO CUBS

TOP 2012 ROOKIE: Brett Jackson, of. The Cubs don't have many upper-level prospects ready to help, but he's an exception as the most talented outfielder in the organization.

BREAKOUT PROSPECT: Marco Hernandez, ss/2b. He's an all-around shortstop with a good chance to stay at the position.

SLEEPER: Gioskar Amaya, inf. He may lack the quickness for shortstop, but he led the Arizona League in hits (77) and ranked second in batting (.377).

SOURCE OF TOP 30 TALENT			
Homegrown	29	Acquired	1
College	10	Trades	1
Junior college	2	Rule 5 draft	0
High school	8	Independent leagues	0
Draft-and-follow	1	Free agents/waivers	0
Nondrafted free agents	0		
International	8		

LF
Garrett Schlecht
Kyung-Min Na

CF
Brett Jackson (1)
Matt Szczur (3)
Jae-Hoon Ha (18)
Taiwan Easterling (28)
Shawon Dunston Jr. (30)
Pin-Chieh Chen
Trey Martin
Elieser Bonne
Kelvin Encarnacion

RF
Reggie Golden (17)
Nelson Perez
John Andreoli

3B
Javier Baez (2)
Junior Lake (8)
Josh Vitters (9)
Jeimer Candelario (20)
Dustin Geiger
Trevor Gretzky
Ricardo Marcano

SS
Marco Hernandez (16)
Wes Darvill
Carlos Penalver
Elliot Soto
Arismendy Alcantara
Luis Acosta

2B
Zeke DeVoss (14)
Logan Watkins (23)
Rubi Silva
Gioskar Amaya
Jeff Bianchi
Matt Cerda

1B
Dan Vogelbach (10)
Justin Bour
Rock Shoulders
Richard Jones
Paul Hoilman

C
Welington Castillo (6)
Steve Clevenger (21)
Micah Gibbs
Neftali Rosario
Rafael Lopez
Justin Marra
Mark Malave

LHP		RHP	
LHSP	**LHRP**	**RHSP**	**RHRP**
Chris Rusin	Jeff Beliveau (24)	Trey McNutt (4)	Rafael Dolis (7)
Brooks Raley	Scott Maine	Dillon Maples (5)	Chris Carpenter (13)
Frank del Valle	John Gaub	Dae-Eun Rhee (11)	Tony Zych (15)
Austin Kirk	Jeffry Antigua	Dallas Beeler (12)	Marcus Hatley (26)
Willengton Cruz	Casey Harman	Robert Whitenack (19)	Casey Weathers (27)
Eric Jokisch	Kyler Burke	Jose Rosario (22)	Kevin Rhoderick
Graham Hicks		Ben Wells (25)	Alberto Cabrera
Brian Smith		Hayden Simpson (29)	Lendy Castillo
		Ryan Searle	Aaron Kurcz
		Yao-Lin Wang	Blake Parker
		Jay Jackson	Kyle Smit
		Starlin Peralta	Larry Suarez
		Luis Liria	A.J. Morris
		Tayler Scott	Frank Batista
		Austin Reed	P.J. Francesco
		Michael Jensen	
		Jose Arias	
		Nick Struck	

2011 BONUSES: $12.0 MILLION

BEST PURE HITTER: The Cubs signed several impressive bats, starting with SS Javier Baez (1). He had the best bat speed in the entire draft. Among the other standout hitters, three are catchers: Neftali Rosario (6), Justin Marra (15) and Rafael Lopez (16).

BEST POWER HITTER: Signed for $1.6 million, 1B Dan Vogelbach (2) won the 2010 Power Showcase, a high school home run derby, and blasted one ball 508 feet. Baez and 1Bs Paul Hoilman (19) and Rock Shoulders (25) all have above-average pop.

FASTEST RUNNER: 2B Zeke DeVoss (3) can run the 60-yard dash in 6.45 seconds and swiped 16 bases in 42 pro games. He's a half-step quicker than OFs Shawon Dunston Jr. (11), Trey Martin (13) and Taiwan Easterling (27).

BEST DEFENSIVE PLAYER: Martin and Easterling have advanced center-field skills. The Cubs believe Baez can stay at shortstop with his average range and plus-plus arm.

BEST FASTBALL: Coming out of the bullpen, RHP Tony Zych (4) operates at 94-97 mph and hits 99. RHP Dillon Maples (14) pitches at 92-96 mph as a starter.

BEST SECONDARY PITCH: Maples has an above-average curveball. RHP Michael Jensen (26) pairs a plus curve with a 91-94 mph fastball.

BEST PRO DEBUT: Hoilman led the short-season Northwest League in homers (17), extra-base hits (30), total bases (126)—but also strikeouts (105). Lopez, who hit .319 with six homers, joined him on the NWL all-star team.

BEST ATHLETE: Dunston and Martin both offer speed, defense and power potential. Easterling caught 108 passes in three years as a wide receiver at Florida State. Maples would have kicked for North Carolina's football team if Chicago hadn't given him a $2.5 million bonus.

MOST INTRIGUING BACKGROUND: The Cubs selected Dunston's father No. 1 overall in the 1982 draft, and he played 18 big league seasons. OF/3B Trevor Gretzky's (7) dad Wayne is the NHL's all-time leading scorer. SS Daniel Lockhart's (10) father Keith played in the majors and signed him and Martin in his first year as a Cubs area scout. Unsigned OF Bradley Zimmer's (23) brother Kyle is a potential first-round pick in 2012, and they'll play together at the University of San Francisco.

CLOSEST TO THE MAJORS: Zych might not need much more than a year in the minors before he can help Chicago's bullpen.

BEST LATE-ROUND PICK: The Cubs gave seven-figure bonuses to Maples and Dunston ($1.275 million). They also are high on the less-costly Martin, Marra, Jensen and Easterling. In the bargain category, RHP P.J. Francescon (40) showed a 90-93 mph fastball after signing for $1,000.

THE ONE WHO GOT AWAY: RHP Ricky Jacquez (39) is 5-foot-9 yet has a 92-97 mph fastball and a hammer curveball. He couldn't be diverted from attending Texas.

ASSESSMENT: In his second draft as owner, Tom Ricketts showed his commitment to development with a club-record $12 million in bonuses. Chicago loaded up on position players and got a premium arm in Maples.

2010 BONUSES: $4.7 MILLION

RHP Hayden Simpson (1) hasn't been healthy since the Cubs stunningly picked him 16th overall, but they pulled a coup by luring OF Matt Szczur (5) away from a career as an NFL wide receiver. RHP Dallas Beeler (41) was another potential steal.

GRADE: C+

2009 BONUSES: $4.0 MILLION

OF Brett Jackson (1) and RHP Trey McNutt (32) are the system's best position and pitching prospects. 3B/2B D.J. LeMahieu (2) beat them both to Chicago, then was traded to the Rockies in December.

GRADE: B

2008 BONUSES: $5.5 MILLION

RHP Andrew Cashner (1) could be a frontline starter if he stays healthy. Five others players have reached the majors—RHPs Chris Carpenter (3), Casey Coleman (15) and Erik Hamren (37), 3B/2B Josh Harrison (6), OF Tony Campana (13)—and INF/OF Ryan Flaherty (1s) and LHP Jeff Beliveau (18) aren't far behind. Flaherty was lost to the Orioles in the Rule 5 draft in December.

GRADE: B

2007 BONUSES: $6.1 MILLION

3B/1B Josh Vitters (1) hasn't developed as rapidly or as well as expected from a No. 3 overall pick. 2B Darwin Barney (4) is the Cubs' second baseman, LHP James Russell (14) has carved out a bullpen role and C Josh Donaldson (1s) and OF Brandon Guyer (5) were used in deals for Rich Harden and Matt Garza.

GRADE: C

Draft analysis by Jim Callis. Numbers in parentheses indicate draft rounds.

1 BRETT JACKSON, OF

Born: Aug. 2, 1988. **B-T:** L-R. **Ht.:** 6-2. **Wt.:** 210.
Drafted: California, 2009 (1st round). **Signed by:** John Bartsch.

BA GRADE
60
MEDIUM

JOHN WILLIAMSON

Undrafted out of high school, Jackson went to college at California, impressed scouts in the Cape Cod League in the summer of 2008 and became a first-round pick the following June. The Cubs believed he had the best bat speed in the 2009 draft, yet were able to get him with the 31st overall pick because teams worried whether he could make consistent contact. Signed for $972,000, he has struck out 320 times in 296 minor league games, but that hasn't kept him from being productive. He has earned in-season promotions in each of his three years as a pro, hitting 20 homers and stealing 21 bases while reaching Triple-A Iowa in 2011. He ended the year by batting .412 for Team USA at the World Cup in Panama. Only minor injuries have slowed him, with a strained ligament in his left pinky costing him three weeks last May and a foot issue relegating him to pinch-hitting duty at the Pan American Games.

With solid to plus tools across the board and the ability to stay in center field, Jackson is a potential all-star. His power stands out the most, as he has the bat speed, loft and strength to drive balls out of the park to all fields. He has become more selective at the plate than he was in college, waiting for pitches he can punish and taking walks when pitchers won't challenge him. Chicago would like to see him get a little more aggressive and attack more often early in the count. He's not a pure hitter, but he does have a compact swing and doesn't get himself out by chasing pitches out of the zone. Some scouts think Jackson's stroke can get too mechanical and believe he swings and misses too much to hit much more than .260 or .270. He pulls off pitches at times, and his strikeout rate spiked to a career-high 30 percent in Triple-A. Jackson isn't a blazer, but he has plus speed that enables him to get the job done on the bases and in the outfield. He knows when to pick his spots as a basestealer, succeeding at a 76 percent rate in the

minors. Likewise, he gets good jumps and takes nice routes in the outfield. He has played all three outfield positions in pro ball, and his average, accurate arm is enough for right field if he moves to a corner. His steady demeanor and work ethic are assets that have rubbed off on his teammates, such as 2007 first-round pick Josh Vitters.

Not only is Jackson the Cubs' top prospect, but he's also the only position player in the upper levels of the system ready to play regularly in the majors. They resisted the temptation to promote him during their disappointing 2011 season, in part because he didn't have to be protected on the 40-man roster this offseason. With Alfonso Soriano and Marlon Byrd due a combined $24.5 million in salaries in 2012, and David DeJesus coming aboard as a free agent, Jackson could open the season in Triple-A. Even if that happens, he should push his way to Wrigley Field in short order. He has the upside of Jim Edmonds at the plate, if not the same Gold Glove ability in center field.

SCOUTING GRADES

Batting: 55.   **Defense:** 55.
Power: 60.   **Arm:** 50.
Speed: 60.

Based on 20-80 scouting scale, where 50 represents major league average, and future projection rather than present tools.

Year	Club (League)	Class	AVG	G	AB	R	H	2B	3B	HR	RBI	BB	SO	SB	CS	OBP	SLG
2009	Cubs (AZL)	R	.455	3	11	6	5	0	1	0	4	3	4	0	0	.533	.636
	Boise (NWL)	SS	.330	24	88	14	29	1	1	1	15	17	20	2	1	.443	.398
	Peoria (MWL)	LoA	.295	26	112	30	33	5	1	7	17	11	32	11	1	.383	.545
2010	Daytona (FSL)	HiA	.316	67	263	56	83	19	8	6	38	43	63	12	7	.420	.517
	Tennessee (SL)	AA	.276	61	228	47	63	13	6	6	28	30	63	18	4	.366	.465
2011	Tennessee (SL)	AA	.256	67	246	45	63	10	3	10	32	45	74	15	6	.373	.443
	Iowa (PCL)	AAA	.297	48	185	39	55	13	2	10	26	28	64	6	1	.388	.551
Minor League Totals			.292	296	1133	237	331	61	22	40	160	177	320	64	20	.393	.491

BaseballAmerica.com

2 JAVIER BAEZ, SS

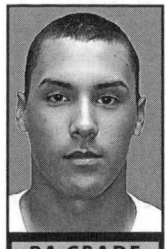

Born: Dec. 1, 1992. **B-T:** R-R. **Ht.:** 6-1. **Wt.:** 205. **Drafted:** HS—Jacksonville, Fla., 2011 (1st round). **Signed by:** Tom Clark.

Born in Puerto Rico, Baez moved to Florida in 2005 and batted .711 with 20 homers as a high school senior last spring. Though the Cubs need pitching, they passed on several college arms to draft him ninth overall last June. He signed for $2.625 million at the Aug. 15 deadline. Baez had the best bat speed in the 2011 draft, prompting comparisons to Gary Sheffield and Hanley Ramirez. In terms of the 20-80 scouting scale, Chicago thinks Baez could develop into a 70 hitter with 65 power. He's still learning that he doesn't have to overswing to do damage. His arm strength gives him a third well above-average tool and may allow him to stay at shortstop. Baez is an average runner with average range who will have to find a new position if he loses a step, with third base perhaps the best long-term fit. Second base, right field and even catcher are other options. Overly aggressive and emotional at times, he'll need time to mature on and off the field. Baez has the highest ceiling in the system and could move quickly. His bat eventually should fit into the No. 3 slot in Chicago's lineup and should provide enough offense for any position. He'll head to low Class A Peoria at age 19.

BA GRADE

65

HIGH

Year	Club (League)	Class	AVG	G	AB	R	H	2B	3B	HR	RBI	BB	SO	SB	CS	OBP	SLG
2011	Cubs (AZL)	R	.333	3	12	2	4	2	0	0	0	0	2	2	0	.333	.500
	Boise (NWL)	SS	.167	2	6	0	1	0	0	0	1	0	2	0	0	.167	.167
Minor League Totals			.278	5	18	2	5	2	0	0	1	0	4	2	0	.278	.389

3 MATT SZCZUR, OF

Born: July 20, 1989. **B-T:** R-R. **Ht.:** 6-1. **Wt.:** 195. **Drafted:** Villanova, 2010 (5th round). **Signed by:** Tim Adkins.

The MVP of the 2009 NCAA football championship subdivision title game, Szczur had NFL aspirations as a wide receiver. After signing him for $100,000 as a 2010 fifth-round pick, the Cubs paid him an additional $1.4 million last March to give up the gridiron. He ranked as the low Class A Midwest League's best defensive outfielder, played in the Futures Game and hit .368 in the playoffs as high Class A Daytona won the Florida State League title. His deal necessitated a spot on the 40-man roster after the season. Szczur is polished for a two-sport player. His plus-plus speed helps him hit for average, makes him a basestealing threat and allows him to run down balls from gap to gap. He has a short, quick swing and strength in his hands and wrists that could translate into average power. Szczur's main needs are to get more patient at the plate and more aggressive on the basepaths. He has worked to improve his arm strength from below-average to solid. Coaches and scouts rave about his makeup as much as his tools. After wearing down from his baseball/football grind in the second half, Szczur could be primed for a breakout. He'll start 2012 at Double-A Tennessee and could reach Chicago in 2013. He should eventually push Brett Jackson to right field.

BA GRADE

60

MEDIUM

Year	Club (League)	Class	AVG	G	AB	R	H	2B	3B	HR	RBI	BB	SO	SB	CS	OBP	SLG
2010	Cubs (AZL)	R	.500	1	2	1	1	0	0	0	0	1	0	1	0	.750	.500
	Boise (NWL)	SS	.397	18	73	17	29	9	0	0	8	6	11	1	0	.439	.521
	Peoria (MWL)	LoA	.192	6	26	6	5	1	1	0	2	3	5	0	0	.300	.308
2011	Peoria (MWL)	LoA	.314	66	274	55	86	15	1	5	27	21	28	17	5	.366	.431
	Daytona (FSL)	HiA	.260	43	173	20	45	7	2	5	19	5	20	7	0	.283	.410
Minor League Totals			.303	134	548	99	166	32	4	10	56	36	64	26	5	.350	.431

4 TREY McNUTT, RHP

Born: Aug. 2, 1989. **B-T:** R-R. **Ht.:** 6-4. **Wt.:** 220. **Drafted:** Shelton State (Ala.) CC, 2009 (32nd round). **Signed by:** Jim Crawford/Al Geddes.

A 32-round steal who fell through the cracks in the 2009 draft, McNutt reached Double-A in his first full pro season but symbolized the Cubs' system-wide pitching woes in his second. Between blisters on two fingers, bruised ribs sustained in an infield collision and bad luck with rain, he worked just 26 innings from mid-May to mid-July. Even when healthy, he battled his command and consistency. McNutt can hit 98 mph with his fastball, though he gets more life and locates it better when he works at 92-94. His power breaking ball, which breaks more like a curveball and has slider velocity, can be equally as devastating. He could use an offspeed pitch to keep hitters off balance, and his changeup is just a work in progress. He needs to worry about working down in the zone rather than trying to blow the ball by hitters. McNutt remained inconsistent in the Arizona Fall League, and he could wind up as a late-inning reliever if he can't improve his changeup

BA GRADE

55

HIGH

and command. If it all comes together, he could be a No. 2 starter, similar to what Chicago hopes for from 2008 first-rounder Andrew Cashner. Ticketed for a return to Tennessee, McNutt could finish 2012 in the majors.

Year	Club (League)	Class	W	L	ERA	G	GS	CG	SV	IP	H	HR	BB	SO	K/9	WHIP	AVG
2009	Cubs (AZL)	R	0	1	0.00	6	4	0	0	7	5	0	3	7	8.6	1.09	.167
	Boise (NWL)	SS	3	0	1.33	7	2	0	0	20	9	1	12	21	9.3	1.03	.132
2010	Peoria (MWL)	LoA	6	0	1.51	13	13	0	0	60	43	0	24	70	10.6	1.12	.202
	Daytona (FSL)	HiA	4	0	2.63	9	9	0	0	41	29	3	9	49	10.8	0.93	.191
	Tennessee (SL)	AA	0	1	5.74	3	3	0	0	16	21	2	4	13	7.5	1.60	.333
2011	Tennessee (SL)	AA	5	6	4.55	23	22	0	0	95	120	5	39	65	6.2	1.67	.319
Minor League Totals			18	8	3.13	61	53	0	0	239	227	11	91	225	8.5	1.33	.252

5 DILLON MAPLES, RHP

Born: May 9, 1992. **B-T:** R-R. **Ht.:** 6-2. **Wt.:** 195. **Drafted:** HS—Southern Pines, N.C., 2011 (14th round). **Signed by:** Billy Swoope.

One of the most talented and most unsignable high school pitchers in the 2011 draft, Maples slid to the 14th round. He seemed likely to attend North Carolina, where he would have played baseball and kicked for the football team, before Chicago stepped in with $2.5 million at the signing deadline. His father Tim was a 1979 second-round pick who reached Double-A in the Orioles system. Maples has a pair of plus pitches in his heavy 92-96 mph fastball and hard curveball. There's little question about the quality of his arm, though scouts worry about his mechanics. Though he's athletic, he has a non-athletic delivery with a short arm action and a stiff, upright finish. That could lead to problems with his command—he locates his curve better than his fastball—and stress on his shoulder. The Cubs don't have any significant concerns and won't make any major adjustments. They'll have him focus on improving his fastball location and developing a changeup. Maples has enough weapons to succeed in low Class A in his pro debut in 2012. As with Trey McNutt, his changeup and command will determine whether he reaches his ceiling as a No. 2 starter or becomes a late-inning reliever.

BA GRADE
55
HIGH

Year	Club (League)	Class	W	L	ERA	G	GS	CG	SV	IP	H	HR	BB	SO	K/9	WHIP	AVG
2011	Did Not Play—Signed Late																

6 WELINGTON CASTILLO, C

Born: April 24, 1987. **B-T:** R-R. **Ht.:** 5-10. **Wt.:** 210. **Signed:** Dominican Republic, 2004. **Signed by:** Jose Serra.

The Cubs always have liked Castillo's arm and power potential, but a lack of work ethic slowed his progress and led to a .232/.275/.386 Double-A performance in 2009. He got the message and improved his effort and conditioning, leading to strong seasons and big league callups in each of the last two years. Thumb and hamstring injuries limited him to 79 games in 2011. Castillo has 28 homers in 131 Triple-A games, with his solid power coming more from strength than bat speed. He doesn't give away as many at-bats as he used to, but his impatient approach probably will prevent him from hitting for a high average. Castillo has well-above-average arm strength and a quick release. He threw out 31 percent of basestealers in 2011, an acceptable rate though also a career low. His receiving and game-calling draw mixed reviews, but he has gotten better. He also has improved his English so he can better communicate with his pitchers. He has next to no speed. Castillo should serve as Geovany Soto's backup in Chicago in 2012. Soto is talented but also inconsistent and getting more expensive, and Castillo will get the chance to show what he might provide as a cheaper alternative.

BA GRADE
50
MEDIUM

Year	Club (League)	Class	AVG	G	AB	R	H	2B	3B	HR	RBI	BB	SO	SB	CS	OBP	SLG
2005	Cubs (DSL)	R	.289	60	204	29	59	14	0	1	28	19	28	1	2	.370	.373
2006	Boise (NWL)	SS	.167	3	6	1	1	0	0	0	0	1	0	0	0	.286	.167
	Cubs (AZL)	R	.192	7	26	4	5	0	0	0	0	1	6	0	0	.250	.192
2007	Peoria (MWL)	LoA	.271	98	317	41	86	11	2	11	44	23	77	1	3	.334	.423
2008	Daytona (FSL)	HiA	.273	33	121	15	33	8	0	0	12	4	23	1	0	.299	.339
	Tennessee (SL)	AA	.298	57	198	25	59	11	0	4	24	14	50	0	0	.362	.414
	Iowa (PCL)	AAA	.200	1	5	0	1	0	0	0	1	0	1	0	0	.200	.200
2009	Tennessee (SL)	AA	.232	95	319	27	74	16	0	11	39	15	71	1	0	.275	.386
2010	Iowa (PCL)	AAA	.255	69	239	35	61	17	1	13	59	19	58	0	2	.317	.498
	Chicago (NL)	MAJ	.300	7	20	3	6	4	0	1	5	1	7	0	0	.333	.650
2011	Daytona (FSL)	HiA	.238	12	42	6	10	3	0	1	7	6	9	0	0	.327	.381
	Chicago (NL)	MAJ	.154	4	13	0	2	0	0	0	0	0	4	0	0	.154	.154
	Cubs (AZL)	R	.667	2	6	2	4	3	0	0	0	3	0	0	0	.778	1.167
	Iowa (PCL)	AAA	.286	61	227	38	65	9	0	15	35	20	57	0	0	.351	.524
Major League Totals			.242	11	33	3	8	4	0	1	5	1	11	0	0	.265	.455
Minor League Totals			.268	498	1710	223	458	92	3	56	249	125	380	4	7	.329	.423

7 RAFAEL DOLIS, RHP

Born: Jan. 10, 1988. **B-T:** R-R. **Ht.:** 6-4. **Wt.:** 215. **Signed:** Dominican Republic, 2004. **Signed by:** Jose Serra/Marino Encarnacion.

The Cubs love to try failed position players on the mound, and their success stories include former catchers Carlos Marmol and Randy Wells. They originally signed Dolis as a shortstop but made him a pitcher before he arrived in the United States in 2006. He hurt his elbow in 2007 and missed 2008 following Tommy John surgery, then claimed a spot on the 40-man roster by hitting 101 mph during instructional league in 2009. Dolis reminds scouts of Marmol, and the similarities became more striking when he became a full-time reliever in 2011. He can make hitters look silly with two pitches, a 93-100 mph fastball with heavy sink and a mid-80s slider with hard bite. His stuff theoretically should have played up in shorter stints, but Dolis' strikeout rate dipped to a career-low 5.9 per nine innings. That's because he focused so much on his command, his biggest shortcoming, that he pounded the bottom of the strike zone and generated tons of groundouts rather than strikeouts. He has a clean high three-quarters delivery that gives him good downward plane with his pitches, but he still needs to throw more strikes. A potential closer if he improves his command, Dolis made his major league debut in late September. He figures to get some Triple-A experience at the start of 2012.

BA GRADE

50

MEDIUM

Year	Club (League)	Class	W	L	ERA	G	GS	CG	SV	IP	H	HR	BB	SO	K/9	WHIP	AVG
2005	Did Not Play																
2006	Cubs (AZL)	R	0	2	8.28	13	3	0	0	25	30	1	16	33	11.9	1.84	.294
2007	Peoria (MWL)	LoA	3	1	1.80	6	0	0	0	30	23	1	16	24	7.2	1.30	.223
2008	Did Not Play—Injured																
2009	Daytona (FSL)	HiA	3	9	3.79	27	25	0	0	100	78	4	53	75	6.8	1.31	.221
2010	Daytona (FSL)	HiA	4	5	2.92	14	13	0	0	71	63	3	30	48	6.1	1.31	.242
	Tennessee (SL)	AA	5	4	4.07	12	12	0	0	55	65	3	27	45	7.3	1.66	.295
2011	Tennessee (SL)	AA	8	5	3.22	51	4	0	17	73	61	2	35	48	5.9	1.32	.227
	Chicago (NL)	MAJ	0	0	0.00	1	0	0	0	1	0	0	1	1	6.8	0.75	.000
Major League Totals			0	0	0.00	1	0	0	0	1	0	0	1	1	6.8	0.75	.000
Minor League Totals			23	26	3.69	123	63	0	17	354	320	14	177	273	6.9	1.41	.245

8 JUNIOR LAKE, SS

Born: March 27, 1990. **B-T:** R-R. **Ht.:** 6-3. **Wt.:** 215. **Signed:** Dominican Republic, 2007. **Signed by:** Jose Serra.

Lake is three days younger than fellow Dominican Starlin Castro, whom he teamed with in the Rookie-level Arizona League in 2008. While Castro has spent the last two years starring in Chicago, Lake has yet to find success above high Class A. The Cubs hope his breakout performance in the Arizona Fall League, where he hit .296 with five homers and a league-best 18 steals in as many attempts, is a sign of things to come. It helped earn him a spot on the 40-man roster after the season. Lake has some of the flashiest tools in the system, starting with what might be the strongest infield arm in the minors. His bat speed and strength give him above-average raw power to all fields, though his lack of patience and tendency to chase breaking pitches undermine him at the plate. After losing a step in 2010, Lake regained his plus speed underway and stole 38 bases in 44 tries. His range also has improved and he's doing a better job of anticipating plays at shortstop, but he may be too big for the position. His hands are fine for the infield, and he ultimately may wind up as a third baseman or right fielder. Though he remained impatient and tailed off toward the end of the fall, Lake's AFL success is encouraging. If he can build on it, he'll find a job in Chicago at a position to be determined. His next task will be to solve Double-A pitching.

BA GRADE

50

HIGH

Year	Club (League)	Class	AVG	G	AB	R	H	2B	3B	HR	RBI	BB	SO	SB	CS	OBP	SLG
2007	Cubs (DSL)	R	.274	62	223	41	61	16	2	3	30	16	53	9	3	.341	.404
2008	Cubs (AZL)	R	.286	47	168	24	48	4	6	2	23	13	42	12	2	.335	.417
2009	Peoria (MWL)	LoA	.248	131	463	71	115	19	7	7	42	18	138	10	7	.277	.365
2010	Daytona (FSL)	HiA	.264	120	394	56	104	18	4	9	46	35	99	13	9	.333	.398
2011	Daytona (FSL)	HiA	.315	49	203	39	64	11	4	6	34	6	49	19	4	.336	.498
	Tennessee (SL)	AA	.248	67	242	41	60	10	2	6	17	13	60	19	2	.300	.380
Minor League Totals			.267	476	1693	272	452	78	25	33	192	101	441	82	27	.315	.401

9 JOSH VITTERS, 3B/1B

BA GRADE
50
HIGH

Born: Aug. 27, 1989. **B-T:** R-R. **Ht.:** 6-2. **Wt.:** 200. **Drafted:** HS—Cypress, Calif., 2007 (1st round). **Signed by:** Denny Henderson.

The third overall choice in the 2007 draft, Vitters hasn't developed as quickly as hoped since signing for $3.2 million. Nevertheless, he reached Double-A at age 20 and had a solid season when he repeated the level in 2011. He batted .360 in the Arizona Fall League and joined the 40-man roster afterward. Some scouts think he has Jeff Conine potential at the plate, while others question whether he can be a quality big league regular. Vitters still shows the short stroke, bat speed, strength and ability to barrel the ball that made him the No. 3 pick. He recognizes pitches well, makes consistent contact and uses the whole field. However, he has yet to develop the patience to draw walks and lay off pitches he can't punish. His 22 walks in 2011 represented a career high. Vitters has shed a reputation for being laid-back and has worked hard to improve his defense. He has a solid arm but fringy quickness, speed and range. He topped Double-A Southern League third basemen with 21 errors in just 100 games. He also saw time at first base during the season and in the outfield in the Arizona Fall League. He still could be Chicago's third baseman of the near future, but so could Javier Baez or Junior Lake. The Cubs don't have an obvious starter for 2012, which Vitters will begin in Triple-A.

Year	Club (League)	Class	AVG	G	AB	R	H	2B	3B	HR	RBI	BB	SO	SB	CS	OBP	SLG
2007	Cubs (AZL)	R	.067	7	30	0	2	0	0	0	2	1	9	0	0	.094	.067
	Boise (NWL)	SS	.190	7	21	2	4	0	0	0	1	2	5	1	1	.261	.190
2008	Peoria (MWL)	LoA	.214	4	14	1	3	3	0	0	1	0	5	0	0	.214	.429
	Boise (NWL)	SS	.328	61	259	38	85	25	2	5	37	13	45	1	3	.365	.498
2009	Peoria (MWL)	LoA	.316	70	269	42	85	12	1	15	46	7	42	4	0	.351	.535
	Daytona (FSL)	HiA	.238	50	189	21	45	7	2	3	22	5	23	2	1	.260	.344
2010	Daytona (FSL)	HiA	.291	28	110	16	32	8	0	3	13	8	22	4	1	.350	.445
	Tennessee (SL)	AA	.223	63	206	28	46	12	0	7	26	13	41	2	0	.292	.383
2011	Tennessee (SL)	AA	.283	129	449	56	127	28	2	14	81	22	54	4	10	.322	.448
Minor League Totals			.277	419	1547	204	429	95	7	47	229	71	246	18	16	.319	.439

10 DAN VOGELBACH, 1B

BRIAN FLEMING

BA GRADE
50
HIGH

Born: Dec. 17, 1992. **B-T:** L-R. **Ht.:** 5-11. **Wt.:** 255. **Drafted:** HS—Fort Myers, Fla., 2011 (2nd round). **Signed by:** Lukas McKnight.

Bryce Harper blasted a 502-foot homer at the 2009 Power Showcase, a high school homer run derby. Vogelbach surpassed that by launching a 508-foot shot while winning the 2010 event, power that earned him $1.6 million as a second-round choice a year later. He and Twins sandwich pick Hudson Boyd led Bishop Verot High (Fort Myers, Fla.) to the Florida state 3-A championship last spring. Vogelbach's plus-plus raw power is all the more impressive because it comes to all fields and he generates it with a very loose, effortless swing. His rhythm, patience and pitch recognition give him the chance to hit for average as well. Vogelbach's bat will have to carry him because he lacks athleticism and speed. He has gotten in better shape since carrying 280 pounds on the showcase circuit in 2010, but he may never be more than an average defender and is a well below-average runner. He takes pride in his defense and is working to improve his footwork around the bag. The Cubs would love to see Vogelbach drop to 240 pounds before he reports to spring training. A potential middle-of-the-order threat, he has enough polish at the plate to make the jump to low Class A in 2012.

Year	Club (League)	Class	AVG	G	AB	R	H	2B	3B	HR	RBI	BB	SO	SB	CS	OBP	SLG
2011	Cubs (AZL)	R	.292	6	24	4	7	3	0	1	6	2	2	1	0	.370	.542
Minor League Totals			.292	6	24	4	7	3	0	1	6	2	2	1	0	.370	.542

11 DAE-EUN RHEE, RHP

BA GRADE
50
HIGH

Born: March 23, 1989. **B-T:** L-R. **Ht.:** 6-2. **Wt.:** 190. **Signed:** Korea, 2007. **Signed by:** Steve Wilson.

Rhee signed for $525,000 out of a Korean high school, and he was so advanced that the Cubs had no qualms about sending him to low Class A at age 19 for his pro debut the following spring. He aced the test, giving up just one run in his first three starts while displaying precocious feel for three average or better pitches. Then he hurt his elbow in his next outing, leading to Tommy John surgery that knocked him out for most of 2009 and left him without his best stuff in 2010. Rhee finally began to regain his previous form in 2011, saving his best for last. He went 3-0, 2.84 in August before posting a 2.25 ERA in two playoff starts, winning the finale to give Daytona the Florida State League championship. Rhee pitched at 88-92 mph for much of the year before adding 2 mph in the final month. He also added more power to his breaking ball, which can get caught in between a curveball and a slider at times but is a solid curve at its best. His changeup is his best pitch at times, featuring both sink and fade. Rhee generally throws strikes and works the bottom of the zone. If he stays healthy and continues to improve, he could become a No. 3 starter.

Year	Club (League)	Class	W	L	ERA	G	GS	CG	SV	IP	H	HR	BB	SO	K/9	WHIP	AVG
2008	Peoria (MWL)	LoA	4	1	1.80	10	10	0	0	40	28	0	16	33	7.4	1.10	.194
2009	Cubs (AZL)	R	0	0	7.71	3	2	0	0	5	4	0	5	3	5.8	1.93	.235
	Boise (NWL)	SS	0	1	11.25	2	2	0	0	4	8	2	1	4	9.0	2.25	.421
2010	Daytona (FSL)	HiA	5	13	5.27	26	25	0	0	114	125	11	40	70	5.5	1.44	.279
2011	Daytona (FSL)	HiA	8	7	4.02	25	17	4	0	128	131	10	43	117	8.2	1.36	.265
Minor League Totals			17	22	4.37	66	56	4	0	291	296	23	105	227	7.0	1.38	.264

12 DALLAS BEELER, RHP

BA GRADE
50
HIGH

Born: June 12, 1989. **B-T:** R-R. **Ht.:** 6-5. **Wt.:** 205. **Drafted:** Oral Roberts, 2010 (41st round). **Signed by:** Ty Nichols.

Beeler began his college career by helping Seminole State (Okla.) reach the 2009 Junior College World Series, then had Tommy John surgery following the season. Expected to miss all of 2010 after transferring to Oral Roberts, he came back at midseason and showed enough for the Cubs to draft him in the 41st round and sign him for $150,000. They handled Beeler carefully in his first full pro season, letting him work as many as five innings only once before June, but he still forced his way to Double-A. Chicago also kept his innings down by shelving him for two weeks when he strained an oblique in late April and for a month when he came down with shoulder tendinitis in late July. Beeler flashed more plus pitches (three) than he had victories (two) in 2011. He throws an 89-93 mph fastball that runs down and in on righthanders, inducing plenty of groundouts. He has a hard curveball that gets slurvy at times, and he also has a changeup with nifty sink. Beeler throws across his body, which creates deception but doesn't prevent him from filling the strike zone. He still needs to refine his command, however. He's a good athlete who helped Jenks (Okla.) High win two Oklahoma state 6-A championships as a wide receiver. The Cubs will turn Beeler loose in 2012, when he's set to open the season back at Tennessee. A potential No. 3 starter, he's battling his brother Chase (a center on the San Francisco 49ers' practice squad) to become the first member of the family to reach the big time in his sport.

Year	Club (League)	Class	W	L	ERA	G	GS	CG	SV	IP	H	HR	BB	SO	K/9	WHIP	AVG
2010	Cubs (AZL)	R	0	3	3.31	8	2	0	0	16	20	0	2	16	8.8	1.35	.303
	Boise (NWL)	SS	0	0	0.00	1	0	0	0	2	2	0	0	2	9.0	1.00	.250
2011	Tennessee (SL)	AA	1	5	4.53	9	9	0	0	52	68	7	7	33	5.7	1.45	.315
	Peoria (MWL)	LoA	1	1	1.66	12	11	0	0	43	35	1	6	35	7.3	0.95	.222
Minor League Totals			2	9	3.18	30	22	0	0	113	125	8	15	86	6.8	1.24	.279

13 CHRIS CARPENTER, RHP

BA GRADE
50
HIGH

Born: Dec. 26, 1985. **B-T:** R-R. **Ht.:** 6-4. **Wt.:** 220. **Drafted:** Kent State, 2008 (3rd round). **Signed by:** Lukas McKnight.

The Tigers took Carpenter in the seventh round of the 2004 draft, but he became the highest prep pick that year to opt for college when he attended Kent State. He had Tommy John surgery as a freshman and a second elbow operation the next year, but regained his stuff and became a third-round pick in 2008. He has been healthy throughout his pro career, with the exception of missing most of last August with a strained oblique. Carpenter was a starter until he got to the Arizona Fall League in 2010, when his fastball jumped to 94-100 mph when he came out of the bullpen. The Cubs kept him in relief and brought him to the big leagues last season, but his control and command regressed and he put up the worst numbers of his pro career. He had trouble adjusting to the routine of a reliever, and he started overthrowing and lost consistency with his mechanics. By the end of the year, Carpenter realized he still could sit in the mid-90s and touch triple digits without selling out for velocity. He had tightened his breaking ball, giving him a consistent hard slider as a second pitch. He showed a changeup with some deception and fade as a starter, but he doesn't use it much as a reliever. Carpenter got back on track and lived in the strike zone when he returned to the AFL following the 2011 season, laying the groundwork to contribute in Chicago this year. He eventually could develop into a set-up man.

Year	Club (League)	Class	W	L	ERA	G	GS	CG	SV	IP	H	HR	BB	SO	K/9	WHIP	AVG
2008	Cubs (AZL)	R	0	0	18.00	1	1	0	0	1	2	0	1	1	9.0	3.00	.500
	Boise (NWL)	SS	4	2	4.22	10	6	0	0	32	32	2	22	24	6.8	1.69	.258
2009	Peoria (MWL)	LoA	4	3	2.44	15	15	1	0	74	55	4	33	60	7.3	1.19	.210
	Daytona (FSL)	HiA	2	1	1.44	5	5	0	0	25	15	1	8	33	11.9	0.92	.163
	Tennessee (SL)	AA	0	3	4.78	7	7	0	0	32	30	0	11	25	7.0	1.28	.246
2010	Tennessee (SL)	AA	8	6	3.16	23	23	0	0	120	118	5	48	100	7.5	1.39	.262
	Iowa (PCL)	AAA	0	0	5.40	3	3	0	0	15	19	3	9	12	7.2	1.87	.317
2011	Tennessee (SL)	AA	1	1	4.38	10	0	0	1	12	10	2	4	6	4.4	1.14	.227
	Chicago (NL)	MAJ	0	0	2.79	10	0	0	0	10	12	1	7	8	7.4	1.97	.316
	Iowa (PCL)	AAA	2	3	6.53	22	0	0	1	30	32	3	23	28	8.3	1.81	.286
Major League Totals			0	0	2.79	10	0	0	0	10	12	1	7	8	7.4	1.97	.316
Minor League Totals			21	19	3.62	96	60	1	2	341	313	20	159	289	7.6	1.38	.246

14 ZEKE DeVOSS, 2B

BA GRADE
50
HIGH

Born: July 17, 1990. **B-T:** B-R. **Ht.:** 5-10. **Wt.:** 175. **Drafted:** Miami, 2011 (3rd round). **Signed by:** Lukas McKnight.

Cubs officials joke that DeVoss became owner Tom Ricketts' favorite player after Ricketts watched him draw three walks and blow up the opposing catcher in a home-plate collision in an August game at Boise. The Red Sox made a run at DeVoss as a 38th-round pick out of high school in 2009, but he opted to attend Miami, then signed for $500,000 as a sophomore-eligible in the third round last summer. He has all the tools to be a leadoff hitter, most notably on-base ability and speed. He ranked fourth in NCAA Division I with 57 walks last spring, and he drew more free passes (33) than he had strikeouts (32) in his pro debut. A switch-hitter, he's adept from both sides of the plate, though he won't hit for much power. He can run the 60-yard dash in 6.45 seconds and knows how to use his speed, swiping 16 bases in 20 tries as a pro. DeVoss split time between second base and the outfield with the Hurricanes, and Chicago deployed him mostly at second. He has the quickness for the position, and his hands and arm are good enough to keep him there, though he made 14 errors in 31 pro games. DeVoss has the wheels and instincts to handle center field if he can't cut it at second base. The Cubs aren't afraid to push players, so DeVoss could wind up in high Class A at some point in 2012.

Year	Club (League)	Class	AVG	G	AB	R	H	2B	3B	HR	RBI	BB	SO	SB	CS	OBP	SLG
2011	Cubs (AZL)	R	.294	4	17	4	5	1	0	0	3	1	4	2	0	.368	.353
	Boise (NWL)	SS	.311	38	132	28	41	8	1	0	14	32	28	14	4	.458	.386
Minor League Totals			.309	42	149	32	46	9	1	0	17	33	32	16	4	.449	.383

15 TONY ZYCH, RHP

BA GRADE
50
HIGH

Born: Aug. 7, 1990. **B-T:** R-R. **Ht.:** 6-3. **Wt.:** 180. **Drafted:** Louisville, 2011 (4th round). **Signed by:** Tim Adkins.

Scouts voted Zych the Cape Cod League's top prospect in 2010, when he led college baseball's premier summer circuit with 12 saves and dealt 97-mph heat during the all-star game. The 2011 draft was unusually deep as well as stocked with college relievers, and the product of the south Chicago suburbs surprisingly lasted until the Cubs pounced on him in the fourth round. They also had drafted him in the 46th round out of high school three years earlier. He signed three days before the Aug. 15 deadline for $400,000 and made four brief appearances afterward. Zych usually pitches at 94-97 and has touched 99, and his fastball seems even quicker because he has a funky delivery. Scouts don't love his arm action, which adds stress to his shoulder, but it gives him deception and doesn't prevent him from throwing strikes. Zych has the upside of a closer, and whether he reaches that ceiling depends on how well he can develop his slider, a mid-80s pitch that flattens out some of the time. He's extremely competitive and athletic, and he saw some action as a middle infielder as a Louisville freshman. Zych should move quickly through the minors, with a chance to reach Double-A by the end of 2012 and Wrigley Field at some point in 2013.

Year	Club (League)	Class	W	L	ERA	G	GS	CG	SV	IP	H	HR	BB	SO	K/9	WHIP	AVG
2011	Cubs (AZL)	R	0	0	4.50	2	0	0	0	2	2	0	1	3	13.5	1.50	.250
	Boise (NWL)	SS	0	0	0.00	2	0	0	0	2	0	0	1	2	9.0	0.50	.000
Minor League Totals			0	0	2.25	4	0	0	0	4	2	0	2	5	11.3	1.00	.143

16 MARCO HERNANDEZ, SS/2B

BA GRADE
55
EXTREME

Born: Sept. 6, 1992. **B-T:** L-R. **Ht.:** 6-0. **Wt.:** 170. **Signed:** Dominican Republic, 2009. **Signed by:** Jose Serra/Jose Estevez.

In 2008, scouts and managers fell in love with the Cubs' Arizona League double-play tandem of Starlin Castro and Junior Lake. That scenario repeated itself three years later, as Hernandez and Gioskar Amaya were two of the AZL's best middle-infield prospects. Amaya hit .377, but Hernandez wasn't far behind at .333 and ranks as the better prospect because he has a better chance to stay at shortstop. A switch-hitter, Hernandez handles the bat well but is better from the left side of the plate. He has enough bat speed and strength for gap power and the plus speed to beat out bunts. He's still learning to use his quickness on the basepaths. His first-step quickness and above-average arm strength give Hernandez the tools to make plays at shortstop. He needs to improve his throwing accuracy but overall is very reliable for a young defender. His .953 fielding percentage would have led AZL shortstops had his timeshare with Amaya not limited his playing time there. Chicago isn't afraid to aggressively promote teenagers, though it's unlikely Hernandez will jump from Arizona all the way to high Class A like Castro did three years ago.

Year	Club (League)	Class	AVG	G	AB	R	H	2B	3B	HR	RBI	BB	SO	SB	CS	OBP	SLG
2010	Cubs 2 (DSL)	R	.272	23	92	10	25	8	0	0	7	6	6	6	5	.316	.359
	Cubs 1 (DSL)	R	.294	46	163	21	48	13	1	1	14	15	21	16	7	.364	.405
2011	Cubs (AZL)	R	.333	51	210	39	70	16	5	2	42	16	29	9	7	.375	.486
Minor League Totals			.308	120	465	70	143	37	6	3	63	37	56	31	19	.360	.432

17 REGGIE GOLDEN, OF

BA GRADE
50
HIGH

Born: Oct. 10, 1991. **B-T:** R-R. **Ht.:** 5-10. **Wt.:** 210. **Drafted:** HS—Wetumpka, Ala., 2010 (2nd round). **Signed by:** Tom Clark.

Golden has one of the highest ceilings among Cubs farmhands, though they knew his development would require patience when they paid him an above-slot $720,000 bonus as a second-rounder in 2010. He was extremely raw coming out of an Alabama high school, and a severe hamstring pull restricted him as a senior and limited him to 15 at-bats in his pro debut. He moved to short-season Boise in 2011 and won't make his full-season debut until this year. Golden's impressive bat speed and physical strength give him well above-average power potential and draw comparisons to a young Kevin Mitchell. He made strides with his approach and discipline last year, pulling off of fewer pitches and drawing more walks, but he still swings and misses a lot. He'll need to improve his pitch recognition if he's going to hit for average. Golden is a good athlete who's slow out of the batter's box but has solid speed once he gets going. He has a very strong arm that plays well in right field, though he sometimes gets out of control and led Northwest League outfielders with six errors in 2011. Golden will advance to low Class A as a 20-year-old, and he'll probably need a full season in Peoria.

Year	Club (League)	Class	AVG	G	AB	R	H	2B	3B	HR	RBI	BB	SO	SB	CS	OBP	SLG
2010	Cubs (AZL)	R	.333	4	15	3	5	1	0	0	1	1	7	1	0	.412	.400
2011	Boise (NWL)	SS	.242	64	231	36	56	10	5	7	39	28	68	5	2	.332	.420
Minor League Totals			.248	68	246	39	61	11	5	7	40	29	75	6	2	.337	.419

18 JAE-HOON HA, OF

BA GRADE
50
HIGH

Born: Oct. 29, 1990. **B-T:** R-R. **Ht.:** 6-1. **Wt.:** 185. **Signed:** Korea, 2008. **Signed by:** Steve Wilson/Aaron Tassano.

Ha has been full of surprises since signing as part of the Cubs' Korean pipeline in 2008. A catcher as an amateur, he debuted as an outfielder before moving behind plate again in instructional league that fall. He developed a mental block about making throws to second base, however, so his catching career ended. Chicago didn't think he was ready for full-season ball as a teenager in 2010, but he batted .317 after arriving in low Class A in late May. Last year, he hit his way to Double-A while establishing himself as the best defensive center fielder in the system. Ha doesn't walk much, but he doesn't chase pitches out of the zone and almost never gives up at-bats. He has a short stroke and some deceptive pop, backspinning enough balls to hit 15 homers a season. He has plus speed but is an adventure on the basepaths, running into outs and getting caught 17 times in 30 steal attempts in 2011. Ha has a quick first step and gets outstanding jumps in center, enabling him to track down balls from gap to gap. He hasn't had any problems throwing in the outfield, and his strong, accurate arm would fit in right field. Ha may not be able to keep the Cubs' center-field job away from Matt Szczur in the long term—and he might not provide enough offense to be a regular on a corner—but should beat him to Chicago.

Year	Club (League)	Class	AVG	G	AB	R	H	2B	3B	HR	RBI	BB	SO	SB	CS	OBP	SLG
2009	Boise (NWL)	SS	.242	65	248	31	60	15	0	2	37	6	31	5	5	.264	.327
2010	Peoria (MWL)	LoA	.317	77	293	36	93	15	4	7	46	10	45	9	4	.334	.468
2011	Daytona (FSL)	HiA	.276	71	294	35	81	15	2	8	47	12	39	7	8	.311	.422
	Tennessee (SL)	AA	.283	61	226	32	64	16	1	3	25	11	28	6	9	.320	.403
Minor League Totals			.281	274	1061	134	298	61	7	20	155	39	143	27	26	.308	.408

19 ROBERT WHITENACK, RHP

BA GRADE
50
HIGH

Born: Nov. 20, 1988 **B-T:** R-R. **Ht.:** 6-5. **Wt.:** 200. **Drafted:** SUNY Old Westbury, 2009 (8th round). **Signed by:** Billy Blitzer.

Few Cubs pitchers enjoyed sustained success in 2011, with Whitenack a rare exception—until he blew out his elbow in late May. The only player ever drafted out of SUNY Old Westbury, he signed for $125,000 as an eighth-rounder in 2009. He finished strong at Daytona in 2010 and needed just four starts there last April to earn a promotion to Double-A. Whitenack added 15 pounds in between the two seasons and his stuff got stronger as well. His fastball jumped from the high 80s to 89-94 mph with a high of 96 while maintaining hard sink. He traded his knuckle-curve for a low-80s slider and kept his effective changeup. With his big frame and long arms, Whitenack throws on a steep downhill plane, consistently finding the strike zone and inducing groundouts. At the rate he was going, he might have pitched his way to Chicago by the end of 2011. Instead, he had Tommy John surgery in June and won't return to the mound until the second half of 2012. The Cubs anxiously await his return because Whitenack looked like a possible No. 3 starter before he went down.

Year	Club (League)	Class	W	L	ERA	G	GS	CG	SV	IP	H	HR	BB	SO	K/9	WHIP	AVG
2009	Boise (NWL)	SS	0	4	4.80	15	12	0	0	54	66	1	20	33	5.5	1.58	.296
2010	Peoria (MWL)	LoA	8	7	4.96	21	20	0	1	103	102	5	30	63	5.5	1.28	.262
	Daytona (FSL)	HiA	3	1	2.04	7	7	0	0	40	32	2	10	28	6.4	1.06	.218
2011	Daytona (FSL)	HiA	3	0	1.17	4	4	0	0	23	11	0	1	25	9.8	0.52	.141
	Tennessee (SL)	AA	4	0	2.39	7	7	0	0	38	32	1	13	22	5.3	1.19	.237
Minor League Totals			18	12	3.77	54	50	0	1	258	243	9	74	171	6.0	1.23	.250

20 JEIMER CANDELARIO, 3B

BA GRADE
55
EXTREME

Born: Nov. 24, 1993. **B-T:** B-R. **Ht.:** 6-1. **Wt.:** 180. **Signed:** Dominican Republic, 2010. **Signed by:** Jose Serra/Marino Encarnacion.

Signed for $500,000 as a 16-year-old in 2010, Candelario had a banner pro debut in the Rookie-level Dominican Summer League last year. He ranked second in RBIs (53), third in hits (84) and fifth in batting (.337), living up to his billing as a player with offensive promise. He has an advanced approach for his age, as he's patient, recognizes pitches well and uses the entire field. He's a switch-hitter with a loose swing and impressive bat speed from both sides of the plate. He projects as a plus hitter whose strong hands should produce at least average power. Candelario has thick legs and below-average speed, and he'll have to watch his conditioning as he gets older. He has the hands and arm strength to play third base, though some scouts wonder if he'll slow down enough and necessitate a move to first base. He needs to do a better job with his footwork and with getting better prepared before the pitcher delivers to the plate. The Cubs have several third-base prospects ahead of him, but they better watch out for Candelario. He'll make his U.S. debut in the Arizona League in June.

Year	Club (League)	Class	AVG	G	AB	R	H	2B	3B	HR	RBI	BB	SO	SB	CS	OBP	SLG
2011	Cubs 2 (DSL)	R	.337	72	249	50	84	16	2	5	53	50	42	4	4	.443	.478
Minor League Totals			.337	72	249	50	84	16	2	5	53	50	42	4	4	.443	.478

21 STEVE CLEVENGER, C

BA GRADE
45
LOW

Born: April 5, 1986. **B-T:** L-R. **Ht.:** 6-0. **Wt.:** 195. **Drafted:** Chipola (Fla.) JC, 2006 (7th round). **Signed by:** Keith Stohr.

Clevenger took a circuitous path to the majors. He began his college career as a shortstop at Southeastern Louisiana in 2005 and planned to transfer to Texas, but a credit snafu led him to Chipola (Fla.) JC, which made him draft-eligible a year earlier than expected. The Cubs signed him for $150,000 as a seventh-rounder in 2006, quickly found his infield actions lacking and converted him to catching in instructional league that fall. It took him six years to climb through the minors before he reached Chicago late last September. Clevenger excels at putting the bat on the ball. He controls the zone, rarely strikes out and has a career .308 average as a pro. He's not a big home run threat, but he can drive balls to the gaps and has done so more frequently in the last two years. As his legs have gotten stronger from catching, he has added power. He has developed nicely behind the plate, with Tennessee manager Brian Harper (a former big league catcher) calling Clevenger one of the best receivers he ever has seen. He has solid arm strength and makes accurate throws, though he erased just 23 percent of basestealers in 2011. He has improved his ability to block balls and manage a pitching staff. Clevenger has below-average speed but has more than most catchers and runs the bases intelligently. He also offers versatility, with the ability to play first or third base if needed. Clevenger profiles more as a quality backup than as a regular, and as a lefthanded hitter he'd be a perfect complement to Geovany Soto in Chicago. However, Welington Castillo is also in the picture, so Clevenger may spend most of 2012 in Triple-A.

Year	Club (League)	Class	AVG	G	AB	R	H	2B	3B	HR	RBI	BB	SO	SB	CS	OBP	SLG
2006	Boise (NWL)	SS	.286	63	220	35	63	8	1	2	21	26	28	5	2	.363	.359
2007	Boise (NWL)	SS	.373	22	83	10	31	9	0	0	18	4	6	0	0	.398	.482
	Daytona (FSL)	HiA	.323	43	164	21	53	8	1	2	24	13	5	0	0	.368	.421
2008	Tennessee (SL)	AA	.247	29	89	5	22	5	1	1	15	10	10	0	0	.314	.360
	Daytona (FSL)	HiA	.313	84	284	36	89	20	0	2	38	39	41	7	3	.393	.405
2009	Tennessee (SL)	AA	.364	26	77	12	28	4	3	1	10	10	8	0	0	.443	.532
	Iowa (PCL)	AAA	.265	68	230	21	61	12	1	0	26	15	31	4	3	.309	.326
2010	Tennessee (SL)	AA	.317	88	271	37	86	24	0	5	47	20	28	0	6	.367	.461
2011	Iowa (PCL)	AAA	.407	25	86	9	35	3	1	3	15	9	7	1	0	.454	.570
	Tennessee (SL)	AA	.295	95	312	42	92	27	3	5	39	35	39	1	0	.363	.449
	Chicago (NL)	MAJ	.250	2	4	1	1	1	0	0	0	0	0	0	0	.400	.500
Major League Totals			.250	2	4	1	1	1	0	0	0	0	0	0	0	.400	.500
Minor League Totals			.308	543	1816	228	560	120	11	21	254	181	203	18	14	.369	.421

22 JOSE ROSARIO, RHP

BA GRADE
50
HIGH

Born: Aug. 29, 1990. **B-T:** R-R. **Ht.:** 6-1. **Wt.:** 170. **Drafted:** Dominican Republic, 2008. **Signed by:** Jose Serra/Carlos Reyes.

Rosario has yet to make it to full-season ball after four years as a pro, including three in the United States, but he'll get there in 2012 after making impressive strides last season. After his fastball worked at 90-93 mph in 2010, it jumped to 93-97 and exploded on hitters last year. One scout saw him throw five consecutive 97-mph heaters in one game. Rosario has good life to go with his velocity, and he also has improved his ability to command his fastball. He has a chance to develop a plus slider, though his is presently more notable for its mid-80s velocity than its bite. It lacks consistency and gets slurvy at times. His changeup is even more rudimentary, and some scouts wonder if he'll develop a deep enough repertoire to remain a starter in the long run. His lack of size also may not be conducive to the durability needed to stay in the rotation, though he generates his velocity with arm speed and not effort. Rosario has the ceiling of a No. 3 starter or a set-up man, but it will take a few more years before the Cubs know exactly what they have in him.

Year	Club (League)	Class	W	L	ERA	G	GS	CG	SV	IP	H	HR	BB	SO	K/9	WHIP	AVG
2008	Cubs 1 (DSL)	R	1	0	5.06	4	0	0	0	5	6	1	4	3	5.1	1.88	.273
2009	Cubs 2 (DSL)	R	2	2	2.49	7	3	0	0	22	12	0	13	28	11.6	1.15	.148
	Cubs (AZL)	R	2	1	4.76	11	1	0	1	17	15	1	6	21	11.1	1.24	.234
	Daytona (FSL)	HiA	0	0	0.00	2	0	0	0	3	1	0	2	3	9.0	1.00	.100
2010	Cubs (AZL)	R	1	2	7.57	11	1	0	0	27	31	2	14	33	10.9	1.65	.277
2011	Boise (NWL)	SS	6	3	3.53	15	7	0	2	64	67	1	18	50	7.1	1.34	.266
Minor League Totals			12	8	4.30	50	12	0	3	138	132	5	57	138	9.0	1.37	.244

23 LOGAN WATKINS, 2B/SS/OF

BA GRADE
45
MEDIUM

Born: Aug. 29, 1989. **B-T:** L-R. **Ht.:** 5-11. **Wt.:** 170. **Drafted:** HS—Goddard, Kan., 2008 (21st round). **Signed by:** Brandon Mozley.

The Cubs fell in love with Watkins' intensity when they were scouting him as a Kansas high schooler, and he has been an organization favorite ever since he signed for $500,000 as a 21st-round pick in 2008. His mental toughness helped him rebound from a dreadful start in 2011, when he hit .122/.235/.149 in his first 20 games in high Class A. He batted .310/.373/.450 the rest of the way and led the Florida State League with 12 triples. Watkins has become less pull-conscious as he has gotten older, spraying line drives to all fields. He has bat speed and is stronger than his 170-pound frame might indicate, capable of hitting 30 doubles a season, but his main job will be to get on base. He's selective but could stand to draw more walks. An all-state quarterback and defensive back as a high school football player, Watkins is a good athlete with plus speed. He's an adept bunter who's getting more proficient at stealing bases, establishing career bests with 21 swipes and an 81 percent success rate last year. His athleticism also makes him a versatile defender. At second base he has plus range, soft hands and solid arm strength. He has gotten the job done in stints at shortstop and center field, and he also has seen time at third base and both outfield corners. Watkins will profile more as a utilityman than as a regular unless he maintains the offensive progress he made in 2011. He'll advance to Double-A this year.

Year	Club (League)	Class	AVG	G	AB	R	H	2B	3B	HR	RBI	BB	SO	SB	CS	OBP	SLG
2008	Cubs (AZL)	R	.325	27	80	15	26	3	0	0	14	20	19	2	0	.462	.363
2009	Boise (NWL)	SS	.326	72	279	48	91	14	2	0	29	27	31	14	7	.389	.391
2010	Peoria (MWL)	LoA	.261	118	440	69	115	15	8	1	30	58	97	19	10	.351	.339
2011	Daytona (FSL)	HiA	.281	125	441	70	124	15	12	5	45	44	97	21	5	.352	.404
Minor League Totals			.287	342	1240	202	356	47	22	6	118	149	244	56	22	.368	.375

24 JEFF BELIVEAU, LHP

BA GRADE
45
MEDIUM

Born: Jan. 17, 1987. **B-T:** L-L. **Ht.:** 6-1. **Wt.:** 190. **Drafted:** Florida Atlantic, 2008 (18th round). **Signed by:** Rolando Pino.

Beliveau won three consecutive Rhode Island state championships at Bishop Hendricken High (Warwick) and was the state's player of the year as a senior in 2005. Undrafted out of high school, he spent two years at the College of Charleston before transferring to Florida Atlantic, where he ranked second in NCAA Division I with 77 walks in as many innings in 2008. The Cubs drafted him in the 18th round that June, signed him for $30,000 and have since polished him into a reliever on the verge of helping their big league club. Beliveau still had more than his share of skeptics despite averaging 12.2 strikeouts per nine innings in his first three pro seasons, but he quieted many of them when he dominated Double-A hitters in 2011. He led Southern League relievers in opponent average (.183) and baserunners per nine innings (8.1) while earning Chicago's minor league pitcher of the year award and a spot on the 40-man roster. Beliveau relentlessly attacks hitters with an 88-91 mph fastball, which generates swings and misses because it looks like it's coming out of his sleeve. He keeps opponents off balance with a deceptive changeup, and also mixes in a curveball that has added depth since he has turned pro. Beliveau's biggest improvement has come with his control, as he led SL relievers in fewest unintentional walks per nine innings (1.6) and didn't give up a single free pass to a lefthander in 100 plate appearances last year. After the season, he had a successful stint with the U.S. World Cup team and pitched briefly in the Arizona Fall League. It may be hard to project Beliveau as a set-up man, but he gets righthanders out and is more than just a lefty specialist. He's more reliable than the Cubs' other top lefty relief prospects, Scott Maine and John Gaub, and should get his first big league opportunity at some point in 2012.

Year	Club (League)	Class	W	L	ERA	G	GS	CG	SV	IP	H	HR	BB	SO	K/9	WHIP	AVG
2008	Cubs (AZL)	R	0	0	13.50	1	0	0	0	1	1	0	1	1	13.5	3.00	.333
	Boise (NWL)	SS	2	1	2.60	13	7	0	0	35	25	1	28	51	13.2	1.53	.202
2009	Peoria (MWL)	LoA	5	4	3.54	29	7	0	3	97	77	5	45	117	10.9	1.26	.216
2010	Peoria (MWL)	LoA	0	0	1.59	6	0	0	0	11	6	1	6	23	18.3	1.06	.162
	Daytona (FSL)	HiA	4	2	2.89	40	0	0	2	53	41	4	23	74	12.6	1.21	.208
2011	Daytona (FSL)	HiA	0	1	0.52	12	0	0	2	17	13	0	6	20	10.4	1.10	.224
	Tennessee (SL)	AA	6	1	1.89	41	0	0	3	57	37	7	13	69	10.9	0.88	.183
Minor League Totals			17	9	2.69	142	14	0	10	271	200	18	122	355	11.8	1.19	.205

25 BEN WELLS, RHP

BA GRADE
50
HIGH

Born: Sept. 10, 1992. **B-T:** R-R. **Ht.:** 6-2. **Wt.:** 220. **Drafted:** HS—Bryant, Ark., 2010 (7th round). **Signed by:** Jim Crawford.

Wells was unknown to all but a few area scouts until shortly before the 2010 draft, when his fastball jumped about 5 mph and he threw a five-inning perfect game in the Arkansas 7-A high school championship game. The Cubs took him in the seventh round and signed him at the deadline for $530,000. Though he faced limited competition as an amateur, he survived against older hitters when he made his pro debut at Boise last summer. Wells' weapon of choice is a heavy sinker that helped him post a 3.8 groundout/air-out ratio in 2011. He threw it mostly at 87-90 mph early in the season before sitting at 90-94 in August. His hard slider shows flashes of becoming a plus pitch and his changeup has a chance to be a solid third offering. While Wells has a soft body, he's athletic and repeats his delivery well, giving him good control. He has uncommon mound presence for a teenager, which will come in handy when he advances to low Class A in 2012.

Year	Club (League)	Class	W	L	ERA	G	GS	CG	SV	IP	H	HR	BB	SO	K/9	WHIP	AVG
2011	Boise (NWL)	SS	4	4	4.66	16	15	0	0	77	83	4	19	53	6.2	1.32	.265
Minor League Totals			4	4	4.66	16	15	0	0	77	83	4	19	53	6.2	1.32	.265

26 MARCUS HATLEY, RHP

BA GRADE
50
HIGH

Born: March 26, 1988. **B-T:** R-R. **Ht.:** 6-5. **Wt.:** 220. **Drafted:** Palomar (Calif.) JC, D/F 2006 (39th round). **Signed by:** Denny Henderson.

The Cubs drafted Hatley as an outfielder out of a California high school in 2006, and that's where he played at Palomar (Calif.) JC the following spring, making just two relief appearances. Yet Chicago signed him as a pitcher for $40,000 as a draft-and-follow. Raw on the mound, Hatley didn't reach full-season ball until 2009, when he blew out his elbow and needed Tommy John surgery. He bounced back and reached Double-A last season. Hatley looks the part of a late-inning reliever. He's big and throws hard, working from 92-97 mph. He can get swings and misses up in the zone with his fastball and down in the zone with his hammer curveball. He also throws a cutter/slider that can be a solid pitch. Hatley's control and command never were his strong suits and aren't all the way back yet. The Cubs opted not to protect him on their 40-man roster, but he could pitch his way into their plans by the end of 2012 and eventually could become a set-up man.

Year	Club (League)	Class	W	L	ERA	G	GS	CG	SV	IP	H	HR	BB	SO	K/9	WHIP	AVG
2007	Cubs (AZL)	R	1	3	3.82	13	6	0	0	38	36	0	12	26	6.2	1.27	.254
	Boise (NWL)	SS	1	0	3.86	3	0	0	1	5	3	1	2	3	5.8	1.07	.167
2008	Boise (NWL)	SS	1	3	5.71	12	6	0	0	35	46	3	21	30	7.8	1.93	.317
2009	Peoria (MWL)	LoA	6	6	4.64	30	16	0	0	95	103	10	41	64	6.1	1.52	.278
2010	Boise (NWL)	SS	0	0	2.45	2	2	0	0	4	2	0	2	4	9.8	1.09	.154
	Cubs (AZL)	R	0	0	0.00	2	2	0	0	3	2	0	0	3	9.0	0.67	.182
	Peoria (MWL)	LoA	0	0	3.38	7	7	0	0	13	14	0	7	13	8.8	1.58	.318
2011	Peoria (MWL)	LoA	2	1	2.35	13	0	0	3	15	9	0	8	21	12.3	1.11	.170
	Daytona (FSL)	HiA	0	0	1.76	13	0	0	4	15	10	0	11	19	11.2	1.37	.192
	Tennessee (SL)	AA	3	0	4.66	22	0	0	4	29	30	2	11	20	6.2	1.41	.278
Minor League Totals			14	13	4.18	117	39	0	12	252	255	16	115	203	7.3	1.47	.266

27 CASEY WEATHERS, RHP

BA GRADE
50
HIGH

Born: June 10, 1985. **B-T:** R-R. **Ht.:** 6-1. **Wt.:** 205. **Drafted:** Vanderbilt, 2007 (1st round). **Signed by:** Damon Iannelli (Rockies).

The Rockies took Weathers eighth overall and signed him for $1.8 million in 2007, and he likely would have gotten to Colorado in 2009 had he not injured his elbow throwing a bullpen session in the Arizona Fall League after the 2008 season. After Tommy John surgery, he missed all of 2009 and has a 5.74 ERA in full-season ball since returning. He came to the Cubs with Ian Stewart in the December trade that sent Tyler Colvin and D.J. LeMahieu to the Rockies. Weathers' command wasn't sharp before he got hurt and is now the chief obstacle he must overcome. He has regained his two power pitches, a live fastball that sits at 95-98 mph and an 86-88 mph slider with good bite. Both can be wildly inconsistent. He also can mix in a below-average changeup. If he can learn to locate his fastball and slider better, Weathers has the stuff to be a late-inning reliever in the majors. He has toned down his high leg kick, so it's not a mechanical issue. Weathers faces a crucial season in 2012, when he could determine whether he's a big league contributor or an eternal puzzle.

Year	Club (League)	Class	W	L	ERA	G	GS	CG	SV	IP	H	HR	BB	SO	K/9	WHIP	AVG
2007	Asheville (SAL)	LoA	0	1	4.61	13	0	0	2	14	6	2	7	19	12.5	0.95	.130
	Modesto (CAL)	HiA	0	0	0.00	1	0	0	0	1	0	0	2	2	18.0	2.00	.000
2008	Tulsa (TL)	AA	2	1	3.05	44	0	0	2	44	34	1	28	54	11.0	1.40	.210
2009	Did Not Play—Injured																
2010	Tri-City (NWL)	SS	0	0	0.00	10	0	0	0	12	2	0	5	21	16.2	0.60	.056
	Modesto (CAL)	HiA	0	1	6.75	20	0	0	4	19	18	2	17	25	12.1	1.88	.250
2011	Tulsa (TL)	AA	2	2	5.32	44	0	0	0	46	32	3	48	48	9.5	1.75	.199
Minor League Totals			4	5	4.20	132	0	0	8	135	92	8	107	169	11.3	1.47	.192

28 TAIWAN EASTERLING, OF

BA GRADE
50
HIGH

Born: Feb. 24, 1989. **B-T:** R-R. **Ht.:** 6-0. **Wt.:** 205. **Drafted:** Florida State, 2011 (27th round). **Signed by:** Tom Clark.

The Marlins drafted Easterling in the sixth round out of a Mississippi high school in 2007, but he turned them down to play football at Florida State. A wide receiver, he caught 108 passes in the three seasons with the Seminoles. He didn't return to the diamond in 2010, going just 3-for-23 (.130) but enticing the Marlins to draft him again, this time in the 31st round. He skipped spring football in 2011 to focus on baseball, played semi-regularly as a redshirt junior and surprised the football program by signing for $150,000 after Chicago selected him in the 27th round. Like Matt Szczur the year before, Easterling surprised the Cubs by how little rust he had after juggling two sports in college. Despite having just 138 at-bats in four years at Florida State, he handled low Class A pitching in his pro debut, showing the hand-eye coordination to repeatedly barrel the ball. The ball explodes off his bat in batting practice, so he has the chance to develop average power. He'll need to improve his plate discipline, though that should come with more experience. Easterling was a plus-plus runner before rupturing his Achilles tendon in February 2009 and has lost maybe a half-step since. He's not particularly quick out of the batter's box but can create havoc on the bases. He's a fearless defender in center field and has solid arm strength to go with his plus range. Chicago can't wait to see how Easterling performs in his first full pro season, which he'll spend in high Class A.

Year	Club (League)	Class	AVG	G	AB	R	H	2B	3B	HR	RBI	BB	SO	SB	CS	OBP	SLG
2011	Cubs (AZL)	R	.500	7	28	10	14	2	2	0	1	1	4	1	2	.517	.714
	Peoria (MWL)	LoA	.277	40	166	18	46	6	1	2	16	8	32	9	4	.305	.361
	Daytona (FSL)	HiA	.200	1	5	0	1	0	0	0	0	0	1	0	0	.200	.200
Minor League Totals			.307	48	199	28	61	8	3	2	17	9	37	10	6	.332	.407

29 HAYDEN SIMPSON, RHP

BA GRADE
50
EXTREME

Born: May 20, 1989. **B-T:** R-R. **Ht.:** 6-0. **Wt.:** 170. **Drafted:** Southern Arkansas, 2010 (1st round). **Signed by:** Jim Crawford.

The Cubs shocked the industry when they made Simpson the 16th overall pick in the 2010 draft, and they have yet to see much return on their $1.06 million investment. He went 35-2, 2.39 in three seasons at Southern Arkansas, and Chicago fell in love with him after seeing him throw 94-97 mph and show three solid or better secondary pitches in an NCAA Division II playoff game. But Simpson didn't pitch professionally in 2010 after coming down with a bad case of mononucleosis that cost him 25 pounds on an already skinny frame, and he hadn't fully regained his strength by the start of spring training. He struck out seven of the 14 batters he faced while touching 90 mph in his first pro game, then never looked that good again during a 1-10, 6.27 debut season. He never complained of soreness, but his fastball resided in the low 80s for most of the year. A postseason MRI revealed he pitched through a stress reaction and a small tear in his elbow, both of which healed on their own. When healthy, Simpson had a pair of hard breaking balls in his curveball and slider, as well as a promising changeup and solid command. The Cubs thought they were drafting a budding Roy Oswalt, but at this point they're just hoping he'll be completely healthy for the 2012 season. They'll determine where to send him after evaluating him in spring training.

Year	Club (League)	Class	W	L	ERA	G	GS	CG	SV	IP	H	HR	BB	SO	K/9	WHIP	AVG
2011	Peoria (MWL)	LoA	1	6	5.72	16	16	0	0	61	76	9	27	46	6.8	1.68	.305
	Cubs (AZL)	R	0	4	8.15	11	9	0	0	18	26	1	11	11	5.6	2.09	.356
Minor League Totals			1	10	6.27	27	25	0	0	79	102	10	38	57	6.5	1.77	.317

30 SHAWON DUNSTON JR., OF

BA GRADE
50
EXTREME

Born: Feb. 5, 1993. **B-T:** L-R. **Ht.:** 6-0. **Wt.:** 170. **Drafted:** HS—San Jose, 2011 (11th round). **Signed by:** Rick Schroeder.

Twenty-nine years after the Cubs selected Shawon Dunston with the No. 1 overall pick in the 1982 draft, they chose his son in the 11th round. Luring Shawon Jr. away from a Vanderbilt scholarship cost them $1.275 million—nearly 10 times his father's $135,000 bonus. Several clubs backed off Dunston when he didn't play well at the beginning of his high school senior season, but Chicago liked what it saw at the end of the spring. He had a bat wrap that hampered him at the plate, but the Cubs ironed his swing out during instructional league. He's raw and needs time to develop, but Chicago sees him becoming a solid hitter with average or better power. No one questions Dunston's speed. He runs the 60-yard dash in 6.55 seconds, allowing him to project as a basestealer and a plus defender in center field. He has a strong arm, though it's not in the same class as his dad's legendary cannon. His passion for the game is evident. Dunston signed at the Aug. 15 deadline and didn't play professionally last summer, so he could make his pro debut at Boise in June.

Year	Club (League)	Class	AVG	G	AB	R	H	2B	3B	HR	RBI	BB	SO	SB	CS	OBP	SLG
2011	Did Not Play—Signed Late																

Chicago White Sox

BY PHIL ROGERS

Since winning the 2005 World Series, few teams have gotten less of a bang for their buck than the White Sox. They've spent more than $600 million on payroll since the 2006 all-star break, more money than any other American League Central team save the Tigers, yet have a 440-445 regular-season record and one playoff victory to show for it.

With his farm system failing to supply impact players, general manager Ken Williams constantly has had to be on the lookout for other people's talent. He has chosen poorly in recent years, hamstringing Chicago with bad contracts for Adam Dunn, Jake Peavy and Alex Rios. After Williams committed $93.5 million to bring back Paul Konerko and add Dunn last offseason, many analysts picked the White Sox to win the AL Central. But they started the season 11-21 and essentially conceded at the trade deadline, when they dealt Edwin Jackson.

Dunn gave them the worst batting average in big league history for a player with 450 plate appearances (.159), Rios had the majors' worst OPS among batting qualifiers (.613) and Peavy delivered just seven wins and 18 starts. That trio still has $103 million remaining on their contracts.

Manager Ozzie Guillen, who was signed through 2012, went public in September with his demands for a contract extension. It was the second year in a row he had pushed his financial desires through the media. The White Sox released him from his contract, receiving two players from the Marlins after Miami signed Guillen to a four-year deal.

Williams called 2011 the most disappointing season of his 11-year tenure as GM, and he said he went to owner Jerry Reinsdorf more than once to ask if the club wanted a change in the front office. Reinsdorf wasn't ready to hand the reins to longtime assistant GM Rick Hahn, so it fell to Williams to pick a new manager. He tabbed special adviser Robin Ventura, who has no managerial experience at any level.

The club could struggle to contend in the immediate future because it has done a poor job of signing and developing its own talent. Chicago has the worst farm system in baseball, and it's no coincidence that it ranks last in draft spending in the last five years ($18.3 million) and has had little presence on the international amateur market in that time.

The White Sox never were a leader in Latin America, but international operations have been in shambles since former senior director of player personnel Dave Wilder and two scouts were caught in

General manager Ken Williams and the White Sox haven't had much success since 2005

TOP 30 PROSPECTS

1. Addison Reed, rhp	16. Jared Mitchell, of
2. Nestor Molina, rhp	17. Andre Rienzo, rhp
3. Trayce Thompson, of	18. Brandon Short, of
4. Jacob Petricka, rhp	19. Josh Phegley, c
5. Keenyn Walker, of	20. Mike Blanke, c
6. Jhan Marinez, rhp	21. Carlos Sanchez, 2b/ss
7. Tyler Saladino, ss	22. Nate Jones, rhp
8. Juan Silverio, 3b	23. Gregori Infante, rhp
9. Osvaldo Martinez, ss	24. Dylan Axelrod, rhp
10. Eduardo Escobar, ss/2b	25. Jose Martinez, of
11. Hector Santiago, lhp	26. Blair Walters, lhp
12. Andy Wilkins, 1b	27. Tyler Kuhn, inf/of
13. Erik Johnson, rhp	28. Kevan Smith, c
14. Charlie Leesman, lhp	29. Jordan Danks, of
15. Jefferson Olacio, lhp	30. Deunte Heath, rhp

a scandal taking kickbacks from prospects in 2008. Chicago made a move to bolster its international efforts in November, hiring Blue Jays director of Latin American operations Marco Paddy.

Whether the White Sox will decide to invest more heavily in the draft remains to be seen. They haven't drafted a truly productive homegrown position player since 16th-rounder Chris Young in 2001. They've had more success with more recent pitching selections such as Daniel Hudson, Addison Reed and Chris Sale.

General Manager: Ken Williams. **Farm Director:** Buddy Bell. **Scouting Director:** Doug Laumann.

Class	Team	League	W	L	Pct	Finish*	Manager(s)
Majors	Chicago White Sox	American	79	83	.488	9th (14)	Ozzie Guillen/Don Cooper
Triple-A	Charlotte Knights	International	69	74	.483	9th (14)	Joe McEwing
Double-A	Birmingham Barons	Southern	71	69	.507	4th (10)	Bobby Magallanes
High A	Winston-Salem Dash	Carolina	69	71	.493	4th (8)	Julio Vinas
Low A	Kannapolis Intimidators	South Atlantic	76	62	.551	5th (14)	Tommy Thompson
Rookie	Great Falls Voyagers	Pioneer	42	34	.553	3rd (8)†	Ryan Newman
Rookie	Bristol White Sox	Appalachian	24	44	.353	t-9th (10)	Pete Rose II

Overall 2011 Minor League Record   354   354   .498 18th (30)

*Finish in overall standings (No. of teams in league). †League champion.

LAST YEAR'S TOP 30

Player, Pos.		Status
1.	Chris Sale, lhp	Majors
2.	Brent Morel, 3b/ss	Majors
3.	Dayan Viciedo, 1b/3b	Majors
4.	Jared Mitchell, of	No. 16
5.	Eduardo Escobar, ss	No. 10
6.	Gregori Infante, rhp	No. 23
7.	Jacob Petricka, rhp	No. 4
8.	Brandon Short, of	No. 18
9.	Trayce Thompson, of	No. 3
10.	Anthony Carter, rhp	Dropped out
11.	Charlie Leesman, lhp	No. 14
12.	Santos Rodriguez, lhp	Dropped out
13.	Addison Reed, rhp	No. 1
14.	Mike Blanke, c	No. 20
15.	Lucas Harrell, rhp	(Astros)
16.	Thomas Royce, rhp	Dropped out
17.	Tyler Flowers, c	Majors
18.	Jordan Danks, of	No. 29
19.	Andy Wilkins, 3b	No. 12
20.	Tyler Saladino, ss	No. 7
21.	Nate Jones, rhp	No. 22
22.	Jhonny Nunez, rhp	Dropped out
23.	Kyle Cofield, rhp	(Pirates)
24.	Miguel Gonzalez, c	Dropped out
25.	Andre Rienzo, rhp	No. 17
26.	Josh Phegley, c	No. 19
27.	Matt Heidenreich, rhp	Dropped out
28.	Jon Gilmore, 3b	Dropped out
29.	Cameron Bayne, rhp	Dropped out
30.	Spencer Arroyo, lhp	Dropped out

BEST TOOLS

Best Hitter for Average	Tyler Kuhn
Best Power Hitter	Trayce Thompson
Best Strike-Zone Discipline	Christian Marrero
Fastest Baserunner	Keenyn Walker
Best Athlete	Jared Mitchell
Best Fastball	Jeff Soptic
Best Curveball	Johnnie Lowe
Best Slider	Addison Reed
Best Changeup	Charlie Leesman
Best Control	Nestor Molina
Best Defensive Catcher	Miguel Gonzalez
Best Defensive Infielder	Eduardo Escobar
Best Infield Arm	Juan Silverio
Best Defensive Outfielder	John Danks
Best Outfield Arm	Jose Martinez

PROJECTED 2015 LINEUP

Catcher	Tyler Flowers
First Base	Andy Wilkins
Second Base	Gordon Beckham
Third Base	Brent Morel
Shortstop	Alexei Ramirez
Left Field	Carlos Quentin
Center Field	Keenyn Walker
Right Field	Trayce Thompson
Designated Hitter	Dayan Viciedo
No. 1 Starter	John Danks
No. 2 Starter	Chris Sale
No. 3 Starter	Gavin Floyd
No. 4 Starter	Nestor Molina
No. 5 Starter	Philip Humber
Closer	Addison Reed

TOP PROSPECTS OF THE DECADE

Year	Player, Pos.	2011 Org.
2002	Joe Borchard, of	Bridgeport (Atlantic)
2003	Joe Borchard, of	Bridgeport (Atlantic)
2004	Joe Borchard, of	Bridgeport (Atlantic)
2005	Brian Anderson, of	Yankees
2006	Bobby Jenks, rhp	Red Sox
2007	Ryan Sweeney, of	Athletics
2008	Aaron Poreda, lhp	Padres
2009	Gordon Beckham, ss	White Sox
2010	Jared Mitchell, of	White Sox
2011	Chris Sale, lhp	White Sox

TOP DRAFT PICKS OF THE DECADE

Year	Player, Pos.	2011 Org.
2002	Royce Ring, lhp	Red Sox
2003	Brian Anderson, of	Yankees
2004	Josh Fields, 3b	Yomiuri (Japan)
2005	Lance Broadway, rhp	Out of baseball
2006	Kyle McCulloch, rhp	Reds
2007	Aaron Poreda, lhp	Padres
2008	Gordon Beckham, ss	White Sox
2009	Jared Mitchell, of	White Sox
2010	Chris Sale, lhp	White Sox
2011	Keenyn Walker, of	White Sox

LARGEST BONUSES IN CLUB HISTORY

Joe Borchard, 2003	$5,300,000
Dayan Viciedo, 2008	$4,000,000
Gordon Beckham, 2008	$2,600,000
Jason Stumm, 1999	$1,750,000
Chris Sale, 2010	$1,656,000

CHICAGO WHITE SOX

TOP 2012 ROOKIE: Addison Reed, rhp. After jumping from low Class A to the majors in 2011, he could spend the entire year in Chicago and possible emerge as the closer.

BREAKOUT PROSPECT: Andy Wilkins, 1b. The White Sox are starting to get excited about his power, and he might not need much more than another season in the minors.

SLEEPER: Mark Haddow, of. He never hit more than six homers in any of his four seasons at UC Santa Barbara, then hit 12 in his pro debut.

SOURCE OF TOP 30 TALENT			
Homegrown	25	Acquired	5
College	14	Trades	3
Junior college	3	Rule 5 draft	0
High school	1	Independent leagues	1
Draft-and-follow	0	Free agents/waivers	1
Nondrafted free agents	0		
International	7		

LF
Brady Shoemaker
Collin Kuhn

CF
Keenyn Walker (5)
Jared Mitchell (16)
Brandon Short (18)
Jordan Danks (29)
Justin Greene

RF
Trayce Thompson (3)
Jose Martinez (25)
Mark Haddow
Nick Ciolli

3B
Juan Silverio (8)
Rangel Ravelo
Jon Gilmore

SS
Tyler Saladino (7)
Osvaldo Martinez (9)
Eduardo Escobar (10)
Marcus Semien
David Herbek
Greg Paiml

2B
Carlos Sanchez (21)
Tyler Kuhn (27)
Ross Wilson
Drew Lee
Daniel Wagner

1B
Andy Wilkins (12)
Christian Marrero
Dan Black
Grant Buckner
Seth Loman

C
Josh Phegley (19)
Mike Blanke (20)
Kevan Smith (28)
Miguel Gonzalez
Martin Medina
Bryce Mosier

LHP

LHSP	LHRP
Hector Santiago (11)	Santos Rodriguez
Charlie Leesman (14)	Donnie Veal
Jefferson Olacio (15)	Matt Wickstat
Blair Walters (26)	Brandon Parrent
Scott Snodgress	
Jose Quintana	
Spencer Arroyo	
Justin Edwards	
Joe Serafin	
Matt Lane	

RHP

RHSP	RHRP
Nestor Molina (2)	Addison Reed (1)
Jacob Petricka (4)	Jhan Marinez (6)
Erik Johnson (13)	Nate Jones (22)
Andre Rienzo (17)	Gregori Infante (23)
Dylan Axelrod (24)	Deunte Heath (30)
Thomas Royse	Ryan Kussmaul
Ryan Buch	Brian Omogrosso
Cameron Bayne	Jeff Soptic
Matthew Heidenreich	Kyle McMillen
Nevin Griffith	Dan Remenowsky
Jean Duque	Brandon Kloess
Chris Bassitt	Anthony Carter
	Steven Upchurch
	Jake Wilson
	Kevin Vance
	Nick McCully

2011   BONUSES: $2.8 MILLION

BEST PURE HITTER: 1B Grant Buckner (26) has present strength and an advanced approach befitting his age (23) and background as the son of a high school coach.

BEST POWER HITTER: With his long levers, 6-foot-6 OF Mark Haddow (24) has tantalized scouts with his power/speed combination but never hit more than six homers in a season at UC Santa Barbara. He had 70 strikeouts in as many games but also hit 12 homers for Rookie-level Great Falls.

FASTEST RUNNER: OF Keenyn Walker (1s), who led national juco players with 70 steals last spring, reminds White Sox officials of Chris Singleton physically and is faster. He's an easy 70 runner on the 20-80 scouting scale who occasionally turns in better times.

BEST DEFENSIVE PLAYER: Walker has the tools to be an above-average center fielder with added polish. SS David Herbek (15) has the quick feet and soft hands for shortstop and should have enough arm strength to stick there.

BEST FASTBALL: Scouts saw RHP Jeff Soptic (3) reached 100 mph as an amateur, and Chicago has seen 101 since he signed. He has erratic control and had only sporadic success in junior college.

BEST SECONDARY PITCH: LHP Blair Walters (11) has a plus breaking ball, a hybrid cutter/slider that doesn't have much depth but has late, hard bite that prevents righthanders from getting comfortable and keeps lefties honest.

BEST PRO DEBUT: Walters was named Pioneer League pitcher of the year, going 9-0, 4.03 with a 72-17 K-BB ratio in 74 innings for Great Falls. C Kevan Smith (7) batted .355/.448/.626. RHP Chris Bassitt (16) had a 1.77 ERA with 42 strikeouts in 36 innings, mostly at low Class A Kannapolis.

BEST ATHLETE: Walker is an athlete, not just a burner. OF Cory Farris (45) was a prep football star in Kentucky, rushing for 2,250 yards as a senior. A teammate of Chicago scouting director Doug Laumann's son Jackson in high school, Farris is raw but has power and speed in his 6-foot, 190-pound frame.

MOST INTRIGUING BACKGROUND: Smith started at quarterback for Pitt as a redshirt freshman. Unsigned OF Zach Regier (49) is the son of White Sox special assignment scout Alan Regier, who was the team's farm director for two years.

CLOSEST TO THE MAJORS: Walters' breaking ball (and lefthandedness) should help him move quickly, especially if he returns to his college role as a reliever. SS Marcus Semien (6) has solid all-around tools and held his own in low Class A.

BEST LATE-ROUND PICK: Walters and Bassitt, who throws a low-90s sinker, both could rise quickly as relievers.

THE ONE WHO GOT AWAY: RHP Ian Gardeck (8, now at Alabama) was drafted higher, but the White Sox made more of a run at physical LHP Ben O'Shea (10), who planned to transfer to NCAA Division II Tampa.

ASSESSMENT: Chicago is the cheapest team when it comes to the draft, ranking 30th in bonus spending in 2011, when it handed out nearly $5 million less than the average team. The White Sox gambled on a lot of high-risk, high-reward types yet signed only one high schooler (C Bryce Mosier, 33).

2010   BONUSES: $3.9 MILLION

LHP Chris Sale (1) was the first player from the 2011 draft to reach the majors, and RHP Addison Reed (3) was the fourth. RHP Jacob Petricka (2), 1B Andy Wilkins (5) and SS Tyler Saladino (7) rank among the best prospects in a thin system.

GRADE: B+

2009   BONUSES: $4.2 MILLION

The two best players drafted by the White Sox were LHP David Holmberg (2), lost in the Edwin Jackson trade with Arizona a year later, and OF Brian Goodwin (17), who didn't sign and became the 34th overall pick in 2011. OF Trayce Thompson (2) has a high ceiling yet remains raw, and OF Jared Mitchell (1) and C Josh Phegley (1s) haven't been healthy.

GRADE: C

2008   BONUSES: $4.7 MILLION

Chicago's best draft in years featured 2B Gordon Beckham (1) and 3B Brent Morel (3), both big league regulars who haven't quite lived up to offensive expectations yet, and RHP Daniel Hudson (5), the key piece in the ill-fated Jackson deal. Unsigned 1B C.J. Cron (44) became a 2011 first-rounder.

GRADE: A

2007   BONUSES: $2.8 MILLION

LHP Aaron Poreda (1) was a bust, but he did reach the majors and was sent to the Padres in a trade for Jake Peavy. RHP John Ely (3) went to the Dodgers in a deal for Juan Pierre. The best prospect still in the system is erratic RHP Nate Jones (5).

GRADE: F

Draft analysis by John Manuel (2011) and Jim Callis (2007-10). Numbers in parentheses indicate draft rounds.

1 ADDISON REED, RHP

Born: Dec. 27, 1988. **B-T:** L-R. **Ht.:** 6-4. **Wt.:** 215.
Drafted: San Diego State, 2010 (3rd round). **Signed by:** George Kachigian.

BA GRADE
55
LOW

BILL MITCHELL

Stephen Strasburg's college closer continues to make a name for himself. Like Daniel Hudson and Chris Sale before him, Reed shot through the White Sox system and was one of the first members of his draft class to reach the majors. A third-round pick signed for $358,200 in 2010, Reed started last year in low Class A Kannapolis and moved one level at a time before getting to Chicago in September. The only 2010 draftees to arrive in the big leagues before him were White Sox teammate Chris Sale, Josh Spence and Chance Ruffin, all relievers. After saving 20 games with a 0.65 ERA in 2009, Reed replaced Strasburg as San Diego State's Friday starter as a junior and went 8-2, 2.50. Though he has the stuff to fit in a rotation, he made just two starts in his pro debut and none last year. He put up crazy minor league numbers in 2011, with a 1.26 ERA, a 111-14 K-BB ratio and a .157 opponent batting average in 78 innings. He wasn't as dominant in the majors, but he did strike out 12 of the 33 hitters he faced, including Miguel Cabrera twice. Reed's younger brother Austin pitches in the Cubs system after signing as a 12th-rounder out of high school in 2010.

Reed has a great pitcher's build and a solid delivery, operating from a three-quarters arm slot. He works quickly and throws strikes, challenging hitters to beat him. He can make them look bad with either his fastball or slider. Reed works at 93-96 mph and touches 98 with a fastball that often runs in on righthanders. His slider grades better than his heater, with some scouts rating it as a plus-plus offering. His slider has late bite and arrives in the low 80s, giving it great separation in velocity from his fastball. It works almost as a changeup. Reed throws a true changeup as well and made strides with the pitch in 2011, though he doesn't have much need for it in relief. He has strong mound presence and a durable arm, two important attributes for a late-inning reliever. While he handled a full workload

SCOUTING GRADES

Fastball: 65.   **Command/**
Slider: 65.   **Control:** 65.
Changeup: 50.   **Delivery:** 60.

Based on 20-80 scouting scale, where 50 represents major league average, and future projection rather than present tools.

in his first full pro season, the White Sox generally gave Reed at least two days off between outings in the minors and didn't pitch him on back-to-back days after he reached the majors. He'll still have to prove he can get the job done on back-to-back days, but with his stuff, that shouldn't be a problem.

Chicago is looking to get younger and cheaper with its starting rotation, and some club officials think Reed could help fill that need. But for now, the White Sox are developing him as a set-up man who ultimately could be used as a closer. They traded Sergio Santos, who had 30 saves in 2011, to the Blue Jays at the Winter Meetings and may move Sale to the rotation in 2012, so their closer's job is wide open. Reed has a terrific chance to win a bullpen role in spring training. If he progresses as rapidly as he did in 2011, it's not out of the question that he could be finishing games for the Sox by the end of the season.

Year	Club (League)	Class	W	L	ERA	G	GS	CG	SV	IP	H	HR	BB	SO	K/9	WHIP	AVG
2010	Great Falls (PIO)	R	1	0	1.80	13	2	0	1	30	17	1	6	44	13.2	0.77	.162
2011	Kannapolis (SAL)	LoA	0	0	1.13	4	0	0	0	8	4	0	1	11	12.4	0.63	.148
	Winston-Salem (CAR)	HiA	2	0	1.59	15	0	0	1	28	21	1	4	39	12.4	0.88	.196
	Birmingham (SL)	AA	0	1	0.87	13	0	0	2	21	10	0	6	33	14.4	0.77	.143
	Charlotte (IL)	AAA	0	0	1.27	11	0	0	2	21	8	2	3	28	11.8	0.52	.114
	Chicago (AL)	MAJ	0	0	3.68	6	0	0	0	7	10	1	1	12	14.7	1.50	.313
Major League Totals			0	0	3.68	6	0	0	0	7	10	1	1	12	14.7	1.50	.312
Minor League Total			3	1	1.41	56	2	0	6	108	60	4	20	155	12.9	0.74	.158

2 NESTOR MOLINA, RHP

Born: Jan. 9, 1989. **B-T:** R-R. **Ht.:** 6-1. **Wt.:** 180. **Signed:** Venezuela, 2006. **Signed by:** Rafael Mancada (Blue Jays).

Originally signed as a third baseman, Molina hit .223/.369/.273 in three seasons in the Rookie-level Venezuelan and Dominican summer leagues and moved to the mound before making his U.S. debut. He made just four starts before 2010 but flourished after moving to the rotation last year, ranking third in the minors in K-BB ratio (9.3), fourth in walk rate (1.1 per nine innings) and ninth in ERA (2.21). The White Sox acquired him from the Blue Jays in a December trade for Sergio Santos. Molina doesn't have a consistent plus pitch, but his entire repertoire plays up because of his superlative command. He has averaged just 1.4 walks per nine innings in five seasons as a pitcher. Molina works both sides of the plate with an 88-93 mph fastball. He had a slurvy breaking ball that he tried to turn in into a slider, but that didn't work and he's now operating with a curveball. He also has a splitter that flashes hard tumble and demonstrates some feel for a straight changeup. Molina is best suited for the back of a rotation and if he keeps up last year's pace, he may find himself in the big leagues at some point in 2012. He could open the season at Double-A Birmingham.

BA GRADE
50
MEDIUM

Year	Club (League)	Class	W	L	ERA	G	GS	CG	SV	IP	H	HR	BB	SO	K/9	WHIP	AVG
2007	Blue Jays 2 (DSL)	R	0	0	0.00	1	0	0	0	1	0	0	1	0	0.0	1.00	.000
2008	Blue Jays 2 (DSL)	R	4	1	0.96	20	0	0	4	37	30	1	5	27	6.5	0.94	.213
2009	Blue Jays (GCL)	R	3	0	1.69	15	2	0	1	37	31	0	4	32	7.7	0.94	.226
	Auburn (NYP)	SS	0	1	1.59	2	0	0	0	6	9	1	1	6	9.5	1.76	.346
2010	Lansing (MWL)	LoA	8	2	3.17	37	2	0	4	77	64	4	20	61	7.2	1.10	.224
	Dunedin (FSL)	HiA	0	0	2.08	2	0	0	0	4	7	0	0	3	6.2	1.62	.350
2011	Dunedin (FSL)	HiA	10	3	2.58	21	18	0	0	108	102	8	14	115	9.6	1.07	.248
	New Hampshire (EL)	AA	2	0	0.41	5	5	0	0	22	12	0	2	33	13.5	0.64	.156
Minor League Totals			27	7	2.21	103	27	0	9	293	255	14	47	277	8.5	1.03	.232

3 TRAYCE THOMPSON, OF

Born: March 15, 1991. **B-T:** R-R. **Ht.:** 6-4. **Wt.:** 200. **Drafted:** HS—Santa Margarita, Calif., 2009 (2nd round). **Signed by:** George Kachigian.

A rare above-slot signing for the White Sox, Thompson got $625,000 as a second-round pick in 2009. Following an abbreviated 2010 season in which a pitch shattered his right thumb, he stayed healthy last year and led the low Class A South Atlantic League with 95 runs while ranking second in the system with 24 homers. His father Mychal is a former No. 1 overall pick in the NBA draft. Older brothers Mychel (Pepperdine) and Klay (Washington State) are college basketball players, with Klay rated as a possible NBA first-rounder. Thompson has the ability to hit long home runs to all fields, thanks to his strength and the loft in his stroke. The length in his swing limits his plate coverage, and, combined with his lack of pitch recognition, leads to frequent strikeouts. His 172 whiffs tied for fifth in the minors in 2011. Thompson isn't just a bomber. He has worked hard on his center-field defense, which some scouts say is better than his bat. His strong arm is a weapon in center field and should play in right, where he'll likely wind up. He's slow out of the batter's box but has average speed when he hits his strides. He shows good instincts on the bases and in the outfield. He may have repeated low Class A, yet Thompson will be just 21 when he advances to high Class A Winston-Salem in 2012. He has the highest offensive ceiling in the system but will have to cut down his strikeouts considerably to reach it.

BA GRADE
55
EXTREME

Year	Club (League)	Class	AVG	G	AB	R	H	2B	3B	HR	RBI	BB	SO	SB	CS	OBP	SLG
2009	Bristol (APP)	R	.188	25	85	8	16	3	1	0	10	4	33	2	0	.247	.247
	Great Falls (PIO)	R	.238	7	21	2	5	0	0	0	0	3	8	1	0	.333	.238
2010	Kannapolis (SAL)	LoA	.229	58	210	28	48	13	3	8	31	21	69	6	4	.302	.433
2011	Kannapolis (SAL)	LoA	.241	136	519	95	125	36	2	24	87	60	172	8	4	.329	.457
Minor League Totals			.232	226	835	133	194	52	6	32	128	88	282	17	8	.314	.424

4 JACOB PETRICKA, RHP

Born: June 5, 1988. **B-T:** R-R. **Ht.:** 6-5. **Wt.:** 170. **Drafted:** Indiana State, 2010 (2nd round). **Signed by:** Mike Shirley.

The White Sox drafted Petricka in the 38th round out of a Minnesota high school in 2006 but didn't sign him, then took him again as a second-rounder in 2010. In between, he had stints at Iowa Western CC and Indiana State and lost a year to Tommy John surgery. He was overpowering in 2011 until he came down with back problems, missed most of June and wasn't as sharp afterward. Radar guns love Petricka, who works in the mid-90s with his fastball and has been clocked at 100 mph. He relies on his velocity at the expense of his other pitches, however. His curveball can be a hammer but often spins to the plate or sails to the screen. His changeup shows promise, though he lacks the confidence to throw it in hitter's counts. Petricka induces a lot of groundballs, a key for pitchers at U.S. Cellular Field. He can get mechanical at times and has spells where he doesn't throw enough strikes. Petricka has the ingredients to develop into an A.J. Burnett type but struggles to make adjustments. Some scouts believe he's destined for the bullpen, where he pitched in the Arizona Fall League. Chicago has more of a need for starters, so he'll get plenty of rope in that role.

BA GRADE
50
HIGH

Year	Club (League)	Class	W	L	ERA	G	GS	CG	SV	IP	H	HR	BB	SO	K/9	WHIP	AVG
2010	Bristol (APP)	R	2	4	2.86	8	8	0	0	35	25	1	7	38	9.9	0.92	.197
	Kannapolis (SAL)	LoA	0	1	3.72	9	0	0	0	10	13	0	8	10	9.3	2.17	.295
2011	Kannapolis (SAL)	LoA	3	1	2.81	8	8	0	0	42	39	0	13	48	10.4	1.25	.255
	Bristol (APP)	R	0	0	0.00	2	1	0	0	4	4	0	0	5	11.3	1.00	.286
	Winston-Salem (CAR)	HiA	4	7	4.39	13	13	0	0	68	71	3	26	46	6.1	1.43	.265
Minor League Totals			9	13	3.48	40	30	0	0	158	152	4	54	147	8.4	1.31	.251

5 KEENYN WALKER, OF

Born: Aug. 12, 1990. **B-T:** B-R. **Ht.:** 6-3. **Wt.:** 195. **Drafted:** Central Arizona JC, 2011 (1st round supplemental). **Signed by:** John Kazanas.

Recruited as a safety by Boise State and some Pacific-10 Conference programs, Walker gave up football after leaving high school. He also turned down the Cubs as a 16th-rounder in 2009 and the Phillies as a 38th-rounder in 2010 before Chicago made him its top pick (47th overall) in 2011. He signed for a slightly over-slot $795,000 after leading national juco players with 70 steals in 73 tries for Central Arizona JC. Walker's plus-plus speed makes him a game-changer on the bases and helps him in center field, but he has a lot of work to do as a hitter. A switch-hitter, he was overmatched from both sides of the plate after reaching low Class A. He swings and misses frequently and has yet to show the gap power as a pro that he displayed in junior college. Walker is still a bit raw defensively, but he has plus range and arm strength for center field. Walker is a potential top-of-the-order force, though he'll need time to refine his offense and defense. Because he played with a wood bat in junior college, the Sox think he could make rapid adjustments to pro pitching in 2012. They'll send him back to Kannapolis with the potential for a midseason promotion.

BILL MITCHELL

BA GRADE
55
EXTREME

Year	Club (League)	Class	AVG	G	AB	R	H	2B	3B	HR	RBI	BB	SO	SB	CS	OBP	SLG
2011	Great Falls (PIO)	R	.333	15	60	16	20	7	1	0	9	7	17	11	5	.431	.483
	Kannapolis (SAL)	LoA	.228	39	162	25	37	1	2	0	15	14	64	10	4	.296	.259
Minor League Totals			.257	54	222	41	57	8	3	0	24	21	81	21	9	.335	.320

6 JHAN MARINEZ, RHP

Born: Aug. 12, 1988. **B-T:** R-R. **Ht.:** 6-1. **Wt.:** 165. **Signed:** Dominican Republic, 2006. **Signed by:** Sandy Nin (Marlins).

Marinez is following the path less taken. He made his major league debut a year prior to pitching in the 2011 Futures Game, three months before the Marlins sent him and shortstop Osvaldo Martinez to the White Sox as compensation for manager Ozzie Guillen. Marinez has battled control problems that have become more pronounced since he strained his elbow during his 2010 big league callup. Marinez is a classic two-pitch reliever, relying almost exclusively on his fastball and slider. He gets easy velocity from a low three-quarters arm slot, with his fastball sitting at 92-96 mph and climbing into the upper 90s. His slider arrives in the mid-80s and can look like his heater until it gets on top of hitters. Marinez sometimes gets under his pitches, causing him to leave them up in the zone. He also has bouts of wildness when he struggles with his release point. He dominates when his location is good. He has to prove he can stay healthy after working just 226 innings in six pro seasons. Scouts see a big-league set-up man or possibly even a closer in Marinez,

BA GRADE
50
HIGH

provided that he can significantly improve his command. He's an ideal project for big league pitching coach Don Cooper, though Marinez will get some time at Triple-A Charlotte before he sees Chicago.

Year	Club (League)	Class	W	L	ERA	G	GS	CG	SV	IP	H	HR	BB	SO	K/9	WHIP	AVG
2006	Marlins (DSL)	R	2	1	7.00	20	2	0	1	36	44	0	26	22	5.5	1.94	.324
2007	Marlins (GCL)	R	0	0	10.80	3	0	0	0	3	5	0	4	4	10.8	2.70	.357
	Marlins (DSL)	R	2	3	4.70	5	5	0	0	23	14	1	19	25	9.8	1.43	.163
2008	Marlins (GCL)	R	1	1	6.11	12	1	0	1	18	21	1	14	18	9.2	1.98	.296
2009	Jupiter (FSL)	HiA	1	1	3.14	29	0	0	1	43	28	4	20	42	8.8	1.12	.185
2010	Florida (NL)	MAJ	1	1	6.75	4	0	0	0	3	3	1	3	3	10.1	2.25	.273
	Jupiter (FSL)	HiA	0	1	1.42	21	1	0	4	25	12	1	14	44	15.6	1.03	.148
	Jacksonville (SL)	AA	1	0	2.16	15	0	0	6	17	9	1	7	20	10.8	0.96	.164
2011	Jacksonville (SL)	AA	3	8	3.57	56	0	0	3	58	47	7	42	74	11.5	1.53	.223
Major League Totals			1	1	6.75	4	0	0	0	3	3	1	3	3	10.1	2.25	.273
Minor League Totals			10	15	4.12	161	9	0	16	223	180	14	146	249	10.0	1.46	.224

7 TYLER SALADINO, SS

Born: July 20, 1989. **B-T:** R-R. **Ht.:** 5-11. **Wt.:** 180. **Drafted:** Oral Roberts, 2010 (7th round). **Signed by:** Clay Overcash.

The White Sox drafted Saladino mostly on his reputation as a hitter, taking him in the seventh round after he hit .381 with 17 homers at Oral Roberts in 2010. He nearly matched that longball total in his first full season as a pro, smashing 16 in high Class A despite missing the first month after breaking a bone in his hand during spring training. He continued to play well in the Arizona Fall League. Saladino doesn't have a standout tool but he's a steady all-around player. He has a line-drive, all-fields approach at the plate, making consistent contact with surprising power. He projects as a possible 30-double/15-homer threat at U.S. Cellular Field. He has average speed and range at shortstop, though his instincts allow him to play above his physical ability. His strong arm would fit at third base if he has to move off shortstop. Ticketed for Double-A in 2012, Saladino faces a shortstop logjam ahead. Alexei Ramirez is entrenched in Chicago, while prospects Osvaldo Martinez and Eduardo Escobar already have reached Triple-A and gotten cups of coffee in the majors. Saladino has a better bat than Martinez and Escobar, and he eventually could help the Sox at second or third base or as an offensive-minded utilityman.

BA GRADE
50
HIGH

Year	Club (League)	Class	AVG	G	AB	R	H	2B	3B	HR	RBI	BB	SO	SB	CS	OBP	SLG
2010	Bristol (APP)	R	.292	13	48	7	14	3	0	1	6	5	12	1	2	.364	.417
	Kannapolis (SAL)	LoA	.309	47	165	40	51	14	1	2	18	22	44	4	2	.397	.442
2011	Winston-Salem (CAR)	HiA	.270	102	397	75	107	26	9	16	55	51	90	7	7	.363	.501
Minor League Totals			.282	162	610	122	172	43	10	19	79	78	146	12	11	.372	.479

8 JUAN SILVERIO, 3B

Born: April 18, 1991. **B-T:** R-R. **Ht.:** 6-1. **Wt.:** 175. **Signed:** Dominican Republic, 2007. **Signed by:** Victor Mateo/Dave Wilder.

The White Sox touted Silverio as a five-tool shortstop when Victor Mateo and Dave Wilder signed him for $600,000 out of the Dominican Republic in 2007. A year later, they learned that Mateo and Wilder were part of a conspiracy to oversell prospects so they could skim their bonus money. Silverio overcame that stigma and three uneven seasons in the lower minors to break through with a solid year at two Class A stops in 2011. Silverio began making adjustments at the plate when he returned to Kannapolis last year. He's still too undisciplined at the plate, but he has a knack for barreling the ball and projects to have average power to both gaps. He's a good athlete with average speed. Silverio has played primarily at third base in the past two seasons. He has a strong arm and can make some spectacular plays, but he has to learn not to try to force difficult throws after making 39 errors in 124 games in 2011. Silverio will open the 2012 season as a 20-year-old, so Chicago can continue to be patient with his development. He may repeat high Class A, at least for the first half. If he doesn't become an everyday third baseman, he has the tools to play the outfield and could become a corner utilityman.

BA GRADE
50
HIGH

Year	Club (League)	Class	AVG	G	AB	R	H	2B	3B	HR	RBI	BB	SO	SB	CS	OBP	SLG
2008	Bristol (APP)	R	.228	59	215	31	49	8	0	4	35	8	56	3	1	.265	.321
2009	White Sox (DSL)	R	.321	61	243	52	78	11	10	8	56	16	47	5	6	.366	.547
2010	Great Falls (PIO)	R	.299	20	87	11	26	9	0	3	16	6	20	3	1	.340	.506
	Kannapolis (SAL)	LoA	.200	63	220	20	44	12	3	4	24	6	57	3	4	.237	.336
2011	Kannapolis (SAL)	LoA	.289	88	329	48	95	29	6	5	58	18	81	4	7	.341	.459
	Winston-Salem (CAR)	HiA	.276	45	170	28	47	10	3	4	27	10	41	2	1	.322	.441
Minor League Totals			.268	336	1264	190	339	79	22	28	216	64	302	20	20	.313	.432

9 OSVALDO MARTINEZ, SS

Born: May 7, 1988. **B-T:** R-R. **Ht.:** 5-10. **Wt.:** 180. **Drafted:** Porterville (Calif.) JC, 2006 (11th round). **Signed by:** Carlos Berroa (Marlins).

After he took a step backward in 2011, the Marlins gave up Martinez as part of the compensation package for manager Ozzie Guillen. They didn't help his development by promoting him twice for a total of six weeks early in the season and giving him just 20 at-bats. He took three bullets in a September 2009 drive-by shooting but recovered to play in the 2010 Futures Game. Martinez lasted as long as he did in the majors because of his defense. He has soft hands and a strong arm, and he uses his first-step quickness to get to a lot of balls. He's a true shortstop who's capable of handling second and third base as well. While Martinez' glove is ahead of his bat, he has a level swing and a good two-strike approach. He's never going to hit for much power but has shown signs of the bat control necessary to handle advanced pitching. He's an aggressive baserunner with slightly above-average speed. Alexei Ramirez blocks Martinez's path in Chicago, just as Hanley Ramirez did in Florida. The White Sox will give him a long look at second base, where Gordon Beckham has stagnated. Martinez will have to show more with the bat to avoid being tagged as a utiltyman.

BA GRADE

45

MEDIUM

Year	Club (League)	Class	AVG	G	AB	R	H	2B	3B	HR	RBI	BB	SO	SB	CS	OBP	SLG
2006	Marlins (GCL)	R	.263	49	171	21	45	4	1	1	21	19	21	7	4	.335	.316
2007	Jupiter (FSL)	HiA	—	1	0	0	0	0	0	0	0	1	0	0	0	1.000	—
	Jamestown (NYP)	SS	.184	38	114	8	21	5	0	0	6	11	25	8	2	.262	.228
2008	Greensboro (SAL)	LoA	.296	85	304	44	90	11	3	6	29	13	46	5	5	.331	.411
2009	Jupiter (FSL)	HiA	.254	130	433	54	110	16	5	1	45	41	51	16	4	.323	.321
2010	Jacksonville (SL)	AA	.302	130	516	90	156	28	4	5	54	49	64	13	9	.372	.401
	Florida (NL)	MAJ	.326	14	43	8	14	4	1	0	2	4	6	1	0	.383	.465
2011	Florida (NL)	MAJ	.130	20	23	0	3	0	0	0	1	0	9	0	0	.130	.130
	New Orleans (PCL)	AAA	.245	88	339	43	83	15	1	3	26	21	57	11	4	.296	.322
Major League Totals			.258	34	66	8	17	4	1	0	3	4	15	1	0	.300	.348
Minor League Totals			.269	521	1877	260	505	79	14	16	181	155	264	60	28	.331	.352

10 EDUARDO ESCOBAR, SS/2B

Born: Jan 5, 1989. **B-T:** B-R. **Ht.:** 5-10. **Wt.:** 165. **Signed:** Venezuela, 2006. **Signed by:** Amador Arias.

A clone of former White Sox manager Ozzie Guillen, Escobar advanced from low Class A in 2009 to Triple-A last year. Chicago promoted him in September but never gave him a start, though he did collect an infield hit against Justin Verlander in his first big league at-bat. Escobar is a ballplayer more than a toolkit, the type of guy managers and teammates want the ball hit to with the game on the line. He covers a lot of ground at shortstop but his solid arm isn't quite enough to pull off all the plays from the hole. He's a vacuum cleaner who makes the routine plays and hangs in well on double plays. While Escobar has quick hands at the plate, he has yet to develop the strength or discipline to be an effective hitter. He flashed some pop in the Arizona Fall League after the 2010 season, but it didn't carry over to Triple-A. He has slightly above-average speed but isn't a real basestealing threat. The arrival of Osvaldo Martinez creates immediate competition for Escobar, though Martinez could be moved to second base. Neither figures to displace Alexei Ramirez in Chicago, and Escobar needs a second season in Charlotte to continue his development as a hitter.

BA GRADE

45

MEDIUM

Year	Club (League)	Class	AVG	G	AB	R	H	2B	3B	HR	RBI	BB	SO	SB	CS	OBP	SLG
2006	Orioles/White Sox (VSL)R		.236	46	123	21	29	3	1	0	17	14	25	7	6	.317	.276
2007	White Sox2 (DSL)	R	.291	64	247	56	72	5	4	0	18	22	45	19	14	.359	.344
2008	Great Falls (PIO)	R	.417	6	24	6	10	2	1	1	4	2	3	1	1	.464	.708
	Kannapolis (SAL)	LoA	.267	60	243	37	65	6	1	0	22	13	65	4	3	.302	.300
2009	Kannapolis (SAL)	LoA	.256	128	464	64	119	10	7	3	41	29	91	20	6	.300	.328
2010	Winston-Salem (CAR)HiA		.285	87	368	57	105	18	8	3	39	23	76	8	5	.327	.402
	Birmingham (SL)	AA	.262	49	202	22	53	8	3	3	22	9	35	3	0	.294	.376
2011	Charlotte (IL)	AAA	.266	137	489	55	130	23	4	4	49	27	104	13	8	.303	.354
	Chicago (AL)	MAJ	.286	9	7	0	2	0	0	0	0	0	1	0	0	.286	.286
Major League Totals			.286	9	7	0	2	0	0	0	0	0	1	0	0	.286	.286
Minor League Totals			.270	577	2160	318	583	75	29	14	212	139	444	75	43	.315	.351

11 HECTOR SANTIAGO, LHP

BA GRADE

45

MEDIUM

Born: Dec. 16, 1987. **B-T:** R-L. **Ht.:** 6-0. **Wt.:** 210. **Drafted:** Okaloosa-Walton (Fla.) CC, D/F 2006 (30th round). **Signed by:** Chuck Fox.

A prototypical sleeper, this blue-collar guy from Newark, N.J. somehow shot from high

Class A to Chicago in a six-week period last season. After signing for $85,000 as a 30th-round draft-and-follow, Santiago spent his first four pro seasons in middle relief. The key to his rapid ascent was was a trip to the Puerto Rican Winter League after the 2010 season, where former Brewers lefty Angel Miranda helped him improve his changeup and develop a screwball. The White Sox sent Santiago back to Winston-Salem for a third straight year but made him a starter, and he came up to the majors for a short stay in July. He struck out Eric Hosmer in his debut and threw 4⅓ scoreless innings the next day before returning to the minors. Santiago's best pitch is a low-90s fastball that spikes as high as 96 mph. His heater straightens out at times, which made the refinement of his changeup and addition of his screwball so important. They give him a pair of average secondary pitches to keep opponents from sitting on his fastball. His mediocre slider wasn't getting the job done. Santiago's control and command waver, and he'll need to throw consistent strikes to stick in the majors. He could be part of Chicago's bullpen in 2012, though the organization may want to send him to Triple-A and continue to develop him as a starter. The White Sox don't have much pitching depth in the high minors, so he should get an opportunity soon no matter what path he takes.

Year	Club (League)	Class	W	L	ERA	G	GS	CG	SV	IP	H	HR	BB	SO	K/9	WHIP	AVG
2007	Bristol (APP)	R	1	1	1.65	17	0	0	0	33	19	1	16	38	10.5	1.07	.176
2008	Kannapolis (SAL)	LoA	5	1	4.06	38	0	0	1	64	57	1	44	83	11.6	1.57	.241
2009	Winston-Salem (CAR)	HiA	4	4	3.88	38	0	0	1	58	54	5	25	66	10.2	1.36	.252
2010	Winston-Salem (CAR)	HiA	4	5	4.15	37	1	0	2	61	63	4	19	61	9.0	1.35	.267
2011	Winston-Salem (CAR)	HiA	2	3	3.68	8	8	0	0	44	38	7	14	43	8.8	1.18	.236
	Chicago (AL)	MAJ	0	0	0.00	2	0	0	0	5	1	0	1	2	3.4	0.38	.059
	Birmingham (SL)	AA	7	5	3.56	15	15	0	0	83	71	4	39	74	8.0	1.32	.235
Major League Totals			0	0	0.00	2	0	0	0	5	1	0	1	2	3.4	0.38	.059
Minor League Totals			23	19	3.65	153	24	0	4	343	302	22	157	365	9.6	1.34	.240

12 ANDY WILKINS, 1B

BA GRADE
50 HIGH

Born: Sept. 13, 1988. **B-T:** L-R. **Ht.:** 6-2. **Wt.:** 225. **Drafted:** Arkansas, 2010 (5th round). **Signed by:** Clay Overcash.

Wilkins is about as subtle as a jackhammer. He's a throwback masher who can hit the ball a country mile, and his power makes him a guy to watch in a system that hasn't developed a 30-homer player since Joe Crede. Wilkins skipped a level in 2011, spending his first full pro season in high Class A and ranking second in the Carolina League with 23 homers. Scouts don't like the way he wraps the bat behind his head, but he still generates enough bat speed to drive high fastballs to the opposite field. He crushes pitches that are down and in. He isn't as dangerous against lefties (.692 OPS last year) but crushed righthanders (.911 OPS). He draws a fair amount of walks and doesn't strike out much for a slugger. Chicago tried Wilkins at third base in his pro debut but moved him across the diamond to first base in 2011. He lacks range and agility at either corner, but he has solid arm strength and can make the routine play at first base. He has below-average speed but is aggressive on the bases. Wilkins will move up to Double-A and if he continues to develop, he ultimately could allow the rebuilding White Sox to entertain offers for Paul Konerko.

Year	Club (League)	Class	AVG	G	AB	R	H	2B	3B	HR	RBI	BB	SO	SB	CS	OBP	SLG
2010	Great Falls (PIO)	R	.307	53	218	37	67	14	1	6	40	33	31	7	2	.396	.463
2011	Winston-Salem (CAR)	HiA	.278	134	493	72	137	33	0	23	89	56	91	2	2	.349	.485
Minor League Totals			.287	187	711	109	204	47	1	29	129	89	122	9	4	.364	.478

13 ERIK JOHNSON, RHP

BA GRADE
50 HIGH

Born: Dec. 30, 1989. **B-T:** R-R. **Ht.:** 6-3. **Wt.:** 240. **Drafted:** California, 2011 (2nd round). **Signed by:** Adam Virchis.

Matched against No. 2 overall pick Danny Hultzen in California's College World Series opener last June, Johnson battled nerves but held Virginia scoreless for three innings in a game the Bears would lose 4-1 after the bullpens got involved. Unlike the polished Hultzen, Johnson is more of a project who will need time to develop. The White Sox, who drafted him in the second round and paid him $450,000, love his strong build and arm plus the fact that he moved into a Friday-starter role as a college freshman and never gave it up. Johnson throws a 90-94 mph fastball that tops out at 96. Chicago believes he could gain velocity as he smooths out his delivery and becomes less of a max-effort guy. Johnson complements his heater with three offerings, the best of which is a hard slider that can be a swing-and-miss pitch. His curveball and changeup were the focus of hard work in instructional league. Johnson's fastball/slider combination makes him a late-inning relief candidate, but the White Sox want to see how he fares as a starter. He could become a mid-rotation option if he refines his fastball command. Johnson pitched only two innings after signing, so 2012 will be a learning experience. He'll probably open the year in low Class A and have an opportunity for a midseason promotion.

Year	Club (League)	Class	W	L	ERA	G	GS	CG	SV	IP	H	HR	BB	SO	K/9	WHIP	AVG
2011	Great Falls (PIO)	R	0	0	4.50	2	0	0	0	2	4	0	1	2	9.0	2.50	.444
Minor League Totals			0	0	4.50	2	0	0	0	2	4	0	1	2	9.0	2.50	.444

14 CHARLIE LEESMAN, LHP

BA GRADE
45
MEDIUM

Born: March 10, 1987. **B-T:** L-L. **Ht.:** 6-4. **Wt.:** 210. **Drafted:** Xavier, 2008 (11th round). **Signed by:** Mike Shirley/Phil Gulley.

It might be time for the White Sox to throw Leesman into the deep water and see if he can swim. He handled a full season in Double-A last year, running his record as a pro to 37-18 after winning just six games in three college seasons at Xavier. Signed for $50,000 as an 11th-round pick in 2008, he continues to impress scouts as a savvy lefthander with four pitches and claimed a spot on the 40-man roster in November. Leesman's fastball sits in the high 80s, spiking to 90 mph, and sets up a plus changeup that he throws in the mid-70s. He uses two breaking balls, with his slider a better pitch than his curveball, but both need work. He also has learned a cut fastball that helps him against righthanders. Leesman moves the ball around well and rarely loses track of the strike zone. Some scouts project him as a back-of-the-rotation starter in the big leagues, but Chicago isn't sure if he has the secondary pitches to succeed with marginal velocity. He'll compete for a job in spring training and might get his first opportunity in the bullpen, though he'll likely open 2012 in Triple-A as a starter.

Year	Club (League)	Class	W	L	ERA	G	GS	CG	SV	IP	H	HR	BB	SO	K/9	WHIP	AVG
2008	Bristol (APP)	R	0	0	0.00	2	0	0	1	5	5	0	1	6	10.1	1.13	.263
	Kannapolis (SAL)	LoA	0	0	0.00	1	1	0	0	5	3	0	2	5	9.6	1.07	.188
2009	Kannapolis (SAL)	LoA	13	5	3.08	27	27	1	0	158	165	4	58	117	6.7	1.41	.275
2010	Winston-Salem (CAR)	HiA	9	4	5.10	17	17	0	0	85	98	6	44	39	4.2	1.68	.294
	Birmingham (SL)	AA	5	2	2.69	11	11	0	0	64	47	1	20	51	7.2	1.05	.210
2011	Birmingham (SL)	AA	10	7	4.03	27	27	0	0	152	150	4	83	113	6.7	1.53	.264
Minor League Totals			37	18	3.63	85	83	1	1	468	468	15	208	331	6.4	1.44	.266

15 JEFFERSON OLACIO, LHP

BA GRADE
50
EXTREME

Born: Jan.16, 1994. **B-T:** L-L. **Ht.:** 6-7. **Wt.:** 230. **Signed:** Dominican Republic, 2010. **Signed by:** Jerry Krause.

As unproductive as the White Sox have been in the Dominican Republic over the last decade, Olacio could get the organization headed in the right direction. He's built along the lines of C.C. Sabathia and has a power arm, though he's as raw as a pitcher can be. Signed for $125,000 after showcasing himself in the Dominican Prospect League in 2010, Olacio came to the United States for minor league spring training last March. He then returned home to play in the Dominican Summer League, where his lack of control was painfully evident. So too was his potential, however, as he struck out 42 in 38 innings and didn't allow a home run. Olacio already has a fastball that's consistently in the low 90s, and Chicago thinks it will get better as he grows into his body. When he was 14, he stood 6-foot-3 but couldn't hit 80 mph. He's still developing a feel for his curveball and changeup, for now trying to get by on his intimidating size and his fastball. Olacio has a max-effort delivery that gives him deception. He'll be tested in the United States in 2012, most likely at Rookie-level Bristol after he spends the first half of the season in extended spring training. Olacio has a high ceiling, but he'll need to refine his secondary pitches and learn to control the inner half of the plate to reach it.

Year	Club (League)	Class	W	L	ERA	G	GS	CG	SV	IP	H	HR	BB	SO	K/9	WHIP	AVG
2011	White Sox (DSL)	R	3	5	5.50	11	11	0	0	38	30	0	38	42	10.0	1.81	.227
Minor League Totals			3	5	5.50	11	11	0	0	38	30	0	38	42	10.0	1.81	.227

16 JARED MITCHELL, OF

BA GRADE
50
EXTREME

Born: Oct. 31, 1988. **B-T:** L-L. **Ht.:** 5-11. **Wt.:** 192. **Drafted:** Louisiana State, 2009 (1st round). **Signed by:** Warren Hughes.

Mitchell still is trying to bounce back from tearing a tendon in his left ankle when he crashed into an outfield fence in spring training in 2010, costing him the entire season. He was considered a potential five-tool player when the White Sox drafted him 23rd overall and signed him for $1.2 million in 2009, but he hasn't been the same guy since his injury. He never got untracked in 2011, hitting better than .231 in only one month and .134 in August, though scouts came away talking about his relentless effort and hustle. Part of national championships in baseball and football at Louisiana State, Mitchell needs to make adjustments in his swing and his approach. He chased high pitches en route to 183 strikeouts last season, the third-highest total in the minors. He's willing to work counts but gets in trouble when he falls behind. He has average raw power, though he'll have to make more contact in order to tap into it. A wide receiver at LSU, Mitchell runs well but isn't the plus-plus runner he was before he hurt his ankle. He's a solid center fielder with an average arm. Some club officials wonder if the collision with the wall two years ago has made him tentative in pursuing balls over his head. Mitchell will return to high Class A to open 2012, and Chicago will try to remain patient.

Year	Club (League)	Class	AVG	G	AB	R	H	2B	3B	HR	RBI	BB	SO	SB	CS	OBP	SLG
2009	Kannapolis (SAL)	LoA	.296	34	115	13	34	12	2	0	10	23	40	5	3	.417	.435
2010	Did Not Play—Injured																
2011	Winston-Salem (CAR)	HiA	.222	129	477	74	106	31	8	9	58	52	183	14	6	.304	.377
Minor League Totals			.236	163	592	87	140	43	10	9	68	75	223	19	9	.327	.389

17 ANDRE RIENZO, RHP

BA GRADE
45
HIGH

Born: June 5, 1988. **B-T:** R-R. **Ht.:** 6-3. **Wt.:** 160. **Signed:** Brazil, 2006. **Signed by:** Orlando Santana.

The White Sox remain intrigued by Rienzo's arm strength, though they didn't see as much improvement as they hoped for last season in his secondary pitches. Chicago opted not to add him to its 40-man roster, and was relieved when other teams decided he was too raw to select in the Rule 5 draft. Rienzo has overpowered lower-level hitters with his fastball, which sits in the low 90s and rarely straightens out. He has better command than his 66 walks in 116 innings last year would indicate. He had trouble finding the strike zone because the White Sox insisted he throw more curveballs and sliders. He still hasn't found a go-to breaking pitch, generally throwing slurves that break early and don't fool hitters. He sometimes telegraphs his changeup, which would be more effective if he could throw something off at and throw it in the high 70s rather than the low 80s. Rienzo will move up to Double-A and needs to make strides rounding out his repertoire in 2012.

Year	Club (League)	Class	W	L	ERA	G	GS	CG	SV	IP	H	HR	BB	SO	K/9	WHIP	AVG
2007	White Sox2 (DSL)	R	1	1	7.63	7	3	0	0	15	16	1	11	22	12.9	1.76	.286
2008	White Sox 2 (DSL)	R	2	1	1.64	5	4	0	0	22	17	0	6	22	9.0	1.05	.218
	White Sox 1 (DSL)	R	3	0	0.96	3	3	0	0	19	15	0	3	22	10.6	0.96	.214
2009	Bristol (APP)	R	2	6	4.14	13	9	0	0	54	55	4	13	49	8.1	1.25	.263
2010	Kannapolis (SAL)	LoA	8	4	3.65	20	18	2	0	101	95	5	32	125	11.1	1.26	.242
2011	Winston-Salem (CAR)	HiA	6	5	3.41	25	22	1	0	116	108	4	66	118	9.2	1.50	.247
Minor League Totals			22	17	3.55	73	59	3	0	327	306	14	131	358	9.8	1.34	.246

18 BRANDON SHORT, OF

BA GRADE
45
HIGH

Born: Sept. 9, 1988. **B-T:** R-R. **Ht.:** 6-1. **Wt.:** 175. **Drafted:** St. John's River (Fla.) CC, 2008 (28th round). **Signed by:** Joe Siers.

Short is one of the better pure hitters in the system and won the Carolina League batting title with a .316 average in 2010, but his numbers suffered when he moved up to Double-A last year. He has a stylish swing from the right side and generates solid gap power to both fields but needs to do a better job of recognizing pitches and controlling the strike zone after giving away too many at-bats to Southern League pitchers. To his credit, Short improved the other phases of his game in 2011. He played a strong center field and did a better job of using his solid speed on the bases. He runs down balls in the alleys and has an average, accurate arm. Because the system is so thin, the White Sox may promote Short to Triple-A in 2012. They gambled and didn't protect him on the 40-man roster, but he could force his way into the big league picture by midseason.

Year	Club (League)	Class	AVG	G	AB	R	H	2B	3B	HR	RBI	BB	SO	SB	CS	OBP	SLG
2008	Bristol (APP)	R	.273	49	183	30	50	13	2	1	23	16	37	14	7	.357	.383
2009	Kannapolis (SAL)	LoA	.284	97	345	56	98	19	3	7	55	27	78	12	1	.342	.417
2010	Winston-Salem (CAR)	HiA	.316	116	491	77	155	31	5	15	79	28	107	7	10	.365	.491
2011	Birmingham (SL)	AA	.262	130	526	75	138	29	5	13	60	36	125	21	9	.318	.411
Minor League Totals			.285	392	1545	238	441	92	15	36	217	107	347	54	27	.343	.434

19 JOSH PHEGLEY, C

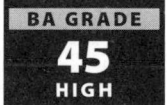

BA GRADE
45
HIGH

Born: Feb. 12, 1988. **B-T:** R-R. **Ht.:** 5-10. **Wt.:** 210. **Drafted:** Indiana, 2009 (1st round supplemental). **Signed by:** Mike Shirley.

If it wasn't for bad luck, Phegley wouldn't have any luck at all. Since signing for $858,600 in the 2009 draft, he has been slowed by a series of injuries and medical woes. A wrist injury prevented him from making a trip to the Arizona Fall league after the 2011 season, but at least he played in 116 games and reached Triple-A. The year before was a nightmare, as Phegley had his spleen removed after medication was unable to control a condition known as idiopathic thrombocytopenic purpura, which results in low blood platelets. He has a level swing and solid two-strike approach, but good fastballs beat him too often. Some scouts think his bat speed will improve as he gets healthier, allowing him to make use of his plus raw power to all fields. Phegley has to hit because he doesn't do much else. He's thick-bodied and lacks athleticism, which limits when he's on the bases or moves behind the plate. He's a below-average receiver with solid arm strength and has nailed 48 percent of basestealers in his pro career. He figures to spend 2012 in Triple-A but should be first in line for a major league promotion if A.J. Pierzynski or Tyler Flowers is sidelined. The toughness he has shown should come in handy making the next step.

Year	Club (League)	Class	AVG	G	AB	R	H	2B	3B	HR	RBI	BB	SO	SB	CS	OBP	SLG
2009	Kannapolis (SAL)	LoA	.224	52	196	27	44	9	0	9	33	11	40	1	1	.277	.408
2010	Bristol (APP)	R	.200	5	15	1	3	1	0	1	2	4	0	0	.333	.267
	Winston-Salem (CAR)	HiA	.292	25	89	16	26	3	0	3	12	7	22	0	0	.337	.427
	Birmingham (SL)	AA	.292	18	72	7	21	4	0	2	13	2	22	0	0	.316	.431
2011	Birmingham (SL)	AA	.242	94	364	43	88	21	2	7	50	23	61	1	2	.292	.368
	Charlotte (IL)	AAA	.241	22	79	9	19	4	0	2	6	8	18	0	0	.326	.367
Minor League Totals			.247	216	815	103	201	42	2	23	115	53	167	2	3	.300	.388

20 MIKE BLANKE, C

BA GRADE
45
HIGH

Born: Oct. 17, 1988. **B-T:** R-R. **Ht.:** 6-4. **Wt.:** 220. **Drafted:** Tampa, 2010 (14th round). **Signed by:** Joe Siers.

Catchers with offensive potential and arm strength are valuable commodities, and Blanke's rise to high Class A in his first full pro season showed what the White Sox think of him. They also sent him to the Arizona Fall League, where he earned compliments for his work behind the plate. Blanke's size leads to some receiving and quickness issues. He made 18 errors in 103 games last season, in part because he often rushes his throws, though he used his strong arm to throw out 37 percent of basestealers. Blanke shows raw power in batting practice but has a long swing and hasn't fully tapped into it in games. He needs to tighten his stroke and do a better job with pitch recognition. As expected for a catcher, he's a well below-average runner. Blanke has grown into his body but he still has some awkwardness that Chicago expects eventually will get smoothed out. Coaches praise his ability to make adjustments. He should see Double-A at some point in 2012.

Year	Club (League)	Class	AVG	G	AB	R	H	2B	3B	HR	RBI	BB	SO	SB	CS	OBP	SLG
2010	Great Falls (PIO)	R	.329	62	240	35	79	20	1	7	43	23	33	0	0	.400	.508
2011	Kannapolis (SAL)	LoA	.259	47	170	22	44	13	1	2	18	11	28	0	0	.311	.382
	Winston-Salem (CAR)	HiA	.236	68	237	25	56	9	0	7	25	22	43	0	0	.303	.363
Minor League Totals			.277	177	647	82	179	42	2	16	86	56	104	0	0	.342	.422

21 CARLOS SANCHEZ, 2B/SS

BA GRADE
45
HIGH

Born: June 29, 1992. **B-T:** B-R. **Ht.:** 5-11. **Wt.:** 175. **Signed:** Venezuela, 2009. **Signed by:** Amador Arias.

The switch-hitter steadily has improved with the bat since signing out of Venezuela in 2009, but it's his play in the field that has captured the White Sox's attention. Kannapolis manager Tommy Thompson, who started his career as a coach/instructor in 1988, says Sanchez is as strong defensively as any second baseman he has seen. He has excellent range to both sides and quick, soft hands. He hangs in well on double plays and has a strong arm that has allowed him to see time on the left side of the infield. Sanchez is a better hitter from the left side of the plate. He has a small-ball game, bunting and protecting the plate, but he'll have to make more contact and draw more walks. He has very little power, so he must focus on getting on base. He has average speed but gets reckless on the bases and runs into too many outs. Sanchez has the upside of an everyday second baseman in the major leagues, though he'll need to add a lot of polish first. He'll still be 19 when he opens 2012 in high Class A.

Year	Club (League)	Class	AVG	G	AB	R	H	2B	3B	HR	RBI	BB	SO	SB	CS	OBP	SLG
2009	White Sox (DSL)	R	.156	22	32	7	5	0	0	0	3	8	10	1	0	.341	.156
2010	White Sox (DSL)	R	.269	52	156	26	42	5	2	1	18	41	26	7	3	.431	.346
2011	Bristol (APP)	R	.250	5	16	4	4	1	0	0	3	5	2	1	2	.500	.313
	Kannapolis (SAL)	LoA	.288	63	264	44	76	10	1	1	27	15	49	7	8	.341	.345
Minor League Totals			.271	142	468	81	127	16	3	2	51	69	87	16	13	.381	.331

22 NATE JONES, RHP

BA GRADE
50
EXTREME

Born: Jan. 28, 1986. **B-T:** R-R. **Ht.:** 6-5. **Wt.:** 190. **Drafted:** Northern Kentucky, 2007 (5th round). **Signed by:** Mike Shirley.

Moved back into the bullpen after spending 2010 as a starter, Jones continued to flash the two pitches that made Bobby Jenks successful with the White Sox: a triple-digit fastball and a knee-buckling curveball. After going on the disabled list in mid-May with shoulder tendinitis, Jones returned to record a 2.49 ERA and 53 strikeouts in 47 innings the rest of the way. While his fastball resides in the mid-90s and his curveball can be a true hammer, there's one important difference between him and Jenks. He never has commanded those weapons the way Jenks did when he was at the top of his game, though Jones is less wild than he was when he entered pro ball in 2007. He still pitches behind in the count too often and has to sacrifice stuff to get the ball over the plate, getting hit harder than he should. He has shortened his delivery in recent years but still has trouble repeating it. Jones has developed a cut fastball that sometimes is more trustworthy than his curveball, and he uses it to keep lefthanders off his fastball. After some work in the Puerto Rican Winter League, he'll probably open the season in Triple-A but could finish it in Chicago.

Year	Club (League)	Class	W	L	ERA	G	GS	CG	SV	IP	H	HR	BB	SO	K/9	WHIP	AVG
2007	Bristol (APP)	R	0	4	5.13	13	10	0	0	47	44	4	29	42	8.0	1.54	.250
2008	Bristol (APP)	R	1	0	1.35	4	1	0	0	7	6	0	2	12	16.2	1.20	.222
	Kannapolis (SAL)	LoA	1	7	6.83	18	10	1	0	57	63	8	35	71	11.3	1.73	.281
	Winston-Salem (CAR)	HiA	0	0	3.38	2	0	0	0	3	1	0	2	1	3.4	1.13	.111
2009	Kannapolis (SAL)	LoA	2	0	2.41	13	0	0	1	19	8	0	9	25	12.1	0.91	.129
	Winston-Salem (CAR)	HiA	2	1	3.65	32	0	0	0	49	44	4	13	43	7.8	1.16	.244
2010	Winston-Salem (CAR)	HiA	11	6	4.08	28	28	1	0	152	176	10	56	109	6.4	1.52	.296
2011	Birmingham (SL)	AA	2	3	3.27	42	0	0	12	63	58	3	27	67	9.5	1.34	.243
Minor League Totals			19	21	4.28	152	49	2	13	397	400	29	173	370	8.4	1.44	.265

23 GREGORI INFANTE, RHP

BA GRADE
45
HIGH

Born: July 10, 1987. **B-T:** R-R. **Ht.:** 6-2. **Wt.:** 185. **Signed:** Venezuela, 2006.
Signed by: Amador Arias.

Infante impressed former White Sox manager Ozzie Guillen by making five scoreless appearances during a September 2010 big league cameo, but never got a big league look last season. In fact he opened 2011 in Double-A, where he allowed just one run (unearned) in 12 appearances before spending the rest of the year in Triple-A. Infante's fastball averaged 96 mph when he was in Chicago, and that was no illusion. He pitches at 94-98 mph but still seeks reliable secondary pitches and command to go with his heat. He has a hard slider that gets groundballs when it's on but tends to be slurvy. He also has a mid-80s changeup that he used more when the White Sox tried to develop him as a starter. He leaves too many pitches up in the strike zone, which is why he doesn't dominate as much as his sheer velocity might indicate he should. After spending the winter pitching in Venezuela, Infante will get a chance to pitch for a major league job in spring training.

Year	Club (League)	Class	W	L	ERA	G	GS	CG	SV	IP	H	HR	BB	SO	K/9	WHIP	AVG
2006	Orioles/White Sox (VSL)	R	0	0	8.61	10	2	0	0	23	25	2	26	17	6.7	2.22	.291
2007	Bristol (APP)	R	2	3	4.01	10	8	0	0	34	25	1	23	33	8.8	1.43	.207
2008	Kannapolis (SAL)	LoA	1	2	6.59	4	3	0	0	14	16	0	12	11	7.2	2.05	.286
	Bristol (APP)	R	4	3	2.66	13	12	0	0	74	63	4	19	57	6.9	1.10	.232
2009	Kannapolis (SAL)	LoA	3	5	3.26	15	15	0	0	88	76	4	37	75	7.6	1.28	.239
	Winston-Salem (CAR)	HiA	1	2	7.84	6	5	0	0	21	18	3	23	10	4.4	1.98	.243
2010	Winston-Salem (CAR)	HiA	1	2	3.48	31	0	0	9	34	32	0	15	35	9.4	1.40	.250
	Birmingham (SL)	AA	2	2	3.42	24	0	0	3	26	23	0	12	34	11.6	1.33	.235
	Chicago (AL)	MAJ	0	0	0.00	5	0	0	0	5	2	0	4	5	9.6	1.29	.133
2011	Birmingham (SL)	AA	2	0	0.00	12	0	0	7	15	7	0	7	14	8.2	0.91	.132
	Charlotte (IL)	AAA	1	4	3.35	34	0	0	4	48	50	5	21	40	7.5	1.47	.263
Major League Totals			0	0	0.00	5	0	0	0	5	2	0	4	5	9.6	1.29	.133
Minor League Totals			17	23	3.82	159	45	0	23	377	335	19	195	326	7.8	1.40	.240

24 DYLAN AXELROD, RHP

BA GRADE
40
LOW

Born: July 30, 1985. **B-T:** R-R. **Ht.:** 6-0. **Wt.:** 195. **Drafted:** UC Irvine, 2007, (30th round). **Signed by:** Brendan Hause (Padres).

Jake Peavy has paid few dividends for Chicago, but his extended professional family led to one bargain. His agent, Barry Axelrod, is the uncle of Dylan, who signed with the White Sox two days after they acquired Peavy at the 2009 trade deadline. Axelrod signed with the Padres for $1,000 as a 30th-rounder in 2007 and was released two years later before heading to the independent Frontier League and hooking up with the Sox. He's a strike-throwing machine who works fast and challenges hitters despite less-than-overwhelming stuff. His fastball runs from 88-91 mph, his slider is average and his changeup is fringy. Axelrod makes it work with his feel for pitching and off-the-charts makeup. He often confuses hitters by pitching backward. His ceiling is limited to a No. 5 starter, but he could find himself alongside Peavy in the big league rotation to open 2012.

Year	Club (League)	Class	W	L	ERA	G	GS	CG	SV	IP	H	HR	BB	SO	K/9	WHIP	AVG
2007	Padres (AZL)	R	0	2	5.40	11	0	0	2	12	15	0	4	15	11.6	1.63	.294
	Fort Wayne (MWL)	LoA	2	1	1.27	10	0	0	0	21	18	0	4	15	6.3	1.03	.237
2008	Lake Elsinore (CAL)	HiA	2	1	5.29	32	0	0	0	49	51	4	19	55	10.0	1.42	.258
	Fort Wayne (MWL)	LoA	1	1	3.62	23	0	0	0	27	26	2	7	25	8.2	1.21	.245
2009	Lake Elsinore (CAL)	HiA	0	0	4.50	11	0	0	0	12	12	0	5	6	4.5	1.42	.245
	Windy City (FRN)	IND	3	1	2.21	22	8	0	6	61	51	4	14	60	8.9	1.07	.226
	Kannapolis (SAL)	LoA	0	0	2.08	2	0	0	0	4	3	0	1	3	6.2	0.92	.158
	Winston-Salem (CAR)	HiA	2	1	1.91	5	5	0	0	28	29	2	4	17	5.4	1.16	.274
2010	Birmingham (SL)	AA	0	1	2.70	2	2	0	0	10	8	0	3	8	7.2	1.10	.216
	Winston-Salem (CAR)	HiA	8	3	1.99	23	13	1	0	99	95	6	12	84	7.6	1.08	.252
2011	Birmingham (SL)	AA	3	2	3.34	11	9	0	0	59	52	1	14	57	8.7	1.11	.237
	Charlotte (IL)	AAA	6	1	2.27	15	15	0	0	91	74	2	21	75	7.4	1.04	.220
	Chicago (AL)	MAJ	1	0	2.89	4	3	0	0	19	18	1	9	19	9.2	1.45	.257
Major League Totals			1	0	2.89	4	3	0	0	19	18	1	9	19	9.2	1.45	.257
Minor League Totals			24	13	2.89	145	44	1	2	414	383	13	94	360	7.8	1.15	.243

25 JOSE MARTINEZ, OF

BA GRADE
45
HIGH

Born: July 25, 1988. **B-T:** R-R. **Ht.:** 6-5. **Wt.:** 170. **Drafted: Signed:** Venezuela, 2006. **Signed by:** Amador Arias.

Martinez flashed five-tool potential when he made his U.S. debut in 2007, but his body never filled out as expected and a torn anterior cruciate ligament in his right knee in 2008 cost him valuable repetitions and some speed. The son of the late White Sox outfielder Carlos Martinez, Jose still catches the eye of scouts. His signature tool is his strong arm, which plays well in right field and resulted in 15 assists last year. He shows off his arm too much, however, which led to 14 errors. Martinez needs to settle down at the plate, too. He makes consistent contact thanks to his bat speed, but he doesn't walk much or make the most of his gap power because he lacks patience. He might top out at 10-15 homers annually because his swing is fairly flat. Martinez has a lost a step and now has fringy speed, though he does cover enough ground in the outfield. Ticketed to start 2012 back in Birmingham, he most realistically projects as a fourth outfielder.

Year	Club (League)	Class	AVG	G	AB	R	H	2B	3B	HR	RBI	BB	SO	SB	CS	OBP	SLG
2006	Orioles/White Sox (VSL)R		.278	54	158	26	44	8	0	4	30	25	29	5	4	.384	.405
2007	Bristol (APP)	R	.282	65	245	34	69	11	3	7	37	22	53	12	2	.348	.437
2008	Kannapolis (SAL)	LoA	.306	39	144	19	44	5	0	2	18	12	26	7	5	.359	.382
2009	DID NOT PLAY-INJURED																
2010	Bristol (APP)	R	.409	6	22	5	9	1	0	1	5	2	3	1	0	.458	.591
	Winston-Salem (CAR)HiA		.242	61	236	28	57	8	1	5	24	17	42	4	1	.295	.347
2011	Winston-Salem (CAR)HiA		.314	80	315	45	99	13	3	5	29	13	44	2	3	.344	.422
	Birmingham (SL)	AA	.295	53	200	19	59	13	1	1	16	15	25	5	2	.344	.385
Minor League Totals			.289	358	1320	176	381	59	8	25	159	106	222	36	17	.345	.402

26 BLAIR WALTERS, LHP

BA GRADE 45 HIGH

Born: Nov. 8, 1989. **B-T:** L-L. **Ht.:** 6-0. **Wt.:** 200. **Drafted:** Hawaii, 2011 (11th round). **Signed by:** Gary Woods.

Confidence can be a huge factor for a pitcher, and Walters demonstrated that by carrying Rookie-level Great Falls to the Pioneer League title in his pro debut last summer. He went on an 11-0 roll (including two playoff wins) as a starter, after working exclusively in the bullpen in his two seasons at Hawaii. He was named Pioneer League pitcher of the year and won the decisive game for the league championship. Pretty heady stuff for a guy who was signed for $25,000 as an 11th-round pick. Walters works mostly off a low-90s fastball with natural sink. Hitters in Rookie ball were baffled by his breaking ball, a combination cutter/slider with late bite. He also has a fringy changeup. Walters mixes his pitches well and rarely makes mistakes up in the zone. He limits damage by throwing strikes and not putting men on base. Though Walters may not be more than a future No. 4 starter, the White Sox want to find out more about him and may give him a nonroster invitation to major league spring training. They won't get too excited until he has success at higher levels, but they're also in need of some pitching prospects who can move quickly. He might get tested in high Class A to open 2012.

Year	Club (League)	Class	W	L	ERA	G	GS	CG	SV	IP	H	HR	BB	SO	K/9	WHIP	AVG
2011	Great Falls (PIO)	R	9	0	4.03	14	13	0	0	74	72	6	17	72	8.8	1.21	.257
Minor League Totals			9	0	4.03	14	13	0	0	74	72	6	17	72	8.8	1.21	.257

27 TYLER KUHN, INF/OF

BA GRADE 45 HIGH

Born: Sept. 9, 1986. **B-T:** L-R. **Ht.:** 5-10. **Wt.:** 185. **Drafted:** West Virginia, 2008 (15th round). **Signed by:** Mike Shirley/Phil Gulley.

Kuhn has hit .314 in four pro seasons but hasn't figured more prominently in the White Sox's plans because he hasn't found a defensive home. He missed winning the Southern League batting title last year by just seven points. His confidence and plate coverage make him feel that he can hit any pitch. He works counts in his favor and has a knack for fouling off pitchers' pitches. Kuhn forces pitchers to challenge him and consistently squares up the ball, hitting line drives all over the field. He has little home run power but uses his solid speed to pile up his share of extra-base hits. Chicago could have used a bat like Kuhn's to spice up their stagnant lineup in 2011, but he has yet to prove he can handle any position well. A shortstop in college, he has played mostly second base and left field as a pro. He also has seen action at third base. He has average arm strength but limited range, and he profiles best offensively and defensively at second. Kuhn figures to open 2012 in Triple-A and await a chance to prove he can be more than an offensive-minded utilityman.

Year	Club (League)	Class	AVG	G	AB	R	H	2B	3B	HR	RBI	BB	SO	SB	CS	OBP	SLG
2008	Great Falls (PIO)	R	.375	62	256	51	96	23	9	3	46	21	35	7	3	.424	.570
2009	Kannapolis (SAL)	LoA	.299	58	221	27	66	10	3	0	27	18	30	19	4	.353	.371
	Winston-Salem (CAR)HiA		.281	68	256	28	72	14	2	0	19	14	38	7	7	.320	.352
2010	Birmingham (SL)	AA	.279	109	384	52	107	17	6	5	50	36	75	6	5	.345	.393
2011	Birmingham (SL)	AA	.341	107	414	61	141	28	10	1	55	39	64	16	5	.401	.464
	Charlotte (IL)	AAA	.297	23	91	9	27	4	1	0	4	5	13	0	2	.327	.363
Minor League Totals			.314	427	1622	228	509	96	31	9	201	133	255	55	26	.368	.428

28 KEVAN SMITH, C

BA GRADE 50 EXTREME

Born: June 28, 1988. **B-T:** R-R. **Ht.:** 6-4. **Wt.:** 240. **Drafted:** Pittsburgh, 2011 (7th round). **Signed by:** Phil Gulley.

Because at 23 he was quite old for Rookie ball, the White Sox expected Smith to get off to a flying start in Rookie ball after signing him for $60,000 as a seventh-round pick. He did even better than that, combining for a 1.074 OPS between the Appalachian and Pioneer leagues last summer. He hit .478 in the playoffs to help Great Falls win the Pioneer League championship. Smith recreated the success he once had on the gridiron, as he earned the starting quarterback job at Pitt as a redshirt freshman in 2007. He set a school record with 202 passing yards in his debut—surpassing even Dan Marino—but he battled arm injuries and fell out of favor with coaches, so he eventually traded in his shoulder pads for catcher's gear. Smith played three seasons of baseball and ranked second in the Big East Conference with a .397 average last spring. He has solid discipline and recognizes pitches well, so he should continue to hit for average. He also has power to all fields. The key for Smith will be how well he can develop as a catcher. He's more athletic and quicker than most backstops, but his lack of experience shows up in his throwing mechanics and his receiving. He has an average arm and threw out 34 percent of pro basestealers. Chicago is intrigued by Smith's maturity and willingness to learn, and could jump him to high Class A for his first full pro season.

Year	Club (League)	Class	AVG	G	AB	R	H	2B	3B	HR	RBI	BB	SO	SB	CS	OBP	SLG
2011	Bristol (APP)	R	.396	26	96	24	38	10	1	7	32	14	14	1	2	.482	.740
	Great Falls (PIO)	R	.318	30	107	22	34	12	2	2	16	14	16	1	0	.417	.523
Minor League Totals			.355	56	203	46	72	22	3	9	48	28	30	2	2	.448	.626

29 JORDAN DANKS, OF

BA GRADE
45
HIGH

Born: Aug. 7, 1986. **B-T:** L-R. **Ht.:** 6-4. **Wt.:** 210. **Drafted:** Texas, 2008 (7th round). **Signed by:** Keith Staab/Derek Valenzuela.

The 2011 season was disappointing for Danks, whose older brother John has won 54 games in five seasons with the White Sox. While fellow Charlotte outfielder Alejandro de Aza and Dayan Viciedo got a chance to show what they could do in Chicago, Jordan spent his second full season in Triple-A. He did set career highs with 14 homers and 18 steals, landing a spot on the U.S. national team for the World Cup in Panama and Pan Am Games in Mexico. Nevertheless, the White Sox declined to add him to their 40-man roster after he finished the season with 51 strikeouts in 101 at-bats. Danks is the best defensive outfielder in the system but has yet to show that he can make a difference with the bat. He has made only incremental progress as a hitter and finished with 150-plus whiffs for the second straight year. He has trouble catching up to good velocity and too often cheats to do so, starting his swing early and chasing bad pitches. Though he has size and strength in his favor, he makes a lot of weak contact to the opposite field. Danks hasn't let his hitting issues derail his overall game. He's one of the top defensive center fielders in the minors, thanks to his plus speed and instincts and average arm. He also has become a proficient if not prolific basestealer. Danks' window to play in the big leagues is closing, and he probably faces another Triple-A assignment to begin 2012.

Year	Club (League)	Class	AVG	G	AB	R	H	2B	3B	HR	RBI	BB	SO	SB	CS	OBP	SLG
2008	Kannapolis (SAL)	LoA	.325	10	40	10	13	4	1	2	7	4	14	1	0	.400	.625
2009	Winston-Salem (CAR)	HiA	.322	30	118	25	38	11	2	3	21	18	32	5	1	.409	.525
	Birmingham (SL)	AA	.243	73	284	50	69	12	1	6	20	37	73	7	3	.337	.356
2010	Charlotte (IL)	AAA	.245	119	445	62	109	27	3	8	42	41	151	15	6	.312	.373
2011	Charlotte (IL)	AAA	.257	133	463	65	119	24	6	14	65	57	155	18	4	.344	.425
Minor League Totals			.258	365	1350	212	348	78	13	33	155	157	425	46	14	.340	.408

30 DEUNTE HEATH, RHP

BA GRADE
45
HIGH

Born: Aug. 8, 1985. **B-T:** R-R. **Ht.:** 6-4. **Wt.:** 215. **Drafted:** Tennessee, 2006 (19th round). **Signed by:** Billy Best (Braves).

Heath was drafted by the Mets out of high school and the Devil Rays and Angels out of Lake City (Fla.) CC before signing with the Braves for $245,000 as a 19th-round pick in 2006. He rode his fastball to Triple-A by the end of 2009, but Atlanta released him the following spring after he was caught in a prostitution sting during spring training. Since signing with the White Sox, club officials and coaches have given him high marks for his conduct. Heath throws 91-95 mph and pushes the upper 90s with his fastball, which features riding life. He backs it up with a slider more notable for its low-80s velocity than its bite. Charlotte needed him in a starter's role last year and he made the most of it, and he pitched well out of the rotation in the Venezuelan League. Chicago prefers him in the bullpen, however, because neither his curveball nor his changeup qualifies as an effective offspeed pitch and his control remains shaky after five years in pro ball. His strong winter performance landed him on the Sox's 40-man roster in November and put him in line to make his major league debut at some point in 2012. Until he throws more strikes, he won't be trusted as more than a middle reliever.

Year	Club (League)	Class	W	L	ERA	G	GS	CG	SV	IP	H	HR	BB	SO	K/9	WHIP	AVG
2007	Rome (SAL)	LoA	2	3	2.03	16	9	0	0	71	59	1	19	47	6.0	1.10	.225
	Myrtle Beach (CAR)	HiA	2	4	5.82	11	11	0	0	56	64	8	31	47	7.6	1.71	.284
2008	Myrtle Beach (CAR)	HiA	9	2	3.11	14	14	1	0	84	78	5	41	53	5.7	1.42	.247
	Mississippi (SL)	AA	4	5	5.56	13	11	0	0	66	76	5	32	46	6.2	1.63	.284
2009	Mississippi (SL)	AA	2	5	4.16	25	12	0	1	80	80	4	38	70	7.9	1.48	.260
	Gwinnett (IL)	AAA	0	1	9.64	7	2	0	0	19	27	2	12	18	8.7	2.09	.325
2010	Birmingham (SL)	AA	2	4	3.12	39	0	0	2	58	49	4	32	84	13.1	1.40	.231
2011	Charlotte (IL)	AAA	4	7	4.73	30	16	0	1	103	98	12	62	117	10.3	1.56	.249
Minor League Totals			25	31	4.25	155	75	1	4	536	531	41	267	482	8.1	1.49	.257

Cincinnati Reds

BY J.J. COOPER

In 2010, the Reds took advantage of one of the weakest divisions in baseball to earn their first playoff appearance in 15 years. But after an offseason in which it stood pat and their two top competitors improved, Cincinnati found itself back in a familiar position—third place, with a record four games under .500.

For the 10th time in 11 years, the Reds finished with a losing record. That disappointing performance left Cincinnati with a difficult question to ponder throughout the winter: Was it just a setback, or is this a team that's best work already is behind it?

The Reds have little choice but to believe that 2011 was the fluke. The core of their team is under contract for 2012 and they once again will have little salary flexibility to make significant additions. If they're to compete with the Brewers and Cardinals, they'll have to make trades or improve from within.

The main culprit for the downturn was the pitching staff. Johnny Cueto emerged as the team's homegrown ace, but Cincinnati dropped to 12th in runs allowed after ranking seventh in 2010. Bronson Arroyo allowed a club-record 46 homers, while Edinson Volquez ranked last among NL pitchers with at least 100 innings with a 5.71 ERA.

While the Reds have one of baseball's better farm systems, they don't have pitching reinforcements available to step in. Their best mound prospect, Daniel Corcino, hasn't pitched above low Class A. Their second-best, 2011 first-round choice Robert Stephenson, is a teenager who has yet to make his pro debut.

By contrast, Cincinnati has more big league-ready position prospects than it has open spots in the lineup. Devin Mesoraco is ready to take over as the team's primary catcher with Ramon Hernandez departing via free agency, but Yonder Alonso may still be on the outside looking in despite posting a .943 OPS in 88 late-season at-bats. His best position is first base, currently occupied by 2010 National League MVP Joey Votto.

If Zack Cozart is fully recovered from Tommy John surgery on his non-throwing elbow, he should be the Reds' starting shortstop. Todd Frazier and Juan Francisco have nothing left to prove in Triple-A but once again will serve as backups.

Mesoraco (2007) and Alonso (2008) continue a strong run of Cincinnati first-round picks that's even more impressive considering the team usually heeds

While other pitchers faltered, Johnny Cueto emerged as a homegrown ace in 2011

MORRIS FOSTOFF

TOP 30 PROSPECTS

1. Devin Mesoraco, c	16. Dave Sappelt, of
2. Billy Hamilton, ss	17. Henry Rodriguez, 2b
3. Yonder Alonso, of/1b	18. Amir Garrett, lhp
4. Yasmani Grandal, c	19. Yorman Rodriguez, of
5. Zack Cozart, ss	20. Gabriel Rosa, 3b
6. Daniel Corcino, rhp	21. Chris Valaika, inf
7. Robert Stephenson, rhp	22. Kyle Waldrop, of
8. Didi Gregorius, ss	23. Ryan Wright, 2b
9. Todd Frazier, 3b/1b/of	24. Sean Buckley, 3b/of
10. Brad Boxberger, rhp	25. Tucker Barnhart, c
11. Neftali Soto, 1b	26. David Vidal, 3b
12. J.C. Sulbaran, rhp	27. Donnie Joseph, lhp
13. Ronald Torreyes, 2b	28. Juan Duran, of
14. Ryan LaMarre, of	29. Jonathan Perez, rhp
15. Tony Cingrani, lhp	30. Kyle Lotzkar, rhp

MLB's bonus recommendations. The Reds' other first-rounders from 2004 through 2009 (Homer Bailey, Jay Bruce, Drew Stubbs, Mike Leake) already are fixtures on the big league club, and catcher Yasmani Grandal (2010) is progressing nicely in the minors.

Cincinnati has been more aggressive in the last two drafts, further fortifying its strong system. The Reds gave Grandal a $3.2 million major league contract as the No. 12 pick and Stephenson a $2 million bonus at No. 27. They also went over slot for several intriguing later-round selections, most notably third baseman Gabriel Rosa, lefthander Amir Garrett and outfielder Kyle Waldrop.

General Manager: Walt Jocketty. **Farm Director:** Bill Bavasi. **Scouting Director:** Chris Buckley.

Class	Team	League	W	L	Pct	Finish*	Manager(s)
Majors	Cincinnati Reds	National	79	83	.488	9th (16)	Dusty Baker
Triple-A	Louisville Bats	International	73	71	.507	8th (14)	Rick Sweet
Double-A	#Carolina Mudcats	Southern	53	86	.381	10th (10)	David Bell
High A	Bakersfield Blaze	California	66	74	.471	7th (10)	Ken Griffey
Low A	Dayton Dragons	Midwest	83	57	.593	1st (16)	Delino DeShields
Rookie	Billings Mustangs	Pioneer	44	32	.579	2nd (8)	Pat Kelly
Rookie	AZL Reds	Arizona	31	25	.554	4th (13)	Jose Nieves
Overall 2011 Minor League Record			350	345	.504	15th (30)	

*Finish in overall standings (No. of teams in league). †League champion.
#Double-A affiliate moves to Pensacola (Southern) in 2012.

LAST YEAR'S TOP 30

Player, Pos.		Status
1.	Aroldis Chapman, lhp	Majors
2.	Billy Hamilton, 2b/ss	No. 2
3.	Devin Mesoraco, c	No. 1
4.	Yonder Alonso, 1b/of	No. 3
5.	Yorman Rodriguez, of	No. 19
6.	Yasmani Grandal, c	No. 4
7.	Juan Francisco, 3b	Majors
8.	Zack Cozart, ss	No. 5
9.	Todd Frazier, of/3b/1b	No. 9
10.	Kyle Lotzkar, rhp	No. 30
11.	Ryan LaMarre, of	No. 14
12.	Drew Cisco, rhp	Dropped out
13.	Donnie Joseph, lhp	No. 27
14.	Chris Valaika, 2b/ss	No. 21
15.	Daniel Corcino, rhp	No. 6
16.	Ismael Guillon, lhp	Dropped out
17.	Junior Arias, ss	Dropped out
18.	Brad Boxberger, rhp	No. 10
19.	Didi Gregorius, ss	No. 8
20.	Dave Sappelt, of	No. 16
21.	Kyle Waldrop, of	No. 22
22.	Ronald Torreyes, inf	No. 13
23.	Henry Rodriguez, 2b	No. 17
24.	Neftali Soto, 1b	No. 11
25.	Sam LeCure, rhp	Majors
26.	Jonathan Correa, rhp	Dropped out
27.	Daryl Thompson, rhp	Dropped out
28.	Juan Duran, of	No. 28
29.	Philippe Valiquette, lhp	(Mariners)
30.	Felix Perez, of	Dropped out

BEST TOOLS

Best Hitter for Average	Yonder Alonso
Best Power Hitter	Neftali Soto
Best Strike-Zone Discipline	Yonder Alonso
Fastest Baserunner	Billy Hamilton
Best Athlete	Billy Hamilton
Best Fastball	Daniel Corcino
Best Curveball	J.C. Sulbaran
Best Slider	Tim Crabbe
Best Changeup	Daniel Renken
Best Control	Justice French
Best Defensive Catcher	Tucker Barnhart
Best Defensive Infielder	Didi Gregorius
Best Infield Arm	Didi Gregorius
Best Defensive Outfielder	Ryan LaMarre
Best Outfield Arm	Yorman Rodriguez

PROJECTED 2015 LINEUP

Catcher	Devin Mesoraco
First Base	Joey Votto
Second Base	Billy Hamilton
Third Base	Todd Frazier
Shortstop	Zack Cozart
Left Field	Yonder Alonso
Center Field	Drew Stubbs
Right Field	Jay Bruce
No. 1 Starter	Johnny Cueto
No. 2 Starter	Aroldis Chapman
No. 3 Starter	Homer Bailey
No. 4 Starter	Daniel Corcino
No. 5 Starter	Mike Leake
Closer	Brad Boxberger

TOP PROSPECTS OF THE DECADE

Year	Player, Pos.	2011 Org.
2002	Austin Kearns, of	Indians
2003	Chris Gruler, rhp	Out of baseball
2004	Ryan Wagner, rhp	Out of baseball
2005	Homer Bailey, rhp	Reds
2006	Homer Bailey, rhp	Reds
2007	Homer Bailey, rhp	Reds
2008	Jay Bruce, of	Reds
2009	Yonder Alonso, 1b	Reds
2010	Todd Frazier, 3b/of	Reds
2011	Aroldis Chapman, lhp	Reds

TOP DRAFT PICKS OF THE DECADE

Year	Player, Pos.	2011 Org.
2002	Chris Gruler, rhp	Out of baseball
2003	Ryan Wagner, rhp	Out of baseball
2004	Homer Bailey, rhp	Reds
2005	Jay Bruce, of	Reds
2006	Drew Stubbs, of	Reds
2007	Devin Mesoraco, c	Reds
2008	Yonder Alonso, 1b	Reds
2009	Mike Leake, rhp	Reds
2010	Yasmani Grandal, c	Reds
2011	Robert Stephenson, rhp	Reds

LARGEST BONUSES IN CLUB HISTORY

Aroldis Chapman, 2010	$16,250,000
Chris Gruler, 2002	$2,500,000
Yorman Rodriguez, 2008	$2,500,000
Homer Bailey, 2004	$2,300,000
Mike Leake, 2009	$2,270,000

CINCINNATI REDS

TOP 2012 ROOKIE: Yonder Alonso, of/1b. He has no obvious opening in the big league lineup, but the Reds need to find room for his bat.

BREAKOUT PROSPECT: Tony Cingrani, lhp. First college senior taken in 2011 draft could be a No. 3 starter if he refines his slider.

SLEEPER: Tim Crabbe, rhp. A 14th-round steal, he has a 92-94 mph fastball and a solid slider.

SOURCE OF TOP 30 TALENT

Homegrown	30	Acquired	0
College	11	Trades	0
Junior College	2	Rule 5 draft	0
High school	10	Independent leagues	0
Draft-and-follow	0	Free agents/waivers	0
Nondrafted free agents	0		
International	7		

LF
Dave Sappelt (16)
Juan Duran (28)
Cody Puckett
Josh Fellhauer

CF
Ryan LaMarre (14)
Denis Phipps
Bryson Smith

RF
Yorman Rodriguez (19)
Kyle Waldrop (22)
Jon Matthews
Steven Selsky

3B
Todd Frazier (9)
Gabriel Rosa (20)
Sean Buckley (24)
David Vidal (26)
Travis Mattair

SS
Billy Hamilton (2)
Zack Cozart (5)
Didi Gregorius (8)
Miguel Rojas
Devin Lohman
Juan Perez

2B
Ronald Torreyes (13)
Henry Rodriguez (17)
Chris Valaika (21)
Ryan Wright (23)
Ty Washington
Brodie Greene
Kris Negron

1B
Yonder Alonso (3)
Neftali Soto (11)
Donald Lutz
Robert Maddox

C
Devin Mesoraco (1)
Yasmani Grandal (4)
Tucker Barnhart (25)
Mark Fleury

LHP

LHSP	LHRP
Tony Cingrani (15)	Donnie Joseph (27)
Amir Garrett (18)	Chris Manno
Ismael Guillon	Jeremy Horst
Tanner Robles	Andrew Bowman
	Matt Fairel
	Blaine Howell

RHP

RHSP	RHRP
Daniel Corcino (6)	Brad Boxberger (10)
Robert Stephenson (7)	Nick Christiani
J.C. Sulbaran (12)	James Allen
Jonathan Perez (29)	Brooks Pinckard
Kyle Lotzkar (30)	Drew Hayes
Tim Crabbe	Pedro Villarreal
Kyle McMyne	Justin Freeman
Daniel Renken	Clayton Shunick
Drew Cisco	Chad Rogers
Josh Smith	Alejandro Chacin
Sal Romano	Erik Miller
Josh Ravin	Brian Pearl
Vaughn Covington	Daniel Wolford
Daniel Tuttle	Pat Doyle
Wes Mugarian	
Radhames Quezeda	
Cole Green	

2011

BEST PURE HITTER: 2B Ryan Wright (5) led the U.S. college national team with a .361 average in the summer of 2010 and hit .301/.351/.536 in his pro debut. He has a smooth stroke for a righthander.

BEST POWER HITTER: 3B Sean Buckley (6) has plus power and bashed 14 homers in 59 games at Rookie-level Billings. 3B Gabriel Rosa (2) doesn't have Buckley's present power, but he has the raw pop to catch up to him in time.

FASTEST RUNNER: The Reds' fastest signee won't get to use his plus-plus speed, because RHP Brooks Pinckard's (10) future is on the mound. OF Jon Matthews (8) and 2B Ty Washington (43) are above-average runners but not burners.

BEST DEFENSIVE PLAYER: Cincinnati will give Rosa the chance to make it at the hot corner, but his range and arm may fit best in right field. Wright has average tools, sure hands and keen instincts at second base, where he made just two errors in 41 pro games.

BEST FASTBALL: RHP Robert Stephenson (1) worked at 94-95 mph all spring and tops out at 97. The Reds love the upside of LHP Amir Garrett (22), who's 6-foot-6 and already reaches 95 mph despite little pitching experience or instruction. LHP Tony Cingrani (3) and RHPs Kyle McMyne (4) and Pinckard can deal in the mid-90s.

BEST SECONDARY PITCH: Stephenson's curveball or Cingrani's changeup.

BEST PRO DEBUT: Buckley was a Pioneer League all-star, while SS Juan Perez (26) earned similar honors in the Rookie-level Arizona League after hitting .316 with 15 steals. OF Bryson Smith (34) batted .368/.470/.611 between the two leagues.

BEST ATHLETE: Garrett has a St. John's basketball scholarship, though his hoops future is cloudy after he was academically ineligible in the fall. The Cubs drafted Pinckard as an outfielder in 2010. Among the position players, Matthews is the best athlete.

MOST INTRIGUING BACKGROUND: Buckley is the son of Reds scouting director Chris. 2B Taylor Wrenn's (27) dad Luke scouts for the Diamondbacks and signed Tino Martinez and Nomar Garciaparra. Unsigned C Jacob Stallings' (42) father Kevin is Vanderbilt's basketball coach. Unsigned OF Shon Carson (44) is a college running back at South Carolina. RHP Austin Robichaux (50) opted to attend Louisiana-Lafayette, where his dad Tony is the head coach.

CLOSEST TO THE MAJORS: Cingrani, who has two solid pitches and can make it as a starter if he improves his slider. RHP James Allen (7) has a 90-94

mph fastball and could progress rapidly as a reliever.

BEST LATE-ROUND PICK: Garrett, who signed a backloaded $1 million deal. Cincinnati also invested $450,000 in RHP Sal Romano (23), who has a promising fastball/curveball combo, and $350,000 in Washington.

THE ONE WHO GOT AWAY: LHP Travis Radke (45) has an 88-92 mph fastball and an advanced feel for pitching. He decided to attend Portland.

ASSESSMENT: The Reds were more aggressive than usual, paying over-slot bonuses to Stephenson, Rosa, Wright, Garrett, Romano and Washington. They got a nice balance of prep and college players, hitters and pitchers.

2010

C Yasmani Grandal (1) is one of the best catching prospects in the game, if only the second-best in the system. OFs Ryan LaMarre (2) and Kyle Waldrop (12) are athletes with upside.

GRADE: B

2009

RHP Mike Leake (1) went straight to the majors and has won 20 games in two seasons. SS Billy Hamilton (2), the fastest man in baseball, became the first minor leaguer in a decade to steal 100 bases. RHP Brad Boxberger (1s) is on the verge of joining the big league bullpen in 2012. Unsigned SS Deven Marrero (17) could be the No. 1 overall pick in the 2012 draft.

GRADE: B+

2008

OF/1B Yonder Alonso (1) has a big league-ready bat and just needs a place to play. RHP Zack Stewart (3) was the key to the Scott Rolen trade with the Blue Jays. OF Dave Sappelt (9) hit .309 in the minors to rush to Cincinnati.

GRADE: B

2007

C Devin Mesoraco (1), 3B/1B/OF Todd Frazier (1s) and SS Zack Cozart (2) all could be Reds regulars in the near future. RHP Jeremy Horst (21) beat the odds and contributed to the Cincinnati bullpen last season.

GRADE: B+

Draft analysis by Jim Callis. Numbers in parentheses indicate draft rounds.

1 DEVIN MESORACO, C

Born: June 19, 1988. **B-T:** R-R. **Ht.:** 6-1. **Wt.:** 220.
Drafted: HS—Punxsutawney, Pa., 2007 (1st round).
Signed by: Jeff Brookens.

BA GRADE
65
LOW

It's not often that a Pennsylvania prospect turns into a first-round pick. There have been just four in the last 10 years: Chris Lubanski (2003), Neil Walker (2004), Mesoraco (2007) and Jesse Biddle (2010). Mesoraco was difficult to scout, because he didn't catch much in high school or on the showcase circuit in 2006 because he was recovering from Tommy John surgery. The short Pennsylvania high school season didn't help either, but he was willing to take extra batting practice or go to workouts whenever teams asked. The Reds signed him for $1.4 million as the 15th overall pick, then watched him struggle with hand and finger injuries while batting .240/.311/.368 through his first three years as a pro. Over the last two seasons, Mesoraco has improved his conditioning and blossomed into one of the more productive catchers in the minors. He hit 26 homers in 2010 and ranked as the Triple-A International League's top position prospect in 2011. Called to Cincinnati in September, he hit his first two big league homers and started for much of the final three weeks.

Mesoraco is the rare catcher who has the potential to be an above-average hitter with above-average power. He has an uppercut swing with a lot of bat speed, plus the ability to turn on a pitch and park it over the fence. He does a better job of using the whole field then he did early in his career, but his power still comes almost solely to his pull side—not one of his homers in 2011 went to right field. Mesoraco has developed the ability to take a pitch on the outer half and line it up the middle, which allows him to hit for average. His selectiveness enables him to work counts to get pitches he can drive. Like most catchers, he has below-average speed. Behind the plate, Mesoraco is an average receiver. He had problems when he wore down at the end of 2010 and struggles occasionally with velocity. He led IL catchers with 10 errors. He's relatively agile and consistently displays average 2.0-second pop times on throws to second base. He threw out 28 percent of basestealers in 2011, down from 41 percent the year before. Mesoraco's biggest impediment has been a series of nagging injuries. Finger and hand injuries have dogged him, but he's not one to beg out of the lineup. The Reds are thrilled with his makeup.

Mesoraco is ready to take over as Cincinnati's everyday catcher and has no obstacles in his path. A potential all-star, Mesoraco will get time to lay claim to a starting job.

SCOUTING GRADES

Batting: 60. **Defense:** 50.
Power: 65. **Arm:** 50.
Speed: 30.

Based on 20-80 scouting scale, where 50 represents major league average, and future projection rather than present tools.

Year	Club (League)	Class	AVG	G	AB	R	H	2B	3B	HR	RBI	BB	SO	SB	CS	OBP	SLG
2007	Reds (GCL)	R	.219	40	137	16	30	4	0	1	8	15	26	2	0	.310	.270
2008	Dayton (MWL)	LoA	.261	83	306	29	80	13	1	9	42	20	64	2	3	.311	.399
2009	Sarasota (FSL)	HiA	.228	92	312	32	71	22	1	8	37	35	76	0	1	.311	.381
2010	Lynchburg (CAR)	HiA	.335	43	158	24	53	11	2	10	31	19	29	2	2	.414	.620
	Carolina (SL)	AA	.294	56	187	42	55	11	3	13	31	18	37	1	0	.363	.594
	Louisville (IL)	AAA	.231	14	52	5	12	3	0	3	13	6	14	0	1	.310	.462
2011	Louisville (IL)	AAA	.289	120	436	60	126	36	2	15	71	52	83	1	1	.371	.484
	Cincinnati (NL)	MAJ	.180	18	50	5	9	3	0	2	6	3	10	0	0	.226	.360
Major League Totals			.180	18	50	5	9	3	0	2	6	3	10	0	0	.226	.360
Minor League Totals			.269	448	1588	208	427	100	9	59	233	165	329	8	8	.344	.455

2 BILLY HAMILTON, SS

Born: Sept. 9, 1990. **B-T:** B-R. **Ht.:** 6-1. **Wt.:** 159. **Drafted:** HS—Taylorsville, Miss., 2009 (2nd round). **Signed by:** Tyler Jennings.

BA GRADE

65
HIGH

Hamilton became the first minor leaguer in a decade to top 100 steals, when he stole 103 bases in 2011. The former Mississippi State wide receiver recruit recovered from hitting .195 through late May to bat .316 afterward, and he moved to shortstop after playing second base in 2010. Hamilton's speed is one of the easiest 80 grades a scout will ever hand out. He regularly outruns pitchouts, slide steps and pickoff throws. He still has plenty of work to do on the rest of his game, however. He's a raw hitter with little power, and he needs to improve his bunting and plate discipline. At the Reds' insistence, he has stuck with switch-hitting and ended up hitting better as a lefty (.721 OPS) than from his natural right side (.648 OPS) in 2011. Hamilton shows excellent range at shortstop, but his hands aren't soft and he lacks the arm strength to make plays deep in the hole. His low arm slot makes many of his throws tail, costing him accuracy. Some scouts believe he'll eventually move to second or center field. Hamilton is an off-the-charts athlete who made significant improvements in the second half of 2011. He'll move up to high Class A Bakersfield and will need at least a couple of more years to develop before he's ready to unleash his speed on the majors.

Year	Club (League)	Class	AVG	G	AB	R	H	2B	3B	HR	RBI	BB	SO	SB	CS	OBP	SLG
2009	Reds (GCL)	R	.205	43	166	19	34	6	3	0	11	11	47	14	3	.253	.277
2010	Billings (PIO)	R	.318	69	283	61	90	13	10	2	24	28	56	48	9	.383	.456
2011	Dayton (MWL)	LoA	.278	135	550	99	153	18	9	3	50	52	133	103	20	.340	.360
Minor League Totals			.277	247	999	179	277	37	22	5	85	91	236	165	32	.338	.373

3 YONDER ALONSO, OF/1B

Born: April 8, 1987. **B-T:** L-R. **Ht.:** 6-2. **Wt.:** 240. **Drafted:** Miami, 2008 (1st round). **Signed by:** Tony Arias.

BA GRADE

60
LOW

An emigree from Cuba, where his father Luis played for the Havana Industriales, Alonso established himself as one of college baseball's best hitters while at Miami. The seventh overall pick in the 2008 draft, he received the most lucrative draft deal in franchise history, a $4.55 million big league contract that included a $2 million bonus. His climb to the majors was slower than the Reds expected, but that's largely because he's blocked by 2010 National League MVP Joey Votto. Alonso is an above-average hitter with a good sense of the strike zone and the ability to hit to all fields. Cincinnati always has believed that he has plus power, which he showed in his limited big league trial in the second half of 2011. While hitting comes easy for Alonso, defense has been an issue. He's adequate at first base, which is really his only viable option. He has some arm strength, but his well below-average speed doesn't play well in left field and he lacks the agility for third base. After hitting .330/.398/.545 in 88 big league at-bats, Alonso is ready for regular playing time with the Reds. They need to find a spot for him to play, either via a trade or by enduring his defensive deficiencies in left field.

Year	Club (League)	Class	AVG	G	AB	R	H	2B	3B	HR	RBI	BB	SO	SB	CS	OBP	SLG
2008	Sarasota (FSL)	HiA	.316	6	19	1	6	1	0	0	2	5	5	0	0	.440	.368
2009	Reds (GCL)	R	.133	6	15	0	2	0	0	0	0	3	1	0	0	.278	.133
	Sarasota (FSL)	HiA	.303	49	175	21	53	13	0	7	38	24	30	0	1	.383	.497
	Carolina (SL)	AA	.295	29	105	12	31	11	0	2	14	14	15	1	0	.372	.457
2010	Carolina (SL)	AA	.267	31	101	19	27	5	0	3	13	19	16	4	2	.388	.406
	Louisville (IL)	AAA	.296	101	406	50	120	31	2	12	56	37	76	9	1	.355	.470
	Cincinnati (NL)	MAJ	.207	22	29	2	6	2	0	0	3	0	10	0	0	.207	.276
2011	Louisville (IL)	AAA	.296	91	358	46	106	24	4	12	56	46	60	6	5	.374	.486
	Cincinnati (NL)	MAJ	.330	47	88	9	29	4	0	5	15	10	21	0	0	.398	.545
Major League Totals			.299	69	117	11	35	6	0	5	18	10	31	0	0	.354	.479
Minor League Totals			.293	313	1179	149	345	85	6	36	179	148	203	20	9	.370	.466

4 YASMANI GRANDAL, C

Born: Nov. 8, 1988. **B-T:** B-R. **Ht.:** 6-2. **Wt.:** 205. **Drafted:** Miami, 2010 (1st round). **Signed by:** Miguel Machado.

Heading into 2007, Grandal was rated the nation's top high school catching prospect, though Devin Mesoraco moved ahead of him on most draft boards. Signed to a $3.2 million major league contract as the 12th overall pick in 2010, he zoomed to Triple-A in his first full pro season. There are a lot of similarities between Grandal and Mesoraco. Both project as catchers who will provide above-average offense and solid defense. Mesoraco is a better athlete and has a tick more power, but Grandal projects to hit for a higher average and has the advantage of being a switch-hitter. He has a balanced approach, controls the strike zone and uses the entire field. Though Grandal racked up 19 passed balls in 90 games in 2011, the Reds still think he'll be an average receiver. He has an average arm and threw out 34 percent of basestealers. He has well below-average speed. Grandal still has work to do on his receiving and could use a full year in Triple-A. By then Mesoraco may be entrenched in Cincinnati, and backup Ryan Hanigan is signed through 2013, which may lead to a trade.

BA GRADE
60
MEDIUM

Year	Club (League)	Class	AVG	G	AB	R	H	2B	3B	HR	RBI	BB	SO	SB	CS	OBP	SLG
2010	Reds (AZL)	R	.286	8	28	4	8	1	0	0	1	4	4	0	1	.394	.321
2011	Bakersfield (CAL)	HiA	.296	56	206	47	61	14	0	10	40	41	57	0	0	.410	.510
	Carolina (SL)	AA	.301	45	156	20	47	15	0	4	26	13	39	0	1	.360	.474
	Louisville (IL)	AAA	.500	4	12	2	6	2	0	0	2	5	1	0	0	.667	.667
Minor League Totals			.303	113	402	73	122	32	0	14	69	63	101	0	2	.401	.488

5 ZACK COZART, SS

Born: Aug. 12, 1985. **B-T:** R-R. **Ht.:** 6-0. **Wt.:** 195. **Drafted:** Mississippi, 2007 (2nd round). **Signed by:** Jerry Flowers.

When the Reds made Cozart a second-round pick in 2007, many scouts thought his pull-heavy approach wouldn't translate to wood bats. The Reds always believed he had potential at the plate, and he put up the best offensive numbers of his career at Triple-A in 2011, then hit well in two weeks in Cincinnati before injuring his left elbow while applying a tag. He had Tommy John surgery but should be ready for spring training because it was his non-throwing elbow. Cozart has solid tools across the board. He's an average hitter with average power who sprays line drives all over the field, and he could fit in the No. 2 spot in the lineup if he drew more walks. He has average speed with the instincts to pick his spots to steal bases. Cozart doesn't have a cannon for an arm, but it's strong enough to make all the plays at shortstop. He also has soft hands and a tick above-average range. Scouts differ on whether he's a first-division regular, but he should get the job done defensively while producing more-than-adequate offense for his position.

BA GRADE
50
SAFE

Year	Club (League)	Class	AVG	G	AB	R	H	2B	3B	HR	RBI	BB	SO	SB	CS	OBP	SLG
2007	Dayton (MWL)	LoA	.239	53	184	28	44	7	2	2	18	11	36	3	1	.288	.332
2008	Dayton (MWL)	LoA	.280	109	418	57	117	20	6	14	49	24	77	3	3	.330	.457
2009	Carolina (SL)	AA	.262	131	462	72	121	29	2	10	59	63	87	10	2	.360	.398
2010	Louisville (IL)	AAA	.255	136	553	91	141	30	4	17	67	40	107	30	4	.310	.416
2011	Louisville (IL)	AAA	.310	77	323	57	100	26	2	7	32	23	51	9	2	.357	.467
	Cincinnati (NL)	MAJ	.324	11	37	6	12	0	0	2	3	0	6	0	0	.324	.486
Major League Totals			.324	11	37	6	12	0	0	2	3	0	6	0	0	.324	.486
Minor League Totals			.270	506	1940	305	523	112	16	50	225	161	358	55	12	.332	.421

6 DANIEL CORCINO, RHP

Born: Aug. 26, 1990 **B-T:** R-R. **Ht.:** 5-11. **Wt.:** 203. **Signed:** Dominican Republic, 2008. **Signed by:** Richard Jimenez.

The Reds announced they were making a big push into the international market in 2008 by signing Yorman Rodriguez and Juan Duran to $4.5 million in bonuses. But it's Corcino who has proven to be the best Latin American they signed that year, a steal at $25,000. Corcino elicits frequent comparisons to Johnny Cueto for his stature, appearance, delivery and stuff. With a 92-94 mph fastball that touches 96, he throws harder than Cueto did at the same point in his career. Corcino doesn't generate much downward plane with his fastball, because he lacks height and throws from a three-quarters arm slot. He has tightened his slider, making it an average pitch, and his 84-85 mph changeup is just as effective. He has a very quick arm and throws strikes, but his delivery involves some effort as he spins off the mound after bringing his arm across his body. Some scouts believe Corcino's stuff and feel for pitching will allow him to become a No. 3 starter,

BA GRADE
55
MEDIUM

while others point to his small stature and delivery and envision him as a back-of-the-rotation option or set-up man. Cueto has become a frontline starter, though he has a better slider. Corcino will make the jump to high Class A in 2012.

Year	Club (League)	Class	W	L	ERA	G	GS	CG	SV	IP	H	HR	BB	SO	K/9	WHIP	AVG
2008	Reds (DSL)	R	6	2	5.29	23	0	0	0	34	37	2	14	26	6.9	1.50	.280
2009	Reds (GCL)	R	0	1	0.00	2	0	0	0	3	5	0	1	2	6.8	2.25	.455
	Billings (PIO)	R	1	4	4.91	20	0	0	3	26	23	2	15	30	10.5	1.48	.245
2010	Billings (PIO)	R	1	3	3.40	9	9	0	0	40	38	2	17	31	7.0	1.39	.245
	Dayton (MWL)	LoA	1	1	4.31	6	6	0	0	31	31	1	15	29	8.3	1.47	.254
2011	Dayton (MWL)	LoA	11	7	3.42	26	26	1	0	139	128	10	34	156	10.1	1.16	.238
Minor League Totals			20	18	3.86	86	41	1	3	273	262	17	96	274	9.0	1.31	.250

7 ROBERT STEPHENSON, RHP

Born: Feb. 24, 1993. **B-T:** R-R. **Ht.:** 6-2. **Wt.:** 182. **Drafted:** HS—Martinez, Calif., 2011 (1st round). **Signed by:** Rich Bordi.

BA GRADE 60 HIGH

It didn't take long for Stephenson to make his pitch for a spot in the first round of the 2011 draft. He threw back-to-back no-hitters in his first two starts, striking out 20 in the second game. After the Reds selected him 27th overall, the Washington recruit waited until the Aug. 15 signing deadline before agreeing to a $2 million bonus. Thanks to his California pedigree, Stephenson is relatively polished for a high school righthander. His fastball made him a first-round pick, as he sits at 92-95 mph and touches 97 mph. His clean delivery allows him to command his fastball and maintain his velocity. He shows the ability to spin a curveball and an understanding of how to throw a changeup, but neither is a consistently effective pitch yet. He also threw a splitter in high school, but Cincinnati has taken it away because of concerns it could lead to elbow problems. Because he's advanced for his age, Stephenson has a chance to make his pro debut at low Class A Dayton. If he starts the year in extended spring training and reports to Rookie-level Billings in June, he'd still be on a normal pace for a high school draftee. He has the upside of a frontline starter but will need time to develop.

Year	Club (League)	Class	W	L	ERA	G	GS	CG	SV	IP	H	HR	BB	SO	K/9	WHIP	AVG
2011	Did Not Play—Signed Late																

8 DIDI GREGORIUS, SS

Born: Feb. 18, 1990. **B-T:** L-R. **Ht.:** 6-1. **Wt.:** 175. **Signed:** Curacao, 2007. **Signed by:** Jim Stoeckel.

BA GRADE 55 HIGH

Signed for $50,000 out of Curacao in 2007, Gregorius looks like quite a bargain. He reached Double-A in 2011, then started at shortstop for the Dutch national team that won the World Cup in Panama. His father Didi and brother Johnny played professionally in Holland and Curacao. Gregorius is a quality athlete whose best attribute is his arm, which rates a 65 on the 20-80 scouting scale thanks to its strength and accuracy. He's a plus defender with good range and a quick first step. His hands are his biggest drawback defensively and contributed to his 21 errors in 80 games in 2011. Being a lefthanded-hitting shortstop is another positive in Gregorius' favor, though he has struggled against lefties throughout his career. His combination of solid bat control, good pitch recognition and plus speed lead some scouts to project him as an above-average hitter. He has well below-average power, however, rarely walks and has yet to show a knack for stealing bases. Because of his solid makeup, the Reds have been comfortable with aggressively promoting Gregorius. He could begin 2011 in Triple-A at age 22, though it's more likely he'll start off at Cincinnati's new Double-A Pensacola affiliate. He has a higher ceiling but more risk than Zack Cozart, whom he'll eventually battle for a big league job.

Year	Club (League)	Class	AVG	G	AB	R	H	2B	3B	HR	RBI	BB	SO	SB	CS	OBP	SLG
2008	Reds (GCL)	R	.155	31	97	6	15	0	0	0	9	10	10	2	1	.241	.155
2009	Sarasota (FSL)	HiA	.254	22	71	8	18	4	0	0	2	1	9	0	0	.274	.310
	Billings (PIO)	R	.314	50	204	28	64	10	1	1	16	12	27	8	6	.363	.387
2010	Dayton (MWL)	LoA	.273	120	501	65	137	16	11	5	41	33	62	16	7	.327	.379
	Lynchburg (CAR)	HiA	.240	7	25	4	6	0	0	0	0	2	6	0	0	.321	.240
2011	Bakersfield (CAL)	HiA	.303	46	188	30	57	12	1	5	28	10	25	8	8	.333	.457
	Carolina (SL)	AA	.270	38	148	18	40	6	3	2	16	9	25	3	2	.312	.392
Minor League Totals			.273	314	1234	159	337	48	16	13	112	77	164	37	24	.322	.370

9 TODD FRAZIER, 3B/1B/OF

Born: Feb. 12, 1986. **B-T:** R-R. **Ht.:** 6-3. **Wt.:** 220. **Drafted:** Rutgers, 2007 (1st round supplemental). **Signed by:** Lee Seras.

The star of the 1998 Little League World Series championship team from Toms River, N.J., Frazier followed his brothers Charles and Jeff into pro ball. Signed for $875,000 as the 34th overall pick in 2007, he has spent most of the past two seasons in Triple-A because of the presence of Scott Rolen in Cincinnati. Frazier's best position is third base, but the Reds have tried him all over the infield and outfield in an attempt to find a spot for his bat. Frazier's most attractive tool is his plus power to all fields. He may never hit for a high average, though, because he has a pronounced arm bar in his swing and is too aggressive at the plate. He has a tick below-average speed but runs the bases well. While Frazier's feel for the game means he can play almost anywhere on the field—he played five different positions in 41 big league games—he profiles best at third base. His actions fit better at the hot corner than in the middle infield, and he has an average, accurate arm. After logging nearly 2,000 minor league at-bats, he's more than ready for the majors. With Rolen still under contract, Frazier still doesn't have a clear shot at a starting job, so for now he'll be a corner utilityman.

BA GRADE

50

LOW

Year	Club (League)	Class	AVG	G	AB	R	H	2B	3B	HR	RBI	BB	SO	SB	CS	OBP	SLG
2007	Billings (PIO)	R	.319	41	160	29	51	6	5	5	25	18	22	3	3	.409	.513
	Dayton (MWL)	LoA	.318	6	22	4	7	3	0	2	5	2	4	0	0	.375	.727
2008	Dayton (MWL)	LoA	.321	30	112	25	36	10	0	7	20	15	28	4	2	.402	.598
	Sarasota (FSL)	HiA	.281	100	366	62	103	20	3	12	54	41	84	8	4	.357	.451
2009	Carolina (SL)	AA	.290	119	451	59	131	40	2	14	68	42	67	7	8	.350	.481
	Louisville (IL)	AAA	.302	16	63	9	19	5	0	2	9	6	12	2	0	.362	.476
2010	Louisville (IL)	AAA	.258	130	480	71	124	32	4	17	66	45	127	14	4	.333	.448
2011	Louisville (IL)	AAA	.260	90	315	47	82	18	1	15	46	34	82	17	4	.340	.467
	Cincinnati (NL)	MAJ	.232	41	112	17	26	5	0	6	15	7	27	1	0	.289	.438
Major League Totals			.232	41	112	17	26	5	0	6	15	7	27	1	0	.289	.438
Minor League Totals			.281	532	1969	306	553	134	15	74	293	203	426	55	25	.354	.477

10 BRAD BOXBERGER, RHP

Born: May 27, 1988. **B-T:** R-R. **Ht.:** 6-2. **Wt.:** 200. **Drafted:** Southern California, 2009 (1st round supplemental). **Signed by:** Rex de la Nuez.

Rod Boxberger was the College World Series MVP and a first-round pick in 1978, and his son nearly matched his draft status 21 years later. Signed for $857,000 as the 43rd overall pick in 2009, Brad fell apart after a midseason promotion and move to the bullpen in 2010. Once he stopped overthrowing in an attempt to rush to the big leagues, he progressed to Triple-A in 2011. Boxberger has learned that when he throws with less effort, his stuff is crisper and he can find the strike zone more consistently. It also helps him maintain his release point, which he lost in 2010. Boxberger's success depends mostly on a 92-95 mph fastball that has sharp cutting action. His average slider is effective when he throws it for strikes. He also throws a fringy changeup but doesn't need it much in his relief role. He also threw a spike curveball when he was a starter but he has junked it since moving to the bullpen. Boxberger's control deserted him in Triple-A and has been an issue during his two years in pro ball. If he can throw strikes like he did in the Arizona Fall League, he has a good chance to earn a big league bullpen job in spring training. He profiles as a set-up man who could close in the right situation.

BA GRADE

50

MEDIUM

NIKOLAUS JOHNSON

Year	Club (League)	Class	W	L	ERA	G	GS	CG	SV	IP	H	HR	BB	SO	K/9	WHIP	AVG
2010	Lynchburg (CAR)	HiA	4	6	3.19	14	13	0	0	62	57	3	20	70	10.2	1.24	.249
	Carolina (SL)	AA	1	4	8.49	22	0	0	0	30	35	4	22	40	12.1	1.92	.289
2011	Carolina (SL)	AA	1	2	1.31	30	0	0	4	34	16	2	13	57	14.9	0.84	.139
	Louisville (IL)	AAA	1	2	2.93	25	0	0	7	28	16	2	15	36	11.7	1.12	.167
Minor League Totals			7	14	3.75	91	13	0	11	154	124	11	70	203	11.9	1.26	.221

11 NEFTALI SOTO, 1B

BA GRADE

50

MEDIUM

Born: Feb. 28, 1989. **B-T:** R-R. **Ht.:** 6-2. **Wt.:** 200. **Drafted:** HS—Manati, P.R., 2007 (3rd round). **Signed by:** Tony Arias.

When the Reds drafted Soto in the third round in 2007, he was considered a polished hitter who might not be able to stick at shortstop. Five seasons later, Soto has bounced from shortstop to third base to catcher and finally to first base. His bat has risen to the occasion, as he tied Paul Goldschmidt for the Double-A Southern League lead with 30 homers in 2011 despite missing a month with a broken bone in his left wrist. His plus power started translating into production once he became less pull-happy. He hit 11 homers in 2009, with nine to left field and none to right. Last year, 10 of his 31 blasts were opposite-field shots. Soto's approach is still undisciplined, as he rarely takes ball four, and some scouts question his ability to handle quality inside fastballs. His value lies mainly in his bat, as he's a well below-average runner and an average-at-best defender. He has a strong arm, though it doesn't get much use at first base. With Joey Votto and Yonder Alonso ahead of him, Soto looks like trade bait. Added to the 40-man roster in November, he's ready for Triple-A.

Year	Club (League)	Class	AVG	G	AB	R	H	2B	3B	HR	RBI	BB	SO	SB	CS	OBP	SLG
2007	Reds (GCL)	R	.303	40	152	18	46	7	5	2	28	11	31	2	0	.355	.454
2008	Billings (PIO)	R	.388	15	67	12	26	10	1	4	11	4	10	1	0	.423	.746
	Dayton (MWL)	LoA	.326	52	218	26	71	15	1	7	36	7	36	1	1	.343	.500
2009	Sarasota (FSL)	HiA	.248	131	505	53	125	21	2	11	57	23	95	1	3	.282	.362
2010	Lynchburg (CAR)	HiA	.268	134	522	73	140	33	2	21	73	32	105	0	0	.319	.460
2011	Carolina (SL)	AA	.272	102	379	70	103	19	3	30	76	25	96	0	1	.329	.575
	Louisville (IL)	AAA	.412	4	17	1	7	0	0	1	4	1	2	0	0	.444	.588
Minor League Totals			.278	478	1860	253	518	105	14	76	285	103	375	5	5	.322	.473

12 J.C. SULBARAN, RHP

BA GRADE
50
HIGH

Born: Nov. 9, 1989. **B-T:** R-R. **Ht.:** 6-1. **Wt.:** 219. **Drafted:** HS—Plantation, Fla., 2008 (30th round). **Signed by:** Tony Arias.

Ever since the Reds' gave him $500,000 as a 30th-rounder in 2008, Sulbaran has shown some of the better stuff in the system but not the performance to match. Maturity issues have been his biggest obstacle, and blister problems also haven't helped. In 2011, he finally took some steps forward, posting career bests in ERA (4.60) and strikeouts per nine innings (10.2) in the high Class A California League, a notorious hitter's haven. Cincinnati managed to get Sulbaran better directed toward home plate in his delivery last year. He still throws across his body but not nearly as much as in the past, and his improved mechanics gave him increased ability to locate pitches to his arm side. After sitting at 89-92 mph with his fastball in previous years, Sulbaran rang up a lot of 93s and 94s and touched 95 in 2011. His fastball has late sink, which makes it more effective. He's still working on his secondary pitches, an erratic curveball that's a plus offering at times and a fringy changeup that gives him a chance against lefthanders. Sulbaran has the stuff to be a No. 3 starter if he can continue to improve his command and mound presence. He'll work on that in Double-A this year.

Year	Club (League)	Class	W	L	ERA	G	GS	CG	SV	IP	H	HR	BB	SO	K/9	WHIP	AVG
2009	Dayton (MWL)	LoA	5	5	5.24	21	21	0	0	93	94	19	51	100	9.7	1.56	.265
2010	Dayton (MWL)	LoA	4	6	4.99	16	15	0	0	79	78	6	49	83	9.4	1.60	.252
2011	Bakersfield (CAL)	HiA	9	6	4.60	26	26	0	0	137	140	10	50	155	10.2	1.39	.264
Minor League Totals			18	17	4.89	63	62	0	0	309	312	35	150	338	9.8	1.50	.261

13 RONALD TORREYES, 2B

BA GRADE
50
HIGH

Born: Sept. 2, 1992. **B-T:** R-R. **Ht.:** 5-7. **Wt.:** 139. **Signed:** Venezuela, 2010. **Signed by:** Jose Fuentes.

For a man who stands 5-foot-7, Torreyes casts a very long shadow. Even before he played a game in the United States, he was a constant topic among Reds officials who had seen him in the Rookie-level Venezuelan Summer League and couldn't wait to tell others what they had witnessed. He lived up to his advanced billing by batting .356 as an 18-year-old in low Class A last year. Torreyes has a knack for centering the ball on the sweet spot in at-bat after at-bat, and his advanced approach belies his youth. While he's an above-average hitter, his small stature leaves him with just 35 power on the 20-80 scouting scale. He makes contact so easily that he draws few walks and he has no better than average speed, so he may not contribute much offensively beyond his high batting average. Torreyes has average range at second base and projects as a slightly above-average defender because he has soft hands and positions himself well. He doesn't really have the arm to play shortstop, though some scouts think he could handle the position as a utilityman. Torreyes will continue to have to prove himself at every stop because of his physical limitations. As the owner of .364 career batting average, he should salivate at the chance to hit in the California League in 2012.

Year	Club (League)	Class	AVG	G	AB	R	H	2B	3B	HR	RBI	BB	SO	SB	CS	OBP	SLG
2010	Reds (VSL)	R	.390	67	241	56	94	20	10	4	33	23	11	23	15	.468	.606
	Reds (AZL)	R	.349	18	83	13	29	7	1	1	11	1	5	2	2	.379	.494
	Dayton (MWL)	LoA	.240	6	25	3	6	2	1	0	2	0	3	0	0	.240	.400
2011	Dayton (MWL)	LoA	.356	67	278	53	99	9	5	3	41	14	19	12	7	.398	.457
Minor League Totals			.364	158	627	125	228	38	17	8	87	38	38	37	24	.419	.517

14 RYAN LaMARRE, OF

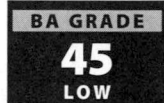

BA GRADE
50
HIGH

Born: Nov. 21, 1988. **B-T:** R-L. **Ht.:** 6-2. **Wt.:** 209. **Drafted:** Michigan, 2010 (2nd round). **Signed by:** Brad Meador.

In any other season, LaMarre's 55 stolen bases would have stood out among Reds farmhands. No one in the system had swiped that many since 1994, but he took a back seat to Billy Hamilton, who led the minors with 103. LaMarre might have been even more prolific if not for a series of minor hamstring injuries. An outstanding athlete, he was the leading tackler on consecutive state-championship football teams in high school and was also a hockey star. He has well above-average speed and shows a feel for getting leads and reading pitchers. LaMarre had a quick bat and shows solid raw power in batting practice, but it hasn't come through in games. Instead he uses a top-of-the-order approach with good selectivity and an all-fields mentality. He also has a knack for laying down bunts. In the field, LaMarre is average defensively in center field with an arm that's strong enough to let him handle right field as well. He got a taste of Double-A at the end of the season, and will head to Pensacola to begin 2012. His bat will determine whether he ends up as a regular or a useful fourth outfielder.

Year	Club (League)	Class	AVG	G	AB	R	H	2B	3B	HR	RBI	BB	SO	SB	CS	OBP	SLG
2010	Dayton (MWL)	LoA	.282	60	227	44	64	11	0	5	29	21	53	18	7	.370	.396
	Lynchburg (CAR)	HiA	.222	8	27	2	6	2	0	1	3	2	4	1	1	.276	.407
2011	Bakersfield (CAL)	HiA	.279	117	445	78	124	17	3	6	47	42	97	52	14	.347	.371
	Carolina (SL)	AA	.267	5	15	3	4	1	0	0	0	3	3	3	0	.421	.333
Minor League Totals			.277	190	714	127	198	31	3	12	79	68	157	74	22	.354	.380

15 TONY CINGRANI, LHP

BA GRADE
50
HIGH

Born: July 5, 1989. **B-T:** L-L. **Ht.:** 6-5. **Wt.:** 205. **Drafted:** Rice, 2011 (3rd round). **Signed by:** Jerry Flowers.

After breaking former big leaguer Tim Byrdak's single-season and career strikeout records at South Suburban (Ill.) JC, Cingrani transferred to Rice and posted an 8.58 ERA in six starts as a junior. He cleaned up his delivery last spring and became a dominant reliever. After the Reds made him the first college senior drafted in 2011 (third round) and signed him for $210,000, they moved him back to the rotation with much better results. He fell 10 innings shy of qualifying for official leadership, but he topped all Rookie-level Pioneer League pitchers with at least 50 innings in ERA (1.75), strikeouts per nine innings (14.0), K-BB ratio (13.3), opponent average (.190) and WHIP (0.80). Cingrani uses his height to get great extension on the mound, making his 92-95 mph fastball look even faster. He also has a solid changeup with late fade that he's willing to throw in any count. He's trying to refine a slider but it's still a fringy pitch at best. Cingrani will need a better breaking ball to stick as a starter as he climbs the ladder, though he already profiles nicely as a late-inning reliever. His delivery has a lot of moving parts that add deception. Because he's already 22, Cingrani may begin his first full pro season in high Class A.

Year	Club (League)	Class	W	L	ERA	G	GS	CG	SV	IP	H	HR	BB	SO	K/9	WHIP	AVG
2011	Billings (PIO)	R	3	2	1.75	13	13	0	0	51	35	1	6	80	14.0	0.80	.190
Minor League Totals			3	2	1.75	13	13	0	0	51	35	1	6	80	14.0	0.80	.190

16 DAVE SAPPELT, OF

BA GRADE
45
LOW

Born: Jan. 2, 1987. **B-T:** R-R. **Ht.:** 5-9. **Wt.:** 195. **Drafted:** Coastal Carolina, 2008 (9th round). **Signed by:** Steve Kring.

Wherever Sappelt has played, he's hit. Whether at Coastal Carolina (where he was nicknamed "Gary Coleman" because of his small stature) or in the minors, he continually has squared up the ball. He won the Southern League batting title with a .361 average in 2010, and he hit better than .300 for all but three days in 2011 before the Reds called him up in August. He struggled for the first time after reaching the big leagues, where pitchers used his aggressiveness against him. There aren't many long-term concerns about Sappelt's bat, however. He can turn on almost any fastball and just needs to prove he also can handle offspeed stuff when pitchers work him away. He doesn't have more than gap power and though he's a slightly above-average runner, he's not much of a basestealer. His speed doesn't fully translate on defense either, because he doesn't read balls well off the bat. He's a below-average defender with a substandard arm in center field, the only position at which he could make it as a regular. Unless he can improve his routes, he faces a future as a fourth outfielder. Cincinnati will give him a chance to make the club as a reserve in spring training, but he also could head back to Triple-A to work on his defense.

Year	Club (League)	Class	AVG	G	AB	R	H	2B	3B	HR	RBI	BB	SO	SB	CS	OBP	SLG
2008	Billings (PIO)	R	.299	62	254	47	76	19	5	7	35	21	45	6	3	.354	.496
2009	Dayton (MWL)	LoA	.269	74	301	44	81	14	7	3	25	23	46	26	11	.322	.392
	Sarasota (FSL)	HiA	.295	62	251	27	74	10	3	4	21	13	29	21	11	.333	.406
2010	Lynchburg (CAR)	HiA	.282	19	71	7	20	5	0	0	4	5	15	6	4	.338	.352
	Carolina (SL)	AA	.361	89	330	53	119	19	8	9	62	31	46	15	13	.416	.548

	Louisville (IL)	AAA	.324	25	108	12	35	8	3	1	8	6	13	4	1	.365	.481
2011	Louisville (IL)	AAA	.313	74	297	40	93	16	3	7	29	30	39	4	4	.377	.458
	Cincinnati (NL)	MAJ	.243	38	107	14	26	8	0	0	5	7	17	1	1	.289	.318
Major League Totals			.243	38	107	14	26	8	0	0	5	7	17	1	1	.289	.318
Minor League Totals			.309	405	1612	230	498	91	29	31	184	129	233	82	47	.362	.459

17 HENRY RODRIGUEZ, 2B

BA GRADE
45
MEDIUM

Born: Feb. 9, 1990. **B-T:** B-R. **Ht.:** 5-10. **Wt.:** 150. **Signed:** Venezuela, 2007. **Signed by:** Tony Arias.

In a system filled with second baseman who can hit, Rodriguez's bat pales only in comparison to Ronald Torreyes' among that group. A switch-hitter who's equally comfortable from either side of the plate, Rodriguez has hit .300 or better in each of the past four seasons to earn a spot on Cincinnati's 40-man roster. He has a repeatable swing from both sides with significantly more power from the right side. His pop goes mainly to the gaps rather than over the fence, and he's at his best when he focuses on using the whole field. He's a slightly above-average runner who steals bases because he knows when to pick his spots. If Rodriguez is going to be a big leaguer, he still has work to do defensively. He doesn't always read balls off the bat properly, leading to late jumps, and struggles with the pivot on double plays. Rodriguez's has enough arm for second base and can hold his own at third base. He also has played shortstop on occasion and could end up as a utilityman if he can improve his defense. He's ready for Triple-A but may end up at Pensacola if Chris Valaika starts 2012 in Louisville.

Year	Club (League)	Class	AVG	G	AB	R	H	2B	3B	HR	RBI	BB	SO	SB	CS	OBP	SLG
2007	Devil Rays/Reds (VSL)	R	.267	54	206	30	55	14	5	3	25	28	29	4	2	.361	.427
	Reds (DSL)	R	.235	7	17	3	4	0	0	0	4	1	1	1	0	.263	.235
2008	Reds (DSL)	R	.240	13	50	5	12	1	0	0	3	7	9	5	1	.328	.260
	D'backs/Reds (DSL)	R	.337	46	181	25	61	8	3	1	18	20	14	16	6	.405	.431
2009	Reds (GCL)	R	.322	42	152	24	49	10	1	1	19	7	18	9	0	.354	.421
2010	Dayton (MWL)	LoA	.307	124	514	76	158	37	3	14	78	22	70	33	13	.337	.473
	Lynchburg (CAR)	HiA	.250	6	24	2	6	0	0	0	4	0	4	0	0	.250	.250
2011	Bakersfield (CAL)	HiA	.340	58	238	37	81	17	0	8	44	14	35	12	7	.378	.513
	Carolina (SL)	AA	.302	69	278	39	84	19	1	5	37	25	43	18	3	.367	.432
Minor League Totals			.307	419	1660	241	510	106	13	32	232	124	223	98	32	.358	.445

18 AMIR GARRETT, LHP

BA GRADE
55
EXTREME

Born: May 3, 1992. **B-T:** L-L. **Ht.:** 6-6. **Wt.:** 190. **Drafted:** HS—Henderson, Nev., 2011 (22nd round). **Signed by:** Clark Crist.

The Reds prefer to stick close to MLB's slot recommendations in the first round, but they're not afraid to get creative later in the draft to add high-ceiling talents. Garrett is their latest high-risk, high-reward signing. Though he has little track record in baseball and will play basketball at St. John's, Cincinnati drafted him in the 22nd round last June and gave him a $1 million bonus. To protect themselves, the Reds took advantage of MLB provisions for two-sport athletes and spread the bonus over five years. Garrett appeared briefly on the high school showcase circuit in 2010 but didn't have a senior season because Henderson (Nev.) International School doesn't field a baseball team. He built up arm strength via a long-toss program and threw in workouts for scouts, creating buzz in May when he displayed a consistent 90-94 mph fastball. Garrett's delivery is extremely raw, which means he can follow a 95-mph fastball with an 86-mph heater. His secondary pitches are more an idea than anything he can use consistently, though he shows flashes of promise with his breaking ball. Cincinnati will have to wait until the end of his school year at St. John's before he returns to baseball next summer, but they're willing to be patient with a tall, athletic lefthander with a strong arm.

Year	Club (League)	Class	W	L	ERA	G	GS	CG	SV	IP	H	HR	BB	SO	K/9	WHIP	AVG
2011	Did Not Play—Signed Late																

19 YORMAN RODRIGUEZ, OF

BA GRADE
55
EXTREME

Born: Aug. 15, 1992. **B-T:** R-R. **Ht.:** 6-3. **Wt.:** 180. **Signed:** Venezuela, 2008. **Signed by:** Tony Arias.

If everything comes together, Rodriguez has the tools to be a big league all-star. He shows off plus power in batting practice, and he also has above-average arm strength and speed. Considering he was just one of three 18-year-old regulars in the low Class A Midwest League last year, he performed reasonably well in his full-season debut. But as intriguing as his upside may be, it's also fair to say that Rodriguez does almost nothing to help a team win at this point in his career. The Reds expected more from a player they invested $2.5 million in 2008, setting a since-broken record for a Venezuelan amateur bonus. Dayton improved both on the field and in the clubhouse when he went home to Venezuela with a shoulder injury in mid-July. Rodriguez has the tools to play center field, but he takes too many poor at-bats into the field, which led to run-ins with Dayton teammates who were upset when he let catchable balls drop in for hits while making minimal effort. He eventually was moved to right field to lessen his defensive damage. It's hard for scouts to get a good handle on his speed because he rarely goes all-out from home to first. Besides growing up, Rodriguez also has to make some adjustments at the plate. He lacks plate discipline, doesn't recognize pitches well and swings and misses too frequently. The biggest boom-or-bust prospect in the system, Rodriguez could return to low Class A in 2012.

Year	Club (League)	Class	AVG	G	AB	R	H	2B	3B	HR	RBI	BB	SO	SB	CS	OBP	SLG
2009	Reds (GCL)	R	.274	22	84	9	23	2	1	0	2	10	23	5	0	.347	.321
	Billings (PIO)	R	.219	46	183	21	40	10	2	3	17	9	61	5	2	.259	.344
2010	Billings (PIO)	R	.339	43	171	25	58	8	3	2	39	8	30	12	2	.361	.456
2011	Dayton (MWL)	LoA	.254	79	280	38	71	10	4	7	40	25	84	20	8	.318	.393
Minor League Totals			.267	190	718	93	192	30	10	12	98	52	198	42	12	.317	.387

20 GABRIEL ROSA, 3B

BA GRADE
50
HIGH

Born: July 2, 1993. **B-T:** R-R. **Ht.:** 6-4. **Wt.:** 186. **Drafted:** HS—Rio Grande, P.R., 2011 (2nd round). **Signed by:** Tony Arias.

The top Puerto Rican position prospect for the 2011 draft, Rosa went 84th overall and turned down a commitment to Bethune-Cookman to sign for an above-slot $500,000. Rosa has good raw power for his age, and he has the frame to get bigger and stronger. But he was picked apart by pitchers in the Rookie-level Arizona League because of his long stride and long swing. Like many young power hitters, he tries to pull the ball too much and needs to learn to go the other way when pitchers work the outer half of the plate. Rosa played outfield and shortstop as an amateur, then saw time exclusively at third base in his pro debut. He has plus arm strength, though his long release means his arm grades out only average. If he can't stick at third base, he projects as a potential right fielder. He currently has slightly above-average speed and he has a good feel for running the bases, though he'll probably lose a step as he fills out. Considering his youth and his struggles in the AZL, Rosa figures to open 2012 in extended spring training before heading to Billings in June.

Year	Club (League)	Class	AVG	G	AB	R	H	2B	3B	HR	RBI	BB	SO	SB	CS	OBP	SLG
2011	Reds (AZL)	R	.245	28	106	17	26	5	3	2	10	8	28	4	3	.314	.406
Minor League Totals			.245	28	106	17	26	5	3	2	10	8	28	4	3	.314	.406

21 CHRIS VALAIKA, INF

BA GRADE
45
MEDIUM

Born: Aug. 14, 1985. **B-T:** R-R. **Ht.:** 6-0. **Wt.:** 215. **Drafted:** UC Santa Barbara, 2006 (3rd round). **Signed by:** Rex de la Nuez.

Valaika's bat seemed strong enough to carry his adequate glove in the lower levels of the minors, but his aggressiveness hasn't paid off with the same kind of power production against more advanced pitching. He has spent most of the past three seasons in Triple-A, getting just 63 big league at-bats in 2010-11. His ceiling has been lowered from an offensive-minded regular at second base to more of a utilityman, but he still can be useful in that role. Valaika has a balanced swing at the plate and could hit .270 with some gap power and a few walks in the big leagues if he got regular at-bats. He's an average defender at second base, the only position at which he could profile as a regular. He throws well enough to handle third base and can play shortstop in brief stints, seeing action at both spots last year. He's a below-average runner. Valaika is as ready as he'll ever be but there's still not a clear spot open for him in Cincinnati. He still has an option remaining, so he could ride the Louisville-Cincinnati shuttle again in 2012.

Year	Club (League)	Class	AVG	G	AB	R	H	2B	3B	HR	RBI	BB	SO	SB	CS	OBP	SLG
2006	Billings (PIO)	R	.324	70	275	58	89	22	4	8	60	24	61	2	2	.387	.520
2007	Dayton (MWL)	LoA	.307	79	300	38	92	20	3	10	56	17	72	1	4	.353	.493
	Sarasota (FSL)	HiA	.253	57	217	26	55	9	1	2	23	13	42	0	3	.310	.332
2008	Sarasota (FSL)	HiA	.363	32	135	20	49	9	0	7	31	7	28	2	0	.393	.585
	Chattanooga (SL)	AA	.301	97	379	58	114	19	1	11	50	28	74	7	4	.352	.443
2009	Louisville (IL)	AAA	.235	95	366	32	86	20	1	6	36	16	76	1	0	.271	.344
2010	Louisville (IL)	AAA	.304	118	424	49	129	28	2	4	53	19	72	3	3	.330	.408
	Cincinnati (NL)	MAJ	.263	19	38	3	10	1	0	1	2	1	9	0	0	.282	.368
2011	Louisville (IL)	AAA	.261	109	417	39	109	18	0	7	37	21	65	1	0	.302	.355
	Cincinnati (NL)	MAJ	.280	14	25	3	7	1	1	0	0	2	3	0	0	.333	.400
Major League Totals			.270	33	63	6	17	2	1	1	2	3	12	0	0	.303	.381
Minor League Totals			.288	657	2513	320	723	145	12	55	346	145	490	17	16	.331	.421

22 KYLE WALDROP, OF

BA GRADE
50
HIGH

Born: Nov. 26, 1991. **B-T:** L-L. **Ht.:** 6-3. **Wt.:** 194. **Drafted:** HS—Fort Myers, Fla., 2010 (12th round). **Signed by:** Greg Zunino.

Like Amir Garrett, Waldrop is another high-ceiling talent who fell in the draft because of his potential commitment to another sport. While Garrett was one of the top basketball recruits in his class, Waldrop always had more potential on the diamond than the gridiron. He was a standout safety and wide receiver who committed to play baseball and football at South Florida until the Reds paid him $500,000 as a 12th-round pick in 2010. Waldrop has a natural lefthanded stroke that helped him to a fine showing as a 19-year-old against older Pioneer League competition. He has average power and speed, with the chance to be a reliable offensive performer once he learns to manage the strike zone. Like many football players who turn to baseball, Waldrop has a below-average arm but can improve it through drills and repetition. He played mostly right field in 2011 and will have to add more arm strength to stick there at higher levels. Waldrop has the potential for solid tools across the board, and he'll work on refining them this year in low Class A.

Year	Club (League)	Class	AVG	G	AB	R	H	2B	3B	HR	RBI	BB	SO	SB	CS	OBP	SLG
2010	Reds (AZL)	R	.214	7	28	1	6	1	0	0	1	1	9	0	0	.241	.250
2011	Billings (PIO)	R	.273	68	278	38	76	22	9	5	29	10	65	4	4	.305	.471
Minor League Totals			.268	75	306	39	82	23	9	5	30	11	74	4	4	.299	.451

23 RYAN WRIGHT, 2B

BA GRADE
45
MEDIUM

Born: Dec. 3, 1989. **B-T:** R-R. **Ht.:** 6-1. **Wt.:** 194. **Drafted:** Louisville, 2011 (5th round). **Signed by:** Joe Katuska.

The Reds have a recent history of drafting productive college middle infielders, with Justin Turner, Paul Janish, Zack Cozart and Chris Valaika all reaching the majors. The latest in that line is Wright, a fifth-round pick last June who signed for a slightly above-slot $225,000. A three-year starter at Louisville who led the U.S. college national team with a .361 average in 2010, he has many similarities to Valaika. As with Valaika, Wright's ultimate role as an everyday second baseman or a utilityman depends on how well his bat develops. His smooth swing allows scouts to project him as a plus hitter, but he has fringy raw power and speed. He gets the most out of his physical ability, however, reaching double figures in both homers and steals as a sophomore and junior. Wright has average range and arm strength at second base, with his sure hands being his best defensive tool. He made only two errors in his 41-game pro debut. His tools may scream utilityman, but his feel for the game allowed him to exceed expectations during his amateur career. He'll probably open his first full pro season in low Class A but could push his way to a midseason promotion.

Year	Club (League)	Class	AVG	G	AB	R	H	2B	3B	HR	RBI	BB	SO	SB	CS	OBP	SLG
2011	Reds (AZL)	R	.318	5	22	4	7	2	1	1	5	0	5	1	2	.375	.636
	Billings (PIO)	R	.298	40	161	28	48	11	2	7	32	9	27	6	1	.348	.522
Minor League Totals			.301	45	183	32	55	13	3	8	37	9	32	7	3	.351	.536

24 SEAN BUCKLEY, 3B/OF

BA GRADE
50
HIGH

Born: Sept. 3, 1989. **B-T:** R-R. **Ht.:** 6-4. **Wt.:** 223. **Drafted:** St. Petersburg (Fla.) JC, 2011 (6th round). **Signed by:** Greg Zunino.

Both Sean and his father, Reds scouting director Chris Buckley, agreed before the 2011 draft it would be best for the son to strike off on his own path in another organization. But other members of Cincinnati's scouting staff grew more and more enamored with Buckley's potential when they evaluated him last spring. When he was still on the board in the sixth round, Reds crosschecker Mark Snipp—who said Sean reminded him of a young Matt Holliday—and others persuaded Chris to take his son. After signing for $125,000, Sean showed that he was anything but a nepotism pick when he hit 14 homers in 59 games to earn all-star honors in the Pioneer League. It was the first year he was fully healthy since 2008, as his first two years in college at South Florida were marred by an allergic reaction to antibiotics and a broken hamate bone in his left hand. Buckley projects to have plus power, including natural pop to the opposite field, though his swing is not as conducive to hitting for average. He's an average runner from home plate to first base but shows plus speed once he gets going. Buckley played third base in his pro debut, but he has fringy range there and spent time in the outfield during instructional league. His strong arm would play well in right field, where he could be a solid defender. He'll spend his first full pro season in low Class A.

Year	Club (League)	Class	AVG	G	AB	R	H	2B	3B	HR	RBI	BB	SO	SB	CS	OBP	SLG
2011	Billings (PIO)	R	.289	59	225	38	65	11	3	14	41	23	73	6	4	.372	.551
Minor League Totals			.289	59	225	38	65	11	3	14	41	23	73	6	4	.372	.551

25 TUCKER BARNHART, C

BA GRADE
45
MEDIUM

Born: Jan. 7, 1991. **B-T:** B-R. **Ht.:** 5-8. **Wt.:** 183. **Drafted:** HS—Brownsburg, Ind., 2009 (10th round). **Signed by:** Rick Sellers.

In a system with two of baseball's best catching prospects in Devin Mesoraco and Yasmani Grandal, Barnhart understandably ranks a distant third. Despite that, he's one of the safer bets among Reds farmhands to have a big league career. His catch-and-throw skills alone should allow him to find a job as at least a backup catcher. Barnhart sets up well behind the plate, is a solid receiver and has a quick release that makes his average arm play up. His fast transfer helped him throw out 47 percent of basestealers in 2011. Barnhart has a lot more work to do as a hitter. Scouts suggest he may need to give up switch-hitting because he's helpless from the right side He doesn't have much power, but he makes line-drive contact and draws walks from the left side. Like many catchers, he's a well below-average runner. Barnhart could prove useful as a lefthanded-hitting catcher with defensive skills. He's ready for high Class A in 2012.

Year	Club (League)	Class	AVG	G	AB	R	H	2B	3B	HR	RBI	BB	SO	SB	CS	OBP	SLG
2009	Reds (GCL)	R	.208	14	48	5	10	2	0	0	6	6	9	0	0	.291	.250
2010	Billings (PIO)	R	.306	35	111	17	34	9	0	0	12	18	25	4	1	.412	.387
2011	Dayton (MWL)	LoA	.273	97	326	47	89	24	2	3	43	37	59	2	1	.344	.387
Minor League Totals			.274	146	485	69	133	35	2	3	61	61	93	6	2	.355	.373

26 DAVID VIDAL, 3B

BA GRADE
50
HIGH

Born: Oct. 23, 1989. **B-T:** R-R. **Ht.:** 5-11. **Wt.:** 193. **Drafted:** Miami Dade JC, 2010 (8th round). **Signed by:** Tony Arias.

Vidal batted .401 with 14 homers as a sophomore at Miami Dade JC in 2010, and he was such a feared hitter that he drew intentional walks with the bases empty. Since signing for $100,000 as an eighth-round pick that spring, he has gained more notoriety with his defense in pro ball. He's a well above-average defender at third base with solid arm strength. Scouts rave about his range and ability to make highlight plays. Though he put together a very productive 2011 season in low Class A, hitting .280 with 20 homers, there's more concern about his bat. He tends to feast on mistakes and will have to improve his selectivity as he climbs the ladder. Trying to hit for power, he pulls off the ball and is susceptible to pitches on the outer half, especially sliders. He does have some strength and hand-eye coordination, so he may be able to provide average power production. He's a below-average runner. Vidal was benched for one of Dayton's playoff games after showing poor effort and sometime pouts when calls don't go his way, but his makeup isn't considered a serious problem. His climb to the big leagues will continue in high Class A this year.

Year	Club (League)	Class	AVG	G	AB	R	H	2B	3B	HR	RBI	BB	SO	SB	CS	OBP	SLG
2010	Billings (PIO)	R	.172	8	29	2	5	0	0	0	0	2	3	0	1	.273	.172
	Reds (AZL)	R	.297	36	145	30	43	13	2	6	34	14	30	0	0	.354	.538
	Dayton (MWL)	LoA	.154	4	13	2	2	1	0	0	2	2	4	0	0	.313	.231
2011	Dayton (MWL)	LoA	.280	127	454	85	127	37	1	20	85	44	111	3	2	.350	.498
Minor League Totals			.276	175	641	119	177	51	3	26	121	62	148	3	3	.346	.487

27 DONNIE JOSEPH, LHP

BA GRADE
45
HIGH

Born: Nov. 1, 1987. **B-T:** L-L. **Ht.:** 6-3. **Wt.:** 190. **Drafted:** Houston, 2009 (3rd round). **Signed by:** Jerry Flowers.

After a dominant 2010 season that saw him climb from low Class A to Double-A in just a couple of months, Joseph turned in one of the worst performances in the system last year. He gave up five runs in one inning in his first appearance and never got his ERA below 6.00. Joseph's troubles didn't come from a lack of stuff. He actually threw harder than he had in past years, sitting at 91-93 mph and touching 96 with his fastball. But as he faced more advanced hitters, Joseph's below-average control caught up to him. His mechanics are pretty ugly, as he whips his head during his delivery and falls off the mound toward third base, making it hard to throw consistent strikes. A tendency to overthrow doesn't help either. He also opens up too soon in his delivery, which turned his slider from a plus pitch to a merely ordinary offering. The Reds still think Joseph has the stuff to be a power reliever if he can improve his mechanics. If not, his effectiveness against lefties (.615 opponent OPS in 2011) should at least make him a lefty specialist. He'll give Double-A another try at the start of 2012.

Year	Club (League)	Class	W	L	ERA	G	GS	CG	SV	IP	H	HR	BB	SO	K/9	WHIP	AVG
2009	Billings (PIO)	R	2	1	0.77	8	0	0	0	12	6	0	4	11	8.5	0.86	.146
	Dayton (MWL)	LoA	2	2	4.35	16	0	0	4	21	13	0	10	31	13.5	1.11	.176
2010	Dayton (MWL)	LoA	2	1	0.78	19	0	0	6	23	13	0	7	40	15.7	0.87	.160
	Lynchburg (CAR)	HiA	0	4	2.31	31	0	0	17	35	23	2	16	56	14.4	1.11	.181
	Carolina (SL)	AA	0	0	5.14	7	0	0	1	7	7	0	2	7	9.0	1.29	.250
2011	Carolina (SL)	AA	1	3	6.94	57	0	0	8	58	67	8	30	66	10.2	1.66	.286
Minor League Totals			8	11	4.10	138	0	0	36	156	129	10	69	211	12.2	1.27	.221

28 JUAN DURAN, OF

BA GRADE
50
EXTREME

Born: Sept. 2, 1991. **B-T:** R-R. **Ht.:** 6-7. **Wt.:** 227. **Signed:** Dominican Republic, 2008. **Signed by:** Tony Arias.

Three years after Reds assistant GM Bob Miller discovered a loophole that allowed the Reds to sign him months before other teams believed he was eligible—at a cost of $2 million—Duran began to show his power in more than just batting-practice displays. He might have the best raw pop in the entire system, though it remains to be seen whether he'll hit enough to make use of it. He struck out in a career-high 38 percent of his plate appearances while making his full-season debut last year. Duran can crush a ball when it's out over the plate and gets his arms extended, but he's overly aggressive and has poor pitch recognition. He rarely gets himself into hitter's counts and doesn't show much feel for hitting. Duran grew six inches in the year he signed, and even now his coordination has yet to catch up. He's a poor left fielder whose .931 fielding percentage ranked last among Midwest League outfielders in 2011. His arm is fringy and his speed is well below average. Scouts who saw him in the MWL didn't think much of his instincts or makeup, as he got benched on multiple occasions for not playing hard. Duran is still light years away from Cincinnati, but he did make enough progress in 2011 to warrant a move up to high Class A.

Year	Club (League)	Class	AVG	G	AB	R	H	2B	3B	HR	RBI	BB	SO	SB	CS	OBP	SLG
2008	Reds (DSL)	R	.215	41	135	15	29	3	4	1	14	24	47	8	5	.340	.319
2009	Reds (GCL)	R	.177	45	164	15	29	7	4	0	17	8	52	0	0	.218	.268
2010	Billings (PIO)	R	.244	54	201	23	49	10	1	6	25	19	71	2	3	.309	.393
2011	Dayton (MWL)	LoA	.264	104	367	48	97	21	2	16	71	34	152	1	4	.329	.463
Minor League Totals			.235	244	867	101	204	41	11	23	127	85	322	11	12	.306	.388

29 JONATHAN PEREZ, RHP

BA GRADE

50

EXTREME

Born: May 3, 1995. **B-T:** R-R. **Ht.:** 6-4. **Wt.:** 195. **Signed:** Venezuela, 2011. **Signed by:** Jose Fuentes.

When the Reds made a big splash in Latin America by signing outfielders Yorman Rodriguez and Juan Duran for a combined $4.5 million, they trumpeted those signings. When Cincinnati inked Perez last summer for $825,000, they initially denied it, even after he posted photos on his Facebook page that showed him in a Reds cap signing the contract. He has yet to make his pro debut, but he did come to the United States for instructional league in the fall. Perez throws an 88-90 mph fastball with good sink, a slow curveball and a changeup that's still in its infant stages. As expected for a 16-year-old, he's a long ways from being ready for full-season ball, but his excellent frame gives him plenty of room for projection as he physically matures. He generates good downhill plane and has a clean delivery that should allow him to develop solid control. Perez will probably begin his pro career in the Venezuelan Summer League next June.

Year	Club (League)	Class	W	L	ERA	G	GS	CG	SV	IP	H	HR	BB	SO	K/9	WHIP	AVG
2011	Did Not Play																

30 KYLE LOTZKAR, RHP

BA GRADE

50

EXTREME

Born: Oct. 24, 1989. **B-T:** R-R. **Ht.:** 6-4. **Wt.:** 200. **Drafted:** HS—Delta, B.C., 2007 (1st round supplemental). **Signed by:** Bill Bychowski.

Lotzkar has been around for so long that he was drafted with a supplemental first-round pick the Reds got for losing free agent Scott Schoeneweis. With the way that Lotzkar burst onto the scene in 2008, blowing away the low Class A hitters for 10 midseason starts as a teenager, he could have made his big league debut by now. Instead, he still hasn't gotten past the Midwest League because injuries have slowed his development. He developed a stress fracture in his elbow in 2008 and had Tommy John surgery the following season. His 67 innings last year were a career high, but he missed more time with a strained hamstring. Lotzkar's stuff didn't hold up as well with his increased workload. After showing a 90-94 mph fastball in 2010, he worked more at 89-91 last season. He also battled control problems, leading the MWL with 15 hit batters in 14 starts. Lotzkar still has a plus curveball, while his changeup remains below average. Though he has progressed much slower than hoped and he's not close to being big league-ready, Cincinnati still opted to protect him on its 40-man roster in November. His stuff likely would play up in the bullpen, and he might be able to stay healthy by working shorter stints. If he can stay on the mound, he'll finally reach high Class A in 2012.

Year	Club (League)	Class	W	L	ERA	G	GS	CG	SV	IP	H	HR	BB	SO	K/9	WHIP	AVG
2007	Reds (GCL)	R	0	2	3.86	7	7	0	0	21	21	2	7	24	10.3	1.33	.263
	Billings (PIO)	R	0	0	1.13	2	2	0	0	8	1	1	3	12	13.5	0.50	.040
2008	Dayton (MWL)	LoA	2	3	3.58	10	10	0	0	38	29	2	24	50	11.9	1.41	.215
2009	Did Not Play—Injured																
2010	Reds (AZL)	R	1	1	3.33	8	6	0	0	24	20	1	12	27	10.0	1.32	.230
	Billings (PIO)	R	2	0	0.45	4	4	0	0	20	8	1	2	33	14.9	0.50	.119
2011	Dayton (MWL)	LoA	3	2	4.32	14	14	0	0	67	51	8	25	72	9.7	1.14	.213
Minor League Totals			8	8	3.39	45	43	0	0	178	130	15	73	218	11.0	1.14	.205

Cleveland Indians

BY BEN BADLER

No matter which side of the ace-pitcher trade market the Indians have been on in the last four years, they haven't come out on top.

In July 2008, Cleveland had a sliding major league club, veterans on the verge of free agency and a farm system in decline. It also had two of baseball's best pitchers in CC Sabathia and Cliff Lee, and would trade both of them within a year to rebuild with young talent. So far, the returns have disappointed.

At the 2008 trade deadline, the Indians dealt Sabathia for Matt LaPorta, Michael Brantley and minor league arms Rob Bryson and Zack Jackson. Neither LaPorta nor Brantley has made much of a difference, and Bryson and Jackson made none.

One year later, Cleveland shipped Lee to the Phillies in another deal that has yielded little impact talent. Carlos Carrasco flashed mid-rotation potential, but he had Tommy John surgery in September and will miss the entire 2012 season. Jason Donald and Lou Marson fit best as backups, while minor league righthander Jason Knapp has had two shoulder surgeries.

Last season, the Indians raced off to the best record in the American League at 30-15 but had fallen to 52-51 when they reversed roles at the deadline. They added Ubaldo Jimenez from the Rockies at the cost of their 2009 and 2010 first-rounders, Alex White and Drew Pomeranz, as well as a pair of prospects, righthander Joe Gardner and first baseman/outfielder Matt McBride. Cleveland limped to an 80-82 finish as Jimenez went 4-4, 5.10 in 11 starts.

The Indians have made some successful trades. Acquiring Carlos Santana from the Dodgers for Casey Blake in 2008 was a steal. Chris Perez was part of a package from the Cardinals for Mark DeRosa in 2009. Justin Masterson, Cleveland's top starting pitcher, and lefty bullpen option Nick Hagadone arrived from the Red Sox in a 2009 trade for Victor Martinez.

Which side of the trade market will Cleveland find itself on in 2012? The offense has an intriguing nucleus with Santana and Asdrubal Cabrera headed into their primes, Shin-Soo Choo poised for a bounce-back year and homegrown hitters Lonnie Chisenhall and Jason Kipnis ready for their first full big league seasons. The rotation, on the other hand, is full of question marks, including Jimenez.

If things don't click for the Indians, they'll likely have to turn back to trade market. The trades of

Carlos Santana has been a steal, but the Indians traded their aces for little return

TOP 30 PROSPECTS

1. Francisco Lindor, ss	16. Trey Haley, rhp
2. Dillon Howard, rhp	17. Mike Rayl, lhp
3. Nick Hagadone, lhp	18. Nick Weglarz, of
4. Chen Lee, rhp	19. LeVon Washington, of
5. Luigi Rodriguez, of	20. Felix Sterling, rhp
6. Zach McAllister, rhp	21. T.J. McFarland, lhp
7. Tony Wolters, ss	22. Hector Rondon, rhp
8. Austin Adams, rhp	23. Josh Judy, rhp
9. Scott Barnes, lhp	24. Bryce Stowell, rhp
10. Zach Putnam, rhp	25. Jesus Aguilar, 1b
11. Elvis Araujo, lhp	26. Chun Chen, c
12. Tyler Sturdevant, lhp	27. Jake Lowery, c/1b
13. Ronny Rodriguez, ss	28. Bryson Myles, of
14. Jake Sisco, rhp	29. Matt Packer, lhp
15. Cord Phelps, 2b/ss	30. Jordan Smith, 3b/of

White and Pomeranz and graduations of Chisenhall and Kipnis have left the system thin of talent. Cleveland's strength in the minors is its relief depth, but Hagadone, Chen Lee, Zach Putnam and Co. aren't going to provide the foundation for a contender.

The Indians' best prospects are years away from contributing. They paid $4.75 million for their first two picks in the 2011 draft, shortstop Francisco Lindor and righthander Dillon Howard, but they're high schoolers with a combined five games of pro experiences. Similarly, Dominican outfielder Luigi Rodriguez and shortstop Tony Wolters have played just 34 games in full-season leagues.

General Manager: Chris Antonetti. **Farm Director:** Ross Atkins. **Scouting Director:** Brad Grant.

Class	Team	League	W	L	Pct	Finish*	Manager(s)
Majors	Cleveland Indians	American	80	82	.494	8th (14)	Manny Acta
Triple-A	Columbus Clippers	International	88	56	.611	1st (14)†	Mike Sarbaugh
Double-A	Akron Aeros	Eastern	73	69	.514	6th (12)	Chris Tremie
High A	#Kinston Indians	Carolina	76	62	.551	2nd (8)	Aaron Holbert
Low A	Lake County Captains	Midwest	53	86	.381	16th (16)	Ted Kubiak
Short-season	Mahoning Valley Scrappers	New York-Penn	41	34	.547	5th (14)	David Wallace
Rookie	AZL Indians	Arizona	30	26	.536	5th (13)	Anthony Medrano
Overall 2011 Minor League Record			361	333	.520	9th (30)	

*Finish in overall standings (No. of teams in league). †League champion. #High Class A affiliate moves to Carolina (Carolina) in 2012.

LAST YEAR'S TOP 30

Player, Pos.		Status
1.	Lonnie Chisenhall, 3b	Majors
2.	Alex White, rhp	Majors
3.	Jason Kipnis, 2b	Majors
4.	Drew Pomeranz, lhp	(Rockies)
5.	Nick Weglarz, of	No. 18
6.	Jason Knapp, rhp	Dropped out
7.	LeVon Washington, of	No. 19
8.	Tony Wolters, ss	No. 7
9.	Joe Gardner, rhp	(Rockies)
10.	Nick Hagadone, lhp	No. 3
11.	Kyle Blair, rhp	Dropped out
12.	Alex Lavisky, c	Dropped out
13.	Felix Sterling, rhp	No. 20
14.	T.J. House, lhp	Dropped out
15.	Hector Rondon, rhp	No. 22
16.	Jordan Henry, of	Dropped out
17.	Zach Putnam, rhp	No. 10
18.	Bryce Stowell, rhp	No. 24
19.	Josh Judy, rhp	No. 23
20.	Cord Phelps, 2b	No. 15
21.	Chen Lee, rhp	No. 4
22.	Chun Chen, c	No. 26
23.	Matt Packer, lhp	No. 29
24.	Kelvin de la Cruz, lhp	Dropped out
25.	Luigi Rodriguez, of	No. 5
26.	Corey Kluber, rhp	Dropped out
27.	Jess Todd, rhp	(Cardinals)
28.	Tyler Holt, of	Dropped out
29.	Rob Bryson, rhp	Dropped out
30.	Giovanny Urshela, 3b	Dropped out

BEST TOOLS

Best Hitter for Average	Francisco Lindor
Best Power Hitter	Jesus Aguilar
Best Strike-Zone Discipline	Jordan Henry
Fastest Baserunner	Luigi Rodriguez
Best Athlete	LeVon Washington
Best Fastball	Austin Adams
Best Curveball	Trey Haley
Best Slider	Chen Lee
Best Changeup	Matt Packer
Best Control	Mike Rayl
Best Defensive Catcher	Roberto Perez
Best Defensive Infielder	Francisco Lindor
Best Infield Arm	Ronny Rodriguez
Best Defensive Outfielder	Tyler Holt
Best Outfield Arm	Carlos Moncrief

PROJECTED 2015 LINEUP

Catcher	Carlos Santana
First Base	Matt LaPorta
Second Base	Asdrubal Cabrera
Third Base	Lonnie Chisenhall
Shortstop	Francisco Lindor
Left Field	Michael Brantley
Center Field	Grady Sizemore
Right Field	Shin-Soo Choo
Designated Hitter	Jason Kipnis
No. 1 Starter	Ubaldo Jimenez
No. 2 Starter	Justin Masterson
No. 3 Starter	Carlos Carrasco
No. 4 Starter	Dillon Howard
No. 5 Starter	Josh Tomlin
Closer	Chris Perez

TOP PROSPECTS OF THE DECADE

Year	Player, Pos.	2011 Org.
2002	Corey Smith, 3b	Dodgers
2003	Brandon Phillips, ss/2b	Reds
2004	Grady Sizemore, of	Indians
2005	Adam Miller, rhp	Indians
2006	Adam Miller, rhp	Indians
2007	Adam Miller, rhp	Indians
2008	Adam Miller, rhp	Indians
2009	Carlos Santana, c	Indians
2010	Carlos Santana, c	Indians
2011	Lonnie Chisenhall, 3b	Indians

TOP DRAFT PICKS OF THE DECADE

Year	Player, Pos.	2011 Org.
2002	Jeremy Guthrie, rhp	Orioles
2003	Michael Aubrey, 1b	Nationals
2004	Jeremy Sowers, lhp	Indians
2005	Trevor Crowe, of	Indians
2006	David Huff (1st round supplemental)	Indians
2007	Beau Mills, 3b/1b	Indians
2008	Lonnie Chisenhall, 3b	Indians
2009	Alex White, rhp	Rockies
2010	Drew Pomeranz, lhp	Rockies
2011	Francisco Lindor, ss	Indians

LARGEST BONUSES IN CLUB HISTORY

Danys Baez, 1999	$4,500,000
Jeremy Guthrie, 2002	$3,000,000
Francisco Lindor, 2011	$2,900,000
Drew Pomeranz, 2010	$2,650,000
Jeremy Sowers, 2004	$2,475,000

CLEVELAND INDIANS

TOP 2012 ROOKIE: Nick Hagadone, lhp. The Indians don't have a starting pitcher or position player likely to make an impact but do have several relievers on the cusp, led by Hagadone.

BREAKOUT PROSPECT: Elvis Araujo, lhp. Araujo has outstanding size and arm strength from the left side, and he stayed healthy in 2011 after missing the previous two seasons.

SLEEPER: Anthony Santander, of. A switch-hitter from Venezuela, he signed for $385,000 last summer and has intriguing all-around tools.

SOURCE OF TOP 30 TALENT			
Homegrown	27	Acquired	3
College	10	Trades	3
Junior college	3	Rule 5 draft	0
High school	6	Independent leagues	0
Draft-and-follow	0	Free agents/waivers	0
Nondrafted free agents	0		
International	8		

LF
Nick Weglarz (18)
Thomas Neal
Tim Fedroff

CF
Luigi Rodriguez (5)
LeVon Washington (19)
Bryson Myles (28)
Tyler Holt
Jordan Henry

RF
Anthony Santander
Carlos Moncrief
Bo Greenwell

3B
Jordan Smith (30)
Dorssys Paulino
Giovanny Urshela
Kyle Bellows
Robel Garcia

SS
Francisco Lindor (1)
Ronnie Rodriguez (13)
Juan Diaz
Jorge Martinez

2B
Tony Wolters (7)
Cord Phelps (15)
Jairo Kelly
Jose Ramirez
Tyler Cannon
Zack MacPhee
Todd Hankins

1B
Jesus Aguilar (25)
Beau Mills

C
Chun Chen (26)
Jake Lowery (27)
Alex Monsalve
Roberto Perez
Eric Haase
Alex Lavisky
Charlie Valerio

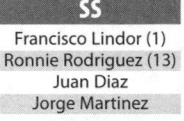
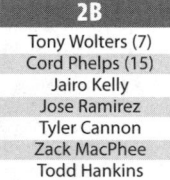

LHP		RHP	
LHSP	**LHRP**	**RHSP**	**RHRP**
Scott Barnes (9)	Nick Hagadone (3)	Dillon Howard (2)	Chen Lee (4)
Elvis Araujo (11)	Tyler Sturdevant (12)	Zach McAllister (6)	Zach Putnam (10)
Mike Rayl (17)	Eric Berger	Austin Adams (8)	Trey Haley (16)
T.J. McFarland (21)	Edgar Pineda	Jake Sisco (14)	Josh Judy (23)
Matt Packer (29)	Kyle Petter	Felix Sterling (20)	Bryce Stowell (24)
Kelvin de la Cruz	Geoff Davenport	Hector Rondon (22)	Cory Burns
Giovanni Soto		Jason Knapp	Paolo Espino
T.J. House		Clayton Cook	Luis Encarnacion
Shawn Morimando		Corey Kluber	Preston Guilmet
Ryan Merritt		Michael Goodnight	Rob Bryson
		Kyle Blair	Cody Allen
		Danny Salazar	Jason Rice
		Will Roberts	Jose Flores
		Cody Anderson	
		Shawn Armstrong	
		Luis DeJesus	
		Jeff Johnson	

2011

BEST PURE HITTER: 3B/OF Jordan Smith (9) hit .420 in two seasons at NCAA Division II St. Cloud State (Minn.), then had a strong debut, hitting .300/.403/.391 with an easy swing and a knack for centering the ball.

BEST POWER HITTER: C/1B Jake Lowery (4) ranked led NCAA Division I with 200 total bases and ranked second with 24 homers in the spring, then led the short-season New York-Penn League with 23 doubles and 30 extra-base hits.

FASTEST RUNNER: SS Francisco Lindor (1) and OF Bryson Myles (6) both have plus speed, with Myles being a bit more explosive. He topped NCAA Division I with 53 steals in the spring.

BEST DEFENSIVE PLAYER: Lindor drew comparisons to Omar Vizquel as an amateur. He has fluid actions, a strong arm and first-rate hands and feet. He has tremendous instincts and the passion to get better.

BEST FASTBALL: RHP Dillon Howard (2) features all three aspects of a quality fastball: above-average velocity at 92-94 mph, late sink and solid command, the last of which is a separator for a high school pitcher. RHP Cody Anderson (14) touched 96 in the spring and sat at 94-95 mph in instructional league. RHP Jake Cisco (3) and RHP Shawn Armstrong (18) have hit 95.

BEST SECONDARY PITCH: The Indians have liked RHP Cody Allen's (23) curveball for several years and also drafted him out of junior college in 2010. Sicso flashes a plus slider.

BEST PRO DEBUT: Allen went 5-1, 1.65 with 75 strikeouts in 55 innings at four levels, including an outing in Double-A. Myles hit .302/.394/.401 with 20 stolen bases in the NY-P, where RHP Will Roberts (5) went 1-3, 3.27 with just seven walks in 41 innings while bumping 94 mph with his fastball.

BEST ATHLETE: Lindor over Myles.

MOST INTRIGUING BACKGROUND: Myles originally signed to play linebacker at Texas Christian. His brother Candon signed with the Pirates as a 12th-rounder. Unsigned RHP Matthew Reckling (RHP) returned to Rice, where the stadium is named after his grandparents, Tommy (a former Owls player) and Isla, the facility's lead donors.

CLOSEST TO THE MAJORS: Allen also has a low-90s fastball and could zip to the majors as a reliever.

BEST LATE-ROUND PICK: Allen. LHP Shawn Morimando (19) shows three average pitches as well as a clean arm and sound delivery. OF Brian Ruiz (41) has athleticism and some power potential.

THE ONE WHO GOT AWAY: The Indians made six-figure overtures to LHPs Stephen Tarpley (8), who wound up at Southern California, and Dillon Peters (20), who headed to Texas.

ASSESSMENT: Lindor is the first prep first-rounder for the Indians since 2001, and the Indians spent $4.75 million to sign him and Howard. This refreshingly young class should help restock a system gutted by the Ubaldo Jimenez trade and big league graduations.

2010

LHP Drew Pomeranz (1) pitched in the big leagues a year after being drafted—but it was for the Rockies after joining them in the Ubaldo Jimenez trade in July. SS Tony Wolters (3) shows promise with the bat.

GRADE: B+

2009

Like Pomeranz, RHP Alex White (1) raced to the majors last year and was part of the Jimenez deal. 2B Jason Kipnis made an instant impact with his bat when he joined Cleveland in July.

GRADE: A

2008

3B Lonnie Chisenhall (1) went from No. 1 on this Top 30 a year ago to the Indians in June. 2B/SS Cord Phelps (3) and RHP Zach Putnam (5) also have reached the majors and have futures as complementary players.

GRADE: B+

2007

Cleveland blew the 13th overall pick on 1B Beau Mills (1) and didn't have second- or third-rounders. Its lone big league hope for this crop is RHP Josh Judy (34).

GRADE: F

Draft analysis by John Manuel (2011) and Jim Callis (2007-10). Numbers in parentheses indicate draft rounds.

1 FRANCISCO LINDOR, SS

Born: Nov. 13, 1993. **B-T:** B-R. **Ht.:** 5-11. **Wt.:** 175.
Drafted: HS—Montverde, Fla., 2011 (1st round).
Signed by: Mike Soper.

BA GRADE
65
HIGH

BILL MITCHELL

Born in Puerto Rico, Lindor moved to the United States at age 12 and couldn't speak English when he arrived at Montverde Academy, an international boarding school in central Florida. In 2009, he captained the U.S. 16-and-under national team that won the gold medal at the World Youth Championships in Taiwan. He hit .500 in 11 games and started laying the groundwork to become a future first-round pick. He further whetted scouts' appetites the following summer on the showcase circuit, highlighted by a surprise victory in the home run derby at the Aflac All-American Game at Petco Park. Though he played a truncated senior season because Montverde failed to qualify for the playoffs, Lindor earned third-team All-America honors in 2011 by hitting .528 in 53 at-bats with six homers and 20 steals. The Indians drafted him eighth overall in June, the first time since 2001 they had spent a first-rounder on a high schooler. He signed at the Aug. 15 deadline for $2.9 million, the largest bonus for a prepster and for a position player in franchise history. Lindor signed too late to play much, but he did hold his own for a week with short-season Mahoning Valley.

Lindor projects as a true shortstop with incredible instincts and advanced feel for the game for his age. He drew comparisons to Omar Vizquel as an amateur and was the best defensive shortstop in the 2011 draft. Lindor is a quality athlete with excellent hands, fluid actions and good footwork. He gets great reads off the bat and shows a knack for being in the right place at the right time. He has plus range with a plus arm and solid fundamentals, giving him all the ingredients to be a star defender. A switch-hitter since he was 13, Lindor has a smooth, line-drive swing and bat speed from both sides of the plate. His best approach comes when he works the ball up the middle. To be a productive offensive player, he'll have to hit for average and get on base at a good clip because his power is mostly to the gaps. He has more pop from the right side and perhaps could hit 10-15 homers per year in his prime. He has a tick above-average speed and has shown flashes of being a plus runner as he has matured and

gotten stronger. While he's not a major basestealing threat, his baserunning should be another positive. He has earned rave reviews from coaches and scouts for his work ethic, maturity and dedication.

Lindor will play his first full pro season at age 18, so the Indians won't rush him. He's talented enough to start 2012 in low Class A Lake County, though with his age and the bitter weather early in the Midwest League season he's not a lock to be there on Opening Day. His feel for the game should help him move quickly relative to other 2011 high school picks. Cleveland's system has a shortage of high-upside players who could develop into above-average regulars, but Lindor is an exception.

SCOUTING GRADES

Batting: 60.   **Defense:** 65.
Power: 40.   **Arm:** 60.
Speed: 55.

Based on 20-80 scouting scale, where 50 represents major league average, and future projection rather than present tools.

Year	Club (League)	Class	AVG	G	AB	R	H	2B	3B	HR	RBI	BB	SO	SB	CS	OBP	SLG
2011	Mahoning Valley (NYP)	SS	.316	5	19	4	6	0	0	0	2	1	5	1	0	.350	.316
Minor League Totals			.316	5	19	4	6	0	0	0	2	1	5	1	0	.350	.316

2 DILLON HOWARD, RHP

Born: July 1, 1992. **B-T:** R-R. **Ht.:** 6-4. **Wt.:** 210. **Drafted:** HS—Searcy, Ark., 2011 (2nd round). **Signed by:** Steve Abney.

Howard established himself as a potential 2011 first-round pick as early as his sophomore year in high school. He didn't quite live up to expectations as a senior last spring, and signability questions helped drop him to the second round. The Indians signed him at the deadline for $1.85 million, the equivalent of mid-first-round money. Howard's best pitch is his lively two-seam fastball, which he runs in the low 90s with plus sink. He can get both groundouts and swings and misses with his two-seamer, and he can mix in a four-seamer that reaches 94 mph and changes hitters' eye level. His No. 2 pitch is an average changeup with good deception that could become a plus offering in time. His breaking ball needs some tightening, as he throws a slurvy curveball with the potential to become average if he learns to stay on top of it. Howard is a solid athlete whose arm works well, though scouts who saw him as an amateur had some concerns about his fastball command. They also raised questions about his mound presence and energy level, though Cleveland doesn't share any of those worries. Howard has the potential to become a frontline starter, though he'll need some time to develop. He'll make his pro debut in low Class A.

BA GRADE

60

HIGH

Year	Club (League)	Class	W	L	ERA	G	GS	CG	SV	IP	H	HR	BB	SO	K/9	WHIP	AVG
2011	Did Not Play—Signed Late																

3 NICK HAGADONE, LHP

Born: Jan. 1, 1986. **B-T:** L-L. **Ht.:** 6-5. **Wt.:** 230. **Drafted:** Washington, 2007 (1st round supplemental). **Signed by:** John Booher (Red Sox).

Hagadone has moved slowly for a college draft pick, but he finally made his big league debut last September, four years after the Red Sox made him a supplemental first-round pick. Tommy John surgery cost him most of 2008 and slowed him in 2009, though he recovered his arm strength quickly upon his return. The Indians sent Victor Martinez to Boston to acquire Hagadone, Justin Masterson and righthander Bryan Price at the 2009 trade deadline. Hagadone's fastball has excellent velocity, typically ranging from 93-96 mph and touching 98. His slider flashes as a plus pitch with late, short break and generates some swings and misses. He's still learning to vary its shape and to throw it to the back foot of righthanders. After walking 6.6 batters per nine innings in 2010, Hagadone sliced his walk rate to 2.8 in the minors last year. He started pitching exclusively out of the stretch, which helped him simplify his delivery and improve his fastball command. If he can maintain the improvements in his control, Hagadone can be a late-inning reliever in the majors. In spring training, he'll get the chance to open 2012 in Cleveland.

BA GRADE

50

MEDIUM

Year	Club (League)	Class	W	L	ERA	G	GS	CG	SV	IP	H	HR	BB	SO	K/9	WHIP	AVG
2007	Lowell (NYP)	SS	0	1	1.85	10	10	0	0	24	14	1	8	33	12.2	0.90	.163
2008	Greenville (SAL)	LoA	1	1	0.00	3	3	0	0	10	5	0	6	12	10.8	1.10	.135
2009	Greenville (SAL)	LoA	0	2	2.52	10	10	0	0	25	13	0	14	32	11.5	1.08	.149
	Lake County (SAL)	LoA	0	1	2.45	5	5	0	0	15	8	0	5	21	12.9	0.89	.163
	Kinston (CAR)	HiA	0	0	5.06	2	2	0	0	5	5	0	5	6	10.1	1.88	.250
2010	Kinston (CAR)	HiA	1	3	2.39	10	10	0	0	38	28	2	29	45	10.8	1.51	.206
	Akron (EL)	AA	2	2	4.50	19	7	0	1	48	44	5	34	44	8.3	1.63	.242
2011	Akron (EL)	AA	2	1	1.59	12	0	0	0	23	14	0	7	24	9.5	0.93	.175
	Columbus (IL)	AAA	4	3	3.35	34	0	0	4	48	42	5	15	53	9.9	1.18	.228
	Cleveland (AL)	MAJ	1	0	4.09	9	0	0	0	11	4	0	6	11	9.0	0.91	.118
Major League Totals			1	0	4.09	9	0	0	0	11	4	0	6	11	9.0	0.91	.118
Minor League Totals			10	14	2.86	105	47	0	5	236	173	13	123	270	10.3	1.25	.201

4 CHEN LEE, RHP

Born: Oct. 21, 1986. **B-T:** R-R. **Ht.:** 5-11. **Wt.:** 175. **Signed:** Taiwan, 2008. **Signed by:** Jason Lee.

Among the more active teams in Taiwan, the Indians tried to sign Lee out of high school. He instead chose to attend college before signing with Cleveland for $400,000 in September 2008. He represented Taiwan at the Olympics that summer and again at the 2009 World Baseball Classic. He has had no trouble handling minor league hitters, averaging 11.0 strikeouts per nine innings in three pro seasons. Lee throws from a low three-quarters arm slot and has more velocity than most pitchers who drop down. His fastball sits at 92-93 mph, hits 95 and has plus movement. His fastball and the deception in his delivery help him miss bats and keep the ball down in the zone. Lee has a solid slider at times but he struggles to stay on top of it because of his low arm slot. He does a nice job of throwing strikes and getting groundballs. With just 32 innings of Triple-A experience, Lee could return to Columbus to begin 2012. He's in line to make his major league debut at some point during the season and projects as a future set-up man.

BA GRADE
50
MEDIUM

Year	Club (League)	Class	W	L	ERA	G	GS	CG	SV	IP	H	HR	BB	SO	K/9	WHIP	AVG
2009	Kinston (CAR)	HiA	4	6	3.35	45	0	0	2	83	67	5	28	97	10.5	1.14	.220
2010	Akron (EL)	AA	5	4	3.22	44	0	0	0	73	59	6	22	82	10.2	1.11	.219
2011	Akron (EL)	AA	2	1	2.50	23	0	0	0	40	27	1	11	56	12.7	0.96	.196
	Columbus (IL)	AAA	4	0	2.27	21	0	0	1	32	26	2	12	43	12.2	1.20	.228
Minor League Totals			15	11	3.01	133	0	0	3	227	179	14	73	278	11.0	1.11	.217

5 LUIGI RODRIGUEZ, OF

Born: Nov. 13, 1992. **B-T:** B-R. **Ht.:** 5-11. **Wt.:** 160. **Signed:** Dominican Republic, 2009. **Signed by:** Lino Diaz.

The Indians used to be one of the leaders in developing Latin American talent, with players such as Victor Martinez, Jhonny Peralta, Fausto Carmona and Rafael Perez coming through the system. That pipeline hasn't been as fruitful in recent years, with Rodriguez one of the few highlights. In his U.S. debut last year, he reached low Class A at age 18. A switch-hitter, Rodriguez tore up the Rookie-level Arizona League last summer, showing the ability to barrel the ball with some gap power. Considering his age, he's understandably raw at the plate, but he has some patience and uses his plus-plus speed to help him leg out hits. He's so fast that he often can outrun his mistakes on the bases and in center field. Signed as a second baseman, Rodriguez didn't have great infield instincts and moved to the outfield one month into his career. He's still improving his reads and routes but should have above-average range in time. He has an average arm. Rodriguez must get strong so he can handle more advanced pitching. He wasn't completely in over his head in the Midwest League, and he'll still be one of the youngest players in the circuit this year.

BA GRADE
50
HIGH

Year	Club (League)	Class	W	L	ERA	G	GS	CG	SV	IP	H	HR	BB	SO	K/9	WHIP	AVG
2009	Kinston (CAR)	HiA	4	6	3.35	45	0	0	2	83	67	5	28	97	10.5	1.14	.220
2010	Akron (EL)	AA	5	4	3.22	44	0	0	0	73	59	6	22	82	10.2	1.11	.219
2011	Akron (EL)	AA	2	1	2.50	23	0	0	0	40	27	1	11	56	12.7	0.96	.196
	Columbus (IL)	AAA	4	0	2.27	21	0	0	1	32	26	2	12	43	12.2	1.20	.228
Minor League Totals			15	11	3.01	133	0	0	3	227	179	14	73	278	11.0	1.11	.217

6 ZACH McALLISTER, RHP

Born: Dec. 8, 1987. **B-T:** R-R. **Ht.:** 6-6. **Wt.:** 240. **Drafted:** HS—Chillicothe, Ill., 2006 (3rd round). **Signed by:** Steve Lemke (Yankees).

McAllister pitched well in the Yankees system up until 2010, when his velocity dropped. At the trade deadline that July, the Indians sent Austin Kearns to New York for a player to be named, which three weeks later became McAllister. Buying low on him could pay off, as he rebounded in 2011 and made four starts in the majors. His father Steve is the Midwest crosschecker for the Diamondbacks. Cleveland gave McAllister a higher leg kick and a little more rotation in his upper half, helping him get more shoulder tilt. The mechanical adjustment helped him get more power to his fastball, which returned to the low 90s and touched 94 mph with sink. He did a better job of staying over the rubber last year and his control improved. Beyond his fastball, the rest of McAllister's repertoire is fringy. He has a changeup and a slurvy slider, also mixing in an occasional curveball as a show-me pitch. McAllister doesn't have huge upside, but he could be a durable back-of-the-rotation starter if everything clicks. The Indians' offseason acquisition of Derek Lowe means they don't have

BA GRADE
45
MEDIUM

any rotation openings, so McAllister could be ticketed for a third season in Triple-A.

Year	Club (League)	Class	W	L	ERA	G	GS	CG	SV	IP	H	HR	BB	SO	K/9	WHIP	AVG
2006	Yankees (GCL)	R	5	2	3.09	11	1	0	0	35	35	1	12	28	7.2	1.34	.259
2007	Staten Island (NYP)	SS	4	6	5.17	16	15	0	0	71	80	3	28	75	9.5	1.51	.286
2008	Charleston, SC (SAL)	LoA	6	3	2.45	10	10	0	0	62	59	3	8	53	7.7	1.07	.245
	Tampa (FSL)	HiA	8	6	1.83	15	14	1	1	89	74	6	13	62	6.3	0.98	.225
2009	Trenton (EL)	AA	7	5	2.23	22	22	0	0	121	98	4	33	96	7.1	1.08	.220
2010	Scranton/W-B (IL)	AAA	8	10	5.09	24	24	1	0	133	165	20	38	88	6.0	1.53	.308
	Columbus (IL)	AAA	1	2	6.88	3	3	0	0	17	20	1	7	11	5.8	1.59	.303
2011	Columbus (IL)	AAA	12	3	3.32	25	25	3	0	155	155	11	31	128	7.4	1.20	.261
	Cleveland (AL)	MAJ	0	1	6.11	4	4	0	0	18	26	1	7	14	7.1	1.87	.338
Major League Totals			0	1	6.11	4	4	0	0	18	26	1	7	14	7.1	1.87	.338
Minor League Totals			51	37	3.47	126	114	5	1	683	686	49	170	541	7.1	1.25	.261

7 TONY WOLTERS, SS

Born: June 9, 1992. **B-T:** L-R. **Ht.:** 5-10. **Wt.:** 165. **Drafted:** HS—Vista, Calif., 2010 (3rd round). **Signed by:** Jason Smith.

Wolters signed for $1.35 million as a third-round pick in 2010, but an injury delayed what would have been his first full pro season. He broke the hamate bone in his right hand during spring training and required surgery. After reporting to Mahoning Valley in June, he led the New York-Penn League with 50 runs. Wolters shows a good feel for working the count with an advanced hitting approach. He makes consistent contact and is at his best when he works the ball back up the middle. While the hamate injury sapped some of his pop, he likely will top out with below-average power and be more of a gap hitter. Wolters is adept on the basepaths, but has fringy speed and isn't quite the threat his 19 steals in 69 games last summer might suggest. He has excellent hands and a strong, accurate arm, and he shows some flair at shortstop. Though he has made strides with his reads and footwork, some scouts think his lack of range ultimately may lead him to second base. He can be more aggressive instead of waiting for the ball to come to him. Wolters will get the chance to remain at shortstop, but he might have a hard time getting time there at Lake County in 2012. Cleveland also could send superior defenders Francisco Lindor and Ronnie Rodriguez there.

BA GRADE
50
HIGH

Year	Club (League)	Class	AVG	G	AB	R	H	2B	3B	HR	RBI	BB	SO	SB	CS	OBP	SLG
2010	Indians (AZL)	R	.211	5	19	2	4	0	0	0	3	2	5	2	0	.286	.211
2011	Mahoning Valley (NYP)	SS	.292	69	267	50	78	10	3	1	20	30	49	19	4	.385	.363
Minor League Totals			.287	74	286	52	82	10	3	1	23	32	54	21	4	.379	.353

8 AUSTIN ADAMS, RHP

Born: Aug. 19, 1986. **B-T:** R-R. **Ht.:** 5-11. **Wt.:** 185. **Drafted:** Faulkner (Ala.), 2009 (5th round). **Signed by:** Chuck Bartlett.

The Brewers drafted Adams as a shortstop in the 27th round in 2008, but he turned them down to return to Faulkner (Ala.), an NAIA program, for his senior season. A two-way star for the Eagles, he didn't become a full-time pitcher until he signed with the Indians for $70,000 as a fifth-round pick in 2009. Adams has outstanding arm strength, as evidenced by a mid-90s fastball that has touched 100 mph. It's by far his best pitch. Both his curveball and slider are average pitches at times, with the slider more advanced largely because of his pure arm speed. His changeup is below average. Adams is still raw as a pitcher but has made mechanical improvements with his lower half thanks in part to his athleticism. He's staying over the rubber better, leading to better balance and weight transfer. He's doesn't throw across his body quite as much as he did in the past, getting better direction to the plate. His walk rate rose to a career-high 4.2 per nine innings when

BA GRADE
50
HIGH

he got to Double-A Akron last year, so he'll need to challenge hitters more. With his one dominant pitch and lack of size, many scouts peg Adams as a future reliever. Cleveland broke him into pro ball in the bullpen but has kept him in the rotation since. He'll move up to Triple-A in 2012.

Year	Club (League)	Class	W	L	ERA	G	GS	CG	SV	IP	H	HR	BB	SO	K/9	WHIP	AVG
2009	Mahoning Valley (NYP)	SS	3	1	4.86	17	0	0	1	37	39	4	15	29	7.1	1.46	.269
2010	Lake County (MWL)	LoA	2	4	3.54	13	8	0	1	53	40	7	21	61	10.3	1.14	—
	Kinston (CAR)	HiA	6	1	1.53	13	12	0	0	59	50	5	15	51	7.8	1.11	.228
2011	Akron (EL)	AA	11	10	3.77	26	26	0	0	136	147	6	63	131	8.7	1.54	.280
Minor League Totals			22	16	3.41	69	46	0	2	285	276	22	114	272	8.6	1.37	.255

9 SCOTT BARNES, LHP

Born: Sept. 5, 1987. **B-T:** L-L. **Ht.:** 6-4. **Wt.:** 185. **Drafted:** St. John's, 2008 (8th round). **Signed by:** John DiCarlo (Giants).

Barnes posted a 2.60 ERA in the lower levels of the Giants system before San Francisco traded him to the Indians for Ryan Garko in July 2009. He struggled in Double-A in 2009 and 2010, then rebounded last year, only to have his season end on July 10 when he tore the anterior-cruciate ligament in his left knee while fielding a bunt. Cleveland added him to its 40-man roster in November. Reports on Barnes' velocity vary, with some scouts seeing an average fastball that tops out in the low 90s while others have seen him reach 96 mph. He has an unorthodox delivery that has some effort, but he's athletic and made improvements repeating his delivery in 2011, which helped his fastball command. His solid slider shows flashes of being a plus pitch, and his changeup could become average with further refinement. Many scouts see Barnes as a reliever, but he could end up as a No. 4 or 5 starter. He's expected to be 100 percent by spring training and could get a big league look in the second half of 2012.

BA GRADE
45
MEDIUM

Year	Club (League)	Class	W	L	ERA	G	GS	CG	SV	IP	H	HR	BB	SO	K/9	WHIP	AVG
2008	Giants (AZL)	R	0	1	3.38	3	0	0	0	5	3	0	4	11	18.6	1.31	.167
	Salem-Keizer (NWL)	SS	0	0	4.76	2	1	0	0	6	6	0	1	11	17.5	1.24	.250
	Augusta (SAL)	LoA	3	2	1.38	6	6	0	0	33	15	0	7	41	11.3	0.67	.133
2009	San Jose (CAL)	HiA	12	3	2.85	18	18	0	0	98	82	7	29	99	9.1	1.13	.227
	Kinston (CAR)	HiA	0	0	2.13	3	3	0	0	13	14	1	6	10	7.1	1.58	.280
	Akron (EL)	AA	2	2	5.68	6	6	0	0	32	35	7	14	29	8.2	1.55	.292
2010	Akron (EL)	AA	6	11	5.22	26	26	0	0	138	126	15	58	127	8.3	1.33	.241
2011	Akron (EL)	AA	1	0	1.64	2	2	0	0	11	5	0	2	17	13.9	0.64	.139
	Columbus (IL)	AAA	7	4	3.68	16	15	0	0	88	80	12	34	90	9.2	1.30	.240
Minor League Totals			31	23	3.87	82	77	0	0	423	366	42	155	435	9.3	1.23	.232

10 ZACH PUTNAM, RHP

Born: July 3, 1987. **B-T:** R-R. **Ht.:** 6-2. **Wt.:** 225. **Drafted:** Michigan, 2008 (5th round). **Signed by:** Derrick Ross.

Like Austin Adams, Putnam was a two-way player in college and focused on pitching once he turned pro. Signed for an above-slot $600,000 as a fifth-round pick in 2008, he pitched in Triple-A for much of the last two seasons before making his big league debut last September. Putnam has effort in his delivery but his athleticism helps him repeat his mechanics and throw strikes with a 90-93 mph fastball that touches 95. He pitches off his fastball and can put hitters away with an above-average splitter, a combination that helps him miss bats and get groundballs. He throws a below-average slider, which puts him in the difficult situation of being a righthanded reliever who can be vulnerable against righthanded hitters. His splitter helps him attack lefties, whom he held to a .547 OPS at Columbus last year, but he's still searching for a weapon against righties, who tagged him for a .712 OPS. Putnam projects as a middle reliever. He should get a chance to fill that role in Cleveland in 2012, possibly as soon as Opening Day.

BA GRADE
45
MEDIUM

Year	Club (League)	Class	W	L	ERA	G	GS	CG	SV	IP	H	HR	BB	SO	K/9	WHIP	AVG
2008	Mahoning Valley (NYP)	SS	0	1	3.72	3	3	0	0	7	7	0	5	8	7.4	1.24	.206
2009	Kinston (CAR)	HiA	2	0	4.13	5	5	0	0	24	22	1	5	23	8.6	1.13	.247
	Akron (EL)	AA	4	2	4.13	33	0	0	2	57	59	2	18	57	9.1	1.36	.261
2010	Akron (EL)	AA	4	1	3.86	20	7	0	3	51	58	2	9	41	7.2	1.31	.286
	Columbus (IL)	AAA	0	1	3.33	17	0	0	0	24	20	2	7	24	8.9	1.11	.222
2011	Columbus (IL)	AAA	6	3	3.65	44	0	0	9	69	61	6	23	68	8.9	1.22	.233
	Cleveland (AL)	MAJ	1	1	6.14	8	0	0	0	7	10	1	0	9	11.0	1.36	.313
Major League Totals			1	1	6.14	8	0	0	0	7	10	1	0	9	11.0	1.36	.312
Minor League Totals			16	8	3.83	122	15	0	14	235	227	13	67	221	8.5	1.25	.251

11 ELVIS ARAUJO, LHP

BA GRADE
50
EXTREME

Born: July 15, 1991. **B-T:** L-L. **Ht.:** 6-6. **Wt.:** 215. **Signed:** Venezuela, 2007. **Signed by:** Otilio Chourio.

Araujo was a long, lanky Venezuelan lefty with a quick arm when he signed with the Indians for $125,000 on his 16th birthday in 2007. He always has had breakout potential because of his projectable body and arm strength. Instead of watching a breakout, however, the Indians' main goal has been to just keep him healthy for a full season. He had Tommy John surgery after his 2008 pro debut that cost him the entire 2009 season, and a setback in his recovery nuked his 2010 campaign as well. He returned to the mound in 2011, flashing the potential Cleveland saw when it first started scouting him. Araujo has gained velocity on his fastball, sitting at 92-94 mph and peaking at 98. His command and secondary pitches both need a lot of work. He shows some feel to spin a mid-80s power slider, which is occasionally above average but needs to get more consistent. His changeup shows flashes but is most often a below-average pitch. Araujo's arm slot wanders from three-quarters to high three-quarters, which costs him command of all his pitches, and he has a tendency to overthrow. He'll remain a starter for now, but because he's been fragile he could end up in a bullpen role down the road. He should make his full-season debut in low Class A this season.

Year	Club (League)	Class	W	L	ERA	G	GS	CG	SV	IP	H	HR	BB	SO	K/9	WHIP	AVG
2008	Indians (DSL)	R	4	2	1.89	14	14	0	0	57	46	0	23	37	5.8	1.21	.230
2009	Did Not Play—Injured																
2010	Did Not Play—Injured																
2011	Indians (AZL)	R	9	1	2.86	13	11	0	0	63	54	2	18	58	8.3	1.14	.228
	Mahoning Valley (NYP)	SS	0	0	8.10	2	2	0	0	7	11	0	7	5	6.8	2.70	.393
Minor League Totals			13	3	2.70	29	27	0	0	127	111	2	48	100	7.1	1.26	.239

12 TYLER STURDEVANT, LHP

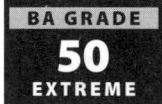

BA GRADE
45
MEDIUM

Born: Dec. 20, 1985. **B-T:** R-L. **Ht.:** 6-1. **Wt.:** 191. **Drafted:** New Mexico State, 2009 (27th round). **Signed by:** Byron Ewing.

A 23rd-round pick in 2009 out of New Mexico State, Sturdevant signed for $2,500 as a 23-year-old senior and since his pitched his way into the Indians' bullpen plans. While he has always been old for his level, he has a strong arm and could have value as a middle-relief option for Cleveland in the near future. Sturdevant has a lanky build and a quick arm that delivers 93-95 mph fastballs, and he touched 97 during the regular season. The Indians clocked him up to 100 mph in the offseason at the Arizona Fall League. His fastball is his out pitch, a lively four-seamer that he keeps down in the zone and is difficult for hitters to lift. Sturdevant has a flat slider but has developed a promising cutter that comes in around the high 80s and touches 90 mph. He'll throw an occasional changeup, but he tends to slow his arm down when he does. Sturdevant will have to sharpen his command to succeed in the big leagues, and he's still more thrower than pitcher. He'll probably open the season in Triple-A but could get a chance to pitch in the Cleveland bullpen at some point in 2012.

Year	Club (League)	Class	W	L	ERA	G	GS	CG	SV	IP	H	HR	BB	SO	K/9	WHIP	AVG
2009	Mahoning Valley (NYP)	SS	2	1	2.75	19	0	0	3	36	34	1	13	42	10.5	1.31	.245
2010	Lake County (MWL)	LoA	3	0	0.76	16	0	0	2	36	17	1	8	56	14.1	0.70	—
	Kinston (CAR)	HiA	3	2	3.72	15	0	0	0	29	28	3	11	35	10.9	1.34	.248
2011	Kinston (CAR)	HiA	4	2	1.98	21	0	0	1	41	31	3	8	44	9.7	0.95	.203
	Akron (EL)	AA	3	1	3.30	19	0	0	2	30	30	2	9	34	10.2	1.30	.270
	Columbus (IL)	AAA	0	0	4.91	2	0	0	1	4	6	0	2	4	9.8	2.18	.353
Minor League Totals			15	6	2.46	92	0	0	9	175	146	10	51	215	11.0	1.12	.223

13 RONNY RODRIGUEZ, SS

BA GRADE
50
EXTREME

Born: April 17, 1992. **B-T:** R-R. **Ht.:** 6-0. **Wt.:** 170. **Signed:** Dominican Republic, 2010. **Signed by:** Ramon Pena/Miguel Valdez.

Rodriguez was Cleveland's top international acquisition in 2010, though he wasn't a typical Latin American amateur signing. Born in the Dominican Republic, he moved to Lawrence, Mass,. when he was 12 and attended high school in the United States. Before he graduated he moved back to the Dominican Republic, and he waited a year for Major League Baseball to determine whether he was subject to the draft or able to sign as a free agent. MLB decided on the latter, and he signed October 2010 for $375,000 as an 18-year-old. He's a good athlete with above-average speed, good range and a 70 arm on the 20-80 scouting scale. Despite those tools, he's still mistake-prone and committed 38 errors in 97 games at shortstop last season, when he made his pro debut as a teenager in low Class A. His throws often sail because he has a tendency to rush his footwork. Rodriguez isn't very physical, but he has a quick bat and surprising raw power for his size. He had 46 extra-base hits in 2011, though Midwest League scouts aren't sure how his pop will play at higher levels. His approach needs a lot of work, as he's a hyper-aggressive hitter who struggles to recognize pitches and get on base. He gets caught out on his front foot too often, causing him to slash at the ball with an uppercut stroke. While Rodriguez's offensive development would benefit from a return to low Class A, the Indians also have Francisco Lindor and Tony Wolters ready to play in the middle infield there.

Year	Club (League)	Class	AVG	G	AB	R	H	2B	3B	HR	RBI	BB	SO	SB	CS	OBP	SLG
2011	Lake County (MWL)	LoA	.246	98	370	41	91	28	7	11	42	13	83	10	7	.274	.449
Minor League Totals			.246	98	370	41	91	28	7	11	42	13	83	10	7	.274	.449

14 JAKE SISCO, RHP

BA GRADE
50
EXTREME

Born: Dec. 9, 1991. **B-T:** R-R. **Ht.:** 6-3. **Wt.:** 185. **Drafted:** Merced (Calif.) JC, 2011 (3rd round). **Signed by:** Don Lyle.

The Giants drafted Sisco in the 37th round out of high school in 2010, but he went to Merced (Calif.) JC and improved his stock. The Indians picked him in the third round last June and signed him for $325,000. He struggled during his introduction to pro ball in the Rookie-level Arizona League. After sitting around 88-90 mph with his fastball in high school, Sisco now throws at 91-92 mph and peaks at 95. He's not quite as polished as Cleveland's 2011 second-round pick, Dillon Howard, but like Howard he also has plus sink on his fastball. Sisco's slider shows signs of becoming a plus pitch, and his curveball has similar promise. He doesn't throw his changeup as often as his other offerings, but he shows occasional feel for it. He's a good athlete who should be able to repeat his delivery, though he had some difficulty throwing strikes in his pro debut. Sisco should head to low Class A to begin his first full pro season.

Year	Club (League)	Class	W	L	ERA	G	GS	CG	SV	IP	H	HR	BB	SO	K/9	WHIP	AVG
2011	Indians (AZL)	R	2	4	5.24	12	8	0	0	34	40	0	17	31	8.1	1.66	.303
Minor League Totals			2	4	5.24	12	8	0	0	34	40	0	17	31	8.1	1.66	.303

15 CORD PHELPS, 2B/SS

Born: Jan. 23, 1987. **B-T:** B-R. **Ht.:** 6-2. **Wt.:** 200. **Drafted:** Stanford, 2008 (3rd round). **Signed by:** Don Lyle.

BA GRADE
45
MEDIUM

Phelps posted a second straight solid offensive season in Triple-A and earned a shot to fill Cleveland's hole at second base in June. He didn't have much success before getting sent back to Columbus, and by the time he returned to the majors in August, Jason Kipnis had laid claim to the second-base job. Phelps has a limited ceiling, but he gets the most out of the tools he has because he has very good instincts. He's a patient hitter who manages his plate appearances well and doesn't chase many pitches out of the strike zone. His hitting mechanics aren't conventional, as he sets up from a deep crouch with low hands, but he doesn't swing and miss much and flashed more power last season than he had in the past. He still projects more as a gap hitter than a home run threat. Phelps is a below-average runner with an average arm, so he doesn't add much on the bases and is limited defensively. Second base is his best position, as he's stretched thin at shortstop and hasn't handled third base well in limited time there. With Kipnis at second, Lonnie Chisenhall at third and Jason Donald established in a utility role, it could be difficult for Phelps to force his way into the Indians' plans. If he can carry his Triple-A success over to the majors, he should be able to find a role as at least an offensive-oriented bench player.

Year	Club (League)	Class	AVG	G	AB	R	H	2B	3B	HR	RBI	BB	SO	SB	CS	OBP	SLG
2008	Indians (GCL)	R	.000	1	3	0	0	0	0	0	1	0	2	0	0	.000	.000
	Mahoning Valley (NYP)	SS	.312	35	141	24	44	10	2	2	21	15	22	4	3	.376	.454
2009	Kinston (CAR)	HiA	.261	130	479	72	125	27	5	4	53	93	97	17	14	.386	.363
2010	Akron (EL)	AA	.296	53	199	25	59	8	3	2	23	15	29	1	4	.346	.397
	Columbus (IL)	AAA	.317	66	243	41	77	20	4	6	31	24	39	3	2	.386	.506
2011	Columbus (IL)	AAA	.294	97	378	51	111	25	4	14	63	51	89	3	6	.376	.492
	Cleveland (AL)	MAJ	.155	35	71	10	11	2	1	1	6	8	17	1	0	.241	.254
Major League Totals			.155	35	71	10	11	2	1	1	6	8	17	1	0	.241	.254
Minor League Totals			.288	382	1443	213	416	90	18	28	192	198	278	28	29	.376	.434

16 TREY HALEY, RHP

Born: June 21, 1990. **B-T:** R-R. **Ht.:** 6-3. **Wt.:** 180. **Drafted:** HS—Nacogdoches, Texas, 2008 (2nd round). **Signed by:** Kevin Cullen.

BA GRADE
50
EXTREME

After signing out of high school for $1.25 million as a second-round pick in 2008, Haley quickly looked like a colossal disappointment. He spent his first two full seasons struggling in low Class A, and by the end of 2010 he had a 6.10 career ERA with more walks (158) than strikeouts (156). The Indians moved him to the bullpen in 2011, a maneuver that has salvaged his career and helped his velocity soar, even as he pitched through a groin injury. Haley showed an 88-92 mph fastball that touched 95 in high school, and he remained in that range as a starter. Last year out of the bullpen, he sat around 95-96 mph with plus sink and reached 100 mph. He has the feel to spin a curveball that's a plus pitch at times, with good depth and power bite. Throwing strikes and controlling his delivery are still obstacles for Haley. He's athletic, which should help him make adjustments, but his mechanics aren't fluid and he's still too wild. He eventually may work from the stretch full-time to simplify his delivery. Haley has the raw stuff to be a late-inning reliever. He'll move up to Double-A to start 2012.

Year	Club (League)	Class	W	L	ERA	G	GS	CG	SV	IP	H	HR	BB	SO	K/9	WHIP	AVG
2008	Indians (GCL)	R	0	0	0.00	1	1	0	0	1	1	0	1	1	9.0	1.00	.000
	Mahoning Valley (NYP)	SS	0	1	54.00	2	1	0	0	1	4	0	6	1	6.8	7.50	.571
2009	Lake County (SAL)	LoA	4	8	5.56	19	16	0	0	78	70	6	65	57	6.6	1.74	.241
2010	Lake County (MWL)	LoA	5	11	5.97	27	26	0	0	116	122	13	86	97	7.5	1.79	—
2011	Lake County (MWL)	LoA	1	1	2.84	8	2	0	1	13	5	0	8	17	12.1	1.03	.125
	Indians (AZL)	R	0	0	0.00	2	1	0	0	3	0	0	0	4	12.0	0.00	.000
	Kinston (CAR)	HiA	1	1	3.77	19	0	0	1	29	25	1	17	27	8.5	1.47	.240
Minor League Totals			10	21	5.58	78	47	0	2	240	226	20	183	204	7.6	1.70	.253

17 MIKE RAYL, LHP

BA GRADE
45
HIGH

Born: Nov. 1, 1988. **B-T:** L-L. **Ht.:** 6-5. **Wt.:** 180. **Drafted:** Palm Beach (Fla.) CC, 2009 (15th round). **Signed by:** Mike Soper.

Rayl was one of the top Florida juco pitching prospects in 2009, but he lasted until the 15th round because of his commitment to Florida. The Indians signed him for $125,000. Rayl gets by more on savvy than stuff, though his pitches ticked up slightly last season. Rayl's fastball improved from the upper 80s at the start of 2011 to sitting at 90 mph and touching 93 by the end. He has started to grow into his lanky frame and learned how to use his legs more in his delivery, which has helped his fastball. He's an adept strike-thrower with good mechanics and mixes his offerings well. His curveball and changeup both have a chance to be average, with the curve better one now. Rayl still has to prove his stuff will play against hitters at higher levels after getting knocked around at high Class A Kinston last August, but he has a chance to become a back-of-the-rotation starter. To begin 2012, he'll probably return to high Class A with the organization's new Carolina affiliate.

Year	Club (League)	Class	W	L	ERA	G	GS	CG	SV	IP	H	HR	BB	SO	K/9	WHIP	AVG
2009	Indians (AZL)	R	1	2	3.74	10	8	0	0	34	36	3	10	41	11.0	1.37	.267
2010	Mahoning Valley (NYP)	SS	2	4	2.81	14	14	0	0	67	57	1	21	56	7.5	1.16	.234
	Lake County (MWL)	LoA	0	0	10.80	1	0	0	0	3	5	0	4	4	10.8	2.70	—
2011	Lake County (MWL)	LoA	5	5	2.83	17	17	0	0	83	66	3	13	84	9.1	0.96	.216
	Kinston (CAR)	HiA	1	3	4.61	8	8	0	0	41	48	6	13	37	8.1	1.49	.293
Minor League Totals			9	14	3.39	50	47	0	0	228	212	13	61	222	8.8	1.20	.246

18 NICK WEGLARZ, OF

BA GRADE
45
HIGH

Born: Dec. 16, 1987. **B-T:** L-L. **Ht.:** 6-3. **Wt.:** 240. **Drafted:** HS—Stevensville, Ont., 2005 (3rd round). **Signed by:** Les Pajari.

Weglarz has been equal parts promising and frustrating, with most of the frustration resulting from injuries. A broken hand wiped out his 2006 season, and he missed time with a stress fracture in his left shin in 2009 and a sprained right thumb in 2010. The worst was yet to come. Weglarz tore the meniscus in his left knee in spring training last year, costing him the season's first two months and hampering him the entire year. He hurt his throwing elbow in August, putting an end to his most disappointing season. Even when not at full health, Weglarz always has shown an excellent batting eye. He lays off pitches out of the strike zone and works counts to draw walks. He has plus raw power but takes a big uppercut swing and gets pull-conscious, with a tendency too fly open early. He's a well below-average runner and a limited left-field defender with a fringy arm. If Weglarz can stay healthy his bat still has value, but he's unlikely to become the middle-of-the-order hitter the Indians were expecting. He should open the year in Triple-A, where he hit well at the end of 2010.

Year	Club (League)	Class	AVG	G	AB	R	H	2B	3B	HR	RBI	BB	SO	SB	CS	OBP	SLG
2005	Burlington (APP)	R	.231	41	147	22	34	11	0	2	13	17	42	2	1	.313	.347
2006	Indians (GCL)	R	.000	1	2	0	0	0	0	0	0	0	2	0	0	.000	.000
2007	Lake County (SAL)	LoA	.276	125	439	75	121	28	0	23	82	82	129	1	1	.395	.497
	Kinston (CAR)	HiA	.143	2	7	1	1	0	0	1	1	1	2	0	0	.250	.571
2008	Kinston (CAR)	HiA	.272	106	375	68	102	20	5	10	41	71	78	9	5	.396	.432
2009	Akron (EL)	AA	.227	105	339	69	77	17	2	16	65	75	78	2	3	.377	.431
2010	Akron (EL)	AA	.285	37	137	21	39	10	0	7	27	22	26	1	0	.387	.511
	Columbus (IL)	AAA	.286	50	175	30	50	17	1	6	20	28	43	2	2	.392	.497
2011	Akron (EL)	AA	.179	41	134	25	24	8	0	3	12	36	43	0	1	.360	.306
Minor League Totals			.255	508	1755	311	448	111	8	68	261	332	443	17	13	.381	.444

19 LEVON WASHINGTON, OF

BA GRADE
50
EXTREME

Born: July 26, 1991. **B-T:** L-R. **Ht.:** 5-11. **Wt.:** 170. **Drafted:** Chipola (Fla.) JC, 2010 (2nd round). **Signed by:** Chuck Bartlett.

Washington has been highly touted since high school, but thus far he hasn't lived up to his billing. The 30th overall pick by the Rays in 2009 out of high school, he didn't sign but didn't qualify academically to play at Florida. He ended up at Chipola (Fla.) JC for the 2010 season, went back into the draft and signed with the Indians for $1.2 million as a second-round pick. Washington struggled in 2011 while battling hip and knee issues. He has good bat speed, quick hands and works the count, but he tinkered with his set-up to bad effect. After his stance got narrow and upright during the season, the Indians had him spread out more like he had in junior college and raised his hand position. He takes a big swing and can become pull-conscious, which doesn't help a player with below-average power. Washington's a 65 runner on the 20-80 scale, though his home-to-first times don't always reflect that. His reads need work in the center field, and his arm has been well below average since shoulder surgery in high school. Washington probably will start the season back in low Class A.

Year	Club (League)	Class	AVG	G	AB	R	H	2B	3B	HR	RBI	BB	SO	SB	CS	OBP	SLG
2010	Indians (AZL)	R	.444	3	9	0	4	0	0	0	3	3	1	1	0	.583	.444
2011	Lake County (MWL)	LoA	.218	79	298	35	65	9	4	4	20	49	89	15	6	.331	.315
Minor League Totals			.225	82	307	35	69	9	4	4	23	52	90	16	6	.340	.319

20 FELIX STERLING, RHP

BA GRADE
50
EXTREME

Born: March 15, 1993. **B-T:** R-R. **Ht.:** 6-3. **Wt.:** 200. **Signed:** Dominican Republic, 2009. **Signed by:** Ramon Pena.

Sterling was one of the best pitchers in the Rookie-level Arizona League in 2010, his first professional season. He went back to the AZL to open 2011, then received a promotion to low Class A in July. Sterling is a physical pitcher whose best attribute is his arm strength. He throws a fastball in the low 90s and gets up to 96 mph. He has a mature frame and a thick lower half, so he doesn't project to have more velocity. While he had little use for a changeup in the past, he threw it more often last season. It's now his No. 2 pitch and shows flashes of becoming a plus pitch. The rest of Sterling's game is still raw. His breaking ball is a slurvy slider with loose, erratic rotation. He can overthrow and come out of his delivery, which hampers his command. Some scouts see Sterling as a reliever, but he'll remain a starter for now. He'll step to high Class A to open 2012.

Year	Club (League)	Class	W	L	ERA	G	GS	CG	SV	IP	H	HR	BB	SO	K/9	WHIP	AVG
2010	Indians (AZL)	R	2	3	3.16	12	11	0	0	51	40	2	20	57	10.0	1.17	.222
2011	Indians (AZL)	R	2	3	4.10	6	4	0	0	26	26	3	8	31	10.6	1.29	.257
	Lake County (MWL)	LoA	2	3	4.14	9	9	0	0	41	31	4	25	35	7.6	1.35	.220
Minor League Totals			6	9	3.71	27	24	0	0	119	97	9	53	123	9.3	1.26	.230

21 T.J. McFARLAND, LHP

BA GRADE
45
HIGH

Born: June 8, 1989. **B-T:** L-L. **Ht.:** 6-3. **Wt.:** 209. **Drafted:** HS—Palos Heights, Ill., 2007 (4th round). **Signed by:** Mike Soper.

McFarland hasn't moved quickly but he has put himself on the radar with consistent performance. Though he lacks overpowering stuff, he has succeeded by sinking the ball and piling up ground-outs. His fastball sits in the high 80s with heavy life and tail, which makes it difficult for hitters to lift. With his large, thick frame, he isn't likely to add velocity, so he'll have to rely on movement and the refinement of his secondary pitches and control. He pitches well off his fastball, moving it in and out. He throws across his body, which isn't ideal but does provide some deception from his low three-quarters arm slot. McFarland's sweeping slider and changeup are both fringy, but he mixes his them well and has good feel for his craft. While his upside is limited, he could be a back-of-the-rotation starter or middle reliever in the majors. His next step is Triple-A.

Year	Club (League)	Class	W	L	ERA	G	GS	CG	SV	IP	H	HR	BB	SO	K/9	WHIP	AVG
2008	Indians (GCL)	R	3	4	5.07	12	10	0	0	55	70	3	15	38	6.2	1.55	.314
2009	Lake County (SAL)	LoA	9	4	3.58	25	23	0	1	121	128	6	42	85	6.3	1.41	.275
2010	Akron (EL)	AA	0	0	11.25	1	1	0	0	4	9	1	2	5	11.3	2.75	.429
	Kinston (CAR)	HiA	11	5	3.13	24	19	1	0	127	121	9	40	92	6.5	1.27	.246
2011	Kinston (CAR)	HiA	0	1	2.25	2	2	0	0	12	9	2	1	12	9.0	0.83	.191
	Akron (EL)	AA	9	9	3.87	25	25	2	0	137	140	9	50	103	6.8	1.38	.265
Minor League Totals			32	23	3.75	89	80	3	1	456	477	30	150	335	6.6	1.38	.269

22 HECTOR RONDON, RHP

BA GRADE
50
EXTREME

Born: Feb. 26, 1988. **B-T:** R-R. **Ht.:** 6-3. **Wt.:** 180. **Signed:** Venezuela, 2004. **Signed by:** Stewart Ruiz.

Rondon moved quickly, reaching Triple-A in 2009 as a 21-year-old. So far that has been the highlight of his professional career. He struggled when he returned to Columbus in 2010 before injuring his elbow. After trying rehab, he finally had Tommy John surgery after the 2010 season, which essentially wiped out his 2011 campaign. Rondon pitched in the Venezuelan League this winter and struggled with his command before he suffered a setback. He had a second surgery on his elbow to repair a fracture and isn't expected to be ready for the start of the 2012 season. At his best, Rondon has shown good command of a lively low-90s fastball that has touched 96 mph. He flashes an average changeup, though his fringy slider never has developed into a legitimate weapon. Rondon is a good athlete who repeats his delivery and fields his position well. When he's healthy again, the Indians will ease him back as a reliever at a Class A stop with the hope that he can be stretched out into a starter's role later in the year. They removed him from the 40-man roster in December.

Year	Club (League)	Class	W	L	ERA	G	GS	CG	SV	IP	H	HR	BB	SO	K/9	WHIP	AVG
2005	Indians1 (DSL)	R	3	3	1.65	15	12	1	1	65	60	2	8	55	7.6	1.04	.230
2006	Indians (GCL)	R	3	4	5.13	11	11	0	0	53	62	6	3	32	5.5	1.23	.286
2007	Lake County (SAL)	LoA	7	10	4.37	27	27	0	0	136	143	13	27	113	7.5	1.25	.269
2008	Kinston (CAR)	HiA	11	6	3.60	27	27	0	0	145	130	12	42	145	9.0	1.19	.239
2009	Akron (EL)	AA	7	5	2.75	15	13	1	0	72	60	3	16	73	9.1	1.06	.227
	Columbus (IL)	AAA	4	5	4.00	12	12	0	0	74	83	8	13	64	7.7	1.29	.282
2010	Columbus (IL)	AAA	1	3	8.53	7	7	0	0	32	48	12	10	33	9.4	1.83	.343
2011	Mahoning Valley (NYP)	SS	0	0	3.00	2	2	0	0	3	3	0	0	2	6.0	1.00	.250
Minor League Totals			36	36	3.91	116	111	2	1	580	589	56	119	517	8.0	1.22	.260

23 JOSH JUDY, RHP

BA GRADE
40
LOW

Born: Feb. 9, 1986. **B-T:** R-R. **Ht.:** 6-4. **Wt.:** 200. **Drafted:** Indiana Tech, 2007 (34th round). **Signed by:** Derrick Ross.

Judy has been quite a find for the Indians as a 34th-round pick signed for $52,500 out of Indiana Tech in 2007. He has averaged at least a strikeout per inning at every full-season minor league stop in the system, and he might be the lone big leaguer out of what was a disastrous draft for Cleveland. He spent most of 2011 in Triple-A, making his major league debut with a scoreless relief inning on May 22 and returning for stints in Cleveland in July and September. Judy throws strikes with a low-90s fastball, getting a lot of deception because of his herky-jerky delivery. He can generate swings and misses with a slider that has late action, though the pitch lacks consistency because he doesn't always stay on top of it. He doesn't have a reliable third pitch to combat lefthanders, who hit him much harder (.834 OPS) than righties did (.581 OPS) last year in Triple-A, a pattern consistent with his career splits. Judy's upside is limited, but he could win a middle-relief job in spring training.

Year	Club (League)	Class	W	L	ERA	G	GS	CG	SV	IP	H	HR	BB	SO	K/9	WHIP	AVG
2007	Indians (GCL)	R	1	2	0.63	9	0	0	0	14	11	0	8	14	8.8	1.33	.204
	Mahoning Valley (NYP)	SS	0	0	0.00	4	1	0	1	11	7	0	3	7	5.7	0.91	.194
2008	Lake County (SAL)	LoA	12	1	3.51	35	0	0	1	74	60	6	25	80	9.7	1.14	.223
	Kinston (CAR)	HiA	0	0	1.93	7	0	0	0	14	12	0	1	17	10.9	0.93	.226
2009	Kinston (CAR)	HiA	0	0	0.00	5	0	0	3	5	4	0	0	7	13.5	0.86	.235
	Akron (EL)	AA	4	3	3.10	36	1	0	11	49	35	2	18	63	11.5	1.07	.198
2010	Akron (EL)	AA	0	0	9.00	2	0	0	0	2	6	0	0	2	9.0	3.00	.545
	Columbus (IL)	AAA	3	0	2.68	38	0	0	2	47	48	5	14	55	10.5	1.32	.262
2011	Columbus (IL)	AAA	6	2	3.12	50	0	0	23	52	44	5	25	60	10.4	1.33	.230
	Cleveland (AL)	MAJ	0	0	7.07	12	0	0	0	14	18	4	4	10	6.4	1.57	.321
Major League Totals			0	0	7.07	12	0	0	0	14	18	4	4	10	6.4	1.57	.321
Minor League Totals			26	8	2.81	186	2	0	41	269	227	18	94	305	10.2	1.19	.229

24 BRYCE STOWELL, RHP

BA GRADE
45
HIGH

Born: Sept. 23, 1986. **B-T:** R-R. **Ht.:** 6-2. **Wt.:** 205. **Drafted:** UC Irvine, 2008 (22nd round). **Signed by:** Jason Smith.

A draft-eligible sophomore in the 2008 draft, Stowell's extra leverage caused him to slide to the 22nd round, where he signed for $725,000. His stock surged along with his velocity in 2010, when he rose from him high Class A to Triple-A while his fastball spiked and touched 100 mph. He tailed off at the end of the season, however, because of an elbow strain that didn't require surgery. During spring training last year, his velocity was down and his mechanics were out of whack. He didn't see any game action until June and spent the last six weeks of the season in Double-A. After working in the mid-90s with his fastball in 2010, Stowell sat in the low 90s and maxed out at 95 last year. He shows an average slider at times but it's inconsistent. He can get away with a little wildness when his fastball is at its best, but regardless of whether his velocity returns, he'll need to throw more strikes and improve his fastball command. Stowell also missed six weeks in 2009 with biceps tendinitis, giving him an arm injury in each of his three pro seasons, so durability is a concern. He'll likely open 2012 in the Triple-A bullpen.

Year	Club (League)	Class	W	L	ERA	G	GS	CG	SV	IP	H	HR	BB	SO	K/9	WHIP	AVG
2009	Lake County (SAL)	LoA	0	0	1.00	3	1	0	0	9	4	1	3	15	15.0	0.78	.133
	Kinston (CAR)	HiA	4	6	5.31	19	6	0	0	61	64	6	34	62	9.1	1.61	.270
2010	Kinston (CAR)	HiA	1	0	1.42	11	0	0	0	25	16	2	8	41	14.6	0.95	.186
	Akron (EL)	AA	1	0	0.00	14	1	0	7	22	15	0	11	33	13.3	1.16	.192
	Columbus (IL)	AAA	1	1	5.49	17	0	0	0	20	11	2	17	28	12.8	1.42	.167
2011	Lake County (MWL)	LoA	0	1	2.60	10	0	0	0	17	8	0	10	26	13.5	1.04	.140
	Mahoning Valley (NYP)	SS	0	0	0.00	1	0	0	1	2	1	0	1	3	13.5	1.00	.143
	Akron (EL)	AA	1	0	1.86	13	0	0	0	19	12	1	10	28	13.0	1.14	.176
Minor League Totals			8	8	3.17	88	8	0	8	176	131	12	94	236	12.1	1.28	.208

25 JESUS AGUILAR, 1B

BA GRADE
45
HIGH

Born: June 30, 1990. **B-T:** R-R. **Ht.:** 6-3. **Wt.:** 241. **Signed:** Venezuela, 2007. **Signed by:** Jesus Mendoza.

Aguilar didn't make much noise in his first three years in the system, but he took a step forward in 2011 when he hit 23 homers between two Class A stops. He continued to produce in the Arizona Fall League, batting .339/.458/.610, then went home to the Venezuelan League to play for Caracas. Aguilar has a massive physical frame, good strength and plus raw power. His best pop comes to center and left-center field, and he generates a lot of loft with his stroke. He relies more on a strength-based swing than bat speed and doesn't always get the bat head out front, but it has worked at the lower levels. He'll need to improve his plate discipline when he faces more advanced pitching. A bottom-of-the-scale runner, Aguilar is a limited athlete and defender at first base. He has an average arm and has made some progress with his footwork, hands and instincts. He's ready to give Double-A a try.

Year	Club (League)	Class	AVG	G	AB	R	H	2B	3B	HR	RBI	BB	SO	SB	CS	OBP	SLG
2008	Indians (DSL)	R	.209	68	235	23	49	12	0	4	45	23	29	4	3	.286	.311
2009	Indians (DSL)	R	.305	55	200	33	61	16	0	5	46	31	24	5	1	.412	.460
2010	Indians (AZL)	R	.259	29	112	15	29	2	1	7	22	5	33	1	1	.293	.482
	Mahoning Valley (NYP)SS		.244	32	123	8	30	9	0	2	17	11	28	2	0	.301	.366
2011	Lake County (MWL)	LoA	.292	95	349	58	102	27	2	19	69	35	98	1	0	.370	.544
	Kinston (CAR)	HiA	.257	31	113	12	29	3	0	4	13	11	28	1	0	.323	.389
Minor League Totals			.265	310	1132	149	300	69	3	41	212	116	240	14	5	.341	.440

26 CHUN CHEN, C

BA GRADE 45 HIGH

Born: Nov. 1, 1988. **B-T:** R-R. **Ht.:** 6-1. **Wt.:** 200. **Signed:** Taiwan, 2007. **Signed by:** Jason Lee.

The Indians are aggressive in Taiwan, where they signed Chen as an 18-year-old in September 2007. After he struggled at Mahoning Valley in 2009, he ditched a leg kick in his swing and had a breakout season at two Class A stops in 2010. His production dipped upon a jump to Double-A in 2011. Chen is an offense-first catcher and has been since his amateur days, though scouts have questions about just how much he'll hit. He has a short swing but is a pull-oriented hitter who doesn't have great bat speed and is often late getting the bat head out front. He has a tendency to leak open and pull off the ball, which hurts him against breaking pitches. The biggest concern right now is with Chen's defense. He ranked second in the Eastern League with 18 passed balls in 82 games and needs to improve his blocking and receiving. He has an average arm and threw out 35 percent of basestealers last year. The thick-bodied Chen has well below-average speed. He'll have to get better defensively even to become a backup catcher, as his bat likely won't play at another position and he doesn't really have the athleticism to fit elsewhere on the diamond. He may return to Double-A in 2012 in an effort to heat his bat up.

Year	Club (League)	Class	AVG	G	AB	R	H	2B	3B	HR	RBI	BB	SO	SB	CS	OBP	SLG
2008	Indians (GCL)	R	.261	38	115	11	30	4	2	3	15	13	29	1	1	.336	.409
2009	Mahoning Valley (NYP)SS		.215	59	195	24	42	15	0	1	19	31	42	9	2	.328	.308
2010	Lake County (MWL)	LoA	.312	58	218	27	68	21	3	6	39	17	38	1	1	.368	.518
	Kinston (CAR)	HiA	.320	52	172	31	55	17	0	6	30	38	36	4	1	.442	.523
2011	Akron (EL)	AA	.262	113	412	58	108	24	3	16	70	43	122	2	1	.330	.451
Minor League Totals			.272	320	1112	151	303	81	8	32	173	142	267	17	6	.357	.446

27 JAKE LOWERY, C/1B

BA GRADE 45 HIGH

Born: July 21, 1990. **B-T:** L-R. **Ht.:** 5-11. **Wt.:** 200. **Drafted:** James Madison, 2011 (4th round). **Signed by:** Bob Mayer.

While many college hitters struggled to adjust to new bat regulations in 2011, Lowery took advantage of the hitter-friendly conditions at James Madison. He led NCAA Division I in runs (80), RBIs (91) and total bases (200) while ranking second in homers (24) and slugging (.797). Drafted 128th overall in June, he signed for $220,000 and topped the New York-Penn League with 23 doubles and 30 extra-base hits. Lowery's best skill is his plate discipline. He has an advanced approach that helps him draw plenty of walks, though he did start to expand his strike zone in the second half of his pro debut He has a strong, compact frame and uses the whole field. Despite his eye-catching numbers in college, he projects to top out at average power. Lowery threw out 43 percent of basestealers last spring and 35 percent in pro ball, and he has a plus arm with excellent carry and accuracy. His receiving and blocking still need a lot of work for him to become an adequate defensive catcher. He also played first base at Mahoning Valley, but moving there would put a lot of additional pressure on his bat. He'll spend his first full pro season in low Class A.

Year	Club (League)	Class	AVG	G	AB	R	H	2B	3B	HR	RBI	BB	SO	SB	CS	OBP	SLG
2011	Mahoning Valley (NYP)SS		.245	69	253	43	62	23	1	6	43	54	56	3	2	.377	.415
Minor League Totals			.245	69	253	43	62	23	1	6	43	54	56	3	2	.377	.415

28 BRYSON MYLES, OF

BA GRADE 45 HIGH

Born: Sept. 18, 1989. **B-T:** R-R. **Ht.:** 5-11. **Wt.:** 230. **Drafted:** Stephen F. Austin State, 2011 (6th round). **Signed by:** Kevin Cullen.

Myles originally intended to play linebacker at Texas Christian, but instead he found his way to Weatherford (Texas) JC, where he went undrafted for two years. He transferred to Stephen F. Austin State for 2011 and hit .411 while leading NCAA Division I with 53 steals. While he was caught 15 times, he swiped 14 more bases than the next-closest finisher. He signed for $112,500 as a sixth-round pick, then hit well in his pro debut at Mahoning Valley. Myles draws physical comparisons to Kirby Puckett because he has a thick, muscular frame with plenty of strength, quick hands and an intriguing combination of plus speed and raw power.

He didn't strike out much in his debut, but he does have an all-out swing that he may have to tone down against more advanced pitchers. Myles gets good marks for his instincts on the bases despite his caught-stealing totals. He's still raw defensively in center field and his below-average arm might end up relegating him to left field. He'll step up to low Class A in 2012.

Year	Club (League)	Class	AVG	G	AB	R	H	2B	3B	HR	RBI	BB	SO	SB	CS	OBP	SLG
2011	Mahoning Valley (NYP)	SS	.302	50	192	36	58	10	3	1	15	24	32	20	7	.394	.401
Minor League Totals			.302	50	192	36	58	10	3	1	15	24	32	20	7	.394	.401

29 MATT PACKER, LHP

BA GRADE
40
MEDIUM

Born: Aug. 28, 1987. **B-T:** L-L. **Ht.:** 6-0. **Wt.:** 200. **Drafted:** Virginia, 2009 (32nd round). **Signed by:** Bob Mayer.

Packer dominated as a Virginia sophomore in 2008, leading NCAA Division I with a 1.14 ERA. His ERA jumped to 4.13 in his junior year, however, and he lasted until the 32nd round of the 2009 draft, where he signed for $50,000. He made quick work of the lower levels of the system and reached Double-A in August of his first full pro season. Packer isn't big but gets downhill plane on an 86-90 mph fastball that peaks at 92 with plus sink. He fills the strike zone and averaged just 1.8 walks per nine innings last year when he returned to Akron. His efficiency helps him get groundballs early in the count and to get ahead of hitters, setting up his above-average changeup. His curveball and a slider are both below-average pitches at this point, with the slider showing more potential. Despite his advanced changeup and lack of a breaking ball, Packer was much more effective against lefthanders (.604 OPS) than righties (.790 OPS) in 2011. He'll make his Triple-A debut in 2012 and could see big league action as a back-of-the-rotation starter.

Year	Club (League)	Class	W	L	ERA	G	GS	CG	SV	IP	H	HR	BB	SO	K/9	WHIP	AVG
2009	Mahoning Valley (NYP)	SS	0	0	2.38	5	0	0	1	11	8	1	1	13	10.3	0.79	.186
2010	Lake County (MWL)	LoA	8	5	1.60	24	13	1	1	96	77	4	13	92	8.7	0.94	—
	Akron (EL)	AA	1	2	3.16	6	5	0	0	37	35	3	9	31	7.5	1.19	.267
2011	Akron (EL)	AA	9	12	4.31	27	27	1	0	169	175	16	33	129	6.9	1.23	.269
Minor League Totals			18	19	3.27	62	45	2	2	313	295	24	56	265	7.6	1.12	.250

30 JORDAN SMITH, 3B/OF

BA GRADE
45
HIGH

Born: July 5, 1990. **B-T:** L-R. **Ht.:** 6-4. **Wt.:** 205. **Drafted:** St. Cloud State (Minn.), 2011 (9th round). **Signed by:** Les Pajari.

Smith hit .420/.480/.772 in two seasons at NCAA Division II St. Cloud State (Minn.) and proved himself against tougher competition by hitting .374 with wood bats in the collegiate Northwoods League in the summer of 2010. After signing for $125,000 as a ninth-round pick last June, he showed why the Indians considered him the most advanced hitter in their 2011 draft class by batting .300 at Mahoning Valley. Smith has a calm, balanced approach at the plate, an easy swing and a knack for centering the baseball. He showed good plate discipline in his first summer of pro ball. His swing can get long at times, however, and scouts have questions about how he'll handle better velocity. Smith has good size and shows average raw power in batting practice, but he offered little pop in his pro debut and employs more of a line-drive stroke than a power swing. He has a lanky frame, so he could grow into more pop with additional strength. A below-average runner with a solid arm, Smith played the outfield as a freshman and moved to third base in 2011. He played both positions in his pro debut and may lack the first-step quickness to remain at the hot corner. He'll open his first full pro season in low Class A.

Year	Club (League)	Class	AVG	G	AB	R	H	2B	3B	HR	RBI	BB	SO	SB	CS	OBP	SLG
2011	Mahoning Valley (NYP)	SS	.300	65	243	36	73	20	1	0	47	35	30	3	1	.403	.391
Minor League Totals			.300	65	243	36	73	20	1	0	47	35	30	3	1	.403	.391

Colorado Rockies

BY JACK ETKIN

When the Rockies' season went south, they dealt ace Ubaldo Jimenez for prospects

Coming off consecutive winning seasons for just the second time ever, the Rockies entered 2011 with playoff expectations. They started the season 11-2, but went just 62-87 afterward in one of the most disappointing performances in the franchise's 19-year history.

Colorado wound up 21 games behind the Diamondbacks in the National League West and just two games ahead of the last-place Padres. The pitching staff shouldered most of the blame, finishing next-to-last in the NL in runs allowed.

In the midst of this season gone wrong, the Rockies  made a seismic trade. They shipped Ubaldo Jimenez, who set franchise records for wins and ERA and threw the franchise's first-ever no-hitter in 2010, to the Indians for four youngsters in July. The two biggest prizes were former first-round picks Drew Pomeranz and Alex White, who finished the season in the big league rotation and should resurface there at some point in 2012.

Several factors led to the Jimenez deal, the most significant being Colorado's desperation to add some pitchers close to being major league-ready.

The Rockies have reaped surprisingly little from their 2006-08 drafts, in which they took a pitcher with their top choice each year. They regrettably picked Greg Reynolds over Evan Longoria with the No. 2 overall selection in 2006, then tabbed Casey Weathers at No. 8 in 2007 and Christian Friedrich at No. 25 in 2008. All three have had injury issues since signing, and the team may not get a single big league regular out of those three drafts.

Colorado also invested a franchise-record $3.9 million bonus in a first-round pitcher in 2009, but Tyler Matzek regressed so much in 2011 that he got demoted to low Class A Asheville and left the team in June for two weeks to work with his youth coach. The Rockies haven't drafted and developed a pitcher who had sustained major league success since selecting Jeff Francis ninth overall in 2002, faring better with arms from their Latin American program such as Jimenez, Jhoulys Chacin and Juan Nicasio.

Marcel Lachemann, who had been a special assistant to O'Dowd and his most trusted advisor, resigned in October because he disagreed with how the organization was developing pitchers. Other staff changes included senior director of baseball operations Jeff Bridich taking over as farm director for Marc Gustafson, who was given a role in the scouting department.

TOP 30 PROSPECTS

1. Drew Pomeranz, lhp	16. Rosell Herrera, ss/3b
2. Nolan Arenado, 3b	17. Jordan Pacheco, c/1b/3b
3. Chad Bettis, rhp	18. Edwar Cabrera, lhp
4. Wilin Rosario, c	19. Hector Gomez, ss
5. Tim Wheeler, of	20. Cristhian Adames, ss
6. Trevor Story, ss/3b	21. Will Swanner, c
7. Tyler Anderson, lhp	22. Rafael Ortega, of
8. Kent Matthes, of	23. Ben Paulsen, 1b
9. Kyle Parker, of	24. Rob Scahill, rhp
10. Josh Rutledge, ss	25. Joe Gardner, rhp
11. Charlie Blackmon, of	26. Jayson Aquino, lhp
12. Tyler Matzek, lhp	27. Tommy Field, 2b/ss
13. D.J. LeMahieu, 3b/2b	28. Parker Frazier, rhp
14. Christian Friedrich, lhp	29. Coty Woods, rhp
15. Peter Tago, rhp	30. Michael Marbry, rhp

Fortunately for Colorado, its most recent drafts look more productive. Even if Matzek turns into a bust, the 2009 crop already has sent Rex Brothers to the big league bullpen and features three of the system's top position prospects in third baseman Nolan Arenado and outfielders Tim Wheeler and Kent Matthes.

The 2010 group includes a promising arm in Chad Bettis and two more bats in Kyle Parker and Josh Rutledge. Potential five-tool shortstop Trevor Story, a supplemental first-rounder, looks like one of the steals of the entire 2011 draft.

General Manager: Dan O'Dowd. **Farm Director:** Jeff Bridich. **Scouting Director:** Bill Schmidt.

Class	Team	League	W	L	Pct	Finish*	Manager(s)
Majors	Colorado Rockies	National	73	89	.451	11th (16)	Jim Tracy
Triple-A	Colorado Springs Sky Sox	Pacific Coast	64	80	.444	15th (16)	Stu Cole
Double-A	Tulsa Drillers	Texas	68	72	.486	5th (8)	Duane Espy
High A	Modesto Nuts	California	74	66	.529	4th (10)	Jerry Weinstein
Low A	Asheville Tourists	South Atlantic	69	70	.496	9th (14)	Joe Mikulik
Short-season	Tri-City Dust Devils	Northwest	44	32	.579	2nd (8)	Fred Ocasio
Rookie	#Casper Ghosts	Pioneer	27	49	.355	8th (8)	Tony Diaz
Overall 2011 Minor League Record			346	369	.484	21st (30)	

*Finish in overall standings (No. of teams in league). †League champion. #Franchise moves to Grand Junction, Colo., in 2012.

LAST YEAR'S TOP 30

Player, Pos.		Status
1.	Tyler Matzek, lhp	No. 12
2.	Wilin Rosario, c	No. 4
3.	Nolan Arenado, 3b	No. 2
4.	Christian Friedrich, lhp	No. 14
5.	Peter Tago, rhp	No. 15
6.	Kyle Parker, of	No. 9
7.	Rex Brothers, lhp	Majors
8.	Juan Nicasio, rhp	Majors
9.	Chad Bettis, rhp	No. 3
10.	Hector Gomez, ss	No. 19
11.	Charlie Blackmon, of	No. 11
12.	Rosell Herrera, ss	No. 16
13.	Albert Campos, rhp	Dropped out
14.	Casey Weathers, rhp	(Cubs)
15.	Rob Scahill, rhp	No. 24
16.	Will Swanner, c	No. 21
17.	Chris Nelson, lnf	Majors
18.	Jordan Pacheco, c	No. 17
19.	Russell Wilson, 2b	Dropped out
20.	Matt Reynolds, lhp	Majors
21.	Tim Wheeler, of	No. 5
22.	Cole Garner, of	Dropped out
23.	Samuel Deduno, rhp	(Padres)
24.	Parker Frazier, rhp	No. 28
25.	Cory Riordan, rhp	Dropped out
26.	Corey Dickerson, of	Dropped out
27.	Edgmer Escalona, rhp	Dropped out
28.	Ben Paulsen, 1b	No. 23
29.	Tommy Field, ss	No. 27
30.	Edwar Cabrera, lhp	No. 18

BEST TOOLS

Best Hitter for Average	Nolan Arenado
Best Power Hitter	Kent Matthes
Best Strike-Zone Discipline	Nolan Arenado
Fastest Baserunner	Rafael Ortega
Best Athlete	Trevor Story
Best Fastball	Chad Bettis
Best Curveball	Nelson Gonzalez
Best Slider	Chad Bettis
Best Changeup	Edwar Cabrera
Best Control	Edwar Cabrera
Best Defensive Catcher	Wilin Rosario
Best Defensive Infielder	Cristhian Adames
Best Infield Arm	Hector Gomez
Best Defensive Outfielder	Rafael Ortega
Best Outfield Arm	Julian Yan

PROJECTED 2015 LINEUP

Catcher	Wilin Rosario
First Base	Kent Matthes
Second Base	Trevor Story
Third Base	Nolan Arenado
Shortstop	Troy Tulowitzki
Left Field	Tim Wheeler
Center Field	Dexter Fowler
Right Field	Carlos Gonzalez
No. 1 Starter	Drew Pomeranz
No. 2 Starter	Jhoulys Chacin
No. 3 Starter	Chad Bettis
No. 4 Starter	Alex White
No. 5 Starter	Tyler Anderson
Closer	Rex Brothers

TOP PROSPECTS OF THE DECADE

Year	Player, Pos.	2011 Org.
2002	Chin-Hui Tsao, rhp	Out of baseball
2003	Aaron Cook, rhp	Rockies
2004	Chin-Hui Tsao, rhp	Out of baseball
2005	Ian Stewart, 3b	Rockies
2006	Ian Stewart, 3b	Rockies
2007	Troy Tulowitzki, ss	Rockies
2008	Franklin Morales, lhp	Red Sox
2009	Dexter Fowler, of	Rockies
2010	Tyler Matzek, lhp	Rockies
2011	Drew Pomeranz, lhp	Rockies

TOP DRAFT PICKS OF THE DECADE

Year	Player, Pos.	2011 Org.
2002	Jeff Francis, lhp	Royals
2003	Ian Stewart, 3b	Rockies
2004	Chris Nelson, ss	Rockies
2005	Troy Tulowitzki, ss	Rockies
2006	Greg Reynolds, rhp	Rockies
2007	Casey Weathers, rhp	Rockies
2008	Christian Friedrich, lhp	Rockies
2009	Tyler Matzek, lhp	Rockies
2010	Kyle Parker, of	Rockies
2011	Tyler Anderson, lhp	Rockies

LARGEST BONUSES IN CLUB HISTORY

Tyler Matzek, 2009	$3,900,000
Greg Reynolds, 2006	$3,250,000
Jason Young, 2000	$2,750,000
Troy Tulowitzki, 2005	$2,300,000
Chin-Hui Tsao, 1999	$2,200,000

COLORADO ROCKIES

TOP 2012 ROOKIE: Drew Pomeranz, lhp. The key to the Ubaldo Jimenez trade, he pitched without his best stuff but showed great poise and consistently threw strikes for the Rockies in September.

BREAKOUT PROSPECT: Cristhian Adames, ss. He had a very solid full-season debut offensively and defensively, playing most of it at age 19.

SLEEPER: Ben Hughes, rhp. The first NCAA Division III player drafted in 2011, he has a fastball that touches 96 mph and a splitter that can be nasty.

SOURCE OF TOP 30 TALENT

Homegrown	26	Acquired	4
College	13	Trades	3
Junior College	0	Rule 5 draft	0
High school	6	Independent leagues	0
Draft-and-follow	0	Free agents/waivers	1
Nondrafted free agents	0		
International	7		

LF
Charlie Blackmon (11)
Dillon Thomas
Corey Dickerson
Chandler Laurent
Jared Simon

CF
Rafael Ortega (22)
Jamie Hoffmann
Delta Cleary
Mike Mitchell

RF
Tim Wheeler (5)
Kent Matthes (8)
Kyle Parker (9)
Carl Thomore
Cole Garner
Brian Rike
Julian Yan

3B
Nolan Arenado (2)
D.J. LeMahieu (13)
Rosell Herrera (16)
Brett Tanos
Joey Wong

SS
Trevor Story (6)
Hector Gomez (19)
Cristhian Adames (20)
Taylor Featherston

2B
Josh Rutledge (10)
Tommy Field (27)
Russell Wilson
Angelys Nina
Tim Smalling
Jimmy Cesario

1B
Jordan Pacheco (17)
Ben Paulsen (23)
Harold Riggins
Mike Zuanich
Matt McBride
Jordan Ribera
Kiel Roling

C
Wilin Rosario (4)
Will Swanner (21)
Lars Davis
Dustin Garneau
Bryce Massanari
Ryan Casteel

LHP

LHSP	LHRP
Drew Pomeranz (1)	Kraig Sitton
Tyler Anderson (7)	Keith Weiser
Tyler Matzek (12)	Ken Roberts
Christian Friedrich (14)	Craig Bennigson
Edwar Cabrera (18)	
Jayson Aquino (26)	
Roberto Padilla	

RHP

RHSP	RHRP
Chad Bettis (3)	Joe Gardner (25)
Peter Tago (15)	Coty Woods (29)
Rob Scahill (24)	Michael Marbry (30)
Parker Frazier (28)	Edgmer Escalona
Ben Hughes	Daniel Turpen
Albert Campos	Juan Gonzalez
Cory Riordan	Stephen Dodson
Chris Jensen	Adam Jorgenson
Josh Slaats	Nelson Gonzalez
Dan Houston	Rafael Suarez
Jefri Hernandez	Vianny Mayo
Josh Sullivan	
Danny Winkler	
Nick Schnaitmann	
Christian Bergman	
Geoff Parker	

2011

BEST PURE HITTER: SS Trevor Story (1s) has quick hands and barrels balls. The Rockies don't have a complex-based team, so they had to send him to the more advanced Rookie-level Pioneer League, where he batted .268/.364/.436 against older competition.

BEST POWER HITTER: OF Carl Thomore (2) gets the nod over OF Dillon Thomas (4) and 1B Harold Riggins (7). 1B Jordan Ribera (21) led NCAA Division I with 27 homers and the Cape Cod League with seven longballs in 2010.

FASTEST RUNNER: Story isn't as quick out of the batter's box, but he's a plus runner under way. He stole 13 bases in 14 tries at Casper.

BEST DEFENSIVE PLAYER: Once again, it's Story. He has smooth actions to go with solid range and above-average arm strength. Colorado was delighted to get a potential five-tool shortstop with the 45th overall pick.

BEST FASTBALL: RHP Ben Hughes (10) usually works in the low 90s and peaked at 96 mph after signing. The St. Olaf (Minn.) product was the highest-drafted NCAA Division III player in 2011. RHP Chris Jensen (6) may have more consistent velocity and tops out at 95.

BEST SECONDARY PITCH: LHP Tyler Anderson (1) keeps hitters off balance with a funky delivery and his ability to command five pitches, most notably a plus changeup. The best breaking balls in the Rockies' draft crop are the solid sliders thrown by Anderson and RHP Danny Winkler (20).

BEST PRO DEBUT: Story, who ranked as the Pioneer League's No. 1 prospect. Riggins hit .278 with eight homers and a Pioneer League-leading 46 walks.

BEST ATHLETE: Story, who has average power to go with the rest of his package. Thomore draws Hunter Pence comparisons because he doesn't look pretty but has average or better tools across the board. SS Taylor Featherston (5) isn't as gifted as Story, but he has good tools for a middle infielder.

MOST INTRIGUING BACKGROUND: Unsigned LHP Brandon Bonilla's (37) father Bobby was a six-time all-star during a 16-year big league career. Unsigned C Tyler Servais' (36) dad Scott and unsigned 2B Drew Stankiewicz's (40) father Andy also played in the majors.

CLOSEST TO THE MAJORS: Anderson, an extremely polished college lefthander.

BEST LATE-ROUND PICK: Winkler, who may profile best as a reliever. He showed a 91-94 mph fastball in the early innings as a starter at Casper. 2B/SS Tim Smalling (15), a college senior signed for $2,500, has what it takes to make it to the [?] as a utilityman.

THE ONE WHO GOT AWAY: Power-hitting [?] O'Brien (3) was the highest unsigned college play[?] the 2011 draft who didn't fail his physical. He nev[?] got close to signing with Colorado and has transferred from Bethune-Cookman to Miami for his senior season. The best long-term prospect not to sign was RHP John Curtiss (30), who has the stuff to become a first-round pick after three years at Texas.

ASSESSMENT: After taking an advanced arm in Anderson, the Rockies took hitters with six of their next seven picks. It's difficult to find quality shortstops, but Colorado got one with promise in Story.

2010

The Rockies are still high on their top two picks, OF Kyle Parker (1) and RHP Peter Tago (1s). But they've been outperformed by RHP Chad Bettis (2), the 2011 high Class A California League pitcher of the year, and SS Josh Rutledge (3), who hit .348 in the same circuit.

GRADE: C+

2009

LHP Tyler Matzek (1) has been a mess, though he started to regroup at the end of last season. LHP Rex Brothers (1s) is Colorado's closer of the future, while 3B Nolan Arenado (2) is the system's best hitting prospect and OF Tim Wheeler (1) ranked second in the minors with 33 homers last year.

GRADE: B+

2008

LHP Christian Friedrich (1) got to Double-A quickly but has stalled there. OF Charlie Blackmon (2) and 2B/SS Tommy Field (24) have made big league cameos, though both may be reserves.

GRADE: C

2007

RHP Casey Weathers (1) was supposed to be a fast-track reliever before Tommy John surgery got in the way, and Colorado traded him to the Cubs in December. The Rockies found three spare parts in C/1B/3B Jordan Pacheco (9), LHP Matt Reynolds (20) and RHP Bruce Billings (30) but failed to land their most talented draftee, LHP Chris Sale (21).

GRADE: C

Draft analysis by Jim Callis. Numbers in parentheses indicate draft rounds.

BA GRADE

65

MEDIUM

DIAMOND IMAGES

: 230.

ned by:

pitched
levels,
strike-
...astern
...rs in 2010, when
...e first college pitcher drafted
... He was the centerpiece of the July deal
... which Cleveland sent him and three other prospects (righthanders Alex White and Joe Gardner, first baseman/outfielder Matt McBride) to the Rockies for Ubaldo Jimenez. Because he couldn't be traded until the one-year anniversary of his signing for $2.65 million, Pomeranz had to spend two weeks in limbo at Cleveland's spring-training complex. He made his first appearance with his new organization at Double-A Tulsa on Aug. 17, 23 days after his last outing. With Colorado GM Dan O'Dowd and assistant GM Bill Geivett in the stands, Pomeranz went out and pitched six perfect innings before allowing two singles in the seventh. He had an emergency appendectomy three days later, then returned to throw three perfect innings in Tulsa's season finale. His 1.78 ERA would have led the minors if he had the innings to qualify. Pomeranz became the fifth player from the 2010 draft to reach the majors, working five scoreless innings against the Reds on Sept. 11 and pitching well in three of his four starts for the Rockies. They were pleased with the way he handled an eventful season but disappointed when he was arrested in mid-October for disturbing the peace in Oxford, Miss.

Pomeranz threw a 91-95 mph fastball at the start of the season in the high Class A Carolina League, where he ranked as the top pitching prospect, but he was down to 87-92 mph by the time he joined the Rockies. His fastball still played well at the lower velocity, because he keeps it down in the zone and his size and long arms add deception to his delivery. When he's back at full strength, he should have a plus fastball. His curveball is his best swing-and-miss pitch, a tight hammer that likewise wasn't as sharp at the end of 2011. He's refining his changeup, but it has a chance to become a solid-average offering. Pomeranz's biggest need is to throw more strikes and locate his pitches with more precision. His delivery isn't the most fluid and has a stabbing motion in the back, which hampers his control and command at times. Unlike many young pitchers who overthrow when they get to the majors, he threw more strikes during his brief big league stint. Considering all the attention focused on him, Pomeranz also showed tremendous poise. He looked and acted like a major league pitcher despite lacking experience and his best stuff.

Pomeranz will get the opportunity to make Colorado's rotation in spring training. At worst he'll begin the year at Triple-A Colorado Springs, but he likely wouldn't be there long. He has better stuff than most lefthanders and projects as a No. 2 starter.

SCOUTING GRADES

Fastball: 60.   **Command/**
Curveball: 65.   **Control:** 55.
Changeup: 55.   **Delivery:** 55.

*Based on 20-80 scouting scale, where
50 represents major league average, and
future projection rather than present tools.*

Year	Club (League)	Class	W	L	ERA	G	GS	CG	SV	IP	H	HR	BB	SO	K/9	WHIP	AVG
2011	Kinston (CAR)	HiA	3	2	1.87	15	15	0	0	77	56	2	32	95	11.1	1.14	.202
	Akron (EL)	AA	0	1	2.57	3	3	0	0	14	10	1	6	17	10.9	1.14	.200
	Tulsa (TL)	AA	1	0	0.00	2	2	0	0	10	2	0	0	7	6.3	0.20	.063
	Colorado (NL)	MAJ	2	1	5.40	4	4	0	0	18	19	0	5	13	6.4	1.31	.271
Major League Totals			2	1	5.40	4	4	0	0	18	19	0	5	13	6.4	1.31	.271
Minor League Totals			4	3	1.78	20	20	0	0	101	68	3	38	119	10.6	1.05	.189

2 NOLAN ARENADO, 3B

BA GRADE

60

MEDIUM

Born: April 16, 1991. **B-T:** R-R. **Ht.:** 6-1. **Wt.:** 205. **Drafted:** HS—El Toro, Calif., 2009 (2nd round). **Signed by:** Jon Lukens.

After missing the first six weeks in 2010 with a groin injury, Arenado broke out in 2011, leading the minors with 122 RBIs and flourishing in the Arizona Fall League. He won AFL MVP honors after batting .388 and leading the league in hits (47), doubles (12) and extra-base hits (18). He also improved on defense, ending talk that his range and first-step quickness would prompt a move from third to first base. Arenado has exceptional hand-eye coordination and very quick, strong hands. He entered pro ball with an advanced two-strike approach and has learned to turn on pitches when he gets the opportunity. His swing has a flat path, but he gets good extension and has shown an increased ability to hit balls with backspin, which should lead to solid or better power. He controls the strike zone well and is starting to draw more walks. Arenado dropped 20 pounds last offseason, resulting in average range at third base despite his lack of quick feet. He has soft hands and plenty of arm strength, with plus accuracy and a quick release from any angle. He's a well below-average runner. Arenado has the work ethic to maintain his defensive skills. He's competitive but can show his youth by getting emotional at times. A potential No. 3 hitter, Arenado should open 2012 in Double-A, with a second-half promotion to the big leagues a possibility. He could be ready for a regular role in Colorado by 2013.

Year	Club (League)	Class	AVG	G	AB	R	H	2B	3B	HR	RBI	BB	SO	SB	CS	OBP	SLG
2009	Casper (PIO)	R	.300	54	203	28	61	15	0	2	22	16	18	5	2	.351	.404
2010	Asheville (SAL)	LoA	.308	92	373	45	115	41	1	12	65	19	52	1	3	.338	.520
2011	Modesto (CAL)	HiA	.298	134	517	82	154	32	3	20	122	47	53	2	1	.349	.487
Minor League Totals			.302	280	1093	155	330	88	4	34	209	82	123	8	6	.346	.483

3 CHAD BETTIS, RHP

BA GRADE

55

MEDIUM

Born: April 26, 1989. **B-T:** R-R. **Ht.:** 6-1. **Wt.:** 210. **Drafted:** Texas Tech, 2010 (2nd round). **Signed by:** Dar Cox.

Bettis started and relieved at Texas Tech, which could be helpful because his ultimate role has yet to be determined. He has had nothing but success as a starter in two pro seasons, going 18-6, 2.70 overall and earning high Class A California League pitcher of the year honors in 2011. He led the league in innings (170), strikeouts (184), WHIP (1.10) and opponent average (.225). Bettis pitches at 94-95 mph with his fastball, easily gets to 98 mph and maintains his velocity in the late innings. His tight slider reaches the upper 80s and gives him a second plus pitch. His height raises concerns that he'll work on a flat plane and have trouble the third time through a lineup unless he develops a softer pitch so he can change speeds as well as locations. That offering likely will be a curveball that's better than his below-average changeup. Bettis is aggressive but did a better job of staying back in his delivery in the second half of the season. He throws strikes and works the bottom of the zone. If his secondary stuff develops, Bettis can become a solid No. 3 starter and perhaps more. If he ends up in the bullpen, he profiles as a possible closer and could rise quickly. He'll open 2012 in Double-A.

Year	Club (League)	Class	W	L	ERA	G	GS	CG	SV	IP	H	HR	BB	SO	K/9	WHIP	AVG
2010	Tri-City (NWL)	SS	4	1	1.12	10	9	0	0	48	44	0	10	39	7.3	1.12	.227
	Asheville (SAL)	LoA	2	0	0.96	3	3	0	0	19	14	1	3	17	8.2	0.91	.209
2011	Modesto (CAL)	HiA	12	5	3.34	27	27	0	0	170	142	10	45	184	9.8	1.10	.225
Minor League Totals			18	6	2.70	40	39	0	0	237	200	11	58	240	9.1	1.09	.224

4 WILIN ROSARIO, C

BA GRADE

55

MEDIUM

Born: Feb. 23, 1989. **B-T:** R-R. **Ht.:** 5-11. **Wt.:** 200. **Signed:** Dominican Republic, 2006. **Signed by:** Rolando Fernandez/Felix Feliz.

Rosario had the best year of his career in 2010, but his season ended in August when he tore the anterior cruciate ligament in his right knee during a rundown play in August. The Rockies brought him back slowly in 2011, sending him back to Double-A, where he didn't hit as well but nevertheless played in his second straight Futures Game and reached the majors for the first time in September. He started 14 of Colorado's final 21 games. Rosario's two carrying tools are his exceptional arm and plus power. He also has good hands and a quick release, enabling him to throw out 41 percent of basestealers in his minor league career and five of the eight who tested him in the big leagues. He still needs work blocking balls, moving laterally and calling a game. Rosario has a short stroke and showed he could hit major league fastballs in September. But too often he sits on fastballs and looks to pull, leaving him vulnerable to breaking pitches. He's also impatient at the plate, so he probably won't hit for a high average. He's a well below-average runner but athletic for a catcher. Rosario never has played in Triple-A and could open 2012 there. Even if he does, he's the Rockies' catcher of the future and should get considerable big league playing time this season.

Year	Club (League)	Class	AVG	G	AB	R	H	2B	3B	HR	RBI	BB	SO	SB	CS	OBP	SLG
2006	Rockies (DSL)	R	.249	62	213	28	53	7	0	3	25	16	56	5	2	.309	.324
2007	Casper (PIO)	R	.209	34	115	11	24	4	0	2	9	11	38	2	2	.283	.296
2008	Casper (PIO)	R	.316	66	263	48	83	15	3	12	49	24	57	4	3	.371	.532
2009	Modesto (CAL)	HiA	.266	58	203	17	54	12	2	4	33	10	55	2	1	.297	.404
2010	Tulsa (TL)	AA	.285	73	270	42	77	13	1	19	52	21	57	1	0	.342	.552
2011	Tulsa (TL)	AA	.249	102	405	52	101	15	3	21	48	19	91	1	2	.284	.457
	Colorado (NL)	MAJ	.204	16	54	6	11	3	1	3	8	2	20	0	0	.228	.463
Major League Totals			.204	16	54	6	11	3	1	3	8	2	20	0	0	.228	.463
Minor League Totals			.267	395	1469	198	392	66	9	61	216	101	354	15	10	.316	.449

5 TIM WHEELER, OF

Born: Jan. 21, 1988. **B-T:** L-R. **Ht.:** 6-4. **Wt.:** 205. **Drafted:** Sacramento State, 2009 (1st round). **Signed by:** Gary Wilson.

BA GRADE

55

MEDIUM

The final pick of 2009's first round, Wheeler signed for a below-slot $900,000 and didn't do much in his first two pro seasons. He surprised the Rockies by finishing second in the minors with 33 homers in 2011, the most by a Tulsa player since Irving Burns hit 36 in 1929. Wheeler hit his 29th homer on July 25 but pressed so much to get to 30 that he didn't reach the milestone until Aug. 24. Wheeler has very flexible, quick hips and generated more power by doing a better job of getting his hands out front to turn on pitches. He can get pull-happy, which was the case during his monthlong homer drought. He tends to drop his head at the plate, resulting in him missing hittable pitches and struggling against lefthanders. He may strike out too much to hit for a high average. Wheeler has solid speed and has played center field in the minors, but he profiles as a corner outfielder in the majors. He has enough arm for right field and should have average range once he refines his reads and routes. He has terrific makeup and runs out every ball. Wheeler will begin 2012 in Triple-A and could reach the majors later in the year. Some scouts see him as a 20-20 player, while others wonder if he'll be a platoon player because he hasn't hit lefties.

Year	Club (League)	Class	AVG	G	AB	R	H	2B	3B	HR	RBI	BB	SO	SB	CS	OBP	SLG
2009	Tri-City (NWL)	SS	.256	68	273	44	70	13	3	5	35	29	60	10	4	.332	.381
2010	Modesto (CAL)	HiA	.249	129	510	88	127	21	6	12	63	60	114	22	8	.341	.384
2011	Tulsa (TL)	AA	.287	138	561	105	161	28	6	33	86	59	142	21	12	.365	.535
Minor League Totals			.266	335	1344	237	358	62	15	50	184	148	316	53	24	.349	.446

6 TREVOR STORY, SS/3B

Born: Nov. 15, 1992. **B-T:** R-R. **Ht.:** 6-1. **Wt.:** 175. **Drafted:** HS—Irving, Texas, 2011 (1st round). **Signed by:** Dar Cox.

BA GRADE

55

HIGH

Octavio Dotel pitched just eight games for Colorado in 2010, but his departure as a free agent gave the Rockies the 45th overall pick in 2011 draft as compensation. They took Story, the first time they used a top-100 choice on a shortstop since taking Troy Tulowitzki seventh overall in 2005, and signed him for $915,000. He ranked as the top prospect in the Rookie-level Pioneer League, where he split time at shortstop with Rosell Herrera and played 15 games at third base. Story has unusual presence for such a young player and a chance to have five average or better tools. He has a solid middle-of-the-field approach, good bat speed and the ability to drive the ball. He could have 20-homer power once he gains size and strength. He makes steady contact but can get overly aggressive and drop his back shoulder and get under balls. Story's above-average speed and instincts give him basestealing ability and solid range at shortstop. He has smooth actions and a plus arm that will play better once he upgrades his footwork. Eight of his 15 errors at Casper came on throws. Story can handle the jump to low Class A Asheville as a 19-year-old. Tulowitzki eventually will block him at shortstop, but Colorado will develop Story there for the time being. He should have enough bat for second or third base if needed.

Year	Club (League)	Class	AVG	G	AB	R	H	2B	3B	HR	RBI	BB	SO	SB	CS	OBP	SLG
2011	Casper (PIO)	R	.268	47	179	37	48	8	2	6	28	26	41	13	1	.364	.436
Minor League Totals			.268	47	179	37	48	8	2	6	28	26	41	13	1	.364	.436

7 TYLER ANDERSON, LHP

Born: Dec. 30, 1989. **B-T:** L-L. **Ht.:** 6-4. **Wt.:** 215. **Drafted:** Oregon, 2011 (1st round). **Signed by:** Jesse Retzlaff.

Drafted in the 50th round by the Twins in 2008, Anderson opted to become part of the resuscitated baseball program at Oregon, where he set school records for strikeouts in a game (14), season (114) and career (285). The Rockies drafted him 20th overall last June, making him the third lefthander they selected in the first round in the last four drafts, following Christian Friedrich (2008) and Tyler Matzek (2009). Anderson signed for $1.4 million at the Aug. 15 deadline, too late to pitch in the minors, and threw just one bullpen session in instructional league before getting shut down with pelvic soreness. Anderson isn't overpowering but succeeds by commanding a deep repertoire. His best pitch is a changeup. He also has two- and four-seam fastballs, which range form 89-93 mph and feature good life, and he throws two breaking balls, with his slider ranking ahead of his curveball. He fills the strike zone and creates deception with the backswing and leg kick in his delivery. The combination of his lefthandedness, stuff and command made Anderson one of the most big league-ready players in the 2011 draft. He may start his career in low Class A, but he may not need more than two years in the minors. He has the upside of a No. 3 starter.

BA GRADE
50
MEDIUM

Year	Club (League)	Class	W	L	ERA	G	GS	CG	SV	IP	H	HR	BB	SO	K/9	WHIP	AVG
2011	Did Not Play—Signed Late																

8 KENT MATTHES, OF

Born: Jan. 8, 1987. **B-T:** R-R. **Ht.:** 6-2. **Wt.:** 215. **Drafted:** Alabama, 2009 (4th round). **Signed by:** Damon Iannelli.

Matthes hobbled through 21 games in 2010 before having surgery on a torn patellar tendon in his left knee, an injury that occurred while working out before spring training. He came back to win the California League MVP award and lead the circuit in slugging (.642) in 2011, though his season ended when a pitch broke his left hand on Aug. 3. Matthes' bat speed and power are as good as any Rockies farmhand's. He has more of a flat than an uphill swing, and his homers tend to be high line drives. He has very strong hands but lacks a fluid, easy stroke. It's better than the aluminum-bat swing he brought into pro ball, which led to excessive strikeouts in his first two pro seasons. Matthes does a good job of covering all quadrants of the strike zone, though he still has to prove he can handle quality offspeed pitches. While he doesn't chase many pitches, he also walks infrequently. Despite his knee injury, Matthes still has solid speed. He has one of the strongest arms in the system and average range, though he sometimes loses focus in right field. Because he signed as a college senior and lost a year to injury, Matthes will be 25 when he gets to Double-A in 2012. Colorado wants to see how he handles more advanced pitching to get a better read on him.

BA GRADE
50
MEDIUM

Year	Club (League)	Class	AVG	G	AB	R	H	2B	3B	HR	RBI	BB	SO	SB	CS	OBP	SLG
2009	Tri-City (NWL)	SS	.289	63	239	39	69	23	1	5	35	21	77	6	4	.364	.456
2010	Asheville (SAL)	LoA	.185	21	81	9	15	7	1	1	11	5	32	0	0	.261	.333
2011	Modesto (CAL)	HiA	.334	93	371	70	124	39	3	23	95	22	80	7	4	.378	.642
Minor League Totals			.301	177	691	118	208	69	5	29	141	48	189	13	8	.359	.541

9 KYLE PARKER, OF

Born: Sept. 30, 1989. **B-T:** R-R. **Ht.:** 6-0. **Wt.:** 200. **Drafted:** Clemson, 2010 (1st round). **Signed by:** Jay Matthews.

The 26th overall pick in 2010, Parker turned down a $2.2 million offer in mid-July that stipulated he immediately give up football. Instead, he signed for $1.4 million at the Aug. 15 deadline and played his final season at quarterback for Clemson. The son of former NFL wide receiver Carl Parker, Kyle is only player in NCAA Division I history to throw 20 touchdown passes and hit 20 homers in the same school year. He sustained broken ribs in his final football game but was ready for spring training. Parker has plus bat speed and strength to go with an aggressive mentality, too aggressive as evidenced by his 133 strikeouts in 117 pro games. His swing gets long and he struggles with breaking balls, notably sliders on the outer half of the plate. He has above-average raw power but will have to tone down his approach to make the most of it. Parker is a below-average runner with solid arm strength and range that fits in right field. Colorado would like to see him show more urgency about maximizing his talent. Making the transition from football to baseball with little time off, Parker was worn out by the end of 2011 but managed to hit .300/.393/.535 in the second half.

BA GRADE
50
MEDIUM

TONY FARLOW

He could put up big numbers in the hitter-friendly California League in 2012.

Year	Club (League)	Class	AVG	G	AB	R	H	2B	3B	HR	RBI	BB	SO	SB	CS	OBP	SLG
2011	Asheville (SAL)	LoA	.285	117	445	75	127	23	1	21	95	48	133	2	0	.367	.483
Minor League Totals			.285	117	445	75	127	23	1	21	95	48	133	2	0	.367	.483

10 JOSH RUTLEDGE, SS

Born: April 21, 1989. **B-T:** R-R. **Ht.:** 6-1. **Wt.:** 190. **Drafted:** Alabama, 2010 (3rd round). **Signed by:** Damon Iannelli.

Though a wrist injury limited Rutledge to 11 games at short-season Tri-City in his 2010 pro debut, he skipped a level to high Class A Modesto in his first full season. After a nondescript .260/.352/.313 first half, he exploded to hit .410/.459/.664 with all nine of his homers in the second half, putting together a 27-game hitting streak. Rutledge has outstanding hand-eye coordination and a compact stroke, albeit with some stiffness. He takes a quick, flat path to the ball and uses the whole field. He has good balance, and improving his load and weight shift in the second half enabled him to center more balls. He has the tools to hit for a high average with at least gap power. A solid runner, he can steal a few bases as well. Rutledge has improved at shortstop, but he has trouble at times making plays on balls to his left and throws from deep in the hole. He has soft hands and the range for shortstop, but his average arm likely will push him to second base. He throws flat-footed too often. Troy Tulowitzki eventually would force him off shortstop anyway, so Rutledge may start seeing some time at second base in 2012. He'll open the year in Double-A with a chance to hit his way to Triple-A if continues to produce like he did at the end of 2011.

BA GRADE 50 MEDIUM

Year	Club (League)	Class	AVG	G	AB	R	H	2B	3B	HR	RBI	BB	SO	SB	CS	OBP	SLG
2010	Tri-City (NWL)	SS	.128	11	39	6	5	0	0	0	4	4	10	1	0	.227	.128
2011	Modesto (CAL)	HiA	.348	113	460	91	160	33	9	9	71	41	91	16	3	.414	.517
Minor League Totals			.331	124	499	97	165	33	9	9	75	45	101	17	3	.399	.487

11 CHARLIE BLACKMON, OF

BA GRADE 50 MEDIUM

Born: July 1, 1986. **B-T:** L-L. **Ht.:** 6-3. **Wt.:** 200. **Drafted:** Georgia Tech, 2008 (2nd round). **Signed by:** Alan Matthews.

Blackmon earned a promotion to the Rockies on June 7 and that night made the first of 14 consecutive starts in left field. A freak injury ended his season a month later, however, when he broke his left foot while rounding second base. Drafted as a pitcher out of high school and junior college, he moved to the outfielder in a college summer league in 2007 and played his way into the second round of the 2008 draft. Blackmon has an easy swing and doesn't strike out often, a trait he carried to the big leagues. He did a better job of handling lefthanders last season and should be able to hit for a solid average. He shows flashes of power, but how much he'll ultimately have is a question. Blackmon may lack the bat speed to catch up to quality fastballs and do a lot of damage. Though he was a center fielder in the minors prior to 2011, he's more of a corner outfielder and will need better than average pop to profile as a regular. Blackmon runs and bunts well. His routes, reads and first-step quickness in the outfield need to improve further, but they have gotten better. He has plus arm strength and has learned to streamline his throwing mechanics. Very focused and aggressive, he plays with an edge. Given Colorado's troubles last year, Blackmon would have played a lot had he not gotten hurt, which would have given the club a better read on whether he'll be more than a fourth outfielder. He should open 2012 in that role for the Rockies.

Year	Club (League)	Class	AVG	G	AB	R	H	2B	3B	HR	RBI	BB	SO	SB	CS	OBP	SLG
2008	Tri-City (NWL)	SS	.338	68	290	42	98	21	5	2	33	16	37	13	7	.390	.466
2009	Modesto (CAL)	HiA	.307	133	550	87	169	34	7	7	69	39	83	30	13	.370	.433
2010	Tulsa (TL)	AA	.297	86	337	53	100	22	4	11	55	32	43	19	7	.360	.484
2011	Colo. Springs (PCL)	AAA	.337	58	243	49	82	19	4	10	49	19	34	12	5	.393	.572
	Colorado (NL)	MAJ	.255	27	98	9	25	1	0	1	8	3	8	5	1	.277	.296
Major League Totals			.255	27	98	9	25	1	0	1	8	3	8	5	1	.277	.296
Minor League Totals			.316	345	1420	231	449	96	20	30	206	106	197	74	32	.376	.475

12 TYLER MATZEK, LHP

BA GRADE 55 EXTREME

Born: Oct. 19, 1990. **B-T:** L-L. **Ht.:** 6-3. **Wt.:** 210. **Drafted:** HS—Capistrano Valley, Calif., 2009 (1st round). **Signed by:** Jon Lukens.

Matzek has become an enigma, something the Rockies didn't expect when they took him 11th overall in 2009 and signed him for a franchise-record $3.9 million. Some clubs rated him as the second-best prospect behind only Stephen Strasburg in that draft, but he hasn't pitched up to it. After he began 2011 in a 10-start swoon in high Class A in 2011, the Rockies demoted him. Following three rough starts in low

Class A, he asked to return home to southern California to work with Lon Fullmer, his youth pitching coach and a disciple of Mike Marshall, the 1974 National League Cy Young Award winner whose ideas about pitching are generally shunned by the baseball establishment. Matzek returned to Asheville after three weeks, going back to the high arm slot he used as an amateur. He had more success, going 5-2, 2.78 with 64 strikeouts in 55 innings, albeit with 35 walks. Matzek remained inconsistent with his fastball velocity, which ranged from 84-96 mph during instructional league. He can sit easily at 92 mph when he gets in a groove, but his mechanics vary. That's particularly evident when he works out of the stretch, as he breaks his hands late and drifts on the mound. He also has problems throwing strikes low in the zone, which may always be an issue because his hand position at the top of his delivery gets him underneath the ball. Matzek also throws a pair of hard breaking balls in his curveball and slider, and he also has a changeup. All of his secondary pitches are hit or miss, though his changeup showed improvement toward the end of instructional league. Matzek still has stuff but ultimately whether he succeeds will come down to command. He must do a better job of getting his fastball in on righthanders. He also needs to trust his pitching coaches and his ability to make pitches. He's a perfectionist and starts working faster when things aren't going well. Matzek can be his own worst enemy, expecting things to go wrong at times and letting negative thoughts affect him when they do. It wouldn't hurt him to tone up his lower half and make it more flexible, which would help his delivery. He'll give high Class A another try in 2012, when Colorado hopes to get a better handle on what exactly he can become.

Year	Club (League)	Class	W	L	ERA	G	GS	CG	SV	IP	H	HR	BB	SO	K/9	WHIP	AVG
2010	Asheville (SAL)	LoA	5	1	2.92	18	18	0	0	89	62	6	62	88	8.9	1.39	.204
2011	Modesto (CAL)	HiA	0	3	9.82	10	10	0	0	33	34	5	46	37	10.1	2.42	.266
	Asheville (SAL)	LoA	5	4	4.36	12	12	0	0	64	45	3	50	74	10.4	1.48	.202
Minor League Totals			10	8	4.64	40	40	0	0	186	141	14	158	199	9.6	1.60	.215

13 D.J. LeMAHIEU, 3B/2B

Born: July 13, 1988. **B-T:** R-R. **Ht.:** 6-4. **Wt.:** 215. **Drafted:** Louisiana State, 2009 (2nd round). **Signed by:** Steve Riha (Cubs).

LeMahieu led 2009 College World Series champion Louisiana State with a .350 average and signed for an above-slot $508,000 as a Cubs second-round pick that summer. He has continued to hit, batting .317 in three minor league seasons, but he has yet to show that he can do enough else to become a big league regular. Chicago's new regime didn't wait to find out, trading him and Tyler Colvin to the Rockies in December for Ian Stewart and 2007 first-rounder Casey Weathers. Though he has impressive size and strength, LeMahieu is content to stay inside pitches and serve them to the opposite field. He rarely turns on balls and drives them for power, with his five homers in 2011 representing a career high. His proponents believe he'll develop into a 40-double/15-homer threat once he does a better job of recognizing which pitches he can drive, but most scouts see him as a singles hitter who doesn't provide enough beyond his batting average. He makes contact so easily that he doesn't draw many walks. LeMahieu's lack of pop wouldn't matter as much if he could stick in the middle infield, where he has spent much of his pro career, but his fringy speed and quickness don't fit at second base or shortstop. His best position is third base, where his soft hands and solid arm make him an average defender, but he'll have to show more power to play every day at the hot corner. LeMahieu spent all of June and most of September with the Cubs, but former manager Mike Quade never gave him much playing time to show what he could do. Though LeMahieu will compete for a job in spring training, Nolan Arenado is clearly Colorado's future at third base.

Year	Club (League)	Class	AVG	G	AB	R	H	2B	3B	HR	RBI	BB	SO	SB	CS	OBP	SLG
2009	Cubs (AZL)	R	.417	3	12	2	5	0	1	0	4	1	3	1	0	.429	.583
	Peoria (MWL)	LoA	.316	38	152	19	48	4	2	0	30	12	22	2	2	.371	.368
2010	Daytona (FSL)	HiA	.314	135	554	63	174	24	5	2	73	29	61	15	7	.346	.386
2011	Tennessee (SL)	AA	.358	50	187	32	67	15	2	2	27	11	22	4	3	.386	.492
	Iowa (PCL)	AAA	.286	58	227	23	65	7	1	3	23	14	27	5	5	.328	.366
	Chicago (NL)	MAJ	.250	37	60	3	15	2	0	0	4	1	12	0	0	.262	.283
Major League Totals			.250	37	60	3	15	2	0	0	4	1	12	0	0	.262	.283
Minor League Totals			.317	284	1132	139	359	50	11	7	157	67	135	27	17	.353	.399

14 CHRISTIAN FRIEDRICH, LHP

Born: July 8, 1987. **B-T:** R-L. **Ht.:** 6-4. **Wt.:** 215. **Drafted:** Eastern Kentucky, 2008 (1st round). **Signed by:** Scott Corman.

The 25th overall pick in the 2008 draft, Friedrich signed for $1.35 million and breezed to high Class A by the end of his first full pro season. But he hasn't progressed as the Rockies have hoped since then, spending the last two years going 9-16, 5.02 in Double-A. After missing a month with elbow inflammation in both 2009 and 2010 and having a strained lat muscle end the latter season, the good news was that Friedrich stayed healthy last year. He relaxed his grip and arm while working on his changeup and realized that he had been muscling his pitches too much. When he had success, Friedrich relied on two plus pitches, an 89-93 mph fastball that touched 95 and a big-breaking curveball. Last year, he lost a tick of velocity on his heater but began to change speeds with it. With more of a finesse fastball approach, he didn't use his curve as much and it suffered. Friedrich has some feel for his decent changeup but doesn't always locate it where he wants. He also mixes in a slider, though it has more rolling action than bite. He did a better of throwing strikes last year but his command must improve. Friedrich learned a lot about pitching in 2011 and the time has come to implement it. Colorado showed its faith by protecting him on its 40-man roster and will send him to Triple-A in 2012.

Year	Club (League)	Class	W	L	ERA	G	GS	CG	SV	IP	H	HR	BB	SO	K/9	WHIP	AVG
2008	Tri-City (NWL)	SS	2	1	3.25	8	8	0	0	36	31	2	8	50	12.5	1.08	.228
	Asheville (SAL)	LoA	0	1	7.50	3	3	0	0	12	14	2	7	15	11.3	1.75	.269
2009	Asheville (SAL)	LoA	3	3	2.18	8	8	0	0	45	35	2	15	66	13.1	1.10	.215
	Modesto (CAL)	HiA	3	2	2.54	14	14	0	0	74	59	3	28	93	11.3	1.17	.215
2010	Tulsa (TL)	AA	3	6	5.05	18	18	0	0	87	100	10	35	78	8.0	1.55	.293
2011	Tulsa (TL)	AA	6	10	5.00	25	25	0	0	133	156	20	43	103	7.0	1.49	.286
Minor League Totals			17	23	4.13	76	76	0	0	388	395	39	136	405	9.4	1.37	.261

15 PETER TAGO, RHP

| BA GRADE |
| **55** |
| EXTREME |

Born: July 5, 1982. **B-T:** R-R. **Ht.:** 6-3. **Wt.:** 180. **Drafted:** HS—Dana Hills, Calif., 2010 (1st round supplemental). **Signed by:** Jon Lukens.

The Rockies selected Tago 47th overall in the 2010 draft with a compensation pick they received for the loss of free agent Jason Marquis. Tago signed for $982,500 hours before the Aug. 16 deadline and didn't begin his pro career until 2011. Colorado kept him in extended spring training, which it typically does with high school pitchers at the outset of their careers to limit their innings and keep them in warmer weather. He had problems repeating his delivery once he got to low Class A in late May, contributing to a 7.07 ERA and 72 walks in 90 innings. Tago has the stuff to become a frontline starter but also has plenty of work to do. His fastball already sits at 90-91 mph and touches 95, and he should find more velocity with more consistent mechanics. His curveball rates ahead of his changeup, though both are works in progress that suffer when he doesn't maintain his release point. Tago has an easy arm action but is still growing into his body, and the Rockies hope he'll settle down once he matures physically. After looking overmatched at Asheville, he'll return there to begin 2012.

Year	Club (League)	Class	W	L	ERA	G	GS	CG	SV	IP	H	HR	BB	SO	K/9	WHIP	AVG
2011	Asheville (SAL)	LoA	3	5	7.07	19	19	0	0	90	88	10	72	58	5.8	1.77	.267
Minor League Totals			3	5	7.07	19	19	0	0	90	88	10	72	58	5.8	1.77	.267

16 ROSELL HERRERA, SS/3B

| BA GRADE |
| **50** |
| HIGH |

Born: Oct. 16, 1992. **B-T:** B-R. **Ht.:** 6-3. **Wt.:** 180. **Signed:** Dominican Republic, 2009. **Signed by:** Rolando Fernandez/Jhonathan Leyba.

The Rockies signed Herrera for $800,000 out of the Dominican Republic in 2009. After he made the his pro debut in the Rookie-level Dominican Summer League in 2010, he was the only DSL player Colorado invited to instructional league that fall. He made his U.S. debut last summer at Casper, where he and Trevor Story shared shortstop and also saw time at third base. A switch-hitter, Herrera is a significantly better hitter with more power from the left side. He doesn't have the same bat speed from the right side. Herrera has a lot of moving parts at the plate but exceptional hand-eye coordination, so he's able to barrel the ball. He can get overly long and loft-happy with his swing, but he toned things down and didn't load up on his back side and whale away as often in the latter stages of 2011. Herrera has average speed and range to go with solid arm strength. He throws from a low angle and doesn't get on top of the ball, costing him accuracy, as does his inconsistent footwork. Already 6-foot-3, he figures to outgrow shortstop and could end up at third base, the outfield or even first base. The Rockies want both him and Story to play regularly at shortstop in 2012, so Herrera probably will go to Tri-City while Story heads to Asheville.

Year	Club (League)	Class	AVG	G	AB	R	H	2B	3B	HR	RBI	BB	SO	SB	CS	OBP	SLG
2010	Rockies (DSL)	R	.237	67	232	27	55	6	1	1	26	24	24	17	8	.323	.284
2011	Casper (PIO)	R	.284	63	243	38	69	6	8	6	34	27	62	5	4	.361	.449
Minor League Totals			.261	130	475	65	124	12	9	7	60	51	86	22	12	.343	.368

17 JORDAN PACHECO, C/1B/3B

| BA GRADE |
| **45** |
| MEDIUM |

Born: Jan. 30, 1986. **B-T:** R-R. **Ht.:** 6-1. **Wt.:** 190. **Drafted:** New Mexico, 2007 (9th round). **Signed by:** Mike Ericson.

Pacheco played second base in college at New Mexico and saw time at shortstop during his 2007 pro debut before moving to catcher the following spring. He spent most of 2010 in high Class A before a season-ending injury to Wilin Rosario gave Pacheco an opportunity in Double-A. He parlayed that and a strong big league camp last spring into a Triple-A assignment in 2011, setting the stage for a September callup. During his first exposure to the big leagues, Pacheco played at first base, third base, catcher and second base.

He'll be a super-utility player going forward, capable of providing offense off the bench and serving as a third catcher. While at Colorado Springs, Pacheco raised doubts about his ability to be an everyday catcher. Problems with his transfer and footwork diminished his throwing accuracy, as he nabbed just 20 percent of basestealers despite solid arm strength. He let his throwing troubles and the challenge of handling a poor pitching staff leak into his offense. Freed of the burden of catching regularly in Colorado, Pacheco had a much improved offensive approach. He did a better job of using all fields and staying back and letting the ball travel deep. He has an uncanny ability to make contact, though his power is limited. Pacheco has fringy speed and infield range, though he does have soft hands and can make the routine play. He'll have a chance in spring training to win a roster spot with the Rockies, who view his bat as a valuable asset.

Year	Club (League)	Class	AVG	G	AB	R	H	2B	3B	HR	RBI	BB	SO	SB	CS	OBP	SLG
2007	Casper (PIO)	R	.292	55	192	27	56	10	2	3	29	21	36	3	1	.380	.411
	Tri-City (NWL)	SS	.258	8	31	5	8	2	0	0	3	1	6	0	0	.324	.323
2008	Tri-City (NWL)	SS	.280	54	214	26	60	8	3	1	35	26	20	3	3	.368	.360
2009	Asheville (SAL)	LoA	.322	117	451	67	145	30	4	13	79	38	44	12	2	.379	.492
2010	Modesto (CAL)	HiA	.321	104	390	59	125	27	3	5	70	54	36	5	6	.407	.444
	Tulsa (TL)	AA	.333	21	78	11	26	5	0	1	19	6	6	1	1	.396	.436
2011	Colo. Springs (PCL)	AAA	.278	97	363	57	101	21	3	3	50	30	48	2	2	.343	.377
	Colorado (NL)	MAJ	.286	21	84	5	24	1	0	2	14	3	9	0	0	.318	.369
Major League Totals			.286	21	84	5	24	1	0	2	14	3	9	0	0	.318	.369
Minor League Totals			.303	456	1719	251	521	103	15	26	285	176	196	26	15	.377	.426

18 EDWAR CABRERA, LHP

BA GRADE

45 MEDIUM

Born: Oct. 10, 1987. **B-T:** L-L. **Ht.:** 6-0. **Wt.:** 160. **Signed:** Dominican Republic, 2008. **Signed by:** Rolando Fernandez/Jhonathan Leyba/Martin Cabrera.

After leading the short-season Northwest League with 87 strikeouts in 73 innings in 2010, his first full year in the United States, Cabrera was even more impressive in his first taste of full-season ball. Splitting 2011 between Asheville and Modesto, he led the minors with 217 whiffs while walking just 41 in 167 innings, earning a spot on Colorado's 40-man roster. Scouts still question how dominant he'll be against more advanced hitters because his out pitch is a superb changeup. He sells his changeup with quality arm speed and has the confidence to throw the pitch in any count. Cabrera's fastball runs from 87-91 mph, and he tends to work the outer half of the plate with it. He'll need to come inside more with his fastball against better hitters so he can set them up for his changeup away. His curveball is below average, though to his credit he focused on trying to improve it in instructional league. Cabrera profiles as a No. 4 or 5 starter in the big leagues. He'll begin 2012 in Double-A and will be pushed because of his age. There are whispers that he spent time in the Twins system before the Rockies signed him in March 2008 and that he's older than 24.

Year	Club (League)	Class	W	L	ERA	G	GS	CG	SV	IP	H	HR	BB	SO	K/9	WHIP	AVG
2008	Rockies (DSL)	R	5	1	0.92	8	8	0	0	49	26	1	18	75	13.9	0.90	.158
	Casper (PIO)	R	0	4	7.80	9	5	0	0	30	38	7	15	38	11.4	1.77	.304
2009	Rockies (DSL)	R	1	0	1.16	7	3	0	0	31	16	0	10	50	14.5	0.84	.145
	Casper (PIO)	R	0	0	3.38	9	1	0	0	21	19	2	12	28	11.8	1.45	.235
2010	Tri-City (NWL)	SS	1	8	3.07	14	14	0	0	73	71	2	24	87	10.7	1.30	.251
2011	Asheville (SAL)	LoA	4	2	3.14	13	13	0	0	86	77	10	18	110	11.5	1.10	.237
	Modesto (CAL)	HiA	4	1	3.56	13	13	0	0	81	78	8	23	107	11.9	1.25	.252
Minor League Totals			15	16	3.15	73	57	0	0	371	325	30	120	495	12.0	1.20	.232

19 HECTOR GOMEZ, SS

BA GRADE

50 HIGH

Born: March 5, 1988. **B-T:** R-R. **Ht.:** 6-2. **Wt.:** 180. **Signed:** Dominican Republic, 2004. **Signed by:** Rolando Fernandez/Felix Feliz/Frank Roa.

Staying healthy has been a problem for Gomez, who has played in just 214 games over the last four seasons. He missed all but one game in 2008 with a stress fracture in his left leg and an elbow injury that required Tommy John surgery, had groin problems in 2009 and a stress fracture in his right leg in 2010. He also had to deal with the death of his son shortly after his birth in June 2010. He and his girlfriend had a healthy son in May 2011, and Gomez was able to play in 102 games despite dealing with back problems. He went home at the end of the minor league season when the Rockies, needing shortstop depth because of several injuries, unexpectedly called him to the big leagues Sept. 16. He made his major league debut that night and went 2-for-4 in his first start the following day. Colorado wrote him in the lineup twice in the next three days, but he had to be scratched because of a sore lower back and didn't play the rest of the season. Gomez has the tools to make all the plays at shortstop, including plus range, soft hands, quick feet and a very strong arm. He did a better job of playing under control in 2011, fielding a career-high .963. At the plate, Gomez has strong hands that whip the bat through the zone quickly and give him good pop for a middle infielder. He's capable of 15 homers per season, though he's such a free swinger that he often gets himself out by chasing pitches. Gomez will open 2012 in Triple-A, with the Rockies once again hoping that he finally can stay on the field for a full season.

Year	Club (League)	Class	AVG	G	AB	R	H	2B	3B	HR	RBI	BB	SO	SB	CS	OBP	SLG
2005	Rockies (DSL)	R	.335	67	242	49	81	16	1	6	43	24	38	15	12	.423	.483
2006	Casper (PIO)	R	.327	50	202	24	66	9	4	5	35	11	26	5	3	.364	.485
	Tri-City (NWL)	SS	.244	12	45	4	11	3	0	0	6	0	14	0	1	.255	.311
2007	Asheville (SAL)	LoA	.266	124	534	89	142	34	8	11	61	29	120	20	10	.309	.421
2008	Modesto (CAL)	HiA	.333	1	3	0	1	0	0	0	0	0	0	0	0	.333	.333
2009	Modesto (CAL)	HiA	.275	83	338	39	93	21	4	7	46	15	68	10	4	.310	.423
2010	Tri-City (NWL)	SS	.246	18	69	8	17	2	1	2	7	5	15	0	3	.293	.391
	Tulsa (TL)	AA	.314	9	35	6	11	4	0	0	3	0	8	0	0	.314	.429
2011	Tulsa (TL)	AA	.235	102	425	46	100	23	6	14	50	19	94	16	4	.272	.416
	Colorado (NL)	MAJ	.333	2	6	1	2	0	0	0	0	1	2	0	0	.429	.333
Major League Totals			.333	2	6	1	2	0	0	0	0	1	2	0	0	.429	.333
Minor League Totals			.276	466	1893	265	522	112	24	45	251	103	383	66	37	.321	.432

20 CRISTHIAN ADAMES, SS

Born: July 26, 1991. **B-T:** B-R. **Ht.:** 6-0. **Wt.:** 160. **Signed:** Dominican Republic, 2007. **Signed by:** Rolando Fernandez/Felix Feliz.

Adames spent two years in the Dominican Summer League before making his U.S. debut in 2010, only to have a broken left thumb end his season in mid-August. He moved up to low Class A as a 19-year-old last season and came on strong in the final month, batting .325/.416/.444. Adames has good balance, loads his hands well and shows some gap power from both sides of the plate. He does a good job of staying inside the ball and for the most part, he doesn't try to do too much. He needs to get stronger and develop a little more plate discipline but should be able to do both. Adames is the best defensive shortstop in the system. His actions are reminiscent of those of former Rockies Gold Glover Neifi Perez, though Adames plays more under control. He has solid range, soft hands and average arm strength, and he makes extremely accurate throws. He can get careless with his footwork at times because he knows he can compensate with his hands and arm. He led South Atlantic League shortstops with a .966 fielding percentage despite his youth. Adames has fringy speed and is still learning to run the bases. He'll move up to high Class A in 2012.

Year	Club (League)	Class	AVG	G	AB	R	H	2B	3B	HR	RBI	BB	SO	SB	CS	OBP	SLG
2008	Rockies (DSL)	R	.262	51	168	22	44	5	0	0	8	18	26	7	8	.339	.292
2009	Rockies (DSL)	R	.231	36	121	17	28	6	0	1	19	18	24	8	3	.340	.306
2010	Casper (PIO)	R	.290	37	145	30	42	9	0	1	15	14	24	4	5	.356	.372
2011	Asheville (SAL)	LoA	.273	108	399	63	109	17	2	8	44	42	74	2	0	.350	.386
Minor League Totals			.268	232	833	132	223	37	2	10	86	92	148	21	16	.347	.353

21 WILL SWANNER, C

Born: Sept. 10, 1991. **B-T:** R-R. **Ht.:** 6-2. **Wt.:** 185. **Drafted:** HS—Carlsbad, Calif., 2010 (15th round). **Signed by:** Jon Lukens.

Swanner hit seven homers in 18 games at Casper in 2010 after signing shortly before the deadline for $490,000 as a 15th-rounder. He returned to the Pioneer League last summer with the goals of improving his plate discipline and his receiving, and made strides in both areas before injuring his left thumb Aug. 13. He missed all but three games the rest of the way and had surgery to repair a torn ulnar collateral ligament in the thumb, knocking him out of instructional league. Swanner hits the ball very hard and has above-average power. In his second stint with Casper, he showed more patience and a better two-strike approach. Making steady contact remains an issue, because he doesn't recognize breaking balls well and still can get overly aggressive at times. Swanner shows leadership qualities behind the plate and has plenty of arm strength. His arm action needs to be shortened, because he has a tendency to pause and unnecessarily reach back for more velocity on his throws. He caught just 19 percent of basestealers last year and also committed nine passed balls in 31 games. His height make it difficult for him to get low enough when blocking balls. Like most catchers, Swanner is a below-average runner. He's ready for full-season ball and will move up to low Class A this year.

Year	Club (League)	Class	AVG	G	AB	R	H	2B	3B	HR	RBI	BB	SO	SB	CS	OBP	SLG
2010	Casper (PIO)	R	.303	18	76	14	23	4	0	7	13	0	33	0	1	.321	.632
2011	Casper (PIO)	R	.264	43	159	33	42	14	1	10	24	20	60	1	2	.357	.553
Minor League Totals			.277	61	235	47	65	18	1	17	37	20	93	1	3	.346	.579

22 RAFAEL ORTEGA, OF

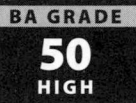

Born: May 15, 1991. **B-T:** L-R. **Ht.:** 5-11. **Wt.:** 160. **Signed:** Venezuela, 2008. **Signed by:** Rolando Fernandez/Francisco Cartaya/Carlos Gomez.

Ortega batted .358 at Casper in a stellar U.S. debut in 2010. His girlfriend gave birth to their first child in Venezuela late in the season, but that did nothing to detract from his focus and high level of play. He's at his best in games and not particularly impressive in spring training, batting practice and the like. Ortega is the fastest runner in a system that lacks a true burner, and he's also the best defensive outfielder among

Rockies farmhands. He's still working on his reads and jumps on the bases after getting caught in 19 of 51 steal attempts last year, but he's a true center fielder with a fearlessness when it comes to going after flyballs at the wall. He also has a strong arm for his position. Ortega hit too many balls in the air early in the 2011 season but worked to level out his swing path and batted .313/.352/.492 in the second half. He's a leadoff hitter who has quick hands and handles the bat well, but he needs to improve his strike-zone awareness. Getting stronger also would help, though he'll never have much power. He'll play in high Class A this year.

Year	Club (League)	Class	AVG	G	AB	R	H	2B	3B	HR	RBI	BB	SO	SB	CS	OBP	SLG
2008	Rockies (DSL)	R	.277	52	188	38	52	4	2	1	11	20	20	17	3	.349	.335
2009	Rockies (DSL)	R	.324	70	256	45	83	7	8	0	39	32	23	39	12	.395	.414
2010	Casper (PIO)	R	.358	71	288	69	103	17	3	7	45	28	42	23	9	.416	.510
2011	Asheville (SAL)	LoA	.294	113	479	77	141	26	8	9	66	28	90	32	19	.335	.438
Minor League Totals			.313	306	1211	229	379	54	21	17	161	108	175	111	43	.370	.434

23 BEN PAULSEN, 1B

BA GRADE
45
MEDIUM

Born: Oct. 27, 1987. **B-T:** L-R. **Ht.:** 6-4. **Wt.:** 205. **Drafted:** Clemson, 2009 (3rd round). **Signed by:** Jay Matthews.

After hitting .303/.346/.449 in his first two pro seasons, Paulsen found Double-A more challenging last season. He still showed his plus raw power, which started to emerge as he hit a career-high 19 homers. But he has a long swing with a lot of moving parts and tends to drift to the ball, raising concerns about whether he can hit more advanced pitching. He batted just .241 in 2011 and did a poor job of controlling the strike zone. While he has some looseness and quickness to his stroke, Paulsen hasn't shown the ability to stay back on pitches and make adjustments. His head would dip when he took his stride, but he started holding the bat at a 45-degree angle in the Arizona Fall League and solved that problem. The change also rid him of a habit of moving his hands in front of his face and not getting loaded in time. He batted just .267/.327/.378 in the offensive-minded AFL, however. Though he's a well below-average runner, Paulsen moves decently around the bag at first base. He has a strong, accurate arm but is tentative with his throwing. He'll move up to Triple-A this year and see if the adjustments he made in the AFL will help.

Year	Club (League)	Class	AVG	G	AB	R	H	2B	3B	HR	RBI	BB	SO	SB	CS	OBP	SLG
2009	Tri-City (NWL)	SS	.280	44	175	28	49	10	2	1	25	12	32	2	1	.325	.377
2010	Modesto (CAL)	HiA	.311	130	498	65	155	29	8	12	83	33	113	5	4	.353	.474
2011	Tulsa (TL)	AA	.241	136	547	69	132	29	4	19	78	40	132	2	3	.296	.413
Minor League Totals			.275	310	1220	162	336	68	14	32	186	85	277	9	8	.323	.433

24 ROB SCAHILL, RHP

BA GRADE
45
MEDIUM

Born: Feb. 15, 1987. **B-T:** L-R. **Ht.:** 6-2. **Wt.:** 220. **Drafted:** Bradley, 2009 (8th round). **Signed by:** Mark Germann.

Scahill worked strictly with a two-seam fastball and slider when he came out of Bradley as an eighth-round pick in 2009, but he has added a four-seamer, curveball and changeup during his three years as a pro. His fastball sits at 93-94 mph and ranges from 92-96, though it lacks much life. His best secondary pitch is his curveball, an average offering at times. Scahill's slider can be an average pitch and peaks at 89 mph, though it needs more depth and he often hangs it in the strike zone. He has worked very hard on his changeup, which is still fringy and his fourth-best pitch. Scahill is aggressive on the mound and has a strong, durable frame that has allowed him to work 317 innings during the last two seasons. He has an extremely clean arm action, though it also means that his delivery lacks deception and allows hitters to see his pitches easily. His command and control are decent but don't help his stuff to play up. Scahill profiles as a No. 4 or 5 starter, though he might wind up as a middle reliever if his secondary pitches don't develop. After spending his second straight offseason in the Arizona Fall League, he'll begin 2012 in the Colorado Springs rotation.

Year	Club (League)	Class	W	L	ERA	G	GS	CG	SV	IP	H	HR	BB	SO	K/9	WHIP	AVG
2009	Tri-City (NWL)	SS	1	4	3.14	15	15	0	0	63	58	2	20	58	8.3	1.24	.245
2010	Modesto (CAL)	HiA	10	7	4.73	27	27	1	0	156	173	9	59	140	8.1	1.49	.284
2011	Tulsa (TL)	AA	12	11	3.92	27	26	1	0	161	164	12	60	104	5.8	1.39	.266
Minor League Totals			23	22	4.12	69	68	2	0	380	395	23	139	302	7.2	1.41	.270

25 JOE GARDNER, RHP

BA GRADE
45
MEDIUM

Born: May 18, 1988. **B-T:** R-R. **Ht.:** 6-4. **Wt.:** 220. **Drafted:** UC Santa Barbara, 2009 (3rd round). **Signed by:** Vince Sagisi (Indians).

An Indians third-round pick in 2009, Gardner had to wait a year to make his pro debut because of a ribcage injury. Once he got started, he quickly established himself as a groundball machine. That was especially evident after he came to the Rockies in the Ubaldo Jimenez trade last July. In six Double-A starts after switching organizations, Gardner posted a 2.48 ERA and a 4.5 groundout/airout ratio. At the time of the deal, Colorado GM Dan O'Dowd said Gardner eventually would move to the bullpen and likened his arm action, body and action on his pitches to those of Sergio Romo. Gardner lives off his 87-92 mph sinker, slinging it from a deceptive low three-quarters arm angle. His other pitches are nothing special, a below-average slider that has more bend than bite and a fringy changeup. His control and command need to improve as well. He struggles to pitch inside to lefthanders and gets jumpy while working out of the stretch. Gardner may remain in the rotation for a little while longer and should open the season in Triple-A.

Year	Club (League)	Class	W	L	ERA	G	GS	CG	SV	IP	H	HR	BB	SO	K/9	WHIP	AVG
2010	Lake County (MWL)	LoA	1	0	3.24	6	6	0	0	25	17	2	11	38	13.7	1.12	.185
	Kinston (CAR)	HiA	12	6	2.65	22	22	0	0	122	85	4	51	104	7.7	1.11	.199
2011	Akron (EL)	AA	7	8	4.99	19	19	0	0	97	108	6	47	60	5.5	1.59	.287
	Tulsa (TL)	AA	3	3	2.48	6	6	0	0	36	31	1	8	22	5.4	1.07	.226
Minor League Totals			23	17	3.49	53	53	0	0	281	241	13	117	224	7.2	1.27	.234

26 JAYSON AQUINO, LHP

BA GRADE

50

EXTREME

Born: Nov. 22, 1992. **B-T:** L-L. **Ht.:** 6-1. **Wt.:** 175. **Signed:** Dominican Republic, 2009. **Signed by:** Rolando Fernandez/Jhonathan Leyba/Frank Roa.

Aquino has dominated the Dominican Summer League in his two years in pro ball, leading the circuit with two shutouts and a 0.71 WHIP in 2010 and ranking third in ERA in both seasons. He was the only players from the Rockies' 2011 DSL team to be invited to instructional league. He has a lean, projectable body and the chance to have a quality three-pitch mix in the future. Aquino already pitches at 88-91 mph with his fastball, touches 92 and throws it for strikes. He worked a lot on his curveball in instructional league. While he doesn't have feel for his curve yet, his ability to spin the ball bodes well for its future. He has good arm speed and decent action on his changeup, even if it's still very inconsistent. Aquino has the potential to become a No. 3 starter but is years from reaching it. He'll make his U.S. debut in 2012, participating in extended spring training before heading to Colorado's new Pioneer League affiliate in Grand Junction.

Year	Club (League)	Class	W	L	ERA	G	GS	CG	SV	IP	H	HR	BB	SO	K/9	WHIP	AVG
2010	Rockies (DSL)	R	4	3	1.02	12	12	2	0	62	35	0	9	59	8.6	0.71	.161
2011	Rockies (DSL)	R	8	2	1.30	14	14	3	0	90	55	1	22	80	8.0	0.86	.175
Minor League Totals			12	5	1.19	26	26	5	0	151	90	1	31	139	8.3	0.80	.169

27 TOMMY FIELD, 2B/SS

BA GRADE

45

MEDIUM

Born: Feb. 22, 1987. **B-T:** R-R. **Ht.:** 5-9. **Wt.:** 175. **Drafted:** Texas State, 2008 (24th round). **Signed by:** Chris Forbes.

Signed for $43,000 as a 28th-round pick in 2008, Field beat the odds and made it to Coors Field three years later. His September callup five days after his Double-A season ended took him by surprise, but injuries decimated the Rockies at shortstop and he started 12 of their final 17 games. He's a grinder who has drawn comparisons to Jamey Carroll, the former Rockie who parlayed his grit into a $6.5 million free-agent deal with the Twins this offseason. Field has surprising power for a 5-foot-9 middle infielder, as he can pull balls out of the park and has hit 32 homers over the last two seasons. He strikes out too much, though, and he has to work on his balance at the plate because he tends to drift too much onto his back leg and pop balls up. Field doesn't really have a plus tool but makes the most of what he has. He has average speed, though he's not a basestealing threat. He was primarily a shortstop until teaming with Hector Gomez and moving to second base at Tulsa in 2011. Field has good range, reliable hands and a solid arm. He profiles as a utility player capable of playing second base, shortstop and third base. He even manned right field for three innings in Colorado. Field will open 2012 in Triple-A and wait for a need to arise with the Rockies.

Year	Club (League)	Class	AVG	G	AB	R	H	2B	3B	HR	RBI	BB	SO	SB	CS	OBP	SLG
2008	Tri-City (NWL)	SS	.247	56	182	34	45	8	2	5	32	42	34	10	6	.403	.396
2009	Asheville (SAL)	LoA	.257	89	304	42	78	17	0	2	32	26	58	8	3	.335	.332
2010	Modesto (CAL)	HiA	.284	124	440	84	125	21	7	15	72	66	114	16	5	.397	.466
2011	Tulsa (TL)	AA	.271	134	472	77	128	22	3	17	61	53	108	9	4	.357	.439
	Colorado (NL)	MAJ	.271	16	48	4	13	0	0	0	3	3	14	0	0	.314	.271
Major League Totals			.271	16	48	4	13	0	0	0	3	3	14	0	0	.314	.271
Minor League Totals			.269	403	1398	237	376	68	12	39	197	187	314	43	18	.372	.418

28 PARKER FRAZIER, RHP

BA GRADE

45

HIGH

Born: Nov. 11, 1988. **B-T:** R-R. **Ht.:** 6-5. **Wt.:** 185. **Drafted:** HS—Tulsa, 2007 (8th round). **Signed by:** Dar Cox.

Frazier required Tommy John surgery in September 2009, but his arm was in such good shape at the time that he was able to return in nine months and become Tri-City's Opening Night pitcher in June 2010. He moved up to Modesto within a month and spent the entire 2011 season there. He's the son of former major league reliever and current Rockies television analyst George Frazier, so it's no surprise that Parker has good feel for pitching. He consistently throws strikes and relies on an 88-92 mph sinker. His slider is an average pitch at times, but it's often slurvy and he falls in love with it too much. His changeup is a below-average offering and won't improve unless he uses it more often. Frazier is a good competitor but can be his own worst enemy, sometimes overthrowing his fastball and leaving it up in the zone. There's a lot of effort in his delivery, which contributed to his elbow injury. Frazier will begin 2012 in Tulsa, his hometown. He has a ceiling as a fifth starter but profiles more as a middle reliever.

Year	Club (League)	Class	W	L	ERA	G	GS	CG	SV	IP	H	HR	BB	SO	K/9	WHIP	AVG
2007	Casper (PIO)	R	3	5	10.07	16	10	0	0	45	78	8	18	22	4.4	2.15	.386
2008	Tri-City (NWL)	SS	5	5	3.83	15	15	0	0	87	94	3	20	47	4.9	1.31	.281
2009	Asheville (SAL)	LoA	10	7	4.48	23	23	1	0	131	158	7	33	98	6.8	1.46	.303
2010	Tri-City (NWL)	SS	1	3	7.52	5	5	0	0	20	28	1	8	15	6.6	1.77	.318
	Modesto (CAL)	HiA	2	2	4.70	9	9	0	0	46	49	1	11	38	7.4	1.30	.269
2011	Modesto (CAL)	HiA	11	11	4.50	27	27	0	0	154	171	15	46	105	6.1	1.41	.281
Minor League Totals			32	33	5.03	95	89	1	0	483	578	35	136	325	6.1	1.48	.299

29 COTY WOODS, RHP

BA GRADE
40
MEDIUM

Born: March 3, 1988. **B-T:** R-R. **Ht.:** 6-2. **Wt.:** 190. **Drafted:** Middle Tennessee State, 2009 (33rd round). **Signed by:** Scott Corman.

Another late-round find for the Rockies, Woods signed for $20,000 as a 33rd-round choice in 2009. He pitched his way into prospect status last season in high Class A, where he had a string of 35⅓ consecutive scoreless innings and gave up just four homers in 78 innings. Woods works from an arm slot that's even lower than a traditional sidearm delivery, and the unusual angle makes his 89-91 mph fastball look a lot quicker. Hitters can't pull his fastball unless he elevates it. He also throws a sweeping slider that his low arm slot also enhances, and he has a surprisingly effective changeup that helped him hold righthanders to a .215 average last year. Against more advanced competition, Woods will have to do a better job of coming inside against lefties, who hit .292 against him in 2011, and throw more strikes in general. Ticketed for Double-A this season, Woods could become a righthanded specialist in the mold of Darren O'Day.

Year	Club (League)	Class	W	L	ERA	G	GS	CG	SV	IP	H	HR	BB	SO	K/9	WHIP	AVG
2009	Casper (PIO)	R	2	1	4.43	17	0	0	2	22	21	1	10	19	7.7	1.39	.244
2010	Casper (PIO)	R	1	0	2.19	8	0	0	3	12	7	1	4	14	10.2	0.89	.171
	Asheville (SAL)	LoA	0	1	2.70	16	0	0	1	27	28	3	2	32	10.8	1.13	.269
2011	Modesto (CAL)	HiA	5	4	2.19	49	0	0	1	78	61	4	33	88	10.2	1.21	.215
Minor League Totals			8	6	2.65	90	0	0	7	139	117	9	49	153	9.9	1.19	.227

30 MICHAEL MARBRY, RHP

BA GRADE
45
HIGH

Born: Sept. 3, 1984. **B-T:** R-R. **Ht.:** 6-3. **Wt.:** 185. **Drafted:** UNC Wilmington, NDFA 2006. **Signed by:** Billy Best (Braves).

A light-hitting shortstop at UNC Wilmington, Marbry signed with the Braves as a nondrafted free agent in 2006 but drew his release after going 3-for-23 (.130) in Rookie ball. He never pitched in four years of college, but Marbry threw off a mound while working as a hitting instructor in 2007 and showed enough arm strength that a friend arranged a tryout with Asheville manager Joe Mikulik and pitching coach Bryan Harvey that summer. Marbry had left to return home when Mikulik called to tell him the Tourists had an opening on their staff because of injury. Marbry since has pitched his way into Colorado's plans, emerging as Modesto's closer in the second half of 2011. Last year, he developed a more explosive delivery and his fastball jumped from 90-93 mph to 93-96. His motion features a lot of effort and some recoil, but it doesn't prevent him from throwing strikes. The key for Marbry will be coming up with a reliable second pitch. He scrapped an ineffective slider and now works with a splitter that will need more velocity to succeed against more advanced hitters. A potential seventh-inning reliever in the majors, Marbry will begin 2012 in Double-A and the Rockies would like to push him because he turned 27 at the end of last season.

Year	Club (League)	Class	W	L	ERA	G	GS	CG	SV	IP	H	HR	BB	SO	K/9	WHIP	AVG
2007	Asheville (SAL)	LoA	0	0	14.54	5	0	0	0	4	10	2	3	2	4.2	3.00	.476
2008	Tri-City (NWL)	SS	2	0	2.01	20	0	0	0	31	33	1	10	21	6.0	1.37	.268
2009	Asheville (SAL)	LoA	5	3	3.46	46	0	0	2	65	67	1	15	54	7.5	1.26	.267
2010	Modesto (CAL)	HiA	3	1	4.28	23	0	0	0	34	38	3	7	39	10.4	1.34	.279
2011	Modesto (CAL)	HiA	5	3	2.92	50	0	0	16	65	58	5	20	66	9.2	1.21	.239
Minor League Totals			15	7	3.44	144	0	0	18	199	206	12	55	182	8.2	1.31	.266

Year	Club (League)	Class	AVG	G	AB	R	H	2B	3B	HR	RBI	BB	SO	SB	CS	OBP	SLG
2006	Braves (GCL)	R	.130	10	23	4	3	1	0	0	0	4	10	0	0	.259	.174
Minor League Totals			.130	10	23	4	3	1	0	0	0	4	10	0	0	.259	.174

Detroit Tigers

BY BEN BADLER

Last year, the Tigers returned to the playoffs for the first time since 2006. While they lost to the Rangers in the American League Championship Series, the makeup of the AL Central and Detroit's major league roster should mean it won't have to wait five years for its next postseason appearance.

The Twins and White Sox tumbled in 2011 and have bleak outlooks in 2012. The Indians improved, though they were still just an 80-win team with significant questions. Better days are ahead for the Royals and their enviable stash of high-upside youngsters, but they don't look ready to go toe-to-toe with Detroit.

Homegrown ace Justin Verlander won the AL pitching triple crown and MVP and Cy Young awards. Yet it was Detroit's offense, which ranked fourth in the majors in scoring, that carried the team.

Miguel Cabrera is on track to become the greatest Venezuelan-born hitter of all time. Victor Martinez and Jhonny Peralta produced in their first seasons under multiyear deals with the Tigers. Draft finds Alex Avila (fifth round, 2008) and Brennan Boesch (third round, 2006) have turned into pleasant offensive surprises, with Avila becoming an all-star last season.

Detroit's farm system is heavier on pitchers than position players, though getting those pitchers acclimated to the big leagues hasn't been easy. Jacob Turner and Andy Oliver both pitched in the majors in 2011, as did a handful of homegrown relievers, though none found much immediate success. Former top prospect Rick Porcello will be just 23 in 2012, but he's coming off two mediocre seasons and already is arbitration-eligible.

Turner, No. 1 on this list for the third straight year, could play a role at the back of the rotation at some point this year, though some scouts aren't sure he's ready yet. He's a prime example of the Tigers willingness to invest in the draft, signing a $5.5 million big league contract as the ninth overall pick in 2009. So is the system's best position prospect, third baseman Nick Castellanos, who set a supplemental first-round record with a $3.45 million bonus in 2010.

The Tigers broke from that blueprint in the 2011 draft, however, ranking next-to-last by spending just $2.9 million. Detroit didn't have a first-round pick in its first draft under scouting director Scott Pleis. The team also has a new farm director. Mike Rojas held the position for less than a year before becoming the

TOM DiPACE

Justin Verlander won both the American League Cy Young and MVP awards

TOP 30 PROSPECTS

1. Jacob Turner, rhp	16. Matt Hoffman, lhp
2. Nick Castellanos, 3b	17. Tyler Stohr, rhp
3. Drew Smyly, lhp	18. Danry Vasquez, of
4. Casey Crosby, lhp	19. Brandon Loy, ss
5. Andy Oliver, lhp	20. Tyler Gibson, of
6. Brenny Paulino, rhp	21. Duane Below, lhp
7. Rob Brantly, c	22. Adam Wilk, lhp
8. Alex Burgos, lhp	23. Luis Marte, rhp
9. James McCann, c	24. Brian Flynn, lhp
10. Avisail Garcia, of	25. Dixon Machado, ss
11. Ramon Lebron, rhp	26. Kevin Eichhorn, rhp
12. Bruce Rondon, rhp	27. Daniel Fields, of
13. Tyler Collins, of	28. Eugenio Suarez, ss
14. Aaron Westlake, 1b	29. Jose Ortega, rhp
15. Brayan Villarreal, rhp	30. Hernan Perez, 2b/ss

big league bullpen coach in July, and infield instructor Dave Owen was promoted to replace him.

Detroit has benefited from its growing international presence, which has yielded several of the best prospects in its system, including Latin American righthanders Brenny Paulino, Bruce Rondon and Ramon Lebron and outfielder Avisail Garcia. The Tigers used a pair of Venezuelans, third baseman Francisco Martinez and righthander Lester Oliveros, in deadline deals to get playoff heroes Doug Fister from the Mariners and outfielder Delmon Young from the Twins.

General Manager: Dave Dombrowski. **Farm Director:** Dave Owen. **Scouting Director:** Scott Pleis.

Class	Team	League	W	L	Pct	Finish*	Manager(s)
Majors	Detroit Tigers	American	95	67	.586	3rd (14)	Jim Leyland
Triple-A	Toledo Mud Hens	International	67	77	.465	11th (14)	Phil Nevin
Double-A	Erie SeaWolves	Eastern	67	75	.472	9th (12)	Chris Cron
High A	Lakeland Flying Tigers	Florida State	64	74	.464	8th (12)	Dave Huppert
Low A	West Michigan Whitecaps	Midwest	70	69	.504	7th (16)	Ernie Young
Short-season	Connecticut Tigers	New York-Penn	39	35	.527	t-6th (14)	Andrew Graham
Rookie	GCL Tigers	Gulf Coast	29	31	.483	7th (15)	Basilio Cabrera
Overall 2011 Minor League Record			336	361	.482	23rd (30)	

*Finish in overall standings (No. of teams in league). †League champion.

LAST YEAR'S TOP 30

Player, Pos.		Status
1.	Jacob Turner, rhp	No. 1
2.	Nick Castellanos, 3b	No. 2
3.	Andy Oliver, lhp	No. 5
4.	Francisco Martinez, 3b	(Mariners)
5.	Daniel Fields, of	No. 27
6.	Casey Crosby, lhp	No. 4
7.	Chance Ruffin, rhp	(Mariners)
8.	Drew Smyly, lhp	No. 3
9.	Avisail Garcia, of	No. 10
10.	Jose Ortega, rhp	No. 29
11.	Andy Dirks, of	Majors
12.	Robbie Weinhardt, rhp	Dropped out
13.	Bruce Rondon, rhp	No. 12
14.	Ryan Strieby, of/1b	Dropped out
15.	Duane Below, lhp	No. 21
16.	Matt Hoffman, lhp	No. 16
17.	Lester Oliveros, rhp	(Twins)
18.	Brayan Villareal, rhp	No. 15
19.	Casper Wells, of	(Mariners)
20.	Bryan Holaday, c	Dropped out
21.	Rob Brantly, c	No. 7
22.	Cale Iorg, ss	Dropped out
23.	Gustavo Nunez, ss	(Pirates)
24.	Danry Vasquez, of	No. 18
25.	Wade Gaynor, 3b	Dropped out
26.	Charlie Furbush, lhp	(Mariners)
27.	Adam Wilk, lhp	No. 22
28.	Dixon Machado, ss	No. 25
29.	Kyle Ryan, lhp	Dropped out
30.	Cole Nelson, lhp	(Twins)

BEST TOOLS

Best Hitter for Average	Nick Castellanos
Best Power Hitter	Nick Castellanos
Best Strike-Zone Discipline	Jamie Johnson
Fastest Baserunner	Ismael Salgado
Best Athlete	Tyler Gibson
Best Fastball	Bruce Rondon
Best Curveball	Casey Crosby
Best Slider	Shawn Teufel
Best Changeup	Jacob Turner
Best Control	Adam Wilk
Best Defensive Catcher	James McCann
Best Defensive Infielder	Dixon Machado
Best Infield Arm	Dixon Machado
Best Defensive Outfielder	Avisail Garcia
Best Outfield Arm	Avisail Garcia

PROJECTED 2015 LINEUP

Catcher	Alex Avila
First Base	Miguel Cabrera
Second Base	Ramon Santiago
Third Base	Nick Castellanos
Shortstop	Jhonny Peralta
Left Field	Brennan Boesch
Center Field	Austin Jackson
Right Field	Avisail Garcia
Designated Hitter	Victor Martinez
No. 1 Starter	Justin Verlander
No. 2 Starter	Jacob Turner
No. 3 Starter	Doug Fister
No. 4 Starter	Max Scherzer
No. 5 Starter	Rick Porcello
Closer	Jose Valverde

TOP PROSPECTS OF THE DECADE

Year	Player, Pos.	2011 Org.
2002	Nate Cornejo, rhp	Out of baseball
2003	Jeremy Bonderman, rhp	Out of baseball
2004	Kyle Sleeth, rhp	Out of baseball
2005	Curtis Granderson, of	Yankees
2006	Justin Verlander, rhp	Tigers
2007	Cameron Maybin of	Padres
2008	Rick Porcello, rhp	Tigers
2009	Rick Porcello, rhp	Tigers
2010	Jacob Turner, rhp	Tigers
2011	Jacob Turner, rhp	Tigers

TOP DRAFT PICKS OF THE DECADE

Year	Player, Pos.	2011 Org.
2002	Scott Moore, ss	Cubs
2003	Kyle Sleeth, rhp	Out of baseball
2004	Justin Verlander, rhp	Tigers
2005	Cameron Maybin, of	Padres
2006	Andrew Miller, lhp	Red Sox
2007	Rick Porcello, rhp	Tigers
2008	Ryan Perry, rhp	Tigers
2009	Jacob Turner, rhp	Tigers
2010	Nick Castellanos, 3b (1st round supp.)	Tigers
2011	James McCann (2nd round)	Tigers

LARGEST BONUSES IN CLUB HISTORY

Jacob Turner, 2009	$4,700,000
Rick Porcello, 2007	$3,580,000
Andrew Miller, 2006	$3,550,000
Eric Munson, 1999	$3,500,000
Nick Castellanos, 2010	$3,450,000

DETROIT TIGERS

TOP 2012 ROOKIE: Jacob Turner, rhp. The system's top prospect will get a chance to take Detroit's No. 5 starter job in spring training.

BREAKOUT PROSPECT: Tyler Collins, of. The 2011 sixth-round pick has hit everywhere he ever has been, including .313/.366/.536 in his pro debut.

SLEEPER: Montreal Robertson, rhp. Area scout Bryson Barber found the 29th-rounder touching 96 mph and throwing a solid slider at obscure Coahoma (Miss.) CC.

SOURCE OF TOP 30 TALENT			
Homegrown	29	Acquired	1
College	9	Trades	1
Junior college	3	Rule 5 draft	0
High school	6	Independent leagues	0
Draft-and-follow	0	Free agents/waivers	0
Nondrafted free agents	0		
International	11		

LF
Tyler Collins (13)
Danry Vasquez (18)
Justin Henry
Brandon Eckerle

CF
Tyler Gibson (20)
Daniel Fields (27)
Jamie Johnson
Ismael Salgado
Chad Wright

RF
Avisail Garcia (10)
Ben Guez
Steven Moya
Jason Krizan
Jeff Holm

3B
Nick Castellanos (2)
Wade Gaynor
Jason King
Adelin Santa
Brett Harrison

SS
Brandon Loy (19)
Dixon Machado (25)
Eugenio Suarez (28)
Audy Ciriaco

2B
Hernan Perez (30)
Brandon Douglas
Corey Jones

1B
Aaron Westlake (14)
Dean Green
Ryan Strieby
Tony Plagman

C
Rob Brantly (7)
James McCann (9)
Bryan Holaday
Curt Casali
Julio Rodriguez

LHP

LHSP	LHRP
Drew Smyly (3)	Matt Hoffman (16)
Casey Crosby (4)	Adam Wilk (22)
Andy Oliver (5)	Austin Wood
Alex Burgos (8)	Kenny Faulk
Duane Below (21)	Ryan Robowski
Brian Flynn (24)	Shawn Teufel
Jay Voss	
Kyle Ryan	

RHP

RHSP	RHRP
Jacob Turner (1)	Ramon Lebron (11)
Brenny Paulino (6)	Bruce Rondon (12)
Kevin Eichhorn (26)	Brayan Villarreal (15)
Thad Weber	Tyler Stohr (17)
Tommy Collier	Luis Marte (23)
Mark Sorensen	Jose Ortega (29)
Josue Carreno	Montreal Robertson
	Robbie Weinhardt
	Michael Morrison
	Jordan Pratt
	Matt Little
	Dan Bennett

2011

BEST PURE HITTER: OF Tyler Collins (6) led NJCAA Division I in hits (105), doubles (34) and homers (19) in the spring, then hit .313/.360/.534 for short-season Connecticut. 1B Aaron Westlake (3) has a feel for hitting and patience to go with his strength.

BEST POWER HITTER: At 6-foot-4 and 235 pounds, Westlake is built for power and led the Southeastern Conference with 11 home runs in league games last spring. 1B Dean Green (11) is even bigger and has similar pop. 3B Jason King (4) is more athletic than either and offers power from both sides.

FASTEST RUNNER: OF Ismael Salgado (16) turned in 3.7-second home-to-first times on drag bunts from the right side of the plate. He runs the 60-yard dash in 6.5-seconds.

BEST DEFENSIVE PLAYER: The Tigers drafted two of college baseball's more accomplished up-the-middle defenders. C James McCann (2), their top pick, has solid tools and good leadership skills. SS Brandon Loy (5) has quality range, hands and arm.

BEST FASTBALL: LHP Brian Flynn (7) was the first pitcher the Tigers drafted. The 6-foot-8, 239-pounder bumps his fastball up to 96 mph and sits in the low 90s.

BEST SECONDARY PITCH: Flynn has flashed a promising slider since scrapping his curveball earlier in the spring. RHP Tommy Collier (22), a Tommy John surgery survivor, has a feel for a power breaking ball.

BEST PRO DEBUT: Flynn went straight to low Class A West Michigan and thrived, going 7-2, 3.46 with 57 strikeouts in 68 innings. Green hit .341/.395/.520 with seven home runs at Connecticut.

BEST ATHLETE: OF Tyler Gibson (16) has strength in his 6-foot-2, 190-pound frame and moves well, turning in 6.65-second 60-yard dash times.

MOST INTRIGUING BACKGROUND: The Tigers went nuts drafting players with relatives who had ties to the club. 2B Colin Kaline's (26) grandfather Al is a Hall of Famer outfielder. RHP Nick Avila's (37) cousin Alex is an all-star catcher for Detroit, and his uncle Al is an assistant GM with the team. C Blaise Salter's (38) uncle Bill Freehan was an all-star catcher. C Tim Chadd's (42) uncle David is the club's vice president for amateur scouting. OF Chretien Matz's (44) uncle Ernie Young is the manager at West Michigan. 1B Andrew Allen's (45) father Rod and OF Brett Impemba's (49) dad Mario are the team's television broadcast team. Kaline, Avila and Matz signed.

CLOSEST TO THE MAJORS: McCann gets the edge over Loy because he has a more advanced bat.

BEST LATE-ROUND PICK: Gibson will get the most attention after signing for $525,000, but watch out for RHP Montreal Robinson (29) and Green.

THE ONE WHO GOT AWAY: RHP Mitch Mormann (25) has tantalizing size at 6-foot-6 and 255 pounds and has reached 96 mph. He returned to Wichita State, where he sat out 2011 as a transfer.

ASSESSMENT: When targets such as righthander Tyler Beede didn't fall to them, the Tigers went the conservative route, signing just three high school players and ranking just 29th in spending. Ten of their first 11 picks were college or juco bats.

2010

Despite not having a first-round pick, Detroit landed its best position prospect (3B Nick Castellanos, 1s), the third player from the 2010 draft class to reach the majors (RHP Chance Ruffin, 1s), a pair of polished LHPs (Drew Smyly, 2; Alex Burgos, 5) and an offensive-minded C (Rob Brantly, 3). Ruffin went to the Mariners in a July trade that delivered Doug Fister and the American League Central title.

GRADE: B+

2009

RHP Jacob Turner (1) and LHPs Andy Oliver (2) and Adam Wilk (11) have pitched in the majors, and top prospect Turner is on the verge of making an impact. The Tigers paid SS Daniel Fields (6) $1.625 million but may have ruined him by rushing him.

GRADE: B+

2008

C Alex Avila (5), the son of assistant GM Al, turned out to be an all-star and no mere nepotism pick. RHP Ryan Perry (1) opened 2009 in Detroit but was dumped on the Nationals for Colin Balester in December. OF Andy Dirks (8) and RHP Robbie Weinhardt (10) also have reached the majors.

GRADE: B+

2007

RHP Rick Porcello (1) has delivered 38 big league wins but hasn't been the frontline pitcher the Tigers paid $7 million for. INF Danny Worth (2), LHP Charlie Furbush (4) and unsigned 3B/2B D.J. LeMahieu (41) all have played in the big leagues. LHP Casey Crosby (5) might make the biggest impact of them all, provided he can stay healthy.

GRADE: C+

Draft analysis by John Manuel (2011) and Jim Callis (2007-10). Numbers in parentheses indicate draft rounds.

1 JACOB TURNER

Born: May 21, 1991. **B-T:** R-R. **Ht.:** 6-5. **Wt.:** 210.
Drafted: HS—St. Louis, 2009 (1st round). **Signed by:** Marty Miller.

BA GRADE

65
MEDIUM

Turner was a dominant high school pitcher both for Westminster Christian Academy (St. Louis) and on the showcase circuit. At the 2008 Aflac All-American Game, he struck out five straight hitters. While at Westminster Christian, he benefited from the tutelage of pitching coach Todd Worrell, a former all-star closer, and also soaked up knowledge from ex-big leaguers Andy Benes and Mike Matheny, who had sons on the team. Though Turner's signability worried some clubs, the Tigers were undeterred and drafted him with the ninth overall pick in 2009. They lured him away from a North Carolina commitment with a $5.5 million big league contract that included a $4.7 million bonus, a record at the time for a prep pitcher. He pitched well at two Class A stops during his first season in pro ball in 2010, then pitched in the Futures Game and made an emergency start in Detroit last July. The first high school pick from the 2009 draft to reach the majors, he returned for two more starts in September.

Turner is still just 20 and extremely polished for his age, showing remarkable feel for pitching and maturity. Big and athletic, he repeats his smooth delivery well and is a prolific strike-thrower, averaging just 2.2 walks per nine innings as a pro. He works from a three-quarters arm slot and gets good angle on his two- and four-seam fastballs. Turner sits at 90-94 mph and touches 95 with late, heavy life, which helps him keep the ball on the ground and in the park. His fastball usually isn't a swing-and-miss pitch but his curveball and his changeup both can miss bats and grade from average to plus. His curveball is a high-70s hammer at times though still inconsistent, and he leaned on it more than his changeup when he got to the big leagues. Some scouts think his changeup could end up being as good or better than his curve. He sells his changeup with deceptive arm speed and, while in the minors, showed a willingness to throw it even when

behind in the count. Turner has a tall, slender frame and will have to continue to strengthen his body to endure the grind of the long pro season. He has had minor elbow and shoulder stiffness early in 2011, but he recovered easily and never has had any major health concerns.

Detroit is looking for a fifth starter and Turner could compete for that job in spring training. He wasn't quite ready when the Tigers called him up in July, but he cruised at Triple-A Toledo after they sent him back down. The most likely scenario is that Turner opens 2012 in Triple-A and arrives in the majors quickly if he gets off to a good start. While he doesn't have the pure stuff of an ace, he has the repertoire and command to be a No. 2 or 3 starter in the big leagues. While he didn't reach Detroit quite as fast as fellow high school first-rounder Rick Porcello, Turner has better stuff and a brighter future.

SCOUTING GRADES

Fastball: 65. **Command/**
Curveball: 60. **Control:** 60.
Changeup: 55. **Delivery:** 60.

Based on 20-80 scouting scale, where 50 represents major league average, and future projection rather than present tools.

Year	Club (League)	Class	W	L	ERA	G	GS	CG	SV	IP	H	HR	BB	SO	K/9	WHIP	AVG
2010	West Michigan (MWL)	LoA	2	3	3.67	11	10	0	0	54	53	4	9	51	8.5	1.15	.245
	Lakeland (FSL)	HiA	4	2	2.93	13	13	0	0	61	53	3	14	51	7.5	1.09	.231
2011	Erie (EL)	AA	3	5	3.48	17	17	0	0	114	102	9	32	90	7.1	1.18	.239
	Toledo (IL)	AAA	1	0	3.12	3	3	0	0	17	15	1	3	20	10.4	1.04	.227
	Detroit (AL)	MAJ	0	1	8.53	3	3	0	0	13	17	3	4	8	5.7	1.66	.315
Major League Totals			0	1	8.53	3	3	0	0	13	17	3	4	8	5.7	1.66	.315
Minor League Totals			10	10	3.36	44	43	0	0	246	223	17	58	212	7.7	1.14	.238

2 NICK CASTELLANOS, 3B

Born: March 4, 1992. **B-T:** R-R. **Ht.:** 6-4. **Wt.:** 195. **Drafted:** HS—Southwest Ranches, Fla., 2010 (1st round supplemental). **Signed by:** Rolando Casanova.

The Tigers lost their 2010 first-round pick after signing Jose Valverde as a free agent prior to the season but still landed one of the top players on their board with their first selection (44th overall). Castellanos slid due to his bonus demands, then signed at the Aug. 16 deadline for a supplemental first-round record $3.45 million. After a slow start in April, Castellanos led the low Class A Midwest League with 158 hits in 2011. Castellanos has a good swing and hitting instincts, gets great extension and uses the opposite field well. Though he hit .312 last year, he also struck out 130 times, in part because he tends to chase pitches He showed more plate discipline and a better approach as the season went on, making in-game adjustments and staying inside the ball better. Castellanos isn't a major home run threat yet but barrels the ball well and tied for second in the MWL with 36 doubles. Once he gets stronger, pulls more pitches and adds more backspin, he should have at least average power and perhaps more. A high school shortstop, he's learning to play third base. He has solid speed, moves well and while there's length to his arm stroke his throws have good carry. Castellanos has all-star potential but needs at least two more years before he's ready for Detroit. He'll head to high Class A Lakeland in 2012.

BA GRADE 60 MEDIUM

Year	Club (League)	Class	AVG	G	AB	R	H	2B	3B	HR	RBI	BB	SO	SB	CS	OBP	SLG
2010	Tigers (GCL)	R	.333	7	24	5	8	2	0	0	3	4	5	0	1	.414	.417
2011	West Michigan (MWL)	LoA	.312	135	507	65	158	36	3	7	76	45	130	3	2	.367	.436
Minor League Totals			.313	142	531	70	166	38	3	7	79	49	135	3	3	.369	.435

3 DREW SMYLY, LHP

Born: June 13, 1989. **B-T:** L-L. **Ht.:** 6-3. **Wt.:** 190. **Drafted:** Arkansas, 2010 (2nd round). **Signed by:** Chris Wimmer.

Smyly parlayed his extra leverage as a draft-eligible sophomore into a $1.1 million bonus as a second-rounder in 2010. Making his pro debut in 2011, he reached Double-A Erie in July and allowed just six earned runs in eight outings. After the season, he threw 17 shutout innings for Team USA at the World Cup and Pan American Games. Smyly has an advanced understanding of how to attack hitters, which allows his average stuff to play up. He throws his fastball at 87-92 mph with slight tailing life, commanding it down in the zone to get grounders. He uses both a curveball and a slider, with scouts split on which is more effective. He also has a splitter-like changeup and a mid-80s cutter that helps him against righthanders. Smyly repeats his easy delivery and maintains a consistent high three-quarters arm slot, making it difficult for hitters to figure out what he's throwing. He redshirted in his first season at Arkansas with a stress fracture in his elbow and missed six weeks early last year with a sore arm, so he has to prove he can handle a starter's workload. The Tigers aren't afraid to fast-track their pitching prospects, and Smyly's polish and performance merit a swift rise. A future No. 3 or 4 starter, he could open 2012 in Triple-A and finish it in the big league rotation.

BA GRADE 55 MEDIUM

Year	Club (League)	Class	W	L	ERA	G	GS	CG	SV	IP	H	HR	BB	SO	K/9	WHIP	AVG
2011	Lakeland (FSL)	HiA	7	3	2.58	14	14	0	0	80	71	1	21	77	8.6	1.15	.241
	Erie (EL)	AA	4	3	1.18	8	7	0	0	46	32	1	15	53	10.4	1.03	.201
Minor League Totals			11	6	2.07	22	21	0	0	126	103	2	36	130	9.3	1.10	.227

4 CASEY CROSBY, LHP

Born: Sept. 17, 1988. **B-T:** R-L. **Ht.:** 6-5. **Wt.:** 200. **Drafted:** HS—Maple Park, Ill., 2007 (5th round). **Signed by:** Marty Miller.

Crosby signed for $748,500 as a fifth-round pick in 2007, then hurt his elbow during instructional league that fall. Tommy John surgery sidelined him for most of 2008 and swelling in his elbow cost him most of 2010, though he didn't require a second operation. His 132 innings in Double-A last year exceeded his previous total of 122 in three pro seasons. Crosby throws two- and four-seam fastballs, working at 92-94 mph with the ability to hit 96. His size helps him get good downhill plane, which leads to swings and misses and groundouts. His curveball flashes plus potential with sharp bite and depth, though at times it can get slurvy. He throws his changeup with good arm speed and sink. Crosby still needs to make significant strides with throwing strikes. He tried to be too fine with his pitches against Double-A hitters. He needs to repeat his mechanics better, and his athleticism should help him make adjustments with his lower half in his delivery. Staying healthy for a full season was a significant step for Crosby, though his health and control issues still may

BA GRADE 55 HIGH

land him in the bullpen. The Tigers will continue to develop him in hopes he can become a No. 2 or 3 starter, though it's possible he could reach the majors in 2012 if used as a reliever. Protected on the 40-man roster in November, he'll advance to Triple-A.

Year	Club (League)	Class	W	L	ERA	G	GS	CG	SV	IP	H	HR	BB	SO	K/9	WHIP	AVG
2008	Tigers (GCL)	R	0	0	0.00	3	3	0	0	5	4	0	3	2	3.9	1.50	.211
2009	West Michigan (MWL)	LoA	10	4	2.41	24	24	0	0	105	70	3	48	117	10.1	1.13	.195
2010	Tigers (GCL)	R	0	1	8.76	3	3	0	0	12	21	1	4	10	7.3	2.03	.382
2011	Erie (EL)	AA	9	7	4.10	25	25	0	0	132	122	11	77	121	8.3	1.51	.253
Minor League Totals			19	12	3.55	55	55	0	0	253	217	15	132	250	8.9	1.38	.237

5 ANDY OLIVER, LHP

BA GRADE
55
HIGH

Born: Dec. 3, 1987. **B-T:** L-L. **Ht.:** 6-3. **Wt.:** 210. **Drafted:** Oklahoma State, 2009 (2nd round). **Signed by:** Chris Wimmer.

Oliver sued the NCAA in 2008 after it suspended him for having an adviser while negotiating with the Twins when they drafted him out of high school. Reinstated after winning the lawsuit, he received a $750,000 settlement and signed for $1.495 million as a second-round pick in 2009. He has pitched in the majors in each of his two pro seasons, but hasn't shown the control or command to survive there. Oliver's best pitch is his 92-96 mph fastball, though his inability to command his heater is one of his biggest obstacles. He couldn't overpower big league hitters, who pounded him when he couldn't locate his fastball. He once had a plus curveball in college, but he now has a below-average slider that doesn't fool lefties. His changeup is inconsistent but shows flashes of becoming an average pitch. The Tigers haven't helped Oliver by rushing him to the big leagues before he was ready. He tinkered too much with his pitches after getting sent back down to Triple-A last June. Like Casey Crosby, Oliver is a power lefty who needs to throw more strikes Scouts seem more optimistic about Crosby's chances to do so. Without a reliable breaking ball, Oliver's bullpen utility might be limited, so Detroit would like him to figure out how to command his fastball and become an effective starter.

Year	Club (League)	Class	W	L	ERA	G	GS	CG	SV	IP	H	HR	BB	SO	K/9	WHIP	AVG
2010	Erie (EL)	AA	6	4	3.61	14	14	0	0	77	74	7	25	70	8.1	1.28	.253
	Detroit (AL)	MAJ	0	4	7.36	5	5	0	0	22	26	3	13	18	7.4	1.77	.310
	Toledo (IL)	AAA	3	4	3.23	9	9	0	0	53	43	6	25	49	8.3	1.28	.226
2011	Detroit (AL)	MAJ	0	1	6.52	2	2	0	0	10	11	3	8	5	4.7	1.97	.289
	Toledo (IL)	AAA	8	12	4.71	26	26	0	0	147	149	15	80	143	8.8	1.56	.272
Major League Totals			0	5	7.11	7	7	0	0	32	37	6	21	23	6.5	1.83	.303
Minor League Totals			17	20	4.12	49	49	0	0	277	266	28	130	262	8.5	1.43	.258

6 BRENNY PAULINO, RHP

BA GRADE
55
EXTREME

Born: Feb. 21, 1993. **B-T:** R-R. **Ht.:** 6-5. **Wt.:** 182. **Signed:** Dominican Republic, 2009. **Signed by:** Carlos Santana/Ramon Perez/Miguel Garcia.

When Paulino was an amateur in the Dominican Republic, he had a mid-to-high 80s fastball and had trouble finding the strike zone. The Tigers saw a tall, skinny righthander with an extremely loose arm and the chance to add considerable velocity, so they signed him for $100,000. His velocity has soared since then, and he emerged as one of the top pitching prospects in the Rookie-level Gulf Coast League in 2011. Paulino has grown taller and gained weight since signing, helping him add roughly 10 mph to his fastball. After touching 95 mph in his 2010 pro debut, he sat at 92-95 mph last year and peaked at 97 while holding his velocity deep into outings. Because his frame has more room to add strength, some scouts believe he could throw even harder in the future. His four-seam fastball has good life, generating swings and misses when he throws it in the strike zone. Paulino's curveball has made strides but is still inconsistent, and his changeup is still below average. His control improved markedly in 2011, though it still has a ways to go and he's prone to bouts of wildness. His long arms help him get angle and leverage from his three-quarters arm slot. Paulino has the frame and arm speed to become a starter with a power arsenal. He'll need to refine his secondary pitches and control to reach his ceiling. Years away from the majors, he'll make the jump to low Class A in 2012.

Year	Club (League)	Class	W	L	ERA	G	GS	CG	SV	IP	H	HR	BB	SO	K/9	WHIP	AVG
2010	Tigers (DSL)	R	1	6	3.88	16	15	0	0	46	34	0	45	55	10.7	1.71	.205
2011	Tigers (GCL)	R	4	3	2.36	11	8	2	0	46	34	1	18	45	8.9	1.14	.202
	Lakeland (FSL)	HiA	0	2	21.94	2	2	0	0	5	9	0	9	7	11.8	3.38	.346
Minor League Totals			5	11	4.16	29	25	2	0	97	77	1	72	107	9.9	1.53	.214

7 ROB BRANTLY, C

Born: July 14, 1989. **B-T:** L-R. **Ht.:** 6-2. **Wt.:** 188. **Drafted:** UC Riverside, 2010 (3rd round). **Signed by:** Steve Pack.

Brantly's performance has been up and down since he signed for $330,300 as a sopho-more-eligible third-round pick in 2010. He was mediocre at low Class A West Michigan in his pro debut but much improved when he opened last season there. He struggled after a July promotion to Lakeland, then hit .388 in 15 Arizona Fall League games. An offensive-oriented catcher with a short lefthanded swing, Brantly has a balanced approach and makes consistent contact to all fields, though he lacks patience. His swing is geared more toward line drives than loft, but he has enough strength to hit 10-15 homers per season. Though he's a well below-average runner, Brantly is athletic for a catcher. He has solid catch-and-throw skills and still is working on his game-calling, blocking and receiving. His quick release helps his average arm play up, and he threw out 36 percent of basesteal-ers last season. The Tigers project Brantly as an everyday catcher, though others see a bat-first backup. He still has to prove he can hit high Class A pitching, but the Tigers may push him to Double-A.

BA GRADE

50

HIGH

Year	Club (League)	Class	AVG	G	AB	R	H	2B	3B	HR	RBI	BB	SO	SB	CS	OBP	SLG
2010	West Michigan (MWL)	LoA	.255	52	188	26	48	10	1	1	21	23	22	2	2	.352	.335
2011	West Michigan (MWL)	LoA	.303	75	284	42	86	16	1	7	44	24	39	2	2	.366	.440
	Lakeland (FSL)	HiA	.219	39	146	16	32	6	0	3	18	5	17	0	0	.239	.322
Minor League Totals			.269	166	618	84	166	32	2	11	83	52	78	4	4	.333	.380

8 ALEX BURGOS, LHP

Born: Dec. 1, 1990. **B-T:** L-L. **Ht.:** 5-11. **Wt.:** 192. **Drafted:** JC of Florida, 2010 (5th round). **Signed by:** Rolando Casanova.

Burgos pitched the JC of Florida to the 2010 Junior College World Series, earning juco all-America honors and then signing for $152,100 as a fifth-round pick. He didn't realize the offseason preparation needed to be physically ready for pro ball, so the Tigers held him back in extended spring training last year until June, after which he was one of the Midwest League's best pitchers. Burgos has a small frame and fairly average stuff, but he mixes five pitches to keep hitters off balance. He throws an 87-93 mph fastball with two-seam action and commands it well. He has nice feel for his changeup, a plus pitch at times. Burgos also has a pair of fringy breaking balls in his curveball and slider, and he also owns a cutter. He eventually may go to just one breaking pitch to focus on its development. He held lefties to a .152/.211/.205 line in 2011. While Burgos has a tiny frame, he's lefthanded and has enough stuff to remain a starter. If he refines his pitches, he has the upside of a No. 3 starter, but more realistically he'll be a No. 4. He'll open 2012 in high Class A.

BA GRADE

50

HIGH

Year	Club (League)	Class	W	L	ERA	G	GS	CG	SV	IP	H	HR	BB	SO	K/9	WHIP	AVG
2010	Tigers (GCL)	R	0	0	1.54	8	0	0	1	12	10	1	3	15	11.6	1.11	.227
2011	West Michigan (MWL)	LoA	6	5	2.19	16	16	0	0	95	63	4	33	89	8.5	1.01	.189
Minor League Totals			6	5	2.12	24	16	0	1	106	73	5	36	104	8.8	1.03	.193

9 JAMES McCANN, C

Born: June 13, 1990. **B-T:** R-R. **Ht.:** 6-1. **Wt.:** 210. **Drafted:** Arkansas, 2011 (2nd round). **Signed by:** Chris Wimmer.

The Tigers gave up their 2011 first-round pick as compensation for free agent Victor Martinez, so their first choice didn't come until No. 76. They took McCann, who signed for $577,900, which was exactly $100,000 over MLB's slot recommendation. While he isn't as advanced offensively as Rob Brantly, McCann gets better reviews for his work behind the plate. He has a strong frame, a solid arm and leadership and game-calling skills. Some scouts who saw him as an amateur labeled him a fringy receiver, but the Tigers believe he's solid in that regard. McCann's bat is his biggest question. His swing can get long and he has trouble catching up to good velocity. He projects as a .260 hitter who can take advantage of mistakes and produce gap power. He's a below-average runner. McCann doesn't have any standout tools, but he has the skills to become a big league regular if his bat develops. If not, his defense makes him a backup option. Where Detroit sends Brantly will affect McCann's 2012 assignment, but he figures to spend his first full pro season in Class A.

BA GRADE

50

HIGH

Year	Club (League)	Class	AVG	G	AB	R	H	2B	3B	HR	RBI	BB	SO	SB	CS	OBP	SLG
2011	Tigers (GCL)	R	.357	5	14	1	5	1	0	1	6	1	1	0	0	.438	.643
	West Michigan (MWL)	LoA	.059	9	34	0	2	1	0	0	1	2	12	0	0	.132	.088
Minor League Totals			.146	14	48	1	7	2	0	1	7	3	13	0	0	.222	.250

10 AVISAIL GARCIA, OF

Born: June 12, 1991. **B-T:** R-R. **Ht.:** 6-4. **Wt.:** 240. **Signed:** Venezuela, 2007. **Signed by:** Alejandro Rodriguez/Pedro Chavez.

Garcia was one of Detroit's top international signings in 2007, receiving a $200,000 bonus. He hit well in the Rookie-level Venezuelan Summer League in his 2008 pro debut, but that was the last time he produced good offensive numbers. The Tigers have pushed him aggressively and he has batted .271/.298/.391 in three seasons in the United States. While scouts haven't come around yet on Garcia's hitting ability, he draws their interest with his big frame and his tools. The ball jumps off Garcia's bat in batting practice, where he shows above-average raw power, though he does it more with strength than pure bat speed. He showed more usable power in 2011 as he learned to get himself better pitches to hit, but he still has a long ways to go in that area. Garcia has poor pitch recognition and struggles against breaking balls, which will limit his on-base percentage and result in a high strikeout rate. He has the physical ability to be a plus defender in right field, running well for his size and possessing an arm that earns 70 grades on the 20-80 scouting scale. Garcia was born eight days before the Padres' Rymer Liriano, a toolsy outfielder who finally put his offensive game together in low Class A last year. The Tigers hope for a similar breakout for Garcia in 2012, when he would be best served returning to high Class A. They protected him on their 40-man roster in November.

BA GRADE 55 EXTREME

Year	Club (League)	Class	AVG	G	AB	R	H	2B	3B	HR	RBI	BB	SO	SB	CS	OBP	SLG
2008	Tigers (VSL)	R	.298	63	245	33	73	12	2	7	34	15	39	7	5	.342	.449
2009	Lakeland (FSL)	HiA	.250	3	8	1	2	0	0	0	0	0	2	0	0	.250	.250
	West Michigan (MWL)	LoA	.264	81	299	36	79	11	2	1	31	8	70	8	7	.289	.324
2010	West Michigan (MWL)	LoA	.281	125	494	58	139	17	4	4	63	20	113	20	4	.313	.356
2011	Lakeland (FSL)	HiA	.264	129	488	53	129	16	6	11	56	18	132	14	5	.297	.389
Minor League Totals			.275	401	1534	181	422	56	14	23	184	61	356	49	21	.308	.375

11 RAMON LEBRON, RHP

BA GRADE 50 HIGH

Born: Feb. 1, 1989. **B-T:** R-R. **Ht.:** 6-1. **Wt.:** 186. **Signed:** Dominican Republic, 2006. **Signed by:** Julian German/Ramon Perez.

Lebron has been a project since he signed out of the Dominican Republic in 2006. He made strides with his stuff and his command in 2011 until a shoulder injury ended his season in early July. When healthy, Lebron has a strong fastball/changeup combination. Though he doesn't have the same velocity or life on his fastball as West Michigan teammate Bruce Rondon, Lebron has a quick arm and a 92-96 mph heater. He backs it up with a potentially above-average changeup that he throws with the same arm speed as his fastball. Lebron keeps his wrist and fingers relaxed when he throws his changeup, which allows him to finish the pitch and give it sink at the end. He also throws a below-average slurve that has curveball rotation and slider angle. Lebron throws across his body, which hampers his control and command as well as puts stress on his arm. The effort in his delivery does add some deception, though, especially to his changeup. Lebron did a better job last year of corralling his emotions on the mound after spiraling out of control in previous seasons. Lebron has the stuff to profile as an impact reliever, though he'll need to learn to throw more strikes to reach that potential. He'll head to high Class A in 2012.

Year	Club (League)	Class	W	L	ERA	G	GS	CG	SV	IP	H	HR	BB	SO	K/9	WHIP	AVG
2007	Tigers (DSL)	R	0	1	10.80	2	2	0	0	3	5	0	3	3	8.1	2.40	.333
2008	Tigers (DSL)	R	2	4	4.31	16	9	0	1	48	40	4	27	51	9.6	1.40	.225
2009	Tigers (GCL)	R	3	4	3.73	12	10	0	0	51	45	1	31	55	9.8	1.62	.249
2010	West Michigan (MWL)	LoA	4	5	6.85	13	13	0	0	47	50	5	39	55	10.5	1.88	.267
	Tigers (GCL)	R	1	0	2.28	11	2	0	0	28	16	0	9	43	14.0	0.90	.167
	Connecticut (NYP)	SS	1	1	8.44	7	0	0	1	11	12	1	10	20	16.9	2.06	.267
2011	West Michigan (MWL)	LoA	3	1	1.83	22	0	0	1	34	18	1	19	44	11.5	1.08	.161
Minor League Totals			14	16	4.38	83	36	0	3	222	186	12	144	271	11.0	1.49	.229

12 BRUCE RONDON, RHP

BA GRADE 50 HIGH

Born: Dec. 9,1990. **B-T:** R-R. **Ht.:** 6-3. **Wt.:** 271. **Signed:** Venezuela, 2007. **Signed by:** German Robles/Pedro Chavez/Miguel Garcia.

Rondon initially tried out for teams as a catcher in Venezuela before his trainer moved him to the mound. He threw in the high 80s when the Tigers signed him in 2007, but his fastball has soared as he has gained nearly 100 pounds since signing. There are few pitchers more uncomfortable to face than Rondon, both because of his electric fastball and his lack of any clue where it's going. His fastball regularly clocks in the mid-90s, ranging from 95-101 mph. It's overpowering not just for its velocity, but also its boring, heavy life. He also throws a slurvy 81-86 mph slider with occasional hard bite. It's effective against lower-level hitters but will need to get shorter and quicker to work against better competition. Rondon struck out 34 percent of the batters he faced in 2011, but he also issued 34 walks, hit five batters and threw 11 wild pitches in 40 innings. He has a max-effort delivery, gets amped up and overthrows, which causes him to lose his release point and his control. Repeating his delivery is difficult because of his lack of athleticism and his weight, which ballooned close to 300 pounds before he shed some excess baggage. Rondon always will be heavy because of his frame, but he'll need to keep his weight in check to reduce his risk of injury. He doesn't need pinpoint command to be successful, but he does need to find the plate in order to realize his potential as a late-inning reliever. He'll advance to high Class A this year.

Year	Club (League)	Class	W	L	ERA	G	GS	CG	SV	IP	H	HR	BB	SO	K/9	WHIP	AVG
2008	Tigers (VSL)	R	2	6	3.58	13	13	1	0	55	48	0	20	34	5.5	1.23	.225
2009	Tigers (GCL)	R	0	1	4.76	3	3	0	0	11	12	0	8	15	11.9	1.76	.267
	Tigers (VSL)	R	0	0	13.50	3	0	0	0	4	5	0	7	4	9.0	3.00	.313
2010	Tigers (GCL)	R	0	0	0.70	24	0	0	15	26	11	1	14	26	9.1	0.97	.133
	Lakeland (FSL)	HiA	0	0	1.35	4	0	0	2	7	2	1	2	7	9.5	0.60	.095
2011	West Michigan (MWL)	LoA	2	2	2.03	41	0	0	19	40	22	0	34	61	13.7	1.40	.164
Minor League Totals			4	9	2.90	88	16	1	36	143	100	2	85	147	9.3	1.29	.195

13 TYLER COLLINS, OF

BA GRADE
50
HIGH

Born: June 6, 1990. **B-T:** L-L. **Ht.:** 5-11. **Wt.:** 205. **Drafted:** Howard (Texas) JC, 2011 (6th round). **Signed by:** Tim Grieve.

Collins hit .404 in 89 at-bats as a Baylor freshman in 2010 before getting declared academically ineligible. He continued to hit after transferring to Howard (Texas) JC, winning national junior college player of the year honors and leading NJCAA Division I in hits (105), doubles (34) and homers (19) while ranking second in batting (.488) and RBIs (82). The Tigers drafted Collins in the sixth round last June, but he made a pit stop in the Texas Collegiate League—where he ranked as the No. 1 prospect—before signing for $210,000. He posted a .902 OPS in his pro debut, then put up similar numbers in the Australian Baseball League during the winter. Collins has some length to his swing, but he finds a way to get the barrel to the ball routinely. He has a quick bat and uses an all-fields approach. Strong and stocky, Collins has average power but not the prototypical pop for a left fielder. His above-average speed allows him to play center field in a pinch, though he still needs to improve his reads and routes. His arm is below average. Some scouts wonder whether Collins is a tweener, but he may end up having enough bat to be an everyday player. He could hit his way to high Class A in his first full pro season.

Year	Club (League)	Class	AVG	G	AB	R	H	2B	3B	HR	RBI	BB	SO	SB	CS	OBP	SLG
2011	Tigers (GCL)	R	.333	1	3	2	1	1	0	0	1	2	0	0	0	.600	.667
	Connecticut (NYP)	SS	.313	42	163	28	51	10	1	8	31	10	17	6	1	.360	.534
Minor League Totals			.313	43	166	30	52	11	1	8	32	12	17	6	1	.366	.536

14 AARON WESTLAKE, 1B

BA GRADE
50
HIGH

Born: Dec. 27, 1988. **B-T:** L-R. **Ht.:** 6-4. **Wt.:** 238. **Drafted:** Vanderbilt, 2011 (3rd round). **Signed by:** Harold Zonder.

A blood-clotting issue forced Westlake to redshirt at Vanderbilt in 2008 and made him draft-eligible as a sophomore two years later. He starred in the Cape Cod League that summer but ultimately didn't sign with the Blue Jays as a 22nd-rounder. He returned to Vandy in 2011 and helped the Commodores to their first-ever College World Series appearance by hitting .344 with a team-high 18 homers. He had a modest pro debut after signing for $310,000 in the third round, missing time late in the summer with a concussion. The Tigers believe Westlake will develop into a power-hitting first baseman. He has a large frame, good strength and can hit the ball out to all fields. He has a smooth stroke, though it gets long at times when pitchers disrupt his timing. He's a patient hitter who would benefit from being more aggressive against fastballs when he's ahead in the count. Westlake is a below-average runner and an adequate defender at first base. He has solid hands, though his glovework needs improvement. He'll play the 2012 season at age 23, so he could get fast-tracked and sent to high Class A.

Year	Club (League)	Class	AVG	G	AB	R	H	2B	3B	HR	RBI	BB	SO	SB	CS	OBP	SLG
2011	Tigers (GCL)	R	.167	5	18	2	3	1	0	1	4	2	6	0	0	.250	.389
	Connecticut (NYP)	SS	.264	27	106	14	28	4	1	2	15	10	23	1	0	.328	.377
Minor League Totals			.250	32	124	16	31	5	1	3	19	12	29	1	0	.316	.379

15 BRAYAN VILLARREAL, RHP

BA GRADE
50
HIGH

Born: May 10, 1987. **B-T:** R-R. **Ht.:** 6-0. **Wt.:** 170. **Signed:** Venezuela, 2005.
Signed by: Ramon Pena.

Villarreal made just one start in his 2007 U.S. debut before he needed Tommy John surgery. He got back to full strength by 2009, and two years later he made the Tigers' Opening Day roster as a reliever. He struggled with Detroit and didn't have much more success when he was demoted in May. Despite a down 2011, Villarreal has a quick arm that produces plenty of velocity. He sits at 90-95 mph with his fastball as a starter, and operates at 93-95 mph when he comes out of the bullpen. He uses both two- and four-seamers, and he gets cutting action at times when he overthrows and gets around the ball. Villarreal also throws a power slider at 86-88 mph, though it has a tendency to break too early, allowing hitters to pick it up. His changeup is a below-average pitch that he rarely uses as a reliever. Whatever his future role, his command will have to improve. His most likely path back to the big leagues is through the bullpen.

Year	Club (League)	Class	W	L	ERA	G	GS	CG	SV	IP	H	HR	BB	SO	K/9	WHIP	AVG
2006	Tigers/Marlins (VSL)	R	0	2	3.48	14	5	0	0	41	35	3	20	23	5.0	1.33	.233
2007	Tigers (GCL)	R	0	0	6.23	1	1	0	0	4	4	0	3	5	10.4	1.62	.235
2008	Tigers (GCL)	R	1	5	3.65	11	6	1	0	37	26	0	11	37	9.0	1.00	.197
	West Michigan (MWL)	LoA	0	1	16.20	1	1	0	0	3	7	1	1	0	0.0	2.40	.438
2009	West Michigan (MWL)	LoA	5	5	2.87	26	16	0	2	103	85	5	34	118	10.3	1.15	.231
2010	Lakeland (FSL)	HiA	7	4	3.47	16	16	1	0	86	73	8	23	90	9.5	1.12	.232
	Erie (EL)	AA	0	4	3.71	8	8	0	0	44	37	6	16	46	9.5	1.21	.231
2011	Detroit (AL)	MAJ	1	1	6.75	16	0	0	0	16	21	3	10	14	7.9	1.94	.323
	Toledo (IL)	AAA	3	5	5.05	17	10	0	0	66	65	6	29	40	5.5	1.42	.261
Major League Totals			1	1	6.75	16	0	0	0	16	21	3	10	14	7.9	1.94	.323
Minor League Totals			16	26	3.77	94	63	2	2	385	332	29	137	359	8.4	1.22	.236

16 MATT HOFFMAN, LHP

BA GRADE
45
MEDIUM

Born: Nov. 18, 1988. **B-T:** L-L. **Ht.:** 6-2. **Wt.:** 195. **Drafted:** HS—Owasso, Okla., 2007 (26th round). **Signed by:** Steve Taylor.

An outfielder at Oklahoma powerhouse Owasso High, Hoffman got on the mound as a senior and ran his fastball up to 92 mph. He lasted until the 26th round of the 2007 draft because of his strong college commitment to Oklahoma, but he signed with the Tigers for $175,000. A full-time reliever since 2010, Hoffman added velocity with the move to the bullpen and now throws 90-95 mph fastballs from a low three-quarters arm slot. He has developed better feel for his slider, which has tight break and good tilt, though it can flatten out and leave him vulnerable to lefthanders. They batted .306 against him in Triple-A last season, and he'll have to do better to cut it in a major league bullpen. Hoffman also mixes in an effective changeup as well. He doesn't have the stuff to miss many bats, but his fastball and ability to keep the ball down allow him to induce groundouts. Hoffman still has somewhat of a crossfire delivery, but he has improved his direction to the plate. His command can waver when he peels off in his delivery, so he has worked to control his momentum going forward. Sent to the Arizona Fall League after the season, he had to leave with a tired arm. Detroit still added him to its 40-man roster and could give him his first big league callup in 2012. His ceiling isn't high, but he could become a useful lefty reliever.

Year	Club (League)	Class	W	L	ERA	G	GS	CG	SV	IP	H	HR	BB	SO	K/9	WHIP	AVG
2008	West Michigan (MWL)	LoA	0	2	4.60	5	2	0	0	16	19	1	14	20	11.5	2.11	.284
	Oneonta (NYP)	SS	3	5	3.05	12	10	0	0	56	49	1	24	44	7.1	1.30	.237
2009	West Michigan (MWL)	LoA	5	0	1.12	7	3	0	1	40	24	1	8	33	7.4	0.79	.169
	Lakeland (FSL)	HiA	3	7	6.79	16	10	1	0	62	79	9	21	32	4.6	1.60	.309
2010	Lakeland (FSL)	HiA	0	1	1.59	16	0	0	3	23	17	1	2	18	7.1	0.84	.215
	Toledo (IL)	AAA	0	0	10.38	3	0	0	0	4	9	1	4	4	8.3	3.00	.474
	Erie (EL)	AA	1	2	7.43	26	0	0	0	27	36	3	20	22	7.4	2.10	.308
2011	Erie (EL)	AA	0	0	54.00	1	0	0	0	0	0	0	2	0	0.0	6.00	.000
	Toledo (IL)	AAA	2	5	3.18	49	0	0	0	62	60	3	23	46	6.6	1.33	.253
Minor League Totals			14	22	4.15	135	25	1	4	291	293	20	118	219	6.8	1.41	.260

17 TYLER STOHR, RHP

BA GRADE
50
HIGH

Born: Sept. 19, 1986. **B-T:** R-R. **Ht.:** 6-2. **Wt.:** 210. **Drafted:** North Florida, 2008 (6th round). **Signed by:** Steve Nichols.

Stohr made seven starts for Army as a freshman, then decided to transfer to North Florida for his sophomore season and transitioned into a closer role there. The son of Cubs pro scout Keith Stohr, Tyler signed with the Tigers for $150,000 as a 2008 sixth-round pick. Tommy John surgery derailed him in 2010, but he made a successful return last year, reaching Double-A and claiming a spot on the 40-man roster. At his best, Stohr has one of the more impressive arsenals in the system. After throwing 90-94 mph early in 2011, he ratcheted his fastball up to 93-97 with good life by midsummer. His slider also improved as the year progressed, getting faster and sharper and becoming a solid offering. There's some effort in Stohr's delivery, which impedes his fastball command. He needs to throw more strikes, though getting another year removed from elbow surgery should help. Once his control improves, he should be able to fill a middle-relief role in Detroit.

Year	Club (League)	Class	W	L	ERA	G	GS	CG	SV	IP	H	HR	BB	SO	K/9	WHIP	AVG
2008	Oneonta (NYP)	SS	0	1	3.98	21	0	0	12	20	17	0	15	24	10.6	1.57	.224
2009	West Michigan (MWL)	LoA	3	4	3.54	52	0	0	19	61	59	2	16	55	8.1	1.23	.254
2010	Lakeland (FSL)	HiA	1	0	0.00	3	0	0	0	5	3	0	4	2	3.6	1.40	.188
2011	Lakeland (FSL)	HiA	1	0	3.45	24	0	0	0	31	24	3	8	23	6.6	1.02	.214
	Erie (EL)	AA	0	2	4.21	20	0	0	3	26	22	3	17	27	9.5	1.52	.234
Minor League Totals			5	7	3.58	120	0	0	34	143	125	8	60	131	8.2	1.29	.236

18 DANRY VASQUEZ, OF

BA GRADE
55
EXTREME

Born: Jan. 8, 1994. **B-T:** L-R. **Ht.:** 6-3. **Wt.:** 176. **Signed:** Venezuela, 2010. **Signed by:** Oscar Garcia/Pedro Chavez.

One of the most aggressive teams in Venezuela, the Tigers scouted Vasquez for two years before signing him for $1.2 million in 2010. That was their largest expenditure ever on a Venezuelan amateur and one that surprised many other teams that were skeptical of his profile. Detroit was more enthusiastic about his bat than any club and was gratified to see him hold his own in the Gulf Coast League last summer at age 17. Vasquez has broad shoulders, a high waist and a skinny frame. He handles the bat well and has a good idea of what he's doing at the plate for his age, hitting line drives to all fields. Gaining strength will be critical for Vasquez, who doesn't have much pop right now. He'll need more than gap power to profile as a corner outfielder, and several scouts question whether he could develop it after seeing him as an amateur. A below-average runner, Vasquez played right field in his pro debut. His fringy arm may be a better fit in left field, though he could develop more arm strength as he matures physically. The Tigers could jump him to low Class A as an 18-year-old, though he'd still be one of the youngest players in the short-season New York-Penn League if they more conservatively sent him to Connecticut.

Year	Club (League)	Class	AVG	G	AB	R	H	2B	3B	HR	RBI	BB	SO	SB	CS	OBP	SLG
2011	Tigers (GCL)	R	.272	54	206	25	56	8	1	2	30	7	34	3	2	.306	.350
Minor League Totals			.272	54	206	25	56	8	1	2	30	7	34	3	2	.306	.350

19 BRANDON LOY, SS

BA GRADE
50
HIGH

Born: May 3, 1990. **B-T:** R-R. **Ht.:** 6-0. **Wt.:** 190. **Drafted:** Texas, 2011 (5th round). **Signed by:** Tim Grieve.

Loy had a reputation as one of college baseball's best defensive shortstops after taking over as Texas' starter as a freshman in 2009, and he enhanced his pro profile by batting .342 last spring. The Tigers selected him in the fifth round and signed him for $212,000. While his improved offense helped, they drafted him for his defense. Loy has excellent footwork, solid range to both sides, sure hands and a strong arm. He makes the routine plays as well as the flashier ones. Loy controls the strike zone well, but his bat is still a question mark for many scouts. He hit two home runs in three years with the Longhorns and has very little power. He's an adept bunter who fits best at the bottom of a lineup. He won't be a big basestealing threat, but he has average speed and is a smart baserunner. Loy will open his first full pro season at one of Detroit's Class A affiliates.

Year	Club (League)	Class	AVG	G	AB	R	H	2B	3B	HR	RBI	BB	SO	SB	CS	OBP	SLG
2011	Tigers (GCL)	R	.333	5	15	3	5	1	0	0	3	4	2	0	0	.474	.400
	Lakeland (FSL)	HiA	.220	12	41	2	9	1	0	0	2	5	8	1	1	.304	.244
Minor League Totals			.250	17	56	5	14	2	0	0	5	9	10	1	1	.354	.286

20 TYLER GIBSON, OF

BA GRADE
50
HIGH

Born: June 17, 1993. **B-T:** L-R. **Ht.:** 6-2. **Wt.:** 190. **Drafted:** HS—Macon, Ga., 2011 (15th round). **Signed by:** Jim Rough.

The Tigers have been among the most aggressive draft spenders but were unusually conservative in 2011. The only player they really splurged on was Gibson, who fell to the 15th round because he was strongly committed to Georgia Tech. The son of Mercer head coach Craig Gibson, Tyler signed at the Aug. 15 deadline for $525,000, the second-highest bonus in Detroit's draft class. He has a smooth lefty stroke with good bat speed. He's a balanced hitter who has added strength to his broad-shouldered frame and hits with good leverage. Area scouts were split on his power potential, with some believing he'll have plus pop and others chalking his high school production to overmatching poor competition. Gibson played shortstop in high school and would have stayed there in college, but he moved to center field in pro ball. He'll have to learn the position and refine his instincts, but his plus speed should give him the range needed for the position. He has fringy arm strength. Talented but raw, Gibson will start 2012 in extended spring training before heading to Connecticut in June.

Year	Club (League)	Class	AVG	G	AB	R	H	2B	3B	HR	RBI	BB	SO	SB	CS	OBP	SLG
2011	Tigers (GCL)	R	.143	4	14	0	2	0	0	0	0	0	9	0	0	.143	.143
Minor League Totals			.143	4	14	0	2	0	0	0	0	0	9	0	0	.143	.143

21 DUANE BELOW, LHP

BA GRADE 40 LOW

Born: Nov. 15, 1985. **B-T:** L-L. **Ht.:** 6-2. **Wt.:** 205. **Drafted:** Lake Michigan CC, 2006 (19th round). **Signed by:** Tom Osowski.

A native of Britton, Mich., about an hour southwest of Comerica Park, Below climbed from the 19th round in 2006 to the majors last July. Signed for $15,000, he was the organization's 2007 minor league pitcher of the year after leading the Midwest League with 13 wins and 160 strikeouts. He succumbed to Tommy John surgery in June 2009 but zoomed was back on the mound at the start of the 2010 season. Some club officials believe his elbow reconstruction and rehab helped Below rededicate himself to his craft. While many pitchers struggle with their command following Tommy John surgery, he came back throwing more strikes than ever. Below's stuff is average at best, but he throws strikes and has good feel for pitching. He throws an 88-93 mph fastball, a high-70s curveball that's average at times and a slider that can get slurvy. His best pitch is a changeup with sink. After spending most of his career as a starter, Below transitioned to the bullpen after making two big league starts. He fits best as a No. 5 starter or swingman.

Year	Club (League)	Class	W	L	ERA	G	GS	CG	SV	IP	H	HR	BB	SO	K/9	WHIP	AVG
2006	Tigers (GCL)	R	2	0	1.60	15	4	0	0	34	27	1	10	30	8.0	1.10	.216
	Oneonta (NYP)	SS	0	0	3.86	2	2	0	0	9	11	0	5	8	7.7	1.71	.282
2007	West Michigan (MWL)	LoA	13	5	2.97	26	26	0	0	146	128	6	58	160	9.9	1.28	.236
2008	Lakeland (FSL)	HiA	8	7	4.46	27	26	0	0	133	144	10	70	126	8.5	1.61	.280
2009	Lakeland (FSL)	HiA	1	4	3.14	6	6	0	0	29	22	4	14	38	11.9	1.26	.208
	Erie (EL)	AA	1	0	1.59	2	2	0	0	11	7	1	6	7	5.6	1.15	.175
2010	Erie (EL)	AA	7	12	4.93	28	28	0	0	126	137	17	37	103	7.4	1.38	.275
2011	Toledo (IL)	AAA	9	4	3.13	18	18	0	0	115	99	12	37	83	6.5	1.18	.232
	Detroit (AL)	MAJ	0	2	4.34	14	2	0	0	29	28	2	11	14	4.3	1.34	.252
Major League Totals			0	2	4.34	14	2	0	0	29	28	2	11	14	4.3	1.34	.252
Minor League Totals			41	32	3.66	124	112	0	0	603	575	51	237	555	8.3	1.35	.251

22 ADAM WILK, LHP

BA GRADE 40 LOW

Born: Dec. 8, 1987. **B-T:** L-L. **Ht.:** 6-2. **Wt.:** 175. **Drafted:** Long Beach State, 2009 (11th round). **Signed by:** Phil Huttmann.

Wilk was the ace on a bad 2009 Long Beach State team, going 7-4, 2.78 for a sub-.500 club. He has gone from an 11th-rounder signed for $68,000 that June to the Tigers' minor league pitcher of the year in 2010 to making his big league debut last May. He rose through the system on his feel for pitching more than his pure stuff. Wilk has the best control among Detroit farmhands and is one of the most prepared pitchers in the system. He's disciplined, knows how to read swings and understands how to mix and locate his pitches to keep hitters off balance. Wilk needs those attributes because his stuff is mostly below average. His fastball ranges from 85-88 mph when he starts, ticks up slightly when he relieves and touches 89-90 mph on occasion. His cutter is his best weapon. Hitters don't have an easy time picking up on its rotation, and it rides in on the handle against righties and hits the end of the bat against lefties. He also mixes in a decent changeup and a fringy curveball. Wilk gets the most out of his limited stuff and could help the Tigers as occasional fifth starter or reliever.

Year	Club (League)	Class	W	L	ERA	G	GS	CG	SV	IP	H	HR	BB	SO	K/9	WHIP	AVG
2009	Oneonta (NYP)	SS	2	0	1.45	7	7	1	0	37	23	0	5	34	8.2	0.75	.173
	West Michigan (MWL)	LoA	2	1	1.49	7	7	0	0	36	30	2	2	33	8.2	0.88	.222
2010	Lakeland (FSL)	HiA	9	5	3.01	24	24	1	0	144	139	8	19	100	6.3	1.10	.250
	Erie (EL)	AA	2	0	1.14	3	3	0	0	24	10	1	5	14	5.3	0.63	.128
2011	Toledo (IL)	AAA	8	6	3.24	18	18	0	0	103	105	15	14	76	6.7	1.16	.262
	Detroit (AL)	MAJ	0	0	5.40	5	0	0	0	13	14	3	3	10	6.8	1.28	.259
Major League Totals			0	0	5.40	5	0	0	0	13	14	3	3	10	6.8	1.28	.259
Minor League Totals			23	12	2.62	59	59	2	0	344	307	26	45	257	6.7	1.02	.236

23 LUIS MARTE, RHP

BA GRADE 45 MEDIUM

Born: Aug. 26, 1986. **B-T:** R-R. **Ht.:** 5-11. **Wt.:** 200. **Signed:** Dominican Republic, 2005. **Signed by:** Ramon Pena.

It took four seasons, but Marte finally mastered Double-A in 2011 and earned a September callup to Detroit, where he held opponents scoreless in three of his four appearances. After the season, he pitched well in the Dominican League. He spent his first four years in pro ball as a starter to give him the innings to work on all of his pitches, but he has taken well to relieving since changing roles in 2010. He throws his fastball at 89-92 mph and it seems faster because it has late life through the zone. His slider is his best secondary pitch, grading as plus at its best, though it tends to get slurvy. He also has a below-average changeup that he doesn't use as much now that he's a reliever. After he was erratic in his first season coming out of the bullpen, Marte showed improved control in 2011. The Tigers have plenty of power arms in their bullpen, but he could give them a different look. He'll get a chance to win a middle-relief job in spring training.

Year	Club (League)	Class	W	L	ERA	G	GS	CG	SV	IP	H	HR	BB	SO	K/9	WHIP	AVG
2006	Tigers (DSL)	R	8	0	1.38	11	11	2	0	65	41	0	15	90	12.5	0.86	.176
2007	Tigers (GCL)	R	2	0	0.75	2	2	1	0	12	8	0	1	12	9.0	0.75	.186
	West Michigan (MWL)	LoA	1	2	2.83	15	2	0	3	35	28	2	11	36	9.3	1.11	.220
2008	Lakeland (FSL)	HiA	3	2	1.98	7	7	0	0	41	29	1	11	41	9.0	0.98	.196
	Erie (EL)	AA	4	4	5.05	10	10	0	0	57	57	8	26	32	5.1	1.46	.264
	Tigers (GCL)	R	0	1	3.60	1	0	0	0	5	5	0	0	5	9.0	1.00	.238
2009	Erie (EL)	AA	5	8	4.02	19	17	0	0	105	106	18	28	84	7.2	1.27	.259
2010	Erie (EL)	AA	2	2	5.06	38	0	0	7	48	44	5	26	53	9.9	1.46	.244
	Toledo (IL)	AAA	0	0	0.00	1	0	0	0	1	1	0	1	0	0.0	2.00	.250
2011	Erie (EL)	AA	3	0	1.70	23	1	0	3	53	29	3	18	68	11.5	0.89	.158
	Toledo (IL)	AAA	1	0	5.40	2	0	0	0	3	3	0	4	2	5.4	2.10	.231
	Detroit (AL)	MAJ	1	0	2.45	4	0	0	0	4	6	0	1	3	7.4	1.91	.375
Major League Totals			1	0	2.45	4	0	0	0	4	6	0	1	3	7.4	1.91	.375
Minor League Totals			29	19	3.19	129	50	3	13	426	351	37	141	423	8.9	1.16	.223

24 BRIAN FLYNN, LHP

BA GRADE
50
HIGH

Born: April 19, 1990. **B-T:** L-L. **Ht.:** 6-8. **Wt.:** 239. **Drafted:** Wichita State, 2011 (7th round). **Signed by:** Chris Wimmer.

A teammate of Matt Hoffman's at Owasso (Okla.) High, Flynn won just eight games in three years at Wichita State, missing 2010 while academically ineligible. Despite his lack of dominance, a 6-foot-8 lefthander with plus velocity is hard to ignore. The Tigers made him the first pitcher they drafted last year, signing him for $125,000 in the seventh round. Flynn's fastball ranges from 88-93 mph and touches 96 with solid life. His heater jumps on hitters quickly because of his size, which also helps him get steep plane on his pitches. Flynn threw a soft, loopy curveball in college until Shockers pitching coach Brent Kemnitz taught him a slider midway through his final season. The pitch has short, cutter-like action at times and the depth of a true slider at others. He still throws the curveball as an occasional show-me pitch and also has a changeup that has yet to develop into a reliable weapon. The Tigers believe Flynn has more projection than a typical college draft pick and will send him to high Class A to begin his first full pro season. If everything comes together, he might develop into a No. 3 starter.

Year	Club (League)	Class	W	L	ERA	G	GS	CG	SV	IP	H	HR	BB	SO	K/9	WHIP	AVG
2011	West Michigan (MWL)	LoA	7	2	3.46	13	13	0	0	68	58	3	23	57	7.6	1.20	.235
Minor League Totals			7	2	3.46	13	13	0	0	68	58	3	23	57	7.6	1.20	.235

25 DIXON MACHADO, SS

BA GRADE
45
HIGH

Born: Feb. 22, 1992. **B-T:** R-R. **Ht.:** 6-0. **Wt.:** 162. **Signed:** Venezuela 2008. **Signed by:** German Robles.

The Tigers signed Machado as soon as he became eligible on July 2, 2008. He was 16 at the time and looked much younger because of his 130-pound build. While he's still a slight-framed teenager, his defense has developed as Detroit hoped. Managers rated him the best defensive shortstop and best infield arm in the Midwest League in 2011, his first year in full-season ball. Machado has good body control, smooth hands and excellent defensive instincts. He shows fine range to both sides and a plus arm with accuracy. He reads hops well and has better decision-making skills in the field than many young shortstops. Machado isn't a burner on the basepaths, but he's an intelligent baserunner with average speed. Whether he'll ever hit is the bigger question. He has 20 power on the 20-80 scouting scale and registered just three extra-base hits in 429 at-bats last season. He added two more in the Arizona Fall League but went just 8-for-68 (.118) there. Machado's swing path is solid and he uses his hands well at the plate, staying inside the ball and using the opposite field. He doesn't strike out much and walks at a surprising clip given his present inability to hurt pitchers. Additional strength will be crucial for Machado, who will advance to high Class A in 2012.

Year	Club (League)	Class	AVG	G	AB	R	H	2B	3B	HR	RBI	BB	SO	SB	CS	OBP	SLG
2009	Tigers (VSL)	R	.205	63	234	41	48	6	1	3	26	32	32	27	6	.310	.278
2010	Tigers (GCL)	R	.261	43	165	22	43	4	3	0	11	14	27	12	3	.315	.321
	Connecticut (NYP)	SS	.292	7	24	4	7	1	0	0	1	3	5	1	2	.393	.333
2011	West Michigan (MWL)	LoA	.235	124	429	47	101	1	2	0	28	46	77	25	5	.314	.247
Minor League Totals			.234	237	852	114	199	12	6	3	66	95	141	65	16	.315	.272

26 KEVIN EICHHORN, RHP

Born: Feb. 6, 1990. **B-T:** R-R. **Ht.:** 6-0. **Wt.:** 175. **Drafted:** HS—Aptos, Calif., 2008 (3rd round). **Signed by:** Darold Brown (Diamondbacks).

Eichhorn's father Mark pitched 11 seasons in the big leagues using a submarine delivery before coaching his son's team to the 2002 Little League World Series. The Diamondbacks drafted Kevin out of high school in the third round in 2008 and signed him for $500,000, and he spent most of his first three seasons as a pro in Rookie ball. In January 2011, Arizona traded him and lefthander Ryan Robowski to get Armando Galarraga from the Tigers. Eichhorn's pitches get varying reviews from scouts, though his stuff mostly grades out around average. He throws from a high three-quarters arm slot and is a good athlete with a sound delivery, which is why he has walked just 2.1 batters per nine innings in his career. Eichhorn throws two- and four-seam fastballs anywhere from 86-92 mph. He has heavy sink on his two-seamer, which helps him get plenty of grounders. He has good feel for his average changeup, which has sink and fade and could become a plus pitch down the road. He throws a big curveball with good depth, but it gets loopy and easier for hitters to pick up. If he can create more power for his curveball, it could jump ahead of his changeup. Eichhorn has little margin for error and gets too careful with his stuff at times. Ticketed for high Class A in 2012, he has the potential to be a back-of-the-rotation starter.

Year	Club (League)	Class	W	L	ERA	G	GS	CG	SV	IP	H	HR	BB	SO	K/9	WHIP	AVG
2008	Missoula (PIO)	R	0	0	6.75	2	0	0	0	3	2	0	1	2	6.8	1.13	.222
2009	Missoula (PIO)	R	0	2	3.38	10	0	0	0	16	13	1	9	25	14.1	1.38	.224
2010	Visalia (CAL)	HiA	0	0	6.35	1	1	0	0	6	9	0	0	5	7.9	1.59	.375
	Missoula (PIO)	R	5	5	4.94	13	13	0	0	75	80	12	15	71	8.6	1.27	.271
	Yakima (NWL)	SS	0	1	4.50	1	1	0	0	6	6	0	3	5	7.5	1.50	.261
2011	West Michigan (MWL)	LoA	11	5	3.61	25	25	2	0	152	148	10	33	109	6.5	1.19	.256
Minor League Totals			16	13	4.10	52	40	2	0	257	258	23	61	217	7.6	1.24	.261

27 DANIEL FIELDS, OF

Born: Jan. 23, 1991. **B-T:** L-R. **Ht.:** 6-2. **Wt.:** 215. **Drafted:** HS—Detroit, 2009 (6th round). **Signed by:** Tom Osowski.

The Tigers have aggressively pushed Fields more than any player in the system. The son of former Tigers hitting coach and current Indians coach Bruce Fields, Daniel gave up a Michigan commitment to sign for $1.625 million as a sixth-round pick in 2009. Detroit threw him into the fire by sending him to high Class A at age 19 for his pro debut, and he predictably struggled. He repeated the Florida State League in 2011 and regressed, though he still was one of the circuit's youngest players. Fields shows some ability to work the count but swings and misses too often. He has average raw power that doesn't play in games because of his lack of contact, and he was more of a gap-to-gap hitter last year. Fields was praised for his athleticism coming out of high school, but scouts now wonder if he has the ability to play a premium position. Drafted as a shortstop, he moved to center field as a pro and may be a better defensive fit in a corner. He's an average runner with a fringy arm. The 2012 season will be critical for Fields to reverse his slide and reclaim his prospect stock. He's still not ready to advance to Double-A.

Year	Club (League)	Class	AVG	G	AB	R	H	2B	3B	HR	RBI	BB	SO	SB	CS	OBP	SLG
2010	Lakeland (FSL)	HiA	.240	109	375	33	90	13	6	8	47	55	119	8	9	.343	.371
2011	Lakeland (FSL)	HiA	.220	124	432	57	95	14	4	8	46	49	133	4	4	.308	.326
Minor League Totals			.229	233	807	90	185	27	10	16	93	104	252	12	13	.325	.347

28 EUGENIO SUAREZ, SS

Born: July 18, 1991. **B-T:** B-R. **Ht.:** 6-0. **Wt.:** 178. **Signed:** Venezuela, 2008. **Signed by:** Alejandro Rodriguez.

Suarez spent his first two years playing in the Venezuelan Summer League and was the Tigers' VSL player of the year in 2010. He made his U.S. debut last year, dominating the Gulf Coast League for two weeks before earning a promotion to Connecticut. Suarez is notable more for his baseball instincts than his raw tools. He has grown two inches since signing but still isn't a physical player. He needs to develop a better two-strike approach but he has quick hands and could become an average hitter with fringy power. Suarez shows flashes of quality defense at shortstop with good range up the middle and a strong arm, but he also committed 24 errors in 70 games last year. Like many young shortstops, he needs to learn to not force throws or rush the double play. He's an average runner. Suarez may not be an everyday player but he has enough potential to be a utility player in the big leagues. He'll step up to low Class A this year.

Year	Club (League)	Class	AVG	G	AB	R	H	2B	3B	HR	RBI	BB	SO	SB	CS	OBP	SLG
2009	Tigers (VSL)	R	.262	57	206	29	54	9	3	1	15	17	32	8	4	.360	.350
2010	Tigers (VSL)	R	.311	61	225	32	70	12	2	1	18	23	44	8	6	.389	.396
2011	Tigers (GCL)	R	.341	12	44	11	15	7	0	2	9	3	4	2	0	.408	.636
	Connecticut (NYP)	SS	.250	58	204	37	51	11	5	5	24	18	43	9	5	.323	.426
Minor League Totals			.280	188	679	109	190	39	10	9	66	61	123	27	15	.362	.406

BaseballAmerica.com

29 JOSE ORTEGA, RHP

Born: Oct. 12, 1988. **B-T:** R-R. **Ht.:** 5-11. **Wt.:** 185. **Signed:** Venezuela, 2006.
Signed by: German Robles.

BA GRADE
45
HIGH

Ortega didn't reach full-season ball until 2010, his fourth year as a pro, but he ended that campaign in Double-A. He spent the entire 2011 season in Triple-A, where his numbers went backwards. A reliever his entire career, Ortega shows promising arm strength but inconsistent secondary pitches and erratic command. He has a small frame with good strength for his size and a quick arm that delivers fastballs from 94-97 mph. He needs to improve his slider, which has short, tight action at times. It gives him a second power pitch when it's on but often gets slurvy. He mixes in a below-average changeup on occasion. Ortega has effort and a head whack in his delivery, which hampers his command. He has a tendency to get amped up and overthrow for the radar gun, which magnifies his control issues. If he can develop average fastball control and tighten his slider, he has middle-relief potential. He'll start 2012 back at Toledo.

Year	Club (League)	Class	W	L	ERA	G	GS	CG	SV	IP	H	HR	BB	SO	K/9	WHIP	AVG
2007	Tigers (VSL)	R	0	0	2.45	10	0	0	0	11	9	1	3	11	9.0	1.09	.209
2008	Tigers (VSL)	R	1	1	2.20	23	0	0	5	45	43	5	15	27	5.4	1.29	.256
2009	Oneonta (NYP)	SS	2	2	3.97	25	0	0	1	34	28	2	23	32	8.5	1.50	.220
2010	West Michigan (MWL)	LoA	0	3	4.56	18	0	0	1	26	28	1	17	22	7.7	1.75	.275
	Lakeland (FSL)	HiA	2	1	0.95	10	0	0	0	19	14	0	7	20	9.5	1.11	.212
	Erie (EL)	AA	1	0	3.04	15	1	0	0	24	22	2	7	19	7.2	1.23	.242
2011	Toledo (IL)	AAA	1	3	6.30	33	0	0	0	50	61	7	27	44	7.9	1.76	.310
Minor League Totals			7	10	3.76	134	1	0	7	208	205	18	99	175	7.6	1.46	.258

30 HERNAN PEREZ, 2B/SS

Born: March 26, 1991. **B-T:** R-R. **Ht.:** 6-1. **Wt.:** 185. **Signed:** Venezuela, 2007.
Signed by: Jesus Garces/Pedro Chavez.

BA GRADE
45
HIGH

When the 2007 international signing period opened on July 2, the Tigers immediately signed Perez for $237,000. While he never has produced much at the plate, he showed some improvements last year and batted .302 in the Arizona Fall League. Detroit protected him on its 40-man roster in November. Perez was one of the Midwest League's better hitters in the first half, batting .306/.349/.427 before wearing down afterward. When he's going well, he's a line-drive hitter with gap power. He's not much of a home run threat but has good pop for a middle infielder and doesn't strike out too much. He has fringy speed but can steal a few bases thanks to his instincts. Perez can play shortstop but spent most of 2011 at second base in deference to Dixon Machado at West Michigan. Perez has fine instincts, sure hands and a strong arm. He's not especially rangy, so he's probably a better fit at second base. He'll need to get stronger to handle the grind of a full season. It's hard to project Perez as a big league regular given his modest track record at the plate, but he eventually could fit a utility role. After two years in low Class A, he's ready for Lakeland.

Year	Club (League)	Class	AVG	G	AB	R	H	2B	3B	HR	RBI	BB	SO	SB	CS	OBP	SLG
2008	Tigers (VSL)	R	.226	68	265	38	60	8	4	1	22	16	35	4	4	.278	.298
2009	West Michigan (MWL)	LoA	.227	12	44	0	10	0	1	0	5	0	8	2	1	.227	.273
	Tigers (GCL)	R	.222	21	81	9	18	9	1	1	9	3	14	2	0	.259	.395
	Lakeland (FSL)	HiA	.264	21	72	7	19	4	1	0	10	3	21	0	0	.289	.347
2010	West Michigan (MWL)	LoA	.235	124	473	45	111	15	0	5	50	25	98	5	1	.273	.298
2011	West Michigan (MWL)	LoA	.258	129	503	69	130	23	3	8	42	38	87	23	6	.314	.364
Minor League Totals			.242	375	1438	168	348	59	10	15	138	85	263	36	12	.287	.328

Houston Astros

BY JOHN MANUEL

After clinging to respectability the previous four seasons, the Astros hope they bottomed out in 2011.

At 56-106, Houston had its worst season ever and lost 100 games for the first time. The club's decline has several obvious causes, such as a dip in Opening Day payroll from $103 million (eighth in MLB) as recently as 2009 to $71 million (20th) in 2011.

Jim Crane paid Drayton McLane $645 million for the team and a 60 percent share in the Houston Regional Sports Network. Crane will get a $35 million rebate from MLB for agreeing to move the Astros to the American League West, likely in 2013.

His first significant move was to fire Ed Wade, general manager since September 2007, and hire Jeff Luhnow as to replace him. As St. Louis' vice president of scouting and player development, Luhnow rebuilt the Cardinals farm system and international operations, and will need to do the same in Houston.

Once a pace-setter in Venezuela, the Astros now hang their Latin program's hat on Jose Altuve, a 5-foot-7 scrapper who led the minors in batting but made little impact in his big league debut. Altuve was one of four players who went from instructional league in 2010 to the majors in 2011, along with David Carpenter, J.D. Martinez and Jimmy Paredes.

Martinez is a rare draft success for Houston, which had a brutal run from 2005-07. In those drafts, the Astros selected only one player with long-term big league value: 2006 sixth-rounder Bud Norris.

Bobby Heck took over as scouting director in 2008 and the organization has made progress, but it has been slow. The organization's emphasis on atheticism and raw tools still could pay dividends, but Heck's drafts have produced just four big leaguers so far: Jason Castro, Jordan Lyles, Martinez and J.B. Shuck. How much of an impact they'll make remains to be seen.

With the big league club foundering and the upper levels of the system still thin, Houston traded outfielders Michael Bourn and Hunter Pence in July for five members of its current Top 10 Prospects. Pence went to the Phillies for four minor leaguers, including first baseman/outfielder Jonathan Singleton (No. 1), righthander Jared Cosart (No. 2) and outfielder Domingo Santana (No. 6). Righthander Paul Clemens (No. 5) and lefty Brett Oberholtzer (No. 7) were acquired in a four-player package from the Braves for Bourn.

The added depth should allow the Astros to slow

Outfielder J.D. Martinez rushed to Houston as part of an overdue rebuilding movement

TOP 30 PROSPECTS

1. Jonathan Singleton, 1b/of	**16.** Ross Seaton, rhp
2. Jarred Cosart, rhp	**17.** J.B. Shuck, of
3. George Springer, of	**18.** Austin Wates, of
4. Jonathan Villar, ss	**19.** Juan Abreu, rhp
5. Paul Clemens, rhp	**20.** Marwin Gonzalez, ss/2b
6. Domingo Santana, of	**21.** Dallas Keuchel, lhp
7. Brett Oberholtzer, lhp	**22.** Jorge DeLeon, rhp
8. Delino DeShields Jr., 2b	**23.** Jio Mier, ss
9. Mike Foltynewicz, rhp	**24.** Tanner Bushue, rhp
10. Telvin Nash, 1b/of	**25.** Mike Kvasnicka, 3b
11. Adrian Houser, rhp	**26.** Jose Cisnero, rhp
12. Nick Tropeano, rhp	**27.** Vince Velasquez, rhp
13. Jake Buchanan, rhp	**28.** Rhiner Cruz, rhp
14. Ariel Ovando, of	**29.** Jack Armstrong Jr., rhp
15. R.J. Alaniz, rhp	**30.** Chris Wallace, c

down the development of young prospects such as shortstop Jonathan Villar and second baseman Delino DeShields Jr. Several players could repeat levels after looking overmatched in 2011, when Houston's affiliates posted an MLB-worst .409 winning percentage in the minors. The Astros have finished 30th in organization winning percentage in three of the last four years.

As a consolation prize for posting baseball's worst record in 2011, Houston holds the No. 1 overall draft pick in 2012. The last time the Astros chose first, in 1992, signability concerns diverted them from Derek Jeter and led them to Phil Nevin.

ORGANIZATION OVERVIEW

General Manager: Jeff Luhnow. **Farm Director:** Fred Nelson. **Scouting Director:** Bobby Heck.

Class	Team	League	W	L	Pct	Finish*	Manager(s)
Majors	Houston Astros	National	56	106	.346	16th (16)	Brad Mills
Triple-A	Oklahoma City RedHawks	Pacific Coast	68	75	.476	11th (16)	Tony DeFrancesco
Double-A	Corpus Christi Hooks	Texas	50	90	.357	8th (8)	Tom Lawless
High A	Lancaster JetHawks	California	55	85	.393	10th (10)	Tom Spencer
Low A	Lexington Legends	South Atlantic	59	79	.428	12th (14)	Rodney Linares
Short-season	Tri-City Valley Cats	New York-Penn	33	42	.440	11th (14)	Stubby Clapp
Rookie	Greeneville Astros	Appalachian	25	43	.368	8th (10)	Omar Lopez
Rookie	GCL Astros	Gulf Coast	20	34	.370	15th (15)	Ed Romero
Overall 2011 Minor League Record			310	448	.409	30th (30)	

*Finish in overall standings (No. of teams in league). †League champion.

LAST YEAR'S TOP 30

Player, Pos.		Status
1.	Jordan Lyles, rhp	Majors
2.	Delino DeShields Jr., of/2b	No. 8
3.	Jonathan Villar, ss	No. 4
4.	Mike Foltynewicz, rhp	No. 9
5.	Jio Mier, ss	No. 23
6.	J.D. Martinez, of	Majors
7.	Jimmy Paredes, inf	Majors
8.	Tanner Bushue, rhp	No. 24
9.	Austin Wates, of	No. 18
10.	Ariel Ovando, of	No. 14
11.	Aneury Rodriguez, rhp	Majors
12.	Vince Velasquez, rhp	No. 27
13.	Telvin Nash, of	No. 10
14.	Mike Kvasnicka, of/3b	No. 25
15.	R.J. Alaniz, rhp	No. 15
16.	Fernando Abad, lhp	Majors
17.	Ross Seaton, rhp	No. 16
18.	J.B. Shuck, of	No. 17
19.	Jay Austin, of	Dropped out
20.	Jorge DeLeon, rhp	No. 22
21.	Ben Heath, c	Dropped out
22.	Henry Villar, rhp	Dropped out
23.	Dallas Keuchel, lhp	No. 21
24.	Kyle Greenwalt, rhp	Dropped out
25.	David Carpenter, rhp	Majors
26.	Chia-Jen Lo, rhp	Dropped out
27.	Brian Bogusevic, of/1b	Majors
28.	Jose Altuve, 2b	Majors
29.	Lance Pendleton, rhp	Dropped out
30.	Zachary Grimmett, rhp	Dropped out

BEST TOOLS

Best Hitter for Average	Jonathan Singleton
Best Power Hitter	Jonathan Singleton
Best Strike-Zone Discipline	J.B. Schuck
Fastest Baserunner	Delino DeShields Jr.
Best Athlete	George Springer
Best Fastball	Jarred Cosart
Best Curveball	Jarred Cosart
Best Slider	Brett Oberholtzer
Best Changeup	Nick Tropeano
Best Control	Jake Buchanan
Best Defensive Catcher	Roberto Pena
Best Defensive Infielder	Jonathan Villar
Best Infield Arm	Jonathan Villar
Best Defensive Outfielder	George Springer
Best Outfield Arm	George Springer

PROJECTED 2015 LINEUP

Catcher	Jason Castro
First Base	Jonathan Singleton
Second Base	Delino DeShields Jr.
Third Base	Jimmy Paredes
Shortstop	Jonathan Villar
Left Field	J.D. Martinez
Center Field	George Springer
Right Field	Domingo Santana
Designated Hitter	Telvin Nash
No. 1 Starter	Bud Norris
No. 2 Starter	Jarred Cosart
No. 3 Starter	Wandy Rodriguez
No. 4 Starter	Jordan Lyles
No. 5 Starter	Paul Clemens
Closer	Mark Melancon

TOP PROSPECTS OF THE DECADE

Year	Player, Pos.	2011 Org.
2002	Carlos Hernandez, lhp	Out of baseball
2003	John Buck, c	Marlins
2004	Taylor Buchholz, rhp	Mets
2005	Chris Burke, 2b	Out of baseball
2006	Jason Hirsh, rhp	Out of baseball
2007	Hunter Pence, of	Phillies
2008	J.R. Towles, c	Astros
2009	Jason Castro, c	Astros
2010	Jason Castro, c	Astros
2011	Jordan Lyles, rhp	Astros

TOP DRAFT PICKS OF THE DECADE

Year	Player, Pos.	2011 Org.
2002	Derick Grigsby, rhp	Out of baseball
2003	Jason Hirsh, rhp (2nd round)	Out of baseball
2004	Hunter Pence, of (2nd round)	Phillies
2005	Brian Bogusevic, lhp	Astros
2006	Max Sapp, c	Out of baseball
2007	*Derek Dietrich, 3b (3rd round)	Rays
2008	Jason Castro, c	Astros
2009	Jio Mier, ss	Astros
2010	Delino DeShields Jr., 2b	Astros
2011	George Springer, of	Astros

*Did not sign.

LARGEST BONUSES IN CLUB HISTORY

Ariel Ovando, 2010	$2,600,000
George Springer, 2011	$2,525,000
Delino DeShields, Jr., 2010	$2,150,000
Chris Burke, 2001	$2,125,000
Jason Castro, 2008	$2,070,000

HOUSTON ASTROS

TOP 2012 ROOKIE: J.B. Shuck, of. If he can handle center field, he'll challenge Jordan Schafer for the job in Houston.

BREAKOUT PROSPECT: Nick Tropeano, rhp. His velocity jumped in his pro debut, and his changeup should overmatch Class A hitters.

SLEEPER: David Martinez, rhp. He needed four years to escape the Rookie-level Venezuelan Summer league, but he worked at 93-96 mph as a reliever last season and even hit 94 mph as a starter.

SOURCE OF TOP 30 TALENT			
Homegrown	21	Acquired	9
College	9	Trades	7
Junior College	0	Rule 5 draft	2
High school	8	Independent leagues	0
Draft-and-follow	0	Free agents/waivers	0
Nondrafted free agents	1		
International	3		

LF
Jake Goebbert
Jordan Scott
Brandon Meredith

CF
George Springer (3)
J.B. Shuck (17)
Austin Wates (18)
Jay Austin
Emilio King
Javaris Reynolds
Brandon Barnes
Justin Gominsky

RF
Domingo Santana (6)
Ariel Ovando (14)
Adam Bailey
Wallace Gonzalez

3B
Mike Kvasnicka (25)
Jonathan Meyer
Matt Duffy

SS
Jonathan Villar (4)
Marwin Gonzalez (20)
Jio Mier (23)
Jose Fernandez

2B
Delino DeShields Jr. (8)
Kiki Hernandez

1B
Jonathan Singleton (1)
Telvin Nash (10)
Kody Hinze
Chase Davidson

C
Chris Wallace (30)
Roberto Pena
Ben Heath
Alfredo Gonzalez
Rene Garcia

LHP

LHSP	LHRP
Brett Oberholtzer (7)	Pat Urckfitz
Dallas Keuchel (21)	Alex Sogard
Kyle Hallock	Mitchell Lambson
Chris Lee	
Wes Musick	
Luis Cruz	
Tommy Shirley	

RHP

RHSP	RHRP
Jarred Cosart (2)	Juan Abreu (19)
Paul Clemens (5)	Jorge DeLeon (22)
Mike Foltynewicz (9)	Rhiner Cruz (28)
Adrian Houser (11)	Josh Zeid
Nick Tropeano (12)	Jason Stoffel
Jake Buchanan (13)	David Martinez
R.J. Alaniz (15)	Arcenio Leon
Ross Seaton (16)	Lucas Harrell
Tanner Bushue (24)	Dayan Diaz
Jose Cisnero (26)	Henry Villar
Vince Velasquez (27)	Chia-Jen Lo
Jack Armstrong Jr. (29)	
Lucas Harrell	
Sergio Perez	
Jonas Dufek	
Juri Perez	
Brandon Culbreth	
Zachary Grimmett	
Tyson Perez	

2011

BEST PURE HITTER: The Astros didn't draft a player whose best tool is his bat, though they believe OF George Springer (1) will hit for average. He cut his strikeout rate at Connecticut from 29 percent in 2010 to 16 percent in 2011.

BEST POWER HITTER: Springer has strength, bat speed and snap in his hands, producing well above-average raw power. 1B Chase Davidson (41) has similar raw power due to his strength.

FASTEST RUNNER: The 6-foot-3, 205-pound Springer is a plus runner, as is OF Javaris Reynolds (7), similarly sized at 6-foot-2, 210.

BEST DEFENSIVE PLAYER: Springer glides to the gaps in center field and owns a plus arm for right if he needs to move. His overall tool packages resembles that of Matt Kemp.

BEST FASTBALL: RHPs Adrian Houser (2) and Jack Armstrong Jr. both flash mid-90s fastballs, with Houser having better command and Armstrong having better life.

BEST SECONDARY PITCH: Houser shows feel for a hard curveball with plus potential. RHP Nick Tropeano (5) has extreme confidence in his changeup, which he throws with late fade and excellent arm speed.

BEST PRO DEBUT: Tropeano had 63 whiffs in 53 innings and a 2.36 ERA at short-season Tri-City. LHP Kyle Hallock (10), signed for just $40,000, had a 2.63 ERA and 61 strikeouts in 62 innings on the same club. Davidson hit .335/.426/.646 at Rookie-level Greeneville with 11 home runs—as many as he hit in three seasons at Georgia.

BEST ATHLETE: Springer and Reynolds, who needs an offensive approach to go with his strength and athleticism.

MOST INTRIGUING BACKGROUND: RHP Buddy Lamothe (40) was hitting 93 mph and attracting draft interest at San Jacinto (Texas) JC before a May 1 diving accident left him with serious neck and spinal cord injuries. Houston picked him anyway, then presented the paralyzed pitcher with a wheelchair-accessible van in August, courtesy of owner Drayton McLane. Armstrong's father Jack started the 1990 All-Star Game for the National League. Houser's father Mike was his high school coach, while his cousin Bob Davis spent eight seasons in the majors as a catcher.

CLOSEST TO THE MAJORS: Springer could move quickly if his bat progresses. Tropeano's changeup gives him a weapon to dominate the lower levels of the minors.

BEST LATE-ROUND PICK: OF Wallace Gonzalez (29) has good athleticism and size (6-foot-5, 230 pounds), and he drew significant college football interest as a tight end. RHP Tyson Perez (17) has a strong curveball to go with a fastball that reaches 92-94 mph at times.

THE ONE WHO GOT AWAY: The family of RHP Gandy Stubblefield (14) loves Texas A&M. The Astros offered the projectable 6-foot-4, 190-pounder second-round money but couldn't keep him from College Station.

ASSESSMENT: Houston values raw athleticism for hitters and tall pitchers, and it drafts accordingly. Springer, Houser and Armstrong hold the keys to this crop.

2010

The Astros had a golden opportunity with three of the first 33 picks, though 2B Delino DeShields Jr. (1), RHP Mike Foltynewicz (1) and 3B Mike Kvasnicka (1s) made only incremental progress in their first full pro seasons.

GRADE: C

2009

Houston's top two choices this year, SS Jio Mier (1) and RHP Tanner Bushue (2), also have been slow to develop. The good news is that OF J.D. Martinez (20) sped to the majors and 1B/OF Telvin Nash (3) has one of the best power bats in the system.

GRADE: C

2008

C Jason Castro (1) missed all of 2011 following knee surgery but still could be a solid regular behind the plate. RHP Jordan Lyles (1s), who has more polish than ceiling, reached the majors at age 20. OF J.D. Shuck (6) has played in Houston as well.

GRADE: C+

2007

In one of the most disastrous drafts ever, the Astros didn't have picks in the first two rounds and failed to sign their three best choices: SS Derek Dietrich (3), OF Brett Eibner (4) and RHP Chad Bettis (8), all of whom went in 2010's second round. They won't get a single big leaguer out of this draft.

GRADE: F

Draft analysis by John Manuel (2011) and Jim Callis (2007-10). Numbers in parentheses indicate draft rounds.

1 JONATHAN SINGLETON, 1B/OF

Born: Sept. 18, 1991. **B-T:** L-L. **Ht.:** 6-2. **Wt.:** 215.
Drafted: HS—Long Beach, 2009 (8th round). **Signed by:** Demerius Pittman (Phillies).

BA GRADE
65
MEDIUM

The Astros scouted Singleton heavily for the 2009 draft, Bobby Heck's second as scouting director. Singleton had a subpar senior season at Millikan High in Long Beach and fell to the eighth round, where he signed with the Phillies for $200,000. Almost immediately, he outperformed his draft round. He tore up the low Class A South Atlantic League in the first half of 2010, and though he cooled off afterward, he still ranked as the circuit's No. 1 prospect at season's end. With Ryan Howard signed through 2016, Philadelphia moved Singleton to left field in instructional league after the 2010 season, then moved him to Houston last July. He accompanied righthanders Jarred Cosart and Josh Zeid and outfielder Domingo Santana in a deal Hunter Pence. One Phillies official said of all the prospects his team has traded the last three years—a group that also includes Carlos Carrasco, Travis d'Arnaud, Kyle Drabek, Anthony Gose and Jonathan Villar—Singleton has the highest upside.

Scouts use words like "explosive" and "impact" when describing Singleton's bat. He has pure hitting skills with emerging home run power. He uses the whole field naturally while showing the bat speed to turn on good fastballs. He has the barrel awareness, hitting rhythm and timing teams want in a middle-of-the-order threat. He draws power from both his lower half and his strong hands and wrists. Singleton's well above-average pop presently plays more as average, as he's too patient at times and lets pitches go by that he should drive. He has advanced pitch recognition for his experience level, though, which should allow his power to grow as he gains experience. The biggest concern will be how he fares against lefthanders. Scouts say he hangs in well against breaking balls for his age, but he batted .248 with no homers against southpaws in 153 at-bats in 2011. While he's not as athletic as his father Herb, who played quarterback for Oregon in the early 1970s, Singleton is "baseball athletic," as one Astros official put it, with good body control and coordination. He's better defensively at first base than in left field, where

his well below-average speed was a hindrance. Houston still could give him some time in left to maintain some versatility but prefers him at first, where he has nimble feet. He has enough arm strength for first base and makes accurate throws. One scout expressed some trepidation that Singleton could get too big and immobile if he doesn't watch his body.

Brett Wallace was the key piece in the deal that sent Roy Oswalt to the Phillies in 2010, but he won't be an impediment to Singleton, the Astros' first baseman and No. 3 hitter of the future. Singleton will start 2012 at Double-A Corpus Christi and could spend the next two seasons in the minors and/or move back to left field if Wallace fulfills his early promise. If Wallace continues to struggle to get to his power, Singleton could take over in Houston in 2013. The best first-base prospect in the minors, he has a chance to hit .300 with 25-30 homers annually.

SCOUTING GRADES

Batting: 60. **Defense:** 50.
Power: 70. **Arm:** 40.
Speed: 30.

Based on 20-80 scouting scale, where 50 represents major league average, and future projection rather than present tools.

Year	Club (League)	Class	AVG	G	AB	R	H	2B	3B	HR	RBI	BB	SO	SB	CS	OBP	SLG
2009	Phillies (GCL)	R	.290	31	100	12	29	9	0	2	12	18	13	1	0	.395	.440
2010	Lakewood (SAL)	LoA	.290	104	376	64	109	25	2	14	77	62	74	9	7	.393	.479
2011	Clearwater (FSL)	HiA	.284	93	320	48	91	14	0	9	47	56	83	3	3	.387	.413
	Lancaster (CAL)	HiA	.333	35	129	20	43	9	1	4	16	14	40	0	0	.405	.512
Minor League Totals			.294	263	925	144	272	57	3	29	152	150	210	13	10	.393	.456

2 JARRED COSART, RHP

Born: May 25, 1990. **B-T:** R-R. **Ht.:** 6-3. **Wt.:** 180. **Drafted:** HS—League City, Texas, 2008 (38th round). **Signed by:** Steve Cohen (Phillies).

BA GRADE

65

HIGH

Shortly after Cosart starred in the 2011 Futures Game—he missed the 2010 contest with elbow tenderness—the Astros acquired him from the Phillies in the Hunter Pence deal. Promoted to Corpus Christi after the trade, he allowed one run or less in five of his seven Double-A starts. Some scouts describe Cosart's delivery as maximum effort, while Houston prefers to call it energetic. All sides agree his quick arm and athleticism produce electric stuff. "You see this little guy out there and then—wham!—the ball explodes out of his hand," said one scout. Cosart's fastball sits around 95 mph and touches 98, and his curveball has excellent shape and upper-70s power when it's on. He also flashes a plus changeup that he throws with good arm speed. Cosart needs to add some strength and control his delivery in order to throw more strikes, which helps explain why someone with dominant stuff averaged a modest 6.3 strikeouts per nine innings in 2011. Some scouts question his durability because of his wiry build and high-effort delivery. Cosart has the stuff to be a No. 1 starter, though he may lack the command, consistency and durability to be a true ace. Ticketed for Double-A to start 2012, he could be a closer in the Brad Lidge mold if starting doesn't work out.

Year	Club (League)	Class	W	L	ERA	G	GS	CG	SV	IP	H	HR	BB	SO	K/9	WHIP	AVG
2009	Phillies (GCL)	R	2	2	2.22	7	5	0	0	24	12	0	7	25	9.2	0.78	.143
2010	Lakewood (SAL)	LoA	7	3	3.79	14	14	1	0	71	60	3	16	77	9.7	1.07	.224
2011	Clearwater (FSL)	HiA	9	8	3.92	20	19	0	0	108	98	7	43	79	6.6	1.31	.243
	Corpus Christi (TL)	AA	1	2	4.71	7	7	0	0	36	33	4	13	22	5.4	1.27	.234
Minor League Totals			19	15	3.83	48	45	1	0	240	203	14	79	203	7.6	1.18	.227

3 GEORGE SPRINGER, OF

Born: Sept. 19, 1989. **B-T:** R-R. **Ht.:** 6-3. **Wt.:** 205. **Drafted:** Connecticut, 2011 (1st round). **Signed by:** John Kosciak/Bobby Heck.

BA GRADE

65

HIGH

Drafted out of high school by the Twins in the 48th round, Springer instead went to Connecticut, honing his raw tools and helping the Huskies reach back-to-back NCAA regionals. He also starred for the U.S. college national team in 2010 before becoming the 11th overall pick last June, the highest-drafted Husky ever. His $2.525 million bonus is the largest in Astros draft history. Springer has a power-speed combination in the Mike Cameron mold and could be a five-tool player if his bat becomes more consistent. His quick hands and strong wrists generate explosive bat speed and above-average power potential. His approach at the plate vacillates between too passive and too aggressive, but he sliced his strikeout rate from 29 percent as a sophomore to 16 percent as a junior. He needs to keep improving his pitch recognition and feel for the strike zone, but he isn't afraid to draw a walk. With his plus speed and arm strength, Springer can play center or right field. His speed also plays on the bases, as he stole 64 bases in 73 tries in his final two college seasons. The most well-rounded position player in the system, Springer could move quickly. He'll start 2012 at low Class A Lexington, with his bat dictating his timetable.

Year	Club (League)	Class	AVG	G	AB	R	H	2B	3B	HR	RBI	BB	SO	SB	CS	OBP	SLG
2011	Tri-City (NYP)	SS	.179	8	28	8	5	3	0	1	3	2	2	4	0	.303	.393
Minor League Totals			.179	8	28	8	5	3	0	1	3	2	2	4	0	.303	.393

4 JONATHAN VILLAR, SS

Born: May 2, 1991. **B-T:** B-R. **Ht.:** 6-1. **Wt.:** 195. **Signed:** Dominican Republic, 2008. **Signed by:** Sal Agostinelli (Phillies).

BA GRADE

65

HIGH

Villar signed for a $105,000 in 2008 with the Phillies, who sent him to the Astros in the Roy Oswalt trade two year later. Teaming with steadier but less toolsy Jose Altuve at high Class A Lancaster and Corpus Christi, Villar had an uneven 2011 season, striking out a system-high 156 times and committing 36 errors. Villar's tools are loud, as he earns 60 and 70 grades on the 20-80 scouting scale for his speed, arm and defensive ability at shortstop. He's flashy, sometimes to a fault, on defense. Some scouts thought he coasted during the regular season, leading to careless errors and empty at-bats, but Villar competed much better in instructional league. He's a switch-hitter with solid gap power, particularly from the right side, but he won't fully tap into it until he stops chasing pitches out of the strike zone. He's more of a slasher while hitting lefthanded. An aggressive basestealer, he led Houston farmhands with 34 thefts in 46 tries in 2011. Villar may be the toolsiest shortstop in the minors other than the Rangers' Jurickson Profar, who's much more polished. The Astros hope to let Villar catch his breath at bit with a return to Double-A, but he could play his way into the major league mix in 2012.

Year	Club (League)	Class	AVG	G	AB	R	H	2B	3B	HR	RBI	BB	SO	SB	CS	OBP	SLG
2008	Phillies (DSL)	R	.271	62	214	37	58	6	3	1	21	30	56	27	8	.367	.341
2009	Phillies (GCL)	R	.277	31	94	14	26	7	1	0	14	13	24	11	2	.364	.372
	Williamsport (NYP)	SS	.231	11	39	6	9	1	1	0	5	4	14	6	0	.302	.308
2010	Lakewood (SAL)	LoA	.272	100	371	61	101	18	4	2	36	26	103	38	13	.332	.358
	Lancaster (CAL)	HiA	.225	32	129	18	29	6	2	3	19	12	50	7	2	.294	.372
2011	Lancaster (CAL)	HiA	.259	47	174	26	45	7	4	4	26	25	56	20	6	.353	.414
	Corpus Christi (TL)	AA	.231	83	324	52	75	16	2	10	26	29	100	14	6	.301	.386
Minor League Totals			.255	366	1345	214	343	61	17	20	147	139	403	123	37	.331	.370

5 PAUL CLEMENS, RHP

Born: Feb. 14, 1988. **B-T:** R-R. **Ht.:** 6-4. **Wt.:** 180. **Drafted:** Louisburg (N.C.) JC, 2008 (7th round). **Signed by:** Billy Best (Braves).

BA GRADE
55
MEDIUM

Clemens broke Javier Lopez's single-game strikeout record at Robinson High (Fairfax, Va.), then took his raw power arm to Louisburg (N.C.) JC before signing with Atlanta as a seventh-rounder in 2008. Astros field coordinator Paul Runge got to know him at the end of his three-decade tenure in the Braves organization and recommended him strongly when Houston made the Michael Bourn trade last July. The Astros also acquired Jordan Schafer and pitchers Brett Oberholtzer and Juan Abreu in the deal. Clemens' fastball sits at 93-96 mph. He has cleaned up his delivery and shortened his arm action over the last few years, helping him find the strike zone more often, but he's still effectively wild. He has improved his direction to the plate, wasting less energy in his high-effort motion. Clemens' secondary pitches have progressed, and his mid-70s downer curve is a plus pitch at times. He also throws a hard cutter/slider hybrid as well as a solid changeup than enables him to handle lefthanders better than righthanders. Houston added Clemens to its 40-man roster in November and intends to keep him as a starter to hone his control and repertoire. He'll begin 2012 back at Triple-A Oklahoma City, where he made his final start of 2011. At worst, his strong arm should make him an effective big league reliever.

Year	Club (League)	Class	W	L	ERA	G	GS	CG	SV	IP	H	HR	BB	SO	K/9	WHIP	AVG
2008	Braves (GCL)	R	1	0	0.00	1	0	0	0	3	1	0	0	2	6.0	0.33	.111
	Danville (APP)	R	3	3	3.39	12	8	0	1	58	57	6	18	57	8.8	1.29	.252
	Rome (SAL)	LoA	0	1	9.00	1	1	0	0	4	7	0	2	0	0.0	2.25	.412
2009	Rome (SAL)	LoA	6	5	5.91	26	11	0	3	85	105	7	49	64	6.8	1.80	.296
2010	Rome (SAL)	LoA	2	0	1.42	8	0	0	1	19	11	1	8	16	7.6	1.00	.164
	Myrtle Beach (CAR)	HiA	0	4	3.69	27	8	0	2	76	83	5	28	65	7.7	1.47	.275
2011	Mississippi (SL)	AA	6	5	3.73	20	20	0	0	109	103	8	44	93	7.7	1.35	.249
	Corpus Christi (TL)	AA	2	1	2.35	5	5	0	0	31	23	3	12	26	7.6	1.14	.200
	Oklahoma City (PCL)	AAA	0	1	15.43	1	1	0	0	5	4	1	6	6	11.6	2.14	.250
Minor League Totals			20	20	4.09	101	54	0	7	389	394	31	167	329	7.6	1.44	.259

6 DOMINGO SANTANA, OF

Born: Aug. 5, 1992. **B-T:** R-R. **Ht.:** 6-5. **Wt.:** 200. **Signed:** Dominican Republic, 2008. **Signed by:** Sal Agostinelli (Phillies).

BA GRADE
60
HIGH

Santana was just 16 when he made his U.S. debut in 2009. He started 2011 as an 18-year old in low Class A with the Phillies, who signed him out of the Dominican for $30,000, and he stayed in the South Atlantic League after getting included in the Hunter Pence trade. Santana had 10 multihit games in his 17 starts for Lexington. Scouts acknowledge Santana's raw hitting approach and most think he'll always have his share of strikeouts. If he makes consistent contact, though, he could become a prototypical right fielder in the Jermaine Dye mold. Santana's combination of tremendous leverage and excellent bat speed creates monstrous raw power. He needs at-bats to see more pitches, learn to identify them and manage the strike zone. He's an average runner, though not a basestealer, and has a plus arm. He has the tools to be an above-average defender in right field. The Astros envision an outfield of the future with J.D. Martinez in left, George Springer in center and Santana in right by the time they become competitive. If Santana cuts down on his strikeouts, he could move rapidly. He has a chance to put up sick numbers in Lancaster in 2012.

Year	Club (League)	Class	AVG	G	AB	R	H	2B	3B	HR	RBI	BB	SO	SB	CS	OBP	SLG
2009	Phillies (GCL)	R	.288	37	118	17	34	6	1	6	28	15	44	3	1	.388	.508
2010	Lakewood (SAL)	LoA	.182	49	165	27	30	10	0	3	16	29	76	5	6	.322	.297
	Williamsport (NYP)	SS	.237	54	186	28	44	9	0	5	20	23	73	4	4	.336	.366
2011	Lakewood (SAL)	LoA	.269	96	350	45	94	29	4	7	32	26	120	4	1	.345	.434
	Lexington (SAL)	LoA	.382	17	68	13	26	4	0	5	21	6	15	1	0	.447	.662
Minor League Totals			.257	253	887	130	228	58	5	26	117	99	328	17	12	.352	.422

7 BRETT OBERHOLTZER, LHP

Born: July 1, 1989. **B-T:** L-L. **Ht.:** 6-2. **Wt.:** 230. **Drafted:** Seminole (Fla.) CC, 2008 (8th round). **Signed by:** Gregg Kilby (Braves).

Oberholtzer grew up in suburban Philadelphia and was a fan of Michael Bourn when Bourn was a Phillies minor leaguer. He introduced himself to Bourn when their paths crossed in spring training when the Braves and Astros played, then he was traded—along with his Double-A road roommate Paul Clemens—for Bourn last July. Oberholtzer combines a four-pitch mix with pitching savvy to try to let hitters get themselves out. He has a No. 4 starter profile with no plus pitch but a durable, innings-eating frame, and he knows his strengths and weaknesses. Oberholtzer pitches inside with his 88-92 mph fastball, and his slider can be an asset when he locates it. He can back-foot it against righthanders and it helps him neutralize lefties. His average curveball has good shape, and his average changeup features solid arm speed. Without a true out pitch, Oberholtzer needs to hone his average control and improve his command of all his pitches. He has some funkiness in his delivery that gives him some deception. He has some similarities to J.A. Happ, another Houston trade acquisition, and to avoid Happ's 2011 struggles Oberholtzer will have to locate his pitches better. He and Clemens are headed to Triple-A in 2012 and will jockey for callup when the Astros need another starter.

BA GRADE

50

MEDIUM

Year	Club (League)	Class	W	L	ERA	G	GS	CG	SV	IP	H	HR	BB	SO	K/9	WHIP	AVG
2008	Braves (GCL)	R	4	1	2.89	10	0	0	0	37	34	1	10	32	7.7	1.18	.241
2009	Danville (APP)	R	6	2	2.01	12	12	1	0	67	46	1	6	56	7.5	0.78	.191
2010	Rome (SAL)	LoA	0	2	1.96	4	4	0	0	23	22	1	5	19	7.4	1.17	.262
	Myrtle Beach (CAR)	HiA	6	6	4.15	22	18	0	2	113	123	7	18	107	8.5	1.25	.279
2011	Mississippi (SL)	AA	9	9	3.74	21	21	1	0	128	119	6	42	93	6.6	1.26	.249
	Corpus Christi (TL)	AA	2	3	5.27	6	6	0	0	27	28	3	10	28	9.2	1.39	.267
Minor League Totals			27	23	3.49	75	61	2	2	395	372	19	91	335	7.6	1.17	.250

8 DELINO DeSHIELDS JR., 2B

Born: Aug. 16, 1992. **B-T:** R-R. **Ht.:** 5-9. **Wt.:** 188. **Drafted:** HS—College Park, Ga. (1st round). **Signed by:** Lincoln Martin.

The son of the big leaguer who once was traded for Pedro Martinez and now manages in the Reds system, DeShields doesn't look like his lithe father. He's built more like Mike Tyson and was a star prep football player before being drafted eighth overall in 2010. Signed for $2.125 million, he struggled in 2011 as the sixth-youngest player in the South Atlantic League. DeShields' youth and inexperience showed in his first full pro season. He didn't make consistent contact but still showed bat speed and strength. He must improve his ability to identify pitches and work counts. He could develop average power, though he mostly drives balls to the gaps for now. DeShields graded as an 80 runner on the 20-80 scouting scale as an amateur, and as a 70 runner as he adjusted to the pro grind, though he's still learning to maximize his speed on the bases. In his first extended time at second base, he improved his footwork and double-play pivot and became more consistent after making seven errors in his first 13 games. He has a fringy arm that will play in center field if he can't stick in the infield. The Astros are encouraged by DeShields' progress and still love his upside. He'll probably head back to low Class A to start the 2012 season.

BA GRADE

60

EXTREME

Year	Club (League)	Class	AVG	G	AB	R	H	2B	3B	HR	RBI	BB	SO	SB	CS	OBP	SLG
2010	Astros (GCL)	R	.111	2	9	3	1	0	0	0	0	1	2	0	0	.200	.111
	Greeneville (APP)	R	.313	16	67	11	21	6	1	0	8	5	18	5	1	.356	.433
2011	Lexington (SAL)	LoA	.220	119	469	73	103	17	2	9	48	52	118	30	11	.305	.322
Minor League Totals			.229	137	545	87	125	23	3	9	56	58	138	35	12	.310	.332

9 MIKE FOLTYNEWICZ, RHP

BA GRADE

55

HIGH

Born: Oct. 7, 1991. **B-T:** R-R. **Ht.:** 6-4. **Wt.:** 200. **Drafted:** HS—Minooka, Ill., 2010 (1st round supplemental). **Signed by:** Troy Hoerner.

The Astros signed the top high school pitcher out of Illinois in back-to-back drafts in Tanner Bushue (second round, 2009) and Foltynewicz (19th overall, 2010). Recipient of a $1.305 million bonus, he lost his first nine decisions as a pro, including six of his first seven starts in 2011. A classic raw Midwestern prep pitcher, Foltynewicz is the best homegrown arm in the system. He combines a good pitcher's frame and athleticism to throw four-seam fastballs that sit in the low 90s and top out at 96 mph. Houston has de-emphasized an 89-93 mph two-seamer and a slider he used in high school, having him use mainly four-seamers and focus on a curveball. The Astros liked how he made the adjustments and had to stay on his catchers to have him throw more curves. Foltynewicz still is learning to throw the curve with power and confidence, but it has plus potential. He has solid feel for an average changeup. He needs to refine his control and command, because he doesn't throw enough strikes or miss enough bats. After adding pitching depth via trades, Houston won't have to rush Foltynewicz. He'll return to Lexington to open 2012 and should get tested by Lancaster's gusting winds and rock-hard infield later in the season. If everything comes together, he can be a No. 3 starter.

Year	Club (League)	Class	W	L	ERA	G	GS	CG	SV	IP	H	HR	BB	SO	K/9	WHIP	AVG
2010	Greeneville (APP)	R	0	3	4.03	12	12	0	0	45	46	3	15	39	7.9	1.37	.272
2011	Lexington (SAL)	LoA	5	11	4.97	26	26	0	0	134	149	10	51	88	5.9	1.49	.289
Minor League Totals			5	14	4.74	38	38	0	0	179	195	13	66	127	6.4	1.46	.285

10 TELVIN NASH, 1B/OF

BA GRADE

50

HIGH

Born: Feb. 20, 1991. **B-T:** R-R. **Ht.:** 6-1. **Wt.:** 230. **Drafted:** HS—Griffin, Ga., 2009 (3rd round). **Signed by:** Lincoln Martin.

A prep teammate of Tim Beckham, the No. 1 overall pick in 2008, Nash was recruited by college football programs before committing to Kennesaw State for baseball. He homered five times in his first 15 games in 2011, his first stab at full-season ball, before a broken hamate bone in his left hand sidelined him for two months. Scouts look for players with a carrying tool, and Nash has one in his well above-average righthanded power. Even after hamate surgery, which usually saps a player's pop, he homered nine times in 210 at-bats. He has good bat speed and even better strength, and his bat will get quicker if he can eliminate a wrap in his swing. That flaw also leads to an excessive amount of strikeouts, though he's not afraid to take a walk. Nash has seen time at both first base and left field but projects as a subpar defender at both spots. He's a well below-average runner with fringy arm strength and iffy hands. With Jonathan Singleton joining the organization, Nash is blocked at first base and will have to work hard to become a passable left fielder. With the Astros moving to the American League, he could be their future DH. If healthy, he could put up huge home run numbers in Lancaster in 2012.

Year	Club (League)	Class	AVG	G	AB	R	H	2B	3B	HR	RBI	BB	SO	SB	CS	OBP	SLG
2009	Astros (GCL)	R	.218	40	142	15	31	10	1	1	20	12	45	1	2	.280	.324
2010	Greeneville (APP)	R	.265	57	200	30	53	12	1	12	39	25	64	1	1	.348	.515
	Tri-City (NYP)	SS	.308	4	13	2	4	1	1	1	1	0	7	0	1	.308	.769
2011	Astros (GCL)	R	.385	5	13	5	5	2	0	0	0	3	2	0	0	.500	.538
	Lexington (SAL)	LoA	.269	73	268	41	72	16	0	14	37	40	103	2	0	.373	.485
Minor League Totals			.259	179	636	93	165	41	3	28	97	80	221	4	4	.347	.465

11 ADRIAN HOUSER, RHP

BA GRADE

50

HIGH

Born: Feb. 2, 1993. **B-T:** R-R. **Ht.:** 6-4. **Wt.:** 205. **Drafted:** HS—Locust Grove, Okla., 2011 (2nd round). **Signed by:** Jim Stevenson.

Houser was the fourth Oklahoma high school pitcher drafted in 2011, and he still went 69th overall. It was a banner year in the state, and Houser was able to lead his Locust Grove High team (coached by his father Mike) to a state 4-A championship as both a pitcher and center fielder. He comes from a baseball family, with a cousin (Bob Davis) who played in the majors and an uncle (James Knott) who pitched briefly in the Mets system. The Astros gave Houser a $530,100 bonus in the second round to dissuade him from attending the University of Oklahoma. He made strides after signing, tossing five shutout innings in his final outing in the Rookie-level Appalachian League and impressing scouts in instructional league. Houser has two pitches that grab scouts' attention, with a low-90s fastball notable both for its sinking life and his ability to run it up to 95 mph, and a hard curveball. He uses a high arm slot and works up and down in the zone with his fastball and curve. As with most young pitchers, he still has work to do with his changeup and fastball command. Houser likely will work on those areas of his game in extended spring training before going to short-season Tri-City in June.

Year	Club (League)	Class	W	L	ERA	G	GS	CG	SV	IP	H	HR	BB	SO	K/9	WHIP	AVG
2011	Astros (GCL)	R	1	2	4.03	6	5	0	0	22	24	0	10	25	10.1	1.52	.273
	Greeneville (APP)	R	1	2	4.56	6	6	0	0	26	25	1	15	19	6.7	1.56	.258
Minor League Totals			2	4	4.31	12	11	0	0	48	49	1	25	44	8.3	1.54	.265

12 NICK TROPEANO, RHP

BA GRADE

50

HIGH

Born: Aug. 27, 1990. **B-T:** R-R. **Ht.:** 6-4. **Wt.:** 205. **Drafted:** Stony Brook, 2011 (5th round). **Signed by:** John Kosciak.

Tropeano ranked as the No. 1 prospect in the Atlantic Collegiate League after his freshman year, then helped lead Cotuit to the Cape Cod League championship in 2010 as the ace of the Kettleers' playoff staff. As a junior he led Stony Brook's emerging program to the America East regular-season title and a 42-12 record. Tropeano has honed a consistent formula, commanding his fastball and an excellent changeup that was one of the finest in the 2011 draft and is the best in the system. Tropeano's changeup is so good—he throws it with deceptive arm speed and achieves quality fade—that he pitched off it too much as an amateur, to the detriment of his fastball and slider. After signing for $155,700 as a fifth-round pick last June, he found more fastball velocity simply by throwing the pitch more often. He pitched at 91-94 mph at times last in the short-season New York-Penn League and sat at 88-92 during instructional league. His slider has modest break and remains his third pitch. Tropeano's fastball command and changeup should help him move quickly, and he could reach high Class A in his first full pro season. The development of his slider will determine whether he remains a starter or moves to the bullpen, where he might be a late-inning asset with his dominant changeup.

Year	Club (League)	Class	W	L	ERA	G	GS	CG	SV	IP	H	HR	BB	SO	K/9	WHIP	AVG
2011	Tri-City (NYP)	SS	3	2	2.36	12	12	0	0	53	42	1	21	63	10.6	1.18	.212
Minor League Totals			3	2	2.36	12	12	0	0	53	42	1	21	63	10.6	1.18	.212

13 JAKE BUCHANAN, RHP

BA GRADE

45

MEDIUM

Born: Sept. 24, 1989. **B-T:** R-R. **Ht.:** 6-0. **Wt.:** 200. **Drafted:** North Carolina State, 2010 (8th round). **Signed by:** J.D. Alleva.

At North Carolina State, Buchanan was a stock 6-foot righthander with an average three-pitch mix. After signing for $120,000 as an eighth-round pick in 2010, his career changed in March, when he decided to start throwing a slider, which soon morphed into a cutter. He also focused on throwing more two-seam fastballs in preparation for an assignment to high Class A. Buchanan didn't thrive at home, posting a 6.86 ERA at the wind tunnel that is Lancaster's Clear Channel Stadium, but he was outstanding on the road with a 2.17 ERA. He did it by pounding the strike zone aggressively with an 87-91 mph fastball that touches 92, featuring the sink to produce a sterling 3.2 groundout/airout ratio with the JetHawks. Buchanan leans heavily on his cutter, using it and his fastball to pitch inside effectively. He also throws a changeup with some fade, and he uses his curveball as an early-count change of pace as well. He's efficient with all his pitches and sequences smartly, helping him shackle lefthanded hitters (.541 OPS in the Cal League). Buchanan doesn't make mistakes in the middle of the plate, allowing him to post the lowest ERA (3.91) ever for a full-time starter in the 16-season history of the Lancaster franchise. Buchanan finished the year with a strong Double-A start and will return to Corpus Christi to see if he can continue to avoid the middle of the plate. He profiles as a workhorse No. 4 or 5 starter.

Year	Club (League)	Class	W	L	ERA	G	GS	CG	SV	IP	H	HR	BB	SO	K/9	WHIP	AVG
2010	Tri-City (NYP)	SS	4	5	4.28	14	14	0	0	61	69	3	11	42	6.2	1.31	.286
2011	Lancaster (CAL)	HiA	5	10	3.91	25	25	1	0	159	157	10	35	102	5.8	1.21	.256
	Corpus Christi (TL)	AA	0	0	1.29	1	1	0	0	7	6	0	1	2	2.6	1.00	.231
Minor League Totals			9	15	3.93	40	40	1	0	227	232	13	47	146	5.8	1.23	.263

14 ARIEL OVANDO, OF

BA GRADE

55

EXTREME

Born: Sept. 15, 1993. **B-T:** L-L. **Ht.:** 6-4. **Wt.:** 190. **Signed:** Dominican Republic, 2010. **Signed by:** Felix Francisco.

The Astros' most successful homegrown Latin American player in 2011 was 5-foot-7 Venezuelan second baseman Jose Altuve, who in many ways is the opposite of the organization's new poster boy for its Latin program, Ovando. Built like a shooting guard or wide receiver, Ovando is 6-foot-4 and still growing. He signed for a franchise-record $2.6 million in 2010 and had high expectations placed upon him from the start. Even in a half-season league, he had trouble staying healthy as nagging ankle, wrist and hamstring injuries cost him at-bats. It was a good lesson on how he'll need to get stronger to survive the minor league grind. Ovando did improve simply by playing in an organized setting for the first time, and the Astros hope to see a jump in performance in 2012, now that he has gone through two instructional leagues and a summer of games. Ovando's carrying tool, his outstanding raw power, was evident in batting practice more than in games. He has excellent leverage in his loose swing and impressed Appalachian League managers with his athleticism. All aspects of his game are raw, from his approach at the plate to his baserunning to his defense. He flashes plus arm strength, though it grades as below-average at times, and has fringy speed. Ovando could repeat Rookie ball or advance to the New York-Penn League after starting this season in extended spring training.

Year	Club (League)	Class	AVG	G	AB	R	H	2B	3B	HR	RBI	BB	SO	SB	CS	OBP	SLG
2011	Greeneville (APP)	R	.235	44	170	16	40	10	3	2	30	12	51	0	0	.283	.365
Minor League Totals			.235	44	170	16	40	10	3	2	30	12	51	0	0	.283	.365

15 R.J. ALANIZ, RHP

BA GRADE

50

HIGH

Born: June 14, 1991. **B-T:** R-R. **Ht.:** 6-4. **Wt.:** 195. **Signed:** HS—La Joya, Texas, NDFA 2009. **Signed by:** Rusty Pendergrass.

Alaniz has better stuff than the typical nondrafted free agent. His high school senior season was canceled in 2009 because of a swine flu outbreak in the Rio Grande Valley. He spent the summer pitching in tryouts and in a league based at Atlanta's East Cobb complex before the Astros signed him for $150,000. Alaniz is far from a finished product but has a chance to develop two plus pitches. His fastball is one of the system's best, sitting at 92-95 mph at times and featuring short, late sink. He uses his heater confidently, with one club official saying, "He likes to grip it and rip it." His belief and control with his fastball helps him keep an aggressive tempo when he's throwing strikes. Alaniz found an effective grip with his changeup as the 2011 season progressed and started to trust it more in the second half. The more he used it, the more he threw it with the same release point and sinking action as his fastball. His changeup is a plus pitch on occasion. Houston considered his curveball the best in the system a year ago; it's a solid pitch at times but lacks consistency. Too often, his curve gets early, loopy action rather than late, sharp break, and he needs to a better job of staying on top of it. Alaniz throws strikes and has gained about 20 pounds since signing, so he's on the path to developing the control and durability to be a workhorse starter. He's also an intriguing possibility as a power reliever. He'll remain in the rotation this year in high Class A.

Year	Club (League)	Class	W	L	ERA	G	GS	CG	SV	IP	H	HR	BB	SO	K/9	WHIP	AVG
2010	Greeneville (APP)	R	6	4	4.21	12	12	0	0	58	65	5	10	42	6.6	1.30	.280
2011	Lexington (SAL)	LoA	7	10	4.44	27	21	0	0	116	111	11	38	96	7.5	1.29	.248
Minor League Totals			13	14	4.36	39	33	0	0	173	176	16	48	138	7.2	1.29	.259

16 ROSS SEATON, RHP

BA GRADE

50

HIGH

Born: Sept. 18, 1989. **B-T:** L-R. **Ht.:** 6-4. **Wt.:** 212. **Drafted:** HS—Houston, 2008 (3rd round supplemental). **Signed by:** Rusty Pendergrass/Mike Burns.

Signed for an over-slot $700,000 as a supplemental third-rounder in 2008, Seaton embodies some of the best and worst elements of the Astros system. In a thin organization, he's taking a long time to develop and hasn't performed well. He's also very young and has been pushed out of necessity, pitching the entire 2011 season in Double-A at age 21 after posting a 6.64 ERA at Lancaster the year before. He was overmatched for much of last year but compiled a 3.43 ERA in the final month after improving his mechanics and getting better extension. Club officials credit Corpus Christi pitching coach Don Alexander with getting Seaton out front more, allowing him to better locate his fastball inside against righthanders. He also quickened his delivery's tempo and shortened his arm action. Seaton pitches with a quality fastball at 91-94 mph. His slider improved along with his mechanics, giving him a second plus pitch at times. His fringy changeup will have to get better for him to combat lefties, who put up an .824 OPS against him last year. Seaton could take a step forward in 2012, when he repeats a level for the first time with what should be an older, more competitive Corpus Christi club.

Year	Club (League)	Class	W	L	ERA	G	GS	CG	SV	IP	H	HR	BB	SO	K/9	WHIP	AVG
2008	Greeneville (APP)	R	0	0	13.50	3	3	0	0	4	8	1	2	4	9.0	2.50	.381
2009	Lexington (SAL)	LoA	8	10	3.29	24	24	1	0	137	137	11	39	88	5.8	1.29	.261
2010	Lancaster (CAL)	HiA	6	13	6.64	28	28	0	0	146	198	22	45	85	5.2	1.66	.327
2011	Corpus Christi (TL)	AA	4	9	5.23	28	28	0	0	155	168	19	47	97	5.6	1.39	.279
Minor League Totals			18	32	5.17	83	83	1	0	442	511	53	133	274	5.6	1.46	.292

17 J.B. SHUCK, OF

BA GRADE

45

MEDIUM

Born: June 18, 1987. **B-T:** L-L. **Ht.:** 5-11. **Wt.:** 195. **Drafted:** Ohio State, 2008 (6th round). **Signed by:** Nick Venuto.

Since Bobby Heck started running the team's draft in 2008, Shuck is one of four Astros picks to reach the majors, joining Jason Castro, Jordan Lyles and J.D. Martinez. Shuck has the lowest ceiling of the group and he's close to reaching it. His ability to be a regular hinges on whether he'll be able to play center field capably. Shuck hits singles, draws walks and leaves scouts wanting more. He has a slashing, contact-oriented approach that enabled him to hit .302 in the minors while striking out just once every 10.2 plate appearances. He also draws a fair share of walks, making him a top-of-the-order option. However, Shuck doesn't do much else. He's a plus-plus runner down the line, but his speed doesn't play that well on the bases or in the field because he lacks instincts and aggressiveness. Though he pitched at Ohio State, he lacks the arm strength to play right field and hasn't distinguished himself in center. Shuck will compete for Houston's center-field job in 2012 and could settle in as a fourth outfielder if he doesn't win it.

Year	Club (League)	Class	AVG	G	AB	R	H	2B	3B	HR	RBI	BB	SO	SB	CS	OBP	SLG
2008	Tri-City (NYP)	SS	.300	65	263	51	79	12	5	4	24	35	34	8	6	.385	.430
2009	Lancaster (CAL)	HiA	.315	133	556	98	175	30	11	1	36	64	55	18	9	.389	.414
2010	Corpus Christi (TL)	AA	.298	101	389	52	116	14	2	2	28	46	56	9	9	.372	.360
	Round Rock (PCL)	AAA	.273	36	139	15	38	2	2	0	7	16	15	7	3	.348	.317
2011	Oklahoma City (PCL)	AAA	.297	108	354	60	105	11	7	0	30	56	30	20	11	.398	.367
	Houston (NL)	MAJ	.272	37	81	9	22	2	1	0	3	11	7	2	0	.359	.321
Major League Totals			.272	37	81	9	22	2	1	0	3	11	7	2	0	.359	.321
Minor League Totals			.302	443	1701	276	513	69	27	7	125	217	190	62	38	.383	.386

18 AUSTIN WATES, OF

BA GRADE
45
MEDIUM

Born: Sept. 2, 1988. **B-T:** R-R. **Ht.:** 6-1. **Wt.:** 179. **Drafted:** Virginia Tech, 2010 (3rd round). **Signed by:** Everett Stull.

The Astros have drafted several college hitters with single-digit draft picks in recent years and still are waiting for one of them to break out. Their top two such selections from 2010, Austin Wates and Mike Kvasnicka, had modest full-season debuts last year. Wates split time between first base and the outfield at Virginia Tech, and Houston likes both his bat and his speed. He played all three outfield positions in 2011, hitting .300 while leading Lancaster in doubles (23) and RBIs (75) while ranking second in steals (26). Considering the offensive nature of the high Class A California League and Lancaster's Clear Channel Stadium, his .413 slugging percentage was a downer. Wates' swing and approach are the issue. He has natural feel for hitting and for making consistent contact, but he inside-outs the ball and is content to shoot singles to center and right field. He has yet to learn to turn on balls consistently and show any pull power, and his swing lacks loft. Wates shows some raw power in batting practice. His plus speed enables him to steal bases and make up for his inexperience in the outfield. He has a decent arm, certainly enough for left or center field. If Wates can stick in center, it will put less pressure on his bat and enhance his profile significantly. He'll work in all three outfield spots again this year in Double-A.

Year	Club (League)	Class	AVG	G	AB	R	H	2B	3B	HR	RBI	BB	SO	SB	CS	OBP	SLG
2010	Astros (GCL)	R	.000	1	3	0	0	0	0	0	0	0	2	0	0	.250	.000
	Tri-City (NYP)	SS	.316	12	38	11	12	2	1	1	6	8	6	9	0	.447	.500
2011	Lancaster (CAL)	HiA	.300	132	526	85	158	23	9	6	75	47	86	26	7	.366	.413
Minor League Totals			.300	145	567	97	170	25	10	7	81	55	94	35	7	.371	.416

19 JUAN ABREU, RHP

BA GRADE
45
MEDIUM

Born: April 8, 1985. **B-T:** 6-0. **Ht.:** 6-0. **Wt.:** 180. **Signed:** Dominican Republic, 2003. **Signed by:** Pedro Silverio (Royals).

The Royals originally signed Abreu and watched him develop one of the best fastballs in their system before a contract snafu let him hit the open market in 2009. The Braves turned him from a minor league free agent find into part of the four-player package they sent to the Astros for Michael Bourn last July. Abreu didn't spend much time in the minors with Houston before making his major league debut, and he got 12 of his 20 big league outs via strikeouts. His violent delivery never will be used in instructional videos, as he has a significant head whack. His arm is quick enough to catch up to the rest of his body, though, and he pumps 93-98 mph fastballs close enough to the strike zone. He also throws a slurvy breaking ball at 78-81 mph. He doesn't have much control, however, and he averaged 5.4 walks per nine innings in the minors. He's hard to hit, so he doesn't always pay for those free passes. The more strikes Abreu throws, the more high-leverage innings he'll earn in Houston. He has a good shot at earning a spot in the big league bullpen in 2012.

Year	Club (League)	Class	W	L	ERA	G	GS	CG	SV	IP	H	HR	BB	SO	K/9	WHIP	AVG
2003	Royals (DSL)	R	0	2	2.25	5	2	0	0	16	16	0	7	10	5.6	1.44	.242
2004	Royals (DSL)	R	2	1	4.06	9	7	0	0	31	22	0	20	33	9.6	1.35	.198
2005	Royals (AZL)	R	2	5	6.88	14	13	0	0	52	72	4	27	52	8.9	1.89	.327
2006	Idaho Falls (PIO)	R	4	2	5.76	20	0	0	2	50	39	4	35	57	10.3	1.48	.223
2007	Did Not Play—Injured																
2008	Burlington (MWL)	LoA	4	4	3.66	22	4	0	7	76	59	6	42	104	12.3	1.32	.214
2009	Wilmington (CAR)	HiA	3	2	1.69	20	0	0	12	21	8	1	14	28	11.8	1.03	.114
	NW Arkansas (TL)	AA	2	2	5.75	16	0	0	4	20	19	3	22	25	11.1	2.02	.247
2010	Myrtle Beach (CAR)	HiA	0	0	8.22	8	0	0	1	15	14	5	8	15	8.8	1.43	.241
	Mississippi (SL)	AA	4	2	3.02	39	0	0	11	45	41	2	22	47	9.5	1.41	.243
2011	Gwinnett (IL)	AAA	4	2	2.25	41	0	0	1	48	34	5	27	68	12.8	1.27	.193
	Oklahoma City (PCL)	AAA	1	0	1.86	7	0	0	3	10	8	0	7	9	8.4	1.55	.235
	Houston (NL)	MAJ	0	0	2.70	7	0	0	0	7	6	1	3	12	16.2	1.35	.231
Major League Totals			0	0	2.70	7	0	0	0	7	6	1	3	12	16.2	1.35	.231
Minor League Totals			26	22	4.23	201	26	0	41	385	332	30	231	448	10.5	1.46	.232

20 MARWIN GONZALEZ, SS/2B

BA GRADE
45
MEDIUM

Born: March 14, 1989. **B-T:** B-R. **Ht.:** 6-1. **Wt.:** 186. **Signed:** Venezuela, 2005. **Signed by:** Hector Ortega (Cubs).

After the Red Sox selected Gonzalez from the Cubs in the major league portion of the Rule 5 draft in December, they traded him to the Astros for Triple-A Rule 5 pick Marco Duarte, a righthander out of the Rockies system. Gonzalez has a chance to stick in Houston, where the middle infield took a hit with the free-agent departure of shortstop Clint Barmes. Gonzalez signed as a 16-year-old out of Venezuela and made a methodical climb up Chicago's system, posting a career-best .742 OPS and reaching Triple-A for the first time in 2011. He chokes up on the bat and has solid bat control, making consistent contact from both sides of the plate. His lack of power and only modest basestealing ability limits his offensive upside. He's an average runner who's above-average under way and has solid defensive tools. Gonzalez played a career-high 99 games at shortstop in 2011 and spent the winter playing second base in Venezuela. His range and arm are likely a bit shy for him to be an ideal everyday shortstop. Gonzalez's defensive versatility enhances his chances to remain in Houston, which has to expose him to waivers and offer him back to the Cubs before it can send him to the minors.

Year	Club (League)	Class	AVG	G	AB	R	H	2B	3B	HR	RBI	BB	SO	SB	CS	OBP	SLG
2006	Cubs (AZL)	R	.198	24	86	9	17	4	1	0	11	8	19	0	2	.266	.267
	Cubs (DSL)	R	.265	18	68	9	18	3	0	4	10	0	14	1	1	.265	.485
2007	Cubs (AZL)	R	.288	17	59	12	17	3	3	1	10	9	10	1	2	.391	.492
2008	Peoria (MWL)	LoA	.224	33	116	6	26	7	0	0	9	3	15	1	1	.240	.284
	Boise (NWL)	SS	.279	65	244	29	68	15	3	0	43	13	36	15	7	.318	.365
2009	Daytona (FSL)	HiA	.241	120	424	43	102	15	4	2	34	26	77	9	8	.287	.309
2010	Daytona (FSL)	HiA	.271	23	85	7	23	3	0	0	5	7	13	7	1	.330	.306
	Tennessee (SL)	AA	.246	86	305	24	75	11	3	4	41	17	40	6	4	.284	.341
2011	Tennessee (SL)	AA	.301	64	216	29	65	18	1	2	20	17	27	4	2	.359	.421
	Iowa (PCL)	AAA	.274	60	197	24	54	12	1	2	19	16	21	3	1	.326	.376
Minor League Totals			.258	510	1800	192	465	91	16	15	202	116	272	47	29	.305	.352

21 DALLAS KEUCHEL, LHP

BA GRADE
40
LOW

Born: Jan. 1, 1988. **B-T:** L-L. **Ht.:** 6-3. **Wt.:** 200. **Drafted:** Arkansas, 2009 (7th round). **Signed by:** Jim Stevenson.

Keuchel won 19 games in three seasons at Arkansas, leading the Razorbacks to the 2009 College World Series, and he's continued to win in pro ball, even in an Astros system all too accustomed to losing. He was the only Houston farmhand to reach 10 victories in 2011. He's a rare lefthanded sinkerballer who pitches inside even though his fastball sits at only 84-87 mph. He has touched 90-91 in the past but generally relies on movement and location. Keuchel mixes up his tempo, at times adding a hitch to his delivery, and also employs a slow curveball to keep hitters off balance. His best pitch is a sinking changeup that has better action than his fastball and grades as solid or better. Righthanders batted .255 against him last year, while lefties hit .305. His overall package compares best to finesse southpaws such as Zane Smith or Doug Davis. Keuchel is extremely durable, working 174 innings in 2010 and 189 last year (including his time in the Arizona Fall League). A potential back-of-the-rotation starter or middle reliever, he'll have to keep proving himself one level at a time. He'll start 2012 back in Triple-A, where he was rocked in four of his seven late-season starts.

Year	Club (League)	Class	W	L	ERA	G	GS	CG	SV	IP	H	HR	BB	SO	K/9	WHIP	AVG
2009	Tri-City (NYP)	SS	2	3	2.70	11	10	0	0	57	52	2	9	44	7.0	1.08	.240
2010	Lancaster (CAL)	HiA	5	8	3.36	19	18	3	0	121	129	10	25	97	7.2	1.28	.273
	Corpus Christi (TL)	AA	2	6	4.70	9	9	0	0	54	59	2	11	36	6.0	1.30	.285
2011	Corpus Christi (TL)	AA	9	7	3.17	20	20	1	0	128	116	9	27	76	5.4	1.12	.244
	Oklahoma City (PCL)	AAA	1	1	7.50	7	7	0	0	36	52	5	12	15	3.8	1.78	.354
Minor League Totals			19	25	3.76	66	64	4	0	395	408	28	84	268	6.1	1.25	.269

22 JORGE DeLEON, RHP

BA GRADE
50
HIGH

Born: Aug. 15, 1987. **B-T:** R-R. **Ht.:** 6-0. **Wt.:** 180. **Signed:** Dominican Republic, 2006. **Signed by:** Sergio Beltre/Julio Linares.

DeLeon signed as a shortstop but never hit, batting .213/.283/.323 in four pro seasons. His arm strength and athleticism made more an easy transition to the mound, and he earned a spot on the 40-man roster after working just 28 innings in his pitching debut in 2010. His performance and stuff varied in 2011, when he served as the closer on a bad Lexington team. When he's on, DeLeon's fastball sits at 93-97 mph and peaks at 98. In other outings, he operates in the low 90s. His slider is even more inconsistent, but at times it's a short downer that grades as an average pitch. More often it's a spinner, and he generally lacks feel for spinning the ball. He has started using a changeup that's too firm but gives hitters something else to think about. DeLeon has a quick arm and high-energy delivery that add some deception. He'll need to prove he can get outs at higher levels when working back-to-back nights, but his 40-man roster spot and big fastball make a call to Houston possible by September. He'll likely start 2012 in high Class A but could open in Double-A if he has a good spring.

Year	Club (League)	Class	W	L	ERA	G	GS	CG	SV	IP	H	HR	BB	SO	K/9	WHIP	AVG
2010	Tri-City (NYP)	SS	2	1	0.64	23	0	0	6	28	26	0	12	29	9.3	1.36	.248
2011	Lexington (SAL)	LoA	6	4	3.42	43	0	0	16	55	48	5	13	51	8.3	1.10	.225
Minor League Totals			8	5	2.48	66	0	0	22	83	74	5	25	80	8.6	1.19	.233

Year	Club (League)	Class	AVG	G	AB	R	H	2B	3B	HR	RBI	BB	SO	SB	CS	OBP	SLG
2006	Astros (DSL)	R	.230	56	183	21	42	8	3	3	19	15	57	5	7	.297	.355
2007	Astros (DSL)	R	.190	52	179	23	34	9	3	2	17	15	41	3	3	.298	.307
2008	Greeneville (APP)	R	.235	32	102	16	24	6	2	1	14	6	24	1	2	.297	.363
2009	Lexington (SAL)	LoA	.187	43	123	14	23	5	1	0	9	3	38	2	2	.219	.244
	Tri-City (NYP)	SS	.242	23	66	7	16	4	2	0	7	4	13	1	0	.296	.364
Minor League Totals			.213	207	653	81	139	32	11	6	66	43	173	12	14	.283	.323

23 JIO MIER, SS

BA GRADE
50
HIGH

Born: Aug. 26, 1990. **B-T:** R-R. **Ht.:** 6-2. **Wt.:** 180. **Drafted:** HS—LaVerne, Calif. (1st round). **Signed by:** Doug Deutsch/Bobby Heck.

The first high school shortstop drafted in 2009, Mier has progressed slowly since going 21st overall and signing for $1,358,000. He entered pro ball with a reputation as a smooth defender at shortstop and raised expectations by slugging .484 while ranking as the No. 1 prospect in the Appalachian League. He hit seven homers in 192 at-bats in his debut but has added just nine more in 915 at-bats since. A good athlete with fringy speed, Mier has above-average defensive tools with soft hands and an accurate, average throwing arm. He improved at making the routine play in 2011, cutting his errors to 22 after making 34 the previous season. He made better decisions and avoided high-risk plays. Mier encouraged the Astros by hitting .280/.392/.453 in the first seven weeks last season, but then he went into a 3-for-31 slump and continued to struggle even after a promotion to extremely hitter-friendly Lancaster. His swing gets long and mechanical, and good fastballs get by him. His best asset at the plate is his patience, as he has drawn 129 walks the last two seasons. He isn't as explosive or athletic as minor league teammates Jonathan Villar or Delino DeShields Jr., and Mier's lack of offensive upside likely limits him to a future utility role. Mier will head back to high Class A to try to shorten up his swing.

Year	Club (League)	Class	AVG	G	AB	R	H	2B	3B	HR	RBI	BB	SO	SB	CS	OBP	SLG
2009	Greeneville (APP)	R	.276	51	192	32	53	7	6	7	32	30	45	10	5	.380	.484
2010	Lexington (SAL)	LoA	.235	131	493	83	116	31	1	2	53	63	107	15	7	.323	.314
2011	Lexington (SAL)	LoA	.245	57	216	39	53	14	0	5	29	37	58	6	2	.354	.380
	Lancaster (CAL)	HiA	.233	57	206	35	48	7	1	2	23	29	54	5	3	.335	.306
Minor League Totals			.244	296	1107	189	270	59	8	16	137	159	264	36	17	.341	.355

24 TANNER BUSHUE, RHP

BA GRADE
50
HIGH

Born: June 20, 1991. **B-T:** R-R. **Ht.:** 6-4. **Wt.:** 180. **Drafted:** HS—Farina, Ill., 2010 (2nd round). **Signed by:** Troy Hoerner.

Like Mike Foltynewicz, Bushue is an Illinois high school product with a lanky pitcher's frame. The similarities end there, however, because Bushue doesn't have Foltynewicz's power repertoire. Bushue's strong suit is his fastball command, which helped him win five of his first six starts last year at Lexington. He pitched off an 88-92 mph fastball that he located to all four quadrants of the strike zone. However, he started wearing down by June, spending six weeks on the disabled list with back spasms, and posted a 7.43 ERA after his return before being shut down in late August. Bushue's curveball is his next-best pitch, and when it's on it's a 12-to-6 breaker with good shape. It can get loopy at times, too. He also throws a slider and changeup, and neither pitch stands out as an effective third offering. Bushue has to add some strength to his frame in order to stay healthy over a full season and to maintain his delivery during games. He could be headed back to Lexington for a third season if he doesn't wow the Astros in spring training, but he has a shot to earn a spot in Lancaster. If he gets stronger and refines his secondary pitches, he could develop into a No. 3 or 4 starter.

Year	Club (League)	Class	W	L	ERA	G	GS	CG	SV	IP	H	HR	BB	SO	K/9	WHIP	AVG
2009	Astros (GCL)	R	1	0	2.42	5	5	0	0	22	18	2	5	19	7.7	1.03	.220
2010	Lexington (SAL)	LoA	7	8	4.11	25	25	0	0	134	129	18	48	114	7.7	1.32	.256
2011	Astros (GCL)	R	0	2	7.88	3	3	0	0	8	14	0	0	7	7.9	1.75	.368
	Lexington (SAL)	LoA	6	6	4.66	16	16	0	0	77	89	13	17	51	5.9	1.37	.284
Minor League Totals			14	16	4.25	49	49	0	0	241	250	33	70	191	7.1	1.33	.267

25 MIKE KVASNICKA, 3B

BA GRADE
45
MEDIUM

Born: Dec. 7, 1988. **B-T:** B-R. **Ht.:** 6-2. **Wt.:** 200. **Drafted:** Minnesota, 2010 (1st round supplemental). **Signed by:** Troy Hoerner.

Kvasnicka's dad Jay was an eighth-round pick in 1988 and reached Triple-A in the Twins system. Mike shot up draft boards in 2010 thanks to his profile as a switch-hitting catcher, even though he only caught part-time in college at Minnesota. The Astros liked his bat more than his potential behind the plate. They considered him one of the best college position players in the 2010 draft and paid him $936,000 as the

33rd overall pick. Kvasnicka hasn't caught as a pro, instead moving to third base, where his size, strong arm and solid athleticism should allow him to be an average defender. However, he made 31 errors in his first full season, and his bat will to have to play better than it did in 2011 for him to become a regular. Houston officials point out that Kvasnicka was playing a new position and is still fairly new to switch-hitting, which he began in 2009. His lefthanded swing is flatter and geared more for line drives, as evidenced by his one home run in 339 at-bats from that side last year. His righty stroke has more natural lift and pop. He's a below-average runner, though he could handle an outfield corner if needed. Scouts outside the organization report they didn't see any plus tools out of Kvasnicka, who wore down in the second half and needs to improve his offseason conditioning to gear up for the 2012 season. If his bat doesn't come around, Houston could move him back behind the plate. For now, he's headed to high Class A to play third base in 2012.

Year	Club (League)	Class	AVG	G	AB	R	H	2B	3B	HR	RBI	BB	SO	SB	CS	OBP	SLG
2010	Tri-City (NYP)	SS	.234	68	261	31	61	10	1	5	36	27	48	2	1	.305	.337
2011	Lexington (SAL)	LoA	.260	128	484	59	126	32	4	4	59	46	106	5	5	.328	.368
Minor League Totals			.251	196	745	90	187	42	5	9	95	73	154	7	6	.320	.357

26 JOSE CISNERO, RHP

BA GRADE
50
HIGH

Born: April 11, 1989. **B-T:** R-R. **Ht.:** 6-3. **Wt.:** 185. **Signed:** Dominican Republic, 2007. **Signed by:** Felix Francisco/Andres Lopez.

Cisnero led the Cal League in strikeouts per nine innings (11.9) while ranking second in opponent average (.246) and sixth in strikeouts (152). However, his 6.06 ERA was the sixth-worst in the league. (Four of the bottom six ERAs belonged to JetHawks pitchers.) Cisnero throws an 87-91 mph two-seamer with fair sink and a 92-94 mph four-seamer that scrapes 97. The more he used his four-seamer last year, the better his velocity got. He lacks command of both fastballs and nibbles too often, leading to deep counts and too many walks. Cisnero has enough velocity and life to challenge hitters more and develop passable control, but he's unlikely ever to have average command with his long arm action. He throws a slider that gets sloppy and hammered at times, and a changeup that doesn't have enough separation from his fastball. Cisnero has a good pitcher's frame and could use a bit more urgency. One scout likened him to Jamie Navarro for his frame, stuff and demeanor. Cisnero could wind up as a No. 4 starter or seventh-inning reliever. He'll escape Lancaster and advance to Double-A in 2012.

Year	Club (League)	Class	W	L	ERA	G	GS	CG	SV	IP	H	HR	BB	SO	K/9	WHIP	AVG
2008	Astros (DSL)	R	0	3	3.10	10	6	0	2	29	18	0	11	34	10.6	1.00	.180
2009	Greeneville (APP)	R	4	2	3.56	13	13	0	0	56	32	5	30	64	10.3	1.11	.165
2010	Lexington (SAL)	LoA	8	6	3.65	26	26	0	0	133	106	11	65	126	8.5	1.29	.221
2011	Lancaster (CAL)	HiA	8	11	6.06	27	27	0	0	123	115	13	75	152	11.1	1.54	.246
Minor League Totals			20	22	4.46	76	72	0	2	341	271	29	181	376	9.9	1.33	.218

27 VINCE VELASQUEZ, RHP

BA GRADE
50
EXTREME

Born: June 7, 1992. **B-T:** B-R. **Ht.:** 6-3. **Wt.:** 185. **Drafted:** HS—Garey, Calif., 2010 (2nd round). **Signed by:** Tim Costic/Bobby Heck.

Velasquez had a strong pro debut after signing for $655,830 as a second-round pick in 2010, but he hasn't pitched in a game since. He needed Tommy John surgery after the season after tearing a ligament in his elbow and missed all of 2011. He also didn't pitch as a high school junior in 2009 because of a stress fracture and strained ligament in his elbow. Velasquez returned in instructional league last fall and looked strong. He still had some rust but showed his full menu of pitches, with the only setback a bout with biceps tendinitis that prompted the Astros to skip his final start. He worked in the low 90s and touched 95 mph with his fastball in instructs, a touch better velocity than he showed prior to surgery. His fastball command was spotty, as is often the case for pitchers coming back from ligament reconstruction. Velasquez's changeup and curveball were sharp and crisp at times, though inconsistent because of his layoff. Houston wants to be careful with him, so he'll probably begin 2012 in extended spring training and stay on a carefully monitored workload. He showed the potential to be a No. 3 starter before he got hurt.

Year	Club (League)	Class	W	L	ERA	G	GS	CG	SV	IP	H	HR	BB	SO	K/9	WHIP	AVG
2010	Greeneville (APP)	R	2	2	3.07	8	6	0	0	29	24	4	5	25	7.7	0.99	.216
2011	Did Not Play—Injured																
Minor League Totals			2	2	3.07	8	6	0	0	29	24	4	5	25	7.7	0.99	.216

28 RHINER CRUZ, RHP

BA GRADE
45
HIGH

Born: Nov. 1, 1986. **B-T:** R-R. **Ht.:** 6-2. **Wt.:** 205. **Signed:** Dominican Republic, 2003. **Signed by:** Ramon Pena (Tigers).

Originally signed by the Tigers in 2003, Cruz was released three years later before signing with the Mets and resuscitating his career. He reached Double-A in 2011 before pitching with Cibao in the Dominican League, where Rick Aponte is the pitching coach. Aponte holds the same job at Rookie-level

Greeneville in the Astros system and provided positive reports on Cruz to Houston's front office, and the club's scouts seconded his enthusiasm. The Astros made Cruz the No. 1 overall pick in the major league portion of the Rule 5 draft in December. Some scouts saw Cruz hit 100 mph during the winter, and the Astros have reports of a consistent high-90s fastball. His sweepy slider sits in the low 80s and improved with Aponte's coaching this winter. Cruz, who pitched for Spain in the 2009 World Cup, has pitched just 59 innings above Class A and has averaged 5.5 walks per nine innings in his career. The Astros have to keep him on their major league roster throughout 2012, or else put him on waivers and offer him back to New York. He factors into the 2012 Houston bullpen.

Year	Club (League)	Class	W	L	ERA	G	GS	CG	SV	IP	H	HR	BB	SO	K/9	WHIP	AVG
2004	Tigers (GCL)	R	0	1	4.78	16	0	0	0	32	37	3	19	26	7.3	1.75	.298
2005	Tigers (GCL)	R	1	0	4.50	14	0	0	1	28	35	5	12	23	7.4	1.68	.299
2006	Did Not Play																
2007	Mets (DSL)	R	0	1	2.70	4	1	0	1	13	8	0	10	18	12.2	1.35	.170
	Mets (GCL)	R	2	0	0.00	4	0	0	0	6	1	0	5	4	6.0	1.00	.056
	Kingsport (APP)	R	1	1	0.71	11	0	0	4	13	7	0	14	13	9.2	1.66	.184
2008	Brooklyn (NYP)	SS	0	0	3.72	6	0	0	1	10	9	1	6	13	12.1	1.55	.243
	Savannah (SAL)	LoA	2	2	5.04	15	0	0	1	30	27	4	14	33	9.8	1.35	.235
2009	Savannah (SAL)	LoA	3	3	1.92	50	0	0	22	61	42	2	31	55	8.1	1.20	.199
2010	St. Lucie (FSL)	HiA	0	5	3.46	51	0	0	6	75	62	6	53	66	7.9	1.53	.232
2011	St. Lucie (FSL)	HiA	2	1	2.77	8	0	0	0	13	9	1	6	18	12.5	1.15	.200
	Binghamton (EL)	AA	3	2	4.14	36	0	0	7	59	43	4	39	51	7.8	1.40	.202
Minor League Totals			14	16	3.44	215	1	0	43	340	280	26	209	320	8.5	1.44	.227

29 JACK ARMSTRONG JR., RHP

BA GRADE
50
EXTREME

Born: Dec. 14, 1989. **B-T:** R-R. **Ht.:** 6-7. **Wt.:** 200. **Drafted:** Vanderbilt, 2011 (3rd round). **Signed by:** Nick Venuto.

Armstrong's father started the All-Star Game for the National League in 1990, his lone winning season in an enigmatic big league career. Armstrong's college career at Vanderbilt was similarly puzzling, and the Astros hope he has more staying power as a pro after signing him for an over-slot $750,000 in the third round of the 2011 draft. He's physically gifted with athleticism and a monster frame. While he was dominant at times in the Cape Cod League in 2009, he was a starter for only one of his three seasons with the Commodores and pitched just 17 innings last spring while battling back problems. Armstrong's fastball can sit in the low 90s and has touched 97 mph in short stints. His hard curveball and his changeup have their moments, too, but he didn't use them as much in 2011 as he had in the past. Armstrong signed too late to pitch and wasn't healthy enough to pitch in games during instructional league games, instead working out in the bullpen. He has much more upside than the back-of-the-rotation college pitchers the Astros have drafted in recent years, such as Jake Buchanan and Dallas Keuchel, but he's far behind them in polish and health. Houston will handle him carefully in his pro debut, worrying more about keeping him on the mound than his level of competition.

Year	Club (League)	Class	W	L	ERA	G	GS	CG	SV	IP	H	HR	BB	SO	K/9	WHIP	AVG
2011	Did Not Play—Signed Late																

30 CHRIS WALLACE, C

BA GRADE
40
MEDIUM

Born: April 27, 1988. **B-T:** R-R. **Ht.:** 6-0. **Wt.:** 205. **Drafted:** Houston, 2010 (16th round). **Signed by:** Rusty Pendergrass.

Wallace attended Cy-Fair High in suburban Houston, playing with Pirates farmhand Robbie Grossman and Nats minor leaguer Caleb Ramsey. He also played with Ramsey in college at Houston, where he hit 19 homers in his final two seasons as the regular catcher. Wallace's 2009 junior season almost ended before it began when he was hit in the face with a pitch in February, and he still wears a protective mask at the plate to protect his reconstructed face. He needed five metal plates and 42 screws to help repair the broken bones. The Astros drafted him as an organizational soldier in 2010, signing him for $5,000 in the 16th round. Wallace ranked third in the system last year with 20 homers and 78 RBIs. He has good strength, the leadership skills for catcher and an outstanding work ethic. He works out at the Astros' local facility all offseason, and his efforts helped reshape his body and prepare him for the pro grind in 2011. His best tool is his solid power, which could become plus if he improves his pitch recognition and patience. He probably strikes out too much to hit for a high average in the big leagues. Behind the plate, he's a solid receiver with the ability to handle a pitching staff. He has a fringy arm and threw out 21 percent of basestealers last year, including just three of 30 in Double-A. He spent one-third of his time as a DH and fits a backup catcher-profile. He'll head back to Corpus Christi in 2012.

Year	Club (League)	Class	AVG	G	AB	R	H	2B	3B	HR	RBI	BB	SO	SB	CS	OBP	SLG
2010	Greeneville (APP)	R	.310	47	171	29	53	6	3	8	32	17	44	3	2	.390	.520
	Tri-City (NYP)	SS	.250	20	68	10	17	2	0	2	8	7	12	1	0	.329	.368
2011	Lexington (SAL)	LoA	.285	66	242	37	69	16	3	14	49	17	52	0	3	.356	.550
	Corpus Christi (TL)	AA	.244	36	123	17	30	4	0	6	29	12	41	1	0	.316	.423
Minor League Totals			.280	169	604	93	169	28	6	30	118	53	149	5	5	.355	.495

Kansas City Royals

BY J.J. COOPER

The Royals' slow slog to respectability sped up in 2011.

That might not be apparent from their final record, 71-91. But this wasn't the same old team that has disappointed Kansas City fans for years. The Royals had their 16th losing season in the last 17 years and once again were out of the playoff race before the all-star break, but this time they did it with youth.

By the end of the season, there were days where Kansas City fielded five rookies in its starting lineup. At times, the bullpen featured just two pitchers with more than a year of big league experience.

Royals position players averaged 25.8 years of age, their youngest since their first year as an expansion team in 1969 and nearly two years younger than any other team in baseball in 2011. Kansas City's pitching staff averaged 26.4 years of age, its youngest since 2000 and again the youngest in the game last season.

More important than birthdates, for the first time in years, the Royals actually fielded a lineup of players whose best days are ahead of them. Rather than aging free-agent acquisitions such as Jose Guillen and Jason Kendall, Kansas City featured a wave of prospects who gave fans something interesting to watch for a change.

The Royals entered 2011 with a farm system not only ranked No. 1 by Baseball America, but also acclaimed as the best baseball had seen in quite a while. Youngsters Eric Hosmer and Mike Moustakas were expected to reach the majors last season, while Johnny Giavotella and Salvador Perez sped up their timetables. It also helped that Alex Gordon, the No. 2 overall pick in 2005 and the franchise's most promising position prospect of the previous generation, finally lived up to expectations with a breakout season.

Kansas City will enter 2012 with a relatively set lineup that it hopes will mature together after ranking sixth in the American League in scoring last year. For the Royals to return to contention, their starting pitching prospects will have to step up after a disappointing 2011. Danny Duffy made it to the majors, but Mike Montgomery and Chris Dwyer both struggled while John Lamb had Tommy John surgery.

Even after acquiring Jonathan Sanchez from the Giants in a November trade, Kansas City had few clear-cut fixtures in its starting rotation. The Royals have plenty of prospects who eventually could fill that void, and they hope that the hiring of former Tigers

Catcher Salvador Perez is among the young core of Royals giving fans hope for the future

TOP 30 PROSPECTS

1. Mike Montgomery, lhp	16. Brian Brickhouse, rhp
2. Bubba Starling, of	17. Noel Arguelles, lhp
3. Wil Myers, of	18. Kevin Chapman, lhp
4. Jake Odorizzi, rhp	19. Tim Melville, rhp
5. Cheslor Cuthbert, 3b	20. Orlando Calixte, ss
6. John Lamb, lhp	21. Clint Robinson, 1b
7. Kelvin Herrera, rhp	22. Will Smith, lhp
8. Jason Adam, rhp	23. Cameron Gallagher, c
9. Chris Dwyer, lhp	24. Mike Antonio, ss
10. Yordano Ventura, rhp	25. Jack Lopez, ss
11. Christian Colon, ss/2b	26. Everett Teaford, lhp
12. Brett Eibner, of	27. Brian Fletcher, of
13. Jeremy Jeffress, rhp	28. Danny Mateo, 2b/3b
14. Elier Hernandez, of	29. Humberto Arteaga, ss
15. Jorge Bonifacio, of	30. David Lough, of

pitching coach Rick Knapp as pitching coordinator will help end their difficulties in developing starting pitchers. Zack Greinke is their lone homegrown starter to post a sub-4.00 ERA since 2000.

Kansas City is in better shape in the bullpen thanks to the arrival of several talented arms in 2011. Former first-round pick Aaron Crow made the All-Star Game as a rookie. Louis Coleman and Greg Holland also had fine rookie seasons, with Nathan Adcock and Everett Teaford contributing in their first year as well. The Royals added Jonathan Broxton in the offseason as well.

General Manager: Dayton Moore. **Farm Director:** Scott Sharp. **Scouting Director:** Lonnie Goldberg.

Class	Team	League	W	L	Pct	Finish*	Manager(s)
Majors	Kansas City Royals	American	71	91	.438	11th (14)	Ned Yost
Triple-A	Omaha Storm Chasers	Pacific Coast	79	63	.556	3rd (16)†	Mike Jirschele
Double-A	Northwest Arkansas Naturals	Texas	73	64	.533	3rd (8)	Brian Poldberg
High A	Wilmington Blue Rocks	Carolina	66	72	.478	6th (8)	Brian Rupp
Low A	Kane County Cougars	Midwest	65	74	.468	12th (16)	Vance Wilson
Rookie	Idaho Falls Chukars	Pioneer	33	43	.434	6th (8)	Brian Buchanan
Rookie	Burlington Royals	Appalachian	24	44	.353	t-9th (10)	Nelson Liriano
Rookie	AZL Royals	Arizona	22	34	.393	11th (13)	Darryl Kennedy
Overall 2011 Minor League Record			362	394	.479	24th (30)	

*Finish in overall standings (No. of teams in league). †League champion.

LAST YEAR'S TOP 30

Player, Pos.	Status
1. Eric Hosmer, 1b	Majors
2. Wil Myers, c	No. 3
3. Mike Moustakas, 3b	Majors
4. John Lamb, lhp	No. 6
5. Mike Montgomery, lhp	No. 1
6. Christian Colon, ss	No. 11
7. Danny Duffy, lhp	Majors
8. Chris Dwyer, lhp	No. 9
9. Aaron Crow, rhp	Majors
10. Brett Eibner, of	No. 12
11. Jason Adam, rhp	No. 8
12. Yordano Ventura, rhp	No. 10
13. Tim Collins, lhp	Majors
14. Tim Melville, rhp	No. 19
15. Cheslor Cuthbert, 3b	No. 5
16. Robinson Yambati, rhp	Dropped out
17. Salvador Perez, c	Majors
18. Johnny Giavotella, 2b	Majors
19. Louis Coleman, rhp	Majors
20. Jarrod Dyson, of	Dropped out
21. Jeff Bianchi, ss	(Cubs)
22. Patrick Keating, rhp	Dropped out
23. Humberto Arteaga, ss	No. 29
24. Orlando Calixte, ss	No. 20
25. David Lough, of	No. 30
26. Derrick Robinson, of	Dropped out
27. Henry Barrera, rhp	Dropped out
28. Clint Robinson, 1b	No. 21
29. Elisaul Pimentel, rhp	Dropped out
30. Kelvin Herrera, rhp	No. 7

BEST TOOLS

Best Hitter for Average	Wil Myers
Best Power Hitter	Bubba Starling
Best Strike-Zone Discipline	Wil Myers
Fastest Baserunner	Terrance Gore
Best Athlete	Bubba Starling
Best Fastball	Yordano Ventura
Best Curveball	Chris Dwyer
Best Slider	Kevin Chapman
Best Changeup	Mike Montgomery
Best Control	Greg Billo
Best Defensive Catcher	Manny Pina
Best Defensive Infielder	Humberto Arteaga
Best Infield Arm	Cheslor Cuthbert
Best Defensive Outfielder	Jarrod Dyson
Best Outfield Arm	Brett Eibner

PROJECTED 2015 LINEUP

Catcher	Salvador Perez
First Base	Eric Hosmer
Second Base	Johnny Giavotella
Third Base	Mike Moustakas
Shortstop	Alcides Escobar
Left Field	Wil Myers
Center Field	Bubba Starling
Right Field	Alex Gordon
Designated Hitter	Billy Butler
No. 1 Starter	Mike Montgomery
No. 2 Starter	Danny Duffy
No. 3 Starter	Jake Odorizzi
No. 4 Starter	John Lamb
No. 5 Starter	Luke Hochevar
Closer	Joakim Soria

TOP PROSPECTS OF THE DECADE

Year	Player, Pos.	2011 Org.
2002	Angel Berroa, ss	Diamondbacks
2003	Zack Greinke, rhp	Brewers
2004	Zack Greinke, rhp	Brewers
2005	Billy Butler, 1b	Royals
2006	Alex Gordon, 3b	Royals
2007	Alex Gordon, 3b	Royals
2008	Mike Moustakas, ss	Royals
2009	Mike Moustakas, 3b	Royals
2010	Mike Montgomery, lhp	Royals
2011	Eric Hosmer, 1b	Royals

TOP DRAFT PICKS OF THE DECADE

Year	Player, Pos.	2011 Org.
2002	Zack Greinke, rhp	Royals
2003	Chris Lubanski, of	Phillies
2004	Billy Butler, of	Royals
2005	Alex Gordon, 3b	Royals
2006	Luke Hochevar, rhp	Royals
2007	Mike Moustakas, ss	Royals
2008	Eric Hosmer, 1b	Royals
2009	Aaron Crow, rhp	Royals
2010	Christian Colon, ss	Royals
2011	Bubba Starling, of	Royals

LARGEST BONUSES IN CLUB HISTORY

Bubba Starling, 2011	$7,500,000
Eric Hosmer, 2008	$6,000,000
Alex Gordon, 2005	$4,000,000
Mike Moustakas, 2007	$4,000,000
Luke Hochevar, 2006	$3,500,000

MINOR LEAGUE DEPTH CHART

KANSAS CITY ROYALS

TOP 2012 ROOKIE: Kelvin Herrera, rhp. A fastball that hits 102 mph and quality secondary stuff have him ready to set up Joakim Soria.

BREAKOUT PROSPECT: Jorge Bonifaco, of. Emilio's little brother has a promising bat and solid tools across the board.

SLEEPER: Edwin Carl, rhp. He was old for Rookie ball at age 22, but that doesn't explain how he averaged 19.0 strikeouts per nine innings last year with a deceptive 91-95 mph fastball.

SOURCE OF TOP 30 TALENT			
Homegrown	27	Acquired	3
College	8	Trades	3
Junior college	0	Rule 5 draft	0
High school	10	Independent leagues	0
Draft-and-follow	0	Free agents/waivers	0
Nondrafted free agents	0		
International	9		

LF
Brian Fletcher (27)
David Lough (30)
Tim Smith
Gabe Gray

CF
Bubba Starling (2)
Brett Eibner (12)
Jarrod Dyson
D'Andre Toney
Terrance Gore
Derrick Robinson
Lane Adams
Jerrell Allen

RF
Wil Myers (3)
Elier Hernandez (14)
Jorge Bonifacio (15)

3B
Cheslor Cuthbert (5)
Mike Antonio (24)
Patrick Leonard
Johnny Whittleman
Nick Cuckovich

SS
Orlando Calixte (20)
Jack Lopez (25)
Humberto Arteaga (29)
Aldaberto Mondesi

2B
Christian Colon (11)
Danny Mateo (28)
Rey Navarro
Justin Trapp
Diego Goris

1B
Clint Robinson (21)

C
Cameron Gallagher (23)
Manny Pina
Julio Rodriguez
Jose Bonilla

LHP

LHSP	LHRP
Mike Montgomery (1)	Kevin Chapman (18)
John Lamb (6)	Everett Teaford (26)
Chris Dwyer (9)	Antonio Cruz
Noel Arguelles (17)	Ryan Verdugo
Will Smith (22)	Buddy Baumann
Justin Marks	Jon Keck
Cesar Ogando	Brandon Sisk
Stephen Lumpkins	Brendan Lafferty
Crawford Simmons	Blaine Hardy

RHP

RHSP	RHRP
Jake Odorizzi (4)	Kelvin Herrera (7)
Jason Adam (8)	Jeremy Jeffress (13)
Yordano Ventura (10)	Edwin Carl
Brian Brickhouse (16)	Patrick Keating
Tim Melville (19)	Leonel Santiago
Kyle Smith	Kendall Volz
Robinson Yambati	Michael Mariot
Jake Junis	Kellen Moen
Mark Binford	Aaron Brooks
Elisaul Pimentel	Matt Murray
Greg Billo	
Tyler Sample	
Matt Ridings	
Brooks Pounders	

2011

BEST PURE HITTER: SS Jack Lopez (16) is the purest player and hitter in the Royals' draft class. He has excellent instincts with a quick swing and good finish, as well as surprising power for a 5-foot-10, 170-pounder.

BEST POWER HITTER: OF Bubba Starling (1) resembles Jeff Francoeur physically and has similar raw power. Above-average righthanded power is 3B Patrick Leonard's (5) best tool.

FASTEST RUNNER: Kansas City emphasized speed and drafted several players quicker than Starling, who's a 70 runner on the 20-80 scouting scale. Five-foot-7 OF Terrance Gore (20) turns in 3.7-second times to first base from the right side of the plate—with 3.9 seconds considered 80 speed. OFs Jerrell Allen (11) and Gabe Gray (35) join Starling as plus-plus runners.

BEST DEFENSIVE PLAYER: Starling has outstanding aptitude to go with his strong arm and plus-plus speed, and could be a Gold Glove center fielder.

BEST FASTBALL: RHP Bryan Brickhouse (3) sits at 92-94 mph and touches 97 with his fastball. His rounded shoulders and 6-foot-0, 209-pound frame elicit physical comparisons to John Wetteland and Jeremy Bonderman.

BEST SECONDARY PITCH: RHP Kyle Smith (4) has excellent feel for spinning a hard slurve. RHP Kellen Moen (7) showed an above-average curveball and changeup as a reliever in college at Oregon.

BEST PRO DEBUT: Former Gulf Coast (Fla.) CC teammates Gore and D'Andre Toney (14) patrolled the outfield together in the Rookie-level Arizona League and both hit .340. Toney showed more pop, with five homers and a .587 slugging percentage. Gore drew 15 walks in 35 games and stole 17 bases without being caught. 3B Nick Cuckovich (17) hit .302/.418/.367 with an AZL-leading 24 steals.

BEST ATHLETE: Starling was the best athlete in the entire draft. He had a football scholarship to play quarterback at Nebraska, which he parlayed into a $7.5 million bonus.

MOST INTRIGUING BACKGROUND: Six-foot-8 LHP Stephen Lumpkins (13) averaged 13 points and eight rebounds the last two seasons at American (D.C.), which doesn't have a baseball program. C Cameron Gallagher's (2) dad Glenn and older brother Austin (currently in the Dodgers system) were both third-round picks. Lopez's father Juan is the Reds' bullpen coach. RHP Ali Williams (34) is distantly related to Hall of Famer Larry Doby, the first black player in the American League.

CLOSEST TO THE MAJORS: Williams, who has touched 96 mph and has a decent slider, could move quickly in the bullpen. Moen has more polish but less fastball.

BEST LATE-ROUND PICK: Lopez, who signed for $750,000. Keep an eye on Gore and the versatile Cuckovich.

THE ONE WHO GOT AWAY: The Royals made late runs at three high school RHPs, signing Jake Junis (29) and Mark Binford (30) but falling short on Nick Piscotty (32). The younger brother of Stanford 3B and 2012 draft prospect Stephen Piscotty, he's headed to Duke.

ASSESSMENT: Kansas City got both superstar potential (Starling) and depth. It went over slot for its next four picks (Gallagher, Brickhouse, Smith, Leonard) and several lower-rounders as well, spending a franchise-record $14.1 million.

2010

SS/2B Christian Colon (1), OF Brett Eibner (2) and RHP Jason Adam (5) didn't tear up the minors in their first full pro seasons, but they still have considerable upside. LHP Kevin Chapman (4) could beat them all to the majors.

GRADE: C+

2009

RHP Aaron Crow (1) went to the All-Star Game as a rookie in 2011, and RHP Louis Coleman (5) also bolstered the bullpen. OF Wil Myers (3) is one of the game's most promising hitting prospects.

GRADE: B+

2008

Kansas City found the right side of its infield in 1B Eric Hosmer (1) and 2B Johnny Giavotella (2), and perhaps its future ace in LHP Mike Montgomery (1s). LHP John Lamb (5) was just as good before succumbing to Tommy John surgery last June.

GRADE: A

2007

3B Mike Moustakas (1) and LHP Danny Duffy (3) are major parts of the Royals' future. Both scuffled as rookies in 2011, while RHP Greg Holland (10) was a revelation in the bullpen with a 1.80 ERA.

GRADE: A

Draft analysis by John Manuel (2011) and Jim Callis (2007-10). Numbers in parentheses indicate draft rounds.

1 MIKE MONTGOMERY, LHP

Born: July 1, 1989. **B-T:** L-L. **Ht.:** 6-4. **Wt.:** 185.
Drafted: HS—Newhall, Calif., 2008 (1st round supplemental). **Signed by:** Dan Ontiveros.

BA GRADE
65
MEDIUM

JOHN WILLIAMSON

In spring training last year, Montgomery made a strong push to make the Royals' Opening Day roster. In the end, Kansas City decided to send him to Omaha to give him some Triple-A experience, with the expectation that he would soon make the trek to the majors. He recorded a 2.45 ERA in his first six starts before struggles with his control and command caught up to him. He went 3-10, 6.11 in his final 22 outings and never got that callup. It was the first on-field hiccup for Montgomery, who quickly established himself as the Royals' best pitching prospect after signing for $988,000 as the 36th overall pick in the 2008 draft. He ranked No. 1 on this list before the 2010 season, when he was spectacular at high Class A Wilmington in April before straining his forearm. Montgomery sat out two months and hasn't missed a start since, though his control hasn't been as sharp. He averaged 2.6 walks per nine innings before he was sidelined and has averaged 3.9 afterward.

As a 6-foot-5 lefthander who generates good downward plane, Montgomery can dominate when he maintains his delivery. He runs his fastball up to 95-96 mph on his best nights and sits at 92-93, overpowering hitters when he commands it. But he struggled to do so in 2011, which left him behind in too many counts. Though Montgomery did a good job of getting out on the front side of his delivery in spring training, he had trouble keeping his mechanics in sync once the season began. While he battled to control his fastball, Kansas City tried to get him to focus more on pitching up and down in the zone and worrying less about working in and out. Even when he struggled, Montgomery was able to locate his plus changeup. He throws the changeup with deceptive arm speed and nice fade, and he keeps it down in the zone. After four pro seasons, Montgomery still is seeking the right grip for his curveball. He tried a spike curveball in spring training and while it showed

SCOUTING GRADES

Fastball: 65.   **Command/**
Curveball: 50.   **Control:** 50.
Changeup: 60.   **Delivery:** 50.

Based on 20-80 scouting scale, where 50 represents major league average, and future projection rather than present tools.

some promise, it also caused forearm discomfort. He shelved it in May and went back to a more traditional curve. That version is slower at 74-76 mph and has big break that often carries it out of the strike zone, and it also lacks consistency. He still has the palmball/curve he used in high school that he can use when he feels he has to throw a strike. Whichever breaking ball Montgomery throws, it's usually his third-best offering and shows only flashes of becoming a plus pitch. He's an intense competitor.

Montgomery's 2011 struggles were disconcerting, but he also was a 22-year-old in the Pacific Coast League and sill has plenty of time to work out his delivery issues. The Royals aren't worried and scouts from other teams see no long-term hiccups. He still projects as a frontline starter and will head to spring training with an outside chance to make the big league club.

Year	Club (League)	Class	W	L	ERA	G	GS	CG	SV	IP	H	HR	BB	SO	K/9	WHIP	AVG
2008	Royals (AZL)	R	2	1	1.69	12	9	0	0	43	31	2	12	34	7.2	1.01	.211
2009	Burlington (MWL)	LoA	2	3	2.17	12	12	0	0	58	42	1	24	52	8.1	1.14	.206
	Wilmington (CAR)	HiA	4	1	2.25	9	9	0	0	52	38	0	12	46	8.0	0.96	.196
2010	Wilmington (CAR)	HiA	2	0	1.09	4	4	0	0	25	14	0	4	33	12.0	0.73	.165
	Royals (AZL)	R	0	1	1.04	3	3	0	0	9	6	0	1	7	7.3	0.81	.207
	NW Arkansas (TL)	AA	5	4	3.47	13	13	0	0	60	56	4	26	48	7.2	1.37	.255
2011	Omaha (PCL)	AAA	5	11	5.32	28	27	0	0	151	157	15	69	129	7.7	1.50	.271
Minor League Totals			20	21	3.43	81	77	0	0	396	344	22	148	349	7.9	1.24	.236

2 BUBBA STARLING, OF

BRACE HEMMELGARN

Born: Aug. 3, 1992. **B-T:** R-R. **Ht.:** 6-4. **Wt.:** 205. **Drafted:** HS—Gardner, Kan., 2011 (1st round). **Signed by:** Blake Davis.

As a high school senior, Starling accounted for 3,167 yards and 39 touchdowns as a quarterback and averaged 28 points per game in basketball. He could have been Nebraska's quarterback of the future, but the Royals signed him for a franchise-record $7.5 million bonus after selecting him fifth overall in the 2011 draft. In an organization that covets premium athletes, Starling is the best of the bunch. He has excellent strength and bat speed and shows plus-plus power in batting practice. While he's not nearly as polished as Eric Hosmer and Mike Moustakas were when the Royals drafted them near the top of the first round out of high school, Starling has shortened his swing enough over the last year that scouts believe he'll hit for average as well. He's a well above-average runner, making him a basestealing threat and giving him plus range in center field. Clocked at 95 mph on the mound, he has a stronger arm than most center fielders. He was cited for underage drinking during instructional league, but the Royals say his makeup isn't a problem. Starling has a huge ceiling but will need more development time than Hosmer or Moustakas did. Starling could make his pro debut at low Class A Kane County, or he could begin 2012 in extended spring training.

BA GRADE 75 EXTREME

Year	Club (League)	Class	AVG	G	AB	R	H	2B	3B	HR	RBI	BB	SO	SB	CS	OBP	SLG
2011	Did Not Play—Signed Late																

3 WIL MYERS, OF

Born: Dec. 10, 1990. **B-T:** R-R. **Ht.:** 6-3. **Wt.:** 190. **Drafted:** HS—High Point, N.C., 2009 (3rd round). **Signed by:** Steve Connelly.

A potential first-round talent in 2009, Myers fell to the third round because of his $2 million asking price, which the Royals paid him. He finished 2010 as one of the top catching prospects in baseball. A year later, he has switched positions and added a little tarnish. He missed a month in 2011 with a knee injury that got infected and didn't hit with as much authority as he had in the past. Myers has the quick hands and raw strength to hit 20-25 homers per year, plus the understanding of the strike zone and the hand-eye coordination to hit for average. He's most comfortable hitting pitches on the outer half, but Double-A pitchers busted him inside with fastballs and he struggled to turn on them. Late in the season, he spread out his feet, which opened him up to handle inside heat better. Myers has average speed and a plus arm, but he's a below-average right fielder for now. He takes poor routes to balls and some scouts were turned off by his low-energy approach, especially when it came to working on his defense. Myers looked like his old self while hitting .360/.481/.674 in the Arizona Fall League and profiles as a possible all-star corner outfielder. He'll return to Northwest Arkansas to begin 2012, seemingly better prepared to handle Double-A pitching this time around.

BA GRADE 65 MEDIUM

Year	Club (League)	Class	AVG	G	AB	R	H	2B	3B	HR	RBI	BB	SO	SB	CS	OBP	SLG
2009	Burlington (APP)	R	.125	4	16	1	2	0	1	1	4	0	3	0	0	.125	.438
	Idaho Falls (PIO)	R	.426	18	68	18	29	7	1	4	14	9	15	2	0	.488	.735
2010	Burlington (MWL)	LoA	.289	68	242	42	70	19	1	10	45	48	55	10	3	.408	.500
	Wilmington (CAR)	HiA	.346	58	205	28	71	18	2	8	38	37	39	2	3	.453	.512
2011	NW Arkansas (TL)	AA	.254	99	354	50	90	23	1	8	49	52	87	9	2	.353	.393
Minor League Totals			.296	247	885	139	262	67	6	27	150	146	199	23	8	.399	.477

4 JAKE ODORIZZI, RHP

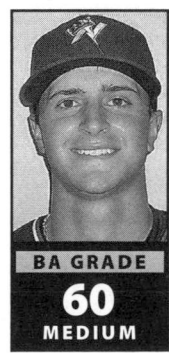

Born: March 27, 1990. **B-T:** R-R. **Ht.:** 6-2. **Wt.:** 175. **Drafted:** HS—Highland, Ill., 2008 (1st round supplemental). **Signed by:** Harvey Kuenn Jr. (Brewers).

Odorizzi starred as a pitcher, shortstop and wide receiver in high school before Milwaukee made him the 32nd overall pick in the 2008 draft and signed him for $1.06 million. He swiftly blossomed into the Brewers' top pitching prospect before they packaged him with Lorenzo Cain, Alcides Escobar and Jeremy Jeffress to acquire Zack Greinke and Yuniesky Betancourt from the Royals in December 2010. When he was in low Class A, Odorizzi's athleticism drew comparisons to Greinke's. Odorizzi sits at 91-93 mph and touches 95 with his fastball, which seems a little firmer because he has a slow, easy delivery with a quick finish. He misses a lot of bats with his heater, which has sinking and running action, and maintains its velocity deep into games. Odorizzi's curveball, slider and changeup all have the potential to be average. His curve has the most upside, and he throws his changeup with conviction. After his promotion to Double-A Northwest Arkansas last July, he tried to be too fine with his pitches, which led to more walks and deeper counts. Odorizzi could pitch

BA GRADE 60 MEDIUM

his way to Triple-A with a dominant spring, but it's more likely that he'll return to Northwest Arkansas for a tuneup. He profiles as a No. 2 or 3 starter once he refines his secondary pitches.

Year	Club (League)	Class	W	L	ERA	G	GS	CG	SV	IP	H	HR	BB	SO	K/9	WHIP	AVG
2008	Brewers (AZL)	R	1	2	3.48	11	4	0	0	21	18	2	9	19	8.3	1.31	.220
2009	Helena (PIO)	R	1	4	4.40	12	10	0	0	47	55	3	9	43	8.2	1.36	.296
2010	Wisconsin (MWL)	LoA	7	3	3.43	23	20	0	1	121	99	7	40	135	10.1	1.15	.220
2011	Wilmington (CAR)	HiA	5	4	2.87	15	15	0	0	78	68	4	22	103	11.8	1.15	.235
	NW Arkansas (TL)	AA	5	3	4.72	12	12	0	0	69	66	13	22	54	7.1	1.28	.254
Minor League Totals			19	16	3.70	73	61	0	1	335	306	29	102	354	9.5	1.22	.242

5 CHESLOR CUTHBERT, 3B

Born: Nov. 16, 1992. **B-T:** R-R. **Ht.:** 5-11. **Wt.:** 194. **Signed:** Nicaragua, 2009. **Signed by:** Orlando Esteves/Juan Lopez.

BA GRADE
60
HIGH

Miguel Sano (Twins) and Gary Sanchez (Yankees) were the big names in the international signing class in 2009, but Cuthbert has been right on their heals since signing for $1.35 million out of Big Corn Island off the coast of Nicaragua. His polish made the Royals comfortable sending him to Kane County last May at age 18, making him the Midwest League's youngest position player. He had a .866 OPS entering August but wore out in the final month. Cuthbert is an advanced hitter for his age. He works deep counts, recognizes breaking balls and uses the entire field. Thanks to his approach, strength and simple swing, he could become a plus hitter with plus power. The Royals also think Cuthbert can become an above-average defender at third base with good hands, solid footwork and an above-average arm. MWL observers wondered if he'd be able to stay at third base since he's a well-below average runner with fringy range and a thick lower half. He'll have to maintain his conditioning and agility to avoid a move across the diamond. With above-average offensive potential and a chance to stick at third base, Cuthbert could emerge as one of the game's better prospects with a solid 2012 season in high Class A. He's on course to reach Kansas City at age 22.

Year	Club (League)	Class	AVG	G	AB	R	H	2B	3B	HR	RBI	BB	SO	SB	CS	OBP	SLG
2010	Royals (AZL)	R	.265	18	68	14	18	3	2	1	5	6	19	1	1	.342	.412
	Idaho Falls (PIO)	R	.233	14	60	10	14	4	1	2	10	3	16	1	0	.281	.433
2011	Kane County (MWL)	LoA	.267	81	300	33	80	13	1	8	51	36	65	2	0	.345	.397
Minor League Totals			.262	113	428	57	112	20	4	11	66	45	100	4	1	.336	.404

6 JOHN LAMB, LHP

Born: July 10, 1990. **B-T:** L-L. **Ht.:** 6-3. **Wt.:** 195. **Drafted:** HS—Laguna Hills, Calif., 2008 (5th round). **Signed by:** Gary Johnson/John Ramey.

BA GRADE
60
HIGH

Lamb's stock dipped when he fractured his pitching elbow in a car accident as a high school senior. The Royals stayed on him, drafted him in 2008's fifth round and signed him for $165,000. He reached Double-A two years later and established himself as one of game's top lefty prospects. Lamb strained an oblique muscle in spring training last year and showed decreased velocity once the season began. Even when his oblique healed, his stuff didn't bounce back and doctors found a torn elbow ligament that required Tommy John surgery in June. Before the surgery, Lamb showed exquisite command of a 90-95 mph fastball and a plus changeup. He also threw an inconsistent curveball that can become an average pitch. Because of his feel for his delivery, the Royals expect he won't take long to regain his command when he returns. He has shown the ability to keep the ball down in the zone and to win without his best stuff. If his pitches come back to what they were before he got hurt, Lamb projects as a solid No. 2 or 3 starter. He was only throwing off flat ground during the offseason and won't return to game action until June at the earliest. It probably will be 2013 before he's fully back to his pre-injury form. Even so, he still could get to the majors before he turns 23.

Year	Club (League)	Class	W	L	ERA	G	GS	CG	SV	IP	H	HR	BB	SO	K/9	WHIP	AVG
2009	Burlington (APP)	R	2	2	3.95	6	6	0	0	27	24	4	9	25	8.2	1.21	.238
	Idaho Falls (PIO)	R	3	1	3.70	8	8	0	0	41	33	4	11	46	10.0	1.06	.217
2010	Burlington (MWL)	LoA	2	3	1.58	8	8	0	0	40	26	2	14	43	9.7	1.08	.188
	Wilmington (CAR)	HiA	6	3	1.45	13	13	0	0	75	59	1	15	90	10.8	0.99	.219
	NW Arkansas (TL)	AA	2	1	5.45	7	7	0	0	33	37	2	13	26	7.1	1.52	.280
2011	NW Arkansas (TL)	AA	1	2	3.09	8	8	0	0	35	33	3	13	22	5.7	1.31	.246
Minor League Totals			16	12	2.86	50	50	0	0	251	212	16	78	252	9.0	1.15	.229

7 KELVIN HERRERA, RHP

Born: Dec. 31, 1989. **B-T:** R-R. **Ht.:** 5-10. **Wt.:** 190. **Signed:** Dominican Republic, 2006. **Signed by:** Daurys Nin/Rafael Vasquez.

Herrera ranked among the Royals' best pitching prospects after he made his U.S. debut in 2008, then lost nearly two years to elbow problems. To get him back on track, Kansas City moved him to the bullpen last year, and it proved to be a perfect fit. While climbing from high Class A to the majors, he threw more innings (70) than he did in 2009-10 as a starter (46). In a system with plenty of intriguing arms, Herrera has the best pure stuff. He has been clocked as high as 102 mph, consistently touches 100 and sits at 95-98 mph with his overpowering fastball. He backs up his heat with a solid curveball and even flashes a plus changeup with late tumbling action, though he doesn't use the changeup as much in a relief role. Herrera's delivery never will be particularly clean, but he has smoothed out the jarring motion he used in past years. While his mechanics don't prevent him from throwing strikes, they do lead to concerns about his long-term health. Herrera followed a two-inning big league cameo with a dominating stint this winter in the Dominican League. He's ready for a set-up role in Kansas City and could be Joakim Soria's eventual successor at closer if he stays healthy.

BA GRADE
55
MEDIUM

Year	Club (League)	Class	W	L	ERA	G	GS	CG	SV	IP	H	HR	BB	SO	K/9	WHIP	AVG
2007	Royals (DSL)	R	4	1	0.84	11	5	0	1	43	30	1	15	50	10.55	1.05	.197
2008	Burlington (APP)	R	2	2	1.42	11	8	0	0	51	48	0	5	45	7.99	1.05	.254
2008	Burlington (MWL)	LoA	2	0	2.13	3	1	0	0	13	13	0	2	7	4.97	1.18	.265
2009	Burlington (MWL)	LoA	1	0	0.00	1	1	0	0	5	3	0	0	1	1.80	0.60	.176
2010	Burlington (MWL)	LoA	2	3	4.35	8	8	0	0	41	38	2	15	40	8.71	1.28	.253
2011	Wilmington (CAR)	HiA	2	1	0.61	8	0	0	1	15	8	1	2	12	7.36	0.68	.160
2011	NW Arkansas (TL)	AA	4	0	1.75	23	0	0	7	36	22	4	6	40	10.00	0.78	.176
2011	Omaha (PCL)	AAA	1	0	2.12	14	0	0	6	17	12	1	7	18	9.53	1.12	.190
2011	Kansas City (AL)	MAJ	0	1	13.50	2	0	0	0	2	2	1	0	0	0.00	1.00	.286
Major League Totals			0	1	13.50	2	0	0	0	2	2	1	0	0	0.00	1.00	.286
Minor League Totals			18	7	1.92	79	23	0	15	220	174	9	52	213	8.71	1.03	.219

8 JASON ADAM, RHP

Born: Aug. 4, 1991. **B-T:** R-R. **Ht.:** 6-4. **Wt.:** 225. **Drafted:** HS—Overland Park, Kan., 2010 (5th round) **Signed by:** Steve Gossett.

The Royals have a renewed emphasis to scout, draft and sign players in their area, such as Adam, whose high school sits 22 miles from Kauffmann Stadium. His inconsistent senior season and commitment to Missouri helped drop him to the fifth round of the 2010 draft, where Kansas City pounced and signed him for $800,000. The Royals sent him to low Class A for his 2011 pro debut, and while he had an up-and-down year, he finished with 5⅔ scoreless innings in the deciding game of the Midwest League quarterfinals. After showing a 95-96 mph fastball during instructional league in 2010, Adam didn't have the same velocity while enduring the grind of starting every fifth day. He pitched at 88-93 mph for much of the season. His curveball shows flashes of being a plus pitch and he locates it well for a 20-year-old, but it lost some of its bite when his velocity dropped. Adam's changeup eventually could give him a third average-or-better pitch. He was glacially slow to the plate at the start of the season and while he improved, he has to get quicker after giving up 27 steals in 30 attempts. Adam didn't dominate in his pro debut, but he did make every start after arriving in Kane County in mid-May. He's a potential No. 3 starter and headed to high Class A.

BA GRADE
55
HIGH

Year	Club (League)	Class	W	L	ERA	G	GS	CG	SV	IP	H	HR	BB	SO	K/9	WHIP	AVG
2011	Kane County (MWL)	LoA	6	9	4.23	21	21	0	0	104	94	9	25	76	6.6	1.14	.235
Minor League Totals			6	9	4.23	21	21	0	0	104	94	9	25	76	6.6	1.14	.235

9 CHRIS DWYER, LHP

Born: April 10, 1988. **B-T:** L-L. **Ht.:** 6-2. **Wt.:** 210. **Drafted:** Clemson, 2009 (4th round). **Signed by:** Steve Connelly.

The Royals viewed Dwyer, a rare draft-eligible freshman, as one of the top lefthanders in the 2009 draft and paid him accordingly, $1.45 million as a fourth-round pick. He made it to Double-A in his first full pro season, but he was shut down that July with a back injury and had control problems when he returned to Northwest Arkansas in 2011. His ERA swelled to 6.96 by mid-July, though he recorded a 3.53 ERA over his final nine starts. When Dwyer was able to throw strikes early in games in 2011, he'd get ahead with a 90-92 mph fastball that touches 94 and set up hitters for his sharp 12-to-6 curveball. But too often, he couldn't find the strike zone because of delivery issues. He had problems locating pitches to his glove side and keeping the ball down in the zone. Dwyer tends to throw across his body and fail to finish his pitches, which takes away some of the bite and effectiveness from his curve. Interestingly, his average changeup was his most consistent pitch last year. Dwyer had delivery issues even when he was going well in 2010 and he must take a step forward with his control if he's going to be the middle-of-the-rotation starter that Kansas City envisions. He'll advance to Triple-A at some point in 2012.

BA GRADE 55 HIGH

Year	Club (League)	Class	W	L	ERA	G	GS	CG	SV	IP	H	HR	BB	SO	K/9	WHIP	AVG
2009	Idaho Falls (PIO)	R	0	0	4.15	4	4	0	0	9	12	1	8	15	15.6	2.31	.324
2010	Wilmington (CAR)	HiA	6	3	2.99	15	15	1	0	84	79	3	33	93	9.9	1.33	.246
	NW Arkansas (TL)	AA	2	1	3.06	4	4	0	0	18	11	2	10	20	10.2	1.19	.175
2011	NW Arkansas (TL)	AA	8	10	5.60	27	27	2	0	141	124	14	78	126	8.0	1.43	.238
Minor League Totals			16	14	4.50	50	50	3	0	252	226	20	129	254	9.1	1.41	.240

10 YORDANO VENTURA, RHP

Born: June 3, 1991. **B-T:** R-R. **Ht.:** 5-11. **Wt.:** 160. **Signed:** Dominican Republic, 2008. **Signed by:** Pedro Silverio.

Ventura is the rare sub-6-foot pitcher who can reach triple digits on the radar gun. Signed for $28,000 out of the Dominican Republic at age 17, he has added nearly 10 mph to his fastball since then as he's gained weight and cleaned up his delivery. While Ventura can throw 100 mph, he's better off when he stops worrying about the radar gun, something that has been a problem for him. When he's trying to throw hard, his delivery becomes much messier with plenty of effort, leading him to spin off the mound and recoil at the end of his follow-through. When he relaxes and throws easier, he stays more in line to the plate. Then he locates his 94-97 mph fastball much better and his curveball shows plus potential rather than becoming the flat spinner he shows when he's overthrowing. His fastball has good late life. Ventura's 79-83 mph changeup is his third-best pitch, but it has late fade and almost unfair separation from his heater. He generally throws strikes but his lack of command leads to his stuff getting hit harder than it should. Ventura has the upside of a frontline starter, though he could wind up in the bullpen if he can't clean up his mechanics. He responds well to being challenged, and the Royals will push him to high Class A at age 20 this season.

BA GRADE 60 EXTREME

Year	Club (League)	Class	W	L	ERA	G	GS	CG	SV	IP	H	HR	BB	SO	K/9	WHIP	AVG
2009	Royals (DSL)	R	0	1	2.78	10	5	0	3	23	28	0	5	11	4.4	1.46	.304
2010	Royals (DSL)	R	0	1	2.31	3	3	0	0	12	9	0	1	13	10.0	0.86	.209
	Royals (AZL)	R	4	2	3.25	14	6	0	0	53	49	3	17	58	9.9	1.25	.236
2011	Kane County (MWL)	LoA	4	6	4.27	19	19	0	0	84	82	8	24	88	9.4	1.26	.258
Minor League Totals			8	10	3.62	46	33	0	3	171	168	11	47	170	8.9	1.25	.254

11 CHRISTIAN COLON, SS/2B

BA GRADE 50 MEDIUM

Born: May 14, 1989. **B-T:** R-R. **Ht.:** 6-1. **Wt.:** 180. **Drafted:** Cal State Fullerton, 2010 (1st round). **Signed by:** Scott Groot.

In 2010, the Royals had the fourth pick in a draft with a clear-cut top three prospects. Colon attracted the Royals because he was willing to sign for MLB's recommended $2.75 million slot bonus and because he gave them a shortstop prospect at a time when the team had no shortstop of the future. Since then, Kansas City has acquired Alcides Escobar in the Zack Greinke trade and Colon has struggled in Double-A. When he was drafted, scouts questioned whether he had a true plus tool outside of his bat. His hitting hasn't lived up to expectations during his short pro career, however. Colon became too pull-happy in his first full pro season, transferring his weight too early and becoming easy pickings for quality breaking balls. He has bat speed and gap power, and he controls the strike zone well, but he's going to have to tone down his approach. Colon will have to hit to make an impact because he's a tick below-average defender at shortstop, largely because of troubles ranging to his right. He has average arm strength and fringy speed. Colon played second base in the Arizona Fall League and showed he could be a plus defender there. He won't move Escobar at shortstop and will have to prove he can out-hit Johnny Giavotella at second base. If he can't, Colon's path to the big leagues may be as a utility infielder. He'll head back to Northwest Arkansas to begin 2012.

Year	Club (League)	Class	AVG	G	AB	R	H	2B	3B	HR	RBI	BB	SO	SB	CS	OBP	SLG
2010	Wilmington (CAR)	HiA	.278	60	245	38	68	12	2	3	30	13	33	2	4	.326	.380
2011	NW Arkansas (TL)	AA	.257	127	491	69	126	14	2	8	61	46	51	17	7	.325	.342
Minor League Totals			.264	187	736	107	194	26	4	11	91	59	84	19	11	.326	.355

12 BRETT EIBNER, OF

BA GRADE
55
HIGH

Born: Dec. 2, 1988. **B-T:** R-R. **Ht.:** 6-4. **Wt.:** 210. **Drafted:** Arkansas, 2010 (2nd round). **Signed by:** Lloyd Simmons.

A fourth-round pick of the Astros out of high school, Eibner turned down pro ball to attend Arkansas. He starred as a two-way player for the Razorbacks, and many teams preferred him as a pitcher whose natural athleticism would help him take off once he focused on the mound. But he wanted to hit, and the Royals agreed to let him do so after signing him for $1.25 million as a second-round pick in 2010. Eibner homered in his first pro at-bat last April, but injured his left thumb diving for a ball the next day and missed two months. Once he returned, he showed excellent bat speed and power potential but also the same propensity to swing and miss too much that plagued him in college. He throws away too many at-bats by chasing pitches out of the zone. When he does work counts to get a pitch he can drive, he has easy plus power. Though he's only a slightly above-average runner, Eibner is a quality center fielder. He has an advanced ability to read balls off the bat, which allows him to take direct routes that give him more range than his speed should allow. His plus arm would fit well in right field if needed and delivered fastballs clocked as high as 97 mph in college. Eibner has four solid tools, but he'll have to improve his contact ability to get to the big leagues. He'll roam center field in high Class A this year.

Year	Club (League)	Class	AVG	G	AB	R	H	2B	3B	HR	RBI	BB	SO	SB	CS	OBP	SLG
2011	Kane County (MWL)	LoA	.213	76	272	46	58	13	2	12	31	48	90	2	3	.340	.408
Minor League Totals			.213	76	272	46	58	13	2	12	31	48	90	2	3	.340	.408

13 JEREMY JEFFRESS, RHP

BA GRADE
55
HIGH

Born: Sept. 21, 1987. **B-T:** R-R. **Ht.:** 6-1. **Wt.:** 185. **Drafted:** HS—South Boston, Va., 2006 (1st round). **Signed by:** Tim McIlvaine (Brewers).

Ever since the Brewers picked him with the 16th pick of the 2006 draft, Jeffress has had one of the best arms in the minors. But six seasons later, he's still is working to harness his overpowering fastball. A pair of drug suspensions for marijuana cost him 150 games and hurt his development. A third suspension would cost him a lifetime ban in the minor leagues, but because he's on the 40-man roster, he can't be suspended for recreational drugs. Acquired in the Zack Greinke trade in December 2010, Jeffress opened last season in Kansas City but his control problems landed him in the minors in mid-May. When he can't throw strikes, he relies too much on his 96-100 mph fastball and hitters can sit on it. His 12-to-6 spike curveball can be a plus pitch, but he struggles to locate it in the strike zone. After his demotion, the Royals tweaked Jeffress' arm slot, moving his hand slightly further away from his head. The adjustment made his curve more of an 11-to-5 breaker and allowed him to command it better. He uses a cutter/slider as his third pitch. Jeffress' lack of control and command limit his ceiling. He has the pure velocity to close games, but he's more likely to be a seventh-inning reliever unless he can find a way to throw more strikes. He'll compete for a spot in Kansas City's crowded bullpen in spring training.

Year	Club (League)	Class	W	L	ERA	G	GS	CG	SV	IP	H	HR	BB	SO	K/9	WHIP	AVG
2006	Brewers (AZL)	R	2	5	5.88	13	4	0	0	34	30	0	25	37	9.9	1.63	.227
2007	West Virginia (SAL)	LoA	9	5	3.13	18	18	0	0	86	62	8	44	95	9.9	1.23	.201
2008	Brevard County (FSL)	HiA	4	6	4.08	15	14	1	0	79	65	5	41	102	11.6	1.34	.226
	Huntsville (SL)	AA	2	1	5.52	4	4	0	0	15	17	2	11	13	8.0	1.91	.298
2009	Huntsville (SL)	AA	1	3	7.57	8	8	0	0	27	26	1	33	34	11.2	2.16	.255
	Brevard County (FSL)	HiA	2	1	2.18	6	5	1	0	33	16	2	22	36	9.8	1.15	.145
2010	Wisconsin (MWL)	LoA	0	0	0.00	5	0	0	0	8	0	0	3	14	15.8	0.38	.000
	Brevard County (FSL)	HiA	0	0	5.40	8	0	0	1	10	10	0	7	14	12.6	1.70	.244
	Huntsville (SL)	AA	1	1	1.26	11	0	0	3	14	8	0	2	15	9.4	0.70	.160
	Milwaukee (NL)	MAJ	1	0	2.70	10	0	0	0	10	8	0	6	8	7.2	1.40	.229
2011	Kansas City (AL)	MAJ	1	1	4.70	14	0	0	1	15	12	1	11	13	7.6	1.50	.222
	Omaha (PCL)	AAA	1	3	7.13	16	3	0	3	24	27	5	18	24	9.0	1.88	.293
	NW Arkansas (TL)	AA	1	3	4.26	9	8	0	0	32	32	2	22	20	5.7	1.71	.271
Major League Totals			2	1	3.91	24	0	0	1	25	20	1	17	21	7.5	1.46	.225
Minor League Totals			24	28	4.22	113	64	2	7	362	293	25	228	404	10.0	1.44	.222

14 ELIER HERNANDEZ, OF

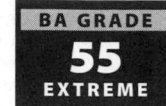

BA GRADE
55
EXTREME

Born: Nov. 21, 1994. **B-T:** R-R. **Ht.:** 6-3. **Wt.:** 200. **Signed:** Dominican Republic, 2011. **Signed by:** Rene Francisco.

As recently as five years ago, the Royals had only one homegrown Latin American prospect among their Top 30 Prospects. The team's renewed emphasis on scouting in that region has paid off with the likes of Cheslor Cuthbert, Kelvin Herrera and Yordano Ventura. Kansas City hopes it found another keeper in 2011 when it signed Hernandez to a $3.05 million bonus that ranked third on the international amateur market last year. He has some of the best bat speed international scouts have seen in recent years. Like many young prospects, he has work to do on his pitch recognition, and he's a ways from tapping into his above-average power potential because his quick swing is more suited to line drives than long flyballs. Hernandez also has excellent quickness—though only average speed—enough arm for right field and solid athleticism. If his bat develops, he could be a potential all-star corner outfielder, but he's years away from realizing that ceiling. Hernandez got his first taste of pro ball with an impressive showing in instructional league. He could make his official U.S. debut in the Rookie-level Arizona League in 2012.

Year	Club (League)	Class	AVG	G	AB	R	H	2B	3B	HR	RBI	BB	SO	SB	CS	OBP	SLG
2011	Did Not Play—Signed 2012 Contract																

15 JORGE BONIFACIO, OF

BA GRADE
55
EXTREME

Born: June 4, 1993. **B-T:** R-R. **Ht.:** 6-0. **Wt.:** 203. **Signed:** Dominican Republic, 2009. **Signed by:** Edis Perez.

Because the Royals have three Rookie-level affiliates, Burlington sometimes get the short end of the talent pool. Kansas City treats Idaho Falls as its most advanced Rookie club and the AZL Royals as its least advanced, with Burlington caught in between. Nevertheless, Burlington did a get a full 2011 season from Bonifacio, one of the system's most promising young outfielders. The brother of big leaguer Emilio Bonifacio, Jorge has a somewhat lengthy swing and a rather noisy setup, yet still makes a healthy amount of contact and hits for power. He profiles as a solid defender in right field with an above-average arm. His worst tool is his speed. He's an average runner now but figures to slow down as he matures physically. The Royals challenged Bonifacio by playing him with their advanced instructional league team in the fall. He handled that assignment with few problems and appears ready for low Class A in 2012.

Year	Club (League)	Class	AVG	G	AB	R	H	2B	3B	HR	RBI	BB	SO	SB	CS	OBP	SLG
2010	Royals (DSL)	R	.335	48	164	22	55	16	2	1	28	26	27	13	5	.429	.476
	Royals (AZL)	R	.211	21	76	9	16	0	5	0	6	6	31	1	2	.271	.342
2011	Burlington (APP)	R	.284	62	236	26	67	20	4	7	30	16	58	5	6	.333	.492
Minor League Totals			.290	131	476	57	138	36	11	8	64	48	116	19	13	.358	.462

16 BRIAN BRICKHOUSE, RHP

BA GRADE
55
HIGH

Born: June 6, 1992. **B-T:** R-R. **Ht.:** 6-0. **Wt.:** 209. **Drafted:** HS—The Woodlands, Texas, 2011 (3rd round). **Signed by:** Brian Rhees.

Brickhouse is the latest in a long line of power pitchers from The Woodlands (Texas) High, following former first-round picks Kyle Drabek and Jameson Taillon. A third-round pick last June, Brickhouse signed for $1.5 million—a higher bonus than nine first-round picks got in the 2011 draft. He's a good friend of Taillon, and watching the No. 2 overall choice in 2010 going through the draft process helped prepare Brickhouse for the spotlight of getting scouted in every start. He's not as physical or athletic as Taillon, but Brickhouse still features a fastball that sits at 92-94 mph and touches 97. He throws both a curveball and a slider, but they're similar enough that they'll likely end up as one breaking ball. The curve shows promise with a tight 11-5 break at times. His changeup needs lots of work, as is the case with many young pitchers. Brickhouse has to refine his delivery to stop collapsing on his front side. When that happens, he shows the ball too early and struggles to control his fastball. Some scouts see Brickhouse as a hard-throwing reliever, but the Royals believe he has the stuff to be a mid-rotation starter. As a relatively polished high school pitcher, he could reach low Class A at some point in 2012, though he'll probably make his pro debut at Idaho Falls.

Year	Club (League)	Class	AVG	G	AB	R	H	2B	3B	HR	RBI	BB	SO	SB	CS	OBP	SLG
2011	Did Not Play—Signed Late																

17 NOEL ARGUELLES, LHP

BA GRADE
50
MEDIUM

Born: Jan. 12, 1990. **B-T:** L-L. **Ht.:** 6-3. **Wt.:** 215. **Signed:** Cuba, 2009. **Signed by:** Rene Francisco.

A member of the Cuban 18-and-under national team, Arguelles defected at the World Junior Championships in Edmonton in July 2008. Seventeen months later, he signed a five-year, $6.9 million big league contract with the Royals that included a $3.4 million bonus. They had to wait more than a year to see him in game action, however, because he developed shoulder soreness and needed surgery to repair his labrum. With Arguelles' track record of performing well at major international tournaments, Kansas City sent him straight to high Class A to make his pro debut. He responded well, as his plus command allowed his fringy stuff to play up. Arguelles' fastball sat at 90 mph and peaked at 93 before he got hurt, but he operated at 87-89 in 2011. His best pitch is his average changeup, which he's not afraid to throw in any count. He also has a tick below-average curveball. The Royals kept him on tight pitch counts as he came back from injury, but he was so efficient that they had to scrap plans to have Michael Mariot piggyback behind him because Mariot wasn't getting enough work. If Arguelles returns to pre-injury form, he could be a No. 3 or 4 starter. If not, his feel for pitching still could get him to the big leagues in a lesser role. He'll head to Double-A in 2012.

Year	Club (League)	Class	W	L	ERA	G	GS	CG	SV	IP	H	HR	BB	SO	K/9	WHIP	AVG
2010	Did Not Play—Injured																
2011	Wilmington (CAR)	HiA	4	5	3.20	21	21	0	0	104	93	6	24	64	5.5	1.13	.245
Minor League Totals			4	5	3.20	21	21	0	0	104	93	6	24	64	5.5	1.13	.245

18 KEVIN CHAPMAN, LHP

BA GRADE
50
MEDIUM

Born: Feb. 19, 1988. **B-T:** L-L. **Ht.:** 6-3. **Wt.:** 219. **Drafted:** Florida, 2010 (4th round). **Signed by:** Colin Gonzales.

When their high school-heavy 2007 and 2008 draft classes started to reach the upper minors, the Royals began emphasizing picking advanced college relievers who could help fill in some holes. Louis Coleman was the first of that group to make the big leagues and Chapman could be the second. He battled injuries through much of his college career at Florida, but after cleaning up his delivery and getting more direct to the plate, he dominated as a junior in 2010. He pitched himself into the fourth round of the draft and signed for $250,000. When Chapman is locating his 93-95 mph fastball, he can succeed using it almost exclusively. His fastball has late sink and tail, and he can cut it as well. He also throws a sweeping slider that can be an average pitch. Lefties get few good swings against him, and he has enough stuff to get righties out as well. Chapman still has control issues at times, partly because he isn't consistent about getting the ball out of his glove promptly. When he doesn't, his arm struggles to catch up to his body and he can't find the strike zone. After reaching Double-A last June, he'll head back there to open this season.

Year	Club (League)	Class	W	L	ERA	G	GS	CG	SV	IP	H	HR	BB	SO	K/9	WHIP	AVG
2010	Wilmington (CAR)	HiA	1	1	5.50	14	0	0	1	18	20	1	8	20	10.0	1.56	.267
2011	Wilmington (CAR)	HiA	0	2	4.84	15	0	0	7	22	24	1	7	40	16.1	1.39	.264
	NW Arkansas (TL)	AA	1	2	4.99	25	0	0	3	40	37	5	21	50	11.3	1.46	.255
Minor League Totals			2	5	5.06	54	0	0	11	80	81	7	36	110	12.4	1.46	.260

19 TIM MELVILLE, RHP

BA GRADE
50
HIGH

Born: Oct. 9, 1989. **B-T:** R-R. **Ht.:** 6-5. **Wt.:** 210. **Drafted:** HS—Wentzville, Mo., 2008 (4th round). **Signed by:** Phil Huttman.

Since signing for a well-over-slot $1.25 million as a fourth-round pick, Melville has climbed significantly slower through the system than fellow 2008 draftee Mike Montgomery. Melville repeated high Class A in 2011 without making huge progress. His fastball still can be a plus pitch but he doesn't always command it, and he doesn't throw it with the conviction expected for someone who works at 92-93 mph and touches 95. He always has nibbled more than scouts would like. Melville's slow curveball lacks consistency, occasionally featuring big break but too often getting loopier than he would like. His changeup is fringy. Scouts outside the organization believe Melville will improve once the Royals give him the freedom to throw a two-seam fastball and a slider. Kansas City wants him to master his current repertoire before he worries about adding more pitches, although it did allow him to start using his slider late in the season. Many high school power pitchers take a while to develop, and the Royals hope that's true with Melville. At this point, his most realistic ceiling may be as a No. 4 or 5 starter or a power reliever. He'll finally make the jump to Double-A this year.

Year	Club (League)	Class	W	L	ERA	G	GS	CG	SV	IP	H	HR	BB	SO	K/9	WHIP	AVG
2009	Burlington (MWL)	LoA	7	7	3.79	21	21	0	0	97	89	10	43	96	8.9	1.36	.245
2010	Wilmington (CAR)	HiA	2	12	4.97	22	22	0	0	112	101	10	54	90	7.2	1.38	.240
	Royals (AZL)	R	0	1	3.86	2	2	0	0	5	4	0	2	6	11.6	1.29	.222
2011	Wilmington (CAR)	HiA	11	10	4.32	29	25	0	0	135	152	7	53	108	7.2	1.51	.287
Minor League Totals			20	30	4.38	74	70	0	0	350	346	27	152	300	7.7	1.42	.260

20 ORLANDO CALIXTE, SS

BA GRADE
55
EXTREME

Born: Feb. 3, 1992. **B-T:** R-R. **Ht.:** 6-0. **Wt.:** 174. **Signed:** Dominican Republic, 2010. **Signed by:** Alvin Cuevas/Hector Pineda.

When the Royals first started scouting Calixte when he was a 15-year-old in 2007, they were able to get a good feel for his power potential and his likelihood of sticking at shortstop. What they couldn't get was a clear idea of who exactly he was. He has to wait nearly two years after he turned 16 to sign because he had swapped identities with his brother. Once MLB determined he was Orlando Calixte (and not Paul Carlixte or Orlando Caxito) and cleared him to sign, Kansas City was happy to land him for $1 million. Calixte impressed the Royals enough last spring that they sent him to low Class A for his U.S. debut. He often looked over his head, especially when pitchers figured out there were few pitches he wouldn't swing at. But he also showed excellent bat speed, and has the strength to eventually have more power than a typical shortstop. Calixte eventually may outgrow the position, but he has sure hands and a solid arm. The question is whether he'll lose a step off his slightly above-average speed and have enough range once he matures physically. He'll head back to Kane County in 2012 to try to gain some confidence.

Year	Club (League)	Class	AVG	G	AB	R	H	2B	3B	HR	RBI	BB	SO	SB	CS	OBP	SLG
2010	Royals (DSL)	R	.227	20	66	10	15	6	0	0	12	13	13	3	1	.350	.318
2011	Kane County (MWL)	LoA	.208	81	289	19	60	5	1	3	31	20	70	11	4	.256	.263
Minor League Totals			.211	101	355	29	75	11	1	3	43	33	83	14	5	.275	.273

21 CLINT ROBINSON, 1B

BA GRADE
45
MEDIUM

Born: Feb. 16, 1985. **B-T:** L-L. **Ht.:** 6-5. **Wt.:** 225. **Drafted:** Troy, 2007 (25th round). **Signed by:** Max Semler.

Even with Eric Hosmer, Mike Moustakas and Wil Myers in the system, Robinson arguably has been the most productive Royals minor leaguer over the last three years. A former 25th-round pick signed for $1,000, he won the Double-A Texas League triple crown by hitting .335-29-98 in 2010. He followed up by batting .326 with a career-high 100 RBIs in 2011, helping lead Omaha to the Pacific Coast League championship. He missed the Triple-A championship game with a sports hernia that required surgery. When Robinson turned pro, he was a dead-pull hitter incapable of taking a ball the other way. Now he uses the whole field and has a very advanced two-strike approach. He's a plus hitter with average power, though his other tools aren't nearly as impressive. His speed rates as a 20 on the 20-80 scouting scale and he's a below-average defender at first base. Robinson throws well enough to play the outfield, but his lack of speed makes that a stretch. He has played just three games in left field in five years as a pro. With Hosmer and Billy Butler entrenched in Kansas City, Robinson is stuck in Triple-A for now. The trade market for first basemen with average power never is particularly heated, so he may have to bide his time in Omaha for a while.

Year	Club (League)	Class	AVG	G	AB	R	H	2B	3B	HR	RBI	BB	SO	SB	CS	OBP	SLG
2007	Idaho Falls (PIO)	R	.336	67	253	39	85	18	1	15	66	19	42	2	0	.388	.593
2008	Burlington (MWL)	LoA	.264	106	379	53	100	22	3	17	64	37	67	0	3	.333	.472
2009	Wilmington (CAR)	HiA	.298	124	436	65	130	31	1	13	57	35	79	4	3	.356	.463
2010	NW Arkansas (TL)	AA	.335	129	477	90	160	41	5	29	98	58	86	4	3	.410	.625
2011	Omaha (PCL)	AAA	.326	134	503	86	164	35	0	23	100	58	88	2	1	.399	.533
Minor League Totals			.312	560	2048	333	639	147	10	97	385	207	362	12	10	.379	.536

22 WILL SMITH, LHP

BA GRADE
45
MEDIUM

Born: July 10, 1989. **B-T:** R-L. **Ht.:** 6-5. **Wt.:** 235. **Drafted:** HS—Newnan, Ga., 2007 (7th round). **Signed by:** Tom Kotchman (Angels).

When the Royals traded Alberto Callaspo to the Angels in July 2010, they received a pair of finesse starters in Sean O'Sullivan and Smith. The latter is a big-bodied lefthander who's not particularly flashy and has three average pitches with average command. Smith's two-seam fastball sits at 88-90 mph, a tick up from what he showed in 2010. He tweaked his two-seam grip midway through last season, adding velocity while not losing any of movement. His four-seamer operates at 91-92 mph and touches 94. His best secondary pitches are his big-breaking curveball and a changeup that's not quite as consistent. He added a slider midway through 2011 to give him a better chance against righthanders. Smith lacks a true strikeout pitch and he lands on a stiff front leg, which affects his control at times. His crossfire delivery helps create some deception, however, and he's equally successful against lefties and righties. Smith projects as a back-of-the-rotation starter if he continues to develop, and he should be at least a long reliever in the big leagues. He'll get a shot at making Kansas City's rotation in spring training but most likely will be sent to Triple-A.

Year	Club (League)	Class	W	L	ERA	G	GS	CG	SV	IP	H	HR	BB	SO	K/9	WHIP	AVG
2008	Orem (PIO)	R	8	2	3.08	16	14	0	0	73	73	6	6	76	9.4	1.08	.253
2009	Cedar Rapids (MWL)	LoA	10	5	3.76	20	19	0	0	115	109	11	24	95	7.4	1.16	.249
2010	R. Cucamonga (CAL)	HiA	2	2	4.58	6	6	0	0	37	36	4	13	31	7.5	1.31	.259
	Salt Lake (PCL)	AAA	2	4	5.60	9	9	0	0	53	65	6	20	40	6.8	1.60	.305
	Arkansas (TL)	AA	1	2	7.23	4	4	0	0	19	33	3	9	8	3.9	2.25	.398
	Wilmington (CAR)	HiA	4	1	2.80	8	8	0	0	55	48	6	4	51	8.4	0.95	.233
2011	NW Arkansas (TL)	AA	13	9	3.85	27	27	2	0	161	171	13	45	108	6.0	1.34	.279
Minor League Totals			40	25	3.96	90	87	2	0	513	535	49	121	409	7.2	1.28	.270

23 CAMERON GALLAGHER, C

BA GRADE
50
HIGH

Born: Dec. 6, 1992. **B-T:** R-R. **Ht.:** 6-3. **Wt.:** 215. **Drafted:** HS—Lancaster, Pa., 2011 (2nd round). **Signed by:** Jim Farr.

When Salvador Perez sped up his timetable to the big leagues and Wil Myers moved from behind the plate to the outfield, the Royals suddenly were left quite thin in minor league catchers. They attempted to rectify that by drafting Gallagher in the second round last June and trading Wilson Betemit to the Tigers for Julio Rodriguez (and minor league lefty Antonio Cruz) a month later. Gallagher's bloodlines didn't hurt: his father Glenn and his brother Austin (currently in the Dodgers system) were both third-round picks. Signed for an over-slot $750,000, Cameron is big for a catcher but has the soft hands to be a good receiver. He also has a strong arm, though he threw out just two of 11 basestealers in his pro debut. Gallagher has offensive promise as well with above-average power potential, though his bat is relatively unrefined. Like most catchers, he's a below-average runner who's sure to slow down as he spends more time behind the plate. Some scouts wonder if he'll end up being too big to stay at catcher, though Kansas City isn't concerned. The last two Pennsylvania high school catchers to succeed (Neil Walker and Devin Mesoraco) were slow starters, so it won't be a surprise if Gallagher takes a while to get acclimated to pro ball. He could see some time in low Class A in his first full pro season, though it's not a given that he'll open 2012 there.

Year	Club (League)	Class	AVG	G	AB	R	H	2B	3B	HR	RBI	BB	SO	SB	CS	OBP	SLG
2011	Royals (AZL)	R	.141	20	78	6	11	0	0	1	7	7	15	0	0	.209	.179
	Idaho Falls (PIO)	R	.200	8	30	2	6	0	0	1	2	3	4	0	0	.273	.300
Minor League Totals			.157	28	108	8	17	0	0	2	9	10	19	0	0	.227	.213

24 MIKE ANTONIO, SS

BA GRADE
50
HIGH

Born: Oct. 26, 1991. **B-T:** R-R. **Ht.:** 6-1. **Wt.:** 186. **Drafted:** HS—New York, 2010 (3rd round). **Signed by:** Dennis Sheehan.

The best player to come out of New York's George Washington High since Manny Ramirez, Antonio signed for $411,000 as a third-round pick in 2010. Though he didn't face much in the way of high school competition, he has adapted well to pro ball. He smacked 10 homers at Burlington last summer and is ready for low Class A at age 20. Antonio has plus power potential with a long swing that will bring both home runs and strikeouts. He'll have to improve his ability to lay off balls off the plate at higher levels. He's an average runner. Because the Royals have a surplus of middle infielders projected to play at Kane County in 2012, Antonio will get to play some third base in addition to his usual position of shortstop. That move will serve him well, as he may outgrow shortstop in the long run. He has good hands, but he tends to bend at the waist rather than his knees, which limits his below-average range. He has a strong if erratic arm that would fit fine at the hot corner, though he needs to be careful about getting on the side of the ball in his release.

Year	Club (League)	Class	AVG	G	AB	R	H	2B	3B	HR	RBI	BB	SO	SB	CS	OBP	SLG
2010	Royals (AZL)	R	.264	40	163	19	43	14	5	1	12	8	31	7	4	.297	.429
2011	Burlington (APP)	R	.262	55	206	30	54	11	0	10	37	17	25	10	5	.322	.461
	Idaho Falls (PIO)	R	.303	8	33	6	10	2	1	1	5	1	6	1	0	.314	.515
Minor League Totals			.266	103	402	55	107	27	6	12	54	26	62	18	9	.311	.453

25 JACK LOPEZ, SS

BA GRADE
50
HIGH

Born: Dec. 16, 1992. **B-T:** R-R. **Ht.:** 5-10. **Wt.:** 170. **Drafted:** HS—Deltona, Fla., 2011 (16th round). **Signed by:** Colin Gonzales.

In the 2011 draft, scouts viewed Lopez as a polished high school middle infielder who could use some time in college to get bigger and stronger. Once the third round passed, the son of Reds bullpen coach Juan Lopez seemed destined to attend Miami. But the Royals took him in the 16th round and signed him at the Aug. 15 deadline for $750,000, matching what they paid second-rounder Cameron Gallagher. Kansas City viewed Lopez as one of the best high school shortstops in the draft, especially at the plate. He has good hand-eye coordination and a more advanced approach than the normal high school draftee. He doesn't have much power now, but he's expected to add strength as he fills out and already has added 10 pounds since last spring. Defensively, Lopez has fine actions, soft hands and a strong enough arm. His speed and range are solid. His game has a lot of similarities to Christian Colon's, though Lopez is more likely to stick at shortstop. He could handle an assignment to low Class A in his first full pro season, but he'll likely stay in Rookie ball because the Royals have a surplus of middle infielders headed to Kane County.

Year	Club (League)	Class	AVG	G	AB	R	H	2B	3B	HR	RBI	BB	SO	SB	CS	OBP	SLG
2011	Did Not Play—Signed Late																

26 EVERETT TEAFORD, LHP

BA GRADE

45

LOW

Born: May 15, 1984. **B-T:** L-L. **Ht.:** 5-11. **Wt.:** 156. **Drafted:** Georgia Southern, 2006 (12th round). **Signed by:** Spencer Graham.

The Royals left Teaford unprotected in the 2009 Rule 5 draft, and to no one's surprise, he went unpicked. But in the two years since, he has improved his stuff and transformed from roster-filler to big leaguer. He showed in 2011 that the improvements he made the year before weren't a fluke. Teaford doesn't have an explanation for why his former 88-90 mph fastball jumped to 90-93. But that increase in velocity made all the difference, helping his average breaking ball and changeup play up. He also throws a cutter at times, and he can vary his arm slot to make life harder on lefthanders. He does a good job of throwing strikes. Teaford worked both out of the bullpen and the rotation in 2011, and figures to serve Kansas City in a swing role in the short term. His ceiling isn't particularly high, but he already has proven he can get big league hitters out.

Year	Club (League)	Class	W	L	ERA	G	GS	CG	SV	IP	H	HR	BB	SO	K/9	WHIP	AVG
2006	Idaho Falls (PIO)	R	5	1	3.71	15	12	0	0	63	54	3	20	51	7.3	1.17	.228
2007	Burlington (MWL)	LoA	6	8	4.68	27	21	0	0	135	147	11	36	84	5.6	1.36	.281
2008	Wilmington (CAR)	HiA	8	6	3.80	28	23	0	1	144	135	15	46	116	7.2	1.25	.246
2009	Wilmington (CAR)	HiA	7	1	2.39	11	11	0	0	64	51	7	12	49	6.9	0.98	.219
	NW Arkansas (TL)	AA	3	7	5.11	16	16	1	0	81	86	12	34	42	4.7	1.48	.269
2010	NW Arkansas (TL)	AA	14	3	3.36	27	12	0	0	99	91	7	32	113	10.3	1.24	.243
	Omaha (PCL)	AAA	0	1	13.50	1	1	0	0	5	8	2	1	4	7.7	1.93	.364
2011	Omaha (PCL)	AAA	3	2	3.34	16	3	0	0	35	23	5	11	33	8.5	0.97	.183
	Kansas City (AL)	MAJ	2	1	3.27	26	3	0	1	44	36	8	14	28	5.7	1.14	.231
Major League Totals			2	1	3.27	26	3	0	1	44	36	8	14	28	5.7	1.14	.231
Minor League Totals			46	29	3.98	141	99	1	1	626	595	62	192	492	7.1	1.26	.250

27 BRIAN FLETCHER, OF

BA GRADE

50

HIGH

Born: Oct. 26, 1988. **B-T:** R-R. **Ht.:** 6-0. **Wt.:** 187. **Drafted:** Auburn, 2010 (18th round). **Signed by:** Sean Gibbs.

The son of former big leaguer Scott Fletcher, Brian turned down the Astros as a 39th-round pick out of high school in 2007, when Brett Eibner did the same. After three years at Auburn, Fletcher went in the 18th round and signed for $275,000, the equivalent of fourth-round money. He doesn't have a conventional approach at the plate, but his style works for him and has produced a .328/.384/.566 numbers in pro ball. While he gets out on his front foot too quickly and pushes his hands through the zone, he manages to square up his share of pitches, which allows his solid power to come through. Some scouts wonder if Fletcher's approach won't work as well against more advanced pitchers, but the Royals aren't going to change him as long as he keeps producing. His aggressiveness at the plate sometimes works against him, though he has a good gameplan with two strikes. Fletcher is a below-average runner, but he does have a feel for when to take an extra base. His below-average arm limits him to left field, and he also could see some time at first base, where his power might profile. Kansas City left Fletcher in low Class A all of last year because he was integral in Kane County's run toward the Midwest League playoffs. With a solid start, his stay in high Class A this year could be shorter.

Year	Club (League)	Class	AVG	G	AB	R	H	2B	3B	HR	RBI	BB	SO	SB	CS	OBP	SLG
2010	Burlington (APP)	R	.313	4	16	4	5	0	0	2	4	1	5	2	0	.353	.688
2011	Kane County (MWL)	LoA	.328	91	341	54	112	31	3	14	60	24	80	4	4	.386	.560
Minor League Totals			.328	95	357	58	117	31	3	16	64	25	85	6	4	.384	.566

28 DANNY MATEO, 2B/3B

BA GRADE

50

HIGH

Born: Aug. 10, 1991. **B-T:** B-R. **Ht.:** 5-11. **Wt.:** 194. **Signed:** Dominican Republic, 2008. **Signed by:** Edis Perez.

Jorge Bonifacio wasn't the only young Latin American to emerge on the Royals prospect scene in 2011. Mateo showed an advanced approach with a sweet swing for a switch-hitter as he flushed away a poor 2010 to rank among the best hitters in the Rookie-level Pioneer League. His lefthanded swing allows him to keep the bat head in the zone for a long time. His righty stroke has no obvious flaws but isn't smooth or refined. The big question for Mateo is whether he'll improve enough at second base to stick there, because he doesn't have enough power potential to profile at third base. He has the tools to be a solid defender at second, with adequate range, reliable hands and a strong arm for the position. His footwork is a mess at times, though that can be explained somewhat by his youth. He's an average runner. Mateo will join a very crowded infield in Kane County in 2012.

Year	Club (League)	Class	AVG	G	AB	R	H	2B	3B	HR	RBI	BB	SO	SB	CS	OBP	SLG
2009	Royals (DSL)	R	.254	61	213	29	54	13	5	2	27	23	37	12	6	.339	.390
2010	Royals (AZL)	R	.218	52	206	19	45	11	5	2	25	10	48	7	1	.256	.350
2011	Idaho Falls (PIO)	R	.348	56	224	33	78	9	4	4	40	17	43	0	1	.389	.478
Minor League Totals			.275	169	643	81	177	33	14	8	92	50	128	19	8	.330	.407

29 HUMBERTO ARTEAGA, SS

BA GRADE

50 HIGH

Born: Jan. 23, 1994. **B-T:** R-R. **Ht.:** 6-0 **Wt.:** 174. **Signed:** Venezuela, 2010. **Signed by:** Orlando Estevez/Richard Castro.

Facing a shortage of young shortstops in the system, the Royals added Orlando Calixte and Arteaga in 2010. Arteaga got a slightly higher bonus at $1.1 million, in part because he was two years younger. And unlike with Calixte, there's no question that Arteaga is a long-term shortstop. His defense is his best attribute, as he has the range, hands and feel for reading balls off the bat to make all the plays at shortstop. He had a fringy arm when he signed, but it's now solid thanks to his diligent work on a throwing program, His quick release and smooth actions help as well. Offensively, he's less gifted than Calixte. Arteaga has very little power and will need to get stronger just to avoid having the bat knocked from his hands at higher levels. He's a slightly below-average runner, so he'll need to become an average hitter to have any offensive value. Scouts from other organizations question whether he can do that. Arteaga's defense will carry him through the lower levels of the minors, but his bat will determine how far he goes. He has years of development ahead and will spend a second season in Rookie ball in 2012.

Year	Club (League)	Class	AVG	G	AB	R	H	2B	3B	HR	RBI	BB	SO	SB	CS	OBP	SLG
2011	Royals (AZL)	R	.254	47	213	30	54	11	2	0	28	9	39	8	2	.290	.324
Minor League Totals			.254	47	213	30	54	11	2	0	28	9	39	8	2	.290	.324

30 DAVID LOUGH, OF

BA GRADE

45 LOW

Born: Jan. 20, 1986. **B-T:** L-L. **Ht.:** 6-0. **Wt.:** 180. **Drafted:** Merceyhurst (Pa.), 2007 (11th round). **Signed by:** Jason Bryan.

Lough is one of the few players who has been around long enough to see the system go from among the game's worst to among the best. Unfortunately for him, the system's improvement has slowed his climb. Added to the 40-man roster after the 2010 season, he spent 2011 repeating Triple-A. He never got very close to making his big league debut, as the arrival of Lorenzo Cain in the Zack Greinke trade and the development of Jarrod Dyson moved Lough down Kansas City's depth chart. A career .299 hitter in the minors, he hits for average, shows average power and is a plus runner. Lough doesn't play center field well enough to be more than an occasional fill-in, and he doesn't hit for enough power to be a regular corner outfielder. His below-average arm makes him best suited for left field. Lough's profile and minor league track record is quite similar to current Royal Mitch Maier's, and his hope is to have a similar career. Lough's path to the big leagues in 2012 still seems blocked by Cain and Dyson.

Year	Club (League)	Class	AVG	G	AB	R	H	2B	3B	HR	RBI	BB	SO	SB	CS	OBP	SLG
2007	Burlington (APP)	R	.337	24	86	15	29	6	0	2	12	4	13	6	1	.380	.477
2008	Burlington (MWL)	LoA	.268	126	488	76	131	21	11	16	62	35	70	12	11	.329	.455
2009	Wilmington (CAR)	HiA	.320	65	222	28	71	15	2	5	30	12	34	6	4	.370	.473
	NW Arkansas (TL)	AA	.331	61	236	41	78	13	2	9	31	12	30	13	4	.371	.517
2010	Omaha (PCL)	AAA	.280	120	460	65	129	15	12	11	58	40	72	14	5	.346	.437
2011	Omaha (PCL)	AAA	.318	114	456	87	145	26	11	9	65	36	49	14	8	.367	.482
Minor League Totals			.299	510	1948	312	583	96	38	52	258	139	268	65	33	.354	.468

Los Angeles Angels

BY MATT EDDY

The Angels handed over the reins—and a hefty checkbook—to new GM Jerry Dipoto

I f you want to know the standard the Angels hold themselves to these days, witness the changes that took place after they completed an 86-76 season.

Los Angeles reeled off its seventh winning season in the last eight, but missed the playoffs in consecutive years for the first time since 2000-01, Mike Scioscia's first two years as manager. What's more, the Rangers repeated as the American League West champion and AL pennant winner, with a former Angel as a driving force.

The Angels' January 2011 trade of Mike Napoli not only skewed the balance of power in the AL West, but it also led to a front-office overhaul. General manager Tony Reagins dealt Napoli and Juan Rivera to the Blue Jays for Vernon Wells— and the full $86 million left on his bloated contract. Toronto then flipped Napoli to Texas, where he led all big league catchers in hitting (.320), on-base percentage (.414), slugging (.631) and homers (30).

Wells had a terrible season, hitting 25 homers but posting a .248 on-base percentage. Jeff Mathis hit .174 after picking up the bulk of the catching duties in Napoli's absence, and Los Angeles plummeted to 10th in the AL in runs scored.

The changes came swiftly. Two days after the season ended, owner Arte Moreno forced Reagins to resign. He later fired farm director Abe Flores and assistant GMs Ken Forsch and Gary Sutherland.

The Angels hired Diamondbacks senior vice president of scouting and player development Jerry Dipoto to replace Reagins in late October. Dipoto retained Ric Wilson as amateur scouting director and hired Red Sox scout Hal Morris as pro scouting director. He also hired Rangers farm director Scott Servais as assistant GM.

Emboldened by a new $3 billion, 20-year local television deal with Fox, the new front office dramatically improved the roster. Dipoto signed the most coveted position player and pitcher on the free agent market, landing Albert Pujols with a 10-year, $254 million contract and then signing C.J. Wilson away from the Rangers for five years and $77.5 million.

Dipoto also upgraded the Angels at catcher, dealing righthander Tyler Chatwood (the system's No. 2 prospect a year ago) to the Rockies for Chris Iannetta, then dealing Mathis to the Blue Jays for Brad Mills.

Chatwood was one of six Angels rookies in 2011. Jordan Walden rode a 98 mph fastball to 32 saves and a place on the AL all-star team, while Mark Trumbo

TOP 30 PROSPECTS

1. Mike Trout, of	**16.** Mike Clevinger, rhp
2. Jean Segura, ss	**17.** Randal Grichuk, of
3. Garrett Richards, rhp	**18.** Cam Bedrosian, rhp
4. Johnny Hellweg, rhp	**19.** Alexi Amarista, 2b/of
5. C.J. Cron, 1b	**20.** Kole Calhoun, of/1b
6. Kaleb Cowart, 3b	**21.** Carlos Ramirez, c
7. Taylor Lindsey, 2b	**22.** Trevor Reckling, lhp
8. Daniel Tillman, rhp	**23.** Donn Roach, rhp
9. Ariel Pena, rhp	**24.** Austin Wood, rhp
10. Nick Maronde, lhp	**25.** Andrew Romine, inf
11. Jeremy Moore, of	**26.** Orangel Arenas, rhp
12. Luis Jimenez, 3b	**27.** Matt Shoemaker, rhp
13. Fabio Martinez, rhp	**28.** A.J. Schugel, rhp
14. Nick Mutz, rhp	**29.** Ryan Brasier, rhp
15. Travis Witherspoon, of	**30.** Loek Van Mil, rhp

belted 29 homers and finished runner-up for AL rookie of the year honors. Unless he learns a new position, however, Trumbo becomes redundant with the acquisition of Pujols.

Last season, the trio of Mathis, Trumbo and Wells extinguished many a rally by combining for a .262 on-base percentage. In 2012, Los Angeles could replace that trio in the lineup with Iannetta, Pujols and elite prospect Mike Trout. Those upgrades, combined with a stout rotation featuring Jered Weaver, Dan Haren, Wilson and Ervin Santana, give the Angels hope of snapping their two-year playoff drought.

General Manager: Jerry Dipoto. **Farm Director:** Scott Servais. **Scouting Director:** Ric Wilson.

Class	Team	League	W	L	Pct	Finish*	Manager(s)
Majors	Los Angeles Angels	American	86	76	.531	6th (14)	Mike Scioscia
Triple-A	Salt Lake Bees	Pacific Coast	62	82	.431	16th (16)	Keith Johnson
Double-A	Arkansas Travelers	Texas	68	69	.496	4th (8)	B.Mosiello/T.Takayoshi/B.Mitchell
High A	Inland Empire 66ers	California	69	71	.493	t-5th (10)	Tom Gamboa
Low A	Cedar Rapids Kernels	Midwest	61	78	.439	14th (16)	Brent Del Chiaro
Rookie	Orem Owlz	Pioneer	46	30	.605	1st (8)	Tom Kotchman
Rookie	AZL Angels	Arizona	28	28	.500	t-6th (13)	Tyrone Boykin
Overall 2011 Minor League Record			334	358	.483	22nd (30)	

*Finish in overall standings (No. of teams in league). †League champion.

LAST YEAR'S TOP 30

Player, Pos.		Status
1.	Mike Trout, of	No. 1
2.	Tyler Chatwood, rhp	(Rockies)
3.	Jean Segura, 2b	No. 2
4.	Hank Conger, c	Majors
5.	Jordan Walden, rhp	Majors
6.	Kaleb Cowart, 3b	No. 6
7.	Garrett Richards, rhp	No. 3
8.	Fabio Martinez, rhp	No. 13
9.	Mark Trumbo, 1b/of	Majors
10.	Cam Bedrosian, rhp	No. 18
11.	Trevor Reckling, lhp	No. 22
12.	Randal Grichuk, of	No. 17
13.	Chevy Clarke, of	Dropped out
14.	Daniel Tillman, rhp	No. 8
15.	Michael Kohn, rhp	Majors
16.	Jeremy Moore, of	No. 11
17.	Andrew Romine, ss	No. 25
18.	Alexi Amarista, 2b	No. 19
19.	Taylor Lindsey, 2b	No. 7
20.	Orangel Arenas, rhp	No. 26
21.	Travis Witherspoon, of	No. 15
22.	Luis Jimenez, 3b	No. 12
23.	Johnny Hellweg, rhp	No. 4
24.	Bobby Cassevah, rhp	Majors
25.	Donn Roach, rhp	No. 23
26.	Ryan Bolden, of	Dropped out
27.	Ysmael Carmona, rhp	Dropped out
28.	Drew Taylor, lhp	Dropped out
29.	Drew Heid, of	Dropped out
30.	Loek Van Mil, rhp	No. 30

BEST TOOLS

Best Hitter for Average	Mike Trout
Best Power Hitter	C.J. Cron
Best Strike-Zone Discipline	Kole Calhoun
Fastest Baserunner	Mike Trout
Best Athlete	Mike Trout
Best Fastball	Johnny Hellweg
Best Curveball	Johnny Hellweg
Best Slider	Ariel Pena
Best Changeup	Lay Batista
Best Control	Orangel Arenas
Best Defensive Catcher	Alberto Rosario
Best Defensive Infielder	Andrew Romine
Best Infield Arm	Kaleb Cowart
Best Defensive Outfielder	Mike Trout
Best Outfield Arm	Angel Castillo

PROJECTED 2015 LINEUP

Catcher	Chris Iannetta
First Base	Albert Pujols
Second Base	Jean Segura
Third Base	Kaleb Cowart
Shortstop	Erick Aybar
Left Field	Mike Trout
Center Field	Peter Bourjos
Right Field	Howard Kendrick
Designated Hitter	C.J. Cron
No. 1 Starter	Jered Weaver
No. 2 Starter	Dan Haren
No. 3 Starter	C.J. Wilson
No. 4 Starter	Ervin Santana
No. 5 Starter	Garrett Richards
Closer	Jordan Walden

TOP PROSPECTS OF THE DECADE

Year	Player, Pos.	2011 Org.
2002	Casey Kotchman, 1b	Rays
2003	Francisco Rodriguez, rhp	Brewers
2004	Casey Kotchman, 1b	Rays
2005	Casey Kotchman, 1b	Rays
2006	Brandon Wood, ss	Pirates
2007	Brandon Wood, ss	Pirates
2008	Brandon Wood, ss	Pirates
2009	Nick Adenhart, rhp	Deceased
2010	Hank Conger, c	Angels
2011	Mike Trout, of	Angels

TOP DRAFT PICKS OF THE DECADE

Year	Player, Pos.	2011 Org.
2002	Joe Saunders, lhp	Diamondbacks
2003	Brandon Wood, ss	Pirates
2004	Jered Weaver, rhp	Angels
2005	Trevor Bell, rhp (1st round supp.)	Angels
2006	Hank Conger, c	Angels
2007	Jon Bachanov, rhp (1st round supp.)	White Sox
2008	Tyler Chatwood, rhp (2nd round)	Angels
2009	Randal Grichuk, of	Angels
2010	Kaleb Cowart, 3b	Angels
2011	C.J. Cron, 1b	Angels

LARGEST BONUSES IN CLUB HISTORY

Jered Weaver, 2004	$4,000,000
Kendry Morales, 2004	$3,000,000
Kaleb Cowart, 2010	$2,300,000
Troy Glaus, 1997	$2,250,000
Joe Torres, 2000	$2,080,000

LOS ANGELES ANGELS

TOP 2012 ROOKIE: Mike Trout, of. Baseball America's 2011 Minor League Player of the Year is on standby in the event Vernon Wells doesn't get back on track.

BREAKOUT PROSPECT: Nick Mutz, rhp. A ninth-round find last June, he already throws two strong pitches and appears none the worse for not pitching collegiately in 2011.

SOURCE OF TOP 30 TALENT			
Homegrown	29	Acquired	1
College	8	Trades	1
Junior college	6	Rule 5 draft	0
High school	7	Independent leagues	0
Drafted/no school	1	Free agents/waivers	0
Nondrafted free agents	1		
International	6		

SLEEPER: Daniel Vargas-Vila, rhp. The 28th-rounder helped pitch West Florida to the NCAA Division II World Series championship, then showed encouraging pitchability and enhanced velocity in his pro debut.

LF	CF	RF
Drew Heid	Mike Trout (1)	Randal Grichuk (17)
Matt Long	Jeremy Moore (11)	Kole Calhoun (20)
Chris Pettit	Travis Witherspoon (15)	Angel Castillo
Clay Fuller	Chevy Clarke	Ryan Bolden
	Tyson Auer	Andrew Ray
	Drew Martinez	

3B	SS	2B	1B
Kaleb Cowart (6)	Andrew Romine (25)	Jean Segura (2)	C.J. Cron (5)
Luis Jimenez (12)	Darwin Perez	Taylor Lindsey (7)	Efren Navarro
Jeremy Cruz	Rolando Gomez	Alexi Amarista (19)	Dillon Baird
Joe Krehbiel	Wendell Soto	Ryan Mount	Jackson Whitley

C
Carlos Ramirez (21)
Alberto Rosario
Abel Baker
Jett Bandy

LHP		RHP	
LHSP	**LHRP**	**RHSP**	**RHRP**
Nick Maronde (10)	Drew Taylor	Garrett Richards (3)	Daniel Tillman (8)
Trevor Reckling (22)	Matt Meyer	Johnny Hellweg (4)	Ariel Pena (9)
Brad Mills	Junior Carlin	Nick Mutz (15)	Fabio Martinez (13)
Max Russell		Mike Clevinger (16)	Donn Roach (23)
Manuel Flores		Cam Bedrosian (18)	Ryan Brasier (29)
Michael Johnson		Austin Wood (24)	Loek Van Mil (30)
		Orangel Arenas (26)	David Carpenter
		Matt Shoemaker (27)	Ryan Chaffee
		A.J. Schugel (28)	Ysmael Carmona
		Daniel Vargas-Vila	Steve Geltz
			Chris Scholl
			Baudilio Lopez
			Jose Perez
			Danny Reynolds
			Logan Odom

2011

BEST PURE HITTER: 1B C.J. Cron (1) is the rare hitter who improved his batting average from 2010 (.431) even after the introduction of less-lively bats in college baseball in 2011 (.434). His knack for hitting may be ahead of his considerable power at this stage.

BEST POWER HITTER: Cron also led NCAA Division I in slugging (.803), then tied for sixth in the Rookie-level Pioneer League in homers (13) despite playing just 34 games because of a dislocated kneecap.

FASTEST RUNNER: OF Drew Martinez (10) is an above-average runner whose speed plays on the bases and in center field.

BEST DEFENSIVE PLAYER: SS Trevor Hairgrove (18) has modest range, but the rest of his tools and actions play well at short.

BEST FASTBALL: The Angels don't shy away from big arms with modest track records, and they drafted several in 2011, led by RHP Austin Wood (6), who has touched 99 mph and sat at 92-96 mph last spring for Southern California. RHPs Mike Clevinger (4) and Nick Mutz (9) work at 93-95 mph and can touch higher in short bursts, while LHP Nick Maronde (3) deals at 90-95.

BEST SECONDARY PITCH: Clevinger and Mutz have swing-and-miss sliders, though both lack consistency. Mutz has made real progress since he signed.

BEST PRO DEBUT: Cron batted .308/.371/.629 in his short stint. 1B Frazier Hall (16) batted .355/.391/.575 with nine homers, ranking third in the Pioneer League in batting. Maronde went 5-0, 2.14 there, striking out 50 in 46 innings.

BEST ATHLETE: There's no true standout athlete in the class, but OF Zach Borenstein (23) moves well for his strong 5-foot-11, 205-pound frame.

MOST INTRIGUING BACKGROUND: Cron's father Chris reached the majors with the Angels in 1991 and managed the Tigers' Double-A club in 2011, while brother Kevin was a third-round pick of the Mariners in June but didn't sign. Mutz didn't play college ball this spring, but he signed for $100,000 after impressing Los Angeles in a workout and in the Cape Cod League. C Matt Scioscia's (45) father Mike manages the Angels and played in the majors. So did Martinez's dad Chito and unsigned OF Domonic Jose's (15) father Felix.

CLOSEST TO THE MAJORS: Maronde gets the nod over Cron, who had surgery on his knee and a torn labrum in his shoulder after the season.

BEST LATE-ROUND PICK: RHP Daniel Vargas-Vila (28) led NCAA Division II in victories at 16-1, 1.86 last spring. He touched 94 mph after signing and used a three-pitch mix to strike out 56 in as many innings at Rookie-level Orem.

THE ONE WHO GOT AWAY: C Wayne Taylor (14) and Jose (15) both opted to attend Stanford. The Angels made a stronger run at Taylor.

ASSESSMENT: Cron's health and bat obviously will help determine how this class pans out. The Angels got plenty of intriguing, low-mileage arms but not many athletes.

2010

The Angels had six picks in the first two rounds, and so far they've liked what they've seen from 3B Kaleb Cowart (1), 2B Taylor Lindsey (1s) and RHP Daniel Tillman (2). On the downside, RHP Cam Bedrosian (1) had Tommy John surgery and OFs Chevy Clarke and Ryan Bolden failed to make our Top 30 list.

GRADE: C

2009

Los Angeles found a superstar in OF Mike Trout (1) with the 25th overall pick. LHP Tyler Skaggs (1s) has a high ceiling, too, and the Angels used him and LHP Patrick Corbin (2) to get Dan Haren from the Diamondbacks. RHP Garrett Richards (1s) has the stuff to also make an impact in the majors. Unsigned LHP Josh Spence (3) already has raced to the big leagues, while OF Jake Locker (10) went on to become an NFL first-round pick.

GRADE: A

2008

The Angels didn't have a first-rounder but found a pair of marginal big leaguers in RHPs Tyler Chatwood (2), traded to the Rockies for Chris Iannetta this offseason, and Michael Kohn (13). Strong-armed but erratic RHP Johnny Hellweg (16) holds the key to this crop.

GRADE: C+

2007

Not only did Los Angeles lack first- and second-round picks, but they also swiftly cut top selection RHP Jon Bachanov (1s) and failed to sign their best choice, RHP Matt Harvey (3), who went seventh overall in 2010. The Angels did get three fringe big leaguers in INF Andrew Romine (5), RHP Mason Tobin (16, since lost in the Rule 5 draft) and 1B Efren Navarro (50).

GRADE: F

Draft analysis by John Manuel (2011) and Jim Callis (2007-10). Numbers in parentheses indicate draft rounds.

1 MIKE TROUT, OF

Born: Aug. 7, 1991. **B-T:** R-R. **Ht.:** 6-1. **Wt.:** 200.
Drafted: HS—Millville, N.J., 2009 (1st round).
Signed by: Greg Morhardt.

BA GRADE

75
LOW

LARRY GOREN

Despite his athleticism, Trout's Northeast pedigree and reported $3.5 million price tag prompted clubs to hedge their bets on draft day in 2009. He waited until pick No. 25 to hear his name called by the Angels, signed for $1.215 million and has made the 22 teams that passed on him regret it ever since. Trout starred in the 2010 Futures Games in Anaheim, going 2-for-4 with a double, and then made his big league debut in the same ballpark less than a year later on July 8, 2011. Trout ranked as the top prospect in all four leagues he played in on his rapid climb up the minor league ladder. He won the batting and on-base percentage titles in the low Class A Midwest (2010) and Double-A Texas (2011) leagues, and he owns a career .338 average and .422 OBP in the minors. Trout capped his wild ride by winning Baseball America Minor League Player of the Year honors in 2011, hitting .326/.414/.544 as the lone teenager in the Texas League.

Strong, broad-shouldered and built like a football safety, Trout has a high baseball IQ and full-throttle approach that allow him to get the absolute most out of his tools, four of which grade as future plusses or better. He combines a rare blend of bat control, strike-zone management, blazing speed and burgeoning power. His running speed continues to garner the most initial attention. He gets down the first-base line in four seconds flat from the right side to grade as a true 80 on the 20-80 scouting scale. Some evaluators believe he may slow to merely a plus runner as he fills out, but others aren't so pessimistic. A dangerous hitter because of his balanced, quick swing and discerning eye, Trout also remembers how pitchers attack him and makes adjustments on the fly. Double-A hurlers had some success pounding him on the inner half with fastballs, but he avoided slumps by looking to drive the ball line to line and using the opposite field when necessary. Trout connected for a career-high 16 home runs in 2011 while playing in unforgiving home parks, and that total only will increase as he learns to turn on more fastballs in hitter's counts. Some scouts project Trout as an annual .300 hitter with 25-plus homers and 40-plus steals. He completes the five-tool picture with plus range in center field, where he reads the ball well off the bat, and an accurate, if only average, arm.

Trout wore down as his season stretched into September, October and November for the first time. He went just 10-for-55 (.182) in 18 games for the Angels in September, then batted .245/.279/.321 in 25 Arizona Fall League games. Just 20, he could win most of the playing time in left field if Vernon Wells continues to freefall. Center field is out of the question so long as future Gold Glover Peter Bourjos roams that pasture. Regardless, Trout's offensive potential makes him a future all-star at any position.

SCOUTING GRADES

Batting: 70.   **Defense:** 70.
Power: 65.   **Arm:** 50.
Speed: 80.

Based on 20-80 scouting scale and future projection rather than present tools. 50 represents major league average.

Year	Club (League)	Class	AVG	G	AB	R	H	2B	3B	HR	RBI	BB	SO	SB	CS	OBP	SLG
2009	Angels (AZL)	R	.360	39	164	29	59	7	7	1	25	18	28	13	2	.418	.506
	Cedar Rapids (MWL)	LoA	.267	5	15	1	4	0	0	0	0	4	6	0	0	.421	.267
2010	Cedar Rapids (MWL)	LoA	.362	81	312	76	113	19	7	6	39	46	52	45	9	.454	.526
	R. Cucamonga (CAL)	HiA	.306	50	196	30	60	9	2	4	19	27	33	11	6	.388	.434
2011	Arkansas (TL)	AA	.326	91	353	82	115	18	13	11	38	45	76	33	10	.414	.544
	Los Angeles (AL)	MAJ	.220	40	123	20	27	6	0	5	16	9	30	4	0	.281	.390
Major League Totals			.220	40	123	20	27	6	0	5	16	9	30	4	0	.281	.390
Minor League Totals			.338	266	1040	218	351	53	29	22	121	140	195	102	27	.422	.508

2 JEAN SEGURA, SS

Born: March 17, 1990. **B-T:** R-R. **Ht.:** 5-10. **Wt.:** 185. **Signed:** Dominican Republic, 2007. **Signed by:** Leo Perez.

After a broken ankle in 2009 and broken finger in 2009, Segura stayed healthy and showed electrifying tools during a 2010 breakout at low Class A Cedar Rapids. But the injury bug returned with a vengeance last year as he missed all but 44 games with a torn hamstring. The Angels still protected him on the 40-man roster in November. Segura matured as a hitter in 2011, demonstrating a willingness to use the entire field and a more patient approach that put him in hitter's counts more frequently. His strength and explosive, quick-twitch actions excite evaluators almost as much as his short, direct swing. His bat is lightning-quick, and he could consistently bat .290 with as many as 20 homers at his peak because he hits all types of pitches. Scouts regard Segura as an above-average runner, though they qualify that grade by describing his body type as "heavy-legged" or "thick." His arm also grades as plus, which prompted the Angels to move Segura from second base to shortstop last year. His hands and throwing accuracy probably won't play at the position long-term. He has average range at both spots. Segura has the arm strength to handle third base, but the Angels would like to keep him in the middle infield. He could play shortstop as he climbs to Double-A, but most expect that he'll man the keystone in the majors, and no later than 2013—if he stays healthy.

BA GRADE
60
MEDIUM

Year	Club (League)	Class	AVG	G	AB	R	H	2B	3B	HR	RBI	BB	SO	SB	CS	OBP	SLG
2007	Angels (DSL)	R	.324	61	219	39	71	5	2	2	31	22	28	22	6	.392	.393
2008	Angels (AZL)	R	.250	11	36	13	9	0	0	0	4	6	5	1	0	.372	.250
2009	Salt Lake (PCL)	AAA	.421	7	19	2	8	2	0	0	2	0	4	0	0	.421	.526
	Orem (PIO)	R	.346	36	162	33	56	10	4	3	21	11	11	11	3	.392	.512
2010	Cedar Rapids (MWL)	LoA	.313	130	515	89	161	24	12	10	79	45	72	50	10	.365	.464
2011	Angels (AZL)	R	.367	8	30	5	11	4	0	1	5	0	3	0	0	.367	.600
	Inland Empire (CAL)	HiA	.281	44	185	26	52	9	4	3	21	15	26	18	6	.337	.422
Minor League Totals			.316	297	1166	207	368	54	22	19	163	99	149	102	25	.370	.449

3 GARRETT RICHARDS, RHP

Born: May 27, 1988. **B-T:** R-R. **Ht.:** 6-3. **Wt.:** 215. **Drafted:** Oklahoma, 2009 (1st round supplemental). **Signed by:** Arnold Brathwaite.

Despite his impressive arsenal of pitchers, Richards lasted 42 picks in the 2009 draft because he ran up a 6.57 ERA in three years at Oklahoma. He has experienced little resistance in the minors, going 27-8, 3.14 in three seasons. He ranked second in the Texas League in wins (12) and opponent average (.233) and third in ERA (3.15) and WHIP (1.14) last year. Richards learned to sacrifice strikeouts for early-contact outs in 2011. He pitches at 94-95 mph with a sinking, tailing two-seam fastball and holds that velocity all game. His four-seam fastball tops out near 99, and he likes to elevate the pitch for swinging strikes and popups. He de-emphasized his 12-to-6 curveball last season to focus on his 84-89 mph slider, which features power tilt and plus potential. Even his sinking, low-80s changeup has its moments. Richards throws across his body to such a degree that sometimes the life on his sinker and changeup are compromised. Improved fastball command and more faith in his changeup would boost Richard's ceiling to No. 2 starter, though a No. 3 profile is the most likely outcome. He allowed runs in six of his seven big league appearances, indicating a need for minor league time, probably at Triple-A Salt Lake at the outset of 2012.

BA GRADE
55
MEDIUM

Year	Club (League)	Class	W	L	ERA	G	GS	CG	SV	IP	H	HR	BB	SO	K/9	WHIP	AVG
2009	Orem (PIO)	R	3	1	1.53	8	8	0	0	35	37	0	4	30	7.6	1.16	.278
2010	Cedar Rapids (MWL)	LoA	8	4	3.41	19	19	2	0	108	92	6	34	108	9.0	1.16	.229
	R. Cucamonga (CAL)	HiA	4	1	3.89	7	7	0	0	35	38	4	9	41	10.6	1.36	.281
2011	Arkansas (TL)	AA	12	2	3.15	22	21	3	0	143	123	10	40	103	6.5	1.14	.233
	Los Angeles (AL)	MAJ	0	2	5.79	7	3	0	0	14	16	4	7	9	5.8	1.64	.291
Major League Totals			0	2	5.79	7	3	0	0	14	16	4	7	9	5.8	1.64	.291
Minor League Totals			27	8	3.14	56	55	5	0	321	290	20	87	282	7.9	1.17	.242

4 JOHNNY HELLWEG, RHP

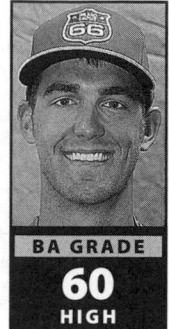

Born: Oct. 29, 1988. **B-T:** R-R. **Ht.:** 6-9. **Wt.:** 210. **Drafted:** Florida CC, 2008 (16th round). **Signed by:** Tom Kotchman.

Signed for $150,000 as a 16th-round selection in 2008, Hellweg walked 129 batters in his first 122 pro innings, most as a reliever. He took off after the Angels shifted him to the rotation at high Class A Inland Empire last June, recording a 2.12 ERA and 80-24 K-BB ratio in 14 starts. Starting every fifth day allowed Hellweg to work on improving his direction to the plate and repeating his arm path during side sessions. Pacing himself also forced him to throttle back his fastball a bit, resulting in dramatically better control. With an effortless delivery, Hellweg tops out near 100 mph and sits at 95-97 with his fastball, which features late sink that induces plenty of grounders. He has improved the command of his low-80s breaking ball, which more often resembles a slider with plus lateral break but occasionally morphs into a knee-buckling curve when he stays on top of the pitch. He tends to throw a changeup with too much velocity, and he used it only sparingly in 2011.

BA GRADE 60 HIGH

Tall and skinny, Hellweg still is growing into his frame and velocity, but if he holds onto his control gains he has No. 2 starter potential. The Angels added him to the 40-man roster in November and Double-A awaits in 2012.

Year	Club (League)	Class	W	L	ERA	G	GS	CG	SV	IP	H	HR	BB	SO	K/9	WHIP	AVG
2008	Angels (AZL)	R	1	0	4.98	14	3	0	0	22	19	1	38	25	10.4	2.63	.224
2009	Angels (AZL)	R	2	1	2.96	18	0	0	6	24	16	0	8	25	9.2	0.99	.186
	Cedar Rapids (MWL)	LoA	0	0	1.35	5	0	0	2	7	4	0	7	7	9.5	1.65	.160
2010	Cedar Rapids (MWL)	LoA	2	4	4.33	41	0	0	16	44	20	2	45	66	13.6	1.49	.133
2011	Inland Empire (CAL)	HiA	6	4	3.73	28	14	0	0	89	75	2	59	113	11.4	1.50	.229
Minor League Totals			11	9	3.83	106	17	0	24	186	134	5	157	236	11.4	1.57	.199

5 C.J. CRON, 1B

Born: Jan. 5, 1990. **B-T:** R-R. **Ht.:** 6-4. **Wt.:** 235. **Drafted:** Utah, 2011 (1st round). **Signed by:** John Gracio.

Cron hit .434 at Utah and led NCAA Division I with an .803 slugging percentage in 2011 while contending with a torn labrum in his right shoulder. The 17th overall pick in June, he signed quickly for $1.467 million and mashed 13 homers in 34 games at Rookie-level Orem before dislocating his right kneecap during a swing. Offseason surgery cleaned up both his shoulder and knee maladies. Cron's plus-plus power could translate to 30 homers at his peak. His bat stays on the same plane as the ball, which prevents him swinging uphill and compromising power for the sake of loft. He uses the whole field and makes adjustments well enough to hit .280 in the big leagues. Pioneer League managers weren't sold on his ability to handle hard stuff inside, though he was considerably dinged up when they saw him. A catcher at Utah prior to his shoulder trouble, Cron projects as an adequate first baseman with an average arm. He's a bottom-of-the-scale runner. Cron's

BA GRADE 55 HIGH

thick, bulky physique turns off some scouts, but nobody will complain as long as he realizes his massive power potential. He could finish the 2012 season in Double-A if he hits the ground running in high Class A.

Year	Club (League)	Class	AVG	G	AB	R	H	2B	3B	HR	RBI	BB	SO	SB	CS	OBP	SLG
2011	Orem (PIO)	R	.308	34	143	30	44	5	1	13	41	10	34	0	0	.371	.629
Minor League Totals			.308	34	143	30	44	5	1	13	41	10	34	0	0	.371	.629

6 KALEB COWART, 3B

Born: June 2, 1992. **B-T:** B-R. **Ht.:** 6-3. **Wt.:** 190. **Drafted:** HS—Adel, Ga., 2010 (1st round). **Signed by:** Chris McAlpin.

Most teams preferred Cowart, the Baseball America 2010 High School Player of the Year, as a pitcher, but the two-way standout aspired to hit. The Angels acceded to his wishes and signed him for $2.3 million as the 18th overall pick in 2010. He began the 2011 season by going 18-for-33 (.545) in his first nine games at Orem but batted .248/.312/.388 the rest of the way. Cowart hits with authority to all fields with plus bat speed, but the natural righthanded hitter still isn't comfortable with his lefty stroke. He lacks the same seamless weight transfer and fluidity with his hands while batting lefthanded, resulting in a muscular, loopy swing. He did hit for power in equal measures from both sides at Orem, actually producing a higher average as a lefty (.295) than as a righty (.247). Scouts expect he'll mature into plus power, though he'll need to improve his selectivity to hit for average. Cowart's athleticism and first-step quickness stand out at

BA GRADE 55 HIGH

third base, though he racked up 16 errors in 66 games, most of them on throws when he failed to set his feet. His plus-plus arm strength affords him plenty of time to make plays on any ball he keeps in front of him. Assuming he refines his lefty swing, Cowart profiles as a starting-caliber third baseman. He's ready for an assignment to low Class A but might need three or four more years to fully develop.

Year	Club (League)	Class	AVG	G	AB	R	H	2B	3B	HR	RBI	BB	SO	SB	CS	OBP	SLG
2010	Angels (AZL)	R	.143	6	21	0	3	0	0	0	4	0	6	0	0	.136	.143
	Orem (PIO)	R	.400	1	5	1	2	0	0	1	3	1	2	0	0	.500	1.000
2011	Orem (PIO)	R	.283	72	283	49	80	12	3	7	40	25	81	11	4	.345	.420
Minor League Totals			.275	79	309	50	85	12	3	8	47	26	89	11	4	.334	.411

7 TAYLOR LINDSEY, 2B

Born: Dec. 2, 1991. **B-T:** L-R. **Ht.:** 6-0. **Wt.:** 195. **Drafted:** HS—Scottsdale, Ariz., 2010 (1st round supplemental). **Signed by:** John Gracio.

**BA GRADE
50
HIGH**

The Angels bucked consensus when they drafted Lindsey 37th overall and signed him for $873,000 in 2010, but he validated that selection by winning Rookie-level Pioneer League MVP honors a year later. He led the league runs (64), hits (105), doubles (28) and extra-base hits (43) while ranking second in batting (.362) and third in slugging (.593). Lindsey ought to continue to hit for high averages with his buggy-whip lefty stroke, especially after learning to take the outside pitch to left field last season. He makes steady contact against both lefties and righties. The Angels love Lindsey's hitting makeup, comparing him to Howard Kendrick because he remains on an even keel whether he collects four hits in a game or none. Lindsey's low hand position and leg kick disrupt his timing against offspeed pitches at times, though he's able to compensate with strong hand-eye coordination. Scouts expect him to grow into average power as he fills out his wiry frame and learns to incorporate his lower half. He's an average defender at second base who ranges well to both sides, though his arm and speed are fringy at best. Lindsey will have to prove his aggressive approach will play at higher levels. He could reach the majors in three years and serve as a top-of-the-order hitter. His journey will continue in low Class A in 2012.

Year	Club (League)	Class	AVG	G	AB	R	H	2B	3B	HR	RBI	BB	SO	SB	CS	OBP	SLG
2010	Angels (AZL)	R	.284	45	194	26	55	12	6	0	18	12	33	8	3	.325	.407
2011	Orem (PIO)	R	.362	63	290	64	105	28	6	9	46	13	46	10	4	.394	.593
Minor League Totals			.331	108	484	90	160	40	12	9	64	25	79	18	7	.366	.519

8 DANIEL TILLMAN, RHP

Born: March 14, 1989. **B-T:** R-R. **Ht.:** 6-1. **Wt.:** 205. **Drafted:** Florida Southern, 2010 (2nd round). **Signed by:** Tom Kotchman.

**BA GRADE
50
HIGH**

In his 2010 pro debut, Tillman led Pioneer League relievers with 13.9 strikeouts per nine innings and a .195 opponent average. The Angels attempted to stretch him out as a starter in low Class A last year, and he went 2-1, 3.09 in five turns. They believe his intensity is better suited for closing, so they returned him to the bullpen for good on May 22. He logged a 2.52 ERA and a 52-20 K-BB ratio afterward in the Midwest, California and Arizona Fall leagues. Tillman pitches with a 92-95 mph fastball with above-average sink and backs it up with a 78-80 mph slider that finishes low in the zone. He delivers both plus pitches with the same motion and the same three-quarters arm slot, adding to their deception. He improved the depth and power on his slider in the AFL, regularly topping out near 84 mph. Tillman has flashed an average changeup from time to time, but he lacks confidence in the pitch because he has spent the bulk of his amateur and pro career in the bullpen. He'll need to throw more strikes at higher levels. Tillman's quick arm and two quality pitches make him a candidate to ride quickly through the minors. He could open 2012 in Double-A and finish 2013 in the big leagues, eventually emerging as a set-up man.

Year	Club (League)	Class	W	L	ERA	G	GS	CG	SV	IP	H	HR	BB	SO	K/9	WHIP	AVG
2010	Orem (PIO)	R	2	2	1.95	22	0	0	10	32	23	0	10	50	13.9	1.02	.195
2011	Cedar Rapids (MWL)	LoA	5	3	2.04	36	5	0	12	66	53	1	32	70	9.5	1.28	.218
	Inland Empire (CAL)	HiA	1	0	4.50	7	0	0	2	8	7	1	2	8	9.0	1.13	.212
Minor League Totals			8	5	2.19	65	5	0	24	107	83	2	44	128	10.8	1.19	.211

9 ARIEL PENA, RHP

BA GRADE

50

HIGH

Born: May 20, 1989. **B-T:** R-R. **Ht.:** 6-3. **Wt.:** 190. **Signed:** Dominican Republic, 2007. **Signed by:** Freddy Rodriguez.

Signed as a 17-year-old, Pena spent three years in Rookie ball and has pitched just four innings above Class A in five pro seasons. After he ranked second in the high Class A California League with 180 strikeouts last year, he earned a place on the Angels' 40-man roster in November. Pena always has shown plus velocity on his fastball and slider, but his shaky command has held him back. He sits at 92-94 mph with his sinker and touches 98 with his four-seamer, showing explosive life when he stays on top of the ball. He throws a hard, late slider at 82-86 mph, getting both called strikes and swings and misses. He flashes a fringy changeup in the low 80s but lacks consistent feel for it. Though he's big and durable, Pena's delivery features enough effort to prompt some scouts to project him as a reliever. He leaves too many pitches up and to his arm side. He jabs at the back of his arm stroke and often loses balance in his delivery, causing his arm to rush to catch up with the rest of his body. Pena can be nearly unhittable when his fastball and slider are working, but he'll have to cut his walk rate (5.3 per nine innings in full-season leagues) to remain a starter. He'll begin 2012 in Double-A.

Year	Club (League)	Class	W	L	ERA	G	GS	CG	SV	IP	H	HR	BB	SO	K/9	WHIP	AVG
2007	Angels (DSL)	R	10	2	2.26	14	14	2	0	80	62	1	32	54	6.1	1.18	.212
2008	Angels (DSL)	R	7	3	1.86	15	15	0	0	97	73	0	26	110	10.2	1.02	.208
2009	Angels (AZL)	R	5	4	3.83	14	6	0	0	49	46	2	15	47	8.6	1.24	.247
2010	R. Cucamonga (CAL)	HiA	0	1	8.71	3	3	0	0	10	10	0	13	8	7.0	2.23	.270
	Cedar Rapids (MWL)	LoA	7	5	3.76	18	18	1	0	103	93	7	60	88	7.7	1.49	.242
2011	Inland Empire (CAL)	HiA	10	6	4.45	27	27	1	0	152	154	10	81	180	10.7	1.55	.264
	Salt Lake (PCL)	AAA	0	0	2.25	1	1	0	0	4	7	0	4	3	6.8	2.75	.389
Minor League Totals			39	21	3.46	92	84	4	0	495	445	20	231	490	8.9	1.37	.240

10 NICK MARONDE, LHP

BA GRADE

50

HIGH

Born: Sept. 5, 1989. **B-T:** B-L. **Ht.:** 6-3. **Wt.:** 205. **Drafted:** Florida, 2011 (3rd round). **Signed by:** Tom Kotchman.

Maronde ran up a 6.15 ERA and lost his rotation spot as a Florida sophomore but rebounded to pitch well in relief in 2011 as the Gators finished runner-up at the College World Series. He signed for $309,600 as a third-round pick and went to the Pioneer League, where he ranked as the top pitching prospect. Maronde returned to starting at Orem, showing above-average velocity, size and the potential for three pitches. He relied heavily on his fastball in college and carried that trend into pro ball, ranging from 90-95 mph and sitting at 92-93 with strong command. He comes right at batters with an up-tempo delivery and has added movement to his four-seam fastball since turning pro. He also improved on a two-seamer that sometimes sinks so dramatically that it resembles a splitter. Maronde flashes an 80-85 mph slider with late break that's untouchable at its best. His fringy changeup plays down because it arrives at the same velocity as his slider. Some scouts project Maronde as a reliever because his strengths lean more toward power than pitchability. The Angels were impressed with his willingness to learn, however, and plan to develop him as a starter. He could jump straight to high Class A for his first full pro season.

Year	Club (League)	Class	W	L	ERA	G	GS	CG	SV	IP	H	HR	BB	SO	K/9	WHIP	AVG
2011	Orem (PIO)	R	5	0	2.14	11	11	0	0	46	36	5	15	50	9.7	1.10	.217
Minor League Totals			5	0	2.14	11	11	0	0	46	36	5	15	50	9.7	1.10	.217

11 JEREMY MOORE, OF

BA GRADE

45

MEDIUM

Born: June 29, 1987. **B-T:** L-R. **Ht.:** 6-1. **Wt.:** 190. **Drafted:** HS—Vivian, La., 2005 (6th round). **Signed by:** Chad MacDonald.

Moore also starred in football, basketball and track in high school, so his baseball skills were unrefined when the Angels drafted him in the sixth round in 2005. He went through the minors one level at a time, and his climb reached its summit with a big league callup last September. He served mostly as a pinch-runner and defensive replacement, going 1-for-8, but did start the season finale. Moore batted .318/.353/.614 with 12 of his 15 homers in June, July and August last year, after a similar second-half surge with Double-A Arkansas in 2010. He saw more pitches in 2011 but still strikes out too much. Moore may never be more than a fringy hitter because he struggles to transfer weight to the front side of his swing, collapsing his backside and creating an uphill bat path. His best tool is plus-plus speed, as evidenced by a minor league-leading 18 triples last year, which also testifies to his average power. He's still learning to steal bases and was caught 10 times in 31 tries in 2011. He's a solid defender in center field who would be stretched as an everyday right fielder because he has a fringy arm. Moore has hit .258 against lefthanders in Double-A and Triple-A, but if spotted against righties in the big leagues he could forge a career as a reserve outfielder because of sturdy supporting tools.

Year	Club (League)	Class	AVG	G	AB	R	H	2B	3B	HR	RBI	BB	SO	SB	CS	OBP	SLG
2005	Angels (AZL)	R	.227	34	110	15	25	3	1	0	11	11	46	12	6	.303	.273
2006	Angels (AZL)	R	.254	41	142	25	36	7	2	3	19	18	37	4	8	.348	.394
2007	Orem (PIO)	R	.272	68	254	50	69	13	6	14	54	19	68	17	5	.329	.535
2008	Cedar Rapids (MWL)	LoA	.240	96	362	47	87	11	12	17	48	21	125	28	10	.284	.478
2009	Arkansas (TL)	AA	.333	7	21	5	7	0	1	2	10	3	7	1	1	.423	.714
	R. Cucamonga (CAL)	HiA	.279	124	470	61	131	20	12	11	58	34	144	17	13	.330	.443
2010	Arkansas (TL)	AA	.303	128	456	72	138	14	10	13	61	39	122	24	10	.358	.463
2011	Salt Lake (PCL)	AAA	.298	113	426	76	127	24	18	15	66	21	114	21	10	.331	.545
	Los Angeles (AL)	MAJ	.125	8	8	3	1	0	0	0	0	0	2	0	0	.125	.125
Major League Totals			.125	8	8	3	1	0	0	0	0	0	2	0	0	.125	.125
Minor League Totals			.277	611	2241	351	620	92	62	75	327	166	663	124	63	.329	.473

12 LUIS JIMENEZ, 3B

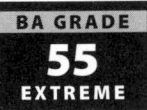

BA GRADE

45

MEDIUM

Born: Jan. 18, 1988. **B-T:** R-R. **Ht.:** 6-1. **Wt.:** 205. **Signed:** Dominican Republic, 2005. **Signed by:** Leo Perez.

Jimenez conquered three levels of the minors in the past two seasons to earn a place on the Angels' 40-man roster in November. He lost the 2009 season to a torn labrum in his throwing shoulder but recovered to reach Double-A in 2011, where he played a career-high 101 games at third base. Jimenez smacked 18 homers and led the Texas League with 40 doubles, but scouts aren't convinced his power will play at higher levels because he's such a free swinger. He gives away too many at-bats now to project more than average power. He does have a quick, smooth stroke, makes enough contact and hits breaking balls well enough, so he should maintain a solid average. His plate coverage makes him dangerous in RBI situations, and he drove in 94 runs to rank second in the TL. Jimenez has recovered his arm strength, but he's a heavy-footed, fringy defender who makes only the routine plays at third base. He'll begin 2012 in Triple-A and could serve as a big league bridge from Alberto Callaspo to 2010 first-rounder Kaleb Cowart.

Year	Club (League)	Class	AVG	G	AB	R	H	2B	3B	HR	RBI	BB	SO	SB	CS	OBP	SLG
2006	Angels (DSL)	R	.284	25	74	12	21	9	1	1	10	7	9	4	0	.341	.473
2007	Angels (DSL)	R	.313	67	256	49	80	19	2	11	55	10	27	16	4	.347	.531
2008	Orem (PIO)	R	.331	66	284	57	94	28	6	15	65	11	45	6	2	.361	.630
2009	Did Not Play—Injured																
2010	Cedar Rapids (MWL)	LoA	.292	43	168	32	49	15	5	2	38	11	27	6	2	.332	.476
	R. Cucamonga (CAL)	HiA	.286	81	318	52	91	31	4	12	43	13	43	15	8	.324	.522
2011	Arkansas (TL)	AA	.290	125	490	62	142	40	1	18	94	27	72	15	6	.335	.486
Minor League Totals			.300	407	1590	264	477	142	19	59	305	79	223	62	22	.339	.525

13 FABIO MARTINEZ, RHP

BA GRADE

55

EXTREME

Born: Oct. 29, 1989. **B-T:** R-R. **Ht.:** 6-3. **Wt.:** 190. **Signed:** Dominican Republic, 2007. **Signed by:** Leo Perez.

Martinez rocketed to No. 6 on this list two years ago on the strength of a mid-90s fastball and gaudy strikeout numbers. He carried elevated strikeout and walk ratios to low Class A in 2010 but missed the final month of the season with shoulder tendinitis. The injury lingered into 2011, and he spent most of the season on the disabled list while attempting to rebuild strength in his shoulder. He returned to action in the Rookie-level Arizona League on Aug. 17, but a comebacker broke a bone in his ankle in just his second relief appearance. He missed instructional league as a result. In a system chock full of hard throwers, Martinez stands out when he's at his best. Using a high arm slot, he throws a 90-96 mph fastball that touches 98. He pairs his heater with a low-80s slider that features extreme horizontal tilt. Martinez pitches to the radar gun and shows little feel for changing speeds, so he hasn't fully embraced a changeup. Busy, hard-to-repeat mechanics do his control and command no favors. Rather than risk losing him in the Rule 5 draft, the Angels added Martinez to the 40-man roster in November. Because he hasn't been at full strength since July 2010, a full and healthy season in high Class A in 2012 would be an accomplishment. Los Angeles hasn't given up on him as a starter, but his power stuff and lack of control and durability eventually may lead him to the bullpen, where he has upside as a closer.

Year	Club (League)	Class	W	L	ERA	G	GS	CG	SV	IP	H	HR	BB	SO	K/9	WHIP	AVG
2007	Angels (DSL)	R	1	2	6.75	13	3	0	1	25	27	0	26	30	10.7	2.09	.270
2008	Angels (DSL)	R	6	1	1.53	13	13	1	0	76	55	1	32	93	11.0	1.14	.202
2009	Angels (AZL)	R	3	2	3.26	14	13	0	0	61	45	1	36	92	13.6	1.34	.197
	Orem (PIO)	R	1	0	3.86	2	2	0	0	7	5	2	2	10	12.9	1.00	.192
2010	Cedar Rapids (MWL)	LoA	7	3	3.92	20	19	0	0	103	80	6	76	141	12.3	1.51	.216
2011	Angels (AZL)	R	0	0	0.00	2	0	0	0	2	2	0	1	2	7.7	1.29	.222
Minor League Totals			18	8	3.34	64	50	1	1	275	214	10	173	368	12.0	1.41	.213

14 NICK MUTZ, RHP

BA GRADE
50
HIGH

Born: June 15, 1990. **B-T:** R-R. **Ht.:** 6-1. **Wt.:** 190. **Drafted:** Cotati, Calif. (no school), 2011 (9th round). **Signed by:** Joel Murrie.

In Ric Wilson's first draft as Angels scouting director in 2011, the club took several big arms with short track records, with Mutz serving as the prime example. He didn't pitch during the spring after leaving Dakota State (S.D.), an NAIA program, following the 2010 season. Working off a tip, Los Angeles worked him out prior to the draft, selected him in the ninth round and signed him for $100,000 in late July after following him in the Cape Cod League. The Angels see Mutz developing as a starter, though they plugged him into Orem bullpen last summer. He ranges from 93-95 mph with his fastball and throws a darting slider that has the makings of a plus pitch. Mutz's arm action is loose and he locates his pitches well down in the zone, especially after the Orem coaching staff helped him streamline his mechanics. He toned down a max-effort delivery and eliminating a head snap. He shows only a rudimentary feel for a changeup, so softening that pitch and improving his fastball command top his to-do list for 2012. Mutz bounced back quickly from multi-inning relief outings, so Los Angeles believes he can handle a starting job in low Class A.

Year	Club (League)	Class	W	L	ERA	G	GS	CG	SV	IP	H	HR	BB	SO	K/9	WHIP	AVG
2011	Orem (PIO)	R	2	3	2.31	12	0	0	2	23	20	4	5	25	9.6	1.07	.230
Minor League Totals			2	3	2.31	12	0	0	2	23	20	4	5	25	9.6	1.07	.230

15 TRAVIS WITHERSPOON, OF

BA GRADE
50
HIGH

Born: April 16, 1989. **B-T:** R-R. **Ht.:** 6-2. **Wt.:** 190. **Drafted:** Spartanburg Methodist (S.C.) JC, 2009 (12th round). **Signed by:** Chris McAlpin.

Witherspoon helped propel Spartanburg Methodist (S.C.) JC to the Junior College World Series in 2009, then signed for $100,000 as a 12th-round draft pick. The Angels had questions about his ability to hit for average, but they took a chance because they like his speed and defensive ability. Among players in the organization, only big leaguer Peter Bourjos can surpass Witherspoon's plus-plus range and instincts in center field. His arm strength is average. Witherspoon puts his speed to good use on the bases, too. He has 76 steals in 88 career attempts, good for an 86 percent success rate. Witherspoon has the athleticism and bat speed to factor as an offensive player if he shortens his swing and enhances his pitch recognition. He gets in the habit of uppercutting the ball, and Los Angeles would prefer that he level his swing and focus on line drives while showing more willingness to take the ball to the opposite field. Witherspoon works as hard as any Angels prospect and should be at least a reserve outfielder in the big leagues. He got a taste of high Class A during the last two weeks of 2011 and will pick up there this season.

Year	Club (League)	Class	AVG	G	AB	R	H	2B	3B	HR	RBI	BB	SO	SB	CS	OBP	SLG
2009	Angels (AZL)	R	.231	5	13	2	3	1	0	0	0	1	3	0	0	.286	.308
	Orem (PIO)	R	.227	58	194	37	44	3	6	6	26	10	61	10	1	.281	.397
2010	Orem (PIO)	R	.309	71	288	57	89	11	3	10	45	24	73	20	0	.365	.472
2011	Cedar Rapids (MWL)	LoA	.245	102	404	60	99	16	4	12	42	36	103	44	9	.313	.394
	Inland Empire (CAL)	HiA	.279	16	68	15	19	4	0	1	10	5	14	2	2	.338	.382
Minor League Totals			.263	252	967	171	254	35	13	29	123	76	254	76	12	.323	.416

16 MIKE CLEVINGER, RHP

BA GRADE
50
HIGH

Born: Dec. 21, 1990. **B-T:** R-R. **Ht.:** 6-4. **Wt.:** 202. **Drafted:** Seminole State (Fla.) JC, 2011 (4th round). **Signed by:** Tom Kotchman.

Clevinger transferred from The Citadel following his freshman year to attend Seminole State (Fla.) JC, returning him closer to his Jacksonville home and making him eligible for the 2011 draft. He also shifted from the rotation to the bullpen, where he racked up 52 strikeouts in 32 innings as a closer for the Trojans. The Angels grabbed Clevinger in the fourth round and signed him for $250,000 in mid-August following his successful run in the Cape Cod League, where he fanned 25 in 20 innings. Clevinger showed high-end velocity in three brief relief outings for Orem, ranging from 92-96 mph. He backed his fastball with a plus hard slider and a changeup that has shown flashes of excellence. He missed instructional league with arm fatigue. Clevinger could move quickly as a reliever, but Los Angeles hasn't ruled out the prospect of starting. He joins sixth-rounder Austin Wood and ninth-rounder Nick Mutz as power righthanders from the 2011 draft who don't have a lot of mileage on their arms. All three could begin the 2012 season together in low Class A.

Year	Club (League)	Class	W	L	ERA	G	GS	CG	SV	IP	H	HR	BB	SO	K/9	WHIP	AVG
2011	Orem (PIO)	R	0	0	2.25	3	0	0	0	4	3	0	2	5	11.3	1.25	.200
Minor League Totals			0	0	2.25	3	0	0	0	4	3	0	2	5	11.3	1.25	.200

17 RANDAL GRICHUK, OF

BA GRADE

50
HIGH

Born: Aug. 13, 1991. **B-T:** R-R. **Ht.:** 6-1. **Wt.:** 195. **Drafted:** HS—Rosenberg, Texas, 2009 (1st round). **Signed by:** Kevin Ham.

Grichuk led the Arizona League with 76 hits after signing for $1.242 million as the 24th overall pick in the 2009 draft, but little has gone right for him since. Injuries have limited him to just 117 games in the last two years. He lost time in 2010 when he tore a ligament in his right thumb in early May and broke his wrist when he ran into an outfield wall in August. His 2011 season got off on the wrong foot when he fouled a ball off his kneecap and cracked it in spring training, and then he sprained the medial collateral ligament in his other knee during a slide in extended spring. He returned to action on July 10 and climbed to high Class A to finish the year. When healthy, Grichuk shows the plus bat speed and strong wrists that got him drafted in the first round, but he needs at-bats to learn to identify breaking balls and iron out his plate discipline. He has the raw pop to hit 25-30 homers annually in the big leagues. Grichuk entered pro ball as a one-dimensional slugger, and he has worked hard to improve his arm strength and defense in right field. Both now grade as average, as does his baserunning. With a clean bill of health, Grichuk is ready to tackle the California League for real in 2012.

Year	Club (League)	Class	AVG	G	AB	R	H	2B	3B	HR	RBI	BB	SO	SB	CS	OBP	SLG
2009	Angels (AZL)	R	.322	53	236	47	76	13	10	7	53	9	64	6	4	.352	.551
2010	Angels (AZL)	R	.327	12	49	7	16	3	2	4	10	3	9	0	0	.365	.714
	Cedar Rapids (MWL)	LoA	.292	52	202	41	59	19	4	7	36	9	50	4	0	.327	.530
2011	Angels (AZL)	R	.333	7	24	2	8	1	1	0	6	2	4	0	0	.357	.458
	Cedar Rapids (MWL)	LoA	.230	32	122	12	28	7	4	2	13	6	29	0	1	.267	.402
	Inland Empire (CAL)	HiA	.283	14	53	13	15	4	2	1	6	0	13	0	0	.316	.491
Minor League Totals			.294	170	686	122	202	47	23	21	124	29	169	10	5	.328	.522

18 CAM BEDROSIAN, RHP

BA GRADE

50
EXTREME

Born: Oct. 2, 1991. **B-T:** R-R. **Ht.:** 6-0. **Wt.:** 205. **Drafted:** HS—Sharpsburg, Ga., 2010 (1st round). **Signed by:** Chris McAlpin.

The Angels tabbed Bedrosian, the son of 1987 National League Cy Young Award winner Steve Bedrosian, with the 29th pick in the 2010 draft and signed him for $1.116 million. Elbow soreness knocked him out of action only a month after signing, and he also missed out on instructional league. Rest and rehab didn't work, so Bedrosian had Tommy John surgery in May after failing to take the hill during spring training. When healthy, Bedrosian pumps 92-94 mph fastballs and touches 96, a testament to a quick arm and impressive lower-body strength. At 6 feet he's on the short side for a righthander, but he repeats his delivery and throws a hard slider that chews up righthanders. As with many high school pitchers, Bedrosian's changeup lags behind his other offerings, but the Angels saw enough promise with the pitch to project him as a starter. He's expected to be healthy in time for spring training, but he may stay behind in extended spring until Rookie leagues begin play in June.

Year	Club (League)	Class	W	L	ERA	G	GS	CG	SV	IP	H	HR	BB	SO	K/9	WHIP	AVG
2010	Angels (AZL)	R	0	2	4.50	5	4	0	0	12	13	0	7	10	7.5	1.67	.283
2011	Did Not Play—Injured																
Minor League Totals			0	2	4.50	5	4	0	0	12	13	0	7	10	7.5	1.67	.283

19 ALEXI AMARISTA, 2B/OF

BA GRADE

45
MEDIUM

Born: April 6, 1989. **B-T:** L-R. **Ht.:** 5-8. **Wt.:** 150. **Signed:** Venezuela, 2007. **Signed by:** Denny Suarez.

Amarista slashed, bunted and ran his way into the Angels' plans in 2009, hitting .319 to win the low Class A Midwest League batting title. He hasn't replicated those gaudy numbers in two years since, but he did earn his first big league callup last April 25. He filled in for injured utilityman Maicer Izturis, who like Amarista hails from Venezuela and is listed at 5-foot-8. Amarista profiles as a lesser version of Izturis because he lacks the veteran's defensive versatility and ability to switch-hit. He has the hands and range to handle the middle infield, but his fringy arm strength fits best at second base. He played every outfield position for Triple-A Salt Lake last season as the Angels broadened his defensive portfolio. Amarista could stand to tighten his strike zone and not give away as many at-bats, but he likes to jump on the first fastball he can handle. His power grades out well-below-average, his swing can get loopy and he doesn't hit the ball the other way well. He's an average runner who draws praise for his high energy level and all-out hustle. Los Angeles sees Amarista as a pesky, offensive-oriented backup who can play four or five positions. He'll head back to Triple-A to wait for his next callup.

Year	Club (League)	Class	AVG	G	AB	R	H	2B	3B	HR	RBI	BB	SO	SB	CS	OBP	SLG
2007	Angels (DSL)	R	.340	65	241	52	82	14	4	5	39	25	23	16	6	.408	.494
2008	Angels (AZL)	R	.332	51	202	46	67	6	4	2	21	29	20	22	14	.416	.431
	Cedar Rapids (MWL)	LoA	.000	1	2	0	0	0	0	0	0	0	1	0	0	.000	.000
2009	Cedar Rapids (MWL)	LoA	.319	125	477	84	152	39	10	4	49	50	61	38	20	.390	.468
2010	R. Cucamonga (CAL)	HiA	.303	72	297	39	90	19	6	4	39	19	42	17	10	.349	.448
	Arkansas (TL)	AA	.288	48	191	25	55	2	1	1	20	13	15	4	1	.332	.325
	Salt Lake (PCL)	AAA	.400	15	65	13	26	6	3	0	9	1	4	4	2	.412	.585
2011	Salt Lake (PCL)	AAA	.292	86	363	49	106	24	5	4	50	22	56	15	8	.337	.419
	Los Angeles (AL)	MAJ	.154	23	52	2	8	3	1	0	5	2	8	0	0	.182	.250
Major League Totals			.154	23	52	2	8	3	1	0	5	2	8	0	0	.182	.250
Minor League Totals			.314	463	1838	308	578	110	33	20	227	159	222	116	61	.373	.443

20 KOLE CALHOUN, OF/1B

BA GRADE 45 MEDIUM

Born: Oct. 14, 1987. **B-T:** L-L. **Ht.:** 5-10. **Wt.:** 200. **Drafted:** Arizona State, 2010 (8th round). **Signed by:** John Gracio.

Calhoun batted .321/.478/.616 with 17 homers in 224 at-bats as an Arizona State senior in 2010 and lasted until the eighth round of the draft because his maxed-out physique left little room for projection. Signed for $36,000, he jumped straight to high Class A in 2011 and hit .324/.410/.547 with 64 extra-base hits, which ranked third in the California League. Calhoun wins admirers not for his raw tools but for his blue-collar approach, plate discipline and professionalism. He sees his share of pitches and knows what he can handle, seldom missing a pitch he can drive. He's confident and doesn't dwell on bad at-bats. Scouts who believe in Calhoun say he compensates for fringy bat speed with a strong, leveraged swing, but he'll still probably be better suited to a reserve role than a starting job. He provides at least average range on the outfield corners and at first base, and his plus arm strength is a good match for right field. Though he grades out as a below-average runner, he swiped 20 bases in 30 tries last year because of strong instincts. He also played 22 games in center field, though a big league team probably would have a better option. Calhoun will head to Double-A in 2012.

Year	Club (League)	Class	AVG	G	AB	R	H	2B	3B	HR	RBI	BB	SO	SB	CS	OBP	SLG
2010	Orem (PIO)	R	.292	56	202	43	59	14	4	7	42	39	45	3	1	.411	.505
2011	Inland Empire (CAL)	HiA	.324	133	512	94	166	36	6	22	99	73	96	20	10	.410	.547
Minor League Totals			.315	189	714	137	225	50	10	29	141	112	141	23	11	.410	.535

21 CARLOS RAMIREZ, C

BA GRADE 45 MEDIUM

Born: March 19, 1988. **B-T:** R-R. **Ht.:** 5-11. **Wt.:** 210. **Drafted:** Arizona State, 2009 (8th round). **Signed by:** John Gracio.

Ramirez drew physical comparisons to Bengie Molina coming out of Arizona State, and he has improved his defensive play to the point that he now profiles as a major league backup. Scouts like Ramirez's quiet set-up, soft hands, sure feet and quick, short arm stroke. He sacrifices his body to block balls in the dirt, and he regularly produces above-average pop times on throws to second base, typically around 1.8-1.9 seconds. However, he threw out just 24 percent of basestealers in 2011. He moves well behind the plate despite poor speed and a thick, stocky frame. Ramirez shows pull-side power when he cheats on fastballs, but he lacks the bat speed to be a factor on offense. He knows his strike zone and seldom goes outside it, usually connecting when he swings. He hits the ball to all fields with a line-drive stroke, though he may struggle to hit for average or draw walks when pitchers at higher levels challenge him with hard stuff. Ramirez will return to Double-A.

Year	Club (League)	Class	AVG	G	AB	R	H	2B	3B	HR	RBI	BB	SO	SB	CS	OBP	SLG
2009	Orem (PIO)	R	.376	42	149	34	56	18	0	7	36	35	26	0	0	.500	.638
2010	Cedar Rapids (MWL)	LoA	.226	77	257	39	58	9	2	9	34	35	72	3	2	.337	.381
2011	Cedar Rapids (MWL)	LoA	.259	31	108	20	28	3	0	3	12	15	17	1	2	.367	.370
	Inland Empire (CAL)	HiA	.348	52	181	28	63	21	0	4	28	16	33	1	0	.403	.530
	Arkansas (TL)	AA	.222	4	9	1	2	0	0	0	1	0	1	1	0	.222	.222
Minor League Totals			.294	206	704	122	207	51	2	23	111	101	149	6	4	.394	.470

22 TREVOR RECKLING, LHP

BA GRADE 45 HIGH

Born: May 22, 1989. **B-T:** L-L. **Ht.:** 6-2. **Wt.:** 205. **Drafted:** HS—Newark, N.J., 2007 (8th round). **Signed by:** Greg Morhardt.

Reckling won Angels minor league pitcher of the year honors when he raced to Double-A as a 19-year-old in 2009, but his 2.93 ERA with Arkansas obscured his walk rate of 5.0 per nine innings. Since then, little has gone right. He has spent the bulk of the past two seasons attempting to tame the Texas League, with mixed results. He didn't pitch after July 11 last year because of a strained elbow ligament. Reckling's fastball has lost velocity since its 2009 peak, and he now sits at 86-88 mph and touches 90 with solid downhill plane and dramatically improved command. Because his fastball is now fringy, he lives and dies with the quality of his secondary stuff. His mid-70s slider induces swings and misses with its late break. His fading changeup rates as his best pitch, in part because his herky-jerky delivery deceives batters. Reckling experimented with different arm angles last year in an effort to recover velocity. Even if his days of working in the low 90s are history, he still may have a future as a reliever. He could start 2012 in Triple-A if his elbow is healthy.

Year	Club (League)	Class	W	L	ERA	G	GS	CG	SV	IP	H	HR	BB	SO	K/9	WHIP	AVG
2007	Angels (AZL)	R	3	1	2.75	9	5	0	2	36	33	2	7	55	13.8	1.11	.236
2008	Cedar Rapids (MWL)	LoA	10	7	3.37	26	26	1	0	152	137	8	59	128	7.6	1.29	.246
2009	R. Cucamonga (CAL)	HiA	1	2	0.95	3	3	0	0	19	9	2	3	16	7.6	0.63	.138
	Arkansas (TL)	AA	8	7	2.93	23	23	1	0	135	118	4	75	106	7.0	1.43	.244
2010	Salt Lake (PCL)	AAA	4	7	8.53	14	14	0	0	70	99	11	50	46	5.9	2.14	.339
	Arkansas (TL)	AA	3	6	4.56	14	14	1	0	79	74	4	35	62	7.1	1.38	.254
2011	Arkansas (TL)	AA	4	7	3.73	17	17	2	0	99	104	11	35	63	5.7	1.40	.274
Minor League Totals			33	37	3.98	106	102	5	2	590	574	42	264	476	7.3	1.42	.260

23 DONN ROACH, RHP

BA GRADE
45
HIGH

Born: Dec. 14, 1989. **B-T:** R-R. **Ht.:** 6-1. **Wt.:** 200. **Drafted:** JC of Southern Nevada, 2010 (3rd round supplemental). **Signed by:** Jeff Scholzen.

Roach won three Nevada state championships at Bishop Gorman High in Las Vegas and attended Arizona as a college freshman before transferring to JC of Southern Nevada for the 2010 season. After he ran up a 6.04 ERA in his 2010 pro debut, the Angels worked on streamlining his mechanics, softening his landing and improving his direction to the plate. He turned in a strong full-season debut with Cedar Rapids in 2011, showing three pitches and finishing second in the minors among qualified relievers with a 3.6 ground-out/airout ratio. Roach sits at 90-92 mph with his fastball, which lives at the bottom of the strike zone. His slurvy breaking ball features high-70s velocity and late tilt at times. Instead of a traditional changeup, he shows strong feel for a splitter. Roach loses control in some outings because his busy delivery can be difficult to repeat. With three pitches and a taste of pro success under his belt, he'll move to the rotation in high Class A this season.

Year	Club (League)	Class	W	L	ERA	G	GS	CG	SV	IP	H	HR	BB	SO	K/9	WHIP	AVG
2010	Orem (PIO)	R	4	1	6.04	16	10	0	0	54	64	6	16	59	9.9	1.49	.294
2011	Cedar Rapids (MWL)	LoA	5	5	3.45	45	0	0	2	70	73	1	20	68	8.7	1.32	.266
Minor League Totals			9	6	4.57	61	10	0	2	124	137	7	36	127	9.2	1.40	.278

24 AUSTIN WOOD, RHP

BA GRADE
50
EXTREME

Born: July 11, 1990. **B-T:** R-R. **Ht.:** 6-4. **Wt.:** 225. **Drafted:** Southern California, 2011 (6th round). **Signed by:** Tim Corcoran.

Wood pitched Cotuit to the Cape Cod League championship in 2010 while leading the circuit in opponent average (.144), ranking second in ERA (0.74) and hitting 99 mph in the all-star game. He's never demonstrated that type of ceiling at any other stop, however. A 36th-round pick of the Astros out of high school in 2008, Wood struggled at Florida State in 2009 and pitched his way out of the St. Petersburg (Fla.) JC rotation in 2010. The Rays drafted him in the fourth round anyway but failed to sign him after his big summer. Wood transferred again, to Southern California, where he went just 5-7, 5.61 as a junior last spring. The Angels spent a sixth-round pick and $180,000 to see if they can help him harness his stuff. Wood pitches at 92-96 mph with his fastball, which gets hit harder than it should because it's fairly straight, and he lacks another pitch to keep opponents honest. His changeup regressed after he made progress with it on the Cape, and his breaking ball is slurvy. His control is as inconsistent as his secondary pitches. Los Angeles will initially use Wood as a starter, though it's not a given that he's ready to succeed in low Class A in 2012.

Year	Club (League)	Class	W	L	ERA	G	GS	CG	SV	IP	H	HR	BB	SO	K/9	WHIP	AVG
2011	Orem (PIO)	R	0	0	20.25	2	0	0	0	1	4	1	0	1	6.8	3.00	.500
Minor League Totals			0	0	20.25	2	0	0	0	1	4	1	0	1	6.8	3.00	.500

25 ANDREW ROMINE, INF

BA GRADE
40
LOW

Born: Dec. 24, 1985. **B-T:** B-R. **Ht.:** 6-1. **Wt.:** 190. **Drafted:** Arizona State, 2007 (5th round). **Signed by:** John Gracio.

Romine's younger brother Austin made his big league debut with the Yankees in September, a year after Andrew first appeared in the majors with the Angels. Their father Kevin spent seven seasons in the big leagues with the Red Sox. Andrew has strong middle-infield defensive skills with average range, speed and arm strength at shortstop, but he hasn't grown much as an offensive player. He hits for a decent average, draws walks and steals his share of bases, but his power is nonexistent. He slugged .346 in extremely hitter-friendly conditions in Salt Lake last year. He comes up short in strength and bat speed, rarely squaring up the ball. His saving grace is that he's a switch-hitter who can handle the bat from the left side, reaching base at a .371 clip as a lefty during the past two seasons in the minors. Romine could fit with a club that needs a proficient defender to back up shortstop as well as second and third base, but his below-average bat limits his ceiling. He'll team up with Alexi Amarista in the Salt Lake middle infield again in 2012.

Year	Club (League)	Class	AVG	G	AB	R	H	2B	3B	HR	RBI	BB	SO	SB	CS	OBP	SLG
2007	Orem (PIO)	R	.286	56	231	38	66	6	6	5	35	16	38	12	4	.337	.429
2008	Cedar Rapids (MWL)	LoA	.260	126	461	79	120	21	4	2	34	55	76	62	18	.347	.336
2009	R. Cucamonga (CAL)	HiA	.278	131	479	68	133	13	9	1	36	51	83	26	11	.351	.349
2010	Arkansas (TL)	AA	.282	106	383	55	108	15	4	3	34	50	66	21	9	.370	.366
	Los Angeles (AL)	MAJ	.091	5	11	0	1	0	0	0	0	0	4	0	0	.091	.091
2011	Salt Lake (PCL)	AAA	.281	105	381	67	107	9	2	4	35	45	87	23	6	.363	.346
	Los Angeles (AL)	MAJ	.125	10	16	2	2	0	0	0	0	1	6	1	0	.176	.125
Major League Totals			.111	15	27	2	3	0	0	0	0	1	10	1	0	.143	.111
Minor League Totals			.276	524	1935	307	534	64	25	15	174	217	350	144	48	.354	.358

26 ORANGEL ARENAS, RHP

BA GRADE 45 HIGH

Born: March 31, 1989. **B-T:** R-R. **Ht.:** 6-0. **Wt.:** 200. **Signed:** Venezuela, 2007. **Signed by:** Denny Suarez.

Arenas and Ariel Pena both began the 2010 season in the Cedar Rapids rotation before their paths diverged. Arenas rocketed to high Class A after nine starts and spent all of 2011 in Double-A, yet the Angels didn't add him to the 40-man roster. Pena, on the other hand, stayed in high Class A in last year but did get protected on the 40-man. The key reason: Pena generates swings and misses with his power fastball and slider, while Arenas lacks an out pitch. Arenas sits at 91-93 mph with plus sinking and tailing action on his fastball. He throws from an easy delivery with a clean arm action that allows him to throw strikes consistently. His sinker would play up with improved secondary stuff, but he throws a spinning slider that hangs as often as it bites. His changeup is too firm and in the same mid-80s range as his slider, so Los Angeles taught him a splitter in instructional league to give him a weapon versus lefthanders. They hit .309/.353/.489 against him last year. The Angels haven't given up on Arenas, but his upside appears to be No. 5 starter or middle reliever.

Year	Club (League)	Class	W	L	ERA	G	GS	CG	SV	IP	H	HR	BB	SO	K/9	WHIP	AVG
2007	Angels (DSL)	R	1	3	2.45	10	4	0	1	33	31	1	6	21	5.7	1.12	.250
2008	Angels (DSL)	R	8	1	1.36	13	13	1	0	86	52	2	25	71	7.4	0.90	.173
2009	Orem (PIO)	R	4	3	4.65	15	15	0	0	70	76	7	18	48	6.2	1.35	.281
2010	Cedar Rapids (MWL)	LoA	4	5	2.01	9	9	0	0	54	41	2	15	36	6.0	1.04	.212
	R. Cucamonga (CAL)	HiA	7	3	4.55	17	17	0	0	97	93	9	45	71	6.6	1.42	.255
2011	Arkansas (TL)	AA	9	10	4.48	25	25	0	0	149	176	12	39	67	4.1	1.45	.296
Minor League Totals			33	25	3.56	89	83	1	1	488	469	33	148	314	5.8	1.26	.254

27 MATT SHOEMAKER, RHP

BA GRADE 40 LOW

Born: Sept. 27, 1986. **B-T:** R-R. **Ht.:** 6-2. **Wt.:** 225. **Signed:** Eastern Michigan, NDFA 2008. **Signed by:** Joel Murrie.

Shoemaker wasn't drafted out of high school in Trenton, Mich., or in four years at Eastern Michigan, even though he was on scouts' radar after solid summer league performances. He waited another four years to create a ripple in pro ball, winning Angels minor league pitcher of the year honors in 2011. He won the Texas League ERA title at 2.48 and led the league in strikeouts (129), WHIP (1.07), opponent average (.228) and complete games (five) as well. After signing as a nondrafted free agent, he takes nothing for granted and is all business on the mound. Shoemaker attacks hitters with three pitches, though none grades better than solid. His fastball ranges from 87-93 mph and parks at 90, featuring a little life and tailing action. He tries to get lefthanders to chase a low-80s splitter under the zone, and he locates the pitch for strikes as well. His slider shows consistent three-quarters break but not a lot of power at 81-82 mph. He has touched 95 mph in short bursts, which combined with command of his splitter and slider could land him in a major league swingman role. The Angels have tried to bump Shoemaker to Triple-A during the past two seasons, but he hasn't cleared the hurdle. He'll get another shot in 2012.

Year	Club (League)	Class	W	L	ERA	G	GS	CG	SV	IP	H	HR	BB	SO	K/9	WHIP	AVG
2008	Angels (AZL)	R	1	0	4.50	3	0	0	1	4	6	0	0	4	9.0	1.50	.353
2009	Cedar Rapids (MWL)	LoA	4	1	3.39	20	5	0	0	64	53	5	23	54	7.6	1.19	.227
	R. Cucamonga (CAL)	HiA	1	0	3.12	3	3	0	0	17	14	2	1	13	6.8	0.87	.212
2010	R. Cucamonga (CAL)	HiA	7	8	4.93	20	20	2	0	122	138	14	39	119	8.8	1.45	.283
	Salt Lake (PCL)	AAA	2	1	5.87	3	2	0	0	15	20	0	8	9	5.3	1.83	.328
2011	Salt Lake (PCL)	AAA	0	2	8.14	4	4	0	0	21	28	3	12	12	5.1	1.90	.326
	Arkansas (TL)	AA	12	5	2.48	23	23	5	0	156	132	17	35	129	7.4	1.07	.228
Minor League Totals			27	17	3.85	76	57	7	1	400	391	41	118	340	7.7	1.27	.255

28 A.J. SCHUGEL, RHP

BA GRADE 45 HIGH

Born: June 27, 1989. **B-T:** R-R. **Ht.:** 6-1. **Wt.:** 190. **Drafted:** Central Arizona JC, 2010 (25th round). **Signed by:** John Gracio.

The Padres took Schugel in the 33rd round of the 2007 draft as a third baseman out of a Colorado high school but didn't sign him. The Angels drafted him in the 25th round three years later and persuaded him to take up pitching full-time after giving him a $40,000 bonus. His father Jeff serves as a pro scout for the club. Schugel pitched sparingly at Central Arizona JC, though he did sit at 92 mph in bullpen sessions. He shows surprising polish for a recently converted pitcher and throws two pitches that project as at least average. Schugel's 89-93 mph fastball features above-average sink and sneaky life, and a clean delivery helps him find the strike zone. His slurvy breaking ball resembles a slider but often lacks definition, while he's still gaining confidence in his below-average changeup. Schugel began 2011 in the Cedar Rapids bullpen and pitched his way into the rotation in mid-June, going 2-2, 2.48 in 12 starts. He continued as a starter after a mid-August promotion to high Class A, where he'll begin the 2012 season.

Year	Club (League)	Class	W	L	ERA	G	GS	CG	SV	IP	H	HR	BB	SO	K/9	WHIP	AVG
2010	Angels (AZL)	R	0	0	1.72	11	0	0	2	16	15	0	5	12	6.9	1.28	.259
	Orem (PIO)	R	2	2	8.59	6	0	0	1	7	8	0	6	9	11.0	1.91	.267
2011	Cedar Rapids (MWL)	LoA	4	3	2.59	25	12	0	1	90	73	2	39	80	8.0	1.24	.220
	Inland Empire (CAL)	HiA	1	2	5.03	4	4	0	0	20	22	1	6	15	6.9	1.42	.278
Minor League Totals			7	7	3.18	46	16	0	4	133	118	3	56	116	7.8	1.31	.236

29 RYAN BRASIER, RHP

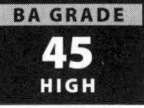

BA GRADE
45
HIGH

Born: Aug. 26, 1987. **B-T:** R-R. **Ht.:** 6-0. **Wt.:** 205. **Drafted:** Weatherford (Texas) JC, 2007 (6th round). **Signed by:** Arnold Brathwaite.

Brasier converted from high school catcher to junior college pitcher at Weatherford (Texas) JC, and the Angels made him a sixth-round pick and signed him for $123,000 in 2007. He worked as a starter in the second half of 2009 and in 2010, throwing a no-hitter in the latter season, but he has spent the bulk of his time in pro ball lighting up radar guns out of the bullpen. Brasier ranges from 92-96 mph and attacks batters with a tailing, sinking fastball that he delivers from a short, quick arm stroke. Brasier did a better job of extending through the front side of his delivery in 2011, getting better location down in the zone. Brasier also has a power slider that often features short, late break away from the sweet spot of opponents' bats. He seldom throws his below-average changeup and doesn't need it in relief. While he finds the strike zone frequently, Brasier still misses his spots often enough to limit his ceiling to that of middle reliever. He'll open the season back in Salt Lake.

Year	Club (League)	Class	W	L	ERA	G	GS	CG	SV	IP	H	HR	BB	SO	K/9	WHIP	AVG
2007	Orem (PIO)	R	1	2	2.08	26	0	0	9	30	22	2	7	26	7.7	0.96	.212
2008	Cedar Rapids (MWL)	LoA	1	3	1.59	23	0	0	9	28	22	0	14	24	7.6	1.27	.210
	Angels (AZL)	R	1	0	3.86	4	0	0	1	5	3	0	1	2	3.9	0.86	.188
	R. Cucamonga (CAL)	HiA	0	0	2.70	3	0	0	1	3	3	0	2	0	0.0	1.50	.300
2009	Arkansas (TL)	AA	2	1	5.56	8	0	0	2	11	13	1	7	6	4.8	1.76	.283
	R. Cucamonga (CAL)	HiA	5	4	5.23	27	14	0	0	98	103	17	32	93	8.5	1.38	.270
2010	Arkansas (TL)	AA	7	12	5.07	28	23	1	0	142	127	28	68	94	6.0	1.37	.242
2011	Arkansas (TL)	AA	0	1	0.71	25	0	0	16	25	18	1	14	26	9.2	1.26	.198
	Salt Lake (PCL)	AAA	2	1	5.00	25	0	0	3	27	26	2	9	26	8.7	1.30	.257
Minor League Totals			19	24	4.28	169	37	1	41	370	337	51	154	297	7.2	1.33	.244

30 LOEK VAN MIL, RHP

BA GRADE
45
HIGH

Born: Sept. 15, 1984. **B-T:** R-R. **Ht.:** 7-1. **Wt.:** 220. **Signed:** Netherlands, 2005. **Signed by:** Howie Norsetter (Twins).

Van Mil pitched a career-high 66 innings in 2011 and turned in his best performance at the Double-A level, but that wasn't enough for him to preserve his spot on the 40-man roster. The Angels outrighted him to the minors in November, and he went unselected in the Rule 5 draft. Los Angeles acquired Van Mil from the Twins in September 2010 for Brian Fuentes. Staying healthy has been a significant obstacle for Van Mil, who at 7-foot-1 is the tallest player in the pro ranks and would surpass the 6-foot-11 Jon Rauch as the tallest in major league history if he makes that jump. Van Mil's stratospheric release point affords him steep plane on his pitches, but his long levers also create problems repeating his delivery. He began to find the strike zone more consistently last year. Van Mil's fastball sinks and tails at 91-93 mph, and batters struggle to square the pitch up. His slurvy slider and sinking changeup both range from 80-84 mph and grade as average when his delivery is in sync. Van Mil has a lot to prove in Triple-A this year.

Year	Club (League)	Class	W	L	ERA	G	GS	CG	SV	IP	H	HR	BB	SO	K/9	WHIP	AVG
2006	Twins (GCL)	R	1	2	3.30	10	8	0	0	44	51	3	17	24	4.9	1.56	.290
2007	Elizabethton (APP)	R	2	2	2.63	13	0	0	0	24	14	0	17	23	8.6	1.29	.171
2008	Beloit (MWL)	LoA	2	2	3.22	28	0	0	3	45	36	5	25	42	8.5	1.37	.221
2009	Fort Myers (FSL)	HiA	0	0	2.86	25	0	0	5	35	29	3	17	23	6.0	1.33	.236
	New Britain (EL)	AA	1	1	2.45	8	0	0	1	7	7	0	6	5	6.1	1.77	.269
2010	Fort Myers (FSL)	HiA	0	1	4.50	3	0	0	0	4	4	0	0	6	13.5	1.00	.267
	New Britain (EL)	AA	1	2	6.37	23	0	0	0	30	40	1	22	21	6.4	2.09	.315
	Arkansas (TL)	AA	0	0	0.00	1	0	0	0	1	0	0	1	0	0.0	1.00	.000
2011	Arkansas (TL)	AA	3	5	2.04	30	1	0	0	66	53	4	23	46	6.2	1.15	.220
Minor League Totals			10	15	3.17	141	9	0	9	255	234	16	128	190	6.7	1.42	.245

Los Angeles Dodgers

BY JIM SHONERD

After two years that have been like a bad dream that wouldn't end for Dodgers fans, there's finally hope that the franchise will be able to move forward in 2012.

In early November, embattled owner Frank McCourt agreed to sell the team and Dodger Stadium through a bankruptcy auction, ending a saga that began when McCourt and wife Jamie, then the team's CEO, announced the end of their marriage in October 2009. What followed were two years of court battles over control of the franchise, first between the McCourts, then between Frank McCourt and Major League Baseball, which accused the couple of taking $189 million out of the team to fund an extravagant lifestyle.

MLB took the fight to McCourt in April by appointing a trustee to oversee the team's day-to-day operations in an attempt to remove him from power. The battle for control of the team's finances continued through the summer, with commissioner Bud Selig rejecting a 17-year, $3 billion television deal with Fox that would have given McCourt a desperately needed influx of cash. McCourt and the league came to an agreement in the offseason creating an orderly process to sell the team.

A season that also included the near-fatal beating of a Giants fan in a Dodger Stadium parking lot on Opening Day and the lowest attendance in 11 years did provide on-field highlights, however. Homegrown players Matt Kemp and Clayton Kershaw blossomed into two of the game's brightest stars. Kershaw won the National League Cy Young Award and pitching triple crown, while Kemp took home Baseball America's Major League Player of the Year award.

Though Los Angeles fell out of the playoff race by midseason, it went 41-28 after the all-star break and managed to finish with a winning 82-79 record under rookie manager Don Mattingly. The farm system provided plenty of contributions, most notably Dee Gordon, who hit .304 and showed spectacular defensive ability at shortstop. Rubby de la Rosa, Javy Guerra, Kenley Jansen and Jerry Sands also showed promise, though de la Rosa needed Tommy John surgery.

With Gordon and Sands graduating to the majors and Trayvon Robinson traded to the Mariners, the system lacks potential impact hitters outside of outfielder Alfredo Silverio. There's plenty more in the pitching pipeline, however, from top prospect Zach Lee to the cadre of arms who pitched at Double-A Chattanooga last year, such as Allen Webster and Nate Eovaldi.

The Dodgers hope to move forward after the end of Frank McCourt's troubled ownership

LARRY GOREN

TOP 30 PROSPECTS

1. Zach Lee, rhp	**16.** Aaron Miller, lhp
2. Allen Webster, rhp	**17.** Ethan Martin, rhp
3. Nate Eovaldi, rhp	**18.** Alex Santana, 3b
4. Alfredo Silverio, of	**19.** Alex Castellanos, of
5. Chris Reed, lhp	**20.** Kyle Russell, of
6. Garrett Gould, rhp	**21.** Scott Van Slyke, of/1b
7. Chris Withrow, rhp	**22.** Angelo Songco, of/1b
8. Josh Lindblom, rhp	**23.** Ryan O'Sullivan, rhp
9. Joc Pederson, of	**24.** Josh Wall, rhp
10. Tim Federowicz, c	**25.** Pratt Maynard, c
11. James Baldwin III, of	**26.** Ivan DeJesus Jr., inf
12. Angel Sanchez, rhp	**27.** Jake Lemmerman, ss
13. Jonathan Garcia, of	**28.** Gorman Erickson, c
14. Scott Barlow, rhp	**29.** O'Koyea Dickson, 1b
15. Shawn Tolleson, rhp	**30.** Blake Smith, of

McCourt's financial woes have taken their toll on the team's ability to bring in amateur talent. Los Angeles spent just $3.5 million on its 2011 draft class, fifth-lowest total in baseball and less than the back-loaded $5.25 million deal it gave Lee alone in 2010.

The Dodgers' once-strong presence in Latin America also has greatly diminished. Just two international signings are among Los Angeles' top 30 prospects, as the team has been relegated to hoping it can strike gold with bargain deals such as the $50,000 it gave Silverio in 2003 or the $15,000 it cost them to land de la Rosa in 2007.

General Manager: Ned Colletti. **Farm Director:** De Jon Watson. **Scouting Director:** Logan White.

Class	Team	League	W	L	Pct	Finish*	Manager(s)
Majors	Los Angeles Dodgers	National	82	79	.509	7th (16)	Don Mattingly
Triple-A	Albuquerque Isotopes	Pacific Coast	70	74	.486	t-8th (16)	Lorenzo Bundy
Double-A	Chattanooga Lookouts	Southern	77	62	.554	3rd (10)	Carlos Subero
High A	Rancho Cucamonga Quakes	California	80	60	.571	2nd (10)	Juan Bustabad
Low A	Great Lakes Loons	Midwest	72	67	.518	6th (16)	John Shoemaker
Rookie	Ogden Raptors	Pioneer	41	35	.539	t-4th (8)	Damon Berryhill
Rookie	AZL Dodgers	Arizona	34	22	.607	3rd (13)†	Jody Reed
Overall 2011 Minor League Record			374	320	.539	3rd (30)	

*Finish in overall standings (No. of teams in league). †League champion.

LAST YEAR'S TOP 30

Player, Pos.		Status
1.	Dee Gordon, ss	Majors
2.	Zach Lee, rhp	No. 1
3.	Rubby de la Rosa, rhp	Majors
4.	Chris Withrow, rhp	No. 7
5.	Allen Webster, rhp	No. 2
6.	Jerry Sands, of/1b	Majors
7.	Scott Elbert, lhp	Majors
8.	Kenley Jansen, rhp	Majors
9.	Ethan Martin, rhp	No. 17
10.	Trayvon Robinson, of	(Mariners)
11.	Leon Landry, of	Dropped out
12.	James Baldwin III, of	No. 11
13.	Aaron Miller, lhp	No. 16
14.	Ivan DeJesus Jr. 2b/ss	No. 26
15.	Kyle Russell, of	No. 20
16.	Josh Lindblom, rhp	No. 8
17.	Nate Eovaldi, rhp	No. 3
18.	Garrett Gould, rhp	No. 6
19.	Brian Cavazos-Galvez, of	Dropped out
20.	Ralson Cash, rhp	Dropped out
21.	Jonathan Garcia, of	No. 13
22.	Pedro Baez, 3b	Dropped out
23.	Scott Schebler, of	Dropped out
24.	Jake Lemmerman, ss	No. 27
25.	Joc Pederson, of	No. 9
26.	Javy Guerra, rhp	Majors
27.	Blake Smith, of	No. 30
28.	Angelo Songco, of	No. 22
29.	Derek Cone, rhp	Dropped out
30.	Luis Vasquez, rhp	Dropped out

BEST TOOLS

Best Hitter for Average	Joc Pederson
Best Power Hitter	Kyle Russell
Best Strike-Zone Discipline	Gorman Erickson
Fastest Baserunner	James Baldwin III
Best Athlete	James Baldwin III
Best Fastball	Nate Eovaldi
Best Curveball	Garrett Gould
Best Slider	Chris Reed
Best Changeup	Allen Webster
Best Control	Zach Lee
Best Defensive Catcher	Tim Federowicz
Best Defensive Infielder	Pedro Baez
Best Infield Arm	Pedro Baez
Best Defensive Outfielder	James Baldwin III
Best Outfield Arm	Blake Smith

PROJECTED 2015 LINEUP

Catcher	Tim Federowicz
First Base	Jerry Sands
Second Base	Ivan DeJesus Jr.
Third Base	Alex Santana
Shortstop	Dee Gordon
Left Field	Joc Pederson
Center Field	Matt Kemp
Right Field	Alfredo Silverio
No. 1 Starter	Clayton Kershaw
No. 2 Starter	Zach Lee
No. 3 Starter	Chad Billingsley
No. 4 Starter	Allen Webster
No. 5 Starter	Nate Eovaldi
Closer	Kenley Jansen

TOP PROSPECTS OF THE DECADE

Year	Player, Pos.	2011 Org.
2002	Ricardo Rodriguez, rhp	Out of baseball
2003	James Loney, 1b	Dodgers
2004	Edwin Jackson, rhp	Cardinals
2005	Joel Guzman, ss/of	Chunichi (Japan)
2006	Chad Billingsley, rhp	Dodgers
2007	Andy LaRoche, 3b	Athletics
2008	Clayton Kershaw, lhp	Dodgers
2009	Andrew Lambo, of	Pirates
2010	Dee Gordon, ss	Dodgers
2011	Zach Lee, rhp	Dodgers

TOP DRAFT PICKS OF THE DECADE

Year	Player, Pos.	2011 Org.
2002	James Loney, 1b	Dodgers
2003	Chad Billingsley, rhp	Dodgers
2004	Scott Elbert, lhp	Dodgers
2005	*Luke Hochevar, rhp (1st round supp.)	Royals
2006	Clayton Kershaw, lhp	Dodgers
2007	Chris Withrow, rhp	Dodgers
2008	Ethan Martin, rhp	Dodgers
2009	Aaron Miller, lhp (1st round supp.)	Dodgers
2010	Zach Lee, rhp	Dodgers
2011	Chris Reed, lhp	Dodgers

*Did not sign.

LARGEST BONUSES IN CLUB HISTORY

Hiroki Kuroda, 2007	$7,300,000
Zach Lee, 2010	$5,250,000
Clayton Kershaw, 2006	$2,300,000
Joel Guzman, 2001	$2,255,000
Ben Diggins, 2000	$2,200,000

MINOR LEAGUE DEPTH CHART

LOS ANGELES DODGERS

TOP 2012 ROOKIE: Nate Eovaldi, rhp. He held his own in the majors at age 21 could join the rotation full-time this year.

BREAKOUT PROSPECT: Scott Barlow, rhp. The sixth-round pick from last year's draft already has added velocity and has feel for a nice four-pitch mix.

SLEEPER: Chris O'Brien, c. The son of former big league catcher Charlie O'Brien has an advanced hitting approach and surprised the Dodgers with his defense after they took him in the 18th round last June.

SOURCE OF TOP 30 TALENT

Homegrown	28	Acquired	2
College	11	Trades	2
Junior College	0	Rule 5 draft	0
High school	14	Independent leagues	0
Draft-and-follow	1	Free agents/waivers	0
Nondrafted free agents	0		
International	2		

LF
Joc Pederson (9)
Scott Van Slyke (21)
Bobby Coyle
Nick Akins

CF
James Baldwin (11)
Noel Cuevas
Leon Landry
Scott Woodward

RF
Alfredo Silverio (4)
Jonathan Garcia (13)
Alex Castellanos (19)
Kyle Russell (20)
Blake Smith (30)
Scott Schebler

3B
Alex Santana (18)
Pedro Baez
Jesus Valdez

SS
Delvis Morales
Justin Sellers
Justin Boudreaux

2B
Ivan DeJesus Jr. (26)
Jake Lemmerman (27)
Elian Herrera
Scott Wingo
Malcolm Holland

1B
Angelo Songco (22)
O'Koyea Dickson (29)
Brian Cavazos-Galvez
Austin Gallagher
Matt Kirkland

C
Tim Federowicz (10)
Pratt Maynard (25)
Gorman Erickson (28)
J.T. Wise
Chris O'Brien
Tyler Ogle

LHP

LHSP	LHRP
Chris Reed (5)	Eric Eadington
Aaron Miller (16)	Cole St. Clair
Mike Antonini	Wilkin de la Rosa
Rick Anton	Jarret Martin
Ryan Christenson	
Greg Wilborn	

RHP

RHSP	RHRP
Zach Lee (1)	Josh Lindblom (8)
Allen Webster (2)	Shawn Tolleson (15)
Nate Eovaldi (3)	Josh Wall (24)
Garrett Gould (6)	Scott McGough
Chris Withrow (7)	Juan Rodriguez
Angel Sanchez (12)	Steven Ames
Scott Barlow (14)	Luis Vasquez
Ethan Martin (17)	Logan Bawcom
Ryan O'Sullivan (23)	Javier Solano
Stephen Fife	Yimi Garcia
Ralston Cash	
Red Patterson	
Derek Cone	
Andres Santiago	
Jon Michael Redding	
Matt Magill	

2011   BONUSES: $3.5 MILLION

BEST PURE HITTER: 1B O'Koyea Dickson (12) has the sound righthanded swing and the bat speed to hit for average. He did exactly that, batting .333 at Rookie-level Ogden. The Dodgers also like the bats of 3B Alex Santana (2) and C Chris O'Brien (18).

BEST POWER HITTER: Dickson smacked 13 homers and led the Pioneer League in slugging at .603. He hit a ball clear out of AT&T Park during a playoff game as a high school sophomore in 2006. Santana has the projectable 6-foot-4 frame and bat speed to match Dickson's power in time.

FASTEST RUNNER: 2B Malcolm Holland (33) can run the 60-yard dash in 6.4-6.5 seconds. SS Justin Boudreaux (14) isn't quite that quick, though he did steal 17 bases without getting caught in 44 pro games.

BEST DEFENSIVE PLAYER: 2B Scott Wingo (11) is a sure-handed defender whose glovework helped South Carolina win its second straight College World Series. Santana has the athleticism and arm strength to be a quality defender at the hot corner.

BEST FASTBALL: Arm strength was the commodity Los Angeles got the most of in this draft. LHP Chris Reed (1) worked at 92-94 mph and hit 96 often as a reliever at Stanford. RHP Garrett Bolt (23) touches 95-96, albeit without much command. RHPs Ryan O'Sullivan (4) and Scott McGough (5) also have fastballs in the same range.

BEST SECONDARY PITCH: Reed has a plus slider and a strong changeup as well, so the Dodgers will develop him as a starter.

BEST PRO DEBUT: Dickson. McGough had a 2.21 ERA and eight saves in low Class A. OF Joey Winker (28) led the Arizona League with 46 RBIs and a .442 on-base percentage, though he was old for a complex league at 21.

BEST ATHLETE: Holland had a scholarship to play defensive back at Boise State. He has middle-of-the-diamond tools, though he lacks the arm for shortstop, and is learning to switch-hit. He's similar to former Dodger Trayvon Robinson, a long-term project who made it to the majors with the Mariners after a July trade.

MOST INTRIGUING BACKGROUND: 2B Stefan Jarrin's (40) grandfather Jaime is Los Angeles' Spanish-language broadcaster and won the Hall of Fame's Frick Award in 1998. O'Sullivan's brother Sean pitches for the Royals. Santana's father Rafael, O'Brien's father Charlie and OF Devin Shines' (38) father Razor all played in the big leagues.

CLOSEST TO THE MAJORS: Reed, though McGough will give him a run as a fast-tracked reliever.

BEST LATE-ROUND PICK: Dickson or O'Brien. Dickson reminds the Dodgers a little bit of Paul Goldschmidt, whom they drafted out of high school. O'Brien had a reputation as being a better hitter than a defender, so his catch-and-throw skills were a pleasant surprise.

THE ONE WHO GOT AWAY: LHP Jamaal Moore (10), a raw athlete whose fastball sits in the high 80s, decided to attend Los Angeles Harbor JC rather than turn pro.

ASSESSMENT: The financially strapped Dodgers ranked 26th in MLB in spending. They went over slot only for Reed, who got a mere $77,000 over MLB's recommendation and will have to carry this draft crop.

2010   BONUSES: $8.0 MILLION

RHP Zach Lee (1), the system's No. 1 prospect, got a $5.25 million bonus—more money than the Dodgers spent on any other total draft from 2007-11. OFs James Baldwin III (4) and Joc Pederson (11) and RHP Shawn Tolleson (30) also have shown well. Unsigned RHP Kevin Gausman (6) will be an early first-rounder in the 2012 draft.

GRADE: C+

2009   BONUSES: $4.0 MILLION

Los Angeles didn't have a first-round selection and didn't get much beyond its top two choices, LHP Aaron Miller (1s) and RHP Garrett Gould (2).

GRADE: C

2008   BONUSES: $4.4 MILLION

The Dodgers pulled off four heists by getting SS Dee Gordon (4), RHPs Nate Eovaldi (11) and Allen Webster (18) and OF/1B Jerry Sands (25) as low as they did. RHP Josh Lindblom (2) pitched well in the big league bullpen last summer, and there's still hope for live-armed RHP Ethan Martin (1).

GRADE: B+

2007   BONUSES: $3.6 MILLION

RHP Chris Withrow (1) has an electric arm but has been exceedingly slow to develop. There may not be another future big leaguer in this crop, unless it's unsigned OF Matt Szczur (38).

GRADE: D

Draft analysis by Jim Callis. Numbers in parentheses indicate draft rounds.

1 ZACH LEE, RHP

Born: Sept. 13, 1991. **B-T:** R-R. **Ht.:** 6-4. **Wt.:** 190.
Drafted: HS—McKinney, Texas, 2010 (1st round).
Signed by: Calvin Jones.

BA GRADE
60
MEDIUM

BILL MITCHELL

When Los Angeles drafted Lee with the 28th overall selection in 2010, the pick was met with plenty of skepticism. Not because of any lack of ability on his part, but rather because it was suspected the budget-conscious Dodgers intended to save money by not signing him. In addition to his prowess on the mound, Lee also was a highly rated quarterback recruit, throwing for 2,565 yards and 31 touchdowns as a senior at McKinney (Texas) High, where his top wide receiver was current Braves prospect Matt Lipka. Lee intended to play both sports for Louisiana State, and he spent the summer of 2010 taking classes at LSU and working out with the football team. Still, Los Angeles believed it could get a deal done. The Dodgers shocked the industry at the Aug. 16 deadline by signing him for $5.25 million, the largest draft bonus in franchise history. They spread the bonus over five years in a heavily backloaded deal that paid him less up front than MLB's slot value for the No. 28 pick ($1,134,000). Lee missed three weeks last May due to elbow tightness that proved to be nothing major, and that was his only real speed bump in an otherwise solid pro debut. He allowed two earned runs or fewer in 19 of his 24 starts at low Class A Great Lakes.

Lee has a deep arsenal and the pitchability to get the most out of it. His fastball generally ranges from 89-93 mph, but he can reach back for more when he needs it, touching as high as 98. He commands his fastball to both sides of the plate, and he also has an advanced feel for manipulating it. He can make his fastball sink or turn it into a cutter has developed into a true weapon. Lee featured a hard curveball that tended to get slurvy in high school, but he worked on developing a curve and slider as separate offerings in 2011. He made huge strides with the slider by the end of the season, allowing him to get in on the hands of lefthanders, whom he held to a .229/.291/.341 line. The curve still shows promising spin and depth at 79-83 mph when it's on, but it continues to come and go. He also features an 81-84 mph changeup that has a chance to be an average pitch down the road.

Lee earns high marks for his poise on the mound and the leadership he showed on Great Lakes' staff, a trait owing to his quarterbacking days. He does a good job of controlling games and doesn't get frustrated when something doesn't go his way. His big, strong frame elicits physical comparisons to Chris Carpenter. His delivery has some crossfire to it, though it also gives him deception. Los Angeles worked on improving his direction to the plate in instructional league, but he doesn't require any major mechanical changes.

The Dodgers considered promoting Lee to high Class A Rancho Cucamonga or even Double-A Chattanooga toward the end of 2011 but elected to let him finish out the year in Great Lakes. He'll likely begin 2012 in high Class A, but he has the polish and the stuff to handle a more aggressive timetable than the usual high school draft pick. Los Angeles believes he'll be a frontline starter and he could arrive in the majors by the end of 2013.

Year	Club (League)	Class	W	L	ERA	G	GS	CG	SV	IP	H	HR	BB	SO	K/9	WHIP	AVG
2011	Great Lakes (MWL)	LoA	9	6	3.47	24	24	0	0	109	101	9	32	91	7.5	1.22	.242
Minor League Totals			9	6	3.47	24	24	0	0	109	101	9	32	91	7.5	1.22	.242

2 ALLEN WEBSTER, RHP

Born: Feb. 10, 1990. **B-T:** R-R. **Ht.:** 6-3. **Wt.:** 185. **Drafted:** HS—Madison, N.C., 2008 (18th round). **Signed by:** Lon Joyce.

The Dodgers converted Webster from shortstop after stealing him in the 18th round of the 2008 draft for $20,000. He quickly has become one of their best pitching prospects, easily handling the challenging high Class A California League and holding his own in Double-A before tiring down the stretch in 2011. Webster shows plus pitches across the board when he has everything working. He has an easy delivery and 90-95 mph fastball that peaks at 97 mph with plenty of sink, helping him generate grounders all day long. He throws both a slider and curveball that are plus pitches at times, though at others he gets caught between the two. He has some trouble staying on top of his curve but it shows sharp three-quarters bite when it's on. Webster's changeup could be his best pitch, featuring sink and fade at 79-83 mph, though some scouts think he tips it off by slowing his arm speed. Los Angeles had him work on honing his armside fastball command in instructional league, but he already shows advanced pitchability for his age. One Dodgers official compares Webster to Derek Lowe, and his stuff gives him the potential to be a No. 2 starter. He'll likely end up back in Double-A to start 2012, with an outside chance of pitching his way into the big league rotation in spring training.

BA GRADE
55
MEDIUM

Year	Club (League)	Class	W	L	ERA	G	GS	CG	SV	IP	H	HR	BB	SO	K/9	WHIP	AVG
2008	Dodgers (GCL)	R	1	1	3.44	12	0	0	1	18	12	1	17	13	6.4	1.58	.197
2009	Dodgers (AZL)	R	2	1	2.08	12	8	0	0	48	35	0	14	56	10.6	1.03	.197
	Ogden (PIO)	R	2	0	3.00	4	3	0	0	21	23	1	4	21	9.0	1.29	.277
2010	Great Lakes (MWL)	LoA	12	9	2.88	26	23	0	0	131	119	6	53	114	7.8	1.31	.239
2011	R. Cucamonga (CAL)	HiA	5	2	2.33	9	9	0	0	54	46	2	21	62	10.3	1.24	.228
	Chattanooga (SL)	AA	6	3	5.04	18	17	1	0	91	101	7	36	73	7.2	1.51	.286
Minor League Totals			28	16	3.27	81	60	1	1	363	336	17	145	339	8.4	1.32	.245

3 NATE EOVALDI, RHP

Born: Feb. 13, 1990. **B-T:** R-R. **Ht.:** 6-3. **Wt.:** 195. **Drafted:** HS—Alvin, Texas, 2008 (11th round). **Signed by:** Chris Smith.

Eovaldi fell to the 11th round of the 2008 draft because he had Tommy John surgery as a high school junior and made a strong commitment to Texas A&M. The Dodgers weren't scared off and signed him for $250,000. After a solid but unspectacular start to his pro career, he took off in 2011, dominating Double-A and making his big league debut at age 21. Eovaldi has a power arsenal, led by a heater that works at 94-98 mph with good downhill angle and occasional late life. His fastball touched triple digits when he came out of the bullpen in the majors. He has a wrist wrap in his arm action that has led to inconsistency, but he did a better job in 2011 of staying over the rubber longer and allowing his arm to clear, helping his fastball command. Eovaldi ditched his curveball after 2010 and developed an 85-91 mph slider that's a plus pitch with tilt and late movement at its best. His changeup is fringy but good enough to keep hitters honest. His key going forward will be to throw more strikes. Some scouts believe Eovaldi fits best as a two-pitch, late-inning reliever, but Los Angeles will keep him a starter. He'll vie for a spot in the big league rotation in spring training.

BA GRADE
55
MEDIUM

Year	Club (League)	Class	W	L	ERA	G	GS	CG	SV	IP	H	HR	BB	SO	K/9	WHIP	AVG
2008	Dodgers (GCL)	R	0	1	1.13	6	0	0	1	8	6	0	3	9	10.1	1.13	.207
	Ogden (PIO)	R	0	0	0.00	1	0	0	0	3	1	0	0	2	6.8	0.38	.125
2009	Great Lakes (MWL)	LoA	3	5	3.27	26	16	0	1	96	95	2	41	71	6.6	1.41	.265
2010	Inland Empire (CAL)	HiA	3	5	4.45	16	14	2	0	85	99	3	33	58	6.1	1.55	.302
	Dodgers (AZL)	R	0	1	4.32	3	3	0	0	8	6	0	4	10	10.8	1.20	.214
	Ogden (PIO)	R	1	0	1.80	1	1	0	0	5	3	0	0	4	7.2	0.60	.167
2011	Chattanooga (SL)	AA	6	5	2.62	20	19	0	0	103	76	3	46	99	8.7	1.18	.203
	Los Angeles (NL)	MAJ	1	2	3.63	10	6	0	0	35	28	2	20	23	6.0	1.38	.230
Major League Totals			1	2	3.63	10	6	0	0	35	28	2	20	23	6.0	1.38	.230
Minor League Totals			13	17	3.30	73	53	2	2	308	286	8	127	253	7.4	1.34	.250

4 ALFREDO SILVERIO, OF

Born: May 6, 1987. **B-T:** R-R. **Ht.:** 6-0. **Wt.:** 205. **Signed:** Dominican Republic, 2003. **Signed by:** Angel Santana.

Silverio has made incremental progress since signing for $50,000 as a 16-year-old. He didn't rise above Class A until 2011, his eighth pro season, but he proved he could handle advanced pitching. He led the Double-A Southern League in total bases (289) and the minors in triples (18) while finishing fifth in the SL batting race (.306). He earned a trip to the Futures Game and a spot on the 40-man roster. Silverio could end up with five average or better tools. He has a quick, powerful swing, generating line drives from gap to gap and average home run power, mostly to his pull side. The biggest difference-maker for him in 2011 was how much he tightened his strike zone, putting together quality at-bats and forcing pitchers to execute pitches to get him out. He never has walked much and still has an aggressive mentality at the plate, but he has shown he can make adjustments. Silverio played all three outfield spots in 2011, seeing the most action in center field. He's a tick above average runner who fits best on a corner. His solid arm strength and throwing accuracy play well in right field. In line to move up to Triple-A Albuquerque in 2012, Silverio can be a solid everyday major league outfielder. He offers an in-house option if Andre Ethier departs via free agency after 2012.

BA GRADE 55 MEDIUM

Year	Club (League)	Class	AVG	G	AB	R	H	2B	3B	HR	RBI	BB	SO	SB	CS	OBP	SLG
2004	Dodgers2 (DSL)	R	.240	59	192	18	46	6	2	1	16	7	36	5	6	.273	.307
2005	Dodgers (DSL)	R	.244	25	82	11	20	2	0	1	14	10	15	2	2	.316	.305
2006	Dodgers (DSL)	R	.276	61	225	36	62	12	6	6	48	18	44	6	3	.335	.462
2007	Dodgers (GCL)	R	.373	51	193	38	72	9	3	6	46	11	32	5	3	.406	.544
2008	Great Lakes (MWL)	LoA	.263	95	376	37	99	15	4	10	45	7	83	6	3	.279	.404
2009	Great Lakes (MWL)	LoA	.284	132	490	75	139	34	6	13	61	26	104	2	5	.320	.457
2010	Inland Empire (CAL)	HiA	.292	95	387	66	113	27	6	12	43	18	63	17	7	.324	.486
	Chattanooga (SL)	AA	.063	4	16	1	1	0	0	0	0	0	3	0	0	.063	.063
2011	Chattanooga (SL)	AA	.306	132	533	90	163	42	18	16	85	30	91	11	12	.340	.542
Minor League Totals			.287	654	2494	372	715	147	45	65	358	127	471	54	41	.322	.460

5 CHRIS REED, LHP

Born: May 20, 1990. **B-T:** L-L. **Ht.:** 6-4. **Wt.:** 195. **Drafted:** Stanford, 2011 (1st round). **Signed by:** Orsino Hill.

After splurging on Zach Lee in 2010, the cash-strapped Dodgers were limited financially in the first round. They took Reed, who posted a 1.23 ERA as Stanford's closer in the spring, with the 16th overall pick. They signed him for $1.589 million, slightly above MLB's slot recommendation, and plan on developing him as a starter. Though Reed made only one start in three seasons at Stanford, he has the repertoire to work in a big league rotation. His fastball ranges from 89-96 mph, with tail and sink on his two-seamer and late boring action on his four-seamer. He throws a late-breaking slider at 85-86, and while it's often a plus pitch is also can get slurvy. He has good feel for a changeup that has action similar to his two-seamer's. Reed earns high marks for his competitiveness and intelligence. Los Angeles was encouraged by how well he repeated his delivery and held his velocity for five innings during a playoff start at Rancho Cucamonga. The Dodgers agreed to allow Reed to return to Stanford over the winter to finish his degree. When he gets back, he'll open his first full pro season back in high Class A. It remains to be seen how his arm will respond to the increased workload, but the ingredients are there for him to move quickly with the ceiling of a No. 2 starter.

BA GRADE 55 MEDIUM

Year	Club (League)	Class	W	L	ERA	G	GS	CG	SV	IP	H	HR	BB	SO	K/9	WHIP	AVG
2011	R. Cucamonga (CAL)	HiA	0	1	7.71	3	3	0	0	7	9	1	4	9	11.6	1.86	.321
Minor League Totals			0	1	7.71	3	3	0	0	7	9	1	4	9	11.6	1.86	.321

6 GARRETT GOULD, RHP

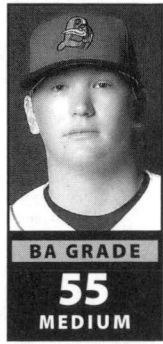

Born: July 19, 1991. **B-T:** R-R. **Ht.:** 6-4. **Wt.:** 190. **Drafted:** HS—Maize, Kan., 2009 (2nd round). **Signed by:** Scott Little.

Though his $900,000 bonus was the largest in the Dodgers' 2009 draft class, Gould spent his first two pro seasons at Rookie-level Ogden before making the move to low Class A in 2011. Gould has a quality three-pitch mix. He commands both sides of the plate with a sinking fastball that ranges from 90-95 mph and sits at 92-93. His curveball is his best pitch, a sharp three-quarters breaker which comes in at 79-83 mph. Gould also has a changeup that plays as a solid third pitch. His command and aggressiveness in the strike zone have improved notably. Gould used to raise some red flags with his mechanics because he landed on a stiff front leg, but he softened it up in 2011 and his whole delivery got cleaner. The Dodgers stressed the need to improve his work ethic and his demeanor on the mound. He responded to the challenge, though he still can do a better job of controlling his emotions. Gould has the weapons to be a mid-rotation starter and possibly more. He'll join Lee again in 2012, this time in high Class A. Gould's pure stuff is a little better, while Lee has more pitchability.

BA GRADE 55 MEDIUM

Year	Club (League)	Class	W	L	ERA	G	GS	CG	SV	IP	H	HR	BB	SO	K/9	WHIP	AVG
2009	Ogden (PIO)	R	0	1	10.13	3	3	0	0	3	4	1	2	4	13.5	2.25	.333
2010	Ogden (PIO)	R	1	4	4.06	13	13	0	0	58	68	4	20	52	8.1	1.53	.292
2011	Great Lakes (MWL)	LoA	11	6	2.40	27	24	0	0	124	102	8	37	104	7.6	1.12	.220
Minor League Totals			12	11	3.03	43	40	0	0	184	174	13	59	160	7.8	1.27	.245

7 CHRIS WITHROW, RHP

Born: April 1, 1989. **B-T:** R-R. **Ht.:** 6-3. **Wt.:** 195. **Drafted:** HS—Midland, Texas, 2007 (1st round). **Signed by:** Calvin Jones.

Withrow had enough hitting ability to play both ways at Baylor had the Dodgers not signed him for $1.35 million as the 20th overall pick in 2007. He's been stuck in Double-A for three years and led the Southern League with 9.1 strikeouts per nine innings in 2011 but recorded consecutive quality starts once all year. Withrow has a riding fastball that sits at 94-95 mph and can reach 98. When he's on, he's able to spin a sharp, downer curveball that rates as a plus pitch, but he has trouble maintaining its consistency and short-arms it. His changeup has nice fading action at 83-86 mph, and while he shows some aptitude for maintaining his arm speed, it's not always a reliable offering. He also throws an 85-88 mph slider early in counts. Scouts don't question Withrow's stuff, but they wonder how well he'll be able to use it. His control and command still need a lot of work, and at times he looks like he's solely concerned with lighting up radar guns. If he ever figures out command, Withrow can be a quality big league starter. Though he's likely headed back to Chattanooga for a fourth stint, Los Angeles protected him on its 40-man roster in November.

BA GRADE 55 HIGH

Year	Club (League)	Class	W	L	ERA	G	GS	CG	SV	IP	H	HR	BB	SO	K/9	WHIP	AVG
2007	Dodgers (GCL)	R	0	0	.500	6	4	0	0	9	5	0	4	13	13.0	1.00	.167
2008	Inland Empire (CAL)	HiA	0	0	4.50	4	0	0	0	4	2	0	6	1	2.3	2.00	.182
2009	Inland Empire (CAL)	HiA	6	6	4.69	19	16	0	0	86	80	3	45	105	10.9	1.45	.252
	Chattanooga (SL)	AA	2	2	3.95	6	6	0	0	27	24	2	12	26	8.6	1.32	.240
2010	Chattanooga (SL)	AA	4	9	5.97	27	27	1	0	130	146	13	69	120	8.3	1.66	.285
2011	Chattanooga (SL)	AA	6	6	4.20	25	25	1	0	129	111	8	75	130	9.1	1.45	.239
Minor League Totals			18	23	4.91	87	78	2	0	385	368	26	211	395	9.2	1.50	.256

8 JOSH LINDBLOM, RHP

Born: June 15, 1987. **B-T:** R-R. **Ht.:** 6-5. **Wt.:** 240. **Drafted:** Purdue, 2008 (2nd round). **Signed by:** Chet Sergo.

Lindblom turned down a $300,000 offer as the Astros' third-round pick out of high school in 2005, then attended Tennessee and Purdue before landing $663,000 from the Dodgers three years later. He struggled as a starter before settling in as a closer in college, and his pro career has followed a similar pattern. Los Angeles returned him to the bullpen in mid-2010 after his velocity dropped off. While he has a starter's repertoire, Lindblom is more comfortable in the bullpen. Now that he's working in relief again, his fastball operates at 91-95 mph with average sink. His breaking pitches are more crisp, with his mid-80s slider showing tilt and generating some swings and misses. He also has a 73-74 mph curveball with average bite and a usable changeup with some downward movement and deception. As a reliever, Lindblom focuses mainly on his fastball and slider. His body is strong and durable, and he has a solid delivery. He shows more confidence coming out

BA GRADE 50 LOW

of the bullpen than he did in the rotation. Some scouts still think Lindblom could develop into a useful starter, but Los Angeles plans to keep him as a reliever after he pitched well in the majors in the final two months. He could work in a number of roles, most likely settling in as a set-up man.

Year	Club (League)	Class	W	L	ERA	G	GS	CG	SV	IP	H	HR	BB	SO	K/9	WHIP	AVG
2008	Great Lakes (MWL)	LoA	0	0	1.86	8	8	0	0	29	14	2	4	33	10.2	0.62	.137
	Jacksonville (SL)	AA	0	0	3.60	1	1	0	0	5	5	0	1	4	7.2	1.20	.263
2009	Chattanooga (SL)	AA	3	5	4.71	14	11	0	0	57	55	4	14	46	7.2	1.20	.250
	Albuquerque (PCL)	AAA	3	0	2.54	20	3	0	1	39	34	3	12	36	8.3	1.18	.236
2010	Albuquerque (PCL)	AAA	3	2	6.54	40	10	0	0	95	143	12	32	84	8.0	1.84	.340
2011	Chattanooga (SL)	AA	1	3	2.13	34	0	0	17	42	30	3	14	54	11.5	1.04	.205
	Los Angeles (NL)	MAJ	1	0	2.73	27	0	0	0	30	21	0	10	28	8.5	1.04	.212
Major League Totals			1	0	2.73	27	0	0	0	30	21	0	10	28	8.5	1.04	.212
Minor League Totals			10	10	4.30	117	33	0	18	268	281	24	77	257	8.6	1.34	.267

9 JOC PEDERSON, OF

Born: April 21, 1992. **B-T:** L-L. **Ht.:** 6-1. **Wt.:** 185. **Drafted:** HS—Palo Alto, Calif., 2010 (11th round). **Signed by:** Orsino Hill.

A two-sport standout as an outfielder and wide receiver in high school, Pederson signed for $600,000 as an 11th-rounder. In his first full year as a pro, he looked overmatched in a brief stint in low Class A before leading the Rookie-level Pioneer League in RBIs (64) and finishing second in on-base percentage (.429) and fourth in batting (.353). His father Stu played eight games for the Dodgers in September 1985. Pederson shows lots of polish for a teenager and plays with a blue-collar mentality. He has a short, sound swing and the chance to be an above-average hitter. He's willing to use all fields, and he got better at pulling inside pitches with more authority in 2011, which should help him get to his average power potential. Pederson saw action at all three outfield positions with Ogden, though he played primarily in left and will end up on a corner in the long term. He has a solid arm with slightly above-average speed. He's an efficient basestealer with good instincts on the basepaths. Pederson will get another crack at the Midwest League in 2012. He'll need time to develop but his talent stands out among the position prospects at the lower levels of the system.

BA GRADE 50 HIGH

Year	Club (League)	Class	AVG	G	AB	R	H	2B	3B	HR	RBI	BB	SO	SB	CS	OBP	SLG
2010	Dodgers (AZL)	R	.000	3	7	1	0	0	0	0	0	4	5	0	0	.417	.000
2011	Great Lakes (MWL)	LoA	.160	16	50	4	8	0	0	0	1	7	9	2	0	.288	.160
	Ogden (PIO)	R	.353	68	266	54	94	20	2	11	64	36	54	24	5	.429	.568
Minor League Totals			.316	87	323	59	102	20	2	11	65	47	68	26	5	.407	.492

10 TIM FEDEROWICZ, C

Born: Aug. 5, 1987. **B-T:** R-R. **Ht.:** 5-11. **Wt.:** 200. **Drafted:** North Carolina, 2008 (7th round). **Signed by:** Quincy Boyd (Red Sox).

The Dodgers entered 2011 sorely lacking in catching prospects. They addressed that need through the draft and by getting Federowicz, who arrived along with righthanders Stephen Fife and Juan Rodriguez in the three-team deal that sent Eric Bedard from the Mariners to the Red Sox in July. Los Angeles sent Trayvon Robinson to Seattle. Federowicz always has been known for his defense more than his bat. His hands work well behind the plate and his ability to block balls stands out as well. He has outstanding receiving skills and a solid, accurate arm. He also draws praise for his game-calling and leadership. Federowicz put up the best numbers of his pro career in his month at hitter-friendly Albuquerque, showing good feel at the plate and loft power he hadn't displayed previously. Most scouts project that he'll hit for a decent average with gap power but nothing more. He gets himself out when he starts pulling off breaking pitches. He has a stocky frame and is a below-average runner, like most catchers. Rod Barajas' departure via free agency enhances Federowicz's chances of opening 2012 in the majors, though it's unlikely the Dodgers would hand him their starting job. His defensive ability may allow him to claim that role down the road.

BA GRADE 45 LOW

Year	Club (League)	Class	AVG	G	AB	R	H	2B	3B	HR	RBI	BB	SO	SB	CS	OBP	SLG
2008	Lowell (NYP)	SS	.244	36	127	14	31	6	0	1	15	19	24	10	3	.338	.315
2009	Greenville (SAL)	LoA	.345	55	226	34	78	19	0	10	34	15	42	1	0	.393	.562
	Salem (CAR)	HiA	.257	51	187	18	48	13	0	4	24	5	22	1	0	.276	.390
2010	Salem (CAR)	HiA	.253	109	407	47	103	34	1	4	61	43	86	1	1	.324	.371
2011	Portland (EL)	AA	.277	90	339	46	94	20	0	8	52	32	63	1	0	.338	.407
	Albuquerque (PCL)	AAA	.325	25	83	17	27	7	0	6	17	15	20	0	0	.431	.627
	Los Angeles (NL)	MAJ	.154	7	13	0	2	0	0	0	1	2	4	0	0	.313	.154
Major League Totals			.154	7	13	0	2	0	0	0	1	2	4	0	0	.313	.154
Minor League Totals			.278	366	1369	176	381	99	1	33	203	129	257	14	4	.341	.424

11 JAMES BALDWIN III, OF

Born: Oct. 10, 1991. **B-T:** L-R. **Ht.:** 6-3. **Wt.:** 190. **Drafted:** HS—Southern Pines, N.C., 2010 (4th round). **Signed by:** Lon Joyce.

Baldwin kept busy at Pinecrest High (Southern Pines, N.C), enjoying standout careers in football and basketball as well as baseball, where he both pitched and played outfield. His father James Jr. pitched 11 seasons in the majors and was Pinecrest's pitching coach, but the son's future is as a position player. The Dodgers signed him away from an Elon commitment for $180,000 after taking him in the fourth round of in 2010. Baldwin is more raw than Joc Pederson, his teammate at Ogden last season, but his tools offer intriguing projection. He's an outstanding athlete with a lean build. Los Angeles projects him as a solid hitter in time, though he still has a ways to go. His swing can get long and he gives at-bats away at times. Baldwin struggled against quality stuff in the Pioneer League and hit just .183/.300/.367 against lefthanders. He has some pop in his bat and he projects to have 20-homer power once he fills out. There's little question about Baldwin's defense. He can be a frontline center fielder, showing the well above-average speed to go and get balls, and he has a strong arm. His quickness makes him a threat on the bases, too. Baldwin likely will need development time at every level, but his tools could be worth the wait. He'll get his first look at full-season ball at Great Lakes in 2012.

Year	Club (League)	Class	AVG	G	AB	R	H	2B	3B	HR	RBI	BB	SO	SB	CS	OBP	SLG
2010	Dodgers (AZL)	R	.274	46	179	25	49	6	2	2	22	9	60	17	3	.313	.363
2011	Ogden (PIO)	R	.250	50	196	47	49	9	3	10	39	18	74	22	5	.348	.480
Minor League Totals			.261	96	375	72	98	15	5	12	61	27	134	39	8	.332	.424

12 ANGEL SANCHEZ, RHP

Born: Nov. 28, 1989. **B-T:** R-R. **Ht.:** 6-3. **Wt.:** 177. **Signed:** Dominican Republic, 2010. **Signed by:** Ezequiel Sepulveda.

Sanchez's route to pro ball was very atypical for a Latin American prospect, as he signed out of a Dominican college. He passed up opportunities to turn pro as a teenager so he could attend Santo Domingo Autonomous University. He was one semester away from graduating when he signed with the Dodgers in July 2010, costing them just $7,500. Sanchez pitched well in his pro debut in low Class A last year, allowing three runs or less in 18 of his 20 outings. He has a power arm, throwing 92-96 mph four-seam fastballs with armside run and sinking two-seamers. His changeup is his best secondary offering, featuring splitter-like action at 80-85 mph. He also has a slurvy curveball that flashes depth and rotation at times but is a work in progress. Sanchez uses a high three-quarters arm slot and, while he can be a little upright finishing his delivery at times, he doesn't have any major mechanical issues. He does need to tighten his command. Sanchez receives praise for his work ethic and how quickly he's picked up English. He's a potential No. 3 starter who could begin moving quickly, possibly reaching Double-A in 2012.

Year	Club (League)	Class	W	L	ERA	G	GS	CG	SV	IP	H	HR	BB	SO	K/9	WHIP	AVG
2011	Great Lakes (MWL)	LoA	8	4	2.82	20	16	0	0	99	72	5	39	84	7.6	1.12	.198
Minor League Totals			8	4	2.82	20	16	0	0	99	72	5	39	84	7.6	1.12	.198

13 JONATHAN GARCIA, OF

Born: Nov. 11, 1991. **B-T:** R-R. **Ht.:** 5-11. **Wt.:** 175. **Drafted:** HS—Yauco, P.R., 2009 (8th round). **Signed by:** Manny Estrada.

Garcia came out of the gate red-hot last season, defying the Midwest League's cold weather by belting seven homers in April to lead the circuit. The rest of his year didn't go as well, as he batted just .218/.281/.376 afterward and finished in a 2-for-23 skid. To his credit, his 19 homers still were an impressive total for a teenager in a tough league for hitters. Garcia's above-average raw power has been his biggest selling point since his high school days, when he was known to put on shows in batting practice but struggle against live pitching. He has strong hands and a quick bat with loft in his stroke, allowing him to hit balls a long way when he connects. However, Garcia struggles to maintain a consistent approach and setup, and thus his swing gets out of sync. He has an aggressive mentality, and opponents found they could exploit him with offspeed pitches. Great Lakes' everyday right fielder last season, Garcia has enough arm strength to play there, but he's already a slightly below-average runner and needs to watch his conditioning. Garcia got his swing back during instructional league, where the Dodgers named him the most improved player in camp. He'll try to carry that momentum into 2012 when he moves up to high Class A.

Year	Club (League)	Class	AVG	G	AB	R	H	2B	3B	HR	RBI	BB	SO	SB	CS	OBP	SLG
2009	Dodgers (AZL)	R	.304	41	138	22	42	16	1	3	21	10	37	4	0	.362	.500
2010	Ogden (PIO)	R	.305	61	239	45	73	19	2	10	40	19	59	4	1	.365	.527
2011	Great Lakes (MWL)	LoA	.228	130	464	58	106	28	2	19	63	34	133	2	1	.290	.420
Minor League Totals			.263	232	841	125	221	63	5	32	124	63	229	10	2	.323	.464

14 SCOTT BARLOW, RHP

BA GRADE
50
HIGH

Born: Dec. 18, 1992. **B-T:** R-R. **Ht.:** 6-4. **Wt.:** 170. **Drafted:** HS—Santa Clarita, Calif., 2011 (6th round). **Signed by:** Dennis Moeller.

The Dodgers believe Barlow could be one of the steals of the 2011 draft. He had a very projectable frame but pitched with a fringy fastball in high school, which is why he lasted until the 194th overall pick. Los Angeles signed him away from a Fresno State commitment for $150,000 in early August. Between the draft and instructional league, Barlow put on some quality weight and his fastball got stronger as well, rising to 90-93 mph and hitting 94. He spins a quality 1-to-7 curveball at 76-78 mph and also shows promise with his slider and changeup, though the changeup lags behind his other pitches. Barlow has a loose, easy arm and throws from a three-quarters angle. He has a clean delivery, with good balance and the ability to generate a nice downhill plane. He receives high marks for his competitiveness and advanced feel for pitching for his age. A potential mid-rotation starter, Barlow will get a chance to begin his first full pro season in low Class A. He only pitched two innings after signing, so he could open 2012 in extended spring training and head to Ogden in June.

Year	Club (League)	Class	W	L	ERA	G	GS	CG	SV	IP	H	HR	BB	SO	K/9	WHIP	AVG
2011	Dodgers (AZL)	R	0	1	27.00	2	0	0	0	2	5	1	2	1	5.4	4.20	.500
Minor League Totals			0	1	27.00	2	0	0	0	2	5	1	2	1	5.4	4.20	.500

15 SHAWN TOLLESON, RHP

BA GRADE
50
HIGH

Born: Jan. 19, 1988. **B-T:** R-R. **Ht.:** 6-2. **Wt.:** 215. **Drafted:** Baylor, 2010 (30th round). **Signed by:** Fred Costello.

Tolleson was a potential first-round pick entering his high school senior season in 2006, but he blew out his elbow and needed Tommy John surgery that March. His injury and bonus demands caused him to go undrafted, so he headed to Baylor, where he battled more elbow problems and inconsistency over the next four years. He went unpicked again as a redshirt sophomore in 2009 and signed for $20,000 as a 30th-round pick in 2010. The Dodgers promptly moved Tolleson to the bullpen and he has done nothing but dominate in pro ball. He has a 1.01 ERA, .198 opponent average and 144-23 K-BB ratio in 98 pro innings, and he reached Double-A in May of his first full pro season. Tolleson's herky-jerky delivery made scouts nervous when he was a starter in college, but it works as a reliever and gives him some deception. He throws a running four-seam fastball at 93-96 mph and has turned his cutter into a weapon as well. He also throws a solid slider, featuring tilt and late bite. His changeup is a below-average pitch but he doesn't need it much as a reliever. Los Angeles believes Tolleson could've pitched in the majors last season if needed. He should make his major league debut in 2012 and has a ceiling as a set-up man.

Year	Club (League)	Class	W	L	ERA	G	GS	CG	SV	IP	H	HR	BB	SO	K/9	WHIP	AVG
2010	Ogden (PIO)	R	1	1	0.63	26	0	0	17	29	17	1	5	39	12.2	0.77	.175
2011	Great Lakes (MWL)	LoA	1	0	0.00	14	0	0	10	15	8	0	4	33	19.8	0.80	.154
	R. Cucamonga (CAL)	HiA	2	0	0.93	5	0	0	3	10	2	1	3	17	15.8	0.52	.061
	Chattanooga (SL)	AA	4	2	1.62	38	0	0	12	44	42	2	11	55	11.2	1.20	.251
Minor League Totals			8	3	1.01	83	0	0	42	98	69	4	23	144	13.3	0.94	.198

16 AARON MILLER, LHP

BA GRADE
50
HIGH

Born: Sept. 18, 1987. **B-T:** L-L. **Ht.:** 6-3. **Wt.:** 200. **Drafted:** Baylor, 2009 (1st round supplemental). **Signed by:** Chris Smith.

Miller and Shawn Tolleson were part of the same Baylor recruiting class, which Baseball America ranked as college baseball's best in 2006. At that point, Miller was more highly regarded as a hitter and the Rockies drafted him as an outfielder in the 11th round. Miller spent most of his first two college seasons in the outfield before becoming a two-way player in 2009, when he pitched his way into the sandwich round. He signed for $889,200 bonus as the Dodgers' top pick that June. Miller had a strong first full season in 2010, despite his fastball dropping to 87-91 mph, but injuries prevented him from building on it. He didn't make his first start until late May and tried to pitch through pain with what turned out to be a sports hernia that wasn't diagnosed until late in the season. His fastball fell another tick to 86-90 mph and he also had trouble finishing his delivery and spinning his slider. In the past, Miller has shown the makings of a mid-rotation starter with a low-90s fastball and a slider with true plus potential. He also has displayed feel for a changeup with sink. Not surprisingly for an inexperienced pitcher, he needs to do a better job of maintaining his arm slot and commanding his pitches. Miller didn't have surgery until late in the year, so Los Angeles will assess his progress in spring training. He would have pitched in Double-A last year if healthy and will head there once he's back at full strength.

Year	Club (League)	Class	W	L	ERA	G	GS	CG	SV	IP	H	HR	BB	SO	K/9	WHIP	AVG
2009	Dodgers (AZL)	R	0	0	6.35	3	3	0	0	6	8	0	2	10	15.9	1.76	.320
	Great Lakes (MWL)	LoA	3	1	2.08	7	7	0	0	30	22	3	10	38	11.3	1.05	.208
2010	Chattanooga (SL)	AA	1	4	7.04	6	6	0	0	23	28	3	18	22	8.6	2.00	.304
	Inland Empire (CAL)	HiA	6	4	2.92	19	17	0	0	102	76	6	48	99	8.8	1.22	.207

2011	Dodgers (AZL)	R	1	0	0.00	1	0	0	0	2	1	0	1	3	13.5	1.00	.143
	R. Cucamonga (CAL)	HiA	3	2	3.97	10	6	0	0	34	37	2	18	30	7.9	1.62	.282
Minor League Totals			14	11	3.52	46	39	0	0	197	172	14	97	202	9.2	1.37	.236

17 ETHAN MARTIN, RHP

BA GRADE
55
EXTREME

Born: June 6, 1989. **B-T:** R-R. **Ht.:** 6-2. **Wt.:** 195. **Drafted:** HS—Toccoa, Ga., 2008 (1st round). **Signed by:** Lon Joyce.

When Martin's high school senior season began in 2008, some teams wanted him for his power and athleticism as a third baseman, while others were attracted to his big arm on the mound. By June, most clubs preferred him as a pitcher and the Dodgers made him the first prep arm taken. The 15th overall choice, he signed for $1.73 million. Martin was raw even by the standards of a high school draft pick and got shelled in high Class A for most of the last two years, but his potential still sticks out. He still throws a mid-90s fastball with life in the zone, and he has an extra gear to get it up to 98 mph. He has a curveball that shows flashes of becoming a plus pitch with good rotation, but it's inconsistent. Last season, he added an 82-84 mph slider that shows occasional tilt and grades as an average offering at times, though it also tends to break too early. He has shown some feel a fading 84-86 mph changeup, which has a chance to be average. Martin's lack of pitchability and command have been his downfall. He rushes his delivery and struggles to repeat it despite efforts to improve his direction and timing. Los Angeles wanted to get Martin out of the unforgiving California League and did so by sending him to Double-A as a reliever late last June. He had a 3.29 ERA in that role for Chattanooga, though he still had trouble finding the zone. Because he has an array of promising pitches, the Dodgers will return him to the rotation in Double-A this year. He maintains the ceiling of a No. 2 starter but has a long way to go.

Year	Club (League)	Class	W	L	ERA	G	GS	CG	SV	IP	H	HR	BB	SO	K/9	WHIP	AVG
2009	Great Lakes (MWL)	LoA	6	8	3.87	27	19	0	1	100	85	4	61	120	10.8	1.46	.232
2010	Inland Empire (CAL)	HiA	9	14	6.35	25	22	1	0	113	120	10	81	105	8.3	1.77	.279
2011	R. Cucamonga (CAL)	HiA	4	4	7.36	16	9	0	0	55	60	8	37	61	10.0	1.85	.291
	Chattanooga (SL)	AA	5	3	4.02	21	3	0	2	40	31	3	29	43	9.6	1.49	.215
Minor League Totals			24	29	5.42	89	53	1	3	309	301	25	208	329	9.6	1.65	.259

18 ALEX SANTANA, 3B

BA GRADE
50
HIGH

Born: Aug. 21, 1993. **B-T:** R-R. **Ht.:** 6-4. **Wt.:** 190. **Drafted:** HS—Cape Coral, Fla., 2011 (2nd round). **Signed by:** Rob Sidwell.

Santana's father Rafael was the everyday shortstop for the 1986 World Series champion Mets and played in seven big league seasons. Alex was a shortstop in high school too, but it quickly became apparent he was outgrowing the position and the Dodgers moved him to third base after signing him for $499,500 as the 73rd overall pick in last year's draft. Santana was just 17 when he signed, making him one of the youngest players in his draft class. He's accordingly raw but has intriguing tools. Santana has plus bat speed and good hands at the plate, giving him above-average power potential. He's still growing into his body, though, and he looks awkward at times. His swing is a little long and Los Angeles wants him to use his legs better. He shows promising pitch recognition, but he still swung and missed too frequently in his pro debut. Santana has the actions and athleticism to stick at third base. He also has a strong arm, though he throws from a low slot and tends to get under the ball. He's not a burner but has decent speed. While Santana could break camp with Great Lakes in 2012, he'll probably stay in extended spring training before getting assigned to Ogden in June.

Year	Club (League)	Class	AVG	G	AB	R	H	2B	3B	HR	RBI	BB	SO	SB	CS	OBP	SLG
2011	Dodgers (AZL)	R	.238	50	189	30	45	10	3	1	19	10	64	8	1	.298	.339
Minor League Totals			.238	50	189	30	45	10	3	1	19	10	64	8	1	.298	.339

19 ALEX CASTELLANOS, OF

BA GRADE
45
MEDIUM

Born: Aug. 4, 1986. **B-T:** R-R. **Ht.:** 5-11. **Wt.:** 180. **Drafted:** Belmont Abbey (N.C.), 2008 (10th round). **Signed by:** Mike Juhl (Cardinals).

In two seasons at Belmont Abbey (N.C.), an NCAA Division II program, Castellanos set school records for career batting average (.408) and single-season hits (97) and doubles (31). The first Crusader drafted since 1972, he signed with the Cardinals for $70,000 as a 10th-round pick in 2008. He set career bests in almost every category while advancing to Double-A in 2011, and St. Louis used him to get a much-need shortstop (Rafael Furcal) from the Dodgers at the July trade deadline. He has a smooth stroke and the ball jumps off his bat, giving him the potential for average power. Offspeed pitches give him problems, however, and he can be beaten by high fastballs as well. Castellanos played second and third base before moving to right field in 2010. He has above-average speed and a strong arm. Los Angeles added Castellanos to their 40-man roster after the season and will send him to Triple-A in 2012. The Dodgers had a D-II product reach the majors last year in Jerry Sands, and Castellanos could be next.

Year	Club (League)	Class	AVG	G	AB	R	H	2B	3B	HR	RBI	BB	SO	SB	CS	OBP	SLG
2008	Johnson City (APP)	R	.298	49	181	42	54	14	4	7	31	8	45	20	2	.354	.536
	Batavia (NYP)	SS	.269	10	26	6	7	2	2	0	4	2	7	0	1	.345	.500
2009	Quad Cities (MWL)	LoA	.270	82	311	51	84	21	4	5	34	20	89	21	4	.336	.412
	Palm Beach (FSL)	HiA	.189	21	53	5	10	1	1	1	2	2	19	0	2	.232	.302
2010	Palm Beach (FSL)	HiA	.270	129	459	62	124	35	7	13	58	38	112	19	9	.339	.462
2011	Springfield (TL)	AA	.319	93	354	72	113	21	4	19	62	24	94	10	1	.379	.562
	Chattanooga (SL)	AA	.322	32	121	30	39	14	4	4	23	15	24	4	1	.406	.603
Minor League Totals			.286	416	1505	268	431	108	26	49	214	109	390	74	20	.352	.490

20 KYLE RUSSELL, OF

BA GRADE 45 MEDIUM

Born: June 27, 1986. **B-T:** L-L. **Ht.:** 6-5. **Wt.:** 195. **Drafted:** Texas, 2008 (3rd round). **Signed by:** Chris Smith.

Russell set single-season (28) and career (57) home run records at Texas. Along the way, he passed up a reported $800,000 offer as the Cardinals' fourth-round pick in 2007. A year later, he landed $410,000 in the third round from the Dodgers. He has more raw power than any hitter in the system, and he draws comparisons to Russell Branyan for his homer and strikeout totals. Russell has a lean frame but generates good leverage and loft in his swing. He swings hard every time, and while he'll punish mistakes, he struggles to make adjustments against quality pitching. He has holes in his stroke and is helpless against lefthanders, who held him to .175/.279/.360 numbers in 2011. Russell might hit 25-30 homers annually in the majors, but it would come with the tradeoff of a subpar average and plenty of strikeouts. He has solid defensive tools in his arm and speed, though he doesn't stand out in right field. Russell moved up to Triple-A late last season and will head back to Albuquerque to start 2012. While his power could lead to big numbers in one of the minors' best launching pads, Los Angeles is eager to see how he'll handle veteran pitching.

Year	Club (League)	Class	AVG	G	AB	R	H	2B	3B	HR	RBI	BB	SO	SB	CS	OBP	SLG
2008	Ogden (PIO)	R	.279	61	219	46	61	13	5	11	46	27	82	4	0	.365	.534
2009	Great Lakes (MWL)	LoA	.272	133	481	90	131	39	7	26	102	72	180	20	5	.371	.545
2010	Inland Empire (CAL)	HiA	.354	53	198	42	70	11	4	16	53	32	64	8	3	.448	.692
	Chattanooga (SL)	AA	.245	76	273	36	67	23	3	10	28	29	113	3	2	.319	.462
2011	Chattanooga (SL)	AA	.259	120	394	61	102	29	4	19	69	45	144	5	1	.342	.497
	Albuquerque (PCL)	AAA	.211	11	38	6	8	2	1	1	3	8	10	1	0	.348	.395
Minor League Totals			.274	454	1603	281	439	117	24	83	301	213	593	41	8	.364	.532

21 SCOTT VAN SLYKE, OF/1B

BA GRADE 45 MEDIUM

Born: July 24, 1986. **B-T:** R-R. **Ht.:** 6-5. **Wt.:** 220. **Drafted:** HS—Ladue, Mo., 2005 (14th round). **Signed by:** Mitch Webster.

Van Slyke has an outstanding pedigree. His father Andy played 13 seasons in the majors, making the All-Star Game three times and winning five straight Gold Gloves as an outfielder. Older brother A.J. played four seasons in the Cardinals system. Scott struggled with a long swing and poor plate discipline in his first look at Double-A in 2010, ending in a demotion that June, but he came back with a vengeance in 2011. He led the Southern League in hitting (.348) and doubles (45) while finishing second in on-base percentage (.427) and slugging (.595). Van Slyke has a nice swing with good wrist action. Once he stopped being as pull-conscious as he'd been in the past, he started showing solid power to all fields. Some scouts still have concerns about his ability to handle inside pitches and quality breaking stuff. A full-time outfielder until 2011, Van Slyke saw time at first base early in the season before moving back to the outfield in June, mostly playing in left field. He showed soft hands at first base and was adequate at both positions, though he didn't stand out at either. He's a fringy runner with a solid arm. The Dodgers added Van Slyke to their 40-man roster after the season to protect him from the Rule 5 draft. He could put up more gaudy numbers at Albuquerque in 2012, with the opportunity for a big league promotion later in the year.

Year	Club (League)	Class	AVG	G	AB	R	H	2B	3B	HR	RBI	BB	SO	SB	CS	OBP	SLG
2005	Dodgers (GCL)	R	.282	24	85	15	24	4	1	2	15	4	19	4	3	.330	.424
2006	Ogden (PIO)	R	.256	45	156	18	40	5	2	2	17	14	41	5	3	.320	.353
2007	Great Lakes (MWL)	LoA	.254	104	351	38	89	18	1	2	35	27	68	4	4	.310	.328
2008	Great Lakes (MWL)	LoA	.148	22	61	4	9	4	0	0	7	12	11	0	0	.280	.213
	Inland Empire (CAL)	HiA	.261	48	176	29	46	9	2	5	26	11	35	7	4	.309	.420
2009	Inland Empire (CAL)	HiA	.294	132	496	75	146	42	4	23	100	61	128	10	7	.373	.534
	Albuquerque (PCL)	AAA	.167	3	6	1	1	0	0	0	0	2	1	0	0	.375	.167
2010	Chattanooga (SL)	AA	.235	65	217	28	51	7	3	4	29	18	37	4	2	.300	.350
	Inland Empire (CAL)	HiA	.307	48	189	34	58	12	2	9	35	17	39	3	1	.368	.534
	Albuquerque (PCL)	AAA	.289	12	38	5	11	4	0	1	5	0	7	0	0	.289	.474
2011	Chattanooga (SL)	AA	.348	130	457	81	159	45	4	20	92	65	100	6	5	.427	.595
Minor League Totals			.284	633	2232	328	634	150	19	68	361	231	486	43	29	.353	.460

22 ANGELO SONGCO, OF/1B

BA GRADE
45
MEDIUM

Born: Sept. 9, 1988. **B-T:** L-R. **Ht.:** 6-0. **Wt.:** 195. **Drafted:** Loyola Marymount, 2009 (4th round). **Signed by:** Bobby Darwin.

Songco had an accomplished three-year career at Loyola Marymount, winning West Coast Conference freshman of the year honors in 2007 and leaving with the second-best career slugging percentage in Lions history at .630. Playing close to home at Rancho Cucamonga last season, Songco blistered the California League, leading the circuit in doubles (48) and ranking second in homers (29). He made nice adjustments against lefthanders, slugging .478 against them in 2011 compared to .346 the year before. Songco holds the bat up high in an open stance. He has power more to the gaps than over the fence, and some scouts question whether he'll have enough pop, regardless of his Cal League home run total. Most of his longballs come to his pull side. Songco spent his first two pro seasons and began 2011 in left field, but his below-average speed and athleticism prompted a move to first base in June. He made strides there and showed he can be a decent first baseman in the future. His subpar arm strength fits better at first base, too. Songco will have to prove himself again this year in Double-A, where how he fares against more advanced pitchers will tell much about his future.

Year	Club (League)	Class	AVG	G	AB	R	H	2B	3B	HR	RBI	BB	SO	SB	CS	OBP	SLG
2009	Great Lakes (MWL)	LoA	.150	33	120	8	18	6	2	1	16	10	28	1	0	.226	.258
	Ogden (PIO)	R	.306	36	144	27	44	11	1	9	29	10	41	0	1	.361	.583
2010	Great Lakes (MWL)	LoA	.274	135	507	87	139	30	6	15	71	51	91	6	1	.344	.446
2011	R. Cucamonga (CAL)	HiA	.313	131	534	110	167	48	4	29	114	42	121	4	3	.367	.581
Minor League Totals			.282	335	1305	232	368	95	13	54	230	113	281	11	5	.345	.499

23 RYAN O'SULLIVAN, RHP

BA GRADE
50
EXTREME

Born: Sept. 5, 1990. **B-T:** R-R. **Ht.:** 6-2. **Wt.:** 190. **Drafted:** Oklahoma City, 2011 (4th round). **Signed by:** Calvin Jones.

After passing on signing with the Giants as a 10th-rounder out of high school, O'Sullivan began his college career at San Diego State in 2009. He injured his elbow in his first appearance of 2010 and didn't pitch again that season. Grade issues prompted him to transfer to Oklahoma City, a top NAIA program, but he didn't get his academic release and had to sit out last spring. After teams scouted O'Sullivan in bullpen sessions, the Dodgers drafted him in the fourth round last June. He didn't completely pass his physical, so he signed for a below-slot $100,000. O'Sullivan has better pure stuff than his older brother Sean, who has been in and out of the Royals rotation. Ryan's fastball ranges from 89-95 mph and sits at 92-93 with average movement. He complements it with a slider, curveball and a circle changeup, with the slider rating as the best of his secondary pitches. His curve is more of a show-me pitch, while his 80-83 changeup has some fade away from righthanders. There's some effort in O'Sullivan's delivery, though it isn't excessive. A potential mid rotation starter if everything comes together, he'll open his first full pro season at one of the Dodgers' Class A affiliates.

Year	Club (League)	Class	W	L	ERA	G	GS	CG	SV	IP	H	HR	BB	SO	K/9	WHIP	AVG
2011	Ogden (PIO)	R	0	1	6.48	3	3	0	0	8	7	1	6	5	5.4	1.56	.250
Minor League Totals			0	1	6.48	3	3	0	0	8	7	1	6	5	5.4	1.56	.250

24 JOSH WALL, RHP

BA GRADE
45
HIGH

Born: Jan. 21, 1987. **B-T:** R-R. **Ht.:** 6-6. **Wt.:** 218. **Drafted:** HS—Walker, La., 2005 (2nd round). **Signed by:** Dennis Moeller.

A second-round pick in 2005, Wall slipped off the prospect radar after six up-and-down seasons as a starter. He looked like a big leaguer at times, but he was prone to losing focus and struggled to maintain consistent stuff. The Dodgers moved him to relief in 2011 and the shorter stints suited him better, as he had his best season as a pro. Wall's fastball velocity varied as a starter but he sits at 95-98 mph coming out of the bullpen. His fastball has some armside movement, though it gets straighter at higher velocities. His slider also has improved, as it's now tighter and harder at 87-90 mph. Wall also owns a curveball he can throw for strikes and a fringy changeup. Some scouts still question his feel for using his secondary pitches, and lefthanders batted .327/.410/.505 against him in 2011. The Dodgers prefer to point to how much he has matured and added him to the 40-man roster to protect him from the Rule 5 draft. Wall has a good delivery and a loose, easy arm, so durability hasn't been a problem. He could be a middle-relief option in Los Angeles in the near future.

Year	Club (League)	Class	W	L	ERA	G	GS	CG	SV	IP	H	HR	BB	SO	K/9	WHIP	AVG
2005	Dodgers (GCL)	R	1	3	3.86	5	4	0	0	14	13	2	8	5	3.2	1.50	.245
2006	Ogden (PIO)	R	3	5	5.86	14	14	0	0	66	80	5	33	41	5.6	1.71	.305
2007	Great Lakes (MWL)	LoA	6	10	4.18	26	24	1	1	129	136	8	48	103	7.2	1.42	.269
2008	Inland Empire (CAL)	HiA	9	6	6.28	27	25	0	0	129	152	12	63	101	7.0	1.67	.297
2009	Inland Empire (CAL)	HiA	5	8	5.98	23	22	0	0	111	135	9	51	77	6.2	1.67	.310
2010	Great Lakes (MWL)	LoA	9	7	4.24	26	26	1	0	153	144	11	68	151	8.9	1.39	.248
2011	Chattanooga (SL)	AA	4	5	3.93	51	0	0	1	69	72	6	27	57	7.5	1.44	.271
Minor League Totals			37	44	5.03	172	115	2	2	671	732	53	298	535	7.2	1.53	.280

25 PRATT MAYNARD, C

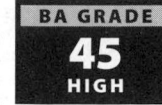

BA GRADE
45
HIGH

Born: Nov. 19, 1989. **B-T:** L-R. **Ht.:** 6-0. **Wt.:** 215. **Drafted:** North Carolina State, 2011 (3rd round). **Signed by:** Clair Rierson.

The Dodgers signed four college catchers out of the 2011 draft, starting with Maynard in the third round for $315,000. He stands out more offensively than defensively at this point. Maynard, who ranked third in NCAA Division I with a North Carolina State-record 64 walks in 2010, has good pitch-recognition skills. He lets balls travel deep in the hitting zone and utilizes the opposite field. He has some fringy power, though it comes mostly in the form of line drives and doubles rather than homers. Maynard will need to stick as a catcher because his bat won't be enough to carry him if he has to move to a corner. He didn't catch every day in college, so he's more raw behind the plate than the typical college draft pick. He shows quality leadership and game-calling abilities, but he needs to soften up his receiving and improve his footwork. Maynard does have solid arm strength and threw out 23 percent of basestealers in his pro debut. An ankle injury limited him to 25 games at Ogden, though he did recover in time to participate in instructional league. He'll move up to one of Los Angeles' Class A affiliates in 2012, most likely Great Lakes.

Year	Club (League)	Class	AVG	G	AB	R	H	2B	3B	HR	RBI	BB	SO	SB	CS	OBP	SLG
2011	Ogden (PIO)	R	.239	25	88	16	21	3	0	2	11	13	24	0	0	.346	.341
Minor League Totals			.239	25	88	16	21	3	0	2	11	13	24	0	0	.346	.341

26 IVAN DeJESUS JR., INF

BA GRADE
40
LOW

Born: May 1, 1987. **B-T:** R-R. **Ht.:** 5-11. **Wt.:** 200. **Drafted:** HS—Guaynabo, P.R., 2005 (2nd round). **Signed by:** Manny Estrada.

DeJesus looked overpowered in his first exposure to the big leagues last April and May, but he righted the ship after returning to Triple-A. He draws comparisons to his father Ivan Sr., who also came up with the Dodgers and played in the majors for 15 seasons. DeJesus has an inside-out swing, producing line drives from gap to gap with solid bat speed. His power output will be limited and he compensates with good on-base skills, as his patient approach produces walks. DeJesus broke his leg during spring training in 2009, costing him most of that season. Never a speedster even before the injury, he's now a tick below-average runner who rarely has tried to steal in the last two seasons. Unlike his father, DeJesus won't carve out a long career as a shortstop. He has good hands, and while his arm is accurate and strong enough to get by at shortstop, he fits best at second base. Since he got hurt, he has played primarily at second while also seeing action at short and third base. He'll have to fight for a job in spring training and may face a third season in Triple-A.

Year	Club (League)	Class	AVG	G	AB	R	H	2B	3B	HR	RBI	BB	SO	SB	CS	OBP	SLG
2005	Dodgers (GCL)	R	.339	33	121	18	41	5	0	0	11	10	22	8	2	.389	.380
	Ogden (PIO)	R	.208	20	72	4	15	1	0	0	3	6	18	3	3	.296	.222
2006	Columbus (SAL)	LoA	.277	126	483	65	134	17	2	1	44	63	85	16	5	.361	.327
2007	Inland Empire (CAL)	HiA	.287	121	428	69	123	22	3	4	52	57	64	11	6	.371	.381
2008	Jacksonville (SL)	AA	.324	128	463	91	150	21	2	7	58	76	81	16	2	.419	.423
2009	Dodgers (AZL)	R	.200	4	10	1	2	1	0	0	3	1	6	0	0	.308	.300
2010	Albuquerque (PCL)	AAA	.296	130	533	89	158	33	2	7	70	32	81	6	1	.335	.405
2011	Los Angeles (NL)	MAJ	.188	17	32	2	6	0	0	0	1	2	11	0	0	.235	.188
	Albuquerque (PCL)	AAA	.310	100	387	61	120	19	2	8	59	45	68	4	1	.389	.432
Major League Totals			.188	17	32	2	6	0	0	0	1	2	11	0	0	.235	.188
Minor League Totals			.298	662	2497	398	743	119	11	27	300	290	425	64	20	.372	.386

27 JAKE LEMMERMAN, SS

BA GRADE
40
MEDIUM

Born: May 4, 1989. **B-T:** R-R. **Ht.:** 6-1. **Wt.:** 192. **Drafted:** Duke, 2010 (5th round). **Signed by:** Lon Joyce.

Lemmerman followed up his Pioneer League MVP season in 2010 with a solid first full year in pro ball, earning a promotion to Double-A in August. He doesn't have anything flashy about his game but he finds a way to get the job done. Lemmerman has a quick, compact swing and grinds out quality at-bats. He went to the Arizona Fall League after last season but fell into a slump when he started trying to do too much and pulled off balls, hitting just .156/.299/.203. He's at his best when he uses the middle of the field, as he has below-average power and needs to avoid trying to muscle up. Lemmerman is a consistent defender whose savvy is his best asset. He's a slightly below-average runner with just enough arm strength to get by at shortstop for now. The Dodgers felt Lemmerman wore down towards the end of last season and that fatigue was another factor in his poor AFL showing. He'll try to bounce back when he returns to Chattanooga to open 2012.

Year	Club (League)	Class	AVG	G	AB	R	H	2B	3B	HR	RBI	BB	SO	SB	CS	OBP	SLG
2010	Ogden (PIO)	R	.363	66	259	69	94	24	2	12	47	31	56	5	4	.434	.610
2011	R. Cucamonga (CAL)	HiA	.293	103	400	71	117	23	2	8	54	47	90	9	3	.379	.420
	Chattanooga (SL)	AA	.234	21	77	11	18	6	0	2	11	8	22	1	0	.318	.390
Minor League Totals			.311	190	736	151	229	53	4	22	112	86	168	15	7	.392	.484

28 GORMAN ERICKSON, C

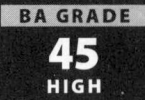

Born: March 11, 1988. **B-T:** B-R. **Ht.:** 6-4. **Wt.:** 220. **Drafted:** San Diego Mesa JC, D/F 2006 (15th round). **Signed by:** Gerric Waller.

The Dodgers signed Erickson for $35,000 in May 2007 as part of the last class of draft-and-follows. He didn't show much offensively in his first four seasons as a pro but turned a corner in 2011, hitting more homers last year (13) than he had in his entire career previously (nine). Erickson always had power potential given his athletic, well-built frame. He has a contact-oriented approach, but his strength and the leverage in his swing give him 15-20 homer potential. Though his average likely will settle in around .250 at the big league level, he has a good eye at the plate and draws a healthy amount of walks. Erickson's size leads some scouts to doubt whether he can stay as a catcher, but others think he blocks balls well and is relatively agile. He has average arm strength and threw out 30 percent of basestealers in 2011. His game-calling improved last year, though his receiving still needs work. As a switch-hitting catcher with pop, Erickson will get every chance to succeed. He got to Double-A last July and will return there to open 2012.

Year	Club (League)	Class	AVG	G	AB	R	H	2B	3B	HR	RBI	BB	SO	SB	CS	OBP	SLG
2007	Dodgers (GCL)	R	.163	18	49	10	8	0	0	0	5	8	16	0	1	.311	.163
	Las Vegas (PCL)	AAA	.000	1	1	0	0	0	0	0	0	0	0	0	0	.000	.000
2008	Dodgers (GCL)	R	.261	29	92	11	24	5	0	2	7	12	17	0	1	.349	.380
	Las Vegas (PCL)	AAA	.000	1	5	0	0	0	0	0	0	0	2	0	0	.000	.000
2009	Ogden (PIO)	R	.305	55	197	40	60	18	1	5	36	24	36	0	0	.378	.482
2010	Great Lakes (MWL)	LoA	.215	82	261	32	56	13	3	2	27	34	45	3	0	.309	.310
2011	R. Cucamonga (CAL)	HiA	.305	63	226	37	69	16	4	6	40	41	42	3	2	.408	.491
	Chattanooga (SL)	AA	.275	41	142	18	39	8	0	7	26	11	22	1	0	.329	.479
Minor League Totals			.263	290	973	148	256	60	8	22	141	130	180	7	4	.352	.409

29 O'KOYEA DICKSON, 1B

Born: Feb. 9, 1990. **B-T:** R-R. **Ht.:** 5-11. **Wt.:** 215. **Drafted:** Sonoma State (Calif.), 2011 (12th round). **Signed by:** Orsino Hill.

After spending two seasons at the JC of San Mateo (Calif.), Dickson led Sonoma State (Calif.) to its second-ever NCAA Division II World Series last spring by batting .341/.438/.565 with a team-high 11 homers. He didn't cool off after signing for $45,000 as a 12th-round pick, leading the Pioneer League in slugging (.603) and finishing sixth in batting (.333). Dickson is strictly a first baseman, so his bat will have to continue carrying him, but it's good enough to give him a chance. He has a sound swing and generates plus bat speed, though his raw power rates as just average. He has some moving parts in his approach that the Dodgers hope to simplify, but he has shown he can drive balls to center field and go the other way. Dickson runs fairly well for his size and is an adequate first baseman. His actions around the bag are fine and he has an average arm. Los Angeles could see him fitting the mold of Paul Goldschmidt, whom they drafted in the 49th round out of high school but didn't sign, though Dickson doesn't have the same power. He'll move up to the Midwest League in 2012, with the Dodgers anxious to see how his bat responds to a much tougher offensive environment.

Year	Club (League)	Class	AVG	G	AB	R	H	2B	3B	HR	RBI	BB	SO	SB	CS	OBP	SLG
2011	Ogden (PIO)	R	.333	48	189	33	63	10	1	13	38	19	44	1	1	.402	.603
Minor League Totals			.333	48	189	33	63	10	1	13	38	19	44	1	1	.402	.603

30 BLAKE SMITH, OF

Born: Dec. 9, 1987. **B-T:** L-R. **Ht.:** 6-2. **Wt.:** 225. **Drafted:** California, 2009 (2nd round). **Signed by:** Fred Costello.

Scouts viewed Smith as a prospect as both an outfielder and pitcher during his college career at California. He showed a plus fastball but was plagued by poor control on the mound, so the Dodgers made him a hitter after signing him for $643,500 as a 2009 second-round pick. He hit 19 homers in his first full pro season and topped that with 20 last year despite missing two months with a sports hernia. Smith has above-average raw power, thanks to his strength, bat speed and ability to load his hands well. He worked to close holes in his swing in 2011, though his aggressive, pull-oriented approach may prevent him from hitting for average. Smith is a fringy runner but a dependable outfielder. He threw 92-94 mph as a pitcher and has a well above-average arm in right field. Los Angeles won't have any reservations about putting Smith back on the mound should his development as a hitter stall, but he'll keep a bat in his hands and move up to Double-A in 2012.

Year	Club (League)	Class	AVG	G	AB	R	H	2B	3B	HR	RBI	BB	SO	SB	CS	OBP	SLG
2009	Dodgers (AZL)	R	.227	6	22	3	5	1	0	0	2	2	9	0	0	.346	.273
	Ogden (PIO)	R	.212	30	104	14	22	7	0	1	12	13	38	0	0	.311	.308
2010	Great Lakes (MWL)	LoA	.281	115	430	77	121	28	2	19	76	49	135	2	3	.363	.488
2011	Dodgers (AZL)	R	.450	6	20	7	9	2	0	4	10	3	1	0	0	.522	1.150
	R. Cucamonga (CAL)	HiA	.294	74	293	59	86	24	0	16	63	32	83	3	2	.359	.539
Minor League Totals			.280	231	869	160	243	62	2	40	163	99	266	5	5	.359	.494

Miami Marlins

BY JAMES BAILEY

Sharing a division with the four-ace Phillies, the Marlins faced an uphill battle going into the 2011 season. First place in the National League East may not have been a realistic goal, but fifth place wasn't the destination most foresaw either. After finishing May in second place, just two games back, the team fell apart.

The Marlins went 5-23 in June, enduring a 1-19 stretch and dropping into last place, which they would escape only briefly later in the year. Manager Fredi Gonzalez resigned near the end of the club's franchise-tying 11-game losing streak, just days short of the one-year anniversary of his hire.

Veteran Jack McKeon, who famously rallied the club to a World Series title after taking over in mid-2003, was unable to replicate the feat. He guided a young roster to a 40-50 record, then stepped aside when Ozzie Guillen was acquired from the White Sox in a trade for prospects Jhan Marinez and Osvaldo Martinez in October. The return of the feisty former Marlins third-base coach stirred up the fan base as the franchise prepared to move into a new stadium for 2012.

Expectations were further stoked when Miami went on a spending spree in December. The Marlins signed free agents Heath Bell, Mark Buehrle and Jose Reyes to contracts worth a total of $191 million, and also made strong runs at Albert Pujols and C.J. Wilson before they inked with the Angels.

Shortly before Guillen's long-rumored arrival, a front-office shakeup saw longtime vice president of player development and scouting Jim Fleming reassigned as a special assistant. Marty Scott, who had been managing the independent Lincoln Saltdogs (American Association), came in as vice president of player development and will oversee the farm system. Scouting director Stan Meek was promoted to vice president of scouting and will continue to run Miami's drafts.

While the organization's spin on the changes was that they were just "a different approach," they were rooted in owner Jeffrey Loria's frustration with the club's lack of major league-ready talent in the system, which he voiced publicly in July. After years of plugging key pieces into the lineup and pitching staff, the upper levels have gone dry. The Marlins rank 29th in draft spending over the last five years ($21.7 million), and that has caught up to them.

Mike Stanton has established himself as a young star, but there's little behind him

MORRIS FOSTOFF

TOP 30 PROSPECTS

1. Christian Yelich, of	16. Jesus Solorzano, of
2. Marcell Ozuna, of	17. Grant Dayton, lhp
3. Jose Fernandez, rhp	18. Michael Brady, rhp
4. Matt Dominguez, 3b	19. Kyle Jensen, of
5. J.T. Realmuto, c	20. A.J. Ramos, rhp
6. Chad James, lhp	21. Kyle Skipworth, c
7. Rob Rasmussen, lhp	22. Mark Canha, 1b/of
8. Noah Perio, 2b	23. Mason Hope, rhp
9. Scott Cousins, of	24. Evan Reed, rhp
10. Adam Conley, lhp	25. Joey O'Gara, rhp
11. Jose Urena, rhp	26. Tom Koehler, rhp
12. Austin Brice, rhp	27. Kevin Mattison, of
13. Ryan Fisher, 3b	28. Josh Hodges, rhp
14. Chris Hatcher, rhp	29. Sandy Rosario, rhp
15. Jose Ceda, rhp	30. Daniel Jennings, lhp

Matt Dominguez failed to win the third-base job in spring training, then missed the start of the year with a fractured elbow. Scott Cousins wasn't the answer when Chris Coghlan went down with a knee injury. Martinez did nothing when given an opportunity.

Finesse starters Tom Koehler and Elih Villanueva, who had blitzed through Double-A in 2010, were woeful in Triple-A and not options when Josh Johnson was lost for the year. The only significant rookie contributions the team got came from backup outfielder Bryan Petersen and relievers Steve Cishek and Mike Dunn.

General Manager: Larry Beinfest. **Farm Director:** Marty Scott. **Scouting Director:** Stan Meek.

Class	Team	League	W	L	Pct	Finish*	Manager(s)
Majors	Florida Marlins	National	72	90	.444	t-12th (16)	Fredi Gonzalez/Jack McKeon
Triple-A	New Orleans Zephyrs	Pacific Coast	69	74	.483	10th (16)	Greg Norton
Double-A	Jacksonville Suns	Southern	70	70	.500	5th (10)	Andy Barkett
High A	Jupiter Hammerheads	Florida State	60	80	.429	12th (12)	Ron Hassey
Low A	Greensboro Grasshoppers	South Atlantic	79	60	.568	t-2nd (14)†	Andy Haines
Short-season	Jamestown Jammers	New York-Penn	35	40	.467	10th (14)	Dave Berg
Rookie	GCL Marlins	Gulf Coast	38	16	.704	1st (15)	Jorge Hernandez
Overall 2011 Minor League Record			351	340	.508	12th (30)	

*Finish in overall standings (No. of teams in league). †League champion.

LAST YEAR'S TOP 30

Player, Pos.		Status
1.	Matt Dominguez, 3b	No. 4
2.	Chad James, lhp	No. 6
3.	Christian Yelich, of	No. 1
4.	Jhan Marinez, rhp	(White Sox)
5.	Osvaldo Martinez, ss	(White Sox)
6.	Brad Hand, lhp	Majors
7.	Scott Cousins, of	No. 9
8.	Kyle Skipworth, c	No. 21
9.	Marcell Ozuna, of	No. 2
10.	Rob Rasmussen, lhp	No. 7
11.	Mike Dunn, lhp	Majors
12.	Jose Ceda, rhp	No. 15
13.	Tom Koehler, rhp	No. 26
14.	Elih Villanueva, rhp	Dropped out
15.	J.T. Realmuto, c	No. 5
16.	Daniel Jennings, lhp	No. 30
17.	Isaac Galloway, of	Dropped out
18.	Bryan Petersen, of	Majors
19.	Steve Cishek, rhp	Majors
20.	Arquimedes Caminero, rhp	Dropped out
21.	Sandy Rosario, rhp	No. 29
22.	Edgar Olmos, lhp	Dropped out
23.	Omar Poveda, rhp	Dropped out
24.	Jake Smolinski, 3b/of	Dropped out
25.	Kevin Cravey, rhp	Dropped out
26.	Noah Perio, ss/2b	No. 8
27.	Ramon Benjamin, lhp	Dropped out
28.	Robert Morey, rhp	Dropped out
29.	Brett Hayes, c	Majors
30.	Joey O'Gara, rhp	No. 25

BEST TOOLS

Best Hitter for Average	Christian Yelich
Best Power Hitter	Marcell Ozuna
Best Strike-Zone Discipline	Jake Smolinski
Fastest Baserunner	Kevin Mattison
Best Athlete	J.T. Realmuto
Best Fastball	Jose Fernandez
Best Curveball	Austin Brice
Best Slider	Rob Rasmussen
Best Changeup	Jose Alvarez
Best Control	Michael Brady
Best Defensive Catcher	J.T. Realmuto
Best Defensive Infielder	Matt Dominguez
Best Infield Arm	Matt Dominguez
Best Defensive Outfielder	Kevin Mattison
Best Outfield Arm	Marcell Ozuna

PROJECTED 2015 LINEUP

Catcher	J.T. Realmuto
First Base	Gaby Sanchez
Second Base	Noah Perio
Third Base	Hanley Ramirez
Shortstop	Jose Reyes
Left Field	Logan Morrison
Center Field	Christian Yelich
Right Field	Mike Stanton
No. 1 Starter	Josh Johnson
No. 2 Starter	Anibal Sanchez
No. 3 Starter	Jose Fernandez
No. 4 Starter	Mark Buehrle
No. 5 Starter	Chad James
Closer	Heath Bell

TOP PROSPECTS OF THE DECADE

Year	Player, Pos.	2011 Org.
2002	Josh Beckett, rhp	Red Sox
2003	Miguel Cabrera, 3b	Tigers
2004	Jeremy Hermida, of	Padres
2005	Jeremy Hermida, of	Padres
2006	Jeremy Hermida, of	Padres
2007	Chris Volstad, rhp	Marlins
2008	Cameron Maybin, of	Padres
2009	Cameron Maybin, of	Padres
2010	Mike Stanton, of	Marlins
2011	Matt Dominguez, 3b	Marlins

TOP DRAFT PICKS OF THE DECADE

Year	Player, Pos.	2011 Org.
2002	Jeremy Hermida, of	Padres
2003	Jeff Allison, rhp	Marlins
2004	Taylor Tankersley, lhp	Mets
2005	Chris Volstad, rhp	Marlins
2006	Brett Sinkbeil, rhp	Pirates
2007	Matt Dominguez, 3b	Marlins
2008	Kyle Skipworth, c	Marlins
2009	Chad James, lhp	Marlins
2010	Christian Yelich, of	Marlins
2011	Jose Fernandez, rhp	Marlins

LARGEST BONUSES IN CLUB HISTORY

Josh Beckett, 1999	$3,625,000
Adrian Gonzalez, 2000	$3,000,000
Livan Hernandez, 1996	$2,500,000
Kyle Skipworth, 2008	$2,300,000
Jason Stokes, 2000	$2,027,000

MIAMI MARLINS

TOP 2012 ROOKIE: Matt Dominguez, 3b. His bat may need some more Triple-A seasoning, but his glove is ready and the Marlins have an opening at the hot corner.

BREAKOUT PROSPECT: Jesus Solorzano, of. The toolsy center fielder will get his first crack at full-season ball.

SLEEPER: Danny Black, ss. The best shortstop prospect in the system, he has a line-drive stroke, plus speed and a strong arm.

SOURCE OF TOP 30 TALENT			
Homegrown	28	Acquired	2
College	14	Trades	2
Junior College	0	Rule 5 draft	0
High school	10	Independent leagues	0
Draft-and-follow	0	Free agents/waivers	0
Nondrafted free agents	0		
International	4		

LF
Christian Yelich (1)
Kyle Jensen (19)
Jake Smolinski
Kentrell Dewitt

CF
Scott Cousins (9)
Jesus Solorzano (16)
Kevin Mattison (27)
Isaac Galloway
Brent Keys

RF
Marcell Ozuna (2)
Jhiomar Veras

3B
Matt Dominguez (4)
Ryan Fisher (13)
Paul Gran
Chase Austin
Josh Adams

SS
Danny Black
Yeison Hernandez
Pedro Mendoza
Yefri Perez

2B
Noah Perio (8)
Ryan Curry
Luis Ortiz
Alfredo Lopez

1B
Mark Canha (22)
Ryan Rieger
Viosergy Rosa
Aaron Senne
Felix Munoz

C
J.T. Realmuto (5)
Kyle Skipworth (21)
Austin Barnes
Wilfredo Gimenez
Jobduan Morales
Tony Caldwell

LHP

LHSP	LHRP
Chad James (6)	Grant Dayton (17)
Rob Rasmussen (7)	Daniel Jennings (30)
Adam Conley (10)	Ramon Benjamin
Jose Alvarez	Wade Korpi
Charlie Lowell	
Edgar Olmos	
Greg Nappo	

RHP

RHSP	RHRP
Jose Fernandez (3)	Chris Hatcher (14)
Jose Urena (11)	Jose Ceda (15)
Austin Brice (12)	Michael Brady (18)
Mason Hope (23)	A.J. Ramos (20)
Joey O'Gara (25)	Evan Reed (24)
Tom Koehler (26)	Sandy Rosario (29)
Josh Hodges (28)	Arquimedes Caminero
Ramon del Orbe	Kevin Cravey
Elih Villanueva	Kyle Kaminska
Omar Poveda	Jacob Esch
Jose Rodriguez	Mike Ojala
Robert Morey	Scott Lyman
Zach Neal	Jose Rosario
Rett Varner	Pete Andrelczyk
Jared Rogers	Corey Madden
Helpi Reyes	Garrett Parcell
Dejai Oliver	James Nygren

DRAFT ANALYSIS

2011

BEST PURE HITTER: 1B Ryan Rieger (7) has a pretty lefthanded swing and keeps the bat in the hitting zone for a long time.

BEST POWER HITTER: OF Jhiomar Veras (15) topped NJCAA Division II with 23 homers in 2011, winning national player of the year honors and leading Western Oklahoma State to a national championship. He also tied for the NCJAA D-II lead with 20 longballs as a freshman.

FASTEST RUNNER: OF Ryan McIntyre (12) has regained his 65 speed on the 20-80 scouting scale. He missed much of the 2010 season after surgery to repair a torn anterior cruciate ligament in his right knee.

BEST DEFENSIVE PLAYER: C/2B Austin Barnes (9) never played behind the plate in high school before moving there at Arizona State. He's agile, has a quick release and threw out 39 percent of basestealers in his pro debut.

BEST FASTBALL: RHP Jose Fernandez (1) was clocked at 94-97 mph throwing his riding four-seam fastball in instructional league. He also has a heavy two-seamer in the low 90s. LHP Adam Conley (2) can hit 97 mph in shorter stints, and he has good sink on his two-seamer. LHP Charlie Lowell (6) and RHPs Scott Lyman (10) and Jacob Esch (11) all can run their fastballs up to 95-96 mph.

BEST SECONDARY PITCH: RHP Mason Hope (5) has a wipeout curveball that qualifies as a plus-plus pitch at times. Fernandez has a pair of power breaking balls in his curveball and slider, and Miami will let him keep throwing both because they don't detract from each other.

BEST PRO DEBUT: RHP James Nygren (33) had a 1.36 ERA, six saves and 34 strikeouts in 33 innings in the Gulf Coast League, though he was old by complex-league standards at 22. Finesse LHP Greg Nappo (18) opened his pro career with 14 scoreless innings at short-season Jamestown and went 3-0, 3.68 in his first four low Class A starts before fading late.

BEST ATHLETE: Barnes is more athletic than most catchers and still retains enough quickness that he played 12 games at second base in his pro debut. Veras has solid speed and arm strength to go with his impressive raw power.

MOST INTRIGUING BACKGROUND: As a Cuban defector, Fernandez has extra appeal to the South Florida market. RHP Dejai Oliver's (8) father Joe caught for 13 seasons in the majors. Barnes' uncle Mike Gallego also spent 13 seasons in the big leagues.

CLOSEST TO THE MAJORS: Conley or Lowell. If Conley refines his slider and/or moves to the bullpen, he should arrive in Miami first.

BEST LATE-ROUND PICK: Veras or Nygren, who throws a 90-92 mph fastball and solid slider for strikes.

THE ONE WHO GOT AWAY: The Marlins made a seven-figure offer to athletic SS Connor Barron (3) but couldn't lure him away from Southern Mississippi. They were close to signing offensive-minded 2B Tyler Palmer (4) before he cut his right hand so severely that it put his career in jeopardy.

ASSESSMENT: Not signing Barron or Palmer left the Marlins with just two position players in the first 11 rounds. Fernandez will try to become the club's first-rounder to make it big since Adrian Gonzalez (2000).

2010

OF Christian Yelich (1) is the Marlins' best prospect, and the next two picks, LHP Rob Rasmussen (2) and C J.T. Realmuto (3), are also off to nice starts. RHP Austin Brice (9) and 3B Ryan Fisher (15) have two of the higher ceilings in the system.

GRADE: B+

2009

LHP Chad James' (1) 10-25 record isn't indicative of his talent. OF Kyle Jensen (12) won the high Class A Florida State League MVP award last year. Offensive-minded 2B Noah Perio (39) was a late-round steal.

GRADE: C

2008

C Kyle Skipworth (1) has been a massive bust so far, though LHP Brad Hand (2) arrived in the majors ahead of schedule. RHP Elih Villanueva (27) also got a cup of coffee last year.

GRADE: C

2007

A big league home run title is in OF Mike Stanton's (2) future. 3B Matt Dominguez has Gold Glove ability but a questionable bat. OF Bryan Petersen (4) and RHP Steve Cishek (5) give the Marlins two more big leaguers from this draft.

GRADE: A

Draft analysis by Jim Callis. Numbers in parentheses indicate draft rounds.

1 CHRISTIAN YELICH, OF

Born: Dec. 5, 1991. **B-T:** L-R. **Ht.:** 6-4. **Wt.:** 189.
Drafted: HS—Westlake Village, Calif., 2010 (1st round). **Signed by:** Tim McDonnell.

BA GRADE

60
MEDIUM

TOM PRIDDY

Yelich is a product of the Westlake High (Westlake Village, Calif.) program that produced big leaguers Matt Franco, Mike Lieberthal, Mike Nickeas and John Snyder. One of the best hitters available in the 2010 draft, he went 23rd overall and signed for an above-slot $1.7 million bonus at the deadline. He spent a week at low Class A Greensboro at the end of his truncated pro debut, then returned there in 2011. Yelich caught fire in the second half, batting .354/.423/.568 with 10 of his 15 homers. His dramatic 15th-inning home run in the opening game of the playoffs set the Grasshoppers on the path to the South Atlantic League title. He finished third in the SAL in batting (.312) and ranked among league leaders in doubles (32), total bases (223), steals (32), on-base percentage (.388) and OPS (.871). The Marlins named him their minor league player of the year.

The Marlins loved Yelich's pure swing in high school and are even more enamored with it now. He's a rhythm hitter with an advanced approach at the plate, already demonstrating an understanding of which pitches to attack and which to let go. He has quick hands, covers the zone well with his long arms and lines balls to all fields. Early in the season, he was getting beat on balls because he wasn't starting his swing soon enough. Once he worked out those timing issues and became more familiar with the league, his confidence and his performance took off. He also learned to condense his strike zone and hone in on pitches he could drive. Yelich has power to center field as well as to his pull side, and while he doesn't project as an elite slugger, he should be a threat for 25 homers annually once he fills out his lanky frame and learns to create more leverage in his swing. His solid-average to plus speed and baserunning acumen are even better than Miami expected. He was caught just five times in 37 steal attempts. He's a glider in the outfield, covering ground with long strides. A first baseman in high school, he played both left and center at Greensboro. At times he still appears to be thinking instead of reacting instinctively in the outfield, but he has put in a lot of extra early work to improve his defense. His raw arm strength is average, though his throwing is hindered by poor mechanics and a long arm stroke, which Miami believes can be ironed out. The organization loves his attitude, work ethic and competitive nature.

Yelich should open 2012 at high Class A Jupiter, surrounded by the same teammates who helped him raise a flag in Greensboro. He's a good bet to advance faster than the rest of them, however, and may not need a full season in the Florida State League. While the Marlins plan to keep giving him time in center field, he projects as a left fielder with better than average range. His swing elicits comparisons to Will Clark and should eventually land him in the No. 3 spot in Miami's order.

SCOUTING GRADES

Batting: 65. **Defense:** 55.
Power: 60. **Arm:** 45.
Speed: 55.

Based on 20-80 scouting scale, where 50 represents major league average, and future projection rather than present tools.

Year	Club (League)	Class	AVG	G	AB	R	H	2B	3B	HR	RBI	BB	SO	SB	CS	OBP	SLG
2010	Marlins (GCL)	R	.375	6	24	3	9	1	1	0	3	2	7	1	0	.423	.500
	Greensboro (SAL)	LoA	.348	6	23	2	8	2	0	0	2	1	6	0	0	.375	.435
2011	Greensboro (SAL)	LoA	.312	122	461	73	144	32	1	15	77	55	102	32	5	.388	.484
Minor League Totals			.317	134	508	78	161	35	2	15	82	58	115	33	5	.389	.482

2 MARCELL OZUNA, OF

Born: Nov. 12, 1990. **B-T:** R-R. **Ht.:** 6-2. **Wt.:** 190. **Signed:** Dominican Republic, 2008. **Signed by:** Sandy Nin.

Ozuna led the short-season New York-Penn League with 21 home runs and 60 RBIs in 2010 despite striking out in 35 percent of his at-bats. He struggled early in 2011 but put it all together in the second half, hitting .310/.371/.585 with 15 homers. He batted .353 with three homers in seven playoff games as Greensboro won the South Atlantic League title. Ozuna wows scouts with his tools, especially his well above-average raw power and bazooka arm. Before 2011, he had lacked plate discipline and shown a particular susceptibility to breaking balls down and out of the zone. After putting in extra time with Grasshoppers hitting coach Kevin Randel and learning to focus on finding pitches he could drive to the middle of the field, Ozuna took a huge step forward. He has slightly above-average speed and was caught only twice in 19 steal attempts last season. He uses his athleticism well in right field, where he shows above-average range and a strong arm, though his throwing accuracy can improve. The Marlins love his infectious enthusiasm for the game. Ozuna will advance to high Class A and attempt to maintain the gains he showed in the second half of 2011. His ability to manage his strike zone will dictate how quickly he moves.

BA GRADE
60
HIGH

Year	Club (League)	Class	AVG	G	AB	R	H	2B	3B	HR	RBI	BB	SO	SB	CS	OBP	SLG
2008	Marlins (DSL)	R	.279	63	233	33	65	14	0	6	43	23	61	8	1	.335	.416
2009	Marlins (GCL)	R	.313	55	214	32	67	22	0	5	39	22	52	4	2	.377	.486
2010	Greensboro (SAL)	LoA	.160	6	25	3	4	0	0	1	2	2	10	0	0	.222	.280
	Jamestown (NYP)	SS	.267	68	270	53	72	11	2	21	60	17	94	3	1	.314	.556
2011	Greensboro (SAL)	LoA	.266	131	496	87	132	28	5	23	71	46	121	17	2	.330	.482
Minor League Totals			.275	323	1238	208	340	75	7	56	215	110	338	32	6	.334	.482

3 JOSE FERNANDEZ, RHP

Born: July 31, 1992. **B-T:** R-R. **Ht.:** 6-3. **Wt.:** 215. **Drafted:** HS—Tampa, 2011 (1st round). **Signed by:** Brian Kraft.

Fernandez fled Cuba in a speedboat with his mother and sister in 2008, finding freedom on their second escape attempt. He learned English after settling in Tampa, where he led Alonso High to two Florida 6-A state championships in three years. The Marlins drafted him 14th overall last June and signed him to an above-slot $2 million bonus at the Aug. 15 deadline. Fernandez offers a power arsenal, starting with a fastball that ranges from 92-95 mph and reaches as high as 97. His two-seamer doesn't sink as much as it bores in on righthanders. His four-seamer has a little run to it but at times comes in too straight. He throws both a sharp-breaking curveball and a hard slider, and he also shows feel for a promising changeup. Fernandez uses his lower half well, getting in position to explode through his hips. While he'll overthrow on occasion, leaving the ball up in the zone, his command projects as average to plus. Despite his size, he's a good athlete. Fernandez will compete for a job in low Class A during his first spring training. He profiles as a No. 2 starter in the big leagues, though he'll need time to develop.

CLIFF WELCH

BA GRADE
60
HIGH

Year	Club (League)	Class	W	L	ERA	G	GS	CG	SV	IP	H	HR	BB	SO	K/9	WHIP	AVG
2011	Marlins (GCL)	R	0	0	0.00	1	1	0	0	2	1	0	1	3	13.5	1.00	.125
	Jamestown (NYP)	SS	0	1	19.29	1	1	0	0	2	4	0	3	4	15.4	3.00	.400
Minor League Totals			0	1	10.38	2	2	0	0	4	5	0	4	7	14.5	2.08	.278

4 MATT DOMINGUEZ, 3B

Born: Aug. 28, 1989. **B-T:** R-R. **Ht.:** 6-1. **Wt.:** 205. **Drafted:** HS—Chatsworth, Calif., 2007 (1st round). **Signed by:** Tim McDonnell.

Dominguez and Chatsworth (Calif.) High teammate Mike Moustakas were both first-round picks in 2007, with Dominguez signing for $1.8 million as the No. 12 choice. The No. 1 prospect on this list a year ago, he entered spring training favored to win a starting job. But he batted just .190 before he was reassigned to minor league camp, where a pitch fractured his left elbow and cost him the first five weeks of the season. Dominguez's calling card always has been his defense. He possesses Gold Glove ability, with good anticipation, quick feet, smooth hands and a strong, accurate arm. He has yet to make the same kind of impact at the plate, however. Dominguez's hand-eye coordination works against him, as he believes he can put the bat on pitches he needs to let go. He gets tied up on the inner half and rarely drives the ball with authority. If he can become more selective and repeat his swing, he could become an average hitter with average power. He has below-

BA GRADE
50
MEDIUM

average speed but good instincts. After making his big league debut in September, Dominguez will challenge for the third-base job again in spring training. He'll likely need some more time at Triple-A New Orleans before his bat is ready.

Year	Club (League)	Class	AVG	G	AB	R	H	2B	3B	HR	RBI	BB	SO	SB	CS	OBP	SLG
2007	Marlins (GCL)	R	.100	5	20	0	2	0	0	0	2	1	2	0	0	.136	.100
	Jamestown (NYP)	SS	.189	10	37	3	7	2	0	1	4	1	12	0	0	.211	.324
2008	Greensboro (SAL)	LoA	.296	88	345	59	102	16	0	18	70	28	68	0	1	.354	.499
2009	Jupiter (FSL)	HiA	.262	103	381	49	100	25	1	11	53	38	68	1	0	.333	.420
	Jacksonville (SL)	AA	.186	31	97	10	18	7	0	2	9	14	24	0	0	.292	.320
2010	Jacksonville (SL)	AA	.252	138	504	61	127	34	2	14	81	56	96	0	2	.333	.411
2011	Jupiter (FSL)	HiA	.167	4	18	0	3	0	0	0	2	1	3	0	0	.250	.167
	Jacksonville (SL)	AA	.133	4	15	1	2	0	0	0	1	3	2	0	0	.316	.133
	New Orleans (PCL)	AAA	.258	87	325	47	84	18	1	12	55	24	50	0	1	.312	.431
	Florida (NL)	MAJ	.244	17	45	2	11	4	0	0	2	2	8	0	0	.292	.333
Major League Totals			.244	17	45	2	11	4	0	0	2	2	8	0	0	.292	.333
Minor League Totals			.255	470	1742	230	445	102	4	58	277	166	325	1	4	.325	.418

5 J.T. REALMUTO, C

Born: March 18, 1991. **B-T:** R-R. **Ht.:** 6-1. **Wt.:** 190. **Drafted:** HS—Midwest City, Okla., 2010 (3rd round). **Signed by:** Steve Taylor.

A star quarterback in high school, Realmuto set national records in 2010 with 88 hits and 119 RBIs while hitting .595 with 28 home runs. The Marlins signed him for $600,000 in the third round that summer and moved him from shortstop to catcher. After they shortened his stride and started his hands in a better hitting position, he batted .299/.351/.519 in the second half of 2011 with all 12 of his homers—including one off a rehabbing Stephen Strasburg. Realmuto projects as a solid hitter, though he gets in trouble at times expanding his zone. He's still learning which pitches to drive and when to pull balls to tap into his average power. A gifted all-around athlete, his plus speed stands out for a catcher. With his agility, soft hands and strong arm, he has the tools to be an above-average defender. He threw out 42 percent of basestealers in 2011 while exhibiting 1.9-second pop times. He needs to get better on blocking pitches and committed 25 passed balls in 76 games, many a result of trying to keep pitches in the strike zone. Realmuto will move a level at a time as he incorporates the many adjustments the Marlins have thrown at him. He has blown by 2008 first-rounder Kyle Skipworth as Miami's catcher of the future.

BA GRADE
55
HIGH

Year	Club (League)	Class	AVG	G	AB	R	H	2B	3B	HR	RBI	BB	SO	SB	CS	OBP	SLG
2010	Marlins (GCL)	R	.175	12	40	2	7	0	0	0	4	7	11	0	1	.298	.175
2011	Greensboro (SAL)	LoA	.287	96	348	46	100	16	3	12	49	26	78	13	6	.347	.454
Minor League Totals			.276	108	388	48	107	16	3	12	53	33	89	13	7	.342	.425

6 CHAD JAMES, LHP

Born: Jan. 23, 1991. **B-T:** L-L. **Ht.:** 6-3. **Wt.:** 185. **Drafted:** HS—Yukon, Okla., 2009 (1st round). **Signed by:** Ryan Wardinsky.

James signed for $1.7 million at the deadline after being selected with the 18th overall pick in the 2009 draft. After going 5-10 at Greensboro in his pro debut, he began 2011 0-13 before winning five of his final seven decisions. His older brother Justin pitched briefly with the 2010 Athletics. After touching 95 mph in low Class A, James' fastball backed up in 2011, ranging from 90-93 mph early in the season and down to 89-91 by the end. The heat and humidity in the Florida State League may have worn him down, and he also sacrificed velocity in an effort to gain more consistency with his delivery and command. His curveball was so unreliable that the Marlins took it away and asked him to focus on his slider, which he locates better. They also asked him to throw his straight changeup more frequently. As a result, he often pitched backward, a learning strategy that contributed to his ups and downs. He committed six errors in 27 starts and needs to field his position better. It's time for James to put everything together and apply the lessons he learned in 2011. Whether his fastball returns will determine if he can reach his ceiling as a mid-rotation starter.

BA GRADE
55
HIGH

Year	Club (League)	Class	W	L	ERA	G	GS	CG	SV	IP	H	HR	BB	SO	K/9	WHIP	AVG
2010	Greensboro (SAL)	LoA	5	10	5.12	24	24	0	0	114	116	3	65	105	8.3	1.58	.269
2011	Jupiter (FSL)	HiA	5	15	3.80	27	27	0	0	149	173	12	51	124	7.5	1.50	.294
Minor League Totals			10	25	4.37	51	51	0	0	264	289	15	116	229	7.8	1.54	.283

7 ROB RASMUSSEN, LHP

Born: April 2, 1989. **B-T:** R-L. **Ht.:** 5-10. **Wt.:** 155. **Drafted:** UCLA, 2010 (2nd round). **Signed by:** Tim McDonnell.

Rasmussen was the No. 3 starter on UCLA's College World Series runner-up team in 2010, pitching behind Gerrit Cole and Trevor Bauer, the first and third picks in the 2011 draft. Rasmussen pitched just seven innings after signing and essentially made his pro debut in 2011, when he posted a 5.91 ERA in April and a 3.26 mark afterward. Rasmussen owns four solid-average pitches with a 90-93 mph fastball, a slider, a curveball and a changeup. His fastball command was poor early in the season, when he worked up in the zone too frequently and wasn't able to get away with it like he did in college. He learned to keep his fastball down and move it all around the zone, and he also did a better job of pitching off his heater. Rasmussen's 84-87 mph slider is his best secondary pitch, though he still needs to improve the angle on it. He gets nice two-plane break on his upper-70s curve. He isn't afraid to work inside. Rasmussen will move up to Double-A Jacksonville in 2012 and may not need much more than another year in the minors. Some Marlins officials see his future as a situational lefty, but he'll continue to start for now.

BA GRADE

50

MEDIUM

Year	Club (League)	Class	W	L	ERA	G	GS	CG	SV	IP	H	HR	BB	SO	K/9	WHIP	AVG
2010	Greensboro (SAL)	LoA	0	0	1.35	5	0	0	0	7	6	0	2	4	5.4	1.20	.240
2011	Jupiter (FSL)	HiA	12	10	3.64	28	27	1	0	148	140	10	71	118	7.2	1.42	.254
Minor League Totals			12	10	3.54	33	27	1	0	155	146	10	73	122	7.1	1.41	.253

8 NOAH PERIO, 2B

Born: Nov. 14, 1991. **B-T:** L-R. **Ht.:** 6-0. **Wt.:** 170. **Drafted:** HS—Concord, Calif., 2009 (39th round). **Signed by:** John Hughes.

Because he was better known as wide receiver/defensive back and had a baseball scholarship from Texas, Perio fell to the 39th round of the 2009 draft. The Marlins made a late push and signed him for $150,000, and he since has blossomed into their top middle-infield prospect. The wiry, athletic Perio makes good contact and keeps the barrel of his bat level and in the zone. While he doesn't strike out a lot, the Marlins would like him to be more selective, looking for pitches to drive and taking more walks. He quit hurrying his lower half and learned to trust his strong hands and wrists, finally tapping into his power and slugging .458 in the second half of 2011. He's an average runner with good instincts, but he won't be a prolific basestealer. Perio began his pro career as a shortstop, but his fringy arm predicated a move to second base, where he has good range but committed 24 errors in 114 games at Greensboro. He has the work ethic to become an average defender. Perio projects as an offensive-minded second baseman, a No. 2 hitter with good pop that will only get better as he fills out. He'll play in high Class A in 2012.

BA GRADE

50

HIGH

Year	Club (League)	Class	AVG	G	AB	R	H	2B	3B	HR	RBI	BB	SO	SB	CS	OBP	SLG
2009	Marlins (GCL)	R	.429	4	14	2	6	1	1	0	5	0	0	1	0	.429	.643
2010	Jamestown (NYP)	SS	.258	59	225	30	58	10	0	0	31	17	25	7	0	.313	.302
2011	Greensboro (SAL)	LoA	.295	119	488	76	144	30	3	6	52	19	64	15	6	.323	.406
Minor League Totals			.286	182	727	108	208	41	4	6	88	36	89	23	6	.322	.378

9 SCOTT COUSINS, OF

Born: Jan. 22, 1985. **B-T:** L-L. **Ht.:** 6-1. **Wt.:** 195. **Drafted:** San Francisco, 2006 (3rd round). **Signed by:** John Hughes.

A two-way star in college, Cousins climbed through the system a level at a time. He earned a September callup in 2010 and made the Marlins' Opening Day roster last year, though he had a poor camp and benefited from an injury to DeWayne Wise. Cousins served as a defensive replacement and pinch-hitter, making his biggest headlines when he flattened Giants catcher Buster Posey on a play at the plate. Hip and ankle injuries nagged Cousins even before a bulging disk in his back ended his season in mid-June. He has solid tools across the board, projecting as a possible .280 hitter with 15-20 homers if he can work his way into the everyday lineup. One of the best athletes in the system, he has the speed to steal 20 bases and enough range to patrol all three outfield spots. His plus arm is strong enough for right field. Cousins' bugaboo throughout his ascent has been a lack of consistency, which was only exacerbated by a bench role. When he's cold, he tends to chase pitches out of the zone. He has the talent to make a bigger impact than he made in 2011, but he'll need better health and an opportunity.

BA GRADE

45

MEDIUM

MIAMI MARLINS

Year	Club (League)	Class	AVG	G	AB	R	H	2B	3B	HR	RBI	BB	SO	SB	CS	OBP	SLG
2006	Jamestown (NYP)	SS	.211	21	90	11	19	1	0	1	6	4	17	3	1	.253	.256
2007	Greensboro (SAL)	LoA	.292	110	421	69	123	25	0	18	74	38	92	16	7	.358	.480
2008	Marlins (GCL)	R	.000	2	6	0	0	0	0	0	0	0	5	0	0	.000	.000
	Jupiter (FSL)	HiA	.304	49	191	35	58	9	2	9	29	20	47	11	3	.370	.513
	Carolina (SL)	AA	.264	27	91	15	24	7	1	1	9	10	28	4	1	.350	.396
2009	Jacksonville (SL)	AA	.263	130	482	60	127	31	11	12	74	42	107	27	9	.323	.448
2010	New Orleans (PCL)	AAA	.285	118	410	74	117	20	5	14	49	32	78	12	4	.336	.461
	Florida (NL)	MAJ	.297	27	37	2	11	2	2	0	2	1	13	0	0	.316	.459
2011	Florida (NL)	MAJ	.135	48	52	5	7	1	0	1	4	6	21	1	1	.224	.212
	Jupiter (FSL)	HiA	.308	5	13	2	4	0	0	0	2	3	4	0	0	.438	.308
	New Orleans (PCL)	AAA	.222	2	9	1	2	0	0	0	1	1	3	0	0	.300	.222
Major League Totals			.202	75	89	7	18	3	2	1	6	7	34	1	1	.260	.315
Minor League Totals			.277	464	1713	267	474	93	19	55	244	150	381	73	25	.338	.450

BA GRADE
50
HIGH

10 ADAM CONLEY, LHP

Born: May 24, 1990. **B-T:** L-L. **Ht.:** 6-3. **Wt.:** 185. **Drafted:** Washington State, 2011 (2nd round). **Signed by:** Gabe Sandy.

Washington State's primary closer as a sophomore, Conley moved into the rotation last spring and impressed the Marlins enough that they popped him in the second round and inked him to a $625,000 bonus. His heavy, two-seam fastball operates at 89-91 mph with good life, and he also throws a 92-94 mph four-seamer that hit 97 mph when he worked out of the bullpen. His sinker has the makings of a plus pitch, as does his straight changeup, which he turns over and fades away from righthanders. He didn't use his slider much in his days as a reliever, so it lags behind his other pitches, often just rolling up to the plate and lacking any snap. Conley has a very quick arm and some deception to his delivery, using a lower arm slot and throwing across his body. Despite the funkiness, he has good command. His frame is wiry and he'll need to get in the weight room to add strength. If Conley can refine his slider, he has a chance to become a solid No. 3 or 4 starter. He may not open 2012 in high Class A, but he should get there by the end of the season.

Year	Club (League)	Class	W	L	ERA	G	GS	CG	SV	IP	H	HR	BB	SO	K/9	WHIP	AVG
2011	Marlins (GCL)	R	0	0	0.00	2	0	0	0	2	1	0	0	2	9.0	0.50	.143
Minor League Totals			0	0	0.00	2	0	0	0	2	1	0	0	2	9.0	0.50	.143

11 JOSE URENA, RHP

BA GRADE
50
HIGH

Born: Sept. 12, 1991. **B-T:** R-R. **Ht.:** 6-3. **Wt.:** 172. **Signed:** Dominican Republic, 2008. **Signed by:** Sandy Nin.

The Marlins inked Urena in 2008 for what appears to be a bargain at $52,000. After spending two seasons in the Rookie-level Dominican Summer League, the lean righthander made his U.S. debut last summer and ranked as the No. 5 prospect in the New York-Penn League. Urena has a nice, loose arm action and a projectable frame. He throws his fastball at 92-94 mph with good life, running it up to 96-97 at times. He'll flash a plus slider on occasion, but it lacks consistent depth and he doesn't get enough swings and misses with it yet. He has a good feel for his changeup, but it too has a ways to progress. Some nights he looks unhittable, and on others he gets caught up trying to overthrow and loses his command. In addition to the usual trials on the field, Urena is still dealing with a significant language barrier. He improved at holding runners and fielding his position last summer. He's a competitor who's not afraid to show a little animation on the hill. Urena should get his first taste of full-season ball this spring at Greensboro.

Year	Club (League)	Class	W	L	ERA	G	GS	CG	SV	IP	H	HR	BB	SO	K/9	WHIP	AVG
2009	Marlins (DSL)	R	3	3	6.75	14	2	0	2	27	36	0	11	15	5.1	1.76	.313
2010	Marlins (DSL)	R	5	6	2.61	13	13	3	0	83	76	2	7	66	7.2	1.00	.241
2011	Jamestown (NYP)	SS	4	7	4.33	15	15	0	0	73	74	4	29	48	5.9	1.42	.264
Minor League Totals			12	16	3.91	42	30	3	2	182	186	6	47	129	6.4	1.28	.262

12 AUSTIN BRICE, RHP

BA GRADE
50
HIGH

Born: June 19, 1992. **B-T:** R-R. **Ht.:** 6-4. **Wt.:** 205. **Drafted:** HS—Pittsboro, N.C., 2010 (9th round). **Signed by:** Joel Matthews.

The top-rated North Carolina high school pitcher in the 2010 draft, Brice passed on an Appalachian State scholarship after the Marlins offered him $205,000 as a ninth-round pick. He made six relief appearances after signing but didn't see serious action until last summer. His 10.2 strikeouts per nine innings paced the Rookie-level Gulf Coast League, but so did his 33 walks. Brice's plus fastball sits at 92-94 mph, reaching as high as 96. He has a natural feel to spin the ball and throws an above-average curveball in the low 80s with downer action. He's gaining a better feel for his changeup and it could blossom into at least an average offering.

Despite his control issues last year, Brice isn't wild. He just hasn't learned how to harness all of his weapons yet, particularly the curve. His arm action is clean and he already has a nice delivery, though he's trying to get a little more compact with his lead arm. He maintains excellent poise on the hill, at times appearing almost stoic. Brice should make his full-season debut at Greensboro this year.

Year	Club (League)	Class	W	L	ERA	G	GS	CG	SV	IP	H	HR	BB	SO	K/9	WHIP	AVG
2010	Marlins (GCL)	R	0	1	4.32	6	0	0	0	8	7	0	7	8	8.6	1.68	.219
2011	Marlins (GCL)	R	6	0	2.96	11	9	0	0	49	32	2	33	55	10.2	1.34	.189
Minor League Totals			6	1	3.16	17	9	0	0	57	39	2	40	63	9.9	1.39	.194

13 RYAN FISHER, 3B

BA GRADE
50
HIGH

Born: April 24, 1988. **B-T:** L-R. **Ht.:** 6-3. **Wt.:** 195. **Drafted:** UC Irvine, 2010 (15th round). **Signed by:** Tim McDonnell.

Primarily a corner outfielder at UC Irvine, where he wasn't an everyday player, Fisher has found a home at the hot corner since signing for $25,000 as a 15th-round pick in 2010. He played some third base at short-season Jamestown in his pro debut, when he led the New York-Penn League with 41 extra-base hits, and move there full-time in 2011, when he topped the system with 58 extra-base hits. Fisher's bat speed gives him solid power and he consistently hits the ball hard—when he hits it. His strikeouts result more from his bat not staying in the zone long enough than from chasing pitches outside of it, and he may always provide more power than average. Fisher struggles versus lefthanders, posting a .638 OPS against them last year compared to an .868 mark against righties. He's at his best when he focuses on driving the ball to left-center. Fisher's speed is a hair below average but he's quick enough to move back to the outfield if necessary. He has the tools to play third base, however, with good range and a solid arm. His feet are getting quicker, though he still has room yet to improve. He has a great work ethic, frequently arriving early for extra drills. Fisher will take his extra-base bat to high Class A in 2012, when he'll work on making better contact and solving southpaws.

Year	Club (League)	Class	AVG	G	AB	R	H	2B	3B	HR	RBI	BB	SO	SB	CS	OBP	SLG
2010	Jamestown (NYP)	SS	.274	67	252	47	69	24	9	8	49	22	77	1	1	.346	.536
2011	Greensboro (SAL)	LoA	.258	129	469	74	121	36	4	18	79	38	137	7	3	.330	.467
Minor League Totals			.264	196	721	121	190	60	13	26	128	60	214	8	4	.336	.491

14 CHRIS HATCHER, RHP

BA GRADE
45
MEDIUM

Born: Jan. 12, 1985. **B-T:** B-R. **Ht.:** 6-2. **Wt.:** 205. **Drafted:** UNC Wilmington, 2006 (5th round). **Signed by:** Joel Matthews.

Hatcher's defensive ability garnered him a September callup as a catcher in 2010, but his light bat led him to become a full-time pitcher in 2011. Despite having made just two previous emergency relief appearances as pro, he made the transition seem effortless and earned a return trip to Florida in mid-July. The arm strength that Hatcher showed behind the plate translates into a 93-95 mph fastball. He has a natural feel for throwing strikes, though there's room to refine his command, particularly down in the zone. He lacks consistency with his tight 84-87 mph slider, which could give him a second above-average pitch. When he gains enough confidence to throw his slider in fastball counts, he'll be able to keep hitters from sitting on his heater. His straight changeup is already usable and has a chance to become an average offering. He utilizes a compact delivery and quick arm action, displaying a confidence on the mound that belies his novice status. Hatcher will go to camp with a shot at winning a job in Miami's relief corps. He may need some time to further refine his secondary pitches, but his upside is as high as any reliever's in the system.

Year	Club (League)	Class	AVG	G	AB	R	H	2B	3B	HR	RBI	BB	SO	SB	CS	OBP	SLG
2006	Jamestown (NYP)	SS	.181	36	127	19	23	4	2	2	17	11	40	3	1	.273	.291
2007	Greensboro (SAL)	LoA	.242	102	356	62	86	23	1	15	50	34	104	8	6	.312	.438
2008	Jupiter (FSL)	HiA	.178	63	202	22	36	12	0	6	28	23	78	3	1	.278	.327
2009	Jupiter (FSL)	HiA	.333	6	18	4	6	1	0	0	2	1	8	0	1	.400	.389
	Jacksonville (SL)	AA	.218	51	156	29	34	9	3	8	27	14	43	1	0	.294	.468
2010	New Orleans (PCL)	AAA	.167	17	48	10	8	1	0	2	10	9	19	0	0	.333	.313
	Jacksonville (SL)	AA	.202	84	267	23	54	9	1	3	26	20	92	1	2	.261	.277
	Florida (NL)	MAJ	.000	5	6	0	0	0	0	0	0	0	2	0	0	.250	.000
Major League Totals			.000	17	6	0	0	0	0	0	0	0	2	0	0	.250	.000
Minor League Totals			.211	385	1178	169	248	59	7	36	160	112	385	17	11	.290	.364

Year	Club (League)	Class	W	L	ERA	G	GS	CG	SV	IP	H	HR	BB	SO	K/9	WHIP	AVG
2009	Jacksonville (SL)	AA	0	0	0.00	1	0	0	0	0	0	0	0	0	0.0	0.00	.000
2010	Jacksonville (SL)	AA	1	0	0.00	1	0	0	0	1	0	0	0	1	9.0	0.00	.000
2011	Jacksonville (SL)	AA	2	1	1.90	42	0	0	6	47	32	2	19	57	10.8	1.08	.192
	Florida (NL)	MAJ	0	0	6.97	11	0	0	0	10	14	2	4	8	7.0	1.74	.341
Major League Totals			0	0	6.97	11	0	0	0	10	14	2	4	8	7.0	1.74	.341
Minor League Totals			3	1	1.85	44	0	0	6	49	32	2	19	58	10.7	1.05	.187

15 JOSE CEDA, RHP

Born: Jan. 28, 1987. **B-T:** R-R. **Ht.:** 6-4. **Wt.:** 275. **Signed:** Dominican Republic, 2004. **Signed by:** Felix Francisco/Randy Smith (Padres).

BA GRADE
45
MEDIUM

Originally signed by the Padres in 2004, Ceda went to the Cubs in a 2006 trade for Todd Walker and came to the Marlins in a 2008 deal for Kevin Gregg. After making his big league debut in September 2010, he took a step back last spring, showing up to camp overweight and getting held out of workouts. He recovered his mojo at New Orleans, where managers tabbed him the best relief prospect in the Pacific Coast League. Ceda's fastball touched 100 mph in the Cubs system and now sits at 95-96 mph, which is plenty. Command has been an issue in the past, but he was able to keep his fastball down in the zone much better as 2011, at least until he was called up. He also improved the location on his solid average slider. Ceda also will work in an occasional splitter, which has developed into a usable third pitch, particularly against lefties. Conditioning is always going to be a concern, and he missed all of 2009 following shoulder surgery. If he can command his pitches like he did in Triple-A last year, Ceda will win a big league bullpen job in spring training. His ceiling is that of a set-up man.

Year	Club (League)	Class	W	L	ERA	G	GS	CG	SV	IP	H	HR	BB	SO	K/9	WHIP	AVG
2005	Padres (DSL)	R	4	2	1.50	13	9	2	2	60	38	2	29	83	12.5	1.12	.174
2006	Padres (AZL)	R	2	0	5.09	8	4	0	0	23	20	1	13	31	12.1	1.43	.235
	Cubs (AZL)	R	0	0	0.75	5	3	0	0	12	6	0	7	21	15.8	1.08	.154
	Boise (NWL)	SS	1	0	3.27	3	3	0	0	11	5	1	2	11	9.0	0.64	.139
2007	Cubs (AZL)	R	0	0	2.45	2	1	0	0	4	2	0	3	3	7.4	1.36	.182
	Peoria (MWL)	LoA	2	2	3.11	21	6	0	0	46	14	1	31	66	12.8	0.97	.093
2008	Daytona (FSL)	HiA	2	2	4.80	15	12	0	0	54	41	4	28	53	8.8	1.27	.212
	Tennessee (SL)	AA	2	1	2.08	22	0	0	9	30	26	2	14	42	12.5	1.32	.234
2009	Did Not Play—Injured																
2010	Greensboro (SAL)	LoA	0	0	4.50	7	0	0	0	8	7	2	1	5	5.6	1.00	.226
	Jacksonville (SL)	AA	4	1	1.39	27	0	0	6	32	18	2	20	45	12.5	1.18	.168
	Florida (NL)	MAJ	0	0	5.19	8	0	0	0	9	8	1	11	9	9.3	2.19	.242
2011	New Orleans (PCL)	AAA	3	1	1.36	36	0	0	24	40	30	1	13	53	12.0	1.08	.201
	Florida (NL)	MAJ	0	1	4.43	17	0	0	0	20	16	1	12	21	9.3	1.38	.211
Major League Totals			0	1	4.66	25	0	0	0	29	24	2	23	30	9.3	1.62	.220
Minor League Totals			20	9	2.69	159	38	2	41	321	207	16	161	413	11.6	1.15	.183

16 JESUS SOLORZANO, OF

Born: Aug. 8, 1990. **B-T:** R-R. **Ht.:** 6-0. **Wt.:** 190. **Signed:** Venezuela, 2009. **Signed by:** Wilmer Castillo.

BA GRADE
50
EXTREME

One of the best athletes in the system, Solorzano spent two years in the Dominican Summer League before making his U.S. debut in 2011. He's an aggressive hitter with gap power, and the ball jumps nicely off his bat. He has raw strength and could develop average to plus power in time. His plate discipline has room to improve, as he's too often tempted by pitches out of the zone, but he makes consistent contact. Solorzano's plus speed gives him basestealing ability and the range to cover center field from gap to gap. He shows good instincts on defense. Mix in a plus arm and he's capable of playing any of the outfield spots, though he'll continue to advance as a center fielder for the immediate future. Solorzano plays with energy to match his exciting package of tools. He'll compete for a spot on the Greensboro roster this spring.

Year	Club (League)	Class	AVG	G	AB	R	H	2B	3B	HR	RBI	BB	SO	SB	CS	OBP	SLG
2009	Marlins (DSL)	R	.109	23	55	6	6	0	1	1	6	5	18	2	1	.219	.200
2010	Marlins (DSL)	R	.286	51	175	22	50	7	2	0	13	11	47	12	3	.365	.349
2011	Marlins (GCL)	R	.299	51	194	34	58	13	4	3	31	13	30	18	7	.355	.454
Minor League Totals			.269	125	424	62	114	20	7	4	50	29	95	32	11	.341	.377

17 GRANT DAYTON, LHP

Born: Nov. 25, 1987. **B-T:** L-L. **Ht.:** 6-2. **Wt.:** 200. **Drafted:** Auburn, 2010 (11th round). **Signed by:** Mark Willoughby.

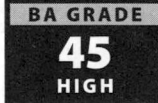

BA GRADE
45
HIGH

Dayton exhibited pinpoint control as a starter at Auburn, where he relied mainly on his fastball and changeup. An 11th-round pick in 2010, he took off last spring after Greensboro pitching coach Willie Glen moved him from the third-base side of the rubber to the first-base side and worked with him to improve his slider. Including the playoffs, Dayton posted a 111-27 K-BB in 79 innings. He's aggressive with his fastball, which sits at 91-94 mph and reaches 96. He beats hitters with it, garnering swings and misses on fastballs in the strike zone. He has good depth on his 81-84 mph slider and has learned to drop it in on the back foot of righthanders. His changeup is serviceable but it's not as good as his other two offerings and he doesn't use it often. Scouts love the way the ball comes easy out of Dayton's hand. He projects as a set-up man more than a situational reliever, and some Marlins officials would like to see what he could do as a starter.

Year	Club (League)	Class	W	L	ERA	G	GS	CG	SV	IP	H	HR	BB	SO	K/9	WHIP	AVG
2010	Marlins (GCL)	R	0	0	0.00	1	0	0	1	1	0	0	0	1	9.0	0.00	.000
	Jamestown (NYP)	SS	1	1	1.26	17	0	0	1	29	18	0	15	23	7.2	1.15	.186
2011	Greensboro (SAL)	LoA	7	1	2.89	49	0	0	5	72	59	5	24	99	12.4	1.16	.223
Minor League Totals			8	2	2.40	67	0	0	7	101	77	5	39	123	10.9	1.14	.211

18 MICHAEL BRADY, RHP

BA GRADE
45
HIGH

Born: March 21, 1987. **B-T:** R-R. **Ht.:** 6-0. **Wt.:** 200. **Drafted:** California, 2009 (24th round). **Signed by:** Robby Corsaro.

Brady hit just .254 as an infielder at California, but he caught the Marlins' eye with his arm strength, which was enough to get him drafted in the 24th round in 2009. Signed for $1,500, he went 3-for-35 in his pro debut before converting to the mound in 2010. He took to the switch immediately and has posted a 1.87 ERA and 106-15 K-BB ratio in two seasons. Brady is a natural strike-thrower with plus command, especially with a 90-93 mph fastball that he can locate with pinpoint precision. His fastball plays better than its velocity, because it takes a little hop at the end and hitters seem to have trouble picking it up. His 83-84 mph slider has a chance to be an above-average pitch, but his changeup is mostly just for show at this point. As expected given his background, Brady fields his position well. He exhibits an even-keel demeanor, never getting too high or too low. He projects as a quality middle reliever or set-up man and could move through the upper levels of the system quickly. He's a candidate to skip a level and open 2012 in Double-A.

Year	Club (League)	Class	W	L	ERA	G	GS	CG	SV	IP	H	HR	BB	SO	K/9	WHIP	AVG
2010	Jamestown (NYP)	SS	1	1	1.59	26	0	0	3	28	17	2	4	25	7.9	0.74	.173
2011	Jacksonville (SL)	AA	0	0	4.50	1	0	0	0	2	3	0	1	0	0.0	2.00	.333
	Greensboro (SAL)	LoA	7	1	1.91	48	0	0	18	61	40	4	10	81	11.9	0.82	.184
Minor League Totals			8	2	1.87	75	0	0	21	92	60	6	15	106	10.4	0.82	.185

Year	Club (League)	Class	AVG	G	AB	R	H	2B	3B	HR	RBI	BB	SO	SB	CS	OBP	SLG
2009	Jamestown (NYP)	SS	.333	4	6	0	2	0	0	0	0	2	2	1	0	.556	.333
	Marlins (GCL)	R	.034	11	29	6	1	0	0	0	2	8	7	0	0	.256	.034
Minor League Totals			.086	15	35	6	3	0	0	0	2	10	9	1	0	.313	.086

19 KYLE JENSEN, OF

BA GRADE
45
HIGH

Born: May 20, 1988. **B-T:** R-L. **Ht.:** 6-4. **Wt.:** 230. **Drafted:** St. Mary's, 2009 (12th round). **Signed by:** John Hughes.

As a college sophomore, Jensen set a St. Mary's record by hitting .421. In his third pro season last year, he won high Class A Florida State League MVP honors after putting on a power display despite a tough home park in Jupiter and virtually no protection in the lineup. Despite being promoted to Double-A with nearly a month remaining, he finished third in the FSL home run chase with 22. Jensen generates his power more with strength than bat speed, though he times pitches well enough to catch up with good fastballs. Scouts question whether he can do as much damage against better pitching, because his swing gets long and he struggles against quality breaking balls. He does use the entire field, an approach that gives him a chance to be an average hitter. He goes to the plate with an idea of what he's looking for and punishes mistakes. While he's a below-average runner and little threat to steal a bag, Jensen isn't a clogger on the bases. He has enough athleticism to do a passable job on the outfield corners, where his range has improved since he signed and he generally makes good reads. His arm is fringy, making him better suited for left field. Jensen likely will return to Jacksonville to begin 2012.

Year	Club (League)	Class	AVG	G	AB	R	H	2B	3B	HR	RBI	BB	SO	SB	CS	OBP	SLG
2009	Jamestown (NYP)	SS	.280	55	182	24	51	10	5	4	24	18	46	3	0	.354	.456
2010	Greensboro (SAL)	LoA	.272	125	470	61	128	26	1	18	86	45	119	5	1	.342	.447
2011	Jupiter (FSL)	HiA	.309	109	391	53	121	20	1	22	66	46	114	0	0	.385	.535
	Jacksonville (SL)	AA	.250	21	80	14	20	1	1	5	10	7	23	1	0	.310	.475
Minor League Totals			.285	310	1123	152	320	57	8	49	186	116	302	9	1	.357	.481

20 A.J. RAMOS, RHP

BA GRADE
45
HIGH

Born: Sept. 20, 1986. **B-T:** R-R. **Ht.:** 5-10. **Wt.:** 210. **Signed:** Texas Tech, 2009 (21st round). **Signed by:** Dennis Cardoza.

Ramos was Texas Tech's Friday-night starter until he tore an elbow ligament as a junior in 2008, requiring Tommy John surgery. He returned in time for the start of his senior season, reclaimed his spot at the front of the Red Raiders rotation and signed with the Marlins for $1,500 as a 21st-round pick. Immediately converted to a reliever after turning pro, he has fanned 12.6 batters per nine innings in three years in the minors. Ramos works mainly with a 91-94 mph fastball that touches 97 and a hard slider, and he'll also mix in an occasional changeup. He's a strike thrower but needs to improve his command within the zone. At 5-foot-10 he's on the short side, and at times he lacks plane on his fastball, which can flatten out. Ramos has tremendous strength in his legs, which helps him generate his velocity. He competes well, though at times can be too much of a perfectionist. After going to the Arizona Fall League in the offseason, he'll advance to Double-A and isn't far away from helping the big league club.

Year	Club (League)	Class	W	L	ERA	G	GS	CG	SV	IP	H	HR	BB	SO	K/9	WHIP	AVG
2009	Jamestown (NYP)	SS	2	2	2.14	25	0	0	9	34	22	0	14	50	13.4	1.07	.182
2010	Greensboro (SAL)	LoA	3	7	3.70	49	0	0	28	58	40	3	32	78	12.0	1.23	.198
2011	Jupiter (FSL)	HiA	1	4	1.78	49	0	0	25	51	37	2	19	71	12.6	1.11	.200
Minor League Totals			6	13	2.65	123	0	0	62	143	99	5	65	199	12.6	1.15	.195

21 KYLE SKIPWORTH, C

BA GRADE
45
HIGH

Born: March 1, 1990. **B-T:** L-R. **Ht.:** 6-4. **Wt.:** 205. **Drafted:** HS—Rubidoux, Calif., 2008 (1st round). **Signed by:** Robby Corsaro.

An offensive star in high school, Skipworth set a California prep record with hits in 18 straight at-bats before signing for $2.3 million as the sixth overall pick in 2008. His bat has never clicked in pro ball, though the Marlins were encouraged when he put up career-best numbers in 2010 and followed with a solid showing in the Arizona Fall League. That prompted the Marlins to jump him a level to Double-A last year, and the offensive gains he had made disappeared. Prone to expanding his strike zone both up and down, Skipworth seems to decide ahead of time that he's going to swing without analyzing the pitch. He has enticing lefthanded power but he doesn't keep his bat in the zone long enough to utilize it. Despite his struggles, he never has given in mentally and stayed focused last year on improving his defense. He has become more sophisticated at calling pitches and has learned to control the rhythm of the game. His receiving has gotten quieter and he blocks balls well. Though he threw out just 23 percent of basestealers in 2011, he has above-average arm strength and average feet. He's a below-average runner, typical of a catcher. Miami retains optimism that at 22 he still has time to put his offensive game together, but he has shown few signs of it. He'll repeat Double-A this season.

Year	Club (League)	Class	AVG	G	AB	R	H	2B	3B	HR	RBI	BB	SO	SB	CS	OBP	SLG
2008	Marlins (GCL)	R	.208	43	159	22	33	6	0	5	21	13	46	2	2	.263	.340
2009	Greensboro (SAL)	LoA	.208	70	264	28	55	14	1	7	37	18	91	1	2	.263	.348
2010	Greensboro (SAL)	LoA	.249	107	397	55	99	17	1	17	59	32	132	1	2	.312	.426
	Jacksonville (SL)	AA	.000	2	7	1	0	0	0	0	0	1	3	0	0	.125	.000
2011	Jacksonville (SL)	AA	.207	106	396	35	82	12	2	11	49	34	143	0	4	.273	.331
Minor League Totals			.220	328	1223	141	269	49	4	40	166	98	415	4	10	.281	.365

22 MARK CANHA, 1B/OF

BA GRADE
45
HIGH

Born: Feb. 15, 1989. **B-T:** R-R. **Ht.:** 6-2. **Wt.:** 195. **Drafted:** California, 2010 (7th round). **Signed by:** John Hughes.

A two-time all-Pacific-10 Conference honoree at California, Canha led the conference with 69 RBIs in 54 games in 2010, enticing the Marlins with his power. They signed him for $300,000 in the seventh round that summer and made a few small adjustments with his swing, helping him reach inside pitches better. The changes helped him rank second in the South Atlantic League leaders with 25 homers last year despite missing four weeks early in the season with a back strain. He was helped by Greensboro's hospitable NewBridge Bank Park, where he batted .306/.427/.611 with 16 homers. Canha generates his power with a short stroke and can drive the ball to the opposite field with authority. He's also patient enough to take a walk if pitches won't challenge him. At times he has a tendency to overstride, and keeping his lower half in check will help him more consistently tap into his power. Canha's speed is below average, which may relegate him to first base, though he has played some left field as well. His range at first is average, but he still needs work around the bag. He has drawn comparisons to former Marlin Josh Willingham, another righty hitter with a similar build. Canha should reach Double-A at some point this year, perhaps even to start the season.

Year	Club (League)	Class	AVG	G	AB	R	H	2B	3B	HR	RBI	BB	SO	SB	CS	OBP	SLG
2010	Marlins (GCL)	R	.176	6	17	3	3	0	0	0	1	2	1	1	1	.286	.176
	Jamestown (NYP)	SS	.264	14	53	7	14	3	1	4	9	6	13	0	0	.339	.585
2011	Greensboro (SAL)	LoA	.276	107	384	72	106	22	0	25	85	59	85	7	3	.374	.529
Minor League Totals			.271	127	454	82	123	25	1	29	95	67	99	8	4	.366	.522

23 MASON HOPE, RHP

BA GRADE
50
EXTREME

Born: June 27, 1992. **B-T:** R-R. **Ht.:** 6-3. **Wt.:** 190. **Drafted:** HS—Broken Arrow, Okla., 2011 (5th round). **Signed by:** Steve Taylor.

Overshadowed in high school by teammate Archie Bradley (the No. 7 overall pick by the Diamondbacks) and rival Dylan Bundy (No. 4 to the Orioles), Hope lasted until the Marlins took him in the fifth round in June. They signed him away from a scholarship to Oklahoma for $250,000. His father Pat, a standout pitcher at Oklahoma State, is enshrined in the Cape Cod League Hall of Fame. Mason has an advanced feel for pitching and pounds the zone with strikes. He gets a good downward angle on his fastball, which sits at

90-93 mph and touches 94. His biting 12-to-6 curveball grades as a plus-plus pitch at times, though it still lacks consistency. When it's on, he can throw it for strikes as well as get hitters to chase it out of the zone. His changeup is still developing but projects as an average pitch. Hope tends to get too deliberate in his delivery at times and could gain velocity if he can quicken it up. He's a fierce competitor. His performance this spring will dictate whether he jumps to low Class A or waits in extended spring training for Jamestown's season to open in June.

Year	Club (League)	Class	W	L	ERA	G	GS	CG	SV	IP	H	HR	BB	SO	K/9	WHIP	AVG
2011	Marlins (GCL)	R	2	0	3.29	7	6	0	0	27	27	0	7	31	10.2	1.24	.237
Minor League Totals			2	0	3.29	7	6	0	0	27	27	0	7	31	10.2	1.24	.237

24 EVAN REED, RHP

Born: Dec. 31, 1985. **B-T:** R-R. **Ht.:** 6-4. **Wt.:** 225. **Drafted:** Cal Poly, 2007 (3rd round). **Signed by:** Todd Guggiana (Rangers).

BA GRADE
45
HIGH

Acquired along with righthander Omar Poveda from the Rangers in a July 2010 deal for Jorge Cantu, Reed tore a ligament in his elbow in his first outing in the Marlins system. He spent most of last year rehabbing from Tommy John surgery, returning to action in the Gulf Coast League in early July. By the end of the season the Marlins were seeing the electric arm they had traded for. A big, strapping horse, Reed has regained his fastball velocity. He's again pitching at 92-95 mph and touching 98. Before he got hurt, he had a hard slider with late tilt that peaked at 90 mph and was absolutely filthy at times. His slider hasn't come all of the way back, though it was getting closer by the end of the season. His control and command still need some fine-tuning, and that was true before his surgery. The Marlins sent Reed to the Arizona Fall League to make up some of his lost innings. A starter early in his pro career, he projects as a set-up man. He has a bullpen mentality all the way, aggressively attacking hitters with his power arsenal. He'll probably open 2012 in Double-A and it may not be long before he's ready to contribute in Miami.

Year	Club (League)	Class	W	L	ERA	G	GS	CG	SV	IP	H	HR	BB	SO	K/9	WHIP	AVG
2007	Spokane (NWL)	SS	0	0	2.04	7	4	0	1	18	9	0	9	23	11.7	1.02	.150
	Clinton (MWL)	LoA	1	1	1.80	4	4	0	0	20	9	0	7	11	5.0	0.80	.136
2008	Frisco (TL)	AA	1	0	0.00	1	1	0	0	5	4	0	3	5.4	0.80	.222
	Clinton (MWL)	LoA	1	0	1.50	2	2	0	0	12	8	0	2	12	9.0	0.83	.190
	Bakersfield (CAL)	HiA	7	10	6.25	23	23	0	0	121	130	14	55	89	6.6	1.53	.273
2009	Bakersfield (CAL)	HiA	2	2	2.96	46	0	0	25	49	44	1	28	65	12.0	1.48	.244
2010	Oklahoma City (PCL)	AAA	1	0	4.50	1	0	0	0	2	1	1	0	2	9.0	0.50	.143
	Frisco (TL)	AA	1	1	1.62	30	0	0	5	39	35	0	13	34	7.8	1.23	.238
	Jacksonville (SL)	AA	0	0	0.00	1	0	0	0	2	1	0	1	1	5.4	1.20	.200
2011	Marlins (GCL)	R	0	0	3.12	8	3	0	0	9	15	0	0	11	11.4	1.73	.395
	Jupiter (FSL)	HiA	0	1	4.02	11	0	0	0	16	9	0	10	13	7.5	1.21	.176
Minor League Totals			14	15	3.95	134	37	0	31	291	265	16	125	264	8.2	1.34	.243

25 JOEY O'GARA, RHP

Born: April 20, 1988. **B-T:** R-R. **Ht.:** 6-7. **Wt.:** 205. **Drafted:** Indiana, 2009 (31st round). **Signed by:** Kevin Ibach.

BA GRADE
45
HIGH

Signed for $60,000 as a 31st-round pick in 2009, O'Gara took an unplanned route to the fast track after tossing five shutout innings in a fill-in start in high Class A in May 2010. After opening that year in extended spring training, he spent the rest of it at Jupiter and moved up to Double-A last spring. O'Gara struggled early with his sinker, at times looking like he was trying to force action on the ball instead of just letting it go. His results improved when he regained the pitch, which runs from 90-92 mph and induces grounders by the bushel. He'll also throw a four-seamer, mostly against lefthanders, and it can get up to 95 mph. His slider lacks consistent depth, often flattening out, which is a particular challenge given his lower arm slot. He has a better feel now for his changeup, which mimics the sinking action of his fastball, though at times he'll slow his body down when throwing it. An intelligent pitcher with a competitive makeup, O'Gara always been a hard worker. He's a candidate for a back-end-of-the-rotation job eventually, but he'll first need to iron out his secondary offerings, possibly back in Jacksonville to begin 2012.

Year	Club (League)	Class	W	L	ERA	G	GS	CG	SV	IP	H	HR	BB	SO	K/9	WHIP	AVG
2009	Jamestown (NYP)	SS	3	4	6.46	15	3	0	0	39	53	4	14	28	6.5	1.72	.338
2010	Jupiter (FSL)	HiA	7	6	3.84	18	16	1	0	96	113	3	19	42	3.9	1.38	.301
2011	Jacksonville (SL)	AA	7	9	4.55	27	27	0	0	158	181	11	45	72	4.1	1.43	.291
Minor League Totals			17	19	4.57	60	46	1	0	293	347	18	78	142	4.4	1.45	.301

26 TOM KOEHLER, RHP

Born: June 29, 1986. **B-T:** R-R. **Ht.:** 6-3. **Wt.:** 235. **Drafted:** Stony Brook, 2008 (18th round). **Signed by:** Steve Payne.

Koehler had enjoyed nothing but success since signing for $1,000 as an 18th-rounder in 2008. He almost made things look too easy in 2010, when he tied for the minor league lead with 16 victories and was honored as the Southern League's top pitcher. He went 5-0, 2.92 in his first nine Triple-A starts last year, but then got away from working off his fastball and finally hit adversity. He posted a 7.56 ERA over his next 12 starts, as he relied too much on his secondary pitches and lost his ability to command the bottom half of the strike zone, before getting back on track in the final month. Koehler doesn't have a huge margin for error and has to set up hitters with his full repertoire and keep the ball down to succeed. He can throw his fastball at 90-94 mph, but it lacks life and gets pounded if he leaves it up in the zone. He also throws a high-80s cutter, a hard spike curveball and a changeup that's a potential plus pitch. He tended to nibble at the strike zone last year rather than attack hitters like he had in the past, and he's going to have to throw more strikes to make it as a back-of-the-rotation starter or long reliever in the majors. His struggles may make him a better pitcher in the long run, though they cost him a chance to make his big league debut last year, when the Marlins went through 11 starting pitchers. Miami did protect him on its 40-man roster in November.

Year	Club (League)	Class	W	L	ERA	G	GS	CG	SV	IP	H	HR	BB	SO	K/9	WHIP	AVG
2008	Jamestown (NYP)	SS	5	5	3.68	15	13	0	0	66	66	0	29	58	7.9	1.44	.261
2009	Greensboro (SAL)	LoA	5	5	3.20	18	18	0	0	98	88	9	39	82	7.5	1.29	.238
	Jupiter (FSL)	HiA	4	1	3.38	6	6	0	0	35	35	0	9	25	6.5	1.27	.271
2010	Jacksonville (SL)	AA	16	2	2.61	28	28	0	0	159	140	11	46	145	8.2	1.17	.241
2011	New Orleans (PCL)	AAA	12	7	4.97	28	28	0	0	150	144	18	79	116	6.9	1.48	.254
Minor League Totals			42	20	3.61	95	93	0	0	508	473	38	202	426	7.5	1.33	.249

27 KEVIN MATTISON, OF

Born: Sept. 20, 1985. **B-T:** L-L. **Ht.:** 6-0. **Wt.:** 180. **Drafted:** UNC Asheville, 2008 (28th round). **Signed by:** Joel Matthews.

Mattison has gone from a $1,000 senior sign in 2008 to a place on Miami's 40-man roster after the 2011 season. The fastest man in the organization, he has averaged 43 stolen bases in his three full pro seasons. He hasn't been as dangerous at the plate, though he put everything together in the first two months of 2011, batting .338/.424/.512. Afterward, however, he hit just .209/.307/.334. He found the spark again in the Arizona Fall League, where he batted .349, ranked among the league leaders in several categories and won the Dernell Stenson Sportsmanship Award. Mattison is at his best when he keeps the ball on the ground and wreaks havoc with his plus-plus speed. To combat his habit of hitting the ball in the air, the Marlins moved him to a heavier bat last spring and drilled into him the virtue of taking a direct path to the top of the ball. They also encouraged him to bunt more frequently. He got in trouble when he reverted to a long, loopy swing that results in too many routine flyouts. Mattison isn't a proficient basestealer yet, making up for poor jumps and instincts with pure speed. He shows plus range in center field as well as an average arm. Mattison hustles constantly and profiles as a fourth outfielder who can fulfill a variety of roles off the bench. He'll get his first taste of Triple-A and possibly the majors in 2012.

Year	Club (League)	Class	AVG	G	AB	R	H	2B	3B	HR	RBI	BB	SO	SB	CS	OBP	SLG
2008	Jamestown (NYP)	SS	.250	70	268	48	67	10	6	4	20	37	71	14	4	.344	.377
2009	Greensboro (SAL)	LoA	.250	95	360	61	90	15	1	15	47	32	81	41	6	.323	.422
2010	New Orleans (PCL)	AAA	.207	7	29	4	6	0	0	0	0	1	7	1	1	.233	.207
	Jupiter (FSL)	HiA	.218	90	362	46	79	13	4	3	29	22	87	44	10	.274	.301
	Jacksonville (SL)	AA	.222	16	45	10	10	4	1	0	1	4	10	4	0	.286	.356
2011	Jacksonville (SL)	AA	.260	130	503	87	131	17	16	8	49	58	127	38	16	.353	.406
Minor League Totals			.244	408	1567	256	383	59	28	30	146	154	383	142	37	.323	.375

28 JOSH HODGES, RHP

Born: June 21, 1991. **B-T:** R-R. **Ht.:** 6-7. **Wt.:** 235. **Drafted:** HS—New Albany, Miss., 2009 (7th round). **Signed by:** Mark Willoughby.

Hodges hit 94 mph in high school but posed a challenge for scouts because he played in a remote northern Mississippi town and didn't face much in the way of competition. The Marlins invested a seventh-round pick and $125,000 in him, knowing he would take time to develop. He has yet to reach full-season ball after three years as a pro, but he turned the corner in 2011 while repeating Jamestown. While he has been clocked as high as 97 mph, Hodges now works mostly at 90-92 mph with his fastball, trading velocity for sink. He's learning he doesn't need to max out on every pitch to be successful. He doesn't yet have good feel for his hard slider, showing a preference for his changeup as his second offering. His delivery is still a little raw and he'll finish too straight up at times, but his arm action is clean and he shows decent command. He's quick to both first base and the plate, and opponents stole just two bases in seven tries against him last year. Hodges took a major step forward in controlling his emotions in 2011, not losing his cool as frequently when hits dropped in, though there were still occasional signs of frustration. He's also understanding better what being a professional athlete entails off the field. A potential No. 3 or 4 starter, Hodges is ready to graduate to full-season ball in Greensboro.

Year	Club (League)	Class	W	L	ERA	G	GS	CG	SV	IP	H	HR	BB	SO	K/9	WHIP	AVG
2009	Marlins (GCL)	R	2	1	4.02	5	2	0	0	16	15	0	8	14	8.0	1.47	.238
	Jamestown (NYP)	SS	1	0	4.50	1	0	0	0	4	5	1	0	6	13.5	1.25	.294
2010	Jamestown (NYP)	SS	3	3	6.04	12	12	0	0	54	57	4	23	38	6.4	1.49	.270
2011	Jamestown (NYP)	SS	8	1	3.39	15	15	0	0	88	90	7	18	50	5.1	1.23	.272
Minor League Totals			14	5	4.36	33	29	0	0	161	167	12	49	108	6.0	1.34	.268

29 SANDY ROSARIO, RHP

BA GRADE

40

MEDIUM

Born: Aug. 22, 1985. **B-T:** R-R. **Ht.:** 6-1. **Wt.:** 170. **Signed:** Dominican Republic, 2004. **Signed by:** Fred Ferreira/Enrique Constante.

Rosario led minor league relievers with 125 strikeouts in 92 innings in 2010, spending most of the season in low Class A but finishing it in Florida. He again got a taste of the big leagues last fall, though his stat line wasn't nearly as gaudy as his previous campaign. Rosario fills the zone with 92-95 mph fastballs, reaching 97 at times, but his four-seamer is fairly straight. When he doesn't locate his heater where he wants to, it gets hit. He's working on a two-seamer that should have more life. Rosario's low-80s slider gives him a potentially solid No. 2 pitch, but he lacks a true offspeed offering to disrupt hitters' timing. Scouts have expressed concern with his long arm action, which interferes with his command and gives hitters a good look at his pitches. A closer in 2011, he profiles more as a seventh-inning arm in the majors. Rosario will contend for a big league job this spring but may need more time in Triple-A.

Year	Club (League)	Class	W	L	ERA	G	GS	CG	SV	IP	H	HR	BB	SO	K/9	WHIP	AVG
2004	Marlins (DSL)	R	3	1	2.89	10	4	0	0	37	34	1	9	32	7.7	1.15	.239
2005	Marlins (DSL)	R	6	3	1.03	14	4	1	0	44	28	0	10	52	10.7	0.87	.178
2006	Marlins (GCL)	R	3	2	2.25	10	6	0	0	40	41	0	10	27	6.1	1.28	.256
2007	Greensboro (SAL)	LoA	0	1	9.82	2	2	0	0	7	11	1	2	7	8.6	1.77	.355
2008	Greensboro (SAL)	LoA	0	0	13.50	1	1	0	0	2	3	0	3	4	18.0	3.00	.375
2009	Jamestown (NYP)	SS	4	2	1.70	9	9	0	0	42	48	1	8	41	8.7	1.32	.277
	Greensboro (SAL)	LoA	3	2	5.13	7	7	0	0	40	57	4	6	36	8.0	1.56	.322
2010	Greensboro (SAL)	LoA	7	2	3.60	43	0	0	3	90	92	9	17	122	12.2	1.21	.263
	Jacksonville (SL)	AA	1	0	0.00	1	0	0	0	2	0	0	0	3	13.5	0.00	.000
	Florida (NL)	MAJ	0	0	54.00	2	0	0	0	1	9	2	1	0	0.0	10.00	.818
2011	Jacksonville (SL)	AA	3	2	4.15	46	0	0	23	48	52	4	17	46	8.7	1.45	.274
	New Orleans (PCL)	AAA	0	1	4.05	7	0	0	4	7	5	0	5	4	5.4	1.50	.217
	Florida (NL)	MAJ	0	0	2.45	4	0	0	0	4	5	0	2	2	4.9	1.91	.313
Major League Totals			0	0	13.50	6	0	0	0	5	14	2	3	2	3.9	3.64	.519
Minor League Totals			30	16	3.26	150	33	1	30	359	371	20	87	374	9.4	1.27	.262

30 DANIEL JENNINGS, LHP

BA GRADE

40

MEDIUM

Born: April 17, 1987. **B-T:** L-L. **Ht.:** 6-3. **Wt.:** 190. **Drafted:** Nebraska, 2008 (9th round). **Signed by:** Bob Oldis.

No relation to the Marlins vice president of player personnel of the same name, Jennings shot to Double-A in his first full season three years ago but has had trouble advancing beyond that level. A 50-game suspension in July 2010 for using a banned over-the-counter stimulant carried over to the start of last season. He had decent success in his third stint in Jacksonville before a mid-June promotion to New Orleans, where his command faltered and his results turned ugly. He had a 7.04 ERA and surrendered three homers in 30 innings after yielding just four in his previous 200. Nevertheless, Miami protected him on its 40-man roster after the season. Jennings gets by with a two-pitch arsenal, mixing a 90-94 mph fastball with a solid to plus slider. He disguises the slider well and is able to give it different looks for lefties and righties. He got in trouble last year when he didn't stay down through the ball in his delivery, which caused his fastball to flatten out. Jennings uses a low arm slot, which makes him tough for lefties to pick up, yet he was much more effective against righties in 2011. He went to the Arizona Fall League to continue working on his delivery and command, and he'll give Triple-A another try this season.

Year	Club (League)	Class	W	L	ERA	G	GS	CG	SV	IP	H	HR	BB	SO	K/9	WHIP	AVG
2008	Jamestown (NYP)	SS	1	4	3.53	13	13	0	0	59	79	2	18	62	9.5	1.65	.321
2009	Greensboro (SAL)	LoA	1	2	2.74	34	0	0	0	49	42	1	21	54	9.9	1.28	.237
	Jupiter (FSL)	HiA	0	0	0.00	8	0	0	6	12	5	0	4	13	10.0	0.77	.132
	Jacksonville (SL)	AA	0	0	0.00	3	0	0	0	2	2	0	1	2	10.8	1.80	.286
2010	Jacksonville (SL)	AA	4	2	2.56	37	0	0	0	53	49	0	26	44	7.5	1.42	.257
2011	Jacksonville (SL)	AA	4	1	3.16	21	0	0	2	26	26	1	11	29	10.2	1.44	.265
	New Orleans (PCL)	AAA	1	3	7.04	24	0	0	2	31	34	3	17	27	7.9	1.66	.301
Minor League Totals			11	12	3.36	140	13	0	10	230	237	7	98	231	9.0	1.45	.272

Milwaukee Brewers

BY TOM HAUDRICOURT

When the Brewers decided to retain Prince Fielder despite his pending free agency and gave up three of their best prospects (Brett Lawrie, Jake Odorizzi, Jeremy Jeffress) as well as youngsters Alcides Escobar and Lorenzo Cain in trades for Zack Greinke and Shaun Marcum, it was obvious they were going all-in for the 2011 season.

And then their chip stack grew and grew.

An improved pitching staff propelled Milwaukee to a franchise-record 96 regular-season victories. The Brewers won their first division title and first playoff series since their World Series season of 1982, dispatching the Diamondbacks in the Division Series before losing to the Cardinals in a six-game National League Championship Series.

Greinke and Marcum lived up to expectations, helping lower the team ERA from 4.58 in 2010 (14th-best in the NL) to 3.63 in 2011 (seventh). Homegrown product Yovani Gallardo remained the staff ace, winning 17 games and becoming the first Milwaukee pitcher to reach 200 strikeouts in three consecutive seasons.

As usual, the offense was productive and led by the formidable 1-2 punch of Ryan Braun and Fielder. Braun was named NL MVP while Fielder finished third in the balloting, but the Brewers could be without both of them to start the 2012 season. Braun faces a possible 50-game suspension after testing positive for elevated levels of testosterone and Fielder is expected to sign elsewhere.

General manager Doug Melvin continued to make astute moves during the season. He picked up Nyjer Morgan from the Nationals at the end of spring training, and Morgan ignited the team with his enthusiasm and delivered the Division Series-winning hit. Melvin also acquired Francisco Rodriguez from the Mets to serve as John Axford's set-up man, and Jerry Hairston from Washington to fill in for an injured Rickie Weeks and a slumping Casey McGehee.

Milwaukee didn't need much help from the minor leagues, though third baseman Taylor Green parlayed a big season at Triple-A into a late-August callup and a spot on the postseason roster. After dropping to 30th in Baseball America's rankings, the farm system rallied in 2011 and showed some promise for the future.

The Brewers won't necessarily have openings for them, but Green, outfielders Logan Schafer and Caleb Gindl and righthander Michael Fiers have proven themselves in Triple-A and could help in 2012.

GEORGE GOJKOVICH

Dealing for Zack Greinke helped push the Brewers to the brink of the World Series

TOP 30 PROSPECTS

1. Wily Peralta, rhp	16. Kentrail Davis, of
2. Taylor Jungmann, rhp	17. David Goforth, rhp
3. Jed Bradley, lhp	18. Martin Maldonado, c
4. Tyler Thornburg, rhp	19. Mark Rogers, rhp
5. Scooter Gennett, 2b	20. Nick Bucci, rhp
6. Logan Schafer, of	21. D'Vontrey Richardson, of
7. Cody Scarpetta, rhp	22. Orlando Arcia, ss
8. Taylor Green, 3b/2b	23. Drew Gagnon, rhp
9. Jorge Lopez, rhp	24. Michael Reed, of
10. Jimmy Nelson, rhp	25. Brooks Hall, rhp
11. Santo Manzanillo, rhp	26. Kyle Heckathorn, rhp
12. Michael Fiers, rhp	27. Eric Farris, 2b/ss
13. Caleb Gindl, of	28. Nick Ramirez, 1b
14. Hunter Morris, 1b	29. Khris Davis, of
15. Yadiel Rivera, ss	30. Amaury Rivas, rhp

Righthander Wily Peralta, the organization's No. 1 prospect, allowed just seven runs in five Triple-A starts at the end of the season and isn't far behind.

To avoid having to trade for more pitching in the future, Milwaukee focused on arms in the draft. It had two of the top 15 choices in 2011, including a compensation pick for failing to sign first-rounder Dylan Covey the previous year. The Brewers used first-rounders on Texas righthander Taylor Jungmann and Georgia Tech lefty Jed Bradley, and also picked up righthanders Jorge Lopez (second round), Drew Gagnon (third) and David Goforth (seventh).

General Manager: Doug Melvin. **Farm Director:** Reid Nichols. **Scouting Director:** Bruce Seid.

Class	Team	League	W	L	Pct	Finish*	Manager(s)
Majors	Milwaukee Brewers	National	96	66	.593	2nd (16)	Ron Roenicke
Triple-A	Nashville Sounds	Pacific Coast	71	73	.493	t-6th (16)	Don Money
Double-A	Huntsville Stars	Southern	64	73	.467	8th (10)	Mike Guerrero
High A	Brevard County Manatees	Florida State	62	76	.449	11th (12)	Jeff Isom
Low A	Wisconsin Timber Rattlers	Midwest	67	72	.482	11th (16)	Matt Erickson
Rookie	Helena Brewers	Pioneer	30	46	.395	7th (8)	Joe Ayrault
Rookie	AZL Brewers	Arizona	17	39	.304	13th (13)	Tony Diggs
Overall 2011 Minor League Record			**311**	**379**	**.451**	**29th (30)**	

*Finish in overall standings (No. of teams in league). †League champion.

LAST YEAR'S TOP 30

Player, Pos.		Status
1.	Jake Odorizzi, rhp	(Royals)
2.	Mark Rogers, rhp	No. 19
3.	Jeremy Jeffress, rhp	(Royals)
4.	Cody Scarpetta, rhp	No. 7
5.	Wily Peralta, rhp	No. 1
6.	Scooter Gennett, 2b/ss	No. 5
7.	Kentrail Davis, of	No. 16
8.	Tyler Thornburg, rhp	No. 4
9.	Eric Farris, 2b	No. 27
10.	Jimmy Nelson, rhp	No. 10
11.	Kyle Heckathorn, rhp	No. 26
12.	Amaury Rivas, rhp	No. 30
13.	Matt Miller, rhp	Dropped out
14.	Erik Komatsu, of	(Nationals)
15.	Caleb Gindl, of	No. 13
16.	Logan Schafer, of	No. 6
17.	Hunter Morris, 1b/3b	No. 14
18.	Eric Arnett, rhp	Dropped out
19.	Andre Lamontagne, rhp	Dropped out
20.	Cody Hawn, 1b	Dropped out
21.	Yadiel Rivera, ss	No. 15
22.	Cameron Garfield, c	Dropped out
23.	Tyler Roberts, c	Dropped out
24.	D'Vontrey Richardson, of	No. 21
25.	Mike McClendon, rhp	Dropped out
26.	Brandon Kintzler, rhp	Dropped out
27.	Nick Bucci, rhp	No. 20
28.	Maverick Lasker, rhp	Dropped out
29.	Lee Haydel, of	Dropped out
30.	Austin Ross, rhp	Dropped out

BEST TOOLS

Best Hitter for Average	Taylor Green
Best Power Hitter	Hunter Morris
Best Strike-Zone Discipline	Nick Shaw
Fastest Baserunner	Reggie Keen
Best Athlete	D'Vontrey Richardson
Best Fastball	Santo Manzanillo
Best Curveball	Cody Scarpetta
Best Slider	Jimmy Nelson
Best Changeup	Dan Meadows
Best Control	Michael Fiers
Best Defensive Catcher	Martin Maldonado
Best Defensive Infielder	Yadiel Rivera
Best Infield Arm	Yadiel Rivera
Best Defensive Outfielder	Logan Schafer
Best Outfield Arm	D'Vontrey Richardson

PROJECTED 2015 LINEUP

Catcher	Jonathan Lucroy
First Base	Hunter Morris
Second Base	Rickie Weeks
Third Base	Taylor Green
Shortstop	Yadiel Rivera
Left Field	Ryan Braun
Center Field	Logan Schafer
Right Field	Corey Hart
No. 1 Starter	Yovanni Gallardo
No. 2 Starter	Zack Greinke
No. 3 Starter	Wily Peralta
No. 4 Starter	Taylor Jungmann
No. 5 Starter	Jed Bradley
Closer	Johh Axford

TOP PROSPECTS OF THE DECADE

Year	Player, Pos.	2011 Org.
2002	Nick Neugebauer, rhp	Out of baseball
2003	Brad Nelson, 1b	Rangers
2004	Rickie Weeks, 2b	Brewers
2005	Rickie Weeks, 2b	Brewers
2006	Prince Fielder, 1b	Brewers
2007	Yovani Gallardo, rhp	Brewers
2008	Matt LaPorta, of	Indians
2009	Alcides Escobar, ss	Royals
2010	Alcides Escobar, ss	Royals
2011	Mark Rogers, rhp	Brewers

TOP DRAFT PICKS OF THE DECADE

Year	Player, Pos.	2011 Org.
2002	Prince Fielder, 1b	Brewers
2003	Rickie Weeks, 2b	Brewers
2004	Mark Rogers, rhp	Brewers
2005	Ryan Braun, 3b	Brewers
2006	Jeremy Jeffress, rhp	Royals
2007	Matt LaPorta, of	Indians
2008	Brett Lawrie, c/3b	Blue Jays
2009	Eric Arnett, rhp	Brewers
2010	*Dylan Covey, rhp	U. of San Diego
2011	Taylor Jungmann, rhp	Brewers

*Did not sign.

LARGEST BONUSES IN CLUB HISTORY

Rickie Weeks, 2003	$3,600,000
Taylor Jungmann, 2011	$2,525,000
Ben Sheets, 1999	$2,450,000
Ryan Braun, 2005	$2,450,000
Prince Fielder, 2002	$2,400,000

MILWAUKEE BREWERS

TOP 2012 ROOKIE: Logan Schafer, of. He doesn't have a clear shot at big league playing time to open the season, but he's a good hitter with fine instincts on the bases and in the outfield.

BREAKOUT PROSPECT: Nick Bucci, rhp. A mainstay on the Canadian national team, he throws strikes with a solid fastball/cutter combination.

SLEEPER: Dan Meadows, lhp. The former 49th-rounder keeps getting outs with his quality changeup.

SOURCE OF TOP 30 TALENT

Homegrown	29	Acquired	1
College	15	Trades	0
Junior college	0	Rule 5 draft	0
High school	9	Independent leagues	0
Draft-and-follow	1	Free agents/waivers	1
Nondrafted free agents	0		
International	4		

LF
Caleb Gindl (13)
Kentrail Davis (16)
Khris Davis (29)
Brock Kjeldgaard
T.J. Mittelstaedt
Lee Haydel

CF
Logan Schafer (6)
D'Vontrey Richardson (21)
Reggie Keen
John Dishon
Malcolm Dowell

RF
Michael Reed (24)
Max Walla
Chad Stang
Raul Mondesi Jr.

3B
Taylor Green (8)
Zelous Wheeler
Shea Vucinich
Mike Walker
Jalen Harris

SS
Yadiel Rivera (15)
Orlando Arcia (22)
Carlos George
Josh Prince
Renaldo Jenkins

2B
Scooter Gennett (5)
Eric Farris (27)
Chris McFarland
Nick Shaw
Mike Brownstein

1B
Hunter Morris (14)
Nick Ramirez (28)
Cody Hawn
Sean Halton

C
Martin Maldonado (18)
Cameron Garfield
Tyler Roberts
Dustin Houle
Shawn Zarraga

LHP

LHSP	LHRP
Jed Bradley (3)	Dan Meadows
Dan Merklinger	Jon Pokorny
Del Howell	Brian Garman
	Efrain Nieves
	Mike Strong

RHP

RHSP	RHRP
Wily Peralta (1)	Santo Manzanillo (11)
Taylor Jungmann (2)	David Goforth (17)
Tyler Thornburg (4)	Mark Rogers (19)
Cody Scarpetta (7)	Mike McClendon
Jorge Lopez (9)	Brandon Kintzler
Jimmy Nelson (10)	Frankie de la Cruz
Michael Fiers (12)	Andre Lamontagne
Nick Bucci (20)	Casey Medlen
Drew Gagnon (23)	Tommy Toledo
Brooks Hall (25)	Robert Wooten
Kyle Heckathorn (26)	Jim Henderson
Amaury Rivas (30)	Adrian Rosario
Austin Ross	
Matt Miller	
Maverick Lasker	
Daniel Keller	
Chad Thompson	
Eric Arnett	

2011

BEST PURE HITTER: 1B Nick Ramirez (4) broke into pro ball by hitting .369 in the Rookie-level Pioneer League, though he found low Class A pitchers much less hospitable (.197).

BEST POWER HITTER: Ramirez, who hit 11 homers between his two stops, has the most present power. C Dustin Houle (8) has the raw strength to pass Ramirez down the road, as does OF Michael Reed (5).

FASTEST RUNNER: When Milwaukee ran its draftees in a 60-yard dash, it was surprised when 6-foot-2, 210-pounder 3B/1B Jalen Harris (41) was the quickest at 6.69 seconds. Reed and OF Malcolm Dowell (9) have similar speed.

BEST DEFENSIVE PLAYER: Houle hasn't spent much time behind the plate, but the Brewers like his soft hands, plus arm and agility. If he can't make it as a catcher, those tools also would play well at third base.

BEST FASTBALL: RHP David Goforth (7) often pitches at 94-97 mph when used as a reliever, and Milwaukee has seen him up to 99. RHP Taylor Jungmann (1) does an excellent job of pitching off his fastball, which sits at 90-94 mph and tops out at 96. LHP Jed Bradley (1) also can reach 96.

BEST SECONDARY PITCH: RHP Jorge Lopez's (2) curveball shows signs of becoming a true out pitch. RHP Drew Gagnon (3) spun a nifty curve in instructional league, while Bradley has a tough slider.

BEST PRO DEBUT: Ramirez, who hit a combined .271/.305/.496 with 32 extra-base hits in 59 games. RHP Casey Medlen (37) had a 3.00 ERA and a 35-5 K-BB ratio in 27 innings in low Class A.

BEST ATHLETE: The Brewers see Reed as a potential five-tool player. Dowell drew interest from college football programs as a defensive back.

MOST INTRIGUING BACKGROUND: Harris was born deaf and had cochlear implants put in his ears as a toddler. 2B Gant Elmore (49) broke into pro ball with Rookie-level Helena, a franchise owned by his father D.G. Unsigned RHP David Lucroy's (29) brother Jonathan starts at catcher for Milwaukee. Unsigned 3B Trent Boras' (30) father Scott is one of baseball's most powerful agents, and his brother Shane signed with the Athletics as a 39th-round pick.

CLOSEST TO THE MAJORS: Jungmann and Bradley could make their pro debuts in high Class A and reach the big leagues before the end of 2013.

BEST LATE-ROUND PICK: Harris has all the tools to become a prototypical third baseman. Medlen has a solid fastball and shows signs of a plus curveball. SS Chris McFarland (18), whom the Brewers signed away

from Rice for $315,000, has a nice package of tools. RHP Chad Thompson (27) lacks consistency but flashes a plus fastball and slider.

THE ONE WHO GOT AWAY: LHP Carlos Rodon (16), who opted to attend North Carolina State, has a nice sinker/slider combination and command.

ASSESSMENT: Milwaukee had two of the top 15 picks and got two of the top college pitchers in Jungmann and Bradley. Lopez, Gagnon and Goforth add more arms to an organization that has struggled to develop its own.

2010

The Brewers didn't sign RHP Dylan Covey (1), though he yielded a consolation pick that turned into Bradley a year later. RHP Tyler Thornburg (3) is moving quickly, and Milwaukee also has hopes for RHP Jimmy Nelson (2), 1B Hunter Morris (4) and SS Yadiel Rivera (9).

GRADE: C

2009

RHP Eric Arnett (1) has been terrible, and OF Kentrail Davis (1s) and Kyle Heckathorn (1s) have developed more slowly than expected. But a couple of late-rounders may salvage this crop: offensive 2B Scooter Gennett (16) and strike-throwing RHP Michael Fiers (22).

GRADE: C

2008

3B Brett Lawrie (1), RHP Jake Odorizzi (1s) and OF/INF Cutter Dykstra (2) were key pieces in trades for Shaun Marcum, Zack Greinke and Nyjer Morgan. The best prospect still in the system is OF Logan Schafer (3).

GRADE: A

2007

1B Matt LaPorta (1) hasn't become the slugger the Brewers envisioned, but they turned him into C.C. Sabathia, who delivered a 2008 playoff berth. This crop has yielded three other big leaguers in C Jonathan Lucroy (3), 2B Eric Farris (4) and since-traded C Eric Fryer (10), and it could have two more in OF Caleb Gindl (5) and RHP Cody Scarpetta (11).

GRADE: C+

Draft analysis by Jim Callis. Numbers in parentheses indicate draft rounds.

1 WILY PERALTA, RHP

Born: May 8, 1989. **B-T:** R-R. **Ht.:** 6-2. **Wt.:** 240.
Signed: Dominican Republic, 2005. **Signed by:**
Fausto Sosa Pena/Fernando Arango.

BA GRADE
60
MEDIUM

BILL MITCHELL

When his handlers were shopping Peralta out of the Dominican Republic in 2005, they tried to sell him as an outfielder with raw power, speed and athleticism. But after the Brewers saw him display a quick arm capable of flashing a 96-mph fastball, they preferred him on the mound. He signed for $450,000 but suffered a significant setback early in his career, missing the entire 2007 season after undergoing Tommy John reconstructive elbow surgery. He has progressed steadily since then, developing into the workhorse pitcher Milwaukee always envisioned. At the outset of 2011, an injury to Zack Greinke gave him the chance to open the season in the Brewers rotation, but Peralta put too much pressure on himself and gave up 15 hits and 10 runs in 10 innings in big league camp. Instead, he returned to Double-A Huntsville after finishing 2010 there and led the Southern League with a 3.46 ERA. He earned a promotion to Triple-A Nashville in August and excelled even more, posting a 2.03 ERA and 40 strikeouts in 31 innings.

With a big, physical frame and a repeatable delivery, Peralta regularly sits at 91-95 mph with his explosive fastball. When he reaches back for a little extra, he can get up to 98. He uses both two-seam and four-seam fastballs, with the two-seamer running down and in to righthanders, jamming them and often breaking their bats. He throws on a downward plane and keeps his fastball down in the zone, inducing grounders when he isn't missing bats. Peralta has developed better command of his secondary pitches, a low-80s slider and a changeup. Most scouts prefer his slider, which has some deception and sharp bite. He has improved his changeup in the last year and it features some good sink, though it still lacks consistency. Peralta has made strides with his control and

SCOUTING GRADES

Fastball: 70. **Command/**
Slider: 60. **Control:** 55.
Changeup: 55. **Delivery:** 60.

Based on 20-80 scouting scale, where 50 represents major league average, and future projection rather than present tools.

command, but he still needs to throw more strikes and improve the location of his secondary pitches. He does a fine job of controlling the running game, permitting just four steals in 11 attempts in 2011. He fields his position well but has been an automatic out as a hitter, surprising considering his background. Peralta's confidence has continued to rise with his success and he displays more poise on the mound than he did early in his career. He's a hard worker who listens to instruction and absorbs it. He has a thick body and conditioning will always be key for him, but to his credit he has been committed in that regard.

Early in his career, when he wasn't getting his secondary pitches over the plate, many observers thought Peralta profiled best a closer or set-up man. The Brewers stuck with him in the rotation and had him keep working on all of his pitches, and now they have a possible No. 2 or 3 starter. He'll get a good look in big league camp in spring training but, barring an injury to a veteran, he'll almost certainly begin 2012 back in Triple-A. Milwaukee believes he'll be big league-ready during the year if needed and definitely if Zack Greinke or Shaun Marcum departs as a free agent after the season.

Year	Club (League)	Class	W	L	ERA	G	GS	CG	SV	IP	H	HR	BB	SO	K/9	WHIP	AVG
2006	Brewers (AZL)	R	2	5	6.63	14	6	0	0	38	51	5	20	28	6.6	1.87	.319
2007	Did Not Play—Injured																
2008	Helena (PIO)	R	1	1	3.07	15	2	0	2	29	23	4	8	36	11.0	1.06	.209
	West Virginia (SAL)	LoA	0	1	10.80	2	2	0	0	5	6	0	3	3	5.4	1.80	.316
2009	Wisconsin (MWL)	LoA	4	4	3.47	27	15	0	1	104	91	5	46	118	10.2	1.32	.235
2010	Brevard County (FSL)	HiA	6	3	3.86	19	17	0	0	105	102	5	40	75	6.4	1.35	.253
	Huntsville (SL)	AA	2	3	3.61	8	8	0	0	42	43	5	24	29	6.2	1.58	.269
2011	Huntsville (SL)	AA	9	7	3.46	21	21	1	0	120	116	9	48	117	8.8	1.29	.243
	Nashville (PCL)	AAA	2	0	2.03	5	5	0	0	31	21	0	11	40	11.6	1.03	.193
Minor League Totals			26	24	3.78	111	76	1	3	474	443	33	200	446	8.5	1.36	.248

2 TAYLOR JUNGMANN, RHP

Born: Dec. 18, 1989. **B-T:** R-R. **Ht.:** 6-6. **Wt.:** 220. **Drafted:** Texas, 2011 (1st round). **Signed by:** Jeremy Booth.

Jungmann was a star almost from the day he arrived at Texas, winning 11 games and pitching a complete-game five-hitter against Louisiana State in the College World Series finals as a freshman. He ranked second in NCAA Division I in wins (13) and opponent average (.165) last spring before going 12th overall in the draft and signing for $2,525,000, the second-largest bonus in club history. Jungman uses his lanky frame to throw downhill easily, working primarily with a fastball that sits at 90-94 mph and tops out at 96. He can get lefthanders and righthanders out with the combination of velocity and life on his heater. He has improved the sharpness and command of his slider, and he continues to work on a changeup that's a tick below average. Some scouts worry that his delivery features a short stride and some effort, but he has smoothed it out some since high school and it doesn't hamper his ability to throw strikes. Jungmann waited until the final minutes before the Aug. 15 signing deadline to come to terms and has yet to make his debut. He got his indoctrination into pro ball during instructional league and likely will start 2012 at high Class A Brevard County. A potential No. 2 starter, he could move quickly through the minors.

BA GRADE
60
MEDIUM

Year	Club (League)	Class	W	L	ERA	G	GS	CG	SV	IP	H	HR	BB	SO	K/9	WHIP	AVG
2011	Did Not Play—Signed Late																

3 JED BRADLEY, LHP

Born: June 12, 1990. **B-T:** L-L. **Ht.:** 6-4. **Wt.:** 225. **Drafted:** Georgia Tech, 2011 (1st round). **Signed by:** Ryan Robinson.

When the Brewers didn't sign 2010 first-rounder Dylan Covey after he was diagnosed with Type 1 diabetes, they received the 15th overall pick in 2011 as compensation. They were pleasantly surprised that Bradley was available there, in part because he was inconsistent right before the draft. He signed for $2 million at the deadline and saw some action in the Arizona Fall League. Bradley got stronger and saw his stuff improve during three years at Georgia Tech. He generally pitches at 88-94 mph, and Milwaukee saw more of the high end of that spectrum with some 96s sprinkled in during instructional league. His low-90s slider gives him a second plus pitch, and he throws his changeup with deceptive arm action and fade. He has a great pitcher's body and a clean, repeatable delivery that allows him to throw strikes. The Brewers believe they picked up a perfect lefthanded complement to Taylor Jungmann in Bradley and see them rising through the system together. They both project as No. 2 starters, figure to make their pro debuts in high Class A and may not need even two full seasons in the minors. The system is short on southpaws, so Bradley was a welcome addition.

BA GRADE
60
MEDIUM

Year	Club (League)	Class	W	L	ERA	G	GS	CG	SV	IP	H	HR	BB	SO	K/9	WHIP	AVG
2011	Did Not Play—Signed Late																

4 TYLER THORNBURG, RHP

Born: Sept. 29, 1988. **B-T:** R-R. **Ht.:** 5-11. **Wt.:** 185. **Drafted:** Charleston Southern, 2010 (3rd round). **Signed by:** Ryan Robinson.

Compared to Tim Lincecum because of his slight frame and pinwheeling delivery, Thornburg has had little difficulty in the lower minors, compiling a 2.48 ERA and 198 strikeouts in 160 innings since signing as a 2010 third-round pick. In his first full pro season, he allowed 12 runs in 12 starts at low Class A Wisconsin and appeared in the Futures Game and held high Class A hitters to a .186 average. Thornburg has been clocked as high as 98 mph when used in relief, but as a starter he usually pitches at 89-92 mph and peaks at 94. His changeup can be his best pitch at times, confounding hitters because it has good fade and he throws it with deceptive arm speed. His 11-to-5 curveball has the potential to be a solid third offering, though his unorthodox mechanics make it difficult to finish the pitch. His delivery is funky but it also leads scouts to wonder if he'll have enough command and durability to remain a starter. The Brewers have no plans to take Thornburg out of the rotation, though his stuff and aggressive nature would play well in a late-inning relief role if needed. A likely No. 3 starter, he'll step up to Double-A to begin 2012 and could surface in Milwaukee at some point in 2013.

BA GRADE
55
MEDIUM

Year	Club (League)	Class	W	L	ERA	G	GS	CG	SV	IP	H	HR	BB	SO	K/9	WHIP	AVG
2010	Helena (PIO)	R	1	0	1.93	9	6	0	1	23	15	2	11	38	14.7	1.11	.179
2011	Wisconsin (MWL)	LoA	7	0	1.57	12	12	2	0	69	49	3	25	76	10.0	1.08	.203
	Brevard County (FSL)	HiA	3	6	3.57	12	12	0	0	68	45	5	33	84	11.1	1.15	.186
Minor League Totals			11	6	2.48	33	30	2	1	160	109	10	69	198	11.1	1.11	.192

5 SCOOTER GENNETT, 2B

BA GRADE

50

MEDIUM

Born: May 1, 1990. **B-T:** L-R. **Ht.:** 5-9. **Wt.:** 165. **Drafted:** HS—Sarasota, Fla., 2009 (16th round). **Signed by:** Tim McIlvaine.

After abandoning a Florida State scholarship to sign for $260,000 as a 16th-round pick in 2009, Gennett has done nothing but hit. He has batted .300 or better in each of his two pro seasons, earning all-star honors in both the low Class A Midwest and high Class A Florida State leagues. He concluded 2011 by finishing second in the Arizona Fall League batting race with a .411 average. Gennett uses an open stance and level swing to consistently stroke line drives to all fields. He makes a lot of contact, though his aggressive nature cuts into his walks and on-base percentage. He has some surprising pop for his size, most of it coming in the form of doubles rather than homers. Gennett has average speed and good baserunning instincts, though he's not much of a threat to steal. A high school shortstop, he still needs considerable work at second base. He has led his leagues' second baseman in errors in each of the last two years, but he has average defensive tools for the position and the work ethic to improve. Gennett has a ceiling as an everyday second baseman with a solid bat, and a fallback option of becoming an offensive-minded utilityman. He'll spend 2012 in Double-A at age 22. With Rickie Weeks signed through 2014 with an option for 2015, the Brewers won't have to rush Gennett.

Year	Club (League)	Class	AVG	G	AB	R	H	2B	3B	HR	RBI	BB	SO	SB	CS	OBP	SLG
2010	Wisconsin (MWL)	LoA	.309	118	482	87	149	39	4	9	55	31	91	14	4	.354	.463
2011	Brevard County (FSL)	HiA	.300	134	556	74	167	20	6	9	51	27	69	11	10	.334	.406
Minor League Totals			.304	252	1038	161	316	59	10	18	106	58	160	25	14	.343	.433

6 LOGAN SCHAFER, OF

BA GRADE

50

MEDIUM

Born: Sept. 8, 1986. **B-T:** L-L. **Ht.:** 6-1. **Wt.:** 175. **Drafted:** Cal Poly, 2008 (3rd round). **Signed by:** Corey Rodriguez.

Schafer followed a breakout 2009 season—he won the Florida State League batting title (.313) and the Brewers' minor league player of the year award—with a lost year in 2010. Between a groin tear that morphed into a sports hernia and a broken right foot, he played in just seven games. He broke his right thumb in big league camp last spring, but returned in mid-May and picked up where he left off two years earlier. Schafer has a simple lefthanded swing, controls the strike zone and makes line-drive contact. He doesn't have much power, but he can drive some balls into the gaps and slugged a career-high .521 after arriving in Triple-A. He has solid speed and good instincts on the bases and in center field. He covers a lot of ground and has an average, accurate arm. He plays with poise and intelligence. Schafer is old for a prospect at 25 but also on the verge of being a reliable contributor in the majors. Nyjer Morgan played a prominent role in Milwaukee's 2011 success, but should he get injured or revert to his 2009 form, the team wouldn't hesitate to promote Schafer. He could end up as a regular with the Brewers sooner than many people might expect.

Year	Club (League)	Class	AVG	G	AB	R	H	2B	3B	HR	RBI	BB	SO	SB	CS	OBP	SLG
2008	Helena (PIO)	R	.240	8	25	4	6	0	1	2	8	5	4	1	0	.355	.560
	West Virginia (SAL)	LoA	.276	43	181	25	50	13	2	0	20	8	42	3	8	.306	.370
2009	Huntsville (SL)	AA	.217	7	23	4	5	0	1	0	0	4	3	1	0	.379	.304
	Brevard County (FSL)	HiA	.313	113	457	76	143	31	6	6	58	38	53	16	8	.369	.446
2010	Brevard County (FSL)	HiA	.174	7	23	7	4	2	0	0	1	4	6	0	0	.286	.261
2011	Brevard County (FSL)	HiA	.306	9	36	4	11	0	0	0	1	5	4	1	1	.390	.306
	Huntsville (SL)	AA	.302	50	189	31	57	9	4	0	19	17	25	10	5	.368	.392
	Nashville (PCL)	AAA	.331	40	169	31	56	13	2	5	23	17	18	5	3	.401	.521
	Milwaukee (NL)	MAJ	.333	8	3	1	1	0	0	0	0	1	1	0	0	.500	.333
Major League Totals			.333	8	3	1	1	0	0	0	0	1	1	0	0	.500	.333
Minor League Totals			.301	277	1103	182	332	68	16	13	130	98	155	37	25	.363	.427

7 CODY SCARPETTA, RHP

Born: Aug. 25, 1988. **B-T:** R-R. **Ht.:** 6-3. **Wt.:** 240. **Drafted:** HS—Guilford, Ill., 2007 (11th round). **Signed by:** Harvey Kuenn Jr.

Scarpetta slipped to the 11th round of the 2007 draft because a torn flexor tendon in his right index finger required surgery. He originally signed for $325,000, but that deal was voided when he needed a second operation. Milwaukee re-signed him for $125,000 but had to place him on its 40-man roster to retain his rights. The Brewers used his fourth and what normally would be his final option to send him to the minors in 2011, but he was granted an extra option. Scarpetta has a pair of plus pitches in a 90-94 mph fastball and a sharp-breaking curveball. He has worked on improving his changeup but it's still a work in progress. At times he gets out of whack with his short-arm delivery and his control and command become erratic, resulting in too many walks. He has worked on smoothing out his lower half to be able to locate his pitches down in the zone with more consistency. He has the raw stuff to be a No. 3 or 4 starter, but Scarpetta could wind up in the bullpen if he can't refine his changeup and control. Now that he has the extra option, he'll spend 2012 in Triple-A.

BA GRADE
50
MEDIUM

Year	Club (League)	Class	W	L	ERA	G	GS	CG	SV	IP	H	HR	BB	SO	K/9	WHIP	AVG
2008	Brewers (AZL)	R	1	0	0.57	6	5	0	0	16	8	0	8	27	15.5	1.02	.154
	Helena (PIO)	R	1	0	3.48	6	3	0	0	21	18	2	8	31	13.5	1.26	.237
2009	Wisconsin (MWL)	LoA	4	11	3.43	26	18	0	0	105	83	5	55	116	9.9	1.31	.217
	Huntsville (SL)	AA	0	0	5.40	1	1	0	0	5	5	1	1	1	1.8	1.20	.263
2010	Brevard County (FSL)	HiA	7	12	3.87	27	27	1	0	128	120	4	67	142	10.0	1.46	.247
2011	Huntsville (SL)	AA	8	5	3.85	23	23	0	0	117	100	8	61	98	7.5	1.38	.234
Minor League Totals			21	28	3.61	89	77	1	0	391	334	20	200	415	9.5	1.36	.231

8 TAYLOR GREEN, 3B/2B

Born: Nov. 2, 1986. **B-T:** L-R. **Ht.:** 5-11. **Wt.:** 200. **Drafted:** Cypress (Calif.) JC, D/F 2005 (25th round). **Signed by:** Bruce Seid.

Green was the Brewers' minor league player of the year in 2007 and was on the list of potential players to be named later in the C.C. Sabathia trade the following year. His career took a downturn after he had surgery on his left wrist in January 2009, costing him half of that season and continued to affect his swing in 2010. He got back on track in 2011, earning Triple-A Pacific Coast League all-star honors, his second organization player of the year award and his first big league callup. His aptitude as a pinch-hitter earned him a spot on Milwaukee's postseason roster. Green has a compact swing, an all-fields approach and solid power. He makes consistent contact and draws his share of walks. Much of his value lies in his bat, because he's a below-average runner with only adequate defensive skills. He doesn't have great range or a fantastic arm at third base, and lacks the quickness desired at second base, but his reliable hands and good instincts allow him to make routine plays. After getting left off the Brewers' 40-man roster after the 2010 season, Green went from Double-A on Opening Day to the National League Championship Series in October. Now he's in position to push his way into Milwaukee's lineup with a strong performance in spring training.

BA GRADE
50
MEDIUM

Year	Club (League)	Class	AVG	G	AB	R	H	2B	3B	HR	RBI	BB	SO	SB	CS	OBP	SLG
2006	Helena (PIO)	R	.231	62	221	36	51	12	1	1	23	29	35	0	1	.328	.308
2007	West Virginia (SAL)	LoA	.327	111	397	68	130	29	2	14	86	51	65	0	5	.406	.516
2008	Brevard County (FSL)	HiA	.289	114	418	46	121	19	0	15	73	61	59	4	2	.382	.443
2009	Wisconsin (MWL)	LoA	.400	6	20	6	8	1	0	1	5	4	4	0	0	.538	.600
	Huntsville (SL)	AA	.258	87	306	34	79	15	0	5	43	33	37	0	2	.330	.356
2010	Huntsville (SL)	AA	.260	113	393	51	102	29	1	13	81	45	67	0	2	.336	.438
2011	Huntsville (SL)	AA	.364	3	11	2	4	1	0	0	3	3	0	0	0	.385	.455
	Nashville (PCL)	AAA	.336	120	420	74	141	36	1	22	88	55	72	1	0	.413	.583
	Milwaukee (NL)	MAJ	.270	20	37	2	10	3	0	0	1	0	6	0	0	.270	.351
Major League Totals			.270	20	37	2	10	3	0	0	1	0	6	0	0	.270	.351
Minor League Totals			.291	616	2186	317	636	142	5	71	402	278	342	5	12	.373	.458

9 JORGE LOPEZ, RHP

Born: Feb. 10, 1993. **B-T:** R-R. **Ht.:** 6-4. **Wt.:** 170. **Drafted:** HS—Cayey, P.R., 2011 (2nd round). **Signed by:** Charlie Sullivan/Manolo Hernandez.

The Brewers figured Lopez would go in the supplemental first round of the 2011 draft, and they were thrilled to grab him with the 70th overall choice and sign him for $690,000. He became Puerto Rico's second-highest drafted pitcher ever, trailing only Braves 2003 sandwich pick Luis Atilano. Also a volleyball and track star in high school, Lopez has a lot of physical projection remaining in his lanky frame and should improve now that he's focusing on baseball. With long arms and a loose delivery, Lopez regularly throws his fastball at 89-91 mph and touches 93. Milwaukee believes he'll throw in the mid-90s once he fills out. He also has an over-the-top curveball that can buckle hitters' knees. He has unusual feel for his curve for a teenager and will throw it in any count. He only has been pitching for three years, so his changeup and command are still works in progress. Lopez has good body control for a lanky youngster, though his arm action can get a little sweepy in the back. Lopez has a ceiling as a No. 2 or 3 starter but a long way to go to get there. He'll probably spend 2012 at Rookie-level Helena and make his full-season debut the following season.

BA GRADE
50
HIGH

Year	Club (League)	Class	W	L	ERA	G	GS	CG	SV	IP	H	HR	BB	SO	K/9	WHIP	AVG
2011	Brewers (AZL)	R	0	0	2.25	4	4	0	0	12	13	0	3	10	7.5	1.33	.265
Minor League Totals			0	0	2.25	4	4	0	0	12	13	0	3	10	7.5	1.33	.265

10 JIMMY NELSON, RHP

Born: June 5, 1989. **B-T:** R-R. **Ht.:** 6-6. **Wt.:** 245. **Drafted:** Alabama, 2010 (2nd round). **Signed by:** Joe Mason.

When first-rounder Dylan Covey was diagnosed with diabetes and opted to attend college, Nelson became Milwaukee's top signee in the 2010 draft as a second-rounder. Used exclusively as a reliever in his pro debut after a heavy workload as an Alabama junior, he had an up-and-down season as a starter in 2011. He did show improvement in the second half, going 6-2, 3.71 in his final 13 starts, and made significant strides in instructional league. Nelson can be an intimidating presence on the mound, with his size and a fastball that he can run up to 97 mph. He has better command when he relies on his two-seamer, a low-90s offering with heavy sink. His 84-86 mph slider that is a plus pitch when he throws it for strikes but he often struggles to keep it in the zone. Nelson's changeup remains a work in progress and a key to his continued development. He has trouble repeating his delivery at times, which negatively affects his control. He has the body and mentality to be a workhorse. The Brewers were excited with Nelson's performance in instructional league and believe he can be a middle-of-the-rotation starter. If not, he profiles well as a late-inning reliever provided he throws more strikes. He could force his way to Double-A at some point in 2012.

BA GRADE
50
HIGH

Year	Club (League)	Class	W	L	ERA	G	GS	CG	SV	IP	H	HR	BB	SO	K/9	WHIP	AVG
2010	Helena (PIO)	R	2	0	3.71	12	0	0	3	27	30	2	13	33	11.1	1.61	.268
2011	Wisconsin (MWL)	LoA	8	9	4.38	26	25	1	0	146	146	9	65	120	7.4	1.45	.266
Minor League Totals			10	9	4.27	38	25	1	3	173	176	11	78	153	8.0	1.47	.267

11 SANTO MANZANILLO, RHP

BA GRADE
50
HIGH

Born: Sept. 20, 1988. **B-T:** R-R. **Ht.:** 6-1. **Wt.:** 218. **Signed:** Dominican Republic, 2005. **Signed by:** Fernando Arango/Fausto Sosa Pena.

When the Brewers signed Manzanillo two months shy of his 17th birthday, he was a raw pitcher with a good arm who had no idea where the ball was going. He walked a stunning 47 batters in 16 innings in his 2006 pro debut and didn't total more strikeouts than walks until 2008. He blew out his elbow and missed the entire 2009 season following Tommy John surgery, then continued to struggle with his control the next year. He finally harnessed his stuff under the tutelage of Brevard County pitching coach Fred Dabney and flourished last year. Manzanillo's lively fastball explodes on hitters, regularly arriving at 94-96 mph and peaking at 99. He has a second power pitch in his mid-80s slider, though it has more cut than bite and is no more than an average offering. His changeup is actually more effective than his slider, because hitters have to gear up to hit his fastball. If Manzanillo can continue to improve his control and command like he has over the past year, he could become a set-up man for Milwaukee in the near future. He was added to the 40-man roster in November, but later that month his status for the spring was clouded when he dislocated his right shoulder in an auto accident in the Dominican Republic. He also fractured his right scapula and is expected to miss spring training.

Year	Club (League)	Class	W	L	ERA	G	GS	CG	SV	IP	H	HR	BB	SO	K/9	WHIP	AVG
2006	Brewers (AZL)	R	0	0	13.22	14	0	0	0	16	14	1	47	13	7.2	3.73	.230
2007	Brewers (AZL)	R	4	4	3.90	14	0	0	1	28	22	1	29	18	5.9	1.84	.214
2008	Helena (PIO)	R	0	1	9.28	13	6	0	1	32	41	3	26	27	7.6	2.09	.318
2009	Did Not Play—Injured																
2010	Wisconsin (MWL)	LoA	1	1	5.77	26	0	0	0	53	58	3	30	40	6.8	1.66	.279
2011	Brevard County (FSL)	HiA	1	0	1.52	28	0	0	10	41	31	2	14	43	9.4	1.09	.200
	Huntsville (SL)	AA	0	1	2.21	20	0	0	7	20	13	2	12	19	8.4	1.23	.181
Minor League Totals			6	7	5.43	115	6	0	19	191	179	12	158	160	7.6	1.77	.246

12 MICHAEL FIERS, RHP

BA GRADE
45
LOW

Born: June 15, 1985. **B-T:** R-R. **Ht.:** 6-2. **Wt.:** 195. **Drafted:** Nova Southeastern (Fla.), 2009 (22nd round). **Signed by:** Charlie Sullivan.

Nova Southeastern (Fla.) already has sent two late-rounders from the 2009 draft to the big leagues, with J.D. Martinez and Fiers making their debuts last season. The Astros drafted Martinez in the 20th round, while Fiers went two rounds later after leading NCAA Division II with 145 strikeouts in 109 innings that spring. Signed for $2,500, he broke into pro ball as a closer and has split the last two years between starting and relieving. Milwaukee's 2011 minor league pitcher of the year after leading the system in wins (13) and ERA (1.86), he made two scoreless relief appearances for the Brewers in September. Fiers pitches from an over-the-top delivery with excellent control, constantly working ahead in the count. He's not overpowering, but there's deception in his delivery and hitters have trouble picking up his pitches. His best pitch is a solid changeup with tailing action that keeps lefthanders at bay. He sets is up with an 88-92 mph fastball more notable for his ability to locate it down in the zone than its velocity. He also mixes in a low-80s slider and a mid-70s curveball. Fiers' 2011 performance has the Brewers projecting him as a back-of-the-rotation starter, though they have no openings in the big leagues. He may open the year in Nashville unless he wins a middle-relief job during spring training.

Year	Club (League)	Class	W	L	ERA	G	GS	CG	SV	IP	H	HR	BB	SO	K/9	WHIP	AVG
2009	Helena (PIO)	R	1	0	1.29	13	0	0	8	21	10	2	1	35	15.0	0.52	.137
	Wisconsin (MWL)	LoA	0	0	0.00	3	0	0	1	6	4	0	2	8	12.0	1.00	.190
	Brevard County (FSL)	HiA	1	0	1.98	6	0	0	2	14	10	2	2	16	10.5	0.88	.204
2010	Brevard County (FSL)	HiA	4	8	3.47	17	15	0	0	93	78	6	23	94	9.1	1.08	.229
	Huntsville (SL)	AA	1	1	3.69	10	4	0	1	32	28	3	9	36	10.2	1.17	.231
2011	Huntsville (SL)	AA	5	3	2.64	22	8	0	5	61	42	7	14	63	9.2	0.91	.189
	Nashville (PCL)	AAA	8	0	1.11	12	10	1	0	65	41	4	22	69	9.6	0.97	.174
	Milwaukee (NL)	MAJ	0	0	0.00	2	0	0	0	2	2	0	3	2	9.0	2.50	.286
Major League Totals			0	0	0.00	2	0	0	0	2	2	0	3	2	9.0	2.50	.286
Minor League Totals			20	12	2.50	83	37	1	17	292	213	24	73	321	9.9	0.98	.201

13 CALEB GINDL, OF

BA GRADE
45
MEDIUM

Born: Aug. 31, 1988. **B-T:** L-L. **Ht.:** 5-9. **Wt.:** 185. **Drafted:** HS—Milton, Fla., 2007 (5th round). **Signed by:** Doug Reynolds.

After having the worst full season of his pro career in 2010, Gindl rebounded with his best in 2011. One of the youngest regulars in the Pacific Coast League at age 22, he set career highs in batting (.307) and on-base percentage (.390). He finished on fire, batting .346/.429/.508 in the final two months. Gindl has a squatty build and doesn't wow anyone with his athleticism, but he has a track record of producing at the plate. His short stroke and discerning eye have made him a career .300 hitter in the minors. The question is whether he has enough pop to profile as a regular corner outfielder. His power comes mostly to the gaps and he never has hit more than 17 homers in a season. Gindl's speed and arm strength are average to fringy, though his instincts help those tools play up. He gets good enough jumps that the Brewers have given him some time in center field, but he's best suited for left. He's a grinder who shows up to play every day. Gindl impressed the staff in big league camp last spring with the way he swung the bat without being intimidated. He has little left to prove in Triple-A, but he'll probably return to Nashville this year because Milwaukee has Ryan Braun and Corey Hart manning its outfield corners. The Brewers protected Gindl on their 40-man roster this offseason.

Year	Club (League)	Class	AVG	G	AB	R	H	2B	3B	HR	RBI	BB	SO	SB	CS	OBP	SLG
2007	Helena (PIO)	R	.372	55	207	40	77	22	3	5	42	20	38	4	4	.420	.580
2008	West Virginia (SAL)	LoA	.307	137	508	86	156	38	4	13	81	63	144	14	5	.388	.474
2009	Brevard County (FSL)	HiA	.277	112	394	61	109	15	3	17	71	57	92	18	4	.363	.459
2010	Huntsville (SL)	AA	.272	128	463	61	126	33	1	9	60	55	78	10	5	.352	.406
2011	Nashville (PCL)	AAA	.307	126	472	84	145	23	5	15	60	63	93	6	5	.390	.472
Minor League Totals			.300	558	2044	332	613	131	16	59	314	258	445	52	23	.378	.466

14 HUNTER MORRIS, 1B

BA GRADE
45
MEDIUM

Born: Oct. 7, 1988. **B-T:** L-R. **Ht.:** 6-4. **Wt.:** 205. **Drafted:** Auburn, 2010 (4th round). **Signed by:** Joe Mason.

Morris turned down the Red Sox as a second-round pick out of high school in 2007, then spent three years at Auburn and signed as a fourth-rounder in 2010. He has the most usable power in the system and clearly is the Brewers' top first-base prospect, but he also has to address a couple of glaring flaws in his game. Morris generates his pop more with strength than bat speed. He does a good job of making consistent contact and is equally dangerous against lefthanders and righthanders. How well his power will play at high levels will depend on his ability to tone down his aggressiveness. He has just 38 walks and a .303 on-base percentage in 201 pro games. Morris will have to produce at the plate, because he didn't show much in brief trials as a third baseman and outfielder, limiting him to first base. He has a lot of work to do defensively after leading Florida State League first basemen with 19 errors last year, many the product of substandard range and footwork. He does have good arm strength for the position. While he's a below-average runner, Morris isn't bad once he gets going. He'll spend 2012 in Double-A, working on his plate discipline and defense.

Year	Club (League)	Class	AVG	G	AB	R	H	2B	3B	HR	RBI	BB	SO	SB	CS	OBP	SLG
2010	Wisconsin (MWL)	LoA	.251	71	291	38	73	19	4	9	44	20	58	7	2	.306	.436
2011	Huntsville (SL)	AA	.353	4	17	6	6	1	1	1	2	0	1	0	0	.353	.706
	Brevard County (FSL)	HiA	.271	126	501	75	136	28	5	19	67	18	84	7	3	.299	.461
Minor League Totals			.266	201	809	119	215	48	10	29	113	38	143	14	5	.303	.457

15 YADIEL RIVERA, SS

BA GRADE
55
EXTREME

Born: May 1, 1992. **B-T:** R-R. **Ht.:** 6-3. **Wt.:** 178. **Drafted:** HS—Caguas, P.R., 2010 (9th round). **Signed by:** Charlie Sullivan.

The Brewers have no doubt about Rivera's ability to one day play shortstop in the big leagues. He makes it look easy at times and was a unanimous choice of Pioneer League managers as the best defensive shortstop in the Rookie league in last summer. He makes all of the routine plays and uses above-average range and arm strength to also produce web gems. He has sure hands and good lateral movement. The question, however, is whether Rivera can generate enough offense to be an everyday player in the majors. He hit just .194 with 34 strikeouts in 32 games at Wisconsin to open the 2011 season, and he ranked second in the Pioneer League with 91 strikeouts in 330 at-bats. He has some pop but it actually works against him because he focuses on trying to hit homers rather than putting the ball in play. His swing gets too long and pull-oriented, and he sometimes has trouble catching up to ordinary fastballs. He's also too aggressive and doesn't draw enough walks for a player whose focus should be getting on base. Rivera has just fringy speed and won't be a basestealing threat. He'll get a second chance at trying to solve low Class A pitching in 2012, but he's going to have to show much more at the plate to profile as a regular.

Year	Club (League)	Class	AVG	G	AB	R	H	2B	3B	HR	RBI	BB	SO	SB	CS	OBP	SLG
2010	Brewers (AZL)	R	.209	49	206	22	43	8	1	0	23	9	72	6	2	.243	.257
2011	Wisconsin (MWL)	LoA	.194	32	103	6	20	2	1	1	5	4	34	0	0	.224	.262
	Helena (PIO)	R	.248	74	330	47	82	14	7	8	38	14	91	7	3	.285	.406
Minor League Totals			.227	155	639	75	145	24	9	9	66	27	197	13	5	.262	.335

16 KENTRAIL DAVIS, OF

BA GRADE
50
HIGH

Born: June 29, 1988. **B-T:** L-R. **Ht.:** 5-9. **Wt.:** 195. **Drafted:** Tennessee, 2009 (1st round supplemental). **Signed by:** Joe Mason.

Considered one of the best college hitters in the 2009 draft, Davis hasn't lived up to that billing since signing for $1.2 million as the 39th overall pick. He struggled when sent to high Class A to make his pro debut in 2010, and again when he returned to Brevard County last season. Davis has the short swing and bat speed to hit for average and power, but he gets too pull-conscious at times and his plate discipline deteriorated in 2011. Some scouts question whether he has enough pop to play on an outfield corner in the majors. Davis has plus speed and uses it well to steal bases, but his defensive instincts are a bit lacking and may prevent him from playing center field at the upper levels. He spent more of last year in right field, though his arm strength is fringy and eventually could relegate him to left field. The Brewers hoped Davis would already have reached Double-A by now, and they'll send him there and hope his bat gets going in 2012.

Year	Club (League)	Class	AVG	G	AB	R	H	2B	3B	HR	RBI	BB	SO	SB	CS	OBP	SLG
2010	Brevard County (FSL)	HiA	.244	33	123	20	30	2	5	0	17	17	28	8	2	.380	.341
	Wisconsin (MWL)	LoA	.335	64	245	44	82	26	5	3	46	31	36	3	1	.421	.518
2011	Brevard County (FSL)	HiA	.245	132	507	76	124	19	8	8	46	37	97	33	8	.317	.361
Minor League Totals			.270	229	875	140	236	47	18	11	109	85	161	44	11	.357	.402

17 DAVID GOFORTH, RHP

BA GRADE
50
HIGH

Born: Oct. 11, 1988. **B-T:** R-R. **Ht.:** 6-0. **Wt.:** 186. **Drafted:** Mississippi, 2011 (7th round). **Signed by:** Joe Mason.

Goforth had mixed results as a starter in college at Mississippi, though his arm strength got him drafted in the 31st round by the Indians as a redshirt sophomore in 2010 and in the seventh round by the Brewers last June. He signed for $100,000 before starring in his pro debut, when he worked exclusively as a reliever. Goforth's four-seam fastball is erratic at times, but when he comes out of the bullpen he throws it comfortably at 94-97 mph and peaks at 99. He has had trouble throwing his secondary pitches for strikes, though he helped himself in that regarded by adding an 88-92 mph cutter last spring. He throws a slider in the mid-80s, but it's often slurvy and Milwaukee would like him to develop a true curveball. He also has a changeup that's a below-average pitch just used for show. A bit undersized, Goforth gets into trouble when he works too high in the strike zone. If he can come up with a solid secondary pitch, he'll profile as a set-up man and possibly a closer. He may spend 2012 as a starter in Class A to get more innings.

Year	Club (League)	Class	W	L	ERA	G	GS	CG	SV	IP	H	HR	BB	SO	K/9	WHIP	AVG
2011	Helena (PIO)	R	0	4	4.43	19	0	0	2	41	44	5	10	42	9.3	1.33	.277
Minor League Totals			0	4	4.43	19	0	0	2	41	44	5	10	42	9.3	1.33	.277

18 MARTIN MALDONADO, C

BA GRADE
45
MEDIUM

Born: Aug. 16, 1986. **B-T:** R-R. **Ht.:** 6-1. **Wt.:** 215. **Drafted:** HS—Naguabo, P.R., 2004 (27th round). **Signed by:** Arnold Cochrane (Angels).

The Brewers always have believed that Maldonado had the defensive skills to play in the major leagues. He just never showed anything with the bat, which is why the Angels released him after he hit .237/.294/.274 in his first three pro seasons, none above Rookie ball. He didn't fare much better in his first four years in the Brewers system before surprisingly breaking out in 2011. He set career highs across the board and benefited from working with hitting coach Sandy Guerrero at Nashville, where he hit .321/.410/.537 in 39 games. Maldonado's work behind the plate remained as good as ever, with managers rating him the best defensive catcher in the Double-A Southern League last year. He used his plus-plus arm to throw out 43 percent of basestealers. He also has soft hands and moves well behind the dish despite being a well below-average runner. In the past, Maldonado found little offensive success with a long swing, overly aggressive approach and a maddening inability to punish mistakes. Whether the gains he made in 2011 are real will determine his future. He got a cup of coffee in Milwaukee in September and is a significantly better defender than the club's two main catchers last year, Jonathan Lucroy and George Kottaras. Maldonado projects as at least a defensive-minded backup and possibly a starter if he continues to hit.

Year	Club (League)	Class	AVG	G	AB	R	H	2B	3B	HR	RBI	BB	SO	SB	CS	OBP	SLG
2004	Angels (AZL)	R	.217	25	60	5	13	1	0	0	4	3	13	2	1	.277	.233
2005	Angels (AZL)	R	.256	27	86	6	22	2	0	0	10	2	9	0	0	.278	.279
	Orem (PIO)	R	.250	9	32	4	8	0	0	1	2	2	6	0	0	.294	.344
2006	Angels (AZL)	R	.222	21	63	9	14	1	1	0	6	7	12	0	2	.329	.270
2007	West Virginia (SAL)	LoA	.221	66	208	20	46	8	0	2	22	14	36	2	0	.309	.288
2008	Brevard County (FSL)	HiA	.266	34	94	8	25	8	0	0	9	8	17	3	1	.352	.351
	Huntsville (SL)	AA	.194	31	98	4	19	2	0	2	8	4	24	0	0	.225	.276
2009	Nashville (PCL)	AAA	.333	7	18	1	6	1	0	0	3	1	2	0	0	.350	.389
	Wisconsin (MWL)	LoA	.105	7	19	1	2	0	0	0	2	2	7	1	0	.182	.105
	Brevard County (FSL)	HiA	.199	81	251	25	50	9	0	2	21	30	51	2	1	.300	.259
2010	Brevard County (FSL)	HiA	.121	10	33	1	4	0	0	0	3	1	8	1	0	.189	.121
	Huntsville (SL)	AA	.252	34	103	9	26	6	0	2	12	9	24	0	2	.347	.369
	Nashville (PCL)	AAA	.253	52	174	19	44	9	0	7	26	14	45	0	1	.309	.425
2011	Huntsville (SL)	AA	.264	64	208	24	55	13	0	3	34	19	56	2	1	.349	.370
	Nashville (PCL)	AAA	.321	39	134	23	43	5	0	8	25	16	21	0	0	.410	.537
	Milwaukee (NL)	MAJ	.000	3	1	0	0	0	0	0	0	0	1	0	0	.000	.000
Major League Totals			.000	3	1	0	0	0	0	0	0	0	1	0	0	.000	.000
Minor League Totals			.238	507	1581	159	377	65	1	27	187	132	331	13	9	.316	.332

19 MARK ROGERS, RHP

BA GRADE
55
EXTREME

Born: Jan. 30, 1986. **B-T:** R-R. **Ht.:** 6-2. **Wt.:** 225. **Drafted:** HS—Mount Ararat, Maine, 2004 (1st round). **Signed by:** Tony Blengino.

After the Brewers gave up Brett Lawrie and Jake Odorizzi in deals for Zack Greinke and Shawn Marcum in December 2010, Rogers entered last season as the organization's top prospect. He was fresh off a September callup, a stunning turnaround for a pitcher who missed the 2007 and 2008 seasons while recovering from a pair of shoulder surgeries. The No. 5 overall pick in the 2004 draft and the recipient of a $2.2 million bonus, he arrived in spring training with a chance to earn a job in the big league rotation. Rogers came down with shoulder stiffness, however, then came down with carpal tunnel syndrome in both wrists after he was sent to Triple-A. Though he tried to work through the issue with physical therapy, he ultimately pitched just 44 innings before having surgery on both wrists. After another lost year for Rogers, Milwaukee is left wondering if he'll ever realize his vast potential. Before his latest setback, he was again regularly throwing his fastball in the mid-90s and touching 97 at times. His 12-to-6 curveball was devastating when he threw it for strikes, and he also threw a hard slider and an inconsistent changeup. Rogers has enough stuff to start, but his durability remains a major concern. His control never has been his strong suit and regressed in 2011. The Brewers are worrying more about his health than his future role at this point, but he seems destined for the bullpen.

Year	Club (League)	Class	W	L	ERA	G	GS	CG	SV	IP	H	HR	BB	SO	K/9	WHIP	AVG
2004	Brewers (AZL)	R	0	3	4.73	9	6	0	0	27	30	0	14	35	11.8	1.65	.294
2005	West Virginia (SAL)	LoA	2	9	5.11	25	20	0	1	99	87	11	70	109	9.9	1.59	.238
2006	Brevard County (FSL)	HiA	1	2	5.07	16	16	0	0	71	68	6	53	96	12.2	1.70	.253
	Brewers (AZL)	R	0	0	2.25	3	3	0	0	4	5	0	2	5	11.3	1.75	.294
2007	Did Not Play—Injured																
2008	Did Not Play—Injured																
2009	Brevard County (FSL)	HiA	1	3	1.67	23	22	0	0	65	46	2	29	67	9.3	1.16	.201
2010	Nashville (PCL)	AAA	0	0	2.08	1	1	0	0	4	3	0	3	3	6.2	1.38	.188
	Huntsville (SL)	AA	6	8	3.71	24	24	0	0	112	86	3	69	111	8.9	1.39	.210
	Milwaukee (NL)	MAJ	0	0	1.80	4	2	0	0	10	2	0	3	11	9.9	0.50	.067
2011	Nashville (PCL)	AAA	0	2	13.20	5	5	0	0	15	21	1	22	12	7.2	2.87	.333
	Brewers (AZL)	R	0	0	4.85	5	3	0	0	13	13	1	5	11	7.6	1.38	.250
	Brevard County (FSL)	HiA	0	3	9.37	5	5	0	0	16	22	4	15	17	9.4	2.27	.301
Major League Totals			0	0	1.80	4	2	0	0	10	2	0	3	11	9.9	0.50	.067
Minor League Totals			10	30	4.57	116	105	0	1	425	381	28	282	466	9.9	1.56	.239

20 NICK BUCCI, RHP

BA GRADE
45
MEDIUM

Born: Aug. 16, 1990. **B-T:** R-R. **Ht.:** 6-2. **Wt.:** 180. **Drafted:** HS—Sarnia, Ont., 2008 (18th round). **Signed by:** Jay Lapp.

Extremely raw when he signed out of Canada for $50,000 as an 18th-round pick in 2008, Bucci has made steady progress and pitched well last year in high Class A at age 20. His experience with Canada's national teams has helped his development, as he contributed to bronze-medal finishes at the 2009 and 2011 World Cups and a championship at the 2011 Pan American Games. Bucci likes to pitch inside with a 90-92 mph fastball that tops out at 94. He added a cutter/slider last season that became a solid pitch at times, and both his downer curveball and sinking changeup have the potential to become average offerings. He did a better job in 2011 of limiting walks and keeping his pitch counts down, allowing him to work a career-high 150 innings. Bucci has a good pitcher's frame and athleticism that enables him to repeat his delivery. He's a hard worker and tough competitor with a reasonable projection of becoming a No. 4 starter. He's ready to pitch in Double-A.

Year	Club (League)	Class	W	L	ERA	G	GS	CG	SV	IP	H	HR	BB	SO	K/9	WHIP	AVG
2008	Brewers (AZL)	R	0	3	7.36	5	4	0	0	11	12	2	2	14	11.5	1.27	.273
2009	Huntsville (SL)	AA	1	0	6.75	3	0	0	0	4	3	2	3	3	6.8	1.25	.231
	Helena (PIO)	R	6	3	4.41	13	12	0	0	69	59	7	21	66	8.6	1.15	.231
2010	Wisconsin (MWL)	LoA	6	7	3.51	26	20	0	1	121	96	12	68	100	7.5	1.36	.220
2011	Brevard County (FSL)	HiA	8	11	3.84	26	25	1	0	150	143	12	51	119	7.1	1.29	.247
Minor League Totals			21	24	3.98	73	61	1	1	355	313	35	144	302	7.7	1.29	.236

21 D'VONTREY RICHARDSON, OF

BA GRADE
50
HIGH

Born: July 30, 1988. **B-T:** R-R. **Ht.:** 6-2. **Wt.:** 215. **Drafted:** Florida State, 2009 (5th round). **Signed by:** Ryan Robinson.

Richardson was limited to 97 games last year by hip and vision problems, not good for a player who needs plenty of development time after a limited baseball career at Florida State. He went to Tallahassee on a football scholarship and set a Seminoles record for the longest run by a quarterback with a 55-yard touchdown in 2008. He would have shifted to defensive back had he not signed with the Brewers for $400,000 as a fifth-round pick the following summer. Richardson is the system's best athlete, but his lack of baseball instincts has limited his success. That has been particularly evident on the basepaths, where he has been caught stealing 28 times in 54 attempts despite above-average speed. After fanning 164 times in his 2010 pro debut, he cut down his swing, though that also reduced his power. He tightened his strike zone and started to make adjustments against breaking balls, lending hope that he can become a tablesetter who can get on base and provide some occasional pop. Richardson also is still learning as a center fielder, needed to improve his reads and jumps to maximize his considerable range. He has a strong arm and has recorded 30 assists in two pro seasons. Ticketed for Double-A this year, he has a long ways to go to reach his ceiling and no guarantee that he'll do so.

Year	Club (League)	Class	AVG	G	AB	R	H	2B	3B	HR	RBI	BB	SO	SB	CS	OBP	SLG
2010	Wisconsin (MWL)	LoA	.243	132	522	78	127	28	8	7	51	58	164	17	15	.331	.368
2011	Brevard County (FSL)	HiA	.284	97	359	47	102	13	7	3	41	22	70	9	13	.327	.384
Minor League Totals			.260	229	881	125	229	41	15	10	92	80	234	26	28	.330	.375

22 ORLANDO ARCIA, SS

Born: Aug. 4, 1994. **B-T:** R-R. **Ht.:** 6-0. **Wt.:** 165. **Signed:** Venezuela, 2010.
Signed by: Fernando Arango.

BA GRADE
55
EXTREME

The Brewers let their Latin American program lapse in the mid-2000s and at one point were the only organization without an academy in the Dominican Republic. They re-opened an academy after the 2009 season and have tried to increase their presence on the international market. The best of Milwaukee's recent finds is Arcia, who signed out of Venezuela for $95,000 in 2010. His brother Oswaldo is a top outfield prospect in the Twins system. Making his pro debut as one of the youngest players in the Rookie-level Dominican Summer League last year, Orlando attracted attention with his live bat. He showed surprising pop at times for a player with such a lanky frame, and his plate discipline was just as impressive. He shows average speed and good instincts on the basepaths. In the field, Arcia displays fine range to both sides and solid footwork around the bag on double plays. He's a very instinctive defender and has enough arm to stay at shortstop. While Arcia will need plenty of time to develop, the early returns on him are intriguing. He should make his U.S. debut this year.

Year	Club (League)	Class	AVG	G	AB	R	H	2B	3B	HR	RBI	BB	SO	SB	CS	OBP	SLG
2011	Brewers (DSL)	R	.294	64	218	47	64	16	1	6	36	30	20	13	4	.386	.459
Minor League Totals			.294	64	218	47	64	16	1	6	36	30	20	13	4	.386	.459

23 DREW GAGNON, RHP

Born: June 26, 1990. **B-T:** R-R. **Ht.:** 6-4. **Wt.:** 195. **Drafted:** Long Beach State,
2011 (3rd round). **Signed by:** Josh Belovsky.

BA GRADE
45
MEDIUM

Gagnon went just 12-24 in three seasons at Long Beach State, but he improved each season and showed a truer glimpse of his potential when he led the Cape Cod League with five wins in the summer of 2010. A third-round pick last June, he went through a dead-arm stage after signing for $340,000 and got roughed up in his pro debut. He threw much better in instructional league and will be ready for Class A ball in 2012. Gagnon has good life on a 90-93 mph fastball that reaches 95 at times. He had issues in the past with his curveball and slider blending into a slurve, but he showed a quality 79-82 mph curve in instructional league. He also has an average changeup, though he's still learning how to put hitters away with his secondary pitches. Gagnon has good mound presence and likes to attack hitters with his fastball. The Brewers envision him become a workhorse who could fit in the No. 4 slot in a rotation.

Year	Club (League)	Class	W	L	ERA	G	GS	CG	SV	IP	H	HR	BB	SO	K/9	WHIP	AVG
2011	Helena (PIO)	R	0	3	8.05	8	7	0	1	19	25	1	10	27	12.8	1.84	.321
Minor League Totals			0	3	8.05	8	7	0	1	19	25	1	10	27	12.8	1.84	.321

24 MICHAEL REED, OF

Born: Nov. 18, 1992. **B-T:** R-R. **Ht.:** 6-0. **Wt.:** 190. **Drafted:** HS—Leander, Texas,
2011 (5th round). **Signed by:** Jeremy Booth.

BA GRADE
50
HIGH

Though the Brewers focused on pitching in the 2011 draft, they also came away with a potential five-tool outfielder when they signed Reed in the fifth round for $500,000. If he hadn't turned pro, he would have played at Mississippi, where his father Benton played football en route to a brief NFL career. Michael has plus speed and raw power. He doesn't get cheated at the plate, though he may have to tone down his swing to hit for average. He has enough range to make center field a possibility, and after throwing 90-mph fastballs as a high school pitcher, he clearly has the arm strength for right field. Some area scouts weren't as high on Reed, considering him a physically maxed-out player who does everything with effort. Milwaukee believes he's much more than that and will send him to low Class A for his first full pro season.

Year	Club (League)	Class	AVG	G	AB	R	H	2B	3B	HR	RBI	BB	SO	SB	CS	OBP	SLG
2011	Brewers (AZL)	R	.232	14	56	11	13	4	2	0	5	5	17	1	0	.295	.375
Minor League Totals			.232	14	56	11	13	4	2	0	5	5	17	1	0	.295	.375

25 BROOKS HALL, RHP

Born: June 26, 1990. **B-T:** R-R. **Ht.:** 6-5. **Wt.:** 194. **Drafted:** HS—Anderson, S.C.,
2009 (4th round). **Signed by:** Ryan Robinson.

BA GRADE
45
MEDIUM

Hall played mostly shortstop in high school, pitching just five innings as a junior and 20 as a senior. That was enough for the Brewers to take him in the fourth round and give him a $700,000 bonus in 2009. He signed late that summer and began each of his two pro seasons in extended spring training. A slew of doubleheaders left Wisconsin needing an extra starter last May, and he pitched so well as a fill-in that he stayed in the rotation for the remainder of the season. Hall touched 95 mph with his fastball in high school, but he has sat at 87-92 mph in pro ball. He improved his fastball command in 2011, consistently driving the ball down in the zone with an over-the-top delivery. His best secondary pitch is a changeup that gives him a weapon against lefthanders, and he also throws a slurvy breaking ball in the low 80s. He's working on adding a cutter to expand his repertoire. Hall doesn't miss a lot of bats, but he stays ahead in the count and pitches to contact. A good competitor who profiles as a back-of-the-rotation starter, he'll begin 2012 in high Class A.

Year	Club (League)	Class	W	L	ERA	G	GS	CG	SV	IP	H	HR	BB	SO	K/9	WHIP	AVG
2010	Brewers (AZL)	R	3	4	5.44	14	7	0	0	46	55	5	16	43	8.4	1.53	.294
2011	Wisconsin (MWL)	LoA	7	5	4.13	19	18	0	0	100	109	7	25	63	5.7	1.34	.279
Minor League Totals			10	9	4.54	33	25	0	0	147	164	12	41	106	6.5	1.40	.284

26 KYLE HECKATHORN, RHP

BA GRADE
45
MEDIUM

Born: June 17, 1988. **B-T:** R-R. **Ht.:** 6-6. **Wt.:** 235. **Drafted:** Kennesaw State, 2009 (1st round supplemental). **Signed by:** Ryan Robinson.

With 2009 first-round pick Eric Arnett looking like a bust, the Brewers would like to get something out of Heckathorn, who signed for $776,000 as the 47th overall pick in the same draft. But he got hit hard in Double-A last year and hasn't shown the same stuff he featured at Kennesaw State, where his fastball sat at 91-94 mph and topped out at 98. Heckathorn mostly pitches at 88-93 mph, relying on sinking and tailing action to get groundouts rather than blowing his fastball by hitters. He throws both his slider and changeup in the mid-80s. His changeup is more effective and moves like his fastball, but he doesn't throw it enough. With a big frame, Heckathorn sometimes struggles with his mechanics, losing his release point and his command. He does a good job of throwing strikes but doesn't always locate his pitches as well as he needs to. He has a bulldog approach to pitching, sometimes to his own detriment. At some point soon, the Brewers might have to move Heckathorn to the bullpen. He'll likely remain in the rotation this year in Double-A to see if he can get over the hump.

Year	Club (League)	Class	W	L	ERA	G	GS	CG	SV	IP	H	HR	BB	SO	K/9	WHIP	AVG
2009	Helena (PIO)	R	0	1	6.04	6	5	0	0	22	30	4	4	15	6.0	1.52	.326
2010	Wisconsin (MWL)	LoA	6	6	2.96	17	13	1	0	85	82	2	23	67	7.1	1.24	.246
	Brevard County (FSL)	HiA	4	0	3.00	8	8	1	0	39	40	1	10	23	5.3	1.28	.265
2011	Brevard County (FSL)	HiA	5	6	3.95	15	15	1	0	80	82	8	21	65	7.3	1.29	.267
	Huntsville (SL)	AA	0	4	7.18	7	7	0	0	36	45	7	17	24	5.9	1.71	.296
Minor League Totals			15	17	4.12	53	48	3	0	262	279	22	75	194	6.7	1.35	.270

27 ERIC FARRIS, 2B/SS

BA GRADE
40
LOW

Born: March 3, 1986. **B-T:** R-R. **Ht.:** 5-10. **Wt.:** 175. **Drafted:** Loyola Marymount, 2007 (4th round). **Signed by:** Corey Rodriguez.

Farris stole 70 bases in 76 tries in high Class A in 2009, but he hasn't run as wild since injuring his right knee in a home-plate collision in April 2010. He earns points for his competitiveness and defensive play, but he has a limited offensive ceiling and doesn't have a clear path to the Brewers. Farris is too aggressive at the plate, especially for a hitter with little power to speak of, which prevents him from getting on base enough to be a true tablesetter. He does make contact and is a good bunter, but he needs to draw more walks. Farris isn't the blazer that 70-steal season might suggest, as he's more of a solid-to-plus runner with excellent instincts. He shows nice range, hands and athleticism at second base, though he lacks the arm strength needed on the left side of the infield, which hurts his potential as a utilityman. Even if he provided more offense, he'd be blocked at second base by Rickie Weeks in Milwaukee. Farris got a one-day callup last July and figures to spent a third straight season in Triple-A.

Year	Club (League)	Class	AVG	G	AB	R	H	2B	3B	HR	RBI	BB	SO	SB	CS	OBP	SLG
2007	Helena (PIO)	R	.326	63	239	34	78	16	2	1	34	16	22	21	5	.369	.423
2008	West Virginia (SAL)	LoA	.293	103	454	73	133	21	4	3	54	24	50	32	10	.332	.377
2009	Brevard County (FSL)	HiA	.298	124	473	68	141	18	1	7	49	29	46	70	6	.341	.385
2010	Brewers (AZL)	R	.250	10	32	5	8	5	0	1	9	1	3	1	0	.257	.500
	Nashville (PCL)	AAA	.274	60	230	28	63	9	1	2	15	9	25	14	2	.311	.348
2011	Milwaukee (NL)	MAJ	.000	1	1	0	0	0	0	0	0	0	0	0	0	.000	.000
	Nashville (PCL)	AAA	.271	134	538	70	146	26	5	6	55	32	70	21	7	.317	.372
Major League Totals			.000	1	1	0	0	0	0	0	0	0	0	0	0	.000	.000
Minor League Totals			.289	494	1966	278	569	95	13	20	216	111	216	159	30	.331	.381

28 NICK RAMIREZ, 1B

BA GRADE
45
MEDIUM

Born: Aug. 1, 1989. **B-T:** L-L. **Ht.:** 6-3. **Wt.:** 225. **Drafted:** Cal State Fullerton, 2011 (4th round). **Signed by:** Josh Belovsky.

Ramirez starred in two roles at Cal State Fullerton, serving as the Titans' primary power threat as well as their closer. He led the team with nine homers and 16 saves last spring before signing for $213,300 as a fourth-round pick. While he showed good feel for a solid mix of four pitches, the Brewers focused on his offensive ability and never really considered drafting him as a pitcher. Ramirez got off to a tremendous start in pro ball, batting .369 with eight homers in 23 games at Helena, before dropping to .197 with three longballs in 36 contests at Wisconsin. Moving forward, Ramirez will need to develop more plate discipline to have success. He has above-average raw power, thanks more to strength than bat speed, though some scouts worry about an arm bar in his swing. His hands work well at the plate and enable him to turn on pitches as well as drive them into the left-center gap. Ramirez has below-average speed and range, but he's an average defender with good hands at first base. He'll return to low Class A to start 2012 but could earn a promotion as soon as he proves he can handle Midwest League pitching.

Year	Club (League)	Class	AVG	G	AB	R	H	2B	3B	HR	RBI	BB	SO	SB	CS	OBP	SLG
2011	Helena (PIO)	R	.369	23	103	23	38	9	0	8	30	2	22	0	1	.383	.689
	Wisconsin (MWL)	LoA	.197	36	137	11	27	12	0	3	23	9	36	0	0	.248	.350
Minor League Totals			.271	59	240	34	65	21	0	11	53	11	58	0	1	.305	.496

29 KHRIS DAVIS, OF

BA GRADE
45
MEDIUM

Born: Dec. 21, 1987. **B-T:** R-R. **Ht.:** 5-11. **Wt.:** 190. **Drafted:** Cal State Fullerton, 2009 (7th round). **Signed by:** Josh Belovsky.

A teammate of Nick Ramirez at Cal State Fullerton, Davis offers some of the best power in the system. He won the Midwest League home run derby and set a Wisconsin franchise record with 22 longballs in 2010, his first full pro season. He followed up by slugging .533 in high Class A last year, though his power dropped off after he was promoted to Double-A in late July. Davis is a streaky hitter, using bat speed to drive the ball to all fields. He'll take a walk when he's pitched around, but he has some holes in his long swing and may not hit for high averages against big league pitching. Davis is a below-average runner and doesn't read balls well in the outfield, though he can make the routine play. His arm is substandard as well—he has two assists in 206 pro games—so he's limited to left field and possibly first base. Davis profiles more as a power bat off the bench than a regular, but he'll have to keep proving he can produce at every level. He'll take another shot at Double-A in 2012.

Year	Club (League)	Class	AVG	G	AB	R	H	2B	3B	HR	RBI	BB	SO	SB	CS	OBP	SLG
2009	Helena (PIO)	R	.000	1	1	0	0	0	0	0	0	0	0	0	0	.000	.000
	Brewers (AZL)	R	.243	10	37	7	9	0	2	2	8	6	11	4	0	.356	.514
2010	Wisconsin (MWL)	LoA	.280	128	457	86	128	26	4	22	72	77	120	17	10	.398	.499
2011	Brevard County (FSL)	HiA	.309	90	304	50	94	21	1	15	68	51	70	10	5	.415	.533
	Huntsville (SL)	AA	.210	35	124	10	26	7	1	2	16	10	23	0	0	.272	.331
Minor League Totals			.278	264	923	153	257	54	8	41	164	144	224	31	15	.386	.488

30 AMAURY RIVAS, RHP

BA GRADE
45
MEDIUM

Born: Dec. 20, 1985. **B-T:** R-R. **Ht.:** 6-2. **Wt.:** 205. **Signed:** Dominican Republic, 2005. **Signed by:** Fernando Arango/Fausto Sosa Pena.

After making his league's all-star game in the previous three seasons, Rivas wasn't as effective when he moved up to Triple-A for the first time last year. He couldn't throw his inconsistent slider for strikes and led the Pacific Coast League with 81 walks. Rivas still has a quality fastball that usually operates in the low 90s with good sink. He can run it up to 94-95 mph but it straightens out and gets hit at higher velocity. He developed feel for his changeup at a young age and it remains his best pitch. Unless Rivas can finally develop a breaking pitch, he probably faces a future as a middle reliever. He doesn't have the stuff to survive repeatedly falling behind in the count like he did in 2011. Rivas has overcome adversity in the past—he missed almost all of 2007 following Tommy John surgery—and has the mental toughness to make the necessary adjustments. He'll return to Nashville this season.

Year	Club (League)	Class	W	L	ERA	G	GS	CG	SV	IP	H	HR	BB	SO	K/9	WHIP	AVG
2005	Brewers (AZL)	R	2	3	6.91	14	6	0	0	42	56	1	16	34	7.3	1.73	.326
2006	Brewers (AZL)	R	1	0	6.43	4	2	0	0	14	17	1	3	12	7.7	1.43	.293
	Helena (PIO)	R	5	4	3.02	10	10	0	0	54	48	6	16	36	6.0	1.19	.236
2007	Brewers (AZL)	R	0	0	3.12	6	6	0	0	9	3	1	4	10	10.4	0.81	.107
2008	West Virginia (SAL)	LoA	8	3	3.50	19	15	0	0	90	83	11	32	70	7.0	1.28	.239
	Brevard County (FSL)	HiA	1	2	4.20	7	6	0	0	30	35	2	11	20	6.0	1.53	.294
2009	Brevard County (FSL)	HiA	13	7	2.98	26	23	0	0	133	109	11	43	123	8.3	1.14	.220
2010	Huntsville (SL)	AA	11	6	3.37	25	25	2	0	142	130	7	55	114	7.2	1.31	.253
2011	Nashville (PCL)	AAA	7	12	4.72	28	28	0	0	151	151	14	81	108	6.5	1.54	.260
Minor League Totals			48	37	3.91	139	121	2	0	663	632	54	261	527	7.2	1.35	.251

Minnesota Twins

BY JOHN MANUEL

When Terry Ryan surprised the Twins by resigning as GM after the 2007 season, he said he felt guilty for leaving such a mess for his successor, Bill Smith. Ryan's last club went 79-83 and had Johan Santana demanding a trade with one year left on his contract.

Smith got little in return when he traded Santana to the Mets, but Minnesota made the most of the roster and farm system Ryan had constructed. The Twins lost the American League Central in Game 163 in 2008, then won the division in 2009 and 2010, built around the brilliance of Joe Mauer and Justin Morneau and low-cost, homegrown complements.

Smith traded for key pieces such as J.J. Hardy and Carl Pavano to plug holes as needed.

Then came 2011, and everything that could go wrong did. Japanese import Tsuyoshi Nishioka and holdovers Alexi Casilla and Trevor Plouffe flopped in the middle infield. The Twins hit with no power, ran poorly, defended worse and paid for their lack of power arms, as the pitching staff complied a 4.60 ERA and an AL-worst 940 strikeouts.

The twin pillars of the lineup also faltered. Morneau has had concussion issues since June 2010 and hit .227 with four homers in 69 games. He's owed $28 million over the next two seasons, which pales in comparison to the $161 million due Mauer over the next seven. Mauer had the worst offensive year of his career (.287, three homers in 82 games) as he recovered from offseason knee surgery, suffered from bilateral leg weakness, came down with pneumonia and had teammates question his toughness in the media.

The combination of a franchise-record $113 million Opening Day payroll and 99 losses led to a return to the past in Minnesota's front office. Owner Jim Pohlad fired Smith in November and brought Ryan back as GM. A special assistant since his resignation, Ryan tabbed Mets special assistant Wayne Krivsky, his former assistant, to be an advisor.

Ryan immediately started reshaping the big league roster, signing Jamey Carroll and Ryan Doumit and allowing Joe Nathan to depart as a free agent. The big league team's fortunes depend most on a return to health by Mauer and Morneau, however

A former scouting director, Ryan built the Twins' player-development model, so don't expect changes there. Vice president of player personnel Mike Radcliff still evaluates the organization's top talents for the draft and its farm system, and has taken the lead in getting the club active in Latin America, spearheading

Terry Ryan returns to his general manager post after four years as a special assistant

TOP 30 PROSPECTS

1. Miguel Sano, 3b/ss	**16.** Adrian Salcedo, rhp
2. Joe Benson, of	**17.** Carlos Gutierrez, rhp
3. Eddie Rosario, 2b/of	**18.** Hudson Boyd, rhp
4. Aaron Hicks, of	**19.** Niko Goodrum, ss
5. Oswaldo Arcia, of	**20.** Max Kepler, of
6. Levi Michael, ss/2b	**21.** Matt Summers, rhp
7. Liam Hendriks, rhp	**22.** Logan Darnell, lhp
8. Kyle Gibson, rhp	**23.** Manuel Soliman, rhp
9. Chris Parmelee, 1b/of	**24.** Tom Stuifbergen, rhp
10. Brian Dozier, ss/2b	**25.** Alex Wimmers, rhp
11. Travis Harrison, 3b/1b	**26.** Lester Oliveros, rhp
12. Madison Boer, rhp	**27.** B.J. Hermsen, rhp
13. Corey Williams, lhp	**28.** Jorge Polanco, inf/of
14. Chris Herrmann, c/of	**29.** Angel Mata, rhp
15. Deolis Guerra, rhp	**30.** Terry Doyle, rhp

the signing of No. 1 prospect Miguel Sano in 2009.

The system isn't as strong as it was when Ryan last was in charge, and 2011 was a rough season for the team's previous three first-round picks. Outfielder Aaron Hicks (2008) had to rally to hit .242 in high Class A, righthander Kyle Gibson (2009) needed Tommy John surgery and righty Alex Wimmers (2010) missed half the year with a bout of wildness after walking the first six batters he faced in an April start.

Wimmers eventually came back to throw seven no-hit innings in his final outing. Minnesota hopes Ryan's return is just as successful.

General Manager: Terry Ryan. **Farm Director:** Jim Rantz. **Scouting Director:** Deron Johnson.

Class	Team	League	W	L	Pct	Finish*	Manager(s)
Majors	Minnesota Twins	American	63	99	.389	14th (14)	Ron Gardenhire
Triple-A	Rochester Red Wings	International	53	91	.368	14th (14)	Tom Nieto
Double-A	New Britain Rock Cats	Eastern	72	70	.507	7th (12)	Jeff Smith
High A	Fort Myers Miracle	Florida State	63	76	.453	10th (12)	Jake Mauer
Low A	Beloit Snappers	Midwest	69	69	.500	8th (16)	Nelson Prada
Rookie	Elizabethton Twins	Appalachian	42	26	.618	2nd (10)	Ray Smith
Rookie	GCL Twins	Gulf Coast	31	29	.517	6th (15)	Ramon Borrego
Overall 2011 Minor League Record			330	361	.478	25th (30)	

*Finish in overall standings (No. of teams in league). †League champion.

LAST YEAR'S TOP 30

Player, Pos.		Status
1.	Kyle Gibson, rhp	No. 8
2.	Aaron Hicks, of	No. 4
3.	Miguel Sano, 3b/ss	No. 1
4.	Joe Benson, of	No. 2
5.	Ben Revere, of	Majors
6.	Liam Hendriks, rhp	No. 7
7.	Alex Wimmers, rhp	No. 25
8.	Adrian Salcedo, rhp	No. 16
9.	Oswaldo Arcia, of	No. 5
10.	Carlos Gutierrez, rhp	No. 17
11.	Max Kepler, of	No. 20
12.	Rene Tosoni, of	Majors
13.	David Bromberg, rhp	Dropped out
14.	Angel Morales, of	Dropped out
15.	Billy Bullock, rhp	(Braves)
16.	Manuel Soliman, rhp	No. 23
17.	Jorge Polanco, ss/2b	No. 28
18.	Chris Parmelee, 1b/of	No. 9
19.	Niko Goodrum, ss/2b	No. 19
20.	Daniel Santana, ss/2b	Dropped out
21.	Eddie Rosario, of	No. 3
22.	Dakota Watts, rhp	Dropped out
23.	Pat Dean, lhp	Dropped out
24.	Trevor Plouffe, ss	Majors
25.	B.J. Hermsen, rhp	No. 27
26.	Bruce Pugh, rhp	Dropped out
27.	Tom Stuifbergen, rhp	No. 24
28.	Anthony Slama, rhp	Dropped out
29.	Scott Diamond, lhp	Dropped out
30.	Brian Dozier, inf	No. 10

BEST TOOLS

Best Hitter for Average	Eddie Rosario
Best Power Hitter	Miguel Sano
Best Strike-Zone Discipline	Brian Dozier
Fastest Baserunner	J.D. Williams
Best Athlete	Joe Benson
Best Fastball	Lester Oliveros
Best Curveball	Hudson Boyd
Best Slider	Kyle Gibson
Best Changeup	Deolis Guerra
Best Control	Liam Hendriks
Best Defensive Catcher	Danny Lehmann
Best Defensive Infielder	Brian Dozier
Best Infield Arm	Niko Goodrum
Best Defensive Outfielder	Aaron Hicks
Best Outfield Arm	Aaron Hicks

PROJECTED 2015 LINEUP

Catcher	Joe Mauer
First Base	Chris Parmelee
Second Base	Eddie Rosario
Third Base	Miguel Sano
Shortstop	Levi Michael
Left Field	Denard Span
Center Field	Aaron Hicks
Right Field	Joe Benson
Designated Hitter	Justin Morneau
No. 1 Starter	Scott Baker
No. 2 Starter	Francisco Liriano
No. 3 Starter	Brian Duensing
No. 4 Starter	Liam Hendriks
No. 5 Starter	Kyle Gibson
Closer	Corey Williams

TOP PROSPECTS OF THE DECADE

Year	Player, Pos.	2011 Org.
2002	Joe Mauer, c	Twins
2003	Joe Mauer, c	Twins
2004	Joe Mauer, c	Twins
2005	Joe Mauer, c	Twins
2006	Francisco Liriano, lhp	Twins
2007	Matt Garza, rhp	Cubs
2008	Nick Blackburn, rhp	Twins
2009	Aaron Hicks, of	Twins
2010	Aaron Hicks, of	Twins
2011	Kyle Gibson, rhp	Twins

TOP DRAFT PICKS OF THE DECADE

Year	Player, Pos.	2011 Org.
2002	Denard Span, of	Twins
2003	Matt Moses, 3b	Out of baseball
2004	Trevor Plouffe, ss	Twins
2005	Matt Garza, rhp	Cubs
2006	Chris Parmelee, of/1b	Twins
2007	Ben Revere, of	Twins
2008	Aaron Hicks, of	Twins
2009	Kyle Gibson, rhp	Twins
2010	Alex Wimmers, rhp	Twins
2011	Levi Michael, ss	Twins

LARGEST BONUSES IN CLUB HISTORY

Joe Mauer, 2001	$5,150,000
Miguel Sano, 2009	$3,150,000
B.J. Garbe, 1999	$2,750,000
Adam Johnson, 2000	$2,500,000
Ryan Mills, 1998	$2,000,000

MINNESOTA TWINS

TOP 2012 ROOKIE: Joe Benson, of. He might be the big league team's best outfield defender already, and his righty bat should fit into the lineup.

BREAKOUT PROSPECT: Corey Williams, lhp. If the Twins keep him in the bullpen, he could rocket through the system.

SLEEPER: Hein Robb, lhp. The South African southpaw has shown three-pitch promise and aptitude.

SOURCE OF TOP 30 TALENT

Homegrown	27	Acquired	3
College	10	Trades	2
Junior college	0	Rule 5 draft	1
High school	8	Independent leagues	0
Draft-and-follow	0	Free agents/waivers	0
Nondrafted free agents	0		
International	9		

LF
Dustin Martin
Brian Dinkelman
Nate Roberts
Daniel Ortiz
Wang-Wei Lin

CF
Aaron Hicks (4)
Max Kepler (20)

RF
Joe Benson (2)
Oswaldo Arcia (5)
Angel Morales
J.D. Williams
Dereck Rodriguez

3B
Miguel Sano (1)
Deibinson Romero

SS
Levi Michael (6)
Brian Dozier (10)
Niko Goodrum (19)
Jorge Polanco (28)
James Beresford
Tyler Grimes
Pedro Florimon

2B
Eddie Rosario (3)
Daniel Santana
Adam Bryant
Aderlin Mejia

1B
Chris Parmelee (9)
Travis Harrison (11)
Lance Ray
Michael Gonzales

C
Chris Herrmann (14)
Danny Lehmann
Matt Koch

LHP

LHSP	LHRP
Logan Darnell (22)	Corey Williams (13)
Hein Robb	Luis Nunez
Pat Dean	Andrew Albers
Edgar Ibarra	Tyler Robertson
Brett Lee	Cole Nelson
Austin Malinowski	Josue Montanez
Steven Gruver	
Jason Wheeler	

RHP

RHSP	RHRP
Liam Hendriks (7)	Deolis Guerra (15)
Kyle Gibson (8)	Carlos Gutierrez (17)
Madison Boer (12)	Matt Summers (21)
Adrian Salcedo (16)	Leser Oliveros (26)
Hudson Boyd (18)	Dakota Watts
Manuel Soliman (23)	Kyle Waldrop
Tom Stuifbergen (24)	Matt Hauser
Alex Wimmers (25)	Bobby Lanigan
B.J. Hermsen (27)	Bruce Pugh
Angel Mata (29)	Josh Burris
Terry Doyle (30)	Tyler Jones
David Bromberg	
Hung Yi Chen	
Trent Higginbotham	
Tim Shibuya	
Kuo-Hua Lo	
Todd Van Steensel	

2011

BEST PURE HITTER: The Twins signed just 10 position players, including their first two picks in SS/2B Levi Michael (1) and 3B/1B Travis Harrison (1s). Michael has a polished approach, having walked more than he struck out in his final two seasons at North Carolina, and a sound swing from both sides of the plate. Harrison has present strength and a pure feel for hitting.

BEST POWER HITTER: Harrison's swing lacks loft, but Minnesota sees so much hard contact that it thinks he'll have plus home run power down the line. He unleashed a 504-foot blast at the 2010 Power Showcase, an international home run derby.

FASTEST RUNNER: Michael struggled with groin and hip issues all spring, muting his bat and plus speed. He stole 15 bases in 16 tries for the Tar Heels.

BEST DEFENSIVE PLAYER: The Twins believe in Michael's above-average defensive tools at shortstop. SS Tyler Grimes (5) has a plus-plus arm and could stick at short if he learns to slow the game down and play a bit more under control.

BEST FASTBALL: Minnesota needs hard throwers and drafted several in RHPs Hudson Boyd (1s), Madison Boer (2) and Matt Summers (4), who all sit in the low 90s. Boyd has the best combination of velocity, durability and control. Summers touches 97 mph in shorter bursts. Out of the bullpen, LHP Corey Williams (3) pitches at 93-94 mph with sink and tailing action.

BEST SECONDARY PITCH: Boyd's power curveball scrapes 80 mph and has sharp, late break. Williams' slider also can be a plus pitch, at times reaching 84-85 mph with cutter action.

BEST PRO DEBUT: The Twins intend for Boer to start in 2012, but he stood out as a reliever last summer, posting 11 saves and a 43-3 K-BB in 25 innings while reaching low Class A Beloit. Summers was similarly dominant at Rookie-level Elizabethton, going 1-1, 0.87 with a 36-5 K-BB ratio in 21 innings.

BEST ATHLETE: Michael has strength, quickness and excellent body control.

MOST INTRIGUING BACKGROUND: OF Dereck Rodriguez (6) is the son of future Hall of Famer Ivan. Unsigned RHP T.J. Oakes (41) joined his father Todd, a pitching coach, at the University of Minnesota.

CLOSEST TO THE MAJORS: Boer, Summers and Williams will race each other to Minnesota. Boer may be slowest of the three if he becomes a starter.

BEST LATE-ROUND PICK: RHP Trent Higginbotham (26), who signed for $195,000, has touched 94 mph with a solid delivery and clean arm. He also has shown a nice breaking ball, though nothing like RHP Josh Burris' (17) 12-to-6 power curve. A converted catcher, Burris throws his fastball in the low 90s and hit 95 mph in instructional league.

THE ONE WHO GOT AWAY: The Twins badly wanted OF James Ramsey (22), whom they compare to Jason Kipnis, but he spurned their $500,000 offer to return to Florida State. Injuries helped push LHP Adam McCreery (14), now at Arizona State, out of the early rounds.

ASSESSMENT: An organization in need of strong arms got an infusion while also adding a pair of high-ceiling hitters. A full return to health for Michael could give Minnesota a much-needed middle-infield bat.

2010   BONUSES: $3.5 MILLION

RHP Alex Wimmers (1) was supposed to be polished, but he completely lost his control for much of his first full pro season. 2B/OF Eddie Rosario (4) won MVP honors in the Rookie-level Appalachian League last summer, hitting a league-best 21 homers.

GRADE: C+

2009   BONUSES: $4.7 MILLION

Another polished RHP, Kyle Gibson (1), made swift progress before having Tommy John surgery last summer. The same fate befell LHP Matt Bashore (1s) as well. SS/2B Brian Dozier (8), the Twins' 2011 minor league player of the year, has picked up some of the slack.

GRADE: C+

2008   BONUSES: $7.3 MILLION

Minnesota has gotten very little out of its three selections before the second round. OF Aaron Hicks (1) and RHP Carlos Gutierrez (1) have developed much slower than expected. RHP Shooter Hunt (1s) had problems throwing strikes before he was lost in the Triple-A phase of the 2011 Rule 5 draft.

GRADE: C

2007   BONUSES: $2.2 MILLION

A career .326 hitter in the minors, OF Ben Revere (1) can hit for average and run but it's unclear whether he can do enough else to be a productive regular. He may be the only big leaguer in this group.

GRADE: C

Draft analysis by John Manuel (2011) and Jim Callis (2007-10). Numbers in parentheses indicate draft rounds.

1 MIGUEL
SANO, 3B/SS

Born: May 11, 1993. **B-T:** R-R. **Ht.:** 6-3. **Wt.:** 232.
Signed: Dominican Republic, 2009. **Signed by:** Fred Guerrero.

BA GRADE
70
HIGH

TONY FARLOW

The Twins built their success in the last decade mostly on the draft and astute acquisitions, with few homegrown contributors from Latin America. Minnesota has struggled to land talent from the Dominican Republic but went all-in in 2009 when Sano came on the open market. Twins scout John Wilson was so overwhelmed while watching him take batting practice, he filmed the session on his phone's camera. Wilson played it for club officials back in Minneapolis and said, "I don't care how old this guy is, we've got to get him." Sano was regarded as the top talent in a 2009 international class that also included Yankees catcher Gary Sanchez and Rangers shortstop Jurickson Profar. It took a lengthy investigation process as well as a bidding war with the Pirates before the Twins snared Sano with a $3.15 million bonus. He spent his first full year in the United States in 2011, ranking as the No. 1 prospect in the Rookie-level Appalachian League and finishing second to teammate Eddie Rosario with 20 homers.

Scouts inside and outside the organization love Sano's easy power. Elizabethton manager Ray Smith, who has been in the Appy League for more than 20 years, says the only players who have come through the circuit and produced similar sound off their bat to Sano are Josh Hamilton and Joe Mauer. A physical specimen, Sano already has added 40 pounds since signing and may not be done growing. He drives balls to all fields effortlessly, incorporating his strong lower half into his swing. Sano regularly expanded his strike zone at the start of the summer, then adjusted. He improved his weight shift and began staying back and trusting his hands. He led the Appy League with 45 extra-base hits, with six of his final 10 homers coming to center field or right. Sano won't stay at shortstop. At 232 pounds, he has outgrown the position and will have to work to maintain his agility to remain at third base. He has a strong arm and sure hands, though sloppy footwork and inexperience at third base led to 15 errors in just 48 games. Minnesota doesn't intend to move him off third base any time soon, but an eventual shift to an outfield corner is possible. If he keeps getting bigger and loses his presently fringy speed, he might have to move to first base.

Sano is ready for his full-season closeup at low Class A Beloit. The Twins usually try to take it slow with their prospects, but he could be an exception if he improves his pitch recognition and cuts down on his strikeouts. He has the highest ceiling of any Minnesota prospect since Joe Mauer and could be in the Twin Cities by 2014, allowing him two full seasons in the minors. Sano profiles as at least a 30-homer threat at third base, a luxury the Twins haven't had since Gary Gaetti's heyday in the late 1980s.

SCOUTING GRADES

Batting: 60.   **Defense:** 50.
Power: 75.   **Arm:** 60.
Speed: 40.

Based on 20-80 scouting scale, where 50 represents major league average, and future projection rather than present tools.

Year	Club (League)	Class	AVG	G	AB	R	H	2B	3B	HR	RBI	BB	SO	SB	CS	OBP	SLG
2010	Twins (DSL)	R	.344	20	64	11	22	2	1	3	10	14	17	2	1	.463	.547
	Twins (GCL)	R	.291	41	148	23	43	14	0	4	19	10	43	2	2	.338	.466
2011	Elizabethton (APP)	R	.292	66	267	58	78	18	7	20	59	23	77	5	4	.352	.637
Minor League Totals			.299	127	479	92	143	34	8	27	88	47	137	9	7	.364	.572

2 JOE BENSON, OF

BA GRADE
55
MEDIUM

Born: March 5, 1988. **B-T:** R-R. **Ht.:** 6-1. **Wt.:** 205. **Drafted:** HS—Joliet, Ill., 2006 (2nd round). **Signed by:** Billy Milos.

Benson has ranked among the Twins' top 15 prospects every year since being drafted 64th overall in 2006, moving in virtual lockstep with '06 first-rounder Chris Parmelee. Signed away from a Purdue football scholarship for $575,000, Benson has battled injuries—including a knee problem that required arthroscopic surgery in 2011—but played in a career-high 135 games and made his major league debut last season. Minnesota still considers Benson a five-tool player, and so do scouts outside the organization. The biggest question is how much contact he'll make. He's too aggressive at times, still struggles with spin and doesn't always handle breaking balls on the outer half well. He improved his walk rate in 2011 by learning to lay off such pitches, and he made more hard contact with a better two-strike approach and a greater willingness to use the entire field. Benson has plus raw power and speed, though his power plays more consistently. He has one of the system's strongest and most accurate arms and is an above-average defender at all three outfield spots. Benson could help the Twins replace free agents Mike Cuddyer and Jason Kubel if they depart. He hasn't played at Triple-A yet, though, so he's probably headed to Rochester.

Year	Club (League)	Class	AVG	G	AB	R	H	2B	3B	HR	RBI	BB	SO	SB	CS	OBP	SLG
2006	Twins (GCL)	R	.260	52	196	30	51	11	5	5	28	21	41	9	10	.335	.444
	Beloit (MWL)	LoA	.263	8	19	2	5	0	0	1	0	6	1	0	.263	.263
2007	Beloit (MWL)	LoA	.255	122	432	73	110	18	8	5	38	49	124	18	16	.347	.368
2008	Beloit (MWL)	LoA	.248	69	254	39	63	16	3	4	27	24	73	17	11	.326	.382
2009	Twins (GCL)	R	.200	2	5	1	1	0	0	0	0	2	0	1	1	.429	.200
	Fort Myers (FSL)	HiA	.285	80	263	46	75	10	3	5	29	46	74	14	7	.414	.403
2010	Fort Myers (FSL)	HiA	.294	21	85	16	25	11	1	4	13	8	21	5	0	.375	.588
	New Britain (EL)	AA	.251	102	374	65	94	20	7	23	49	39	115	14	9	.336	.527
2011	Twins (GCL)	R	.222	3	9	2	2	1	0	0	0	2	2	1	1	.364	.333
	New Britain (EL)	AA	.285	111	400	69	114	28	4	16	67	56	109	13	9	.388	.495
	Minnesota (AL)	MAJ	.239	21	71	3	17	6	1	0	2	3	21	2	2	.270	.352
Major League Totals			.239	21	71	3	17	6	1	0	2	3	21	2	2	.270	.352
Minor League Totals			.265	570	2037	343	540	115	31	62	252	247	565	93	64	.359	.443

3 EDDIE ROSARIO, 2B/OF

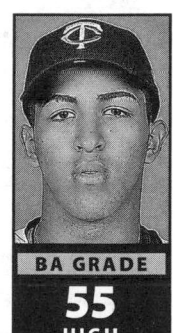

BA GRADE
55
HIGH

Born: Sept. 28, 1991. **B-T:** L-R. **Ht.:** 6-0. **Wt.:** 177. **Drafted:** HS—Guayama, P.R., 2010 (4th round). **Signed by:** Hector Otero.

Though he had a strong debut in the Rookie-level Gulf Coast League in 2010, Rosario wasn't assigned to a full-season roster to start 2011, instead languishing in extended spring training. He couldn't have been more ready for the Appalachian League, winning co-MVP honors while leading the circuit in runs (71), triples (nine), homers (21, three shy of the Appy record), total bases (181) and slugging (.670). The Twins love Rosario's swing and were less surprised by his batting average than by his power. He's balanced at the plate, has above-average bat speed and a short swing with surprising strength, helping him drive the ball from pole to pole. While he's not a slugger, he should have average to plus power down the line. Rosario has above-average speed as well, though his baserunning lacks polish. He shows average range and arm strength in center field, and he encouraged Minnesota with his play after moving to second base in instructional league. Rosario will need repetitions at second, but his arm, athleticism and quickness give him a chance to stay there. He'll report to spring training as a second baseman ticketed for Beloit this year. If it all works out, the Twins will have their best offensive second baseman since Chuck Knoblauch.

Year	Club (League)	Class	AVG	G	AB	R	H	2B	3B	HR	RBI	BB	SO	SB	CS	OBP	SLG
2010	Twins (GCL)	R	.294	51	194	34	57	9	2	5	26	16	28	22	5	.343	.438
2011	Elizabethton (APP)	R	.337	67	270	71	91	9	9	21	60	27	60	17	6	.397	.670
Minor League Totals			.319	118	464	105	148	18	11	26	86	43	88	39	11	.375	.573

4 AARON HICKS, OF

BA GRADE
55
HIGH

Born: Oct. 2, 1989. **B-T:** B-R. **Ht.:** 6-2. **Wt.:** 185. **Drafted:** HS—Long Beach, 2008 (1st round). **Signed by:** John Leavitt.

A natural athlete, Hicks doubled as a hard-throwing pitcher in high school and is a scratch golfer who jokes that he has had to start golfing lefthanded to get other Twins farmhands to play against him. Signed for $1.78 million as the 14th overall pick in 2008, he still hadn't solved high Class A three years later. Hicks' tools still stand out, starting with a plus-plus throwing arm that remains the best in the system. He's a good center fielder with above-average range. Offensive consistency is Hicks' biggest issue. His lefthanded swing remains too long and loopy, and he hit .234 against righthanders in 2011 (including the Arizona Fall League). He draws plenty of walks but hasn't tapped into his average raw power, and his basestealing skills aren't efficient enough for him to take advantage of his plus speed. Minnesota has discussed having Hicks bat solely righthanded, but enough of its instructors and scouts believe in his athleticism and aptitude for him to continue switch-hitting. Club officials believe he'll blossom late like Torii Hunter and Denard Span did and hope the breakout carries him to Double-A in 2012.

Year	Club (League)	Class	AVG	G	AB	R	H	2B	3B	HR	RBI	BB	SO	SB	CS	OBP	SLG
2008	Twins (GCL)	R	.318	45	173	32	55	10	4	4	27	28	32	12	2	.409	.491
2009	Beloit (MWL)	LoA	.251	67	251	43	63	15	3	4	29	40	55	10	8	.353	.382
2010	Beloit (MWL)	LoA	.279	115	423	86	118	27	6	8	49	88	112	21	11	.401	.428
2011	Fort Myers (FSL)	HiA	.242	122	443	79	107	31	5	5	38	78	110	17	9	.354	.368
Minor League Totals			.266	349	1290	240	343	83	18	21	143	234	309	60	30	.377	.407

5 OSWALDO ARCIA, OF

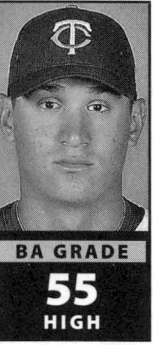

BA GRADE
55
HIGH

Born: May 9, 1991. **B-T:** L-R. **Ht.:** 6-0. **Wt.:** 221. **Signed:** Venezuela, 2007. **Signed by:** Jose Leon.

Though Arcia has yet to get past Class A, Minnesota protected him on its 40-man roster because he has one of the system's most potent bats. He won Appalachian League MVP honors in 2010 after hitting .375/.424/.672 to top the circuit in all three categories. He hurt his right elbow last year, limiting him to DH duty in April and requiring surgery that sidelined him for two months, but he held his own at Fort Myers once he returned. With a lefthanded stance that evokes Bob Abreu, he has the strength and bat speed to make hard contact to all fields. He has plus raw power and doesn't need to square balls up to drive them. Unlike Abreu, Arcia doesn't draw a lot of walks. He has slowed down as he has gotten bigger and stronger, necessitating a move from center field to right. He regained his plus arm strength after the surgery and remains raw defensively. Arcia is pushing his way into Minnesota's big league picture sooner than later. For 2012, Arcia will start back at Fort Myers and make his way to Double-A at some point.

Year	Club (League)	Class	AVG	G	AB	R	H	2B	3B	HR	RBI	BB	SO	SB	CS	OBP	SLG
2008	Twins (DSL)	R	.293	61	229	38	67	12	4	4	36	16	27	8	7	.343	.432
2009	Twins (GCL)	R	.275	44	167	20	46	11	2	5	24	15	18	8	0	.337	.455
2010	Elizabethton (APP)	R	.375	64	259	47	97	21	7	14	51	19	67	4	4	.424	.672
2011	Beloit (MWL)	LoA	.352	20	71	18	25	8	1	5	18	9	16	2	2	.420	.704
	Twins (GCL)	R	.500	2	8	1	4	1	1	0	1	0	1	0	0	.500	.875
	Fort Myers (FSL)	HiA	.263	59	213	27	56	14	2	8	32	9	53	1	1	.300	.460
Minor League Totals			.312	250	947	151	295	67	17	36	162	68	182	23	14	.362	.532

6 LEVI MICHAEL, SS/2B

BA GRADE
55
HIGH

Born: Feb. 9, 1991. **B-T:** B-R. **Ht.:** 5-10. **Wt.:** 180. **Drafted:** North Carolina, 2011 (1st round). **Signed by:** Ricky Taylor.

Michael graduated high school a semester early, bypassing the 2009 draft and playing second base in an infield with future big leaguers Dustin Ackley and Kyle Seager on North Carolina's College World Series team that spring. Michael shifted to third base as a sophomore and shortstop as a junior, He helped lead the Tar Heels back to Omaha in 2011 despite an ankle sprain and a more serious hip/groin soft-tissue injury that initially was misdiagnosed. His maladies helped drop him to the Twins' pick at No. 30, where he signed for $1.175 million. A polished switch-hitter, Michael has a disciplined approach that helped him walk more than he struck out in each of his final two college seasons. He has enough power to keep pitchers honest, projecting to hit plenty of doubles with 10-12 homers annually. Michael is both quick and fast when healthy, with the ability to steal bases and the footwork and agility to stay in the middle infield. He has smooth actions to go with solid arm strength and range. Some scouts consider him better suited for second base, but Minnesota likes him as a shortstop. Michael's injuries were significant enough to keep him from making his pro debut and playing in instructional league. Assuming he's healthy in the spring, he'll play shortstop in a talented Beloit infield that also will include Miguel Sano at third base and Eddie Rosario at second. Michael is the Twins' best long-term answer at shortstop.

Year	Club (League)	Class	AVG	G	AB	R	H	2B	3B	HR	RBI	BB	SO	SB	CS	OBP	SLG
2011	Did Not Play—Signed Late																

7 LIAM HENDRIKS, RHP

BA GRADE

50

LOW

Born: Feb. 10, 1989. **B-T:** R-R. **Ht.:** 6-1. **Wt.:** 190. **Signed:** Australia, 2007. **Signed by:** Howard Norsetter.

One of the highlights of the Twins' extensive Australian efforts, Hendriks reached the majors in 2011 after overcoming a litany of obstacles. He has had two knee surgeries (one before he signed on his 18th birthday) and an emergency appendectomy that kept him from participating in the 2010 Futures Game. He bounced back to work a career-high 163 innings last season and appeared in the prospect showcase in July. Hendriks fits Minnesota's mold as a four-pitch/command starter. His fastball often sits at 86-92 mph and peaks at 94. He uses both two- and four-seamers, complementing his sinker with a solid slider. When he's in rhythm, Hendriks peppers the bottom of the zone and commands his fastball to his arm side, allowing him to induce weak contact with his slider and above-average changeup on the other side of the plate. He also mixes in a curveball as a fourth pitch. He's a strong competitor and good athlete, both owing in part to his family's Australian rules football background. Hendriks could use more Triple-A time, but he's ready for a back-of-the-rotation gig in Minnesota if the opportunity arises. He has an outside chance of becoming a No. 3 starter.

Year	Club (League)	Class	W	L	ERA	G	GS	CG	SV	IP	H	HR	BB	SO	K/9	WHIP	AVG
2007	Twins (GCL)	R	4	2	2.05	10	10	0	0	44	41	2	11	52	10.6	1.18	.241
2008	Did Not Play--Injured																
2009	Elizabethton (APP)	R	2	0	3.71	3	3	0	0	17	19	0	1	13	6.9	1.18	.271
	Beloit (MWL)	LoA	3	5	3.51	11	11	0	0	67	73	3	15	62	8.4	1.32	.278
2010	Beloit (MWL)	LoA	2	1	1.32	6	6	0	0	34	16	0	4	39	10.3	0.59	.138
	Fort Myers (FSL)	HiA	6	3	1.93	13	12	1	0	75	63	2	8	66	8.0	0.95	.225
2011	New Britain (EL)	AA	8	2	2.70	16	15	2	0	90	85	5	18	81	8.1	1.14	.248
	Rochester (IL)	AAA	4	4	4.56	9	9	0	0	49	52	0	3	30	5.5	1.11	.277
	Minnesota (AL)	MAJ	0	2	6.17	4	4	0	0	23	29	3	6	16	6.2	1.50	.312
Major League Totals			0	2	6.17	4	4	0	0	23	29	3	6	16	6.2	1.50	.312
Minor League Totals			29	17	2.78	68	66	3	0	376	349	12	60	343	8.2	1.09	.244

8 KYLE GIBSON, RHP

BA GRADE

50

MEDIUM

Born: Oct. 23, 1987. **B-T:** R-R. **Ht.:** 6-6. **Wt.:** 210. **Drafted:** Missouri, 2009 (1st round). **Signed by:** J.R. DiMercurio/Mike Ruth.

Gibson was primed to go high in the 2009 draft before a stress fracture in his forearm sidelined him in May. That allowed the Twins to get him with the No. 22 overall pick, and they signed him for $1.85 million. No. 1 on this list a year ago after reaching Triple-A in his first pro season, Gibson returned to Rochester and gradually wore down. After doctors diagnosed a muscle strain and a ligament tear in his elbow in July, he had Tommy John surgery. Before he got hurt, Gibson pitched with a 91-92 mph fastball with late sink and threw it for consistent strikes. He manipulates his fastball well, making it run, sink or cut at will and using it to set up his pair of above-average secondary pitches. Both his changeup and slider can generate swings and misses. As the season progressed, his fastball lost velocity and his slider lost sharpness, and it became obvious he was hurt. He may not pitch until the second half of 2012 at the earliest, and Minnesota likely won't get a great read on Gibson until 2013, when he'll be 25. If his stuff and above-average control return, he should be able to establish himself as a solid No. 2 or 3 starter.

Year	Club (League)	Class	W	L	ERA	G	GS	CG	SV	IP	H	HR	BB	SO	K/9	WHIP	AVG
2010	Fort Myers (FSL)	HiA	4	1	1.87	7	7	1	0	43	33	2	12	40	8.3	1.04	.213
	New Britain (EL)	AA	7	5	3.68	16	16	1	0	93	91	5	22	77	7.5	1.22	.259
	Rochester (IL)	AAA	0	0	1.72	3	3	0	0	16	12	0	5	9	5.2	1.09	.214
2011	Rochester (IL)	AAA	3	8	4.81	18	18	0	0	95	109	11	27	91	8.6	1.43	.282
Minor League Totals			14	14	3.68	44	44	2	0	247	245	18	66	217	7.9	1.26	.258

9 CHRIS PARMELEE, 1B/OF

Born: Feb. 24, 1988. **B-T:** L-L. **Ht.:** 6-1. **Wt.:** 230. **Drafted:** HS—Chino Hills, Calif., 2006 (1st round). **Signed by:** John Leavitt.

Signed for $1.5 million as the 20th overall pick in 2006, Parmelee has been linked almost ever since with Joe Benson, Minnesota's second-rounder that June. They've become friends and have been teammates virtually throughout their pro careers. They made their big league debuts together Sept. 6, and Parmelee was the Twins' hottest hitter in the final month. Parmelee has made several adjustments to his swing throughout his career and found a groove working with Double-A hitting coach Tom Brunansky in 2011. Parmelee's stroke is less uphill now and he has become less homer-conscious, making him a solid hitter with pop to both gaps. He has home run power to his pull side. He continues to struggle against lefthanders, posting a .597 OPS against them in 146 Double-A at-bats last year. Parmelee also has improved his body, adding agility that has made him a better defender at first base, and has an above-average arm. If it weren't for his well below-average speed, the outfield would be more of a possibility, but he's limited to reserve duty out there. Club officials like how Parmelee has matured. With Justin Morneau's concussion issues, Parmelee gives Minnesota an in-house option for first base. He'll have to improve against lefties to be more than a second-division regular or platoon player.

BA GRADE 50 MEDIUM

Year	Club (League)	Class	AVG	G	AB	R	H	2B	3B	HR	RBI	BB	SO	SB	CS	OBP	SLG
2006	Twins (GCL)	R	.279	45	154	29	43	7	4	8	32	23	47	3	3	.369	.532
	Beloit (MWL)	LoA	.227	11	22	2	5	1	0	0	2	5	9	0	2	.370	.273
2007	Beloit (MWL)	LoA	.239	128	447	56	107	23	5	15	70	46	137	8	4	.313	.414
2008	Beloit (MWL)	LoA	.239	69	226	41	54	10	3	14	49	52	83	3	1	.385	.496
2009	Fort Myers (FSL)	HiA	.258	123	422	61	109	27	1	16	73	65	109	2	2	.359	.441
2010	Fort Myers (FSL)	HiA	.338	22	80	9	27	2	1	2	17	13	11	0	1	.430	.463
	New Britain (EL)	AA	.275	111	411	51	113	25	2	6	44	43	70	3	2	.341	.389
2011	New Britain (EL)	AA	.287	142	530	76	152	30	5	13	83	68	94	0	1	.366	.436
	Minnesota (AL)	MAJ	.355	21	76	8	27	6	0	4	14	12	13	0	0	.443	.592
Major League Totals			**.355**	**21**	**76**	**8**	**27**	**6**	**0**	**4**	**14**	**12**	**13**	**0**	**0**	**.443**	**.592**
Minor League Totals			**.266**	**651**	**2292**	**325**	**610**	**125**	**21**	**74**	**370**	**315**	**560**	**19**	**16**	**.355**	**.436**

10 BRIAN DOZIER, SS/2B

Born: May 15, 1987. **B-T:** R-R. **Ht.:** 5-11. **Wt.:** 190. **Drafted:** Southern Mississippi, 2009 (8th round). **Signed by:** Earl Winn.

A four-year starter at Southern Mississippi, Dozier overcame a broken collarbone as a senior to return to action in the 2009 College World Series and bat .349 in his pro debut after signing for $30,000. He was named the Twins' 2011 minor league player of the year after leading the system in nine offensive categories, including on-base percentage (.399), slugging (.491), extra-base hits (54) and steals (24). Skilled and savvy, Dozier gets the most out of his solid athleticism and endears himself to managers with his grinding style. He has gotten stronger as a pro and has natural hitting tempo and barrel-to-ball ability. His plate discipline, bat control and speed help him fit the profile of a No. 2 hitter. He's an outstanding bunter and fine baserunner with average speed. Dozier is a fundamentally sound middle infielder with an average arm and plus range. He's an instinctive player who gets good hops and makes all the routine plays. His tools profile him as a second baseman, but his intangibles should allow him to stick at shortstop. Dozier is similar to Jamey Carroll, whom the Twins signed for two years and $6.75 million this offseason. He could replace Carroll in Minnesota at the end of that contract, or learn under him as a utility player before that. Either way, Dozier figures to start 2012 in Triple-A.

BA GRADE 50 MEDIUM

Year	Club (League)	Class	AVG	G	AB	R	H	2B	3B	HR	RBI	BB	SO	SB	CS	OBP	SLG
2009	Twins (GCL)	R	.286	5	14	1	4	0	0	0	0	2	1	0	0	.375	.286
	Elizabethton (APP)	R	.353	53	218	38	77	17	0	0	14	23	26	3	0	.417	.431
2010	Beloit (MWL)	LoA	.278	39	151	24	42	7	1	0	17	16	16	6	1	.347	.338
	Fort Myers (FSL)	HiA	.274	93	350	44	96	11	1	5	42	44	41	10	4	.352	.354
2011	Fort Myers (FSL)	HiA	.322	49	180	32	58	11	5	2	22	27	20	13	4	.423	.472
	New Britain (EL)	AA	.318	78	311	60	99	22	7	7	34	28	46	11	7	.384	.502
Minor League Totals			**.307**	**317**	**1224**	**199**	**376**	**68**	**14**	**14**	**129**	**140**	**150**	**43**	**16**	**.382**	**.420**

11 TRAVIS HARRISON, 3B/1B

BA GRADE 55 HIGH

Born: Oct. 17, 1992. **B-T:** R-R. **Ht.:** 6-1. **Wt.:** 215. **Drafted:** HS—Tustin, Calif., 2011 (1st round supplemental). **Signed by:** John Leavitt.

Southern California's Tustin High has produced three big league all-stars in Heath Bell, Shawn Green and Mark Grace, and Harrison's career there ranks with any of theirs. He hit 33 homers at Tustin and several tape-measure shots on the showcase circuit, including a 504-foot shot at Tropicana Field in the 2010 Power Showcase. He spurned a Southern California scholarship when he signed for $1.05 million as the 50th overall pick in the 2011 draft. The Twins took Harrison for his bat. He's a baseball rat who eschews batting gloves and has a feel for the barrel. He doesn't have much of a stride and has enough strength to pull it off, leading to a balanced, line-drive swing. As he learns to loft the ball, he's expected to hit for above-average home run power. His swing and strength remind some club officials of Paul Goldschmidt. Harrison isn't a fluid athlete and is limited to a corner spot. He'll get time at third base but is expected to move to first eventually. He's a below-average runner but not a clogger. Harrison likely will start 2012 in extended spring training before debuting at Elizabethton.

Year	Club (League)	Class	AVG	G	AB	R	H	2B	3B	HR	RBI	BB	SO	SB	CS	OBP	SLG
2011	Did Not Play—Signed Late																

12 MADISON BOER, RHP

BA GRADE
50
HIGH

Born: Nov. 9, 1989. **B-T:** R-R. **Ht.:** 6-3. **Wt.:** 228. **Drafted:** Oregon, 2011 (2nd round). **Signed by:** Trevor Brown.

Boer grew up in Eden Prairie, a Minneapolis suburb, and was lured out of state by Oregon's resuscitated baseball program. He made 26 starts and picked up eight saves in three seasons for the Ducks. The Twins grabbed him in the second round of the 2011 draft and signed him for $405,000. He dominated in his pro debut, working in relief after pitching 99 innings in the spring. Boer has the type of strong arm the organization sorely needs. As a college starter, he showed a 90-93 mph fastball. As a reliever, he works at 93-94 and peaks at 96. His fastball has good sink, and he complements it with a mid-80s slider that is an out pitch at times. He worked with a splitter at Oregon but incorporated a straight changeup after his debut. Minnesota intends to use Boer as a starter in 2012, both to get him comfortable with the changeup and to see if he can stay in the role. He'll open the season at Beloit. Reaching the big leagues could function as a homecoming for Boer, whose parents still live about a half-hour from Target Field.

Year	Club (League)	Class	W	L	ERA	G	GS	CG	SV	IP	H	HR	BB	SO	K/9	WHIP	AVG
2011	Elizabethton (APP)	R	2	1	2.60	15	0	0	9	17	13	1	2	31	16.1	0.87	.203
	Beloit (MWL)	LoA	0	0	6.75	8	0	0	2	8	12	0	1	12	13.5	1.63	.343
Minor League Totals			2	1	3.91	23	0	0	11	25	25	1	3	43	15.3	1.11	.253

13 COREY WILLIAMS, LHP

BA GRADE
50
HIGH

Born: July 4, 1990. **B-T:** L-L. **Ht.:** 6-1. **Wt.:** 208. **Drafted:** Vanderbilt, 2011 (3rd round). **Signed by:** Earl Winn.

After redshirting as a freshman, Williams pitched 100 innings in college between two seasons at Vanderbilt and one summer in the Valley League. His sophomore year was cut short when a line drive broke his right kneecap, and he nevertheless threw the hitter out at first base in a highlight play that generated lots of attention on YouTube. Healthy in 2011, Williams forced his way to the front of the Commodores' deep bullpen, becoming the moment-of-truth reliever for a team that made its first-ever College World Series appearance. His fresh arm, excellent size and hard stuff from the left side make him particularly intriguing for the Twins, who may send him out as a starter in 2012 after signing him for an over-slot $575,000 as a third-rounder. Williams' fastball sits at 89-92 mph and regularly hits 93-94, and Minnesota believes he could add velocity as he gets more consistent work. His fastball has natural tailing action and some sink as well, and he has a feel for cutting it when he needs to. His changeup is in its early stages, and he throws both a curveball and a hard slider that has cutter shape and action. Williams' competitiveness suited him well for relieving, and the Twins hope they can channel his high-energy delivery into a starting role. Williams also could move quickly if he goes to the bullpen. How he handles longer stints in spring training will determine his 2012 role and assignment, but he's certain to make a Class A roster.

Year	Club (League)	Class	W	L	ERA	G	GS	CG	SV	IP	H	HR	BB	SO	K/9	WHIP	AVG
2011	Elizabethton (APP)	R	1	1	3.86	7	0	0	1	12	12	0	5	11	8.5	1.46	.261
Minor League Totals			1	1	3.86	7	0	0	1	12	12	0	5	11	8.5	1.46	.261

14 CHRIS HERRMANN, C/OF

BA GRADE
45
MEDIUM

Born: Nov. 24, 1987. **B-T:** L-R. **Ht.:** 6-0. **Wt.:** 195. **Drafted:** Miami, 2009 (6th round). **Signed by:** Hector Otero.

Herrmann attended a pair of Texas junior colleges and saw time at third base, outfield and catcher. The Orioles drafted him in the 10th round in 2008 out of Alvin CC, but instead of signing he went to Miami. The Hurricanes used him some at third base but mostly in the outfield and at DH. He led Miami in batting with a .341 average in 2009, and his offensive polish prompted the Twins to push him aggressively after drafting him in the sixth round that June. He jumped to high Class A for his full-season debut in 2010 and made catcher his main position for the first time. Predictably he struggled, but he bounced back nicely last year, hitting his way out of Fort Myers and earning a promotion to Double-A. The organization's best catching prospect, Herrman features good athletic ability for a backstop, average speed that allows him to man either outfield corner and a polished offensive approach. His biggest offensive drawbacks are his flat swing plane and below-average power potential. Defensively, he has a slightly above-average arm and good technique that he used to throw out 38 percent of basestealers last season. He blocks balls well. His inexperience shows up most in his game-calling and handling of a pitching staff. Joe Mauer's injury-plagued season and the offensive ineptitude of his replacements highlighted Minnesota's need for catching help, and Herrmann is the best answer. He's headed for his first taste of Triple-A and isn't far from getting a shot to be Mauer's backup.

Year	Club (League)	Class	AVG	G	AB	R	H	2B	3B	HR	RBI	BB	SO	SB	CS	OBP	SLG
2009	Elizabethton (APP)	R	.297	59	236	45	70	14	1	7	30	33	40	2	2	.391	.453
2010	Fort Myers (FSL)	HiA	.219	107	356	34	78	17	3	2	30	41	74	3	2	.310	.301
2011	Fort Myers (FSL)	HiA	.310	24	87	14	27	5	1	1	16	15	6	1	0	.404	.425
	New Britain (EL)	AA	.258	97	337	53	87	14	5	7	46	64	68	9	3	.380	.392
Minor League Totals			.258	287	1016	146	262	50	10	17	122	153	188	15	7	.361	.377

15 DEOLIS GUERRA, RHP

BA GRADE

50 HIGH

Born: April 17, 1989. **B-T:** R-R. **Ht.:** 6-5. **Wt.:** 245. **Signed:** Venezuela, 2005. **Signed by:** Rafael Bournigal (Mets).

The Bill Smith Era ended with Carlos Gomez having given the Twins the greatest return among the prospects acquired from the Mets in the Johan Santana trade in 2008. In Gomez's case, that meant one year of starting for Minnesota before getting dealt to the Brewers for one year of J.J. Hardy. The book isn't completely closed on the Santana deal, however, thanks to Guerra's second-half turnaround in 2011. Originally signed for $700,000 by the Mets, he has a 5.55 ERA as a Twin. His 2011 ERA sat at 9.00 on June 1, when he made his 10th and final start for New Britain. After moving to the bullpen, he posted a 2.77 ERA, .191 opponent average and 65-13 K-BB ratio in 52 innings. Guerra often pitched backward as a starter but attacks hitters as a reliever. He uses his fastball to set up his plus changeup instead of the other way around. Guerra's fastball bumped up from 90-92 to 92-94 mph once he moved to the bullpen. His sinking, fading changeup remains a weapon. His curveball, once a glaring weakness, now grades as fringy and gets some swings and misses. Guerra has starter's stuff but needed the move to the bullpen to give him the aggressiveness he lacked. He'll challenge for a spot in Minnesota's revamped bullpen in 2012.

Year	Club (League)	Class	W	L	ERA	G	GS	CG	SV	IP	H	HR	BB	SO	K/9	WHIP	AVG
2006	Hagerstown (SAL)	LoA	6	7	2.20	17	17	0	0	82	59	3	37	64	7.1	1.18	.208
	St. Lucie (FSL)	HiA	1	1	6.14	2	2	0	0	7	9	1	6	5	6.1	2.05	.290
2007	St. Lucie (FSL)	HiA	2	6	4.01	21	20	0	0	90	80	9	25	66	6.6	1.17	.240
2008	Fort Myers (FSL)	HiA	11	9	5.47	26	25	1	0	130	138	12	71	71	4.9	1.61	.272
2009	Fort Myers (FSL)	HiA	6	8	4.69	16	15	0	0	86	95	6	25	57	5.9	1.39	.278
	New Britain (EL)	AA	6	3	5.17	12	11	1	0	63	62	4	17	49	7.0	1.26	.258
2010	New Britain (EL)	AA	2	10	6.24	19	19	1	0	102	127	14	37	67	5.9	1.60	.308
	Rochester (IL)	AAA	0	3	6.84	5	4	0	0	25	35	5	8	18	6.5	1.72	.337
2011	New Britain (EL)	AA	8	7	5.59	37	10	0	1	95	102	11	28	95	9.0	1.37	.273
Minor League Totals			42	54	4.95	155	123	3	1	680	707	65	254	492	6.5	1.41	.269

16 ADRIAN SALCEDO, RHP

BA GRADE

50 HIGH

Born: April 24, 1991. **B-T:** R-R. **Ht.:** 6-4. **Wt.:** 175. **Signed:** Dominican Republic, 2007. **Signed by:** Fred Guerrero.

Salcedo announced himself as a prospect when he walked just three batters in 62 innings during his 2009 U.S. debut. His polish prompted Minnesota to accelerate him to high Class A in 2010 when it needed a spot starter, and his first full Class A load came at Beloit last year. He posted a 2.93 ERA in a career-high 135 innings, though his stuff failed to take a step forward. Early in games, Salcedo works off a 90-93 mph fastball, which helps his fringy changeup play up. Both pitches have late sink and generate groundballs. Salcedo has some feel for spinning a breaking ball, which varies between a curve and a slider and features sharp break at times. As he gains strength, it should become an average pitch as well. While he doesn't have true command, he's an excellent athlete who throws a ton of strikes. Salcedo doesn't maintain his stuff deep into games, often falling into the upper 80s with his fastball after a couple of innings. He's a dedicated runner with tremendous work ethic, and the Twins hope he can add strength as he ages. He'll have a more permanent place in the Fort Myers rotation in 2012 and projects as a back-of-the-rotation starter.

Year	Club (League)	Class	W	L	ERA	G	GS	CG	SV	IP	H	HR	BB	SO	K/9	WHIP	AVG
2008	Twins (DSL)	R	4	4	1.65	12	12	0	0	65	47	1	8	50	6.9	0.84	.198
2009	Twins (GCL)	R	3	2	1.46	11	10	0	0	62	60	1	3	58	8.5	1.02	.241
2010	Fort Myers (FSL)	HiA	1	3	6.26	6	6	0	0	27	42	3	8	16	5.3	1.83	.378
	Elizabethton (APP)	R	4	3	3.27	16	8	0	1	66	55	3	10	65	8.9	0.98	.230
2011	Beloit (MWL)	LoA	6	6	2.93	29	20	1	0	135	131	4	27	92	6.1	1.17	.252
Minor League Totals			18	18	2.76	74	56	1	1	355	335	12	56	281	7.1	1.10	.247

17 CARLOS GUTIERREZ, RHP

BA GRADE
45
MEDIUM

Born: Sept. 22. 1986. **B-T:** R-R. **Ht.:** 6-3. **Wt.:** 225. **Drafted:** Miami, 2008 (1st round). **Signed by:** Hector Otero.

So far, the Twins haven't gotten the returns they hoped for on their 2008 draft class. First-round outfielder Aaron Hicks is stumbling in Class A and sandwich-round righthander Shooter Hunt was lost in the Triple-A phase of the 2011 Rule 5 draft. Drafted in between them and signed for $1.29 million, Gutierrez hasn't raced to the majors like he was expected to as a college reliever. He spent much of his first two pro seasons as a starter because Minnesota wanted to give him innings to refine his slider and changeup. He appeared to take off when moved back to the bullpen in 2010, but his control wavered last year after he went on the disabled list with a sore shoulder in July. He gave up 11 runs and 18 hits in his last 14 innings. Gutierrez's fastball can be electric. At times it sits at 93-96 mph with late turbo sink, generating tons of groundballs. Its liveliness makes it difficult for him to command, and advanced hitters started laying off it. Instead of trusting his slider and changeup when that happens, Gutierrez keeps going back to the sinker. As a result, his slider has regressed. Both of his secondary pitches are below average, and his cross-body delivery and tailing action on his fastball make it tough for him to locate pitches to his arm side. A slow tempo and low-energy mound presence haven't helped Gutierrez, who nevertheless was added to the 40-man roster in November. He'll have a chance to win a big league job in March but more likely will return to Triple-A.

Year	Club (League)	Class	W	L	ERA	G	GS	CG	SV	IP	H	HR	BB	SO	K/9	WHIP	AVG
2008	Fort Myers (FSL)	HiA	3	1	2.10	16	0	0	1	26	23	0	7	19	6.7	1.17	.240
2009	Fort Myers (FSL)	HiA	2	3	1.32	11	10	0	0	55	37	1	22	33	5.4	1.08	.192
	New Britain (EL)	AA	1	3	6.19	22	6	0	0	52	62	6	24	32	5.5	1.64	.300
2010	New Britain (EL)	AA	5	8	4.57	32	16	0	2	122	136	7	50	81	6.0	1.52	.291
	Rochester (IL)	AAA	0	0	2.25	2	0	0	0	4	5	0	2	6	13.5	1.75	.333
2011	Rochester (IL)	AAA	2	3	4.62	43	0	0	0	62	60	2	31	57	8.2	1.46	.246
Minor League Totals			13	18	4.07	126	32	0	3	321	323	16	136	228	6.4	1.43	.264

18 HUDSON BOYD, RHP

BA GRADE
55
EXTRME

Born: Oct. 18, 1992. **B-T:** R-R. **Ht.:** 6-2. **Wt.:** 278. **Drafted:** HS—Fort Myers, Fla., 2011 (1st round supplemental). **Signed by:** Billy Corrigan.

Boyd starred at two Fort Myers, Fla., area high schools during his prep career, first at South Fort Myers and then at Bishop Verot as a senior. He teamed with Cubs second-rounder Dan Vogelbach to lead Bishop Verot to the Florida 3-A state championship in 2011, with Boyd pitching a shutout in the semifinals and delivering the game-winning single with two out in the bottom of the seventh in the title game. The Twins, whose Florida operations are based in Fort Myers, had followed him for years. They drafted him 55th overall and bought him out of a Florida commitment with a $1 million bonus. Boyd's jumbo frame elicits comparisons to Bartolo Colon and Jonathan Broxton. After a summer layoff waiting to sign, he reported to instructional league at a whopping 278 pounds. He hired Kyle Gibson's wife, a nutritionist, to improve his diet, and he hoped to get back to 235-240 pounds by spring training. At his best, Boyd incorporates his lower half well into his delivery and maintains his velocity deep into games, usually working at 90-94 mph with his fastball. He topped out at 91 in instructional league. His power curveball features upper-70s velocity and tight, sharp action, giving him a second plus pitch. His arm action is fairly clean. Boyd didn't need a changeup much in high school, but Minnesota has a strong tradition of teaching the pitch and he'll strive to improve his arm speed and find a grip that works for him. If Boyd can keep his body in check, he could emerge as one of the system's best starting pitching prospects. He's likely to open 2012 in extended spring training before making his pro debut in Rookie ball in June.

Year	Club (League)	Class	W	L	ERA	G	GS	CG	SV	IP	H	HR	BB	SO	K/9	WHIP	AVG
2011	Did Not Play—Signed Late																

19 NIKO GOODRUM, SS

BA GRADE
55
EXTREME

Born: Feb. 28, 1992. **B-T:** B-R. **Ht.:** 6-3. **Wt.:** 177. **Drafted:** HS—Fayetteville, Ga., 2010 (2nd round). **Signed by:** Jack Powell.

Goodrum played alongside man-child Miguel Sano in the Appalachian League last year, and the two couldn't be more different. Lean and high-waisted, Goodrum is far from having filled out. His father has the physique of an NFL lineman, however, so the Twins don't think Niko still will look like a greyhound in five years. For now, he's a fast-twitch, raw athlete with the range and arm for shortstop. He has a cannon—edging Tyler Grimes as the system's best infield arm—and fast, soft hands. His size eventually may make his actions too long for short, however. He's an above-average runner under way, so some scouts see him as a center fielder in the Dexter Fowler mold. A switch-hitter, Goodrum has a sound swing from both sides and surprising strength considering his present build. It's easy to dream on his leverage and strength producing average to plus power down the line. At times his swing gets long, and he needs at-bats to improve his pitch recognition. He got better in that regard as the season progressed and finished strong, hitting .341 in August. His overall game lacks consistency thanks to his inexperience. Goodrum works hard and is an organization favorite, but the crowded infield scene in the lower levels of the system could force him to return to Elizabethton for 2012.

Year	Club (League)	Class	AVG	G	AB	R	H	2B	3B	HR	RBI	BB	SO	SB	CS	OBP	SLG
2010	Twins (GCL)	R	.161	36	118	10	19	4	0	0	5	9	34	4	2	.219	.195
2011	Elizabethton (APP)	R	.275	59	204	39	56	10	3	2	20	21	56	8	1	.352	.382
Minor League Totals			.233	95	322	49	75	14	3	2	25	30	90	12	3	.304	.314

20 MAX KEPLER, OF

BA GRADE
55
EXTREME

Born: Feb. 10, 1993. **B-T:** L-L. **Ht.:** 6-4. **Wt.:** 190. **Signed:** Germany, 2009. **Signed by:** Mike Radcliff.

The son of Polish and American ballet dancers, Kepler isn't German but was born and raised in Berlin and played for Germany in the World Cup in Panama last fall. While Germany went 0-7 at the tournament, he went 8-for-23 (.348) with a homer. Kepler signed for $800,000 in 2009, setting a record for a European amateur position player, and he graduated from high school in Florida in 2010 while also playing in the Gulf Coast League. He's a fluid athlete with solid swing mechanics, though he has to adjust to pro pitching and quality velocity, significant hurdles for a European amateur. He's still developing the natural hitting rhythm and timing that come with experience. He's starting to gain more power as he adds strength, and he'll need to show more of that down the line. Signed as a center fielder, Kepler has started to fill out and has slowed down to an average runner. He'll have to work to remain a center fielder and even mixed in some time at first base last summer. Still a teenager, he's raw defensively with a fringy arm that may limit him to left field if he can't play center. Kepler will have to show improvement in spring training to earn a full-season assignment, and he may be headed for a repeat of the Appalachian League in 2012.

Year	Club (League)	Class	AVG	G	AB	R	H	2B	3B	HR	RBI	BB	SO	SB	CS	OBP	SLG
2010	Twins (GCL)	R	.286	37	140	15	40	6	1	0	11	13	27	6	1	.346	.343
2011	Elizabethton (APP)	R	.262	50	191	29	50	11	3	1	24	23	54	1	1	.347	.366
Minor League Totals			.272	87	331	44	90	17	4	1	35	36	81	7	2	.347	.356

21 MATT SUMMERS, RHP

BA GRADE
50
HIGH

Born: Aug. 17, 1989. **B-T:** L-R. **Ht.:** 6-1. **Wt.:** 199. **Drafted:** UC Irvine, 2011 (4th round). **Signed by:** John Leavitt.

Summers was a two-way prep standout in the Scottsdale, Ariz., area. He helped Cactus Shadows win the Arizona 4-A state championship as a sophomore in 2006, then starred at Chaparral. He wound up at UC Irvine and continued to play both ways as a freshman and sophomore, eventually emerging as more of a pitcher. His fastball reached 97 mph when he worked out of the bullpen in the Cape Cod League in the summer of 2010. He became the Anteaters' ace in 2011, throwing a no-hitter against Long Beach State in May but losing twice to Virginia in super-regional action. After signing for a slot bonus of $171,900 as a fourth-rounder, Summers dominated the Appy League as a reliever. The Twins were just holding down his workload, though, and have incorporated a windup into his delivery with plans to start him in 2012. He has an unusually short arm action and may wind up back in the bullpen as a result. He lost some fastball velocity last summer, pitching at 90-92 mph with Elizabethton, but he was back around 94-96 in instructional league. His straight changeup emerged as a weapon in his debut, and he struck out 16 of the 25 lefthanders he faced without allowing a hit. He also throws an upper-80s cutter that gets in on the hands of lefties. His slurvy curveball has some power, reaching 77-78 mph at times. If the plans to start him stick, he'll head to low Class A to open his first full pro season.

Year	Club (League)	Class	W	L	ERA	G	GS	CG	SV	IP	H	HR	BB	SO	K/9	WHIP	AVG
2011	Elizabethton (APP)	R	1	1	0.87	20	0	0	6	21	11	0	5	36	15.7	0.77	.153
Minor League Totals			1	1	0.87	20	0	0	6	21	11	0	5	36	15.7	0.77	.153

22 LOGAN DARNELL, LHP

BA GRADE
45
MEDIUM

Born: Feb. 2, 1989. **B-T:** L-L. **Ht.:** 6-2. **Wt.:** 215. **Drafted:** Kentucky, 2010 (6th round). **Signed by:** Earl Winn.

A reliever for two seasons at Kentucky, Darnell got a chance to start in 2009 in the Alaska League, then posted a 5.50 ERA as a junior, falling out of the Wildcats' rotation. Minnesota signed him for $125,000 as a sixth-rounder. He reminds some scouts of Brian Duensing in terms of his stuff and pitch selection. Darnell isn't afraid to work inside, especially against righthanders, even if he lacks a dominant fastball. He isn't a soft-tosser, going after hitters with an 88-92 mph fastball that he controls well, though he's short of having true fastball command. He has improved his feel for using his fastball and setting up his changeup, which is a plus pitch at times and ranks as his best offering. Hitters can't just sit on the changeup because he has a pair of decent breaking balls in his curveball and slider. While neither is a consistent swing-and-miss pitch, he can throw both for strikes in fastball counts. He has more faith in the slider. Darnell got hit hard when promoted to Double-A last year and figures to start 2012 back in New Britain.

Year	Club (League)	Class	W	L	ERA	G	GS	CG	SV	IP	H	HR	BB	SO	K/9	WHIP	AVG
2010	Elizabethton (APP)	R	2	3	2.08	11	5	0	0	35	28	2	6	32	8.3	0.98	.220
2011	Beloit (MWL)	LoA	2	2	3.78	6	6	0	0	33	24	1	8	24	6.5	0.96	.192
	Fort Myers (FSL)	HiA	8	3	4.17	15	15	0	0	86	95	6	25	46	4.8	1.39	.286
	New Britain (EL)	AA	1	1	5.58	5	5	0	0	31	38	3	4	20	5.9	1.37	.317
Minor League Totals			13	9	3.94	37	31	0	0	185	185	12	43	122	5.9	1.23	.263

23 MANUEL SOLIMAN, RHP

BA GRADE 50 HIGH

Born: Aug. 11, 1989. **B-T:** R-R. **Ht.:** 6-2. **Wt.:** 185. **Signed:** Dominican Republic, 2007. **Signed by:** Fred Guerrero.

Soliman signed with Minnesota as a corner infielder, but after hitting .199 in two seasons in the Rookie-level Dominican Summer League, he agreed to give pitching a try. In his 2010 U.S. debut, he finished second in the Appalachian League with 74 strikeouts. He led the Twins system with 120 whiffs last season. Soliman has a live arm and mostly works at 88-92 mph with his fastball, touching 94. His fastball straightens out when he elevates it, making him prone to homers. His hand speed allows him to spin the ball well, giving him a curveball that's solid at its best and also the potential to add a bit more velocity. His changeup is below-average but has potential. Soliman's inexperience shows on many levels, from repeating his delivery to fielding his position to setting up hitters. He didn't earn a spot on Minnesota's 40-man roster after the season, but he proved too raw to be lost in the Rule 5 draft. The Twins will promote him to high Class A for 2012.

Year	Club (League)	Class	AVG	G	AB	R	H	2B	3B	HR	RBI	BB	SO	SB	CS	OBP	SLG
2007	Twins (DSL)	R	.189	63	201	22	38	4	0	4	16	26	46	5	3	.305	.269
2008	Twins (DSL)	R	.211	58	185	26	39	11	2	1	26	30	39	2	1	.332	.308
Minor League Totals			.199	121	386	48	77	15	2	5	42	56	85	7	4	.318	.288

Year	Club (League)	Class	W	L	ERA	G	GS	CG	SV	IP	H	HR	BB	SO	K/9	WHIP	AVG
2009	Twins (DSL)	R	6	2	2.15	14	14	0	0	71	66	0	20	55	7.0	1.21	.244
2010	Elizabethton (APP)	R	5	2	3.48	12	12	0	0	65	47	5	21	74	10.3	1.05	.201
2011	Beloit (MWL)	LoA	7	11	3.97	28	25	1	0	136	128	17	50	120	7.9	1.31	.250
Minor League Totals			18	15	3.38	54	51	1	0	272	241	22	91	249	8.2	1.22	.237

24 TOM STUIFBERGEN, RHP

BA GRADE 50 HIGH

Born: Sept. 26, 1988. **B-T:** R-R. **Ht.:** 6-3. **Wt.:** 261. **Signed:** Netherlands, 2006. **Signed by:** Andy Johnson.

If international baseball can be called the "bright lights"—and compared to Class A it certainly can be—then it's evident Stuifbergen is at his best in the spotlight. He tossed 17 scoreless innings for the Netherlands at the World Cup in Panama last fall, helping his nation win its first-ever gold medal in international play. Working in relief, he touched 94 mph with his fastball and flashed a plus curveball that he picked up from another Dutch righty, Hall of Famer Bert Blyleven. Stuifbergen also threw four shutout innings in the Netherlands' upset victory against the Dominican Republic in the 2009 World Baseball Classic. In the minors, however, Stuifbergen has been plenty hittable. He usually pitches with an 86-91 mph sinker and a solid curveball, along with an average changeup. He has a feel for changing speeds and pounds the strike zone, but the quality of his stuff is too inconsistent. He'll have to tone up his big frame, and maturity and consistency in his work habits and approach to the game would help as well. Stuifbergen ended his regular season with five solid innings in a spot start in Triple-A, but he was left off the 40-man roster in November. He'll have to earn a spot in Double-A during spring training.

Year	Club (League)	Class	W	L	ERA	G	GS	CG	SV	IP	H	HR	BB	SO	K/9	WHIP	AVG
2007	Twins (GCL)	R	0	0	2.19	7	0	0	0	12	6	0	3	9	6.6	0.73	.140
2008	Did Not Play—Injured																
2009	Elizabethton (APP)	R	5	2	3.28	13	13	1	0	80	79	4	6	69	7.8	1.07	.257
	Fort Myers (FSL)	HiA	0	0	10.13	1	1	0	0	3	5	0	1	3	10.1	2.25	.385
2010	Beloit (MWL)	LoA	6	4	2.98	19	17	0	0	94	99	5	23	88	8.5	1.30	.273
2011	Fort Myers (FSL)	HiA	5	9	4.40	23	22	1	0	117	151	10	19	75	5.8	1.46	.319
	Rochester (IL)	AAA	1	0	1.80	1	1	0	0	5	4	1	0	5	9.0	0.80	.200
Minor League Totals			17	15	3.60	64	54	2	0	310	344	20	52	249	7.2	1.28	.282

25 ALEX WIMMERS, RHP

BA GRADE 50 EXTREME

Born: Nov. 1, 1988. **B-T:** L-R. **Ht.:** 6-1. **Wt.:** 208. **Drafted:** Ohio State, 2010 (1st round). **Signed by:** Jay Weitzel.

Wimmers was supposed to be a prime example of what the Twins seek in pitchers when they signed him for $1.332 million as the 21st overall pick in the 2010 draft. He dominated in four high Class A starts in his pro debut, but Wimmers came to spring training last year unprepared physically, had a setback with a hamstring pull and, in the words of one club official, "All hell broke loose." Back at Fort Myers, he couldn't find the plate. In his first start, he walked six straight hitters and added three wild pitches while throwing just four of

28 pitches for strikes. Minnesota put him on the disabled list and went to work rebuilding his confidence to try to cure his case of Rick Ankiel disease. Wimmers went through extended spring training and returned to game action in July. His season ended on a triumphant note when he tossed a seven-inning no-hitter at Jupiter, walking two and striking out five. Wimmers' fastball sat in the upper 80s in that appearance, and the Twins attribute the lower velocity to his inability to build arm strength during his bouts of wildness. He had pitched at 88-92 mph in the past. He still showed good arm speed on his above-average straight changeup, his best pitch, and threw strikes with his curveball. He showed mental toughness by coming through his difficulties to end the season on a high note. Wimmers was able to find the plate in instructional league and should return to high Class A in 2012 to make the next step in his comeback.

Year	Club (League)	Class	W	L	ERA	G	GS	CG	SV	IP	H	HR	BB	SO	K/9	WHIP	AVG
2010	Fort Myers (FSL)	HiA	2	0	0.57	4	4	0	0	16	6	0	5	23	13.2	0.70	.113
2011	Fort Myers (FSL)	HiA	2	3	4.20	12	4	1	1	41	28	5	22	39	8.6	1.23	.189
	Twins (GCL)	R	0	0	0.00	1	0	0	0	1	0	0	1	1	9.0	1.00	.000
Minor League Totals			4	3	3.14	17	8	1	1	57	34	5	28	63	9.9	1.08	.167

26 LESTER OLIVEROS, RHP

Born: May 28, 1988. **B-T:** R-R. **Ht.:** 6-0. **Wt.:** 225. **Signed:** Venezuela, 2005. **Signed by:** Ramon Pena (Tigers).

Former general manager Bill Smith took a lot of criticism for the Johan Santana trade with the Mets, but the Matt Garza-Jason Bartlett deal with the Rays was arguably worse. The key player the Twins got in that move was Delmon Young, who had a fine 2010 season but otherwise never lived up to his billing. Last August, Minnesota shipped Young to the Tigers for Oliveros and lefthander Cole Nelson. Oliveros reached the majors with Detroit in July and got back with Minnesota in August and September. He has the system's best fastball, an indictment of the system's lack of power arms but also a testament to Oliveros' 93-96 mph heater. He's stocky and strong-bodied, with a full-effort delivery that hinders his control. His future role will depend on his secondary stuff. For now, he has a fringy changeup and a below-average slider that breaks early. The Twins believe his slider can improve and were encouraged by Oliveros' strong winter ball performance in Venezuela. He has a chance to earn innings in the big league bullpen in 2012.

Year	Club (League)	Class	W	L	ERA	G	GS	CG	SV	IP	H	HR	BB	SO	K/9	WHIP	AVG
2006	Tigers/Marlins (VSL)	R	1	3	2.72	20	2	0	4	40	29	2	20	46	10.4	1.24	.193
2007	Tigers (VSL)	R	2	0	1.41	27	0	0	19	38	25	0	13	59	13.9	0.99	.181
2008	Oneonta (NYP)	SS	1	2	1.74	15	0	0	4	21	15	1	6	34	14.8	1.02	.197
	Lakeland (FSL)	HiA	1	1	4.22	5	0	0	0	11	12	0	9	3	2.5	1.97	.293
2009	Lakeland (FSL)	HiA	4	2	4.17	34	0	0	2	54	53	5	16	58	9.7	1.28	.249
	Toledo (IL)	AAA	0	0	0.00	1	0	0	0	2	2	0	1	3	13.5	1.50	.250
2010	Lakeland (FSL)	HiA	0	1	1.89	20	0	0	9	19	13	0	6	24	11.4	1.00	.194
	Erie (EL)	AA	1	2	4.97	24	0	0	14	25	20	3	21	36	12.8	1.62	.217
2011	Erie (EL)	AA	2	0	0.53	10	0	0	0	17	11	0	4	28	14.8	0.88	.193
	Toledo (IL)	AAA	1	3	6.43	22	0	0	5	28	37	7	17	26	8.4	1.93	.316
	Detroit (AL)	MAJ	0	0	5.63	9	0	0	0	8	8	0	4	4	4.5	1.50	.258
	Rochester (IL)	AAA	0	0	3.00	2	0	0	0	3	2	1	0	4	12.0	0.67	.182
	Minnesota (AL)	MAJ	0	0	4.05	10	0	0	0	13	13	0	7	9	6.1	1.50	.277
Major League Totals			0	0	4.64	19	0	0	0	21	21	0	11	13	5.5	1.50	.269
Minor League Totals			13	14	3.21	180	2	0	57	258	219	19	113	321	11.2	1.29	.226

27 B.J. HERMSEN, RHP

Born: Dec. 1, 1989. **B-T:** R-R. **Ht.:** 6-6. **Wt.:** 236. **Drafted:** HS—Manchester, Iowa, 2008 (6th round). **Signed by:** Mark Wilson.

Hermsen was a multisport athlete at West Delaware High (Manchester, Iowa), earning all-star honors in football (as a quarterback), basketball and as both a pitcher and shortstop in baseball. He signed for a $650,000 bonus as a sixth-round pick in 2008. He had his best year as a pro in 2011, finishing the year in high Class A and leading the system with 11 wins. Hermsen doesn't have a plus pitch and profiles as a back-of-the-rotation innings-eater if his fastball velocity improves. His best trait is his fastball command, which is average and still can improve. He smoothed out some rough edges in his delivery and got more aggressive last year with the aid of pitching coordinator Eric Rasmussen. Those changes helped Hermsen touch 90 mph at Fort Myers after his promotion, though he often works at 82-88 mph. He throws a fringy curveball and an improving changeup, but neither consistently puts away hitters. Twins officials are united in agreement that he has excellent makeup and competitiveness, but they're split on his future, with some wondering if he'll ever throw with the power befitting his big body. Hermsen is headed back to high Class A to open 2012.

Year	Club (League)	Class	W	L	ERA	G	GS	CG	SV	IP	H	HR	BB	SO	K/9	WHIP	AVG
2009	Twins (GCL)	R	6	2	1.35	10	10	1	0	53	32	0	4	42	7.1	0.68	.171
2010	Beloit (MWL)	LoA	4	6	5.00	12	12	1	0	72	85	6	15	46	5.8	1.39	.295
	Elizabethton (APP)	R	2	2	3.32	8	6	0	0	38	39	2	4	39	9.2	1.13	.257

Year	Club (League)		W	L	ERA	G	GS	CG	SV	IP	H	HR	BB	SO	K/9	WHIP	AVG
2011	Beloit (MWL)	LoA	11	7	3.10	21	20	1	0	125	131	10	31	81	5.8	1.30	.271
	Fort Myers (FSL)	HiA	2	1	4.39	5	5	0	0	27	34	1	6	20	6.8	1.50	.312
Minor League Totals			25	18	3.38	56	53	3	0	315	321	19	60	228	6.5	1.21	.263

28 JORGE POLANCO, INF/OF

BA GRADE
50
EXTREME

Born: July 5, 1993. **B-T:** B-R. **Ht.:** 5-11. **Wt.:** 165. **Signed:** Dominican Republic, 2009. **Signed by:** Fred Guerrero.

When Minnesota signed Dominicans Polanco and Miguel Sano as part of the same international class in 2009, it probably hoped to keep them moving in tandem. They broke into pro ball together in the Dominican Summer League, and arrived in the United States together on July 4, 2010. But Polanco, who's significantly less physical than Sano, hasn't hit enough to keep pace. He has baseball skills and flashes the tools to be a potential everyday shortstop, with good hands, infield actions and instincts. He also has an average arm that could get better as he gets stronger. He played six positions in 2011: shortstop, third base, second base and all three outfield spots. Polanco lacks the strength to repeat his swing or defensive actions over the grind of everyday play. His swing mechanics are good enough for him to make consistent contact, but he doesn't project to hit for much power. He's an above-average runner once he gets going, but his lack of blazing speed further limits his offensive upside. The Twins think they'll have a player if Polanco gains strength. He's headed back to Rookie ball in 2012.

Year	Club (League)	Class	AVG	G	AB	R	H	2B	3B	HR	RBI	BB	SO	SB	CS	OBP	SLG
2010	Twins (DSL)	R	.250	18	60	5	15	2	0	0	7	6	9	1	3	.309	.283
	Twins (GCL)	R	.223	34	103	12	23	5	0	1	12	12	9	2	4	.299	.301
2011	Twins (GCL)	R	.250	51	172	21	43	8	3	1	16	15	24	6	4	.319	.349
Minor League Totals			.242	103	335	38	81	15	3	2	35	33	42	9	11	.311	.322

29 ANGEL MATA, RHP

BA GRADE
50
EXTREME

Born: Dec. 3, 1992. **B-T:** R-R. **Ht.:** 6-2. **Wt.:** 227. **Signed:** Venezuela, 2010. **Signed by:** Jose Leon.

The Twins signed Mata in January 2010, and he led their Dominican Summer League club with 54 strikeouts in 59 innings in 2010. He came to the United States last year and would have ranked second in the Gulf Coast League with a 1.46 ERA if he hadn't fallen nine innings short of qualifying. Mata has yet to give up a home run as a pro, thanks to a heavy 88-92 mph fastball that peaks at 94. His arm works well and he throws with ease. Mata's fastball has so much life that he doesn't have great command of it yet, nor does he have great body control, both understandable flaws given his age and size. His changeup and curveball are present below-average pitches and neither projects to become a plus offering. His success will hinge on improving his fastball command so that his secondary stuff plays up. He's headed to Elizabethton in 2012.

Year	Club (League)	Class	W	L	ERA	G	GS	CG	SV	IP	H	HR	BB	SO	K/9	WHIP	AVG
2010	Twins (DSL)	R	1	5	2.12	13	10	1	0	59	50	0	15	54	8.2	1.10	.230
2011	Twins (GCL)	R	0	1	1.46	12	11	0	0	37	23	0	19	30	7.3	1.14	.184
Minor League Totals			1	6	1.87	25	21	1	0	96	73	0	34	84	7.8	1.11	.213

30 TERRY DOYLE, RHP

BA GRADE
40
LOW

Born: Nov. 2, 1985. **B-T:** R-R. **Ht.:** 6-4. **Wt.:** 225. **Drafted:** Boston College, 2008 (37th round). **Signed by:** Chuck Fox (White Sox).

Doyle earned a math degree at Boston College and would be teaching that subject if he hadn't signed with the White Sox for $1,000 as a 37th-round pick in 2008. Left unprotected by Chicago, Doyle landed with Minnesota in December as the second pick in the major league Rule 5 draft. The Twins saw Doyle throw well in the Arizona Fall League, where he went 4-0, 1.98 in eight starts and held batters to a .135 average in 27 innings. They also saw that the more he pitched last season, the harder he threw, reaching the mid-90s during the AFL's Rising Stars Game. Counting his AFL stint, he worked 200 innings in 2011. Doyle often pitches backward and uses breaking pitches to set up his fastball, which usually sits in the high 80s. He throws four pitches for strikes, including a biting slider and an upper-70s changeup. He works fast, making it difficult for batters to adjust. Doyle has a chance to stick as a long reliever or fifth starter for a club that lost 99 games in 2011 and for an organization that values pitchers with command. If he doesn't, Rule 5 guidelines mandate that Minnesota has to expose him to waivers and offer him back to Chicago for half his $50,000 draft price.

Year	Club (League)	Class	W	L	ERA	G	GS	CG	SV	IP	H	HR	BB	SO	K/9	WHIP	AVG
2008	Bristol (APP)	R	1	2	1.88	10	0	0	0	24	27	0	3	27	10.1	1.25	.278
2009	Great Falls (PIO)	R	5	1	2.98	12	10	0	0	57	51	1	15	75	11.8	1.15	.244
2010	Kannapolis (SAL)	LoA	4	2	0.96	7	7	0	0	47	31	2	12	58	11.1	0.91	.187
	Winston-Salem (CAR)	HiA	8	8	3.71	20	20	0	0	121	115	13	34	99	7.3	1.23	.249
2011	Winston-Salem (CAR)	HiA	1	5	2.84	11	11	0	0	73	71	3	11	49	6.0	1.12	.252
	Birmingham (SL)	AA	7	5	3.24	15	15	2	0	100	91	8	22	73	6.6	1.13	.241
Minor League Totals			26	23	2.94	75	63	3	0	423	386	27	97	381	8.1	1.14	.242

New York Mets

BY MATT EDDY

Though Jose Reyes became the first Met in the franchise's 50 seasons to win the National League batting title, New York still finished in fourth place in the NL East at 77-85. Reyes turned in a career year, batting .337/.384/.493 with 39 stolen bases, then fled to the Marlins as a free agent in December, signing a six-year, $106 million deal.

Losing Reyes will blunt the Mets' offensive attack, certainly, but the 2011 club quietly had its most productive season at cavernous Citi Field. New York finished second in on-base percentage (.335) and sixth in the NL in scoring, actually totaling five more runs than the division-champion Phillies despite spotting Philadelphia a 45-homer advantage. The Mets certainly would have scored even more runs had injuries not cost Reyes (hamstring) a month, Daniel Murphy (knee) and David Wright (back) two months each and Ike Davis (ankle) all but 36 games.

Barring the import of an impact position player, the Mets must rely on the talent already at hand because the upper levels of the system are void of blue-chip hitting talent. On the positive side, Lucas Duda's .852 OPS led all major league rookies with 300 plate appearances, while Ruben Tejeda and Josh Thole played well in the second half of their sophomore seasons.

The pitching side of the equation, however, is much more complicated because Citi Field masks the staff's deficiencies. During the three years of the park's existence, the Mets have compiled a 3.65 ERA at home compared to 4.60 on the road. New York's 4.19 ERA ranked 13th in the NL in 2011, sinking any hopes the club had to contend.

The organization may be able to address its pitching woes from within because its top prospects are righthanders Zack Wheeler and Matt Harvey, the sixth and seventh overall picks in the 2009 and '10 drafts. Both enjoyed strong seasons in high Class A, and both used power fastball/breaking ball repertoires to strike out more than 10 batters per nine innings.

Righthanders Jeurys Familia, Jenrry Mejia and Michael Fulmer also bring heat in the mid-90s, though Mejia will miss the start of 2012 after having Tommy John surgery last May. The system hasn't had multiple power arms like this since the days of Paul Wilson, Bill Pulsipher and Jason Isringhausen in the mid-1990s.

First-year general manager Sandy Alderson emphasized the future over the present in the trades that sent Carlos Beltran to the Giants (for Wheeler) and Francisco Rodriguez to the Brewers (to ensure that the

Lucas Duda gave the Mets one of baseball's best rookies in 2011, with a .852 OPS

ED WOLFSTEIN

TOP 30 PROSPECTS

1. Zack Wheeler, rhp	16. Zach Lutz, 3b/1b
2. Matt Harvey, rhp	17. Domingo Tapia, rhp
3. Brandon Nimmo, of	18. Juan Urbina, lhp
4. Jeurys Familia, rhp	19. Darrell Ceciliani, of
5. Cesar Puello, of	20. Darin Gorski, lhp
6. Jenrry Mejia, rhp	21. Phillip Evans, ss
7. Kirk Nieuwenhuis, of	22. Juan Lagares, of
8. Michael Fulmer, rhp	23. Josh Edgin, lhp
9. Reese Havens, 2b	24. Chris Schwinden, rhp
10. Wilmer Flores, ss	25. Bradley Marquez, of
11. Jordany Valdespin, ss/2b	26. Logan Verrett, rhp
12. Matt den Dekker, of	27. Jack Leathersich, lhp
13. Cory Mazzoni, rhp	28. Robert Carson, lhp
14. Aderlin Rodriguez, 3b	29. Josh Satin, 3b/2b
15. Cory Vaughn, of	30. Danny Muno, ss

closer's $17.5 option for 2012 didn't vest). New York also took a more progressive approach in the draft, spending $6.8 million on bonuses after shelling out a combined $7.8 million in the previous two drafts.

In their first draft under scouting director Chad MacDonald, the Mets exceeded MLB's bonus recommendations for 11 of the club's signees, including their top two picks, outfielder Brandon Nimmo and Fulmer. MacDonald left after the season to become an assistant GM with the Padres, so New York promoted pro scout Tommy Tanous, a former Blue Jays crosschecker, to replace him.

General Manager: Sandy Alderson. **Farm Director:** Adam Wogan. **Scouting Director:** Tommy Tanous.

Class	Team	League	W	L	Pct	Finish*	Manager(s)
Majors	New York Mets	National	77	85	.475	10th (16)	Terry Collins
Triple-A	Buffalo Bisons	International	61	82	.427	12th (14)	Tim Teufel
Double-A	Binghamton Mets	Eastern	65	76	.461	10th (12)	Wally Backman
High A	St. Lucie Mets	Florida State	72	68	.514	6th (12)	Pedro Lopez
Low A	Savannah Sand Gnats	South Atlantic	79	60	.568	t-2nd (14)	Ryan Ellis
Short-season	Brooklyn Cyclones	New York-Penn	45	29	.608	2nd (14)	Rich Donnelly
Rookie	Kingsport Mets	Appalachian	39	29	.574	t-4th (10)	Frank Fultz
Rookie	GCL Mets	Gulf Coast	27	29	.482	8th (15)	Luis Rojas
Overall 2011 Minor League Record			388	373	.510	11th (30)	

*Finish in overall standings (No. of teams in league). †League champion.

LAST YEAR'S TOP 30

Player, Pos.		Status
1.	Jenrry Mejia, rhp	No. 6
2.	Wilmer Flores, ss	No. 10
3.	Cesar Puello, of	No. 5
4.	Matt Harvey, rhp	No. 2
5.	Kirk Nieuwenhuis, of	No. 7
6.	Reese Havens, 2b	No. 9
7.	Lucas Duda, of/1b	Majors
8.	Fernando Martinez, of	Majors
9.	Aderlin Rodriguez, 3b	No. 14
10.	Brad Holt, rhp	Dropped out
11.	Juan Urbina, lhp	No. 18
12.	Robert Carson, lhp	No. 28
13.	Jeurys Familia, rhp	No. 4
14.	Darrell Ceciliani, of	No. 19
15.	Cory Vaughn, of	No. 15
16.	Dillon Gee, rhp	Majors
17.	Erik Goeddel, rhp	Dropped out
18.	Steve Matz, lhp	Dropped out
19.	Zach Lutz, 3b	No. 16
20.	Robbie Shields, ss	Dropped out
21.	Brad Emaus, 3b/2b	(Rockies)
22.	Mark Cohoon, lhp	Dropped out
23.	Matt den Dekker, of	No. 12
24.	Armando Rodriguez, rhp	Dropped out
25.	Jordany Valdespin, 2b/ss	No. 11
26.	Jefry Marte, 3b	Dropped out
27.	Kyle Allen, rhp	Dropped out
28.	Manny Alvarez, rhp	Dropped out
29.	Blake Forsythe, c	Dropped out
30.	Pedro Beato, rhp	Majors

BEST TOOLS

Best Hitter for Average	Juan Lagares
Best Power Hitter	Zach Lutz
Best Strike-Zone Discipline	Danny Muno
Fastest Baserunner	Pedro Zapata
Best Athlete	Bradley Marquez
Best Fastball	Zack Wheeler
Best Curveball	Zack Wheeler
Best Slider	Matt Harvey
Best Changeup	Darin Gorski
Best Control	Darin Gorski
Best Defensive Catcher	Albert Cordero
Best Defensive Infielder	Wilfredo Tovar
Best Infield Arm	Aderlin Rodriguez
Best Defensive Outfielder	Matt den Dekker
Best Outfield Arm	Cesar Puello

PROJECTED 2015 LINEUP

Catcher	Josh Thole
First Base	Ike Davis
Second Base	Reese Havens
Third Base	David Wright
Shortstop	Ruben Tejada
Left Field	Lucas Duda
Center Field	Brandon Nimmo
Right Field	Cesar Puello
No. 1 Starter	Zack Wheeler
No. 2 Starter	Matt Harvey
No. 3 Starter	Jon Niese
No. 4 Starter	Jeurys Familia
No. 5 Starter	Michael Fulmer
Closer	Jenrry Mejia

TOP PROSPECTS OF THE DECADE

Year	Player, Pos.	2011 Org.
2002	Aaron Heilman, rhp	Pirates
2003	Jose Reyes, ss	Mets
2004	Kazuo Matsui, ss	Rakuten (Japan)
2005	Lastings Milledge, of	White Sox
2006	Lastings Milledge, of	White Sox
2007	Mike Pelfrey, rhp	Mets
2008	Fernando Martinez, of	Mets
2009	Fernando Martinez, of	Mets
2010	Jenrry Mejia, rhp	Mets
2011	Jenrry Mejia, rhp	Mets

TOP DRAFT PICKS OF THE DECADE

Year	Player, Pos.	2011 Org.
2002	Scott Kazmir, lhp	Angels
2003	Lastings Milledge, of	White Sox
2004	Philip Humber, rhp	White Sox
2005	Mike Pelfrey, rhp	Mets
2006	Kevin Mulvey, rhp (2nd round)	Diamondbacks
2007	Eddie Kunz, rhp (1st round supp.)	Padres
2008	Ike Davis, 1b	Mets
2009	Steve Matz, lhp (2nd round)	Mets
2010	Matt Harvey, rhp	Mets
2011	Brandon Nimmo, of	Mets

LARGEST BONUSES IN CLUB HISTORY

Mike Pelfrey, 2005	$3,550,000
Philip Humber, 2004	$3,000,000
Matt Harvey, 2010	$2,525,000
Scott Kazmir, 2002	$2,150,000
Brandon Nimmo, 2011	$2,100,000

NEW YORK METS

TOP 2012 ROOKIE: Jordany Valdespin, ss/2b. The speedy, slash-hitting middle infielder may bridge the gap between present (Daniel Murphy/Justin Turner) and future (possibly Reese Havens) at second base.

BREAKOUT PROSPECT: Juan Lagares, of. He batted .349 during the regular season and kept hitting in Arizona Fall League (.303 in 66 at-bats).

SLEEPER: Chase Huchingson, lhp. The sidewinding lefty tops out at 94 mph but needs to refine a second pitch to profile as situational reliever.

SOURCE OF TOP 30 TALENT			
Homegrown	29	Acquired	1
College	14	Trades	1
Junior college	1	Rule 5 draft	0
High school	5	Independent leagues	0
Draft-and-follow	0	Free agents/waivers	0
Nondrafted free agents	0		
International	9		

LF
Juan Lagares (22)
Mike Baxter
Travis Taijeron

CF
Brandon Nimmo (3)
Matt den Dekker (12)
Darrell Ceciliani (19)
Bradley Marquez (25)
Joe Tuschak
Pedro Zapata
Eudy Pina

RF
Cesar Puello (5)
Kirk Nieuwenhuis (7)
Cory Vaughn (15)
Rafael Fernandez

3B
Wilmer Flores (10)
Zach Lutz (16)
Josh Satin (29)
Jefry Marte

SS
Wilfredo Tovar
Juan Carlos Gamboa

2B
Reese Havens (9)
Jordany Valdespin (11)
Phillip Evans (21)
Danny Muno (30)
Robbie Shields
Luis Nieves
Chad Zurcher

1B
Aderlin Rodriguez (14)
Allan Dykstra
Cole Frenzel

C
Albert Cordero
Cam Maron
Mike Nickeas
Blake Forsythe
Jose Garcia
Jeff Diehl
Xorge Carrillo

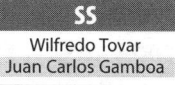
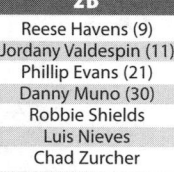

LHP

LHSP	LHRP
Juan Urbina (18)	Josh Edgin (23)
Darin Gorski (20)	Jack Leathersich (27)
Robert Carson (28)	Chase Huchingson
Steve Matz	Eric Niesen
Mark Cohoon	Brandon Sage
Alex Panteliodis	Jeremy Gould
Carlos Vazquez	Hamilton Bennett
Angel Cuan	

RHP

RHSP	RHRP
Zack Wheeler (1)	Jenrry Mejia (6)
Matt Harvey (2)	Brad Holt
Jeurys Familia (4)	Armando Rodriguez
Michael Fulmer (8)	Erik Goeddel
Cory Mazzoni (13)	Rafael Montero
Domingo Tapia (17)	Adrian Rosario
Chris Schwinden (24)	Josh Stinson
Logan Verrett (26)	Kyle Allen
Jeremy Hefner	Tyler Pill
Greg Peavey	Luis Mateo
Akeel Morris	Nick Carr
Matt Budgell	John Church
Christian Montgomery	Brandon Moore
Robert Gsellman	Taylor Whitenton
Yohan Almonte	Tyson Seng
John Gant	

2011

BEST PURE HITTER: OF Brandon Nimmo (1) has a selective approach to go with a smooth lefthanded swing and good barrel awareness. SS Danny Muno (8) also has a good game plan and won the short-season New York-Penn League batting title with a .355 average.

BEST POWER HITTER: The Mets see Nimmo as a plus hitter for both average and power, along the lines of Andre Ethier.

FASTEST RUNNER: OF Bradley Marquez (16) can fly from the right side of the plate to first base in 4.0 seconds. He draws Jose Reyes comparisons because of his speed, wiry build and dreadlocks. Nimmo and OF Joe Tuschak (6) are above-average runners.

BEST DEFENSIVE PLAYER: Marquez is raw but has the wheels to run down everything in center field. Nimmo has good center-field tools, though he's 6-foot-3 and could wind up outgrowing the position.

BEST FASTBALL: RHP Michael Fulmer (1) can maintain a 94 mph fastball for several innings and touch 97. RHP Cory Mazzoni (2) also hit 97 while easing into pro ball as a reliever, though he works at 90-94 mph as a starter, his role going forward. LHP Jack Leathersich (5) operated at 88-92 mph as a college starter, then jumped to 92-96 as a pro reliever.

BEST SECONDARY PITCH: Leathersich also flashed a plus-plus curveball coming out of the bullpen, prompting short-season Brooklyn pitching coach Frank Viola to compare him to John Franco. RHP Logan Verrett (3) has an above-average slider.

BEST PRO DEBUT: Muno, who also led the NY-P with a .466 on-base percentage. In 13 innings at Brooklyn, Leathersich posted a 0.71 ERA and 26 strikeouts. OF Travis Taijeron topped the NY-P in slugging (.557).

BEST ATHLETE: Marquez, who's also a wide receiver at Texas Tech. His deal with the Mets allows him to play both sports for two years before choosing. Nimmo has a more well-rounded package of baseball skills, and Tuschak also shows all-around ability.

MOST INTRIGUING BACKGROUND: Unsigned LHP Sean Buckle (49) fractured a vertebrae in his neck while diving for a Frisbee in April. He already has beaten the odds by walking again, and he hopes to eventually play for Loyola Marymount. RHP Tyler Pill's (4) brother Brett made his big league debut with the Giants in September.

CLOSEST TO THE MAJORS: As a lefthanded reliever with two above-average pitches, Leathersich may not need much minor league seasoning.

BEST LATE-ROUND PICK: Marquez or SS Phillip Evans (15), an offensive-minded player whose instincts allow him to play above his tools. RHP Christian Montomgery (11) had a 90-95 mph fastball and a hard curveball in the summer of 2010 before his stuff regressed last spring.

THE ONE WHO GOT AWAY: New York hoped to steal a late-round lefthander, but couldn't land Kenny Matthews (12, now at Cal State Fullerton) or A.J. Reed (25, Kentucky). OF Mason Robbins (20, Southern Mississippi) and SS Casey Turgeon (22, Florida) could be early-round picks after three years of college.

ASSESSMENT: Under new GM Sandy Alderson and scouting director Chad MacDonald, the Mets finally decided to worry more about upside than money. They invested in several high-ceiling high school players.

2010

RHP Matt Harvey (1) reached Double-A in his first pro season and may reach New York in his second. OFs Cory Vaughn (4) and Matt den Dekker (5) are off to nice starts, too.

GRADE: B

2009

The Mets lacked a first-round pick and their top two choices, LHP Steve Matz (2) and 2B Robbie Shields (3), have been waylaid by Tommy John surgery. The best hopes for this crop are OF Darrell Ceciliani (4) and LHP Darin Gorski (7).

GRADE: D

2008

Ike Davis (1) may become the franchise's best homegrown first baseman ever. 2B Reese Havens (1) also has a promising bat but can't stay healthy. OF Kirk Nieuwenhuis (3) could become a regular in New York, and INF Josh Satin (6) and RHP Chris Schwinden (22) got there last September.

GRADE: B+

2007

The Mets didn't have a first-rounder and blew two sandwich picks on RHP Eddie Kunz (1s) and LHP Nathan Vineyard (1s). But they salvaged this draft with OF/1B Lucas Duda (7) and RHP Dillon Gee (21), who had strong rookies seasons in 2011.

GRADE: B

Draft analysis by Jim Callis. Numbers in parentheses indicate draft rounds.

1 ZACK WHEELER, RHP

Born: May 30, 1990. **B-T:** R-R. **Ht.:** 6-4. **Wt.:** 185.
Drafted: HS—Dallas, Ga., 2009 (1st round). **Signed by:** Sean O'Connor (Giants).

BA GRADE

60

MEDIUM

BILL NICHOLS

The Mets acquired Wheeler from the offense-starved Giants in a straight-up trade for Carlos Beltran on July 27. "We were looking for big upside," said first-year general manager Sandy Alderson, who eschewed offers of two or three players from other clubs because he favored quality over quantity. Wheeler delivered on that front in 2011, ranking as the high Class A California League's No. 4 prospect with San Jose prior to the trade and then running up a 31-to-5 strikeout-to-walk ratio for high Class A St. Lucie afterward. The sixth overall pick in the 2009 draft, Wheeler signed with the Giants for $3.3 million, which still stands as the largest bonus San Francisco has paid an amateur pitcher. That's saying something for an organization that also drafted Matt Cain, Tim Lincecum and Madison Bumgarner in the first round. Wheeler turned in a fully healthy season in 2011 after a persistent cracked-fingernail issue limited him to just 59 innings during his 2010 pro debut. He struck out 10.1 batters per nine innings in 2011, pairing with righthander Matt Harvey (10.3) to give the Mets two of the 23 minor league ERA qualifiers who cracked double digits—and righty Jeurys Familia (9.6) just missed giving the organization three such power pitchers. All three will pitch at Double-A or higher in 2012.

Wheeler hit 97 mph with his first pitch for St. Lucie and consistently pitched at 93-95 for the Mets. He has a loose, easy arm action and throws from a high three-quarters arm slot. He complements his plus fastball with a mid- to high-70s downer curveball that buckles knees and helps him neutralize righthanders. They hit a mere .199 and slugged .292 against him between his two high Class A stops. He has a decent mid-80s changeup that sinks and fades, but improved arm action would help him sell the pitch more effectively. He also unveiled a mid- to high-80s cutter/slider as a potential weapon to get inside against lefties, who batted .283 and slugged .452 against him. Wheeler did a better job locating the ball down in the zone in 2011, though like many young power pitchers his overall

SCOUTING GRADES

Fastball: 70.	**Command/**
Curveball: 60.	**Control:** 50.
Changeup: 50.	**Delivery:** 50.

Based on 20-80 scouting scale and future projection rather than present tools. 50 represents major league average.

command needs sharpening, and it could stand in the way of him reaching frontline starter potential. On the other hand, his control improved dramatically after he reverted to his high school pitching mechanics in July, reinstituting a higher leg kick and bringing his hands to a higher position before breaking them. From July 16 to the end of the season he walked just seven batters in 38 innings (1.7 per nine), compared to 45 walks in 77 innings (5.3) beforehand.

At the time of his trade, Wheeler's command wasn't as advanced as other recent Giants first-round prep pitchers such as Cain or Bumgarner. But his raw stuff—plus-plus fastball, plus curve, chance for an average changeup and/or cutter—gives him No. 2 starter potential when paired with just average command. Still just 22, Wheeler will head to Double-A Binghamton to begin 2012 and could finish the year in Triple-A Buffalo. Expect to see him in Queens at some point in 2013.

Year	Club (League)	Class	W	L	ERA	G	GS	CG	SV	IP	H	HR	BB	SO	K/9	WHIP	AVG
2010	Augusta (SAL)	LoA	3	3	3.99	21	13	0	0	59	47	0	38	70	10.7	1.45	.218
2011	San Jose (CAL)	HiA	7	5	3.99	16	16	0	0	88	74	7	47	98	10.0	1.38	.224
	St. Lucie (FSL)	HiA	2	2	2.00	6	6	0	0	27	26	0	5	31	10.3	1.15	.252
Minor League Totals			12	10	3.68	43	35	0	0	174	147	7	90	199	10.3	1.36	.227

2 MATT HARVEY, RHP

Born: March 17, 1989. **B-T:** R-R. **Ht.:** 6-4. **Wt.:** 210. **Drafted:** North Carolina, 2010 (1st round). **Signed by:** Marlin McPhail.

Harvey signed for $2.525 million as the 2010 draft's seventh overall pick. He began his pro career in style by leading the high Class A Florida State League with 92 strikeouts through June 20, his last start before earning a promotion to Double-A. He overcame a rough beginning at Binghamton to go 5-1, 3.26 over his final nine starts while notching a 50-19 strikeout-walk ratio in 47 innings. Harvey dominated high Class A hitters with a 92-94 mph fastball that clocks as high as 98. He locates his fastball to both sides of the plate and with good life down in the zone. His two-seamer runs in on the hands of righthanders. His No. 2 pitch is a plus 81-84 mph slider, and he also likes to throw a 12-to-6 curveball to catch opponents off guard. He got by without a changeup in the FSL but began throwing one in earnest in Double-A. His changeup features late fade but remains a bit firm in the mid-80s. Harvey holds his velocity deep into starts but has below-average command and presently lacks a reliable changeup, so evaluators project him as anywhere from a No. 2 starter to a high-leverage reliever. How he addresses those concerns as he pitches in Triple-A in 2012 will determine where he fits best.

BA GRADE
60
MEDIUM

MARC LEVINE

Year	Club (League)	Class	W	L	ERA	G	GS	CG	SV	IP	H	HR	BB	SO	K/9	WHIP	AVG
2011	St. Lucie (FSL)	HiA	8	2	2.37	14	14	0	0	76	67	5	24	92	10.9	1.20	.238
	Binghamton (EL)	AA	5	3	4.53	12	12	0	0	60	58	4	23	64	9.7	1.36	.254
Minor League Totals			13	5	3.32	26	26	0	0	136	125	9	47	156	10.3	1.27	.246

3 BRANDON NIMMO, OF

Born: March 17, 1993. **B-T:** L-R. **Ht.:** 6-3. **Wt.:** 185. **Drafted:** HS—Cheyenne, Wyo., 2011 (1st round). **Signed by:** Jim Reeves.

The 13th overall pick in June, Nimmo made history as the only first-round pick ever from the state of Wyoming, which has no high school baseball. He signed for $2.1 million at the Aug. 15 deadline and logged 10 games in Rookie ball, connecting for his first two pro home runs in late August. Nimmo starred in football and also was an accomplished sprinter in high school, but his baseball skills aren't as raw as his background suggests. He has an advanced feel for the strike zone and the quick, compact lefthanded swing to become a plus hitter. The Mets believe he'll add strength to his physical frame and grow into at least solid power, but they're content to let that develop naturally. His swing doesn't have natural loft or pull, and they won't change him. Nimmo tore the anterior cruciate ligament in his right knee while playing football, but he's still a plus runner. His long strides enable him to cover lots of ground in center field, where he's an average defender with a decent arm. New York believes Nimmo's outstanding makeup will allow him to maximize his raw tools. It could also mean he's ready for an assignment to low Class A Savannah to begin 2012.

BA GRADE
60
HIGH

Year	Club (League)	Class	AVG	G	AB	R	H	2B	3B	HR	RBI	BB	SO	SB	CS	OBP	SLG
2011	Mets (GCL)	R	.241	7	29	5	7	0	0	2	4	3	9	0	0	.313	.448
	Kingsport (APP)	R	.111	3	9	0	1	0	0	0	0	3	5	0	0	.333	.111
Minor League Totals			.211	10	38	5	8	0	0	2	4	6	14	0	0	.318	.368

4 JEURYS FAMILIA, RHP

Born: Oct. 10, 1989. **B-T:** R-R. **Ht.:** 6-3. **Wt.:** 185. **Signed:** Dominican Republic, 2007. **Signed by:** Ramon Pena/Ismael Cruz/Marcelino Vallejo.

Familia earned Mets minor league pitcher of the year honors in a breakout 2009 and then represented the franchise at the 2010 Futures Game, even though his performance that season (5.58 ERA, 1.58 WHIP) seemed incongruous with the honor. He began rounding into form late in 2010 and then dominated the Florida State League for six starts in 2011 before earning a bump to Double-A, where he pitched well before and after missing a month with shoulder tendinitis. Familia touches 99 mph with his fastball and pitches comfortably at 92-96 mph with natural cutting action down in the zone. At the behest of former pitching coordinator Rick Tomlin, Familia stands taller in his delivery now and has eliminated a crouch that caused his arm path to swing away from his body in 2010. He now generates more plane on his pitches, including a mid-80s breaking ball that features inconsistent spin but flashes average three-quarters break. His fringy changeup features some sinking action and works well enough to keep batters off his fastball. Below-average control might ultimately limit Familia's upside to mid-rotation starter or power reliever, but he could be just half a season away from a callup. He joined the 40-man roster after the season and will open 2012 in Triple-A.

BA GRADE
55
HIGH

Year	Club (League)	Class	W	L	ERA	G	GS	CG	SV	IP	H	HR	BB	SO	K/9	WHIP	AVG
2008	Mets (GCL)	R	2	2	2.79	11	11	0	0	52	46	2	13	38	6.6	1.14	.232
2009	Savannah (SAL)	LoA	10	6	2.69	24	23	0	0	134	109	3	46	109	7.3	1.16	.221
2010	St. Lucie (FSL)	HiA	6	9	5.58	24	24	0	0	121	117	7	74	137	10.2	1.58	.257
2011	St. Lucie (FSL)	HiA	1	1	1.49	6	6	0	0	36	21	1	8	36	8.9	0.80	.171
	Binghamton (EL)	AA	4	4	3.49	17	17	0	0	88	85	10	35	96	9.9	1.37	.249
Minor League Totals			23	22	3.57	82	81	0	0	431	378	23	176	416	8.7	1.29	.235

5 CESAR PUELLO, OF

BA GRADE
55
HIGH

Born: April 1, 1991. **B-T:** R-R. **Ht.:** 6-2. **Wt.:** 195. **Signed:** Dominican Republic, 2007. **Signed by:** Ramon Pena/Ismael Cruz/Marciano Alvarez.

Puello continues to impress scouts and minor league managers with his broad range of tools and his physicality. During his two years of full-season ball, he has shown marked improvement in the second half. In 2011, he hit .230/.289/.337 through June 15 and .294/.344/.474 afterward. The Mets protected him on their 40-man roster in November. The ball jumps off Puello's bat to all fields, and his plus strength and bat speed could translate into 20 homers annually down the road. He hit a career-high 10 homers in 2011 after going deep only once the year before. His last six bombs went to left field, indicating that he has learned to turn on the ball. Puello still gets himself out too much because he struggles to recognize breaking balls, but scouts believe he can clean up his plate discipline enough to hit about .275. Puello has solid speed but got caught nine times in 28 steal attempts in 2011. He has seen time in center field and takes good routes, but most observers prefer him in right field. He has a strong, accurate arm. If he can learn to lay off pitches he can't drive, Puello can become a first-division regular in right field. His youth and strong work ethic will work in his favor when he tackles Double-A at age 21.

Year	Club (League)	Class	AVG	G	AB	R	H	2B	3B	HR	RBI	BB	SO	SB	CS	OBP	SLG
2008	Mets (GCL)	R	.305	40	151	24	46	6	0	1	17	5	32	13	5	.350	.364
2009	Kingsport (APP)	R	.296	49	196	37	58	10	0	5	23	10	51	15	5	.373	.423
2010	Savannah (SAL)	LoA	.292	109	404	80	118	22	1	1	34	32	82	45	10	.375	.359
2011	St. Lucie (FSL)	HiA	.259	117	441	67	114	21	5	10	50	18	103	19	9	.313	.397
Minor League Totals			.282	315	1192	208	336	59	6	17	124	65	268	92	29	.349	.384

6 JENRRY MEJIA, RHP

BA GRADE
55
HIGH

Born: Oct. 11, 1989. **B-T:** R-R. **Ht.:** 6-0. **Wt.:** 205. **Signed:** Dominican Republic, 2007. **Signed by:** Ramon Pena/Ismael Cruz/Sandy Rosario.

When Mejia made New York's 2010 Opening Day roster, he was the youngest player in the big leagues at age 20. He saw only sporadic work out of the bullpen and eventually pitched his way back to Double-A. He began 2011 in the Buffalo rotation but succumbed to Tommy John surgery in May after just five starts. Despite a smallish build, Mejia featured plus-plus velocity at 94-96 mph and the best fastball life in the system prior to his elbow injury. With natural cutting action, his fastball induces plenty of weak contact. Mejia also threw a firm changeup in the mid-80s that behaved like a splitter and gave him a second plus offering. His high-70s curveball needed refinement but showed signs of becoming an above-average pitch as well. Mejia's command suffers from an inconsistent release point, an issue exacerbated by all the missed time. He's totaled just 203 innings in the last three years as a result of injuries, including finger (2009) and shoulder (2010) strains. Mejia could get back on a mound at some point during spring training and return to game action in May or June. Assuming a full recovery, his ceiling remains unchanged: No. 2 starter or late-inning reliever.

Year	Club (League)	Class	W	L	ERA	G	GS	CG	SV	IP	H	HR	BB	SO	K/9	WHIP	AVG
2007	Mets (DSL)	R	2	3	2.47	14	7	0	1	44	24	0	27	47	9.7	1.17	.160
2008	Mets (GCL)	R	2	0	0.60	3	3	1	0	15	9	0	3	15	9.0	0.80	.164
	Brooklyn (NYP)	SS	3	2	3.49	11	11	0	0	57	42	4	23	52	8.3	1.15	.209
2009	St. Lucie (FSL)	HiA	4	1	1.97	9	9	0	0	50	41	0	16	44	7.9	1.13	.217
	Binghamton (EL)	AA	0	5	4.47	10	10	0	0	44	44	2	23	47	9.5	1.51	.263
2010	Mets (GCL)	R	0	0	3.00	1	1	0	0	3	4	0	1	3	9.0	1.67	.333
	St. Lucie (FSL)	HiA	0	0	0.00	1	1	0	0	4	1	0	0	7	15.8	0.25	.077
	Binghamton (EL)	AA	2	0	1.32	6	6	1	0	27	19	0	14	26	8.6	1.21	.200
	Buffalo (IL)	AAA	0	0	1.13	1	1	0	0	8	5	1	1	9	10.1	0.75	.200
	New York (NL)	MAJ	0	4	4.62	33	3	0	0	39	46	3	20	22	5.1	1.69	.289
2011	Buffalo (IL)	AAA	1	2	2.86	5	5	0	0	28	16	1	14	21	6.7	1.06	.168
Major League Totals			0	4	4.62	33	3	0	0	39	46	3	20	22	5.1	1.69	.289
Minor League Totals			14	13	2.66	61	54	2	1	281	205	8	122	271	8.7	1.17	.205

7 KIRK NIEUWENHUIS, OF

Born: Aug. 7, 1987. **B-T:** L-R. **Ht.:** 6-3. **Wt.:** 215. **Drafted:** Azusa Pacific (Calif.), 2008 (3rd round). **Signed by:** Fred Mazuca.

A torn labrum in his non-throwing shoulder rendered Nieuwenhuis unable to swing a bat after June 9, so he had season-ending surgery in July to remedy the issue. Prior to the injury, the former NAIA standout had enhanced his power production and walk rate in Triple-A, where he had posted career highs in on-base percentage (.403) and slugging (.505). It was an easy decision for the Mets to place him on their 40-man roster following the season. Nieuwenhuis has no carrying tool, but he also has no glaring weakness. He rips line drives to all fields and possesses solid bat speed, but his elevated strikeout rate and trouble with lefthanders limit his offensive potential. Nieuwenhuis might top out near .275 with 12-15 homers at his best, though his strong batting eye ought to translate to a good OBP. He makes all the routine plays in center field, though fringe-average speed probably limits him to a corner long term, particularly in spacious Citi Field. He has the average arm strength to handle all three spots. Nieuwenhuis may lack the range to play center every day and the power to hold down a corner spot in the big leagues, but he profiles as a near-perfect fourth outfielder.

BA GRADE
50
MEDIUM

Year	Club (League)	Class	AVG	G	AB	R	H	2B	3B	HR	RBI	BB	SO	SB	CS	OBP	SLG
2008	Brooklyn (NYP)	SS	.277	74	285	34	79	15	5	3	29	29	70	11	7	.348	.396
2009	St. Lucie (FSL)	HiA	.274	123	482	91	132	35	5	16	71	53	118	16	4	.357	.467
	Binghamton (EL)	AA	.406	8	32	8	13	3	1	1	2	4	9	1	1	.472	.656
2010	Binghamton (EL)	AA	.289	94	394	81	114	35	2	16	60	30	93	13	7	.337	.510
	Buffalo (IL)	AAA	.225	30	120	10	27	8	1	2	17	11	39	0	0	.295	.358
2011	Buffalo (IL)	AAA	.298	53	188	33	56	17	2	6	14	32	59	5	2	.403	.505
Minor League Totals			.280	382	1501	257	421	113	16	44	193	159	388	46	21	.354	.465

8 MICHAEL FULMER, RHP

Born: March 15, 1993. **B-T:** R-R. **Ht.:** 6-3. **Wt.:** 200. **Drafted:** HS—Edmond, Okla., 2011 (1st round supplemental). **Signed by:** Steve Gossett.

The state of Oklahoma boasted its best-ever crop of high school pitching talent in 2011, so Fulmer took a back seat to Dylan Bundy and Archie Bradley, the fourth and seventh overall picks in the draft. Fulmer went 44th overall and signed for an above-slot $937,500 in late July before logging four appearances in the Rookie-level Gulf Coast League. People who have watched Fulmer pitch often use the word "aggressive" to describe him. He attacks the opposition with 92-97 mph heat that explodes through the zone. He imparts natural tailing action on his fastball, making him difficult to square up. He added about 5 mph to his fastball as a senior, and his slider followed suit, jumping to 83-85 mph. It's a swing-and-miss pitch to lefties and righties alike because of its depth and power. Fulmer dominated with just a fastball and breaking ball in high school and has no usable changeup at this stage. At 6-foot-3 and 200 pounds, he has little physical projection remaining and could benefit from tightening his physique. Fulmer will work to enhance his changeup and feel for pitching in 2012, perhaps at short-season Brooklyn following extended spring training. He has the upside of a No. 2 starter but will require time and patience to get there.

BA GRADE
55
HIGH

TOM DiPACE

Year	Club (League)	Class	W	L	ERA	G	GS	CG	SV	IP	H	HR	BB	SO	K/9	WHIP	AVG
2011	Mets (GCL)	R	0	1	10.13	4	3	0	0	5	9	0	4	10	16.9	2.44	.346
Minor League Totals			0	1	10.13	4	3	0	0	5	9	0	4	10	16.9	2.44	.346

9 REESE HAVENS, 2B

Born: Oct. 20, 1986. **B-T:** L-R. **Ht.:** 6-1. **Wt.:** 195. **Drafted:** South Carolina, 2008 (1st round). **Signed by:** Marlin McPhail.

Taken four picks after Ike Davis in the first round of the 2008 draft, Havens has yet to play a full season since signing for $1.41 million. He missed all but 32 games in 2010 because a protruding rib irritated his oblique area. He had surgery to shave the rib following that season, but the procedure kept him out until late May. He also dealt with back trouble and played in just 61 games in 2011. Havens has performed whenever healthy, batting .301/.379/.505 with 12 homers in 279 Double-A at-bats the last two seasons. He swings through pitches at times but makes enough line-drive contact to hit .280 in the big leagues. He drives balls to the middle of the field, which may cap his home runs at 15 annually but ought to produce plenty of doubles. Havens played shortstop until 2010 before shifting seamlessly to second base, where his average range and arm make him a steady defender. He's a below-average runner. Scratched from an Arizona Fall League

BA GRADE
50
HIGH

assignment, Havens returned home to begin his conditioning program. The Mets figured he would have played his way on to their 40-man roster by now, but they added him anyway after the season. They have no long-term second baseman standing in his way—Ruben Tejada profiles best at shortstop and Justin Turner as a utility player—so a full season in Triple-A ought to earn Havens a look in Queens.

Year	Club (League)	Class	AVG	G	AB	R	H	2B	3B	HR	RBI	BB	SO	SB	CS	OBP	SLG
2008	Brooklyn (NYP)	SS	.247	23	85	13	21	6	2	3	11	11	27	3	1	.340	.471
2009	St. Lucie (FSL)	HiA	.247	97	360	53	89	19	1	14	52	55	73	3	2	.361	.422
2010	St. Lucie (FSL)	HiA	.281	14	57	9	16	2	1	3	7	8	18	0	1	.369	.509
	Binghamton (EL)	AA	.338	18	68	12	23	2	1	6	12	6	15	0	2	.400	.662
2011	St. Lucie (FSL)	HiA	.273	3	11	1	3	2	0	0	2	2	5	0	0	.385	.455
	Binghamton (EL)	AA	.289	58	211	37	61	15	1	6	26	27	59	2	0	.372	.455
Minor League Totals			.269	213	792	125	213	46	6	32	110	109	197	8	6	.366	.463

10 WILMER FLORES, SS

Born: Aug. 6, 1991. **B-T:** R-R. **Ht.:** 6-3. **Wt.:** 175. **Signed:** Venezuela, 2007. **Signed by:** Sandy Johnson/Ismael Cruz/Robert Alfonzo.

Signed for $750,000 in 2007, Flores already has played 459 games in the United States at age 20, the vast majority of them as a teenager. The Florida State League's youngest regular in 2010 and second-youngest in 2011, he saw his OPS drop from .739 to .689 in his second stint with St. Lucie. Despite his struggles, New York placed him on its 40-man roster in November. Flores stays inside the ball well and uses the whole field, but he almost makes too much contact for his own good. He won't fully tap into his offensive potential unless he learns to recognize and lay off pitches he can't drive. His natural power stroke carries the ball to center and right-center, which has suppressed his home run totals thus far. As he fills out his lean frame he could develop 20-homer power, which would be special at shortstop—but scouts give Flores no chance to stay up the middle. He's a well below-average runner with heavy feet and substandard range. He reads balls well off the bat and has an average arm, which could keep him on an infield corner. Flores played third base last winter in the Venezuelan League, which is a more natural fit for his skills. His power production must take a giant step forward for his bat to profile there, however. He should reach Double-A in 2012 before he turns 21.

BA GRADE

50 HIGH

Year	Club (League)	Class	AVG	G	AB	R	H	2B	3B	HR	RBI	BB	SO	SB	CS	OBP	SLG
2008	Kingsport (APP)	R	.310	59	245	36	76	12	4	8	41	12	28	2	1	.352	.490
	Savannah (SAL)	LoA	.400	1	5	1	2	0	0	0	0	0	2	0	0	.400	.400
	Brooklyn (NYP)	SS	.267	8	30	3	8	1	0	0	1	1	7	0	0	.290	.300
2009	Savannah (SAL)	LoA	.264	125	488	44	129	20	2	3	36	22	72	3	3	.305	.332
2010	Savannah (SAL)	LoA	.278	66	277	30	77	18	2	7	44	23	37	2	1	.342	.433
	St. Lucie (FSL)	HiA	.300	67	277	32	83	18	1	4	40	9	40	2	4	.324	.415
2011	St. Lucie (FSL)	HiA	.269	133	516	52	139	26	2	9	81	27	68	2	2	.309	.380
Minor League Totals			.280	459	1838	198	514	95	11	31	243	94	254	11	11	.321	.394

11 JORDANY VALDESPIN, SS/2B

BA GRADE

45 MEDIUM

Born: Dec. 23, 1987. **B-T:** L-R. **Ht.:** 6-0. **Wt.:** 190. **Signed:** Dominican Republic, 2007. **Signed by:** Ramon Pena/Ismael Cruz/Marciano Alvarez.

Carlos Beltran mentored Valdespin during spring training, warning him that opportunity might pass him by if he did not shape up. To his credit, Valdespin quieted criticism of his immaturity by turning in his finest offensive season. With 15 homers and 33 steals, he was one of the Double-A Eastern League's most dynamic power/speed talents at the time of his early-August promotion to Triple-A. Though he lacks much of a plan at the plate, Valdespin makes enough contact to hit perhaps .270 one day, though a low walk rate will hurt his on-base percentage. He has just enough power to get himself in trouble. He's at his best when he's slashing doubles and triples into the gaps and putting his solid-average speed to good use, rather than wildly uppercutting and selling out for power. Valdespin hasn't demonstrated the concentration level to hold down shortstop on a regular basis, but his average range and arm strength play well at second base, his primary position prior to 2011. He rubs some scouts the wrong way because he doesn't always give 100 percent, but as a lefthanded batter who flashes enough ability to hit, run, field and throw, he could have a future as a utility player or fringe starter at second base.

Year	Club (League)	Class	AVG	G	AB	R	H	2B	3B	HR	RBI	BB	SO	SB	CS	OBP	SLG
2007	Mets (DSL)	R	.245	43	139	23	34	4	3	1	16	24	26	8	4	.369	.338
2008	Mets (GCL)	R	.284	34	134	23	38	6	3	3	22	7	10	9	2	.319	.440
2009	Savannah (SAL)	LoA	.322	39	152	30	49	9	3	3	18	11	32	7	2	.366	.480
	Mets (DSL)	R	.333	4	15	0	5	0	2	0	5	3	1	1	1	.421	.600
	Mets (GCL)	R	.174	6	23	0	4	0	0	0	0	1	3	1	0	.208	.174
	Brooklyn (NYP)	SS	.279	18	68	10	19	3	1	1	5	5	16	4	3	.338	.397
2010	St. Lucie (FSL)	HiA	.289	65	270	40	78	16	3	6	33	8	45	13	10	.323	.437
	Binghamton (EL)	AA	.232	28	112	8	26	8	0	0	8	2	23	4	2	.243	.304
2011	Binghamton (EL)	AA	.297	107	404	62	120	24	3	15	51	21	68	33	14	.341	.483
	Buffalo (IL)	AAA	.280	27	107	7	30	8	0	2	9	4	25	4	4	.304	.411
Minor League Totals			.283	371	1424	203	403	78	18	31	167	86	249	84	42	.330	.428

12 MATT DEN DEKKER, OF

BA GRADE 45 MEDIUM

Born: Aug. 10, 1987. **B-T:** L-L. **Ht.:** 6-1. **Wt.:** 205. **Drafted:** Florida, 2010 (5th round). **Signed by:** Les Parker.

Den Dekker turned in his finest offensive season in college as a senior, batting .352 with 13 homers at Florida in 2010, and he needed less than a year to reach Double-A after turning pro. He had batted a cumulative .310/.374/.488 in 94 Class A games, but his average plummeted to .235 at Binghamton as the strikeouts piled up. He finished with 156 whiffs in 139 games, though the Mets believe he's a more nuanced hitter than he showed last season. They think den Dekker got caught between being too passive and too aggressive as Binghamton's primary leadoff hitter. He turns on inside fastballs on occasion, but for the most part he's a gap hitter with below-average power. Den Dekker's value is tied to his defensive range and his speed, both of which are plus tools and crucial to the success of any center fielder. He reads balls well off the bat and takes proper routes He unleashes accurate throws with carry, using average arm strength. Despite his raw speed, den Dekker is a modest stolen-base threat because he's faster underway than on his first step. He profiles as a fringe starter in center or, more likely, a strong outfield reserve.

Year	Club (League)	Class	AVG	G	AB	R	H	2B	3B	HR	RBI	BB	SO	SB	CS	OBP	SLG
2010	Mets (GCL)	R	.278	5	18	2	5	2	0	0	5	2	5	0	0	.350	.389
	Savannah (SAL)	LoA	.346	27	104	21	36	10	0	0	15	9	28	3	0	.404	.471
2011	St. Lucie (FSL)	HiA	.296	67	267	54	79	19	8	6	36	24	65	12	5	.362	.494
	Binghamton (EL)	AA	.235	72	272	49	64	13	3	11	32	27	91	12	5	.312	.426
Minor League Totals			.278	171	661	126	184	47	11	17	88	62	189	27	10	.347	.460

13 CORY MAZZONI, RHP

BA GRADE 50 HIGH

Born: Oct. 19, 1989. **B-T:** R-R. **Ht.:** 6-1. **Wt.:** 190. **Drafted:** North Carolina State, 2011 (2nd round). **Signed by:** Marlin MacPhail.

Mazzoni arrived at North Carolina State as a strong-armed but raw Pennsylvania prep product, and he blossomed into staff ace as a junior in 2011, ranking third in NCAA Division I with 137 strikeouts in 115 innings. After he signed quickly for $437,500 as a second-round pick, Mazzoni eased into pro ball as a reliever. Mets scouts saw Mazzoni's stuff improve dramatically over the course of the Atlantic Coast Conference season, and he pitched at 93-97 mph out of the bullpen after turning pro. His fastball doesn't have excessive life, but he locates the ball down in the zone and backs it up with a late-breaking 82-85 mph slider. Working in one-inning relief stints every five days, he didn't have occasion to throw his splitter, a fringe-average pitch he treats as a changeup. Mazzoni sat more comfortably at 90-94 mph as a starter in college, and that's the role the Mets plan to develop him in this season. He profiles as a back-of-the-rotation arm or perhaps a quality set-up man, and he could advance quickly to the big leagues in the latter role.

Year	Club (League)	Class	W	L	ERA	G	GS	CG	SV	IP	H	HR	BB	SO	K/9	WHIP	AVG
2011	Brooklyn (NYP)	SS	1	0	0.00	6	1	0	0	6	5	0	2	10	15.0	1.17	.238
	St. Lucie (FSL)	HiA	1	1	2.57	6	0	0	0	7	7	1	1	8	10.3	1.14	.250
Minor League Totals			2	1	1.38	12	1	0	0	13	12	1	3	18	12.5	1.15	.245

14 ADERLIN RODRIGUEZ, 3B

BA GRADE 50 HIGH

Born: Nov. 18, 1991. **B-T:** R-R. **Ht.:** 6-3. **Wt.:** 210. **Signed:** Dominican Republic, 2008. **Signed by:** Ismael Cruz.

In the five years the Mets have affiliated with Savannah, no player can match the 17 homers Rodriguez hit last year for the Sand Gnats, and he belted two more in the playoffs as they advanced to the finals. But after he hit .312 in Rookie ball in 2010, Rodriguez's average dropped 91 points in low Class A as he made few adjustments to the way pitchers attacked him. Looking to pull the ball almost exclusively, he often crushes middle-in fastballs for plus-plus power but is vulnerable to pitches in any other region of the strike zone. With a wide stance and no stride, Rodriguez has sound balance and basic-pitch recognition skills, lending hope that he can one day recover his feel for hitting. With heavy feet and a mature body, he's a 20 runner on the 20-80 scouting scale whose stiff infield actions leave plenty of doubt as to whether he can stick at third base. He has necessary arm strength for the position, but he committed 44 errors in 127 games last season. Scouts see a move to first base in Rodriguez's future. He's still only 20, so he has ample time to make adjustments.

Year	Club (League)	Class	AVG	G	AB	R	H	2B	3B	HR	RBI	BB	SO	SB	CS	OBP	SLG
2009	Mets (GCL)	R	.290	17	62	5	18	3	0	1	10	9	15	1	1	.389	.387
2010	Kingsport (APP)	R	.312	61	250	44	78	22	0	13	48	15	43	3	1	.352	.556
	Savannah (SAL)	LoA	.200	8	30	3	6	1	0	1	11	6	10	0	0	.333	.333
2011	Savannah (SAL)	LoA	.221	131	516	59	114	23	2	17	78	29	106	2	1	.265	.372
Minor League Totals			.252	217	858	111	216	49	2	32	147	59	174	6	3	.302	.425

15 CORY VAUGHN, OF

BA GRADE
50
HIGH

Born: May 1, 1989. **B-T:** R-R. **Ht.:** 6-3. **Wt.:** 225. **Drafted:** San Diego State, 2010 (4th round). **Signed by:** Fred Mazuca.

Vaughn's father Greg made four all-star teams and hit 355 home runs during a 15-year major league career. A taint of promise unfulfilled followed Cory through his days at San Diego State, not dispelling until he turned pro and led the New York-Penn League with a .557 slugging percentage in 2010. His first full pro season didn't resonate as loudly. Vaughn went deep just four times in a half-season with Savannah while playing in a home park that features fewer home runs than any other South Atlantic League yard—though he did go deep off Hickory's Roman Mendez at the league's all-star game. Vaughn hit a more representative nine homers in 210 at-bats after a promotion to St. Lucie. Scouts think he has enough natural loft and strength to hit for solid power down the road, though he doesn't incorporate his lower half much in his swing, leaving his arms to do all the work. His hitting set-up features a bat waggle reminiscent of Gary Sheffield, if not as exaggerated, Vaughn's two-strike approach has improved drastically in pro ball to the point where his strikeout rate is manageable so long as his power develops. He swings through enough pitches, however, to limit his hitting potential. Vaughn exhibits strong outfield fundamentals, if only average range, and could handle either left or right field with his average arm. A Type 1 diabetic, he wears an insulin pump while playing to regulate his body's sugar levels. He ought to finish 2012 in Double-A, even if it takes him half a season to get there.

Year	Club (League)	Class	AVG	G	AB	R	H	2B	3B	HR	RBI	BB	SO	SB	CS	OBP	SLG
2010	Brooklyn (NYP)	SS	.307	72	264	45	81	14	5	14	56	34	63	12	5	.396	.557
2011	Savannah (SAL)	LoA	.286	68	245	33	70	14	2	4	30	36	64	8	5	.405	.408
	St. Lucie (FSL)	HiA	.219	63	210	29	46	8	1	9	29	23	53	2	3	.308	.395
Minor League Totals			.274	203	719	107	197	36	8	27	115	93	180	22	13	.375	.459

16 ZACH LUTZ, 3B/1B

BA GRADE
45
HIGH

Born: June 3, 1986. **B-T:** R-R. **Ht.:** 6-1. **Wt.:** 222. **Drafted:** Alvernia (Pa.), 2007 (5th round). **Signed by:** Scott Hunter.

The 2007 NCAA Division III player of the year as a senior at Alvernia (Pa.) in 2007—where his father Yogi served as head coach—Lutz fractured a bone in his left foot while making a backhand play during the first inning of his first pro game that summer. The injury served as a harbinger of things to come. Lutz appeared in just 25 games during his first two seasons as he dealt with further problems in his left ankle, not making his full-season debut until 2009. More ankle and foot woes limited him to half-seasons in 2009 and 2010, and his litany of injuries last season included two concussions, a hamstring injury and a broken left ring finger. When healthy, Lutz hits the ball as hard as any Mets farmhand and ranks as the system's most advanced power prospect. He has served notice of his offensive potential by batting .292/.384/.544 with 29 homers in 127 games at the Double-A and Triple-A levels during the last two years. He has the bat speed and strength to hit for at least average power in the big leagues. He shortens his swing with two strikes, so he may hit for an acceptable average too. He throws well enough to play third base but his myriad lower-body injuries have robbed him of his range, to the point where it's no better than fringy. His speed is well below-average. If he can stay healthy, Lutz could serve as a big league power source as soon as this season.

Year	Club (League)	Class	AVG	G	AB	R	H	2B	3B	HR	RBI	BB	SO	SB	CS	OBP	SLG
2007	Brooklyn (NYP)	SS	.000	1	2	0	0	0	0	0	0	0	0	0	0	.000	.000
2008	Brooklyn (NYP)	SS	.333	24	72	9	24	4	0	3	12	14	12	0	2	.442	.514
2009	St. Lucie (FSL)	HiA	.284	99	356	46	101	19	2	11	62	50	72	1	1	.381	.441
	Binghamton (EL)	AA	.207	8	29	0	6	1	0	0	2	5	7	0	0	.324	.241
2010	Mets (GCL)	R	.316	5	19	2	6	1	0	1	4	1	4	0	0	.350	.526
	St. Lucie (FSL)	HiA	.000	1	4	0	0	0	0	0	0	0	2	0	0	.000	.000
	Binghamton (EL)	AA	.289	61	225	42	65	14	0	17	42	33	63	0	2	.389	.578
	Buffalo (IL)	AAA	.300	5	20	3	6	4	0	1	9	2	3	0	0	.364	.650
2011	St. Lucie (FSL)	HiA	.000	2	8	0	0	0	0	0	1	1	2	0	0	.111	.000
	Buffalo (IL)	AAA	.295	61	220	38	65	12	0	11	31	27	70	0	0	.380	.500
Minor League Totals			.286	267	955	140	273	55	2	44	163	133	235	1	5	.380	.486

17 DOMINGO TAPIA, RHP

BA GRADE
50
EXTREME

Born: Dec. 16, 1991. **B-T:** R-R. **Ht.:** 6-4. **Wt.:** 186. **Signed:** Dominican Republic, 2009. **Signed by:** Rafael Perez/Ismael Cruz/Jose Rosario.

Tapia signed in February 2009 but didn't enter pro ball until the following season, which he began in the Rookie-level Dominican Summer League until resolving a visa issue. His fastball topped out at 96 mph in his debut and touched triple digits on multiple occasions in 2011, showing true plus-plus velocity and heavy life. Tapia pitches at 96-98 mph and locates his heater on both sides of the plate. His fringy changeup shows occasional fade but improved throughout the season. His loopy curveball has farther to go, but he can spin the ball when he stays on top of it. Tall and lean, Tapia has room to fill out. He shows strong control for a hard-throwing teenager, though he doesn't induce as many swings and misses as one would expect from his radar-gun readings. The development of a second quality pitch would make Tapia one of New York's best prospects, and without it he probably fits best as a groundball-oriented reliever. He's ready for low Class A.

Year	Club (League)	Class	W	L	ERA	G	GS	CG	SV	IP	H	HR	BB	SO	K/9	WHIP	AVG
2010	Mets1 (DSL)	R	0	1	3.09	3	3	0	0	12	8	0	5	5	3.9	1.11	.195
	Mets (GCL)	R	4	3	3.45	10	10	0	0	47	49	0	10	29	5.6	1.26	.269
2011	Kingsport (APP)	R	5	5	3.78	11	11	0	0	50	50	3	16	30	5.4	1.32	.258
	Brooklyn (NYP)	SS	1	0	0.00	1	1	0	0	6	5	0	0	6	9.0	0.83	.227
Minor League Totals			10	9	3.38	25	25	0	0	115	112	3	31	70	5.5	1.25	.255

18 JUAN URBINA, LHP

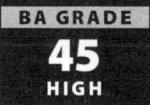

BA GRADE
50
EXTREME

Born: May 31, 1993. **B-T:** L-L. **Ht.:** 6-2. **Wt.:** 170. **Signed:** Venezuela, 2009. **Signed by:** Sandy Johnson/Ramon Pena/Ismael Cruz/Robert Alfonzo.

The Mets signed Urbina for $1.2 million in 2009, paying out a larger sum to him than any international amateur in club history save for Fernando Martinez, who signed for $1.3 million four years earlier. New York used Urbina's signing to make up for a lack of a first-round pick in the 2009 draft. He's the son of former all-star closer Ugueth Urbina, convicted and incarcerated in his native Venezuela on two counts of attempted murder. Juan's ERA jumped nearly a full run as he climbed a step up the ladder from the Gulf Coast League in 2010 to Rookie-level Kingsport in 2011, but the silver lining is that he improved dramatically after a rough start. He went 4-3, 4.00 in his final seven starts, notching 34 strikeouts and eight walks in 36 innings. Tall, lean and loose, Urbina pitches at 88-89 mph with the promise of more fastball velocity as he fills out. The Mets also project him to have a more consistent slider in time, but the pitch flattens out too much now when he gets around it. No such problems exist with his plus changeup, which he sells with his arm speed. Urbina leans heavy on the projection side of the scale now, with the upside of a No. 3 starter or more provided he finds more velocity and a tighter breaking ball. Not many international bonus babies spend three years in short-season leagues, so Urbina probably will head to low Class A on a strict pitch count in 2012.

Year	Club (League)	Class	W	L	ERA	G	GS	CG	SV	IP	H	HR	BB	SO	K/9	WHIP	AVG
2010	Mets (GCL)	R	5	3	5.03	11	11	0	0	48	54	5	14	38	7.1	1.41	.284
2011	Kingsport (APP)	R	4	6	5.95	12	12	0	0	56	68	9	20	49	7.9	1.57	.300
Minor League Totals			9	9	5.52	23	23	0	0	104	122	14	34	87	7.5	1.50	.293

19 DARRELL CECILIANI, OF

BA GRADE
45
HIGH

Born: June 22, 1990. **B-T:** L-L. **Ht.:** 6-1. **Wt.:** 220. **Drafted:** Columbia Basin (Wash.) CC, 2009 (4th round). **Signed by:** Jim Reeves.

Ceciliani won the short-season New York-Penn League batting title by hitting .351 in 2010, but he lost all momentum last season when he landed on the disabled list in April with a hamstring injury. He hardly looked like the same hitter when he returned in May, batting just .245 in the first half. Ceciliani finally caught fire in August, when he hit .320 with 16 walks and nine extra-base hits in 25 games, and he stayed hot for the low Class A South Atlantic League playoffs. He helped carry Savannah to the finals by hitting .394 with two triples while reaching base 19 times in eight games. Ceciliani served as the Sand Gnats' primary leadoff hitter, and that's the role he fits best because he lines the ball to all fields and works deep counts. He improved both his walk rate (to 11 percent) and stolen-base percentage (to 76 percent) substantially in 2011. He has enough power to run into 10 homers on an annual basis, but his swing is geared more for singles and doubles. Ceciliani doesn't possess blazing speed or incredible range in center field—both tools grade as average—though he takes clean routes to the ball. His arm grades as below average and his throws feature limited carry, making him a better fit for left or center field. After finishing last year in style, Ceciliani stands poised for a shot at high Class A in 2012.

Year	Club (League)	Class	AVG	G	AB	R	H	2B	3B	HR	RBI	BB	SO	SB	CS	OBP	SLG
2009	Kingsport (APP)	R	.234	42	158	29	37	6	0	2	13	13	31	14	2	.313	.310
2010	Brooklyn (NYP)	SS	.351	68	271	56	95	19	12	2	35	24	56	21	14	.410	.531
2011	Savannah (SAL)	LoA	.259	109	421	62	109	23	4	4	40	52	96	25	8	.351	.361
Minor League Totals			.284	219	850	147	241	48	16	8	88	89	183	60	24	.363	.406

20 DARIN GORSKI, LHP

BA GRADE
45
HIGH

Born: Oct. 6, 1987. **B-T:** L-L. **Ht.:** 6-4. **Wt.:** 210. **Drafted:** Kutztown (Pa.), 2009 (7th round). **Signed by:** Scott Hunter.

Ryan Vogelsong and Gorski made 2011 an exceptional year for pitchers from Kutztown (Pa.), an NCAA Division II program. Vogelsong signed a minor league deal with the Giants and went on to make the all-star team and finish fourth in the National League ERA race. Gorski began the year in St. Lucie's bullpen, turned a doubleheader spot start into a full-time gig and won Florida State League pitcher of the year honors. He led the team to the FSL finals, topping the league in ERA (2.08) and WHIP (1.00) while ranking third in strikeouts per nine innings (9.1). Gorski had shown strikeout stuff in past seasons, but his command improved dramatically in 2011. He learned to set up hitters by working his tailing 90-91 mph to both sides of the plate. Working well in concert with his fastball is his 80-81 mph changeup, a plus offering he can throw to get swings and misses or called strikes. Gorski's slider tops out near 78 mph and sometimes features average depth, though he throws plenty of spinners when he doesn't stay on top of it. A physical lefty who pitches without fear and takes his preparation seriously, Gorski has all the ingredients needed to profile as a No. 5 starter.

Year	Club (League)	Class	W	L	ERA	G	GS	CG	SV	IP	H	HR	BB	SO	K/9	WHIP	AVG
2009	Brooklyn (NYP)	SS	3	4	4.91	13	11	0	0	62	51	6	26	50	7.2	1.24	.220
2010	Savannah (SAL)	LoA	6	8	4.58	25	18	0	3	114	125	12	43	109	8.6	1.47	.280
2011	St. Lucie (FSL)	HiA	11	3	2.08	27	21	3	1	139	109	11	29	140	9.1	1.00	.212
Minor League Totals			20	15	3.54	65	50	3	4	315	285	29	98	299	8.5	1.22	.239

21 PHILLIP EVANS, SS

BA GRADE
45
HIGH

Born: Sept. 10, 1992. **B-T:** R-R. **Ht.:** 5-10. **Wt.:** 185. **Drafted:** HS—Carlsbad, Calif., 2011 (15th round). **Signed by:** Fred Mazuca.

Evans appeared to be headed to San Diego State after a disappointing senior year at La Costa Canyon High (Carlsbad, Calif.) put him on the bubble for the top three rounds of the 2011 draft. He fell to the 15th round, but the Mets liked him enough to sign him for $650,000, the equivalent of sandwich-round money. He appeared in nine games between New York's three lowest affiliates, playing his way on to Brooklyn's playoff roster and going 0-for-1 in his lone postseason appearance. Evans opened eyes during instructional league with his mature approach and strong, compact body, evoking memories of a young Dan Uggla. Evans' simple, repeatable righthanded swing is geared to hit for average. Though he's not overly physical, he may grow into fringe-average power because he has strong forearms. A shortstop in high school, he's a below-average runner who probably fits best at second base because his range and arm are merely adequate. He might just have the offensive potential to make the switch. The Mets laud Evans' work ethic and instincts, which could earn him a trip to low Class A to begin 2012.

Year	Club (League)	Class	AVG	G	AB	R	H	2B	3B	HR	RBI	BB	SO	SB	CS	OBP	SLG
2011	Mets (GCL)	R	.333	4	15	3	5	2	0	0	1	2	3	0	1	.412	.467
	Kingsport (APP)	R	.364	3	11	3	4	2	0	0	3	1	2	0	0	.417	.545
	Brooklyn (NYP)	SS	.125	2	8	1	1	0	0	0	0	0	0	0	0	.125	.125
Minor League Totals			.294	9	34	7	10	4	0	0	4	3	5	0	1	.351	.412

22 JUAN LAGARES, OF

BA GRADE
45
HIGH

Born: March 17, 1989. **B-T:** R-R. **Ht.:** 6-1. **Wt.:** 175. **Signed:** Dominican Republic, 2006. **Signed by:** Ismael Cruz/Juan Mercado.

Signed as a shortstop out of the Dominican Republic in 2006, Lagares didn't draw much positive attention, either offensively or defensively, until he shifted to the other side of the defensive spectrum by taking up left field in 2009. He dealt with a chronic shoulder injury that season and then missed the final six weeks of 2010 with a broken ankle. Lagares showed no ill effects last season, when he ranked fifth in the minors in hitting at .349. He led the Florida State League with a .338 average at the time of his July 21 promotion to Double-A, and he batted .370 for Binghamton to close out the regular season. The Mets protected him on their 40-man roster after he hit .303 in the Arizona Fall League. A career .254 hitter entering 2011, Lagares owes his startling turnaround to an improved rate of hard contact and better strike-zone discipline. He still gets in trouble by connecting with fastballs outside of his comfort zone. With quick hands and a level bat path, Lagares is geared more for gap power than for home run juice, and he could top out near 15 homers in a good year. He moves well in the outfield, though his speed is fringy and not ideal for anything but a corner. His below-average arm plays best in left. Though his track record is not extensive and he'll be 23 this season, Lagares has shown a knack for barreling the ball and could grow into a fringe outfield starter or quality reserve.

Year	Club (League)	Class	AVG	G	AB	R	H	2B	3B	HR	RBI	BB	SO	SB	CS	OBP	SLG
2006	Mets (DSL)	R	.255	57	204	36	52	7	8	3	33	23	48	12	5	.339	.412
2007	Savannah (SAL)	LoA	.210	83	281	26	59	12	6	2	16	18	64	11	7	.262	.317
2008	Savannah (SAL)	LoA	.254	46	181	14	46	9	0	2	17	8	28	3	4	.285	.337
	Brooklyn (NYP)	SS	.250	19	72	8	18	7	0	1	7	1	10	1	3	.280	.389
2009	Mets (GCL)	R	.208	6	24	1	5	1	0	0	1	1	4	1	0	.240	.250
	Savannah (SAL)	LoA	.274	47	168	23	46	6	2	0	13	6	42	9	4	.305	.333
2010	Savannah (SAL)	LoA	.300	67	290	42	87	13	9	5	39	7	44	18	2	.318	.459
	St. Lucie (FSL)	HiA	.233	33	133	16	31	5	0	2	16	2	18	7	3	.248	.316
2011	St. Lucie (FSL)	HiA	.338	82	308	51	104	15	6	7	49	21	47	5	6	.380	.494
	Binghamton (EL)	AA	.370	38	162	21	60	11	3	2	22	5	29	10	2	.391	.512
Minor League Totals			.279	478	1823	238	508	86	34	24	213	92	334	77	36	.317	.403

23 JOSH EDGIN, LHP

BA GRADE
45
HIGH

Born: Dec. 17, 1986. **B-T:** L-L. **Ht.:** 6-1. **Wt.:** 225. **Drafted:** Francis Marion (S.C.), 2010 (30th round). **Signed by:** Marlin McPhail.

"I love this guy," one scout from outside the organization said of Edgin. "He's a major league reliever and a fast mover." That's high praise for a player taken in the 50th and 30th round in successive drafts from an NCAA Division II program. He spend two years at Ohio State before transferring to Francis Marion (S.C.), turning down the Braves in 2009 to return for his senior season. Signed for $2,000, Edgin decimated lefthanded batters at the Class A level in 2011, holding them to a .169 average with one extra-base hit (a double) and 27 strikeouts in 65 at-bats. The Mets believe Edgin profiles as more than a situational reliever, however, because he has a 92-94 mph sinker and an average slider. He allowed just two home runs last year because he works down in the zone and keeps the ball on the ground. He employs a drop-and-drive delivery with a short arm action, which lends him ample deception. Edgin has a ceiling as a set-up man and could be just a half-season away from New York if he maintains his rapid pace of development.

Year	Club (League)	Class	W	L	ERA	G	GS	CG	SV	IP	H	HR	BB	SO	K/9	WHIP	AVG
2010	Kingsport (APP)	R	0	1	2.84	18	0	0	3	32	28	2	12	41	11.7	1.26	.231
	Savannah (SAL)	LoA	0	0	0.00	2	0	0	0	3	3	0	0	5	15.0	1.00	.273
2011	Savannah (SAL)	LoA	1	0	0.87	24	0	0	16	31	14	0	10	41	11.9	0.77	.135
	St. Lucie (FSL)	HiA	2	1	2.06	25	0	0	11	35	30	2	13	35	9.0	1.23	.233
Minor League Totals			3	2	1.88	69	0	0	30	101	75	4	35	122	10.9	1.09	.205

24 CHRIS SCHWINDEN, RHP

BA GRADE
40
LOW

Born: Sept. 22, 1986. **B-T:** R-R. **Ht.:** 6-3. **Wt.:** 215. **Drafted:** Fresno Pacific, 2008 (22nd round). **Signed by:** Doug Thurman.

The Mets' September rotation featured two righthanders drafted out of college after the 20th round. Dillon Gee, a 21st-round selection in 2007, logged 161 innings for New York and enjoyed the Citi Field experience with a 3.17 ERA at home (compared with 5.74 away). Taken one year and one round later than Gee, Schwinden opened 2011 in the Binghamton bullpen, earning a promotion to Triple-A in mid-April to cover for the promoted Pat Misch. Schwinden struck out nine in his first start for the Bisons and didn't look back, allowing eight runs in his first seven starts. He faded down the stretch with a 5.54 ERA over his final 10 starts, but his strikeout rate remained firm and New York called him up in September. Like Gee, Schwinden pitches at 89-90 mph and his stuff is fringy across the board, but he throws strikes with four pitches and attacks hitters' weaknesses. The addition of a cutter to go with a four-seam fastball that scrapes 93 mph has allowed Schwinden to work both sides of the plate. He improved the power and shape of a mid-70s curve last season, though his changeup remains shaky. He's an extreme flyball pitcher who will benefit from Citi Field's generous outfield dimensions. Schwinden fits best as a No. 5 starter whose pitchability always will outstrip his raw stuff, but he ought to get plenty of opportunity in the near term with New York given its thin rotation.

Year	Club (League)	Class	W	L	ERA	G	GS	CG	SV	IP	H	HR	BB	SO	K/9	WHIP	AVG
2008	Brooklyn (NYP)	SS	4	1	2.01	14	8	0	0	63	53	3	12	70	10.1	1.04	.233
2009	Savannah (SAL)	LoA	9	6	3.28	21	17	0	0	115	126	6	15	88	6.9	1.22	.279
	St. Lucie (FSL)	HiA	1	0	3.97	2	2	0	0	11	12	0	3	4	3.2	1.32	.279
2010	St. Lucie (FSL)	HiA	3	0	1.83	7	2	0	0	34	34	2	5	23	6.0	1.14	.258
	Binghamton (EL)	AA	4	7	5.56	17	14	1	0	79	100	8	19	69	7.8	1.50	.306
2011	Binghamton (EL)	AA	0	0	0.00	2	0	0	0	3	2	0	0	5	15.0	0.67	.200
	Buffalo (IL)	AAA	8	8	3.95	26	26	0	0	146	138	14	48	134	8.3	1.28	.250
	New York (NL)	MAJ	0	2	4.71	4	4	0	0	21	23	1	6	17	7.3	1.38	.274
Major League Totals			0	2	4.71	4	4	0	0	21	23	1	6	17	7.3	1.38	.274
Minor League Totals			29	22	3.61	89	69	1	0	452	465	33	102	393	7.8	1.26	.267

25 BRADLEY MARQUEZ, OF

BA GRADE

50
EXTREME

Born: Dec. 14, 1992. **B-T:** R-R. **Ht.:** 6-1. **Wt.:** 185. **Drafted:** HS—Odessa, Texas, 2011 (16th round). **Signed by:** Max Semler.

Intrigued by Marquez's athleticism and speed, the Mets will allow him to play wide receiver for Texas Tech for two years before he must decide whether he wants to pursue baseball or football. A 16th-round pick last June, he signed for $325,000 at the Aug. 15 deadline. Under MLB provisions for two-sport athletes, New York will spread his bonus over three years, and the club also agreed to pay his tuition for two years. A running back at Odessa (Texas) High, Marquez rushed for 2,210 yards and 29 touchdowns as a senior, and he also was a Texas state finalist in the long jump. His top-of-the-scale speed translates to the baseball diamond, where he can get from home to first base in 4.0 seconds from the right side of the plate. He played shortstop in high school, but scouts envision him fitting best in center field because of his ability to cover so much ground. Marquez has a clean swing he uses to slash line drives into the gaps and then run. He has below-average power, but that's OK given his positional profile and projected role as leadoff batter. Marquez has a passion for baseball and sold New York on his makeup. Now all he needs is repetitions on diamond, which will be curtailed by his football commitment. Marquez didn't participate in instructional league and won't rejoin the Mets until his academic year ends in May. He'll make his pro debut in the Gulf Coast League after some time in extended spring training.

Year	Club (League)	Class	AVG	G	AB	R	H	2B	3B	HR	RBI	BB	SO	SB	CS	OBP	SLG
2011	Did not play—Signed late																

26 LOGAN VERRETT, RHP

BA GRADE

45
HIGH

Born: June 19, 1990. **B-T:** R-R. **Ht.:** 6-2. **Wt.:** 180. **Drafted:** Baylor, 2011 (3rd round). **Signed by:** Max Semler.

Verrett attracted first-round buzz with a strong 2010 Cape Cod League performance, but he fell to the third round last June after a solid if unspectacular junior year at Baylor. He reeled off a 27-inning scoreless streak toward the end of the college season after starting the year slowly. He signed at the Aug. 15 deadline for $425,000 and will make his pro debut in 2012 at one of New York's Class A affiliates. Verrett's best pitch is a slider that can reach the mid-80s. Just as significant, he throws it both for strikes and as an effective swing-and-miss pitch at the back foot of lefthanders. Verrett's fastball typically ranges from 88-92 mph and touches 94, albeit with limited life. He didn't throw a changeup much at Baylor and his is a rudimentary offering with some sinking action. He's a solid athlete who repeats his delivery, so further development of his changeup isn't out of the question. Verrett ultimately may fit best in the bullpen, where his fastball would play up a tick, but the Mets plan to develop him as a starter for now.

Year	Club (League)	Class	W	L	ERA	G	GS	CG	SV	IP	H	HR	BB	SO	K/9	WHIP	AVG
2011	Did not play—Signed late																

27 JACK LEATHERSICH, LHP

BA GRADE

45
HIGH

Born: July 14, 1990. **B-T:** R-L. **Ht.:** 5-11. **Wt.:** 205. **Drafted:** Massachusetts-Lowell, 2011 (5th round). **Signed by:** Art Pontarelli.

Leathersich ranked second among all NCAA Division II pitchers with 12.7 strikeouts per nine innings in 2011 and became the first Massachusetts-Lowell player drafted since Marlins 29th-rounder Aaron Easton in 2004. After signing him for $110,000, the Mets shifted Leathersich to the bullpen with Brooklyn, where he made one- or two-inning relief appearances every five days. He struck out 26 of the 47 batters he faced while allowing just six hits. Leathersich sat at 88-92 mph as a starter in college but ran his heater up to 96 with good life as a reliever. His curveball has big, hard break and graded as a plus-plus pitch at times in short bursts out of the Cyclones bullpen. Leathersich has below-average command and little feel for a changeup at this stage. Add in mechanical concerns—he throws across his body and his arm recoils after release—and he may be limited to a relief role. New York intends to develop Leathersich as a starter, but his potential as an impact lefty reliever could hasten a role switch and put him on the fast track.

Year	Club (League)	Class	W	L	ERA	G	GS	CG	SV	IP	H	HR	BB	SO	K/9	WHIP	AVG
2011	Brooklyn (NYP)	SS	0	0	0.71	9	0	0	1	13	6	0	3	26	18.5	0.71	.136
Minor League Totals			0	0	0.71	9	0	0	1	13	6	0	3	26	18.5	0.71	.136

28 ROBERT CARSON, LHP

BA GRADE

45
HIGH

Born: Jan. 23, 1989. **B-T:** L-L. **Ht.:** 6-3. **Wt.:** 220. **Drafted:** HS—Hattiesburg, Miss., 2007 (14th round). **Signed by:** Benny Latino.

A 21-year-old Carson vaulted to Double-A for the second half of the 2010 season, whereupon Eastern League batters lit him up for an 8.32 ERA over 10 starts. He made incremental improvements in a return engagement last year but still carries a 5.95 ERA through 177 innings for Binghamton. A tall and broad-shouldered lefty, Carson can look terrific in bullpen sessions, but that same pitcher doesn't always appear in games because he tends to guide the ball rather than letting it fly. His game is all about power. He pitches at 92 mph and touches 95 with a tailing fastball—he hit 97 mph as a reliever in the Arizona Fall League—while mixing in plenty of high-80s cutters. Carson's performance against Double-A lefties doesn't speak well to the quality of his low-80s slider or his ability to set up batters—they've hit .297 and slugged .453 against him. He'll show an average changeup on occasion, though he lacks much feel for the pitch. The Mets like Carson's athleticism and arm strength, and they protected him on their 40-man roster after his AFL stint. He'll need to improve his slider and his command to earn more than a cursory look in the big leagues.

Year	Club (League)	Class	W	L	ERA	G	GS	CG	SV	IP	H	HR	BB	SO	K/9	WHIP	AVG
2007	Mets (GCL)	R	1	0	5.00	4	1	0	0	9	8	1	5	9	9.0	1.44	.216
2008	Mets (GCL)	R	1	0	1.57	5	5	0	0	23	11	0	6	25	9.8	0.74	.143
	Kingsport (APP)	R	2	3	1.76	6	6	0	0	31	29	1	18	21	6.2	1.53	.274
2009	Savannah (SAL)	LoA	8	10	3.21	25	25	2	0	132	139	4	45	90	6.2	1.40	.270
2010	St. Lucie (FSL)	HiA	7	5	4.17	17	16	0	0	86	98	5	33	69	7.2	1.52	.287
	Binghamton (EL)	AA	1	6	8.32	10	10	0	0	49	68	7	23	30	5.5	1.87	.343
2011	Binghamton (EL)	AA	4	11	5.05	25	24	0	0	128	154	14	55	91	6.4	1.63	.299
Minor League Totals			24	35	4.31	92	87	2	0	458	507	32	185	335	6.6	1.51	.284

29 JOSH SATIN, 3B/2B

BA GRADE
40
LOW

Born: Dec. 23, 1984. **B-T:** R-R. **Ht.:** 6-2. **Wt.:** 200. **Drafted:** California, 2008 (6th round). **Signed by:** Doug Thurman.

Satin failed to hit .300 for California as either a sophomore or junior, but he broke out in a big way as a senior in 2008, batting .379/.500/.723 with 18 homers. He signed quickly for $25,000 as a sixth-round pick and defied the odds by making his big league debut last September. He took home Mets minor league player of the year honors in 2011 after batting .323/.411/.495 with 12 homers and 43 doubles at the upper levels of the system. Scouts never have loved Satin's tools, but he has produced results in pro ball, with the caveat that he's been old for each level. Satin works counts, patiently waiting for pitches he can drive into the gaps. He occasionally shows home run power to his pull side. He can handle different types of pitches and is a good situational hitter, but he strikes out too much to hit more than .275 or so. Satin has played more games at second base than anywhere else, but he's a well below-average runner who has the hands but not the quickness for the keystone. His arm is average and accurate, and the Mets made third and first base his primary positions during the second half of 2011. He also played left field in the Venezuelan League in the offseason. Satin could help a National League club in a bench role, serving as a pinch-hitter and multi-positional fill-in.

Year	Club (League)	Class	AVG	G	AB	R	H	2B	3B	HR	RBI	BB	SO	SB	CS	OBP	SLG
2008	Kingsport (APP)	R	.583	3	12	3	7	2	0	1	2	1	2	0	0	.615	1.000
	Brooklyn (NYP)	SS	.280	45	143	21	40	10	2	4	13	16	28	0	1	.350	.462
2009	Savannah (SAL)	LoA	.284	125	440	62	125	38	0	7	60	73	103	0	3	.385	.418
	St. Lucie (FSL)	HiA	.364	7	22	6	8	2	0	1	5	5	7	0	0	.464	.591
2010	St. Lucie (FSL)	HiA	.316	58	209	27	66	15	0	5	35	30	50	1	5	.406	.459
	Binghamton (EL)	AA	.308	79	286	49	88	24	1	7	39	36	71	1	0	.395	.472
2011	Binghamton (EL)	AA	.325	94	338	60	110	35	2	11	60	57	91	2	2	.423	.538
	Buffalo (IL)	AAA	.317	38	145	17	46	8	0	1	16	14	33	1	2	.381	.393
	New York (NL)	MAJ	.200	15	25	3	5	1	0	0	2	1	11	0	0	.259	.240
Major League Totals			.200	15	25	3	5	1	0	0	2	1	11	0	0	.259	.240
Minor League Totals			.307	449	1595	245	490	134	5	37	230	232	385	5	13	.397	.467

30 DANNY MUNO, SS

BA GRADE
45
HIGH

Born: Feb. 9, 1989. **B-T:** B-R. **Ht.:** 5-11. **Wt.:** 175. **Drafted:** Fresno State, 2011 (8th round). **Signed by:** Doug Thurman.

Muno served as starting shortstop and offensive catalyst for Fresno State's 2008 national championship team as a freshman. He shifted to third base as a Bulldogs senior in 2011 but moved back to shortstop with Brooklyn after signing for $10,000 as a Mets eighth-round pick. He won the New York-Penn League batting (.355) and on-base (.466) crowns, also sharing the league lead with 23 doubles while driving the Cyclones into the playoffs. Muno launched the ball out of Citi Field during one batting-practice session, but power probably will be the least of his tools. He knows the strike zone and has the bat speed from both sides of the plate to hit for a solid average, though not all scouts trust that he'll be physical enough to be anything than a fringy offensive player. He's a slightly above-average runner with strong baserunning instincts. Muno makes the routine plays at shortstop but lacks the range to hold down the position on an everyday basis. He has ample arm strength for either second or third base. His overall package of tools profiles best at second base or in a utility role. After his excellent pro debut, he could jump to high Class A in 2012.

Year	Club (League)	Class	AVG	G	AB	R	H	2B	3B	HR	RBI	BB	SO	SB	CS	OBP	SLG
2011	Brooklyn (NYP)	SS	.355	59	220	45	78	23	3	2	24	43	39	9	4	.466	.514
Minor League Totals			.355	59	220	45	78	23	3	2	24	43	39	9	4	.466	.514

New York Yankees

BY JOHN MANUEL

Since becoming general manager of the Yankees in 1998, Brian Cashman has overseen a franchise that has missed the playoffs only once while winning 100 games six times and earning four World Series championships. Yet it's impossible to evaluate Cashman's tenure or the team's success without acknowledging its financial advantages.

New York ranked second in major league payroll in 1998 and first every season since, spending $2.4 billion on players. It had $200 million-plus payrolls for the last seven consecutive seasons. When the Yankees don't sign a big-name free agent they want such as

Cliff Lee—who spurned them for the Phillies last offseason—it's considered an upset.

New York's finances make it possible for it to owe 10 players a total of $167 million for 2012, from Curtis Granderson at $10 million to Alex Rodriguez at $29 million. But even the Yankees need low-cost players to supplement those eight-figure big leaguers. Minor league guru Mark Newman, pro scouting director Billy Eppler and scouting director Damon Oppenheimer have done their part to that end.

In 2011, New York's best rookies were products of its Latin American program. Ivan Nova's 16 wins led all big league rookies, while Eduardo Nunez started a total of 81 games at four different positions. Top prospect Jesus Montero made a quick impact in September and positioned himself for a full-time role in 2012 as a DH and part-time catcher.

The big league roster included key pro scouting pickups Bartolo Colon and Freddy Garcia in the rotation and Cory Wade in the bullpen. Oppenheimer draftees Brett Gardner, Ian Kennedy (in Arizona after being used in a December 2009 trade for Granderson) and David Robertson enjoyed all-star-caliber seasons. The latter two are part of a productive 2006 Yankees draft class that has sent 10 players to the majors.

New York has more on the way, starting with Montero, righthander Dellin Betances (another 2006 draftee) and Mexican lefty Manny Banuelos. Montero might not catch for many organizations, but he still might for the Yankees, who look more for offense from their backstops. With few attractive pitching options on the free-agent market, New York could turn to Banuelos or Betances in 2012. And at the other end of the spectrum, Yankees affiliates won championships in the Rookie-level Gulf Coast and short-season New York-Penn leagues.

It wasn't all great news for New York on the player-

Rookie righthander Ivan Nova emerged as New York's second-best starting pitcher

TOP 30 PROSPECTS

1. Jesus Montero, c	16. D.J. Mitchell, rhp
2. Manny Banuelos, lhp	17. Bryan Mitchell, rhp
3. Dellin Betances, rhp	18. Brandon Laird, 3b/of
4. Gary Sanchez, c	19. Zoilo Almonte, of
5. Mason Williams, of	20. Tyler Austin, 3b/1b
6. Dante Bichette Jr., 3b	21. David Phelps, rhp
7. Ravel Santana, of	22. Zach Nuding, rhp
8. Austin Romine, c	23. Mark Montgomery, rhp
9. J.R. Murphy, c/3b	24. Jake Cave, of
10. Slade Heathcott, of	25. Claudio Custodio, ss
11. Brett Marshall, rhp	26. David Adams, 2b
12. Cito Culver, ss	27. Nik Turley, lhp
13. Ramon Flores, of/1b	28. Greg Bird, c/1b
14. Angelo Gumbs, 2b	29. Chase Whitley, rhp
15. Adam Warren, rhp	30. Branden Pinder, rhp

development front. Righthander Andrew Brackman, a 2007 first-round pick who collected nearly $6 million on the big league deal he signed and made just three major league appearances, didn't have his $2.2 million option for 2012 picked up after a terrible season. He contemplated quitting baseball and has gone 15-29, 5.11 as a pro. And outside of Banuelos, the Yankees continue to struggle to develop lefties.

But on Cashman's watch, New York has been the majors' most consistent winner and produced its share of homegrown talent. As the GM begins a new three-year contract, it's easy to say that he has earned it.

ORGANIZATION OVERVIEW

General Manager: Brian Cashman. **Farm Director:** Pat Roessler. **Scouting Director:** Damon Oppenheimer.

Class	Team	League	W	L	Pct	Finish*	Manager(s)
Majors	New York Yankees	American	97	65	.599	1st (14)	Joe Girardi
Triple-A	Scranton/WB Yankees	International	73	69	.514	7th (14)	Dave Miley
Double-A	Trenton Thunder	Eastern	68	73	.482	8th (12)	Tony Franklin
High A	Tampa Yankees	Florida State	74	64	.536	5th (12)	Luis Sojo
Low A	Charleston RiverDogs	South Atlantic	55	85	.393	t-13th (14)	Aaron Ledesma
Short-season	Staten Island Yankees	New York-Penn	45	28	.616	1st (14)†	Tom Slater
Rookie	GCL Yankees	Gulf Coast	37	23	.617	3rd (15)†	Carlos Mendoza
Overall 2011 Minor League Record			352	342	.507	13th (30)	

*Finish in overall standings (No. of teams in league). †League champion.

LAST YEAR'S TOP 30

Player, Pos.		Status
1.	Jesus Montero, c	No. 1
2.	Gary Sanchez, c	No. 4
3.	Dellin Betances, rhp	No. 3
4.	Manny Banuelos, lhp	No. 2
5.	Andrew Brackman, rhp	Dropped out
6.	Austin Romine, c	No. 8
7.	Hector Noesi, rhp	Majors
8.	Eduardo Nunez, ss/3b	Majors
9.	Slade Heathcott, of	No. 10
10.	Brandon Laird, 3b	No. 18
11.	Brett Marshall, rhp	No. 11
12.	Adam Warren, rhp	No. 15
13.	Ivan Nova, rhp	Majors
14.	J.R. Murphy, c	No. 9
15.	Mason Williams, of	No. 5
16.	David Phelps, rhp	No. 21
17.	Graham Stoneburner, rhp	Dropped out
18.	D.J. Mitchell, rhp	No. 16
19.	Melky Mesa, of	Dropped out
20.	Corban Joseph, 2b	Dropped out
21.	Cito Culver, ss	No. 12
22.	David Adams, 2b	No. 26
23.	Bryan Mitchell, rhp	No. 17
24.	Jose A. Ramirez, rhp	Dropped out
25.	Angelo Gumbs, ss	No. 14
26.	Jeremy Bleich, lhp	Dropped out
27.	Daniel Brewer, of	Dropped out
28.	Tommy Kahnle, rhp	Dropped out
29.	Chase Whitley, rhp	No. 29
30.	Pat Venditte, rhp/lhp	Dropped out

BEST TOOLS

Best Hitter for Average	Jesus Montero
Best Power Hitter	Jesus Montero
Best Strike-Zone Discipline	Ramon Flores
Fastest Baserunner	Mason Williams
Best Athlete	Mason Williams
Best Fastball	Dellin Betances
Best Curveball	Dellin Betances
Best Slider	Mark Montgomery
Best Changeup	Manny Banuelos
Best Control	Nik Turley
Best Defensive Catcher	Austin Romine
Best Defensive Infielder	Cito Culver
Best Infield Arm	Cito Culver
Best Defensive Outfielder	Mason Williams
Best Outfield Arm	Ravel Santana

PROJECTED 2015 LINEUP

Catcher	Austin Romine
First Base	Mark Teixeira
Second Base	Robinson Cano
Third Base	Alex Rodriguez
Shortstop	Eduardo Nunez
Left Field	Brett Gardner
Center Field	Mason Williams
Right Field	Curtis Granderson
Designated Hitter	Jesus Montero
No. 1 Starter	CC Sabathia
No. 2 Starter	Manny Banuelos
No. 3 Starter	Ivan Nova
No. 4 Starter	Dellin Betances
No. 5 Starter	Phil Hughes
Closer	David Robertson

TOP PROSPECTS OF THE DECADE

Year	Player, Pos.	2011 Org.
2002	Drew Henson, 3b	Out of baseball
2003	Jose Contreras, rhp	Phillies
2004	Dioner Navarro, c	Dodgers
2005	Eric Duncan, 3b	Cardinals
2006	Phil Hughes, rhp	Yankees
2007	Phil Hughes, rhp	Yankees
2008	Joba Chamberlain, rhp	Yankees
2009	Austin Jackson, of	Tigers
2010	Jesus Montero, c	Yankees
2011	Jesus Montero, c	Yankees

TOP DRAFT PICKS OF THE DECADE

Year	Player, Pos.	2011 Org.
2002	Brandon Weeden, rhp (2nd round)	Out of baseball
2003	Eric Duncan, 3b	Cardinals
2004	Phil Hughes, rhp	Yankees
2005	C.J. Hughes, ss	Out of baseball
2006	Ian Kennedy, rhp	Diamondbacks
2007	Andrew Brackman, rhp	Yankees
2008	*Gerrit Cole, rhp	Pirates
2009	Slade Heathcott, of	Yankees
2010	Cito Culver, ss	Yankees
2011	Dante Bichette Jr., 3b	Yankees

*Did not sign.

LARGEST BONUSES IN CLUB HISTORY

Hideki Irabu, 1997	$8,500,000
Jose Contreras, 2002	$6,000,000
Andrew Brackman, 2007	$3,350,000
Gary Sanchez, 2009	$3,000,000
Willy Mo Pena, 1999	$2,440,000

NEW YORK YANKEES

TOP 2012 ROOKIE: Jesus Montero, c. His righthanded power should fit nicely in a lineup loaded with lefthanded bats.

BREAKOUT PROSPECT: Tyler Austin, 3b/1b. A career .350 hitter as a pro, he's ready for the full-season stage.

SLEEPER: Matt Tracy, lhp. A two-way player at Mississippi, Tracy is the rare senior sign with upside, hitting 94 mph at times.

SOURCE OF TOP 30 TALENT			
Homegrown	30	Acquired	0
College	7	Trades	0
Junior college	2	Rule 5 draft	0
High school	14	Independent leagues	0
Draft-and-follow	0	Free agents/waivers	0
Nondrafted free agents	0		
International	7		

LF
Ramon Flores (13)
Ben Gamel
Abe Almonte

CF
Mason Williams (5)
Ravel Santana (7)
Slade Heathcott (10)
Daniel Lopez
Eduardo Sosa

RF
Zoilo Almonte (19)
Jake Cave (24)
Yeicok Calderon
Melky Mesa
Daniel Brewer
Kelvin DeLeon
Justin James

3B
Dante Bichette Jr. (6)
Brandon Laird (18)
Rob Segedin
Zach Wilson

SS
Cito Culver (12)
Claudio Custodio (25)
Jose Pirela

2B
Angelo Gumbs (14)
David Adams (26)
Jose Rosario
Corban Joseph
Kelvin Castro

1B
Tyler Austin (20)
Greg Bird (28)
Matt Duran
Rob Lyerly
Austin Jones

C
Jesus Montero (1)
Gary Sanchez (4)
Austin Romine (8)
J.R. Murphy (9)
Isaias Tejeda
Kyle Higashioka

LHP	
LHSP	**LHRP**
Manny Banuelos (2)	Cesar Cabral
Nik Turley (27)	Matt Tracy
Daniel Camarena	Kramer Sneed
Evan DeLuca	
Evan Rutckyj	
Jeremy Bleich	
Chaz Hebert	

RHP	
RHSP	**RHRP**
Dellin Betances (3)	Mark Montgomery (23)
Brett Marshall (11)	Chase Whitley (29)
Adam Warren (15)	Branden Pinder (30)
D.J. Mitchell (16)	George Kontos
Bryan Mitchell (17)	Tommy Kahnle
David Phelps (21)	Kevin Whelan
Zach Nuding (22)	Brad Meyers
Graham Stoneburner	Caleb Cotham
Jordan Cote	Shane Greene
Jairo Heredia	Phil Wetherell
Mickey O'Brien	Zach Arneson
Jose A. Ramirez	Dan Burawa
Taylor Morton	Brett Gerritse
Rookie Davis	Rob Paullus
Hayden Sharp	Adam Smith
Joey Maher	

RHP/LHP
Pat Venditte

2011   BONUSES: $6.3 MILLION

BEST PURE HITTER: 3B Dante Bichette Jr. (1s), the club's top pick, got off to a slow start before his natural timing and bat-to-ball skills took over. He was named Rookie-level Gulf Coast League MVP after hitting .342/.446/.505.

BEST POWER HITTER: The Yankees emphasized pop in this draft and got it from both sides of the plate. Bichette has strength and OF Jake Cave (6) has fast hands, but lefthanded-hitting C/1B Greg Bird (4) has the most raw power. Signed for $1.1 million, the largest bonus in New York's draft class, he fits in the system with other bat-first catchers such as Jesus Montero, Gary Sanchez and J.R. Murphy.

FASTEST RUNNER: Cave, who has above-average speed, is the best of a pedestrian lot of runners.

BEST DEFENSIVE PLAYER: Cave threw 94 mph off the mound and fits the right-field profile. The Yankees believe Bichette not only will stay in the infield but also will be an asset defensively at third base. He has solid hands, a plus arm and the agility to defend bunts.

BEST FASTBALL: RHPs Phil Wetherell (8) and Zach Arneson (9) both project as relievers, with fastballs that sit at 92-95 mph. Physical RHP Rookie Davis (14) has touched 94.

BEST SECONDARY PITCH: RHP Mark Montgomery (11) posted a 0.89 ERA at Longwood and showed why as a pro, using a slider that grades as a major league plus pitch already. LHP Daniel Camarena (20) shows promising spin and shape with his curveball.

BEST PRO DEBUT: Bichette. Montgomery struck out 51 in 28 innings, picking up 15 saves and posting a 1.91 ERA while spending most of his time at low Class A Charleston. RHP Branden Pinder (16) recorded a 1.16 ERA and 14 saves for short-season New York-Penn League champion Staten Island, striking out 38 in 31 innings.

BEST ATHLETE: Cave, who was recruited as a two-way player by Louisiana State. It cost $800,000 to sign him away from the Tigers.

MOST INTRIGUING BACKGROUND: Bichette's father Dante Sr. hit 274 major league homers and is now a nationally ranked senior tennis player. OF Justin James (13) is the son of former big league outfielder Dion, who played for the Yankees for four seasons.

CLOSEST TO THE MAJORS: Montgomery and Pinder should hop on the fast track. Bichette should progress quicker than a typical high school hitter.

BEST LATE-ROUND PICK: Montgomery and Pinder. Camarena, who signed for $335,000, has the

makings of a four-pitch mix as well as aptitude. Davis earned $550,000 because of his arm strength.

THE ONE WHO GOT AWAY: For the second time in four years, New York lost a second-rounder because of medical concerns; LHP Sam Stafford (2) returned to Texas and hopes to have a better future than Scott Bittle, who eventually made six pro appearances before the Cardinals released him in 2011. RHP Mathew Troupe (17) reminds the Yankees a bit of Ian Kennedy and wound up at Arizona.

ASSESSMENT: The Yankees went young, not signing a college player in the first seven rounds. Their draftees have a lot of upside but will require patience.

2010   BONUSES: $6.7 MILLION

OF Mason Williams (4) had a breakthrough 2011, ranking as the top prospect in the New York-Penn League. SS Cito Culver (1) and 2B Angelo Gumbs (2) haven't progressed as rapidly but are also promising athletes.

GRADE: B

2009   BONUSES: $7.6 MILLION

New York likes what it has seen from OF Slade Heathcott (1) and C/3B J.R. Murphy (2)—when they've been able to stay healthy. RHPs Adam Warren (4) is ready to help the Yankees as a middle reliever or trade fodder.

GRADE: C

2008   BONUSES: $5.1 MILLION

New York failed to sign RHPs Gerrit Cole (1), who went No. 1 overall three years later, or Scott Bittle (2). Their top signee, LHP Jeremy Bleich (1s), hasn't been the same since labrum surgery in 2010. 2B David Adams (3) has had injury issues too. This crop's best current hope is RHP Brett Marshall (6).

GRADE: D

2007   BONUSES: $8.0 MILLION

C Austin Romine (2) may be New York's catcher of the future, but it has to wonder what might have been. The Yankees paid nearly $6 million for two big league innings from Andrew Brackman (1) and declined to pick up his option this offseason. RHPs Chris Carpenter (18) and Drew Storen (34) and OF Eric Thames (39) all reached the majors after declining to sign with New York.

GRADE: C

Draft analysis by John Manuel (2011) and Jim Callis (2007-10). Numbers in parentheses indicate draft rounds.

1 JESUS MONTERO, C

Born: Nov. **28, 1989. B-T:** R-R. **Ht.:** 6-4. **Wt.:** 235.
Signed: Venezuela, 2006. **Signed by:** Carlos Rios/
Ricardo Finol.

BA GRADE
70
LOW

TOMASSO DeROSA

Montero should be ready for the New York spotlight, because few prospects have received such scrutiny in the minor leagues. It started as soon as he signed out of Venezuela in 2006 for $2 million. His bonus later was reduced to $1.65 million, and the scout who signed him, Carlos Rios, was fired for receiving kickbacks on international deals. Montero rifled through the lower levels of the minor leagues before spending the last two seasons at Triple-A Scranton/Wilkes-Barre. Scouts thought he looked bored in 2011 before his first callup to the majors. He sizzled in September, slugging two homers against the Orioles in his fourth game and earning a spot on New York's postseason roster.

No organization has produced offensive catchers like the Yankees, and club officials admit they prioritize hitting ability in their catchers more than most organizations do. Montero fits New York's profile. One of the more accomplished righthanded hitting prospects to come around in years, Montero combines hand-eye coordination with an innate ability to get the fat part of the bat on the ball. While he's not a walk machine, he has gained a better feel for the strike zone with experience. His front-foot swing isn't for everyone, but his tremendous strength makes it work and he projects to hit .290-.300 with well above-average power. His natural swing path produces excellent pop to the opposite field, and he should be able to exploit the dimensions at Yankee Stadium. Defensively, Montero continues to work hard to overcome his huge frame, and his offensive production makes him more palatable behind the plate. Despite plenty of attention from catching coordinator Julio Mosquera, Montero never will grade better than below-average as a receiver. New York believes that will be acceptable, citing Posada's career. Montero did cut his passed balls from 15 in 2010 to seven last season, when his .997 fielding per-

SCOUTING GRADES

Batting: 65.   **Defense:** 40.
Power: 70.   **Arm:** 50.
Speed: 25.

Based on 20-80 scouting scale, where 50 represents major league average, and future projection rather than present tools.

centage led International League backstops. Despite solid arm strength, he threw out just 21 percent of the 93 basestealers who tested him in 2011. His long throwing stroke costs him consistency and accuracy. He's a well below-average runner who's prone to hitting into double plays.

Montero's righthanded power fits well into a New York lineup that overly relies on the aging Derek Jeter and Alex Rodriguez from that side of the plate. Montero is ready to catch 50 or so games a year while also getting regular at-bats at DH. His defense probably would be too much of a liability for him to catch any more. He should get 400-500 big league plate appearances in 2012 and follow Robinson Cano as New York's next homegrown all-star position player.

Year	Club (League)	Class	AVG	G	AB	R	H	2B	3B	HR	RBI	BB	SO	SB	CS	OBP	SLG
2007	Yankees (GCL)	R	.280	33	107	13	30	6	0	3	19	12	18	0	0	.366	.421
2008	Charleston (SAL)	LoA	.326	132	525	86	171	34	1	17	87	37	83	2	1	.376	.491
2009	Tampa (FSL)	HiA	.356	48	180	26	64	15	1	8	37	14	26	0	0	.406	.583
	Trenton (EL)	AA	.317	44	167	19	53	10	0	9	33	14	21	0	0	.370	.539
2010	Scranton/W-B (IL)	AAA	.289	123	453	66	131	34	3	21	75	46	91	0	0	.353	.517
2011	Scranton/W-B (IL)	AAA	.288	109	420	52	121	19	1	18	67	36	98	0	0	.348	.467
	New York (AL)	MAJ	.328	18	61	9	20	4	0	4	12	7	17	0	0	.406	.590
Major League Totals			.328	18	61	9	20	4	0	4	12	7	17	0	0	.406	.590
Minor League Totals			.308	489	1852	262	570	118	6	76	318	159	337	2	1	.366	.501

2 MANNY BANUELOS, LHP

Born: March 13, 1991. **B-T:** L-L. **Ht.:** 5-11. **Wt.:** 155. **Signed:** Mexico. 2008. **Signed by:** Lee Sigman.

Signed out of Mexico as a command-oriented lefthander, Banuelos has seen his stuff evolve since, and it was on full display in big league camp in 2011. He struck out 14 in 13 innings while making a bid for a big league role. He instead spent the entire season in the minors, pitching a career-high 130 innings and reaching Triple-A but also leading the system with 71 walks. Banuelos beats hitters with three plus pitches when he's at his best, getting swings and misses in the strike zone like an ace. His fastball sits at 89-94 mph and touches 96. His curveball has some downer action and power, often parking at 79-80 mph, and he has good arm speed on his fading changeup. The Yankees believe Banuelos is still learning how to harness his quick arm and improved stuff, and he needs to be pitch-efficient rather than going for strikeouts. He struggles at times to locate his fastball to his glove side, which made him vulnerable against righthanders, who hit .285 against him in 2011. Banuelos has shown frontline stuff and flashed true command, tantalizing yet failing to put it all together. He should make his big league debut in 2012, probably before September. He has the upside to be New York's best homegrown pitcher since Andy Pettitte.

BA GRADE 65 MEDIUM

Year	Club (League)	Class	W	L	ERA	G	GS	CG	SV	IP	H	HR	BB	SO	K/9	WHIP	AVG
2008	Yankees (GCL)	R	4	1	2.57	12	3	0	0	42	32	3	13	37	7.9	1.07	.208
2009	Charleston (SAL)	LoA	9	5	2.67	25	19	0	0	108	88	4	28	104	8.7	1.07	.219
	Tampa (FSL)	HiA	0	0	0.00	1	0	0	0	1	0	0	0	2	18.0	0.00	.000
2010	Yankees (GCL)	R	0	0	1.80	2	2	0	0	5	1	0	3	6	10.8	0.80	.063
	Tampa (FSL)	HiA	0	3	2.23	10	10	0	0	44	38	1	14	62	12.6	1.17	.230
	Trenton (EL)	AA	0	1	3.52	3	3	0	0	15	15	2	8	17	10.0	1.50	.273
2011	Trenton (EL)	AA	4	5	3.59	20	20	0	0	95	94	7	52	94	8.9	1.53	.263
	Scranton/W-B (IL)	AAA	2	2	4.19	7	7	1	0	34	36	2	19	31	8.1	1.60	.277
Minor League Totals			19	17	3.02	80	64	1	0	345	304	19	137	353	9.2	1.28	.237

3 DELLIN BETANCES, RHP

Born: March 23, 1988. **B-T:** R-R. **Ht.:** 6-8. **Wt.:** 260. **Drafted:** HS—New York, 2006 (8th round). **Signed by:** Cesar Presbott/Brian Barber.

In late September, Betances became the 10th player from the Yankees' 2006 draft class to appear in the majors. A New York City product, he signed for $1 million, a record for the eighth round at the time. He has developed slowly and had surgery to reinforce an elbow ligament in 2009, but he has matured into a physical power pitcher with swing-and-miss stuff. Betances works at 91-95 mph with his fastball and can get it up to 97, delivering it on a steep downhill plane. At times he throws his four-seamer with natural cutting action. He throws a fair amount of strikes with his heater but has a harder time harnessing his power curveball, which sits in the low 80s. New York always has believed in Betances' changeup, a solid pitch that flashed above average less frequently in 2011 than it had in 2010. His stiff delivery and modest athleticism prevent him from repeating his delivery and throwing consistent quality strikes. Betances threw a career-best 136 innings in 2011, and his lack of command was exposed a bit at higher levels. His stuff is so good, he could still be effective merely with average control, much like A.J. Burnett. Betances will return to Triple-A to start 2012.

BA GRADE 65 HIGH

Year	Club (League)	Class	W	L	ERA	G	GS	CG	SV	IP	H	HR	BB	SO	K/9	WHIP	AVG
2006	Yankees (GCL)	R	0	1	1.16	7	7	0	0	23	14	1	7	27	10.4	0.90	.173
2007	Staten Island (NYP)	SS	1	2	3.60	6	6	0	0	25	24	0	17	29	10.4	1.64	.255
2008	Yankees (GCL)	R	0	1	8.53	3	2	0	0	6	13	0	3	6	8.5	2.53	.406
	Charleston (SAL)	LoA	9	4	3.67	22	22	0	0	115	87	9	59	135	10.5	1.27	.208
2009	Tampa (FSL)	HiA	2	5	5.48	11	11	0	0	44	48	2	27	44	8.9	1.69	.277
2010	Tampa (FSL)	HiA	8	1	1.77	14	14	0	0	71	43	1	19	88	11.2	0.87	.169
	Trenton (EL)	AA	0	0	3.77	3	3	0	0	14	10	3	3	20	12.6	0.91	.200
2011	Trenton (EL)	AA	4	6	3.42	21	21	0	0	105	86	7	55	115	9.8	1.34	.219
	Scranton/W-B (IL)	AAA	0	3	5.14	4	4	1	0	21	16	2	15	27	11.6	1.48	.208
	New York (AL)	MAJ	0	0	6.75	2	1	0	0	3	1	0	6	2	6.8	2.63	.125
Major League Totals			0	0	6.75	2	1	0	0	3	1	0	6	2	6.8	2.63	.125
Minor League Totals			24	23	3.49	91	90	1	0	426	341	25	205	491	10.4	1.28	.217

4 GARY SANCHEZ, C

Born: Dec. 2, 1992. **B-T:** R-R. **Ht.:** 6-2. **Wt.:** 195. **Signed:** Dominican Republic, 2009. **Signed by:** Raymon Sanchez/Victor Mata.

Signed for $3 million, Sanchez ranked as the Rookie-level Gulf Coast League's No. 1 prospect in a banner 2010 pro debut, then led low Class A Charleston with 17 homers in 82 games in 2011. He was suspended for two weeks in late May for insubordination and missed the final three weeks of the season with a sprained left thumb. Sanchez has a purer swing and more patience at the plate than Jesus Montero, to whom he's often compared. Sanchez has similar raw power, too, and scouts project him as a plus hitter in terms of both average and pop. He's willing to go deep into counts looking for a pitch to drive, which can lead to strikeouts. He struggles to handle breaking balls offensively and defensively, and some scouts reported that he stopped calling for them behind the plate. Sanchez led the South Atlantic League with 26 passed balls in just 60 games, and some scouts believe he's a lost cause as a receiver. He does have plus arm strength and threw out 31 percent of basestealers. He's a well below-average runner, like many catchers. A combination of money, immaturity and hype didn't help Sanchez, but he was one of the SAL's youngest players. He'll probably return to Charleston in 2012. If he doesn't improve defensively, he'll have to hit like Montero to remain a catcher long-term.

BA GRADE 60 HIGH

Year	Club (League)	Class	AVG	G	AB	R	H	2B	3B	HR	RBI	BB	SO	SB	CS	OBP	SLG
2010	Yankees (GCL)	R	.353	31	119	25	42	11	0	6	36	11	28	1	1	.419	.597
	Staten Island (NYP)	SS	.278	16	54	8	15	2	0	2	7	3	16	1	1	.333	.426
2011	Charleston (SAL)	LoA	.256	82	301	49	77	16	1	17	52	36	93	2	1	.335	.485
Minor League Totals			.283	129	474	82	134	29	1	25	95	50	137	4	3	.356	.506

5 MASON WILLIAMS, OF

Born: Aug. 21, 1991. **B-T:** L-R. **Ht.:** 6-0. **Wt.:** 150. **Drafted:** HS—Winter Garden, Fla., 2010 (4th round). **Signed by:** Jeff Deardorff.

Williams got the highest bonus in the Yankees' 2010 draft class, signing for $1.45 million in the fourth round to turn down his commitment to South Carolina. In his first extended taste of pro ball last summer, he led the short-season New York-Penn League in steals (28) and ranked second in batting (.349) to spark Staten Island to its sixth championship in 13 years. He ranked as the NY-P's top prospect. While he's not overly physical, Williams has the system's best all-around tools. He has a lively body with athleticism to spare and surprising strength. While at times he's a slasher, he has good natural timing and barrels balls consistently. His bat is quick enough for him to hit quality velocity. As Williams quiets his hands and uses his legs better, he could develop average power because his swing path has a little bit of loft. He's a prototypical center fielder with raw 80 speed on the 20-80 scouting scale, easy range and an average throwing arm. He still must add polish to his baserunning, basestealing and route-running in addition to his swing. Williams could be the Yankees' next great homegrown center fielder. He'll get his first full-season test in Charleston in 2012. He's on the verge of passing Slade Heathcott within the system but will have to watch Ravel Santana coming up behind him.

BA GRADE 60 HIGH

Year	Club (League)	Class	AVG	G	AB	R	H	2B	3B	HR	RBI	BB	SO	SB	CS	OBP	SLG
2010	Yankees (GCL)	R	.222	5	18	0	4	0	0	0	0	1	4	1	2	.263	.222
2011	Staten Island (NYP)	SS	.349	68	269	42	94	11	6	3	31	20	41	28	12	.395	.468
Minor League Totals			.341	73	287	42	98	11	6	3	31	21	45	29	14	.387	.453

6 DANTE BICHETTE JR., 3B

Born: Sept. 26, 1992. **B-T:** R-R. **Ht.:** 6-1. **Wt.:** 215. **Drafted:** HS—Orlando, 2011 (1st round supplemental). **Signed by:** Jeff Deardorff.

The son of the former all-star outfielder of the same name, Dante Jr. is a baseball rat who hit .640 as a high school senior and became the Yankee's top 2011 draft pick (51st overall). He signed quickly for $750,000 and adjusted on the fly after a slow start to pro ball, lowering his hands and quickening his swing. He earned top-prospect and MVP honors in the Gulf Coast League and led his team to the championship. Like his father, Bichette combines righthanded power and underrated athletic ability. He's an advanced hitter with good hand-eye coordination, present strength and above-average bat speed. He doesn't sell out for power, uses the whole field and has a mature two-strike approach. While area scouts considered Bichette a lock to move to the outfield while he was an amateur, he impressed New York with his agility, arm strength and aptitude at third base. He's an average runner. His work ethic impresses coaches and opponents alike, and he

BA GRADE 60 HIGH

should have the makeup to handle the Big Apple. Bichette's passion for the game helped him make a name for himself with his strong debut. He could move quickly, and if J.R. Murphy remains a catcher, the Yankees don't have another third-base prospect ahead of him. Bichette is ready to advance to low Class A in 2012.

Year	Club (League)	Class	AVG	G	AB	R	H	2B	3B	HR	RBI	BB	SO	SB	CS	OBP	SLG
2011	Yankees (GCL)	R	.342	52	196	33	67	17	3	3	47	30	41	3	3	.446	.505
	Staten Island (NYP)	SS	.143	2	7	1	1	0	0	1	1	1	2	0	1	.250	.571
Minor League Totals			.335	54	203	34	68	17	3	4	48	31	43	3	4	.440	.507

7 RAVEL SANTANA, OF

Born: May 1, 1992. **B-T:** R-R. **Ht.:** 6-2. **Wt.:** 175. **Signed:** Dominican Republic, 2008. **Signed by:** Victor Mata/Juan Rosario.

Signed for just $150,000 in November 2008, Santana made his U.S. debut in 2011 after spending two seasons in the Rookie-level Dominican Summer League. He ranked right behind Dante Bichette as the No. 2 prospect in the Gulf Coast League, ranking third in the league in slugging (.568) and fourth in homers (nine) despite missing the final two weeks after breaking his ankle in two places and damaging ligaments on Aug. 13. Wiry, lean and athletic, Santana could wind up with above-average or better tools across the board. His best present tool is his arm, which rates at least a 70 and earns some 80 grades on the 20-80 scouting scale. He's at least a plus runner and he plays an above-average center field. Santana's offensive ceiling is considerable, thanks to excellent bat speed, strength and loft in his swing and a willingness to use the whole field. He showed plus power as the season went along, gaining confidence as his pitch recognition improved.

BA GRADE 60 HIGH

He does have problems making contact against good breaking balls, though he made encouraging adjustments. Santana is one level behind Mason Williams and could move to right field if they wind up on the same roster. The Yankees expect Santana will be healthy enough for an assignment to Staten Island in June.

Year	Club (League)	Class	AVG	G	AB	R	H	2B	3B	HR	RBI	BB	SO	SB	CS	OBP	SLG
2009	Yankees 1 (DSL)	R	.207	7	29	4	6	2	1	0	3	4	8	1	0	.324	.345
	Yankees 2 (DSL)	R	.239	43	138	27	33	6	0	5	25	22	35	7	3	.361	.391
2010	Yankees 2 (DSL)	R	.322	63	199	46	64	10	1	10	38	35	38	22	5	.440	.533
2011	Yankees (GCL)	R	.296	41	162	43	48	11	3	9	29	17	40	10	3	.361	.568
Minor League Totals			.286	154	528	120	151	29	5	24	95	78	121	40	11	.390	.496

8 AUSTIN ROMINE, C

Born: Nov. 22, 1988. **B-T:** R-R. **Ht.:** 6-0. **Wt.:** 220. **Drafted:** HS—Lake Forest, Calif., 2007 (2nd round). **Signed by:** David Keith.

Romine became the third member of his family to reach the majors, following dad Kevin and older brother Andrew. He debuted in front of his parents and against his brother's team, the Angels, in September. It made for a positive end to a challenging season in which he missed much of June with a concussion and two weeks in August with a back injury. In an organization full of bat-first catchers, Romine sticks out for his athletic ability and solid defensive tools. Flexible and agile, he's a sound receiver who has added polish with experience. While he has plus arm strength, he's inconsistent with his throwing accuracy and has caught just 23 percent of basestealers in each of the last two seasons. Like his arm, Romine's raw power rates as above-average but doesn't play that well in games. His high leg kick results in streaky offensive production. He has become a poor runner and seemed to play with less energy in 2011. Some scouts thought Romine

BA GRADE 50 LOW

got stale repeating Double-A in 2011 and will watch closely to see if he responds to a promotion to Triple-A in 2012. His defense still could make him New York's long-term future catcher, with the offensive upside of a .270 hitter with 10 homers annually.

Year	Club (League)	Class	AVG	G	AB	R	H	2B	3B	HR	RBI	BB	SO	SB	CS	OBP	SLG
2007	Yankees (GCL)	R	.500	1	2	2	1	1	0	0	1	1	1	0	0	.667	1.000
2008	Charleston (SAL)	LoA	.300	104	407	66	122	24	1	10	49	25	56	3	0	.344	.437
2009	Tampa (FSL)	HiA	.276	118	442	61	122	28	3	13	72	29	78	11	5	.322	.441
2010	Trenton (EL)	AA	.268	115	455	61	122	31	0	10	69	37	94	2	0	.324	.402
2011	Trenton (EL)	AA	.286	85	336	43	96	13	0	6	47	32	60	2	2	.351	.378
	Scranton/W-B (IL)	AAA	.133	4	15	1	2	0	0	0	1	0	3	0	0	.133	.133
	New York (AL)	MAJ	.158	9	19	2	3	0	0	0	0	1	5	0	0	.200	.158
Major League Totals			.158	9	19	2	3	0	0	0	0	1	5	0	0	.200	.158
Minor League Totals			.281	427	1657	234	465	97	4	39	239	124	292	18	7	.333	.415

9 J.R. MURPHY, C/3B

BA GRADE

55

HIGH

Born: May 13, 1991. **B-T:** R-R. **Ht.:** 5-11. **Wt.:** 195. **Drafted:** HS—Bradenton, Fla., 2009 (2nd round). **Signed by:** Jeff Deardorff/Brian Barber.

The Yankees love offensive-minded catchers, and they paid Murphy $1.25 million in the second round of the 2009 draft to keep him from attending Miami. He outplayed Gary Sanchez offensively and defensively while sharing time with him at catcher in Charleston in 2011, earning a promotion to high Class A Tampa. His season ended shortly afterward in July when he fouled a ball off his left foot, breaking a bone. New York is trying to find a place for Murphy's bat, as he offers a balanced swing and consistent line-drive, gap-to-gap power. He projects to hit 10-15 homers annually with his present swing, which has a fairly flat path. A solid athlete and average runner, Murphy has improved defensively. He has gained average arm strength through better mechanics and a long-toss program, and he also has quickened his release. He threw out 24 percent of basestealers in 2011. He's still a fringy receiver and blocker but has made enough progress to stay in the catching conversation. He also saw time at third base in 2011, and his fringy speed also makes the outfield corners a possibility. Murphy's total package resembles that of 16-year big leaguer Todd Zeile. Murphy is ticketed for a return to high Class A, where he'll keep catching while getting reps at third and possibly in the outfield.

Year	Club (League)	Class	AVG	G	AB	R	H	2B	3B	HR	RBI	BB	SO	SB	CS	OBP	SLG
2009	Yankees (GCL)	R	.333	9	33	4	11	2	0	1	7	3	8	0	0	.405	.485
2010	Charleston (SAL)	LoA	.255	87	330	46	84	15	2	7	54	36	64	4	5	.327	.376
2011	Charleston (SAL)	LoA	.297	63	256	31	76	23	0	6	32	19	38	2	0	.343	.457
	Tampa (FSL)	HiA	.259	23	85	8	22	6	0	1	14	2	9	0	0	.270	.365
Minor League Totals			.274	182	704	89	193	46	2	15	107	60	119	6	5	.330	.409

10 SLADE HEATHCOTT, OF

BA GRADE

60

EXTREME

Born: Sept. 28, 1990. **B-T:** L-L. **Ht.:** 6-0. **Wt.:** 197. **Drafted:** HS—Texarkana, Texas, 2009 (1st round). **Signed by:** Mark Batchko/Tim Kelly.

Heathcott had an alcohol problem and a troubled family life in high school, yet he also was a two-way star who overcame a football-related knee injury to lead Texas High (Texarkana, Texas) to a state 4-A championship as a senior in 2009. The Yankees selected him 29th overall that June and signed him for $2.2 million. He has sought treatment for his alcohol use, but his career has been slowed by two surgeries on his throwing shoulder. Heathcott reminds New York of Brett Gardner, with the potential to hit for more power if he can become more patient and work himself into more hitter's counts. His injuries have cost him development time needed to improve his pitch selection. He's an explosive athlete whose energy level ingratiates him to teammates, managers and scouts. Heathcott's best present tools are his plus-plus speed and his defense, as he plays center field like a free safety. He's still an unrefined basestealer and needs to tame his aggressiveness in several phases of the game. His second shoulder operation, to reattach part of his previously repaired labrum, likely will cost him some of his formerly above-average arm strength. Heathcott has gotten his life in order, and the Yankees consider his makeup a plus. He'll report to high Class A in 2012 and see if his shoulder can hold up to a full season of play.

Year	Club (League)	Class	AVG	G	AB	R	H	2B	3B	HR	RBI	BB	SO	SB	CS	OBP	SLG
2009	Yankees (GCL)	R	.100	3	10	0	1	0	0	0	0	1	2	0	0	.182	.100
2010	Charleston (SAL)	LoA	.258	76	298	48	77	16	3	2	30	42	101	15	10	.359	.352
2011	Charleston (SAL)	LoA	.271	52	210	36	57	11	4	4	16	19	57	6	7	.342	.419
	Tampa (FSL)	HiA	.600	1	5	2	3	0	0	1	1	0	1	0	0	.600	1.200
Minor League Totals			.264	132	523	86	138	27	7	7	47	62	161	21	17	.351	.382

11 BRETT MARSHALL, RHP

BA GRADE

50

HIGH

Born: March 22, 1990. **B-T:** R-R. **Ht.:** 6-0. **Wt.:** 195. **Drafted:** HS—Baytown, Texas, 2008 (6th round). **Signed by:** Steve Boros.

Marshall was the highest-paid player in the Yankees' draft class in 2008, when they failed to sign first-rounder Gerrit Cole and second-rounder Scott Bittle. Marshall and Triple-A righties D.J. Mitchell and David Phelps should provide a decent return from that draft crop. Marshall just finished his first full, healthy season, nearly doubling his previous career high for innings with 140. Two years after Tommy John surgery, he didn't miss a start in 2011. Once envisioned as a power pitcher, Marshall fits more of a sinker/slider profile these days. He has toned down his delivery since signing and repeats it fairly well, allowing him to throw his fastball, slider and changeup for strikes. His fastball sat in the low 90s for much of last season, and the days of him boasting to club officials that he'd hit 100 one day appear to be behind him. His heater is more notable for its movement, especially down in the strike zone, than its velocity. Marshall gave up just two homers his last 55 innings, quite a feat for a 6-footer who doesn't get natural downward plane on his pitches. His slider and changeup are solid secondary pitches, and New York still plans on introducing a curve to his repertoire at some point. That may happen in 2012, when he'll move up to Double-A. He has the upside of a No. 3 starter.

Year	Club (League)	Class	W	L	ERA	G	GS	CG	SV	IP	H	HR	BB	SO	K/9	WHIP	AVG
2008	Yankees (GCL)	R	0	0	0.00	3	3	0	0	6	2	0	2	8	12.0	0.67	.087
2009	Charleston (SAL)	LoA	3	6	5.56	17	17	0	0	87	98	7	37	60	6.2	1.55	.290
2010	Yankees (GCL)	R	0	0	2.25	2	1	0	0	8	6	0	4	8	9.0	1.25	.194
	Charleston (SAL)	LoA	4	2	2.50	13	13	1	0	72	52	2	22	56	7.0	1.03	.199
	Tampa (FSL)	HiA	0	0	4.50	1	1	0	0	4	5	0	0	6	13.5	1.25	.294
2011	Tampa (FSL)	HiA	9	7	3.78	27	26	0	0	140	142	6	48	114	7.3	1.35	.271
Minor League Totals			16	15	3.88	63	61	1	0	318	305	15	113	252	7.1	1.32	.255

12 CITO CULVER, SS

BA GRADE
50
HIGH

Born: Aug. 26, 1992. **B-T:** B-R. **Ht.:** 6-0. **Wt.:** 185. **Drafted:** HS—Rochester, N.Y., 2010 (1st round). **Signed by:** Matt Hyde.

Any player New York drafts in the first round will have to deal with joining baseball's most scrutinized organization. The Yankees believe Culver thrives on it, as he's already dealt with hairier situations. His father Christopher Sr. broke into the family home in March 2008 and set it aflame, and he's currently imprisoned after being found guilty of arson and burglary. The club got to know Culver well prior to drafting him 32nd overall and signing him for $954,000 as a 17-year-old, and has strong conviction in his ability to play shortstop. The adjective most often used to describe his infield play, from observers inside and outside the organization, is "smooth." He has textbook actions, plus arm strength, excellent hands and solid range despite fringy speed. He should cut down on his errors (he made 17 in 67 games last year) as he gains experience. A switch-hitter, Culver will have to get stronger to hit enough to be a regular. His lefthanded swing remains a work in progress, as he hit .224 from that side in 2011, compared to .324 as a righty. He doesn't drive the ball on a consistent basis. He'll be the everyday shortstop at Charleston in 2012, once again teaming with fellow 2010 draft pick Angelo Gumbs at second base. Culver's glove should get him to the big leagues, but his bat will determine if he winds up as an everyday player.

Year	Club (League)	Class	AVG	G	AB	R	H	2B	3B	HR	RBI	BB	SO	SB	CS	OBP	SLG
2010	Yankees (GCL)	R	.269	41	160	21	43	7	1	2	18	13	41	6	3	.320	.363
	Staten Island (NYP)	SS	.186	15	43	2	8	1	0	0	8	10	1	1		.340	.209
2011	Staten Island (NYP)	SS	.250	69	276	40	69	14	2	2	33	30	57	10	0	.323	.337
Minor League Totals			.251	125	479	63	120	22	3	4	51	51	108	17	4	.323	.334

13 RAMON FLORES, OF/1B

BA GRADE
50
HIGH

Born: March 26, 1992. **B-T:** L-L. **Ht.:** 6-2. **Wt.:** 180. **Signed:** Venezuela, 2008. **Signed by:** Ricardo Finol.

Still listed at 5-foot-10 and 150 pounds, his size when he signed at age 16 four years ago, Flores now stands closer to 6-foot-2 and 180 pounds. He has made significant strides as a prospect, becoming one of the system's best pure hitters thanks to his advanced approach and keen strike-zone judgment. Flores' swing was evident when he was an amateur in Venezuela, with some scouts considering him his nation's top hitter in its 2008 international signing class. His overall game elicits comparisons to players such as Luis Gonzalez and Gerardo Parra. Flores' raw power is just average, but he gets to it regularly because of his plate discipline. He has an easy, natural swing and uses the whole field consistently, and he's not fazed by lefthanders. He has good instincts at the plate and on the bases, where he's a solid baserunner. Because his speed is below-average and his arm is fringy, Flores is best suited for left field and has played some first base as well. He will start 2012 in high Class A and could advance quickly because of his offensive polish.

Year	Club (League)	Class	AVG	G	AB	R	H	2B	3B	HR	RBI	BB	SO	SB	CS	OBP	SLG
2009	Yankees 2 (DSL)	R	.256	11	39	8	10	0	3	1	5	11	5	0	1	.423	.487
	Yankees (GCL)	R	.196	51	158	14	31	5	1	0	14	22	35	7	5	.303	.241
2010	Tampa (FSL)	HiA	.250	8	28	0	7	0	0	0	2	0	5	0	0	.250	.250
	Yankees (GCL)	R	.329	43	158	33	52	10	4	2	22	28	22	4	1	.436	.481
	Charleston (SAL)	LoA	.250	14	48	3	12	3	0	0	2	3	15	1	0	.294	.313
2011	Charleston (SAL)	LoA	.265	125	468	59	124	26	2	11	59	61	93	13	2	.353	.400
Minor League Totals			.263	252	899	117	236	44	10	14	104	125	175	25	9	.357	.380

14 ANGELO GUMBS, 2B

BA GRADE
50
HIGH

Born: Oct. 13, 1992. **B-T:** R-R. **Ht.:** 5-11. **Wt.:** 195. **Drafted:** HS—Torrance, Calif., 2010 (2nd round). **Signed by:** Dave Keith.

Raw and athletic when the Yankees drafted him in the second round, Gumbs showed interesting flashes playing second base alongside fellow 2010 draftee Cito Culver in Staten Island last summer. The two likely will be teammates for the foreseeable future, and while they have some similarities, their tools and strengths are vastly different. Culver is a pure shortstop with classic infield actions. Gumbs was new to the right side of the infield, having split time between shortstop and outfield in high school, and struggled with the transition. His throwing mechanics are inconsistent, and his footwork and agility may not cut it in the middle infield. He's a better raw athlete than Culver, though, with more explosiveness, speed and strength. That comes through most at the plate, where Gumbs shows the ability to drive the ball to all fields. He could have average power down the road. He's still raw offensively and not selective enough, but the Yankees are confident in his aptitude to make adjustments as he gains experience. He's a veteran of MLB's Urban Youth Academy in Compton, Calif., and New York likes his makeup. If Gumbs can't cut it in the infield, he'll head to the outfield, where his speed and raw arm strength should be assets. The Yankees could field an all-prospect infield at Charleston in 2012 with Tyler Austin at first base, Gumbs at second, Culver at short and Dante Bichette Jr. at third.

Year	Club (League)	Class	AVG	G	AB	R	H	2B	3B	HR	RBI	BB	SO	SB	CS	OBP	SLG
2010	Yankees (GCL)	R	.192	7	26	1	5	1	0	0	0	1	3	3	0	.222	.231
2011	Staten Island (NYP)	SS	.264	51	197	32	52	11	4	3	29	20	57	11	7	.332	.406
Minor League Totals			.256	58	223	33	57	12	4	3	29	21	60	14	7	.320	.386

15 ADAM WARREN, RHP

Born: Aug. 25, 1987. **B-T:** R-R. **Ht.:** 6-2. **Wt.:** 215. **Drafted:** North Carolina, 2009 (4th round). **Signed by:** Scott Lovekamp.

Warren went 32-4 in college at North Carolina, and four of his 2009 teammates already have reached the major leagues. He had a breakthrough year in 2010, jumping to Double-A to end his first full pro season, but had a modest 2011 campaign in his first run at Triple-A. He didn't get a win after June 20, losing his final six decisions even though his peripheral stats improved as the year progressed. Warren pitches off his 89-93 mph fastball and touches 94-95 fairly regularly. He has quickened his tempo as a pro and has incorporated his legs more into his delivery to improve his velocity from his amateur days. Warren's slider also has gotten better and is a solid pitch at times. His curveball and changeup remain fringy, and his key will be throwing them for strikes to keep hitters from sitting on his heat. His command of his secondary pitches improved in the second half of 2011, but when he missed, he was vulnerable to home runs. He gave up 13 longballs last year after yielding just four in 2010. Warren profiles as a back-of-the-rotation starter, and for the Yankees he's more important as depth than as a key part of their future. He could get a chance to earn a long-relief role in 2012, but more likely he'll return to Triple-A.

Year	Club (League)	Class	W	L	ERA	G	GS	CG	SV	IP	H	HR	BB	SO	K/9	WHIP	AVG
2009	Staten Island (NYP)	SS	4	2	1.43	12	12	0	0	57	49	1	10	50	7.9	1.04	.236
2010	Tampa (FSL)	HiA	7	5	2.22	15	15	0	0	81	72	2	17	67	7.4	1.10	.235
	Trenton (EL)	AA	4	2	3.15	10	10	0	0	54	49	2	16	59	9.8	1.20	.232
2011	Scranton/W-B (IL)	AAA	6	8	3.60	27	27	1	0	152	145	13	53	111	6.6	1.30	.249
Minor League Totals			21	17	2.85	64	64	2	0	344	315	18	96	287	7.5	1.19	.241

16 D.J. MITCHELL, RHP

Born: May 13, 1987. **B-T:** R-R. **Ht.:** 6-0. **Wt.:** 160. **Drafted:** Clemson, 2008 (10th round). **Signed by:** Scott Lovekamp.

Wins don't matter much for minor league pitchers, but Mitchell has 38 victories in three pro seasons. He's keeping himself in the mix as a possible starter despite being dogged by assumptions that he's headed for the bullpen. While his slender frame hasn't filled out much since he signed for $400,000 as a 10th-rounder in 2008, he has logged 452 innings, establishing a strong track record as a durable sinker-slider pitcher. Mitchell prefers to pound the bottom half of the zone with an 89-91 mph fastball and a solid slider more notable for getting grounders than swings-and-misses. His sinking changeup has improved during the last two seasons, as he proved by holding lefthanders to a .684 OPS in 2011 (versus .677 for righthanders). He also owns a curveball that grades out a bit better than his slider, with fairly sharp, late bite when it's right. Mitchell keeps the ball in the ballpark, a must because he isn't a strikeout pitcher. While he has accomplished more than any other member of New York's 2008 draft class, he has a back-of-the-rotation ceiling at best. In an organization focused on impact, his greatest contributions still are expected to come as a middle reliever who can produce a groundout when needed. Protected on the 40-man roster in November, he's likely to return to Triple-A for 2012 unless the Yankees sell high on him in an offseason trade.

Year	Club (League)	Class	W	L	ERA	G	GS	CG	SV	IP	H	HR	BB	SO	K/9	WHIP	AVG
2009	Charleston (SAL)	LoA	4	1	1.95	6	6	0	0	37	31	1	6	42	10.2	1.00	.228
	Tampa (FSL)	HiA	8	6	2.87	19	18	1	0	103	93	1	38	83	7.2	1.27	.245
2010	Trenton (EL)	AA	11	4	4.06	23	22	0	0	133	128	11	57	96	6.5	1.39	.254
	Scranton/W-B (IL)	AAA	2	0	3.57	3	3	0	0	18	19	0	7	16	8.2	1.47	.271
2011	Scranton/W-B (IL)	AAA	13	9	3.18	28	24	3	0	161	155	10	63	112	6.2	1.35	.256
Minor League Totals			38	20	3.28	79	73	4	0	452	426	23	171	349	6.9	1.32	.252

17 BRYAN MITCHELL, RHP

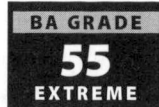

BA GRADE
55
EXTREME

Born: April 19, 1991. **B-T:** L-R. **Ht.:** 6-2. **Wt.:** 193. **Drafted:** HS—Hamlet, N.C., 2009 (16th round). **Signed by:** Scott Lovekamp.

The Yankees gave Mitchell (no relation to D.J.) an $800,000 bonus as a 16th-rounder in 2009 and still love his stuff. They're trying to be patient with his growing pains, which included a serious bout of homesickness after he signed and command issues in each of the last two seasons. Mitchell has a live arm with frontline stuff that he hasn't learned to control. He's not overly physical but has a quick arm and excellent athleticism, and he produces two pitches that have true plus potential. His curveball already is an above-average offering and ranks among the best in the system. It's a true power downer that sits at 80-82 mph. Mitchell's fastball sits at 93-94 mph at times and gets swings and misses when it's around the strike zone, thanks to its late sinking, tailing action. He has lost development time to his late signing in 2009 and to an abdominal strain in 2010, and he has walked 4.5 batters per nine innings in two years as a pro. He'll have to do much better than that as he jumps to full-season ball at Charleston in 2012.

Year	Club (League)	Class	W	L	ERA	G	GS	CG	SV	IP	H	HR	BB	SO	K/9	WHIP	AVG
2010	Yankees (GCL)	R	2	1	3.67	10	9	0	0	42	28	2	22	36	7.8	1.20	.190
	Staten Island (NYP)	SS	0	1	6.75	1	1	0	0	4	7	0	1	3	6.8	2.00	.368
2011	Staten Island (NYP)	SS	1	3	4.09	14	14	0	0	62	65	5	31	59	8.6	1.56	.275
Minor League Totals			3	5	4.02	25	24	0	0	107	100	7	54	98	8.2	1.43	.249

18 BRANDON LAIRD, 3B/1B/OF

BA GRADE
45
LOW

Born: Sept. 11, 1987. **B-T:** R-R. **Ht.:** 6-1. **Wt.:** 215. **Drafted:** Cypress (Calif.) JC, 2007 (27th round). **Signed by:** Dave Keith.

The Double-A Eastern League MVP in 2010, Laird came back to earth a bit last season, though the younger brother of veteran catcher Gerald Laird did make his major league debut in July with a pinch-hit single against the Athletics. He returned to New York as a September callup. However, Laird was exposed by Triple-A pitchers in a way that hadn't happened before. He always has been an aggressive hitter, and more advanced pitchers took advantage. He almost hit more homers than he had walks, and he struggled with quality breaking balls from righthanders, who limited him to a .672 OPS in Triple-A. He has the strength to hit for power to all fields and still mashes lefthanders, against whom he had an .810 OPS. Laird has helped himself by adding some defensive value as his career has progressed. Managers rated him the International League's best defensive third baseman in 2011. He isn't flashy but he's dependable and makes the routine plays, and he's also more than capable at first base. He saw some time in left field last year, though his below-average speed limits him there. Laird's best role with the Yankees would be as a righthanded-hitting corner reserve, though he could be a second-division regular if traded elsewhere. He'll fight for that bench role in New York this year.

Year	Club (League)	Class	AVG	G	AB	R	H	2B	3B	HR	RBI	BB	SO	SB	CS	OBP	SLG
2007	Yankees (GCL)	R	.339	45	168	27	57	14	1	8	29	6	26	0	0	.367	.577
2008	Charleston (SAL)	LoA	.273	122	454	71	124	31	1	23	86	40	86	1	0	.334	.498
2009	Tampa (FSL)	HiA	.266	124	451	53	120	20	4	13	75	39	75	1	1	.329	.415
2010	Trenton (EL)	AA	.291	107	409	73	119	22	2	23	90	38	84	2	2	.355	.523
	Scranton/W-B (IL)	AAA	.246	31	122	13	30	6	0	2	12	4	27	0	0	.268	.344
2011	Scranton/W-B (IL)	AAA	.260	123	462	51	120	27	0	16	69	17	84	0	0	.288	.422
	New York (AL)	MAJ	.190	11	21	3	4	0	0	0	1	3	4	0	0	.292	.190
Major League Totals			.190	11	21	3	4	0	0	0	1	3	4	0	0	.292	.190
Minor League Totals			.276	552	2066	288	570	120	8	85	361	144	382	4	3	.326	.465

19 ZOILO ALMONTE, OF

BA GRADE
45
MEDIUM

Born: June 10, 1989. **B-T:** B-R. **Ht.:** 6-0. **Wt.:** 205. **Signed:** Dominican Republic, 2005. **Signed by:** Carlos Rios/Ramon Valdivia.

The Yankees' Almonte prospects run from A to Z. Abe Almonte ranked 30th on this list in our 2009 Handbook and had a 34-game hitting streak in high Class A last season. His teammate in the first half at Tampa, Zoilo Almonte, hadn't played his way into prospect status before 2011, striking out 130 times in his lone year at the full-season level. He broke out last year, making more consistent contact and bashing a career-high 15 homers. Almonte doesn't have one carrying tool but offers a solid package. He has added 40 pounds since signing in 2005, and now has the strength and bat speed to generate at least average power. A switch-hitter, he has improved his pitch recognition with more experience. Almonte is an above-average defender in left field and has the arm strength to be an average defender in right as well. His speed is fringy, and likely limits him to an outfield corner as a starter, but he'll continue playing center field in the minors and should have a future as a fourth outfielder if his bat falls short of a corner profile. Almonte plays with energy and has many ways to help a team win. How much progress he continues to make with the bat as he returns to Double-A in 2012 will determine if he has a future as a regular. New York believes in him enough to have added him to its 40-man roster in November.

Year	Club (League)	Class	AVG	G	AB	R	H	2B	3B	HR	RBI	BB	SO	SB	CS	OBP	SLG
2006	Yankees1 (DSL)	R	.219	53	192	28	42	6	3	6	36	28	52	4	3	.320	.375
2007	Yankees (GCL)	R	.268	50	190	25	51	11	2	3	24	9	35	2	2	.307	.395
2008	Yankees (GCL)	R	.239	57	180	24	43	7	1	5	20	13	35	3	0	.291	.372
2009	Staten Island (NYP)	SS	.274	69	259	43	71	20	1	7	39	31	58	15	7	.355	.440
2010	Charleston (SAL)	LoA	.278	58	227	33	63	13	2	10	35	21	65	7	6	.341	.485
	Tampa (FSL)	HiA	.261	63	238	26	62	10	3	3	26	23	65	8	1	.322	.366
2011	Tampa (FSL)	HiA	.293	70	259	38	76	15	3	12	54	31	60	14	4	.368	.514
	Trenton (EL)	AA	.251	46	175	23	44	11	1	3	23	14	45	4	1	.309	.377
Minor League Totals			.263	466	1720	240	452	93	16	49	257	170	415	57	24	.330	.421

20 TYLER AUSTIN, 3B/1B

BA GRADE
50
HIGH

Born: Sept. 6, 1991. **B-T:** R-R. **Ht.:** 6-2. **Wt.:** 200. **Drafted:** HS—Conyers, Ga., 2010 (13th round). **Signed by:** Darryl Monroe.

A decorated amateur player, Austin was an Aflac All-American the summer after his junior year in high school. But 2010 was an epic year in Georgia with five prepsters drafted in the first round, and he got a bit lost in the shuffle. He wound up dropping to the 13th round and signed for $130,000, then broke his left wrist when he was hit by a pitch in his second pro game. His bat proved too advanced for the Gulf Coast League last summer, so New York promoted him to Staten Island, where he batted .429 in the playoffs to help the Little Yanks win the title. Strong and physical, Austin has above-average pull power and a fairly advanced approach. He's not afraid to work counts or use the whole field. He's a solid athlete with average speed and excellent instincts that helped him steal 20 bases (including the postseason) while being caught only once in 2011. Austin's future value is tied into his defense. He was primarily a catcher in high school but hasn't caught as a pro, instead working at third and first base. His arm, which is a tick above-average, is his best defensive attribute. His newness at third showed as he made 11 errors in just 29 games (playoffs included). Austin's shaky instincts and footwork at third contributed to his miscues, and he'll likely to play a lot more first base down the line. That's likely to happen this year in low Class A. Austin's speed gives him a chance to man an outfield corner as well.

Year	Club (League)	Class	AVG	G	AB	R	H	2B	3B	HR	RBI	BB	SO	SB	CS	OBP	SLG
2010	Yankees (GCL)	R	.000	2	2	0	0	0	0	0	0	0	1	0	0	.500	.000
2011	Yankees (GCL)	R	.390	20	82	13	32	8	1	3	22	5	16	11	0	.438	.622
	Staten Island (NYP)	SS	.323	27	96	16	31	10	1	3	14	10	23	7	0	.402	.542
Minor League Totals			.350	49	180	29	63	18	2	6	36	15	40	18	0	.420	.572

21 DAVID PHELPS, RHP

BA GRADE
45
MEDIUM

Born: Oct. 9, 1986. **B-T:** R-R. **Ht.:** 6-2. **Wt.:** 185. **Drafted:** Notre Dame, 2008 (14th round). **Signed by:** Mike Gibbons.

Phelps has progressed as far as any member of New York's 2008 draft class. He rocketed to Triple-A in 2010, then hit his first speed bump in pro ball last summer, when he wound up missing two months with shoulder discomfort. He just needed rest as it turned out, and he came back to give up just two earned runs and one walk in his final 19 innings. Phelps resembles Adam Warren in that he profiles as a back-of-the-rotation starter, and his future upside depends mostly on his ability to throw his secondary pitches for strikes in fastball counts. Phelps works off a fastball that sits in the low 90s and touches 95. He also has a solid curveball, fringy slider and decent changeup. Like Warren, he tried to mix in his secondary stuff more often and paid for it when he missed against Triple-A hitters. After giving up just six homers in 158 innings in 2010, Phelps surrendered 11 in 107 innings last season. He generally challenges hitters rather than nibbling, and his control ranks among the best in the system. He'd be a candidate for a callup in a different organization, but with New York he's playing a waiting game. A November addition to the 40-man roster, he's likely headed back for a third stint in Triple-A in 2012.

Year	Club (League)	Class	W	L	ERA	G	GS	CG	SV	IP	H	HR	BB	SO	K/9	WHIP	AVG
2008	Staten Island (NYP)	SS	8	2	2.72	15	15	0	0	73	67	4	18	52	6.4	1.17	.245
2009	Charleston (SAL)	LoA	10	3	2.80	19	19	0	0	113	117	9	25	90	7.2	1.26	.272
	Tampa (FSL)	HiA	3	1	1.17	7	7	0	0	38	34	1	6	32	7.5	1.04	.234
2010	Trenton (EL)	AA	6	0	2.04	14	14	0	0	88	63	2	23	84	8.6	0.97	.199
	Scranton/W-B (IL)	AAA	4	2	3.07	12	11	0	0	70	76	4	13	57	7.3	1.27	.274
2011	Scranton/W-B (IL)	AAA	6	6	3.19	18	18	1	0	107	115	11	26	90	7.5	1.31	.278
	Yankees (GCL)	R	1	1	0.00	2	2	0	0	7	4	0	1	5	6.4	0.71	.154
Minor League Totals			38	15	2.61	87	86	1	0	497	476	31	112	410	7.4	1.18	.253

22 ZACH NUDING, RHP

BA GRADE
50
HIGH

Born: March 29, 1990. **B-T:** R-R. **Ht.:** 6-4. **Wt.:** 260. **Drafted:** Weatherford (Texas) JC, 2010 (30th round). **Signed by:** Mark Batchko.

Big and strong, Nuding draws physical comparisons to Josh Johnson. He doesn't have

Johnson's upside, but he does have a big body and a big arm. He wasn't drafted out of high school, then selected by the Pirates in the 37th round after his freshman year at Weatherford (Texas) JC in 2009. After a second turn at Weatherford and in the Texas Collegiate League, he signed with the Yankees for $265,000 as a 30th-rounder in 2010. Nuding has one of the best fastballs in the system, sitting at 93 mph and ranging from 90-96. When he's at his best, he uses his size to deliver his heater with tough angle and plane, and he has shown the ability to throw strikes to both sides of the plate. Nuding doesn't have the cleanest arm action or delivery, yet he repeats his release point and consistently has heavy sink on his fastball. He pitches off it effectively and gets into trouble when hitters don't have to respect his slider and changeup. His low-80s slider has some depth and is his better secondary pitch. His inconsistent changeup shows late fade when it's on, which wasn't often in his first full pro season. He'll spend 2012 in high Class A and faces a future as a hard-throwing reliever if his secondary pitches don't become more reliable.

Year	Club (League)	Class	W	L	ERA	G	GS	CG	SV	IP	H	HR	BB	SO	K/9	WHIP	AVG
2010	Yankees (GCL)	R	0	1	4.50	1	1	0	0	2	4	0	1	2	9.0	2.50	.400
2011	Charleston (SAL)	LoA	7	6	4.48	20	20	0	0	98	87	11	44	82	7.5	1.33	.232
	Yankees (GCL)	R	0	0	2.57	3	1	0	0	7	6	0	0	8	10.3	0.86	.214
	Tampa (FSL)	HiA	0	0	0.00	1	1	0	0	3	3	0	1	1	3.0	1.33	.273
Minor League Totals			7	7	4.24	25	23	0	0	110	100	11	46	93	7.6	1.32	.236

23 MARK MONTGOMERY, RHP

BA GRADE
50
HIGH

Born: Aug. 30, 1990. **B-T:** R-R. **Ht.:** 5-11. **Wt.:** 205. **Drafted:** Longwood, 2011 (11th round). **Signed by:** Scott Lovekamp.

Montgomery wasn't heavily recruited out of high school and originally signed with NCAA Division I independent Longwood as a shortstop. He was a two-way player as a freshman before becoming a full-time pitcher as a sophomore. That summer in the Coastal Plain League, his low-80s slider started drawing rave reviews for its tilt and tight rotation. It earned him a $65,000 bonus as an 11th-round pick and allowed him to dominate in both college (0.89 ERA, 14.2 K/9) and pro ball (1.91 ERA, 16.2 K/9) in 2011. Montgomery struck out the side in three of his four outings at Staten Island, then had a five-strikeout inning in his first game with Charleston, as his slider was too sharp for Gary Sanchez to handle. (For comparison's sake, there never has been a five-strikeout inning in the major leagues, and the South Atlantic League hadn't had one since 1997.) Montgomery's slider is already a plus pitch by big league standards, and the Yankees will put him on the fast track as they did with David Robertson. His fastball sits at 91-92 mph and touches 94, though at 5-foot-11, he has some issues with his heater coming in flat without much downhill plane. His slider alone could make him a major leaguer, however. If like Robertson he gains velocity as a pro, Montgomery could be a late-inning force in New York. He could jump to Double-A to open his first full big league season.

Year	Club (League)	Class	W	L	ERA	G	GS	CG	SV	IP	H	HR	BB	SO	K/9	WHIP	AVG
2011	Staten Island (NYP)	SS	0	0	2.25	4	0	0	1	4	3	0	2	10	22.5	1.25	.200
	Charleston (SAL)	LoA	0	0	1.85	22	0	0	14	24	17	0	11	41	15.2	1.15	.183
Minor League Totals			0	0	1.91	26	0	0	15	28	20	0	13	51	16.2	1.16	.185

24 JAKE CAVE, OF

BA GRADE
50
HIGH

Born: Dec. 7, 1992. **B-T:** L-L. **Ht.:** 6-0. **Wt.:** 179. **Drafted:** HS—Hampton, Va., 2011 (6th round). **Signed by:** Scott Lovekamp.

Cave received the second-largest signing bonus in New York's 2011 draft class— $800,000 in the sixth round—thanks to his tools, athletic ability and strong commitment as a two-way player to Louisiana State. He helped his cause with a strong summer performance, ranking as the No. 1 prospect in the collegiate Coastal Plain League. The CPL hadn't allowed high schoolers in the league before 2011, and he hit .326/.432/.442 with wood bats. Cave's fast hands produce a whippy swing with plus raw power. His pitch recognition is somewhat raw, and he was susceptible to breaking balls in the summer, so he'll have to make adjustments. Cave played first base in high school and in the CPL in part to save his arm, which delivers fastballs clocked as high as 94 mph. He's an above-average runner, so he should be able to move to the outfield in pro ball. It's possible he could see time in center field, though he profiles better in right. Cave is headed to extended spring training to start 2012 and could earn an assignment to Staten Island.

Year	Club (League)	Class	AVG	G	AB	R	H	2B	3B	HR	RBI	BB	SO	SB	CS	OBP	SLG
2011	Yankees (GCL)	R	.000	1	1	0	0	0	0	0	0	1	0	0	0	.500	.000
Minor League Totals			.000	1	1	0	0	0	0	0	0	1	0	0	0	.500	.000

25 CLAUDIO CUSTODIO, SS

BA GRADE
50
EXTREME

Born: Oct. 30, 1990. **B-T:** R-R. **Ht.:** 5-10. **Wt.:** 150. **Signed:** Dominican Republic, 2010. **Signed by:** Victor Mata/Angel Ovalles.

Custodio was part of a prospect-laden Gulf Coast League championship club in 2011, sharing time at shortstop with Jose Rosario. Even though he didn't play every day and had a lower leg injury end his season early, Custodio led the GCL with 46 runs and 26 steals in 39 games. After originally using a false identity (Claudio Baez) and age, Custodio was going to sign with the Royals until they backed out and he inked with the Yankees for $300,000 in April 2010. Custodio stands out for his hitting ability from the right side, as he has quick hands that produce solid bat speed. He still tends to cheat to try to lift balls and hit for power, but he's patient and isn't afraid to draw a walk, and he showed aptitude in flattening out his swing. Custodio has quick-twitch athleticism and above-average speed, as well as the tools and instincts to play shortstop. He was error-prone in 2011 thanks to a scattershot arm, a problem New York considers correctable. One club official compared him to Robert Andino with a better shot to stay at shortstop. Already 21, Custodio could handle the jump to full-season ball in 2012 but the Yankees won't do that at the expense of playing time for Cito Culver and Angelo Gumbs. More likely, Custodio and Rosario will team up again at Staten Island.

Year	Club (League)	Class	AVG	G	AB	R	H	2B	3B	HR	RBI	BB	SO	SB	CS	OBP	SLG
2010	Yankees 1 (DSL)	R	.217	61	203	46	44	9	3	5	36	30	38	14	3	.328	.365
2011	Yankees (GCL)	R	.325	39	157	46	51	9	1	1	19	22	40	26	2	.433	.414
Minor League Totals			.264	100	360	92	95	18	4	6	55	52	78	40	5	.374	.386

26 DAVID ADAMS, 2B

BA GRADE

50

EXTREME

Born: May 15, 1987. **B-T:** R-R. **Ht.:** 6-1. **Wt.:** 202. **Drafted:** Virginia, 2008 (3rd round). **Signed by:** Scott Lovekamp.

Though Adams has played in just 68 games during the last two seasons, New York still protected him on its 40-man roster in November. As senior vice president of baseball operations Mark Newman said, "I haven't seen a guy yet have his career end because of a broken foot." Adams' injured himself sliding into second base in May 2010. He was initially diagnosed with a high ankle sprain, and it wasn't until July that doctors discovered a broken bone at the joint where his right foot meets the ankle. The Mariners used the injury as a pretext to back out of a trade that would have sent Cliff Lee to the Yankees for a package that included Adams and Jesus Montero. Lee went to the Rangers instead and Adams has hardly been seen since. He played one game at Tampa last April, then sat out for two months before a rehab stint in the Gulf Coast League. He returned to high Class A in late July but didn't last three weeks before pain returned and New York shut him down. When healthy, Adams is an offensive second baseman who has arm strength and the ability to turn the double play well. He has solid gap power and enough juice to project to hit 10-15 homers annually. He has played some third base in the past, and it remains to be seen if his injury problems will diminish his already fringy range at second base. He might lose a step from his below-average speed as well. The Yankees want to keep him at second base, but the main priority at first will be for him to remain healthy. He'll head to Double-A when he's ready in 2012.

Year	Club (League)	Class	AVG	G	AB	R	H	2B	3B	HR	RBI	BB	SO	SB	CS	OBP	SLG
2008	Staten Island (NYP)	SS	.257	67	257	45	66	19	2	4	31	32	57	8	2	.350	.393
2009	Charleston (SAL)	LoA	.290	67	259	32	75	23	2	0	34	35	49	8	4	.385	.394
	Tampa (FSL)	HiA	.281	65	231	37	65	17	6	7	41	26	39	3	4	.360	.498
2010	Trenton (EL)	AA	.309	39	152	31	47	15	3	3	32	18	31	5	2	.393	.507
2011	Tampa (FSL)	HiA	.308	12	52	6	16	3	0	0	4	4	8	0	2	.368	.365
	Yankees (GCL)	R	.429	17	56	13	24	9	0	1	11	5	10	2	1	.469	.643
Minor League Totals			.291	267	1007	164	293	86	13	15	153	120	194	26	15	.375	.447

27 NIK TURLEY, LHP

BA GRADE

45

HIGH

Born: Sept. 11, 1989. **B-T:** L-L. **Ht.:** 6-6. **Wt.:** 230. **Drafted:** HS—Studio City, Calif., 2008 (50th round). **Signed by:** Stuart Smothers.

Turley played at toney Harvard-Westlake High (Studio City, Calif.) and was committed to Brigham Young after graduating in 2008. Because he's a Mormon, many scouts expected him to attend BYU and go on a two-year mission. Instead, he signed for $150,000 after the Yankees drafted him in the 50th round. He comes from an athletic family: his mother skiied for BYU, while three brothers played college sports, including Kurt, a former Cougars righthander. Turley's career took a while to get going, as he began each of his first three pro seasons in Rookie ball. He was just starting to hit his stride in 2011 when he took a line drive off his pitching hand in his second start following a promotion to high Class A, breaking a bone and ending his season. He had been Charleston's best starter in the first half and didn't allow an earned run in his final four starts there. Despite a late growth spurt that has seen him add two inches and 30 pounds since signing, Turley has the system's best control. His fastball is the least of his pitches, sitting in the upper 80s at times and in the low 90s at others. It's effective at average velocity because of his height and angle to the plate. He could throw harder as he irons out his delivery, which has some stiffness. His above-average curveball has good shape and his changeup also has its moments. Turley should return to high Class A in 2012 and has a back-of-the-rotation ceiling.

Year	Club (League)	Class	W	L	ERA	G	GS	CG	SV	IP	H	HR	BB	SO	K/9	WHIP	AVG
2008	Yankees (GCL)	R	2	1	1.13	4	1	0	0	8	6	0	0	13	14.6	0.75	.207
2009	Yankees (GCL)	R	2	3	2.82	11	10	0	0	54	45	1	23	46	7.6	1.25	.228

Year	Club (League)	Class			ERA	G	GS	CG	SV	IP	H	HR	BB	SO	K/9	WHIP	AVG
2010	Yankees (GCL)	R	0	2	0.84	3	2	0	0	11	11	0	2	9	7.6	1.22	.239
	Staten Island (NYP)	SS	4	4	4.38	12	12	1	0	62	57	0	29	47	6.9	1.39	.259
2011	Charleston (SAL)	LoA	4	6	2.51	15	15	0	0	82	70	8	21	82	9.0	1.11	.224
	Tampa (FSL)	HiA	0	0	6.14	2	2	0	0	7	11	1	1	5	6.1	1.64	.344
Minor League Totals			12	16	3.09	47	42	1	0	224	200	10	76	202	8.1	1.23	.239

28 GREG BIRD, C/1B

BA GRADE
50
EXTREME

Born: Nov. 9, 1992. **B-T:** L-R. **Ht.:** 6-3. **Wt.:** 215. **Drafted:** HS—Aurora, Colo., 2011 (4th round). **Signed by:** Steve Kametko.

Bird played at Grandview High (Aurora, Colo.) with righthander Kevin Gausman, who's now at Louisiana State and is expected to be a 2012 first-round pick as a draft-eligible sophomore. Gausman's presence brought some attention to Bird, who made a name for himself last spring, hitting .553 with 12 home runs as Colorado's high school baseball player of the year. Committed to Arkansas, Bird went in the fourth round of the 2011 draft and spent the summer in the California Collegiate League. He hit .273/.446/.494, reinforcing the Yankees' strong conviction that he'll hit for power as a pro. They signed him for $1.1 million, more than they paid any other draftee last year. New York not only believes in Bird's lefthanded pop but also thinks he has a chance to catch, which wasn't the industry consensus. He has some arm strength, but he's big for the position and not terribly athletic or agile. The Yankees love offense-first catchers, but he's behind the likes of Jesus Montero, Gary Sanchez and J.R. Murphy at a similar stage of development. Bird will need time to adjust to catching as a pro and many area scouts believed he'll have to move to first base. They weren't totally sold on his hitting ability because his swing can get long at times, but it's hard not to like his strength and bat speed, not to mention his ability to loft and backspin balls. He's a well below-average runner. Bird will work on his defense in extended spring training to begin 2012.

Year	Club (League)	Class	AVG	G	AB	R	H	2B	3B	HR	RBI	BB	SO	SB	CS	OBP	SLG
2011	Yankees (GCL)	R	.083	4	12	0	1	0	0	0	0	1	4	0	0	.154	.083
Minor League Totals			.083	4	12	0	1	0	0	0	0	1	4	0	0	.154	.083

29 CHASE WHITLEY, RHP

BA GRADE
45
HIGH

Born: June 14, 1989. **B-T:** R-R. **Ht.:** 6-4. **Wt.:** 220. **Drafted:** Troy, 2010 (15th round). **Signed by:** D.J. Svihlik.

David Robertson's success has the Yankees on the lookout for the next Robertson. Whitley is a candidate who has moved quickly since signing for $68,000 as a 15th-round pick in 2010. Primarily a third baseman in college, he also closed at Troy and has a future as a big league reliever. His position-player background is part of the reason for his funky, high-elbow arm action, which gives him some deception. Whitley's fastball is unremarkable at 89-91 mph, so he'll have to be precise with his command at higher levels to make it work. His secondary stuff sets him apart, as both his changeup and slider are plus pitches at their best. He throws his changeup with confidence, good arm speed and late sink. His low-80s slider also generates some swings and missed. Whitley was New York's best performer in the Arizona Fall League after the 2011 season and could push for a role in the majors at some point this year.

Year	Club (League)	Class	W	L	ERA	G	GS	CG	SV	IP	H	HR	BB	SO	K/9	WHIP	AVG
2010	Staten Island (NYP)	SS	4	2	1.31	28	0	0	15	34	18	0	15	44	11.5	0.96	.157
	Tampa (FSL)	HiA	0	0	3.00	2	0	0	0	3	1	1	0	6	18.0	0.33	.100
2011	Tampa (FSL)	HiA	0	1	1.68	23	0	0	6	48	41	2	10	40	7.4	1.06	.233
	Trenton (EL)	AA	3	4	3.38	19	1	0	1	43	46	6	19	37	7.8	1.52	.280
Minor League Totals			7	7	2.17	72	1	0	22	128	106	9	44	127	8.9	1.17	.228

30 BRANDEN PINDER, RHP

BA GRADE
45
HIGH

Born: Jan. 26, 1989. **B-T:** R-R. **Ht.:** 6-3. **Wt.:** 210. **Drafted:** Long Beach State, 2011 (16th round). **Signed by:** Jeff Patterson.

Pinder attended Santa Ana (Calif.) JC for two seasons before transferring to Long Beach State, where he struggled for most of the next two years. The Yankees took him as a senior sign in the 16th round last June and were delighted to find they had landed a hard-throwing reliever for $60,000. Slipped into a bullpen role after starting in college, Pinder picked up velocity and attacked hitters confidently with two pitches. His fastball, a fairly pedestrian 88-91 mph offering at Long Beach State, jumped to 93-94 mph consistently in pro ball. It helped set up his slider, which shows flashes of becoming a plus pitch. Pinder varies the spin on his breaking ball, sometimes favoring a sweepier slider and at other times adding some depth. Both versions found the strike zone and eluded bats all summer. Pinder used a changeup in college but figures to stay with his two-pitch mix in his new role. He should see high Class A at some point in 2012.

Year	Club (League)	Class	W	L	ERA	G	GS	CG	SV	IP	H	HR	BB	SO	K/9	WHIP	AVG
2011	Staten Island (NYP)	SS	2	2	1.16	24	0	0	14	31	16	1	5	38	11.0	0.68	.152
Minor League Totals			2	2	1.16	24	0	0	14	31	16	1	5	38	11.0	0.68	.152

Oakland Athletics

BY JIM SHONERD

This time, the window didn't close on the Athletics. It never opened.

Oakland's success in the early 2000s, which gave rise to the best-seller "Moneyball," was led by a home-grown trio of aces in Tim Hudson, Mark Mulder and Barry Zito. With those three on board, the A's made the playoffs every season from 2000-2003. The window started to close when Hudson and Mulder were traded after the 2004 season, and Oakland has made the postseason only once since, in 2006, which was also their last winning season.

Following the free-agent departure of Zito after 2006 and then Dan Haren (acquired in the Mulder deal) after 2007, the A's tried to retool their pitching staff and stockpile talent for another run at contention. But by the time "Moneyball" became a movie in 2011, Oakland had become an afterthought in the American League West.

With a young staff led by Brett Anderson and Trevor Cahill, the A's led the AL in ERA in 2010. They finished third in 2011 despite losing Anderson and Dallas Braden for most of the season with injuries. Gio Gonzalez blossomed into an all-star and won 16 games, yet Oakland finished 74-88 and 22 games behind the Rangers. Manager Bob Geren lost his job in June and was replaced by Bob Melvin.

Continuing a familiar theme, the team was done in by a woeful offense. Trade acquisitions Chris Carter (No. 1 on this list two years ago) and Michael Taylor were expected to form the heart of the lineup by 2011, but neither has been able to break through. The A's did have 2008 first-round pick Jemile Weeks reach the majors in June and lead the team in hitting (.303), but the club ranked 12th in the AL in both scoring and homers and was unable to capitalize on its pitching.

Continued uncertainty about the team's future home further complicates its outlook. The A's still hope to move to a new ballpark in San Jose in 2014 or 2015, but they must negotiate an agreement with the Giants, who claim San Jose is in their territory.

Such a move would boost the A's resources, but in the short term, GM Billy Beane saw the cost of his pitching staff beginning to rise while his offense remained unable to fuel a contender. It was time to start over—again.

So in December, Beane dealt Cahill and Craig Breslow to the Diamondbacks for three prospects, headlined by righthander Jarrod Parker, who immediately moved into the top spot on this list. Outfielder Collin

Jemile Weeks gave the A's a spark last year, but Oakland still needs more hitters

TOP 30 PROSPECTS

1. Jarrod Parker, rhp	16. Steve Parker, 3b/1b
2. Sonny Gray, rhp	17. Andrew Carignan, rhp
3. Michael Choice, of	18. Ryan Cook, rhp
4. Grant Green, of/ss	19. Blake Treinen, rhp
5. Jermaine Mitchell, of	20. Josh Donaldson, c/3b
6. Michael Taylor, of	21. Rob Gilliam, rhp
7. Chris Carter, 1b	22. Eric Sogard, ss/3b
8. Aaron Shipman, of	23. Justin Souza, rhp
9. B.A. Vollmuth, 3b	24. Chris Bostick, ss/2b
10. Bobby Crocker, of	25. Chih-Fang Pan, 2b
11. Collin Cowgill, of	26. Renato Nunez, 3b
12. Adrian Cardenas, of/2b/3b	27. Michael Ynoa, rhp
13. A.J. Griffin, rhp	28. Ryan Ortiz, c
14. Max Stassi, c	29. Ian Krol, lhp
15. Yordy Cabrera, ss	30. Beau Taylor, c

Cowgill and reliever Ryan Cook could provide immediate help, though they're complementary players.

Oakland will have to do a better job of signing and developing talent. The A's landed a potential frontline arm by taking Sonny Gray with the 18th overall pick in June, yet spent just $3.1 million overall on their 2011 draft class, the third-lowest figure in baseball. They also haven't been as active in Latin America after getting burned by Dominican righthander, Michael Ynoa, who signed for a club-record $4.25 million in 2008 but rarely has been healthy since.

General Manager: Billy Beane. **Farm Director:** Keith Lieppman. **Scouting Director:** Eric Kubota.

Class	Team	League	W	L	Pct	Finish*	Manager(s)
Majors	Oakland Athletics	American	74	88	.457	10th (14)	B. Geren/B. Melvin
Triple-A	Sacramento River Cats	Pacific Coast	88	56	.611	1st (16)	Darren Bush
Double-A	Midland RockHounds	Texas	63	77	.450	6th (8)	Steve Scarsone
High A	Stockton Ports	California	75	65	.536	3rd (10)	Webster Garrison
Low A	Burlington Bees	Midwest	76	62	.551	4th (16)	Aaron Nieckula
Short-season	Vermont Lake Monsters	New York-Penn	39	36	.520	t-6th (14)	Rick Magnante
Rookie	AZL Athletics	Arizona	27	29	.482	8th (13)	Marcus Jensen
Overall 2011 Minor League Record			368	324	.532	5th (30)	

*Finish in overall standings (No. of teams in league). †League champion.

LAST YEAR'S TOP 30

Player,	Pos.	Status
1.	Grant Green, ss	No. 4
2.	Chris Carter, 1b/of	No. 7
3.	Michael Choice, of	No. 3
4.	Tyson Ross, rhp	Majors
5.	Jemile Weeks, 2b	Majors
6.	Max Stassi, c	No. 14
7.	Aaron Shipman, of	No. 8
8.	Yordy Cabrera, ss	No. 15
9.	Ian Krol, lhp	No. 29
10.	Michael Taylor, of	No. 6
11.	Corey Brown, of	(Nationals)
12.	Josh Donaldson, c	No. 20
13.	Fautino de los Santos, rhp	Majors
14.	Clay Mortensen, rhp	(Rockies)
15.	Adrian Cardenas, 2b/3b	No. 12
16.	Renato Nunez, 3b	No. 26
17.	Sean Doolittle, of/1b	Dropped out
18.	Chad Lewis, 3b	Dropped out
19.	Jonathan Joseph, rhp	Dropped out
20.	Pedro Figueroa, lhp	Dropped out
21.	Eric Sogard, inf	No. 22
22.	Danny Farquhar, rhp	(Blue Jays)
23.	Trystan Magnuson, rhp	(Blue Jays)
24.	Steve Parker, 3b	No. 16
25.	Michael Ynoa, rhp	No. 27
26.	Ryan Ortiz, c	No. 28
27.	Matt Thomson, rhp	Dropped out
28.	Rashun Dixon, of	Dropped out
29.	Tony Thompson, 3b	Dropped out
30.	Conner Crumbliss, 2b/of	Dropped out

BEST TOOLS

Best Hitter for Average	Grant Green
Best Power Hitter	Michael Choice
Best Strike-Zone Discipline	Conner Crumbliss
Fastest Baserunner	Jermaine Mitchell
Best Athlete	Aaron Shipman
Best Fastball	Jarrod Parker
Best Curveball	Sonny Gray
Best Slider	Jarrod Parker
Best Changeup	A.J. Griffin
Best Control	A.J. Griffin
Best Defensive Catcher	Max Stassi
Best Defensive Infielder	Tyler Ladendorf
Best Infield Arm	Yordy Cabrera
Best Defensive Outfielder	Jermaine Mitchell
Best Outfield Arm	Collin Cowgill

PROJECTED 2015 LINEUP

Catcher	Kurt Suzuki
First Base	Chris Carter
Second Base	Jemile Weeks
Third Base	B.A. Vollmuth
Shortstop	Cliff Pennington
Left Field	Michael Choice
Center Field	Jermaine Mitchell
Right Field	Grant Green
Designated Hitter	Michael Taylor
No. 1 Starter	Jarrod Parker
No. 2 Starter	Gio Gonzalez
No. 3 Starter	Brett Anderson
No. 4 Starter	Sonny Gray
No. 5 Starter	Dallas Braden
Closer	Andrew Bailey

TOP PROSPECTS OF THE DECADE

Year	Player, Pos.	2011 Org.
2002	Carlos Pena, 1b	Cubs
2003	Rich Harden, rhp	Athletics
2004	Bobby Crosby, ss	Out of baseball
2005	Nick Swisher, of	Yankees
2006	Daric Barton, 1b	Athletics
2007	Travis Buck, of	Indians
2008	Daric Barton, 1b	Athletics
2009	Brett Anderson, lhp	Athletics
2010	Chris Carter, 1b/of	Athletics
2011	Grant Green, ss	Athletics

TOP DRAFT PICKS OF THE DECADE

Year	Player, Pos.	2011 Org.
2002	Nick Swisher, of	Yankees
2003	Brad Sullivan, rhp	Out of baseball
2004	Landon Powell, c	Athletics
2005	Cliff Pennington, ss	Athletics
2006	Trevor Cahill, rhp (2nd round)	Athletics
2007	James Simmons, rhp	Athletics
2008	Jemile Weeks, 2b	Athletics
2009	Grant Green, ss	Athletics
2010	Michael Choice, of	Athletics
2011	Sonny Gray, rhp	Athletics

LARGEST BONUSES IN CLUB HISTORY

Michael Ynoa, 2008	$4,250,000
Mark Mulder, 1998	$3,200,000
Grant Green, 2009	$2,750,000
Renato Nunez, 2010	$2,200,000
Michael Choice, 2010	$2,000,000

OAKLAND ATHLETICS

TOP 2012 ROOKIE: Jarrod Parker, rhp. The key to the Trevor Cahill trade could immediately replace him in Oakland's rotation.

BREAKOUT PROSPECT: Blake Treinen, rhp. It's not often a guy who throws a heavy 92-97 mph sinker lasts until the seventh round.

SLEEPER: Nick Rickles, c. Combining solid defense and power potential, he could be a steal from the 14th round of the 2011 draft.

SOURCE OF TOP 30 TALENT

Homegrown	21	Acquired	9
College	13	Trades	9
Junior college	0	Rule 5 draft	0
High school	5	Independent leagues	0
Draft-and-follow	0	Free agents/waivers	0
Nondrafted free agents	0		
International	3		

LF
Adrian Cardenas (12)
Royce Consigli
Myrio Richard

CF
Michael Choice (3)
Grant Green (4)
Jermaine Mitchell (5)
Aaron Shipman (8)
Bobby Crocker (10)
Collin Cowgill (17)
Vicmal de la Cruz
Dayton Alexander
Dusty Robinson

RF
Michael Taylor (6)
Jai Miller
Rashun Dixon
Josh Whitaker
Jeremy Barfield
Kelvin Rojas
Sanber Pimentel

3B
B.A. Vollmuth (9)
Yordy Cabrera (15)
Steve Parker (16)
Renato Nunez (26)
Chad Lewis

SS
Chris Bostick (24)
Sean Jamieson
Josh Horton
Wilfredo Solano

2B
Eric Sogard (22)
Chih-Fang Pan (25)
Conner Crumbliss

1B
Chris Carter (7)
Tony Thompson
Mike Spina

C
Max Stassi (14)
Josh Donaldson (20)
Ryan Ortiz (28)
Beau Taylor (30)
Nick Rickles
Anthony Recker
Josh Leyland

LHP

LHSP	LHRP
Ian Krol (29)	Pedro Figueroa
Carlos Hernandez	Omar Duran
Jake Brown	Trey Barham
Chris Lamb	Ben Hornbeck
Eric Potter	A.J. Huttenlocker
	Sean Doolittle

RHP

RHSP	RHRP
Jarrod Parker (1)	Andrew Carignan (17)
Sonny Gray (2)	Ryan Cook (18)
A.J. Griffin (13)	Rob Gilliam (21)
Blake Treinen (19)	Justin Souza (23)
Michael Ynoa (27)	Neil Wagner
Graham Godfrey	Tanner Peters
Matt Thomson	Nathan Kilcrease
T.J. Walz	Josh Lansford
Dan Straily	Pedro Vidal
Blake Hassebrock	Zach Thornton
Colin O'Connell	
Tyler Vail	
Shawn Haviland	
Jonathan Joseph	

2011

BEST PURE HITTER: SS/2B Chris Bostick (44)—the only prep player the A's signed—ranked as the No. 2 prospect in the New York Collegiate League before signing for $125,000. He has a unique feel for the barrel of the bat and hit .442 with eight extra-base hits in 14 games in the Rookie-level Arizona League.

BEST POWER HITTER: 3B B.A. Vollmuth (3) has strength and leverage in his swing, helping him hit 40 homers in three seasons at Southern Mississippi.

FASTEST RUNNER: The A's didn't draft a true burner. OF Chad Oberacker (25) is a plus runner and efficient basestealer (42-for-50 in college, 13-for-15 at short-season Vermont).

BEST DEFENSIVE PLAYER: C Beau Taylor's (5) receiving skills allowed him to handle pitchers at low Class A Burlington. Athletic SS Sean Jamieson (17) enhances his average range, hands and arm with good instincts.

BEST FASTBALL: RHPs Sonny Gray (1) and Blake Treinen (7) do it differently, but both touch 97 mph. The 5-foot-11 Gray sits at 90-94 and likes to work up in the zone. The 6-foot-4 Treinen will get a chance to start but dominated in relief in his debut with 36 strikeouts in 30 innings.

BEST SECONDARY PITCH: Gray's high heat sets up his power curveball, the best in the 2011 draft. He has excellent feel for and control of his breaking ball, which has downer action.

BEST PRO DEBUT: Gray put up a 0.45 ERA and 18 strikeouts in 20 Double-A innings. Oakland was pleased with college RHPs Tanner Peters (16), who had 11 saves and a 1.35 ERA with 33 strikeouts in 27 innings at Vermont, and T.J. Walz (13), who went 4-1, 1.99 with 43 whiffs in 41 innings while getting to low Class A.

BEST ATHLETE: OF Bobby Crocker (4) edges Bostick with his combination of size (6-foot-3, 215 pounds), speed and strength.

MOST INTRIGUING BACKGROUND: Treinen went from pitching on the junior varsity at an NAIA school in Kansas to attending Arkansas solely as a student to becoming a legitimate prospect at South Dakota State. Unsigned C Brett Geren's (42) father Bob played in the majors and managed the A's until they fired him last June. 2B Shane Boras's (39) dad Scott is a powerful agent, and the Brewers drafted his brother Trent. OF Dayton Alexander (6) is a cousin of Shane Victorino. Unsigned OF Brandon Magee (21) is a linebacker at Arizona State.

CLOSEST TO THE MAJORS: Gray could make his big league debut in 2012.

BEST LATE-ROUND PICK: Bostick. The A's also like Walz, Peters and RHP Nathan Kilcrease (30), the 5-foot-6 former Alabama ace who has an average fastball, feel for spinning a breaking ball and moxie to spare.

THE ONE WHO GOT AWAY: LHP Jace Fry (9) touched 96 mph as a high schooler in the summer collegiate West Coast League, where he ranked as the No. 1 prospect. He opted to attend Oregon.

ASSESSMENT: No one—least of all the A's—thought Gray would make it to the 18th pick. Offense-starved Oakland also landed some intriguing college bats and complemented them with a late find in Bostick.

2010

OF Michael Choice (1) led the high Class A California League with 30 homers in his first full pro season. The A's also have high hopes for the bats of SS Yordy Cabrera (2) and OF Aaron Shipman (3).

GRADE: B

2009

Last season was tumultuous for this crop's three best prospects. Grant Green (1) moved to center field in an attempt to expedite his bat, while C Max Stassi (4) and LHP Ian Krol (7) were beset by injuries.

GRADE: C+

2008

2B Jemile Weeks (1) finally stayed healthy in 2011 and became one of the few bright spots in Oakland's lineup. RHP Tyson Ross (2) also has played in the majors. RHP Brett Hunter (7) has worked just 137 innings since signing for $1.1 million.

GRADE: B

2007

OF Grant Desme (2) had a 30-30 season in 2009, then entered the priesthood. RHP James Simmons (1) and OF/LHP Sean Doolittle (1s) are two more A's draftees who have had injury issues. Oakland found four big leaguers in RHP Sam Demel (3), traded for Conor Jackson; RHP Andrew Carignan (5); and LHP Daniel Schlereth (8) and OF Colin Cowgill (29), who didn't sign. Neither did OF Gary Brown (12), now the crosstown Giants' No. 1 prospect.

GRADE: D

Draft analysis by John Manuel (2011) and Jim Callis (2007-10). Numbers in parentheses indicate draft rounds.

1 JARROD PARKER, RHP

Born: Nov. 24, 1988. **B-T:** R-R. **Ht.:** 6-1. **Wt.:** 195. **Drafted:** HS Norwell, Ind., 2007 (1st round). **Signed by:** Mike Daughtry (Diamondbacks).

BA GRADE

65

MEDIUM

BILL MITCHELL

The Athletics have had one of the American League's best young pitching staffs in recent years. But the team wasn't on track to contend before those arms started getting expensive, so Oakland's front office took the long view after the 2011 season and sought to cash in on some of its coveted pitchers. In December, the A's traded homegrown all-star Trevor Cahill and Craig Breslow to the Diamondbacks for prospects Parker, Collin Cowgill and Ryan Cook. The ninth overall pick in the 2007 draft, Parker signed for $2.1 million. He breezed through the lower minors and reached Double-A as a 20-year-old in 2009. Elbow tightness sidelined him that July, shortly after he pitched in the Futures Game. After rest and rehab didn't solve the problem, Parker had Tommy John surgery in October 2009 and missed the entire 2010 season. He came back strong last year, making 26 starts in Double-A and ranking second in the Southern League in opponent average (.236) and fifth in ERA (3.79). He was excellent in the SL playoffs, allowing two runs in two starts as Mobile won the championship. Called up to Arizona in September, he made his major league debut with 5⅔ scoreless innings against the Dodgers on Sept. 27. He also earned a spot on the Diamondbacks' postseason roster.

Parker has streamlined mechanics that allow him to get excellent velocity out of a smaller frame. The ball jumps out of his hand and he was able to touch the upper 90s before his surgery. These days, he usually works in the mid-90s and peaks at 96 mph with his four-seam fastball. He developed his two-seamer into a real weapon in the second half of last season, operating in low 90s with good sink. Parker gets swings and misses with a slider and a changeup, both of which he throws at 81-86 mph. His slider rated as a well above-average offering with tilt and depth before he got hurt, though it's more of

SCOUTING GRADES

Fastball: 65.   **Command/**
Slider: 60.   **Control:** 55.
Changeup: 55.   **Delivery:** 60.

Based on 20-80 scouting scale, where 50 represents major league average, and future projection rather than present tools.

a plus pitch now. He has very good touch with his changeup, a solid offering with a chance to get better. He also can mix in an average curveball that's more of a show-me pitch. Parker is an outstanding athlete who regained his easy delivery after his elbow reconstruction. He works with a quick tempo, and scouts noticed he was more mature on the mound last season.

Parker has true frontline-starter potential and isn't far from reaching it. The A's aren't afraid to install talented youngsters in their big league rotation, and he'll get the opportunity to earn a starting job in spring training. If Oakland continues to deal more of their established arms, Parker and 2011 first-rounder Sonny Gray may headline their rotation of the future. In an ideal world, Parker and Gray will hit their stride as the A's move into a new ballpark, wherever and whenever that might happen.

Year	Club (League)	Class	W	L	ERA	G	GS	CG	SV	IP	H	HR	BB	SO	K/9	WHIP	AVG
2008	South Bend (MWL)	LoA	12	5	3.44	24	24	0	0	118	113	8	33	117	8.9	1.24	.251
2009	Visalia (CAL)	HiA	1	0	0.95	4	4	0	0	19	12	0	4	21	9.9	0.84	.179
	Mobile (SL)	AA	4	6	3.68	16	16	0	0	78	82	2	34	74	8.5	1.48	.272
2010	Did Not Play—Injured																
2011	Mobile (SL)	AA	11	8	3.79	26	26	0	0	131	112	7	55	112	7.7	1.28	.236
	Arizona (NL)	MAJ	0	0	0.00	1	1	0	0	6	4	0	1	1	1.6	0.88	.211
Major League Totals			0	0	0.00	1	1	0	0	6	4	0	1	1	1.6	0.88	.211
Minor League Totals			28	19	3.49	70	70	0	0	346	319	17	126	324	8.4	1.29	.247

2 SONNY GRAY, RHP

Born: Nov. 7, 1989. **B-T:** R-R. **Ht.:** 5-11. **Wt.:** 180. **Drafted:** Vanderbilt, 2011 (1st round). **Signed by:** Matt Ranson.

Gray could've been a top-two-rounds pick coming out of high school in 2008, but an ankle injury and a Vanderbilt commitment dropped him to the Cubs in the 27th round. He went on to lead Vanderbilt to its first-ever College World Series in 2011 and became the third recent Commodores ace to become a first-rounder. Following in the footsteps of David Price (2007) and Mike Minor (2009), Gray went 18th overall last June and signed for $1.54 million. Gray is undersized but has the arsenal to make up for it. He gets sink and run on his 90-94 mph fastball, can reach back and hit 97 and has a feel for moving it around the strike zone. He has a second plus pitch in his curveball, which rated as the best in the 2011 draft. It has late, sharp 1-to-7 break, and he'll throw it in any count. Gray's changeup lags behind his other offerings, but it has some sink. He tended to spin off a bit in his delivery, but the A's got him to stay more on line to the plate during instructional league. They love his competitiveness and pitching IQ. Gray dominated at Double-A Midland in his brief pro debut, and he'll likely open his first full pro season there. He has a chance to pitch his way to Oakland by season's end, and he eventually could be a No. 2 starter in the big leagues.

BA GRADE
60
MEDIUM

Year	Club (League)	Class	W	L	ERA	G	GS	CG	SV	IP	H	HR	BB	SO	K/9	WHIP	AVG
2011	Athletics (AZL)	R	0	1	4.50	1	1	0	0	2	4	0	0	2	9.0	2.00	.444
	Midland (TL)	AA	1	0	0.45	5	5	0	0	20	15	0	6	18	8.1	1.05	.214
Minor League Totals			1	1	0.82	6	6	0	0	22	19	0	6	20	8.2	1.14	.241

3 MICHAEL CHOICE, OF

Born: Nov. 10, 1989. **B-T:** R-R. **Ht.:** 6-0. **Wt.:** 215. **Drafted:** Texas-Arlington, 2010 (1st round). **Signed by:** Armann Brown.

Choice set Texas-Arlington's career home run record at 34 and led NCAA Division I with 76 walks in 2010, setting the stage for going 10th overall in the draft that June. Signed for $2 million, he has kept on rolling. In his first full year in pro ball, he led the high Class A California League with 30 homers and then hit .318/.423/.667 with six more longballs in the Arizona Fall League. Choice has leverage in his swing and electrifying bat speed, giving him light-tower power to all fields. He struggles at times with breaking pitches, but his strikeouts rate did drop as the 2011 season went on. The A's have worked to eliminate some moving parts in his swing, particularly in his lower half. He also has gotten better at pitch recognition and selection. Choice was bothered by a hamstring problem during the season, inhibiting his solid speed, but he can take an extra base and has a chance to stick in center field. He has an average arm and has improved his jumps on balls. Choice will be given every opportunity to continue playing center as he advances, with Double-A his next stop. Where he eventually settles in the majors will be dictated by Oakland's needs, and he'll easily have the power to play a corner.

BA GRADE
55
MEDIUM

Year	Club (League)	Class	AVG	G	AB	R	H	2B	3B	HR	RBI	BB	SO	SB	CS	OBP	SLG
2010	Athletics (AZL)	R	.000	3	7	1	0	0	0	0	0	2	2	0	0	.222	.000
	Vancouver (NWL)	SS	.284	27	102	20	29	10	2	7	26	15	43	6	1	.388	.627
2011	Stockton (CAL)	HiA	.285	118	467	79	133	28	1	30	82	61	134	9	5	.376	.542
Minor League Totals			.281	148	576	100	162	38	3	37	108	78	179	15	6	.376	.550

4 GRANT GREEN, OF/SS

Born: Sept. 27, 1987. **B-T:** R-R. **Ht.:** 6-3. **Wt.:** 180. **Drafted:** Southern California, 2009 (1st round). **Signed by:** J.T. Stotts.

Signed for $2.75 million as the 13th overall pick in the 2009 draft, Green has hit .304/.353/.463 as a pro. He won MVP honors at the 2011 Futures Game but the biggest news of his season came a week later, when the A's shifted him from shortstop to center field. Though he had essentially no outfield experience, the move was the quickest way to get his bat to the majors. Green is a natural hitter with a smooth, wristy swing. His power dropped off in 2011, so the A's had him spread out his stance and gave him a firm base when he went to the Arizona Fall League. He responded by hitting five homers and slugging .551 in 26 AFL games. Green had to learn his new position on the fly, though he has the athleticism to handle center field and shows solid range. His average arm was a question mark at shortstop but not an issue in center field. He's working to stretch his arm out to make the longer throws required there. Green got a taste of Triple-A at the end of last season, when he appeared in seven playoff games for Sacramento and hit .296, and he'll be back there

BA GRADE
55
MEDIUM

to open 2012. While his bat may be his lone plus tool, it will get him to the big leagues. He could crash the Oakland outfield before the end of the season.

Year	Club (League)	Class	AVG	G	AB	R	H	2B	3B	HR	RBI	BB	SO	SB	CS	OBP	SLG
2009	Stockton (CAL)	HiA	.316	5	19	2	6	1	0	0	3	1	5	1	0	.350	.368
2010	Stockton (CAL)	HiA	.318	131	548	107	174	39	6	20	87	38	117	9	5	.363	.520
2011	Midland (TL)	AA	.291	127	530	76	154	33	1	9	62	39	119	6	8	.343	.408
Minor League Totals			.304	263	1097	185	334	73	7	29	152	78	241	16	13	.353	.463

5 JERMAINE MITCHELL, OF

Born: Nov. 2, 1984. **B-T:** L-L. **Ht.:** 6-0. **Wt.:** 205. **Drafted:** UNC Greensboro, 2006 (5th round). **Signed by:** Neil Avent.

Mitchell hit .362 and stole 14 bases in 37 games at short-season Vancouver in his 2006 pro debut, but he rarely played like that again during the next four years. He began figuring things out in 2010 before exploding last year, when he batted .332/.430/.530, ranking fifth in the minors in on-base percentage and earning a spot on Oakland's 40-man roster. He credits Hall of Famer Rickey Henderson, now an A's roving instructor, for helping him relax and understand the leadoff man's role. Mitchell has always had electric tools, highlighted by his plus-plus speed. He has a discerning eye at the plate and a short, quick swing. While he won't hit many home runs, he produces line drives to all fields. He has become more confident looking for pitches to drive rather than just trying to make contact. Mitchell still is learning to maximize his speed on the bases. He covers plenty of ground in center field and has an average, accurate arm. After playing through a sore knee all year, Mitchell had offseason surgery to repair a torn meniscus. The six-month rehab may keep him out of spring training, where he would have competed for an outfield job in Oakland. It's only expected to be a short-term setback, however, and he should make his big league debut in 2012.

BA GRADE
50
MEDIUM

Year	Club (League)	Class	AVG	G	AB	R	H	2B	3B	HR	RBI	BB	SO	SB	CS	OBP	SLG
2006	Vancouver (NWL)	SS	.362	37	138	23	50	7	2	3	23	22	27	14	6	.460	.507
2007	Kane County (MWL)	LoA	.288	122	431	79	124	20	5	8	58	74	115	24	8	.390	.413
2008	Stockton (CAL)	HiA	.244	114	422	55	103	20	3	10	49	54	116	23	6	.338	.377
2009	Stockton (CAL)	HiA	.247	124	450	63	111	15	6	3	34	73	128	17	10	.350	.327
2010	Stockton (CAL)	HiA	.309	78	304	68	94	21	7	10	32	51	86	21	9	.413	.523
	Midland (TL)	AA	.223	37	121	16	27	3	3	0	11	19	41	2	6	.331	.298
	Sacramento (PCL)	AAA	.182	3	11	1	2	1	0	0	2	1	3	1	0	.250	.273
2011	Midland (TL)	AA	.355	74	304	67	108	15	13	10	50	54	65	14	13	.453	.589
	Sacramento (PCL)	AAA	.302	56	232	48	70	14	3	5	28	39	47	13	5	.401	.453
Minor League Totals			.286	645	2413	420	689	116	42	49	287	387	628	129	63	.386	.429

6 MICHAEL TAYLOR, OF

Born: Dec. 19, 1985. **B-T:** R-R. **Ht.:** 6-5. **Wt.:** 256. **Drafted:** Stanford, 2007 (5th round). **Signed by:** Joey Davis (Phillies).

Taylor came to the A's after the 2009 season in a deal with the Blue Jays for Brett Wallace, an offshoot of the trade that sent Roy Halladay to the Phillies for Taylor, Travis d'Arnaud and Kyle Drabek. Taylor hit 16 homers in Triple-A in 2011 to earn a September callup. Taylor played at Stanford, where hitters are groomed to hit to all fields, even at the expense of power. Five years later, the A's still are trying to get him to be more aggressive about driving pitches. He has the bat speed and strength to hit balls over the fence in any direction. Oakland also has worked on putting him into a better position to hit, in particular getting his front foot down sooner. He controls the strike zone well. Taylor saw action in center field as recently as 2010, but he's an average runner who fits better in right field. His arm is slightly above average. The A's are rebuilding their outfield after Coco Crisp, David DeJesus and Josh Willingham all left as free agents. Taylor, who spent the winter interning at a Bay Area sports radio station, should have an opportunity to seize a big league job in spring training.

BA GRADE
50
MEDIUM

Year	Club (League)	Class	AVG	G	AB	R	H	2B	3B	HR	RBI	BB	SO	SB	CS	OBP	SLG
2007	Williamsport (NYP)	SS	.227	66	233	30	53	14	0	6	33	23	53	8	2	.300	.365
2008	Lakewood (SAL)	LoA	.361	67	249	40	90	12	3	10	64	30	43	10	3	.441	.554
	Clearwater (FSL)	HiA	.329	65	243	36	80	27	1	9	38	19	46	5	6	.380	.560
2009	Reading (EL)	AA	.333	86	318	59	106	22	4	15	65	35	51	18	4	.408	.569
	Lehigh Valley (IL)	AAA	.282	30	110	15	31	6	1	5	19	13	19	3	1	.359	.491
2010	Sacramento (PCL)	AAA	.272	127	464	59	126	26	6	6	78	51	92	16	5	.348	.392
2011	Sacramento (PCL)	AAA	.272	93	349	51	95	16	0	16	64	46	80	14	5	.360	.456
	Oakland (AL)	MAJ	.200	11	30	4	6	0	0	1	1	5	11	0	0	.314	.300
Major League Totals			.200	11	30	4	6	0	0	1	1	5	11	0	0	.314	.300
Minor League Totals			.296	534	1966	310	581	123	15	67	347	218	384	74	26	.371	.476

7 CHRIS CARTER, 1B

Born: Dec. 18, 1986. **B-T:** R-R. **Ht.:** 6-4. **Wt.:** 245. **Drafted:** HS—Las Vegas, 2005 (15th round). **Signed by:** George Kachigian/Joe Butler (White Sox).

Traded by the White Sox for Carlos Quentin and then by the Diamondbacks in a package for Dan Haren in December 2007, Carter has been knocking on the door to the majors since his Double-A Texas League MVP season in 2009. He has yet to break through, batting just .167 with three homers and 41 strikeouts in 114 at-bats with Oakland the last two years. He missed nearly two months last season with a sprained left wrist but recovered to have a productive season in Triple-A. Carter has a short, easy swing with strength to spare. He can hit tape-measure home runs to all fields when he connects, but connecting continues to be a problem. He swings and misses frequently, and while he'll take walks when teams pitch around him, he gets too passive at times. He needs to be more aggressive early in counts when he gets balls he can drive. Carter's athleticism and speed are below average, so he's limited defensively. He played mostly first base in 2011 after seeing action at the outfield corners and third base in the past. He has average arm strength. Carter will be in the mix for the A's first-base and DH jobs. He doesn't have much left to gain from another year in Triple-A, and Oakland desperately needs his power.

BA GRADE

50

MEDIUM

Year	Club (League)	Class	AVG	G	AB	R	H	2B	3B	HR	RBI	BB	SO	SB	CS	OBP	SLG
2005	Bristol (APP)	R	.283	65	233	33	66	17	0	10	37	17	64	2	1	.350	.485
2006	Kannapolis (SAL)	LoA	.130	13	46	4	6	3	0	1	5	5	17	0	0	.231	.261
	Great Falls (PIO)	R	.299	69	251	37	75	21	1	15	59	34	70	4	4	.398	.570
2007	Kannapolis (SAL)	LoA	.291	126	467	84	136	27	3	25	93	67	112	3	2	.383	.522
2008	Stockton (CAL)	HiA	.259	137	506	101	131	32	4	39	104	77	156	4	0	.361	.569
2009	Midland (TL)	AA	.337	125	490	108	165	41	2	24	101	82	119	13	5	.435	.576
	Sacramento (PCL)	AAA	.259	13	54	7	14	2	0	4	14	3	14	0	1	.293	.519
2010	Sacramento (PCL)	AAA	.258	125	465	92	120	29	2	31	94	73	138	1	1	.365	.529
	Oakland (AL)	MAJ	.186	24	70	8	13	1	0	3	7	7	21	1	0	.256	.329
2011	Stockton (CAL)	HiA	.333	6	24	3	8	0	0	3	7	4	8	0	0	.429	.708
	Sacramento (PCL)	AAA	.274	75	296	55	81	18	2	18	72	42	85	5	1	.366	.530
	Oakland (AL)	MAJ	.136	15	44	2	6	0	0	0	0	2	20	0	0	.174	.136
Major League Totals			.167	39	114	10	19	1	0	3	7	9	41	1	0	.226	.254
Minor League Totals			.283	754	2832	524	802	190	14	170	586	404	783	32	15	.379	.540

8 AARON SHIPMAN, OF

Born: Jan. 27, 1992. **B-T:** L-L. **Ht.:** 6-0. **Wt.:** 175. **Drafted:** HS—Quitman, Ga., 2010 (3rd round). **Signed by:** Matt Ranson.

RODGER WOOD

Shipman learned the game from his father Robert, who was a 10th-round pick of the Tigers in 1987 and coached him in high school. His stock soared shortly before the 2010 draft, in which he received $500,000 in the third round. Playing against older competition in the short-season New York-Penn League last year, he got off to a slow start but hit .293/.418/.320 in August. Shipman is an outstanding athlete with plus-plus speed. He has quick wrists and the A's believe he'll add some gap power as he gets stronger. Despite his youth, he's one of the most patient hitters in the system, to the point that Oakland would like him to be a little more aggressive. He already has a good idea of how to read pitchers, stealing 17 bases in 20 tries last season. Though Shipman saw more time in left field in 2011, he's a true center fielder who gets good jumps and takes proper routes. He has solid arm strength and accuracy. Ticketed for the low Class A Midwest League, Shipman will face another challenging offensive environment in 2012. Even if he doesn't develop much home run power, he has all the tools to be a major league center fielder and leadoff hitter.

BA GRADE

55

EXTREME

Year	Club (League)	Class	AVG	G	AB	R	H	2B	3B	HR	RBI	BB	SO	SB	CS	OBP	SLG
2010	Athletics (AZL)	R	.118	4	17	2	2	0	0	0	2	0	6	3	0	.118	.118
2011	Vermont (NYP)	SS	.254	63	201	34	51	8	1	0	19	42	39	17	3	.385	.303
Minor League Totals			.243	67	218	36	53	8	1	0	21	42	45	20	3	.368	.289

9 B.A. VOLLMUTH, 3B

Born: Dec. 23, 1989. **B-T:** R-R. **Ht.:** 6-3. **Wt.:** 220. **Drafted:** Southern Mississippi, 2011 (3rd round). **Signed by:** Kelcey Mucker.

As a freshman, Vollmuth helped Southern Mississippi make its first College World Series appearance in 2009. He went on to hit 32 homers over the next two seasons and became a third-round pick last June, signing for $304,200 shortly before the deadline. Above-average power is easily Vollmuth's biggest selling point. He has a smooth swing, is direct to the ball and generates loft to all fields. Though he's already 6-foot-3 and 220 pounds, the A's believe he still has room to add more strength. He's a streaky hitter prone to strikeouts, so he may not hit for a high average. A shortstop in his first two college seasons, Vollmuth moved to third base last spring and will continue there in pro ball. He shows nice hands and an arm strong enough for the left side of the infield. He needs to learn proper positioning, which should come with more experience. He's a below-average runner. Vollmuth fits the mold of a power-hitting third baseman. He's a candidate to skip a level and go straight to high Class A Stockton for his first full pro season.

BA GRADE
50
HIGH

Year	Club (League)	Class	AVG	G	AB	R	H	2B	3B	HR	RBI	BB	SO	SB	CS	OBP	SLG
2011	Athletics (AZL)	R	.148	8	27	3	4	0	0	1	2	3	6	0	0	.281	.259
	Vermont (NYP)	SS	.500	4	14	8	7	4	1	0	6	2	3	0	1	.588	.929
Minor League Totals			.268	12	41	11	11	4	1	1	8	5	9	0	1	.388	.488

10 BOBBY CROCKER, OF

Born: May 1, 1990. **B-T:** R-R. **Ht.:** 6-3. **Wt.:** 215. **Drafted:** Cal Poly, 2011 (4th round). **Signed by:** Jermaine Clark.

Crocker showed potential as a pitcher in high school, though his tools as an everyday player stood out more and prompted the A's to take him as an outfielder in the 38th round of the 2008 draft. He turned them down and spent three seasons at Cal Poly before Oakland redrafted him in the fourth round last June. He signed for $198,000. Crocker has a physical frame and intriguing raw power, but his approach doesn't tap into it. He has a flat swing plane and hits line drives with authority to all fields. The A's would like to see him add some loft to his stroke and start pulling more balls. Staying inside the ball exceptionally well, he has good feel for going the other way. He's a disciplined hitter and isn't afraid to hit with two strikes. Though Crocker saw most of his time in right field in his pro debut, his above-average speed may play in center. He has fringy arm strength. Oakland loves his work ethic and energy. If Crocker doesn't stick in center, he'll have to produce more power to fit on a corner. He'll open his first full pro season in Class A.

BA GRADE
50
HIGH

Year	Club (League)	Class	AVG	G	AB	R	H	2B	3B	HR	RBI	BB	SO	SB	CS	OBP	SLG
2011	Athletics (AZL)	R	.261	24	88	14	23	4	3	0	4	5	22	2	2	.316	.375
	Vermont (NYP)	SS	.322	32	118	19	38	5	0	3	15	8	22	6	1	.367	.441
Minor League Totals			.296	56	206	33	61	9	3	3	19	13	44	8	3	.345	.413

11 COLLIN COWGILL, OF

BA GRADE
45
LOW

Born: May 22, 1986. **B-T:** R-L. **Ht.:** 5-9. **Wt.:** 185. **Drafted:** Kentucky, 2008 (5th round). **Signed by:** Matt Haas (Diamondbacks).

The A's drafted Cowgill in the 29th round in 2007, when he was coming off a broken hamate bone that kept him out all season at Kentucky. He decided to go back to school as a fourth-year junior and landed with the Diamondbacks, but Oakland finally grabbed him as part of the Trevor Cahill deal in December. Cowgill put together the best season of his pro career in 2011, earning Triple-A Pacific Coast League all-star recognition and a late July callup to Arizona. He filled the fourth outfielder role for the National League West champs and earned a spot on the postseason roster. Cowgill is the prototypical grinder, the kind of player every manager wants on his team. He has a big bat wrap in his approach that leaves him vulnerable to quality fastballs, and his sweepy upper-body swing leads to struggles with breaking balls too. Yet he makes consistent contact, providing line drives to go with some sneaky power and a fair amount of walks. Cowgill is an above-average runner who can steal bases, succeeding on 34 of 39 attempts last year. He's a solid to plus defender at all three outfield positions and has a strong, accurate arm. He's sometimes compared to Cody Ross for his gamer mentality and bats right/throws left profile. Cowgill may never be a big league regular but should carve out a career as a useful fourth outfielder. He'll compete for a job in the A's new-look outfield in spring training.

Year	Club (League)	Class	AVG	G	AB	R	H	2B	3B	HR	RBI	BB	SO	SB	CS	OBP	SLG
2008	Yakima (NWL)	SS	.304	20	79	21	24	3	1	11	28	12	17	5	0	.415	.785
	South Bend (MWL)	LoA	.249	50	201	31	50	13	3	1	17	25	61	1	0	.346	.358
2009	Visalia (CAL)	HiA	.277	61	220	39	61	9	5	6	36	29	49	11	4	.373	.445

2010	Mobile (SL)	AA	.285	131	502	89	143	34	4	16	83	57	73	25	9	.360	.464
2011	Reno (PCL)	AAA	.354	98	395	95	140	24	8	13	70	51	63	30	3	.430	.554
	Arizona (NL)	MAJ	.239	36	92	8	22	3	0	1	9	8	28	4	2	.300	.304
Major League Totals			.239	36	92	8	22	3	0	1	9	8	28	4	2	.300	.304
Minor League Totals			.299	360	1397	275	418	83	21	47	234	174	263	72	16	.383	.490

12 ADRIAN CARDENAS, OF/2B/3B

BA GRADE
45
MEDIUM

Born: Oct. 10, 1987. **B-T:** L-R. **Ht.:** 6-0. **Wt.:** 205. **Drafted:** HS—Miami, 2006 (1st round supplemental). **Signed by:** Miguel Machado (Phillies).

In 2006, Cardenas was Baseball America's High School Player of the Year and the 37th overall pick in the draft. Signed by the Phillies for $925,000, he came to the A's along with Josh Outman and outfield prospect Matt Spencer in a July 2008 trade for Joe Blanton. Cardenas has hit .303 in the minors, but his power never has developed and he has just 29 homers in six pro seasons. That has become more of a problem now that it has become apparent that he can't stick in the middle infield. Cardenas has a fluid, effortless swing and sprays the ball all over the field. He has an innate understanding of how pitchers are trying to attack him. He makes consistent contact but doesn't drive the ball very often. Cardenas spent most of his first four pro seasons at shortstop and second base, but he lacks true middle-infield actions. His speed, quickness and range are all fringy. He improved his ability to turn the double play in 2011, but he played more in left field than anywhere else. He had no outfield experience at any level before last season. While his routes aren't perfect, he catches what he gets to and has an average arm. At this point, he doesn't profile as a regular at any position and looks more like a line drive-hitting utilityman. He could get a chance to serve that role in Oakland at some point this year.

Year	Club (League)	Class	AVG	G	AB	R	H	2B	3B	HR	RBI	BB	SO	SB	CS	OBP	SLG
2006	Phillies (GCL)	R	.318	41	154	22	49	5	4	2	21	17	28	13	3	.384	.442
2007	Lakewood (SAL)	LoA	.295	127	499	70	147	30	2	9	79	47	80	20	1	.354	.417
2008	Clearwater (FSL)	HiA	.307	68	261	44	80	11	6	4	23	28	42	16	0	.371	.441
	Stockton (CAL)	HiA	.278	15	72	11	20	1	0	1	10	1	14	1	0	.297	.333
	Midland (TL)	AA	.279	26	86	12	24	4	0	0	7	15	10	0	1	.392	.326
2009	Midland (TL)	AA	.326	79	325	56	106	26	2	3	55	38	44	5	4	.392	.446
	Sacramento (PCL)	AAA	.251	51	183	23	46	15	2	1	24	17	29	3	2	.317	.372
2010	Midland (TL)	AA	.345	51	194	36	67	15	0	3	32	33	23	4	6	.436	.469
	Sacramento (PCL)	AAA	.267	58	210	30	56	8	1	1	21	17	28	2	2	.320	.329
2011	Sacramento (PCL)	AAA	.314	127	491	70	154	28	4	5	51	47	56	13	6	.374	.418
Minor League Totals			.303	643	2475	374	749	143	21	29	323	260	354	77	31	.368	.413

13 A.J. GRIFFIN, RHP

BA GRADE
50
HIGH

Born: Jan. 28, 1988. **B-T:** R-R. **Ht.:** 6-5. **Wt.:** 215. **Drafted:** San Diego, 2010 (13th round). **Signed by:** Eric Martins.

Griffin was a closer for his first two seasons at San Diego, amassing 28 saves, before moving into the rotation as a junior in 2009. The A's returned Griffin to the bullpen in his 2010 pro debut to limit his innings. He got back to starting in his first full pro season and saw action at all four full-season levels, tying for the most strikeouts (156) in the system and striking out eight over six innings in a spot start for Sacramento on June 12. Griffin isn't overpowering, pitching at 89-92 mph with his fastball, but he makes up for it with feel and quality secondary stuff. He has outstanding fastball command, knows when he should add and subtract velocity and has strong pitching acumen. His above-average changeup rates as his best pitch, featuring sinking action and quality arm speed, and he'll throw it in any count. He can also spin a solid downer curveball. Griffin repeats his high three-quarters delivery well. He has a real competitive streak, sometimes to a fault, as Oakland would like him to control his emotions on the mound better. Coming off his whirlwind 2011 season, Griffin is expected to open 2012 in Double-A, where he'll try to continue on his track to be a mid-rotation starter.

Year	Club (League)	Class	W	L	ERA	G	GS	CG	SV	IP	H	HR	BB	SO	K/9	WHIP	AVG
2010	Athletics (AZL)	R	0	0	0.00	4	0	0	0	5	1	0	0	6	10.8	0.20	.063
	Vancouver (NWL)	SS	1	1	2.95	20	0	0	15	21	14	0	7	27	11.4	0.98	.184
2011	Burlington (MWL)	LoA	4	0	1.56	8	8	0	0	52	36	2	5	46	8.0	0.79	.187
	Stockton (CAL)	HiA	5	3	3.57	12	12	0	0	71	64	8	14	82	10.4	1.10	.246
	Sacramento (PCL)	AAA	0	1	3.00	1	1	0	0	6	6	1	2	8	12.0	1.33	.273
	Midland (TL)	AA	2	3	6.47	6	6	0	0	32	39	6	11	20	5.6	1.56	.293
Minor League Totals			12	8	3.32	51	27	0	15	187	160	17	39	189	9.1	1.06	.229

14 MAX STASSI, C

BA GRADE
50
HIGH

Born: March 15, 1991. **B-T:** R-R. **Ht.:** 5-10. **Wt.:** 205. **Drafted:** HS—Yuba City, Calif., 2009 (4th round). **Signed by:** Jermaine Clark.

Stassi had pedigree and promise when the A's signed him for $1.5 million in 2009, a record for the fourth round at the time. His great-great uncle Myril Hoag played 13 years in the majors; his father Jim played in the minors; and older brother Brock was a 33rd-round pick by the Phillies in 2011. Stassi rarely has been at full strength over his two full seasons in the minors, bothered by right shoulder problems. He was playing through pain and limited to DH duty last season before being shut down in May for surgery. When he's healthy, Stassi has a compact swing with solid power, along with a feel for hitting and using the middle of the field. He was able to DH again during instructional league and showed the same bat speed he had in the past, but he hadn't resumed catching. He hasn't caught in a game since the end of the 2010 season, and the A's are hopeful his arm strength bounces back after the operation. He had a solid arm in the past and was a quality receiver, showing agility and soft hands. He has below-average speed. Stassi was on a throwing program in the fall and continued rehabbing over the winter. The A's hope to get Stassi a fresh start in high Class A this year. He could be an impact bat at catcher and still has time to catch up as he'll play all of 2012 as a 21-year-old.

Year	Club (League)	Class	AVG	G	AB	R	H	2B	3B	HR	RBI	BB	SO	SB	CS	OBP	SLG
2009	Athletics (AZL)	R	.000	1	1	0	0	0	0	0	0	1	1	0	0	.500	.000
	Vancouver (NWL)	SS	.286	13	49	3	14	4	0	0	8	2	11	0	0	.340	.367
2010	Kane County (MWL)	LoA	.229	110	411	54	94	21	1	13	51	45	141	3	3	.310	.380
2011	Stockton (CAL)	HiA	.231	31	121	22	28	6	0	2	19	16	22	1	1	.331	.331
Minor League Totals			.234	155	582	79	136	31	1	15	78	64	175	4	4	.318	.368

15 YORDY CABRERA, SS

BA GRADE
50
HIGH

Born: Sept. 3, 1990. **B-T:** R-R. **Ht.:** 6-4. **Wt.:** 200. **Drafted:** HS—Lakeland, Fla., 2010 (2nd round). **Signed by:** Trevor Schaffer.

Cabrera spent his early years in the Dominican Republic, but he moved to the U.S. at age 14 to join his father Basilio, who played seven seasons in the Tigers organization and manages Detroit's Rookie-level Gulf Coast League squad. He signed with the A's for $1.25 million as the 60th overall pick in 2010, and he was the oldest high school player in his draft class at nearly 20. Cabrera battled inconsistency throughout his first full pro season. He tinkered with how far to spread out his feet in his stance and how much of a leg kick to use, and he tended to come off balance in his swing. He also pressed and tried to do too much, leading him to chase bad pitches. He found a better comfort level in instructional league after the season. His home run totals from last season don't show it, but he does have above-average power potential. Scouts outside the organization look at his big frame and think Cabrera will have to move to third base, but Oakland remains committed to developing him as a shortstop. He was too inconsistent in 2011, making great plays and then booting routine ones, and his 38 errors were the second-most among Midwest League shortstops. He has plenty of arm strength and threw in the low to mid-90s as a pitcher in high school, so third base might be his best fit. Cabrera will try to keep his momentum from instructional league going as he moves up to high Class A in 2012.

Year	Club (League)	Class	AVG	G	AB	R	H	2B	3B	HR	RBI	BB	SO	SB	CS	OBP	SLG
2010	Athletics (AZL)	R	.188	5	16	3	3	1	0	0	0	4	5	0	0	.350	.250
2011	Burlington (MWL)	LoA	.231	101	359	59	83	21	5	6	47	31	110	23	6	.297	.368
Minor League Totals			.229	106	375	62	86	22	5	6	47	35	115	23	6	.299	.363

16 STEVE PARKER, 3B/1B

BA GRADE
45
MEDIUM

Born: Sept. 3, 1987. **B-T:** L-R. **Ht.:** 6-2. **Wt.:** 200. **Drafted:** Brigham Young, 2009 (5th round). **Signed by:** Jeremy Schied.

Parker was the Mountain West Conference co-freshman of the year in 2007, sharing the award with Stephen Strasburg. He hasn't had to face Strasburg since turning pro, and the pitchers he has seen haven't slowed him down. Parker ranked fifth in the Texas League in both hits (144) and walks (69) last season, earning a promotion to Triple-A at the tail end of just his second full year in the minors. Parker has a simple swing that's direct to the ball when he's going well, though it can get long and loopy at times. He has a capable feel for hitting and should keep putting up solid averages as he moves up, but his power might only be barely acceptable for a corner player. He'll probably settle in around 15-20 homers per year, but to get there, the A's want him to be more aggressive and swing with intent more consistently. He doesn't make much hard contact whenever he goes the other way. Parker cut down on his errors at the hot corner, going from 33 in 2010 to 20 last season, but he still tied for the most among TL third basemen. Despite the miscues, Oakland was encouraged by how hard he worked on his defense, and they believe he can become an average third baseman. The A's put him on a throwing program and he ironed out the unorthodox throwing motion he had in college, giving him a quality arm for the left side of the infield. Even if Parker has only fringy power for a third baseman, his bat should earn him a shot at the majors, possibly as soon as 2012, which he'll begin in Triple-A.

Year	Club (League)	Class	AVG	G	AB	R	H	2B	3B	HR	RBI	BB	SO	SB	CS	OBP	SLG
2009	Athletics (AZL)	R	.214	3	14	2	3	2	0	0	2	1	6	0	0	.267	.357
	Kane County (MWL)	LoA	.244	70	254	27	62	11	2	5	39	25	55	1	4	.312	.362
2010	Stockton (CAL)	HiA	.296	139	524	102	155	38	5	21	98	84	105	3	1	.392	.508
2011	Midland (TL)	AA	.286	132	504	72	144	30	2	10	74	69	107	1	1	.373	.413
	Sacramento (PCL)	AAA	.320	5	25	4	8	0	0	0	2	2	6	0	0	.370	.320
Minor League Totals			.282	349	1321	207	372	81	9	36	215	181	279	5	6	.369	.438

17 ANDREW CARIGNAN, RHP

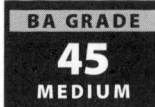

BA GRADE
45
MEDIUM

Born: July 23, 1986. **B-T:** R-R. **Ht.:** 5-11. **Wt.:** 205. **Drafted:** North Carolina, 2007 (5th round). **Signed by:** Neil Avent.

Andrew Bailey was Carignan's set-up man at Double-A Midland in 2008. While Bailey has gone on to become an all-star closer in Oakland, Carignan's career got stuck in neutral. He missed most of 2009 due to soreness in his forearm, followed by surgery to remove bone spurs from his elbow. He returned to the mound in 2010 but wasn't the same, then had to fight through a pulled oblique muscle early in 2011. After all of his time on the sidelines, he emerged last season as a more polished pitcher, and he rocketed from high Class A to the majors. Carignan has a fastball with late life at 94-96 mph. More of a thrower in the past, he now shows a much better understanding of using a gameplan and executing pitches. He also does a better job of staying on line in his delivery, maintaining a consistent release point and moving the ball around the zone. He complements his heater with a knockout slider at 84-86 mph and a decent changeup that he isn't afraid to mix in. After breaking through last season, Carignan will enter 2012 with a chance to make Oakland's bullpen.

Year	Club (League)	Class	W	L	ERA	G	GS	CG	SV	IP	H	HR	BB	SO	K/9	WHIP	AVG
2007	Kane County (MWL)	LoA	1	1	2.03	12	0	0	4	13	6	0	11	19	12.8	1.28	.136
2008	Stockton (CAL)	HiA	1	1	0.90	9	0	0	4	10	5	0	5	17	15.3	1.00	.147
	Midland (TL)	AA	3	3	2.22	46	0	0	24	53	36	4	39	67	11.4	1.42	.196
2009	Stockton (CAL)	HiA	0	0	4.50	2	0	0	0	2	1	0	3	2	9.0	2.00	.167
2010	Stockton (CAL)	HiA	3	3	6.27	30	0	0	0	33	28	2	34	44	12.0	1.88	.228
2011	Stockton (CAL)	HiA	1	0	0.00	9	0	0	5	11	4	0	2	12	9.8	0.55	.108
	Midland (TL)	AA	0	0	3.18	11	0	0	3	11	10	1	3	15	11.9	1.15	.238
	Sacramento (PCL)	AAA	0	0	2.16	13	0	0	0	17	11	1	7	19	10.3	1.08	.186
	Oakland (AL)	MAJ	0	0	4.26	6	0	0	0	6	8	1	2	5	7.1	1.58	.276
Major League Totals			0	0	4.26	6	0	0	0	6	8	1	2	5	7.1	1.58	.276
Minor League Totals			9	8	2.94	132	0	0	40	150	101	8	104	195	11.7	1.37	.191

18 RYAN COOK, RHP

BA GRADE
45
MEDIUM

Born: June 30, 1987. **B-T:** R-R. **Ht.:** 6-3. **Wt.:** 200. **Drafted:** Southern California, 2008 (27th round). **Signed by:** Hal Kurtzman (Diamondbacks).

Cook never posted a sub-5.00 ERA in three seasons at Southern California, but he showed enough promise for the Diamondbacks to give him an $80,000 bonus after they took him in the 27th round of the 2008 draft. He had middling success as a starter in the lower minors before moving to the bullpen and zooming from Double-A to the majors last season, and the A's got him in the December deal that sent Trevor Cahill to Arizona. Cook showed better stuff in shorter stints, though no one expected it to jump as much as it did. He worked with an 89-93 mph fastball as a starter and suddenly had a consistent 95-97 mph heater as a reliever, topping out at 101. His fastball has riding four-seam life. Cook can miss bats with a hard splitter that he throws at 88-91 mph. He also has an 85-88 mph slider with more lateral movement than depth. He can throw the slider for strikes, but he doesn't always command it in the strike zone. Improved overall command is Cook's biggest need. After a taste of the big leagues, he'll contend for a role in Oakland's bullpen.

Year	Club (League)	Class	W	L	ERA	G	GS	CG	SV	IP	H	HR	BB	SO	K/9	WHIP	AVG
2008	Yakima (NWL)	SS	2	2	4.64	7	7	0	0	33	37	4	11	23	6.3	1.45	.272
2009	South Bend (MWL)	LoA	11	11	3.66	25	25	0	0	143	140	5	44	103	6.5	1.29	.265
2010	Reno (PCL)	AAA	0	0	10.80	1	1	0	0	5	7	1	2	5	9.0	1.80	.333
	Visalia (CAL)	HiA	4	7	4.24	20	20	0	0	108	110	3	36	100	8.3	1.35	.263
	Mobile (SL)	AA	1	1	2.89	3	3	0	0	19	13	1	10	12	5.8	1.23	.200
2011	Mobile (SL)	AA	1	4	2.25	34	0	0	13	44	28	2	14	50	10.2	0.95	.179
	Reno (PCL)	AAA	0	1	2.12	14	0	0	6	17	13	0	8	12	6.4	1.24	.224
	Arizona (NL)	MAJ	0	1	7.04	12	0	0	0	8	11	0	8	7	8.2	2.48	.333
Major League Totals			0	1	7.04	12	0	0	0	8	11	0	8	7	8.2	2.48	.333
Minor League Totals			19	26	3.74	104	56	0	19	369	348	16	125	305	7.4	1.28	.252

19 BLAKE TREINEN, RHP

BA GRADE
50
HIGH

Born: June 30, 1988. **B-T:** R-R. **Ht.:** 6-4. **Wt.:** 215. **Drafted:** South Dakota State, 2011 (7th round). **Signed by:** Kevin Mello.

Treinen took a circuitous route to pro ball. He began his college career in 2007 on the junior varsity at Baker (Kan.), an NAIA program, before attending Arkansas without playing baseball in 2008. Then he was off to South Dakota State, where he sat out 2009 because of NCAA transfer rules. Treinen showed impressive arm strength in 2010 and was a 23rd-round pick of the Marlins, but they backed off after a physical raised concerns about his shoulder. Treinen went 7-3, 3.00 as a senior in 2011 and went in the seventh round, making him South Dakota State's highest-drafted player since 1985. Signed for $52,500, Treinen has a physical frame and hard stuff to go with it. He throws a heavy, sinking fastball at 92-97 mph. He complements the heater with an 82-86 mph slider with late, sharp break. He also throws a changeup, but it's definitely his third option and he doesn't fully trust it at this point. Treinen didn't need his changeup much while working as a reliever in his pro debut, but he'll go back to starting in 2012 and Oakland will make sure to emphasize it. He could be a No. 3 starter if his changeup comes around. Treinen has solid mechanics, using a standard three-quarters arm slot. He'll turn 24 next season, so Oakland may look to move him quickly and send him to high Class A.

Year	Club (League)	Class	W	L	ERA	G	GS	CG	SV	IP	H	HR	BB	SO	K/9	WHIP	AVG
2011	Athletics (AZL)	R	0	0	0.00	3	0	0	0	3	3	0	1	7	21.0	1.33	.250
	Burlington (MWL)	LoA	1	1	3.67	18	0	0	2	27	20	1	7	29	9.7	1.00	.202
Minor League Totals			1	1	3.30	21	0	0	2	30	23	1	8	36	10.8	1.03	.207

20 JOSH DONALDSON, C/3B

BA GRADE

45

MEDIUM

Born: Dec. 8, 1985. **B-T:** R-R. **Ht.:** 6-0. **Wt.:** 220. **Drafted:** Auburn, 2007 (1st round supplemental). **Signed by:** Bob Rossi (Cubs).

Donaldson is the last player remaining in the A's organization from the four-prospect package received in the July 2008 trade that sent Rich Harden to the Cubs. Donaldson repeated Triple-A in 2011, improving on his batting average from 2010 and having another solid year in terms of power. Overly aggressive in the past, he cut down on his swing and started managing at-bats rather than just trying to crank home runs. He has a feel for taking balls the other way and at least average raw power, which stands out behind the plate. Donaldson was an infielder until his sophomore year at Auburn, when he moved to catching, and he saw intermittent action at third base last season. The A's liked what they saw from him at the hot corner and consider him an option there, but he's still primarily a catcher. He has a strong arm that's viable at either spot. He moves well blocking balls behind the plate, though his 14 errors were the most among Pacific Coast League catchers. He's a below-average runner but not bad for a catcher. In spring training, Donaldson will compete for the job as Kurt Suzuki's backup in Oakland. A third season in Triple-A wouldn't do much for his development.

Year	Club (League)	Class	AVG	G	AB	R	H	2B	3B	HR	RBI	BB	SO	SB	CS	OBP	SLG
2007	Cubs (AZL)	R	.182	4	11	1	2	2	0	0	0	2	4	0	1	.308	.364
	Boise (NWL)	SS	.346	49	162	37	56	11	2	9	35	37	34	6	2	.470	.605
2008	Peoria (MWL)	LoA	.217	63	235	27	51	13	0	6	23	17	41	7	1	.276	.349
	Stockton (CAL)	HiA	.330	47	188	37	62	13	2	9	39	17	29	0	2	.391	.564
2009	Midland (TL)	AA	.270	124	455	67	123	37	1	9	91	80	92	7	2	.379	.415
2010	Sacramento (PCL)	AAA	.238	86	294	52	70	14	1	18	67	45	79	3	1	.336	.476
	Oakland (AL)	MAJ	.156	14	32	1	5	1	0	1	4	2	12	0	0	.206	.281
2011	Sacramento (PCL)AAA		.261	115	444	79	116	28	0	17	70	51	100	13	4	.344	.439
Major League Totals			.156	14	32	1	5	1	0	1	4	2	12	0	0	.206	.281
Minor League Totals			.268	488	1789	300	480	118	6	68	325	249	379	36	13	.360	.455

21 ROB GILLIAM, RHP

BA GRADE

50

HIGH

Born: Nov. 29, 1987. **B-T:** R-R. **Ht.:** 6-1. **Wt.:** 195. **Drafted:** UNC Greensboro, 2009 (8th round). **Signed by:** Neil Avent.

A's area scout Neil Avent was once an assistant coach at UNC Greensboro, and Oakland has drafted five of its players since 2006. One of them was Gilliam, who worked mostly as a reliever in college and posted a 5.76 ERA as a junior. Scouts still liked his arm, though, and he received $105,000 from Oakland as a ninth-rounder in 2009. The A's believe Gilliam's rough 2011 season was another case of him showing better stuff than his numbers indicate, though he did tie A.J. Griffin for the most strikeouts in the system with 156. Gilliam has a 92-96 mph fastball, though it lacks movement. He found a new grip for his slider last season and it made a real difference for him, creating sharp, late break. His changeup is a work in progress, but he does show some feel for it and it has fading action. Gilliam still is learning the mental side of being a starter, especially when it comes to damage control and continuing to battle after giving up runs. Oakland lowered his arm slot slightly in instructional league, and he has good balance and direction in his delivery. Gilliam will move up to Double-A in 2012, and he could develop into a mid-rotation starter or power reliever.

Year	Club (League)	Class	W	L	ERA	G	GS	CG	SV	IP	H	HR	BB	SO	K/9	WHIP	AVG
2009	Athletics (AZL)	R	0	1	0.00	2	0	0	0	3	4	0	0	2	6.0	1.33	.286
	Vancouver (NWL)	SS	2	0	5.19	6	0	0	0	9	9	1	5	11	11.4	1.62	.290
2010	Kane County (MWL)	LoA	7	6	3.89	24	18	0	0	111	105	7	35	101	8.2	1.26	.253
2011	Stockton (CAL)	HiA	12	7	5.04	28	28	0	0	164	165	24	48	156	8.5	1.30	.263
Minor League Totals			21	14	4.55	60	46	0	0	287	283	32	88	270	8.5	1.29	.260

22 ERIC SOGARD, SS/3B

BA GRADE

45

MEDIUM

Born: May 22, 1986. **B-T:** L-R. **Ht.:** 5-10. **Wt.:** 190. **Drafted:** Arizona State, 2007 (2nd round). **Signed by:** Dave Lottsfeldt (Padres).

Sogard, whose younger brother Alex pitches in the Astros system, was a .371 career hitter in three seasons at Arizona State. He netted $400,000 from the Padres as the 81st overall pick in 2007, and he has hit at every level of the minors. He and Kevin Kouzmanoff came to Oakland in a January 2010 trade that sent Aaron Cunningham and Scott Hairston to San Diego. Sogard's tools don't blow people away, but he has hitting ability. He has a quick swing, rarely gets fooled and sprays line drives all over the field. He has some gap power and showed an improved ability to turn on pitches when he got the chance last season. He controls the strike zone and puts together quality at-bats more consistently than any hitter in the system. He has walked more than he has struck out throughout his minor league career. The A's shifted Sogard to shortstop late in 2010, and he was Sacramento's full-time shortstop last season until he was called up to the majors last July. Sogard's average speed and fringy arm strength make him a better fit at second base, where he played for most of his first four pro seasons. He has put in a lot of work with A's infield coach Mike Gallego, and his ability to handle second, short and third base enhances his utility profile. Sogard will get a chance to fill that role for Oakland in 2012.

Year	Club (League)	Class	AVG	G	AB	R	H	2B	3B	HR	RBI	BB	SO	SB	CS	OBP	SLG
2007	Portland (PCL)	AAA	.000	1	3	0	0	0	0	0	0	0	3	0	0	.250	.000
	Eugene (NWL)	SS	.256	31	125	20	32	9	0	2	18	19	16	4	2	.354	.376
	Fort Wayne (MWL)	LoA	.253	22	83	7	21	2	0	2	15	6	13	2	2	.308	.349
2008	Lake Elsinore (CAL)	HiA	.308	133	536	97	165	42		10	87	79	62	16	7	.394	.453
2009	San Antonio (TL)	AA	.293	117	457	79	134	25	3	6	51	58	47	10	6	.370	.400
2010	Sacramento (PCL)	AAA	.300	137	514	82	154	28	6	5	65	75	68	14	9	.391	.407
	Oakland (AL)	MAJ	.429	4	7	0	3	0	0	0	0	2	1	0	1	.556	.429
2011	Sacramento (PCL)	AAA	.298	79	315	55	94	16	2	5	37	40	34	13	3	.381	.410
	Oakland (AL)	MAJ	.200	27	70	7	14	3	0	2	4	4	13	0	0	.243	.329
Major League Totals			.221	31	77	7	17	3	0	2	4	6	14	0	1	.277	.338
Minor League Totals			.295	520	2033	340	600	122	14	30	273	277	243	59	29	.380	.413

23 JUSTIN SOUZA, RHP

Born: Oct. 22, 1985. **B-T:** R-R. **Ht.:** 6-1. **Wt.:** 185. **Drafted:** Sacramento CC, 2006 (9th round). **Signed by:** Stacey Pettis (Mariners).

BA GRADE
45
MEDIUM

Souza looked to be on the verge of a breakout season after coming over from the Mariners in a trade for Jack Hannahan in 2009, but he was shut down late in 2010 with an elbow injury that required surgery. He also had to face the adversity of his younger brother dying of cystic fibrosis in January 2011. Once Souza joined Midland's bullpen last May, he looked like the pitcher the A's had gotten excited about in the fall of 2009. He pitches at 92-95 mph with his fastball and can dial it up to 97, though it's fairly straight. His slider and changeup can be major league quality when they're on, but he needs them to be more consistent. He can get the slider up to 86 mph, while the changeup has some depth to it at 83-85 mph. Souza was aggressive and controlled the strike zone when he was going well last year, though his command could still be tightened. Teams have toyed with using him as a starter in the past, but those days are over, given that his medical history also includes shoulder issues. Souza will return to Triple-A to open 2011 and could be an option in the big league bullpen in the near future, though he'll have to regain a place on the 40-man roster after losing it at the end of 2010.

Year	Club (League)	Class	W	L	ERA	G	GS	CG	SV	IP	H	HR	BB	SO	K/9	WHIP	AVG
2006	Everett (NWL)	SS	2	2	4.99	17	0	0	1	31	32	5	13	33	9.7	1.47	.267
2007	Wisconsin (MWL)	LoA	5	5	4.73	49	3	0	2	91	119	12	8	58	5.7	1.39	.304
2008	Wisconsin (MWL)	LoA	3	3	3.69	30	0	0	4	39	36	3	13	40	9.2	1.26	.247
	Tacoma (PCL)	AAA	0	0	2.08	2	0	0	0	4	4	0	0	3	6.2	0.92	.235
	High Desert (CAL)	HiA	2	1	4.31	12	5	0	0	40	46	5	13	39	8.8	1.49	.293
2009	West Tenn (SL)	AA	6	6	3.35	20	14	0	0	78	73	4	18	62	7.2	1.17	.247
	Midland (TL)	AA	0	2	10.35	5	5	0	0	20	32	1	10	13	5.9	2.10	.368
2010	Midland (TL)	AA	2	2	3.38	28	0	0	6	40	35	1	20	38	8.6	1.38	.230
	Sacramento (PCL)	AAA	0	0	8.00	5	0	0	0	9	8	2	6	7	7.0	1.56	.242
2011	Midland (TL)	AA	1	0	1.33	14	0	0	1	20	9	2	2	17	7.5	0.54	.125
	Sacramento (PCL)	AAA	3	1	4.85	26	0	0	0	43	43	8	11	31	6.5	1.27	.264
Minor League Totals			24	22	4.38	208	27	0	14	415	437	43	114	341	7.4	1.33	.267

24 CHRIS BOSTICK, SS/2B

Born: March 24, 1993. **B-T:** R-R. **Ht.:** 5-11. **Wt.:** 185. **Drafted:** HS—Rochester, N.Y., 2011 (44th round). **Signed by:** Matt Higginson.

BA GRADE
50
HIGH

Oakland signed only one high school player from last year's draft, and they may have made it count by landing Bostick. After getting picked in the 44th round, he spent last summer hitting .413/.503/.652 against older competition in the New York Collegiate League. The A's signed him in late July for $125,000. More advanced than a typical Northeast prep product, Bostick wowed the organization with his approach and how quickly he adjusted to the pro game. He consistently barrels balls and hits line drives from gap to gap, with a chance to develop some home run power as he gets older. Bostick has the potential to stick at short-stop and shows good instincts for the position, though he may wind up at second base. His arm action is a little long, but he's accurate and can make the throws from shortstop. Though his infield actions can be a little rough, he's a good athlete with above-average speed. Bostick might be advanced enough to handle an assignment to low

Class A Burlington for his first full season. He's a few years away but shows promise as a well-rounded player.

Year	Club (League)	Class	AVG	G	AB	R	H	2B	3B	HR	RBI	BB	SO	SB	CS	OBP	SLG
2011	Athletics (AZL)	R	.442	14	52	13	23	6	1	1	5	3	12	4	0	.482	.654
Minor League Totals			.442	14	52	13	23	6	1	1	5	3	12	4	0	.482	.654

25 CHIH-FANG PAN, 2B

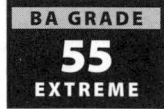

BA GRADE
50
HIGH

Born: Nov. 12, 1990. **B-T:** L-R. **Ht.:** 6-1. **Wt.:** 170. **Signed:** Taiwan, 2010. **Signed by:** Adam Hislop.

Pan has done nothing but hit since coming to the United States in 2010. He was short-season Vermont's leading hitter at .336 last season before he had to leave in late August to return to Taiwan to try out for the national team. Otherwise he would've risked losing his exemption from military service. Pan uses the kind of running, floating swing typical of Asian hitters, and he has an innate ability to square balls up and hit them from foul line to foul line. With the way he swings with his feet moving and front side leaking, he'll look bad at times, but he has solid bat speed and consistently hits line drives. He fits as a top-of-the-order hitter, as he runs well and has limited home run power. Pan was signed as a shortstop but spent most of his time at second base last year. His range and arm strength were questionable at shortstop, but he can be a plus defender at second. He has a short, quick release on his throws and is impressive turning double plays. Pan will at least move up to low Class A to open 2012, with an outside chance at playing his way to high Class A during spring training.

Year	Club (League)	Class	AVG	G	AB	R	H	2B	3B	HR	RBI	BB	SO	SB	CS	OBP	SLG
2010	Athletics (AZL)	R	.331	43	157	31	52	9	4	0	11	13	24	3	4	.386	.439
2011	Vermont (NYP)	SS	.336	37	143	22	48	4	0	1	22	12	27	8	4	.386	.385
Minor League Totals			.333	80	300	53	100	13	4	1	33	25	51	11	8	.386	.413

26 RENATO NUNEZ, 3B

BA GRADE
55
EXTREME

Born: April 4, 1994. **B-T:** R-R. **Ht.:** 6-1. **Wt.:** 185. **Signed:** Venezuela, 2010. **Signed by:** Julio Franco.

The A's scouted Nunez for three years before signing him for $2.2 million once he became eligible on July 2, 2010. In his pro debut in the Dominican Summer League, he didn't post dominant numbers and was plagued by injuries, the most notable a concussion after being hit in the head with a pitch. Nunez has a balanced swing with tremendous bat control and a good swing path. Oakland believes he'll have power to all fields and he shows leverage in his swing, but it hasn't translated into results yet outside of batting practice. Nunez didn't focus much on his defense before signing and has some catching up to do on that side of the ball. He spent a lot of time working on his foot speed and agility last year, and they're getting closer to average. He has solid hands and average arm strength. The A's brought Nunez to the United States in the fall for instructional league. He didn't have much success on the field there, but they didn't expect him to and the purpose was more to get his feet wet than anything else. He'll return to the States in 2012 for spring training and then an assignment to the Rookie-level Arizona League.

Year	Club (League)	Class	AVG	G	AB	R	H	2B	3B	HR	RBI	BB	SO	SB	CS	OBP	SLG
2011	Athletics (DSL)	R	.268	53	194	20	52	12	0	5	28	6	42	1	2	.301	.407
Minor League Totals			.268	53	194	20	52	12	0	5	28	6	42	1	2	.301	.407

27 MICHAEL YNOA, RHP

BA GRADE
50
EXTREME

Born: Sept. 24, 1991. **B-T:** R-R. **Ht.:** 6-7. **Wt.:** 210. **Signed:** Dominican Republic, 2008. **Signed by:** Raymond Abreu.

The A's ponied up $4.25 million to sign Ynoa in 2008, a bonus that remains the largest in franchise history and was the largest ever for a Latin American amateur at the time. Arm injuries have limited him to all of nine innings in the three full years since. He missed the 2011 regular season rehabbing from Tommy John surgery, but he did get back on the mound in the fall at the team's Dominican complex. Ynoa's talent is apparent whenever he does pitch, but those times have been too few and far between. In the fall, he pitched at 92-94 mph with downhill angle on his fastball. He wasn't going all out when he threw his curveball, but it did show tight rotation. In the past, he had a curve that dropped off the table with late break. He also has a changeup with good arm speed and late sink. His mechanics are smooth and balanced. If healthy, Ynoa will pitch in the Arizona League or at Vermont in 2012. He still has frontline potential, but it's time he gets on the mound and shows it.

Year	Club (League)	Class	W	L	ERA	G	GS	CG	SV	IP	H	HR	BB	SO	K/9	WHIP	AVG
2009	Did Not Play—Injured																
2010	Athletics (AZL)	R	0	1	5.00	3	3	0	0	9	6	1	4	11	11.0	1.11	.188
2011	Did Not Play—Injured																
Minor League Totals			0	1	5.00	3	3	0	0	9	6	1	4	11	11.0	1.11	.187

28 RYAN ORTIZ, C

BA GRADE
45
HIGH

Born: Sept. 29, 1987. **B-T:** R-R. **Ht.:** 6-3. **Wt.:** 195. **Drafted:** Oregon State, 2009 (6th round). **Signed by:** Jim Coffman.

Ortiz' first full pro season in 2010 was interrupted by surgery on his throwing shoulder that August, and he didn't get back into games until late last May. When he did, he made quick work of the California League and made his Double-A debut in July. He already had an advanced feel for hitting and the ability to go to the opposite field. He used to be more of an upright swinger, and last season he started using his legs more. He was able to get down to the ball and drive it, and he has enough raw power to be a 20-homer threat. Ortiz's bat is ahead of his defense, which needs plenty of polish. He'll have to do a better job of getting down and blocking balls, and scouts aren't impressed with his receiving. He allowed 17 passed balls in just 68 games behind the plate in 2011. Ortiz showed an average arm before his surgery, but it hadn't come back last season, when he threw out just 17 percent of basestealers. He does receive high marks for his ability to handle a pitching staff. Ortiz's bat will give him a chance as long as he stays at catcher. He's a below-average runner, and his value will plummet if he ever has to move to another position. He'll return to Double-A to start 2012.

Year	Club (League)	Class	AVG	G	AB	R	H	2B	3B	HR	RBI	BB	SO	SB	CS	OBP	SLG
2009	Vancouver (NWL)	SS	.258	48	151	25	39	12	1	4	24	26	29	3	0	.388	.430
2010	Stockton (CAL)	HiA	.277	58	188	35	52	12	1	8	35	36	47	1	0	.394	.479
2011	Stockton (CAL)	HiA	.340	28	97	17	33	5	0	4	21	21	22	2	0	.455	.515
	Midland (TL)	AA	.237	47	152	19	36	4	0	2	14	21	40	2	0	.357	.303
Minor League Totals			.272	181	588	96	160	33	2	18	94	104	138	8	0	.393	.427

29 IAN KROL, LHP

BA GRADE
45
HIGH

Born: May 9, 1991. **B-T:** L-L. **Ht.:** 6-1. **Wt.:** 186. **Drafted:** HS—Naperville, Ill., 2009 (7th round). **Signed by:** Kevin Mello.

Signed for $925,000 as a seventh-round pick in 2009, Krol led the Midwest League in ERA (2.65) in his first full pro season. Injuries and off-field problems prevented him from building on that in 2011. Elbow soreness kept him on the shelf until midseason, when he began rehabbing in the Arizona League. His comeback was short-lived, however, as the A's was suspended Krol for making derogatory comments on Twitter, including a homophobic slur. It wasn't the first time he has had issues. He was suspended from his high school team his senior year for being found in the presence of alcohol. When he gets back on the mound in 2012, the A's expect Krol to be the same pitcher he was in 2010. He doesn't have an overpowering fastball, but his curveball and changeup can both be plus pitches. His heater works at 88-89 mph and peaks at 91, playing up because it has good life and he commands it to both sides of the plate. He can get swings and misses with his 11-to-5 curveball, and his changeup features sinking and tailing movement. Krol has quality mound presence, though his lack of projection leads scouts to believe his best-case scenario is as a mid-rotation starter.

Year	Club (League)	Class	W	L	ERA	G	GS	CG	SV	IP	H	HR	BB	SO	K/9	WHIP	AVG
2009	Athletics (AZL)	R	0	0	0.00	1	1	0	0	1	0	0	0	0	0.0	0.00	.000
	Vancouver (NWL)	SS	0	1	8.10	3	1	0	0	3	6	0	1	4	10.8	2.10	.375
2010	Kane County (MWL)	LoA	9	4	2.65	24	23	0	0	119	98	5	19	91	6.9	0.99	.223
	Stockton (CAL)	HiA	1	0	3.66	4	4	0	0	20	18	3	9	20	9.2	1.37	.247
2011	Athletics (AZL)	R	0	0	0.00	3	3	0	0	5	0	0	0	6	10.8	0.00	.000
Minor League Totals			10	5	2.80	35	32	0	0	148	122	8	29	121	7.4	1.02	.223

30 BEAU TAYLOR, C

BA GRADE
45
HIGH

Born: Feb. 13, 1990. **B-T:** L-R. **Ht.:** 6-0. **Wt.:** 200. **Drafted:** Central Florida, 2011 (5th round). **Signed by:** Trevor Schaffer.

Taylor batted .337 as a three-year starter at Central Florida and backstopped the Knights to their first NCAA regional appearance in seven years as a junior in 2011. He earned a $147,600 bonus as a fifth-rounder and handled himself well as he was pushed to low Class A in his pro debut. Taylor came to pro ball with a bit of an unorthodox approach and a wide open batting stance. That style had worked for him, but the A's got him to be more conventional in instructional league. That allowed him to see pitches better and get in better position to handle them. He uses all fields with a line-drive stroke but won't hit for a ton of power, and he hit just 16 homers over his college career. Taylor still has to learn the finer points of calling pitches, but the A's have liked what they've seen of his catching from a technical standpoint. He's agile and a solid receiver. His arm strength is solid and plays up thanks to great footwork, helping him throw out 39 percent of basestealers in his first summer in pro ball. He's a below-average runner. With Max Stassi ticketed for high Class A, Taylor likely will head back to Burlington to start his first full pro season.

Year	Club (League)	Class	AVG	G	AB	R	H	2B	3B	HR	RBI	BB	SO	SB	CS	OBP	SLG
2011	Vermont (NYP)	SS	.111	5	18	1	2	0	0	0	1	0	4	0	0	.111	.111
	Burlington (MWL)	LoA	.293	43	147	16	43	7	2	0	17	18	34	1	3	.367	.367
Minor League Totals			.273	48	165	17	45	7	2	0	18	18	38	1	3	.342	.339

Philadelphia Phillies

BY MATT FORMAN

The story of the 2011 Phillies wasn't supposed to end the way it did, or as early as it did.

Philadelphia planned to ride its Phearsome Phoursome to a parade down Broad Street. Instead, the season ended nine victories and four weeks earlier than anticipated, and the organization's fears were suddenly realized.

Though the Phillies took their fifth straight National League East title, won a franchise-record 102 games and finished with the best record in baseball for the second straight year, losing to the Cardinals in the NL Division Series made 2011 a disappointment. Anything short of a World Series crown would have been, as Philadelphia entered the postseason as the prohibitive favorite.

The 2011 season also marked the end of an era. Only 10 players remained from the 2008 squad that won it all, and come 2012, only five members of the core that changed the franchise's fortunes might remain.

The most successful stretch in Phillies history doesn't have to end—Roy Halladay, Ryan Howard, Cliff Lee and Chase Utley are all signed through 2013 or longer—but as GM Ruben Amaro Jr. said during his season-in-review news conference, "change is good." For the second consecutive year, Amaro stressed the need for Philadelphia to get younger.

"We did it with our pitching staff, and we have to do it with our position players," Amaro said. "It's a young game played by young players, and hopefully we can get younger."

That will be easier said than done. During the last four seasons, the Phillies have used their farm system to bolster its major league roster. They've traded 17 prospects to acquire Joe Blanton, Halladay, Lee, Roy Oswalt and Hunter Pence, leaving the system bereft of high-end, impact talent, though there's still quality depth.

The move too get younger will start with Domonic Brown, who was No. 1 on this list a year ago but no longer qualifies. He could be joined in Philadelphia in 2012 by three of the system's best prospects, hard-throwing relievers Phillippe Aumont and Justin De Fratus and slick-fielding shortstop Freddy Galvis.

With Brown's graduation to the big leagues, right-hander Trevor May ascended to become the organization's clear-cut top prospect. First baseman Jonathan Singleton and righthander Jarred Cosart would have competed for that No. 1 spot had they not been included in the Pence trade with the Astros.

In an effort to replenish the system, scouting direc-

Domonic Brown graduated to the majors but has yet to establish himself in Philadelphia

DAVID SCHOFIELD

TOP 30 PROSPECTS

1. Trevor May, rhp	**16.** Ervis Manzanillo, lhp
2. Jesse Biddle, lhp	**17.** Julio Rodriguez, rhp
3. Sebastian Valle, c	**18.** Kyrell Hudson, of
4. Jonathan Pettibone, rhp	**19.** Harold Garcia, 2b
5. Phillippe Aumont, rhp	**20.** Larry Greene, of
6. Freddy Galvis, ss	**21.** Perci Garner, rhp
7. Justin De Fratus, rhp	**22.** Austin Hyatt, rhp
8. Brody Colvin, rhp	**23.** Mitchell Walding, ss
9. Jiwan James, of	**24.** Leandro Castro, of
10. Maikel Franco, 3b	**25.** Joe Savery, lhp
11. Roman Quinn, ss	**26.** Austin Wright, lhp
12. Lisalberto Bonilla, rhp	**27.** Zach Collier, of
13. Carlos Tocci, of	**28.** J.C. Ramirez, rhp
14. Cesar Hernandez, 2b	**29.** Adam Morgan, lhp
15. Aaron Altherr, of	**30.** Michael Schwimer, rhp

tor Marti Wolever took several projectable high-ceiling, fast-twitch athletes in the 2011 draft, including outfielders Larry and Tyler Greene (no relation) and shortstops Roman Quinn and Mitch Walding.

Assistant GM for player development Chuck LaMar, in that post since 2008, resigned in early September. He left amid rumors of personality conflicts, despite the admirable job he performed at developing blue-chip prospects. The Phillies hired Joe Jordan, whose drafts as Orioles scouting director the last seven years included Zach Britton and Matt Wieters, to replace LaMar but without the assistant GM title.

General Manager: Ruben Amaro Jr. **Farm Director:** Joe Jordan. **Scouting Director:** Marti Wolever.

Class	Team	League	W	L	Pct	Finish*	Manager(s)
Majors	Philadelphia Phillies	National	102	60	.630	1st (16)	Charlie Manuel
Triple-A	Lehigh Valley Iron Pigs	International	80	64	.556	4th (14)	Ryne Sandberg
Double-A	Reading Phillies	Eastern	74	68	.521	5th (12)	Mark Parent
High A	Clearwater Threshers	Florida State	75	63	.543	3rd (12)	Dusty Wathan
Low A	Lakewood BlueClaws	South Atlantic	68	69	.496	10th (14)	Chris Truby
Short-season	Williamsport Crosscutters	New York-Penn	43	33	.566	4th (14)	Mickey Morandini
Rookie	GCL Phillies	Gulf Coast	27	32	.458	t-9th (15)	Rolando de Armas
Overall 2011 Minor League Record			367	329	.527	7th (30)	

*Finish in overall standings (No. of teams in league). †League champion.

LAST YEAR'S TOP 30

Player, Pos.	Status
1. Domonic Brown, of	Majors
2. Jonathan Singleton, 1b/of	(Astros)
3. Brody Colvin, rhp	No. 8
4. Jarred Cosart, rhp	(Astros)
5. Trevor May, rhp	No. 1
6. Sebastian Valle, c	No. 3
7. Jiwan James, of	No. 9
8. Jesse Biddle, lhp	No. 2
9. Domingo Santana, of	(Astros)
10. Aaron Altherr, of	No. 15
11. Vance Worley, rhp	Majors
12. Antonio Bastardo, lhp	Majors
13. Scott Mathieson, rhp	(Yomiuri/Japan)
14. Phillippe Aumont, rhp	No. 5
15. Justin De Fratus, rhp	No. 7
16. Tyson Gillies, of	Dropped out
17. J.C. Ramirez, rhp	No. 28
18. Jonathan Pettibone, rhp	No. 4
19. Cesar Hernandez, 2b	No. 14
20. Freddy Galvis, ss	No. 6
21. Perci Garner, rhp	No. 21
22. Harold Garcia, 2b	No. 19
23. Josh Zeid, rhp	(Astros)
24. Austin Hyatt, rhp	No. 22
25. Julio Rodriguez, rhp	No. 17
26. Matt Rizzotti, 1b	Dropped out
27. Leandro Castro, of	No. 24
28. Kelly Dugan, of	Dropped out
29. Kevin Walter, rhp	Dropped out
30. Cameron Rupp, c	Dropped out

BEST TOOLS

Best Hitter for Average	Harold Garcia
Best Power Hitter	Larry Greene
Best Strike-Zone Discipline	Mike Rizzotti
Fastest Baserunner	Roman Quinn
Best Athlete	Jiwan James
Best Fastball	Phillippe Aumont
Best Curveball	Phillippe Aumont
Best Slider	Justin De Fratus
Best Changeup	Austin Hyatt
Best Control	Jonathan Pettibone
Best Defensive Catcher	Tuffy Gosewisch
Best Defensive Infielder	Freddy Galvis
Best Infield Arm	Freddy Galvis
Best Defensive Outfielder	Jiwan James
Best Outfield Arm	Jiwan James

PROJECTED 2015 LINEUP

Catcher	Sebastian Valle
First Base	Ryan Howard
Second Base	Chase Utley
Third Base	Maikel Franco
Shortstop	Freddy Galvis
Left Field	Domonic Brown
Center Field	Shane Victorino
Right Field	Hunter Pence
No. 1 Starter	Cliff Lee
No. 2 Starter	Roy Halladay
No. 3 Starter	Cole Hamels
No. 4 Starter	Trevor May
No. 5 Starter	Vance Worley
Closer	Jonathan Papelbon

TOP PROSPECTS OF THE DECADE

Year	Player, Pos.	2011 Org.
2002	Marlon Byrd, of	Cubs
2003	Gavin Floyd, rhp	White Sox
2004	Cole Hamels, lhp	Phillies
2005	Ryan Howard, 1b	Phillies
2006	Cole Hamels, lhp	Phillies
2007	Carlos Carrasco, rhp	Indians
2008	Carlos Carrasco, rhp	Indians
2009	Domonic Brown, of	Phillies
2010	Domonic Brown, of	Phillies
2011	Domonic Brown, of	Phillies

TOP DRAFT PICKS OF THE DECADE

Year	Player, Pos.	2011 Org.
2002	Cole Hamels, lhp	Phillies
2003	Tim Moss, 2b (3rd round)	Out of baseball
2004	Greg Golson, of	Yankees
2005	Mike Costanzo, 3b (2nd round)	Reds
2006	Kyle Drabek, rhp	Blue Jays
2007	Joe Savery, lhp	Phillies
2008	Anthony Hewitt, 3b/of	Phillies
2009	Kelly Dugan, of (2nd round)	Phillies
2010	Jesse Biddle, lhp	Phillies
2011	Larry Greene, of	Phillies

LARGEST BONUSES IN CLUB HISTORY

Gavin Floyd, 2001	$4,200,000
Pat Burrell, 1998	$3,150,000
Brett Myers, 1999	$2,050,000
Cole Hamels, 2002	$2,000,000
Chase Utley, 2000	$1,780,000

PHILADELPHIA PHILLIES

TOP 2012 ROOKIE: Justin De Fratus, rhp. The most big league-ready of the Phillies' upper-minors relievers, he can make an impact similar to what Mike Stutes did last year.

BREAKOUT PROSPECT: Ervis Manzanillo, lhp. He's still raw and unpolished, but he flashes three plus pitches.

SLEEPER: Ethan Stewart, lhp. A 47th-round pick out of New Mexico JC in 2010, the Canadian has a physical frame and a loose arm.

SOURCE OF TOP 30 TALENT

Homegrown	28	Acquired	2
College	6	Trades	2
Junior college	1	Rule 5 draft	0
High school	12	Independent leagues	0
Draft-and-follow	0	Free agents/waivers	0
Nondrafted free agents	0		
International	9		

LF
Larry Greene (20)
Leandro Castro (24)
Zach Collier (27)
Miguel Alvarez

CF
Jiwan James (9)
Carlos Tocci (13)
Kyrell Hudson (18)
Tyson Gillies
Brian Pointer
Gauntlett Eldemire

RF
Aaron Altherr (15)
Kelly Dugan
Anthony Hewitt

3B
Maikel Franco (10)
Mitchell Walding (23)
Carlos Rivero
Cody Asche
Harold Martinez
Jeremy Barnes

SS
Freddy Galvis (6)
Roman Quinn (11)
Tyler Greene
Gustavo Gonzalez
Edgar Duran

2B
Cesar Hernandez (14)
Harold Garcia (19)
Carlos Perdomo

1B
Cody Overbeck
Darin Ruf
Matt Rizzotti

C
Sebastian Valle (3)
Logan Moore
Cameron Rupp
Tuffy Gosewisch

LHP

LHSP	LHRP
Jesse Biddle (2)	Joe Savery (25)
Ervis Manzanillo (16)	Jacob Diekman
Austin Wright (26)	Frank Gailey
Adam Morgan (29)	Mario Hollands
Ethan Stewart	James Birmingham
Bryan Morgado	Jay Johnson
Lino Martinez	
Matt Way	
Nick Hernandez	
Braden Shull	

RHP

RHSP	RHRP
Trevor May (1)	Phillippe Aumont (5)
Jonathan Pettibone (4)	Justin De Fratus (7)
Brody Colvin (8)	J.C. Ramirez (28)
Lisalberto Bonilla (12)	Michael Schwimer (30)
Julio Rodriguez (17)	Juan Sosa
Perci Garner (21)	B.J. Rosenberg
Austin Hyatt (22)	Colby Shreve
David Buchanan	Eric Pettis
Kevin Walter	Mike Cisco
Tyler Cloyd	Colton Murray
Garett Claypool	Kenny Giles
Roman Oviedo	Mike Nesseth
Jonathan Musser	Ebelin Lugo
	Tyler Knigge
	Ryan Duke

2011

BEST PURE HITTER: SS Mitchell Walding (5) has the lefthanded swing, bat speed and approach to make an impact at the plate once he fills out his 6-foot-3, 195-pound frame. SS Roman Quinn (2) should be able to beat out plenty of hits with his speed, and he's trying to tap into it even more by learning to switch-hit.

BEST POWER HITTER: Extremely physical at 6-foot-1 and 230 pounds, OF Larry Greene (1s) had some of the best raw power in the entire draft. 3B Harold Martinez (2) has plus power potential but an inconsistent amateur track record as a hitter.

FASTEST RUNNER: Quinn was the fastest player in the draft. He can slap the ball and get to first base in 3.6 seconds from the left side of the plate, and he reminds the Phillies of their 2003 fourth-round pick, Michael Bourn. They'll try Quinn at shortstop, where he has average hands and a plus arm, with center field as his fallback.

BEST DEFENSIVE PLAYER: Though C Logan Moore (9) moved from third base to behind the plate just last spring, he quickly has picked up impressive catch-and-throw skills. Martinez is an athletic defender with a strong arm at third base.

BEST FASTBALL: RHP Kenny Giles (7) is still figuring out his command and secondary pitches, but he can run his fastball to 99 mph and usually deals at 94-96.

BEST SECONDARY PITCH: LHP Austin Wright (8) used his nasty curveball to strike out 85 hitters in 68 pro innings. He sets his curve up with a plus fastball that sits in the low 90s.

BEST PRO DEBUT: Wright was the revelation of Philadelphia's draft, pitching his way to low Class A, where he posted a 2.67 ERA in seven starts. RHP Ryan Duke (25) used a solid fastball/slider combo to post a 0.78 ERA and limit opponents to a .128 average in two stops.

BEST ATHLETE: Quinn received all-state basketball recognition as a point guard at Florida's 2-A level. Walding accounted for 3,041 yards and 26 touchdowns in 13 games as a high school senior quarterback. SS Tyler Greene (11) still has to translate his tools into skills, but he has intriguing all-around ability.

MOST INTRIGUING BACKGROUND: Unsigned 2B Andrew Amaro (47) is the stepbrother of Phillies GM Ruben Amaro. Unsigned OF Ryan Garvey's (15) father Steve was a 10-time all-star and the 1974 National League MVP. 1B Mike Marshall's (30) dad Mike made an All-Star Game appearance, and Moore's father Brad got a cup of coffee in Philadelphia.

CLOSEST TO THE MAJORS: Wright will be on the fast track if he throws enough strikes. Giles could join him if he can refine his slider and command.

BEST LATE-ROUND PICK: Tyler Greene or RHP Colton Murray (13), who profiles as a possible set-up man with his low-90s fastball and solid slider.

THE ONE WHO GOT AWAY: Garvey has the chance to have an impact bat, but he turned down third-round money to attend Southern California.

ASSESSMENT: The Phillies had a typical Phillies draft, taking high-ceiling athletes such as the Greenes (no relation), Quinn and Walding. The early returns on Wright also have been promising.

2010

LHP Jesse Biddle (1), a hometown product, has drawn some comparisons to Andy Pettitte. The rest of this draft class has been slow to develop.

GRADE: C

2009

The Phillies didn't have a first-round pick but got a first-round bat in 1B/OF Jonathan Singleton (8), the key piece in the Hunter Pence trade in July. RHP Brody Colvin (7) regressed last season but still has a high ceiling, as does OF Aaron Altherr (9).

GRADE: B

2008

RHPs Vance Worley (3) and Mike Stutes (11) were valuable members of Philadelphia's pitching staff last year, RHP Michael Schwimer (14) joined them in September, and RHPs Jonathan Pettibone (3s) and Trevor May (4) may not be far behind. OF Anthony Gose (2) and RHPs Jason Knapp (2) and Jarred Cosart (38) were used in deals for Roy Halladay, Cliff Lee and Pence. It doesn't matter that the top picks, OFs Anthony Hewitt (1) and Zach Collier (1s), have struggled.

GRADE: B+

2007

This crop has yielded four big leaguers in LHP Joe Savery (1), OF Michael Taylor (5) and RHPs Justin De Fratus (11) and Brian Schlitter (16), but the prize is C Travis d'Arnaud (1s). He and Taylor were part of the Halladay trade. OF Jiwan James (22) is an impressive athlete.

GRADE: B+

Draft analysis by Jim Callis. Numbers in parentheses indicate draft rounds.

1 TREVOR MAY, RHP

Born: Sept. 23, 1989. **B-T:** R-R. **Ht.:** 6-5. **Wt.:** 215.
Drafted: HS—Kelso, Wash., 2008 (4th round). **Signed by:** Dave Ryles.

BA GRADE
60
HIGH

CLIFF WELCH

The Phillies like strong-armed high school right-handers and have drafted several players from the Pacific Northwest in recent years. May fits into both demographics, and he signed for $375,000 as a fourth-round pick in 2008, when he ranked as the top prospect in Washington. Since then, May slowly has climbed through the system, moving from projectable package to Philadelphia's top prospect. After cruising through his first two pro seasons, he opened 2010 in high Class A Clearwater but struggled with his command and control. Then-farm director Chuck LaMar demoted him to low Class A Lakewood that July at the suggestion of senior advisor and former GM Pat Gillick, and May responded by carrying the BlueClaws to their second consecutive South Atlantic League title. He dominated during his return to the Florida State League in 2011, cutting his walk rate in half and leading the minors with 12.4 strikeouts per nine innings. His 208 whiffs topped the FSL and ranked third in the minors. The Phillies named him their minor league pitcher of the year.

Scouts compare May to Chris Carpenter because of his size and swing-and-miss stuff. May's best pitch is his 90-95 mph fastball, which has heavy life and great angle, and he holds his velocity deep into games. He has worked to add a two-seamer to his arsenal, though his high three-quarters arm slot produces natural armside run. He gained consistency with his secondary offerings in 2011, particularly with his changeup. His No. 2 pitch is a 74-78 mph downer curveball, which was his best weapon in high school, but he overthrows it at times. His changeup sits at 80-82 mph and shows above-average potential with sink, though he occasionally slows down his arm speed when he throws it. Philadelphia introduced a slider to give May a fourth pitch, and he started throwing it during bullpen sessions in the second half of 2011. The progression of his command and offspeed stuff has resulted from his improved ability to repeat his delivery. The Phillies

SCOUTING GRADES

Fastball: 65.   **Command/**
Curveball: 60.   **Control:** 40.
Changeup: 55.   **Delivery:** 50.

Based on 20-80 scouting scale, where 50 represents major league average, and future projection rather than present tools.

worked to simplify his motion and get his limbs going in the same direction, and now there are no concerns. May had a tendency to fall in love with strikeouts in the past, but now they're coming more as a natural result of his stuff and aptitude. He induces a lot of whiffs on high fastballs out of the zone, which will be harder to get against more advanced competition. He also works a lot of deep counts and needs to do a better job of getting ahead of hitters. He's a durable innings-eater who's still growing into his 6-foot-5 frame.

Despite spending the last three seasons in A-ball, May still will be age-appropriate as a 22-year-old with Double-A Reading in 2012. If his command continues to improve, he could become a No. 2 starter, and he should be at least a solid mid-rotation workhorse. With Philadelphia's starting staff set for the immediate future, May won't have to be rushed, but he could help as early as 2013.

Year	Club (League)	Class	W	L	ERA	G	GS	CG	SV	IP	H	HR	BB	SO	K/9	WHIP	AVG
2008	Phillies (GCL)	R	1	1	3.75	5	2	0	0	12	11	0	7	11	8.3	1.50	.256
2009	Lakewood (SAL)	LoA	4	1	2.56	15	15	0	0	77	58	3	43	95	11.1	1.31	.211
2010	Clearwater (FSL)	HiA	5	5	5.01	16	14	0	0	70	53	7	61	90	11.6	1.63	.212
	Lakewood (SAL)	LoA	7	3	2.91	11	11	0	0	65	51	3	20	92	12.7	1.09	.214
2011	Clearwater (FSL)	HiA	10	8	3.63	27	27	3	0	151	121	8	67	208	12.4	1.24	.221
Minor League Totals			27	18	3.55	74	69	3	0	376	294	21	198	496	11.9	1.31	.217

2 JESSE BIDDLE, LHP

DAVID SCHOFIELD

Born: Oct. 22, 1991. **B-T:** L-L. **Ht.:** 6-4. **Wt.:** 225. **Drafted:** HS—Philadelphia, 2010 (1st round). **Signed by:** Eric Valent.

Biddle pitched his high school ball at Germantown Friends School, 20 minutes away from Citizens Bank Park. The Phillies sent scouts to every one of his starts in 2010 before drafting him 27th overall and signing him away from an Oregon commitment for $1.16 million. In his first full pro season, he was the third-youngest pitcher in the South Atlantic League. Biddle sat at 92-94 mph as a high school senior but has had inconsistent fastball velocity as a pro. He settled in at 87-90 mph during the second half of 2011, but he has remained effective because of his secondary pitches. After not needing one in high school, he has developed a changeup with fade that flashes plus potential. He also throws a sharp curveball with so much break that he struggles throwing it for strikes. Down the line, Philadelphia might reintroduce a slider he used in high school. He throws across his body and needs to improve his fastball command. He has the work ethic to do so. A strong projectable lefthander, Biddle has No. 3 starter potential. He'll make the jump to high Class A in 2012.

BA GRADE

55
HIGH

Year	Club (League)	Class	W	L	ERA	G	GS	CG	SV	IP	H	HR	BB	SO	K/9	WHIP	AVG
2010	Phillies (GCL)	R	3	1	4.32	9	9	1	0	33	35	2	9	41	11.1	1.32	.263
	Williamsport (NYP)	SS	1	0	2.61	3	3	0	0	10	5	0	11	9	7.8	1.55	.152
2011	Lakewood (SAL)	LoA	7	8	2.98	25	24	0	0	133	104	5	66	124	8.4	1.28	.219
Minor League Totals			11	9	3.21	37	36	1	0	177	144	7	86	174	8.9	1.30	.225

3 SEBASTIAN VALLE, C

Born: July 24, 1990. **B-T:** R-R. **Ht.:** 6-1. **Wt.:** 170. **Signed:** Mexico, 2006. **Signed by:** Sal Agostinelli.

Phillies international supervisor Sal Agostinelli worked out Valle in his hometown of Los Mochis, Mexico, and came away uninspired. But he still followed the raw catcher closely in tournaments and eventually signed him for $30,000. Valle has flourished since and played in the Futures Game in 2011, when he was the Florida State League's youngest everyday catcher. Employing a high leg kick, Valle generates impressive bat speed with his quick hands and explosive wrists, leading to above-average raw power. He's overly aggressive and he gets pull-happy, making his swing long at times. When he's on, he stays inside the ball well and works the opposite field. He posted just a .589 OPS in the second half of 2011 as his defensive responsibilities took a toll on his body. An athletic backstop, Valle moves well behind the plate with solid blocking and receiving skills. His solid arm and improved footwork produce 1.9-second pop times and enabled him to throw out 32 percent of FSL basestealers. Valle is the Phillies' catcher of the future, though he'll likely continue to move one level at a time.

BA GRADE

50
MEDIUM

Year	Club (League)	Class	AVG	G	AB	R	H	2B	3B	HR	RBI	BB	SO	SB	CS	OBP	SLG
2007	Phillies (DSL)	R	.284	54	176	29	50	13	1	2	25	29	26	4	4	.398	.403
2008	Phillies (GCL)	R	.281	48	167	27	47	15	0	2	18	12	31	0	0	.341	.407
2009	Williamsport (NYP)	SS	.307	50	192	25	59	15	5	6	40	10	41	0	0	.335	.531
	Lakewood (SAL)	LoA	.223	45	157	16	35	12	1	1	15	16	37	1	2	.313	.331
2010	Lakewood (SAL)	LoA	.255	117	447	51	114	28	1	16	74	27	101	3	2	.298	.430
2011	Clearwater (FSL)	HiA	.284	91	348	34	99	19	2	5	40	13	84	0	0	.312	.394
Minor League Totals			.272	405	1487	182	404	102	10	32	212	107	320	8	8	.325	.418

4 JONATHAN PETTIBONE, RHP

Born: July 19, 1990. **B-T:** L-R. **Ht.:** 6-5. **Wt.:** 200. **Drafted:** HS—Yorba Linda, Calif., 2008 (3rd round supplemental). **Signed by:** Darrell Conner.

A Southern California recruit, Pettibone was thought to be unsignable in 2008, but fellow California high school product Cole Hamels helped persuade him to join the Phillies for $500,000 as a third-round pick. Pettibone's father Jay pitched briefly in the majors and played under current Philadelphia manager Charlie Manuel at Double-A Orlando in 1984. After finishing 2010 on a strong note, Jonathan took the biggest step forward of any Phillies farmhand last year. Pettibone pitches to both sides of the plate with a 90-94 mph fastball that touches 95, and he maintains his velocity deep into games. His 81-84 mph changeup gives him a second plus pitch. He has the best command in the system, and his advanced feel for pitching allowed the Phillies to give him a two-seam fastball earlier than they do with most pitchers. He has made progress with his two-seamer and improved the depth of his 80-83 mph slider, though he doesn't throw it often. He has a smooth, repeatable delivery and a clean arm action that produces easy velocity. Of the Phillies' top pitching

BA GRADE

50
MEDIUM

prospects, Pettibone is the best bet to reach his ceiling, which is as a mid-rotation starter. He'll join Trevor May at the front of Reading's rotation in 2012.

Year	Club (League)	Class	W	L	ERA	G	GS	CG	SV	IP	H	HR	BB	SO	K/9	WHIP	AVG
2008	Phillies (GCL)	R	0	1	0.00	1	1	0	0	1	3	0	1	0	0.0	4.00	.600
2009	Williamsport (NYP)	SS	2	4	5.35	9	8	0	0	35	37	0	16	36	9.2	1.50	.261
2010	Lakewood (SAL)	LoA	8	6	3.49	24	23	1	0	131	114	10	41	84	5.8	1.18	.237
2011	Clearwater (FSL)	HiA	10	11	2.96	27	27	0	0	161	149	5	34	115	6.4	1.14	.248
Minor League Totals			20	22	3.42	61	59	1	0	329	303	15	92	235	6.4	1.20	.247

5 PHILLIPPE AUMONT, RHP

Born: Jan. 7, 1989. **B-T:** L-R. **Ht.:** 6-7. **Wt.:** 255. **Drafted:** HS—Gatineau, Quebec, 2007 (1st round). **Signed by:** Wayne Norton (Mariners).

The centerpiece of the December 2009 Cliff Lee trade that also brought Tyson Gillies and J.C. Ramirez from the Mariners, Aumont signed for $1.9 million as the 11th overall pick in 2007. The Phillies initially made him a starter in 2010 but he floundered in that role, especially with his mechanics. The extra innings did help him learn more about pitching, which showed when he progressed to Triple-A Lehigh Valley as a reliever in 2011. Aumont has the system's best two-pitch combination, with both his fastball and curveball grading as plus-plus pitches. His heavy fastball sits at 93-96 mph and touches 98 with great sink, while his knee-buckling 78-80 mph curveball has sharp, late break. He also throws an 84-87 mph changeup that looks like a splitter, though he doesn't use it much in relief. While he can be overpowering at times, Aumont has a herky-jerky delivery that results in wavering command. There are some concerns about his attitude and competitiveness. If Aumont can do a better job of locating his pitches and controlling his emotions, he has the stuff to become a closer. Philadelphia protected him on its 40-man roster this offseason and will give him an outside shot to make the big league team in spring training. He'll likely open 2012 in Triple-A.

BA GRADE
55
HIGH

Year	Club (League)	Class	W	L	ERA	G	GS	CG	SV	IP	H	HR	BB	SO	K/9	WHIP	AVG
2008	Wisconsin (MWL)	LoA	4	4	2.75	15	8	0	2	56	46	4	19	50	8.1	1.17	.224
2009	High Desert (CAL)	HiA	1	2	3.24	29	0	0	12	33	24	3	12	35	9.5	1.08	.195
	West Tenn (SL)	AA	1	4	5.09	15	0	0	4	18	21	1	11	24	12.2	1.81	.292
2010	Reading (EL)	AA	1	6	7.43	11	11	0	0	50	55	4	38	38	6.9	1.87	.284
	Clearwater (FSL)	HiA	2	5	4.48	16	10	1	1	72	74	6	42	77	9.6	1.60	.270
2011	Reading (EL)	AA	1	5	2.32	25	0	0	4	31	23	2	11	41	11.9	1.10	.195
	Lehigh Valley (IL)	AAA	1	0	3.18	18	0	0	3	23	21	0	14	37	14.7	1.54	.244
Minor League Totals			11	26	4.21	129	29	1	26	282	264	20	147	302	9.6	1.46	.246

6 FREDDY GALVIS, SS

Born: Nov. 14, 1989. **B-T:** B-R. **Ht.:** 5-9. **Wt.:** 170. **Signed:** Venezuela, 2006. **Signed by:** Sal Agostinelli.

The Phillies have raved about Galvis' defensive exploits since they saw him as a 14-year-old in Venezuela, and they signed him two years later for $90,000. Always one of the youngest position players in his leagues, he reached Triple-A at age 21 in 2011, when he was named Phillies minor league position player of the year. Galvis is arguably the best defensive shortstop in the minors. He has plus range despite fringy pure speed, and he also has excellent hands, an above-average arm and incredible instincts. Slightly built, he went through a strength training program last offseason that helped him set career highs across the board in 2011. A switch-hitter who sprays line drives, Galvis makes consistent contact but never will hit for much power and profiles as a No. 8 hitter. He has improved at bunting and moving runners. Philadelphia praises his intelligence and makeup. Galvis' role will likely be determined by how much his bat continues to progress. Most scouts think his defensive wizardry will make him an everyday player, but some think he's no more than a second-division regular. He's in line for more Triple-A seasoning.

BA GRADE
50
MEDIUM

Year	Club (League)	Class	AVG	G	AB	R	H	2B	3B	HR	RBI	BB	SO	SB	CS	OBP	SLG
2007	Williamsport (NYP)	SS	.203	38	143	20	29	5	1	0	7	10	20	9	4	.255	.252
2008	Lakewood (SAL)	LoA	.238	127	458	59	109	12	1	3	42	39	58	14	7	.300	.288
2009	Phillies (GCL)	R	.276	7	29	6	8	1	0	0	0	1	4	1	1	.300	.310
	Clearwater (FSL)	HiA	.247	63	251	29	62	8	2	1	15	10	43	6	3	.280	.307
	Reading (EL)	AA	.197	16	61	6	12	0	0	1	5	2	7	0	1	.222	.246
2010	Reading (EL)	AA	.233	138	502	58	117	16	4	5	48	30	89	15	4	.276	.311
2011	Reading (EL)	AA	.273	104	422	63	115	22	4	8	35	28	68	19	11	.326	.400
	Lehigh Valley (IL)	AAA	.298	33	121	15	36	6	1	0	8	3	18	4	2	.315	.364
Minor League Totals			.246	526	1987	256	488	70	13	18	160	123	307	68	33	.292	.321

7 JUSTIN DE FRATUS, RHP

BA GRADE

50
MEDIUM

Born: Oct. 21, 1987. **B-T:** B-R. **Ht.:** 6-4. **Wt.:** 215. **Drafted:** Ventura (Calif.) JC, 2007 (11th round). **Signed by:** Tim Kissner.

De Fratus hit 94 mph while at Ventura (Calif.) JC, but his fastball sometimes dipped into the mid-80s by the third or fourth inning. After turning pro, he benefited from a full-time pitching coach and daily routine, both of which he lacked as an amateur. He took off in 2010, when he hit 98 mph in the Florida State League all-star game and served as Team USA's closer in the Pan Am qualifying tournament, and made his big league debut this September. De Fratus' fastball sits at 92-95 mph with slight sinking action. His 82-85 mph sweeping slider has come a long way, advancing from a fringy offering to a true plus pitch, but some scouts think he uses it too frequently. He also has a low-80s changeup. De Fratus has thrown strikes since he signed, though he wasn't able to pinpoint his pitches as effectively in 2011 as he had in the past. He has the bulldog mentality and short memory required to work the late innings. Sometimes compared to Brad Lidge, De Fratus figures to play a significant role in Philadelphia's 2012 bullpen. He has the stuff and makeup to become a set-up man.

Year	Club (League)	Class	W	L	ERA	G	GS	CG	SV	IP	H	HR	BB	SO	K/9	WHIP	AVG
2007	Phillies (GCL)	R	2	3	4.30	10	8	0	0	46	51	1	3	34	6.7	1.17	.273
2008	Williamsport (NYP)	SS	6	5	3.67	14	14	1	0	83	87	1	25	74	8.0	1.34	.260
2009	Lakewood (SAL)	LoA	5	6	3.19	36	12	0	3	110	108	3	16	101	8.3	1.13	.258
2010	Clearwater (FSL)	HiA	2	0	1.79	29	0	0	15	40	31	1	11	43	9.6	1.04	.215
	Reading (EL)	AA	1	0	2.19	20	0	0	6	25	17	2	5	28	10.2	0.89	.195
2011	Reading (EL)	AA	4	0	2.10	23	0	0	8	34	28	1	14	43	11.3	1.22	.224
	Lehigh Valley (IL)	AAA	2	3	3.73	28	0	0	7	41	35	3	11	56	12.3	1.12	.230
	Philadelphia (NL)	MAJ	1	0	2.25	5	0	0	0	4	1	0	3	3	6.8	1.00	.083
Major League Totals			1	0	2.25	5	0	0	0	4	1	0	3	3	6.8	1.00	.083
Minor League Totals			22	17	3.18	160	34	1	39	380	357	12	85	379	9.0	1.16	.246

8 BRODY COLVIN, RHP

BA GRADE

55
HIGH

Born: Aug. 14, 1990. **B-T:** R-R. **Ht.:** 6-4. **Wt.:** 195. **Drafted:** HS—Lafayette, La., 2009 (7th round). **Signed by:** Mike Stauffer.

A sandwich-round talent whose commitment to Louisiana State clouded his sign-ability, Colvin signed for $900,000 as a seventh-rounder in 2009. The No. 3 prospect and top pitcher on this list a year ago, he took a big step backward in 2011. He reported to spring training in poor condition, then struggled to stay healthy with back and groin injuries hampering him throughout the season. His stuff wasn't as sharp and his command wavered. When he's healthy, Colvin's fastball sits at 92-94 mph and peaks at 96 with sink. He shows signs of two above-average secondary offerings, a sharp curveball in the upper 70s and an 83-85 mph changeup. Since he was in high school, he has had a long arm circle with a hook and wrap in the back of his motion. He also throws significantly across his body. When everything was going well, there was little reason to alter Colvin's mechanics, but that's no longer the case. Because of his delivery concerns, some scouts say Colvin is destined for the bullpen. Others think his stuff will rebound and he should remain in the rotation, where he has No. 2 starter upside. He'll likely will return to Clearwater to regain his confidence at the start of 2012.

Year	Club (League)	Class	W	L	ERA	G	GS	CG	SV	IP	H	HR	BB	SO	K/9	WHIP	AVG
2009	Phillies (GCL)	R	0	0	0.00	1	0	0	0	2	0	0	1	2	9.0	0.50	.000
2010	Lakewood (SAL)	LoA	6	8	3.39	27	27	0	0	138	138	7	42	120	7.8	1.30	.258
2011	Clearwater (FSL)	HiA	3	8	4.71	22	21	0	0	117	131	10	42	78	6.0	1.48	.289
Minor League Totals			9	16	3.96	50	48	0	0	257	269	17	85	200	7.0	1.38	.271

9 JIWAN JAMES, OF

Born: April 11, 1989. **B-T:** B-R. **Ht.:** 6-4. **Wt.:** 195. **Drafted:** HS—Williston, Fla., 2007 (22nd round). **Signed by:** Chip Lawrence.

James was an all-state baseball, basketball and football player at his Florida high school. He was signed for $150,000 in the 22nd round in 2007 by Chip Lawrence, the same scout who unearthed Domonic Brown one year earlier. An incredible athlete, he evokes images of Brown with his wiry frame. James spent his first two years in pro ball as a pitcher before he suffered a stress reaction in his forearm, prompting a move to the outfield in 2009. A switch-hitter, James is much better from his natural left side, from which he's starting to show home run power during batting practice. He's a slap hitter from the right side, and though the Phillies won't abandon it yet, James eventually may hit solely lefthanded. In 2011, he had a .721 OPS against lefties compared to .608 against righties. He struggles to recognize offspeed pitches and gives at-bats away. James is a plus-plus defender in centerfield and gets great reads off the bat. He has an above-average arm and above-average speed, but he needs to work on getting better reads as a baserunner. The No. 7 prospect on this list a year ago, James still has a high ceiling but needs to make adjustments offensively to become an everyday player. After passing through the Rule 5 draft unscathed, he'll spend 2012 in Double-A.

BA GRADE

55

HIGH

Year	Club (League)		Class	W	L	ERA	G	GS	CG	SV	IP	H	HR	BB	SO	K/9	WHIP	AVG
2007	Phillies (GCL)		R	0	4	7.71	9	8	0	0	33	45	7	15	14	3.9	1.84	.321
2008	Did Not Play—Injured																	
Minor League Totals				0	4	7.71	9	8	0	0	33	45	7	15	14	3.9	1.84	.321

Year	Club (League)	Class	AVG	G	AB	R	H	2B	3B	HR	RBI	BB	SO	SB	CS	OBP	SLG
2009	Williamsport (NYP)	SS	.264	30	121	15	32	4	3	1	13	11	22	7	4	.336	.372
2010	Lakewood (SAL)	LoA	.270	133	556	85	150	26	6	5	64	35	132	33	20	.321	.365
2011	Clearwater (FSL)	HiA	.268	130	526	76	141	26	6	4	38	40	120	31	16	.327	.363
Minor League Totals			.268	293	1203	176	323	56	15	10	115	86	274	71	40	.325	.365

10 MAIKEL FRANCO, 3B

Born: Aug. 26, 1992. **B-T:** R-R. **Ht.:** 6-1. **Wt.:** 189. **Signed:** Dominican Republic, 2010. **Signed by:** Sal Agostinelli.

Franco wasn't flashy in workouts as an amateur, and his 7.7-second 60-yard dash time scared teams away. Phillies international supervisor Sal Agostinelli saw that his tools stood out more in game situations, and signed Franco for $100,000. He was one of the short-season New York-Penn League's top hitters in 2011, though he was overmatched when promoted to low Class A in August. Franco has one of the highest ceilings among Philadelphia's position prospects. He has an unconventional arm-bar swing, but his great bat speed and hand-eye coordination produce above-average power. He's aggressive at the plate, gets pull-happy at times and needs a better two-strike approach. Though he has trimmed down since signing, Franco has a thick body and is a well below-average runner. His plus arm, good agility and smooth actions should allow him to stay at third base. The Phillies initially tried putting Franco behind the plate because of his arm strength, and he could revisit catching down the line. Philadelphia hasn't developed a homegrown third baseman since Scott Rolen, and Franco doesn't have much competition in the system to be the next one. He'll return to Lakewood in 2012, when he'll be one of the youngest players in full-season ball at age 19.

DAVID SCHOFIELD

BA GRADE

55

HIGH

Year	Club (League)	Class	AVG	G	AB	R	H	2B	3B	HR	RBI	BB	SO	SB	CS	OBP	SLG
2010	Phillies (GCL)	R	.222	51	194	23	43	11	2	2	29	16	46	0	0	.292	.330
2011	Lakewood (SAL)	LoA	.123	17	65	6	8	2	0	1	6	1	15	0	0	.149	.200
	Williamsport (NYP)	SS	.287	54	202	19	58	17	1	2	38	25	30	0	0	.367	.411
Minor League Totals			.236	122	461	48	109	30	3	5	73	42	91	0	0	.307	.347

11 ROMAN QUINN, SS

BA GRADE

55

HIGH

Born: May 14, 1993. **B-T:** B-R. **Ht.:** 5-9. **Wt.:** 165. **Drafted:** HS—Port St. Joe, Fla., 2011 (2nd round). **Signed by:** Aaron Jersild.

The Phillies drafted Quinn 66th overall last June and signed him away from his commitment to Florida State for $775,000 several hours before the Aug. 16 deadline. Scouts flocked to see Quinn, the fastest player in the 2011 draft, at the relatively remote town of Port St. Joe on the Florida panhandle. A star basketball player in high school, he's a true top-of-the-scale runner with game-changing speed and incredible first-step quickness. His game draws comparisons to that of Michael Bourn, Philadelphia's 2003 fourth-round pick, and he physically resembles Jimmy Rollins with his compact frame. Quinn toyed with switch-hitting as an amateur and never fully committed to it after struggling at the East Coast Pro Showcase in 2010, but the Phillies think he can swing it from both sides. He's a natural righthanded hitter with surprising pop for his size, and he has shown improvement from the left side. Scouts aren't sure what position best fits Quinn, but Philadelphia is dedicated to developing him as a shortstop, where he shows a strong arm, average hands and good instincts. His speed will allow him to play center field if he doesn't stick at short. Quinn is still raw but has the potential to move quickly, and he could advance to low Class A in 2012 after opening the year in extended spring training.

Year	Club (League)	Class	AVG	G	AB	R	H	2B	3B	HR	RBI	BB	SO	SB	CS	OBP	SLG
2011	Did Not Play—Signed Late																

12 LISALBERTO BONILLA, RHP

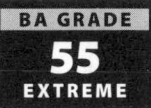

BA GRADE
55
HIGH

Born: June 6, 1990. **B-T:** B-R. **Ht.:** 6-1. **Wt.:** 171. **Signed:** Dominican Republic, 2008. **Signed by:** Sal Agostinelli.

Bonilla hadn't made much noise since he was an unheralded international signing in 2008, He joined Lakewood last May and moved into the rotation a month later when an injury created an opening. He responded by exceeding expectations and rocketing up the list of Phillies pitching prospects. With a loose, quick arm, Bonilla has a 91-94 mph fastball that touches 95. Philadelphia initially was reluctant to use him as a starter because it wanted him to pitch off his fastball with greater frequency and not rely as much on his plus 82-84 mph changeup. At times he went entire outings without using the changeup, which diminished his effectiveness but helped his development. Bonilla's 78-82 mph slider grades out as fringy now but shows flashes of being a swing-and-miss pitch. Wiry and athletic, he has a smooth delivery, though there's a slight head wag and some recoil at the end of his release. Depending on the development of his slider, Bonilla has a chance to be a mid-rotation starter, but he could also serve as a late-inning reliever. He'll advance to high Class A in 2012.

Year	Club (League)	Class	W	L	ERA	G	GS	CG	SV	IP	H	HR	BB	SO	K/9	WHIP	AVG
2009	Phillies (DSL)	R	6	2	1.41	11	11	2	0	70	48	2	16	76	9.8	0.91	.189
2010	Phillies (GCL)	R	2	1	1.95	6	6	0	0	32	32	3	5	38	10.6	1.14	.246
	Williamsport (NYP)	SS	1	3	6.49	10	3	0	0	26	33	5	12	18	6.2	1.71	.308
2011	Lakewood (SAL)	LoA	4	5	2.80	26	15	1	4	106	91	8	29	95	8.1	1.13	.229
Minor League Totals			13	11	2.68	53	35	3	4	235	204	18	62	227	8.7	1.13	.230

13 CARLOS TOCCI, OF

BA GRADE
55
EXTREME

Born: Aug. 23, 1995. **B-T:** R-R. **Ht.:** 6-3. **Wt.:** 160. **Signed:** Venezuela, 2011. **Signed by:** Sal Agostinelli.

After shining at an MLB-sponsor showcase in April, Tocci emerged as one of the most intriguing prospects in the 2011 international class. He also was one of the youngest and had to wait until late August to sign on his 16th birthday for $759,000—one of the highest bonuses the Phillies ever have given an international amateur. If he carried 30 more pounds on his frame, scouts say he would have signed for three times as much and been considered the equivalent of a first-round talent in the draft. Tocci has a stick-figure body with narrow shoulders and scouts aren't sure how his body will fill out, which clouds his future position and offensive potential. His swing tends to get long and loopy in batting practice, but he shortens up in games and makes quick adjustments. He presently has gap-to-gap power and uses the whole field well. He looks like a pure center fielder and also has the arm strength for right field. He has plus speed and uncanny instincts on the bases. It's a matter of eating properly and lifting weights for Tocci to add strength to his frame, and his potential seems limitless. His professional career will begin in the Rookie-level Gulf Coast League this season.

Year	Club (League)	Class	AVG	G	AB	R	H	2B	3B	HR	RBI	BB	SO	SB	CS	OBP	SLG
2011	Did Not Play—Signed 2012 Contract																

14 CESAR HERNANDEZ, 2B

BA GRADE
45
MEDIUM

Born: May 23, 1990. **B-T:** B-R. **Ht.:** 5-10. **Wt.:** 160. **Signed:** Venezuela, 2006. **Signed by:** Sal Agostinelli.

Signed on the same day (July 2, 2006) as fellow Venezuelan infielder Freddy Galvis, Hernandez hasn't moved as quickly but has a better chance to make an impact with his bat. After getting added to the 40-man roster following the 2010 season, he made the jump from short-season to Williamsport to high Class A. He hit just .177 through mid-May while getting acclimated, then batted .296/.333/.371 the rest of the way. A switch-hitter, Hernandez is significantly better from the left side. He has a line-drive approach and the bat speed to develop gap-to-gap power once he adds some strength to his slight frame. He understands the strike zone and shows the ability to barrel the ball, though he lacks patience and gets himself out by chasing pitches. He has plus speed and runs the bases well, making him a threat to steal. Defensively, Hernandez has an above-average arm and smooth actions, but he tends to be passive and sometimes is too stationary at second base. Scouts compare him to Placido Polanco, a steady performer and grinder. After his strong second half, Hernandez should make the jump to Double-A in 2012. Chase Utley is signed for two more seasons, so the Phillies don't have to rush Hernandez.

Year	Club (League)	Class	AVG	G	AB	R	H	2B	3B	HR	RBI	BB	SO	SB	CS	OBP	SLG
2007	Phillies (VSL)	R	.276	54	181	32	50	7	8	2	21	11	30	6	4	.328	.436
2008	Phillies (VSL)	R	.315	60	197	31	62	7	6	1	24	33	22	19	7	.412	.426
2009	Phillies (GCL)	R	.267	41	150	21	40	5	1	0	18	17	20	13	5	.351	.313
2010	Williamsport (NYP)	SS	.325	65	255	36	83	13	2	0	23	26	27	32	6	.390	.392
2011	Clearwater (FSL)	HiA	.268	119	421	47	113	7	4	4	37	23	80	23	10	.306	.333
Minor League Totals			.289	339	1204	167	348	39	21	7	123	110	179	93	32	.352	.374

15 AARON ALTHERR, OF

Born: Jan. 14, 1991. **B-T:** R-R. **Ht.:** 6-5. **Wt.:** 190. **Drafted:** HS—Avondale, Ariz., 2009 (9th round). **Signed by:** Brad Holland.

BA GRADE
55
EXTREME

The Phillies have taken plenty of high-risk, high-reward toolsy outfielders in recent drafts, and Altherr fits that prototype perfectly. A star basketball player in high school, he's still raw as a baseball player. He offers exciting potential but his prospect status is based more on projection than production. He opened 2011 in low Class A but had trouble stringing together consistent at-bats, so he spent the second half repeating Williamsport. His build and upside have led scouts to compare him to a righthanded-hitting Domonic Brown. Altherr is still growing into a lanky frame supported by size-16 shoes and is learning body control. For such a big, young hitter, he takes a short path to the ball, allowing him to make hard contact. He has good plate coverage but is a free swinger. He has added strength and projects to have average to plus power. Altherr has spent time in center field but profiles best in right field, where his above-average arm will play. He has plus speed once he gets going and has good baserunning ability. He'll give Lakewood another try this year.

Year	Club (League)	Class	AVG	G	AB	R	H	2B	3B	HR	RBI	BB	SO	SB	CS	OBP	SLG
2009	Phillies (GCL)	R	.214	28	84	10	18	3	0	1	11	8	15	6	1	.283	.286
2010	Phillies (GCL)	R	.304	27	115	12	35	6	1	1	15	3	22	10	3	.331	.400
	Williamsport (NYP)	SS	.287	28	94	11	27	7	3	0	10	8	13	2	3	.350	.426
2011	Lakewood (SAL)	LoA	.211	41	147	20	31	6	0	1	15	11	47	12	0	.272	.272
	Williamsport (NYP)	SS	.260	71	269	41	70	12	2	5	31	13	52	25	4	.302	.375
Minor League Totals			.255	195	709	94	181	34	6	8	82	43	149	55	11	.304	.354

16 ERVIS MANZANILLO, LHP

Born: Aug. 25, 1991. **B-T:** L-L. **Ht.:** 6-1. **Wt.:** 170. **Signed:** Venezuela, 2009. **Signed by:** Sal Agostinelli.

BA GRADE
50
HIGH

Manzanillo didn't start playing baseball until he was 16 and signed about a year and a half later out of Venezuela. He reached low Class A in his third pro season, and while his statistics weren't loud, he might have better pure stuff than Lakewood teammate Jesse Biddle, who ranks No. 2 on this list. Manzanillo is still rough around the edges and searching for consistency. Thin-framed and athletic, he needs to add strength but has a live, loose arm. His fastball sits at 90-93 mph and touches 95 with late life, though he struggles with command and overthrows at times. He shows feel for two secondary pitches, a slurvy curveball and changeup. Both are fringy offerings now but could be plus pitches, and their development will determine Manzanillo's future. He has some tilt in his delivery and needs to get downhill more to achieve better plane on his pitches. He throws slightly across his body and his arm action is a little long in the back. Scouts say Manzanillo compares favorably to Antonio Bastardo. He should advance to high Class A and pitch alongside Biddle again in 2012.

Year	Club (League)	Class	W	L	ERA	G	GS	CG	SV	IP	H	HR	BB	SO	K/9	WHIP	AVG
2009	Phillies (VSL)	R	0	4	5.03	13	6	0	0	34	31	0	27	32	8.5	1.71	.258
2010	Phillies (GCL)	R	3	0	2.16	7	7	0	0	33	21	1	11	33	8.9	0.96	.183
	Williamsport (NYP)	SS	1	2	6.29	6	6	0	0	24	19	4	18	23	8.5	1.52	.202
2011	Lakewood (SAL)	LoA	8	7	5.02	26	25	0	0	118	114	5	71	105	8.0	1.56	.257
Minor League Totals			12	13	4.71	52	44	0	0	210	185	10	127	193	8.3	1.49	.240

17 JULIO RODRIGUEZ, RHP

Born: Aug. 29, 1990. **B-T:** R-R. **Ht.:** 6-4. **Wt.:** 195. **Drafted:** HS—Gurabo, P.R., 2008 (8th round). **Signed by:** Chip Lawrence.

BA GRADE
45
MEDIUM

Rodriguez may have been the most anonymous member of Clearwater's talented 2011 rotation, but he also posted the best numbers, leading the Florida State League with 16 wins and ranking second in ERA (2.76) and strikeouts (168). His stuff isn't as nasty as his numbers might indicate, as he lacks a present average pitch. With his big frame, Rodriguez has a limber body with long limbs that yields a herky-jerky delivery. His arm works well and his motion creates deception, and hitters at the lower levels haven't been able to square up his pitches. Inconsistent with his fastball velocity in the past, Rodriguez mostly sat at 87-90 mph last year, with natural late cut adding to his effectiveness. He has a loopy 65-72 mph curveball that induces swings and misses, along with a sharper 73-76 mph slider. He also throws a 77-78 mph changeup. When he gets downhill in delivery, Rodriguez's pitches are very tough to pick up. He tends to get under the ball and work up in the zone, which could get him into trouble against better competition. He has good control but not fine command. With his pitchability, Rodriguez has a chance to be a back-end starter, but he'll have to continue to prove himself at every level. After starring for Puerto Rico at the World Cup in October—he struck out 15 and didn't allow an earned run in nine innings—he'll will move to Double-A this season.

Year	Club (League)	Class	W	L	ERA	G	GS	CG	SV	IP	H	HR	BB	SO	K/9	WHIP	AVG
2008	Phillies (GCL)	R	0	1	12.19	7	0	0	0	10	18	3	6	8	7.0	2.32	.383
2009	Phillies (GCL)	R	1	2	3.08	11	8	0	0	50	36	6	14	56	10.1	1.01	.197
2010	Williamsport (NYP)	SS	2	2	2.65	7	5	0	0	34	25	2	15	36	9.5	1.18	.200
	Lakewood (SAL)	LoA	5	1	1.44	13	7	0	0	56	32	2	22	90	14.4	0.96	.160
2011	Clearwater (FSL)	HiA	16	7	2.76	27	27	0	0	157	102	13	56	168	9.7	1.01	.186
Minor League Totals			24	13	2.87	65	47	0	0	307	213	26	113	358	10.5	1.06	.193

18 KYRELL HUDSON, OF

BA GRADE
55
EXTREME

Born: Dec. 6, 1990. **B-T:** R-R. **Ht.:** 6-1. **Wt.:** 185. **Drafted:** HS—Vancouver, Wash., 2009 (3rd round). **Signed by:** Tim Kissner.

Hudson's inconsistent effort as a high schooler frustrated some area scouts, but Phillies scouting director Marti Wolever saw him at his best in a game shortly before the 2009 draft, when Hudson homered and made several diving catches. Philadelphia took him in the third round and paid a $475,000 bonus to sign him away from Oregon State, where he would have played baseball and football (as a wide receiver). A tremendous athlete, Hudson struggled offensively in his first two professional seasons, but he held his own in a return to Williamsport. Hudson always has had bat speed and a good swing path, and he started squaring the ball consistently in 2011. He started to show signs of recognizing pitches and improving his plate discipline. Hudson has gap-to-gap power and could hit for average if he learns to bunt. A plus-plus runner underway, he doesn't get out of the box well but his speed plays on the bases, where he's almost arrogantly aggressive. He's a plus-plus defender with great closing ability in center field, and he could play in the big leagues right now defensively. He also has an above-average arm. Hudson has breakout potential and will advance to low Class A this season.

Year	Club (League)	Class	AVG	G	AB	R	H	2B	3B	HR	RBI	BB	SO	SB	CS	OBP	SLG
2009	Phillies (GCL)	R	.162	10	37	3	6	2	0	0	6	3	9	2	0	.225	.216
2010	Williamsport (NYP)	SS	.173	49	156	13	27	5	0	0	15	5	45	11	3	.205	.205
2011	Williamsport (NYP)	SS	.275	68	269	31	74	11	4	1	18	18	63	28	11	.322	.357
Minor League Totals			.232	127	462	47	107	18	4	1	39	26	117	41	14	.275	.294

19 HAROLD GARCIA, 2B

BA GRADE
45
MEDIUM

Born: Oct. 25, 1986. **B-T:** B-R. **Ht.:** 5-11. **Wt.:** 164. **Signed:** Venezuela, 2004. **Signed by:** Jesus Mendez.

Signed out of Venezuela eight years ago, Garcia spent four years in pro ball before reaching a full-season league. Once he got there in 2009, he quickly starting rising up the ranks of the system. He played on Lakewood's South Atlantic League championship team in 2009 and broke a 59-year-old Florida State League record by hitting in 37 consecutive games in 2010. After retaining him on their 40-man roster, the Phillies expect a breakout season from Garcia in 2011, but he tore the anterior cruciate ligament in his right knee in his 12th game. He returned to take batting practice and grounders during instructional league and should be fully healthy in 2012. Garcia is a switch-hitter who has proven his ability to barrel the ball. He has solid gap power and sprays the ball to all fields. Before the knee injury, he had average speed and played solid defense at second base, where he has an average arm and decent hands. He has a chance to be an everday player, though he profiles best as a hard-working utilityman with some pop. Now 25, Garcia will have to move quickly and will get that chance from Philadelphia.

Year	Club (League)	Class	AVG	G	AB	R	H	2B	3B	HR	RBI	BB	SO	SB	CS	OBP	SLG
2005	Phillies (VSL)	R	.226	23	62	11	14	5	1	0	2	7	15	4	2	.342	.339
2006	Phillies (VSL)	R	.273	44	99	21	27	5	2	2	13	20	20	4	4	.450	.424
2007	Phillies (VSL)	R	.296	49	169	35	50	10	1	2	28	12	26	9	2	.383	.402
2008	Clearwater (FSL)	HiA	.000	2	2	0	0	0	0	0	0	0	2	0	0	.333	.000
	Phillies (GCL)	R	.299	50	174	35	52	12	5	5	21	20	32	17	2	.402	.511
2009	Lakewood (SAL)	LoA	.291	118	444	64	129	21	5	8	55	29	100	42	12	.350	.414
2010	Clearwater (FSL)	HiA	.335	46	179	27	60	13	3	3	32	12	37	17	6	.397	.492
	Reading (EL)	AA	.281	55	231	27	65	9	2	5	32	15	57	12	5	.340	.403
2011	Reading (EL)	AA	.300	12	50	5	15	3	0	2	4	2	11	2	1	.327	.480
Minor League Totals			.292	399	1410	225	412	78	19	27	187	117	300	107	34	.372	.432

20 LARRY GREENE, OF

BA GRADE
55
EXTREME

Born: Feb. 10, 1993. **B-T:** L-R. **Ht.:** 6-1. **Wt.:** 230. **Drafted:** HS—Nashville, Ga., 2011 (1st round supplemental). **Signed by:** Aaron Jersild.

Greene had an offer to play linebacker for Alabama's football team and committed to play baseball Chipola (Fla.) JC. He turned down both after the Phillies drafted him 39th overall last June and offered him $1 million. Greene generated some first-round buzz with his incredible raw power and batting-practice displays during the spring, though struggles with premium velocity on the showcase circuit and an injured ankle during his senior year slightly dropped his stock. He draws comparisons to Russell Branyan, another lefthanded power hitter from south Georgia, and Philadelphia likens his total package to Jonathan Singleton, the key to the Hunter Pence trade with the Astros last July. The difference is that Greene offers more power and is a better defender than Singleton, if not as polished a hitter. Greene played center field in high school but fits better in left with his fringy speed and average arm. He didn't see game action during instructional league because he had a groin injury. He likely will start 2012 in extended spring training.

Year	Club (League)	Class	AVG	G	AB	R	H	2B	3B	HR	RBI	BB	SO	SB	CS	OBP	SLG
2011	Did Not Play—Signed Late																

21 PERCI GARNER, RHP

BA GRADE
55
HIGH

Born: Dec. 13, 1988. **B-T:** R-R. **Ht.:** 6-3. **Wt.:** 225. **Drafted:** Ball State, 2010 (2nd round). **Signed by:** Nate Dion.

A two-time all-state quarterback at Dover (Ohio) High, Garner passed for 8,800 yards and 86 touchdowns during his prep career before heading to Ball State with the intention of playing football. But he never got on the field as a third-string quarterback before switching to baseball full-time after ranking as the No. 2 prospect in the Great Lakes League during the summer of 2009. He quickly moved into Ball State's rotation and shot up draft boards the following spring, going 77th overall and signing for $470,700 in 2010. Still unrefined, Garner has thrown just 34 innings in two pro seasons because he has had a tender arm and oblique strain. When he has taken the mound, he has shown a 92-94 mph fastball that touches 96 and features late life. He has added consistency to his sharp 79-82 mph curveball, while his low-80s changeup has come a long way. His ability to develop reliable secondary pitches will determine whether he remains a starter or moves to the bullpen in the long run. Garner has smoothed out his delivery and is starting to understand his mechanics better, which should help. The Phillies hope to get him a full season of innings in low Class A in 2012.

Year	Club (League)	Class	W	L	ERA	G	GS	CG	SV	IP	H	HR	BB	SO	K/9	WHIP	AVG
2010	Williamsport (NYP)	SS	0	2	18.00	2	2	0	0	4	8	1	1	1	2.3	2.25	.400
2011	Williamsport (NYP)	SS	1	1	1.20	8	4	0	1	30	29	0	9	30	9.0	1.27	.252
Minor League Totals			1	3	3.18	10	6	0	1	34	37	1	10	31	8.2	1.38	.274

22 AUSTIN HYATT, RHP

BA GRADE
45
MEDIUM

Born: May 23, 1986. **B-T:** R-R. **Ht.:** 6-2. **Wt.:** 180. **Drafted:** Alabama, 2009 (15th round). **Signed by:** Mike Stauffer.

Hyatt's hometown Braves took him in the 23rd round out of a suburban Atlanta high school, but he opted to attend Alabama, from where the Phillies signed him for $2,500 as a fifth-year senior in 2009. He has starred in the minors, earning Florida State League most valuable pitcher honors in 2010 and leading the Double-A Eastern League with 171 strikeouts last year. He gets by more on command and deception than overpowering stuff, similar to Julio Rodriguez. Hyatt adds and subtracts from his 87-93 mph fastball that gets occasional sink, but he tends to leave it up in the zone. He relies heavily on his plus 75-78 mph changeup with parachute tumble. He has worked hard to develop his slider, a 76-80 mph offering with occasional sharp bite. Hyatt has a high-effort delivery and there are some concerns about his arm action, which also inhibits hitters from seeing the ball well. Depending on the development of his slider, Hyatt could be used as a back-end starter, though likely not in Philadelphia's rotation unless it comes in an emergency situation. He'll advance to Triple-A to open this season.

Year	Club (League)	Class	W	L	ERA	G	GS	CG	SV	IP	H	HR	BB	SO	K/9	WHIP	AVG
2009	Williamsport (NYP)	SS	3	0	0.66	17	5	0	6	54	26	1	12	81	13.4	0.70	.141
	Lakewood (SAL)	LoA	0	0	7.71	1	1	0	0	5	5	0	2	8	15.4	1.50	.278
2010	Clearwater (FSL)	HiA	11	5	3.04	23	21	0	0	124	100	5	35	156	11.3	1.09	.220
	Reading (EL)	AA	1	0	4.91	4	4	0	0	22	21	4	9	25	10.2	1.36	.247
2011	Reading (EL)	AA	12	6	3.85	28	28	0	0	154	136	20	49	171	10.0	1.20	.235
Minor League Totals			27	11	3.20	73	59	0	6	360	288	30	107	441	11.0	1.10	.218

23 MITCHELL WALDING, SS

BA GRADE
50
HIGH

Born: Sept. 10, 1992. **B-T:** L-R. **Ht.:** 6-3. **Wt.:** 195. **Drafted:** HS—Stockton, Calif., 2011 (5th round). **Signed by:** Joey Davis.

Walding was a two-sport high school star, accounting for 3,041 yards and 26 touchdowns during his senior season as a quarterback, but he flew under the radar as a northern California prep baseball product. Scouts couldn't get extended looks at him because he didn't participate in many summer showcases while preparing for football season, and he missed several weeks last spring with a stress fracture in his right foot. The Phillies snagged him in the fifth round and followed him in the West Coast League, where he ranked as the the No. 2 prospect in the wood-bat summer college circuit. Philadelphia signed him away from a commitment to Oregon for $800,000. Walding still is growing into his broad-shouldered body and adding strength to his frame. He has a smooth lefthanded swing and generates above-average bat speed that could lead to plus power down the line. Walding played shortstop in high school and moves well laterally despite his large frame, but he profiles best at third base. He has good hands to go with solid arm strength and speed. Walding will likely start 2012 in extended spring training and make his pro debut at Williamsport in June.

Year	Club (League)	Class	AVG	G	AB	R	H	2B	3B	HR	RBI	BB	SO	SB	CS	OBP	SLG
2011	Did Not Play—Signed Late																

24 LEANDRO CASTRO, OF

BA GRADE
45
MEDIUM

Born: June 15, 1989. **B-T:** R-R. **Ht.:** 5-11. **Wt.:** 175. **Signed:** Dominican Republic, 2007. **Signed by:** Sal Agostinelli.

Unlike the high-upside outfielders that fill the Phillies system, Castro doesn't have any loud skills, but he also doesn't have many holes in his game. He has shown consistent hitting ability, though he played just 56 games last year before being shut down in mid-June with a deep bone bruise and a stress fracture in his left leg. Castro generates great bat speed with his explosive hands, but he has a pronounced arm bar in his swing, which gets long at times. He has plus raw power, though he also tries to muscle up fastballs and gives away at-bats. Castro does everything aggressively, almost to a fault, which he'll have to tone down as he advances. He's a solid-average runner with a strong arm, giving him a chance to play all three outfield positions. He can play center field in a pinch but doesn't have enough speed to stick there long term, and he likely won't hit for enough power to play a corner, so he profiles as a second-division regular or fourth outfielder. He'll return to high Class A to being this season, with a chance to advance to Double-A later in the year.

Year	Club (League)	Class	AVG	G	AB	R	H	2B	3B	HR	RBI	BB	SO	SB	CS	OBP	SLG
2007	Phillies (DSL)	R	.278	59	223	41	62	3	5	6	37	26	39	24	9	.362	.417
2008	Phillies (GCL)	R	.298	44	161	25	48	9	1	3	19	4	25	9	4	.317	.422
2009	Lakewood (SAL)	LoA	.152	22	66	9	10	4	0	0	6	5	15	2	1	.230	.212
	Williamsport (NYP)	SS	.316	66	256	48	81	19	5	7	43	13	49	18	9	.351	.512
2010	Lakewood (SAL)	LoA	.257	124	502	78	129	27	9	10	81	34	92	22	13	.305	.406
2011	Clearwater (FSL)	HiA	.277	56	231	38	64	11	3	10	31	5	33	10	2	.304	.481
Minor League Totals			.274	371	1439	239	394	73	23	36	217	87	253	85	38	.320	.432

25 JOE SAVERY, LHP

BA GRADE
45
MEDIUM

Born: Nov. 4, 1985. **B-T:** L-L. **Ht.:** 6-3. **Wt.:** 215. **Drafted:** Rice, 2007 (1st round). **Signed by:** Steve Cohen.

Savery's path in pro ball has been tumultuous and unique, as he has gone from first-round pick to suspect back to prospect and from pitcher to hitter to back to the mound. In 2011, he was named Phillies minor league hitter of the month in April—and its pitcher of the month in August before making his big league debut in September. A two-way star at Rice, Savery looked like a top-five pick in the 2007 draft before he had minor shoulder surgery that contributed to him sliding to the 19th pick, where Philadelphia signed him for $1,372,500. He made it to Triple-A in his second full pro season but went 1-12 there in 2010 as his command deteriorated and his fastball velocity dropped into the low 80s. He had more success at the plate that season, hitting .348 in 46 at-bats, and the Phillies decided to make him a full-time outfielder/first baseman in instructional league. Savery began 2011 in high Class A and was hitting .320 in late May when Clearwater ran out of pitchers in a 23-inning game. He pitched two innings of scoreless relief and showed enough promise that Philadelphia used him as a two-way player in Double-A. He regained the 92-94 mph fastball he had at Rice, as rest and a shorter arm action made a significant difference. He focused primarily on pitching in Triple-A and the majors, showing a plus 81-84 mph slider with late bite. Savery missed more bats and threw more strikes as a reliever than he did as a starter, and he has an inside track for a bullpen job with the Phillies in 2012. He's better suited to that role than as a position player, as he has the hand-eye coordination to hit for average but lacks power.

Year	Club (League)	Class	AVG	G	AB	R	H	2B	3B	HR	RBI	BB	SO	SB	CS	OBP	SLG
2008	Clearwater (FSL)	HiA	.231	4	13	2	3	2	0	0	1	1	0	0	0	.286	.385
2009	Reading (EL)	AA	.235	21	34	6	8	2	0	0	1	2	3	0	0	.278	.294
	Lehigh Valley (IL)	AAA	.167	4	6	1	1	0	0	0	0	1	1	0	0	.286	.167
2010	Lehigh Valley (IL)	AAA	.348	23	46	3	16	3	0	1	6	0	10	0	0	.348	.478
2011	Clearwater (FSL)	HiA	.307	54	205	22	63	9	3	2	25	21	28	0	2	.368	.410
	Reading (EL)	AA	.200	16	35	2	7	3	0	1	6	3	8	0	0	.263	.371
	Lehigh Valley (IL)	AAA	.400	9	5	0	2	0	0	0	1	0	2	0	0	.400	.400
	Philadelphia (NL)	MAJ	—	4	0	0	0	0	0	0	0	0	0	0	0	—	—
Major League Totals			—	4	0	0	0	0	0	0	0	0	0	0	0	—	—
Minor League Totals			.291	131	344	38	100	19	3	4	40	28	52	0	2	.342	.398

PHILADELPHIA PHILLIES

Year	Club (League)	Class	W	L	ERA	G	GS	CG	SV	IP	H	HR	BB	SO	K/9	WHIP	AVG
2007	Williamsport (NYP)	SS	2	3	2.73	7	7	0	0	26	22	0	13	22	7.5	1.33	.214
2008	Clearwater (FSL)	HiA	9	10	4.13	27	24	0	0	150	171	10	60	122	7.3	1.54	.286
2009	Reading (EL)	AA	12	4	4.41	21	20	1	0	112	111	13	53	77	6.2	1.46	.262
	Lehigh Valley (IL)	AAA	4	2	4.38	7	7	1	0	39	42	0	24	19	4.4	1.69	.286
2010	Lehigh Valley (IL)	AAA	1	12	4.66	28	19	0	0	127	154	13	51	67	4.7	1.61	.303
2011	Clearwater (FSL)	HiA	0	0	0.00	1	0	0	0	2	2	0	0	1	4.5	1.00	.250
	Reading (EL)	AA	1	0	1.00	6	0	0	0	9	7	0	0	14	14.0	0.78	.212
	Lehigh Valley (IL)	AAA	4	0	1.80	18	0	0	2	25	23	0	6	26	9.4	1.16	.258
	Philadelphia (NL)	MAJ	0	0	0.00	4	0	0	0	3	1	0	0	2	6.8	0.38	.125
Major League Totals			0	0	0.00	4	0	0	0	3	1	0	0	2	6.8	0.38	.125
Minor League Totals			33	31	4.08	115	77	2	2	491	532	36	207	348	6.4	1.50	.279

26 AUSTIN WRIGHT, LHP

BA GRADE
45
HIGH

Born: Sept. 26, 1989. **B-T:** L-L. **Ht.:** 6-4. **Wt.:** 235. **Drafted:** Mississippi, 2011 (8th round). **Signed by:** Mike Stauffer.

Wright was on the prospect radar for a long time as an amateur, getting drafted in the 23rd round twice (out of an Illinois high school by the Pirates, and out of Chipola, Fla., JC by the Red Sox) before the Phillies took him in the eighth round last June. Amateur scouts considered Wright a tease, as he showed interesting arm strength and stuff but raised concerns about his command and makeup. Signed for $125,000, he seemed to turn a corner in his pro debut, posting solid numbers and reaching low Class A. Wright's fastball operates at 90-93 mph, and he has a sharp, late-breaking low-80s curveball that almost looks like a slider. Despite not throwing many changeups in college, he shows some feel for the pitch. Wright needs to work on throwing quality strikes and repeating his delivery. He has the stuff to move quickly, especially in a bullpen role, and he has the upside of a set-up man. If his changeup looks good during spring training, Philadelphia will allow him to develop as a starter. Like Mike Stutes and Vance Worley did coming out of the 2008 draft, Wright has a chance to begin his first full pro season in Double-A.

Year	Club (League)	Class	W	L	ERA	G	GS	CG	SV	IP	H	HR	BB	SO	K/9	WHIP	AVG
2011	Williamsport (NYP)	SS	3	1	3.38	8	7	1	0	35	30	1	13	44	11.4	1.24	.231
	Lakewood (SAL)	LoA	1	2	2.67	7	7	0	0	34	29	2	9	41	11.0	1.13	.238
Minor League Totals			4	3	3.03	15	14	1	0	68	59	3	22	85	11.2	1.19	.234

27 ZACH COLLIER, OF

BA GRADE
45
HIGH

Born: Aug. 27, 1989. **B-T:** L-L. **Ht.:** 6-2. **Wt.:** 185. **Drafted:** HS—Chino Hills, Calif., 2008 (1st round supplemental). **Signed by:** Darrell Conner.

Collier moved up draft boards in 2008 after homering off a 93-mph fastball from his summer-ball teammate, Twins first-rounder Aaron Hicks. The Phillies considered taking Collier with their first-round pick instead of Anthony Hewitt in 2008, and took Collier 10 slots later at No. 34, where he signed for $1.02 million. Some teams were scared away by a 2006 surgical procedure on Collier's heart to improve blood flow. He was unable to handle low Class A pitching in 2009, then missed all of 2010 after having two surgeries on his right hand. He finally showed the potential he flashed in high school again last year, but shortly after the season ended he was suspended for 50 games after testing positive for amphetamines. Collier has good plate coverage and the ball jumps off his bat, though he cuts himself off and doesn't use his lower half well, which limits his power. He has plus speed and is a good baserunner, with an average arm. Collier is an energetic player who makes everything look easy. He has missed a significant amount of playing time and is behind the developmental curve, but he has enough tools to develop into a useful fourth outfielder at the major league level.

Year	Club (League)	Class	AVG	G	AB	R	H	2B	3B	HR	RBI	BB	SO	SB	CS	OBP	SLG
2008	Phillies (GCL)	R	.271	37	129	15	35	9	1	0	19	17	28	5	0	.347	.357
2009	Lakewood (SAL)	LoA	.218	82	298	40	65	16	7	0	32	23	80	13	7	.275	.319
	Williamsport (NYP)	SS	.226	34	137	21	31	10	1	1	13	9	42	7	0	.280	.336
2010	Did not play—Injured																
2011	Lakewood (SAL)	LoA	.255	112	416	50	106	24	6	1	36	40	99	35	13	.328	.349
Minor League Totals			.242	265	980	126	237	59	15	2	100	89	249	60	20	.308	.339

28 J.C. RAMIREZ, RHP

BA GRADE
45
HIGH

Born: Aug. 16, 1988. **B-T:** R-R. **Ht.:** 6-5. **Wt.:** 200. **Signed:** Nicaragua, 2005. **Signed by:** Luis Molina/Nemesio Porras (Mariners).

Acquired along with Phillippe Aumont and Tyson Gillies in the Cliff Lee trade with the Mariners in December 2009, Ramirez has spent most of his time in the Phillies system at Reading. He has the size and strength to remain a starter, but he has yet to develop the polish or secondary stuff that will enable him to stay in that role. Ramirez largely has survived on one pitch, a heavy 92-94 mph fastball with sink that generates weak contact. He throws an 83-85 mph short slider that has tightened up, but he struggles to find a consistent arm slot with the offering. He needs to do a better job of staying on top of the slider, as he often gets on the side of the ball or tries to overthrow it. He also throws a below-average 81-84 mph changeup. Ramirez has struggled with command, though he's usually around the plate. He doesn't miss many bats and needs to throw more quality strikes. The Phillies will continue developing him as a starter in 2012, though he profiles best as a sinker-slider reliever.

Year	Club (League)	Class	W	L	ERA	G	GS	CG	SV	IP	H	HR	BB	SO	K/9	WHIP	AVG
2006	Mariners (VSL)	R	5	1	1.66	14	13	1	0	65	43	0	35	56	7.8	1.20	.191
2007	Everett (NWL)	SS	3	7	4.30	15	15	0	0	75	61	3	43	73	8.7	1.38	.211
2008	Wisconsin (MWL)	LoA	6	9	4.14	25	22	0	0	124	112	9	38	113	8.2	1.21	.239
2009	High Desert (CAL)	HiA	8	10	5.12	28	27	1	0	142	153	18	53	111	7.0	1.45	.276
2010	Clearwater (FSL)	HiA	4	3	4.06	11	11	0	0	64	63	2	17	55	7.7	1.24	.259
	Reading (EL)	AA	3	4	5.45	13	13	1	0	78	89	11	24	60	7.0	1.45	.291
2011	Reading (EL)	AA	11	13	4.50	26	26	3	0	144	144	15	55	89	5.6	1.38	.258
Minor League Totals			40	47	4.34	132	127	6	0	693	665	58	265	557	7.2	1.34	.252

29 ADAM MORGAN, LHP

BA GRADE
45
HIGH

Born: Feb. 27, 1990. **B-T:** L-L. **Ht.:** 6-1. **Wt.:** 195. **Drafted:** Alabama, 2011 (3rd round). **Signed by:** Mike Stauffer.

As a freshman at Alabama, Morgan in 2009 pitched alongside fellow Phillies farmhand Austin Hyatt in the Crimson Tide rotation. Morgan spent each of the next two seasons as a weekend starter and struggled with consistency, mixing flashes of brilliance with low points. He quickly signed for $250,000 as a third-round pick last June, then pitched well for Williamsport. When he's on, he reminds some scouts of Cliff Lee with his arm action and delivery, though he doesn't have Lee's stuff or command. Morgan's fastball sits at 88-92 mph and touches 94, but the pitch flattens out occasionally. He throws two breaking balls, an 82-84 mph slider and an upper-70s curveball, though they sometimes blend together. The slider shows flashes of becoming a plus pitch. He also has an average low-80s changeup. Morgan lands on a stiff front leg in his delivery that prevents him from working downhill at times. The development of his secondary stuff and his ability to command it will determine his future role. He's a durable starter with back-end rotation potential, and he has a chance to move quickly. He'll likely open 2012 in high Class A.

Year	Club (League)	Class	W	L	ERA	G	GS	CG	SV	IP	H	HR	BB	SO	K/9	WHIP	AVG
2011	Williamsport (NYP)	SS	3	3	2.01	11	11	0	0	54	42	2	14	43	7.2	1.04	.206
Minor League Totals			3	3	2.01	11	11	0	0	54	42	2	14	43	7.2	1.04	.206

30 MICHAEL SCHWIMER, RHP

BA GRADE
40
LOW

Born: Feb. 19, 1986. **B-T:** R-R. **Ht.:** 6-8. **Wt.:** 240. **Drafted:** Virginia, 2008 (14th round). **Signed by:** Paul Murphy.

Many big league relievers begin their pro careers as starters, but Schwimer has worked exclusively out of the bullpen in four years at Virginia and four with the Phillies. Undrafted as a college junior, he signed for $5,000 after setting a Cavaliers record with 14 saves as a senior in 2008. He has moved quickly, reaching Double-A at the end of his first full pro season and Philadelphia at the end of 2011. With his super-sized frame, Schwimer creates good downhill plane with his pitches, and his long arms and legs add deception to his delivery. His fastball sits at 89-92 mph, and while he can throw harder, he prefers to operate in his lower register. He relies heavily on his solid 80-84 mph slider, which he'll throw in any count. He also throws a 79-82 mph splitter as a changeup. Schwimer is a thinking man's pitcher who keeps detailed logs of every outing and has a rating system for his performances. While he doesn't have the upside of a late-inning reliever, he should fit nicely in middle relief for the Phillies in 2012.

Year	Club (League)	Class	W	L	ERA	G	GS	CG	SV	IP	H	HR	BB	SO	K/9	WHIP	AVG
2008	Williamsport (NYP)	SS	0	2	1.96	22	0	0	8	41	33	0	15	62	13.5	1.16	.217
2009	Clearwater (FSL)	HiA	2	1	2.85	48	0	0	20	60	44	2	19	82	12.3	1.05	.204
	Reading (EL)	AA	2	1	7.71	5	0	0	0	5	7	0	2	7	13.5	1.93	.350
2010	Reading (EL)	AA	5	3	3.60	32	0	0	11	40	34	5	14	58	13.1	1.20	.225
	Lehigh Valley (IL)	AAA	2	2	1.35	16	0	0	0	20	16	1	7	18	8.1	1.15	.213
2011	Lehigh Valley (IL)	AAA	9	1	1.85	47	0	0	10	68	51	4	22	86	11.4	1.07	.203
	Philadelphia (NL)	MAJ	1	1	5.02	12	0	0	0	14	15	2	7	16	10.0	1.53	.278
Major League Totals			1	1	5.02	12	0	0	0	14	15	2	7	16	10.0	1.53	.278
Minor League Totals			20	10	2.50	170	0	0	49	234	185	12	79	313	12.0	1.13	.214

Pittsburgh Pirates

BY JOHN PERROTTO

The Pirates have committed to building from within and spending generously on scouting and player development since Bob Nutting ousted Kevin McClatchy as the franchise's chairman prior to the 2007 season.

Pittsburgh has spent $47.6 million in the draft during Neal Huntington's four years as GM, including a major league-record $17 million last June in a haul that included No. 1 overall pick Gerrit Cole ($8 million) and second-rounder Josh Bell ($5 million). The Pirates have also been as aggressive in Latin America—they signed Mexican righthander Luis Heredia for $2.6 million in 2010— as they have been since legendary scout Howie Haak became a pioneer in that part of the world in the late 1950s.

However, all of that bonus money has yet to make an impact at the major league level. Pittsburgh's run of consecutive losing seasons now stands at 19, a record for a North American sports franchise, after it surprisingly occupied first place in the National League Central in late July only to lose 43 of its final 62 games. Of the club-record 52 players who saw action for the Pirates last season, only Pedro Alvarez and Chase d'Arnaud were signed as amateurs during the Huntington regime.

Pittsburgh counted on Alvarez as a major building block when they drafted him with the second overall pick in 2008 and gave him a $6.3 million major league contract. Now he's a question mark after batting .191/.272/.289 with four homers in 262 plate appearances last year. D'Arnaud looked overmatched in his big league debut, hitting .217/.242/.287.

The Pirates have used the strategy of exceeding MLB's bonus recommendations in the later rounds to sign pitchers away from solid college commitments. While that has stocked the lower levels of the system with live arms, none are close to big league ready. The heavy concentration on pitchers also has left Pittsburgh with few impact hitting prospects beyond Bell and fellow outfielder Starling Marte.

Nutting and club president Frank Coonelly are happy with the organization's progress and, to be fair, Huntington stepped into quite a mess when he replaced Dave Littlefield in September 2007. Huntington received a three-year contract extension in September that takes him through the 2014 season with a club option for 2015. Afterward, he did some rearranging in the front office.

Farm director Kyle Stark and scouting director Greg Smith both were promoted to assistant GM.

The Pirates have high hopes for Josh Bell, part of their record-setting 2011 draft class

TOP 30 PROSPECTS

1. Gerrit Cole, rhp	**16.** Rudy Owens, lhp
2. Jameson Taillon, rhp	**17.** Justin Wilson, lhp
3. Josh Bell, of	**18.** Jarek Cunningham, 2b
4. Starling Marte, of	**19.** Victor Black, rhp
5. Luis Heredia, rhp	**20.** Gorkys Hernandez, of
6. Kyle McPherson, rhp	**21.** Zack Von Rosenberg, rhp
7. Tony Sanchez, c	**22.** Ramon Cabrera, c
8. Robbie Grossman, of	**23.** Zack Dodson, lhp
9. Stetson Allie, rhp	**24.** Yamaico Navarro, inf/of
10. Jeff Locke, lhp	**25.** Matt Curry, 1b
11. Alex Dickerson, 1b	**26.** Evan Chambers, of
12. Bryan Morris, rhp	**27.** Alen Hanson, ss/2b
13. Colton Cain, lhp	**28.** Brandon Cumpton, rhp
14. Nick Kingham, rhp	**29.** Mel Rojas Jr., of
15. Clay Holmes, rhp	**30.** Jose Osuna, 1b/of

Stark will oversee all elements of medical, physical, mental, personnel and player development at the major and minor league levels, while Smith will be in charge of all elements of the scouting operation at the amateur, professional and international levels.

Tyrone Brooks went from baseball-operations director to player personnel director and will now lead the professional and international (non-Latin America) scouting efforts. Area scout Larry Broadway took over as farm director and Joe DelliCarri moves up from assistant scouting director to amateur scouting director and will run Pittsburgh's drafts.

General Manager: Neal Huntington. **Farm Director:** Larry Broadway. **Scouting Director:** Joe DelliCarri.

Class	Team	League	W	L	Pct	Finish*	Manager(s)
Majors	Pittsburgh Pirates	National	72	90	.444	t-12th (16)	Clint Hurdle
Triple-A	Indianapolis Indians	International	76	68	.528	6th (14)	Dean Treanor/Jeff Branson
Double-A	Altoona Curve	Eastern	64	77	.454	11th (12)	P.J. Forbes
High A	Bradenton Marauders	Florida State	74	63	.540	4th (12)	Carlos Garcia
Low A	West Virginia Power	South Atlantic	69	69	.500	8th (14)	Gary Robinson
Short-season	State College Spikes	New York-Penn	31	44	.413	12th (14)	Kimera Bartee
Rookie	GCL Pirates	Gulf Coast	34	26	.567	4th (15)	Tom Prince
Overall 2011 Minor League Record			348	347	.501	16th (30)	

*Finish in overall standings (No. of teams in league). †League champion.

LAST YEAR'S TOP 30

Player, Pos.		Status
1.	Jameson Taillon, rhp	No. 2
2.	Tony Sanchez, c	No. 7
3.	Stetson Allie, rhp	No. 9
4.	Starling Marte, of	No. 4
5.	Luis Heredia, rhp	No. 5
6.	Bryan Morris, rhp	No. 12
7.	Rudy Owens, lhp	No. 16
8.	Jeff Locke, lhp	No. 10
9.	Zack Von Rosenberg, rhp	No. 21
10.	Chase d'Arnaud ss/2b	Majors
11.	Andrew Lambo, of	Dropped out
12.	Diego Moreno, rhp	Dropped out
13.	Colton Cain, lhp	No. 13
14.	Gorkys Hernandez, of	No. 20
15.	Justin Wilson, lhp	No. 17
16.	Victor Black, rhp	No. 19
17.	Nate Baker, lhp	Dropped out
18.	Zack Dodson, rhp	No. 23
19.	Ramon Aguero, rhp	Dropped out
20.	Alex Presley, of	Majors
21.	Quincy Latimore, of	Dropped out
22.	Jordy Mercer, inf	Dropped out
23.	Mel Rojas Jr., of	No. 29
24.	Josh Rodriguez, ss/2b	Dropped out
25.	Robbie Grossman, of	No. 8
26.	Daniel Moskos, lhp	Dropped out
27.	Pedro Ciriaco, ss	Dropped out
28.	Aaron Pribanic, rhp	Dropped out
29.	Matt Hague, 1b	Dropped out
30.	Josh Harrison, 3b/2b	Majors

BEST TOOLS

Best Hitter for Average	Starling Marte
Best Power Hitter	Josh Bell
Best Strike-Zone Discipline	Robbie Grossman
Fastest Baserunner	Alen Hanson
Best Athlete	Starling Marte
Best Fastball	Gerrit Cole
Best Curveball	Jameson Taillon
Best Slider	Gerrit Cole
Best Changeup	Kyle McPherson
Best Control	Kyle McPherson
Best Defensive Catcher	Tony Sanchez
Best Defensive Infielder	Pedro Ciriaco
Best Infield Arm	Jordy Mercer
Best Defensive Outfielder	Gorkys Hernandez
Best Outfield Arm	Starling Marte

PROJECTED 2015 LINEUP

Catcher	Tony Sanchez
First Base	Alex Dickerson
Second Base	Neil Walker
Third Base	Pedro Alvarez
Shortstop	Chase d'Arnaud
Left Field	Andrew McCutchen
Center Field	Starling Marte
Right Field	Josh Bell
No. 1 Starter	Gerrit Cole
No. 2 Starter	Jameson Taillon
No. 3 Starter	Luis Heredia
No. 4 Starter	James McDonald
No. 5 Starter	Kyle McPherson
Closer	Stetson Allie

TOP PROSPECTS OF THE DECADE

Year	Player, Pos.	2011 Org.
2002	J.R. House, c	Long Island (Atlantic)
2003	John Van Benschoten, rhp	Padres
2004	John Van Benschoten, rhp	Padres
2005	Zach Duke, lhp	Diamondbacks
2006	Neil Walker, c	Pirates
2007	Andrew McCutchen, of	Pirates
2008	Andrew McCutchen, of	Pirates
2009	Pedro Alvarez, 3b	Pirates
2010	Pedro Alvarez, 3b	Pirates
2011	Jameson Taillon, rhp	Pirates

TOP DRAFT PICKS OF THE DECADE

Year	Player, Pos.	2011 Org.
2002	Bryan Bullington, rhp	Hiroshima (Japan)
2003	Paul Maholm, lhp	Pirates
2004	Neil Walker, c	Pirates
2005	Andrew McCutchen, of	Pirates
2006	Brad Lincoln, rhp	Pirates
2007	Daniel Moskos, lhp	Pirates
2008	Pedro Alvarez, 3b	Pirates
2009	Tony Sanchez, c	Pirates
2010	Jameson Taillon, rhp	Pirates
2011	Gerrit Cole, rhp	Pirates

LARGEST BONUSES IN CLUB HISTORY

Gerrit Cole, 2011	$8,000,000
Jameson Taillon, 2010	$6,500,000
Pedro Alvarez, 2008	$6,000,000
Josh Bell, 2011	$5,000,000
Bryan Bullington, 2002	$4,000,000

PITTSBURGH PIRATES

TOP 2012 ROOKIE: Justin Wilson, lhp. His velocity jumped when he went to the bullpen, and if he stays there he could help the Pirates in short order.

BREAKOUT PROSPECT: Mel Rojas Jr., of. Pittsburgh thinks his five-tool talent will start to show now that he has a full season of pro ball under his belt.

SOURCE OF TOP 30 TALENT			
Homegrown	26	Acquired	4
College	8	Trades	4
Junior college	2	Rule 5 draft	0
High school	10	Independent leagues	0
Draft-and-follow	1	Free agents/waivers	0
Nondrafted free agents	0		
International	5		

SLEEPER: Tyler Waldron, rhp. He flashes three solid pitches and reached high Class A in his first full pro season.

LF	CF	RF
Robbie Grossman (8)	Starling Marte (4)	Josh Bell (3)
Adalberto Santos	Gorkys Hernandez (20)	Harold Ramirez
Quincy Latimore	Evan Chambers (26)	Dan Grovatt
	Mel Rojas Jr. (29)	Andrew Lambo
	Taylor Lewis	
	Candon Myles	

3B	SS	2B	1B
Elevys Gonzalez	Jordy Mercer	Jarek Cunningham (18)	Alex Dickerson (11)
Jeremy Farrell	Pedro Ciriaco	Yamaico Navarro (24)	Matt Curry (25)
Daniel Gamache	Drew Maggi	Alen Hanson (27)	Jose Osuna (30)
	Gustavo Nunez	Josh Rodriguez	Matt Hague
		Brock Holt	
		Jodaneli Carvajal	

C
Tony Sanchez (7)
Ramon Cabrera (22)
Carlos Paulino
Samuel Gonzalez
Charlie Cutler
Eric Fryer
Matt Pagnozzi
Ryan Hornback

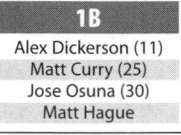

LHP		RHP	
LHSP	**LHRP**	**RHSP**	**RHRP**
Jeff Locke (10)	Justin Wilson (17)	Gerrit Cole (1)	Stetson Allie (9)
Colton Cain (13)	Zac Fuesser	Jameson Taillon (2)	Bryan Morris (12)
Rudy Owens (16)	Aaron Poreda	Luis Heredia (5)	Victor Black (19)
Zack Dodson (23)	Orlando Castro	Kyle McPherson (6)	Jared Hughes
Nate Baker		Nick Kingham (14)	Duke Welker
		Clay Holmes (15)	Diego Moreno
		Zack Von Rosenberg (21)	Casey Sadler
		Brandon Cumpton (28)	Ryan Beckman
		Tyler Waldron	Eliecier Cardenas
		Ryan Hafner	
		Tyler Glasnow	
		Jake Burnette	
		Phillip Irwin	
		Aaron Pribanic	
		Jeff Inman	
		Colten Brewer	
		Jason Creasy	
		Jordan Cooper	
		Matt Benedict	

2011   BONUSES: $17.0 MILLION

BEST PURE HITTER: OF Josh Bell (2) was one of the best pure hitters in the draft, and he does his damage from both sides of the plate. A switch-hitter since age 5, he has a mature approach and repeatedly makes sweet-spot contact. 1B Alex Dickerson (3) was one of the top college hitters available.

BEST POWER HITTER: Bell has bat speed and strength, and he should have plus power once he gets more balanced and uses his legs more in his swing. Dickerson, who won the Big Ten Conference triple crown in 2010, has slightly above-average pop.

FASTEST RUNNER: OFs Taylor Lewis (10) and Candon Myles (12) both have plus speed and can run the 60-yard dash in 6.6 seconds. Lewis stole 16 bases in 20 attempts in his pro debut.

BEST DEFENSIVE PLAYER: C Ryan Hornback (27) has solid catch-and-throw skills, agility and leadership ability. 2B/SS Kirk Singer (29) has good middle-infield actions, soft hands and a plus arm.

BEST FASTBALL: RHP Gerrit Cole (1) had the draft's most electric arm in 2008, when he was a Yankees first-round pick out of high school, and again this year, when he went No. 1 overall. His fastball ranges from 93-98 mph and has peaked at 102 mph. He touched 100 in his first outing in instructional league. The Pirates also invested in several big high school righthanders, and 6-foot-5, 210-pound Clay Holmes (6) already can hit 94 mph.

BEST SECONDARY PITCH: Cole's slider grades as a plus-plus pitch at times, as does his changeup. The best curveball belongs to RHP Tyler Glasnow (5).

BEST PRO DEBUT: Most of Pittsburgh's top picks signed late, though Dickerson batted .313/.393/.493 at short-season State College.

BEST ATHLETE: Lewis or Myles. Lewis has more present strength, while Myles was a college football prospect as a wide receiver.

MOST INTRIGUING BACKGROUND: Myles' brother Bryson signed with the Indians as a sixth-round pick after leading NCAA Division I with 53 steals in the spring.

CLOSEST TO THE MAJORS: Cole got his first taste of pro competition in the Arizona Fall League and could make his official debut in Double-A. Bell has the bat to move quickly for a high schooler.

BEST LATE-ROUND PICK: Lewis and Myles immediately became two of the best athletes in the Pirates system. RHP Matt Benedict (30) opened eyes in instructional league with an 89-92 mph fastball, average curveball and feel for a changeup.

THE ONE WHO GOT AWAY: High school OF Aaron Brown (17) starred against older players in the California Collegiate League this summer, then turned down third-round money to attend Pepperdine. Pittsburgh took fliers on several other prep standouts, including RHPs Brandon Platts (13, now at Missouri) and Kody Watts (15, Portland), LHP Eric Skoglund (16, Central Florida) and SS Trea Turner (20, North Carolina State)

ASSESSMENT: The Pirates continued to be as aggressive as any team in the draft. They set bonus records for total spending ($17 million), a single player ($8 million for Cole), a non-first-rounder ($5 million for Bell) and a ninth-rounder ($1.2 million for Holmes).

2010   BONUSES: $11.9 MILLION

RHP Jameson Taillon (1) has been everything the Pirates hoped he would be, but their other bonus baby, RHP Stetson Allie (2), is off to a rough start. RHP Nick Kingham (4) is another intriguing arm.

GRADE: B+

2009   BONUSES: $8.9 MILLION

C Tony Sanchez (1) had fared very well since being a surprise No. 4 overall pick before regressing in 2011. RHP Victor Black (1s) has a strong arm but hasn't stayed healthy, and seven-figure investments in RHP Zack Von Rosenberg (6) and LHP Colton Cain (8) have yet to look wise.

GRADE: C

2008   BONUSES: $9.8 MILLION

3B Pedro Alvarez (1) raced to Pittsburgh but hasn't become the offensive force he was billed as. INF Chase d'Arnaud (4) also underwhelmed in his first exposure to the majors, though OF Robbie Grossman (6) led the minors in runs and walks last year.

GRADE: B+

2007   BONUSES: $4.5 MILLION

The Pirates may never live down taking LHP Daniel Moskos (1) over Matt Wieters at No. 4, but at least Moskos was an effective big league reliever in 2011. So was LHP Tony Watson (9), though the highlight of this draft is RHP Kyle McPherson (14).

GRADE: C

Draft analysis by Jim Callis. Numbers in parentheses indicate draft rounds.

1 GERRIT COLE, RHP

Born: Sept. 8, 1990. **B-T:** R-R. **Ht.:** 6-4. **Wt.:** 220.
Drafted: UCLA, 2011 (1st round). **Signed by:** Rick Allen.

BA GRADE
70
MEDIUM

BILL MITCHELL

Cole had as good an arm as any pitcher in the 2008 draft, and the Yankees made him the 28th overall pick out of Orange (Calif.) Lutheran. Though he grew up as a huge Yankees fan, he never entered into negotiations with the team and instead opted to attend UCLA because he and his parents felt the college experience would help him gain maturity. Cole believes the three years he spent in Westwood did indeed help him grow as a pitcher and a person. He helped the Bruins reach the finals of the 2010 College World Series. Despite dominant stuff, he had just one winning season in three years at UCLA, going 6-8, 3.31 with a 119-24 K-BB ratio in 114 innings last spring. The Pirates made him the No. 1 overall choice in the 2011 draft and gave him a draft-record $8 million bonus at the Aug. 15 signing deadline. An example of how well regarded he is as a person came when one of the first texts he received after drafted came from Damon Oppenheimer, the Yankees scouting director he had spurned three years earlier. Cole should represent an upgrade on Pittsburgh's checkered history with the top draft pick: Jeff King (1986), Kris Benson (1996) and Bryan Bullington (2002).

Cole signed too late to play in the minors but did participate in the Arizona Fall League, where he lit up radar guns with a fastball that reached as high as 102 mph. That wasn't a fluke because he throws as hard as anybody in pro ball. He usually worked at 93-98 mph at UCLA, with better command when he stayed at the low end of that range. As he gains experience, he could throw harder while doing a better job of locating his fastball. Cole also has a wipeout slider that drops off the table just as it reaches home plate. It's a true swing-and-miss pitch that earns plus-plus grades at times. So too does his changeup, though it's less reliable than his slider. Cole's biggest challenge is to become more consistent with his delivery. Though he has enviable mechanics when he is right, he has spells where he begins flying open with his front shoulder and loses command of his pitches. He also has a tendency to drive too much off his back leg, which causes his front foot to land hard

and also affects his ability to put his pitches where he wants. Cole has the athleticism that will allow him to repeat his delivery, and the size and strength to be a workhorse at the top of a rotation. He's an intelligent young man with the reputation of being extremely coachable.

Cole is advanced enough to make his pro debut at Double-A Altoona, though the Pirates may send him to high Class A Bradenton until the weather warms up. He could push his way to Triple-A Indianapolis before the end of 2012 and shouldn't need much more than a year in the minors before he can help Pittsburgh. He's one of the few pitching prospects in baseball with legitimate ace potential.

SCOUTING GRADES

Fastball: 80.   **Command/**
Slider: 70.   **Control:** 55.
Changeup: 65. **Delivery:** 65.

Based on 20-80 scouting scale, where 50 represents major league average, and future projection rather than present tools

---

Year	Club (League)	Class	W	L	ERA	G	GS	CG	SV	IP	H	HR	BB	SO	K/9	WHIP	AVG
2011	Did Not Play—Signed Late																

2 JAMESON TAILLON, RHP

Born: Nov. 18, 1991. **B-T:** R-R. **Ht.:** 6-6. **Wt.:** 226. **Drafted:** HS—The Woodlands, Texas, 2010 (1st round). **Signed by:** Trevor Haley.

The Pirates took Taillon with the No. 2 overall pick in the 2010 draft and insist they would have selected him over No. 1 choice Bryce Harper. After signing him for $6.5 million, then the second-highest bonus in draft history, they kept him on tight pitch and inning counts in his 2011 pro debut. Taillon's size gives him outstanding leverage on his pitches and causes his fastball, which sits at 95-97 mph and reaches 99 mph, to get on hitters quickly. He also has a 12-to-6 curveball that can be unhittable as well as a slider that's both his third-best pitch and a plus offering. Taillon's changeup is still a work in progress and he didn't get a chance to work on it much in 2011. Pittsburgh had him throw approximately 80 percent fastballs to gain better command of his heater to both sides of the plate. He gets high marks for his competiveness and intelligence. Taillon will begin 2012 in high Class A, and the Pirates will allow him to work deeper into games and use his secondary pitches more often. They won't rush him, but he's talented enough to knock on the door to Pittsburgh late in 2013 and eventually become a No. 1 starter.

Year	Club (League)	Class	W	L	ERA	G	GS	CG	SV	IP	H	HR	BB	SO	K/9	WHIP	AVG
2011	West Virginia (SAL)	LoA	2	3	3.98	23	23	0	0	93	89	9	22	97	9.4	1.20	.249
Minor League Totals			2	3	3.98	23	23	0	0	93	89	9	22	97	9.4	1.20	.249

3 JOSH BELL, OF

Born: Aug. 14, 1992. **B-T:** B-R. **Ht.:** 6-4. **Wt.:** 195. **Drafted:** HS—Dallas, 2011 (2nd round). **Signed by:** Mike Leuzinger.

The Pirates rated Bell as the sixth-best prospect in the 2011 draft, but he was considered virtually unsignable because his mother is a professor at Texas-Arlington and wanted him to attend Texas. Pittsburgh took him with the first pick in the second round and shocked the industry by signing him for $5 million, the biggest draft bonus ever outside of the first round. A switch-hitter since he was 5, Bell has quick hands, wiry strength and outstanding power potential. He'll be a huge home run threat once he adds more balance and incorporates his legs more into his swing. With his mature approach and ability to make consistent hard contact, he should hit for average as well. He's an intelligent player who should learn to work counts and post high on-base percentages. Bell is still refining his defense and baserunning. A high school center fielder, he has average speed and a solid arm which figure to land him in right field. Bell likely will start his pro career at low Class A West Virginia. The Pirates are careful not to rush players, but Bell's advanced hitting skills and raw power may cause him to force the issue. Bell profiles as a No. 3 hitter and could see the major leagues before the end of 2014.

Year	Club (League)	Class	AVG	G	AB	R	H	2B	3B	HR	RBI	BB	SO	SB	CS	OBP	SLG
2011	Did Not Play—Signed Late																

4 STARLING MARTE, OF

Born: Oct. 9, 1988. **B-T:** R-R. **Ht.:** 6-2. **Wt.:** 184. **Signed:** Dominican Republic, 2007. **Signed by:** Rene Gayo/Chino Valdez.

The Pirates signed Marte for $85,000 in 2007 and his stock has risen dramatically since he arrived in the United States in 2009. A career .309/.366/.453 hitter, he led the Double-A Eastern League in batting (.332), hits (178) and doubles (38) in 2011 while drawing comparisons to Austin Jackson. Pittsburgh added him to its 40-man roster in November. Marte shows four strong tools and Pittsburgh is optimistic that there's more power in his bat. He uses his well above-average speed to beat out hits, though he's still learning to maximize it on the bases, where he can get too aggressive. He chases fewer breaking balls than he used to, but he needs to improve his plate discipline. If Marte gets more selective and starts using his lower half more, he could show more pop. He's good enough right now to be an above-average defensive center fielder in the major leagues with outstanding range and a strong arm. His passion for the game and flair for the dramatic are evident. Marte will begin 2012 in Triple-A Indianapolis and almost certainly will make his major league debut at some point later in the season. He's so good defensively in center field that he eventually could push all-star Andrew McCutchen to left. If Marte continues to add power, he could be an all-star.

PITTSBURGH PIRATES

Year	Club (League)	Class	AVG	G	AB	R	H	2B	3B	HR	RBI	BB	SO	SB	CS	OBP	SLG
2007	Pirates (DSL)	R	.220	45	132	27	29	4	1	1	11	10	29	16	2	.307	.288
2008	Pirates (DSL)	R	.296	65	257	53	76	10	2	9	44	16	53	20	8	.367	.455
2009	Pirates (GCL)	R	.000	2	7	1	0	0	0	0	0	0	1	0	0	.000	.000
	West Virginia (SAL)	LoA	.312	54	221	41	69	9	5	3	34	12	55	24	7	.377	.439
	Lynchburg (CAR)	HiA	1.000	1	2	0	2	0	0	0	1	0	0	0	0	1.000	1.000
2010	Pirates (GCL)	R	.346	8	26	6	9	3	0	2	5	1	6	4	1	.393	.692
	Bradenton (FSL)	HiA	.315	60	222	41	70	16	5	0	33	12	59	22	8	.386	.432
2011	Altoona (EL)	AA	.332	129	536	91	178	38	8	12	50	22	100	24	12	.370	.500
Minor League Totals			.309	364	1403	260	433	80	21	27	178	73	303	110	38	.366	.453

5 LUIS HEREDIA, RHP

BA GRADE
60
HIGH

Born: Aug. 10, 1994. **B-T:** R-R. **Ht.:** 6-6. **Wt.:** 205. **Signed:** Mexico, 2010. **Signed by:** Rene Gayo/Chino Valdez/Kyle Stark.

The top Latin American pitcher on the amateur market in 2010, Heredia signed out of Mexico for $2.6 million, the most Pittsburgh ever has given an international free agent. The Pirates took the extraordinary step of having him begin his career in the Rookie-level Gulf Coast League as a 16-year-old because they considered him too advanced for the Rookie-level Dominican Summer League. They carefully monitored Heredia's workload by giving him at least five days off between starts and never allowing him to pitch more than three innings in a game. Heredia added fastball velocity in his first pro season, settling at 92-93 mph and topping out at 96. His curveball can be a swing-and-miss pitch but lacks consistency, and his changeup also shows flashes of becoming a plus offering. For such a young, tall pitcher, he repeats his mechanics on a surprisingly consistent basis. Extremely mature for a teenager, he quickly learned to speak fairly fluent English and bought a house in Bradenton, Fla., to be near Pittsburgh's training base. Heredia remains very raw and will likely stay behind in extended spring training again in 2012 before reporting to short-season State College in June. He has the upside of a frontline starter, though pinning down his ETA in the big leagues is difficult because he's still just 17.

Year	Club (League)	Class	W	L	ERA	G	GS	CG	SV	IP	H	HR	BB	SO	K/9	WHIP	AVG
2011	Pirates (GCL)	R	1	2	4.75	12	11	0	0	30	28	3	19	23	6.8	1.55	.257
Minor League Totals			1	2	4.75	12	11	0	0	30	28	3	19	23	6.8	1.55	.257

6 KYLE McPHERSON, RHP

BA GRADE
50
MEDIUM

Born: Nov. 11, 1987. **B-T:** R-R. **Ht.:** 6-4. **Wt.:** 220. **Drafted:** Mobile (Ala.), 2007 (14th round). **Signed by:** Darren Mazeroski.

McPherson has come a long way since going 1-7, 6.02 in 2007 at Mobile (Ala.), an NAIA program where he primarily played the infield before getting drafted in the 14th round that June. He pitched his way onto the 40-man roster after the 2010 season and won the Pirates' minor league pitcher of the year award in 2011, when he ranked first in the system in strikeouts (142) and second in wins (12) and ERA (2.96). McPherson knows how to pitch, racking up strikeouts by changing speeds and commanding his entire repertoire. He has gotten stronger since coming into pro ball and his fastball now sits in the low 90s and reaches 95 mph. He can spot it to all four quadrants of the strike zone. McPherson has very good arm action on his changeup that allows him to get a number of swings and misses. He also has a 10-to-4 curveball that has its moments, but he tends to overthrow it, which causes it to flatten out. He has a clean delivery that he repeats easily, allowing him to pinpoint his pitches. McPherson handled the jump to Double-A easily in 2011 and could break camp with Indianapolis in 2012. Projected as a middle-of-the-rotation starter, he may reach Pittsburgh by the end of the season.

Year	Club (League)	Class	W	L	ERA	G	GS	CG	SV	IP	H	HR	BB	SO	K/9	WHIP	AVG
2007	Pirates (GCL)	R	4	2	2.61	12	10	0	0	52	47	3	10	35	6.1	1.10	.246
	State College (NYP)	SS	0	1	6.28	3	3	0	0	14	20	1	3	6	3.8	1.60	.323
2008	State College (NYP)	SS	1	3	4.37	15	7	0	1	56	52	10	5	41	6.6	1.02	.240
2009	West Virginia (SAL)	LoA	5	2	4.94	13	8	0	0	51	53	3	6	32	5.6	1.16	.269
	State College (NYP)	SS	4	3	2.99	13	13	0	0	75	70	5	11	57	6.8	1.08	.248
2010	West Virginia (SAL)	LoA	9	9	3.59	26	21	0	0	118	96	14	31	124	9.5	1.08	.216
	Bradenton (FSL)	HiA	0	0	0.00	2	0	0	0	4	2	0	0	7	15.8	0.50	.133
2011	Bradenton (FSL)	HiA	4	1	2.89	12	12	1	0	72	62	4	6	60	7.5	0.95	.227
	Altoona (EL)	AA	8	5	3.02	16	16	0	0	89	75	7	21	82	8.3	1.07	.226
Minor League Totals			35	26	3.48	112	90	1	1	531	477	47	93	444	7.5	1.07	.237

7 TONY SANCHEZ, C

Born: May 20, 1988. **B-T:** R-R. **Ht.:** 6-0. **Wt.:** 213. **Drafted:** Boston College, 2009 (1st round). **Signed by:** Chris Kline.

The Pirates stunned most draft analysts by selecting Sanchez with the No. 4 overall pick in the 2009 draft, a decision made in part because he would sign quickly for $2.5 million. Regarded as a quality defender behind the plate but with a questionable bat, he surprisingly hit .312/.413/.494 in his first two pro seasons before struggling in Double-A in 2011. He also was benched for three games after criticizing Eastern League umpires on Twitter. With his strong arm, receiving skills and feel for working with pitchers, Sanchez has Gold Glove ability. However, his defense slipped in 2011 as he got sloppy with his footwork and lost some accuracy on his throws. He erased just 22 percent of basestealers. Sanchez also regressed offensively, as his swing got long and he got too pull-conscious. He projects as an average hitter with moderate power and the willingness to draw walks. Sanchez's defensive ability gives him a chance to be a frontline major league catcher. Pittsburgh once hoped he would be ready to take over in 2012 with Ryan Doumit and Chris Snyder leaving as free agents, but that isn't going to happen. Instead, Sanchez almost certainly will start the season back at Altoona, and he may not arrive in the majors before mid-2013.

BA GRADE

50

MEDIUM

Year	Club (League)	Class	AVG	G	AB	R	H	2B	3B	HR	RBI	BB	SO	SB	CS	OBP	SLG
2009	State College (NYP)	SS	.308	4	13	2	4	1	0	0	1	1	2	0	0	.357	.385
	West Virginia (SAL)	LoA	.316	41	155	29	49	15	1	7	46	21	34	1	0	.415	.561
	Lynchburg (CAR)	HiA	.200	3	10	2	2	2	0	0	1	1	4	0	0	.385	.400
2010	Bradenton (FSL)	HiA	.314	59	207	31	65	17	0	4	35	28	41	2	1	.416	.454
2011	Altoona (EL)	AA	.241	118	402	46	97	14	1	5	44	47	76	5	5	.340	.318
Minor League Totals			.276	225	787	110	217	49	2	16	127	98	157	8	6	.376	.404

8 ROBBIE GROSSMAN, OF

Born: Sept. 16, 1989. **B-T:** B-L. **Ht.:** 6-0. **Wt.:** 205. **Drafted:** HS—Cypress, Texas, 2008 (6th round). **Signed by:** Mike Leuzinger.

Grossman appeared headed to the University of Texas until the Pirates enticed him to sign for $1 million as a sixth-round pick in 2008. He had only sporadic success before 2011, when he repeated high Class A and led the minors with 104 walks and 127 runs. He was the first minor leaguer to reach triple digits in both categories in the same season since Nick Swisher in 2004. Grossman took off after he improved his selectivity at the plate, putting him in hitter's counts where he can do damage. He hit 13 homers after totaling just nine in his first two full pro seasons, and 11 of those came from the left side of the plate—from which he didn't start hitting until he was a high school senior. Despite his breakthrough, many scouts still are skeptical as to whether he can become a plus hitter for average or power at the major league level. He has slightly above-average speed and even better instincts on the bases. Though he has played some center field in the minors, he spent most of 2011 in right field, where he showed average range and arm strength. Grossman still has to prove his breakout wasn't the result of repeating a level, and many scouts see him as more of a tweener than an everyday big leaguer in center or right field. He did tear up the Arizona Fall League, finishing first in walks (20) and second in homers (seven) before fracturing the hamate bone in his right hand. The injury could hamper him in 2012, when he'll head to Double-A once he's ready.

BA GRADE

50

MEDIUM

Year	Club (League)	Class	AVG	G	AB	R	H	2B	3B	HR	RBI	BB	SO	SB	CS	OBP	SLG
2008	Pirates (GCL)	R	.188	5	16	3	3	1	0	0	1	4	7	1	0	.381	.250
2009	West Virginia (SAL)	LoA	.266	116	451	83	120	21	2	5	42	75	164	35	12	.373	.355
2010	Bradenton (FSL)	HiA	.245	125	470	84	115	29	3	4	50	66	118	15	8	.344	.345
2011	Bradenton (FSL)	HiA	.294	134	490	127	144	34	2	13	56	104	111	24	10	.418	.451
Minor League Totals			.268	380	1427	297	382	85	7	22	149	249	400	75	30	.380	.383

9 STETSON ALLIE, RHP

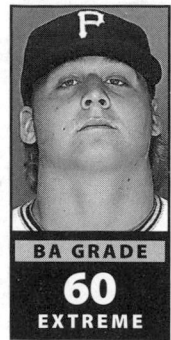

Born: March 13, 1991. **B-T:** R-R. **Ht.:** 6-2. **Wt.:** 219. **Drafted:** HS--Lakewood, Ohio, 2010 (2nd round). **Signed by:** Brian Tracy.

The two most-live arms in the 2010 draft belonged to Jameson Taillon and Allie, and the Pirates landed them both. Signed for $2.25 million as a second-rounder, Allie lacks Taillon's polish and it showed when he had problems finding the strike zone in his pro debut last summer. Allie can reach triple digits with his fastball, though it usually sits at 93-97 mph. His best pitch is a mid-80s slider with sharp, late break that makes it difficult for hitters to read. Allie has yet to prove he can throw strikes with either pitch, however. He had serious bouts of wildness in extended spring training and walked more than a batter an inning at State College. Pittsburgh eventually shifted Allie from the starting rotation to the bullpen in an attempt to take some pressure off him, but it didn't help. If he's going to remain a starter, he'll also have to refine a changeup. Allie is a real wild card at this point. He has the stuff to be a frontline starter or a lockdown closer, and he prefers the latter role. Yet his career will be stuck in neutral or worse until he gains some semblance of command. He figures to remain in extended spring training at the outset of 2012 before returning to State College.

BA GRADE
60
EXTREME

Year	Club (League)	Class	W	L	ERA	G	GS	CG	SV	IP	H	HR	BB	SO	K/9	WHIP	AVG
2011	State College (NYP)	SS	0	2	6.58	15	7	0	0	26	20	1	29	28	9.7	1.88	.208
Minor League Totals			0	2	6.58	15	7	0	0	26	20	1	29	28	9.7	1.88	.208

10 JEFF LOCKE, LHP

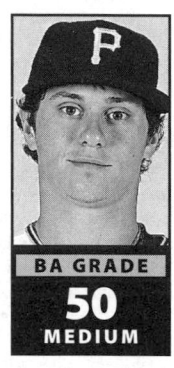

Born: Nov. 20, 1987. **B-T:** L-L. **Ht.:** 6-1. **Wt.:** 214. **Drafted:** HS—Conway, N.H., 2006 (2nd round). **Signed by:** Lonnie Goldberg (Braves).

Locke is trying to follow in the footsteps of such New Hampshire-born pitchers as Mike Flanagan, Bob Tewksbury, Chris Carpenter and Brian Wilson. Acquired with Charlie Morton and outfield prospect Gorkys Hernandez in the 2009 Nate McLouth trade with the Braves, Locke was the player the Pirates coveted the most. He finished the 2012 season in their rotation. Locke doesn't overpower hitters, with his fastball sitting at 89-90 mph and topping out at 92. He gets outs with it, though, because he commands it to both sides of the plate. He backs up his fastball with a solid curveball that he's willing to throw while behind in the count, and a changeup that keeps getting better. Locke has good aptitude for pitching and solid mound presence. Some scouts have questioned his durability because he's not big, but he hasn't missed a start in four full pro seasons and worked 170 innings in 2011. Considering he has made just five starts at the Triple-A level, Locke likely will spend the majority of 2012 at Indianapolis and contend for a full-time job in the Pittsburgh rotation the following year. He projects as an eventual No. 3 or 4 starter.

BA GRADE
50
MEDIUM

Year	Club (League)	Class	W	L	ERA	G	GS	CG	SV	IP	H	HR	BB	SO	K/9	WHIP	AVG
2006	Braves (GCL)	R	4	3	4.22	10	5	0	0	32	38	4	5	38	10.7	1.34	.299
2007	Danville (APP)	R	7	1	2.66	13	11	0	1	61	48	2	8	74	10.9	0.92	.213
2008	Rome (SAL)	LoA	5	12	4.06	25	24	1	0	140	150	6	38	113	7.3	1.35	.269
2009	Myrtle Beach (CAR)	HiA	1	4	5.52	10	10	0	0	46	47	1	26	43	8.5	1.60	.272
	Lynchburg (CAR)	HiA	4	4	4.08	17	17	0	0	82	98	4	18	56	6.2	1.42	.305
2010	Bradenton (FSL)	HiA	9	3	3.54	17	17	0	0	86	82	6	14	83	8.7	1.11	.248
	Altoona (EL)	AA	3	2	3.59	10	10	0	0	58	57	5	12	56	8.7	1.20	.257
2011	Altoona (EL)	AA	7	8	4.03	23	22	0	0	125	118	9	46	114	8.2	1.31	.251
	Indianapolis (IL)	AAA	1	2	2.22	5	5	0	0	28	25	1	9	25	7.9	1.20	.240
	Pittsburgh (NL)	MAJ	0	3	6.48	4	4	0	0	17	21	3	10	5	2.7	1.86	.323
Major League Totals			0	3	6.48	4	4	0	0	17	21	3	10	5	2.7	1.86	.323
Minor League Totals			41	39	3.85	130	121	1	1	657	663	38	176	602	8.2	1.28	.262

11 ALEX DICKERSON, 1B

BA GRADE
50
MEDIUM

Born: May 26, 1990. **B-T:** L-L. **Ht.:** 6-3. **Wt.:** 235. **Drafted:** Indiana, 2011 (3rd round). **Signed by:** Jerry Jordan.

Dickerson had an outstanding college career, winning the Big Ten Conference triple crown in 2010 and tying Indiana's career home run record with 47. The Pirates were thrilled to get him in the third round of the 2011 draft, where they signed him for $380,700. With his advanced approach to hitting, he made an easy transition to pro ball. Dickerson uses the whole field and has the raw strength to hit the ball out to any part of the park. He's also willing to take a walk if pitchers won't challenge him, and projects as a solid hitter with slightly above-average power. Dickerson played left field in college, but his lack of speed and range prompted Pittsburgh to immediately move him to first base in pro ball. Though he made six errors in 34 games, he can become an adequate defender in time. He may skip a level and jump to high Class A for his first full pro season. The Pirates haven't had a 30-homer first baseman since Jason Thompson in 1982 and don't have any can't-miss prospects at the position, so the path to Pittsburgh is wide open for Dickerson.

Year	Club (League)	Class	AVG	G	AB	R	H	2B	3B	HR	RBI	BB	SO	SB	CS	OBP	SLG
2011	State College (NYP)	SS	.313	41	150	25	47	16	1	3	19	16	28	0	0	.393	.493
Minor League Totals			.313	41	150	25	47	16	1	3	19	16	28	0	0	.393	.493

12 BRYAN MORRIS, RHP

BA GRADE
50
HIGH

Born: March 28, 1987. **B-T:** R-R. **Ht.:** 6-3. **Wt.:** 220. **Drafted:** Motlow State (Tenn.) CC, 2006 (1st round). **Signed by:** Marty Lamb (Dodgers).

The 26th overall pick in the 2006 draft, Morris is the last player remaining in the organization from the ill-fated Jason Bay/Manny Ramirez deal at the July 2008 trade deadline. The Pirates gave up Bay and received Andy LaRoche and Morris from the Dodgers and Craig Hansen and Brandon Moss from the Red Sox. Morris entered 2011 on track to crack Pittsburgh's rotation at some point during the season, but a disappointing performance in spring training got him sent back to Double-A for a second season. Things got worse, as he strained an oblique in mid-April and missed a month, then became a full-time reliever in mid-June. Morris' raw stuff plays better when he comes out of the bullpen, as he throws a 90-95 mph fastball and a mid-80s slider. The latter is a plus pitch when it features sharp break. He no longer has to worry about mastering a changeup that never came easy to him. He should be more durable, too, after missing time with Tommy John surgery in 2007, biceps tendinitis in 2008 and foot surgery in 2009. Morris has the personality for relief work, as he pitches aggressively and no longer will have to hold anything in reserve like he did as a starter. He still needs to do a better job of throwing strikes, but he'll go to Triple-A to start the season and could make his major league debut by September. He has the arm to be a set-up man in the big leagues, and perhaps even a closer.

Year	Club (League)	Class	W	L	ERA	G	GS	CG	SV	IP	H	HR	BB	SO	K/9	WHIP	AVG
2006	Ogden (PIO)	R	4	5	5.13	14	14	0	0	60	64	3	40	79	11.9	1.74	.267
2007	Did Not Play—Injured																
2008	Great Lakes (MWL)	LoA	2	4	3.20	17	17	1	0	82	74	5	31	72	7.9	1.29	.247
	Hickory (SAL)	LoA	0	2	5.02	3	3	0	0	14	17	2	12	11	6.9	2.02	.288
2009	Lynchburg (CAR)	HiA	4	9	5.57	15	15	0	0	73	87	2	34	32	4.0	1.67	.295
2010	Bradenton (FSL)	HiA	3	0	0.60	8	8	0	0	45	37	0	7	40	8.1	0.99	.220
	Altoona (EL)	AA	6	4	4.25	19	16	0	0	89	87	9	31	84	8.5	1.33	.258
2011	Altoona (EL)	AA	3	4	3.35	35	6	0	3	78	72	2	33	64	7.4	1.35	.252
Minor League Totals			22	28	3.89	111	79	1	3	440	438	23	188	382	7.8	1.42	.260

13 COLTON CAIN, LHP

BA GRADE
50
HIGH

Born: Feb. 5, 1991. **B-T:** L-L. **Ht.:** 6-3. **Wt.:** 225. **Drafted:** HS—Waxahachie, Texas 2009 (8th round). **Signed by:** Mike Leuzinger.

One of several pitchers the Pirates have signed to over-slot bonuses in the last three drafts, Cain received an eighth-round-record $1.125 million in 2009 to pass up a scholarship from Texas. He also was a slugging first baseman at Waxahachie (Texas) High, the alma mater of golf immortal Byron Nelson, but Pittsburgh believed he had a brighter future on the mound. He signed too late to play in 2009 and spent much of 2010 rehabilitating from offseason back surgery, but last year he started to show what he can do. Cain throws a fastball that sits in the low 90s with good movement. He's still refining an 11-to-5 curveball and a changeup. What separates Cain from many young pitchers is his fearlessness, as he attacks hitters inside and will throw any pitch in any count. He does a good job of keeping the ball down and hides the ball well in his delivery, giving him deception with his pitches. He throws across his body and with some effort, yet it doesn't hamper his control. His stocky frame is built for durability. Cain will pitch in high Class A this year and likely move up one level at a time, putting him in line to reach Pittsburgh in 2015. He could develop into a No. 3 or 4 starter.

Year	Club (League)	Class	W	L	ERA	G	GS	CG	SV	IP	H	HR	BB	SO	K/9	WHIP	AVG
2010	Pirates (GCL)	R	0	1	3.77	4	4	0	0	14	12	1	5	15	9.4	1.19	.214
	State College (NYP)	SS	1	1	5.03	11	9	0	0	34	23	2	14	32	8.5	1.09	.189
2011	West Virginia (SAL)	LoA	6	8	3.64	24	19	0	0	106	92	6	31	81	6.9	1.16	.234
Minor League Totals			7	10	3.96	39	32	0	0	155	127	9	50	128	7.4	1.14	.222

14 NICK KINGHAM, RHP

BA GRADE
50
HIGH

Born: Nov. 8, 1991. **B-T:** R-R. **Ht.:** 6-5. **Wt.:** 233. **Drafted:** HS—Las Vegas, 2010 (4th round). **Signed by:** Larry Broadway.

Another over-slot high school pitcher, Kingham signed for $480,000 as a fourth-round pick in 2010 and turned down a commitment to Oregon. He saw his first extensive pro action last summer, when his 2.15 ERA ranked third in the short-season New York-Penn League (and first among teenagers). Kingham has a long, projectable body and his 91-93 mph fastball appears even quicker because he pitches on a steep downhill plane. He figures to add a little more velocity once his body fills out. Kingham has an advanced changeup, which gives him a leg up on most young pitchers, and is working on tightening up his inconsistent curveball. He controls his body well for such a big pitcher and has a smooth delivery, which gives him good control and command. He'll get his first taste of full-season ball in low Class A this year and eventually could be a No. 3 starter in the big leagues.

Year	Club (League)	Class	W	L	ERA	G	GS	CG	SV	IP	H	HR	BB	SO	K/9	WHIP	AVG
2010	Pirates (GCL)	R	0	0	0.00	2	0	0	0	3	3	0	0	2	6.0	1.00	.273
2011	State College (NYP)	SS	6	2	2.15	15	15	0	0	71	63	5	15	47	6.0	1.10	.238
Minor League Totals			6	2	2.07	17	15	0	0	74	66	5	15	49	6.0	1.09	.239

15 CLAY HOLMES, RHP

BA GRADE
55
EXTREME

Born: March 27, 1993. **B-T:** R-R. **Ht.:** 6-5. **Wt.:** 210. **Drafted:** HS—Slocomb, Ala., 2011 (9th round). **Signed by:** Darren Mazeroski.

The Pirates have paid out the highest bonuses in draft history in the first (Gerrit Cole, $8 million), second (Josh Bell, $5 million), eighth (Colton Cain, $1.125 million) and ninth (Holmes, $1.2 million) rounds. Holmes was able to land a seven-figure bonus because he not only had a big league body and fastball, but he also was the valedictorian of his high school class and strongly committed to Auburn. Holmes already sits at 90-93 mph with good sink on his heater, and he could add more velocity as he fills out his lanky frame. His best secondary pitch is a spike curveball with 12-to-6 break, though it's a bit inconsistent at this point. Holmes' changeup is in the rudimentary stages, but he's a quick learner. His biggest need will be to develop control and command, the result of a delivery that features significant effort. He'll likely begin the 2012 season in extended spring training to get better acclimated to pro ball before making his debut in the Gulf Coast or New York-Penn League in June.

Year	Club (League)	Class	W	L	ERA	G	GS	CG	SV	IP	H	HR	BB	SO	K/9	WHIP	AVG
2011	Did Not Play—Signed Late																

16 RUDY OWENS, LHP

BA GRADE
45
MEDIUM

Born: Dec. 18, 1987. **B-T:** L-L. **Ht.:** 6-3. **Wt.:** 225. **Drafted:** Chandler-Gilbert (Ariz.) CC, D/F 2006 (28th round). **Signed by:** Ted Williams.

Part of the Pirates' last class of draft-and-follows, Owens signed for $390,000 in the spring of 2007. After doing little in his first two pro seasons, he won Pittsburgh's minor league pitcher of the year award in both 2009 and 2010. He became an Altoona legend in the latter season by pitching the Curve to the Eastern League title while wearing a perm reminiscent of 1970s pitchers such as Mark Fidrych, Ross Grimsley and Randy Jones. Altoona even held a Rudy Owens Perm Cap promotion last year. However, Owens wasn't feted in Triple-A in 2011, getting knocked around before he was shut down in August with shoulder fatigue. The Pirates still protected him on their 40-man roster after the season. After showing a 90-93 mph fastball down the stretch the year before, he had a hard time getting it above the mid-80s. Inconsistent mechanics and his tired shoulder contributed to the drop in velocity, which rendered his secondary pitches less effective because they lacked much separation from his fastball. He throws a slurvy curveball and a changeup that have improved but are still fringy. Owens, who has a realistic ceiling as a No. 4 starter, will go back to Indianapolis to start 2012.

Year	Club (League)	Class	W	L	ERA	G	GS	CG	SV	IP	H	HR	BB	SO	K/9	WHIP	AVG
2007	Pirates (GCL)	R	1	4	5.32	6	4	0	0	22	20	1	8	17	7.0	1.27	.238
2008	State College (NYP)	SS	3	6	4.97	15	13	0	0	58	63	2	13	45	7.0	1.31	.269
2009	West Virginia (SAL)	LoA	10	1	1.70	19	19	0	0	101	71	8	15	91	8.1	0.85	.197
	Lynchburg (CAR)	HiA	1	1	3.86	6	6	0	0	23	29	3	2	22	8.5	1.33	.305
2010	Altoona (EL)	AA	12	6	2.46	26	26	0	0	150	124	11	23	132	7.9	0.98	.226
2011	Indianapolis (IL)	AAA	9	7	5.05	21	21	0	0	112	129	10	32	71	5.7	1.43	.289
Minor League Totals			36	25	3.44	93	89	0	0	466	436	35	93	378	7.3	1.13	.246

17 JUSTIN WILSON, LHP

BA GRADE
45
MEDIUM

Born: Aug. 18, 1987. **B-T:** L-L. **Ht.:** 6-2. **Wt.:** 221. **Drafted:** Fresno State, 2008 (5th round). **Signed by:** Sean Campbell.

Wilson capped one of the most improbable runs in College World Series history by winning the title game for Fresno State in 2008. He enjoyed playoff success again two years later, when he was named MVP of the Eastern League postseason by contributing 13 shutout innings to Altoona's championship. He struggled in Triple-A last year, though, so the Pirates moved him to the bullpen in the final month to get him back on track. Wilson earned a spot on the 40-man roster after he was a revelation in relief, hitting the upper 90s in short stints after topping out at 95 mph as a starter. The Pirates still believe he can be an effective starter if he improves the command of his fastball, which normally sits in the low 90s with life. He also throws a big-breaking curveball and a changeup with some fade. Pittsburgh faces a decision in spring training: keep Wilson in the bullpen, where he could help immediately at the big league level, or put him back in the rotation, where he'd likely need a second full year at Indianapolis. His arm action makes it difficult for him to throw strikes consistently, which ultimately may point him to relief.

Year	Club (League)	Class	W	L	ERA	G	GS	CG	SV	IP	H	HR	BB	SO	K/9	WHIP	AVG
2009	Lynchburg (CAR)	HiA	6	8	4.50	26	26	0	0	116	118	14	55	94	7.3	1.49	.262
2010	Altoona (EL)	AA	11	8	3.09	27	26	0	0	143	109	4	71	134	8.5	1.26	.215
2011	Indianapolis (IL)	AAA	10	8	4.13	30	21	0	3	124	121	12	67	94	6.8	1.51	.254
Minor League Totals			27	24	3.85	83	73	0	3	383	348	30	193	322	7.6	1.41	.243

18 JAREK CUNNINGHAM, 2B

BA GRADE
50
HIGH

Born: Dec. 25, 1989. **B-T:** R-R. **Ht.:** 6-1. **Wt.:** 190. **Drafted:** HS—Spokane, Wash., 2008 (18th round). **Signed by:** Greg Hopkins.

Cunningham has hit better than most Pirates position prospects since singing for $100,000 as an 18th-round pick in 2008. But he has had trouble staying healthy. He tore the anterior cruciate ligament in his left knee as a high school senior, missing the season but avoiding surgery when the ACL reattached itself. He wasn't as fortunate when he tore it again during a conditioning drill, requiring an operation that cost him all of 2009. After making it through the 2010 season, he was hit in the head by a pitch last July 15, sustaining a concussion and missing most of the final seven weeks. Cunningham has outstanding pop for a middle infielder, true plus power that he generates to all fields. He hit 15 homers in 80 games in the pitcher-friendly Florida State League last year. The ball jumps off his bat when he makes sweet spot contact. He lacks plate discipline, however, which could be his fatal flaw as he works his way through the system. He swings and misses a lot, and he often chases pitches outside the zone. Despite his knee injuries, Cunningham still has solid speed and some scouts wonder why he doesn't run more often. A shortstop in high school and primarily a third baseman in his pro debut, he shifted to second base following his second knee surgery. He has good range and arm strength, and he's a tick above-average at turning the double play. Cunningham will begin 2012 in Double-A. He has the tools to be Ian Kinsler Lite if his health and strike-zone judgment don't sabotage his chances.

Year	Club (League)	Class	AVG	G	AB	R	H	2B	3B	HR	RBI	BB	SO	SB	CS	OBP	SLG
2008	Pirates (GCL)	R	.318	43	148	20	47	11	1	5	22	14	26	2	1	.385	.507
2009	Did Not Play—Injured																
2010	West Virginia (SAL)	LoA	.258	121	488	72	126	37	7	12	49	30	132	11	7	.309	.436
2011	Bradenton (FSL)	HiA	.258	80	310	53	80	23	6	15	51	17	82	5	2	.320	.516
	Pirates (GCL)	R	.400	2	5	2	2	0	0	0	0	0	0	0	0	.571	.400
Minor League Totals			.268	246	951	147	255	71	14	32	122	61	240	18	10	.327	.473

19 VICTOR BLACK, RHP

BA GRADE
50
HIGH

Born: May 23, 1988. **B-T:** R-R. **Ht.:** 6-4. **Wt.:** 208. **Drafted:** Dallas Baptist, 2009 (1st round supplemental). **Signed by:** Mike Leuzinger.

Black was one of the harder throwers available in the 2009 draft, and the Pirates used a supplemental first-round pick on him after his fastball was clocked consistently at 94-96 mph at Dallas Baptist. He comes from an athletic family as his three sisters all played NCAA Division I volleyball, and that athleticism adds to his intrigue. He pitched just five innings in 2010 while battling shoulder and biceps problems, and those issues delayed the start of his 2011 season until late May. Pittsburgh moved him to the bullpen when he got back on the mound, and he pitched well enough to earn a promotion to high Class A in August. Black's fastball sat at 91-93 mph last year, though he should show more velocity once the Pirates take him off a tight leash. He had shown a hard slider with good tilt in the past, but that too has yet to come all the way back. He also throws a changeup. Besides regaining his former stuff, Black also must do a better job of finding the strike zone after averaging 5.0 walks per nine innings during his brief pro career. Pittsburgh is anxious to see what he can do if he's fully healthy at Bradenton at 2012, hoping he can become a set-up man or maybe more down the road.

Year	Club (League)	Class	W	L	ERA	G	GS	CG	SV	IP	H	HR	BB	SO	K/9	WHIP	AVG
2009	State College (NYP)	SS	1	2	3.45	13	7	0	1	31	26	0	15	33	9.5	1.31	.213
2010	West Virginia (SAL)	LoA	0	0	9.64	2	2	0	0	5	3	1	5	8	15.4	1.71	.176
2011	West Virginia (SAL)	LoA	2	1	5.28	22	0	0	1	29	30	0	16	23	7.1	1.59	.268
	Bradenton (FSL)	HiA	1	0	4.05	5	0	0	0	7	8	1	4	5	6.8	1.80	.333
Minor League Totals			4	3	4.65	42	9	0	2	72	67	2	40	69	8.7	1.49	.244

20 GORKYS HERNANDEZ, OF

BA GRADE
45
MEDIUM

Born: Sept. 7, 1987. **B-T:** R-R. **Ht.:** 6-0. **Wt.:** 186. **Signed:** Venezuela, 2005. **Signed by:** Ramon Pena (Tigers).

Hernandez was involved in two significant trades in his first four pro seasons. The Tigers shipped him and Jair Jurrjens to the Braves in exchange for Edgar Renteria after the 2007 season. In June 2009, Atlanta packaged Hernandez with Jeff Locke and Charlie Morton to get Nate McLouth from the Pirates. Hernandez has a minor league batting title (Gulf Coast League, 2006) and MVP award (low Class A Midwest

League, 2007) on his résumé and has made Top 10 Prospects lists in all three organizations, but he has stalled in the Pittsburgh system because he doesn't provide enough offense. Hernandez's best tool is his center-field defense. He has exceptional range, makes tough plays look easy and has a strong, accurate arm. His plus speed doesn't play as well on the bases, as he's vulnerable to good pickoff moves and hasn't been a prolific basestealer since his MWL days. Hernandez showed some improved strength and gap power last season in Triple-A, but he still doesn't impact the ball or get on base with enough consistency. He's blocked in the majors by Andrew McCutchen and has Starling Marte coming up behind him, so Hernandez may never play regularly in the majors unless he's part of a third trade.

Year	Club (League)	Class	AVG	G	AB	R	H	2B	3B	HR	RBI	BB	SO	SB	CS	OBP	SLG
2005	Tigers (DSL)	R	.265	63	211	44	56	10	0	4	19	30	38	10	10	.377	.370
2006	Tigers (GCL)	R	.327	50	205	41	67	9	2	5	23	10	27	20	4	.356	.463
2007	W. Michigan (MWL)	LoA	.293	124	481	84	141	25	5	4	50	36	69	54	11	.344	.391
2008	Myrtle Beach (CAR)	HiA	.264	100	406	75	107	23	6	5	42	48	79	20	4	.348	.387
2009	Mississippi (SL)	AA	.316	52	212	33	67	11	2	0	19	15	54	10	8	.361	.387
	Altoona (EL)	AA	.262	86	344	45	90	14	2	3	31	24	76	9	8	.312	.340
2010	Altoona (EL)	AA	.266	92	368	45	98	11	4	2	26	33	95	17	3	.333	.334
2011	Indianapolis (IL)	AAA	.283	126	424	48	120	25	9	1	40	35	91	21	9	.348	.392
Minor League Totals			.281	693	2651	415	746	128	30	24	250	231	529	161	57	.345	.379

21 ZACK VON ROSENBERG, RHP

BA GRADE
45
MEDIUM

Born: Sept. 24, 1990. **B-T:** R-R. **Ht.:** 6-5. **Wt.:** 208. **Drafted:** HS—Zachary, La., 2009 (6th round). **Signed by:** Jerome Cochran.

Von Rosenberg was a legendary high school pitcher in Louisiana, winning the state championship game in each of his four years split between two schools. A quality athlete, he planned to pitch at Louisiana State and also punt for the Tigers' football team. Rated the 41st-best player in the 2009 draft by Baseball America, he fell to the sixth round because of signability questions but turned pro for $1.2 million. Von Rosenberg hasn't yet to live up to his hype, going 6-15, 4.90 in three pro seasons. As they do with many of their young pitchers, the Pirates have had him focus on honing his fastball command. He has thrown strikes but hasn't missed many bats with an 86-90 mph fastball that he can sink or cut. Once he began adding in his curveball in the latter stages of last season, he pitched much better, finishing with six perfect innings in his final start. He also throws a slider and changeup, though he has yet to establish a plus pitch that can carry him at upper levels. He'll move up to high Class A in 2012 and try to show that he can become more than a back-of-the-rotation starter.

Year	Club (League)	Class	W	L	ERA	G	GS	CG	SV	IP	H	HR	BB	SO	K/9	WHIP	AVG
2009	Pirates (GCL)	R	0	0	0.00	1	1	0	0	1	0	0	0	1	9.0	0.00	.000
2010	State College (NYP)	SS	1	6	3.20	13	13	0	0	59	60	4	13	39	5.9	1.24	.267
2011	West Virginia (SAL)	LoA	5	9	5.73	27	25	0	0	126	143	19	23	114	8.2	1.32	.290
Minor League Totals			6	15	4.90	41	39	0	0	186	203	23	36	154	7.5	1.29	.282

22 RAMON CABRERA, C

BA GRADE
45
MEDIUM

Born: Nov. 5, 1989. **B-T:** B-R. **Ht.:** 5-8. **Wt.:** 194. **Signed:** Venezuela, 2008. **Signed by:** Rene Gayo/Rodolfo Petit.

Cabrera's father Alex played for the 2000 Diamondbacks and has gone on to spend 11 seasons in Japan. Ramon isn't a slugger like his father, but he won the high Class A Florida State League batting title last season with a .343 average. He also was the FSL's toughest batter to strike out, fanning just once every 13.1 plate appearances. A switch-hitter, Cabrera slashes line drives to the gaps from both sides of the plate. The question is how much more power he can develop and how much his defense can improve. He focuses on making contact and isn't much of a home run threat, having hit just 10 in 1,051 pro at-bats. Though he has a square frame, Cabrera is agile behind the plate and moves surprisingly well on the bases. He also shows good feel for calling a game. However, his arm is average at best and his throws can be scattershot. He threw out just 13 percent of basestealers and committed 14 passed balls in 78 games last year. Keeping his body in shape may always be a struggle. Cabrera will have to keep proving himself at every level to make it to the majors, with Double-A his next challenge.

Year	Club (League)	Class	AVG	G	AB	R	H	2B	3B	HR	RBI	BB	SO	SB	CS	OBP	SLG
2008	Pirates (VSL)	R	.264	56	178	24	47	16	0	3	22	28	27	5	0	.367	.404
2009	Pirates (VSL)	R	.312	20	77	10	24	6	0	2	19	12	11	1	2	.400	.468
	Pirates (GCL)	R	.291	37	127	15	37	11	1	1	16	16	16	2	1	.372	.417
2010	West Virginia (SAL)	LoA	.269	90	342	49	92	14	4	1	40	22	42	3	4	.312	.342
2011	Bradenton (FSL)	HiA	.343	92	327	46	112	25	4	3	53	38	29	5	1	.410	.471
Minor League Totals			.297	295	1051	144	312	72	9	10	150	116	125	16	8	.366	.411

23 ZACK DODSON, LHP

BA GRADE
50
HIGH

Born: July 23, 1990. **B-T:** L-L. **Ht.:** 6-2. **Wt.:** 191. **Drafted:** HS—Castroville, Texas, 2009 (4th round). **Signed by:** Trevor Haley.

Dodson was one of four high school pitchers paid above-slot bonuses by the Pirates in the 2009 draft, getting $600,000 to walk away from a Baylor scholarship. A two-way star, he went 10-0, 1.20 and hit 11 homers as a high school senior. Dodson isn't as physical as some of Pittsburgh's other pitching prospects, but his athleticism and arm speed allow him to run his fastball up to 94 mph. He generally sits at 88-91 mph with his heater, which features nice life that makes it difficult for hitters to square up. He also has a solid curveball that's getting better, and the next item on his agenda is to develop a more reliable changeup. Dodson's mechanics sometimes lose consistency, but when he keeps his delivery contact, he's able to pound the strike zone. He missed two months in 2011 with a broken pitching hand, though he returned to go 4-1, 1.97 in the final month in low Class A. A possible No. 3 or 4 starter, Dodson has pitched just 152 innings since signing but may approach that total in high Class A this year.

Year	Club (League)	Class	W	L	ERA	G	GS	CG	SV	IP	H	HR	BB	SO	K/9	WHIP	AVG
2009	Pirates (GCL)	R	0	0	0.00	1	0	0	0	1	0	0	0	1	9.0	0.00	.000
2010	State College (NYP)	SS	2	6	4.84	15	13	0	0	58	57	2	27	41	6.4	1.46	.265
2011	Pirates (GCL)	R	0	1	4.15	3	3	0	0	9	8	1	3	7	7.3	1.27	.235
	State College (NYP)	SS	0	1	4.58	4	4	0	0	18	22	2	4	13	6.6	1.47	.310
	West Virginia (SAL)	LoA	6	4	2.57	13	13	0	0	67	61	3	15	46	6.2	1.14	.246
Minor League Totals			8	12	3.74	36	33	0	0	152	148	8	49	108	6.4	1.30	.259

24 YAMAICO NAVARRO, INF/OF

BA GRADE
45
MEDIUM

Born: Oct. 31, 1987. **B-T:** R-R. **Ht.:** 5-11. **Wt.:** 170. **Signed:** Dominican Republic, 2005. **Signed by:** Pablo Lantigua (Red Sox).

Navarro was traded twice in 2011, going from the Red Sox to the Royals for Mike Aviles in July, then to the Pirates in exchange for righthander Brooks Pounders and infielder Diego Goris in December. Navarro has the makings of a good offensive middle infielder with outstanding bat speed, some pop, the willingness to work counts and enough quickness to steal an occasional base. However, he's beginning to play his way off shortstop as his range is diminishing. Navarro still has the quick feet to play second base and the arm strength to play third base on a regular basis, though his bat doesn't profile at the hot corner. He has played every position in pro ball except for catcher and pitcher. Boston tired of Navarro's lack of conditioning or consistent effort, and Kansas City didn't wait long to unload him as well. In Pittsburgh, he'll get the opportunity to make the big league team in a super-utility role, but he may be running out of chances if his work ethic doesn't improve. His brother Raul is a shortstop in the Diamondbacks system.

Year	Club (League)	Class	AVG	G	AB	R	H	2B	3B	HR	RBI	BB	SO	SB	CS	OBP	SLG
2006	Red Sox (DSL)	R	.279	53	201	29	56	13	5	3	37	21	29	5	3	.344	.438
2007	Lowell (NYP)	SS	.289	62	225	36	65	10	1	5	37	22	52	12	6	.357	.409
2008	Greenville (SAL)	LoA	.280	83	325	46	91	14	4	7	54	29	73	3	2	.341	.412
	Lancaster (CAL)	HiA	.348	42	181	33	63	13	2	4	23	12	30	3	2	.393	.508
2009	Lowell (NYP)	SS	.238	5	21	1	5	1	0	0	2	2	3	0	2	.304	.286
	Salem (CAR)	HiA	.319	23	94	10	30	9	0	4	17	6	12	2	2	.373	.543
	Portland (EL)	AA	.185	39	135	16	25	6	2	2	11	14	28	5	1	.270	.304
2010	Portland (EL)	AA	.274	88	329	49	90	19	3	8	55	42	53	16	5	.358	.422
	Pawtucket (IL)	AAA	.283	16	53	8	15	4	0	3	6	5	6	2	1	.339	.528
	Boston (AL)	MAJ	.143	20	42	4	6	0	0	0	5	2	17	0	0	.174	.143
2011	Pawtucket (IL)	AAA	.258	34	128	25	33	8	2	5	13	17	25	3	2	.362	.469
	Boston (AL)	MAJ	.216	16	37	6	8	2	0	1	3	3	9	0	0	.275	.351
	Omaha (PCL)	AAA	.272	25	92	11	25	3	1	2	9	7	18	3	4	.317	.391
	Kansas City (AL)	MAJ	.304	6	23	2	7	1	0	0	6	2	5	0	0	.346	.348
Major League Totals			.206	42	102	12	21	3	0	1	14	7	31	0	0	.250	.265
Minor League Totals			.279	470	1784	264	498	100	20	43	264	177	329	54	30	.348	.430

25 MATT CURRY, 1B

BA GRADE
45
MEDIUM

Born: July 27, 1988. **B-T:** L-R. **Ht.:** 6-1. **Wt.:** 217. **Drafted:** Texas Christian, 2010 (16th round). **Signed by:** Mike Leuzinger.

Despite hitting .339 with 18 homers for Texas Christian in 2010, Curry lasted until the 16th round of the draft because he was a bad-bodied college senior who had no value beyond his bat. He has continued to produce since signing for $2,000, leading State College with seven homers in his pro debut and then starting 2011 by batting .361/.477/.671 in the first two months at West Virginia. The Pirates were so impressed that they jumped him to Altoona, making him their first prospect to skip high Class A since Andrew McCutchen in 2006. Curry met his match against Double-A pitching, having trouble with breaking balls and lefthanders. An aggressive hitter who likes to pull the ball with an uppercut stroke, he may need to tone down his approach. Nevertheless, his power and willingness to draw walks make him one of the more intriguing offensive prospects in the system. Though he's a well below-average runner with limited range, he handles himself well enough on the bases and around the bag at first base. How well he adjusts when he returns to Altoona in 2012 will tell a great deal about his future.

Year	Club (League)	Class	AVG	G	AB	R	H	2B	3B	HR	RBI	BB	SO	SB	CS	OBP	SLG
2010	State College (NYP)	SS	.299	58	197	36	59	14	0	7	29	39	47	7	5	.421	.477
2011	West Virginia (SAL)	LoA	.361	46	155	39	56	15	3	9	34	35	29	6	2	.477	.671
	Altoona (EL)	AA	.242	87	302	38	73	16	3	6	39	33	90	1	1	.320	.374
Minor League Totals			.287	191	654	113	188	45	6	22	102	107	166	14	8	.390	.476

26 EVAN CHAMBERS, OF

BA GRADE
50
HIGH

Born: March 24, 1989. **B-T:** R-R. **Ht.:** 5-11. **Wt.:** 216. **Drafted:** Hillsborough (Fla.) CC, 2009 (3rd round). **Signed by:** Matt Wondolowski.

Chambers has one of the highest offensive ceilings in the system, but whether he can reach it remains in question after he has hit .238 in three pro seasons. Built like Kirby Puckett, he packs plenty of strength and raw power. He has quick wrists and generates good backspin on the ball. His patience is evidenced by his 212 walks in 299 pro games. However, Chambers also has several issues at the plate. He sits on fastballs and is too pull-conscious, leaving him vulnerable to breaking balls or pitches on the outer half. He has no two-strike approach and hasn't shown any ability to make adjustments. He also can become overly selective and let too many hittable pitches pass by. The stocky Chambers has deceptively good speed and even better first-step quickness, which enables him to steal bases and get good jumps in center field. His arm also rates above-average. Chambers has been moving up one step at a time and will face a telling challenge in Double-A this year.

Year	Club (League)	Class	AVG	G	AB	R	H	2B	3B	HR	RBI	BB	SO	SB	CS	OBP	SLG
2009	State College (NYP)	SS	.245	58	200	45	49	15	0	4	22	50	78	6	0	.393	.380
2010	West Virginia (SAL)	LoA	.239	116	415	71	99	21	2	12	52	92	116	35	17	.384	.386
2011	Bradenton (FSL)	HiA	.234	125	436	57	102	24	2	11	55	70	131	20	12	.350	.374
Minor League Totals			.238	299	1051	173	250	60	4	27	129	212	325	61	29	.372	.380

27 ALEN HANSON, SS/2B

BA GRADE
50
HIGH

Born: Oct. 22, 1992. **B-T:** R-R. **Ht.:** 5-11. **Wt.:** 152. **Signed:** Dominican Republic, 2009. **Signed by:** Rene Gayo/Ellis Pena.

Hanson opened plenty of eyes with his outstanding athleticism while making his U.S. debut in 2011. He led the Rookie-level Gulf Coast League with seven triples and finished second with 24 steals while teaming with fellow Dominican Jodaneli Cavajal to form an outstanding double-play package. Hanson's most obvious tool is his plus speed, which makes him a factor on the bases and gives him good range. His only drawback on defense is a slightly below-average arm that hinders him from making the long throw from the hole at shortstop. He also saw action at second base last season and that may be his future home. Hanson has an advanced feel for hitting for a foreign teenager. He has good hand-eye coordination and a grasp of the strike zone, along with a line-drive stroke and some gap power. After making a cameo at State College in September, he'll probably return there after opening 2012 in extended spring training.

Year	Club (League)	Class	AVG	G	AB	R	H	2B	3B	HR	RBI	BB	SO	SB	CS	OBP	SLG
2010	Pirates (DSL)	R	.324	68	244	48	79	10	7	2	28	22	37	20	8	.383	.447
2011	Pirates (GCL)	R	.263	52	198	42	52	13	7	2	35	21	34	24	6	.352	.429
	State College (NYP)	SS	.200	3	10	1	2	0	0	0	0	1	2	0	0	.273	.200
Minor League Totals			.294	123	452	91	133	23	14	4	63	44	73	44	14	.367	.434

28 BRANDON CUMPTON, RHP

BA GRADE
45
MEDIUM

Born: Nov. 16, 1988. **B-T:** R-R. **Ht.:** 6-2. **Wt.:** 199. **Drafted:** Georgia Tech, 2010 (9th round). **Signed by:** Greg Schilz.

Cumpton went 31-3 in high school and won back-to-back Georgia 4-A state championships before having an up-and-down career at Georgia Tech. Despite his uneven performance and questions some teams had about his durability, the Pirates drafted him in the ninth round in 2010 and have been pleased with his development. Cumpton pitches at 89-93 mph with his fastball and has answered the stamina concerns by holding his velocity deep into games. He relies heavily on his heater, throwing it for strikes on both sides of the plate and showing some glove-side life. He has tightened up his curveball to give him a second solid pitch. The next step is refining a changeup. Cumpton throws a lot of strikes but his control is significantly sharper than his command. While some scouts think he'd be better served in middle relief, where his pitches would play up, Pittsburgh believes he has a chance to reach the majors as a No. 3 or 4 starter. He'll make the jump to Double-A this season.

Year	Club (League)	Class	W	L	ERA	G	GS	CG	SV	IP	H	HR	BB	SO	K/9	WHIP	AVG
2010	State College (NYP)	SS	0	1	2.53	4	3	0	0	11	8	0	5	6	5.1	1.22	.200
2011	West Virginia (SAL)	LoA	7	4	4.30	13	12	0	0	67	60	6	18	48	6.4	1.16	.240
	Bradenton (FSL)	HiA	3	3	3.66	13	12	0	0	66	73	6	12	42	5.7	1.28	.280
Minor League Totals			10	8	3.88	30	27	0	0	144	141	12	35	96	6.0	1.22	.256

29 MEL ROJAS JR., OF

BA GRADE
50
HIGH

Born: May 24, 1990. **B-T:** B-R. **Ht.:** 6-3. **Wt.:** 209. **Drafted:** Wabash Valley (Ill.) CC, 2009 (3rd round). **Signed by:** Anthony Wycklendt.

Mel Rojas Sr. pitched for 10 years in the majors, but Mel Jr. decided to be a position player after seeing his father's career derailed by shoulder problems. The son turned down offers out of the Dominican Republic and redshirted for a year at Wabash Valley (Ill.) CC before going from virtual unknown to third-round pick in 2009. He led all national juco players with 61 steals while hitting .398 with 12 homers before signing for $423,900. The Pirates viewed him as a potential five-tool talent, but it hasn't translated well in his first two years in pro ball. Rojas is a switch-hitter with size, strength and bat speed. He has an inconsistent approach, however, getting pull-conscious at times and trying to slap the ball at others. He flies open in his stance, making it difficult to handle pitches on the outer half. He's more productive from the left side of the plate, batting just .200/.260/.281 against southpaws in 2011. Rojas has solid but not blazing speed and isn't the same basestealing threat he was at Wabash Valley, getting caught 14 times in 37 steal attempts last year. He glides to balls in center field and has a good arm for the position. The learning curve in pro ball has proven steep so far for Rojas, who will go to high Class A this season. Pittsburgh still likes his upside even if he's moving slower than expected.

Year	Club (League)	Class	AVG	G	AB	R	H	2B	3B	HR	RBI	BB	SO	SB	CS	OBP	SLG
2010	State College (NYP)	SS	.207	43	164	19	34	7	0	0	14	21	42	7	3	.309	.250
2011	West Virginia (SAL)	LoA	.246	131	508	66	125	16	7	5	46	46	119	23	14	.312	.335
Minor League Totals			.237	174	672	85	159	23	7	5	60	67	161	30	17	.311	.314

30 JOSE OSUNA, 1B/OF

BA GRADE
50
HIGH

Born: Dec. 12, 1992. **B-T:** R-R. **Ht.:** 6-3. **Wt.:** 213. **Signed:** Venezuela, 2009. **Signed by:** Rene Gayo/Rodolfo Petit.

Osuna was considered one of the top young pitching prospects in Venezuela as a 15-year-old but his velocity took a mysterious dip in 2009, so many teams decided against bidding on him. The Pirates saw potential in Osuna's bat, however, and signed him for $275,000. It seems like a prudent decision, as he has shown plus power in his limited pro experience. Osuna has loft to his swing and the type of bat speed and leverage that should allow him to hit plenty of balls out of the park once he body matures. Unlike most young power hitters, he understands the strike zone and doesn't chase many bad pitches. Osuna is not overly athletic, though, and his lack of speed and range will limit him to either first base or left field. His arm is fringy, too. Pittsburgh has a dearth of power-hitting prospects, so he'll get the opportunity to hit his way to the big leagues. He's polished enough at the plate to be able to handle low Class A as a teenager in 2012.

Year	Club (League)	Class	AVG	G	AB	R	H	2B	3B	HR	RBI	BB	SO	SB	CS	OBP	SLG
2010	Pirates (VSL)	R	.251	64	215	33	54	16	0	10	43	19	35	2	4	.325	.465
2011	Pirates (GCL)	R	.331	48	178	28	59	14	3	4	32	18	21	3	2	.400	.511
	State College (NYP)	SS	.250	2	8	2	2	1	0	0	1	1	0	0	0	.333	.375
Minor League Totals			.287	114	401	63	115	31	3	14	76	38	56	5	6	.359	.484

St. Louis Cardinals

BY DERRICK GOOLD

The Cardinals had less than 72 hours to enjoy the improbability of their World Series championship before the inevitability of their future interrupted the celebrations.

Good thing they had been planning ahead.

Two days after St. Louis dispatched the Rangers in Game Seven of a riveting World Series, three-time MVP and St. Louis icon Albert Pujols became a free agent for the first time as a pro. The next morning, manager Tony LaRussa resigned after 33 years in the dugout, the final 16 with the Cardinals.

St. Louis offered Pujols what would have been the  third-largest contract in major league history, but the Angels trumped it with a 10-year, $254 million deal that he accepted in December. The departures of LaRussa and Pujols hasten the franchise's steady identity shift from a veteran-studded roster to a streamlined one with higher-paid core players at the top and a growing stream of less expensive youngsters ready to provide increased impact.

The first hints of that impact came late in 2011 as St. Louis overcame a 10½-game deficit on Aug. 25 to win the National League wild card on the final day of the regular season. Several contributors in that unexpected run were either developed by the Cardinals or acquired in exchange for their prospects.

St. Louis put the finishing touches on its title thanks to the heroics of NL Championship Series and World Series MVP David Freese, a St. Louis native acquired as a Class A third baseman from the Padres in exchange for Jim Edmonds. Allen Craig homered three times in the World Series, including the go-ahead shot in Game Seven. He was one of seven homegrown players on the field when he caught the final out of the series finale.

Jason Motte finished that game and closed out five postseason victories. After signing a four-year contract extension in July, Jaime Garcia went 3-0 in September and pitched seven shutout innings of Game Two of the World Series. Colby Rasmus, three times the system's top-ranked prospect, stalled but was dealt to the Blue Jays for key pieces Octavio Dotel, Edwin Jackson and Marc Rzepczynski.

As they searched for a new manager, the Cardinals put an emphasis on a leader comfortable with integrating and nurturing youth. They chose Mike Matheny, who won three Gold Gloves as a St. Louis catcher and most recently served as a special assistant in player development for the club.

Postseason hero Allen Craig was part of a Cardinals roster full of homegrown talent

TOP 30 PROSPECTS

1. Shelby Miller, rhp	16. Joe Kelly, rhp
2. Carlos Martinez, rhp	17. John Gast, lhp
3. Oscar Taveras, of	18. C.J. McElroy, of
4. Zack Cox, 3b	19. Adron Chambers, of
5. Kolten Wong, 2b	20. Tony Cruz, c
6. Tyrell Jenkins, rhp	21. Adam Reifer, rhp
7. Lance Lynn, rhp	22. Brandon Dickson, rhp
8. Eduardo Sanchez, rhp	23. David Kopp, rhp
9. Matt Adams, 1b	24. Cody Stanley, c
10. Jordan Swaggerty, rhp	25. Victor DeLeon, rhp
11. Trevor Rosenthal, rhp	26. Adam Ottavino, rhp
12. Matt Carpenter, 3b	27. Boone Whiting, rhp
13. Ryan Jackson, ss	28. Seth Blair, rhp
14. Maikel Cleto, rhp	29. Lance Jeffries, of
15. Charlie Tilson, of	30. Sam Freeman, lhp

Matheny, who has no managerial experience, inherits not only most of a roster that won the 11th championship title in franchise history but also perhaps St. Louis' best crop of minor league talent in over two decades. That group is headlined by righthanders Shelby Miller and Carlos Martinez, outfielder Oscar Taveras and third baseman Zack Cox.

The man responsible for assembling much of the talent, vice president of scouting and player development Jeff Luhnow, left to become the Astros' GM. He had fortified the farm system and resuscitated international operations since coming aboard in 2003.

General Manager: John Mozeliak. **Farm Director:** John Vuch. **Scouting Director:** Dan Kantrovitz.

Class	Team	League	W	L	Pct	Finish*	Manager(s)
Majors	St. Louis Cardinals	National	90	72	.556	4th (16)	Tony LaRussa
Triple-A	Memphis Redbirds	Pacific Coast	77	66	.538	4th (16)	Chris Maloney
Double-A	Springfield Cardinals	Texas	62	78	.443	7th (8)	Ron Warner
High A	Palm Beach Cardinals	Florida State	68	70	.493	7th (12)	Luis Aguayo
Low A	Quad Cities River Bandits	Midwest	81	56	.591	2nd (16)†	Johnny Rodriguez
Short-season	Batavia Muckdogs	New York-Penn	37	38	.493	8th (14)	Dann Bilardello
Rookie	Johnson City Cardinals	Appalachian	45	23	.662	1st (10)†	Mike Shildt
Rookie	GCL Cardinals	Gulf Coast	31	24	.564	5th (15)	Steve Turco
Overall 2011 Minor League Record			401	355	.530	6th (30)	

*Finish in overall standings (No. of teams in league). †League champion.

LAST YEAR'S TOP 30

Player,	Pos.	Status
1.	Shelby Miller, rhp	No. 1
2.	Zack Cox, 3b	No. 4
3.	Carlos Martinez, rhp	No. 2
4.	Tyrell Jenkins, rhp	No. 6
5.	Allen Craig, of/1b	Majors
6.	Lance Lynn, rhp	No. 7
7.	Eduardo Sanchez, rhp	No. 8
8.	Seth Blair, rhp	No. 28
9.	Jordan Swagerty, rhp	No. 10
10.	Joe Kelly, rhp	No.16
11.	Matt Carpenter, 3b	No. 12
12.	Daniel Descalso, 2b/3b	Majors
13.	John Gast, lhp	No. 17
14.	Fernando Salas, rhp	Majors
15.	Adam Reifer, rhp	No. 21
16.	Maikel Cleto, rhp	No. 14
17.	Adron Chambers, of	No. 19
18.	David Kopp, rhp	No. 23
19.	P.J. Walters, rhp	(Blue Jays)
20.	Francisco Samuel, rhp	Dropped out
21.	Pete Kozma, ss	Dropped out
22.	Blake King, rhp	(Astros)
23.	Mark Hamilton, 1b	Dropped out
24.	Oscar Taveras, of	No. 3
25.	Tony Cruz, c	No. 20
26.	Bryan Anderson, c	Dropped out
27.	Adam Ottavino, rhp	No. 26
28.	Daryl Jones, of	(Reds)
29.	Steven Hill, c	Dropped out
30.	Ryan Jackson, ss	No. 13

BEST TOOLS

Best Hitter for Average	Oscar Taveras
Best Power Hitter	Matt Adams
Best Strike-Zone Discipline	Matt Carpenter
Fastest Baserunner	C.J. McElroy
Best Athlete	Tyrell Jenkins
Best Fastball	Shelby Miller
Best Curveball	Carlos Martinez
Best Slider	Jordan Swagerty
Best Changeup	John Gast
Best Control	Boone Whiting
Best Defensive Catcher	Tony Cruz
Best Defensive Infielder	Ryan Jackson
Best Infield Arm	Pete Kozma
Best Defensive Outfielder	Shane Robinson
Best Outfield Arm	Tommy Pham

PROJECTED 2015 LINEUP

Catcher	Yadier Molina
First Base	Allen Craig
Second Base	Kolten Wong
Third Base	David Freese
Shortstop	Ryan Jackson
Left Field	Matt Holliday
Center Field	Jon Jay
Right Field	Oscar Taveras
No. 1 Starter	Shelby Miller
No. 2 Starter	Adam Wainwright
No. 3 Starter	Jaime Garcia
No. 4 Starter	Carlos Martinez
No. 5 Starter	Tyrell Jenkins
Closer	Jason Motte

TOP PROSPECTS OF THE DECADE

Year	Player, Pos.	2011 Org.
2002	Jimmy Journell, rhp	Out of baseball
2003	Dan Haren, rhp	Angels
2004	Blake Hawksworth, rhp	Dodgers
2005	Anthony Reyes, rhp	Indians
2006	Anthony Reyes, rhp	Indians
2007	Colby Rasmus, of	Blue Jays
2008	Colby Rasmus, of	Blue Jays
2009	Colby Rasmus, of	Blue Jays
2010	Shelby Miller, rhp	Cardinals
2011	Shleby Miller, rhp	Cardinals

TOP DRAFT PICKS OF THE DECADE

Year	Player, Pos.	2011 Org.
2002	Calvin Hayes, ss (3rd round)	Out of baseball
2003	Daric Barton, 1b	Athletics
2004	Chris Lambert, rhp	Out of baseball
2005	Colby Rasmus, of	Blue Jays
2006	Adam Ottavino, rhp	Cardinals
2007	Pete Kozma, ss	Cardinals
2008	Brett Wallace, 1b	Astros
2009	Shelby Miller, rhp	Cardinals
2010	Zack Cox, 3b	Cardinals
2011	Kolten Wong, 2b	Cardinals

LARGEST BONUSES IN CLUB HISTORY

J. D. Drew, 1998	$3,000,000
Shelby Miller, 2009	$2,875,000
Rick Ankiel, 1999	$2,500,000
Chad Hutchinson, 1998	$2,300,000
Zack Cox, 2010	$2,000,000

ST. LOUIS CARDINALS

TOP 2012 ROOKIE: Lance Lynn, rhp. The hard-throwing righty had a strong turn in October and could blossom as a set-up man or spot starter.

BREAKOUT PROSPECT: Ryan Jackson, ss. He has the slick glove and is gaining the respectable bat to solve a lingering riddle for the Cardinals—who's their shortstop of the future?

SLEEPER: Breyvic Valera, 2b. The switch-hitting Venezuelan has a knack for squaring the ball and uses the whole field, and he has the speed to rocket into prominence this summer.

SOURCE OF TOP 30 TALENT			
Homegrown	29	Acquired	1
College	16	Trades	1
Junior college	3	Rule 5 draft	0
High school	5	Independent leagues	0
Draft-and-follow	0	Free agents/waivers	0
Nondrafted free agents	1		
International	4		

LF
Lance Jeffries (30)
Anthony Garcia
Nick Martini
Virgil Hill
Aaron Luna
Jermaine Curtis
Dutch Deol

CF
Charlie Tilson (15)
C.J. McElroy (18)
Adron Chambers (19)
Erik Komatsu
Tommy Pham
Shane Robinson
D'Marcus Ingram

RF
Oscar Taveras (3)
Nick Longmire
Michael Swinson
Chris Swauger
Amaury Capellan

3B
Zack Cox (4)
Matt Carpenter (12)
Roberto de la Cruz
Packy Elkins
Sam Tuivailala

SS
Ryan Jackson (13)
Pete Kozma
Matt Williams
Ronny Gil
Cesar Valera

2B
Kolten Wong (5)
Breyvic Valera
Kenny Peoples
Greg Garcia
Starlin Rodriguez
Tyler Rahmatulla
Jose Garcia

1B
Matt Adams (9)
Mark Hamilton
Steven Hill
Jonathan Rodriguez
Xavier Scruggs

C
Tony Cruz (20)
Cody Stanley (24)
Bryan Anderson
Robert Stock
Nick Derba
Audry Perez
Adam Ehrlich

LHP	
LHSP	**LHRP**
John Gast (17)	Sam Freeman (30)
Nick Additon	Justin Wright
Kevin Siegrist	Daniel Miranda
Kyle Hald	Nick Greenwood
Tyler Lyons	Nick Gillung
Hector Hernandez	
Anthony Ferrara	

RHP	
RHSP	**RHRP**
Shelby Miller (1)	Lance Lynn (7)
Carlos Martinez (2)	Eduardo Sanchez (8)
Tyrell Jenkins (6)	Jordan Swagerty (10)
Trevor Rosenthal (11)	Adam Reifer (21)
Maikel Cleto (14)	Brandon Dickson (22)
Joe Kelly (16)	David Kopp (23)
Victor DeLeon (25)	Chuckie Fick
Adam Ottavino (26)	Keith Butler
Boone Whiting (27)	Jorge Rondon
Seth Blair (28)	Tyler Mills
Sam Gaviglio	Richard Castillo
Eric Fornataro	Brian Broderick
Deryk Hooker	Kevin Jacob
Kevin Thomas	Chris Costantino
Scott Gorgen	Brandon Creath
	Chase Reid

2011
BONUSES: $4.6 MILLION

BEST PURE HITTER: 2B Kolten Wong (1) batted .335 at low Class A Quad Cities. He has a short, quick lefthanded swing with a line-drive approach and tremendous control of the strike zone.

BEST POWER HITTER: OF Lance Jeffries (10) has bat speed, an uppercut stroke and a strong, compact frame that prompts comparisons to Ron Gant.

FASTEST RUNNER: OF C.J. McElroy (3) runs the 60-yard dash in under 6.4 seconds, giving him 75-80 speed on the 20-80 scouting scale. OF Charlie Tilson (2) is a 65 runner.

BEST DEFENSIVE PLAYER: Tilson is an instinctive center fielder with a slightly above-average arm. Wong also made an impression with his glovework, and managers rated him the best defensive second baseman in the Midwest League.

BEST FASTBALL: RHP Tyler Mills (9) worked at 94-96 mph in his first outing for Michigan last spring, but he wore down and sat at 88-92 by the end of the season. RHP Kevin Jacob (31) showed a 97-99 mph fastball in the Alaska League two summers ago but has worked in the low 90s since a shoulder injury that didn't require surgery. RHP Brandon Creath (44) maintained a 90-95 mph fastball all year.

BEST SECONDARY PITCH: LHP Daniel Miranda (8) may get to the big leagues on the strength of his changeup alone.

BEST PRO DEBUT: Wong, who led Quad Cities to the MWL championship. Miranda led the New York-Penn League with 15 saves, while RHP Todd McInnis (25) rode his curveball to top the short-season circuit in WHIP (0.94).

BEST ATHLETE: McElroy would have played wide receiver at Houston if he hadn't turned pro. He rushed for 1,523 yards and accounted for 28 touchdowns as a high school senior, and he finished seventh at the Texas 5-A track meet in the long jump.

MOST INTRIGUING BACKGROUND: A month after selecting C Casey Rasmus (36), St. Louis sent his older brother Colby (their 2005 first-round pick) to the Blue Jays in a trade that paid off with a playoff berth. McElroy's father Chuck and unsigned C Kyle Arnsberg's (40) dad Brad pitched in the big leagues.

CLOSEST TO THE MAJORS: Wong might not need much more than a full season in the minors before he's ready. Among the pitchers, it's Miranda or Sam Gaviglio (5), who gets a lot of grounders with his sinker and changeup.

BEST LATE-ROUND PICK: With power, speed and arm strength, Jeffries has more tools than a typical 10th-rounder. SS Matt Williams (15) has solid offen-sive and defensive ability.

THE ONE WHO GOT AWAY: Power-hitting C Aramis Garcia (20) is a Cardinals fan, but that wasn't enough to sway him from going to Florida International.

ASSESSMENT: St. Louis targeted up-the-middle athletes and speed, kicking off with Wong, Tilson, McElroy and SS Kenny Peoples (4). The Cardinals found two late-rounders who fit that profile in Jeffries and Williams.

2010
BONUSES: $6.7 MILLION

3B Zack Cox's (1) hitting ability took him to Double-A in his first full pro season. RHP Tyrell Jenkins (1s) is a high-upside starter, while RHP Jordan Swagerty (2) could beat Cox to St. Louis.

GRADE: B

2009
BONUSES: $5.4 MILLION

RHP Shelby Miller (1) is the system's best pitching prospect since Rick Ankiel and has developed exactly as hoped. As a bonus, the Cardinals found a power arm in RHP Joe Kelly (3), their possible shortstop of the future in Ryan Jackson (3) and three late-round steals in 3B Matt Carpenter (13), RHP Trevor Rosenthal (21) and 1B Matt Adams (23).

GRADE: A

2008
BONUSES: $5.5 MILLION

1B Brett Wallace (1) wasn't able to play third base and hasn't provided an impact bat, but St. Louis got value from the pick by trading him and OF Shane Peterson (2) to get Matt Holliday from the Athletics. RHP Lance Lynn (1s) contributed out of the bullpen to the Cardinals' World Series championship run. OF Alex Castellanos (10) brought a much-needed shortstop in Rafael Furcal in a July deal with the Dodgers.

GRADE: C+

2007
BONUSES: $4.6 MILLION

It's not often that a single draft produces nine big leaguers though not a single impact player, but this one did with SS/2B Pete Kozma (1); RHPs Clay Mortensen (1s), Jess Todd (2) and Brian Broderick (21); INF Daniel Descalso (3); 1B/C Steven Hill (13); OFs Andrew Brown (18) and Adron Chambers (38); and C Tony Cruz (26). Mortensen and Todd became part of trades for Holliday and Mark DeRosa.

GRADE: C

Draft analysis by Jim Callis. Numbers in parentheses indicate draft rounds.

1 SHELBY
MILLER, RHP

Born: Oct. 10, 1990. **B-T:** R-R. **Ht.:** 6-3. **Wt.:** 195.
Drafted: HS—Brownwood, Texas, 2009 (1st round).
Signed by: Ralph Garr Jr.

BA GRADE
70
MEDIUM

JERRY HALE

The Cardinals' most-heralded righthanded pitching prospect in nearly two decades, Miller spent most of the summer hearing from coaches how he needed to embrace his secondary pitches for the good of his development. It was only halfway through the season that pitching coordinator Dyar Miller wondered: "What if he doesn't? Maybe the fastball is good (enough) to get him there." Miller may be able to ride his fastball all the way to the majors, where he's expected to arrive in the near future. The 19th overall pick in 2009, he became the first high school pitcher selected in the first five rounds by St. Louis since 2005 and the first prep arm taken in the first round by the club since 1991. Signed for $2.875 million, Miller hasn't wilted under the hype. In his two full pro seasons, he has ranked as the No. 1 pitching prospect in each of his three leagues. His only difficulty came in August, when an alcohol-related incident led to a week-long suspension. The Cardinals were pleased with how he responded. In his final start of the year, he struck out nine in eight scoreless innings to punctuate what St. Louis hopes was a season of maturation both on and off the mound.

Miller embraces his Texas gunslinger lineage and has the heat and mound presence to match. His overpowering fastball cooks consistently in the mid-90s and spikes to 97 mph. The fastball comes with late sinking and boring life that's just as notable as its velocity, and the ease of his delivery makes it seem to explode on hitters. Both Miller's curveball and changeup could become plus pitches with further refinement. His curveball has tight drop and his mid-80s changeup has nice fade that allows it to slide in on lefthanders. The Cardinals hoped his midseason jump to Double-A Springfield would reinforce their insistence that he utilize his secondary offerings more often and effectively. For a while he pitched with an offspeed pitch quota, even if his curve and changeup got hit, and both came out the better for it. True to the organization's preference, Miller has pitches that invite meek contact, and he has

proven economical even when he gets fastball-happy. Throughout the 2011 season, he showed improved stamina and sustained velocity. As his frame continues to fill out, he'll be able to maintain his power and his command later into games. He's a good athlete who might have punted in college had he followed through on a baseball scholarship from Texas A&M.

Set for his third consecutive nonroster invitation to big league camp, Miller could open the season in the Triple-A Memphis rotation if he has a strong spring. He'll have to display increased dexterity with his secondary pitches to succeed at the highest levels. He could earn a callup to St. Louis late in the 2012 season and claim a permanent job in the majors in 2013. He's an ace-caliber starter and the most talented pitcher the Cardinals have developed since Rick Ankiel.

SCOUTING GRADES

Fastball: 75.   **Command/**
Curveball: 60.   **Control:** 60.
Changeup: 60.   **Delivery:** 65.

Based on 20-80 scouting scale, where 50 represents major league average, and future projection rather than present tools.

Year	Club (League)	Class	W	L	ERA	G	GS	CG	SV	IP	H	HR	BB	SO	K/9	WHIP	AVG
2009	Quad Cities (MWL)	LoA	0	0	6.00	2	2	0	0	3	5	0	2	2	6.0	2.33	.357
2010	Quad Cities (MWL)	LoA	7	5	3.62	24	24	0	0	104	97	7	33	140	12.1	1.25	.243
2011	Palm Beach (FSL)	HiA	2	3	2.89	9	9	0	0	53	40	2	20	81	13.8	1.13	.204
	Springfield (TL)	AA	9	3	2.70	16	16	0	0	87	72	2	33	89	9.2	1.21	.229
Minor League Totals			18	11	3.17	51	51	0	0	247	214	11	88	312	11.4	1.22	.232

2 CARLOS MARTINEZ, RHP

Born: Sept. 21, 1991. **B-T:** R-R. **Ht.:** 6-0. **Wt.:** 165. **Signed:** Dominican Republic, 2010. **Signed by:** Juan Mercado.

The Red Sox originally signed the righthander then known as Carlos Matias for $160,000 in 2009, but he failed to pass an MLB investigation because his name didn't match his paperwork. The Cardinals helped him piece together the required proof, then signed him for $1.5 million in June 2010. In his first season in the United States, he pitched in the 2011 Futures Game and reached high Class A Palm Beach at age 19. Martinez has an easy delivery, an overpowering fastball and plenty of bravado. His four-seam fastball routinely sits in the upper 90s and reaches 100 mph, even late in games. He also can fire a sinker at 92-93 mph. After he was pushed to high Class A, his mechanics faltered and his command followed. Martinez has a devastating curveball at times, but it was more loopy after he got to Palm Beach. He also has a changeup that features some fade but loses effectiveness when he throws it too hard. Some scouts wonder if his size lends itself to the durability needed in a starter, though he does have wiry strength. Martinez will return to high Class A to get his delivery and command back on track. Once he does, St. Louis may have a hard time holding him back. He has the ingredients to become a frontline starter or a closer.

BA GRADE

65

HIGH

Year	Club (League)	Class	W	L	ERA	G	GS	CG	SV	IP	H	HR	BB	SO	K/9	WHIP	AVG
2010	Cardinals (DSL)	R	3	2	0.76	12	12	1	0	59	28	1	14	78	11.9	0.71	.144
2011	Quad Cities (MWL)	LoA	3	2	2.33	8	8	0	0	39	27	1	14	50	11.6	1.06	.196
	Palm Beach (FSL)	HiA	3	3	5.28	10	10	0	0	46	49	2	30	48	9.4	1.72	.269
Minor League Totals			9	7	2.63	30	30	1	0	144	104	4	58	176	11.0	1.13	.202

3 OSCAR TAVERAS, OF

Born: June 19, 1992. **B-T:** L-L. **Ht.:** 6-2. **Wt.:** 180. **Signed:** Dominican Republic, 2008. **Signed by:** Juan Mercado.

Another product of the Cardinals' revived presence in Latin America, Taveras signed for $145,000 as a 16-year-old Dominican. Not yet 20, he won the Midwest League batting title in 2011 with a .386 average, the highest in the low Class A circuit since Deacon Jones hit .409 in 1956. The verb most often used to describe Taveras' game is "barrel," because of his preternatural ability to get good wood on pitches in all areas of the strike zone. His fluid mechanics and superb hand-eye coordination aid a swing that stays balanced as it sweeps through the zone. He's an aggressive swinger but doesn't strike out much. His line drives to the gap hint at the average power he'll have as he matures. Taveras has played all three outfield positions, though his average speed and solid arm will point him toward right field. He remained at Quad Cities all year because his baserunning and defense weren't ready for a promotion, and at times his effort waned. St. Louis shipped him to the Arizona Fall League as the second-youngest player there. He started slowly but caught up quick. He could make the leap to Double-A in 2012, and if his power continues to develop, he'll profile as a No. 3 hitter.

BA GRADE

60

HIGH

Year	Club (League)	Class	AVG	G	AB	R	H	2B	3B	HR	RBI	BB	SO	SB	CS	OBP	SLG
2009	Cardinals (DSL)	R	.257	65	237	35	61	13	8	1	42	28	36	9	4	.338	.392
2010	Cardinals (GCL)	R	.167	7	30	1	5	1	0	0	2	1	5	1	0	.194	.200
	Johnson City (APP)	R	.322	53	211	39	68	13	3	8	43	12	41	8	5	.362	.526
2011	Quad Cities (MWL)	LoA	.386	78	308	52	119	27	5	8	62	32	52	1	4	.444	.584
Minor League Totals			.322	203	786	127	253	54	16	17	149	73	134	19	13	.381	.496

4 ZACK COX, 3B

Born: May 9, 1989. **B-T:** L-R. **Ht.:** 6-0. **Wt.:** 215. **Drafted:** Arkansas, 2010 (1st round). **Signed by:** Jay Catalano.

Cox parlayed his status as the best pure hitter in the 2010 draft and his extra leverage as a sophomore into a $3.2 million big league contract that included a $2 million bonus. He quickly reached Double-A in his first full pro season, batting .335/.388/.500 in his final 61 games after a slow start that resulted from him bending too much at his waist, cheating to reach outside pitches and growing vulnerable to inside ones. A more upright stance allowed him to pull pitches with more power. Scouts believe he'll continue to hit for average, though whether he'll have more than average power is a subject of debate. Cox has the arm to handle third, though he'll need to continue to refine his footwork to enhance his range. He's a below-average runner. Cox will begin 2012 in Double-A with the expectation that he'll be in Triple-A by midseason. A potential No. 3 hitter, he could earn his first big league callup in September, though David Freese looms ahead of him.

BA GRADE

55

MEDIUM

Year	Club (League)	Class	AVG	G	AB	R	H	2B	3B	HR	RBI	BB	SO	SB	CS	OBP	SLG
2010	Cardinals (GCL)	R	.400	4	15	0	6	1	0	0	1	1	3	0	0	.471	.467
2011	Palm Beach (FSL)	HiA	.335	42	164	22	55	8	0	3	20	11	29	2	1	.380	.439
	Springfield (TL)	AA	.293	93	352	54	103	19	0	10	48	29	69	0	1	.355	.432
Minor League Totals			.309	139	531	76	164	28	0	13	69	41	101	2	3	.366	.435

5 KOLTEN WONG, 2B

BA GRADE
55
MEDIUM

Born: Oct. 10, 2010. **B-T:** L-R. **Ht.:** 5-9. **Wt.:** 190. **Drafted:** Hawaii, 2011 (1st round). **Signed by:** Matt Swanson.

Twenty-five years after they last drafted a second baseman in the first round (Luis Alicea), the Cardinals did it again because they were so smitten with Wong's bat. He had won the MVP award in the wood-bat Cape Cod League in 2010 before hitting .378 at Hawaii last spring. The 23rd overall pick last June, Wong signed quickly for $1.3 million and helped Quad Cities win the Midwest League title. Wong's small frame hides a compact swing with pop and his innate ability to hit for average. He uncoils to generate line drives from corner to corner and could grow into 15-homer power. He has the ability to bunt or hit-and-run, and the patience to draw walks. Wong is not a burner, but he's aggressive and instinctual enough to steal a few bases with slightly above-average speed. He has a plus arm for second base, along with solid range and improving footwork. St. Louis may send Wong to Double-A for his first full pro season. Wong could become the Cardinals' first all-star second baseman since Tommy Herr in 1985. He could be big league-ready by 2013.

Year	Club (League)	Class	AVG	G	AB	R	H	2B	3B	HR	RBI	BB	SO	SB	CS	OBP	SLG
2011	Quad Cities (MWL)	LoA	.335	47	194	39	65	15	2	5	25	21	24	9	5	.401	.510
Minor League Totals			.335	47	194	39	65	15	2	5	25	21	24	9	5	.401	.510

6 TYRELL JENKINS, RHP

BA GRADE
60
HIGH

Born: July 20, 1992. **B-T:** R-R. **Ht.:** 6-4. **Wt.:** 180. **Drafted:** HS—Henderson, Texas, 2010 (1st round supplemental). **Signed by:** Ralph Garr Jr.

Jenkins could have been running routes as a Baylor wide receiver instead of strong-arming Rookie-level Johnson City to the Appalachian League title. A four-sport star in high school, he turned down a football scholarship to sign for $1.3 million as the 50th overall pick in the 2010 draft. The youngest player in Johnson City, he drew plaudits from scouts as the league's best pitching prospect. Jenkins has a lithe and loose but raw delivery that was all high leg kick and arm when he came out of high school. It has become traditional, as he uses his legs more and puts less stress on his arm, also resulting in improved command. He works both sides of the plate with his fastball, sitting at 91-93 mph and touching 95-96. Jenkins abandoned his slider, favoring a 12-to-6 curveball with tighter spin. He also is developing a changeup. The Cardinals are setting a path that could put him two levels behind Carlos Martinez. More time in extended spring is possible in 2012, though a stretch in low Class A is the goal. He'll require patience but ultimately could develop into a frontline starter.

Year	Club (League)	Class	W	L	ERA	G	GS	CG	SV	IP	H	HR	BB	SO	K/9	WHIP	AVG
2010	Johnson City (APP)	R	0	0	0.00	2	2	0	0	3	2	0	2	2	6.0	1.33	.200
2011	Johnson City (APP)	R	4	2	3.86	11	11	0	0	56	63	3	13	55	8.8	1.36	.296
Minor League Totals			4	2	3.66	13	13	0	0	59	65	3	15	57	8.7	1.36	.291

7 LANCE LYNN, RHP

BA GRADE
50
SAFE

Born: May 12, 1987. **B-T:** R-R. **Ht.:** 6-5. **Wt.:** 250. **Drafted:** Mississippi, 2008 (1st round supplemental). **Signed by:** Jay Catalano.

Lynn made his name as a workhorse who never missed a scheduled start after signing for $938,000 as a 2008 sandwich pick, but he was a revelation as a reliever in the majors. His performance was reminiscent, in short bursts, of his 16-strikeout start in the Triple-A playoffs in 2010. After straining his oblique in early August, he returned to earn victories in the National League Championship Series and World Series. As a minor league starter, Lynn mixed a darting 88-92 mph sinker, a curveball that could get loopy and a so-so changeup. As a reliever, he became more aggressive with a four-seam fastball that sits around 93 mph and zooms as high as 98 with late life. He also developed a harder, sharper curve that gave him a true second weapon. He also has created more downhill plane with less rotation on his delivery, an adjustment that has improved his command. The Cardinals have five starters returning in 2012, earmarking Lynn for set-up duty.

Year	Club (League)	Class	W	L	ERA	G	GS	CG	SV	IP	H	HR	BB	SO	K/9	WHIP	AVG
2008	Batavia (NYP)	SS	1	0	0.96	6	4	0	0	19	12	0	4	22	10.6	0.86	.179
	Quad Cities (MWL)	LoA	0	1	2.25	2	2	0	0	8	8	2	2	7	7.9	1.25	.258
2009	Palm Beach (FSL)	HiA	0	0	2.30	5	2	0	0	16	16	0	3	17	9.8	1.21	.276
	Springfield (TL)	AA	11	4	2.92	22	22	0	0	126	117	5	51	98	7.0	1.33	.251
	Memphis (PCL)	AAA	0	0	2.70	1	1	0	0	7	5	0	3	9	12.2	1.20	.200
2010	Memphis (PCL)	AAA	13	10	4.77	29	29	0	0	164	164	21	62	141	7.7	1.38	.259
2011	Memphis (PCL)	AAA	7	3	3.84	12	12	0	0	75	79	2	25	64	7.7	1.39	.279
	St. Louis (NL)	MAJ	1	1	3.12	18	2	0	1	35	25	3	11	40	10.4	1.04	.203
Major League Totals			1	1	3.12	18	2	0	1	35	25	3	11	40	10.4	1.04	.203
Minor League Totals			32	18	3.69	77	72	0	0	414	401	30	150	358	7.8	1.33	.257

8 EDUARDO SANCHEZ, RHP

Born: Feb. 16, 1989. **B-T:** R-R. **Ht.:** 5-11. **Wt.:** 170. **Signed:** Venezuela, 2005. **Signed by:** Enrique Brito.

Less than a year after pitching a perfect inning in the 2010 Futures Game, Sanchez made quick work of his major league debut and validated a new frontier for the Cardinals with each pitch. He received a cameo at closer and settled in as a hard-throwing set-up man before a shoulder injury in mid-June all but ended his season. Sanchez's stuff is far more imposing than his reed-thin frame. He repeatedly delivers 94-95 mph fastballs and can reach back for upper-90s heat. His fastball has natural movement that he exploits further by commanding the pitch to both sides of the plate and down in the strike zone. Sanchez's hard, quick slider handcuffs righthanders, who hit .136 with 24 strikeouts in 59 at-bats against him in the majors. He can dominate big leaguers as long as he's throwing strikes, which becomes a problem at times. Sanchez's shoulder soreness relented late in the season, though St. Louis left him off its playoff roster. He won't need surgery and should have a normal offseason. He should make the big league bullpen in 2012, with his role to be determined.

BA GRADE
50
LOW

Year	Club (League)	Class	W	L	ERA	G	GS	CG	SV	IP	H	HR	BB	SO	K/9	WHIP	AVG
2006	Cardinals (VSL)	R	1	2	8.71	19	2	0	0	31	47	3	24	38	11.0	2.29	.351
2007	Cardinals (GCL)	R	0	1	1.50	7	0	0	3	6	2	0	6	7	10.5	1.33	.100
	Johnson City (APP)	R	2	1	1.17	12	0	0	5	15	8	0	3	22	12.9	0.72	.154
2008	Quad Cities (MWL)	LoA	5	1	2.86	24	5	0	1	57	40	1	25	55	8.7	1.15	.209
2009	Palm Beach (FSL)	HiA	0	1	1.44	19	0	0	3	25	12	2	5	26	9.4	0.68	.146
	Springfield (TL)	AA	2	0	2.70	41	0	0	10	50	32	4	20	56	10.1	1.04	.187
2010	Springfield (TL)	AA	1	1	3.12	24	0	0	11	26	22	2	8	27	9.3	1.15	.232
	Memphis (PCL)	AAA	0	0	1.67	26	0	0	3	27	19	2	12	31	10.3	1.15	.200
2011	Memphis (PCL)	AAA	1	0	0.00	2	0	0	0	3	0	0	0	3	9.0	0.00	.000
	Springfield (TL)	AA	0	1	4.15	3	0	0	0	4	3	0	2	3	6.2	1.15	.200
	St. Louis (NL)	MAJ	3	1	1.80	26	0	0	5	30	14	1	16	35	10.5	1.00	.144
Major League Totals			3	1	1.80	26	0	0	5	30	14	1	16	35	10.5	1.00	.144
Minor League Totals			12	8	3.17	177	7	0	36	244	185	14	105	268	9.9	1.19	.214

9 MATT ADAMS, 1B

Born: Aug. 31, 1988. **B-T:** L-R. **Ht.:** 6-3. **Wt.:** 230. **Drafted:** Slippery Rock (Pa.), 2009 (23rd round). **Signed by:** Brian Hopkins.

Adams starred at Slippery Rock (Pa.), leading NCAA Division II in hitting (.495) in 2009 while setting school records for single-season and career (.454) batting average. Signed for $25,000 as a 23rd-round pick, he moved from catcher to first base and hasn't stopped hitting. He won the Texas League MVP award in 2011, setting a Springfield record with 32 homers and leading the Double-A circuit with 101 RBIs and a .566 slugging percentage. Adams has a hulking frame but doesn't rely solely on muscle to catapult his moonshot homers. He has a compact swing that doesn't need an uppercut or loop to create distance. A coach called the stroke fool-proof because it gives him the ability to punish more than mistakes. One scout likened him to Freddie Freeman with more power and less defense. Though he's big and has below-average speed and quickness, Adams has improved defensively and shows soft hands and an accurate arm. There's a starting spot waiting for Adams in Triple-A, and his long-term future brightened when Albert Pujols signed with the Angels. Adams won't have to move to the outfield to battle for a big league job in 2013.

BA GRADE
50
MEDIUM

Year	Club (League)	Class	AVG	G	AB	R	H	2B	3B	HR	RBI	BB	SO	SB	CS	OBP	SLG
2009	Johnson City (APP)	R	.365	32	115	15	42	6	0	6	25	9	20	0	0	.406	.574
	Batavia (NYP)	SS	.346	31	130	16	45	11	0	4	27	11	21	0	0	.394	.523
2010	Quad Cities (MWL)	LoA	.310	121	464	71	144	41	0	22	88	33	78	5	1	.355	.541
2011	Springfield (TL)	AA	.300	115	463	80	139	23	2	32	101	40	90	0	1	.357	.566
Minor League Totals			.316	299	1172	182	370	81	2	64	241	93	209	5	2	.365	.552

10 JORDAN SWAGERTY, RHP

Born: July 14, 1989. **B-T:** B-R. **Ht.:** 6-2. **Wt.:** 175. **Drafted:** Arizona State, 2010 (2nd round). **Signed by:** Aaron Krawiec.

Though few pitchers in the system sport as much closer pedigree as Swagerty, he began 2011 with a standout turn as a starter in Class A. The Cardinals wanted to give him regular innings and time to develop his pitches. Only when his innings started to climb did St. Louis shift him to the bullpen, where he posted a 1.64 ERA and 29 strikeouts in 27 innings. St. Louis graded Swagerty's breaking ball as the best curveball in the 2010 draft. It's actually more of a hybrid that he calls a slider, but the mid-80s offering that breaks down and away from righthanders is nasty by any name. His time as a starter allowed him to become more effective with his fastball and add a useful changeup. When he comes out of the bullpen, his heater sits at 92-94 mph and touches 96. Swagerty has some funkiness in his delivery and a slight build. Both lead to concerns about his durability, questions somewhat dispelled by his stamina in 12 starts. Swagerty soared through three levels in 2011, finishing the season as a Double-A closer. The Cardinals remain intrigued by him as a starter, though expediting him as a reliever would cut development time. He has the upside of a No. 3 starter or closer.

BA GRADE

50 MEDIUM

Year	Club (League)	Class	W	L	ERA	G	GS	CG	SV	IP	H	HR	BB	SO	K/9	WHIP	AVG
2011	Quad Cities (MWL)	LoA	3	1	1.50	5	5	0	0	30	18	2	2	30	9.0	0.67	.178
	Palm Beach (FSL)	HiA	2	2	1.82	22	7	0	5	54	42	1	16	52	8.6	1.07	.214
	Springfield (TL)	AA	0	0	2.89	9	0	0	3	9	8	1	5	7	6.8	1.39	.222
Minor League Totals			5	3	1.83	36	12	0	8	94	68	4	23	89	8.6	0.97	.204

11 TREVOR ROSENTHAL, RHP

BA GRADE

50 MEDIUM

Born: May 29, 1990. **B-T:** R-R. **Ht.:** 6-2. **Wt.:** 190. **Drafted:** Cowley County (Kan.) CC, 2009 (21st round). **Signed by:** Aaron Looper.

Like Shelby Miller and Lance Lynn before him, Rosenthal asserted his ascending status with a postseason gem. The broad-shouldered righty threw a complete-game, four-hit shutout in the Midwest League's Western Division Championship Series in September. He struck out three, didn't walk a batter and got 14 of his 27 outs on the ground. He punctuated his breakout playoff run with a win in the title clincher, during which he touched 98 mph. Unheralded coming out of Cowley County (Kan.) CC as a 21st-round pick in 2009, the Missouri native signed for $65,000. Rosenthal earned an invitation to the Cardinals' top-prospect camp last spring on potential, then quickly added production to that promise, striking out 11 in his first MWL start. Rosenthal has an athletic frame built for logging innings and a simple, repeatable delivery that aids his power and control. Last season he added zip to his stuff, sitting regularly at 91-95 mph with a heavy sinker. He also throws a biting slider that he can use effectively in the strike zone. His changeup shows life but is still in the early stages of development. Rosenthal will look to prove his worth as a frontline starter with Palm Beach in 2012.

Year	Club (League)	Class	W	L	ERA	G	GS	CG	SV	IP	H	HR	BB	SO	K/9	WHIP	AVG
2009	Cardinals (GCL)	R	4	1	4.88	14	0	0	0	24	25	0	10	26	9.8	1.46	.269
2010	Johnson City (APP)	R	3	0	2.25	10	6	0	1	32	23	1	7	30	8.4	0.94	.200
2011	Quad Cities (MWL)	LoA	7	7	4.11	22	22	1	0	120	111	7	39	133	9.9	1.25	.247
Minor League Totals			14	8	3.88	46	28	1	1	176	159	8	56	189	9.6	1.22	.242

12 MATT CARPENTER, 3B

BA GRADE

50 MEDIUM

Born: Nov. 26, 1985. **B-T:** L-R. **Ht.:** 6-3. **Wt.:** 200. **Drafted:** Texas Christian, 2009 (13th round). **Signed by:** Aaron Krawiec.

One of the final cuts in big league camp last spring, Carpenter won praise and playing time with his keen eye and live bat throughout exhibition play. He made his St. Louis debut in June, getting a brief 15 at-bat sip of the majors. Drafted as a fifth-year senior out of Texas Christian and signed for a $1,000 bonus, he's aware that time and age aren't on his side. Talent is. Carpenter led the system with a .418 on-base percentage in 2010 and followed that with a .417 OBP in 2011. His lack of batting gloves and his early-bird workouts got attention during spring training, but he projects as a high-average hitter because of a quick, elegant swing and advanced feel for the strike zone. He stopped swinging from a standstill and added a weight shift that elevated his power and led to 44 extra-base hits in 2011, including 29 doubles. He could hit 15 homers annually as an everyday player in the majors. Carpenter is a below-average runner but he can make some slick plays at third base when he gets moving. His arm and range at third are adequate, and he's working to become more comfortable on his backhand. He's pinched with David Freese in St. Louis and Zack Cox closing from behind him. Carpenter hasn't played the outfield in pro ball but he may get a look there in spring training in hopes that added versatility could help him win a spot on the big league bench.

Year	Club (League)	Class	AVG	G	AB	R	H	2B	3B	HR	RBI	BB	SO	SB	CS	OBP	SLG
2009	Batavia (NYP)	SS	.469	9	32	9	15	3	0	0	3	4	2	0	1	.541	.563

			AVG	G	AB	R	H	2B	3B	HR	RBI	BB	SO	SB	CS	OBP	SLG
	Quad Cities (MWL)	LoA	.295	29	105	11	31	6	2	0	10	17	13	2	0	.405	.390
	Palm Beach (FSL)	HiA	.219	32	114	13	25	6	1	2	9	10	24	1	0	.286	.342
2010	Palm Beach (FSL)	HiA	.283	28	99	17	28	5	2	1	16	26	14	0	1	.441	.404
	Springfield (TL)	AA	.316	105	396	76	125	26	3	12	53	64	88	11	2	.412	.487
2011	St. Louis (NL)	MAJ	.067	7	15	0	1	1	0	0	0	4	4	0	0	.263	.133
	Memphis (PCL)	AAA	.300	130	434	61	130	29	3	12	70	84	68	5	4	.417	.463
Major League Totals			.067	7	15	0	1	1	0	0	0	4	4	0	0	.263	.133
Minor League Totals			.300	333	1180	187	354	75	11	27	161	205	209	19	8	.408	.451

13 RYAN JACKSON, SS

Born: May 10, 1988. **B-T:** R-R. **Ht.:** 6-3. **Wt.:** 180. **Drafted:** Miami, 2009 (5th round). **Signed by:** Mike Elias.

When Nick Punto visited Springfield on a rehab assignment last summer, he saw one hitch in Jackson's otherwise fine defense. Jackson had a habit of pausing to wait on a better hop, an approach that works fine in college but is too slow at higher levels. Punto worked with him because Jackson is headed to those higher levels. He has validated his reputation as the best defensive college shortstop in the 2009 draft. He's a nimble fielder with a high baseball IQ and strong instincts, and his footwork and accuracy give him an above-average arm. Some scouts think he can play defensively in the majors right now. Jackson helped his cause in 2011 by answering some questions about his bat. He improved his ability to make sharp contact by maintaining his strength and swing all year long. He hit a career-high 11 homers and ranked among the Texas League leaders in doubles (34) and total bases (221). He's a fringy runner and little threat to steal. Jackson continued to swing a productive bat in the Arizona Fall League and projects as a big league regular if he continues to do so. He'll advance to Triple-A and could break into the majors in a utility role in 2012.

Year	Club (League)	Class	AVG	G	AB	R	H	2B	3B	HR	RBI	BB	SO	SB	CS	OBP	SLG
2009	Batavia (NYP)	SS	.216	67	245	29	53	4	1	0	14	29	37	4	3	.297	.241
2010	Quad Cities (MWL)	LoA	.272	84	302	47	82	13	2	2	27	48	63	6	7	.366	.348
	Palm Beach (FSL)	HiA	.291	41	148	14	43	10	1	1	8	11	21	3	2	.342	.392
2011	Springfield (TL)	AA	.278	135	533	65	148	34	3	11	73	44	91	2	0	.334	.415
Minor League Totals			.265	327	1228	155	326	61	7	14	122	132	212	15	12	.336	.361

14 MAIKEL CLETO, RHP

Born: May 1, 1989. **B-T:** R-R. **Ht.:** 6-3. **Wt.:** 235. **Signed:** Dominican Republic, 2006. **Signed by:** Ramon Pena (Mets).

Cleto made his major league debut last June, six months after St. Louis acquired him from Seattle in exchange for Brendan Ryan. Originally signed by the Mets, he became a Mariner in a three-team, 12-player deal that sent Franklin Gutierrez to Seattle and J.J. Putz to New York in December 2008. The Cardinals traded for Cleto because they coveted his raw velocity. The strapping righty had a flamboyant delivery and a habit of flying open or falling to the side of the mound in an attempt to increase his velocity. By getting him to keep his front shoulder closed and, in the words of pitching coordinator Dyar Miller, "throw more like a Ferris Wheel than merry-go-round," Cleto pitched more under control in 2011 without sacrificing heat. In one May start, Cleto hit 102 mph and topped 100 a dozen times, per the opponent's radar gun. The Cardinals had him hitting 101. His fastball sits at 95-99 mph with late life, though he leaves it over the middle of the plate too often. He also throws a big-breaking, mid-80s slider that he also struggles to harness. What he calls his changeup is more of a 90-92 mph two-seam fastball that doesn't have enough separation from his four-seamer. Cleto has spent most of his pro career as a starter, but his lack of fine control or command and an offspeed pitch makes it likely that his long-term role will be as a fire-breathing reliever. He figures to open 2012 in Triple-A and be on call if St. Louis needs help in either role.

Year	Club (League)	Class	W	L	ERA	G	GS	CG	SV	IP	H	HR	BB	SO	K/9	WHIP	AVG
2007	Mets (GCL)	R	1	2	5.03	11	4	0	1	34	34	2	25	28	7.4	1.74	.270
2008	Savannah (SAL)	LoA	5	11	4.25	25	22	1	0	136	140	8	34	81	5.4	1.28	.268
	St. Lucie (FSL)	HiA	0	1	9.00	1	1	0	0	5	5	1	2	1	1.8	1.40	.278
2009	Mariners (AZL)	R	0	1	13.50	1	0	0	0	1	3	0	1	1	13.5	6.00	.500
	Clinton (MWL)	LoA	0	3	5.33	8	8	0	0	25	35	4	11	24	8.5	1.82	.321
2010	High Desert (CAL)	HiA	4	9	6.16	23	21	0	0	102	125	10	44	83	7.3	1.65	.305
2011	Palm Beach (FSL)	HiA	1	1	2.48	5	5	0	0	29	20	2	10	33	10.2	1.03	.190
	Springfield (TL)	AA	2	2	3.93	7	6	0	0	34	40	2	12	36	9.4	1.51	.301
	Memphis (PCL)	AAA	3	3	4.29	13	13	0	0	71	57	6	43	66	8.3	1.40	.218
	St. Louis (NL)	MAJ	0	0	12.46	3	0	0	0	4	7	2	4	6	12.5	2.54	.333
Major League Totals			0	0	12.46	3	0	0	0	4	7	2	4	6	12.5	2.54	.333
Minor League Totals			18	33	4.75	94	80	1	1	438	459	35	182	353	7.3	1.46	.272

15 CHARLIE TILSON, OF

BA GRADE
50
HIGH

Born: Dec. 2, 1992. **B-T:** L-L. **Ht.:** 5-11. **Wt.:** 175. **Drafted:** HS—Winnetka, Ill., 2011 (2nd round). **Signed by:** Kris Gross.

The Chicago-area prep star caught the Cardinals' eye and radically enhanced his draft status with a star turn at the 2010 Area Code Games. In three games, he stole seven bases and hit the lone homer in the wood-bat tournament. He also finished fourth overall in the SPARQ testing designed to gauge power, speed, agility and endurance. Though Tilson was a top student with a commitment to Illinois, St. Louis drafted him in the second round last June and signed him at the Aug. 15 deadline for $1.275 million. Scouts who saw Tilson outside of the Area Code Games view him as a bundle of unsharpened tools in need of tutelage. He's a lefty contact hitter with potential for a line-drive swing. He has the legs, rather than power, to produce extra bases. His speed rates a 65 on the 20-80 scouting scale, and his baserunning will get better with experience. Though he's one of several center fielders they drafted in 2011, the Cardinals will give Tilson priority access to the position because his range, instincts and arm all are better than average for the position. He may begin 2012 in extended spring training, though it's not out of the question that he could force his way to low Class A at some point during the year.

Year	Club (League)	Class	AVG	G	AB	R	H	2B	3B	HR	RBI	BB	SO	SB	CS	OBP	SLG
2011	Cardinals (GCL)	R	.167	4	12	2	2	0	0	0	1	2	3	1	0	.286	.167
	Johnson City (APP)	R	.467	4	15	2	7	2	0	0	4	1	1	0	0	.500	.600
Minor League Totals			.333	8	27	4	9	2	0	0	5	3	4	1	0	.400	.407

16 JOE KELLY, RHP

BA GRADE
50
HIGH

Born: June 9, 1988. **B-T:** R-R. **Ht.:** 6-1. **Wt.:** 165. **Drafted:** UC Riverside, 2009 (3rd round). **Signed by:** Jeff Ishii.

During consecutive starts at Palm Beach in May, Kelly took no-hit bids into the eighth inning. Both of his gems were microcosms of his potential. He overwhelmed hitters with a power sinker, coaxed 24 groundouts in 15 total innings, had fits of wildness (walking five in one start) and hit a few batters. "I want to go inside to every hitter at least once," he explains. "Eventually I'll get strikes." Kelly's 2011 season took a downturn after May, as he worked just 12 innings in June due to circumstances and because he didn't pitch well following a promotion to Double-A in July. He set a UC Riverside career record with 24 saves but the Cardinals launched him as a starter to get innings. What was a temporary assignment has become his means to advancement. Kelly sports upper-register velocity, sitting around 93-94 mph with his fastball and touching 98 as a starter. He hit 100 mph working as a reliever in 2010. His fastball has darting sink, and he succeeds when getting grounders rather than strikeouts. When he commands his fastball, he's able to better utilize his hard slider and his changeup. His slider has some bite to it, but his command of the pitch can be flighty. He also has a curveball that's mostly just for show. Kelly's wiry frame and long-arm delivery may not fit a starter's workload and eventually could recast him as a classic sinker/slider reliever. He'll return to the Springfield rotation in 2012 to get innings to work on command to give him grounders and ownership of the inside edge of the plate.

Year	Club (League)	Class	W	L	ERA	G	GS	CG	SV	IP	H	HR	BB	SO	K/9	WHIP	AVG
2009	Batavia (NYP)	SS	2	3	4.75	16	2	0	1	30	33	0	11	30	8.9	1.45	.273
2010	Quad Cities (MWL)	LoA	6	8	4.62	26	18	0	1	103	103	3	45	92	8.0	1.43	.265
2011	Palm Beach (FSL)	HiA	5	2	2.60	12	11	0	0	73	56	1	34	62	7.7	1.24	.215
	Springfield (TL)	AA	6	4	5.01	11	11	0	0	59	70	7	25	51	7.7	1.60	.306
Minor League Totals			19	17	4.17	65	42	0	2	266	262	11	115	235	8.0	1.42	.263

17 JOHN GAST, LHP

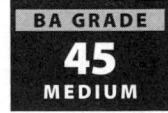

BA GRADE
45
MEDIUM

Born: Feb. 16, 1989. **B-T:** L-L. **Ht.:** 6-1. **Wt.:** 195. **Drafted:** Florida State, 2010 (6th round). **Signed by:** Mike Elias.

Jaime Garcia was so enamored with the pickoff move Gast flashed during a couple of major league exhibition games last spring that he sought out pointers from the prospect. Gast has a deceptive, accurate and whip-quick delivery to first base—traits that also serve him well when he comes to the plate. The lefty put another successful season between him and the questions that cost him in college, reaching Double-A in his first full year as a pro. The Rangers made Gast a fifth-round pick out of high school in 2007, but he opted to have Tommy John surgery and reignite his draft stock at Florida State. He rushed back from injury and his performance suffered with the Seminoles. A 6-0, 1.54 pro debut after signing for $140,000 reset his status. Gast has good poise and a fluid delivery. Some scouts describe him as a finesse lefty, though he has a fastball that ranges from 87 mph all the way up to 93. He mixes it with a hard curveball that falls out of the zone and a changeup that is blossoming into a plus pitch. While he's able to locate his fastball, command remains the primary focus in his development. It wasn't there in college and has been sporadic in pro ball. After Gast makes a cameo in big league camp, a return to Springfield is likely for the system's top lefty starter prospect. He has a ceiling as a No. 3 starter but more likely will fit into the No. 4 slot in a major league rotation.

Year	Club (League)	Class	W	L	ERA	G	GS	CG	SV	IP	H	HR	BB	SO	K/9	WHIP	AVG
2010	Batavia (NYP)	SS	6	0	1.54	8	6	0	0	35	27	1	8	36	9.3	1.00	.227
2011	Palm Beach (FSL)	HiA	5	4	3.95	13	12	1	0	82	85	7	28	59	6.5	1.38	.272
	Springfield (TL)	AA	4	4	4.08	13	13	1	0	79	80	9	33	54	6.1	1.42	.266
Minor League Totals			15	8	3.58	34	31	2	0	196	192	17	69	149	6.8	1.33	.262

18 C.J. MCELROY, OF

BA GRADE
50
HIGH

Born: May 29, 1993. **B-T:** R-R. **Ht.:** 5-10. **Wt.:** 180. **Drafted:** HS—League City, Texas, 2011 (3rd round). **Signed by:** Ralph Garr Jr.

Before he agreed on a $510,000 bonus last summer, McElroy took batting practice at Busch Stadium and mingled with major leaguers. Sitting at a locker assigned to him in the clubhouse, he talked about his baseball vs. football dilemma. "Baseball is in my family," he said. "It's in my blood." It's now his future. The son of longtime major-league reliever Chuck McElroy, C.J. was one of the fleetest talents in the 2011 draft and a multisport threat. As a senior at Clear Creek High (League City, Texas)—the alma mater of Jay Buhner and former Cardinals first-rounder Mark McCormick—McElroy rushed for 1,523 yards and scored 28 touchdowns, stole 33 bases and finished seventh in the long jump at the Texas state 5-A finals. He committed to play football at Houston, where he would have been a wide receiver. St. Louis clocked him at 6.37 seconds in the 60-yard dash, giving him 75-80 speed on the 20-80 scouting scale, and he stole eight bases in 23 pro games. McElroy's quickness gives him plenty of range in center field and helps him compensate for a below-average arm. He shows promising instincts and jumps both in the outfield on the bases. McElroy has a reliable righthanded swing that should translate to pro ball. He won't offer much power, but he recognizes pitches well and can handle good fastballs. He's earmarked for extended spring training but could play his way into a full-season assignment at some point in 2012.

Year	Club (League)	Class	AVG	G	AB	R	H	2B	3B	HR	RBI	BB	SO	SB	CS	OBP	SLG
2011	Cardinals (GCL)	R	.228	23	79	10	18	2	1	0	7	7	15	8	2	.303	.278
Minor League Totals			.228	23	79	10	18	2	1	0	7	7	15	8	2	.303	.278

19 ADRON CHAMBERS, OF

BA GRADE
45
MEDIUM

Born: Oct. 8, 1986. **B-T:** L-L. **Ht.:** 5-10. **Wt.:** 185. **Drafted:** Pensacola (Fla.) JC, 2007 (38th round). **Signed by:** Steve Turco.

As the Cardinals made their late September run for a wild-card berth, Chambers emerged as more than a courtesy callup. In the span of five days, he drove in the winning run in the 11th inning against the Phillies and drilled a bases-loaded triple against the Mets. He saw 16 pitches total in those at-bats, fouling off nine of them. Four days later, he scored on a wild pitch for a walkoff win against the Cubs. A former wide receiver and cornerback at Mississippi State, Chambers was dismissed from school in 2006 after being charged with simple assault and indecent exposure. He reinvented himself the next spring as a baseball player at Pensacola (Fla.) JC, with St. Louis offering him a tryout if he could get to Memphis within 24 hours. He bought a bus ticket, showed enough to get drafted in the 38th round and earn a $40,000 bonus and hasn't had to look back. Chambers has taken his best tool, above-average speed, and outfitted it with a polished game. He profiles as a leadoff type with a feisty approach at the plate and a sharpened sense of the strike zone. He emphasizes contact over power, especially against lefthanders. A quarterback and pitcher in high school, Chambers has plus arm strength and can handle all three spots in the outfield. His September audition positioned him for a chance to serve on the Cardinals' bench as a spare outfielder and tactical speedster in 2012.

Year	Club (League)	Class	AVG	G	AB	R	H	2B	3B	HR	RBI	BB	SO	SB	CS	OBP	SLG
2007	Johnson City (APP)	R	.279	36	111	16	31	7	1	0	10	10	21	6	5	.362	.360
2008	Quad Cities (MWL)	LoA	.238	95	336	56	80	13	7	3	25	33	66	13	8	.322	.345
2009	Palm Beach (FSL)	HiA	.283	122	448	66	127	17	16	1	46	47	96	21	12	.370	.400
2010	Springfield (TL)	AA	.282	75	252	52	71	9	5	5	27	31	50	8	4	.376	.417
	Memphis (PCL)	AAA	.290	37	69	11	20	0	1	1	8	9	18	6	1	.390	.362
2011	Memphis (PCL)	AAA	.277	128	426	73	118	19	5	10	44	53	90	22	13	.368	.415
	St. Louis (NL)	MAJ	.375	18	8	2	3	0	1	0	4	0	1	0	0	.375	.625
Major League Totals			.375	18	8	2	3	0	1	0	4	0	1	0	0	.375	.625
Minor League Totals			.272	493	1642	274	447	65	35	20	160	183	341	76	43	.361	.391

20 TONY CRUZ, C

BA GRADE
40
LOW

Born: Aug. 18, 1986. **B-T:** R-R. **Ht.:** 5-11. **Wt.:** 205. **Drafted:** Palm Beach (Fla.) CC, 2007 (26th round). **Signed by:** Charlie Gonzalez.

Each offseason, the move the Cardinals try to make first is signing (or, in some cases, re-signing) a backup for starter Yadier Molina. Cruz ended their search early after getting a cameo in the majors in 2011 and winning the trust of the rotation and coaching staff. During a 2007 tryout for the Cardinals, Cruz arrived as a third baseman, spent an inning behind the plate and left with a new route to the majors. Each year, he has improved defensively while losing some but not too much of his proficiency at the plate. Cruz has good bat speed and a level swing built for average. He uses the whole field and if he got regular at-bats in the majors, he could hit 10 homers per season. Cruz's crash course in catching in the minors has helped him blossom with agile feet and an average, accurate arm. He threw out 31 percent of basestealers last year, including two of four in the majors. While he has below-average speed like most catchers, Cruz can adroitly handle first and third base and isn't lost in the outfield, giving him more versatility than past St. Louis backup catchers. He also wasn't flummoxed by pinch-hit appearances in the big leagues, going 4-for-15 with two walks. His temp work in the majors and studious approach in pregame planning gives him the edge in competition this spring with Bryan Anderson for the job as Molina's caddy.

Year	Club (League)	Class	AVG	G	AB	R	H	2B	3B	HR	RBI	BB	SO	SB	CS	OBP	SLG
2007	Cardinals (GCL)	R	.375	7	32	8	12	5	0	0	4	1	7	1	0	.382	.531
	Johnson City (APP)	R	.280	6	25	2	7	2	0	2	2	2	2	1	0	.333	.600
	Batavia (NYP)	SS	.375	4	16	2	6	1	0	0	4	0	5	0	0	.412	.438
	Quad Cities (MWL)	LoA	.282	49	195	26	55	10	1	5	34	17	25	3	1	.338	.421
2008	Palm Beach (FSL)	HiA	.279	89	351	41	98	22	3	8	58	19	50	3	0	.316	.427
2009	Springfield (TL)	AA	.220	110	404	44	89	25	2	10	48	34	85	1	0	.281	.366
2010	Palm Beach (FSL)	HiA	.282	46	181	21	51	16	1	1	25	19	33	0	2	.348	.398
	Springfield (TL)	AA	.289	40	149	26	43	10	0	6	20	17	30	0	0	.363	.477
	Memphis (PCL)	AAA	.214	4	14	2	3	0	0	1	1	1	1	0	0	.267	.429
2011	Memphis (PCL)	AAA	.262	45	149	13	39	5	1	4	25	11	31	0	1	.315	.389
	St. Louis (NL)	MAJ	.262	38	65	8	17	5	0	0	6	6	13	0	1	.333	.338
Major League Totals			.262	38	65	8	17	5	0	0	6	6	13	0	1	.333	.338
Minor League Totals			.266	400	1516	185	403	96	8	37	221	121	269	9	4	.320	.413

21 ADAM REIFER, RHP

BA GRADE

45 MEDIUM

Born: June 3, 1986. **B-T:** R-R. **Ht.:** 6-2. **Wt.:** 195. **Drafted:** UC Riverside, 2007 (11th round). **Signed by:** Jeff Ishii.

What set up to be a breakout year for the hard-throwing reliever turned instead into a lost summer when Reifer leapt from the mound to field a bunt in mid-April. He shredded a ligament in his right knee and required reconstructive surgery that ended his season. Given good health, Reifer sports pure heat. He has touched 98 mph throughout his pro career, though he has found more command and success by dialing back his fastball to 93-96. His fastball cuts, especially against lefties. Reifer has a slider that can be overpowering when he locates it in the strike zone, and he was developing a splitter before he got hurt. His control has improved markedly in the last two years, though he hasn't dominated minor league hitters as much as his stuff would indicate he should. He battled bone spurs and elbow tendinitis at UC Riverside in 2007, when he was a teammate of Joe Kelly, but lingering questions about Reifer's durability vanished after he thrived as a worker-bee reliever in 2009 and 2010. The Cardinals are confident enough in his health to keep him on the 40-man roster and believe he'll be 100 percent for spring training. He'll likely begin 2012 in Triple-A but could contribute in St. Louis later in the season. He has a ceiling as a set-up man.

Year	Club (League)	Class	W	L	ERA	G	GS	CG	SV	IP	H	HR	BB	SO	K/9	WHIP	AVG
2007	Did Not Play—Injured																
2008	Batavia (NYP)	SS	2	1	2.97	32	0	0	22	30	18	2	15	41	12.2	1.09	.162
2009	Palm Beach (FSL)	HiA	4	7	4.47	54	0	0	21	48	51	2	24	50	9.3	1.55	.270
2010	Springfield (TL)	AA	3	1	3.00	51	0	0	17	54	53	2	15	52	8.7	1.26	.252
	Memphis (PCL)	AAA	1	0	0.00	1	0	0	0	1	0	0	1	0	0.0	1.00	.000
2011	Memphis (PCL)	AAA	0	1	1.42	5	0	0	0	6	7	1	1	1	1.4	1.26	.318
Minor League Totals			10	10	3.41	143	0	0	60	140	129	7	56	144	9.3	1.32	.242

22 BRANDON DICKSON, RHP

BA GRADE

40 LOW

Born: Nov. 3, 1984. **B-T:** R-R. **Ht.:** 6-5. **Wt.:** 190. **Signed:** Tusculum (Tenn.), NDFA 2006. **Signed by:** Scott Nichols.

Undrafted and unassuming, Dickson found himself in uncharted waters last spring when the Cardinals pulled him into the competition to replace injured Adam Wainwright in the major league rotation. The lanky righty was a longshot candidate, but St. Louis coaches were intrigued by his durability, easy delivery and one trait that always gets noticed in the organization—the ability to get groundballs. Dickson spent most of the year in Triple-A, echoing his 2010 performance as Memphis' most reliable starter, though he did pitch eight innings in the big leagues. Dickson garnered little attention coming out of Tusculum (Tenn.), an NCAA Division II program, and it took a teammate to urge the Cardinals to give him a tryout. He has climbed steadily through the minors because he has easily repeatable mechanics and keeps the ball down in the strike zone. He has a classic, biting sinker that sits at 89-91 mph when he starts and has touched 93 mph when he relieves. His height and high arm angle help his sinker, and he has become more adept at moving it to both sides of the plate. Dickson has improved his command of a hard curveball that he can throw when behind in the count, and he also has a changeup that plays nicely off his fastball because it too features some sink. He has nothing left to prove in Triple-A and will get a chance to make the big league team this spring as a long reliever.

Year	Club (League)	Class	W	L	ERA	G	GS	CG	SV	IP	H	HR	BB	SO	K/9	WHIP	AVG
2006	Johnson City (APP)	R	1	0	6.35	9	0	0	1	11	16	1	6	15	11.9	1.94	.320
2007	Quad Cities (MWL)	LoA	11	7	3.50	31	23	0	1	144	148	9	41	84	5.3	1.31	.260
2008	Palm Beach (FSL)	HiA	7	8	3.51	23	17	1	1	115	119	7	37	66	5.2	1.35	.269
	Springfield (TL)	AA	3	2	6.75	6	6	0	0	29	42	3	16	21	6.4	1.98	.347
2009	Springfield (TL)	AA	8	10	3.78	28	20	1	0	148	160	12	50	112	6.8	1.42	.280
2010	Memphis (PCL)	AAA	11	8	3.23	28	27	0	0	167	180	11	53	137	7.4	1.40	.276
2011	Memphis (PCL)	AAA	9	8	3.95	26	25	1	0	157	169	22	32	124	7.1	1.28	.277
	St. Louis (NL)	MAJ	0	0	3.24	4	1	0	0	8	9	2	3	7	7.6	1.44	.290
Major League Totals			0	0	3.24	4	1	0	0	8	9	2	3	7	7.6	1.44	.290
Minor League Totals			49	44	3.75	151	118	3	3	772	834	65	235	559	6.5	1.38	.277

23 DAVID KOPP, RHP

BA GRADE
45
MEDIUM

Born: Oct. 22, 1985. **B-T:** R-R. **Ht.:** 6-3. **Wt.:** 205. **Drafted:** Clemson, 2007 (2nd round). **Signed by:** Mike Shildt.

A 2011 season that began with a spot on the 40-man roster and included a rocky twist through the Springfield rotation ended where Kopp felt he belonged all along: the bullpen. After going 2-5, 7.98 in nine starts, he posted a 2.50 ERA as a Double-A reliever, though he later got hit hard in that role in stints in Triple-A and the Arizona Fall League. Coming out of the bullpen betters suits Kopp, who missed chunks of his first two full pro seasons with shoulder irritation. He feels less inhibited by the need to throw starter's innings and his stuff takes a step forward. Kopp went from averaging 91-92 mph on his sinking fastball as a starter to working at 94-95 as a reliever. He started throwing his three-quarters breaking ball more often in the low 80s and with more bite. He was able to focus on those two pitches and not worry about refining his changeup once he left the rotation. Kopp has a career 8.18 ERA in Triple-A, and he'll start 2012 by returning there. If he can correct the command that faltered in the AFL, he has a chance to eventually become a big league set-up man.

Year	Club (League)	Class	W	L	ERA	G	GS	CG	SV	IP	H	HR	BB	SO	K/9	WHIP	AVG
2007	Batavia (NYP)	SS	0	1	0.00	2	2	0	0	4	3	0	3	3	6.8	1.50	.200
2008	Palm Beach (FSL)	HiA	1	3	3.76	10	6	0	1	38	38	1	15	30	7.0	1.38	.262
	Cardinals (GCL)	R	0	0	4.91	2	2	0	0	4	2	0	0	2	4.9	0.55	.154
2009	Springfield (TL)	AA	1	1	6.43	5	5	0	0	21	29	3	11	6	2.6	1.90	.337
	Palm Beach (FSL)	HiA	5	3	3.12	15	13	0	0	69	67	3	26	58	7.5	1.34	.262
2010	Memphis (PCL)	AAA	0	5	8.63	5	5	0	0	24	38	4	11	12	4.5	2.04	.365
	Springfield (TL)	AA	12	4	3.05	21	21	1	0	121	126	9	39	78	5.8	1.36	.279
2011	Springfield (TL)	AA	3	5	5.95	23	9	0	4	65	76	12	25	40	5.5	1.55	.288
	Memphis (PCL)	AAA	0	0	7.00	8	0	0	0	9	13	1	5	8	8.0	2.00	.342
Minor League Totals			22	22	4.33	91	63	1	5	355	392	33	135	237	6.0	1.48	.286

24 CODY STANLEY, C

BA GRADE
45
HIGH

Born: Dec. 21, 1988. **B-T:** L-R. **Ht.:** 5-10. **Wt.:** 190. **Drafted:** UNC Wilmington, 2010 (4th round). **Signed by:** Mike Juhl.

For a catcher who was considered completely raw behind the plate when he signed as a fourth-round pick in 2010, Stanley evolved into a comforting and capable presence at catcher last season for Quad Cities standout pitchers Carlos Martinez, Trevor Rosenthal and Boone Whiting. Stanley has proven a quick learner, radically enhancing his average footwork and agility behind the plate. His arm strength is more fringy than average, yet he threw out 39 percent of basestealers last year. He moves well enough to occasionally fill in as an outfielder. All that said, Stanley's most marketable trait is his bat. He hit eight homers in the final two months of last season as his lefthanded swing grew from gap power to legitimate pull power. He also can drive some balls to the opposite-field gap, though he doesn't control the strike zone well enough to hit for a high average. If everything comes together, Stanley could be a .260 hitter who provides 10-15 homers and decent defense as a major league regular. He'll be reunited in high Class A this year with most of the batterymates he thrived with at Quad Cities.

Year	Club (League)	Class	AVG	G	AB	R	H	2B	3B	HR	RBI	BB	SO	SB	CS	OBP	SLG
2010	Johnson City (APP)	R	.321	53	209	34	67	12	5	5	39	21	30	8	1	.380	.498
	Quad Cities (MWL)	LoA	.250	2	4	1	1	0	0	1	2	0	2	0	0	.200	1.000
2011	Quad Cities (MWL)	LoA	.264	101	379	54	100	24	2	11	66	27	92	4	2	.317	.425
Minor League Totals			.284	156	592	89	168	36	7	17	107	48	124	12	3	.339	.454

25 VICTOR DeLEON, RHP

Born: April 19, 1992. **B-T:** R-R. **Ht.:** 6-2. **Wt.:** 190. **Signed:** Dominican Republic, 2009. **Signed by:** Juan Mercado.

DeLeon's statistics from his 2011 U.S. debut didn't sizzle, but the number that matters most for him did: 98. He was able to show that his fastball could operate consistently at 94-96 mph and peak at 98. His control and command waver when he reaches back for more velocity. His frame could add some strength, which would enhance his stamina as well as the consistency of his heater. DeLeon's secondary pitches are still works in progress. He's still developing feel for his slider and his changeup, and he throws the latter pitch too hard to get enough separation from his fastball. He's still learning to find the strike zone on a regular basis, too. DeLeon is extremely raw but has one of the best arms in the lower levels of the system. The short-term plan is to keep him as a starter so that he can get the innings and experience he needs more than anything else right now. He could develop into a workhorse starter with a plus fastball or a power reliever.

Year	Club (League)	Class	W	L	ERA	G	GS	CG	SV	IP	H	HR	BB	SO	K/9	WHIP	AVG
2010	Cardinals (DSL)	R	4	3	2.76	14	8	1	0	49	39	5	26	40	7.3	1.33	.225
2011	Cardinals (GCL)	R	0	6	4.47	10	9	0	0	50	56	2	24	30	5.4	1.59	.290
Minor League Totals			4	9	3.62	24	17	1	0	99	95	7	50	70	6.3	1.46	.260

26 ADAM OTTAVINO, RHP

Born: Nov. 22, 1985. **B-T:** R-R. **Ht.:** 6-5. **Wt.:** 230. **Drafted:** Northeastern, 2006 (1st round). **Signed by:** Kobe Perez.

There was a growing sense late in the 2011 season that the best move for Ottavino and the Cardinals would be a separation. Like longtime roommates, both sides had grown irritated. The first sign of an armistice came in November when St. Louis returned him to the 40-man roster a year after irking him by leaving him off. The 30th overall pick in the 2006 draft and recipient of a $950,000 bonus, Ottavino remains an attractive though beguiling talent. His frame and stamina are carbon copies of the starters the Cardinals rely on in the majors. He has a low-90s two-seam fastball and a four-seamer in the mid-90s. His slurvy breaking ball and sinking changeup aren't particularly sharp. Cursed by inconsistent mechanics early in his pro career, Ottavino has improved but start-to-start inconsistency still foils his advancement. He has spent the last three seasons in Triple-A, missing much of 2010 with a sore shoulder. That July, St. Louis announced he would require surgery to repair a torn labrum. He sought a second opinion and decided to follow advice that the irritation would subside with rest and rehab. Ottavino has advocates in the organization and some think a move to the bullpen could unlock his potential. The Cardinals will give him a look as a reliever during spring training.

Year	Club (League)	Class	W	L	ERA	G	GS	CG	SV	IP	H	HR	BB	SO	K/9	WHIP	AVG
2006	State College (NYP)	SS	2	2	3.14	6	6	0	0	29	23	1	13	26	8.2	1.26	.211
	Quad Cities (MWL)	LoA	2	3	3.44	8	8	0	0	37	28	3	19	38	9.3	1.28	.211
2007	Palm Beach (FSL)	HiA	12	8	3.08	27	27	1	0	143	130	10	63	128	8.0	1.35	.239
2008	Springfield (TL)	AA	3	7	5.23	24	24	1	0	115	133	16	52	96	7.5	1.60	.291
2009	Memphis (PCL)	AAA	7	12	4.75	27	27	0	0	144	141	12	82	119	7.4	1.55	.261
2010	Memphis (PCL)	AAA	5	3	3.97	9	9	0	0	48	43	5	12	43	8.1	1.15	.239
	St. Louis (NL)	MAJ	0	2	8.46	5	3	0	0	22	37	5	9	12	4.8	2.06	.370
2011	Memphis (PCL)	AAA	7	8	4.85	26	25	0	0	141	154	14	71	120	7.7	1.60	.284
Major League Totals			0	2	8.46	5	3	0	0	22	37	5	9	12	4.8	2.06	.370
Minor League Totals			38	43	4.29	127	126	2	0	657	652	61	312	570	7.8	1.47	.260

27 BOONE WHITING, RHP

Born: Aug. 20, 1989. **B-T:** R-R. **Ht.:** 6-1. **Wt.:** 175. **Drafted:** Centenary, 2010 (18th round). **Signed by:** Matt Blood.

Before he emerged as the most reliable member of the rotation that pitched Quad Cities to the 2011 Midwest League title, Whiting had to begin where few aces do—in the bullpen. Pegged as a long reliever after signing for $30,000 as an 18th-round pick in 2010, he seized a June opening in the River Bandits' six-man rotation. He wound up leading the minors in WHIP (0.89) and the MWL in opponent average (.191). A heady pitcher with meticulous pregame prep and notes on opponents, Whiting is a typical Cardinals small-college find. He changes hitters' eye level by mixing 86-91 mph fastballs at the top of the strike zone with swing-and-miss sliders. He also has a changeup with good deception and splitter action. Whiting has the best command in the system, spotting his pitches to all four corners of the strike zone. He also throws batters off with his over-the-top delivery. He'll advance to High Class A, where a spot in the rotation is waiting for him with no early-season bullpen work necessary.

Year	Club (League)	Class	W	L	ERA	G	GS	CG	SV	IP	H	HR	BB	SO	K/9	WHIP	AVG
2010	Johnson City (APP)	R	5	3	3.50	13	9	0	0	54	54	6	5	68	11.3	1.09	.250
2011	Quad Cities (MWL)	LoA	5	2	2.41	30	14	0	4	120	82	8	24	122	9.2	0.89	.191
Minor League Totals			10	5	2.75	43	23	0	4	174	136	14	29	190	9.8	0.95	.211

28 SETH BLAIR, RHP

BA GRADE
50
EXTREME

Born: March 3, 1989. **B-T:** R-R. **Ht.:** 6-2. **Wt.:** 185. **Drafted:** Arizona State, 2010 (1st round supplemental). **Signed by:** Aaron Krawiec.

One of the traits that drew the Cardinals to Blair with the 46th overall pick in the 2010 draft was the one that failed him most in his pro debut last summer: start-to-start reliability. He posted a 5.70 ERA in the second half of the Midwest League season, averaging barely four innings per start while walking 30 batters in 36 innings. He spent three weeks on the disabled list in August to rest and reboot, then was suspended before the MWL playoffs for a violation of organization policy. As the Pacific-10 Conference pitcher of the year in 2010 and during successful stints in the Cape Cod League, Blair had demonstrated consistency and blistering stuff. At his best, he has a fastball that hums at 92-94 mph and touches 96 with good sink, though he often worked at 88-93 mph in low Class A. His curveball has the makings of a plus pitch, while his changeup lags far behind. Blair's command and concentration betrayed him throughout 2011. One observer described him as "pitching distracted," and both his velocity and control suffered. Blair still has the stuff to become a No. 3 starter if he can improve his focus and stop sabotaging himself.

Year	Club (League)	Class	W	L	ERA	G	GS	CG	SV	IP	H	HR	BB	SO	K/9	WHIP	AVG
2011	Quad Cities (MWL)	LoA	6	3	5.29	21	21	0	0	82	79	9	62	70	7.7	1.73	.259
Minor League Totals			6	3	5.29	21	21	0	0	82	79	9	62	70	7.7	1.73	.259

29 LANCE JEFFRIES, OF

BA GRADE
50
EXTREME

Born: March 28, 1993. **B-T:** R-R. **Ht.:** 5-9. **Wt.:** 185. **Drafted:** HS—St. Louis, 2011 (10th round). **Signed by:** Kris Gross.

A St. Louis native, Jeffries wore No. 4 for years before changing, like so many other local youths, to No. 5 because of Albert Pujols. A self-professed baseball nut, Jeffries is a product of a local Boys & Girls Club, where he developed as a toolsy center fielder. He committed to Iowa Western CC and wasn't considered a tough sign, yet he lasted until the 10th round of the 2011 draft before turning pro for $95,000. Jeffries generates significant bat speed from the right side of the plate and has at least average power potential, though he'll need to level an uppercut swing. He has plus speed that he flashed during a workout at Busch Stadium. ("Like a dream," he called taking batting practice at the Cardinals' home.) He used that quickness to swipe 10 bases in 34 pro games, and it also serves him well in center and right field. Jeffries has sound outfield instincts and an arm that delivered 90-mph fastballs in high school. Area scouts said his stacked, compact frame reminded them of former all-star Ron Gant. Jeffries is one several raw, young Cardinals outfield prospects. He'll probably start 2012 in extended spring and move to short-season Batavia in June.

Year	Club (League)	Class	AVG	G	AB	R	H	2B	3B	HR	RBI	BB	SO	SB	CS	OBP	SLG
2011	Cardinals (GCL)	R	.256	44	125	20	32	8	2	1	19	15	48	12	5	.363	.376
Minor League Totals			.256	44	125	20	32	8	2	1	19	15	48	12	5	.363	.376

30 SAM FREEMAN, LHP

BA GRADE
40
MEDIUM

Born: June 24, 1987. **B-T:** R-L. **Ht.:** 5-11. **Wt.:** 170. **Drafted:** Kansas, 2008 (32nd round). **Signed by:** Joe Almaraz.

A full, healthy season removed from Tommy John surgery, Freeman is poised to pick up where he left off as a rising lefty specialist. A wiry athlete, he spent most of 2011 trying to regain arm strength, watching his velocity return steadily to the high 80s and finally to 90-91 mph. He took to Venezuela for extra innings this winter, earning a spot as the lone minor league lefty on the Cardinals' 40-man roster by allowing one earned run in 15 appearances. Once a fleet-footed outfielder, Freeman became a full-time starter at Kansas a year before signing for $10,000 as a 32nd-round pick in 2008. Despite his inexperience, he reached Double-A in his first full pro season while not allowing an extra-base hit to a lefty. Elbow soreness halted his progress that July, and he didn't return to the mound until 21 months later. Freeman pitches mainly off his fastball. Neither his sweeping curveball nor his tailing changeup was effective in 2011, in part because he slows his arm when he delivers his offspeed pitches. His control and command have never been his strong suits, though St. Louis hopes he'll gain more feel for pitching as he puts his elbow reconstruction further behind him. Freeman will get an extended look in big league camp this spring and is positioned to be a late-inning reliever in Triple-A and the first lefty specialist summoned by the Cardinals.

Year	Club (League)	Class	W	L	ERA	G	GS	CG	SV	IP	H	HR	BB	SO	K/9	WHIP	AVG
2008	Johnson City (APP)	R	4	1	3.70	20	0	0	2	24	23	2	12	34	12.6	1.44	.250
	Palm Beach (FSL)	HiA	0	0	0.00	1	0	0	0	2	0	0	1	4	18.0	0.50	.000
2009	Palm Beach (FSL)	HiA	2	1	1.64	26	0	0	1	33	18	0	13	30	8.2	0.94	.157
	Springfield (TL)	AA	0	1	3.52	15	0	0	1	23	19	6	14	17	6.7	1.43	.241
2010	Did Not Play—Injured																
2011	Palm Beach (FSL)	HiA	0	0	4.00	7	0	0	0	9	8	0	4	7	7.0	1.33	.258
	Springfield (TL)	AA	2	2	3.03	52	0	0	3	59	53	5	28	52	7.9	1.37	.240
Minor League Totals			8	5	2.93	121	0	0	7	151	121	13	72	144	8.6	1.28	.222

San Diego Padres

BY MATT EDDY

The two-year reign of Jed Hoyer as Padres general manager ended abruptly in November when he left to take the same position with the Cubs, taking vice president of scouting and player development Jason McLeod with him. Hoyer and McLeod reunited with Chicago's new president of baseball operations Theo Epstein, for whom they served as top lieutenants with the Red Sox.

Josh Byrnes, yet another former Epstein disciple, replaced Hoyer in San Diego. He joined the Padres following the 2010 season after being fired as Diamondbacks GM that July. Byrnes has an extensive professional history with San Diego CEO Jeff Moorad, and so do other members of the reconstituted front office.

When he was team president of the Diamondbacks, Moorad hired Byrnes for his first GM gig in October 2005. Newly minted Padres assistant GMs A.J. Hinch and Chad MacDonald also worked with Moorad and Byrnes in Arizona. MacDonald left his post as Mets scouting director in November to join San Diego.

A restocked farm system may be Hoyer's lasting legacy with the Padres. San Diego built depth quickly through a pair of trades that returned top prospects for veterans Adrian Gonzalez and Mike Adams. A third deal yielded Cameron Maybin, the 10th overall pick in the 2005 draft who finally came into his own, stealing 40 bases and providing quality defense in center field.

The young players received for Gonzalez and Adams could provide a greater impact. First baseman Anthony Rizzo ranks as the Padres' top prospect after a breakout season in which he hit .331/.404/.652 with 26 homers in 93 Triple-A games.

Rizzo came from Boston along with righthander Casey Kelly and center fielder Reymond Fuentes in exchange for Gonzalez. Kelly teamed with lefty Robbie Erlin and righty Joe Wieland, the price the Rangers paid for Adams, to head the playoff rotation for Double-A Texas League-champion San Antonio.

San Diego also has fortified its system by spending what it takes to acquire top draft talent. Under Moorad, the Padres spent $24.4 million on bonuses in the 2009-11 drafts, an expenditure that ranks ninth in MLB. They have doled out three of the four largest bonuses in franchise history during that time, to 2009 No. 3 overall pick Donavan Tate ($6.25 million), 2011 second-rounder Austin Hedges ($3 million) and 2011 first-rounder Joe Ross ($2.75 million).

For the big league club, life after Gonzalez proved as

Rookie lefty Cory Luebke provided a rare bright spot for the last-place Padres

TOP 30 PROSPECTS

1. Anthony Rizzo, 1b	16. Miles Mikolas, rhp
2. Rymer Liriano, of	17. Jace Peterson, ss
3. Casey Kelly, rhp	18. Reymond Fuentes, of
4. Cory Spangenberg, 2b	19. Edinson Rincon, 3b
5. Austin Hedges, c	20. Jason Hagerty, c
6. Jedd Gyorko, 3b	21. Matt Lollis, rhp
7. Joe Wieland, rhp	22. Donavan Tate, of
8. Robbie Erlin, lhp	23. Pedro Hernandez, lhp
9. Joe Ross, rhp	24. Jeudy Valdez, ss
10. Keyvius Sampson, rhp	25. Jose DePaula, lhp
11. Jaff Decker, of	26. Adys Portillo, rhp
12. Juan Oramas, lhp	27. Mike Kelly, rhp
13. James Darnell, 3b/of	28. Anthony Bass, rhp
14. Simon Castro, rhp	29. Brad Brach, rhp
15. Blake Tekotte, of	30. Vince Belnome, 2b/1b

bleak as expected. San Diego followed a surprising 92-win campaign in 2010 with a 71-91 effort that landed them in last place in the National League West.

A pair of rookies provided some of the few pleasant surprises. Lefthander Cory Luebke blossomed at age 26, opening the season in the bullpen before forcing his way into the rotation, where the 2007 supplemental first-round pick went 5-8, 3.31 with 111 strikeouts in 101 innings over 17 starts. The Padres' top offensive performer was 27-year-old Jesus Guzman, who signed as a minor league free agent and hit .312/.369/.478 in 247 at-bats while filling it at all four corners.

General Manager: Josh Byrnes. **Farm Director:** Randy Smith. **Scouting Director:** Jaron Madison.

Class	Team	League	W	L	Pct	Finish*	Manager(s)
Majors	San Diego Padres	National	71	91	.438	t-14th (16)	Bud Black
Triple-A	Tucson Padres	Pacific Coast	65	79	.451	t-13th (16)	Terry Kennedy
Double-A	San Antonio Missions	Texas	94	46	.671	1st (8)†	Doug Dascenzo
High A	Lake Elsinore Storm	California	69	71	.493	t-5th (10)†	Carlos Lezcano/Phil Plantier
Low A	Fort Wayne Tincaps	Midwest	69	70	.496	9th (16)	Shawn Wooten
Short-season	Eugene Emeralds	Northwest	46	30	.605	1st (8)	Pat Murphy
Rookie	AZL Padres	Arizona	23	33	.411	10th (13)	Jim Gabella
Overall 2011 Minor League Record			366	329	.527	8th (30)	

*Finish in overall standings (No. of teams in league). †League champion.

LAST YEAR'S TOP 30

Player, Pos.	Status
1. Casey Kelly, rhp	No. 3
2. Anthony Rizzo, 1b	No. 1
3. Simon Castro, rhp	No. 14
4. Reymond Fuentes, of	No. 18
5. Matt Lollis, rhp	No. 21
6. Cory Luebke, lhp	Majors
7. Jaff Decker, of	No. 11
8. Donavan Tate, of	No. 22
9. Drew Cumberland, ss/2b	Dropped out
10. Jason Hagerty, c	No. 20
11. Jedd Gyorko, 3b	No. 6
12. James Darnell, 3b	No. 13
13. Logan Forsythe, 2b	Majors
14. Blake Tekotte, of	No. 15
15. Jeremy Hefner, rhp	(Mets)
16. Edinson Rincon, 3b	No. 19
17. Juan Oramas, lhp	No. 12
18. Rymer Liriano, of	No. 2
19. Jose DePaula, lhp	No. 25
20. Keyvius Sampson, rhp	No. 10
21. Zach Cates, rhp	Dropped out
22. Anthony Bass, rhp	No. 28
23. Adys Portillo, rhp	No. 26
24. Everett Williams, of	Dropped out
25. Johnny Barbato, rhp	Dropped out
26. Jerry Sullivan, rhp	Dropped out
27. George Kontos, rhp	(Yankees)
28. Jeudy Valdez, 2b/ss	No. 24
29. Nick Schmidt, lhp	(Rockies)
30. Brad Brach, rhp	No. 29

BEST TOOLS

Best Hitter for Average	Jedd Gyorko
Best Power Hitter	Anthony Rizzo
Best Strike-Zone Discipline	Cory Spangenberg
Fastest Baserunner	Reymond Fuentes
Best Athlete	Jace Peterson
Best Fastball	Adys Portillo
Best Curveball	Casey Kelly
Best Slider	Simon Castro
Best Changeup	Robbie Erlin
Best Control	Joe Wieland
Best Defensive Catcher	Austin Hedges
Best Defensive Infielder	Beamer Weems
Best Infield Arm	Jeudy Valdez
Best Defensive Outfielder	Rico Noel
Best Outfield Arm	Rymer Liriano

PROJECTED 2015 LINEUP

Catcher	Austin Hedges
First Base	Anthony Rizzo
Second Base	Cory Spangenberg
Third Base	Chase Headley
Shortstop	Jace Peterson
Left Field	Jedd Gyorko
Center Field	Cameron Maybin
Right Field	Rymer Liriano
No. 1 Starter	Mat Latos
No. 2 Starter	Casey Kelly
No. 3 Starter	Cory Luebke
No. 4 Starter	Joe Wieland
No. 5 Starter	Robbie Erlin
Closer	Huston Street

TOP PROSPECTS OF THE DECADE

Year	Player, Pos.	2011 Org.
2002	Sean Burroughs, 3b	Diamondbacks
2003	Xavier Nady, of	Diamondbacks
2004	Josh Barfield, 2b	Phillies
2005	Josh Barfield, 2b	Phillies
2006	Cesar Carrillo, rhp	Lancaster (Atlantic)
2007	Cedric Hunter, of	Padres
2008	Chase Headley, 3b	Padres
2009	Kyle Blanks, 1b	Padres
2010	Donavan Tate, of	Padres
2011	Casey Kelly, rhp	Padres

TOP DRAFT PICKS OF THE DECADE

Year	Player, Pos.	2011 Org.
2002	Khalil Greene, ss	Out of baseball
2003	Tim Stauffer, rhp	Padres
2004	Matt Bush, ss	Rays
2005	Cesar Carrillo, rhp	Lancaster (Atlantic)
2006	Matt Antonelli, 3b	Nationals
2007	Nick Schmidt, lhp	Padres
2008	Allan Dykstra, 1b	Mets
2009	Donavan Tate, of	Padres
2010	*Karsten Whitson, rhp	U. of Florida
2011	Cory Spangenberg, 2b	Padres

*Did not sign.

LARGEST BONUSES IN CLUB HISTORY

Donavan Tate, 2009	$6,250,000
Matt Bush, 2004	$3,150,000
Austin Hedges, 2011	$3,000,000
Joe Ross, 2011	$2,750,000
Mark Phillips, 2000	$2,200,000

SAN DIEGO PADRES

TOP 2012 ROOKIE: Anthony Rizzo, 1b. After retaining his rookie eligibility by three at-bats, the young slugger will be back in San Diego with a retooled swing.

BREAKOUT PROSPECT: Miles Mikolas, rhp. With two plus pitches, including mid-90s heat, and strong control, he could be among the Padres' first 2012 callups.

SLEEPER: Luis Domoromo, of. Scouts love his smooth lefty swing and quiet setup, but will he develop the power to profile in left field?

SOURCE OF TOP 30 TALENT

Homegrown	25	Acquired	5
College	9	Trades	5
Junior college	2	Rule 5 draft	0
High school	6	Independent leagues	0
Draft-and-follow	0	Free agents/waivers	0
Nondrafted free agents	0		
International	8		

LF
Jaff Decker (11)
Luis Domoromo
Everett Williams
Kyle Gaedele
Dan Robertson
Corey Adamson
Franmil Reyes

CF
Blake Tekotte (15)
Reymond Fuentes (18)
Donavan Tate (22)
Alberth Martinez
Rico Noel

RF
Rymer Liriano (2)
Jose Dore
Yoan Alcantara
Lee Orr

3B
Jedd Gyorko (6)
James Darnell (13)
Vince Belnome (30)
Duanel Jones

SS
Jace Peterson (17)
Beamer Weems

2B
Cory Spangenberg (4)
Jeudy Valdez (24)
Drew Cumberland
Andy Parrino
Jonathan Galvez
Casey McElroy

1B
Anthony Rizzo (1)
Edinson Rincon (19)
Matt Clark
Nate Frieman

C
Austin Hedges (5)
Jason Hagerty (20)
Luis Martinez
Rodney Daal
Jose Ruiz

LHP

LHSP	LHRP
Robbie Erlin (8)	Mike Watt
Juan Oramas (12)	
Pedro Hernandez (23)	
Jose DePaula (25)	
Andrew Werner	
Mark Hardy	

RHP

RHSP	RHRP
Casey Kelly (3)	Miles Mikolas (16)
Joe Wieland (7)	Adys Portillo (26)
Joe Ross (9)	Anthony Bass (28)
Keyvius Sampson (10)	Brad Brach (29)
Simon Castro (14)	Nick Vincent
Matt Lollis (21)	Kevin Quackenbush
Mike Kelly (27)	Matt Stites
Matt Andriese	Justin Hancock
Johnny Barbato	Erik Hamren
Jorge Reyes	Eugenio Reyes
Cody Hebner	Genison Reyes
Zach Cates	Jason Ray
Burch Smith	
Matt Wisler	
Jerry Sullivan	
Mark Pope	
Colin Rea	
Matt Banham	

2011 BONUSES: $11.0 MILLION

BEST PURE HITTER: 2B Cory Spangenberg (1) lived up to his reputation as one of the best bats available in the draft by batting .316 in his pro debut, much of it in low Class A. He has a sweet lefthanded swing, extraordinary hand-eye coordination and the speed to beat out infield hits.

BEST POWER HITTER: Defense is C Austin Hedges' (2) ticket, but after he signed for $3 million, he also put on a show in batting practice at Petco Park. He drove a ball off the back wall in center field and another into the second deck.

FASTEST RUNNER: Spangenberg has legitimate plus-plus speed, with SS Jace Peterson (1s) a half-step behind him.

BEST DEFENSIVE PLAYER: Hedges is a plus-plus receiver with quick and smooth footwork that helps his solid arm strength play up. He also has the take-charge makeup to be a star behind the plate.

BEST FASTBALL: RHP Joe Ross (1) worked at 93-95 mph in instructional league and has topped out at 96. He commands his heater to both sides of the plate and down in the strike zone. RHP Cody Hebner (4) has hit 97 mph.

BEST SECONDARY PITCH: RHP Matt Andriese (3) baffled short-season Northwest League hitters with his changeup, recording a 1.51 ERA and 42 strikeouts in as many innings. RHP Mark Pope's (5) slider is the best breaking ball in this crop.

BEST PRO DEBUT: Spangenberg batted .316/.419/.418 with 25 steals, but RHP Kevin Quackenbush (8) put up even better numbers. Signed to the lowest bonus ($5,000) in the draft's first 10 rounds, he had a 0.64 ERA, 18 saves and 71 strikeouts in 42 innings between two levels.

BEST ATHLETE: Peterson doubled as a defensive back at McNeese State. He's a smooth shortstop with arm strength, speed and some pop.

MOST INTRIGUING BACKGROUND: Kyle Gaedele's (6) great-uncle Eddie was the shortest player in big league history at 3-foot-7, part of a publicity stunt dreamed up by Hall of Fame owner Bill Veeck. Ross' brother Tyson pitches for the Athletics. 2B Cody Gabella (43) was reunited with his father Jim, who manages San Diego's Rookie-level Arizona League affiliate.

CLOSEST TO THE MAJORS: Quackenbush. Hitters just don't get good looks at his fastball, which he throws on a downhill angle at 92-95 mph.

BEST LATE-ROUND PICK: Offensive-minded 2B Casey McElroy (11) or RHPs Burch Smith (14) and Matt Stites (17), who have hit 94 mph.

THE ONE WHO GOT AWAY: San Diego had 27 picks in the first 23 rounds and signed all of them except for C Brett Austin (1s), a switch-hitter with power. He turned down $1.65 million to go to North Carolina State.

ASSESSMENT: The Padres spent a franchise record on bonuses, loading up on intriguing up-the-middle players and arms. They also may have found one of the draft's bigger bargains in Quackenbush.

2010 BONUSES: $4.3 MILLION

In his first full year of pro ball, 3B Jedd Gyorko (2) won batting titles in the California and Arizona Fall leagues. LHP Josh Spence (9) was the second player from the 2010 draft to reach the majors. Failing to sign RHP Karsten Whitson (1) resulted in a compensation pick in 2011 that became Spangenberg.

GRADE: C+

2009 BONUSES: $9.1 MILLION

OFs Donavan Tate (1) and Everett Williams (2) have been profound disappointments and wiped each other out in an outfield collision last year. The Padres recovered in the later rounds, finding RHPs Keyvius Sampson (4), Miles Mikolas (7) and Matt Lollis (15) and C Jason Hagerty (5).

GRADE: C+

2008 BONUSES: $5.4 MILLION

San Diego blew its top choice on 1B Allan Dykstra (1) and didn't sign 2B Jason Kipnis (4) and LHP Sean Gilmartin (31), the latter a 2011 first-rounder. The Padres did land five big leaguers in 2B Logan Forsythe (1s), 3B James Darnell (2), OF Blake Tekotte (3) and RHPs Anthony Bass (5) and Brad Brach (42). OF Jaff Decker (1s) is one of their best hitting prospects.

GRADE: C+

2007 BONUSES: $5.9 MILLION

The Padres had six selections before the second round and hit on just one—LHP Cory Luebke (1s)—but they rallied late to get seven big leaguers. Of that group, only C Luis Martinez (12) and INF Andy Parrino (26) remain with San Diego. INF Eric Sogard (2) and RHPs Corey Kluber (4) and Brandon Gomes (17) were traded, while the Padres lost SS Lance Zawadzki (4) on waivers and released RHP Dylan Axelrod (30).

GRADE: C+

Draft analysis by Jim Callis. Numbers in parentheses indicate draft rounds.

1 ANTHONY
RIZZO, 1B

Born: Aug. 8, 1989. **B-T:** L-L. **Ht.:** 6-3. **Wt.:** 220.
Drafted: HS—Parkland, Fla., 2007 (6th round).
Signed by: Laz Gutierrez (Red Sox).

BA GRADE

60

MEDIUM

BILL MITCHELL

The Red Sox paid an above-slot $325,000 bonus to sign Rizzo as a sixth-round pick in 2007, and he made his full-season debut in style by hitting .373 in 21 games at low Class A the following April. His season came to a sudden halt when he was diagnosed with limited stage classical Hodgkin's lymphoma, but doctors declared him cancer free that November and he bounced back to hit .297/.368/.461 at two Class A stops in 2009. He emerged as Boston's top offensive prospect in 2010, when he spent most of the year in Double-A and swatted 42 doubles and 25 homers. The Red Sox dealt him—along with 2008 and '09 first-rounders Casey Kelly and Reymond Fuentes—to acquire Adrian Gonzalez that December. Rizzo led all Triple-A players with a 1.159 OPS through June 5, when San Diego called him up at age 21 because it had seen enough of Jorge Cantu and Brad Hawpe at first base. Rizzo went 3-for-7 with a double, triple, homer and four walks in his first three big league games, but he soon fell on hard times and went back to Tucson on July 21 having gone 11-for-91 (.121) in San Diego. He went on to rank second in the Pacific Coast League in slugging (.652) and fifth in hitting (.331) before returning to the Padres and starting eight games in September.

He's not Gonzalez, but Rizzo isn't far away from succeeding him as the most dangerous hitter in San Diego's lineup. To do so, he'll have to make adjustments after big league pitchers were able to exploit the length and uppercut in his swing with quality fastballs up in the zone. He needs to stay on top of the ball and level out his stroke to make more contact and hit more line drives. Rizzo started to pull inside pitches for power in Double-A, and he hit 23 of his 27 homers in 2011 to right or right-center field—but that's the most difficult way for a power hitter to thrive at spacious Petco Park. Strikeouts always will be a byproduct of Rizzo's plus power, though he led all big league rookies with at least 100 plate appearances with a 14 percent walk rate. Like many lefty power hitters, Rizzo struggles versus southpaws—he hit .245/.312/.409 against them in Double-A and Triple-A—but his strike-zone awareness should enable him to hit for a decent average. He receives solid to plus grades for his defense at first base, though he's a below-average runner, as expected for a player his size.

Rizzo could make the Padres with a strong spring-training performance, but more likely San Diego will send the 22-year-old back to Triple-A to work out the kinks in his swing. Once he does so, he could develop into a .270 hitter capable of producing 30 homers and a healthy amount of walks on an annual basis.

SCOUTING GRADES

Batting: 50.   **Defense:** 55.
Power: 65.   **Arm:** 55.
Speed: 35.

Based on 20-80 scouting scale and future projection rather than present tools. 50 represents major league average.

Year	Club (League)	Class	AVG	G	AB	R	H	2B	3B	HR	RBI	BB	SO	SB	CS	OBP	SLG
2007	Red Sox (GCL)	R	.286	6	21	6	6	0	0	1	3	1	2	0	0	.375	.429
2008	Greenville (SAL)	LoA	.373	21	83	9	31	6	0	0	11	3	15	0	0	.402	.446
2009	Greenville (SAL)	LoA	.298	64	245	40	73	21	0	9	42	25	60	2	1	.365	.494
	Salem (CAR)	HiA	.295	55	200	23	59	16	0	3	24	25	39	2	0	.371	.420
2010	Salem (CAR)	HiA	.248	29	117	26	29	12	0	5	20	16	32	3	0	.333	.479
	Portland (EL)	AA	.263	107	414	66	109	30	0	20	80	45	100	7	1	.334	.481
2011	Tucson (PCL)	AAA	.331	93	356	64	118	34	1	26	101	43	89	7	6	.404	.652
	San Diego (NL)	MAJ	.141	49	128	9	18	8	1	1	9	21	46	2	1	.281	.242
Major League Totals			.141	49	128	9	18	8	1	1	9	21	46	2	1	.281	.242
Minor League Totals			.296	375	1436	234	425	119	1	64	281	158	337	21	8	.366	.514

2 RYMER LIRIANO, OF

Born: June 20, 1991. **B-T:** R-R. **Ht.:** 6-0. **Wt.:** 230. **Signed:** Dominican Republic, 2007. **Signed by:** Felix Francisco/Randy Smith.

For the second straight year, Liriano slumped early before thriving after an in-season demotion. In 2011, he overcame a 7-for-55 (.127) start at high Class A Lake Elsinore to win the low Class A Midwest League MVP award. He finished third in the MWL batting race (.319), crushed 50 extra-base hits and ranked third in the minors with 66 steals. Among Padres farmhands, only 2009 No. 3 overall pick Donavan Tate can approach Liriano's overall collection of tools. He whips the bat through the zone, drives the ball to the middle of the field and has the strength and bat plane necessary to hit 25 homers one day. His pitch-recognition skills improved dramatically with Fort Wayne as he saw a steady diet of breaking balls, and he now projects as a solid hitter. Liriano has a quick first step and regularly gets down the line in fewer than 4.2 seconds from the right side, giving him plus speed. Strong instincts make him a plus basestealer, though scouts expect he'll lose a step as he fills out his thick frame. His average range and well above-average arm strength fit well in right field. Liriano combined promise and performance like nobody else in the system in 2011, earning a spot on the 40-man roster. A future first-division right fielder, he'll try to solve high Class A in 2012.

BA GRADE 65 HIGH

Year	Club (League)	Class	AVG	G	AB	R	H	2B	3B	HR	RBI	BB	SO	SB	CS	OBP	SLG
2008	Padres (DSL)	R	.198	67	232	34	46	13	1	9	37	28	106	9	5	.296	.379
2009	Padres (AZL)	R	.350	50	197	44	69	8	1	8	44	15	52	14	5	.398	.523
2010	Fort Wayne (MWL)	LoA	.191	50	188	21	36	11	1	2	20	10	54	11	6	.234	.293
	Eugene (NWL)	SS	.271	53	203	35	55	13	6	0	12	17	53	17	7	.335	.394
	Lake Elsinore (CAL)	HiA	.220	14	50	3	11	2	0	1	6	5	12	3	0	.291	.320
2011	Lake Elsinore (CAL)	HiA	.127	15	55	8	7	1	1	0	6	6	13	1	1	.213	.182
	Fort Wayne (MWL)	LoA	.319	116	455	81	145	30	8	12	62	47	95	65	20	.383	.499
Minor League Totals			.267	365	1380	226	369	78	18	32	187	128	385	120	44	.334	.420

3 CASEY KELLY, RHP

Born: Oct. 4, 1989. **B-T:** R-R. **Ht.:** 6-3. **Wt.:** 195. **Drafted:** HS—Sarasota, Fla., 2008 (1st round). **Signed by:** Anthony Turco (Red Sox).

Kelly viewed himself as a shortstop when the Red Sox paid him a franchise draft-record $3 million as the 30th overall pick in 2008. He hit just .219 in his first two pro seasons before finally acceding to Boston's wishes in 2010 that he become a full-time pitcher. He performed well enough to join Anthony Rizzo as the centerpieces of the trade that sent Adrian Gonzalez to Boston. Kelly's fastball ranges from 88-92 to 93-95 mph, with heavy sink that helps it play as an above-average pitch even at lower velocities. That sinking action helped him post the second-best groundout/airout ratio (1.9) in the Double-A Texas League in 2011. He repeats a clean, compact arm action that has aided the development of his secondary pitches. Kelly improved his control and consistency with his breaking ball when he repeated Double-A. His 11-to-5 curveball added depth and velocity, grading as a plus pitch more often, though his changeup took a small step back. He entices batters to swing over his mid-80s change when he throws it from the same arm slot as his fastball. He lives in the bottom of the strike zone, allowing just 18 homers in 48 Double-A starts. Kelly doesn't miss enough bats to profile as a pure ace, but with the potential for three solid to plus pitches, he fits the description of a No. 2 starter to a tee.

BA GRADE 60 MEDIUM

Year	Club (League)	Class	W	L	ERA	G	GS	CG	SV	IP	H	HR	BB	SO	K/9	WHIP	AVG
2009	Salem (CAR)	HiA	1	4	3.09	8	8	0	0	47	33	4	7	35	6.8	0.86	.196
	Greenville (SAL)	LoA	6	1	1.12	9	9	0	0	48	32	0	9	39	7.3	0.85	.184
2010	Portland (EL)	AA	3	5	5.31	21	21	0	0	95	118	10	35	81	7.7	1.61	.307
2011	San Antonio (TL)	AA	11	6	3.98	27	27	0	0	142	153	8	46	105	6.6	1.40	.278
Minor League Totals			21	16	3.82	65	65	0	0	332	336	22	97	260	7.0	1.30	.263

Year	Club (League)	Class	AVG	G	AB	R	H	2B	3B	HR	RBI	BB	SO	SB	CS	OBP	SLG
2008	Red Sox (GCL)	R	.173	27	98	10	17	5	0	1	9	6	34	1	0	.229	.255
	Lowell (NYP)	SS	.344	9	32	5	11	5	1	0	4	0	8	0	1	.344	.563
2009	Red Sox (GCL)	R	.214	8	28	4	6	1	0	2	6	3	10	1	0	.290	.464
	Greenville (SAL)	LoA	.224	32	134	18	30	7	1	1	10	16	39	0	1	.305	.313
2011	San Antonio (TL)	AA	.350	10	20	1	7	2	0	1	2	0	4	0	0	.350	.600
Minor League Totals			.228	86	312	38	71	20	2	5	31	25	95	2	2	.286	.353

4 CORY SPANGENBERG, 2B

Born: March 16, 1991. **B-T:** L-R. **Ht.:** 6-0. **Wt.:** 185. **Drafted:** Indian River (Fla.) JC, 2011 (1st round). **Signed by:** Willie Bosque.

A Pennsylvania prep product, Spangenberg spent his freshman year at Virginia Military Institute before transferring to Indian River (Fla.) JC for 2011. He quickly gained acclaim as one of the best hitters in the draft, went 10th overall and signed four days later for $1.863 million. He ranked as the short-season Northwest League's top position prospect and batted .381 in the final month at Fort Wayne. Spangenberg knows the strike zone, barrels the ball consistently and smokes line drives to all fields. He could be an annual .300 hitter, though he'll have to maintain balance and add loft to his swing to hit for more than fringe-average power. His hips tend to drift when he gets anxious and he sometimes struggles with inside pitches when his stance gets too wide, both easily correctable blemishes. Spangenberg figures to collect his share of infield hits and stolen bases with his plus-plus speed, a true 70 tool on the 20-80 scouting scale. He played third base in junior college but profiles better at second base because of a slinging arm action and below-average present power. He runs well enough to handle center field if the infield doesn't work out. Spangenberg could develop into a lesser version of Dustin Ackley. He'll open his first full season in high Class A and likely finish it at Double-A San Antonio.

Year	Club (League)	Class	AVG	G	AB	R	H	2B	3B	HR	RBI	BB	SO	SB	CS	OBP	SLG
2011	Eugene (NWL)	SS	.384	25	86	20	33	10	0	1	20	31	15	10	4	.545	.535
	Fort Wayne (MWL)	LoA	.286	47	189	35	54	7	1	2	24	14	42	15	4	.345	.365
Minor League Totals			.316	72	275	55	87	17	1	3	44	45	57	25	8	.419	.418

5 AUSTIN HEDGES, C

Born: Aug. 18, 1992. **B-T:** R-R. **Ht.:** 6-1. **Wt.:** 190. **Drafted:** HS—San Juan Capistrano, Calif., 2011 (2nd round). **Signed by:** Josh Emmerick.

The 82nd overall pick in June, Hedges waited until the Aug. 15 deadline before signing for $3 million, which would have been a second-round record had the Pirates' Josh Bell not pulled down $5 million that same night. Scouts regarded Hedges, an A student with a strong UCLA commitment, as one of the best defensive high school catchers in recent draft history. Amateur opponents rarely bothered running on Hedges, whose arm plays as a 70 on the 20-80 scouting scale because of solid strength and clean, quick mechanics that produce pop times as quick as 1.78 seconds. He receives plus-plus grades for his receiving, blocking, quiet setup and leadership qualities, but scouts disagree on his offensive potential. Those who like Hedges' bat give him a chance to be an average hitter with average pop, while others think his overly aggressive approach will hinder him. He showcased stunning raw power during a batting-practice session at Petco Park. Though he's agile for his size, he's a below-average runner like most catchers. Hedges showed up to instructional league with a more physical build than he had in high school, and the Padres think he could be ready for full-season ball in 2012. He may be four years away from the big leagues, where he could be a future Gold Glove winner.

Year	Club (League)	Class	AVG	G	AB	R	H	2B	3B	HR	RBI	BB	SO	SB	CS	OBP	SLG
2011	Padres (AZL)	R	.313	5	16	3	5	0	0	1	4	5	1	1	0	.500	.500
	Eugene (NWL)	SS	.100	4	10	0	1	1	0	0	0	2	3	0	0	.250	.200
Minor League Totals			.231	9	26	3	6	1	0	1	4	7	4	1	0	.412	.385

6 JEDD GYORKO, 3B

Born: Sept. 23, 1988. **B-T:** R-R. **Ht.:** 5-10. **Wt.:** 195. **Drafted:** West Virginia, 2010 (2nd round). **Signed by:** Andrew Salvo.

While scouts rated Gyorko as one of the best bats in the 2010 draft, he nevertheless lasted 59 picks. In his first full year in 2011, he led the minors with 192 hits and ranked second with 114 RBIs. He might have won the high Class A California League triple crown had he not been promoted in July, so he settled for batting titles in the Cal (.365) and Arizona Fall (.437) leagues. Gyorko manages the strike zone well and uses a short, balanced swing that allows him to hit all types of pitching, so he should continue to hit for high averages. He's a sound situational hitter because he shortens up with two strikes, and he's not afraid to go outside his zone in key spots. Though he hits the ball with authority to the opposite field, his overall power potential is just average. Gyorko has soft hands, strong footwork and average arm strength at third base. As long as he maintains his current physique and fringy range, he probably can stay at the hot corner. He's a well below-average runner. Gyorko's line-drive stroke figures to play well at Petco Park, where flyballs go to die. He's Chase

Headley's likely successor in San Diego, possibly as soon as 2013 if Headley becomes too expensive. Gyorko will head back to Double-A to begin 2012.

Year	Club (League)	Class	AVG	G	AB	R	H	2B	3B	HR	RBI	BB	SO	SB	CS	OBP	SLG
2010	Eugene (NWL)	SS	.330	26	106	16	35	6	0	5	18	9	26	1	1	.383	.528
	Fort Wayne (MWL)	LoA	.284	42	162	19	46	11	0	2	23	19	31	1	0	.366	.389
2011	Lake Elsinore (CAL)	HiA	.365	81	340	78	124	35	2	18	74	38	64	11	3	.429	.638
	San Antonio (TL)	AA	.288	59	236	41	68	12	0	7	40	26	50	1	0	.358	.428
Minor League Totals			.323	208	844	154	273	64	2	32	155	92	171	14	4	.392	.518

7 JOE WIELAND, RHP

Born: Jan. 21, 1990. **B-T:** R-R. **Ht.:** 6-3. **Wt.:** 175. **Drafted:** HS—Reno, Nev., 2008 (4th round). **Signed by:** Butch Metzger (Rangers).

Wieland carried a 4.52 ERA through 231 innings at two Class A stops in the Rangers system in 2009-10, undercutting his reputation as a strike-thrower with a three-pitch mix. He nullified those concerns with a breakout 2011 season in which he advanced to Double-A and ranked fifth in the minors with a 1.97 ERA and 7.1 K-BB ratio. He threw a no-hitter on July 29, two days before Texas traded him and lefty Robbie Erlin to the Padres for Mike Adams. Wieland sits at 88-92 mph and paints the corners with a fastball more notable for its precise location than life. He operated at 93 mph and touched 95 during the Texas League playoffs while working with extra rest. His secondary pitches are often as effective as his heat. Wieland's mid-70s curveball features consistent 12-to-6 break, while his 83-84 mph changeup sinks and fades. He occasionally throws a low-80s slider for a different look to his glove side, sometimes favoring it over his curve. He's so quick to the plate that just 12 baserunners attempted to steal against him in 2011. Wieland profiles as a classic No. 4 starter, but his exquisite control suggests he could be a No. 3. Ticketed for Triple-A, he may be ready for a big league audition at some point in 2012.

BA GRADE
55
MEDIUM

Year	Club (League)	Class	W	L	ERA	G	GS	CG	SV	IP	H	HR	BB	SO	K/9	WHIP	AVG
2008	Rangers (AZL)	R	5	1	1.44	13	7	0	0	44	32	2	8	41	8.5	0.92	.200
2009	Hickory (SAL)	LoA	4	6	5.31	19	18	0	0	83	102	7	24	73	7.9	1.52	.299
2010	Hickory (SAL)	LoA	7	4	3.34	15	15	2	0	89	84	4	15	71	7.2	1.11	.251
	Bakersfield (CAL)	HiA	4	3	5.19	11	10	0	0	59	67	6	10	62	9.5	1.31	.283
2011	Myrtle Beach (CAR)	HiA	6	3	2.10	14	13	1	0	86	78	7	4	96	10.1	0.96	.240
	Frisco (TL)	AA	4	0	1.23	7	7	1	0	44	35	2	11	36	7.4	1.05	.217
	San Antonio (TL)	AA	3	1	2.77	5	5	0	0	26	23	0	6	18	6.2	1.12	.240
Minor League Totals			33	18	3.28	84	75	4	0	430	421	28	78	397	8.3	1.16	.254

8 ROBBIE ERLIN, LHP

Born: Oct. 8, 1990. **B-T:** L-L. **Ht.:** 6-0. **Wt.:** 175. **Drafted:** HS—Scotts Valley, Calif., 2009 (3rd round). **Signed by:** Butch Metzger (Rangers).

Erlin led the low Class A South Atlantic League with a 2.12 ERA as a 19-year-old in 2010, and his encore was even more impressive. He needed just nine starts to earn a promotion to Double-A in 2011, when he ranked second in the minors in K-BB ratio (9.6) and fourth in WHIP (0.95). He and Joe Wieland switched Texas League dugouts following the July 31 trade that sent Mike Adams from the Padres to the Rangers. Erlin's secondary pitches, superb control and easy delivery give him more upside than the typical pitcher with an 89-91 mph fastball that tops out at 93. He works both corners with his fastball, rarely straying out of the zone, not even with two strikes. Batters don't see the ball well out of his hand, making his fading changeup a deadly weapon, especially when it arrives anywhere from 12-15 mph slower than his fastball. Erlin buckles knees with a tight downer curveball in the low 70s. If anything, his control is too sharp and leaves him vulnerable to homers. Like Wieland, Erlin is a control-oriented, flyball pitcher who will benefit from Petco Park. His stuff may not play as well in smaller parks, but his overall profile suggests solid mid-rotation starter. He'll team with Wieland again in 2011, this time in Tucson.

BA GRADE
55
MEDIUM

Year	Club (League)	Class	W	L	ERA	G	GS	CG	SV	IP	H	HR	BB	SO	K/9	WHIP	AVG
2009	Rangers (AZL)	R	0	0	2.25	3	0	0	0	4	5	0	1	9	20.3	1.50	.294
2010	Hickory (SAL)	LoA	6	3	2.12	28	17	0	1	115	89	9	17	125	9.8	0.92	.213
2011	Myrtle Beach (CAR)	HiA	3	2	2.14	9	9	0	0	55	25	7	5	62	10.2	0.55	.132
	Frisco (TL)	AA	5	2	4.32	11	10	0	0	67	73	9	7	61	8.2	1.20	.282
	San Antonio (TL)	AA	1	0	1.38	6	6	0	0	26	26	2	4	31	10.7	1.15	.265
Minor League Totals			15	7	2.61	57	42	0	1	266	218	27	34	288	9.7	0.95	.222

9 JOE ROSS, RHP

Born: May 21, 1993. **B-T:** R-R. **Ht.:** 6-3. **Wt.:** 185. **Drafted:** HS—Oakland, 2011 (1st round). **Signed by:** Noah Jackson.

BA GRADE

60

HIGH

Like Padres second-rounder Austin Hedges, Ross turned down a UCLA commitment in exchange for a big bonus at the Aug. 15 deadline, signing for $2.75 million as the 2011 draft's 25th overall pick. He first threw to Hedges during the summer of 2010 as both played on the high school showcase circuit, and they teamed up again during Ross' Aug. 28 pro debut. Ross' older brother Tyson has spent parts of the past two seasons on the Athletics pitching staff. His fastball sat at 91-93 mph during the spring and at 93-95 in short outings during instructional league, topping out at 96 in both settings. He could sit in the upper registers of that range as he fills out his lean frame. His athleticism and smooth mechanics allow him to throw strikes and locate the ball down in the zone. The Padres love his clean arm action and strong aptitude for throwing a changeup, which projects as a plus pitch. His 11-to-5 curveball has its moments but has farther to go than his changeup. A potential frontline starter, Ross probably will team up again with Hedges in low Class A for their first full pro seasons. The Padres believe Ross has more maturity and feel for pitching coming out of high school than Keyvius Sampson or Johnny Barbato did as their most prized pitchers from the previous two drafts.

Year	Club (League)	Class	W	L	ERA	G	GS	CG	SV	IP	H	HR	BB	SO	K/9	WHIP	AVG
2011	Padres (AZL)	R	0	0	0.00	1	0	0	0	1	2	0	0	0	0.0	2.00	.400
Minor League Totals			0	0	0.00	1	0	0	0	1	2	0	0	0	0.0	2.00	.400

10 KEYVIUS SAMPSON, RHP

Born: Jan. 6, 1991. **B-T:** R-R. **Ht.:** 6-0. **Wt.:** 185. **Drafted:** HS—Ocala, Fla., 2009 (4th round). **Signed by:** Rob Sidwell.

BA GRADE

55

HIGH

The Padres stole Sampson with the 114th pick in 2009, selecting him with the third choice on the draft's second day after he softened his bonus demands. Signed for $600,000, he pitched effectively at short-season Eugene in 2010, but his season was marred by a labrum tear in his shoulder as well as late-season elbow soreness. Healthy in 2011, he stifled Midwest League competition, finishing second in opponent average (.192) and third in strikeouts (143). Sampson's fastball sits at 90-92 mph and peaks at 95, exploding out of his hand with late running action. He wraps his wrist on the back side of his arm stroke, showing the ball to his opponent, but his arm is so quick that his control seems unaffected and his fastball grades as plus. He sells his plus changeup with strong arm speed, and it helped him hold MWL lefties to a .191 average. Sampson's curveball is clearly his third-best pitch because it lacks bite and power, sitting in the low 70s. Plus athleticism allows him to repeat his delivery, which features some effort. An improved breaking ball would enhance Sampson's profile, but he still has a chance to be a mid-rotation starter or late-inning reliever. He's ready for high Class A.

Year	Club (League)	Class	W	L	ERA	G	GS	CG	SV	IP	H	HR	BB	SO	K/9	WHIP	AVG
2009	Padres (AZL)	R	0	0	3.00	2	1	0	0	3	1	0	0	3	9.0	0.33	.111
	Eugene (NWL)	SS	0	0	3.60	2	1	0	0	5	3	0	3	5	9.0	1.20	.176
2010	Eugene (NWL)	SS	3	3	3.56	10	10	0	0	43	35	4	17	58	12.1	1.21	.226
2011	Fort Wayne (MWL)	LoA	12	3	2.90	24	24	0	0	118	81	8	49	143	10.9	1.10	.192
Minor League Totals			15	6	3.09	38	36	0	0	169	120	12	69	209	11.1	1.12	.199

11 JAFF DECKER, OF

BA GRADE

50

MEDIUM

Born: Feb. 23, 1990. **B-T:** L-L. **Ht.:** 5-10. **Wt.:** 190. **Drafted:** HS—Peoria, Ariz., 2008 (1st round supplemental). **Signed by:** Dave Lottsfeldt.

Decker experienced immediate pro success after signing for $892,000 as the 42nd overall pick in the 2008 draft. He won the Rookie-level Arizona League MVP award in his pro debut and followed that by leading the Midwest League in OPS (.956) as a teenager in 2009. Decker slipped for the first time in 2010, batting .195 in the first half in high Class A before rallying to slug 14 homers in the second half. Promoted to Double-A last season, he led the Texas League with 103 walks but hit just .236. The Padres believe Decker eventually will be a solid to plus hitter because his lefty swing is short and to the point. He was too selective at times last year while waiting for a perfect pitch and racked up 145 strikeouts, third-most in the TL. Extended hitting slumps result when his stride and hands get out of sync. Decker doesn't necessarily look the part of power hitter with a short, stocky build, but he can drive the ball from left-center to right field and projects to have at least fringy power. He has thinned out since turning pro and now features deceptive athleticism. He plays a strong left field and throws well. San Diego asked Decker to run more in 2011 and he swiped 15 bases in 20 attempts, though he's a fringy runner at best. He appears destined for a return to San Antonio in 2012, and if he hits for either more average or more power, he has a shot at regular play in the big leagues.

Year	Club (League)	Class	AVG	G	AB	R	H	2B	3B	HR	RBI	BB	SO	SB	CS	OBP	SLG
2008	Padres (AZL)	R	.352	49	159	51	56	11	2	5	34	55	36	9	1	.523	.541
	Eugene (NWL)	SS	.200	3	10	2	2	0	0	0	0	2	5	0	0	.333	.200
2009	Fort Wayne (MWL)	LoA	.299	104	358	78	107	25	2	16	64	85	92	10	6	.442	.514
2010	Lake Elsinore (CAL)	HiA	.262	79	290	53	76	14	2	17	58	47	80	5	4	.374	.500
2011	San Antonio (TL)	AA	.236	133	496	90	117	29	2	19	92	103	145	15	5	.373	.417
Minor League Totals			.273	368	1313	274	358	79	8	57	248	292	358	39	16	.411	.475

12 JUAN ORAMAS, LHP

BA GRADE

50

MEDIUM

Born: May 11, 1990. **B-T:** L-L. **Ht.:** 5-10. **Wt.:** 215. **Signed:** Mexico, 2006. **Signed by:** Robert Rowley.

Signed out of Mexico at age 16, Oramas spent two years in the Rookie-level Dominican Summer League and another in the Mexican League, where he finished second with a 2.31 ERA as a teenager in 2009, before ever playing in the United States. He didn't wait long to make his mark, coming within two outs of pitching a perfect game for Lake Elsinore in just his fourth U.S. start. Held back in extended spring training with a back injury in 2011, he didn't throw his first pitch for San Antonio until May 21, but he rounded into form quickly. Among Texas League pitchers with at least 100 innings, Oramas ranked fourth in K-BB ratio (3.6) and WHIP (1.21). His stuff grades out as average to a tick above across the board, and he hides the ball well, locates his pitches and varies arm slots to induce swings and misses. Oramas touches 94 mph with his fastball but typically sits at 89-92 and works both sides of the plate, occasionally dropping his arm slot versus lefthanders. He flashes tight rotation on a mid-70s curveball and more often shows feel for a low-80s changeup and fade. Both secondary pitches have average potential. While nothing about Oramas' repertoire screams future star, he commands three pitches and could pitch at the back of a big league rotation. The Padres added him to the 40-man roster in November. An assignment to the high altitude of Tucson in 2012 could stir memories of his summer in the Mexican League.

Year	Club (League)	Class	W	L	ERA	G	GS	CG	SV	IP	H	HR	BB	SO	K/9	WHIP	AVG
2007	Padres (DSL)	R	2	3	3.81	16	5	0	0	54	39	1	20	63	10.4	1.09	.196
2008	Padres (DSL)	R	3	2	1.02	19	5	0	3	53	23	0	24	70	11.9	0.89	.125
2009	Mexico City (MEX)	AAA	9	1	2.31	25	14	0	0	90	72	4	44	89	8.9	1.29	.219
2010	Fort Wayne (MWL)	LoA	0	1	1.20	5	0	0	0	15	9	0	3	25	15.0	0.80	.176
	Lake Elsinore (CAL)	HiA	7	3	3.00	24	21	0	0	84	64	10	26	90	9.6	1.07	.209
2011	Tucson (PCL)	AAA	0	1	14.73	1	1	0	0	4	7	3	1	4	9.8	2.18	.389
	San Antonio (TL)	AA	10	5	3.10	19	18	0	0	105	99	10	28	102	8.8	1.21	.249
Minor League Totals			31	16	2.76	109	64	0	3	404	313	28	146	443	9.9	1.14	.209

13 JAMES DARNELL, 3B/OF

BA GRADE

50

MEDIUM

Born: Jan. 19, 1987. **B-T:** R-R. **Ht.:** 6-2. **Wt.:** 195. **Drafted:** South Carolina, 2008 (2nd round). **Signed by:** Anthony Byrd.

Darnell developed a cyst in his right hand during his Double-A debut in 2010, and the injury sapped his power and forced him out of action for five weeks at midseason. He redeemed himself in 2011 with a huge half-season with San Antonio. His 1.038 OPS ranked third in the Texas League at the time of his July 3 promotion to Tucson. Darnell completed his bounceback year with a September callup to San Diego, where he started 10 games at third base for an ailing Chase Headley and one in left field. His season ended with a dislocated left shoulder that required surgery to repair the capsule around the joint. Darnell's future value is tied to his bat, and he helped his cause by turning on more early-count fastballs last year. He connected for a career-high 24 homers across three levels, showing an enhanced ability to pull the ball. Some scouts think he's vulnerable to pitches away because he's too pull-conscious, though the strength in his hands translates to his swing and allows him to hit with authority to all fields. Darnell's glovework improved at third base, but he still projects as below-average defender there because he lacks flexibility, range and throwing accuracy. The Padres introduced him to left field in 2011 and he took to it immediately because of his sneaky athleticism. He's a below-average runner with average arm strength. Darnell will continue to play both third and left field in Triple-A to start 2012, and positional flexibility might be his ticket to the big leagues in an organization that has depth on the corners.

Year	Club (League)	Class	AVG	G	AB	R	H	2B	3B	HR	RBI	BB	SO	SB	CS	OBP	SLG
2008	Eugene (NWL)	SS	.373	16	67	9	25	6	1	2	15	11	12	1	1	.462	.582
2009	Fort Wayne (MWL)	LoA	.329	66	222	40	73	17	2	7	38	57	51	5	5	.468	.518
	Lake Elsinore (CAL)	HiA	.294	60	235	40	69	18	2	13	43	30	38	3	1	.377	.553
2010	Fort Wayne (MWL)	LoA	.360	7	25	5	9	4	0	1	8	5	4	0	0	.500	.640
	San Antonio (TL)	AA	.265	101	373	46	99	21	1	10	50	44	64	2	0	.348	.408
2011	San Antonio (TL)	AA	.333	76	288	62	96	25	1	17	62	52	48	2	1	.434	.604
	Tucson (PCL)	AAA	.261	35	134	20	35	4	0	6	17	16	30	0	0	.344	.425
	San Diego (NL)	MAJ	.222	18	45	2	10	2	0	1	7	5	7	1	0	.294	.333
Major League Totals			.222	18	45	2	10	2	0	1	7	5	7	1	0	.294	.333
Minor League Totals			.302	361	1344	222	406	95	7	56	233	215	247	13	8	.401	.508

14 SIMON CASTRO, RHP

BA GRADE
55
HIGH

Born: April 9, 1988. **B-T:** R-R. **Ht.:** 6-4. **Wt.:** 227. **Signed:** Dominican Republic, 2006. **Signed by:** Randy Smith/Felix Francisco.

Castro jumped from short-season ball to Double-A in the span of two seasons, winning the Midwest League strikeout crown in 2009 and then finishing runner-up in the Texas League ERA race a year later. He seemed poised for big things in 2011 as he tackled Triple-A for the first time, but his bubble burst early. Castro landed on the disabled list with a lat injury after six starts for Tucson yielded a 10.17 ERA. He recovered somewhat after a demotion to Double-A in June, and he closed out the season with a 2.53 ERA and a 35-5 K-BB ratio over his final seven starts. Castro always has pitched with a long arm action, but he struggled to repeat his mechanics for much of 2011. He got out of whack, failed to extend on the front side of his delivery and also recoiled his arm. Castro's velocity dipped into the low 90s early before he recovered to pitch at 92-94 mph and touch 96 with tailing action. His slider showed its trademark late bite and 82-84 mph velocity at times, though just as often it resembled a slurve. His mid-80s changeup could become a fringy pitch with more refinement. One of the organization's most dogged workers, Castro could benefit from his first dose of failure in the long run. If he rediscovers his two plus pitches and control, he still profiles as a mid-rotation starter or set-up man.

Year	Club (League)	Class	W	L	ERA	G	GS	CG	SV	IP	H	HR	BB	SO	K/9	WHIP	AVG
2006	Padres (DSL)	R	1	3	4.63	12	12	0	0	47	40	2	21	58	11.2	1.31	.219
2007	Padres (AZL)	R	2	6	6.22	14	12	0	0	51	61	4	30	55	9.8	1.80	.298
2008	Eugene (NWL)	SS	2	3	3.99	15	15	0	0	65	54	3	29	64	8.8	1.27	.223
2009	Fort Wayne (MWL)	LoA	10	6	3.33	28	27	1	0	140	118	9	37	157	10.1	1.10	.226
2010	San Antonio (TL)	AA	7	6	2.92	24	23	0	0	130	107	8	36	107	7.4	1.10	.223
	Portland (PCL)	AAA	0	1	7.84	2	2	0	0	10	16	1	6	6	5.2	2.13	.333
2011	Tucson (PCL)	AAA	2	2	10.17	6	6	0	0	26	37	5	18	21	7.4	2.14	.333
	San Antonio (TL)	AA	5	6	4.33	16	16	0	0	89	95	9	16	73	7.4	1.24	.271
Minor League Totals			29	33	4.24	117	113	1	0	558	528	41	193	541	8.7	1.29	.247

15 BLAKE TEKOTTE, OF

BA GRADE
50
MEDIUM

Born: May 24, 1987. **B-T:** L-R. **Ht.:** 5-11. **Wt.:** 175. **Drafted:** Miami, 2008 (3rd round). **Signed by:** Rob Sidwell.

Tekotte enhanced all aspects of his game while repeating Double-A in 2011, drawing more walks, stealing more bases and hitting for more power. He received two callups to San Diego but hit a mere .176 and struck out 21 times in 34 at-bats. With San Antonio, Tekotte hit 19 homers and stole 36 bases, second-most in the Texas League, and the Padres want him to continue to focus on the speed aspects of his game. He's a plus runner who glides to the ball in center field and has solid range. He has a below-average arm but gets to balls quickly. Tekotte's .393 on-base percentage last year established a career high and ranked third in the TL. While he generally employs a quick, line-drive stroke from the left side, he falls into funks when he sells out for power, as he did in the big leagues. For sustained success he'll need to line the ball into the gaps and use his speed. Tekotte does most of his damage versus righthanders, against whom he has hit .275/.384/.507 in 450 Double-A at-bats, but he makes enough contact against lefties and fields well enough to remain relevant as a potential center-field regular. The presence of Cameron Maybin in San Diego ultimately might force Tekotte into a reserve role. He'll have to outperform Chris Denorfia and veteran free agent import Mark Kotsay to win that job with the 2012 Padres.

Year	Club (League)	Class	AVG	G	AB	R	H	2B	3B	HR	RBI	BB	SO	SB	CS	OBP	SLG
2008	Eugene (NWL)	SS	.285	47	193	43	55	15	0	6	29	27	45	7	4	.379	.456
2009	Fort Wayne (MWL)	LoA	.258	134	530	83	137	24	5	13	56	68	97	30	12	.345	.396
2010	Lake Elsinore (CAL)	HiA	.310	59	203	41	63	17	1	8	27	36	46	22	8	.419	.522
	San Antonio (TL)	AA	.250	67	268	44	67	8	7	10	37	26	63	6	9	.324	.444
2011	San Diego (NL)	MAJ	.176	19	34	1	6	1	1	0	1	4	21	2	1	.263	.265
	San Antonio (TL)	AA	.285	106	414	77	118	27	2	19	67	67	108	36	12	.393	.498
Major League Totals			.176	19	34	1	6	1	1	0	1	4	21	2	1	.263	.265
Minor League Totals			.274	413	1608	288	440	91	15	56	216	224	359	101	45	.368	.453

16 MILES MIKOLAS, RHP

BA GRADE
50
MEDIUM

Born: Aug. 23, 1988. **B-T:** R-R. **Ht.:** 6-5. **Wt.:** 220. **Drafted:** Nova Southeastern (Fla.), 2009 (7th round). **Signed by:** Rob Sidwell.

While at Nova Southeastern (Fla.), an NCAA Division II program, Mikolas attracted attention from scouts for his 6-foot-5 frame and fastball velocity. The Padres signed him for $125,000 out of the seventh round of the 2009 draft, and he abandoned starting once he reached full-season ball the next year. Mikolas frequently shows two plus pitches and average control while working in relief, which makes him a good bet to reach his ceiling. He has walked just 1.7 batters per nine innings in 137 pro appearances. Mikolas dials his fastball up to 98 mph to put batters away but most frequently pitches at 93-96 mph. His heater does lack life and can be turned around when it catches too much of the plate. His hard, downer curveball features tight rotation in the mid-70s and gives righthanders fits. He doesn't show much aptitude for a changeup, so San Diego has no plans to move him from the bullpen. Mikolas could begin 2012 in Triple-A, with a big league callup to follow if he pitches well.

Year	Club (League)	Class	W	L	ERA	G	GS	CG	SV	IP	H	HR	BB	SO	K/9	WHIP	AVG
2009	Eugene (NWL)	SS	1	8	5.94	15	11	0	0	53	77	1	9	39	6.6	1.62	.332
2010	Fort Wayne (MWL)	LoA	6	3	2.20	60	0	0	13	82	76	3	15	78	8.6	1.11	.240
2011	Lake Elsinore (CAL)	HiA	3	0	1.13	34	0	0	12	40	31	1	9	42	9.5	1.01	.214
	San Antonio (TL)	AA	1	0	1.67	28	0	0	9	32	29	0	6	27	7.5	1.08	.240
Minor League Totals			11	11	2.87	137	11	0	34	207	213	5	39	186	8.1	1.22	.261

17 JACE PETERSON, SS

BA GRADE
55
HIGH

Born: May 9, 1990. **B-T:** L-R. **Ht.:** 6-0. **Wt.:** 197. **Drafted:** McNeese State, 2011 (1st round supplemental). **Signed by:** Kevin Ellis.

Peterson starred in four sports in high school before paring down to baseball and football at McNeese State and, finally, to just baseball after turning pro with the Padres. San Diego selected him 58th overall last June and signed him for $624,600. A defensive back in football, Peterson never had concentrated full-time on baseball, but that wasn't necessarily evident from his performance during his pro debut. Batting leadoff and playing shortstop every day for Eugene, he led the Northwest League with 50 walks while finishing second with 39 steals and third with 48 runs. Observers were smitten with his athleticism, intensity and leadership qualities. Peterson manages the strike zone well and uses a short, low-maintenance lefty swing, though his stroke lacks the loft to hit for more than fringy power. He has slightly above-average speed, and his strong baserunning instincts make him a stolen-base threat. Peterson still is learning the finer points of playing shortstop, such as timing hops and positioning his feet, but no one doubts he'll work hard to smooth his rough edges to become perhaps a solid defender. He has average arm strength, though he sacrifices carry on throws because he cuts off his arm path. The Padres have him working on a long-toss program to work out the stiffness, a common trait among ex-football players. Peterson could hit about .270 with a dozen homers and 30 steals at his peak, more than enough production to play shortstop regularly if his glove is up to the task.

Year	Club (League)	Class	AVG	G	AB	R	H	2B	3B	HR	RBI	BB	SO	SB	CS	OBP	SLG
2011	Eugene (NWL)	SS	.243	73	276	48	67	9	5	2	27	50	53	39	10	.360	.333
Minor League Totals			.243	73	276	48	67	9	5	2	27	50	53	39	10	.360	.333

18 REYMOND FUENTES, OF

BA GRADE
50
HIGH

Born: Feb. 12, 1991. **B-T:** l-l. **Ht.:** 6-0. **Wt.:** 160. **Drafted:** HS—Manati, P.R., 2009 (1st round). **Signed by:** Edgar Perez (Red Sox).

A cousin to six-time all-star Carlos Beltran, Fuentes became just the sixth Puerto Rican to be drafted in the first round when the Red Sox selected him 28th overall in 2009. He joined the Padres along with Anthony Rizzo and Casey Kelly in the trade that sent Adrian Gonzalez to Boston in December 2010. One of the youngest regulars in the California League last year, Fuentes showed plus speed and athleticism while stealing 41 bases, fourth-most in the circuit, but his game suffered from overall immaturity. He needs to focus on playing hard for an entire season, gaining strength and refining his skills as a leadoff batter. That means improving his pitch recognition, enhancing his on-base percentage, shortening his swing to hit more line drives and bunting for the occasional hit. He has below-average present power but could have decent pop once he fills out his 160-pound frame. Fuentes' speed plays well on the bases and in center field, where he glides to the ball with plus range. His arm grades as below-average. Fuentes' bat must improve for him to profile as more than second-division regular or a reserve. He could earn a promotion to Double-A with a solid spring training.

Year	Club (League)	Class	AVG	G	AB	R	H	2B	3B	HR	RBI	BB	SO	SB	CS	OBP	SLG
2009	Red Sox (GCL)	R	.290	40	145	16	42	6	2	1	14	7	24	9	5	.331	.379
2010	Greenville (SAL)	LoA	.270	104	374	59	101	15	5	5	41	25	87	42	5	.328	.377
2011	Lake Elsinore (CAL)	HiA	.275	124	510	84	140	15	9	5	45	44	117	41	14	.342	.369
Minor League Totals			.275	268	1029	159	283	36	16	11	100	76	228	92	24	.335	.373

19 EDINSON RINCON, 3B

BA GRADE
50
HIGH

Born: Aug. 11, 1990. **B-T:** R-R. **Ht.:** 6-1. **Wt.:** 221. **Signed:** Dominican Republic, 2007. **Signed by:** Randy Smith/Felix Francisco.

The Padres regard Rincon as a paradigm for their Latin American prospects because he manages the strike zone better than many players his age, foreign or domestic. He cracked 13 home runs in low Class A in 2010 but did so while hitting a meager .250 in 511 at-bats. Promoted to high Class A last year, he batted .336/.391/.509 with eight homers through the end of June, but a broken hamate bone in his left hand scuttled his second half. San Diego believes Rincon has at least average potential as a hitter. His strong swing features loft and produces consistent hard contact but also opens a hole in the upper regions of his strike zone. When he connects, he hits the ball as far as any Padres farmhand. Rincon is a third baseman in name only and faces a shift to an outfield corner or first base. A bottom-of-the-scale runner, he has stiff actions and slow feet at the hot corner.

He committed 18 errors in just 39 games at third last year, good for an .835 fielding average. Rincon's arm is strong but erratic. He'll head back to Lake Elsinore in 2012, partially in deference to Double-A third baseman Jedd Gyorko, and still has time on his side at age 21. San Diego added him to its 40-man roster in November.

Year	Club (League)	Class	AVG	G	AB	R	H	2B	3B	HR	RBI	BB	SO	SB	CS	OBP	SLG
2007	Padres (DSL)	R	.295	33	122	14	36	7	0	2	15	17	26	2	1	.383	.402
	Padres (AZL)	R	.178	15	45	6	8	1	0	0	0	7	11	0	0	.302	.200
2008	Padres (AZL)	R	.308	23	65	8	20	1	1	0	19	14	18	0	0	.429	.354
2009	Eugene (NWL)	SS	.300	70	267	47	80	18	3	7	47	46	60	5	0	.415	.468
2010	Fort Wayne (MWL)	LoA	.250	132	511	72	128	35	1	13	69	44	95	1	2	.315	.399
2011	Lake Elsinore (CAL)	HiA	.329	74	298	54	98	24	1	8	50	32	59	1	1	.394	.497
	Padres (AZL)	R	.300	3	10	0	3	0	0	0	1	1	1	0	0	.364	.300
Minor League Totals			.283	350	1318	201	373	86	6	30	201	161	270	9	4	.367	.426

20 JASON HAGERTY, C

Born: Sept. 13, 1987. **B-T:** B-R. **Ht.:** 6-3. **Wt.:** 220. **Drafted:** Miami, 2009 (5th round). **Signed by:** Rob Sidwell.

BA GRADE
50
HIGH

Hagerty didn't catch much during his final two years at Miami in deference to Yasmani Grandal, and his inexperience behind the plate often shines through. He spent the bulk of his first two pro seasons at the Class A level, while Grandal zoomed from the 12th overall pick in 2010 to Triple-A in the Reds system last year. Hagerty spent six weeks in Double-A at the conclusion of last season, but his bat slowed under the duress of catching 90 games. He threw out 30 percent of the 117 basestealers to test him, pairing average arm strength with a quick release and accuracy. He's often too rigid when receiving and blocking, and he may lack a catcher's prototypically soft hands. Hagerty will be forgiven his defensive lapses if he develops the 20-homer power of which he's capable. A switch-hitter, he shows a more discerning eye and makes more contact from the right side but has significantly more power from the left. Hagerty cracked all nine of his home runs and slugged .490 while batting lefthanded in 2011. He works deep counts and takes walks, but he doesn't run well or project to make enough contact to hit more than .260 or so. Hagerty profiles as a starting catcher because of his power, but most clubs would prefer a stronger defender in a backup role.

Year	Club (League)	Class	AVG	G	AB	R	H	2B	3B	HR	RBI	BB	SO	SB	CS	OBP	SLG
2009	Eugene (NWL)	SS	.225	47	173	34	39	12	0	6	26	26	47	0	0	.335	.399
	Portland (PCL)	AAA	.133	5	15	3	2	1	0	0	1	2	4	0	0	.235	.200
2010	Fort Wayne (MWL)	LoA	.302	122	431	74	130	35	3	14	74	88	104	2	1	.423	.494
2011	Lake Elsinore (CAL)	HiA	.311	68	257	53	80	25	2	8	47	26	62	3	2	.386	.518
	San Antonio (TL)	AA	.231	36	130	15	30	6	1	1	18	14	40	0	1	.318	.315
Minor League Totals			.279	278	1006	179	281	79	6	29	166	156	257	5	4	.383	.456

21 MATT LOLLIS, RHP

Born: Sept. 11, 1990. **B-T:** R-R. **Ht.:** 6-9. **Wt.:** 280. **Drafted:** Riverside (Calif.) CC, 2009 (15th round). **Signed by:** Pete DeYoung.

BA GRADE
50
HIGH

Signed for $100,000 out of the 15th round of the 2009 draft, Lollis zoomed to high Class A in time for the California League playoffs a year later. His fell off the pace with a return engagement to Lake Elsinore in 2011, running up a 5.57 ERA through 16 starts before landing in the Storm bullpen for most of July and August. As a reliever he posted a shiny 36-8 K-BB ratio but still compiled a 3.82 ERA. The 6-foot-9 Lollis pitches at 92-93 mph and peaks at 97 out of the bullpen, but his long levers lead to timing issues with his frontside arm action. He struggles to stay on line to the plate, alternately flying off toward first base or cutting his arm action off prematurely. Lollis' deep repertoire gives San Diego hope he can grow into a mid-rotation starter. His mid-70s knuckle-curve, low-80s slurve and changeup all have shown flashes of being average to a tick above. Some scouts outside the organization believe Lollis' future is in the bullpen, where he can focus on throwing mid-90s gas while sharpening only one of his secondary pitches.

Year	Club (League)	Class	W	L	ERA	G	GS	CG	SV	IP	H	HR	BB	SO	K/9	WHIP	AVG
2009	Padres (AZL)	R	0	0	5.19	6	0	0	0	9	11	1	2	7	7.3	1.50	.297
2010	Eugene (NWL)	SS	2	2	2.86	6	6	0	0	35	21	0	8	24	6.2	0.84	.175
	Fort Wayne (MWL)	LoA	5	2	1.66	9	9	0	0	54	47	3	13	45	7.5	1.10	.234
2011	Lake Elsinore (CAL)	HiA	4	8	5.35	31	19	0	1	119	135	12	45	114	8.6	1.51	.285
Minor League Totals			11	12	4.02	52	34	0	1	217	214	16	68	190	7.9	1.30	.257

22 DONAVAN TATE, OF

Born: Sept. 27, 1990. **B-T:** R-R. **Ht.:** 6-3. **Wt.:** 200. **Drafted:** HS—Cartersville, Ga., 2009 (1st round). **Signed by:** Ash Lawson.

BA GRADE
55
EXTREME

Tate pulled down a franchise-record $6.25 million bonus as the third overall pick in the 2009 draft, but he hasn't played enough subsequently to showcase his true abilities. Beset by injuries and other setbacks, he has played in just 64 pro games since signing. Tate sustained a sports hernia and a broken jaw after turning pro in 2009, and then concussion-like symptoms, a shoulder strain and a stomach virus in 2010. An assignment to Fort Wayne in 2011 lasted for six games until he collided with teammate Everett Williams and hyperextended his knee. His season later ended prematurely with a right wrist injury that sapped his power and required surgery. Tate also failed two drug tests in 2011, both related to synthetic marijuana. He served a 25-game suspension, and the penalty would have totaled 50 games had he not received half credit for attending substance-abuse counseling following the first failed test. When on the field, Tate still demonstrates the same plus raw tools he did as an amateur: bat speed, running speed, arm strength and center-field range. He swiped 19 bases and hit .288 while showing an improved ability to manage the strike zone. His bat tends to loop through the strike zone, so unless he corrects his path he may never hit for a high average. He'll take another pass at low Class A in 2012 and still has a shot at developing into productive regular.

Year	Club (League)	Class	AVG	G	AB	R	H	2B	3B	HR	RBI	BB	SO	SB	CS	OBP	SLG
2010	Padres (AZL)	R	.222	25	90	19	20	5	0	2	10	15	41	7	1	.336	.344
2011	Fort Wayne (MWL)	LoA	.316	6	19	3	6	2	0	0	2	4	3	2	2	.435	.421
	Eugene (NWL)	SS	.283	33	127	24	36	8	4	0	20	25	32	17	5	.406	.409
Minor League Totals			.263	64	236	46	62	15	4	2	32	44	76	26	8	.382	.386

23 PEDRO HERNANDEZ, LHP

BA GRADE
45
MEDIUM

Born: April 12, 1989. **B-T:** L-L. **Ht.:** 5-10. **Wt.:** 200. **Signed:** Venezuela, 2006. **Signed by:** Yfrain Linares.

The most obscure of the six players the Padres added to the 40-man roster in November, Hernandez always has shown a quality changeup and strong command. His prospect status began to take hold when his fastball velocity began to creep up halfway through the 2010 season. Signed at age 18 out of Venezuela, he initially topped out near 87 mph. He now touches 95 on occasion, sits in the low 90s and works both sides of the plate with a riding fastball. Batters don't see the ball well against the short and stocky Hernandez, which helps his low-80s changeup play up. His 78-82 mph slider/cutter doesn't elicit much praise, but it could be a fringy third offering in time. Hernandez may not have a deep enough repertoire to start in the big leagues, but he could grow into a nifty southpaw reliever capable of handling lefties and righties. After getting knocked around in four Triple-A starts last year, he'll return to Tucson at some point in 2012, perhaps to open the season.

Year	Club (League)	Class	W	L	ERA	G	GS	CG	SV	IP	H	HR	BB	SO	K/9	WHIP	AVG
2007	Padres (DSL)	R	0	1	2.03	9	0	0	1	13	12	1	4	13	8.8	1.20	.245
2008	Padres (DSL)	R	7	2	1.42	14	8	0	0	63	50	2	6	74	10.5	0.88	.216
2009	Padres (AZL)	R	4	0	3.78	7	5	0	0	33	33	2	4	31	8.4	1.11	.260
	Eugene (NWL)	SS	0	2	9.92	6	4	0	0	16	31	4	4	15	8.3	2.14	.408
2010	Fort Wayne (MWL)	LoA	4	3	4.04	29	13	0	0	100	122	6	17	79	7.1	1.39	.295
2011	Lake Elsinore (CAL)	HiA	5	0	2.70	15	6	0	0	57	52	3	6	44	7.0	1.02	.239
	Tucson (PCL)	AAA	2	1	6.00	4	4	0	0	18	28	3	6	7	3.5	1.89	.364
	San Antonio (TL)	AA	3	2	3.48	9	8	0	0	41	39	4	10	43	9.4	1.19	.245
Minor League Totals			25	11	3.55	93	48	0	1	343	367	25	57	306	8.0	1.24	.272

24 JEUDY VALDEZ, SS

BA GRADE
45
MEDIUM

Born: May 5, 1989. **B-T:** R-R. **Ht.:** 5-10. **Wt.:** 185. **Signed:** Dominican Republic, 2005. **Signed by:** Felix Francisco.

Valdez earned a spot on the Padres' 40-man roster following the 2010 season despite batting just .247/.302/.380 while repeating low Class A. His breadth of tools and positional flexibility tantalized San Diego and might have held similar cachet for other teams in the Rule 5 draft. Valdez started 2011 by hitting .211 through early May, then picked up the pace and batted .314/.361/.523 with 14 homers in 421 at-bats the rest of the way. He still struggles to identify breaking pitches from righthanders, so he doled out most of his damage versus lefties (1.130 OPS compared to .723 against righties). He finished the year with 59 extra-base hits and has more pop than most middle infielders. He's also an above-average runner who has racked up 34 steals in each of the past two seasons. Valdez slid over from second base to play shortstop full-time in 2011 for the first time since short-season ball. He made flashy plays on occasion, but stiff, robotic actions and concentration lapses led to a multitude of errors. Valdez finished with a lower fielding percentage (.941) than any Cal League regular, though his plus arm definitely plays on the left side of the infield. Any gains he makes in the batter's box this year in Double-A will improve his odds to become a regular middle infielder or hard-hitting utility player.

Year	Club (League)	Class	AVG	G	AB	R	H	2B	3B	HR	RBI	BB	SO	SB	CS	OBP	SLG
2006	Padres (DSL)	R	.238	47	168	29	40	7	2	0	10	15	44	12	6	.319	.304
2007	Padres (AZL)	R	.281	47	192	31	54	7	4	3	30	15	44	11	3	.346	.406
2008	Eugene (NWL)	SS	.227	59	216	35	49	10	2	5	22	18	64	3	4	.293	.361
2009	Fort Wayne (MWL)	LoA	.212	49	193	25	41	11	2	1	14	17	51	11	3	.283	.306
	Padres (AZL)	R	.318	12	44	8	14	3	2	0	6	6	10	3	2	.400	.477
2010	Fort Wayne (MWL)	LoA	.247	132	527	81	130	34	3	10	76	43	115	34	14	.302	.380
2011	Lake Elsinore (CAL)	HiA	.295	122	516	93	152	37	7	15	92	31	108	34	11	.339	.481
Minor League Totals			.259	468	1856	302	480	109	22	34	250	145	436	108	43	.318	.396

25 JOSE DePAULA, LHP

BA GRADE
45
MEDIUM

Born: March 4, 1990. **B-T:** L-L. **Ht.:** 6-1. **Wt.:** 170. **Signed:** Dominican Republic, 2006. **Signed by:** Felix Francisco.

Midwest League scouts regarded DePaula as Fort Wayne's top pitching prospect in 2010, but he struggled through the early going in 2011 after a promotion to high Class A. Through his first eight starts for Lake Elsinore, DePaula allowed 49 hits and 32 runs in 31 innings while pitching through shoulder soreness that ultimately landed him on the disabled list for two weeks. He pitched much more effectively for the final three months, going 7-2, 4.28 in 15 starts, so the Padres added him to the 40-man roster to shield him from the Rule 5 draft. It helped that he won both his California League playoff starts, tossing 13 shutout innings. When right, DePaula sits at 88-90 mph and tops out at 94 with his fastball, which plays up because his motion is smooth and effortless. His low-80s curveball features tight break at its best, though his changeup has further to go. DePaula's fastball/curve mix makes him a natural fit as a lefty situational reliever if his changeup doesn't develop. He held Cal League lefties to a .225/.275/.333 batting line last season and stands poised to tackle Double-A.

Year	Club (League)	Class	W	L	ERA	G	GS	CG	SV	IP	H	HR	BB	SO	K/9	WHIP	AVG
2007	Padres (DSL)	R	2	5	2.44	14	13	0	0	66	52	0	21	78	10.6	1.10	.208
2008	Padres (AZL)	R	4	3	3.57	13	13	0	0	53	61	2	9	56	9.5	1.32	.288
2009	Eugene (NWL)	SS	1	0	2.79	2	2	0	0	10	9	0	2	10	9.3	1.14	.243
2010	Fort Wayne (MWL)	LoA	8	5	3.27	20	14	0	0	85	71	7	20	69	7.3	1.07	.222
2011	Lake Elsinore (CAL)	HiA	10	5	5.22	26	23	0	0	112	129	4	37	87	7.0	1.48	.282
Minor League Totals			25	18	3.81	75	65	0	0	326	322	13	89	300	8.3	1.26	.252

26 ADYS PORTILLO, RHP

BA GRADE
55
EXTREME

Born: Dec. 21, 1991. **B-T:** R-R. **Ht.:** 6-2. **Wt.:** 240. **Signed:** Venezuela, 2008. **Signed by:** Yfrain Linares/Felix Feliz/Randy Smith.

The Padres won a bidding war for Portillo, signing the 16-year-old Venezuelan for $2 million in 2008 because they loved his big arm and projectable frame. They were right about his velocity (he touched 100 mph in 2011) and physicality (he has added 40 pounds since signing), though positive results have yet to materialize. He has gone 6-26, 5.83 in 51 pro appearances while walking 124 batters in 199 innings. He struck out a career-high 10.6 batters per nine innings in low Class A last year, but he also finished with a 1.75 WHIP. Portillo sits at 94-96 mph with his riding four-seam fastball, and he holds that velocity now that he has filled out his lower half. He can dominate with just his fastball when he hits his spots, but that can be a challenge because he so often falls out of his delivery, which also inhibits his ability to command his secondary stuff. He throws a slow, rolling curveball and a floating changeup, both of which have a long way to go to qualify even as below-average. San Diego simplified Portillo's mechanics in instructional league, streamlining his deliberate windup and outfitting him with a slider/cutter to replace the curve. He should be able to do a better job of working down in the zone if he stays more on line to the plate. Portillo turns 20 in 2012 and could earn a bump to high Class A given his encouraging turn in the Venezuelan League in the offseason. The Padres love his work ethic, and if he refines a second pitch and his control he could be a future closer candidate.

Year	Club (League)	Class	W	L	ERA	G	GS	CG	SV	IP	H	HR	BB	SO	K/9	WHIP	AVG
2009	Padres (AZL)	R	1	9	5.13	13	12	0	0	53	67	2	28	44	7.5	1.80	.321
2010	Eugene (NWL)	SS	2	6	4.79	14	14	0	0	62	55	2	40	62	9.0	1.53	.241
	Fort Wayne (MWL)	LoA	0	0	4.50	1	0	0	0	2	2	1	1	1	4.5	1.50	.286
2011	Fort Wayne (MWL)	LoA	3	11	7.11	23	20	0	0	82	89	10	55	97	10.6	1.75	.278
Minor League Totals			6	26	5.83	51	46	0	0	199	213	15	124	204	9.2	1.69	.279

27 MIKE KELLY, RHP

BA GRADE
50
HIGH

Born: Sept. 6, 1992. **B-T:** R-R. **Ht.:** 6-4. **Wt.:** 185. **Drafted:** HS—West Boca Raton, Fla., 2011 (1st round supplemental). **Signed by:** Willie Bosque.

Kelly played both ways at West Boca Raton (Fla.) High, but scouts determined that his tall, broad frame and arm strength were more suited to pitching at the professional level. Viewed as a sure-fire first-round pick heading into his senior year, he fell short of expectations as he struggled to stay tall in his delivery. Kelly's fastball hit 94 mph at times but sat mostly at 89-92, which coupled with inconsistent secondary pitches dropped him into the supplemental round in June. Taken 48th overall by the Padres, he signed for a slightly below-slot $718,000 after not completely passing his physical. He had a minor shoulder issue that didn't require surgery and isn't a long-term concern. Kelly shows the makings of curveball with depth but hasn't worked much with a changeup. Area scouts believed both could become average offerings because of his athleticism. Kelly hadn't recovered his high-end velocity by instructional league, so he's probably destined to begin 2012 in extended spring training and make his pro debut at Eugene in June.

Year	Club (League)	Class	W	L	ERA	G	GS	CG	SV	IP	H	HR	BB	SO	K/9	WHIP	AVG
2011	Did Not Play—Signed Late																

28 ANTHONY BASS, RHP

Born: Nov. 1, 1987. **B-T:** R-R. **Ht.:** 6-2. **Wt.:** 190. **Drafted:** Wayne State (Mich.), 2008 (5th round). **Signed by:** Jeff Stewart.

Bass topped the California League in ERA (3.13) and WHIP (1.09) in 2010, then handled the jump to Double-A well enough last season for San Diego to call him up for a spot start on June 13. He continues to add velocity in pro ball, working his way up to a steady 90-93 mph in a starting role—and he peaked at 96 coming out of the bullpen for the Padres in the second half of 2011. Bass also has improved a mid-80s slider that grades as average at times, but he hasn't taken to a changeup. He doesn't command either his fastball or slider well enough to escape being pigeonholed as a reliever. His delivery features a stabbing motion in the back, and some scouts believe this inhibits his ability to throw quality strikes. Bass kept the ball down in the big leagues but didn't miss many bats. If that pattern holds, he'll be relegated to a low-leverage relief role.

Year	Club (League)	Class	W	L	ERA	G	GS	CG	SV	IP	H	HR	BB	SO	K/9	WHIP	AVG
2008	Eugene (NWL)	SS	2	2	2.10	25	0	0	7	34	25	3	14	41	10.8	1.14	.197
2009	Fort Wayne (MWL)	LoA	9	3	2.19	18	18	0	0	90	79	5	25	69	6.9	1.15	.235
	Lake Elsinore (CAL)	HiA	3	0	3.51	10	8	0	0	33	33	3	14	20	5.4	1.41	.266
2010	Lake Elsinore (CAL)	HiA	8	7	3.13	27	27	0	0	132	124	9	20	109	7.4	1.09	.248
	Portland (PCL)	AAA	0	1	7.94	1	1	0	0	6	7	1	3	3	4.8	1.76	.333
2011	San Antonio (TL)	AA	6	4	3.75	13	13	0	0	70	62	6	21	62	8.0	1.19	.242
	Tucson (PCL)	AAA	1	0	1.80	1	1	0	0	5	6	0	0	3	5.4	1.20	.300
	San Diego (NL)	MAJ	2	0	1.68	27	3	0	0	48	41	3	21	24	4.5	1.28	.236
Major League Totals			2	0	1.68	27	3	0	0	48	41	3	21	24	4.5	1.28	.236
Minor League Totals			29	17	3.01	95	68	0	7	371	336	27	97	307	7.5	1.17	.243

29 BRAD BRACH, RHP

Born: April 12, 1986. **B-T:** R-R. **Ht.:** 6-6. **Wt.:** 210. **Drafted:** Monmouth, 2008 (42nd round). **Signed by:** Jim Bretz.

Brach's amazing journey from a 42nd-round pick who signed for $1,000 to a dominating minor league closer culminated in an Aug. 31 callup to San Diego. He set a California League record with 41 saves in 2010 and has converted 112 of 120 save chances (93 percent) in the minors with a sparkling 7.3 K-BB ratio. Brach works quickly and pitches from a three-quarters arm slot, pumping a heavy 92-93 mph fastball that reaches 95. His velocity has climbed dramatically since 2009, when he sat mostly at 88-90 with Fort Wayne. Brach throws across his body and short-arms the ball from the extreme third-base side of the rubber, providing a difficult look for righthanders. Batters from both sides of the plate saw Brach well in the big leagues, where he got touched for a .300 average. To remedy his problems he'll need to improve the quality of his short, low-80s slider or his splitter. Unless he can better his performance versus lefties, Brach probably fits best in middle relief.

Year	Club (League)	Class	W	L	ERA	G	GS	CG	SV	IP	H	HR	BB	SO	K/9	WHIP	AVG
2008	Padres (AZL)	R	1	1	2.01	17	0	0	4	22	21	0	5	33	13.3	1.16	.250
2009	Fort Wayne (MWL)	LoA	3	3	1.27	60	0	0	33	64	36	1	11	82	11.6	0.74	.164
2010	Lake Elsinore (CAL)	HiA	5	2	2.47	62	0	0	41	66	50	6	11	74	10.1	0.93	.207
2011	San Antonio (TL)	AA	2	2	2.25	42	0	0	23	44	32	3	5	64	13.1	0.84	.198
	Tucson (PCL)	AAA	1	3	3.90	25	0	0	11	28	28	1	7	30	9.8	1.27	.264
	San Diego (NL)	MAJ	0	2	5.14	9	0	0	0	7	9	0	7	11	14.1	2.29	.300
Major League Totals			0	2	5.14	9	0	0	0	7	9	0	7	11	14.1	2.29	.300
Minor League Totals			12	11	2.22	206	0	0	112	223	167	11	39	283	11.4	0.92	.205

30 VINCE BELNOME, 2B/1B

Born: March 11, 1988. **B-T:** L-R. **Ht.:** 5-11. **Wt.:** 205. **Drafted:** West Virginia, 2009 (28th round). **Signed by:** Adam Bourassa.

Belnome led the Northwest and California leagues in walks in his first two pro seasons, and he might have repeated the feat in the Texas League last year had he not suffered an abdominal injury. He hits the ball to all fields with a smooth lefty stroke and has plus pitch recognition, so he projects as at least an average hitter. Belnome's natural swing path takes the ball to left and center field, so he rarely pulls the ball for power, and he hit 13 of his first 14 homers for San Antonio to the opposite field. He's a below-average runner who played mostly third base until he reached San Antonio, where he shifted to second in deference to James Darnell and then Gyorko. Belnome is nothing special at either spot, though he has enough arm strength handle any infield post. He could serve a National League club as a regular pinch-hitter and roving infield sub.

Year	Club (League)	Class	AVG	G	AB	R	H	2B	3B	HR	RBI	BB	SO	SB	CS	OBP	SLG
2009	Eugene (NWL)	SS	.297	65	236	53	70	16	1	10	44	52	55	0	0	.431	.500
	Fort Wayne (MWL)	LoA	.500	10	32	4	16	3	1	0	10	4	5	1	0	.556	.656
2010	Lake Elsinore (CAL)	HiA	.273	135	498	81	136	31	1	16	84	102	136	4	1	.397	.436
2011	San Antonio (TL)	AA	.333	75	267	56	89	19	1	17	62	47	59	0	5	.432	.603
Minor League Totals			.301	285	1033	194	311	69	4	43	200	205	255	5	6	.418	.500

San Francisco Giants

BY ANDY BAGGARLY

The Giants officially remained in contention until the final week of the 2011 season, but for all practical purposes, their World Series rings were knocked off their fingers on May 25. That's when Buster Posey, their cleanup-hitting catcher and reigning National League rookie of the year, sustained three torn ankle ligaments and a fractured leg in a vicious home-plate collision with the Marlins' Scott Cousins.

Injuries would hit nearly all of San Francisco's starting position players, and those who remained healthy had major crashes in performance. The result was the lowest-scoring offense in the major leagues and a club malnourished for clutch hits.  The Giants hit .173 with two outs and runners in scoring position, the lowest figure by a big league team in the three decades for which data is available.

Even Carlos Beltran, viewed as the biggest bat on the trade market, missed three weeks with a hand injury after arriving in a July 27 deal. San Francisco was in first place on the day of the trade, but Beltran's impact wasn't felt until September, and by then the damage was done. The Giants went 11-18 in August, their most losses in a month in four years, and the Diamondbacks passed them to claim the NL West.

The Giants still managed to finish 86-76, almost solely because of a top-flight pitching staff that included a resurgent season from Tim Lincecum, another stalwart year from Matt Cain and a very solid first full campaign for Madison Bumgarner. The staff also witnessed the surprising emergence of first-time all-star Ryan Vogelsong, who returned from Japan to blossom 10 years after San Francisco traded him to the Pirates for Jason Schmidt.

But the rotation is getting more expensive to keep together, and the Giants' pitching factory under vice president of player personnel Dick Tidrow is beginning to stall. They sacrificed their only elite pitching prospect, Zack Wheeler, to the Mets for Beltran—who became a free agent after the season and can't bring draft-pick compensation because his contract forbid offering him arbitration.

The current strength of San Francisco's system is in position players, led by speedster Gary Brown and longball threat Tommy Joseph. Brandon Belt, who graduated to the majors in 2011, could make an impact for years to come.

However, the Giants don't have another can't-miss position player like Posey in the system. He's determined to catch again and club officials will relent to

After catcher Buster Posey was lost for the season, the Giants struggled to score runs

TOP 30 PROSPECTS

1. Gary Brown, of	**16.** Chris Dominguez, 3b
2. Tommy Joseph, c/1b	**17.** Ricky Oropesa, 1b
3. Heath Hembree, rhp	**18.** Chuckie Jones, of
4. Joe Panik, ss	**19.** Chris Marlowe, rhp
5. Francisco Peguero, of	**20.** Mike Kickham, lhp
6. Andrew Susac, c	**21.** Clayton Blackburn, rhp
7. Eric Surkamp, lhp	**22.** Jesus Galindo, of
8. Kyle Crick, rhp	**23.** Josh Osich, lhp
9. Ehire Adrianza, ss	**24.** Ray Black, rhp
10. Hector Sanchez, c	**25.** Stephen Harrold, rhp
11. Charlie Culberson, 2b	**26.** Adalberto Mejia, lhp
12. Brett Pill, 1b/2b	**27.** Roger Kieschnick, of
13. Conor Gillaspie, 3b	**28.** Adam Duvall, 3b
14. Hector Correa, rhp	**29.** Leonardo Fuentes, of
15. Jarrett Parker, of	**30.** Rafael Rodriguez, of

his wishes, but they've talked about moving their best hitter out of harm's way in the not too distant future. Catcher may be the richest position in the system, with Joseph, Susac and Hector Sanchez.

The farm system was a priority for managing partner Bill Neukom, who was forced out by other partners in a palace coup in September. In the new management structure, club president Larry Baer was elevated to CEO and will report directly to the investors. The reorganization wasn't expected to impact Brian Sabean, baseball's longest-tenured general manager with his current club.

General Manager: Brian Sabean. **Farm Director:** Fred Stanley. **Scouting Director:** John Barr.

Class	Team	League	W	L	Pct	Finish*	Manager(s)
Majors	San Francisco Giants	National	86	76	.531	6th (16)	Bruce Bochy
Triple-A	Fresno Grizzlies	Pacific Coast	65	79	.451	t-13th (16)	Steve Decker
Double-A	Richmond Flying Squirrels	Eastern	76	66	.535	3rd (12)	Dave Machemer
High A	San Jose Giants	California	90	50	.643	1st (10)	Andy Skeels
Low A	Augusta GreenJackets	South Atlantic	70	68	.507	7th (14)	Lipso Nava
Short-season	Salem-Keizer Volcanoes	Northwest	34	42	.447	7th (8)	Tom Trebelhorn
Rookie	AZL Giants	Arizona	41	15	.732	1st (13)	Mike Goff
Overall 2011 Minor League Record			376	320	.540	2nd (30)	

*Finish in overall standings (No. of teams in league). †League champion.

LAST YEAR'S TOP 30

Player, Pos.	Status
1. Brandon Belt, 1b/of	Majors
2. Zack Wheeler, rhp	(Mets)
3. Gary Brown, of	No. 1
4. Francisco Peguero, of	No. 5
5. Ehire Adrianza, ss	No. 9
6. Brandon Crawford, ss	Majors
7. Thomas Neal, of	(Indians)
8. Charlie Culberson, 2b	No. 11
9. Eric Surkamp, lhp	No. 7
10. Tommy Joseph, c/1b	No. 2
11. Rafael Rodriguez, of	No. 30
12. Jarrett Parker, of	No. 15
13. Jose Casilla, rhp	Dropped out
14. Roger Kieschnick, of	No. 27
15. Chris Dominguez, 3b	No. 16
16. Conor Gillaspie, 3b	No. 13
17. Mike Kickham, lhp	No. 20
18. Chuckie Jones, of	No. 18
19. Heath Hembree, rhp	No. 3
20. Jake Dunning, rhp	Dropped out
21. Jorge Bucardo, rhp	Dropped out
22. Jason Stoffel, rhp	(Astros)
23. Nick Noonan, 2b	Dropped out
24. Juan Perez, of	Dropped out
25. Ryan Verdugo, lhp	(Royals)
26. Ydwin Villegas, ss	Dropped out
27. Darren Ford, of	(Mariners)
28. Johnny Monell, c	Dropped out
29. Henry Sosa, rhp	(Astros)
30. Clayton Tanner, lhp	(Reds)

BEST TOOLS

Best Hitter for Average	Gary Brown
Best Power Hitter	Chris Dominguez
Best Strike-Zone Discipline	Conor Gillaspie
Fastest Baserunner	Gary Brown
Best Athlete	Gary Brown
Best Fastball	Heath Hembree
Best Curveball	Eric Surkamp
Best Slider	Stephen Harrold
Best Changeup	Eric Surkamp
Best Control	Eric Surkamp
Best Defensive Catcher	Hector Sanchez
Best Defensive Infielder	Ehire Adrianza
Best Infield Arm	Chris Dominguez
Best Defensive Outfielder	Gary Brown
Best Outfield Arm	Francisco Peguero

PROJECTED 2015 LINEUP

Catcher	Buster Posey
First Base	Tommy Joseph
Second Base	Joe Panik
Third Base	Pablo Sandoval
Shortstop	Brandon Crawford
Left Field	Brandon Belt
Center Field	Gary Brown
Right Field	Melky Cabrera
No. 1 Starter	Tim Lincecum
No. 2 Starter	Matt Cain
No. 3 Starter	Madison Bumgarner
No. 4 Starter	Kyle Crick
No. 5 Starter	Eric Surkamp
Closer	Brian Wilson

TOP PROSPECTS OF THE DECADE

Year	Player, Pos.	2011 Org.
2001	Jerome Williams, rhp	Angels
2002	Jerome Williams, rhp	Angels
2003	Jesse Foppert, rhp	Out of baseball
2004	Merkin Valdez, rhp	Rangers
2005	Matt Cain, rhp	Giants
2006	Matt Cain, rhp	Giants
2007	Tim Lincecum, rhp	Giants
2008	Angel Villalona, 3b/1b	Giants
2009	Madison Bumgarner, lhp	Giants
2010	Buster Posey, c	Giants
2011	Brandon Belt, 1b	Giants

TOP DRAFT PICKS OF THE DECADE

Year	Player, Pos.	2011 Org.
2001	Brad Hennessey, rhp	Astros
2002	Matt Cain, rhp	Giants
2003	David Aardsma, rhp	Mariners
2004	Eddy Martinez-Esteve, of (2nd round)	Mariners
2005	Ben Copeland, of (4th round)	Indians
2006	Tim Lincecum, rhp	Giants
2007	Madison Bumgarner, lhp	Giants
2008	Buster Posey, c	Giants
2009	Zack Wheeler, rhp	Mets
2010	Gary Brown, of	Giants
2011	Joe Panik, ss	Giants

LARGEST BONUSES IN CLUB HISTORY

Buster Posey, 2008	$6,200,000
Zack Wheeler, 2009	$3,300,000
Rafael Rodriguez, 2008	$2,550,000
Angel Villalona, 2006	$2,100,000
Tim Lincecum, 2006	$2,025,000

SAN FRANCISCO GIANTS

TOP 2012 ROOKIE: Heath Hembree, rhp. After leading the minors with 38 saves in his first full pro season, he could be helping set up games by midseason.

BREAKOUT PROSPECT: Mike Kickham, lhp. Blisters hampered him in his first extended taste of pro ball, but he's still a southpaw with a plus fastball/slider combination.

SLEEPER: Cody Hall, rhp. A 19th-round pick last June, he hit 95 mph and showed improved fastball command in instructional league.

SOURCE OF TOP 30 TALENT			
Homegrown	29	Acquired	1
College	17	Trades	1
Junior college	0	Rule 5 draft	0
High school	5	Independent leagues	0
Draft-and-follow	0	Free agents/waivers	0
Nondrafted free agents	0		
International	7		

LF
Leonardo Fuentes (29)
Nick Liles
Wendell Fairley
Justin Christian

CF
Gary Brown (1)
Chuckie Jones (18)
Jesus Galindo (22)
Juan Perez
Tyler Graham
Chris Lofton
Kentrell Hill

RF
Francisco Peguero (5)
Jarrett Parker (15)
Roger Kieschnick (27)
Rafael Rodriguez (30)
Christian Diaz
Brett Krill

3B
Conor Gillaspie (13)
Chris Dominguez (16)
Adam Duvall (28)
Jose Cuevas
Garrett Buechele

SS
Joe Panik (4)
Ehire Adrianza (9)
Carter Jurica
Ydwin Villegas
Kelby Tomlinson
Cristian Otero
Travious Relaford

2B
Charlie Culberson (11)
Ryan Cavan
Nick Noonan
Carlos Willoughby
Jean Delgado

1B
Brett Pill (12)
Ricky Oropesa (17)
Angel Villalona
Josh Mazzola
Luke Anders

C
Tommy Joseph (2)
Andrew Susac (6)
Hector Sanchez (10)
Johnny Monell
Joe Staley
Drew Stiner
Eric Sims
Jeff Arnold

LHP

LHSP	LHRP
Eric Surkamp (7)	Josh Osich (23)
Mike Kickham (20)	Bryce Bandilla
Adalberto Mejia (26)	Chuck Lofgren
	Aaron King

RHP

RHSP	RHRP
Kyle Crick (8)	Heath Hembree (3)
Clayton Blackburn (21)	Hector Correa (14)
Justin Fitzgerald	Chris Marlowe (19)
Seth Rosin	Ray Black (24)
Joan Gregorio	Stephen Harrold (25)
Shawn Sanford	Cody Hall
Chris Heston	Edward Concepcion
Daryl Maday	Jose Casilla
Michael Main	Steve Edlefsen
Derek Law	Jake Dunning
Kendry Flores	Brett Bochy
Joe Biagini	Jose Valdez
	Dan Otero
	Armando Paniagua
	Jacob Dunnington
	Reinier Roibal

2011   BONUSES: $6.3 MILLION

BEST PURE HITTER: SS Joe Panik (1) proved he could hit with wood when he batted .297 in the Cape Cod League in the summer of 2010, and he proved it again when he won the short-season Northwest League batting title with a .341 average in his pro debut. He makes consistent hard contact with a short lefthanded swing.

BEST POWER HITTER: C Andrew Susac (2) has more usable power than 1B Ricky Oropesa (3), who has more raw strength but also swings and misses a lot. They also starred in the Cape League in 2010, with Susac pacing the circuit in slugging (.500) and Oropesa tying for the lead in homers (seven).

FASTEST RUNNER: OF Kentrell Hill (10) and SS Travious Relaford (44) both have well above-average speed and can run the 60-yard dash in 6.5 seconds.

BEST DEFENSIVE PLAYER: Panik isn't flashy, but he's a reliable shortstop with good hands. SS Kelby Tomlinson (12) and Cristian Otero (18) may have better pure tools at the position. C Drew Stiner (43) has a plus-plus arm and solid receiving skills.

BEST FASTBALL: The Giants landed five pitchers in the first seven rounds who are capable of reaching 97 mph: RHPs Kyle Crick (1s), Chris Marlowe (5) and Ray Black (7) and LHPs Bryce Bandilla (4) and Josh Osich (6). Crick holds his velocity the longest and is the best bet of the group to remain a starter.

BEST SECONDARY PITCH: Marlowe has a hard breaking ball that tops out at 84 mph and generates swings and misses.

BEST PRO DEBUT: Panik was the NWL MVP and also led the league in runs (49), hits (82), RBIs (54) and total bases (126). OF Shawn Payne (35) led the league with a .431 on-base percentage and stole 21 bases. RHP Clayton Blackburn (16) had a 1.08 ERA and a 30-3 K-BB ratio in 33 innings in the Rookie-level Arizona League.

BEST ATHLETE: Hill and Relaford have arm strength to go with their speed, though they're works in progress at the plate.

MOST INTRIGUING BACKGROUND: 3B Garrett Buechele's (14) father Steve and Relaford's cousin Desi each played 11 seasons in the big leagues. Unsigned 2B Benny Sosnick's (49) brother Matt is an agent.

CLOSEST TO THE MAJORS: Panik. Bandilla, Marlowe and Black could move fast as relievers.

BEST LATE-ROUND PICK: Blackburn got lost in the shadow of an extraordinary crop of Oklahoma high school pitchers this spring, but area scout Daniel Murray and crosschecker Arnold Brathwaite did a nice job of staying on him and gauging his signability.

Inked for $150,000, Blackburn throws four pitches for strikes, including a 91-93 mph sinker.

THE ONE WHO GOT AWAY: RHP Tyler Leslie (15), who's raw but can reach 94 mph, headed to the JC of Southern Nevada. RHP Andrew Triggs (21), a sinker/slider guy, shocked San Francisco by opting to pursue a master's degree at Southern California instead of turning pro.

ASSESSMENT: Despite not picking until No. 29 overall, the Giants got a pair of potential quality up-the-middle regulars in Panik and Susac, and supplemented them with a promising group of power arms.

2010   BONUSES: $4.1 MILLION

OF Gary Brown (1) should be patrolling center field at AT&T Park in the very near future. RHP Heath Hembree (5) led the minors with 38 saves last year and could beat him to San Francisco.

GRADE: B+

2009   BONUSES: $6.3 MILLION

The Giants got two potential blue-chip talents in RHP Zack Wheeler (1) and OF/1B Brandon Belt (5), though they may rue trading Wheeler for Carlos Beltran last summer. C/1B Tommy Joseph (2) made impressive strides offensively and defensively in 2011.

GRADE: B+

2008   BONUSES: $9.1 MILLION

C Buster Posey (1) led San Francisco to a 2010 World Series title as a rookie, and his future is no less bright even after a broken leg ruined his encore. 3B Conor Gillaspie (1s), SS Brandon Crawford (4) and LHP Eric Surkamp (6) all have reached the majors and could be solid contributors.

GRADE: A

2007   BONUSES: $7.4 MILLION

The Giants had six picks before the second round and may hit on just one of them, but that one was LHP Madison Bumgarner (1). They also used RHP Tim Alderson (1) in a deal for Freddy Sanchez before Alderson's value nose-dived. 2B Charlie Culberson (1s) is one of the system's grittiest players, while LHPs Dan Runzler (9) and Joe Paterson (10, lost in the Rule 5 draft) and RHP Steve Edlefsen made it to the majors as relievers.

GRADE: A

Draft analysis by Jim Callis. Numbers in parentheses indicate draft rounds.

1 GARY BROWN, OF

Born: Sept. 28, 1988. **B-T:** R-R. **Ht.:** 6-0. **Wt.:** 185.
Drafted: Cal State Fullerton, 2010 (1st round).
Signed by: Brad Cameron.

BA GRADE
60
MEDIUM

LARRY GOREN

How much does Giants GM Brian Sabean value Brown? When the Mets asked for the speedy center fielder in exchange for Carlos Beltran in July, Sabean parted with top pitching prospect Zack Wheeler instead. The 24th overall pick in the 2010 draft and recipient of a $1.45 million bonus, Brown certainly enhanced his worth with a smashing first full pro season. He played in the Futures Game, batted .336 at San Jose and set a franchise record with a California League-leading 188 hits. He established himself as a force atop the lineup, stealing 53 bases while knocking in 80 runs from the leadoff spot. He also crushed lefthanders (.459/.531/.685). Brown starred despite entering 2011 with just a dozen games of pro experience after signing at the Aug. 16 deadline the year before. "A lot of guys have talent, but you wonder if they're going to show up to play every day," San Jose manager Andy Skeels said. "Gary certainly did. He competes and he finds ways to beat you. That, to me, weighs very favorably and heavily on whether he'll have what it takes to succeed at the major league level."

Choking up on the bat and with his hands pinned against his side, Brown sets up like a slap hitter. But he loads quickly, has explosive wrists and bat speed, loves to shoot the gaps and flashes surprising pull power. His value, though, is in his ability to make consistent contact and to wreak havoc when he gets on base. He's a true 80 runner on the 20-80 scouting scale. Brown expressed disappointment that he was caught stealing 19 times in 2011, saying he improved later in the season after working on his slide mechanics. San Francisco would like to see him work on his bunting skills, as well as recognize when a pitcher is wild and work deeper counts more consistently, which should lead to more walks. For a leadoff man, Brown has a knack for producing with runners on base, though sometimes his aggressiveness works against him when he neglects to use the opposite field. Coaches believe he has the talent and smarts to make adjustments as he faces higher-level pitching. Brown's speed also is a huge asset in center field, where he can play shallow because of his ability to go back on balls over his head. His arm strength is a tick above average and his throws are accurate. He gunned down four runners at the plate for San Jose

Brown remained in high Class A, even though it was apparent by late April that he could have handled a quick promotion like Buster Posey and Brandon Belt had in previous years. He struggled over 11 games in the Arizona Fall League, hitting .220/.278/.300. Following the Giants' November trade for Melky Cabrera, they figure to continue to avoid rushing Brown. He'll likely start 2012 at Double-A Richmond, though if he gets off to a hot start again, San Francisco won't hesitate to promote him to Triple-A Fresno. If the Giants contend again, he's a candidate for a callup in September—if not earlier—to provide some energy with his speed. By 2013, Brown should push Cabrera to an outfield corner and become a fixture in center field and the leadoff spot for San Francisco for years to come.

SCOUTING GRADES

Batting: 60. **Defense:** 70.
Power: 40. **Arm:** 55.
Speed: 80.

Based on 20-80 scouting scale, where 50 represents major league average, and future projection rather than present tools.

Year	Club (League)	Class	AVG	G	AB	R	H	2B	3B	HR	RBI	BB	SO	SB	CS	OBP	SLG
2010	Giants (AZL)	R	.182	6	22	6	4	1	0	0	0	4	5	2	0	.333	.227
	Salem-Keizer (NWL)	SS	.136	6	22	2	3	0	1	0	2	2	7	0	1	.259	.227
2011	San Jose (CAL)	HiA	.336	131	559	115	188	34	13	14	80	46	77	53	19	.407	.519
Minor League Totals			.323	143	603	123	195	35	14	14	82	52	89	55	20	.398	.498

2 TOMMY JOSEPH, C/1B

Born: July 16, 1991. **B-T:** R-R. **Ht.:** 6-1. **Wt.:** 210. **Drafted:** HS—Scottsdale, Ariz., 2009 (2nd round). **Signed by:** Chuck Hensley.

Joseph was one of the best power-hitting prospects in the 2009 draft and signed for an over-slot $712,500 in the second round. After a lackluster 2010 pro debut, Joseph did better offensively after jumping to high Class A in 2011. More impressively, he made major defensive improvements, earning San Jose's defensive player of the year award and leading the California League by throwing out 37 percent of basestealers. Joseph's short, direct swing generates plenty of backspin and gives him plus power to all fields. He needs to improve his approach and plate discipline in order to cut down on his strikeouts and hit for a higher average. His power will play at first base, where he has seen time, but Joseph now looks like he'll be able to stay at catcher after making huge strides blocking balls and cleaning up his footwork. He has plus arm strength and accuracy but just an average

BA GRADE
55
MEDIUM

BARRY COLLA

release. Giants coaches say his acumen and game-calling skills might be second only to Buster Posey in the organization. Joseph is a below-average runner but his lack of speed is easier to overlook if he remains behind the plate. If San Francisco decides to move Posey to a less grueling position, Joseph has the tools to take over behind the plate. If not, he can fit in the lineup at first base. He'll begin 2012 in Double-A.

Year	Club (League)	Class	AVG	G	AB	R	H	2B	3B	HR	RBI	BB	SO	SB	CS	OBP	SLG
2010	Augusta (SAL)	LoA	.236	117	436	46	103	22	1	16	68	26	116	0	0	.290	.401
2011	San Jose (CAL)	HiA	.270	127	514	80	139	33	2	22	95	29	102	1	0	.317	.471
Minor League Totals			.255	244	950	126	242	55	3	38	163	55	218	1	0	.304	.439

3 HEATH HEMBREE, RHP

Born: Jan. 13, 1989. **B-T:** R-R. **Ht.:** 6-4. **Wt.:** 205. **Drafted:** College of Charleston, 2010 (5th round). **Signed by:** Jeremy Cleveland.

Hembree lasted until the fifth round of the 2010 draft because he didn't have much of a track record with scouts. He missed his senior year of high school after tearing up his knee playing football and pitched just 29 innings in two seasons of NCAA Division I baseball (South Carolina in 2008, College of Charleston in 2010) sandwiched around one at Spartanburg Methodist (S.C.) JC. In his first full pro season, he led the minors with 38 saves and reached Double-A. Hembree consistently works at 93-96 mph without having to muscle the ball. His fastball has explosive movement and he likes to work up the ladder, overpowering hitters at the letters. His slider has the makings of a plus pitch, while his changeup is a work in progress. Hembree won't get away with as many mistakes

BA GRADE
55
MEDIUM

BARRY COLLA

up in the zone against big leaguers, and he'll have to throw more strikes. He maintains his composure on the mound, a good attribute for a future closer. Hembree's stuff and cool under pressure demeanor have prompted the Giants to compare him to Brian Wilson. He has an easygoing personality and probably wears socks that actually match, so he's no Wilson clone, but he's likely to be pitching in meaningful, late-inning situations in the near future. Hembree will open 2012 in the minors but could be setting up Wilson by the all-star break.

Year	Club (League)	Class	W	L	ERA	G	GS	CG	SV	IP	H	HR	BB	SO	K/9	WHIP	AVG
2010	Giants (AZL)	R	0	0	0.82	12	0	0	3	11	9	0	0	22	18.0	0.82	.220
2011	San Jose (CAL)	HiA	0	0	0.73	26	0	0	21	25	16	1	12	44	16.1	1.14	.182
	Richmond (EL)	AA	1	1	2.83	28	0	0	17	29	20	1	13	34	10.7	1.15	.194
Minor League Totals			1	1	1.68	66	0	0	41	64	45	2	25	100	14.0	1.09	.194

4 JOE PANIK, SS

Born: Oct. 30, 1990. **B-T:** L-R. **Ht.:** 6-1. **Wt.:** 195. **Drafted:** St. John's, 2011 (1st round). **Signed by:** John DiCarlo.

Panik signed for $1,116,000 just days after the Giants drafted him 29th overall last June. He took the field seemingly trying to prove a point to scouts who felt he was an overdraft, winning short-season Northwest League MVP honors and earning a spot in the Arizona Fall League's Rising Stars Game. He led the NWL in hitting (.341), runs (49), hits (82), RBIs (54) and total bases (126). Panik's bat is his only standout tool and his intelligence and competitiveness make up for the rest. He's aggressive early in the count but very disciplined with two strikes. He has terrific bat control and reads pitchers well. He crowds the plate and jumps on pitchers who try to pound him inside, showing solid gap power. Some scouts think Panik profiles better as a second baseman, but he has good hands and positions himself well. His arm isn't a cannon, but his throws have good carry

BA GRADE
55
MEDIUM

along with tremendous accuracy. He's an average runner but is sharp-witted on the bases too—no surprise for a player who had a 3.81 GPA as a finance major. San Francisco would love for Panik to take over second base in 2013 after Freddy Sanchez's contract expires. Panik will stay at shortstop in his first full pro season, likely jumping to high Class A to begin the year.

Year	Club (League)	Class	AVG	G	AB	R	H	2B	3B	HR	RBI	BB	SO	SB	CS	OBP	SLG
2011	Salem-Keizer (NWL)	SS	.341	69	270	49	92	10	3	6	54	28	25	13	5	.401	.467
Minor League Totals			.341	69	270	49	92	10	3	6	54	28	25	13	5	.401	.467

5 FRANCISCO PEGUERO, OF

Born: June 1, 1988. **B-T:** R-R. **Ht.:** 5-11. **Wt.:** 186. **Signed:** Dominican Republic, 2006 **Signed by:** Pablo Peguero.

BARRY COLLA

BA GRADE

55

MEDIUM

The most tooled-up player in the system, Peguero missed nearly two months in 2011 after requiring arthroscopic surgery on his left knee at the close of spring training. He batted .312/.332/.445 when he returned, nearly matching his previous career numbers, and was running much better by season's end. Peguero goes to the plate in attack mode. He covers the zone well and doesn't get overpowered by premium velocity. His hyper-aggressiveness figures to be exploited as he advances, so it's important that he learns to work counts and hunt pitches. Peguero hasn't hit many homers in the minors, but the ball jumps off his bat and his power is still emerging. The Giants moved him from center to right field, where his well above-average arm is a terrific fit, in 2011. He's a plus defender and started to play with more confidence on his knee later in the year, taking more aggressive angles on balls. Dave Machemer, who managed him two years apart in low Class A and Double-A, says Peguero is a dramatically improved player with much greater on-field awareness. If he continues to file away the rough edges, he could be an asset at AT&T Park, where right field is extra tricky. He made up some at-bats in the Dominican Winter League and will head to Triple-A in April.

Year	Club (League)	Class	AVG	G	AB	R	H	2B	3B	HR	RBI	BB	SO	SB	CS	OBP	SLG
2006	Giants (DSL)	R	.275	56	182	24	50	10	3	4	16	6	37	3	2	.307	.429
2007	Giants (DSL)	R	.294	69	235	51	69	12	2	1	17	15	39	25	5	.341	.374
2008	Augusta (SAL)	LoA	.261	50	180	23	47	2	4	2	15	12	43	15	1	.309	.350
	Salem-Keizer (NWL)	SS	.307	50	202	33	62	11	4	2	28	9	43	10	3	.349	.431
2009	Salem-Keizer (NWL)	SS	.394	17	71	14	28	3	1	0	12	3	9	7	0	.421	.465
	Augusta (SAL)	LoA	.340	58	238	28	81	12	4	1	34	5	39	15	5	.359	.437
2010	San Jose (CAL)	HiA	.329	122	510	78	168	19	16	10	77	18	88	40	22	.358	.488
2011	San Jose (CAL)	HiA	.324	16	68	12	22	2	0	2	9	7	8	4	0	.387	.441
	Richmond (EL)	AA	.309	71	285	34	88	12	6	5	37	5	45	8	1	.318	.446
Minor League Totals			.312	509	1971	297	615	83	40	27	245	80	351	127	39	.344	.436

6 ANDREW SUSAC, C

Born: March 22, 1990. **B-T:** R-R. **Ht.:** 6-1. **Wt.:** 200. **Drafted:** Oregon State, 2011 (2nd round). **Signed by:** Matt Woodward.

BA GRADE

55

MEDIUM

Susac wrote a paper in grade school about how his dream job would be to play for the Giants. By the time he was a standout at Sacramento's Jesuit High, the feeling was mutual. He was set on attending Oregon State, so San Francisco didn't get him until 2011. Considered the top college catcher available and a potential first-rounder, he lasted 86 picks after he fractured the hamate bone in his left wrist and floated a big price tag. He signed for $1.1 million—just $16,000 less than first-rounder Joe Panik. Employing a high leg kick, Susac has plus power and generates the kinds of backspin home runs that keep carrying until they clear the fence. But he tends to turn out his hips as he loads and jumps at the ball, which will lead to strikeouts on breaking pitches until he makes adjustments. Susac profiles as a solid defensive catcher with above-average arm strength. He's athletic for a catcher, with quick feet and average speed. Though he signed at the Aug. 15 deadline and hasn't made his pro debut, Susac likely firmed up an assignment to high Class A with an impressive stint in instructional league. With plenty of catching in the system ahead of him, there's no need to put Susac on the fast track. His performance may force the issue anyway.

Year	Club (League)	Class	AVG	G	AB	R	H	2B	3B	HR	RBI	BB	SO	SB	CS	OBP	SLG
2011	Did Not Play—Signed Late																

7 ERIC SURKAMP, LHP

Born: July 16, 1987. **B-T:** L-L. **Ht.:** 6-5. **Wt.:** 220. **Drafted:** North Carolina State, 2008 (6th round). **Signed by:** Pat Portugal.

Surkamp was zooming toward the Double-A Eastern League's pitching triple crown in August when the Giants suddenly needed a starter for the pennant race after Jonathan Sanchez sprained his ankle. Surkamp gave up one run in six innings in his first big league start against the Astros, then beat the Padres twice before badly losing his command in his final three outings. He didn't make it out of the first inning on Sept. 24, when the defending World Series champions officially were eliminated at Arizona. Surkamp's fastball sits in the upper 80s and touches 91, but he had success with it in Double-A because he attacked hitters inside—something he didn't do enough in the big leagues. His two-seamer tails and sinks and induces groundballs. He uses his plus curveball with two strikes to finish off hitters and his solid changeup plays well against righthanders. Surkamp also continues to experiment with a cutter. The key to his success is his ability to locate his pitches. After surgery in 2010 to repair a torn labrum in his hip, he has re-established himself as a durable presence. GM Brian Sabean said after the season that Surkamp wasn't ready for the majors. A solid back-of-the-rotation starter for the future, he'll hone his craft in Triple-A to begin 2012.

BA GRADE 50 LOW

Year	Club (League)	Class	W	L	ERA	G	GS	CG	SV	IP	H	HR	BB	SO	K/9	WHIP	AVG
2008	Giants (AZL)	R	0	0	2.70	2	0	0	0	3	3	0	0	7	18.9	0.90	.231
	Salem-Keizer (NWL)	SS	0	2	6.43	5	4	0	0	14	20	1	5	16	10.3	1.79	.351
2009	Augusta (SAL)	LoA	11	5	3.30	23	23	2	0	131	129	6	39	169	11.6	1.28	.257
2010	San Jose (CAL)	HiA	4	2	3.11	17	17	1	0	101	79	5	22	108	9.6	1.00	.218
2011	Richmond (EL)	AA	10	4	2.02	23	22	1	0	142	110	5	44	165	10.4	1.08	.213
	San Jose (CAL)	HiA	1	0	0.00	1	1	0	0	6	4	0	1	5	7.5	0.83	.190
	San Francisco (NL)	MAJ	2	2	5.74	6	6	0	0	27	32	1	17	13	4.4	1.84	.311
Major League Totals			2	2	5.74	6	6	0	0	27	32	1	17	13	4.4	1.84	.311
Minor League Totals			26	13	2.85	71	67	4	0	398	345	17	111	470	10.6	1.15	.234

8 KYLE CRICK, RHP

Born: Nov. 30, 1992. **B-T:** L-R. **Ht.:** 6-4. **Wt.:** 225. **Drafted:** HS—Sherman, Texas, 2011 (1st round supplemental). **Signed by:** Todd Thomas.

The Giants are seldom wrong when they spend a high draft pick on a high school pitcher. Crick, a 2011 sandwich pick who signed for $900,000, has every bit as much projection as Matt Cain did nearly a decade ago. Not only does he have size and athleticism, but Crick also has a low-mileage arm. He didn't concentrate on pitching until his senior season, spending more time as a first baseman and a defensive end in football. Crick's fastball already sits easily in the low 90s and reaches as high as 97, and he has the chance to throw even harder once he cleans up his delivery and gets more on line to the plate. He has long, powerful legs and uses them to drive off the mound. His slider is his best secondary pitch, though it features more sweep than bite. At times he throws a curveball with good depth and tilt, but not consistently for strikes. His changeup is in the early stages and he also has tried throwing a forkball. His command is a work in progress as well. Though the young Texan is a long ways off, with Zack Wheeler gone in the Carlos Beltran trade, Crick is the best power arm in a system that usually knows what to do with them. He has the ceiling of a No. 2 starter.

BA GRADE 55 HIGH

BILL MITCHELL

Year	Club (League)	Class	W	L	ERA	G	GS	CG	SV	IP	H	HR	BB	SO	K/9	WHIP	AVG
2011	Giants (AZL)	R	1	0	6.43	7	0	0	0	7	9	0	8	8	10.3	2.43	.321
Minor League Totals			1	0	6.43	7	0	0	0	7	9	0	8	8	10.3	2.43	.321

9 EHIRE ADRIANZA, SS

Born: August 21, 1989. **B-T:** B-R. **Ht.:** 6-0. **Wt.:** 168. **Signed:** Venezuela, 2006. **Signed by:** Ciro Villalobos.

Adrianza, the nephew of Marlins manager Ozzie Guillen, turned a tough 2011 season into a positive. He needed surgery after tearing a left thumb ligament while sliding into a base toward the end of spring training. He didn't take the field until mid-May and hit worse at low Class A Augusta than he had in 2009. He fared better once he got to San Jose, hitting .300/.375/.470 after batting .256/.333/.348 there in 2010. There never has been any doubt that Adrianza can be a star defender with his plus range, soft hands, ultra-quick transfer and accurate arm. His bat continues to be the question. Adrianza needs to add strength, though he doesn't get the lumber knocked out of his hands. He can turn around a fastball from his natural right side but lengthens his swing from the left, where he tries to rotate and cheat on pitches on the inner half of the plate. He draws his share of walks but needs to make more contact considering his lack of power. He's an average runner with smarts on the basepaths and a quick first step. With another plus defender, Brandon Crawford, ahead of him in organization, Adrianza will need to progress quickly at Double-A in 2012 carve out a place as an everyday player in majors. Otherwise, he'll end up as a defense-first utilityman.

BA GRADE 50 MEDIUM

Year	Club (League)	Class	AVG	G	AB	R	H	2B	3B	HR	RBI	BB	SO	SB	CS	OBP	SLG
2006	Giants (DSL)	R	.156	44	122	17	19	2	1	0	7	24	31	3	2	.311	.189
2007	Giants (DSL)	R	.241	66	249	44	60	17	2	0	30	41	31	23	6	.351	.325
2008	Fresno (PCL)	AAA	.500	2	6	2	3	1	0	0	0	2	1	0	0	.625	.667
	Giants (AZL)	R	.255	15	55	13	14	4	0	1	6	7	4	0	1	.349	.382
	Salem-Keizer (NWL)	SS	.400	1	5	3	2	0	0	0	0	0	1	0	0	.400	.400
2009	Augusta (SAL)	LoA	.258	117	388	54	100	15	3	2	46	42	66	7	1	.333	.327
2010	San Jose (CAL)	HiA	.256	124	445	70	114	22	5	3	35	47	87	33	15	.333	.348
2011	Augusta (SAL)	LoA	.231	38	143	18	33	10	1	3	17	18	32	3	2	.315	.378
	San Jose (CAL)	HiA	.300	56	230	34	69	24	3	3	27	23	46	5	1	.375	.470
Minor League Totals			.252	463	1643	255	414	95	15	12	168	204	299	74	28	.340	.350

10 HECTOR SANCHEZ, C

Born: Nov. 17, 1989. **B-T:** S-R. **Ht.:** 5-11. **Wt.:** 225. **Signed:** Venezuela, 2006. **Signed by:** Ciro Villalobos.

No player moved through the system in 2011 quicker than Sanchez, an intriguing switch-hitter with ever-improving receiving skills. He began the year in high Class A, was aggressively promoted to Triple-A in mid-June and made his big league debut a month later while the Giants were desperate to audition catchers following Buster Posey's season-ending leg injury. Sanchez wasn't ready for full-time duty in the majors but held his own. Sanchez has a strong body and solid defensive ability. He has above-average arm strength, a quick release and good accuracy, enabling him to post 1.9-second pop times and erase 34 percent of basestealers in 2011. He blocks balls well and though his English is limited, pitchers enjoy throwing to him. A better hitter from the left side, Sanchez has an advanced two-strike approach and trusts his hands to let the ball get deep. He doesn't get fooled by quality breaking stuff. Though he makes consistent contact, he possesses just gap power and doesn't run well. He may not be another Posey and he may lack the high ceiling of Tommy Joseph or Andrew Susac. But Sanchez profiles well as a big league backup who can contribute offensively and defensively, and he could fill that role in 2012.

BA GRADE 50 MEDIUM

Year	Club (League)	Class	AVG	G	AB	R	H	2B	3B	HR	RBI	BB	SO	SB	CS	OBP	SLG
2007	Giants (DSL)	R	.286	44	119	10	34	10	0	4	18	19	15	2	2	.401	.471
2008	Giants (DSL)	R	.348	55	207	40	72	14	3	4	63	36	29	4	1	.458	.502
2009	Giants (AZL)	R	.299	33	117	13	35	8	1	1	22	16	21	0	0	.403	.410
2010	Augusta (SAL)	LoA	.274	89	310	29	85	20	1	5	31	28	50	0	2	.336	.394
2011	Fresno (PCL)	AAA	.261	46	153	15	40	9	0	1	26	13	22	0	1	.315	.340
	San Jose (CAL)	HiA	.302	52	212	31	64	14	1	11	58	11	49	0	1	.338	.533
	San Francisco (NL)	MAJ	.258	13	31	0	8	2	0	0	1	3	6	0	0	.324	.323
Major League Totals			.258	13	31	0	8	2	0	0	1	3	6	0	0	.324	.323
Minor League Totals			.295	319	1118	138	330	75	6	26	218	123	186	6	7	.373	.443

11 CHARLIE CULBERSON, 2B

BA GRADE 50 MEDIUM

Born: April 10, 1989. **B-T:** R-R. **Ht.:** 6-1. **Wt.:** 191. **Drafted:** HS—Calhoun, Ga., 2007 (1st round supplemental). **Signed by:** Sean O'Connor.

Culberson's father Charles was the Giants' 16th-round pick in 1984 and coached in the

White Sox system. His grandfather Leon played in the major leagues, and he's also related to the Sislers (Hall of Famer George, former all-star Dick, big leaguer Dave). Culberson's baseball bloodlines manifest themselves in his hard-nosed approach and competitiveness. He looks the part of a big leaguer and coaches love the way he comes to play every day. A surprise supplemental first-round pick in 2007, Culberson had a breakout 2010 season in high Class A but had a rough transition to Double-A last year. He responded by working harder and was instrumental in helping Richmond reach the Eastern League finals as a wild-card team. Culberson is a streaky hitter who rakes against lefties but misses fastballs and overstrides when he goes cold. He has trouble laying off sliders even when he's in a hot streak, and he's aggressive to a fault. When everything falls into place, the ball jumps off his bat. Despite average speed, he is an opportunistic runner with good instincts on the bases. After struggling at shortstop and third base earlier in his pro career, Culberson has found his niche at second base. He's a solid defender with better arm strength and ability to turn double plays than most players at his position. Culberson might require a little more time to blossom, but scouts like his body, strength and aptitude. Though he still has youth on his side, he'll need to make progress to avoid being passed by 2011 first-rounder Joe Panik. Added to the 40-man roster in November, Culberson may repeat Double-A at the beginning of 2012.

Year	Club (League)	Class	AVG	G	AB	R	H	2B	3B	HR	RBI	BB	SO	SB	CS	OBP	SLG
2007	Giants (AZL)	R	.286	46	161	32	46	8	5	1	16	19	38	19	1	.374	.416
2008	Augusta (SAL)	LoA	.234	81	282	31	66	11	2	3	27	18	57	6	6	.290	.319
2009	Augusta (SAL)	LoA	.246	132	509	71	125	19	3	2	36	33	110	15	4	.303	.306
2010	San Jose (CAL)	HiA	.290	128	503	80	146	28	4	16	71	33	99	25	5	.340	.457
2011	Richmond (EL)	AA	.259	137	553	69	143	34	2	10	56	22	129	14	4	.293	.382
Minor League Totals			.262	524	2008	283	526	100	16	32	206	125	433	79	22	.314	.375

12 BRETT PILL, 1B/2B

Born: Sept. 9, 1984. **B-T:** R-R. **Ht.:** 6-3. **Wt.:** 233. **Drafted:** Cal State Fullerton, 2006 (7th round). **Signed by:** Ray Krawczyk.

Pill was a lightly regarded prospect who pushed his way onto the Giants' 40-man roster by driving in 109 runs in Double-A in 2009. When he had an unremarkable Triple-A season in 2010, San Francisco designated him for assignment and he went unclaimed on waivers. Pill responded by forcing the issue yet again, hitting a career-high 25 homers and driving in 107 runs when he returned to Fresno last year. The run-starved Giants were so motivated to carve out a September roster space for Pill that they released outfielder Aaron Rowand and ate the $14 million owed him. Pill didn't disappoint, becoming just the second player in franchise history to homer in each of his first two big league games. He's a durable performer who has a simple swing, easy power and the ability to make consistent contact. He's an advanced hitter who uses the whole field in RBI situations. He likes to get his arms extended and will have to make adjustments to inside pitches. He also could stand to draw more walks and do a better job of recognizing pitches beneath the strike zone. Pill runs well for a big man once he gets going. He's an above-average first baseman with good actions and soft hands. He played some second base at Fresno, but he's little more than an emergency option there. With Brandon Belt and Aubrey Huff in the big leagues, San Francisco isn't sure how Pill will fit in the near future. But they certainly won't remove him from 40-man roster again. The Mets drafted his brother Tyler, a righthander, in the fourth round last June.

Year	Club (League)	Class	AVG	G	AB	R	H	2B	3B	HR	RBI	BB	SO	SB	CS	OBP	SLG
2006	Salem-Keizer (NWL)	SS	.220	60	223	37	49	16	0	5	35	22	39	3	2	.296	.359
2007	Augusta (SAL)	LoA	.269	137	536	72	144	47	1	10	91	38	81	4	2	.321	.416
2008	San Jose (CAL)	HiA	.266	131	458	73	122	32	0	9	65	33	85	5	2	.321	.395
2009	Connecticut (EL)	AA	.298	139	527	71	157	37	1	19	109	37	72	6	3	.348	.480
2010	Fresno (PCL)	AAA	.275	140	520	63	143	34	0	16	84	30	65	7	2	.319	.433
2011	Fresno (PCL)	AAA	.312	133	536	82	167	36	3	25	107	25	54	6	6	.341	.530
	San Francisco (NL)	MAJ	.300	15	50	7	15	3	2	2	9	2	8	0	1	.321	.560
Major League Totals			.300	15	50	7	15	3	2	2	9	2	8	0	1	.321	.560
Minor League Totals			.279	740	2800	398	782	202	5	84	491	185	396	31	17	.328	.445

13 CONOR GILLASPIE, 3B

Born: July 18, 1987. **B-T:** L-R. **Ht.:** 6-1. **Wt.:** 201. **Drafted:** Wichita State, 2008 (1st round supplemental). **Signed by:** Hugh Walker.

Gillaspie is a hard-nosed competitor who takes the game very seriously. After making some rocky first impressions during a mandated September callup shortly after he signed for $970,000 as the 37th overall pick in 2008, he has endeared himself to many members of the organization. That group includes Giants manager Bruce Bochy, who called him the most improved player in the system when Gillaspie made it back to San Francisco last year, this time on merit. He always has had supreme contact and pitch-recognition skills, along with the ability to turn around quality fastballs. He hits for average with some gap power and a healthy amount of walks, using a short, line-drive stroke that requires little maintenance. At worst, he projected as a valuable lefthanded bat off the bench. But Gillaspie has raised his stock by making huge strides at third base, tirelessly working to clean up his footwork and improve his throwing accuracy. While fielding roughly the same amount of chances in three successive seasons, he has cut his errors from 27 to 17 to 11. Fresno manager Steve Decker estimated that Gillaspie made at least 20 diving plays for him in 2011. In limited looks, Gillaspie has been adequate at first base but has struggled with reads and jumps in left field. He might not be a candidate to take Pablo Sandoval's job, but he should be ready to bring a little fire to the Giants' bench in 2012.

Year	Club (League)	Class	AVG	G	AB	R	H	2B	3B	HR	RBI	BB	SO	SB	CS	OBP	SLG
2008	Giants (AZL)	R	.273	6	22	2	6	3	0	0	7	3	1	0	1	.360	.409
	Salem-Keizer (NWL)	SS	.268	18	71	4	19	4	0	0	8	9	13	2	0	.350	.324
	San Francisco (NL)	MAJ	.200	8	5	1	1	0	0	0	0	2	0	0	0	.429	.200
2009	San Jose (CAL)	HiA	.286	126	469	62	134	31	2	4	67	55	68	2	3	.364	.386
2010	Richmond (EL)	AA	.287	132	491	57	141	25	8	8	67	37	67	0	4	.335	.420
2011	Fresno (PCL)	AAA	.297	124	428	63	127	22	6	11	61	66	79	9	9	.389	.453
	San Francisco (NL)	MAJ	.263	15	19	2	5	0	0	1	2	2	1	0	0	.333	.421
Major League Totals			.250	23	24	3	6	0	0	1	2	4	1	0	0	.357	.375
Minor League Totals			.288	406	1481	188	427	85	16	23	210	170	228	13	17	.361	.414

14 HECTOR CORREA, RHP

BA GRADE
45
MEDIUM

Born: March 8, 1988. **B-T:** R-R. **Ht.:** 6-3. **Wt.:** 176. **Drafted:** HS—Hatillo, P.R., 2006 (4th round). **Signed by:** Carlos Berroa (Marlins).

Correa showed a strong arm in the lower levels of the Marlins system, but he had shoulder issues that cost him the entire 2009 season and he couldn't make it past low Class A. The Giants hadn't forgotten their strong reports from the days when he was hitting 95 mph from a loose, easy delivery, so they turned a roster crunch into a positive in the spring of 2010. San Francisco sent Jack Taschner to the Pirates for Ronny Paulino, then flipped Paulino to Florida for Correa. It took awhile, but Correa's shoulder came around in 2011 and he was back to punching tickets on two levels. He flashes mid-90s velocity while sitting at 91-92 mph with his fastball. He also sells a plus changeup that overwhelmed Class A hitters, whom he limited to a .141 average before a midseason promotion to Double-A, where he also fared well. His slider is a below-average offering, but he has gotten by with his other two pitches and ability to throw strikes. Correa is a good athlete with a lean, strong frame and plus makeup. He averaged nearly two innings per appearance last year, and because his changeup makes him so effective against lefthanders, the Giants may look to stretch him out as a starter. They protected him on their 40-man roster this offseason.

Year	Club (League)	Class	W	L	ERA	G	GS	CG	SV	IP	H	HR	BB	SO	K/9	WHIP	AVG
2006	Marlins (GCL)	R	1	2	1.76	10	5	0	0	41	38	1	15	38	8.3	1.29	.244
2007	Greensboro (SAL)	LoA	1	5	9.29	8	8	0	0	31	55	7	16	20	5.8	2.3	.401
	Jamestown (NYP)	SS	6	2	3.22	11	11	0	0	59	61	5	13	83	12.7	1.26	.261
2008	Greensboro (SAL)	LoA	0	1	6.30	4	4	0	0	10	15	1	1	9	8.1	1.6	.326
	Marlins (GCL)	R	0	0	13.50	1	1	0	0	3	5	0	2	2	6.7	2.63	.357
2009	Did Not Play—Injured																
2010	Augusta (SAL)	LoA	5	3	4.12	32	0	0	1	44	39	3	16	58	11.9	1.26	.239
2011	San Jose (CAL)	HiA	3	1	1.93	20	0	0	2	42	20	4	12	37	7.9	0.76	.141
	Richmond (EL)	AA	4	1	3.20	23	0	0	1	39	33	3	12	32	7.3	1.14	.236
Minor League Totals			20	15	3.86	109	29	0	4	268	266	24	87	279	9.4	1.32	.258

15 JARRETT PARKER, OF

BA GRADE
50
HIGH

Born: Jan. 1, 1989. **B-T:** L-L. **Ht.:** 6-3. **Wt.:** 190. **Drafted:** Virginia, 2010 (2nd round). **Signed by:** John DiCarlo.

Aside from Francisco Peguero, Parker may have the best blend of speed and power in the system. He's still learning to transform his talents, though. Once regarded as a first-round talent, he fell to the Giants in the second round of the 2010 draft after he hit .188 in the Cape Cod League and struggled with inconsistency in his junior year at Virginia. His first full pro season was more of the same, as he led San Jose with 74 walks but also paced the club by a wide margin with 144 strikeouts in 486 at-bats. Parker, who stands straight up at the plate, has trouble maintaining a consistent strike zone and has yet to solve lefthanders. He isn't much of a battler with two strikes. But he's ready to turn on fastballs and is capable of carrying a club when he's not overthinking at the plate. Parker, moved from center field to right to accommodate Gary Brown at San Jose, doesn't always look assured when he settles under flyballs. His plus speed helps him recover from bad jumps and allows him to steal bases. Arm strength isn't an asset, though. Parker ended the year with a confidence boost after a solid showing in the California League playoffs, making him likely to graduate to Double-A in 2012.

Year	Club (League)	Class	AVG	G	AB	R	H	2B	3B	HR	RBI	BB	SO	SB	CS	OBP	SLG
2011	San Jose (CAL)	HiA	.253	127	486	81	123	25	3	13	61	74	144	20	5	.360	.397
Minor League Totals			.253	127	486	81	123	25	3	13	61	74	144	20	5	.360	.397

16 CHRIS DOMINGUEZ, 3B

BA GRADE

50

HIGH

Born: Nov. 22, 1986. **B-T:** R-R. **Ht.:** 6-5. **Wt.:** 235. **Drafted:** Louisville, 2009 (3rd round). **Signed by:** Kevin Christman.

A power-hitting third baseman with the arm strength of a big league closer, Dominguez did enough damage in the California League in the first two months last year to earn a midseason promotion to Double-A Richmond. But after he started fast as Richmond's cleanup hitter, his lack of selectivity got exploited by more advanced pitchers and he hit just .213/.239/.353 in the second half. Dominguez has the most raw power in the system but is prone to overswinging and chasing pitches. He has a dead-pull approach and doesn't keep his hands back well against breaking balls. Dominguez doesn't have superlative range but can play deeper than most third basemen because of his cannon arm and handles anything within his reach. He played some first base in instructional league, too. Dominguez has below-average speed and range but moves better than most 240-pounders. For a big man, he has impressive stamina and wants to play every inning of every game. If Dominguez doesn't make enough contact to reach the majors, the Giants always could stick him on the mound. It wouldn't be the first time vice president of player personnel Dick Tidrow got his mitts on a strong-armed infielder. Before that happens, Dominguez will give Double-A another shot this year.

Year	Club (League)	Class	AVG	G	AB	R	H	2B	3B	HR	RBI	BB	SO	SB	CS	OBP	SLG
2009	Giants (AZL)	R	.306	9	36	8	11	2	0	2	8	3	9	1	0	.375	.528
	Salem-Keizer (NWL)	SS	.254	47	181	31	46	5	1	9	32	9	57	11	2	.298	.442
2010	Augusta (SAL)	LoA	.272	137	559	85	152	32	4	21	101	35	133	14	7	.326	.456
2011	San Jose (CAL)	HiA	.291	63	258	40	75	10	1	11	40	18	73	8	2	.337	.465
	Richmond (EL)	AA	.244	78	295	35	72	22	2	7	45	9	78	1	5	.272	.403
Minor League Totals			.268	334	1329	199	356	71	8	50	226	74	350	35	16	.314	.446

17 RICKY OROPESA, 1B

BA GRADE

50

HIGH

Born: Dec. 15, 1989. **B-T:** L-R. **Ht.:** 6-3. **Wt.:** 225. **Drafted:** Southern California, 2011 (3rd round). **Signed by:** Michael Kendall.

One look at Oropesa's thick forearms and it's obvious what he brings to the table. The slugging first baseman led the Cape Cod League with seven homers in 2010 and is tied for fifth place with Morgan Ensberg on Southern California's all-time homer list with 40. Already well regarded by Giants scouts, Oropesa reinforced Carlos Pena comparisons with a two-homer, five-RBI game in front of them at California. San Francisco drafted him in the third round last June and signed him in August for an above-slot $550,000. Oropesa's lefthanded swing is fluid and powerful but not especially compact. Though he doesn't chase as many pitches as his lofty strikeout totals as an amateur might indicate, he has trouble with breaking balls and figures to be challenged against lefthanders. Recruited as a two-way player by the Trojans, Oropesa has a strong arm but lacks the hands or range to play third base, giving him a narrow avenue to the big leagues. He's no better than a station-to-station runner as well. Once projected as a top-50 pick, Oropesa turned his draft disappointment into motivational fuel in instructional league and into the weight room over the winter. Growing up in the Inland Empire region of southern California, the first T-ball team he played on was the Giants. He'll be issued a slightly bigger orange and black San Jose uniform to start his pro career.

Year	Club (League)	Class	AVG	G	AB	R	H	2B	3B	HR	RBI	BB	SO	SB	CS	OBP	SLG
2011	Did Not Play—Signed Late																

18 CHUCKIE JONES, OF

BA GRADE

55

EXTREME

Born: July 28, 1992. **B-T:** R-R. **Ht.:** 6-3. **Wt.:** 235. **Drafted:** HS—Boonville, Mo., 2010 (7th round). **Signed by:** Hugh Walker.

The best-case scenario has Jones someday turning his ample physical gifts into a standout, two-way center fielder in the mold of Matt Kemp. But first, the Giants need to keep him on the field. Just two games into his 2011 season at Salem-Keizer, he required an appendectomy that forced him to miss a month. He struggled upon his return, so he'll probably return to the Northwest League for his third pro season. Jones has youth on his side, though. A three-sport standout in high school and Missouri's Gatorade baseball player of the year in 2010, the 6-foot-3, 235-pounder is built like a Big Ten linebacker and possesses above-average speed and arm strength. The former quarterback has big-time raw power, and though he's a long way from making dependable contact, he has shown a willingness to work counts and take walks. Jones acquitted himself well while playing all three outfield positions in instructional league, though he's still learning to make the most of his quickness on the bases and on defense. He didn't play on showcase teams and hasn't been exposed to much quality coaching as an amateur, so he has everything to learn. The same was true of Kemp.

Year	Club (League)	Class	AVG	G	AB	R	H	2B	3B	HR	RBI	BB	SO	SB	CS	OBP	SLG
2010	Giants (AZL)	R	.279	46	165	25	46	7	4	5	17	20	61	6	2	.360	.461
2011	Salem-Keizer (NWL)	SS	.218	41	124	19	27	6	0	2	9	15	48	4	2	.322	.315
Minor League Totals			.253	87	289	44	73	13	4	7	26	35	109	10	4	.343	.398

19 CHRIS MARLOWE, RHP

BA GRADE
50
HIGH

Born: Oct. 26, 1989. **B-T:** R-R. **Ht.:** 6-1. **Wt.:** 175. **Drafted:** Oklahoma State, 2011 (5th round). **Signed by:** Daniel Murray.

Marlowe uses an athletic delivery to get the most out of his smallish frame, he throws a cartoonish breaking ball and posted flat-out ridiculous college strikeout totals—all of which inspired one heck of a comparison by a Giants official who saw him in instructional league: "He's got a lot of things going on, like Tim Lincecum." Marlowe is a much more of a project than Lincecum was when he entered pro ball, though. A 21st-round pick of the Blue Jays in 2010, Marlowe transferred from Navarro (Texas) JC to Oklahoma State rather than turn pro. He struck out 71 in just 41 innings as the Cowboys' closer last spring, but he also walked 34, hit eight batters and threw seven wild pitches. San Francisco drafted him in the fifth round and signed him for $145,000. Marlowe's best pitch is a breaking ball that has the velocity of a slider (81-84 mph) and the big break of a curveball, and it's alternately described as both. He relies on it too much and will be under orders to throw more fastballs as a pro. There's no reason for him to avoid his heater, which sits at 92-95 mph and has been clocked as high as 97. Though Marlowe struggled when asked to pitch on consecutive days in college, any concerns over his stamina were assuaged when scouting director John Barr saw him strike out 12 in five innings against Texas. San Francisco may use him as a starter in the lower minors to get him innings, but Marlowe's future is in the bullpen. If he can harness his stuff, he could become a big league set-up man or possibly a closer. Though he'll probably open in low Class A, he could move rapidly.

Year	Club (League)	Class	W	L	ERA	G	GS	CG	SV	IP	H	HR	BB	SO	K/9	WHIP	AVG
2011	Giants (AZL)	R	1	0	0.00	3	0	0	0	3	3	0	1	5	15.0	1.33	.231
Minor League Totals			1	0	0.00	3	0	0	0	3	3	0	1	5	15.0	1.33	.231

20 MIKE KICKHAM, LHP

BA GRADE
50
HIGH

Born: Dec. 12, 1988. **B-T:** L-L. **Ht.:** 6-4. **Wt.:** 220. **Drafted:** Missouri State, 2010 (6th round). **Signed by:** Hugh Walker.

There's a lot to like about Kickham, but his first full pro season was an unsatisfying experience. The Giants had high hopes for the physical lefty, who received an above-slot $410,000 as a draft-eligible sophomore in the sixth round of the 2010 draft. He's a product of a Missouri State program that has pumped out big league pitchers Ross Detweiler, Jeff Gray, Shaun Marcum, Matt Palmer, John Rheinecker, Brett Sinkbeil and Brad Ziegler in the last decade. His twin brother Dan also pitched for the Bears and signed with the Tigers as a 33rd-rounder last summer. Kickham pitches in the low 90s and can touch 94 mph with fastball, giving him more velocity than most lefty starters. He also shows good feel for a true four-pitch blend that includes a plus slider, solid curveball and emerging changeup. All those attributes pointed Kickham toward the fast track, and he was ticketed to begin 2011 in high Class A. But Kickham dealt with a recurring blister issue, so the Giants started him at low Class A in mid-May and he didn't exactly dominate the league. At least he finished strong, with a 2.23 ERA in the final month of the regular season and a strong playoff start. Kickham has no right to complain about pitcher's fielding practice this spring after making six errors in just 23 chances last year. If he can put the blisters behind him, he should get back on track at San Jose and has the ceiling of a No. 3 starter.

Year	Club (League)	Class	W	L	ERA	G	GS	CG	SV	IP	H	HR	BB	SO	K/9	WHIP	AVG
2010	Giants (AZL)	R	0	0	11.57	3	0	0	0	2	4	0	2	3	11.6	2.57	.400
2011	Augusta (SAL)	LoA	5	10	4.11	21	21	0	0	112	112	9	37	103	8.3	1.33	.261
Minor League Totals			5	10	4.26	24	21	0	0	114	116	9	39	106	8.4	1.36	.264

21 CLAYTON BLACKBURN, RHP

BA GRADE
50
HIGH

Born: Jan. 6, 1993. **B-T:** L-R. **Ht.:** 6-3. **Wt.:** 220. **Drafted:** HS—Edmond, Okla., 2011 (16th round). **Signed by:** Daniel Murray.

Blackburn got a bit overlooked last spring as Oklahoma had its deepest crop of high school pitching ever. The Sooner State produced two top-seven picks in Dylan Bundy (Orioles) and Archie Bradley (Diamondbacks), as well as three other prep arms who went in the first two rounds. The Giants liked Blackburn's feel for pitching and had an accurate read on his signability despite what many teams believed was an unshakable commitment to Oklahoma. Sure enough, he inked a $150,000 deal and immediately went to work in the Rookie-level Arizona League, where he put together a scintillating pro debut. Blackburn throws his low-90s sinker to both sides of the plate and shows good feel for spinning a curveball and locating his changeup. He has the makings of a slider, too. He has a precocious ability to throw strikes and to take something off his fastball at times to control opponents' bat speed. His pitches have good life down in the zone, as evidenced by his 3.1 groundout/airout ratio in the AZL. Blackburn has a sturdy build and doesn't look particularly athletic, but his high three-quarters delivery is sound and repeatable. He'll have to work on his conditioning in order to maintain his stamina through a full season. Blackburn should be able to handle an assignment to low Class A in 2011. He's a potential No. 3 or 4 starter who's already making area scout Daniel Murray and Midwest supervisor Arnold Brathwaite look smart.

Year	Club (League)	Class	W	L	ERA	G	GS	CG	SV	IP	H	HR	BB	SO	K/9	WHIP	AVG
2011	Giants (AZL)	R	3	1	1.08	12	6	0	0	33	16	2	3	30	8.1	0.57	.140
Minor League Totals			3	1	1.08	12	6	0	0	33	16	2	3	30	8.1	0.57	.140

22 JESUS GALINDO, OF

BA GRADE
50
HIGH

Born: Aug. 23, 1990. **B-T:** B-R. **Ht.:** 5-11. **Wt.:** 175. **Signed:** Venezuela, 2009. **Signed by:** Ciro Villalobos.

Galindo spent two years in the Rookie-level Dominican Summer League learning to switch-hit before club officials decided he was ready to be challenged Stateside in 2011. He turned into something more than a slap-and-dash hitter from the left side, though there was never any doubt about the dash part. It was no accident that Galindo led the Northwest League in runs (49) and steals (47). He combines tremendous speed with excellent instincts and fearlessness on the basepaths. He swiped third base eight times and his gumption reminded Salem-Keizer manager Tom Trebelhorn of another aggressive speedster he managed in the NWL more than three decades ago—a guy by the name of Rickey Henderson. Galindo doesn't have the overall hitting ability to become another Rickey, but he has gotten stronger and is making more line-drive contact. He'll never have much power, so he needs to focus on putting the ball on the ground and getting on base. While not a physical presence, Galindo has a strong arm and maximizes his speed in center field by getting good jumps. Though he isn't immune to clanking a ball off his glove, he profiles as an above-average defender. Galindo probably will begin 2011 terrorizing catchers in the South Atlantic League.

Year	Club (League)	Class	AVG	G	AB	R	H	2B	3B	HR	RBI	BB	SO	SB	CS	OBP	SLG
2009	Giants (DSL)	R	.244	58	168	49	41	5	2	0	16	37	49	22	4	.404	.298
2010	Giants (DSL)	R	.246	63	167	46	41	6	0	0	23	35	30	43	7	.385	.281
2011	Salem-Keizer (NWL)	SS	.276	62	239	49	66	9	3	2	20	25	46	47	8	.353	.364
Minor League Totals			.258	183	574	144	148	20	5	2	59	97	125	112	19	.378	.321

23 JOSH OSICH, LHP

BA GRADE
50
EXTREME

Born: Sept. 3, 1988. **B-T:** L-L. **Ht.:** 6-3. **Wt.:** 230. **Drafted:** Oregon State, 2011 (6th round). **Signed by:** Matt Woodward.

Osich was positioned to go in the first two rounds of the 2011 draft before his velocity disappeared in the last month of the college season because of elbow and back discomfort. He was pulled from an NCAA regional playoff game after one inning the day before the draft, and he also had a history of arm problems that included Tommy John surgery in 2010. After taking Oregon State teammate Andrew Susac in the second round, the Giants couldn't pass up Osich when he was still available in the sixth. He signed for $450,000, the equivalent of second-round money, in August after he passed his physical. When healthy last spring, Osich threw a heavy 93-95 mph fastball that peaked at 97. He can get outs with both his changeup and slider, though he didn't throw his breaking ball much last year, perhaps a concession to his health issues. He was at his best on April 30, when he threw the Beavers' first no-hitter since 1947 to beat No. 3 overall pick Trevor Bauer and UCLA. San Francisco believes Osich just might have hit a dead-arm phase in his recovery last June, but limited him to rehab work in instructional league just to be cautious. Osich has all the equipment to be a No. 2 starter if he could stay healthy. He'll probably begin his pro career in relief as the Giants watch his innings, and it's easier to project that as his long-term role.

Year	Club (League)	Class	W	L	ERA	G	GS	CG	SV	IP	H	HR	BB	SO	K/9	WHIP	AVG
2011	Did Not Play—Signed Late																

24 RAY BLACK, RHP

BA GRADE
50
EXTREME

Born: June 26, 1990. **B-T:** R-R. **Ht.:** 6-2. **Wt.:** 205. **Drafted:** Pittsburgh, 2011 (7th round). **Signed by:** John DiCarlo.

Aside from supplemental first-rounder Kyle Crick, Black might have the highest ceiling among the passel of power arms the Giants took in the 2011 draft. But after signing for $225,000 as a seventh-rounder, he also has the furthest to go. He missed his high school senior season with an elbow injury that required Tommy John surgery. He redshirted in his first season at Pittsburgh and pitched just 37 innings over the last two college seasons. Black's stuff is undeniable, starting with a fastball that operates at 94-96 mph and features natual movement. At its best, his mid-80s slider can be a plus-plus pitch. But Black is more often wild than not, and he posted a 6.30 ERA with 26 walks in 20 innings at Pitt last spring. His shoulder flies open when he overthrows and he can't be relied upon to throw strikes. In other words, he's the kind of project the Giants love to give pitching coordinator Bert Bradley and vice president of player personnel Dick Tidrow. Black also has battled knee problems, so he'll be developed as a reliever. There's no telling how he'll hold up when used on consecutive days. If he finds the strike zone often enough in the spring, Black will make his pro debut in low Class A.

Year	Club (League)	Class	W	L	ERA	G	GS	CG	SV	IP	H	HR	BB	SO	K/9	WHIP	AVG
2011	Did Not Play—Signed Late																

25 STEPHEN HARROLD, RHP

BA GRADE
45
MEDIUM

Born: March 12, 1989. **B-T:** R-R. **Ht.:** 6-1. **Wt.:** 200. **Drafted:** UNC Wilmington, 2010 (12th round). **Signed by:** Jeremy Cleveland.

Though his progress was obscured somewhat by Heath Hembree's outstanding season, Harrold also established himself as a relief arm to watch. In his first full pro season, he clicked with pitching coach Steve Kline at Augusta, where he recorded a 1.54 ERA and 16 saves before a late-July promotion. His high Class A numbers weren't as pretty, but he gave up eight runs in his first round outings and recovered to post a 2.79 ERA afterward. He also was the best among the bunch of pitchers the Giants sent to the Arizona Fall League. Harrold throws consistent 92-94 mph fastballs from a high three-quarters slot. He commands a lockdown slider that rates as the best in the system. His main needs are to work on a changeup to combat lefthanders and to throw more strikes. If he can do that, he could reprise Sergio Romo's role someday soon in the San Francisco bullpen. Harrold should reach Double-A, if not higher, in 2012.

Year	Club (League)	Class	W	L	ERA	G	GS	CG	SV	IP	H	HR	BB	SO	K/9	WHIP	AVG
2010	Giants (AZL)	R	1	0	0.00	4	0	0	0	7	5	0	2	6	7.4	0.95	.200
	Salem-Keizer (NWL)	SS	1	1	2.78	18	0	0	7	23	17	2	5	28	11.1	1.0	.202
2011	Augusta (SAL)	LoA	4	3	1.54	38	0	0	16	41	29	4	17	39	8.6	1.12	.200
	San Jose (CAL)	HiA	1	0	5.48	19	0	0	0	23	24	3	13	24	9.4	1.61	.261
Minor League Totals			7	4	2.68	79	0	0	23	94	75	9	37	97	9.3	1.19	.217

26 ADALBERTO MEJIA, LHP

BA GRADE
50
EXTREME

Born: June 20, 1993. **B-T:** L-L. **Ht.:** 6-3. **Wt.:** 195. **Signed:** Dominican Republic, 2011. **Signed by:** Pablo Peguero.

After spending $849,000 on international amateur bonuses in 2010, a figure that ranked 27th among the 30 organizations, the Giants doled out $750,000 for Dominican pitchers Mejia and Simon Mercedes last offseason. Mejia, who signed for $350,000, combines a projectable frame and loose arm with an advanced feel for pitching. In his pro debut, he recorded the fourth-best K-BB ratio (8.9) and sixth-best ERA (1.42) in the Dominican Summer League. He further impressed coaches who worked with him in instructional league. Though he's still growing into his body, Mejia is athletic and coordinated. For now he pitches at 87-90 mph and touches 92 with his fastball, and there's plenty of room for projection in his slender frame. He has some deception in his delivery and effectively sells his changeup. His breaking ball is still just a slurve, however. Despite his youth, Mejia is calm and confident on the mound. Though a case can be made for a full-season assignment at Augusta, San Francisco has a surplus of young pitching and probably will send him to the Arizona or Northwest League.

Year	Club (League)	Class	W	L	ERA	G	GS	CG	SV	IP	H	HR	BB	SO	K/9	WHIP	AVG
2011	Giants (DSL)	R	5	2	1.42	13	13	0	0	76	58	0	8	71	8.4	0.87	.209
Minor League Totals			5	2	1.42	13	13	0	0	76	58	0	8	71	8.4	0.87	.209

27 ROGER KIESCHNICK, OF

BA GRADE
45
MEDIUM

Born: Jan. 21, 1987. **B-T:** L-R. **Ht.:** 6-3. **Wt.:** 229. **Drafted:** Texas Tech, 2008 (3rd round). **Signed by:** Todd Thomas.

Kieschnick led the Giants system with 23 home runs in his 2009 pro debut, but consecutive injury-plagued seasons have knocked the shine off his prospect status. He still has some nice tools, though he'll have to re-establish himself as a durable performer if he hopes to join fellow 2008 draftees Buster Posey, Conor Gillaspie and Brandon Crawford in San Francisco. The Giants did add Kieschnick to their 40-man roster in November. He spent last offseason rehabbing a stress fracture in his lower back and was starting to turn a corner last summer before more stiffness and discomfort locked up his swing in August. With Richmond fighting to make the playoffs, San Francisco shut him down toward the end pf the season. Kieschnick has a big stroke that matches his strapping build and he attacks pitches when he's ahead in the count. He has holes in his swing and lacks patience, so he may never hit for a high average, which will be the tradeoff for his above-average raw power. When healthy, Kieschnick runs well for his size and provides quality defense in right field, where his strong arm is an asset. He's an all-out competitor who pays little heed to outfield walls and gives a consistent effort even when he's playing in pain. If he repeats Double-A again, it'll signal that he had a disappointing spring.

Year	Club (League)	Class	AVG	G	AB	R	H	2B	3B	HR	RBI	BB	SO	SB	CS	OBP	SLG
2009	San Jose (CAL)	HiA	.296	131	517	86	153	37	8	23	110	36	130	9	1	.345	.532
2010	Richmond (EL)	AA	.251	60	223	21	56	8	3	4	23	18	55	2	3	.305	.368
2011	Richmond (EL)	AA	.255	126	459	71	117	22	5	16	65	34	121	13	7	.307	.429
Minor League Totals			.272	317	1199	178	326	67	16	43	198	88	306	24	11	.323	.462

28 ADAM DUVALL, 3B

Born: Sept. 4, 1988. **B-T:** R-R. **Ht.:** 6-1. **Wt.:** 205. **Drafted:** Louisville, 2010 (11th round). **Signed by:** Kevin Christman.

Duvall signed for just $2,500 as an 11th-rounder, he was old for low Class A at age 22 and his at-bats aren't likely to be found on an instructional video. But he just keeps hitting baseballs over the fence and grabbed the Giants' attention by hitting 22 homers at Augusta last year. He took home MVP honors at the South Atlantic League all-star game and probably would have topped 100 RBIs if he didn't miss three weeks with a hamstring injury. Duvall doesn't use his legs enough in his swing but takes a balanced, direct path to the ball. He has established himself as one of the better fastball hitters in the system. A shortstop at Louisville, he had a miserable time while making 27 errors at third base last year, mostly on rushed, high throws. He has average range and arm strength to go with fringy speed. San Francisco has tried him at second base, in the hopes he might just become a poor man's Jeff Kent, but he spent most of instructional league trying to improve at third. Duvall will head to high Class A in 2012, with the chance for a midseason promotion if he continues to hit home runs.

Year	Club (League)	Class	AVG	G	AB	R	H	2B	3B	HR	RBI	BB	SO	SB	CS	OBP	SLG
2010	Salem-Keizer (NWL)	SS	.245	54	192	30	47	10	1	4	18	14	45	2	3	.318	.370
2011	Augusta (SAL)	LoA	.285	116	431	69	123	30	4	22	87	59	98	4	4	.385	.527
Minor League Totals			.273	170	623	99	170	40	5	26	105	73	143	6	7	.365	.478

29 LEONARDO FUENTES, OF

Born: Nov. 29, 1992. **B-T:** R-R. **Ht.:** 6-3. **Wt.:** 185. **Signed:** Colombia, 2009. **Signed by:** Daniel Mavarez/Joe Salermo.

Before Edgar Renteria became a World Series MVP for the Giants, he made another big contribution to the organization. He placed a persuasive call to his countryman Fuentes, who was highly pursued by the Rangers, Yankees and other clubs attracted to his strength, bat speed and short, balanced swing. Adding him was a good start for scouting director John Barr, who's trying to make Latin American inroads beyond the Dominican Republic and Venezuela, where the prices for top teenage talent have skyrocketed. San Francisco still isn't sure what its $280,000 investment in Fuentes will yield, but he made enough progress as a power-hitting corner outfielder to earn a spot in the Arizona League as an 18-year-old last year. He struck out 55 times in 179 at-bats but the contact he did make was loud. Fuentes packed on 25 pounds in a year's time and offers lots of raw power. He's a below-average runner who profiles best in left field, though he probably has enough arm to see spot duty in right. Fuentes is still another year away from being ready for full-season ball.

Year	Club (League)	Class	AVG	G	AB	R	H	2B	3B	HR	RBI	BB	SO	SB	CS	OBP	SLG
2010	Giants (DSL)	R	.240	61	200	32	48	14	1	4	33	25	73	3	5	.340	.380
2011	Giants (AZL)	R	.257	46	179	28	46	13	1	5	31	10	55	1	1	.306	.425
Minor League Totals			.248	107	379	60	94	27	2	9	64	35	128	4	6	.325	.401

30 RAFAEL RODRIGUEZ, OF

Born: July 13, 1992. **B-T:** R-R. **Ht.:** 6-5. **Wt.:** 200. **Signed:** Dominican Republic, 2009. **Signed by:** Felix Peguero/Pablo Peguero.

No wonder the Giants got scared off spending big bucks on international free agents. Rodriguez has been a major disappointment in two years since receiving a $2.55 million bonus, the largest in club history for an international amateur. That exceeded the $2.1 million they gave Angel Villalona, whose career was derailed when he was charged in the fatal shooting of a bar patron in the Dominican Republic. At least there still is a glimmer of hope for Rodriguez, who once was compared to a teenage Dave Winfield but hit just one home run and slugged .297 in low Class A last year. He uses his long arms to cover the zone well and finds a way to put the ball in play with two strikes, but he chases bad pitches early in the count. Still just a teenager growing into his body, he gets frustrated with his at-bats. San Francisco coaches have worked with him to get his bat started a little earlier and to better control the barrel. Thought to have the tools of a prototypical right fielder, Rodriguez has to find a way to tap into his power. He's erratic in the outfield, though he does have a strong arm and deceptive speed. He'll almost assuredly repeat low Class A in 2012.

Year	Club (League)	Class	AVG	G	AB	R	H	2B	3B	HR	RBI	BB	SO	SB	CS	OBP	SLG
2009	Giants (AZL)	R	.299	35	127	25	38	8	0	0	19	16	23	5	4	.392	.362
2010	Salem-Keizer (NWL)	SS	.163	12	43	3	7	0	1	0	4	3	12	1	0	.250	.209
	Giants (AZL)	R	.301	32	123	20	37	6	0	2	14	5	23	4	2	.323	.398
2011	Augusta (SAL)	LoA	.236	96	364	39	86	15	2	1	30	24	69	1	6	.284	.297
Minor League Totals			.256	175	657	87	168	29	3	3	67	48	127	11	12	.311	.323

Seattle Mariners

BY CONOR GLASSEY

At first glance, the Mariners' 2011 season wasn't much better than the year before, which was arguably the worst in franchise history. They finished 67-95, the third-worst record in baseball last year, had a 17-game losing streak and wound up in the American League West cellar for the sixth time in eight years. Not coincidentally, the team drew fewer than 2 million fans for the first time in a full season since 1992.

Seattle's leadership believes things are moving in the right direction, though. After bottoming out in 2010, the major league team showed enough promising signs last year that general manager Jack Zduriencik earned a contract extension before his third season at the helm had ended.

Former GM Bill Bavasi left the Mariners saddled with bad contracts and a gutted farm system. Zduriencik has preached rebuilding through player development, and he has stayed true to the plan despite the pain involved and a major league-high 18 rookies did appear in Seattle last year.

The most notable were Dustin Ackley and Michael Pineda, who join Felix Hernandez as franchise cornerstones. In just his second pro season, Ackley took over at second base and hit .273/.348/.417. Pineda pitched a perfect inning in the All-Star Game and led all rookies with 173 strikeouts in 171 innings.

The rookie parade also featured intriguing storylines. Tom Wilhelmsen made it to the big leagues after quitting baseball in 2005 and taking four years off, working as a bartender and traveling. Steve Delabar was a substitute teacher after the Padres released him in 2008, then worked out for the Mariners in April, signed a minor league contract and reached Seattle in September. Alex Liddi became the first player born and raised in Italy to play in the majors.

The Mariners reaped benefits from their deals at the trade deadline, when they were among the most aggressive sellers in the game. They added big leaguers Casper Wells and Charlie Furbush and a pair of quality prospects in third baseman Francisco Martinez and righthander Chance Ruffin when they shipped Doug Fister and David Pauley to the Tigers. Seattle also landed outfielder Trayvon Robinson from the Dodgers and outfielder Chih-Hsien Chiang from the Red Sox in a three-way deal that sent Erik Bedard and 2008 first-round pick Josh Fields to Boston.

The strength of the system now clearly lies with its pitching, a fact that became even more pronounced when Seattle used the No. 2 overall pick in the draft on polished lefthander Danny Hultzen. In November,

Michael Pineda led all rookies with 173 strikeouts over 171 innings last season

TOP 30 PROSPECTS

1. Taijuan Walker, rhp	16. Carter Capps, rhp
2. Danny Hultzen, lhp	17. Victor Sanchez, rhp
3. James Paxton, lhp	18. Tyler Marlette, c
4. Nick Franklin, ss/2b	19. Forrest Snow, rhp
5. Jose Campos, rhp	20. Jabari Blash, of
6. Francisco Martinez, 3b	21. Brandon Maurer, rhp
7. Chance Ruffin, rhp	22. John Hicks, c
8. Tom Wilhelmsen, rhp	23. Marcus Littlewood, c/ss/2b
9. Vinnie Catricala, 3b/1b/of	24. Chih-Hsien Chiang, of
10. Phillips Castillo, of	25. Carlos Triunfel, ss
11. Brad Miller, ss	26. Mauricio Robles, lhp
12. Guillermo Pimentel, of	27. Steven Proscia, 3b/1b
13. Erasmo Ramirez, rhp	28. Johermyn Chavez, of
14. Alex Liddi, 3b/ss	29. Rich Poythress, 1b
15. Stephen Pryor, rhp	30. Cavan Cohoes, ss

the Mariners hired Padres director of player personnel Chris Gwynn as farm director. Replacing Pedro Grifol, who now will manage the club's high Class A High Desert affiliate, Gwynn will oversee the development of Hultzen, Taijuan Walker, James Paxton and Co.

Tragedy struck the organization in the offseason, when toolsy young outfielder Greg Halman was stabbed to death on Nov. 21 at home in his native Netherlands. His younger brother Jason was taken into custody and placed under psychiatric observation while authorities decided how to proceed.

General Manager: Jack Zduriencik. **Farm Director:** Chris Gwynn. **Scouting Director:** Tom McNamara.

Class	Team	League	W	L	Pct	Finish*	Manager(s)
Majors	Seattle Mariners	American	67	95	.414	13th (14)	Eric Wedge
Triple-A	Tacoma Rainiers	Pacific Coast	70	74	.486	t-8th (16)	Daren Brown
Double-A	Jackson Generals	Southern	68	72	.486	6th (10)	Jim Pankovits
High A	High Desert Mavericks	California	59	81	.421	9th (10)	Jose Moreno
Low A	Clinton LumberKings	Midwest	63	76	.453	13th (16)	J. Azuaje/E. Menchaca
Short-season	Everett AquaSox	Northwest	37	39	.487	4th (8)	Scott Steinmann
Rookie	Pulaski Mariners	Appalachian	32	36	.471	6th (10)	Rob Mummau
Rookie	AZL Mariners	Arizona	25	31	.446	9th (13)	Jesus Azuaje
Overall 2011 Minor League Record			354	409	.464	28th (30)	

*Finish in overall standings (No. of teams in league). †League champion.

LAST YEAR'S TOP 30

Player, Pos.		Status
1.	Dustin Ackley, 2b	Majors
2.	Michael Pineda, rhp	Majors
3.	Nick Franklin, ss/2b	No. 4
4.	Taijuan Walker, rhp	No. 1
5.	Guillermo Pimentel, of	No. 12
6.	Mauricio Robles, lhp	No. 26
7.	Johermyn Chavez, of	No. 28
8.	Marcus Littlewood, ss	No. 23
9.	Kyle Seager, inf	Majors
10.	Dan Cortes, rhp	(Free agent)
11.	Greg Halman, of	(Deceased)
12.	Josh Lueke, rhp	(Rays)
13.	Alex Liddi, 3b/1b	No. 14
14.	Ramon Morla, 3b	Dropped out
15.	Rich Poythress, 1b/3b	No. 29
16.	Carlos Triunfel, ss	No. 25
17.	Blake Beavan, rhp	Majors
18.	Matt Mangini, 3b/1b	(Rays)
19.	Martin Peguero, ss	Dropped out
20.	Phillips Castillo, of	No. 10
21.	Stephen Pryor, rhp	No. 15
22.	James Jones, of	Dropped out
23.	Jordan Shipers, lhp	Dropped out
24.	Josh Fields, rhp	(Red Sox)
25.	Carlos Peguero, of	Majors
26.	Tom Wilhelmsen, rhp	No. 8
27.	Steve Baron, c	Dropped out
28.	Erasmo Ramirez, rhp	No. 13
29.	Mickey Wiswall, 1b/3b	Dropped out
30.	Yoervis Medina, rhp	Dropped out

BEST TOOLS

Best Hitter for Average	Vinnie Catricala
Best Power Hitter	Alex Liddi
Best Strike-Zone Discipline	Vinnie Catricala
Fastest Baserunner	Jamal Austin
Best Athlete	Taijuan Walker
Best Fastball	Taijuan Walker
Best Curveball	James Paxton
Best Slider	Chance Ruffin
Best Changeup	Danny Hultzen
Best Control	Danny Hultzen
Best Defensive Catcher	Steve Baron
Best Defensive Infielder	Gabriel Noriega
Best Infield Arm	Carlos Triunfel
Best Defensive Outfielder	Daniel Carroll
Best Outfield Arm	Johermyn Chavez

PROJECTED 2015 LINEUP

Catcher	John Jaso
First Base	Justin Smoak
Second Base	Dustin Ackley
Third Base	Francisco Martinez
Shortstop	Nick Franklin
Left Field	Vinnie Catricala
Center Field	Trayvon Robinson
Right Field	Phillips Castillo
Designated Hitter	Guillermo Pimentel
No. 1 Starter	Felix Hernandez
No. 2 Starter	Taijuan Walker
No. 3 Starter	Michael Pineda
No. 4 Starter	Danny Hultzen
No. 5 Starter	James Paxton
Closer	Jose Campos

TOP PROSPECTS OF THE DECADE

Year	Player, Pos.	2011 Org.
2002	Ryan Anderson, lhp	Out of baseball
2003	Rafael Soriano, rhp	Yankees
2004	Felix Hernandez, rhp	Mariners
2005	Felix Hernandez, rhp	Mariners
2006	Jeff Clement, c	Pirates
2007	Adam Jones, of	Orioles
2008	Jeff Clement, c	Pirates
2009	Greg Halman, of	Deceased
2010	Dustin Ackley, of/1b	Mariners
2011	Dustin Ackley, 2b	Mariners

TOP DRAFT PICKS OF THE DECADE

Year	Player, Pos.	2011 Org.
2002	*John Mayberry Jr., of	Phillies
2003	Adam Jones, ss (1st round supp.)	Orioles
2004	Matt Tuiasosopo, ss (3rd round)	Mariners
2005	Jeff Clement, c	Pirates
2006	Brandon Morrow, rhp	Blue Jays
2007	Phillippe Aumont, rhp	Phillies
2008	Josh Fields, rhp	Red Sox
2009	Dustin Ackley, of	Mariners
2010	Taijuan Walker, rhp (1st round supp.)	Mariners
2011	Danny Hultzen, lhp	Mariners

*Did not sign.

LARGEST BONUSES IN CLUB HISTORY

Danny Hultzen, 2011	$6,350,000
Dustin Ackley, 2009	$6,000,000
Ichiro Suzuki, 2001	$5,000,000
Jeff Clement, 2005	$3,400,000
Victor Sanchez, 2011	$2,500,000

SEATTLE MARINERS

TOP 2012 ROOKIE: Danny Hultzen, lhp. The No. 2 overall pick in the 2011 draft could make his pro debut as a member of the big league rotation.

BREAKOUT PROSPECT: Carter Capps, rhp. With a fastball that flirts with triple digits and a filthy slider, he could move quickly if deployed as a reliever.

SLEEPER: Andrew Carraway, rhp. He pounds the zone with three average pitches and keeps his team in every game.

SOURCE OF TOP 30 TALENT			
Homegrown	24	Acquired	6
College	9	Trades	5
Junior college	1	Rule 5 draft	0
High school	6	Independent leagues	0
Independent/drafted	1	Free agents/waivers	1
Nondrafted free agents	0		
International	7		

LF
Vinnie Catricala (9)
Guillermo Pimentel (12)
Jabari Blash (20)
Julio Morban
Cory Scammel
Jake Shaffer

CF
James Zamarripa
Jamal Austin
Daniel Carroll
Denny Almonte
Nathan Melendres

RF
Phillips Castillo (10)
Chih-Hsien Chiang (24)
Johermyn Chavez (28)
Alfredo Morales
Mike Wilson
James Jones
Mike McGee
Gabriel Guerrero

3B
Francisco Martinez (6)
Alex Liddi (14)
Steven Proscia (27)
Ramon Morla
Mario Martinez
Yordi Calderon
Stefen Romero

SS
Nick Franklin (4)
Brad Miller (11)
Carlos Triunfel (25)
Cavan Cohoes (30)
Ketel Marte
Gabriel Noriega
Bryan Brito

2B
Martin Peguero
Dan Paolini
Dillon Hazlett

1B
Rich Poythress (29)
Mickey Wiswall
Dennis Raben
Ji-Man Choi

C
Tyler Marlette (18)
John Hicks (22)
Marcus Littlewood (23)
Steve Baron
Jack Marder
Michael Dowd
Luke Guarnaccia

LHP

LHSP	LHRP
Danny Hultzen (2)	Mauricio Robles (26)
James Paxton (3)	Brian Moran
Jordan Shipers	Phillippe Valiquette
Cameron Hobson	Lucas Luetge
Anthony Fernandez	Nick Valenza
Jimmy Gillheeney	Ryan Kiel

RHP

RHSP	RHRP
Taijuan Walker (1)	Chance Ruffin (7)
Jose Campos (5)	Tom Wilhelmsen (8)
Erasmo Ramirez (13)	Stephen Pryor (15)
Carter Capps (16)	Carson Smith
Victor Sanchez (17)	Steve Delabar
Forrest Snow (19)	Jonathan Arias
Brandon Maurer (21)	Tyler Blandford
Andrew Carraway	Tyler Burgoon
Yoervis Medina	Richard White
Mayckol Guaipe	George Mieses
Ambioris Hidalgo	Steven Hensley
Stephen Landazuri	Stephen Kohlscheen
Jose Torres	Richard Vargas
Gabe Saquilon	Cody Weiss

2011   BONUSES: $11.3 MILLION

BEST PURE HITTER: SS Brad Miller (2) was the Atlantic Coast Conference batting champion and player of the year last spring. Using a stance similar to Craig Counsell's, he hit .415 at low Class A Clinton. Miller has good hands and keeps the bat in the hitting zone a long time.

BEST POWER HITTER: C Tyler Marlette (5) homered in the 2010 Aflac All-American game at Petco Park, then showed power to all fields during his senior season. He displayed upper-deck power during a workout at Safeco Field shortly after signing.

FASTEST RUNNER: OF Jamal Austin's (13) speed earns 80 grades on the 20-80 scouting scale. He stole 20 bases in the Rookie-level Appalachian League.

BEST DEFENSIVE PLAYER: The Mariners drafted three catchers in the first 12 rounds and like C John Hicks (4) for his intangibles as well as average catch-and-throw skills.

BEST FASTBALL: RHP Carter Capps (3s) entered the spring as the nation's top NCAA Division II prospect and he touched 99 mph in the Cape Cod League as a reliever.

BEST SECONDARY PITCH: LHP Danny Hultzen (1) has a premium changeup and a slider that he locates to both sides of the plate. RHP Carson Smith (8) has durability concerns, but scouts don't question his two-plane slider with late tilt.

BEST PRO DEBUT: Hultzen's college teammate at Virginia, 3B Steven Proscia (7), took advantage of high Class A High Desert and batted .303/.319/568 with 12 home runs (11 at home).

BEST ATHLETE: Hultzen hit .314 with 18 steals in three seasons as Virginia's ace and DH.

MOST INTRIGUING BACKGROUND: SS Cavan Cohoes (9) attended Patch High, a school for children of American military personnel in Germany. The first player ever drafted from that nation, he's the son of an Air Force pilot. Unsigned 1B Andrew Grifol's (49) older brother Pedro was Seattle farm director and will manage High Desert in 2012. Unsigned 1B Kevin Cron's (3) dad Chris played briefly in the majors and his brother C.J. signed with the Angels as the 20th overall pick in the 2011 draft. LHP Kyle Hunter (31) is related to Hall of Fame shortstop Luke Appling.

CLOSEST TO THE MAJORS: Hultzen debuted in the Arizona Fall League and could make his pro debut as a member of the Mariners rotation.

BEST LATE-ROUND PICK: C Jack Marder (16), a converted infielder, looked good enough in his first full-time duty behind the plate to earn a $200,000 bonus. If Austin hits, he could be very interesting.

RHP Richard White (23) from the Virgin Islands is raw, but was up to 98 mph in a pre-draft workout.

THE ONE WHO GOT AWAY: Cron (3) could develop into a clone of his older brother C.J., who had some of the best power in the 2011 draft. Kevin headed to Texas Christian.

ASSESSMENT: Seattle spent big on Hultzen and Miller with their first two picks, and if Capps maintains his premium velocity he could move quickly as a reliever. This class should bolster the system's pitching and catching depth.

2010   BONUSES: $4.9 MILLION

RHP Taijuan Walker (1) and LHP James Paxton (4) have been even better than advertised and rate as two of Seattle's top three prospects. RHP Ryne Stanek (3) has similar talent but didn't sign and should be a first-rounder in 2013.

GRADE: B+

2009   BONUSES: $10.9 MILLION

One of the best college hitters in years, budding star 2B Dustin Ackley (1) became a big league regular midway through his second pro season. INF Kyle Seager (3) and LHP Anthony Vasquez (18) also reached the majors quickly. SS/2B Nick Franklin (1) and 3B/1B/OF Vinnie Catricala (10) give the Mariners two more promising bats.

GRADE: A

2008   BONUSES: $4.3 MILLION

This crop may not yield a big leaguer. RHP Josh Fields (1) signed late and fizzled before getting used in the three-team Erik Bedard trade last July that brought Trayvon Robinson and Chih-Hsien Chiang to Seattle. RHPs Aaron Pribanic (3) and Brett Lorin (5) were part of a 2009 deal with the Pirates for Jack Wilson and Ian Snell.

GRADE: F

2007   BONUSES: $4.5 MILLION

RHP Phillippe Aumont (1) has been inconsistent, but the Mariners got value out of him by including him when they stole Cliff Lee from the Phillies in a December 2009 trade. RHP Shawn Kelley (13) has been a useful bullpen piece, and 1B/3B Matt Mangini (1s) also made the majors before getting released in 2011.

GRADE: C+

Draft analysis by John Manuel (2011) and Jim Callis (2007-10). Numbers in parentheses indicate draft rounds.

1 TAIJUAN WALKER, RHP

Born: Aug. 13, 1992. **B-T:** R-R. **Ht.:** 6-4. **Wt.:** 195.
Drafted: HS—Yucaipa, Calif., 2010 (1st round supplemental). **Signed by:** John Ramey.

BA GRADE
70
HIGH

CHRIS PROCTOR

Walker spent most of his time at Yucaipa (Calif.) High focusing on basketball. He averaged 21 points and 15 rebounds per game as a senior, earning the nickname "Skywalker" thanks to his dunking ability, a nickname he has stitched into his glove. When he played baseball, he mostly played shortstop, with Diamondbacks prospect Matt Davidson manning third base to his right. It wasn't until the end of Walker's junior year that he really began to pitch. He created significant buzz in the fall of 2009 that carried over into the spring of his senior season. The Mariners selected him with their first pick (43rd overall) in the 2010 draft and signed him for $800,000. Walker, who was 17 when he was drafted, blew opponents and evaluators away in his first full pro season. Seattle held him in extended spring until May and shut him down when he approached 100 innings in August. In between, he ranked as the No. 1 prospect in the low Class A Midwest League and was named Mariners minor league pitcher of the year.

Walker has an ideal frame and athleticism for a pitcher. He's long and loose with strong legs, square shoulders and room for projection remaining. He gets sharp downhill plane on an electric fastball that sits at 91-95 mph and tops out at 98. He significantly improved his fastball command and his curveball during his three months at Clinton. He didn't throw a curve when the Mariners signed him, but they got him to scrap his slider and now he has a low-80s hammer with sharp 12-to-6 break. Walker's biggest goal last season was to improve his changeup. He has a circle change that grades as average and gives him a chance for a third plus offering. He throws it from the same slot and with the same arm speed as his fastball. Walker's control and command still need some polishing but are more advanced than expected. He has excellent feel for spotting his fastball and isn't afraid to own the inner half of the plate. Walker's superb athleticism is obvious when he's on the mound. He repeats his effortless delivery well and maintains his velocity

deep into games. He's working to make his mechanics more consistent and tweaked a few things in 2011, including adding a slight hip rotation at his balance point. Walker also holds runners and fields his position well. He's a tough competitor, a sponge for information and a hard worker. He moved to Peoria, Ariz., this offseason to work out regularly at the Mariners' spring-training facility.

Walker, who will be 19 for most of the 2012 season, may open the year at high Class A High Desert, which would be close to where he grew up. On the other hand, some club officials want to skip Walker straight to Double-A. The Mariners are already in good shape at the top of their rotation with Felix Hernandez and Michael Pineda, but Walker profiles as another potential ace and could be in the big leagues by the end of 2013.

SCOUTING GRADES

Fastball: 75. **Command/**
Curveball: 60. **Control:** 60.
Changeup: 55. **Delivery:** 65.

Based on 20-80 scouting scale, where 50 represents major league average, and future projection rather than present tools.

Year	Club (League)	Class	W	L	ERA	G	GS	CG	SV	IP	H	HR	BB	SO	K/9	WHIP	AVG
2010	Mariners (AZL)	R	1	1	1.29	4	0	0	0	7	2	0	3	9	11.6	0.71	.087
2011	Clinton (MWL)	LoA	6	5	2.89	18	18	1	0	97	69	4	39	113	10.5	1.12	.202
Minor League Totals			7	6	2.78	22	18	1	0	104	71	4	42	122	10.6	1.09	.195

2 DANNY HULTZEN, LHP

Born: Nov. 28, 1989. **B-T:** L-L. **Ht.:** 6-3. **Wt.:** 200. **Drafted:** Virginia, 2011 (1st round). **Signed by:** Mike Moriarty.

The Diamondbacks made seven-figure overtures to Hultzen after drafting him in the 10th round out of high school in 2008, but he opted to attend Virginia. A two-way player for the Cavaliers, he led them to their first two College World Series berths and set school records for career wins (32) and strikeouts (395). While most clubs expected the Mariners to take a hitter with the No. 2 overall pick in the 2011 draft, they opted for Hultzen and gave him an $8.5 million big league contract that included a club-record $6.35 million bonus. Hultzen combines quality stuff and lots of polish. His fastball sits at 91-93 mph and reaches 96. He has an outstanding changeup and a solid slider that he can spot on both sides of the plate. He commands all three of his offerings well. Hultzen entered pro ball with an extreme knee bend in his delivery. Seattle left his full windup alone but got him to stand taller out of the stretch to prevent his secondary pitches from flattening out.

BA GRADE 65 MEDIUM

He also lands closed and throws across his body, but that doesn't bother the Mariners because it adds deception. As advanced as any player in the 2011 draft, Hultzen posted a 1.40 ERA in six Arizona Fall League starts. He has the upside of a No. 2 starter and will get a shot to make the big league rotation in spring training.

Year	Club (League)	Class	W	L	ERA	G	GS	CG	SV	IP	H	HR	BB	SO	K/9	WHIP	AVG
2011	Did Not Play—Signed Late																

3 JAMES PAXTON, LHP

Born: Nov. 6, 1988. **B-T:** L-L. **Ht.:** 6-4. **Wt.:** 220. **Drafted:** Grand Prairie (American Association), 2010 (4th round). **Signed by:** Brian Williams/Jesse Kapellusch.

The Blue Jays drafted Paxton 37th overall out of Kentucky in 2009 but couldn't sign him. Team president Paul Beeston told a Toronto newspaper he had negotiated directly with Paxton's adviser, Scott Boras, which effectively ended Paxton's college eligibility. His stuff wasn't as sharp when he pitched in the independent American Association before the 2010 draft, so he slid to the fourth round. The Mariners finally signed him last March for $942,500, which looks like a steal after he dominated and reached Double-A in his pro debut. Paxton is the rare power lefthander who combines high strikeout totals with above-average groundball rates. His fastball sits at 91-95 mph and peaks at 98. He can pitch up in the zone effectively but has just as much faith in his two-seam fastball as he does his four-seamer. He can use his plus 76-79 mph curveball to get ahead in counts or put away hitters. His changeup made a lot of progress after he switched to a circle grip in

BA GRADE 60 MEDIUM

2011, and should be at least solid in the future. Paxton's arm action gets long in the back, allowing batters to see the ball and limiting his command when he gets out of sync. His delivery was very slow when he entered pro ball, but he worked hard to cut his time to the plate from 1.6-2.0 seconds to 1.3-1.4. Paxton could return to Double-A to start the season to avoid the cold early-season weather at Triple-A Tacoma. He has a No. 2 starter ceiling and could reach Seattle at some point in 2012.

Year	Club (League)	Class	W	L	ERA	G	GS	CG	SV	IP	H	HR	BB	SO	K/9	WHIP	AVG
2010	Grand Prairie (A-A)	IND	1	2	4.24	4	4	0	0	17	15	1	7	18	9.5	1.29	—
2011	Clinton (MWL)	LoA	3	3	2.73	10	10	0	0	56	45	1	30	80	12.9	1.34	.225
	Jackson (SL)	AA	3	0	1.85	7	7	0	0	39	28	2	13	51	11.8	1.05	.201
Minor League Totals			6	3	2.37	17	17	0	0	95	73	3	43	131	12.4	1.22	.215

4 NICK FRANKLIN, SS/2B

Born: March 2, 1991. **B-T:** B-R. **Ht.:** 6-1. **Wt.:** 180. **Drafted:** HS—Altamonte Springs, Fla., 2009 (1st round). **Signed by:** Chuck Carlson.

The 27th overall selection in the 2009 draft, Franklin signed for $1.28 million and set a Clinton record and led the Midwest League with 23 homers in his first full pro season. His 2011 season was a bit rockier, as a teammate's bat flew out of the cage during batting practice and struck Franklin in the jaw, resulting in a concussion. While on the disabled list, he had bouts with food poisoning and mononucleosis. He returned to steal the show in the Arizona Fall League's Rising Stars Game, going 4-for-5 with two doubles and an opposite-field homer off No. 1 overall pick Gerrit Cole. Franklin is a rare switch-hitting middle infielder with solid power. He utilizes a coiling leg kick that triggers an aggressive hip turn, allowing him to get the most of his size. He has good hand-eye coordination and hits the ball with authority to all parts of the park. He's much more productive batting lefthanded, and some scouts think he'd be best served by abandoning his righthanded

BA GRADE 55 MEDIUM

swing. He's an average runner with fine instincts on the bases. Franklin's defense draws mixed reviews. His range and actions work at shortstop, but some evaluators feel his instincts and fringy arm would fit better at second base. He played both positions last year. With Dustin Ackley at second base, the Mariners would love for Franklin to stay at shortstop. He should reach Triple-A during 2012.

Year	Club (League)	Class	AVG	G	AB	R	H	2B	3B	HR	RBI	BB	SO	SB	CS	OBP	SLG
2009	Mariners (AZL)	R	.302	10	43	6	13	2	0	1	4	1	6	0	0	.318	.419
	Everett (NWL)	SS	.400	6	20	4	8	2	1	0	2	1	2	1	0	.429	.600
2010	Clinton (MWL)	LoA	.281	129	513	89	144	22	7	23	65	50	123	25	10	.351	.485
	West Tenn (SL)	AA	.667	1	3	3	2	0	0	0	0	1	1	0	0	.750	.667
2011	High Desert (CAL)	HiA	.275	64	258	50	71	10	5	5	20	31	56	13	1	.356	.411
	Mariners (AZL)	R	.091	3	11	1	1	0	0	0	0	0	6	0	0	.091	.091
	Jackson (SL)	AA	.325	21	83	13	27	3	2	2	6	6	18	5	3	.371	.482
Minor League Totals			.286	234	931	166	266	39	15	31	97	90	212	44	14	.353	.460

5 JOSE CAMPOS, RHP

Born: July 27, 1992. **B-T:** R-R. **Ht.:** 6-4. **Wt.:** 200. **Signed:** Venezuela, 2009. **Signed by:** Emilio Carrasquel/Patrick Guerrero.

Campos tried to join the Cardinals, but it never became official because his parents refused to sign the contract. When the Mariners offered slightly more money at $115,000, he signed with them in January 2009. A cousin of big leaguers Alcides and Kelvim Escobar, Campos led the short-season Northwest League in ERA (2.32) and strikeouts (85) in his U.S. debut. Campos' fastball operates at 92-95 mph and has been clocked as high as 98. For a youngster, he has advanced feel for pitching off his fastball and locating it. His heater has deception, angle and life. Just a thrower when he got to Everett last summer, he grew as a pitcher. His hard curveball and his changeup show flashes of becoming plus pitches. They lack consistency but improved as he cleaned up his delivery. Earlier in 2011, he was landing stiff and upright, throwing with just his arm. Now he lands on a softer front leg and gets more extension out front. He shows great poise on the mound and fills the strike zone. Campos is yet another frontline starting pitching prospect in Seattle's stable. He'll head to low Class A, where he'll give Clinton another ace to follow in Taijuan Walker's footsteps.

BA GRADE
60
HIGH

Year	Club (League)	Class	W	L	ERA	G	GS	CG	SV	IP	H	HR	BB	SO	K/9	WHIP	AVG
2009	Mariners (VSL)	R	1	3	5.73	13	4	0	1	33	38	3	16	23	6.3	1.64	.297
2010	Mariners (VSL)	R	8	2	3.16	13	12	1	0	57	49	0	19	59	9.3	1.19	.231
2011	Everett (NWL)	SS	5	5	2.32	14	14	0	0	81	66	4	13	85	9.4	0.97	.214
Minor League Totals			14	10	3.26	40	30	1	1	171	153	7	48	167	8.8	1.17	.236

6 FRANCISCO MARTINEZ, 3B

Born: Sept. 1, 1990. **B-T:** R-R. **Ht.:** 6-1. **Wt.:** 180. **Signed:** Venezuela, 2007. **Signed by:** Alejandro Rodriguez/Pedro Chavez (Tigers).

When the Mariners shipped Doug Fister and David Pauley to the Tigers in July, Seattle got four players in return. Charlie Furbush, Chance Ruffin and Casper Wells already have reached the majors, but Martinez was the key to the deal. He made the jump to Double-A at age 20 last year and looked like he belonged. Martinez has all the raw tools to fit the profile of an everyday third baseman, with the added bonus of plus speed. Live-bodied and athletic, he has excellent bat speed and a knack for hitting the ball on the screws. The ball explodes off his bat when he gets extended and makes contact, and he projects as a .275 hitter with 15-20 homers annually. Martinez shows soft hands and solid arm strength at third base. He must continue to refine all parts of his game, such as improving his feel for the strike zone, improving his jumps on the bases and becoming more reliable on defense (he made 35 errors in 2011). With Martinez, Vinnie Catricala and Alex Liddi, the Mariners have a logjam at third base in the upper minors. Martinez is the best prospect and the best hot-corner defender of that group, so the position should be his at Tacoma in 2012. Seattle protected him on the 40-man roster in November.

BA GRADE
55
MEDIUM

Year	Club (League)	Class	AVG	G	AB	R	H	2B	3B	HR	RBI	BB	SO	SB	CS	OBP	SLG
2008	Tigers (VSL)	R	.321	68	249	32	80	4	0	1	23	28	28	20	10	.394	.349
2009	Tigers (GCL)	R	.222	43	153	21	34	9	0	2	23	5	38	11	1	.256	.320
	Lakeland (FSL)	HiA	.167	6	18	1	3	0	0	0	2	0	3	1	0	.167	.167
2010	Lakeland (FSL)	HiA	.271	89	340	47	92	17	1	3	29	28	71	12	5	.330	.353
2011	Erie (EL)	AA	.282	91	348	63	98	14	4	7	46	19	80	7	8	.319	.405
	Jackson (SL)	AA	.310	33	129	20	40	7	3	3	23	4	24	3	2	.326	.481
Minor League Totals			.281	330	1237	184	347	51	8	16	146	84	244	54	26	.329	.373

7 CHANCE RUFFIN, RHP

Born: Sept. 8, 1988. **B-T:** R-R. **Ht.:** 6-1. **Wt.:** 185. **Drafted:** Texas, 2010 (1st round supplemental). **Signed by:** Tim Grieve (Tigers).

Like his father Bruce, Ruffin starred at Texas, went in the top 50 picks as a free-agent compensation choice and reached the majors in his first full pro season. He led NCAA Division I in strikeouts per nine innings (13.5) while ranking second in ERA (1.11) and third in saves (14) in 2010 before signing with the Tigers for $1.15 million. The fourth player from the 2010 draft to get to the big leagues, he was the player to be named in the Doug Fister trade in July. Ruffin is undersized but has quality stuff and a fearless mound presence. His best pitch is a wipeout slider that has two-plane break and usually ranges from 81-83 mph. His fastball sits between 92-95 mph with late life, giving him a second plus pitch. He also has a slurvy 76-78 mph curveball he can mix in to give hitters a different look. He'll need to tighten his control and command, which weren't as sharp as advertised as he flew threw the minors. With his size, stuff, makeup and alma mater, he elicits comparisions to Huston Street. Ruffin pitched exclusively in the majors after the trade and may stick there to open the 2012 season. He has the upside of a closer but likely will settle into a middle-relief role this year.

BA GRADE
50
LOW

Year	Club (League)	Class	W	L	ERA	G	GS	CG	SV	IP	H	HR	BB	SO	K/9	WHIP	AVG
2011	Erie (EL)	AA	3	3	2.12	31	0	0	10	34	23	2	16	43	11.4	1.15	.190
	Detroit (AL)	MAJ	0	0	4.91	2	0	0	0	4	5	2	0	3	7.4	1.36	.313
	Toledo (IL)	AAA	0	0	1.84	13	0	0	9	15	14	1	6	17	10.4	1.36	.241
	Seattle (AL)	MAJ	1	0	3.86	13	0	0	0	14	13	2	9	15	9.6	1.57	.245
Major League Totals			1	0	4.08	15	0	0	0	18	18	4	9	18	9.2	1.53	.261
Minor League Totals			3	3	2.03	44	0	0	19	49	37	3	22	60	11.1	1.21	.207

8 TOM WILHELMSEN, RHP

Born: Dec. 16, 1983. **B-T:** R-R. **Ht.:** 6-6. **Wt.:** 230. **Drafted:** HS—Tucson, 2002 (7th round). **Signed by:** Brian Johnson (Brewers).

Wilhelmsen walked away from the game in 2005 after being suspended by the Brewers for the entire 2004 season following a positive test for marijuana. After four years of traveling the world and working as a bartender in Tucson, he wanted to give baseball another shot. He went to the independent Golden League in 2009 before reuniting with Mariners GM Jack Zduriencik, who drafted him as Milwaukee's scouting director in 2002. Wilhelmsen capped his improbable story by opening 2011 in Seattle. Wilhelmsen's best pitch is his fastball, which usually arrives at 93-95 mph and tops out at 98. He backs it up with a 12-to-6 curveball that features good velocity (76-78 mph) and depth. When he started off slowly in the big leagues, the Mariners sent him down to Double-A to work on his changeup as a starter. The changeup improved and has some fade, but it's still fringy and he's not a rotation option for the long term. But the extra work as a starter helped Wilhelmsen repeat his delivery, get consistent downward plane on his fastball and gain confidence. Once he returned to Seattle in August, Wilhelmsen posted a 2.35 ERA and a 22-4 K-BB ratio in 23 innings. He enters 2012 as one of the Mariners' top set-up men and will get a shot at closing if something happens to Brandon League.

BA GRADE
50
LOW

Year	Club (League)	Class	W	L	ERA	G	GS	CG	SV	IP	H	HR	BB	SO	K/9	WHIP	AVG
2003	Brewers (AZL)	R	0	1	4.50	2	2	0	0	4	5	0	4	4	9.0	2.25	—
	Beloit (MWL)	LoA	5	5	2.76	15	15	1	0	88	78	6	27	63	6.4	1.19	—
2004	Did Not Play—Restricted List																
2005	Did Not Play																
2006	Did Not Play																
2007	Did Not Play																
2008	Did Not Play																
2009	Tucson (GBL)	IND	0	0	6.00	11	0	0	2	12	15	0	4	13	9.8	1.58	—
2010	Mariners (AZL)	R	0	0	0.60	5	3	0	0	15	4	0	2	22	13.2	0.40	.078
	Everett (NWL)	SS	1	0	3.68	3	3	0	0	15	14	1	2	14	8.6	1.09	.255
	Clinton (MWL)	LoA	6	1	2.23	7	6	1	0	44	33	1	15	37	7.5	1.08	.198
2011	Jackson (SL)	AA	4	5	5.49	14	12	0	0	61	66	8	26	40	5.9	1.52	.282
	Seattle (AL)	MAJ	2	0	3.31	25	0	0	0	33	25	2	13	30	8.3	1.16	.210
Major League Totals			2	0	3.31	25	0	0	0	33	25	2	13	30	8.3	1.16	.210
Minor League Totals			16	12	3.34	46	41	2	0	227	200	16	76	180	7.1	1.22	.231

9 VINNIE CATRICALA, 3B/1B/OF

Born: Oct. 31, 1988. **B-T:** R-R. **Ht.:** 6-2. **Wt.:** 210. **Drafted:** Hawaii, 2009 (10th round). **Signed by:** Tim Reynolds.

Signed for $90,000 as a 10th-round pick in 2009, Catricala hit .302/.380/.490 in his first two pro seasons before breaking out last year. The Mariners' minor league player of the year, he ranked second in the minors in extra-base hits (77) and total bases (313), third in hits (182), fourth in batting (.349) and sixth in OPS (1.022). He raised his production following a late-June promotion to Double-A. Catricala has a lean, strong frame to go with a sound approach and pure hitting ability. He has the shortest swing in the system, a compact yet powerful stroke with above-average bat speed. He has the tools to hit for solid average and power while also drawing a healthy amount of walks. Catricala has fringy speed and arm strength and he's still in search of a defensive home. He's not reliable at third base, where he made 14 errors in 54 games last year, and is better suited for first base or left field. He saw time at all three spots in 2011. If he keeps hitting like this, the Mariners will make room for him in their lineup. With Justin Smoak in Seattle and Francisco Martinez joining the system, Catricala may wind up in left field. He could begin 2012 in Triple-A.

BA GRADE
50
MEDIUM

Year	Club (League)	Class	AVG	G	AB	R	H	2B	3B	HR	RBI	BB	SO	SB	CS	OBP	SLG
2009	Pulaski (APP)	R	.301	59	219	33	66	14	2	8	40	18	34	6	1	.363	.493
2010	Clinton (MWL)	LoA	.302	135	496	90	150	41	0	17	79	56	112	7	3	.386	.488
2011	High Desert (CAL)	HiA	.351	71	282	56	99	19	1	14	61	33	45	8	3	.421	.574
	Jackson (SL)	AA	.347	62	239	45	83	29	3	11	45	24	47	9	1	.420	.632
Minor League Totals			.322	327	1236	224	398	103	6	50	225	131	238	30	8	.397	.536

10 PHILLIPS CASTILLO, OF

Born: Feb. 2, 1994. **B-T:** R-R. **Ht.:** 6-2. **Wt.:** 190. **Signed:** Dominican Republic, 2010. **Signed by:** Patrick Guerrero/Franklin Taveras Jr./Bob Engle.

Castillo signed in July 2010 for $2.2 million, at the time a franchise record for a foreign amateur. He followed in the footsteps of Guillermo Pimentel by raking in the Arizona League as a 17-year-old last summer, tying for the league lead with 18 doubles and recording an .848 OPS. Castillo's offensive production will carry him. He produces above-average bat speed with a seemingly effortless swing and the ball jumps off his bat. He has good balance at the plate and an understanding of the strike zone, though he tends to be overly aggressive. As he becomes stronger and learns to be more patient, it's not hard to envision him anchoring the middle of a lineup. The other parts of Castillo game are understandably raw. He's still learning to read pickoff moves and take proper routes in the outfield. He's a fringy runner who might lose a step as he fills out his large, athletic frame. He could wind up in right field if his average arm improves as he gets stronger. Castillo will require time to develop but his bat should be worth the wait. He'll likely follow the same path as Pimentel, starting 2012 in extended spring training to smooth out his rough edges before joining Everett or Rookie-level Pulaski in June.

BA GRADE
60
EXTREME

Year	Club (League)	Class	AVG	G	AB	R	H	2B	3B	HR	RBI	BB	SO	SB	CS	OBP	SLG
2011	Mariners (AZL)	R	.300	48	170	36	51	18	5	1	27	15	61	8	5	.366	.482
Minor League Totals			.300	48	170	36	51	18	5	1	27	15	61	8	5	.366	.482

11 BRAD MILLER, SS

BA GRADE
50
MEDIUM

Born: Oct. 18, 1989. **B-T:** L-R. **Ht.:** 6-2. **Wt.:** 185. **Drafted:** Clemson, 2011 (2nd round). **Signed by:** Garrett Ball.

While many college hitters saw their stats decline when the NCAA switched to less-lively bats in 2011, Miller put together his best season at Clemson, hitting .395/.498/.559 to win Atlantic Coast Conference player of the year honors. A two-time member of the U.S. college national team, he went 62nd overall in the draft and signed for $750,000. Miller is a hard-nosed player who always has a plan at the plate. He has an unconventional set-up with his hands held above his head, though not as extreme as Craig Counsell. Once Miller's swing gets going, however, his hands get into a good launch position and his barrel stays in the hitting zone for a long time. He consistently squares up lefties and righties alike and sprays the ball to all parts of the park. He batted .415 when he joined Clinton for 14 games at the end of the season. He'll never be confused for a slugger, but does have enough power to hit 30 doubles and 10 homers annually. Miller has a tick above-average speed and it plays up because he's instinctive and runs the bases well. He struggles defensively at times and had to move to DH in 2010, when he made 31 errors. His footwork isn't always fluid and at times he drops his elbow on throws, causing the ball to tail away from the first baseman. However, his makeup and work ethic give him a chance to remain at shortstop. If not, he should be able to shift to second base, and at worst he's a utility infielder with a lefthanded bat. He'll spend his first full pro season in high Class A.

Year	Club (League)	Class	AVG	G	AB	R	H	2B	3B	HR	RBI	BB	SO	SB	CS	OBP	SLG
2011	Clinton (MWL)	LoA	.415	14	53	9	22	4	1	0	7	4	9	1	0	.458	.528
Minor League Totals			.415	14	53	9	22	4	1	0	7	4	9	1	0	.458	.528

12 GUILLERMO PIMENTEL, OF

BA GRADE
55
EXTREME

Born: Oct. 5, 1992. **B-T:** L-L. **Ht.:** 6-1. **Wt.:** 180. **Signed:** Dominican Republic, 2009. **Signed by:** Patrick Guerrero/Bob Engle/Luis Scheker.

Pimentel signed for $2 million in 2009 and quickly validated the hype, ranking as the Arizona League's No. 1 prospect in 2010 and smacking 11 homers at Pulaski last summer. He has 30-homer potential thanks to his developing strength, quick hands and athletic actions. He shows well above-average power to his pull side and natural lift in his swing. He'll need to improve his pitch recognition, show more patience at the plate and learn how to make adjustments on the fly. Pimentel's ultimate value is tied to his bat because he's limited to left field because of his below-average speed, range and arm strength. Still raw in many facets of the game, he must improve his routes in the outfield and his baserunning skills. Managers also would like to see him play with more fire, as he seems to just go through the motions at times. Pimentel will get his first shot at a full-season ball at Clinton in 2012.

Year	Club (League)	Class	AVG	G	AB	R	H	2B	3B	HR	RBI	BB	SO	SB	CS	OBP	SLG
2010	Mariners (AZL)	R	.250	51	184	20	46	7	6	6	31	5	58	5	1	.276	.451
2011	Pulaski (APP)	R	.265	65	245	33	65	10	0	11	46	15	73	4	1	.308	.441
Minor League Totals			.259	116	429	53	111	17	6	17	77	20	131	9	2	.295	.445

13 ERASMO RAMIREZ, RHP

BA GRADE
50
MEDIUM

Born: May 2, 1990. **B-T:** R-R. **Ht.:** 5-11. **Wt.:** 180. **Signed:** Nicaragua, 2007. **Signed by:** Bob Engle/Ubaldo Heredia.

Ramirez has shot through the system since signing out of Nicaragua in September 2007. He skipped a level to begin 2011 in Double-A at age 20, and he finished the season in Triple-A. It's easier for pitchers to advance when they have above-average control, and he rarely gives a hitter a free pass. While he fills the strike zone, he needs to sharpen his command. He sometimes catches too much of the plate and needs to learn when it's smarter to get hitters to chase. Using an effortless delivery, Ramirez throws a 90-94 fastball. It lacks plane because he's short and he loads up on his backside in his delivery. When he misses up, his fastball gets hammered because it's flat. Ramirez has good feel for his secondary pitches, a slurvy 10-4 breaking ball and a solid changeup, but both need further refinement. Though he's short, he's built like a tank and has proven durable while throwing 304 innings over the last two seasons. He's extremely competitive and can reach back for a little extra when he needs a strikeout late in the game. With his happy-go-lucky nature and obvious love for the game, Ramirez could be a fan favorite in Seattle. He'll likely start 2012 back in Tacoma and projects as a back-of-the rotation workhorse.

Year	Club (League)	Class	W	L	ERA	G	GS	CG	SV	IP	H	HR	BB	SO	K/9	WHIP	AVG
2008	Mariners (VSL)	R	4	1	2.86	13	11	1	0	63	67	2	9	46	6.6	1.21	.276
2009	Mariners (VSL)	R	11	1	0.51	14	13	0	0	88	54	1	5	80	8.2	0.67	.174
2010	Clinton (MWL)	LoA	10	4	2.97	26	23	1	1	152	142	13	21	117	6.9	1.07	.248
2011	Jackson (SL)	AA	7	6	4.73	19	19	0	0	110	127	10	19	81	6.6	1.32	.285
	Tacoma (PCL)	AAA	3	2	5.10	7	7	0	0	42	51	4	13	35	7.4	1.51	.304
Minor League Totals			35	14	3.10	79	73	2	1	455	441	30	67	359	7.1	1.12	.254

14 ALEX LIDDI, 3B/SS

BA GRADE
50
MEDIUM

Born: Aug. 14, 1988. **B-T:** R-R. **Ht.:** 6-4. **Wt.:** 230. **Signed:** Italy, 2005. **Signed by:** Wayne Norton/Mario Mazzotti.

Though six Italian-born players already had played in the big leagues, Liddi became the first born and raised in Italy to reach the majors when he got there in September. His promotion capped a season in which he ranked third in the Triple-A Pacific Coast League with 30 homers and 273 total bases. His game is quite similar to that of Mark Reynolds, as both have plus raw power but not enough other tools to be a viable everyday option for a contending team. As with Reynolds, Liddi's biggest problem is making contact. His 187 strikeouts between Triple-A and the majors were the fourth most in pro ball in 2011. (Reynolds was second with 196 whiffs.) Liddi is a below-average hitter who doesn't recognize pitches well or make adjustments at the plate, limiting his usable power to 15-20 homers annually in the majors. He's a well below-average runner with stiff infield actions. He did loosen up some last year and started 21 games at shortstop for Tacoma, and he does have plus arm strength. He led PCL third basemen with 18 errors in 115 games last year but had just one miscue in 14 big league contests. Despite his flaws as a player, Liddi is lauded for his makeup and hard work. He could beat out Kyle Seager and Chone Figgins for Seattle's starting job at third base in 2012, and should be able to contribute at least as a power bat off the bench.

Year	Club (League)	Class	AVG	G	AB	R	H	2B	3B	HR	RBI	BB	SO	SB	CS	OBP	SLG
2006	Mariners (AZL)	R	.313	47	182	31	57	13	6	3	25	12	48	9	2	.355	.500
	Wisconsin (MWL)	LoA	.184	11	38	4	7	1	0	0	2	1	8	0	1	.200	.211
2007	Wisconsin (MWL)	LoA	.240	113	400	41	96	28	3	8	52	36	123	5	4	.308	.385
2008	Wisconsin (MWL)	LoA	.244	125	447	65	109	26	4	6	53	42	115	17	5	.313	.360
2009	High Desert (CAL)	HiA	.345	129	493	97	170	44	5	23	104	53	122	10	6	.411	.594
2010	West Tenn (SL)	AA	.281	134	502	78	141	37	8	15	92	50	145	5	7	.353	.476
2011	Tacoma (PCL)	AAA	.259	138	559	121	145	32	3	30	104	61	170	5	1	.332	.488
	Seattle (AL)	MAJ	.225	15	40	7	9	3	0	3	6	3	17	1	0	.295	.525
Major League Totals			.225	15	40	7	9	3	0	3	6	3	17	1	0	.295	.525
Minor League Totals			.277	697	2621	437	725	181	29	85	432	255	731	51	26	.344	.465

15 STEPHEN PRYOR, RHP

BA GRADE
50
MEDIUM

Born: July 23, 1989. **B-T:** R-R. **Ht.:** 6-6. **Wt.:** 225. **Drafted:** Tennessee Tech, 2010 (5th round). **Signed by:** Alvin Rittman.

After showing one of the system's best fastballs in his 2010 pro debut, Pryor looked ready to zoom through the system. He got of to a slow start last season, missing the first four weeks with elbow tendinitis and posting a 19.29 ERA in his first nine appearances in high Class A. He rallied and was lights out from June through the end of the season, recording a 1.88 ERA and 51 strikeouts in 38 innings while reaching Double-A. Pryor has a big, intimidating build and the stuff to match. His heavy fastball operates at 93-95 mph and gets as high as 98. He worked on keeping his fastball down in the zone in 2011, though he can elevate it for a punchout. He throws a hard downer curveball at 80-82 mph, but the biggest factor in his second-half success was the addition of a nasty 87-91 mph cutter. Even with his extra-large frame, Pryor has good body control and loosened up his delivery a little bit in the second half of the season. The Mariners have a collection of power arms in front of him, but if he continues on his roll, he could join the big league bullpen at some point in 2012.

Year	Club (League)	Class	W	L	ERA	G	GS	CG	SV	IP	H	HR	BB	SO	K/9	WHIP	AVG
2010	Everett (NWL)	SS	0	0	0.49	11	0	0	4	18	7	0	7	26	12.8	0.76	.119
	Clinton (MWL)	LoA	0	2	3.71	12	0	0	1	17	17	0	6	29	15.4	1.35	.250
2011	High Desert (CAL)	HiA	1	0	7.67	22	0	0	4	27	28	2	26	34	11.3	2.00	.264
	Jackson (SL)	AA	2	1	1.19	17	0	0	6	23	9	0	7	27	10.7	0.71	.123
Minor League Totals			3	3	3.60	62	0	0	15	85	61	2	46	116	12.3	1.26	.199

16 CARTER CAPPS, RHP

BA GRADE
50
HIGH

Born: Aug. 7, 1990. **B-T:** R-R. **Ht.:** 6-5. **Wt.:** 220. **Drafted:** Mount Olive (N.C.), 2011 (3rd round supplemental). **Signed by:** Garrett Ball.

Capps was a catcher in high school, then redshirted his first year at Mount Olive (N.C.) before moving to the mound in 2010. He dominated NCAA Division II hitters as a starter for two seasons, winning his first 24 decisions before taking a loss during the 2011 D-II College World Series. Drafted 121st overall in June, he went to the Cape Cod League—making his first airplane trip—and posted a 0.39 ERA in relief before signing for $500,000. Capps' sinking fastball sits in the low 90s when he starts, but rises to 94-97 mph when he comes out of the bullpen. There were reports that he touched 99 mph in the Cape. He gets some swings and misses with a 79-83 mph slider and flashes an average changeup in the same range. His changeup has nice fade and he throws it with the same arm speed as his fastball, but he's still developing it after rarely using it in college. Capps has an unconventional delivery that doesn't use his 6-foot-5, 220-pound frame to his advantage. He has a long stride that drops him way down in his delivery, and he also throws across his body from a low three-quarters arm angle. The Mariners tried to raise his arm slot a bit in instructional league. Despite his unorthodox mechanics, Capps usually throws strikes. He has a quiet confidence and could move quickly as a reliever. His fresh arm and ability to hold velocity deep into games bode well for his potential as a starter, while his unrefined changeup and delivery point more toward the bullpen. He could start his first full pro season in high Class A.

Year	Club (League)	Class	W	L	ERA	G	GS	CG	SV	IP	H	HR	BB	SO	K/9	WHIP	AVG
2011	Clinton (MWL)	LoA	1	1	6.00	4	4	0	0	18	19	1	10	21	10.5	1.61	.284
Minor League Totals			1	1	6.00	4	4	0	0	18	19	1	10	21	10.5	1.61	.284

17 VICTOR SANCHEZ, RHP

BA GRADE
55
EXTREME

Born: Jan. 30, 1995. **B-T:** R-R. **Ht.:** 6-1. **Wt.:** 200. **Signed:** Venezuela, 2011. **Signed by:** Luis Martinez/Emilio Carrasquel/Bob Engle.

The Mariners are one of the biggest players on the international market, and they landed the best pitcher in the 2011 class in Sanchez. It cost them $2.5 million, the most they've ever spent on a foreign amateur. Venezuelan scouts viewed him as the nation's top prospect since he was 13 and the second-youngest player on Venezuela's 14-and-under team at the COPABE Pan American championships in 2008. That squad also included Blue Jays righthander Ardonys Cardona and Rangers second baseman Rougned Odor. Sanchez struck out eight in a five-inning no-hitter against Ecuador, missing a perfect game when he hit a batter. He has a stout, muscular frame with sloped shoulders and large hands. He already shows impressive velocity, sitting at 92-94 in instructional league. He has a loose arm with an easy delivery, and his athleticism helps him throw his fastball for strikes to both sides of the plate. Sanchez's advanced feel for pitching stands out. He already flashes an above-average changeup and shows the ability to spin a breaking ball as well. He threw a hard slider before signing but has worked with his curveball more since turning pro. His curve has sharp break and he locates it well. Sanchez's body is relatively filled out and he won't gain much more velocity as he gets older. His relatively short stature also limits the plane on his fastball, which can flatten out at times and become hittable. Sanchez likely will begin 2012 in extended spring training to work on the nuances of pitching before reporting to the Arizona League at age 17 in June.

Year	Club (League)	Class	W	L	ERA	G	GS	CG	SV	IP	H	HR	BB	SO	K/9	WHIP	AVG
2011	Did Not Play—Signed 2012 Contract																

18 TYLER MARLETTE, C

BA GRADE
50
HIGH

Born: Jan. 23, 1993. **B-T:** R-R. **Ht.:** 5-11. **Wt.:** 195. **Drafted:** HS—Oviedo, Fla., 2011 (5th round). **Signed by:** Rob Mummau.

Marlette was a high-profile player on the prep showcase circuit in 2010, winning MVP honors at the Aflac All-America game after homering at Petco Park. A fifth-round pick last June, he gave up a Central Florida commitment to sign for an over-slot $650,000. He continued to show power in big league parks after he signed, hitting several balls into the left-field upper deck during batting practice at Safeco Field. On the showcase circuit, Marlette had a tendency to get pull-happy and leak open on his front side. He did a better job of staying closed last spring and displayed plus power to all fields. He struck out 13 times without a walk in his brief pro debut, and how much he'll hit for average is tied to his ability to maintain a more disciplined approach. Marlette's offense is ahead of his defense. Though he has above-average arm strength, his receiving needs a lot of work. He's a grinder who will put in the work to improve. He has below-average speed, though that doesn't matter at his position. Marlette plays with a lot of confidence and is a sparkplug in the clubhouse. He's likely headed for extended spring training and then Everett in 2012.

Year	Club (League)	Class	AVG	G	AB	R	H	2B	3B	HR	RBI	BB	SO	SB	CS	OBP	SLG
2011	Pulaski (APP)	R	.156	12	45	4	7	2	0	0	2	0	13	0	0	.156	.200
Minor League Totals			.156	12	45	4	7	2	0	0	2	0	13	0	0	.156	.200

19 FORREST SNOW, RHP

BA GRADE
50
HIGH

Born: Dec. 30, 1988. **B-T:** R-R. **Ht.:** 6-6. **Wt.:** 195. **Drafted:** Washington, 2010 (36th round). **Signed by:** Joe Ross.

In the 51-year history of the draft, only 18 players signed out of the 36th round have made it to the big leagues. Seattle had the best of that group in Raul Ibanez and has another 36th-rounder knocking on the door with Snow. Both his high school coach (Dana Papasedero from Lakeside High in Seattle) and college pitching coach (Washington's Joe Ross) scout for the Mariners, who drafted him in the 44th round out of high school before signing him for $20,000 after three up-and-down years with the Huskies. Snow quickly turned a corner as a pro, showing improved stuff almost immediately. He threw a 93-95 mph fastball as a reliever in his pro debut, then worked at 88-92 mph as a starter last year. He throws his sinking heater to both sides of the plate and uses his height to get a steep downhill plane. He did a better job of pitching off his fastball in 2011, setting up his best pitch, a changeup he calls "The Snowflake." It's already an above-average pitch and has plus-plus potential. He throws two breaking balls, though both his curveball and slider are below average. His high three-quarters arm slot theoretically would lend itself more to a curve, though his slider would pair better with his sinker if he winds up in the bullpen. Snow repeats his delivery well, doesn't have any significant mechanical issues and owns solid control. He could fill nearly any role on a big league pitching staff. After climbing to Triple-A in his first full pro season then pitching in the Arizona Fall League, he could reach Seattle in 2012.

Year	Club (League)	Class	W	L	ERA	G	GS	CG	SV	IP	H	HR	BB	SO	K/9	WHIP	AVG
2010	Everett (NWL)	SS	0	0	0.00	10	0	0	3	25	8	0	9	26	9.2	0.67	.104
	Clinton (MWL)	LoA	0	1	1.35	15	0	0	6	20	9	1	7	26	11.7	0.80	.132
2011	Clinton (MWL)	LoA	2	7	3.62	13	13	1	0	75	62	4	19	71	8.6	1.08	.223
	High Desert (CAL)	HiA	2	3	8.10	6	6	0	0	33	49	7	13	20	5.4	1.86	.350
	Tacoma (PCL)	AAA	1	2	5.35	9	2	0	0	35	34	4	10	36	9.2	1.25	.256
Minor League Totals			5	13	4.01	53	21	1	9	189	162	16	58	179	8.5	1.17	.233

20 JABARI BLASH, OF

BA GRADE

50

HIGH

Born: July 4, 1989. **B-T:** R-R. **Ht.:** 6-4. **Wt.:** 195. **Drafted:** Miami Dade JC, 2010 (8th round). **Signed by:** Mike Tosar.

Blash took a winding route to pro ball. The White Sox drafted the Virgin Islands native out of high school in 2007 in the 29th round, but he turned them down to attend Alcorn State. Academically ineligible in 2008, he transferred to Miami Dade JC for the following season and emerged as one of Florida's top juco talents. The Rangers selected him in the ninth round of the 2009 draft but he again didn't sign, and his 2010 season ended early when he was kicked off the team in April. The Mariners took him in the eighth round two months later and he finally signed for $140,000. Blash stands out immediately for his chiseled physique, and one Northwest League manager compared him to a stronger version of Eric Davis last summer. Blash's strength shows up at the plate, as he led the NWL in extra-base hits (30) and slugging (.574) after faltering in the first half in the Midwest League. His swing gets too long at times and he has some holes on the outer half of the plate, so he may not hit for a high average. Blash is still raw for a 22-year-old. He has a good eye at the plate but can be too passive and gets himself into a lot of two-strike counts. His prospect status hinges solely on his bat, because he's a fringy runner and left fielder with an average arm. He gets careless at times with his defense. How Blash handles his second shot at low Class A in 2012 will tell a great deal about his future.

Year	Club (League)	Class	AVG	G	AB	R	H	2B	3B	HR	RBI	BB	SO	SB	CS	OBP	SLG
2010	Pulaski (APP)	R	.266	32	109	21	29	6	1	5	20	13	44	1	1	.362	.477
2011	Clinton (MWL)	LoA	.218	42	124	13	27	5	1	3	13	38	43	5	2	.401	.347
	Everett (NWL)	SS	.292	57	195	26	57	16	3	11	43	28	65	10	3	.393	.574
Minor League Totals			.264	131	428	60	113	27	5	19	76	79	152	16	6	.388	.484

21 BRANDON MAURER, RHP

BA GRADE

50

EXTREME

Born: July 3, 1990. **B-T:** R-R. **Ht.:** 6-5. **Wt.:** 200. **Drafted:** HS—Orange, Calif., 2008 (23rd round). **Signed by:** Tim Reynolds.

A case of strep throat caused Maurer to miss the 2007 Area Code Games before his senior year, but he got plenty of looks pitching in the same Orange (Calif.) Lutheran High rotation as Gerrit Cole. While Cole went in the first round of the 2008 draft—and would go No. 1 overall in 2011 after three years at UCLA—Maurer slipped to the 23rd round, where the Mariners bought him out of a Long Beach State commitment with a $150,000 bonus. He has filled out nicely since then and still has a springy, loose body. Maurer's fastball sits at 91-94 mph and gets as high as 97. He mixes in a solid slider with plus potential and shows feel for a changeup and a curveball that could both be average in time. He pounds the strike zone with all of his pitches, showing average control and working with an extremely quick tempo. Maurer has pitched just 185 innings in four pro seasons because he has had trouble staying healthy. A sore elbow limited him to 15 innings in 2010, and a shoulder strain held him to 79 frames last year. The good news is that he has avoided surgery, and to his credit, he moved to the Phoenix area this offseason so he can workout at the Mariners' spring training facility. Though he still throws with some effort, Maurer has smoothed out his delivery since signing. If he can stay healthy and get stretched out, the best-case scenario is that he becomes a No. 2 starter. If he can't handle bigger workloads, he still could be valuable as a late-inning reliever. He'll probably open the season in high Class A.

Year	Club (League)	Class	W	L	ERA	G	GS	CG	SV	IP	H	HR	BB	SO	K/9	WHIP	AVG
2008	Mariners (AZL)	R	1	2	3.09	8	5	0	0	23	20	1	8	25	9.6	1.20	.247
2009	Pulaski (APP)	R	3	4	3.61	13	12	1	0	67	67	4	18	51	6.8	1.26	.266
2010	Mariners (AZL)	R	0	1	1.64	4	4	0	0	11	8	0	2	14	11.5	0.91	.205
	Clinton (MWL)	LoA	0	1	2.08	2	0	0	0	4	5	1	0	6	12.5	1.15	.294
2011	Clinton (MWL)	LoA	1	3	3.41	7	6	0	0	37	28	2	14	44	10.7	1.14	.211
	High Desert (CAL)	HiA	2	4	6.38	9	7	0	0	42	47	8	11	37	7.9	1.37	.275
Minor League Totals			7	15	3.98	43	34	1	0	185	175	16	53	177	8.6	1.23	.253

22 JOHN HICKS, C

BA GRADE

45

MEDIUM

Born: Aug. 31, 1989. **B-T:** R-R. **Ht.:** 6-2. **Wt.:** 190. **Drafted:** Virginia, 2011 (4th round). **Signed by:** Mike Moriarty.

When the Mariners selected Dustin Ackley second overall in 2009, they then took two of his North Carolina teammates with early picks: third baseman Kyle Seager in the third round and lefthander Brian Moran in the seventh round. They did something similar last June, choosing Danny Hultzen at No. 2 and two of his Virginia teammates, Hicks in the fourth round and third baseman Steven Proscia in the seventh. A product of the same Goochland (Va.) High program that spawned Justin Verlander, Hicks signed for $240,000. He didn't become a full-time catcher until 2011, when he helped the Cavaliers to the College World Series semifinals by tying Proscia for the team lead with eight homers and 59 RBIs. Hicks doesn't have one carrying tool, but he has all-around potential to go with tremendous makeup and leadership qualities. He has gap power and a contact-oriented approach at the plate, though he would benefit from working deeper counts and drawing more walks. He's more athletic than most catchers, albeit still with below-average speed. Hicks has average arm strength and threw out 44 percent of basestealers in his pro debut. He has the potential to be an average receiver once he gets some more experience. Hicks has to stay behind the plate to have value because his bat isn't potent enough for another position. He'll open his first full pro season in high Class A.

Year	Club (League)	Class	AVG	G	AB	R	H	2B	3B	HR	RBI	BB	SO	SB	CS	OBP	SLG
2011	Clinton (MWL)	LoA	.309	38	139	21	43	9	2	2	26	5	17	2	3	.331	.446
Minor League Totals			.309	38	139	21	43	9	2	2	26	5	17	2	3	.331	.446

23 MARCUS LITTLEWOOD, C/SS/2B

BA GRADE
50
EXTREME

Born: March 18, 1992. **B-T:** B-R. **Ht.:** 6-3. **Wt.:** 200. **Drafted:** HS—St. George, Utah, 2010 (2nd round). **Signed by:** Chris Pelekoudas.

Littlewood came to pro ball with above-average on-field maturity and instincts, thanks to two stints with U.S. national teams and the fact that his father Mike played briefly in the Brewers system and is the head coach at NCAA Division II Dixie State (Utah). The Mariners invested a 2010 second-round pick and $900,000 in Littlewood, but the early returns last year were disappointing. He hit just .158/.236/.211 at Clinton and didn't fare much better after a demotion to Everett. He was supposed to have a mature approach and control of the strike zone, but he fanned 104 times in 328 at-bats. A switch-hitter, he still could hit for a solid average with 10-15 homers annually if everything clicks. Littlewood embraced the opportunity to enhance his defensive value when Seattle asked him to move to catcher. A below-average runner, he didn't have the range for shortstop or the quickness for second base, the two positions he played in 2011. His above-average arm strength and his agility should work behind the plate. He worked with catching coordinator Roger Hansen during the season to prepare for making the full transition in instructional league. The move will take some pressure off Littlewood's bat. If he hits, he can be an everyday player. If he doesn't, he still can be a backup—an option that wouldn't exist had he remained in the middle infield. Seattle may keep Littlewood in extended spring training at the start of 2012 so he can focus on his catching.

Year	Club (League)	Class	AVG	G	AB	R	H	2B	3B	HR	RBI	BB	SO	SB	CS	OBP	SLG
2011	Clinton (MWL)	LoA	.158	27	95	7	15	0	1	1	6	10	23	0	1	.236	.211
	Everett (NWL)	SS	.206	62	233	45	48	13	1	8	30	45	81	3	3	.337	.373
Minor League Totals			.192	89	328	52	63	13	2	9	36	55	104	3	4	.309	.326

24 CHIH-HSIEN CHIANG, OF

BA GRADE
45
MEDIUM

Born: Feb. 21, 1988. **B-T:** L-R. **Ht.:** 6-2. **Wt.:** 170. **Signed:** Taiwan, 2005. **Signed by:** Jon Deeble (Red Sox).

Seattle was an aggressive seller at the 2011 trade deadline. After the Mariners sent Doug Fister and David Pauley to the Tigers, they engaged the Dodgers and Red Sox in a three-way trade. In exchange for giving Erik Bedard and minor league righthander Josh Fields to Boston, Seattle got Trayvon Robinson from Los Angeles and Chiang from the Sox. Chiang hit .273/.319/.422 in his first five pro seasons and didn't take off until he got a better handle on his diabetes before the 2011 season. He played with more energy and consistency, leading the Double-A Eastern League in slugging (.648) and earning a trip to the Futures Game. Chiang is an aggressive hitter with pop to the gaps and some home run power to the pull side. His bat and power still don't grade out as more than average, which makes it hard to project him as a regular. A former second baseman, Chiang is an average defender with solid arm strength in right field. He's a below-average runner with a thick lower half. He's one of 10 outfielders on the Mariners' 40-man roster, which will make it tough for him to find playing time in Tacoma. He could return to Jackson after his disappointing showing following the trade.

Year	Club (League)	Class	AVG	G	AB	R	H	2B	3B	HR	RBI	BB	SO	SB	CS	OBP	SLG
2006	Red Sox (GCL)	R	.287	33	122	12	35	8	2	1	12	4	11	2	0	.318	.410
	Lowell (NYP)	SS	.278	9	36	6	10	0	3	1	8	2	9	1	0	.308	.528
2007	Greenville (SAL)	LoA	.262	97	355	35	93	27	2	5	41	22	81	1	1	.310	.392
2008	Lancaster (CAL)	HiA	.303	83	320	47	97	19	2	9	59	18	52	2	1	.337	.459
2009	Salem (CAR)	HiA	.264	85	299	37	79	21	3	6	38	24	48	2	1	.323	.415
2010	Portland (EL)	AA	.260	121	438	54	114	35	1	11	65	31	64	2	0	.312	.420
2011	Portland (EL)	AA	.340	88	321	68	109	37	4	18	76	25	61	6	2	.402	.648
	Jackson (SL)	AA	.208	32	130	11	27	7	0	0	10	6	30	1	2	.255	.262
Minor League Totals			.279	548	2021	270	564	154	17	51	309	132	356	17	7	.329	.448

25 CARLOS TRIUNFEL, SS

BA GRADE
45
MEDIUM

Born: Feb. 27, 1990. **B-T:** R-R. **Ht.:** 5-11. **Wt.:** 200. **Signed:** Dominican Republic, 2006. **Signed by:** Bob Engle/Patrick Guerrero.

Though it seems like Triunfel has been around forever, he'll turn just 22 in February and already has made it to Triple-A. Signed for $1.3 million in 2006, he hasn't lived up to the expectations that came with that bonus. Triunfel has impressive hand-eye coordination and bat control which allow him to hit for average, but he doesn't do much else. He's too aggressive at the plate and gets himself out by putting tough pitches in play instead of working counts. He has some strength but it doesn't translate into in-game power because he focuses on making contact rather than waiting for a pitch he can drive. Scouts long have thought that Triunfel would become too thick in the lower half to remain at shortstop, but he got slimmer and showed better agility in 2011. He's still a below-average runner, however. His best tool is his cannon for an arm. Triunfel likely will end up as a utilityman who can play anywhere in the infield. He was added to the 40-man roster in November but will begin 2012 back in Tacoma.

Year	Club (League)	Class	AVG	G	AB	R	H	2B	3B	HR	RBI	BB	SO	SB	CS	OBP	SLG
2007	Wisconsin (MWL)	LoA	.309	43	152	18	47	8	2	0	14	5	23	4	8	.342	.388
	Mariners (AZL)	R	.273	3	11	1	3	0	0	0	3	0	1	0	0	.231	.273
	High Desert (CAL)	HiA	.288	50	208	32	60	10	2	0	22	12	31	3	4	.333	.356
2008	High Desert (CAL)	HiA	.287	108	436	75	125	20	4	8	49	30	52	30	9	.336	.406
2009	West Tenn (SL)	AA	.231	7	26	2	6	1	0	0	4	1	2	0	0	.286	.269
	Mariners (AZL)	R	.250	4	16	0	4	1	0	0	4	0	2	1	0	.250	.313
2010	West Tenn (SL)	AA	.257	129	470	51	121	12	1	7	42	13	54	2	8	.286	.332
2011	Jackson (SL)	AA	.281	105	395	45	111	22	2	6	35	25	71	5	7	.340	.392
	Tacoma (PCL)	AAA	.279	27	111	7	31	6	1	0	10	2	17	1	0	.302	.351
Minor League Totals			.278	476	1825	231	508	80	12	21	183	88	253	46	36	.320	.370

26 MAURICIO ROBLES, LHP

BA GRADE
45
MEDIUM

Born: March 5, 1989. **B-T:** L-L. **Ht.:** 5-10. **Wt.:** 205. **Signed:** Venezuela, 2006. **Signed by:** German Robles (Tigers).

Acquired along with Luke French from the Tigers at the 2009 trade deadline in exchange for Jarrod Washburn, Robles pitched well in his first full season with the Mariners and ranked No. 6 on this list a year ago. But 2011 was essentially a lost year for the Venezuelan lefty. He had bone chips removed from his elbow in March and never was quite right upon returning. Instead of sitting at 91-94 mph with his fastball, like he had in the past, Robles pitched at 89-91. His secondary pitches also slipped after he previously showed flashes of a plus changeup and average curveball. Though he has displayed enough pitches to start, his control never has been good—he has averaged 5.0 walks per nine innings as a pro—and he lost his margin for error in 2011. Robles still could make it as a No. 4 or 5 starter if his stuff recovers, and he always could find a home in the bullpen. How he looks in spring training will determine how Seattle handles him in 2012.

Year	Club (League)	Class	W	L	ERA	G	GS	CG	SV	IP	H	HR	BB	SO	K/9	WHIP	AVG
2006	Tigers/Marlins (VSL)	R	0	1	3.38	14	0	0	0	16	17	0	16	20	11.3	2.06	.279
2007	Tigers (VSL)	R	3	6	3.26	14	14	0	0	69	60	4	27	83	10.8	1.26	.237
2008	West Michigan (MWL)	LoA	5	3	2.66	23	16	0	0	91	54	2	54	79	7.8	1.18	.176
2009	West Michigan (MWL)	LoA	4	4	4.63	11	11	0	0	56	45	6	27	71	11.3	1.28	.221
	Lakeland (FSL)	HiA	4	2	3.60	7	7	0	0	35	34	3	14	40	10.3	1.37	.256
	High Desert (CAL)	HiA	3	2	2.78	7	6	0	0	32	23	1	19	34	9.5	1.30	.202
2010	West Tenn (SL)	AA	6	6	4.11	22	22	0	0	114	102	10	51	120	9.5	1.34	.239
	Tacoma (PCL)	AAA	3	1	3.54	5	5	0	0	28	19	2	20	34	10.9	1.39	.188
2011	High Desert (CAL)	HiA	0	2	12.41	4	4	0	0	12	19	2	11	9	6.6	2.43	.373
	Jackson (SL)	AA	0	1	4.15	2	2	0	0	9	7	1	8	6	6.2	1.73	.219
	Tacoma (PCL)	AAA	1	2	8.74	4	4	0	0	11	7	3	14	8	6.4	1.85	.189
Minor League Totals			29	30	3.91	113	91	0	0	474	387	34	261	504	9.6	1.37	.225

27 STEVEN PROSCIA, 3B/1B

BA GRADE
45
MEDIUM

Born: June 26, 1990. **B-T:** R-R. **Ht.:** 6-2. **Wt.:** 210. **Drafted:** Virginia, 2011 (7th round). **Signed by:** Mike Moriarty.

In high school, Proscia was a standout football player at national powerhouse Don Bosco Prep (Ramsey, N.J.), playing on both sides of the ball for a nationally ranked team that won state championships in 2006 and 2007. His gridiron mentality is evident on the diamond, as he's a blue-collar grinder who started every game but one during his three college seasons at Virginia. After signing for $160,000 as a seventh-round pick in 2011, he had no trouble adapting to pro ball, even with an aggressive assignment to high Class A. Offensively, Proscia fits the bill at third base. He has above-average power potential with bat speed, a swing that stays in the hitting zone a long time and the ability to lift the ball and create good backspin. Proscia has feel for the strike zone, but he can get too aggressive at the plate and drew just four walks in 44 pro games. He did hit 12 homers, though 11 of them came at extremely hitter-friendly High Desert. Proscia has a thick, muscular build and is better coming in on balls than he is moving laterally. He has solid arm strength but may profile best defensively as a corner utility guy rather than as a regular at the hot corner. The speed of the pro game and High Desert's fast infield helped contribute to Proscia making 10 errors in 28 games at third. He has fringy speed but runs the bases aggressively. He may return to high Class A to being 2012 in order to work on his defense.

Year	Club (League)	Class	AVG	G	AB	R	H	2B	3B	HR	RBI	BB	SO	SB	CS	OBP	SLG
2011	High Desert (CAL)	HiA	.303	44	185	28	56	11	1	12	42	4	33	3	3	.319	.568
Minor League Totals			.303	44	185	28	56	11	1	12	42	4	33	3	3	.319	.568

28 JOHERMYN CHAVEZ, OF

BA GRADE
45
HIGH

Born: Jan. 26, 1989. **B-T:** R-R. **Ht.:** 6-3. **Wt.:** 220. **Signed:** Venezuela, 2005. **Signed by:** Rafael Moncada (Blue Jays).

Arriving with Brandon League in the December 2009 trade that sent Brandon Morrow to Toronto, Chavez finished second in the California League with 32 homers in his first season in the Seattle system. His second was a different story, as he ranked second-to-last among Double-A Southern League qualifiers with a .216 average. Chavez always has been prone to strikeouts and streakiness. When he's confident and on a roll, everything seems to come easy to him, but those times were few and far between with Jackson. He looked uncomfortable and out of sync at the plate. He's still learning to recognize pitches and too often chases breaking balls out of the zone, negating his strength. He profiles as a below-average hitter with plus power potential. Chavez is a below-average runner, but he's a good athlete who plays average defense and fits the right-field profile with the best outfield arm in the system. His 18 assists ranked second in the SL last year. He'll take another crack at solving Double-A pitching in 2012.

Year	Club (League)	Class	AVG	G	AB	R	H	2B	3B	HR	RBI	BB	SO	SB	CS	OBP	SLG
2006	Pulaski (APP)	R	.276	36	105	19	29	9	0	0	18	9	23	1	2	.371	.362
2007	Blue Jays (GCL)	R	.301	50	176	29	53	12	2	6	21	20	50	7	2	.389	.494
2008	Lansing (MWL)	LoA	.211	115	402	40	85	20	2	7	39	25	128	9	5	.272	.323
2009	Lansing (MWL)	LoA	.283	134	508	87	144	22	6	21	89	40	137	10	6	.346	.474
2010	High Desert (CAL)	HiA	.315	136	534	109	168	30	7	32	96	52	131	6	9	.387	.577
2011	Jackson (SL)	AA	.216	126	439	47	95	16	4	13	50	49	124	6	9	.312	.360
Minor League Totals			.265	597	2164	331	574	109	21	79	313	195	593	39	33	.341	.445

29 RICH POYTHRESS, 1B

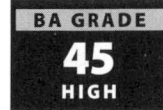

BA GRADE
45
HIGH

Born: Aug. 11, 1987. **B-T:** R-R. **Ht.:** 6-4. **Wt.:** 235. **Drafted:** Georgia, 2009 (2nd round). **Signed by:** Garrett Ball.

After breaking Gordon Beckham's Georgia school record with 86 RBIs in 2009, Poythress led the minors with 130 RBIs the following year. He also ranked second in the California League in slugging (.580) and third in homers (31). His 2011 encore wasn't as impressive, as his numbers plummeted in Double-A. He did make strides in the second half, batting .316/.396/.455. Poythress' swing is built more for line drives than homers and his power comes mostly to the opposite field. He does have strength and can turn around anyone's fastball, as evidenced by the homers he hit against hard-throwing Chris Archer (Rays), Matt Bush (Rays) and Paul Clemens (Astros). He has a solid approach at the plate but ultimately may not produce enough offense to profile as an everyday player at first base. Poythress played some third base in college and in pro ball, but first base is his only option at the upper levels. He has good footwork around the bag and an average arm for the position. He's a bottom-of-the-scale runner and no threat on the bases. Poythress will try to show more power when he repeats Double-A in 2012.

Year	Club (League)	Class	AVG	G	AB	R	H	2B	3B	HR	RBI	BB	SO	SB	CS	OBP	SLG
2009	Mariners (AZL)	R	.300	6	20	4	6	0	0	1	6	5	6	0	0	.462	.450
	West Tenn (SL)	AA	.230	26	87	11	20	2	0	1	9	15	24	1	0	.337	.287
2010	High Desert (CAL)	HiA	.315	123	476	88	150	33	0	31	130	52	100	3	2	.381	.580
2011	Jackson (SL)	AA	.267	122	450	50	120	28	3	11	64	50	82	2	3	.347	.416
Minor League Totals			.287	277	1033	153	296	63	3	44	209	122	212	6	5	.364	.481

30 CAVAN COHOES, SS

BA GRADE
50
EXTREME

Born: May 3, 1993. **B-T:** R-R. **Ht.:** 6-2. **Wt.:** 185. **Drafted:** HS—Stuttgart, Germany, 2011 (9th round). **Signed by:** Wayne Norton.

Although a few other teams were on him, the biggest surprise in the 2011 draft came when the Mariners turned to Germany for their ninth-round pick. Cohoes, whose family is from Ohio, was eligible because he attended a U.S. high school on the Patch Barracks, where his father Chris is an Air Force pilot. His grandfather, Rex Leach, ranks fifth all-time in Ohio high school basketball scoring—one spot behind LeBron James. The first player ever drafted out of Germany, Cohoes nursed a left quadriceps injury after signing for $650,000 and it lingered, keeping him out of instructional league. When healthy, he shows intriguing tools and raw potential. He has a wiry, athletic frame and plus speed and arm strength. Ohio State also wanted him to run track if he made it to campus, and Kent State would have given him a shot on the mound had he signed there. He has the tools to stick at shortstop or make it in center field, his main position in Germany. Cohoes has bat speed and a fluid swing, though his stroke can get out of sync, typical for someone with his limited experience. Given his background, Seattle will need to take things slowly with Cohoes. He'll start 2012 in extended spring training before easing into pro ball in the Arizona League in June.

Year	Club (League)	Class	AVG	G	AB	R	H	2B	3B	HR	RBI	BB	SO	SB	CS	OBP	SLG
2011	Did Not Play—Signed Late																

Tampa Bay Rays

BY BILL BALLEW

If there were any remaining doubters regarding the Rays' way of doing business, the 2011 season should leave nothing more than the sound of chirping crickets. Despite rebuilding the bullpen and filling big holes on the major league roster, general manager Andrew Friedman proved once again that even teams in the American League East can do more with less.

With an Opening Day payroll of $41 million—a fraction of the $203 million spent by the Yankees and the $162 million paid by the Red Sox—Tampa Bay reached the playoffs for the third time in four years with a furious finish. The Rays became the first team in baseball history to make the postseason by overcoming a nine-game deficit in September. They won 17 of their final 25 games and caught Boston for the AL wild card on the final day of the regular season.

Under the direction of manager Joe Maddon, Tampa Bay won again with pitching and defense. Rays pitchers limited opponents to a .234 average, the lowest by an AL team since the league adopted the DH in 1973. Tampa Bay allowed the fewest runs, made the fewest errors (a franchise-record 73) and had the best defensive efficiency in the circuit.

The Rays had looked at 2011 as a rebuilding a year. They lost four-time all-star Carl Crawford, franchise career home run leader Carlos Pena and 2010 AL saves leader Rafael Soriano to free agency and traded Jason Bartlett and 2008 AL Championship Series MVP Matt Garza to further lower their payroll.

The farm system continued to provide reinforcements. Jeremy Hellickson replaced Garza in the rotation, winning 13 games and Baseball America's Rookie of the Year award. Desmond Jennings filled the void left by Crawford in left field in the final two months, hitting 10 homers and stealing 20 bases. Matt Moore made three regular-season appearances and gave a preview of coming attractions by shutting out the Rangers for seven innings in the Division Series.

While Tampa Bay continued to win in the majors, it also restocked its system. The Rays received five youngsters from the Cubs for Garza, including three quality prospects in shortstop Hak-Ju Lee, righthander Chris Archer and outfielder Brandon Guyer.

The exodus of seven free agents gave Tampa Bay 10 compensation draft choices and an unprecedented 12 picks in the first two rounds. The Rays' first two picks weren't supposed to get to them, high school righthander Taylor Guerrieri at No. 24 and Louisiana

CLIFF WELCH

Jeremy Hellickson won Rookie of the Year a season after Minor League Player of the Year

TOP 30 PROSPECTS

1. Matt Moore, lhp	16. Parker Markel, rhp
2. Hak-Ju Lee, ss	17. Albert Suarez, rhp
3. Chris Archer, rhp	18. Tyler Goeddel, 3b
4. Taylor Guerrieri, rhp	19. Matt Bush, rhp
5. Alex Colome, rhp	20. Blake Snell, lhp
6. Alex Torres, lhp	21. Braulio Lara, lhp
7. Tim Beckham, ss	22. Stephen Vogt, c/of/1b
8. Enny Romero, lhp	23. Wilking Rodriguez, rhp
9. Drew Vettleson, of	24. Lenny Linsky, rhp
10. Mikie Mahtook, of	25. Brandon Martin, ss
11. Brandon Guyer, of	26. Kes Carter, of
12. Jake Hager, ss	27. Justin O'Conner, c
13. Derek Dietrich, ss	28. Felipe Rivero, lhp
14. Ryan Brett, 2b	29. Tyler Bortnick, 2b
15. Luke Bailey, c	30. Jake Thompson, rhp

State outfielder Mikie Mahtook at No. 31, and they continued to blend college and prep talent afterward.

Friedman said the draft is more important to his franchise than any other. Baseball's new collective bargaining agreement will make it tougher on Tampa Bay, because as long as it continues to win, it will pick toward the bottom of the draft and receive a relatively small bonus cap. Nevertheless, the Rays have no choice but to build from within, particularly after owner Stuart Sternberg questioned Tampa's viability as a major league market when the team struggled to attract fans during its playoff drive.

General Manager: Andrew Friedman. **Farm Director:** Mitch Lukevics. **Scouting Director:** R.J. Harrison.

Class	Team	League	W	L	Pct	Finish*	Manager(s)
Majors	Tampa Bay Rays	American	91	71	.562	4th (14)	Joe Maddon
Triple-A	Durham Bulls	International	80	62	.563	3rd (14)	Charlie Montoyo
Double-A	Montgomery Biscuits	Southern	65	74	.468	7th (10)	Billy Gardner
High A	Charlotte Stone Crabs	Florida State	64	75	.460	9th (12)	Jim Morrison
Low A	Bowling Green Hot Rods	Midwest	77	63	.550	5th (16)	Brady Williams
Short-season	Hudson Valley Renegades	New York-Penn	37	39	.487	9th (14)	Jared Sandberg
Rookie	Princeton Rays	Appalachian	30	38	.441	7th (10)	Mike Johns
Rookie	GCL Rays	Gulf Coast	24	36	.400	13th (15)	Joe Alvarez
Overall 2011 Minor League Record			377	387	.493	19th (30)	

*Finish in overall standings (No. of teams in league). †League champion.

LAST YEAR'S TOP 30

Player, Pos.		Status
1.	Jeremy Hellickson, rhp	Majors
2.	Matt Moore, lhp	No. 1
3.	Desmond Jennings, of	Majors
4.	Jake McGee, lhp	Majors
5.	Josh Sale, of	Dropped out
6.	Alex Torres, lhp	No. 6
7.	Alex Colome, rhp	No. 5
8.	Justin O'Conner, c	No. 27
9.	Drew Vettleson, of	No. 9
10.	Jake Thompson, rhp	No. 30
11.	Enny Romero, lhp	No. 8
12.	Nick Barnese, rhp	Dropped out
13.	Ty Morrison, of	Dropped out
14.	Braulio Lara, lhp	No. 17
15.	Tim Beckham, ss	No. 7
16.	Alex Cobb, rhp	Majors
17.	Luke Bailey, c	No. 15
18.	Yoel Araujo, of	Dropped out
19.	Joe Cruz, rhp	Dropped out
20.	Zach Quate, rhp	Dropped out
21.	Todd Glaesmann, of	Dropped out
22.	Derek Dietrich, ss	No. 13
23.	Ryan Brett, 2b	No. 14
24.	Scott Shuman, rhp	Dropped out
25.	Wilking Rodriguez, rhp	No. 23
26.	Kevin Kiermaier, of	Dropped out
27.	Hector Guevara, 2b	Dropped out
28.	Leslie Anderson, of/1b	Dropped out
29.	Kyle Lobstein, lhp	Dropped out
30.	Stephen Vogt, c/of/1b	No. 22

BEST TOOLS

Best Hitter for Average	Drew Vettleson
Best Power Hitter	Derek Dietrich
Best Strike-Zone Discipline	Tyler Bortnick
Fastest Baserunner	Hak-Ju Lee
Best Athlete	Ty Morrison
Best Fastball	Matt Moore
Best Curveball	Matt Moore
Best Slider	Chris Archer
Best Changeup	Marquis Fleming
Best Control	Matt Moore
Best Defensive Catcher	Mark Thomas
Best Defensive Infielder	Hak-Ju Lee
Best Infield Arm	Tim Beckham
Best Defensive Outfielder	Kevin Kiermaier
Best Outfield Arm	Brandon Guyer

PROJECTED 2015 LINEUP

Catcher	Luke Bailey
First Base	Ben Zobrist
Second Base	Jake Hager
Third Base	Evan Longoria
Shortstop	Hak-Ju Lee
Left Field	Matt Joyce
Center Field	Desmond Jennings
Right Field	B.J. Upton
Designated Hitter	Tim Beckham
No. 1 Starter	Matt Moore
No. 2 Starter	David Price
No. 3 Starter	James Shields
No. 4 Starter	Jeremy Hellickson
No. 5 Starter	Jeff Niemann
Closer	Chris Archer

TOP PROSPECTS OF THE DECADE

Year	Player, Pos.	2011 Org.
2002	Josh Hamilton, of	Rangers
2003	Rocco Baldelli, of	Out of baseball
2004	B.J. Upton, ss	Rays
2005	Delmon Young, of	Tigers
2006	Delmon Young, of	Tigers
2007	Delmon Young, of	Tigers
2008	Evan Longoria, 3b	Rays
2009	David Price, lhp	Rays
2010	Desmond Jennings, of	Rays
2011	Matt Moore, lhp	Rays

TOP DRAFT PICKS OF THE DECADE

Year	Player, Pos.	2011 Org.
2002	B.J. Upton, ss	Rays
2003	Delmon Young, of	Tigers
2004	Jeff Niemann, rhp	Rays
2005	Wade Townsend, rhp	Out of baseball
2006	Evan Longoria, 3b	Rays
2007	David Price, lhp	Rays
2008	Tim Beckham, ss	Rays
2009	*LeVon Washington, of	Indians
2010	Josh Sale, of	Rays
2011	Taylor Guerrieri, rhp	Rays

*Did not sign.

LARGEST BONUSES IN CLUB HISTORY

Matt White, 1996	$10,200,000
Rolando Arrojo, 1997	$7,000,000
Tim Beckham, 2008	$6,150,000
David Price, 2007	$5,600,000
B.J. Upton, 2002	$4,600,000

TAMPA BAY RAYS

TOP 2012 ROOKIE: Matt Moore, lhp. After capping an impressive campaign with a playoff victory over the Rangers, all he needs is an opening in the rotation.

BREAKOUT PROSPECT: Albert Suarez, rhp. He has been sidetracked by Tommy John surgery and a bout with Lyme disease, but he has regained his 93-94 mph fastball and sharp curveball.

SOURCE OF TOP 30 TALENT			
Homegrown	25	Acquired	5
College	7	Trades	4
Junior college	1	Rule 5 draft	0
High school	11	Independent leagues	0
Draft-and-follow	0	Free agents/waivers	1
Nondrafted free agents	0		
International	6		

SLEEPER: Granden Goetzman, of. The 75th overall selection in the 2011 draft has a loose, compact swing and draws comparisons to Hunter Pence and Jayson Werth.

LF
Josh Sale
Cody Rogers
Chris Murrill

CF
Mikie Mahtook (10)
Kes Carter (26)
Granden Goetzman
Ty Morrison
Johnny Eierman
James Harris
Yoel Araujo
Kevin Kiermaier

RF
Drew Vettleson (9)
Brandon Guyer (11)
Todd Glaesmann
K.D. Kang
Brett Nommensen

3B
Tim Beckham (7)
Derek Dietrich (13)
Tyler Goeddel (18)
Riccio Torrez
Cesar Perez
Taylor Motter

SS
Hak-Ju Lee (2)
Jake Hager (12)
Brandon Martin (25)
Juniel Querecuto

2B
Ryan Brett (14)
Tyler Bortnick (29)
Shawn O'Malley
Hector Guevara
Cole Figueroa
Robby Price

1B
Jeff Malm
John Alexander
Russ Canzler
Cameron Seitzer
Phil Wunderlich
Leslie Anderson

C
Luke Bailey (15)
Stephen Vogt (22)
Justin O'Conner (27)
Robinson Chirinos
Jose Lobaton
Mark Thomas
Oscar Hernandez
Nevin Ashley
Jake DePew
Matt Rice

LHP	
LHSP	**LHRP**
Matt Moore (1)	Frank de los Santos
Alex Torres (6)	Josh Satow
Enny Romero (8)	Adam Liberatore
Blake Snell (20)	Sergio Espinosa
Braulio Lara (21)	Jimmy Patterson
Felipe Rivero (28)	C.J. Riefenhauser
Grayson Garvin	Justin Woodall
Kyle Lobstein	
Ryan Carpenter	

RHP	
RHSP	**RHRP**
Chris Archer (3)	Parker Markel (16)
Taylor Guerrieri (4)	Matt Bush (19)
Alex Colome (5)	Lenny Linsky (24)
Albert Suarez (17)	Dane de la Rosa
Wilking Rodriguez (23)	Josh Lueke
Jake Thompson (30)	Scott Shuman
Nick Barnese	Zach Quate
Jeff Ames	Jake Floethe
Jason McEachern	Marquis Fleming
Joe Cruz	
Victor Mateo	
Shane Dyer	
Jacob Faria	

BEST PURE HITTER: Rays scouts love everything about SS Jake Hager (1), starting with his bat. He's a baseball rat with a good approach and handsy, line-drive swing. He uses the whole field and has impressive consistency.

BEST POWER HITTER: Tampa Bay has several power prospects, including OFs Mikie Mahtook (1) and Granden Goetzman (2) and 1B John Alexander (8). Mahtook has the best mix of present strength and power.

FASTEST RUNNER: Goetzman turns in 6.5-second times in the 60-yard dash but ranks third in this class behind OFs Johnny Eierman (3), a 6.4 runner in the 60, and James Harris (1s).

BEST DEFENSIVE PLAYER: 3B Tyler Goeddel (1s) earned the second-highest bonus in the Rays' crop ($1.5 million) for his all-around tools. The Rays really love his defense, including his strong, accurate arm and athletic infield actions. He can handle shortstop but fits better at third, where Riccio Torrez (4) also stands out. SS Brandon Martin (1s) is another quality defender

BEST FASTBALL: RHP Taylor Guerrieri (1) ranked only behind top-seven picks Dylan Bundy and Archie Bradley as having the best pure stuff in the high school class. Guerrieri's fastball sits at 93-96 mph when he's at his best.

BEST SECONDARY PITCH: Guerrieri has two plus secondary pitches in a cutter that has touched 91-92 mph and a true power curve in the low 80s. RHP Lenny Linsky (2) has a mid-80s slider that can reach 89.

BEST PRO DEBUT: The Rays have history with LHP Ryan Carpenter (7), who they also selected out of high school. He threw well after signing, going 2-1, 0.76 with 26 strikeouts in 24 innings at short-season Hudson Valley. 3B/SS Taylor Motter (17) was a Rookie-level Appalachian League all-star after hitting .323/.436/.481 with 22 stolen bases.

BEST ATHLETE: Harris and Goetzman. Eierman and Alexander have fast-twitch athleticism as well.

MOST INTRIGUING BACKGROUND: C Matt Rice (9) was a Rhodes Scholar finalist in 2010. 1B Cam Seitzer's (11) father Kevin led the American League in hits in 1987 and batted .295 over 12 big league seasons. He's now the Royals' hitting coach. Goeddel's older brother Erik pitches in the Mets system.

CLOSEST TO THE MAJORS: Mahtook, who's making his debut in the Arizona Fall League.

BEST LATE-ROUND PICK: Motter fits the utility infielder profile well. Seitzer has offensive upside as he taps into the power in his 6-foot-5, 220-pound frame. He hit 11 homers at Rookie-level Princeton after hitting four in the spring for Oklahoma.

THE ONE WHO GOT AWAY: 3B/RHP J.D. Davis (5) will play both ways at Cal State Fullerton. Tampa Bay drafted him for his power and might have tried him at catcher. Speedy OF Tanner English (13) couldn't resist the lure of two-time College World Series champion South Carolina.

ASSESSMENT: Having a record 12 picks in the first two rounds ensured the Rays a haul of talent. They got several of the athletic prep players they're known for, tempered by safer college bets such as Mahtook and LHP Grayson Garvin (1s).

2010   BONUSES: $7.2 MILLION

In a prelude to its 2011 draft bonanza, Tampa Bay had five picks in the first two rounds. OF Josh Sale (1) and C Justin O'Conner (1) are off to slow starts with the bat, but OF Drew Vettleson (1s), RHP Jake Thompson (2), SS Derek Dietrich (2) and 2B Ryan Brett (3) all have performed well.

GRADE: C+

2009   BONUSES: $4.0 MILLION

The Rays crippled their draft by failing to sign their top two choices, OF LeVon Washington (1) and 3B Kenny Diekroeger (2). They tried to compensate by paying over-slot bonuses to land OF Todd Glaesmann (3), C Luke Bailey (4), 1B Jeff Malm (5) and LHP Kevin James (9), but only Bailey cracks our Top 30 Prospects list.

GRADE: D

2008   BONUSES: $9.9 MILLION

SS Tim Beckham (1) showed renewed signs of life in 2011, but he may never live up to the expectations of being the No. 1 overall choice. He could be the only big leaguer in this group, too.

GRADE: C

2007   BONUSES: $8.0 MILLION

Tampa Bay did much better with this No. 1 overall selection, tabbing LHP David Price (1). Remarkably, LHP Matt Moore (8) might be better.

GRADE: A

Draft analysis by John Manuel (2011) and Jim Callis (2007-10).
Numbers in parentheses indicate draft rounds.

1 MATT MOORE, LHP

Born: June 18, 1989. **B-T:** L-L. **Ht.:** 6-2. **Wt.:** 205. **Drafted:** HS—Moriarty, N.M., 2007 (8th round). **Signed by:** Jack Powell.

BA GRADE
75
SAFE

CLIFF WELCH

After leading the minors in strikeouts in 2009 and 2010, Moore brought even more to the table in 2011. He went a combined 12-3, 1.92 between Double-A Montgomery and Triple-A Durham, threw a no-hitter in June and pitched a perfect inning in the Futures Game. He finished second in the minors in ERA, strikeouts (a career-high 210) and opponent average (.184). Moore then distinguished himself further following a September callup. He won his first major league start with five shutout innings at Yankee Stadium, then two-hit the Rangers over seven shutout innings to win the opening game of the American League Division Series. Not bad for an eighth-round pick out of a New Mexico high school who signed for $115,000 in 2007. Moore was the top prep prospect in a state that's not heavily scouted, and he fell through the cracks.

There's no question that Moore is the top pitching prospect in baseball. He reported to Double-A in April as equal parts thrower and pitcher before refining his mechanics and improving the quality of his secondary offerings. Moore has displayed an electric arm with easy action since he signed with the Rays. His fastball sits at 93-95 mph and touches 97 when he reaches back for a little extra. He has significantly upgraded his fastball command and now pounds the lower reaches of the strike zone on both sides of the plate. His curveball is also a plus-plus pitch, especially when he keeps his fingers above the ball and creates sharp, quick break and late bite. When he didn't stay on top of his curve at the Futures Game, it morphed into a nasty 86-87 mph slider. Moore gained a better feel in 2011 for his changeup, a pitch he throws with good arm speed to create deception and fade. His changeup is often a plus pitch and allows him to control opponents' bat speed and work deeper into games. Moore's an intelligent pitcher with tremendous mound presence, and he wasn't bothered by the challenges Tampa Bay

SCOUTING GRADES

Fastball: 70. **Command/**
Curveball: 70. **Control:** 60.
Changeup: 60. **Delivery:** 65.

Based on 20-80 scouting scale, where 50 represents major average, and future projection rather than present tools.

presented him with during his taste of the big leagues. He controls the running game well, as only eight of 14 basestealers succeeded against him in 2011.

With above-average or better grades in every facet of his game, Moore is an ace waiting to happen. Scouts say he has better pure stuff than David Price, whom the Rays selected 244 picks ahead of him in the 2007 draft. Moore doesn't have anything left to prove in the minors, where he has gone 28-21, 2.64 with 700 strikeouts in 497 innings. Despite his minimal big league experience, the Rays locked him up for the long term in December, giving him a five-year, $14 million contract that includes another $26 million in options for 2017-19.

Year	Club (League)	Class	W	L	ERA	G	GS	CG	SV	IP	H	HR	BB	SO	K/9	WHIP	AVG
2007	Princeton (APP)	R	0	0	2.66	8	3	0	0	20	12	1	16	29	12.8	1.38	.160
2008	Princeton (APP)	R	2	2	1.66	12	12	0	0	54	30	0	19	77	12.8	0.90	.154
2009	Bowling Green (SAL)	LoA	8	5	3.15	26	26	0	0	123	86	6	70	176	12.9	1.27	.195
2010	Charlotte (FSL)	HiA	6	11	3.36	26	26	0	0	145	109	7	61	208	12.9	1.18	.210
2011	Montgomery (SL)	AA	8	3	2.20	18	18	1	0	102	68	8	28	131	11.5	0.94	.187
	Durham (IL)	AAA	4	0	1.37	9	9	0	0	53	33	3	18	79	13.5	0.97	.179
	Tampa Bay (AL)	MAJ	1	0	2.89	3	1	0	0	9	9	1	3	15	14.5	1.29	.243
Major League Totals			1	0	2.89	3	1	0	0	9	9	1	3	15	14.5	1.29	.243
Minor League Totals			28	21	2.64	99	94	1	0	497	338	25	212	700	12.7	1.11	.190

2 HAK-JU LEE, SS

Born: Nov. 4, 1990. **B-T:** L-R. **Ht.:** 6-2. **Wt.:** 180. **Signed:** South Korea, 2008. **Signed by:** Steve Wilson (Cubs).

Signed for $725,000 by the Cubs in 2008, Lee was a huge part of the eight-player Matt Garza trade last January. He overcame chicken pox at the start of the 2011 season to hit safely in his first 14 games at high Class A Charlotte. He played in his second straight Futures Game before moving up to Double-A for the final month. An exciting player who employs speed and quickness in all aspects of his game, Lee has impressive footwork, plus range and an uncanny ability to read balls. Managers have rated him the best defensive shortstop in his league the past two years, and he has soft hands, a strong arm and a quick release. Using a line-drive stroke, Lee finished third in the Florida State League with a .318 average in 2011. He slapped the ball to the opposite field early in the season before becoming more proficient at turning on pitches. While his home run power is limited, his speed produces doubles and triples. He's learning how to read pitchers in order to become a better basestealer and could swipe 30-plus bases annually in the big leagues. Lee is a pure shortstop who should emerge as a starter and possibly an all-star. He'll return to Montgomery to open 2012 and could reach Tampa Bay by mid-2013.

BA GRADE 60 MEDIUM

Year	Club (League)	Class	AVG	G	AB	R	H	2B	3B	HR	RBI	BB	SO	SB	CS	OBP	SLG
2009	Boise (NWL)	SS	.330	68	264	56	87	14	2	2	33	31	50	25	8	.399	.420
2010	Peoria (MWL)	LoA	.282	122	485	85	137	22	4	1	40	49	86	32	7	.354	.351
2011	Charlotte (FSL)	HiA	.318	97	400	82	127	16	11	4	23	42	72	28	14	.389	.443
	Montgomery (SL)	AA	.190	24	100	16	19	1	4	1	7	11	22	5	2	.272	.310
Minor League Totals			.296	311	1249	239	370	53	21	8	103	133	230	90	31	.368	.392

3 CHRIS ARCHER, RHP

Born: Sept. 26, 1988. **B-T:** R-R. **Ht.:** 6-3. **Wt.:** 180. **Drafted:** HS—Clayton, N.C., 2006 (5th round). **Signed by:** Bob Mayer (Indians).

Archer struggled for three years in the Indians system before joining the Cubs in a trade for Mark DeRosa in December 2008. By the time he was included in the Matt Garza trade last January, Archer ranked as Chicago's No. 1 prospect. Despite an uneven showing in his first season in the Rays system, he recorded a 3.25 ERA over the final three months. Archer has impressive size and a quick arm that generates a power fastball/slider combo. His heater resides at 90-95 mph and touches 97 with run and sink. He falls in love with his plus-plus slider, an 86-88 mph offering with incredible tilt and good depth. He'll need to improve his below-average changeup in order to remain a starter. He struggles at times to repeat his delivery, which leads to control issues. He led the Double-A Southern League with 18 wild pitches and ranked third with 80 walks in 2011. Archer has the stuff to challenge hitters and succeed in the front half of a major league rotation. He also would have what it takes to become a closer. He'll open 2012 in Durham and should make his big league debut at some point during the year.

BA GRADE 60 HIGH

Year	Club (League)	Class	W	L	ERA	G	GS	CG	SV	IP	H	HR	BB	SO	K/9	WHIP	AVG
2006	Indians (GCL)	R	0	3	7.45	7	6	0	0	19	17	1	17	21	9.8	1.76	.224
	Burlington (APP)	R	0	0	10.80	1	0	0	0	2	2	1	1	1	5.4	1.80	.333
2007	Indians (GCL)	R	1	7	5.64	12	11	0	0	53	56	4	21	48	8.2	1.46	.271
	Lake County (SAL)	LoA	0	0	9.00	1	0	0	0	4	5	0	3	5	11.3	2.00	.333
2008	Lake County (SAL)	LoA	4	8	4.29	27	27	0	0	115	92	8	84	106	8.3	1.53	.220
2009	Peoria (MWL)	LoA	6	4	2.81	27	26	0	0	109	78	0	66	119	9.8	1.32	.202
2010	Daytona (FSL)	HiA	7	1	2.86	15	14	0	0	72	54	4	26	82	10.2	1.11	.202
	Tennessee (SL)	AA	8	2	1.80	13	13	0	0	70	48	2	39	67	8.6	1.24	.198
2011	Montgomery (SL)	AA	8	7	4.42	25	25	0	0	134	136	11	80	118	7.9	1.61	.266
	Durham (IL)	AAA	1	0	0.69	2	2	0	0	13	11	0	6	12	8.3	1.31	.224
Minor League Totals			35	32	3.77	130	124	0	0	592	499	31	343	579	8.8	1.42	.229

4 TAYLOR GUERRIERI, RHP

Born: Dec. 1, 1992. **B-T:** R-R. **Ht.:** 6-3. **Wt.:** 195. **Drafted:** HS—Columbia, S.C., 2011 (1st round). **Signed by:** Brad Matthews.

Guerrieri had one of the best arms in the 2011 draft, yet the Rays were able to nab him with the 24th overall pick. He slid somewhat because of questions regarding his makeup that arose after he switched high schools for his senior year. Tampa Bay believed the situation was overblown and signed him for $1.6 million at the Aug. 15 deadline. Guerrieri has matured physically in the last year, allowing him to repeat his mechanics more consistently and adding 6-7 mph to his fastball. With a clean arm action and a high three-quarters arm slot, he delivers easy gas. His fastball sits at 93-96 mph with good life and has been clocked up to 98. It sinks and runs when he throws to the right side of the plate and features heavy sink when he works the left side. Guerrieri's 11-to-5 curveball, which he throws with his middle finger tucked under his index finger, is also a power pitch in the low 80s. He also throws a cutter and changeup that show promise despite being rarely used in high school. Improving his overall command is his main priority. Guerrieri has the potential to become a frontline starter, and the Rays have an impressive track record of developing young pitchers. He'll probably open 2012 in extended spring training and make his pro debut at Rookie-level Princeton in June.

BA GRADE
65
EXTREME

Year	Club (League)	Class	W	L	ERA	G	GS	CG	SV	IP	H	HR	BB	SO	K/9	WHIP	AVG
2011	Did Not Play—Signed Late																

5 ALEX COLOME, RHP

Born: Dec. 31, 1988. **B-T:** R-R. **Ht.:** 6-2. **Wt.:** 185. **Signed:** Dominican Republic, 2007. **Signed by:** Eddy Toledo.

The nephew of former Rays reliever Jesus Colome, Alex spent three seasons in short-season league before making his full-season debut in 2010. He pitched a career-high 158 innings and reached Double-A in 2011, when he ranked second in the system with 12 wins. He finished with a strong relief stint in the Venezuelan League, and Tampa Bay protected him on its 40-man roster. Colome reminds scouts of his uncle with his electric arm. He throws a sinking fastball that sits at 93-95 mph and touches 97 with armside run. His heater doesn't have a lot of deception but comes out of his hand easily. He complements it with a sharp curveball with good rotation and a fringy upper-80s slider with decent tilt. Colome has impressive late fade on his changeup at times. Because Colome is long-limbed, his arm slot can get out of sync, leading to a lack of fastball command. He overthrows on occasion and goes for strikeouts, which limits his effectiveness. While the Rays believe Colome can develop into at least a No. 3 starter, he may be better suited as a reliever if he can't refine his changeup and command. He'll remain in the rotation for now when he returns to Montgomery to open 2012.

BA GRADE
55
MEDIUM

Year	Club (League)	Class	W	L	ERA	G	GS	CG	SV	IP	H	HR	BB	SO	K/9	WHIP	AVG
2007	Devil Rays (DSL)	R	1	6	2.97	14	11	0	0	39	30	1	31	50	11.4	1.55	.208
2008	Princeton (APP)	R	0	5	6.80	12	11	0	0	46	50	5	26	52	10.1	1.64	.272
2009	Hudson Valley (NYP)	SS	7	4	1.66	15	15	2	0	76	46	0	32	94	11.1	1.03	.174
2010	Bowling Green (MWL)	LoA	6	6	3.95	22	22	1	0	114	98	14	45	118	9.3	1.25	--
	Charlotte (FSL)	HiA	0	0	2.25	1	1	0	0	4	5	0	0	8	18.0	1.25	.333
2011	Charlotte (FSL)	HiA	9	5	3.66	19	19	1	0	106	78	8	44	92	7.8	1.15	.214
	Montgomery (SL)	AA	3	4	4.15	9	9	1	0	52	41	5	28	31	5.4	1.33	.219
Minor League Totals			26	30	3.70	92	88	5	0	437	348	33	206	445	9.2	1.27	.220

6 ALEX TORRES, LHP

Born: Dec. 8, 1987. **B-T:** L-L. **Ht.:** 5-10. **Wt.:** 175. **Signed:** Venezuela, 2005. **Signed by:** Carlos Porte (Angels).

Acquired along with Sean Rodriguez and first-base prospect Matt Sweeney in the Scott Kazmir trade with the Angels in August 2009, Torres encountered a roller-coaster ride when he got to Triple-A for the first time in 2011. He gave up five earned runs in his first six starts, then 25 in his next six before posting a 2.17 ERA the rest of the way. He pitched five shutout innings against the Blue Jays to earn his first big league win in a crucial victory on Sept. 24. Torres has the potential for three plus pitches, which helped him lead the International League with 156 strikeouts and rank fourth with a 3.08 ERA. Though he's not a big guy, he generates lively low-90s fastballs with his strong lower half. He has an above-average changeup with good depth that he'll throw in any count. His curveball has the makings of a plus offering but he struggles to maintain his feel for it. Torres throws

BA GRADE
55
MEDIUM

across his body, which provides movement and deception for his pitches, but it also leads to control woes when he fails to repeat his mechanics. He topped the IL with 83 walks. Provided he can harness his control and command, Torres can be a No. 3 starter. Tampa Bay's rotation is crowded, so he'll return to Durham to start 2012.

Year	Club (League)	Class	W	L	ERA	G	GS	CG	SV	IP	H	HR	BB	SO	K/9	WHIP	AVG
2005	Angels (DSL)	R	4	2	1.52	9	9	1	0	53	23	2	23	87	14.7	0.86	.122
2006	Angels (AZL)	R	2	5	4.29	14	9	0	1	50	42	1	36	47	8.4	1.55	.235
2007	Angels (AZL)	R	1	0	4.76	4	0	0	0	6	4	0	8	3	4.8	2.12	.190
2008	Angels (AZL)	R	4	0	1.54	4	4	0	0	23	11	1	10	24	9.3	0.90	.153
	R. Cucamonga (CAL)	HiA	3	2	3.91	10	10	0	0	53	52	1	29	62	10.5	1.53	.264
2009	R. Cucamonga (CAL)	HiA	10	3	2.74	21	19	0	0	121	93	4	63	124	9.2	1.29	.217
	Arkansas (TL)	AA	3	1	2.77	5	5	0	0	26	23	0	17	25	8.7	1.54	.245
	Montgomery (SL)	AA	0	2	3.12	2	2	0	0	9	7	1	5	7	7.3	1.38	.219
2010	Montgomery (SL)	AA	11	6	3.47	27	27	0	0	143	136	9	70	150	9.5	1.44	.256
2011	Durham (IL)	AAA	9	7	3.08	27	27	1	0	146	134	7	83	156	9.6	1.48	.249
	Tampa Bay (AL)	MAJ	1	1	3.38	4	0	0	0	8	8	0	7	9	10.1	1.88	.258
Major League Totals			1	1	3.38	4	0	0	0	8	8	0	7	9	10.1	1.88	.258
Minor League Totals			47	28	3.08	123	112	2	1	631	525	26	344	685	9.8	1.38	.230

7 TIM BECKHAM, SS

Born: Jan. 27, 1990. **B-T:** R-R. **Ht.:** 6-0. **Wt.:** 190. **Drafted:** HS—Griffin, Ga., 2008 (1st round). **Signed by:** Milt Hill.

The No. 1 overall pick in the 2008 draft and recipient of a Rays draft-record $6.15 million bonus, Beckham lost luster by hitting .263/.332/.371 in his first three pro seasons. He boosted his stock in 2011, making solid progess in the upper minors at age 21 and appearing in his first Futures Game. His .736 OPS was his career best, and his 12 homers matched his previous career total. Beckham took a step forward offensively once he improved his pitch recognition and started swinging at more strikes. While he must continue to refine his approach, he didn't give away as many at-bats and showed hints of plus power potential. He also displayed more mental and physical maturity and looked more confident. Most scouts say that Beckham won't be able to stay in the middle infield because he has a thick lower half and fringy speed and range. He does have an above-average arm and has gotten more consistent making routine plays, but he's probably going to wind up on an infield or outfield corner. While Beckham remains a work in progress, he could still develop into a big league regular. He'll spend most of 2012 in Durham and may start to see time at positions other than shortstop.

BA GRADE

50

MEDIUM

Year	Club (League)	Class	AVG	G	AB	R	H	2B	3B	HR	RBI	BB	SO	SB	CS	OBP	SLG
2008	Princeton (APP)	R	.243	46	177	30	43	12	0	2	14	13	43	5	1	.297	.345
	Hudson Valley (NYP)	SS	.333	2	6	5	2	1	0	0	0	2	1	1	0	.556	.500
2009	Bowling Green (SAL)	LoA	.275	125	491	58	135	33	4	5	63	34	116	13	10	.328	.389
2010	Charlotte (FSL)	HiA	.256	123	465	68	119	23	5	5	57	62	119	22	14	.346	.359
2011	Montgomery (SL)	AA	.275	107	418	82	115	25	2	7	57	39	91	15	4	.339	.395
	Durham (IL)	AAA	.255	24	106	12	27	3	2	5	13	3	29	2	1	.282	.462
Minor League Totals			.265	427	1663	255	441	97	13	24	204	153	399	58	30	.331	.382

8 ENNY ROMERO, LHP

Born: Jan. 24, 1991. **B-T:** L-L. **Ht.:** 6-3. **Wt.:** 198. **Signed:** Dominican Republic, 2008. **Signed by:** Eddy Toledo.

A product of the Rays' increased presence in Latin America, Romero led the Rookie-level Appalachian League with a 1.95 ERA in his 2010 U.S. debut. In his first taste of full-season ball in 2011, he ranked second in the low Class A Midwest League with 11.1 strikeouts per nine innings. Romero is an extremely projectable lefthander. He already throws 92-97 mph fastballs with armside run with a whip-like delivery that looks effortless, and his lanky frame has lots of room to fill out. He also throws a firm curveball in the low 80s. His curve lacks consistency, though when it's on, it breaks straight down from his high three-quarters arm slot. Romero's changeup shows promise but he struggles to command it. Scouts believe his command issues with his secondary pitches stem from his inability to repeat his delivery, which could improve as he matures physically. Following in the footsteps of David Price and Matt Moore, Romero is Tampa Bay's latest high-ceiling lefty. He won't develop as quickly as they did, but Romero has a chance to be a frontline starter. If he can't harness his secondary pitches, he could be a late-inning reliever. He figures to spend the entire 2012 season in high Class A.

BA GRADE

55

HIGH

MEGAN STRARMAN PHOTOGRAPHY

Year	Club (League)	Class	W	L	ERA	G	GS	CG	SV	IP	H	HR	BB	SO	K/9	WHIP	AVG
2008	Rays (DSL)	R	1	0	2.76	10	0	0	0	16	11	0	8	20	11.0	1.16	.175
2009	Rays (GCL)	R	2	4	4.81	11	4	0	0	39	38	2	21	33	7.6	1.50	.255
2010	Princeton (APP)	R	4	1	1.95	13	13	0	0	69	51	2	14	72	9.3	0.94	.204
	Hudson Valley (NYP)	SS	1	0	1.80	1	1	0	0	5	1	0	5	4	7.2	1.20	.071
2011	Bowling Green (MWL)	LoA	5	5	4.26	26	26	0	0	114	104	9	68	140	11.1	1.51	.245
Minor League Totals			13	10	3.54	61	44	0	0	244	205	13	116	269	9.9	1.32	.228

9 DREW VETTLESON, OF

Born: July 19, 1991. **B-T:** L-R. **Ht.:** 6-0. **Wt.:** 196. **Drafted:** HS—Silverdale, Wash., 2010 (1st round supplemental). **Signed by:** Paul Kirsch.

BA GRADE
55
HIGH

The Rays sent their top three 2010 draft picks to Princeton last summer, and supplemental first-round pick Vettleson outperformed first-rounders Josh Sale and Justin O'Conner. Vettleson batted .343/.406/.571 through July before running out of gas in the final month. Signed for $845,000, he drew attention as a switch-pitcher in high school, but his pure hitting ability meant his future would be as an everyday player. For a young player, Vettleson has an impressive, disciplined approach at the plate. He displays outstanding hand-eye coordination and barrels the ball easily with solid bat control. He does a good job of going with pitches and using the entire field. Though somewhat lean, he should develop average or better power as his body continues to mature. Vettleson's speed rates a tick above-average but plays up thanks to his excellent baserunning instincts. He also runs well in the outfield and has solid arm strength that should allow him to stay in right field at higher levels. He'll need to get stronger to deal with the grind of a full pro season. Tampa Bay has plenty of outfield options, meaning there's no need to rush Vettleson. He's at least three years from reaching the majors but should be worth the wait. His methodical ascension will continue in 2012 with a promotion to low Class A Bowling Green.

Year	Club (League)	Class	AVG	G	AB	R	H	2B	3B	HR	RBI	BB	SO	SB	CS	OBP	SLG
2011	Princeton (APP)	R	.282	61	234	33	66	13	4	7	40	27	53	20	6	.357	.462
Minor League Totals			.282	61	234	33	66	13	4	7	40	27	53	20	6	.357	.462

10 MIKIE MAHTOOK, OF

Born: Nov. 30, 1989. **B-T:** R-R. **Ht.:** 6-1. **Wt.:** 200. **Drafted:** Louisiana State, 2011 (1st round). **Signed by:** Rickey Drexler.

BA GRADE
55
HIGH

A star quarterback in high school, Mahtook turned down the Marlins as a 39th-rounder in 2008 to attend Louisiana State. He helped the Tigers win the 2009 College World Series as a freshman. Last spring, he led the Southeastern Conference in hitting (.383) and steals (29) while reaching base in all 56 games he played. The Rays were delighted he was available with the 31st overall pick in June and signed him for $1.15 million at the Aug. 15 deadline. Mahtook plays baseball with a football mentality and possesses the power/speed combination to make an impact in the majors. Employing a deep crouch in his stance, he makes consistent hard contact and drives the ball well to all fields. He has a short swing with good weight transfer and extension that generate backspin and distance on his hits. He's a slightly above-average runner who played center field in two of his three seasons at LSU, though he may be limited to left field if he loses a step once his body fully matures. His arm is the least of his tools but still rates as average. Mahtook received his first taste of pro ball in the Arizona Fall League, where he hit .338/.410/.544 to demonstrate yet again that he's an advanced hitter who could move quickly. He'll make his official pro debut in high Class A.

Year	Club (League)	Class	AVG	G	AB	R	H	2B	3B	HR	RBI	BB	SO	SB	CS	OBP	SLG
2011	Did Not Play—Signed Late																

11 BRANDON GUYER, OF

BA GRADE
50
MEDIUM

Born: Jan. 26, 1986. **B-T:** R-R. **Ht.:** 6-1. **Wt.:** 210. **Drafted:** Virginia, 2007 (5th round). **Signed by:** Billy Swoope (Cubs).

Guyer had an impressive first season in the Rays system after arriving from the Cubs in the Matt Garza trade. He tied for second in the International League in runs (78) and ranked fourth in on-base percentage (.384) and fifth in hitting (.312) and slugging (.521). He also hit a two-run homer off Zach Britton in his first big league at-bat in May, and went deep again against Derek Holland in September. Guyer offers an impressive combination of speed and power. He has an ideal body and a smooth swing that produces solid pop from gap to gap. A career .297 hitter in the minors, he should hit for average in the big leagues once he tightens his strike zone and shows more patience looking for pitches he can drive. Guyer has plus speed and is a constant threat to take the extra base. He could steal 20 bases annually in the majors. He's capable of playing all three outfield spots, and with above-average arm strength and good carry on his throws, he fits nicely in right field. Guyer is ready to become a big league regular and is just waiting for an opening in Tampa Bay.

Year	Club (League)	Class	AVG	G	AB	R	H	2B	3B	HR	RBI	BB	SO	SB	CS	OBP	SLG
2007	Cubs (AZL)	R	.222	17	72	10	16	4	1	1	5	5	16	6	2	.309	.347
	Boise (NWL)	SS	.268	19	71	9	19	1	0	0	14	6	9	5	0	.346	.282
2008	Peoria (MWL)	LoA	.269	88	327	55	88	27	3	14	38	19	63	22	7	.331	.498
2009	Daytona (FSL)	HiA	.347	73	265	40	92	16	3	2	32	24	34	23	2	.407	.453
	Tennessee (SL)	AA	.190	57	189	22	36	12	2	1	14	10	33	7	5	.236	.291
2010	Tennessee (SL)	AA	.344	102	369	76	127	39	6	13	58	27	51	30	3	.398	.588
2011	Durham (IL)	AAA	.312	107	388	78	121	29	5	14	61	35	79	16	6	.384	.521
	Tampa Bay (AL)	MAJ	.195	15	41	7	8	1	0	2	3	1	9	0	0	.214	.366
Major League Totals			.195	15	41	7	8	1	0	2	3	1	9	0	0	.214	.366
Minor League Totals			.297	463	1681	290	499	128	20	45	222	126	285	109	25	.360	.477

12 JAKE HAGER, SS

BA GRADE
50
HIGH

Born: March 4, 1993. **B-T:** R-R. **Ht.:** 6-1. **Wt.:** 180. **Drafted:** HS—Las Vegas, 2011 (1st round). **Signed by:** Jayson Durocher.

Hager profiles perfectly as a Rays prospect with all-out hustle that enables him to produce at a consistently high level. After Tampa Bay took him with its third first-round pick (No. 32) overall last June, he signed quickly for $963,000 and played 47 pro games. A baseball rat with a nonstop motor, Hager does a little bit of everything even if he doesn't possess any plus tools. He uses his hands very well at the plate, allowing him to wait on pitches and make consistent contact to all fields. He has good power for a middle infielder and could hit upwards of 15 homers annually at higher levels. He's an average runner with good instincts but won't be a big basestealing threat. Hager moves well at shortstop but does not have great range, which could necessitate a shift to second or third base down the road. His hands are soft and sure, and he has good actions and plus arm strength. Having gotten off to a solid start to his pro career, Hager is expected to open his first full pro season in low Class A at age 19.

Year	Club (League)	Class	AVG	G	AB	R	H	2B	3B	HR	RBI	BB	SO	SB	CS	OBP	SLG
2011	Princeton (APP)	R	.269	47	193	29	52	11	1	4	17	9	26	5	7	.305	.399
Minor League Totals			.269	47	193	29	52	11	1	4	17	9	26	5	7	.305	.399

13 DEREK DIETRICH, SS

BA GRADE
50
HIGH

Born: July 18, 1989. **B-T:** L-R. **Ht.:** 6-0. **Wt.:** 197. **Drafted:** Georgia Tech, 2010 (2nd round). **Signed by:** Milt Hill.

The top pick (third round) in a 2007 Astros draft that will live in infamy, Dietrich turned down Houston to attend Georgia Tech and became a second-rounder three years later. He progressed as hoped during his first full pro season in 2011, leading Rays farmhands with 22 homers and ranking second in the Midwest League with 60 extra-base hits and 241 total bases. Dietrich generates above-average power from the left side of the plate with his quick hands and natural strength. He tries to muscle the ball out of the park on occasion, which adds uppercut and length to his swing, reducing his effectiveness. To his credit, he worked hard over the course of last season on making more consistent line-drive contact and improving his plate discipline, though he still struck out 128 times. A shortstop during his first two pro seasons, Dietrich doesn't have the range or quick-twitch athleticism to remain at the position at higher levels. He has soft hands and good arm strength, which make him a candidate at third base and possibly second. He's a below-average runner but not a liability on the bases. Dietrich does many things well and has a chance to develop into a productive big league regular. Next on his agenda is a full season in high Class A.

Year	Club (League)	Class	AVG	G	AB	R	H	2B	3B	HR	RBI	BB	SO	SB	CS	OBP	SLG
2010	Hudson Valley (NYP)	SS	.279	45	179	33	50	12	2	3	20	11	42	2	2	.340	.419
2011	Bowling Green (MWL)	LoA	.277	127	480	73	133	34	4	22	81	38	128	5	7	.346	.502
Minor League Totals			.278	172	659	106	183	46	6	25	101	49	170	7	9	.344	.480

14 RYAN BRETT, 2B

BA GRADE
50
HIGH

Born: Oct. 9, 1991. **B-T:** R-R. **Ht.:** 5-9. **Wt.:** 180. **Drafted:** HS—Burien, Wash., 2010 (3rd round). **Signed by:** Paul Kirsch.

Tabbed by the Rays as the most improved player in their extended spring-training program, Brett continued to make strides when he headed to Princeton in June. He teamed there with Josh Sale and Drew Vettleson, fellow Seattle-area high school players selected by Tampa Bay in the first three rounds of the 2010 draft. A switch-hitter in high school, Brett had made steady contact while swinging exclusively from the right side as a pro. He repeats his smooth, compact stroke swing and controls the strike zone well. He's capable of driving balls in the gaps and puts his plus speed to work on the bases. Scouts considered Brett's defense choppy during his 2010 pro debut, and he led Appalachian League second basemen with 18 errors last year. His hands aren't particularly soft and his arm is a tick below average, but he does have excellent instincts and quickness. He also has made significant strides on his double-play pivot. Brett is a grinder with impressive drive. He'll graduate to low Class A this year to form a double-play combination with 2011 first-rounder Jake Hager.

Year	Club (League)	Class	AVG	G	AB	R	H	2B	3B	HR	RBI	BB	SO	SB	CS	OBP	SLG
2010	Rays (GCL)	R	.303	27	89	8	27	5	2	0	9	8	17	12	3	.364	.404
2011	Princeton (APP)	R	.300	61	240	42	72	22	5	3	24	26	24	21	3	.370	.471
Minor League Totals			.301	88	329	50	99	27	7	3	33	34	41	33	6	.369	.453

15 LUKE BAILEY, C

BA GRADE
50
HIGH

Born: March 11, 1991. **B-T:** R-R. **Ht.:** 6-0. **Wt.:** 210. **Drafted:** HS—LaGrange, Ga., 2009 (4th round). **Signed by:** Milt Hill.

Teams regarded Bailey as the top high school catching prospect in the 2009 draft until he blew out his elbow while pitching and needed Tommy John surgery. He fell to the fourth round but still signed for $750,000, the equivalent of sandwich-round money. The Rays turned him loose in low Class A last year, though a wrist injury cost him most of the final month. Bailey has plus bat speed and raw power—25 of his 55 hits went for extra bases in 2011—but struggled offensively for most of the season. His long uppercut swing limits the time his bat stays in the hitting zone, which has resulted in strikeouts in 31 percent of his pro plate appearances. Scouts believe he can improve by leveling his stroke and focusing on making more contact. Bailey runs well for a catcher and has has above-average athleticism and agility behind the plate. He proved he has put his elbow reconstruction behind him by throwing out 40 percent of basestealers last year, displaying plus arm strength and accuracy. He also has soft hands and the ability to block balls in the dirt. Tampa Bay applauds Bailey for the progress he has made the past two years. He's slated to open 2012 in high Class A.

Year	Club (League)	Class	AVG	G	AB	R	H	2B	3B	HR	RBI	BB	SO	SB	CS	OBP	SLG
2010	Rays (GCL)	R	.182	42	137	18	25	8	0	5	14	17	47	0	0	.298	.350
2011	Bowling Green (MWL)	LoA	.223	74	247	26	55	17	1	7	35	18	89	5	1	.294	.385
Minor League Totals			.208	116	384	44	80	25	1	12	49	35	136	5	1	.296	.372

16 PARKER MARKEL, RHP

BA GRADE
50
HIGH

Born: Sept. 15, 1990. **B-T:** R-R. **Ht.:** 6-4. **Wt.:** 220. **Drafted:** Yavapai (Ariz.) JC, 2010 (39th round). **Signed by:** Jayson Durocher.

A 39th-round pick in 2010 who signed for $75,000, Markel has some of the best arm strength in the system. A reliever at Yavapai (Ariz.) JC and in his pro debut, he moved into the rotation last summer at short-season Hudson Valley and didn't allow an earned run in his first 29⅔ innings. Markel's fastball ranges from 92-97 mph with heavy sink and armside run, though it moves so much that he has trouble commanding it. He throws an 81-84 mph changeup with fade and deceptive arm speed, and he trusts that pitch more than his breaking stuff. His 82-86 mph slider is a plus pitch at times, as is his curveball with good depth. Markel's doesn't maintain his low three-quarters delivery, leading to a wandering arm slot and intermittent command. He also doesn't stride much or get over his front side well, and his velocity tends to decrease over the course of a game. Most scouts believe those flaws will lead Markel back to the bullpen, but the Rays are intrigued by his repertoire and will keep him as a starter for now. Though raw, he has tremendous upside in either role. He'll open 2012 in low Class A.

Year	Club (League)	Class	W	L	ERA	G	GS	CG	SV	IP	H	HR	BB	SO	K/9	WHIP	AVG
2010	Rays (GCL)	R	2	0	1.74	7	0	0	0	10	8	0	3	13	11.3	1.06	.222
2011	Hudson Valley (NYP)	SS	3	4	3.14	13	13	0	0	57	42	3	23	44	6.9	1.13	.207
Minor League Totals			5	4	2.93	20	13	0	0	68	50	3	26	57	7.6	1.12	.209

17 ALBERT SUAREZ, RHP

BA GRADE
50
HIGH

Born: Oct. 8, 1989. **B-T:** R-R. **Ht.:** 6-2. **Wt.:** 185. **Signed:** Venezuela, 2006. **Signed by:** Ronnie Blanco.

One of the top righthanders in the system, Suarez has flown under the radar because of physical issues. He missed much of 2009 and the first three months of 2010 after Tommy John surgery, and he was sidelined until late July last year with Lyme disease. When healthy, he has shown a fluid delivery as well as a knack for getting hitters out. Suarez' fastball returned last summer to its previous velocity of 93-94 mph, and he throws it on a steep downhill plane. He also has good feel for a sharp curveball and a changeup that could be at least an average pitch. He has maintained his control and command despite his repeated stints on the disabled list. Suarez has tremendous makeup with a strong desire to get better. He has handled his setbacks well and picked up where he left off with little delay. The Rays hope Suarez can pitch an entire season in 2012 and believe he has the ability to develop into a middle-of-the-rotation starter. Though he has only 58 innings in full-season ball, he could reach Double-A at some point this year.

Year	Club (League)	Class	W	L	ERA	G	GS	CG	SV	IP	H	HR	BB	SO	K/9	WHIP	AVG
2007	Did Not Play																
2008	Princeton (APP)	R	0	2	3.92	11	9	0	0	44	41	3	7	37	7.6	1.10	.232
2009	Hudson Valley (NYP)	SS	1	0	2.79	2	2	0	0	10	8	1	2	4	3.7	1.03	.222
2010	Rays (GCL)	R	0	0	1.00	3	3	0	0	9	4	0	1	8	8.0	0.56	.129
	Bowling Green (MWL)	LoA	2	5	3.89	12	11	0	0	42	38	5	16	30	6.5	1.30	.252
2011	Rays (GCL)	R	0	0	1.38	4	4	0	0	13	10	0	5	10	6.9	1.15	.213
	Charlotte (FSL)	HiA	1	1	2.76	4	3	0	0	16	13	1	3	7	3.9	0.98	.210
Minor League Totals			4	8	3.24	36	32	0	0	133	114	10	34	96	6.5	1.11	.226

18 TYLER GOEDDEL, 3B

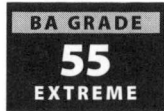

BA GRADE
55
EXTREME

Born: Oct. 20, 1992. **B-T:** R-R. **Ht.:** 6-4. **Wt.:** 180. **Drafted:** HS—Mountain View, Calif., 2011 (1st round supplemental). **Signed by:** Brian Morrison.

Little did Goeddel know when he participated in the Perfect Game National Showcase in June 2010 that he was performing on the same field his future employer calls home. During his brief stint at Tropicana Field and for the past two years in high school, he showed the ability to be a premier player with his easy athleticism and lean, projectable body. The brother of Mets minor league righthander Erik Goeddel, Tyler turned down a scholarship to follow in his sibling's footsteps at UCLA to sign for $1.5 million as the 41st overall selection in last June's draft. His bonus was nearly twice MLB's guideline for his slot and more than what the Rays paid three of the four players they drafted ahead of him. Goeddel employs a tall stance at the plate and tends to wrap the bat yet generates excellent bat speed with his aggressive swing. He barrels the ball consistently and drives pitches from gap to gap, with scouts believing he will hit for above-average power as his body matures. A shortstop in high school who projects as a third baseman in pro ball, Goeddel has the tools to play virtually anywhere on the field. He has plus speed and arm strength, sure hands and moves well for a player his size. Because he didn't sign until the Aug. 15 deadline, Goeddel has yet to make his pro debut. He'll do so at Princeton in June.

Year	Club (League)	Class	AVG	G	AB	R	H	2B	3B	HR	RBI	BB	SO	SB	CS	OBP	SLG
2011	Did Not Play—Signed Late																

19 MATT BUSH, RHP

BA GRADE
50
HIGH

Born: Feb. 8, 1986. **B-T:** R-R. **Ht.:** 5-10. **Wt.:** 180. **Drafted:** HS—San Diego, 2005 (1st round). **Signed by:** Tim McWilliam (Padres).

Bush's legacy once looked like it would be as the biggest bust ever among No. 1 overall picks in the baseball draft, but he has evolved over the past two years while converting from shortstop to pitcher in his third organization. A money-saving choice by the Padres in 2004—though he did get $3.15 million—he got into off-field trouble before he ever played a game and hit just .219/.294/.276 in four seasons. San Diego tried to move him to the mound in 2007, but he injured his elbow after seven games and needed Tommy John surgery. He missed all of 2008 and was sold to the Blue Jays in February 2009, only to get released two months later violating team guidelines. The Rays signed him in January 2010 and sent him to the Winning Inning Baseball Academy in Clearwater, Fla., the same place where Josh Hamilton cleaned up his life. An oblique strain and a sore arm limited Bush to 15 innings in 2010, and he had surgery on the radial nerve in his upper arm after the season. Tampa Bay added him to the 40-man roster after that season, and he repaid the team with an impressive Double-A showing in 2011. Using a 94-97 mph fastball and a hard, tight curveball, he averaged 13.8 strikeouts per nine innings. He also has a slurvy slider and a changeup that are far from quality offerings and he doesn't need them much in short relief. Bush's biggest need is to improve his control and command so his stuff can overpower more advanced hitters. He also needs to prove he can handle a heavier workload, as the Rays never used him with fewer than two days of rest last year. Though he's short, he gets decent plane on his pitches and works the bottom of the zone by repeating his clean delivery. He has good balance and fields his position well with his above-average athleticism. Bush's makeup no longer appears to be a problem and the expectations of being a No. 1 overall choice are in the distant past. He could help in the big league bullpen at some point in 2012, though he also could start the season back in Montgomery.

Year	Club (League)	Class	AVG	G	AB	R	H	2B	3B	HR	RBI	BB	SO	SB	CS	OBP	SLG
2004	Padres (AZL)	R	.181	21	72	12	13	2	1	0	10	11	17	4	1	.302	.236
	Eugene (NWL)	SS	.222	8	27	1	6	2	0	0	3	2	9	0	0	.276	.296
2005	Fort Wayne (MWL)	LoA	.221	126	453	56	100	13	3	2	32	33	76	8	4	.279	.276
2006	Fort Wayne (MWL)	LoA	.268	21	71	8	19	3	0	0	7	6	13	13	2	.333	.310
	Padres (AZL)	R	.000	1	1	1	0	0	0	0	1	3	0	0	0	.750	.000
2007	Lake Elsinore (CAL)	HiA	.204	29	98	8	20	2	1	1	17	16	21	1	0	.310	.276
Minor League Totals			.219	206	722	86	158	22	5	3	70	71	136	26	7	.294	.276

Year	Club (League)	Class	W	L	ERA	G	GS	CG	SV	IP	H	HR	BB	SO	K/9	WHIP	AVG
2007	Padres (AZL)	R	1	0	1.23	6	0	0	0	7	5	0	2	16	19.6	0.95	.192
	Fort Wayne (MWL)	LoA	0	0	0.00	1	0	0	0	0	0	0	0	0	0.0	0.00	.000
2008	Did Not Play—Injured																
2009	Did Not Play																
2010	Rays (GCL)	R	1	0	1.69	4	1	0	0	5	2	0	1	8	13.5	0.56	.100
	Charlotte (FSL)	HiA	0	0	4.32	6	0	0	1	8	7	1	2	12	13.0	1.08	.219
2011	Montgomery (SL)	AA	5	3	4.83	36	0	0	5	50	48	5	24	77	13.8	1.43	.251
Minor League Totals			7	3	4.14	53	1	0	6	72	62	6	29	113	14.2	1.27	.230

20 BLAKE SNELL, LHP

BA GRADE 50 HIGH

Born: Dec. 4, 1992. **B-T:** L-L. **Ht.:** 6-4. **Wt.:** 180. **Drafted:** HS—Shoreline, Wash., 2011 (1st round supplemental). **Signed by:** Paul Kirsch.

Homeschooled until his senior year of high school, Snell attracted lots of interest when his sinking fastball touched 94 mph last spring. The Rays took him with their seventh choice (52nd overall) in the 2011 draft and signed him for $684,000. In his pro debut, Snell showed the ability to get groundouts by keeping his 88-92 mph sinker down in the zone. Some scouts question whether he'll add much more velocity, because he has narrow, sloping shoulders and a wiry frame. He relies heavily on his fastball and will need to improve both his curveball and changeup, both of which grade as below average. He has tried different grips on his secondary pitches, and he'll have to use them and throw them for strikes more often. A potential No. 3 or 4 starter, Snell showed impressive mound presence while having the best debut among the top picks Tampa Bay sent to the Rookie-level Gulf Coast League last summer. The Rays traditionally handle high school pitchers with care, so he'll probably move up one level to Princeton for 2012.

Year	Club (League)	Class	W	L	ERA	G	GS	CG	SV	IP	H	HR	BB	SO	K/9	WHIP	AVG
2011	Rays (GCL)	R	1	2	3.08	11	8	0	0	26	30	0	11	26	8.9	1.56	.291
Minor League Totals			1	2	3.08	11	8	0	0	26	30	0	11	26	8.9	1.56	.291

21 BRAULIO LARA, LHP

BA GRADE 50 HIGH

Born: Dec. 20, 1988. **B-T:** L-L. **Ht.:** 6-1. **Wt.:** 185. **Signed:** Dominican Republic, 2008. **Signed by:** Junior Ramirez.

The 2011 season served as a learning experience for Lara. After leading his Rookie-level Dominican Summer League team in strikeouts in 2008 and 2009 and ranking second in the Appalachian League in ERA in 2010, he discovered that hitters at higher levels have better knowledge of the strike zone and will take advantage of mistakes. He recorded just five quality starts in 25 outings while battling his control and command, though he did throw more strikes in the final two months. Lara's best pitch is a 92-95 mph four-seam fastball that has above-average movement and appears to jump on hitters. He also throws a two-seamer to jam lefthanders, who hit only .212 against him last year (compared to .283 for righties). While he lacks consistent feel for his curveball and changeup, he earned credit for working diligently on them in 2011. Lara has a smooth and easy delivery when he throws fastballs but has difficulty maintaining the same fluidity with his secondary pitches. How he improves in that regard will determine whether he remains a starter or moves to the bullpen. He'll stay in the rotation when he climbs to high Class A in 2012.

Year	Club (League)	Class	W	L	ERA	G	GS	CG	SV	IP	H	HR	BB	SO	K/9	WHIP	AVG
2008	Rays (DSL)	R	2	2	3.97	17	3	0	0	34	28	1	21	39	10.3	1.44	.220
2009	Rays (DSL)	R	5	3	3.58	13	8	1	0	55	52	2	21	58	9.4	1.32	.242
2010	Princeton (APP)	R	6	4	2.18	13	13	1	0	66	49	2	25	58	7.9	1.12	.200
2011	Bowling Green (MWL)	LoA	5	11	4.94	25	25	0	0	120	117	10	55	111	8.3	1.43	.259
Minor League Totals			18	20	3.89	68	49	2	0	276	246	15	122	266	8.7	1.33	.237

22 STEPHEN VOGT, C/OF/1B

BA GRADE 45 MEDIUM

Born: Nov. 1, 1984. **B-T:** L-R. **Ht.:** 6-3. **Wt.:** 215. **Drafted:** Azusa Pacific (Calif.), 2007 (12th round). **Signed by:** Jake Wilson.

The 27-year-old Vogt doesn't have the pedigree to rank among the top-tier prospects in a deep system like Tampa Bay's. At the same time, he has a productive bat and the versatility to play four positions, and he continues to prove he has a future at the major league level. After winning the Florida State League batting (.345) and slugging (.511) titles in 2010, he encored by leading Rays farmhands with 105 RBIs and winning the organization's minor league player of the year award last season. Signed for $6,000 as a 12th-round pick in 2007, Vogt has excellent hand-eye coordination and hitting instincts. He uses the entire field and has learned to drive the ball with his strong hands. He should have at least average power. Vogt would have more value if he projected as an everyday catcher, but most scouts see that as a stretch. He's a fringy receiver with average arm strength, and he threw out 30 percent of basestealers in 2011. He tore the labrum in his throwing shoulder in 2009 and missed most of that season. He's a well below-average runner who's adequate at first base or on the outfield corners. Tampa Bay added Vogt to its 40-man roster in November and should find a role in the majors at some point this year for a player who has the makeup and ability to produce at multiple positions.

Year	Club (League)	Class	AVG	G	AB	R	H	2B	3B	HR	RBI	BB	SO	SB	CS	OBP	SLG
2007	Hudson Valley (NYP)	SS	.300	70	240	40	72	8	0	4	48	31	31	6	1	.371	.383
2008	Columbus (SAL)	LoA	.291	113	392	57	114	22	3	6	54	47	48	6	1	.368	.408
2009	Charlotte (FSL)	HiA	.171	10	35	0	6	2	0	0	3	2	4	0	1	.216	.229
2010	Charlotte (FSL)	HiA	.345	106	368	56	127	31	3	8	47	31	46	3	1	.399	.511
2011	Montgomery (SL)	AA	.301	97	386	52	116	21	6	13	85	30	51	4	2	.344	.487
	Durham (IL)	AAA	.290	31	124	15	36	14	1	4	20	4	29	0	0	.305	.516
Minor League Totals			.305	427	1545	220	471	98	13	35	257	145	209	19	6	.362	.453

23 WILKING RODRIGUEZ, RHP

Born: March 2, 1990. **B-T:** R-R. **Ht.:** 6-3. **Wt.:** 211. **Signed:** Venezuela, 2007. **Signed by:** Ronnie Blanco.

BA GRADE
50
HIGH

Rodriguez has one of the better arms in system but has been overshadowed throughout his pro career. That didn't change in 2011, when he missed the first half of the season with a shoulder injury that didn't require surgery. Rodriguez has a 90-95 fastball with natural tailing action that makes it difficult for opponents to barrel. He can add and subtract velocity from his heater, too. His 76-78 mph curveball shows the potential to be an above-average offering, as he throws it with tight spin at times. He has made strides with his changeup but does not throw it as often as he should, especially if he hopes to remain a starter. Despite his size, Rodriguez uses a drop-and-drive delivery to work the bottom of the zone. He throws strikes but gets hit if he leaves his pitches up. Rodriguez owns just a 6-20 record in the United States, but the Rays believe he's on the verge of a breakthrough if he can stay healthy in 2012. They added him to the 40-man roster in November and will send him to high Class A.

Year	Club (League)	Class	W	L	ERA	G	GS	CG	SV	IP	H	HR	BB	SO	K/9	WHIP	AVG
2007	Devil Rays/Reds (VSL)	R	3	2	1.95	17	0	0	2	32	23	1	14	28	7.8	1.1	.200
2008	Rays (VSL)	R	0	1	3.71	10	8	0	0	27	26	3	6	29	9.8	1.20	.260
2009	Princeton (APP)	R	1	6	3.21	13	13	0	0	56	44	5	12	52	8.4	1.00	.213
2010	Bowling Green (MWL)	LoA	4	10	4.23	22	19	0	0	106	109	11	28	93	7.9	1.3	.263
2011	Hudson Valley (NYP)	SS	1	1	6.48	2	2	0	0	8	10	0	2	9	9.7	1.4	.303
	Bowling Green (MWL)	LoA	0	3	4.66	9	9	0	0	37	38	3	14	34	8.3	1.42	.266
Minor League Totals			9	23	3.82	73	51	0	2	266	250	23	76	245	8.3	1.22	.247

24 LENNY LINSKY, RHP

Born: March 4, 1990. **B-T:** R-R. **Ht.:** 6-2. **Wt.:** 220. **Drafted:** Hawaii, 2011 (2nd round). **Signed by:** Jake Wilson.

BA GRADE
50
HIGH

Linsky was one of the better relievers in the college ranks in 2011, posting a 1.30 ERA and a Hawaii-record 14 saves while leading the Rainbows to their first regular-season Western Athletic Conference title in 19 years. The 12th of Tampa Bay's record 12 picks in the first two rounds, he signed for $392,400 as the 89th overall pick. Linsky has closer potential. He works off a 92-94 mph fastball that touches 96. He throws from a three-quarters arm slot, giving his fastball impressive sinking action that causes hitters to swing over the top. He mixes the heater with a mid-80s slider that reaches 89 mph. His slider has great deception since it looks much like his fastball when it comes out of his hand. Linsky's pitches are tough to elevate, as evidenced by the fact that he allowed just three extra-base hits during his junior season. He sometimes has difficulty with his mechanics, opening up too soon and getting under his pitches, which cause them to flatten out. Linsky reached low Class A at the end of his pro debut and should move quickly through the minors.

Year	Club (League)	Class	W	L	ERA	G	GS	CG	SV	IP	H	HR	BB	SO	K/9	WHIP	AVG
2011	Hudson Valley (NYP)	SS	3	0	1.46	12	0	0	3	25	19	2	6	27	9.9	1.01	.207
	Bowling Green (MWL)	LoA	0	0	0.00	4	0	0	0	5	3	0	1	3	5.8	0.86	.188
Minor League Totals			3	0	1.23	16	0	0	3	29	22	2	7	30	9.2	0.99	.204

25 BRANDON MARTIN, SS

BA GRADE
50
HIGH

Born: Aug. 24, 1993. **B-T:** R-R. **Ht.:** 5-11. **Wt.:** 175. **Drafted:** HS—Corona, Calif., 2011 (1st round supplemental). **Signed by:** Jake Wilson.

Quality defensive shortstops were a rare commodity in the 2011 draft, but the Rays found one with the 38th overall pick. Thanks to adding muscle by dedicating himself to a workout program, Martin made huge progress at the plate as a high school senior last spring. He has a quick bat and a line-drive swing that should allow him to hit for average with good pop for a middle infielder. He's an average runner who can steal a few bases, but it's with his glove that Martin really shines. He makes highlight-reel plays with the leather with his quick-twitch athleticism. He has plus range and soft, reliable hands to go with an above-average arm with excellent carry on his throws. His actions aren't always smooth, though Tampa Bay believes he can iron them out. Martin is likely to spend his first full pro season at Princeton.

Year	Club (League)	Class	AVG	G	AB	R	H	2B	3B	HR	RBI	BB	SO	SB	CS	OBP	SLG
2011	Rays (GCL)	R	.255	19	47	10	12	1	0	1	3	7	12	5	3	.386	.340
Minor League Totals			.255	19	47	10	12	1	0	1	3	7	12	5	3	.386	.340

26 KES CARTER, OF

BA GRADE
50
HIGH

Born: March 3, 1990. **B-T:** L-L. **Ht.:** 6-2. **Wt.:** 205. **Drafted:** Western Kentucky, 2011 (1st round supplemental). **Signed by:** James Bonnici.

The highest-drafted player in the 92-year history of Western Kentucky's baseball program, Carter went 56th overall in the 2011 draft. He was the Rays' eighth pick and signed quickly for $625,000, but played in just three games before his pro debut ended because of shin splints. Injuries have been an issue for Carter, who injured his hip in the Coastal Plain League in the summer of 2010 and was hampered by a strained calf last spring. When healthy, the athletic Carter flashes all five tools. He has a smooth lefthanded stroke and worked hard in college on developing a middle-away approach and better plate discipline. He should have at least average power once he starts turning on more pitches, though he'll have to make more consistent contact against lefthanders. Carter's speed is a tick above average, and he uses his solid instincts to get good jumps on the bases and in the outfield. He may not stick in center fielder in the majors, but his strong, accurate arm easily fits in right field. Carter could return to his college stomping grounds in Bowling Green for his first full pro season.

Year	Club (League)	Class	AVG	G	AB	R	H	2B	3B	HR	RBI	BB	SO	SB	CS	OBP	SLG
2011	Hudson Valley (NYP)	SS	.231	3	13	2	3	0	0	0	1	2	1	0	0	.333	.231
Minor League Totals			.231	3	13	2	3	0	0	0	1	2	1	0	0	.333	.231

27 JUSTIN O'CONNER, C

BA GRADE
50
EXTREME

Born: March 31, 1992. **B-T:** R-R. **Ht.:** 6-2. **Wt.:** 190. **Drafted:** HS—Muncie, Ind., 2010 (1st round). **Signed by:** James Bonnici.

Before his high school senior season in 2010, O'Conner drew interest as a slugging third baseman and power-armed righthander. He moved behind the plate that spring and became the top prep catching prospect in the draft, going 31st overall and signing for $1.025 million. He has made strides defensively but has struggled more than anticipated with the bat, hitting .183/.266/.351 in two years in Rookie ball. O'Conner has plus bat speed and raw power, with 17 of his 28 hits last season going for extra bases. But he struggles with his balance as well as his plate discipline, and he struck out in 40 percent of his plate appearances in 2011, the worst rate in the Appalachian League. O'Conner also topped the Appy League by throwing out 36 percent of basestealers, a testament to his plus-plus arm strength. He has quick feet and impressive leadership skills. He's still learning the mechanical aspects of catching, but he has the drive and determination to make it work. Though O'Conner has below-average speed, he's faster than the typical catcher. He may never hit for a high average, but provided he finds a way to make more consistent contact, he has the potential to be a starting catcher at the big league level. He should reach low Class A at some point in 2012.

Year	Club (League)	Class	AVG	G	AB	R	H	2B	3B	HR	RBI	BB	SO	SB	CS	OBP	SLG
2010	Rays (GCL)	R	.211	48	161	18	34	13	0	3	29	18	46	1	0	.301	.348
2011	Princeton (APP)	R	.157	48	178	18	28	8	0	9	29	17	78	4	1	.234	.354
Minor League Totals			.183	96	339	36	62	21	0	12	58	35	124	5	1	.266	.351

28 FELIPE RIVERO, LHP

BA GRADE
50
EXTREME

Born: July 5, 1991. **B-T:** L-L. **Ht.:** 6-0. **Wt.:** 151. **Signed:** Venezuela, 2008. **Signed by:** Ronnie Blanco.

Rivero is the latest strong-armed lefthander to come through Princeton, following the path blazed by Matt Moore (2008) and Enny Romero (2010). Rivero made his U.S. debut there last year, placing eighth in the Appalachian League by averaging 8.5 strikeouts per nine innings. A quality athlete with a quick arm, he throws his fastball at 93-94 mph, which is 3-4 mph higher than when he broke into pro ball in

2009. He also has a plus curveball with late, sharp break and an average changeup that improved over the course of the 2011 season. Romero displayed advanced feel for pitching at Princeton, mixing his pitches effectively without depending too much on any particular offering. He gets into trouble when he leaves his pitches up in the zone and gave up seven homers in 14 outings last year, including one in each of his first four appearances. He improved his command as the season progressed, doing a better job of pounding the bottom of the zone in the second half. Rivero's spring-training performance will determine whether he begins 2012 at Bowling Green or Hudson Valley.

Year	Club (League)	Class	W	L	ERA	G	GS	CG	SV	IP	H	HR	BB	SO	K/9	WHIP	AVG
2009	Rays (VSL)	R	6	4	3.74	16	0	0	1	34	38	0	12	25	6.7	1.49	.286
2010	Rays (VSL)	R	3	3	2.09	14	9	0	2	52	46	1	10	44	7.7	1.08	.243
2011	Princeton (APP)	R	3	3	4.62	14	12	0	0	60	64	7	13	57	8.5	1.28	.264
Minor League Totals			12	10	3.52	44	21	0	3	146	148	8	35	126	7.8	1.26	.262

29 TYLER BORTNICK, 2B

BA GRADE
45
MEDIUM

Born: July 3, 1987. **B-T:** R-R. **Ht.:** 5-11. **Wt.:** 185. **Drafted:** Coastal Carolina, 2009 (16th round). **Signed by:** Brad Matthews.

It should come as no surprise that Bortnick became a favorite of Rays manager Joe Maddon during spring training last year. Maddon not only appreciated how Bortnick performed on the field but also the way he went about his business. He's a true hustle player who gets the most out of his fringe to average tools across the board. Signed for $5,000 as a 16th-round pick in 2009, Bortnick hits line drives from gap to gap. He has the best plate discipline in the system, which allowed him to draw more walks (79) than strikeouts (67) in 2011, and also to hit lefthanders (.301) and righthanders (.308) equally well. He has some gap power and is an excellent bunter. He combined average speed, a quick first step and keen instincts to steal 43 bases in 47 attempts last year. A shortstop in college before he moved to second and then third base as a senior, Bortnick has seen action at all three positions as a pro but played exclusively at the keystone last season. He has a strong arm and solid range for the position, and he does a nice job of turning the double play. Bortnick has all the makings of a solid utility infielder at the major league level, and he wouldn't hurt a team if he had to start at second base for an extended period. After he played in the Arizona Fall League, a full season in Double-A is on his immediate horizon.

Year	Club (League)	Class	AVG	G	AB	R	H	2B	3B	HR	RBI	BB	SO	SB	CS	OBP	SLG
2009	Hudson Valley (NYP)	SS	.300	65	217	37	65	17	4	4	26	27	38	24	8	.386	.470
2010	Bowling Green (MWL)	LoA	.303	113	406	72	123	32	2	8	45	63	67	39	14	.408	.451
	Charlotte (FSL)	HiA	.206	12	34	4	7	3	0	1	9	5	10	2	0	.300	.382
2011	Charlotte (FSL)	HiA	.306	132	474	96	145	34	7	4	70	79	67	43	4	.428	.432
Minor League Totals			.301	322	1131	209	340	86	13	17	150	174	182	108	26	.409	.445

30 JAKE THOMPSON, RHP

BA GRADE
45
MEDIUM

Born: Aug. 8, 1989. **B-T:** R-R. **Ht.:** 6-0. **Wt.:** 246. **Drafted:** Long Beach State, 2010 (2nd round). **Signed by:** Robbie Moen.

Thompson ranked as the top pitching prospect in the short-season New York-Penn League in his 2010 pro debut, then skipped a level and placed fourth in the Florida State League in ERA (2.90) in his first full pro season. Yet for a college product, he has had to make considerable adjustments. He has lacked consistency with his pitches, struggling at times to locate his fastball and to maintain the feel for his changeup. He also missed May last year with elbow tightness, but he showed no ill effects once he returned. Thompson's fastball resides in the low 90s with average movement. He complements it with a promising mid-80s slider and a changeup that can elicit some swings and misses. He doesn't miss nearly as many bats as he should with that stuff, averaging just 4.4 strikeouts per nine innings in 2011. Thompson doesn't get hit hard, though, keeping the ball down and getting groundballs. He also exhibits good mound presence. While Thompson doesn't have a high ceiling, he could be a serviceable starter in the back of a major league rotation and is ready for Double-A.

Year	Club (League)	Class	W	L	ERA	G	GS	CG	SV	IP	H	HR	BB	SO	K/9	WHIP	AVG
2010	Hudson Valley (NYP)	SS	2	1	1.35	10	7	0	0	40	28	0	6	33	7.4	0.85	.200
	Charlotte (FSL)	HiA	2	0	0.00	2	2	0	0	11	2	0	2	6	4.9	0.36	.059
2011	Charlotte (FSL)	HiA	5	7	2.90	22	22	0	0	115	114	4	37	56	4.4	1.32	.267
Minor League Totals			9	8	2.34	34	31	0	0	166	144	4	45	95	5.2	1.14	.240

Texas Rangers

BY MATT FORMAN

One game, one strike, is all that separated the Rangers from winning their first World Series and completing the organization's transformation.

Texas twice squandered a two-run lead to the Cardinals in Game Six of the World Series, then couldn't rebound in Game Seven. The Rangers hadn't lost consecutive games in 47 trips to the ballpark, but they couldn't overcome the St. Louis buzzsaw and became the first team since the 1991-92 Braves to drop back-to-back World Series.

Despite the disappointment at the end of October, there's no doom and gloom in Arlington. The Rangers  remain positioned to extend their run of playoff appearances, thanks to a young core and one of the game's deepest farm systems.

Since Jon Daniels took over as GM following the 2005 season, the Rangers have become a model organization for scouting and player development. Interestingly, Texas still hasn't had many homegrown talents contribute at the big league level, as the bulk of the club's nucleus—Elvis Andrus, Adrian Beltre, Nelson Cruz, Josh Hamilton, Neftali Feliz, Matt Harrison, Colby Lewis, Mike Napoli, Alexi Ogando—was plucked from other teams.

The farm system provided the talent to upgrade the bullpen with midseason trades for Mike Adams and Koji Uehara. It should continue to be productive, with lefthander Martin Perez, outfielder Leonys Martin and righthanders Neil Ramirez and Tanner Scheppers on the verge of landing big league roles.

To keep the talent flowing, the Rangers have poured resources into Latin America. They have become one of the most aggressive franchises in that arena and spent nearly $20 million in bonuses for international players in 2011. That total included $5 million for Martin (part of a $15.6 million big league contract), $4.95 million for Dominican outfielder Nomar Mazara, $3.45 million for Dominican first baseman/outfielder Ronald Guzman and $1.5 million for Venezuelan lefthander Yohander Mendez.

Texas already had a strong international presence in their system. Their top prospects are shortstop Jurickson Profar (Curacao) and Perez (Venezuela), with Martin (Cuba), second baseman Rougned Odor (Venezuela), catcher Jorge Alfaro (Colombia) and third baseman Christian Villanueva (Mexico) not far behind.

The Rangers weren't as assertive in the 2011 draft, as their scouting staff viewed the class as weaker than the industry consensus did. They ranked 22nd in

Texas' strong presence in Latin America has yielded prospects like Martin Perez

ANDREW WOOLLEY

TOP 30 PROSPECTS

1. Jurickson Profar, ss	16. Tanner Scheppers, rhp
2. Martin Perez, lhp	17. Luis Sardinas, ss
3. Mike Olt, 3b	18. Luke Jackson, rhp
4. Leonys Martin, of	19. Roman Mendez, rhp
5. Neil Ramirez, rhp	20. Barret Loux, rhp
6. Cody Buckel, rhp	21. Will Lamb, lhp
7. Jorge Alfaro, c	22. Kevin Matthews, lhp
8. Christian Villanueva, 3b	23. Kellin Deglan, c
9. Rougned Odor, 2b	24. Jake Skole, of
10. Matt West, rhp	25. Tomas Telis, c
11. Leury Garcia, ss	26. David Perez, rhp
12. Jordan Akins, of	27. Odubel Herrera, 2b
13. Ronald Guzman, 1b/of	28. Michael Kirkman, lhp
14. Robbie Ross, lhp	29. Miguel de los Santos, lhp
15. Justin Grimm, rhp	30. Nomar Mazara, of

draft spending with $4.2 million last year, selecting lefthanders Kevin Matthews and Will Lamb and toolsy outfielder Zach Cone with their first three picks.

After the season, farm director Scott Servais left to become the Angels' assistant GM and join former teammate Jerry Dipoto's new regime. To replace Servais, Texas hired former Astros GM and farm director Tim Purpura, who had been an executive vice president with Minor League Baseball. More departures may be inevitable, as Rangers assistant GM Thad Levine and senior director of player personnel A.J. Preller are considered future GM candidates.

ORGANIZATION OVERVIEW

General Manager: Jon Daniels. **Farm Director:** Tim Purpura. **Scouting Director:** Kip Fagg.

Class	Team	League	W	L	Pct	Finish*	Manager(s)
Majors	Texas Rangers	American	96	66	.593	2nd (14)	Ron Washington
Triple-A	Round Rock Express	Pacific Coast	87	57	.604	2nd (16)	Bobby Jones/Spike Owen
Double-A	Frisco RoughRiders	Texas	79	61	.564	2nd (8)	Steve Buechele
High A	Myrtle Beach Pelicans	Carolina	72	67	.518	3rd (8)	Jason Wood
Low A	Hickory Crawdads	South Atlantic	79	58	.577	1st (14)	Bill Richardson
Short-season	Spokane Indians	Northwest	35	41	.461	6th (8)	Tim Hulett
Rookie	AZL Rangers	Arizona	38	18	.679	2nd (13)	Hector Ortiz
Overall 2011 Minor League Record			390	302	.564	1st (30)	

*Finish in overall standings (No. of teams in league). †League champion.

LAST YEAR'S TOP 30

Player, Pos.		Status
1.	Martin Perez, lhp	No. 2
2.	Jurickson Profar, ss	No. 1
3.	Tanner Scheppers, rhp	No. 16
4.	Robbie Erlin, lhp	(Padres)
5.	Engel Beltre, of	Dropped out
6.	Michael Kirkman, lhp	No. 28
7.	Mike Olt, 3b	No. 3
8.	Luis Sardinas, ss	No. 17
9.	Jake Skole, of	No. 24
10.	Miguel de los Santos, lhp	No. 29
11.	David Perez, rhp	No. 26
12.	Christian Villanueva, 3b	No. 8
13.	Roman Mendez, rhp	No. 19
14.	Wilmer Font, rhp	Dropped out
15.	Leury Garcia, ss	No. 11
16.	Kellin Deglan, c	No. 23
17.	Jorge Alfaro, c	No. 7
18.	Justin Grimm, lhp	No. 15
19.	Robbie Ross, lhp	No.14
20.	Miguel Velazquez, of	(Brewers)
21.	Luke Jackson, rhp	No. 18
22.	Joe Wieland, rhp	(Padres)
23.	Fabio Castillo, rhp	Dropped out
24.	Barret Loux, rhp	No. 20
25.	Jared Hoying, of	Dropped out
26.	Jose Felix, c	Dropped out
27.	Neil Ramirez, rhp	No. 5
28.	Cody Buckel, rhp	No. 6
29.	Josh Richmond, of	Dropped out
30.	Jake Brigham, rhp	Dropped out

BEST TOOLS

Best Hitter for Average	Jurickson Profar
Best Power Hitter	Mike Olt
Best Strike-Zone Discipline	Jurickson Profar
Fastest Baserunner	Leury Garcia
Best Athlete	Jordan Akins
Best Fastball	Matt West
Best Curveball	Martin Perez
Best Slider	Matt West
Best Changeup	Miguel de los Santos
Best Control	Cody Buckel
Best Defensive Catcher	Kellin Deglan
Best Defensive Infielder	Jurickson Profar
Best Infield Arm	Leury Garcia
Best Defensive Outfielder	Engel Beltre
Best Outfield Arm	Jordan Akins

PROJECTED 2015 LINEUP

Catcher	Jorge Alfaro
First Base	Mike Napoli
Second Base	Jurickson Profar
Third Base	Adrian Beltre
Shortstop	Elvis Andrus
Left Field	Josh Hamilton
Center Field	Leonys Martin
Right Field	Nelson Cruz
Designated Hitter	Ian Kinsler
No. 1 Starter	Neftali Feliz
No. 2 Starter	Alexi Ogando
No. 3 Starter	Martin Perez
No. 4 Starter	Derek Holland
No. 5 Starter	Matt Harrison
Closer	Matt West

TOP PROSPECTS OF THE DECADE

Year	Player, Pos.	2011 Org.
2002	Hank Blalock, 3b	Out of baseball
2003	Mark Teixeira, 3b	Yankees
2004	Adrian Gonzalez, 1b	Red Sox
2005	Thomas Diamond, rhp	Twins
2006	Edinson Volquez, rhp	Reds
2007	John Danks, lhp	White Sox
2008	Elvis Andrus, ss	Rangers
2009	Neftali Feliz, rhp	Rangers
2010	Neftali Feliz, rhp	Rangers
2011	Martin Perez, lhp	Rangers

TOP DRAFT PICKS OF THE DECADE

Year	Player, Pos.	2011 Org.
2002	Drew Meyer, ss	Out of baseball
2003	John Danks, lhp	White Sox
2004	Thomas Diamond, rhp	Twins
2005	John Mayberry Jr., of	Phillies
2006	Kasey Kiker, lhp	Rangers
2007	Blake Beavan, rhp	Mariners
2008	Justin Smoak, 1b	Mariners
2009	*Matt Purke, lhp	Nationals
2010	Jake Skole, of	Rangers
2011	Kevin Matthews, lhp	Rangers

*Did not sign.

LARGEST BONUSES IN CLUB HISTORY

Leonys Martin, 2011	$5,000,000
Nomar Mazara, 2011	$4,950,000
Mark Teixeira, 2001	$4,500,000
Justin Smoak, 2008	$3,500,000
Ronald Guzman, 2011	$3,450,000

TEXAS RANGERS

TOP 2012 ROOKIE: Leonys Martin, of. The Cuban defector is a plus hitter with the defensive chops to handle center field, and he could be in the Opening Day lineup.

BREAKOUT PROSPECT: Jordan Akins, of. With incredible raw tools and arguably as much upside as any player in the system, he was the talk of Texas' instructional league camp last fall.

SLEEPER: Luis Marte, ss. Signed for $215,000 out of the Dominican Republic in 2010, he's a wiry athlete with five-tool potential.

SOURCE OF TOP 30 TALENT

Homegrown	29	Acquired	1
College	3	Trades	1
Junior college	0	Rule 5 draft	0
High school	10	Independent leagues	0
Independent/drafted	1	Free agents/waivers	0
Drafted free agents	1		
International	14		

LF
Jared Hoying

CF
Leonys Martin (4)
Jordan Akins (12)
Zach Cone
Engel Beltre
Ryan Strausborger
Desmond Henry
Teodoro Martinez
Eduar Pinto

RF
Jake Skole (24)
Nomar Mazara (30)
Joey Butler
Josh Richmond
Rashard Harlin
Chris Grayson

3B
Mike Olt (3)
Christian Villanueva (8)
Tommy Mendonca
Drew Robinson
Smerling Lantigua

SS
Jurickson Profar (1)
Leury Garcia (11)
Luis Sardinas (17)
Luis Marte
Alberto Triunfel
Greg Miclat

2B
Rougned Odor (9)
Odubel Herrera (27)
Hanser Alberto
Nick Urbanus
Santiago Chirino

1B
Ronald Guzman (13)
Andrew Clark
Mike Bianucci
Matt Leeds

C
Jorge Alfaro (7)
Kellin Deglan (23)
Tomas Telis (25)
Yefry Castillo
Joe Maloney

LHP

LHSP	LHRP
Martin Perez (2)	Michael Kirkman (28)
Robbie Ross (14)	Miguel de los Santos (29)
Will Lamb (21)	Jimmy Reyes
Kevin Matthews (22)	Joe Ortiz
Victor Payano	Ben Snyder
Yohander Mendez	Greg Williams
Christopher Hanna	

RHP

RHSP	RHRP
Neil Ramirez (5)	Matt West (10)
Cody Buckel (6)	Tanner Scheppers (16)
Justin Grimm (15)	David Perez (25)
Luke Jackson (18)	Wilmer Font
Roman Mendez (19)	Justin Miller
Barrett Loux (20)	Randy Henry
Kyle Hendricks	Jacob Brigham
Nick Tepesch	Connor Sadzeck
Kyle Castro	Johan Yan
Nick Martinez	Carlos Melo
Santo Perez	Fabio Castillo
Abel de los Santos	Cody Eppley
Jose Valdespina	Mark Hamburger
Carlos Pimentel	Francisco Mendoza
Wilfredo Boscan	Ryan Kelly
Richard Alvarez	Jerad Eickhoff
	Taylor Dennis
	Nick Martinez

2011   BONUSES: $4.2 MILLION

BEST PURE HITTER: OF Chris Grayson (13), who hit .364 at Lee (Tenn.), an NAIA program, has a solid lefthanded swing with strength.

BEST POWER HITTER: OF Zach Cone (1s) has plus raw power but hasn't figured out how to bring it to games. 1B Matt Leeds (31) hit 18 homers with the less-lively college bats last spring and has above-average pop.

FASTEST RUNNER: The strength of the Rangers' position-player class is speed. Cone is a plus runner but lags behind OFs Desmond Henry (4) and Saquan Johnson (28), who have run 6.3-second 60-yard dashes.

BEST DEFENSIVE PLAYER: Cone has the tools to be a difference-maker in center field but needs to improve his routes and get back to the plus arm he showed prior to last spring. Henry has similar potential, with less arm strength.

BEST FASTBALL: LHP Will Lamb (2) has a fresh arm after playing outfield and relieving at Clemson and touched 98 repeatedly this summer. He needs to gain strength but could sit in the mid-90s as a starter. Just 6-foot-1 and 170 pounds, RHP Taylor Dennis (34) uses a whippy arm to peak at 96 mph.

BEST SECONDARY PITCH: LHP Kevin Matthews (1) has excellent athleticism and spins a tight curveball while flashing an advanced changeup. RHP Jerad Eickhoff (15) has an above-average curveball.

BEST PRO DEBUT: RHP Kyle Hendricks (8) used a 90-93 mph fastball, solid changeup and two breaking balls to strike out 38 and post a 2.02 ERA in 36 innings, including a start at Double-A. Lamb thrived after a late promotion to low Class A Hickory, going 3-2, 2.67 with 70 strikeouts in 61 innings (including the playoffs).

BEST ATHLETE: Cone, Henry and Johnson are all quality athletes.

MOST INTRIGUING BACKGROUND: Cone and OF Jonathan Taylor (33) collided in the outfield while playing for Georgia on March 6, leaving Taylor partially paralyzed. The Rangers picked Taylor on area scout Ryan Coe's recommendation to honor Taylor's rehabilitation efforts, and he went to Arlington for an American League Division Series game. His condition has improved, as he's able to sit up and has some movement in his toes.

CLOSEST TO THE MAJORS: Lamb and Hendricks.

BEST LATE-ROUND PICK: Johnson has significant upside but is raw. RHP Nick Martinez (18) was primarily a second baseman at Fordham, pitching just 26 innings, but showed a strong arm after signing and hit 94 mph.

THE ONE WHO GOT AWAY: Three single-digit picks didn't get signed, and Texas made strong runs at RHP Brandon Woodruff (5), now at Mississippi State, and C Max Pentecost (7), now at Kennesaw State. OF Derek Fisher (6) took his premium talent to Virginia but was never close to signing.

ASSESSMENT: The Rangers didn't share the consensus view that the draft was deep and went off the consensus board at the top with Matthews. The class lacks impact bats and took a hit when Woodruff, Fisher and Pentecost didn't sign.

2010   BONUSES: $8.5 MILLION

The first three picks—OF Jake Skole (1), C Kellin Deglan (1), RHP Luke Jackson (1s)—haven't progressed as quickly as the next three—3B Mike Olt (1s), RHP Cody Buckel (2) and OF Jordan Akins (3)—but all of them have upside. So does RHP Justin Grimm (5).

GRADE: B

2009   BONUSES: $4.7 MILLION

Texas agreed with LHP Matt Purke (1) on a $6 million bonus, but MLB killed the deal. LHP Robbie Erlin helped bring Mike Adams from the Padres in trade last July. RHP Tanner Scheppers (1s) is nearly ready to help the big league bullpen.

GRADE: B

2008   BONUSES: $7.4 MILLION

1B Justin Smoak (1) has struggled in the majors but that hasn't matter to the Rangers, who used him as the centerpiece of a 2010 deal for Cliff Lee that led to the franchise's first World Series appearance. RHP Joe Wieland also was traded, for Adams. RHP Cody Eppley (43) reached the big leagues last year.

GRADE: B

2007   BONUSES: $6.6 MILLION

This draft already has produced six big leaguers: OF Julio Borbon (1s) and 1B Mitch Moreland (17), still with Texas; RHPs Blake Beavan (1) and Josh Lueke (16), part of the Lee trade; RHP Tommy Hunter (1s), used in a deal for Koji Uehara last July; and LHP Drew Pomeranz (12), who didn't sign and went No. 4 overall in the 2007 draft. After making great progress in 2011, RHPs Neil Ramirez (1s) and Matt West (2) may arrive in Texas shortly.

GRADE: B

Draft analysis by John Manuel (2011) and Jim Callis (2007-10).
Numbers in parentheses indicate draft rounds.

1 JURICKSON PROFAR, SS

Born: Feb. 20, 1993. **B-T:** B-R. **Ht.:** 6-0. **Wt.:** 170.
Signed: Curacao, 2009. **Signed by:** Mike Daly/Chu Halabi/Jose Felomina.

BA GRADE
70
MEDIUM

TOM PRIDDY

Signed for a then-franchise international record $1.55 million out of Curacao in 2009, Profar headlines the Rangers' deep crop of Latin American talent. He has been on the prospect radar since he was 11 and starred on the 2004 Little League World Series championship team from Curacao. He tossed six shutout innings while allowing one hit and striking out 12 against Mexico in the international finals, then went 2-for-3 with a homer in a 5-2 defeat of California in the championship contest. The following year, he led Curacao to a runner-up finish at the LLWS, again tossing six scoreless innings in the international final, this time against Japan. Profar attracted more interest as an amateur as a pitcher than a position player, as he showed a low 90s fastball and above-average breaking ball. Texas believed he could play shortstop and would have enough bat for the position, and now it's reaping the benefits. In 2011, Profar was named the low Class A South Atlantic League's MVP and smoked a pinch-hit triple off Twins farmhand Kyle Gibson in the Futures Game. At age 18, he was the youngest player in both settings.

Still young and skinny, Profar offers a rare combination of present five-tool ability and additional projection. A natural righthanded hitter, he didn't start switch-hitting until after he signed, but he has a smooth swing and great bat speed from both sides. His swing has more leverage and loft from the right side, and scouts are split on his future power projection. Some see only gap power while others predict 20-plus homers annually once he fills out. He's the best pure hitter in the system and has exceptional strike-zone awareness for his age. Profar has average speed that plays up on the bases and in the field because of his elite instincts. He's electrifying defensively, with plus range and arm strength to go along with soft hands and a quick release. Sometimes he plays a little fast in the field and is overly aggressive, but that should be cured with experience. He's intelligent, mature for his age, has great aptitude and speaks four languages (Dutch, English, Spanish and Papiamento, a Portuguese-based creole). One scout compared him to Hanley Ramirez with Dustin Pedroia's makeup.

He wants to reach the big leagues as quickly as his hero, Elvis Andrus, who debuted in Texas four months shy of his 21st birthday. That would Profar in the majors at the end of the 2013 season, which is ambitious but not impossible. He'll open 2012 at high Class A Myrtle Beach at age 19. With Andrus entrenched at shortstop, Profar probably won't break in with the Rangers at that position. Some club officials expected him to eventually wind up at third, but that won't happen either with Adrian Beltre signed through at least 2015. He could slide over to second base and push Ian Kinsler to another position, but Texas won't force a move before it's necessary. Profar has all the ingredients to be a future superstar no matter where he plays.

SCOUTING GRADES

Batting: 65. **Defense:** 65.
Power: 55. **Arm:** 65.
Speed: 55.

Based on 20-80 scouting scale, where 50 represents major league average, and future projection rather than present tools.

Year	Club (League)	Class	AVG	G	AB	R	H	2B	3B	HR	RBI	BB	SO	SB	CS	OBP	SLG
2010	Spokane (NWL)	SS	.250	63	252	42	63	19	0	4	23	28	46	8	3	.323	.373
2011	Hickory (SAL)	LoA	.286	115	430	86	123	37	8	12	65	65	63	23	9	.390	.493
Minor League Totals			.273	178	682	128	186	56	8	16	88	93	109	31	12	.366	.449

2 MARTIN PEREZ, LHP

Born: April 4, 1991. **B-T:** L-L. **Ht.:** 6-0. **Wt.:** 178. **Signed:** Venezuela, 2007. **Signed by:** Rafic Saab/Manny Batista/Don Welke.

Since signing for $580,000 in 2007, Perez has rocketed through the system and developed into one of the game's premier lefthanded pitching prospects. He reached Double-A at age 18 and finally mastered that level in his third stint at Frisco last year, then was the youngest pitcher in the Triple-A Pacific Coast League when he was promoted there in mid-July. Scouts rave about Perez's picture-perfect delivery and arm action that evoke comparisons to fellow Venezuelan lefty Johan Santana. There aren't many pitchers who can match Perez's pure stuff, as he has the makings of three above-average pitches. His lively fastball sits at 90-96 mph with sink, though he needs to work on establishing it more early in counts. He also throws a plus-plus 80-82 mph fading changeup and a sharp 73-77 mph curveball with good depth. Wavering command and inconsistency with his secondary pitches have held Perez back slightly. The Rangers have discussed adding a slider to give him a breaking ball that he can better control. Despite his smallish frame, they aren't worried about his durability. For all the attention given to his struggles in his first two years in Double-A and in his 10 PCL starts, Perez got to Triple-A at age 20. He needs additional seasoning at Round Rock but should contribute in Texas at some point in 2012. Added to the 40-man roster in Nobember, he profiles as a No. 2 starter.

BA GRADE

65 MEDIUM

Year	Club (League)	Class	W	L	ERA	G	GS	CG	SV	IP	H	HR	BB	SO	K/9	WHIP	AVG
2008	Spokane (NWL)	SS	1	2	3.65	15	15	0	0	62	66	3	28	53	7.7	1.52	.274
2009	Hickory (SAL)	LoA	5	5	2.31	22	14	0	1	94	82	3	33	105	10.1	1.23	.236
	Frisco (TL)	AA	1	3	5.57	5	5	0	0	21	29	2	5	14	6.0	1.62	.326
2010	Frisco (TL)	AA	5	8	5.96	24	23	0	0	100	117	12	50	101	9.1	1.68	.290
2011	Frisco (TL)	AA	4	2	3.16	17	16	1	0	88	80	6	36	83	8.5	1.31	.245
	Round Rock (PCL)	AAA	4	4	6.43	10	10	0	0	49	72	4	20	37	6.8	1.88	.343
Minor League Totals			20	24	4.22	93	83	1	1	413	446	30	172	393	8.6	1.50	.276

3 MIKE OLT, 3B

Born: Aug. 27, 1988. **B-T:** R-R. **Ht.:** 6-2. **Wt.:** 210. **Drafted:** Connecticut, 2010 (1st round supplemental). **Signed by:** Jay Heafner.

The fourth and final of Texas' selections in the first and sandwich rounds of the 2010 draft, Olt was the lone college pick and viewed as a safer choice. Signed for $717,300, he quickly established himself as the best prospect of the bunch and might have won the high Class A Carolina League MVP award in his first full pro season if he hadn't broken his collarbone in a home-plate collision in June. He made up for lost time by hitting .349/.433/.764 in the Arizona Fall League. Olt offers the increasingly rare combination of plus righthanded power and plus defense at third base. Sturdy and physically mature, he has great bat speed and impressive raw thunder. He projects as an average hitter, as he occasionally gets out front and struggles with quality offspeed stuff. Despite his selective approach, he strikes out often, Initially a shortstop in college at Connecticut, Olt plays the hot corner with fluid actions and soft hands. He has a plus arm and while he's a below-average runner, he has good first-step quickness and average range. With Adrian Beltre signed through at least 2015, Olt likely won't break in with Texas at third base. He has the athleticism to play left field, and he could be used as a blue-chip trade commodity. He'll spend 2012 at Frisco, where he should post massive power numbers.

BA GRADE

60 MEDIUM

Year	Club (League)	Class	AVG	G	AB	R	H	2B	3B	HR	RBI	BB	SO	SB	CS	OBP	SLG
2010	Spokane (NWL)	SS	.293	69	263	57	77	16	1	9	43	40	77	6	0	.390	.464
2011	Rangers (AZL)	R	.214	4	14	2	3	0	0	1	4	1	5	0	0	.267	.429
	Myrtle Beach (CAR)	HiA	.267	69	240	39	64	15	0	14	42	48	70	0	1	.387	.504
Minor League Totals			.279	142	517	98	144	31	1	24	89	89	152	6	1	.386	.482

4 LEONYS MARTIN, OF

BA GRADE

60

HIGH

Born: March 6, 1988. **B-T:** L-R. **Ht.:** 6-1. **Wt.:** 180. **Signed:** Cuba, 2011. **Signed by:** Chu Halabi/Jose Fernandez/Don Welke.

Martin backed up Yoennis Cespedes on Cuba's 2009 World Baseball Classic, then garnered attention by flashing five-tool ability in Cuban pro league games. After defecting at the 2010 FISU World Championships in Taiwan, he signed with the Rangers last May. His $15.6 million major league contract is the second-largest deal ever given to a Cuban defector. He was promoted to Texas when Nelson Cruz went on the disabled list in September and remained with the club for the American League Division Series. Martin profiles as a prototypical leadoff hitter. He's not a burner, but he has above-average speed that plays up because of his instincts. He's a plus hitter with lightning-quick bat speed and a sound approach at the plate. He shows above-average raw power in batting practice but has gap power during games. His swing can get long at times, so the Rangers worked to shorten his path to the ball. Martin is a quality defender in center field, with easy range and a plus-plus arm. He bulked up too much to impress scouts and is better served when his body is loose and athletic. Martin will have a chance to compete for the starting center-field job during spring training. If he wins it, Texas can save some wear and tear on Josh Hamilton by shifting the former MVP to left field.

Year	Club (League)	Class	AVG	G	AB	R	H	2B	3B	HR	RBI	BB	SO	SB	CS	OBP	SLG
2011	Rangers (AZL)	R	.267	4	15	2	4	0	2	0	1	1	6	0	1	.313	.533
	Frisco (TL)	AA	.348	29	112	24	39	9	2	4	24	15	8	10	8	.435	.571
	Round Rock (PCL)	AAA	.263	40	175	27	46	7	1	0	17	11	24	9	2	.316	.314
	Texas (AL)	MAJ	.375	8	8	2	3	1	0	0	0	0	1	0	0	.375	.500
Major League Totals			.375	8	8	2	3	1	0	0	0	0	1	0	0	.375	.500
Minor League Totals			.295	73	302	53	89	16	5	4	42	27	38	19	11	.362	.421

5 NEIL RAMIREZ, RHP

BA GRADE

55

MEDIUM

Born: May 25, 1989. **B-T:** R-R. **Ht.:** 6-3. **Wt.:** 185. **Drafted:** HS—Virginia Beach, Va., 2007 (1st round supplemental). **Signed by:** Russ Ardolina

Ramirez's stock dropped slightly after an up-and-down senior high school season in 2007, but he still went 44th overall in the draft and received a $1 million bonus. Inconsistency plagued him early in his pro career too, as he spent his first two full seasons at low Class A Hickory. After spending last offseason working out at the team's training facility, he spent most of a breakout 2011 season in Triple-A. Ramirez's fastball sits at 92-94 mph and touches 96 with good angle, while his swing-and-miss curveball ranges from 74-78 mph. Scouts previously projected Ramirez as a back-end reliever, but the development of his changeup last year gives him No. 2 starter upside. His mid-80s changeup now gives him a potential third plus pitch. Drafted with a raw drop-and-drive delivery and a short arm circle, Ramirez now has a tall-and-fall approach and has lengthened his arm action, resulting a more consistent release point. His control and command still need improvement, however. There are some concerns about his high back elbow, but his prototypical frame and delivery lend themselves to durability. The Rangers say he's the system's hardest worker. Protected on the 40-man roster in November, Ramirez should be at least a mid-rotation innings eater. He'll likely open 2012 back at Round Rock but has the potential to contribute in the majors immediately, especially if Texas wants to use him in a late-inning relief role.

Year	Club (League)	Class	W	L	ERA	G	GS	CG	SV	IP	H	HR	BB	SO	K/9	WHIP	AVG
2008	Spokane (NWL)	SS	1	2	2.66	13	13	0	0	44	25	5	29	52	10.6	1.23	.166
2009	Hickory (SAL)	LoA	3	6	4.75	18	14	0	0	66	58	8	41	56	7.6	1.49	.235
2010	Hickory (SAL)	LoA	10	8	4.43	28	26	1	0	140	150	14	37	142	9.1	1.33	.281
2011	Myrtle Beach (CAR)	HiA	0	0	0.00	1	1	0	0	5	1	0	1	9	17.4	0.43	.063
	Frisco (TL)	AA	1	0	1.89	6	6	0	0	19	13	1	8	24	11.4	1.11	.194
	Round Rock (PCL)	AAA	4	3	3.63	18	18	0	0	74	63	6	35	86	10.4	1.32	.229
Minor League Totals			19	19	3.90	84	78	1	0	349	310	34	151	369	9.5	1.32	.240

6 CODY BUCKEL, RHP

Born: June 18, 1992. **B-T:** R-R. **Ht.:** 6-0. **Wt.:** 183. **Drafted:** HS—Simi Valley, Calif., 2010 (2nd round). **Signed by:** Todd Guggiana.

The Rangers haven't been afraid of taking undersized pitchers in recent drafts, including the 6-foot Buckel. He opted to forego a Pepperdine commitment to sign for $590,000 as a second-round pick in 2010. He opened his first full season in extended spring training and then the Hickory bullpen before going 7-2, 2.04 with a 104-19 K-BB ratio in 17 starts. Buckel's intelligence, mechanics and quirkiness are reminiscent of those of his best friend—Trevor Bauer, the No. 3 overall choice in the 2011 draft and his offseason workout partner. As with Bauer, Buckel's unorthodox and torque-heavy delivery creates deception. While he doesn't have overpowering stuff, he has a deep four-pitch mix, outstanding pitchability and a fiercely competitive nature. Buckel's fastball sits at 88-92 mph and touches 94 with armside run. He also throws a plus changeup, an average curveball with big break that he learned from Barry Zito and a short cutter/slider that induces grounders. Some scouts still worry about his size and durability, though his athleticism should help him. Buckel doesn't have incredible upside, but he has a low floor and could become a solid No. 3 starter. He'll headline Myrtle Beach's 2012 rotation and may move quickly because of his advanced feel for pitching.

BA GRADE
50
MEDIUM

Year	Club (League)	Class	W	L	ERA	G	GS	CG	SV	IP	H	HR	BB	SO	K/9	WHIP	AVG
2010	Rangers (AZL)	R	0	0	0.00	4	0	0	0	5	2	0	1	9	16.2	0.60	.125
2011	Hickory (SAL)	LoA	8	3	2.61	23	17	0	0	97	83	7	27	120	11.2	1.14	.229
Minor League Totals			8	3	2.48	27	17	0	0	102	85	7	28	129	11.4	1.11	.225

7 JORGE ALFARO, C

Born: June 11, 1993. **B-T:** R-R. **Ht.:** 6-2. **Wt.:** 185. **Signed:** Colombia, 2010. **Signed by:** Rodolfo Rosario/Don Welke.

Alfaro didn't get much exposure as an infielder in his native Colombia, so he moved to the Dominican Republic and started catching. Though raw, he showed enough ability to handle the position to earn a Colombian-record $1.3 million bonus. He was the second-youngest player in the short-season Northwest League last summer, behind teammate Rougned Odor. Athletic and strong, Alfaro stands out for his plus-plus raw power and his cannon arm. With impressive bat speed, hip rotation and extension, he puts on shows in batting practice. Like most young players, he can be overly aggressive and let his swing get long. There are concerns about his hitting ability and whether he'll make enough contact, but he shows pitch-recognition skills. His plate discipline still needs improvement after he walked four times in 45 games last year. Alfaro has top-of-the-scale raw arm strength and good accuracy, but he has a tendency to rush throws and get sloppy with his footwork. That's why he threw out just 22 percent of basestealers in 2011. With refinement, he projects as an above-average defender. Alfaro moves well laterally and is more athletic than most catchers, and he even has fringy speed. He's still learning to deal with success and failure. With the potential to be a middle-of-the-order, middle-of-the-diamond player, Alfaro has one of the highest ceilings in the system. He'll advance to low Class A in 2012.

BA GRADE
60
EXTREME

Year	Club (League)	Class	AVG	G	AB	R	H	2B	3B	HR	RBI	BB	SO	SB	CS	OBP	SLG
2010	Rangers (DSL)	R	.221	48	172	18	38	5	2	1	23	5	48	1	4	.278	.291
2011	Spokane (NWL)	SS	.300	45	160	18	48	9	1	6	23	4	54	1	0	.345	.481
Minor League Totals			.259	93	332	36	86	14	3	7	46	9	102	2	4	.310	.383

8 CHRISTIAN VILLANUEVA, 3B

Born: June 19, 1991. **B-T:** R-R. **Ht.:** 5-11. **Wt.:** 180. **Signed:** Mexico, 2008. **Signed by:** Bill McLaughlin/Mike Daly.

Rangers international scouting director Mike Daly saw Villanueva star for Mexico at the 2008 Junior World Championships, and Texas signed him two weeks later. Coming from a family of baseball players, he always played shortstop as an amateur but moved to third base after injuring his knee in 2009 and starting to fill out. Villanueva has a short, compact swing with a balanced load and good bat control. He has an advanced approach at the plate, though he can get pull-happy at times. There are mixed opinions on his power, as he presently has line-drive sock but some scouts see at least average potential. He doesn't project as a basestealer, but he has sneaky quickness and instincts that allowed him to swipe 32 bases last year. Villanueva is equally as impressive at third base as Mike Olt. An easy plus defender, Villanueva has soft hands and easy actions. Despite average speed, he has a solid range thanks to his first-step quickness and instincts. He has above-average

BA GRADE
60
HIGH

arm with good carry and accuracy. Scouts compare Villanueva to fellow countryman Vinny Castilla. With Adrian Beltre in Texas and Olt ahead of him in the system, Villanueva spent time during instructional league at second base, where there would be reduced pressure on his bat. He'll play in high Class A in 2012.

Year	Club (League)	Class	AVG	G	AB	R	H	2B	3B	HR	RBI	BB	SO	SB	CS	OBP	SLG
2009	Rangers 2 (DSL)	R	.208	8	24	2	5	1	0	0	3	6	5	1	0	.375	.250
2010	Rangers (AZL)	R	.314	51	188	30	59	14	1	2	35	13	42	6	2	.365	.431
2011	Hickory (SAL)	LoA	.278	126	467	78	130	30	3	17	84	37	86	32	6	.338	.465
Minor League Totals			.286	185	679	110	194	45	4	19	122	56	133	39	8	.347	.448

9 ROUGNED ODOR, 2B

BA GRADE

55

HIGH

Born: Feb. 3, 1994. **B-T:** L-R. **Ht.:** 5-11. **Wt.:** 170. **Signed:** Venezuela, 2011 **Signed by:** Rafic Saab/Mike Daly.

The nephew of Indians Double-A hitting coach Rouglas Odor, Rougned was a top international target for his sweet swing, but scouts initially were scared away by his smallish stature and speed. After he improved his speed and showed impressive polish in game action, the Rangers signed him for $425,000 in January. Five months later, he made his debut as the youngest player in the Northwest League, where he ranked as No. 7 prospect at age 17. Odor doesn't have elite-level tools, but what he has plays up because of his instincts, intelligence and swagger. He controls the bat head well and his incredibly quick hands allow him to make late adjustments. Though not big, he has gap power and gets good natural backspin on the ball that could lead to more pop. He hangs in against lefthanders and can bunt. Initially signed as a shortstop, Odor handled the switch to second base smoothly and has the arm to play on either side of the bag. He has smooth actions, good range and a nose for the ball. He's a solid runner. Depending on how much his power develops, Odor could develop into a solid regular or more. He has a chance to move quickly and may not be challenged until he reaches the higher minors. He'll spend 2012 in low Class A.

Year	Club (League)	Class	AVG	G	AB	R	H	2B	3B	HR	RBI	BB	SO	SB	CS	OBP	SLG
2011	Spokane (NWL)	SS	.262	58	233	33	61	9	3	2	29	13	37	10	4	.323	.352
Minor League Totals			.262	58	233	33	61	9	3	2	29	13	37	10	4	.323	.352

10 MATT WEST, RHP

BA GRADE

55

HIGH

Born: Nov. 21, 1988. **B-T:** R-R. **Ht.:** 6-1. **Wt.:** 215. **Drafted:** HS—Bellaire, Texas, 2007 (2nd round) **Signed by:** Randy Taylor.

Drafted as a third baseman in the second round of the 2007 draft, West tested positive for a performance-enhancing substance and was handed a 50-game suspension less than two months after signing for $400,000. He never put it together at the plate, hitting .241/.344/.364 over four seasons and topping out at low Class A. He quickly took to pitching in 2011, earning a spot on the 40-man roster and comparisons to fellow position player-turned-closer Jason Motte for his compact frame and power stuff. With perhaps better pure stuff than Motte, West profiles as a lockdown closer. Using his incredibly quick arm from a three-quarters arm slot, he pumps 94-96 mph fastballs with good life and touches triple digits. His heater can flatten out at higher velocities. Some scouts confuse his 82-84 mph wipeout slider for a power curveball because of its depth. He's also developing a changeup and shows some feel for it despite his inexperience. West has above-average command and control, walking just one batter in 26 innings at short-season Spokane. He has a completely different personality on the mound, as he's fearless in the way he goes after hitters. West will open 2012 in high Class A. If he continues to impress like he did in his pitching debut, his pair of plus-plus pitches could take him to Texas by September.

Year	Club (League)	Class	AVG	G	AB	R	H	2B	3B	HR	RBI	BB	SO	SB	CS	OBP	SLG
2007	Rangers (AZL)	R	.301	29	103	21	31	1	4	0	17	9	21	1	3	.397	.388
2008	Spokane (NWL)	SS	.258	67	240	48	62	12	0	4	30	26	68	1	0	.367	.358
2009	Hickory (SAL)	LoA	.234	135	471	61	110	29	2	5	55	54	136	12	4	.336	.335
2010	Hickory (SAL)	LoA	.223	115	391	52	87	25	2	13	48	38	125	7	2	.326	.396
Minor League Totals			.241	346	1205	182	290	67	8	22	150	127	350	21	9	.344	.364

Year	Club (League)	Class	W	L	ERA	G	GS	CG	SV	IP	H	HR	BB	SO	K/9	WHIP	AVG
2011	Spokane (NWL)	SS	1	2	3.12	23	0	0	9	26	23	3	1	35	12.1	0.92	.242
	Myrtle Beach (CAR)	HiA	0	0	0.00	1	0	0	0	1	1	0	0	0	0.0	1.00	.250
Minor League Totals			1	2	3.00	24	0	0	9	27	24	3	1	35	11.7	0.93	.242

11 LEURY GARCIA, SS

Born: March 18, 1991. **B-T:** B-R. **Ht.:** 5-7. **Wt.:** 153. **Signed:** Dominican Republic, 2007. **Signed by:** Jesus Ovalle.

If he were a few inches taller or in a system that had less middle-of-the-diamond talent, Garcia would get more attention because few shortstop prospects can match his three plus-plus tools: speed, range, and arm strength. He spent 2011 in the high Class A Carolina League, where some scouts said he showed better defensive ability than more heralded Manny Machado (Orioles) and Andrelton Simmons (Braves). Small and compact, Garcia makes more than his share of plays with incredible side-to-side range and impressive arm strength, though he also plays the game too fast and occasionally loses focus. Defensive consistency would assure him an everyday big league role despite questions about his bat. Garcia would benefit from being more vanilla at the plate, hitting the ball on the ground and working counts. He has a flat swing and won't ever have power, but he should hit enough to hold his own. His top-of-the-scale speed makes him a huge basestealing threat. Garcia could play a variety of positions and break into the big leagues as a super-utility player. He hasn't had a breakout season yet but keeps making consistent strides. His next step is Double-A.

Year	Club (League)	Class	AVG	G	AB	R	H	2B	3B	HR	RBI	BB	SO	SB	CS	OBP	SLG
2008	Rangers (AZL)	R	.209	41	129	17	27	3	3	0	14	8	40	12	3	.250	.279
2009	Hickory (SAL)	LoA	.232	83	276	28	64	6	3	1	18	18	64	19	6	.288	.286
2010	Rangers (AZL)	R	.500	6	18	5	9	2	0	0	2	4	4	4	2	.591	.611
	Hickory (SAL)	LoA	.262	89	359	57	94	5	4	3	22	23	57	47	9	.307	.323
2011	Myrtle Beach (CAR)	HiA	.256	109	442	65	113	19	5	3	38	28	100	30	12	.306	.342
Minor League Totals			.251	328	1224	172	307	35	15	7	94	81	265	112	32	.301	.321

12 JORDAN AKINS, OF

Born: April 19, 1992. **B-T:** R-R. **Ht.:** 6-4. **Wt.:** 192. **Drafted:** HS—Locust Grove, Ga., 2010 (3rd round). **Signed by:** Ryan Coe.

Akins spurned a football scholarship from Georgia for the chance to play two sports at Central Florida, but he turned that down to sign with the Rangers for $350,000 as a third-round pick in 2010. A premium fast-twitch athlete, he was an explosive quarterback/wide receiver/defensive back/kick returner who didn't play much baseball. He struggled in his pro debut, then made strides last summer and was the star of instructional league in the fall. Though raw, Akins shows flashes of five plus tools that he's just starting to translate into baseball skills. He has light-tower raw power, drawing crowds during batting practice, but his swing can flatten out and he needs to be more consistent keeping the bat head in the zone. He has a quick path to the ball and a smooth stroke, though he needs to improve his pitch recognition. With plus-plus speed, Akins has good range in center field and takes proper routes to the ball. He also has an above-average arm. He should be able to stick in center field, where he spent most of last year, but he could end up in right field as he fills out. Though he's not as big, he reminds some scouts of Mike Stanton for his football background, elite athleticism and raw power. The Rangers hope Akins can handle a promotion to low Class A to open 2012.

Year	Club (League)	Class	AVG	G	AB	R	H	2B	3B	HR	RBI	BB	SO	SB	CS	OBP	SLG
2010	Rangers (AZL)	R	.187	36	107	14	20	3	2	0	8	5	35	5	1	.241	.252
2011	Rangers (AZL)	R	.283	48	180	37	51	12	4	2	31	6	42	13	2	.312	.428
Minor League Totals			.247	84	287	51	71	15	6	2	39	11	77	18	3	.285	.362

13 RONALD GUZMAN, 1B/OF

Born: Oct. 20, 1994. **B-T:** R-R. **Ht.:** 6-5. **Wt.:** 205. **Signed:** Dominican Republic, 2011. **Signed by:** Willy Espinal/Mike Daly.

Guzman was part of the Rangers' costly 2011 international class, and most scouts considered him the amateur market's top hitter. He signed for $3.45 million last July and the industry consensus is that he's a better hitter and player than fellow Dominican Nomar Mazara, who got $4.95 million. While he doesn't have the same raw power as Mazara, Guzman makes more contact and has a better approach. Guzman led his Dominican team to a championship at the Reviving Baseball in Inner Cities tournament in 2010, then played in the Under Armour All-America Game at Wrigley Field that summer. He projects to have above-average raw power, though his pop doesn't yet show in game action. He has a fluid, easy swing with good balance, though he has a deep load with his hands. Despite average bat speed, he has a good bat path and keeps the head in the zone for a long time. Guzman is below-average runner, though the Rangers hope he'll get faster as he adds strength to his lanky frame. International reports suggested he had good instincts in left field, but during instructional league he worked out primarily at first base and looked raw there. His arm strength is below average. Guzman graduated from high school before signing and earns rave reviews for his makeup and aptitude. He'll likely make his pro debut in the Arizona League next summer, though Texas could be aggressive and send him to Spokane.

Year	Club (League)	Class	AVG	G	AB	R	H	2B	3B	HR	RBI	BB	SO	SB	CS	OBP	SLG
2011	Did Not Play—Signed 2012 Contract																

14 ROBBIE ROSS, LHP

Born: June 24, 1989. **B-T:** L-L. **Ht.:** 5-11. **Wt.:** 185. **Drafted:** HS—Lexington, Ky., 2008 (2nd round). **Signed by:** Jon Poloni.

BA GRADE
50
MEDIUM

Ross catapulted his draft stock in 2008 by outdueling Brett DeVall, who went on to be a Braves sandwich-round pick. The Rangers took Ross in the second round and signed him for $1.575 million. After a tough second half in the California League in 2010, he benefited when Texas moved its high Class A affiliate to the more pitcher-friendly Carolina League last year. He led the circuit in ERA (2.26) and opponent average (.227), earning a promotion to Double-A after Robbie Erlin and Joe Wieland were traded. Ross racks up his share of strikeouts and generates plenty of weak contact. He attacks the zone with an 88-93 mph fastball, and he can cut it or run it. His slider can flatten out when he gets under it but flashes above-average potential. He throws an average changeup that's inconsistent. Scouts don't love the effort in Ross' delivery, as he employs a high leg kick and throws across his body, but it does create deception. He has good control but needs to work on refining command, specifically locating his fastball on the outside corner against righthanders. Some scouts think Ross is best suited for the bullpen, but he'll get an extended look as a starter. He'll return to Frisco in 2012.

Year	Club (League)	Class	W	L	ERA	G	GS	CG	SV	IP	H	HR	BB	SO	K/9	WHIP	AVG
2009	Spokane (NWL)	SS	4	4	2.66	15	15	0	0	74	68	5	17	76	9.2	1.14	.240
2010	Hickory (SAL)	LoA	8	7	2.59	16	16	0	0	94	89	2	20	62	5.9	1.16	.245
	Bakersfield (CAL)	HiA	4	4	5.37	11	11	0	0	52	67	4	17	49	8.5	1.62	.305
2011	Myrtle Beach (CAR)	HiA	9	4	2.26	21	20	1	0	123	102	1	28	98	7.2	1.05	.227
	Frisco (TL)	AA	1	1	2.61	6	6	0	0	38	33	5	5	36	8.5	1.00	.231
Minor League Totals			26	20	2.88	69	68	1	0	382	359	17	87	321	7.6	1.17	.246

15 JUSTIN GRIMM, RHP

Born: Aug. 16, 1988. **B-T:** R-R. **Ht.:** 6-3. **Wt.:** 175. **Drafted:** Georgia, 2010 (5th round). **Signed by:** Ryan Coe.

BA GRADE
55
HIGH

Rangers scouting director Kip Fagg was the team's national crosschecker when he first saw Grimm pitch as a high schooler, and he always liked Grimm's athleticism, frame and the way the ball exploded out of his hand. The Red Sox drafted Grimm in the 13th round out of high school, but he opted to attend Georgia, where he showed flashes of brilliance but went 6-12, 5.80 in three college seasons. Fagg never doubted Grimm's upside and met with him twice before the 2010 draft, finally getting his man with a fifth-round pick and an above-slot $825,000 bonus. A long-toss advocate, Grimm works his fastball at 92-96 mph with late sinking life. His power curveball gives him a second plus offering. The development of his circle changeup last year was a key to his success and gives him a chance to remain a starter. Texas has worked with Grimm to refine and repeat his delivery, which contains considerable effort. He has mid-rotation potential, though he could also fill a late-inning relief role with his velocity playing up out of the bullpen. He'll advance to Double-A in 2012.

Year	Club (League)	Class	W	L	ERA	G	GS	CG	SV	IP	H	HR	BB	SO	K/9	WHIP	AVG
2011	Hickory (SAL)	LoA	2	1	3.40	9	9	0	0	50	45	5	18	54	9.7	1.25	.247
	Myrtle Beach (CAR)	HiA	5	2	3.39	16	16	0	0	90	84	2	30	73	7.3	1.26	.247
Minor League Totals			7	3	3.39	25	25	0	0	141	129	7	48	127	8.1	1.26	.247

16 TANNER SCHEPPERS, RHP

Born: Jan. 17, 1987. **B-T:** R-R. **Ht.:** 6-4. **Wt.:** 200. **Drafted:** St. Paul (American Association), 2009 (1st round supplemental). **Signed by:** Derek Lee.

BA GRADE
55
HIGH

Scheppers missed Fresno State's 2008 College World Series championship run and dropped to the second round of that year's draft because of shoulder issues. He declined to sign with the Pirates and resurfaced in independent ball in 2009, then signed with the Rangers for $1.25 million as a sandwich-rounder. After he pitched exclusively in relief to limit his innings in 2010, Texas hoped to develop him as a starter last year. Instead, a herniated disk in his back pushed him back into the bullpen. Scheppers has lost some of his shine, but he still has value as a late-inning reliever. He has a 95-98 mph fastball that can touch triple digits, though it's often described as soft because it's straight and hitters see it well. His downer curveball with two-plane break gives him a second plus pitch. He also has a fringy slider and a below-average changeup. Scheppers has a herky-jerky delivery that he rushes through, affecting the consistency of his release point. He needs to make mechanical adjustments to help his control and his deception. With his electric fastball/curve combination, Scheppers could be a future closer or set-up man. He figures to open 2012 with his third stint in Triple-A.

Year	Club (League)	Class	W	L	ERA	G	GS	CG	SV	IP	H	HR	BB	SO	K/9	WHIP	AVG
2009	St. Paul (A-A)	IND	1	1	3.32	4	4	0	0	19	17	1	11	20	9.5	1.47	.243
2010	Frisco (TL)	AA	0	0	0.82	6	0	0	2	11	3	1	0	19	15.5	0.27	.079
	Oklahoma City (PCL)	AAA	1	3	5.48	30	7	0	4	69	82	5	30	71	9.3	1.62	.297
2011	Round Rock (PCL)	AAA	2	0	4.35	11	1	0	2	21	23	0	12	20	8.7	1.69	.295
	Frisco (TL)	AA	2	1	3.13	17	0	0	0	23	18	1	9	24	9.4	1.17	.212
Minor League Totals			5	4	4.44	64	8	0	8	124	126	7	51	134	9.8	1.43	.264

17 LUIS SARDINAS, SS

BA GRADE
55
EXTREME

Born: May 16, 1993. **B-T:** B-R. **Ht.:** 6-1. **Wt.:** 150. **Signed:** Venezuela, 2009.
Signed by: Mike Daly/Rafic Saab/Pedro Avila.

Texas signed two Latin American shortstops for seven figures in 2009, Jurickson Profar ($1.55 million) and Sardinas ($1.2 million). While Profar has generated more attention and ranks No. 1 on this list, Sardinas may have better raw tools. But he hasn't been able to stay healthy and doesn't have the same polish. A broken finger delayed his 2010 pro debut, and a dislocated shoulder on a swing and miss during instructional league that fall led to surgery and limited him to just 14 games last year. While scouts don't necessarily think of Sardinas as injury-prone, they do question his durability and slight frame. A quick-twitch athlete, he reminds the Rangers of a young Tony Fernandez. Sardinas is a plus-plus runner with first-step quickness and lateral agility, giving him better speed and range than Profar. Sardinas has above-average arm strength and smooth actions in the field. As a switch-hitter with impressive hand-eye coordination, he offers a similar offensive package to Profar. Sardinas is skinny but not weak, and he has some whip in his swing that produces gap power, though he occasionally tries too hard to muscle up in his swing. His bat takes a good path to the ball, though it's better from the right side, and he would benefit from staying on top of the ball more often. Texas would like to see Sardinas advance to low Class A in 2012 and stay healthy for the entire season.

Year	Club (League)	Class	AVG	G	AB	R	H	2B	3B	HR	RBI	BB	SO	SB	CS	OBP	SLG
2010	Rangers (AZL)	R	.311	26	103	22	32	4	0	0	8	7	15	8	2	.363	.350
2011	Rangers (AZL)	R	.308	14	52	11	16	2	1	0	7	4	10	2	1	.367	.385
Minor League Totals			.310	40	155	33	48	6	1	0	15	11	25	10	3	.364	.361

18 LUKE JACKSON, RHP

BA GRADE
50
HIGH

Born: Aug. 24, 1991. **B-T:** R-R. **Ht.:** 6-2. **Wt.:** 187. **Drafted:** HS—Fort Lauderdale, Fla., 2010 (1st round supplemental). **Signed by:** Juan Alvarez.

Jackson didn't get the same attention as fellow Sunshine State prep products Karsten Whitson and A.J. Cole, but he offered better pure velocity and arguably more projection than any Florida high schooler in the 2010 draft class. Jackson didn't start pitching seriously until he was a high school freshman. Rangers scouts liked his athleticism and big arm, so they took him with a supplemental first-rounder and signed him for $1.545 million. After beginning 2011 in extended spring training, he made his pro debut in low Class A, where his performance was inconsistent but his stuff was steady. Jackson's fastball sits at 91-94 mph and touches 97, and his quick arm action produces late jump. His curveball is a plus pitch at times, especially when he stays on top of it and tightens its rotation. He also has a changeup with solid potential. With a high leg kick and hand break, Jackson has a rocking delivery that creates some deception, though he needs to repeat it better and not slow down while throwing his secondary pitches. He has a lot of work to do with his control and command. Jackson could profile as a No. 2 starter if everything breaks right. He'll advance to high Class A this year.

Year	Club (League)	Class	W	L	ERA	G	GS	CG	SV	IP	H	HR	BB	SO	K/9	WHIP	AVG
2011	Hickory (SAL)	LoA	5	6	5.64	19	19	0	0	75	83	9	48	78	9.4	1.75	.276
Minor League Totals			5	6	5.64	19	19	0	0	75	83	9	48	78	9.4	1.75	.276

19 ROMAN MENDEZ, RHP

BA GRADE
50
HIGH

Born: July 25, 1990. **B-T:** R-R. **Ht.:** 6-2. **Wt.:** 191. **Signed:** Dominican Republic, 2007. **Signed by:** Luciano del Rosario (Red Sox).

The Rangers saw plenty of Mendez as an amateur free agent, as he grew up in San Pedro de Marcoris, not far from their complex in the Dominican Republic. Their scouts liked his wiry-strong frame and whippy arm, but he signed with the Red Sox for $125,000 in 2007. Texas targeted Mendez in several trade discussions with Boston and eventually got him as the main piece in the Jarrod Saltalamacchia trade in July 2010. First baseman Chris McGuiness and since-released catcher Michael Thomas also came to the Rangers in the deal. Mendez's fastball ranges from 92-98 mph and sits around 94-95 when he's on. He can add boring, running and cutting action with his quick arm action. He has a slider with good tilt that flashes as a plus pitch, and he mixes in a solid changeup. He has worked on a splitter that shows good bite, but he doesn't often use it in games. Mendez throws across his body and slings the ball from a three-quarters arm slot, which leads to varying release points and some control issues. He did cut his walk rate from 4.8 per nine innings in 2010 to 3.5 last year. The development of his secondary stuff and command will determine his future role, as some scouts see Mendez as a mid-rotation starter and others view him as a late-inning reliever. Added to the 40-man roster in the offseason, he should start 2012 in high Class A.

Year	Club (League)	Class	W	L	ERA	G	GS	CG	SV	IP	H	HR	BB	SO	K/9	WHIP	AVG
2008	Red Sox (DSL)	R	3	1	2.65	11	11	0	0	51	43	1	16	46	8.1	1.16	.222
2009	Red Sox (GCL)	R	2	3	1.99	12	10	0	0	50	33	1	8	47	8.5	0.83	.184
2010	Greenville (SAL)	LoA	0	2	11.40	6	6	0	0	15	29	5	10	18	10.8	2.60	.392
	Lowell (NYP)	SS	2	3	4.36	8	8	0	0	33	31	5	19	35	9.5	1.52	.240

Year	Club (League)	Class	W	L	ERA	G	GS	CG	SV	IP	H	HR	BB	SO	K/9	WHIP	AVG
	Spokane (NWL)	SS	1	1	2.31	3	3	0	0	12	19	2	3	13	10.0	1.89	.373
2011	Hickory (SAL)	LoA	9	1	3.31	26	20	0	1	117	117	7	45	130	10.0	1.38	.259
Minor League Totals			17	11	3.47	66	58	0	1	277	272	21	101	289	9.4	1.34	.252

20 BARRET LOUX, RHP

BA GRADE 50 HIGH

Born: April 6, 1989. **B-T:** R-R. **Ht.:** 6-5. **Wt.:** 215. **Signed:** Texas A&M, 2010. **Signed by:** Randy Taylor.

Considered a supplemental-round talent in the 2010 draft, Loux went sixth overall to the Diamondbacks in part because he agreed to a below-slot $2 million bonus. Things got complicated when he failed Arizona's physical, prompting the team to back out of the deal. Major League Baseball decided to grant Arizona a compensation pick in the 2011 draft and make Loux a free agent to settle the situation. Despite medical concerns about his shoulder and elbow that dated back to high school, the Rangers had thought highly of Loux all along and signed him in November 2010 for $312,000, roughly third-round money. In his first year as a pro, Loux threw 109 innings in high Class A before being shut down for precautionary reasons in August. He has a big, sturdy frame and an easy low-90s fastball that touches 96 mph, though it's somewhat straight. The development of Loux's secondary stuff will determine his future role, as some scouts see him as a mid-rotation starter and others project him as a middle reliever. He shows feel for a fading changeup that's a plus pitch at times, and he throws two breaking balls that are both inconsistent. His curveball was his best pitch in high school but hasn't been as sharp since he had surgery to remove bone chips from his elbow at Texas A&M, and his slider has some power to it at 82-84 mph. He'll open 2012 in Double-A and could move quickly if shifted to a relief role.

Year	Club (League)	Class	W	L	ERA	G	GS	CG	SV	IP	H	HR	BB	SO	K/9	WHIP	AVG
2011	Myrtle Beach (CAR)	HiA	8	5	3.80	21	21	0	0	109	106	6	34	127	10.5	1.28	.252
Minor League Totals			8	5	3.80	21	21	0	0	109	106	6	34	127	10.5	1.28	.252

21 WILL LAMB, LHP

BA GRADE 50 HIGH

Born: Sept. 9, 1990. **B-T:** L-L. **Ht.:** 6-6. **Wt.:** 180. **Drafted:** Clemson, 2011 (2nd round). **Signed by:** Chris Kemp.

Lamb was a two-way player at Clemson, hitting .348/.389/.471 and posting a 1-1, 5.11 line (mostly in relief) as a junior in 2011. While some scouts thought he could stick in center field because of his above-average speed and defensive chops, Texas thought he could utilize his long levers and athleticism on the mound. Chris Kemp, who had coached at nearby Spartanburg Methodist (S.C.) JC before becoming a Rangers area scout, had seen Lamb pitch as much as anyone and liked him. Texas popped him in the second round and signed him for $430,200. Lamb has a live, loose arm that generates fastballs that sit at 92-95 mph and touch 98. He also shows a low-80s slider with bite and power that's an above-average pitch at its best. He didn't use his changeup much at Clemson, but it could be a solid offering with time. Lamb uses his size to his advantage and gets good downward plane on the ball. He has a tall, skinny frame and needs to bulk up. He also throws significantly across his body, and once he tones that down, it should help the consistency of his secondary stuff. The Rangers like Lamb's makeup and competitiveness, and they'll develop him as a starter. He'll begin his first full pro season in high Class A.

Year	Club (League)	Class	W	L	ERA	G	GS	CG	SV	IP	H	HR	BB	SO	K/9	WHIP	AVG
2011	Spokane (NWL)	SS	1	1	3.89	12	7	0	0	37	35	3	23	42	10.2	1.57	.248
	Hickory (SAL)	LoA	2	0	0.48	4	4	0	0	19	10	0	8	20	9.6	0.96	.156
Minor League Totals			3	1	2.75	16	11	0	0	56	45	3	31	62	10.0	1.37	.220

22 KEVIN MATTHEWS, LHP

BA GRADE 50 HIGH

Born: Nov. 29, 1992. **B-T:** R-L. **Ht.:** 5-11. **Wt.:** 180. **Drafted:** HS—Richmond Hill, Ga., 2011 (1st round). **Signed by:** Ryan Coe.

The Rangers have dipped into the Southeast frequently in recent drafts and went back again in 2011, making Matthews their first-round pick and signing him away from a Virginia commitment for $936,000. Small but athletic and strong, Matthews impressed club officials who watched him throw down a 360-dunk before the draft despite his 5-foot-11 frame. Some scouts compared him to Texas 2006 first-rounder Kasey Kiker in terms of size and stuff, but Matthews is much more athletic, has better makeup and played against tougher high school competition. He has a quick arm and runs his fastball up to 95 mph, though he usually sits at 88-92. He has a tight curveball that already grades as a solid pitch and a changeup that's advanced for his age. As Matthews logged innings during his pro debut and instructional league, his arm slot started to creep down, and it will be important for him to stay on top of the ball to generate downward plane. To help in that regard, the Rangers had had him work with a full windup in instructional league, which also helped him stay in a straight line to the plate. There's some effort in his delivery, so he may be destined for the bullpen, but he'll remain in the rotation for the foreseeable future. Texas hopes Matthews can advance to low Class A after opening his first full pro season in extended spring training.

Year	Club (League)	Class	W	L	ERA	G	GS	CG	SV	IP	H	HR	BB	SO	K/9	WHIP	AVG
2011	Rangers (AZL)	R	1	0	1.50	7	3	0	0	12	10	1	5	12	9.0	1.25	.222
	Spokane (NWL)	SS	0	3	2.70	5	5	0	0	17	14	0	13	18	9.7	1.62	.222
Minor League Totals			1	3	2.20	12	8	0	0	29	24	1	18	30	9.4	1.47	.222

23 KELLIN DEGLAN, C

BA GRADE
50
HIGH

Born: June 3, 1992. **B-T:** L-R. **Ht.:** 6-2. **Wt.:** 188. **Drafted:** HS—Langley, B.C., 2010 (1st round). **Signed by:** Gary McGraw.

Despite attending a secondary school that didn't have a baseball team, Deglan faced quality amateur competition as a member of Canada's junior national team. Strong performances against pro players during extended spring training exhibitions in 2010 boosted his draft stock, and the Rangers signed him for $1 million after taking him 22nd overall that June. Deglan met expectations in 2011 by keeping his head above water in low Class A. While his numbers weren't impressive, the defensive strides he made have the Rangers optimistic about his future. Deglan has a strong, accurate arm and quick release capable of producing 1.8-second pop times, though he threw out just 21 percent of basestealers last year. He must improve his blocking and receiving, but he could develop into an above-average defender. Texas raves about his makeup, aptitude and feel for the game, and he did a nice job handling the Hickory pitching staff. Deglan's bat will determine whether he's an everyday player or a backup. He has a nice lefthanded swing and above-average raw power, though it plays as alley power during games. He needs to do a better job of staying back on pitches, as he's too often fooled by offspeed stuff. He's not afraid to work a walk, but his long arms add length to his swing and diminish his ability to make consistent contact. Deglan likely will return to low Class A this year in an attempt to jump-start his bat.

Year	Club (League)	Class	AVG	G	AB	R	H	2B	3B	HR	RBI	BB	SO	SB	CS	OBP	SLG
2010	Rangers (AZL)	R	.286	10	28	5	8	0	1	0	5	2	7	0	0	.355	.357
	Spokane (NWL)	SS	.159	22	82	7	13	2	0	1	4	7	21	0	0	.222	.220
2011	Hickory (SAL)	LoA	.227	89	291	39	66	15	1	6	39	34	91	2	0	.320	.347
Minor League Totals			.217	121	401	51	87	17	2	7	48	43	119	2	0	.303	.322

24 JAKE SKOLE, OF

BA GRADE
50
HIGH

Born: Jan 7, 1992. **B-T:** L-R. **Ht.:** 6-1. **Wt.:** 192. **Drafted:** HS—Roswell, Ga., 2010 (1st round). **Signed by:** Ryan Coe.

The younger brother of 2011 Nationals fifth-round pick Matt Skole, a slugging third baseman out of Georgia Tech, Jake turned down a two-sport commitment to the Yellow Jackets to turn pro the year before. He signed for $1.56 million as the 15th overall pick in 2010. After focusing on football in high school, Skole started to better understand his swing in his first full pro season. He has shown more power than initially expected, and some scouts now think he could hit 20 or more homers on an annual basis in the big leagues. He projects as a solid hitter who can take the ball to all fields, but he works a lot of deep counts and will chase offspeed stuff, leading to 138 whiffs in 2011. An ankle injury he sustained playing football hurt his speed, which was once considered plus but hasn't fully come back. He's a smart and aggressive baserunner. Though Skole gets good jumps and takes fine routes in center field, his body has thickened and he likely won't have the closing speed to play up the middle in the future. A move to an outfield corner would put more pressure on his bat. His throwing ticked up a notch last year, from solid to above-average. He's ready for high Class A.

Year	Club (League)	Class	AVG	G	AB	R	H	2B	3B	HR	RBI	BB	SO	SB	CS	OBP	SLG
2010	Rangers (AZL)	R	.286	8	28	7	8	2	0	0	5	5	5	3	0	.394	.357
	Spokane (NWL)	SS	.254	57	201	29	51	9	2	2	27	23	52	6	4	.327	.348
2011	Hickory (SAL)	LoA	.264	124	424	76	112	14	6	9	62	65	138	21	14	.366	.389
Minor League Totals			.262	189	653	112	171	25	8	11	94	93	195	30	18	.356	.375

25 TOMAS TELIS, C

BA GRADE
50
HIGH

Born: June 18, 1991. **B-T:** B-R. **Ht.:** 5-8. **Wt.:** 175. **Signed:** Venezuela, 2007. **Signed by:** Edgar Suarez.

Telis initially attracted scouting interest as a middle infielder, but the Rangers moved him behind the plate immediately after signing him for $130,000 in 2007 because of his thick torso and strong lower half. He had Tommy John surgery in 2010 that kept him out for most of the season, and Texas kept his throwing workload down last year by having him split time behind the plate with Kellin Deglan at Hickory. Telis' arm has bounced back well, though it's just fringy and he detracts from it with inconsistent mechanics. He erased just 19 percent of basestealers in low Class A. He still has a lot of work to do behind the plate, as he struggles receiving velocity and movement, and he doesn't block balls in the dirt well. With short arms and a stocky build, Telis doesn't necessarily look the part, but he can rake and rivals Jurickson Profar as the system's pure hitter. A switch-hitter, Telis is significantly better from the left side. Though he's ultra-aggressive, Telis' has strong hand-eye coordination that allows him to consistently barrel the ball. He has a line-drive swing and projects to have more gap than over-the-fence power. Telis could be a bat-first backstop, though scouts wonder if he'll be able to stay behind the plate full-time, so he might end up splitting time between catcher and DH. He'll get more playing time at catcher in 2012, when he advances to high Class A and Deglan returns to Hickory.

Year	Club (League)	Class	AVG	G	AB	R	H	2B	3B	HR	RBI	BB	SO	SB	CS	OBP	SLG
2008	Rangers 1 (DSL)	R	.299	62	234	44	70	14	1	1	36	25	16	10	1	.374	.380
2009	Rangers (AZL)	R	.322	46	183	30	59	11	5	2	28	4	15	8	1	.333	.470
	Spokane (NWL)	SS	.400	7	20	4	8	1	0	2	2	0	4	0	0	.400	.750
2010	Rangers (DSL)	R	.326	37	144	22	47	7	1	2	35	6	16	4	1	.351	.431
2011	Hickory (SAL)	LoA	.297	115	461	67	137	28	0	11	69	18	35	12	6	.329	.430
Minor League Totals			.308	267	1042	167	321	61	7	18	170	53	86	34	9	.345	.432

26 DAVID PEREZ, RHP

BA GRADE
55
EXTREME

Born: Dec. 20, 1992. **B-T:** R-R. **Ht.:** 6-5. **Wt.:** 200. **Signed:** Dominican Republic, 2009. **Signed by:** Rodolfo Rosario.

After signing for $425,000 in 2009, Perez starred in the Dominican Summer League the following year. He then dominated during extended spring training in 2011, so Texas decided to push him to the Northwest League. He was the circuit's youngest pitcher, an 18-year-old facing predominantly college-aged hitters. He recorded eight swinging strikeouts in the first three innings of his U.S. debut but couldn't retire another batter in that appearance. The problems in that start continued for the remainder of the season, as he lost his release point, his control and his confidence as he struggled to repeat his delivery. Despite his struggles, Perez has a lofty ceiling with a projectable 6-foot-5 frame and a live arm. His fastball ranges from 90-96 mph, touching 98 on occasion. His long limbs and impressive extension make his heater explode on hitters. His curveball has risen from 69-72 mph to 75-78, and the harder offering has good depth and bite, though he falls in love with it at times. His changeup regressed last year, but that was the least of his problems. Perez did a better job of harnessing his stuff in instructional league, so he could make a jump to low Class A with a strong spring training.

Year	Club (League)	Class	W	L	ERA	G	GS	CG	SV	IP	H	HR	BB	SO	K/9	WHIP	AVG
2010	Rangers (DSL)	R	4	4	1.41	14	14	0	0	70	50	0	8	68	8.7	0.83	.201
2011	Spokane (NWL)	SS	1	4	8.60	13	9	0	0	30	25	2	29	43	12.8	1.78	.223
Minor League Totals			5	8	3.59	27	23	0	0	100	75	2	37	111	10.0	1.12	.208

27 ODUBEL HERRERA, 2B

BA GRADE
50
HIGH

Born: Dec. 29, 1991. **B-T:** L-R. **Ht.:** 5-11. **Wt.:** 165. **Signed:** Venezuela, 2008. **Signed by:** Rafic Saab.

Though he doesn't look the part with thick legs and a barrel chest, Herrera was a star volleyball player in Venezuela and has a 40-inch vertical jump. He knew his future was on the diamond, though, and he signed with the Rangers for $160,000 in 2008. Herrera moved from shortstop to second base when he made his U.S. debut in 2010. Last year, he ranked fifth in the South Atlantic League in hitting at age 19, and he batted .339 over the final three months. Herrera doesn't have loud tools, but he's a gritty gamer who has the fastest bat in the system. He has a short, compact swing with great hip rotation and a knack for making hard contact. He presently has gap power but might grow into more as he adds strength, though home runs won't ever be a significant part of his game. Herrera has the athleticism, instincts and arm strength to handle shortstop in a pinch, though he fits best at second base, where he's a solid defender with soft hands and good movements around the bag. He could end up being a utility player down the line. Herrera has above-average speed and runs the bases well. He'll continue as Jurickson Profar's double-play partner in high Class A this year.

Year	Club (League)	Class	AVG	G	AB	R	H	2B	3B	HR	RBI	BB	SO	SB	CS	OBP	SLG
2009	Rangers 2 (DSL)	R	.280	58	207	47	58	9	1	0	24	39	39	21	10	.399	.333
2010	Rangers (AZL)	R	.337	48	178	33	60	7	4	0	31	16	27	8	5	.394	.421
	Spokane (NWL)	SS	.222	4	9	0	2	1	0	0	0	0	1	0	0	.222	.333
2011	Hickory (SAL)	LoA	.306	119	464	72	142	26	3	3	56	24	78	34	11	.349	.394
Minor League Totals			.305	229	858	152	262	43	8	3	111	79	145	63	26	.371	.385

28 MICHAEL KIRKMAN, LHP

BA GRADE
45
LOW

Born: Sept. 18, 1986. **B-T:** L-L. **Ht.:** 6-4. **Wt.:** 195. **Drafted:** HS—Lake City, Fla., 2005 (5th round). **Signed by:** Guy DeMutis.

Kirkman hardly looked like a prospect five years ago, when he couldn't get the ball over the plate and his fastball dropped below 80 mph at times. He rehabbed a hamstring injury that slowed his progress and worked closely with pitching coordinator Keith Comstock to turn his career around. He reached the big leagues in 2010 and contributed to the Rangers' World Series run, but he spent most of 2011 in Triple-A. He opened last season in the Round Rock rotation before moving back to the bullpen in May. Though he has the durability and the assortment of secondary pitches needed to start, Kirkman profiles best as a reliever. That's because he doesn't have enough command to make up for his lack of a dominant pitch and he doesn't control the running game well. Kirkman's arm generates 91-94 mph fastballs that are a tick higher in short stints, and his slider gives him a second plus offering. He also throws a changeup and a curveball that are average. His long, herky-jerky delivery creates some deception, especially against lefthanders, but it also can cause his command to falter. Kirkman will compete for a spot in the Texas bullpen in spring training.

Year	Club (League)	Class	W	L	ERA	G	GS	CG	SV	IP	H	HR	BB	SO	K/9	WHIP	AVG
2005	Rangers (AZL)	R	3	1	3.44	14	9	0	0	52	51	0	19	58	10.0	1.34	.249
2006	Clinton (MWL)	LoA	0	3	6.98	6	6	0	0	19	23	0	24	22	10.2	2.43	.303
	Rangers (AZL)	R	1	2	13.20	8	4	0	0	15	21	0	27	8	4.8	3.20	.333
2007	Spokane (NWL)	SS	1	4	7.00	9	6	0	0	27	33	2	25	24	8.0	2.15	.306
	Clinton (MWL)	LoA	0	1	7.43	5	2	0	0	13	17	1	12	12	8.1	2.18	.304
2008	Spokane (NWL)	SS	1	1	0.00	2	2	0	0	10	7	0	2	9	8.1	0.90	.184
	Clinton (MWL)	LoA	4	3	4.36	15	14	0	0	74	78	8	23	58	7.0	1.36	.269
2009	Bakersfield (CAL)	HiA	4	1	2.06	8	7	0	0	48	43	1	18	54	10.1	1.27	.244
	Frisco (TL)	AA	5	7	4.19	18	18	0	0	97	93	9	43	64	6.0	1.41	.254
2010	Oklahoma City (PCL)	AAA	13	3	3.09	24	22	0	0	131	115	8	68	130	8.9	1.40	.235
	Texas (AL)	MAJ	0	0	1.65	14	0	0	0	16	9	0	10	16	8.8	1.16	.161
2011	Round Rock (PCL)	AAA	3	3	5.05	27	7	0	1	73	87	6	37	84	10.4	1.70	.295
	Texas (AL)	MAJ	1	1	6.59	15	0	0	0	27	26	5	12	21	6.9	1.39	.250
Major League Totals			1	1	4.74	29	0	0	0	44	35	5	22	37	7.6	1.31	.219
Minor League Totals			35	29	4.29	136	97	0	1	560	568	35	298	523	8.4	1.55	.263

29 MIGUEL DE LOS SANTOS, LHP

BA GRADE
50
HIGH

Born: July 10, 1988. **B-T:** L-L. **Ht.:** 6-1. **Wt.:** 205. **Signed:** Dominican Republic, 2006. **Signed by:** Danilo Trancoso.

Though de los Santos has been in the Rangers system for six seasons, he has logged just 274 innings in pro ball and only 28 above Class A. He had Tommy John surgery in 2007 and visa issues kept him in the Rookie-level Dominican Summer League in 2009. Last year, he came down with biceps tendinitis during spring training and a shoulder strain in May. De los Santos made up for lost time in the Arizona Fall League, but he still has a lot of work to do. His fastball sits at 89-92 mph and touches 94, but he doesn't command it consistently. He's most effective when he can pitch down in the zone with his fastball, which plays off his Bugs Bunny changeup with tornado action and two-plane depth. He has a tendency to use his devastating changeup too much, though. His sharp curveball was his best secondary offering when he signed, but it's now more of an 11-to-5 breaker than a true downer. De los Santos has the stuff to start, but he projects as a late-inning reliever because of command issues and funky mechanics. He'll get another shot at Double-A in 2012.

Year	Club (League)	Class	W	L	ERA	G	GS	CG	SV	IP	H	HR	BB	SO	K/9	WHIP	AVG
2006	Rangers (DSL)	R	0	1	1.59	13	4	0	0	34	16	1	15	48	12.7	0.91	.136
2007	Rangers (DSL)	R	0	0	0.00	1	0	0	0	3	0	0	2	6.8	0.00	.000
	Rangers (AZL)	R	0	1	6.35	3	3	0	0	6	7	0	3	6	9.5	1.76	.292
2008	Rangers (AZL)	R	0	2	4.67	10	10	0	0	35	28	2	18	54	14.0	1.33	.217
2009	Rangers 2 (DSL)	R	1	1	1.41	22	0	0	12	32	8	0	22	70	19.7	0.94	.074
2010	Spokane (NWL)	SS	2	0	1.69	7	7	0	0	32	13	0	20	50	14.1	1.03	.116
	Hickory (SAL)	LoA	2	2	3.99	12	6	0	0	38	27	3	24	62	14.6	1.33	.199
2011	Frisco (TL)	AA	1	3	8.04	6	6	0	0	28	27	4	17	38	12.2	1.57	.265
	Rangers (AZL)	R	0	0	3.00	1	1	0	0	3	4	0	1	7	21.0	1.67	.308
	Myrtle Beach (CAR)	HiA	6	3	3.82	13	12	0	0	64	46	2	28	97	13.7	1.16	.195
Minor League Totals			12	13	3.58	88	49	0	12	274	176	12	148	434	14.3	1.18	.179

30 NOMAR MAZARA, OF

BA GRADE
50
EXTREME

Born: April 26, 1995. **B-T:** L-L. **Ht.:** 6-4. **Wt.:** 200. **Signed:** Dominican Republic, 2011. **Signed by:** Rodolfo Rosario/Mike Daly.

The subject of many big-ticket rumors prior to the July 2 international signing frenzy in 2011, Mazara signed for $4.95 million. That set a new record for an international amateur, surpassing the $4.25 million the Athletics spent on Michael Ynoa in 2008. The Rangers thought Mazara offered as much power potential as any Latin American prospect in recent years. He put on epic batting-practice displays that left scouts in awe in the months leading up to his signing. Mazara was showcased judiciously in the Dominican Republic and often didn't face live pitching, so many teams had concerns about his bat and ability to make consistent contact. He employed a massive leg kick reminiscent of Juan Gonzalez as an amateur. The Rangers tried to tame it during instructional league and the change should help Mazara free up his lower half, though it inhibits his ability to track pitches. He has a projectable body with lanky limbs and a strong frame, helping him generate natural loft and backspin. His arm is presently average but could improve as he adds strength to his frame. Texas sees him playing right field, though he's still raw defensively. He's a fringy runner. Club officials laud his makeup. Mazara isn't as advanced as fellow Dominican bonus baby Ronald Guzman and will take longer to develop, but the raw power is exciting. He'll debut in the Arizona League in June.

Year	Club (League)	Class	AVG	G	AB	R	H	2B	3B	HR	RBI	BB	SO	SB	CS	OBP	SLG
2011	Did Not Play—Signed 2012 Contract																

Toronto Blue Jays

BY NATHAN RODE

Blue Jays general manager Alex Anthopoulos has been on the job for just two years, and already he has presided over a dramatic makeover of his organization. Toronto still has to settle for the title of the best fourth-place team in baseball, which it has held for the last four seasons, including the final two under the reign of former GM J.P. Ricciardi. But the Jays are getting better in baseball's toughest division, and Anthopoulos has brought in as much young talent as any GM since he took over in October 2009.

His first big move was to deal Roy Halladay to the

Phillies for three blue-chip prospects: Kyle Drabek, Travis d'Arnaud and Michael Taylor. Drabek ranked as Toronto's No. 1 prospect a year ago before graduating to the majors (where he struggled mightily) and has been succeeded by d'Arnaud. Taylor was flipped immediately to the Athletics for Brett Wallace, who was traded seven months later to the Astros for outfielder Anthony Gose, who now ranks No. 2 in the organization.

Anthopoulos continually has shown a deft touch on the trade market. He has acquired Yunel Escobar, Brandon Morrow and Colby Rasmus for the big league club without giving up anyone who was a key part of the franchise's future. He miraculously dumped Vernon Wells and the $86 million remaining on his contract on the Angels and got Mike Napoli back in the deal, though Anthopoulos then traded Napoli for Frank Francisco.

The GM's best move may turn out to be the December 2010 deal that sent Shaun Marcum to the Brewers for Brett Lawrie, who should be Toronto's third baseman for years to come. Lawrie ranked as the Triple-A Pacific Coast League's top prospect in 2011 before hitting .293/.373/.580 in two months in the majors.

The influx of young talent has extended to the farm system as well, thanks to the Blue Jays' aggressive approach to the draft and international markets. Toronto spent a club-record $11.6 million on the 2010 draft and nearly matched that with $11 million in 2011, even after first-round pick Tyler Beede turned down a $2.4 million offer to attend Vanderbilt.

The 2010 draft stocked the system with several promising pitchers, including five who rank in the top 10 in the deep system.

Toronto has asserted itself just as much internationally, starting with a $10 million major league contract

Canadian Brett Lawrie made a strong impression in his major league debut

TOP 30 PROSPECTS

1. Travis d'Arnaud, c	**16.** Dwight Smith Jr., of
2. Anthony Gose, of	**17.** Kevin Comer, rhp
3. Jake Marisnick, of	**18.** Adonys Cardona, rhp
4. Daniel Norris, lhp	**19.** Kellen Sweeney, 3b
5. Justin Nicolino, lhp	**20.** Joe Musgrove, rhp
6. Aaron Sanchez, rhp	**21.** Jacob Anderson, of
7. Noah Syndergaard, rhp	**22.** David Cooper, 1b
8. Deck McGuire, rhp	**23.** Michael Crouse, of
9. Drew Hutchison, rhp	**24.** Marcus Knecht, of
10. Asher Wojciechowski, rhp	**25.** Christopher Hawkins, of
11. Matt Dean, 3b	**26.** John Stilson, rhp
12. A.J. Jimenez, c	**27.** Dickie Joe Thon, ss
13. Adeiny Hechavarria, ss	**28.** Chad Jenkins, rhp
14. Carlos Perez, c	**29.** Christian Lopes, ss
15. Moises Sierra, of	**30.** Roberto Osuna, rhp

for Cuban shortstop Adeiny Hechavarria in April 2010. The Blue Jays also have handed out seven-figure deals to Venezuelan righthander Adonis Cardona ($2.8 million in 2010), Venezuelan outfielder Wilmer Becerra and Dominican shortstop Dawel Lugo ($1.3 million each in 2011) and paid $1.5 million for the rights to Mexican righthander Roberto Osuna last August.

The White Sox took note, hiring away Marco Paddy, who had been Toronto's director of Latin American operations the last five years. The Jays replaced him with former Mets supervisor of Latin American operations Ismael Cruz.

General Manager: Alex Anthopoulos. **Farm Director:** Charlie Wilson. **Scouting Director:** Andrew Tinnish.

Class	Team	League	W	L	Pct	Finish*	Manager(s)
Majors	Toronto Blue Jays	American	81	81	.500	7th (14)	John Farrell
Triple-A	Las Vegas 51s	Pacific Coast	71	73	.493	t-6th (16)	Marty Brown
Double-A	New Hampshire Fisher Cats	Eastern	77	65	.542	2nd (12)†	Sal Fasano
High A	Dunedin Blue Jays	Florida State	79	61	.564	1st (12)	Clayton McCullough
Low A	Lansing Lugnuts	Midwest	77	60	.562	3rd (16)	Mike Redmond
Short-season	Vancouver Canadians	Northwest	39	37	.513	3rd (8)†	John Schneider
Rookie	Bluefield Blue Jays	Appalachian	40	28	.588	3rd (10)	Dennis Holmberg
Rookie	GCL Blue Jays	Gulf Coast	27	32	.458	t-9th (15)	Omar Malave
Overall 2011 Minor League Record			410	356	.535	4th (30)	

*Finish in overall standings (No. of teams in league). †League champion.

LAST YEAR'S TOP 30

Player, Pos.		Status
1.	Kyle Drabek, rhp	Majors
2.	Brett Lawrie, 2b	Majors
3.	Deck McGuire, rhp	No. 8
4.	Anthony Gose, of	No. 2
5.	Travis d'Arnaud, c	No. 1
6.	Zach Stewart, rhp	(White Sox)
7.	Asher Wojciechowski, rhp	No. 10
8.	J.P. Arencibia, c	Majors
9.	Carlos Perez, c	No. 14
10.	Aaron Sanchez, rhp	No. 6
11.	Jake Marisnick, of	No. 3
12.	Eric Thames, of	Majors
13.	Adeiny Hechavarria, ss	No. 13
14.	Griffin Murphy, lhp	Dropped out
15.	Chad Jenkins, rhp	No. 28
16.	Dickie Joe Thon, ss	No. 27
17.	Henderson Alvarez, rhp	Majors
18.	Kellen Sweeney, 3b	No. 19
19.	Adonys Cardona, rhp	No. 18
20.	Justin Nicolino, lhp	No. 5
21.	David Cooper, 1b	No. 22
22.	K.C. Hobson, 1b	Dropped out
23.	Moises Sierra, of	No. 15
24.	Noah Syndergaard, rhp	No. 7
25.	Drew Hutchison, rhp	No. 9
26.	Christopher Hawkins, 3b/of	No. 25
27.	Marcus Knecht, of	No. 24
28.	Gabriel Cenas, 3b	Dropped out
29.	Gustavo Pierre, ss	Dropped out
30.	Brad Mills, lhp	(Angels)

BEST TOOLS

Best Hitter for Average	Travis d'Arnaud
Best Power Hitter	Travis d'Arnaud
Best Strike-Zone Discipline	David Cooper
Fastest Baserunner	Anthony Gose
Best Athlete	Jake Marisnick
Best Fastball	Noah Syndergaard
Best Curveball	Aaron Sanchez
Best Slider	Deck McGuire
Best Changeup	Justin Nicolino
Best Control	Drew Hutchison
Best Defensive Catcher	A.J. Jimenez
Best Defensive Infielder	Adeiny Hechavarria
Best Infield Arm	Adeiny Hechavarria
Best Defensive Outfielder	Anthony Gose
Best Outfield Arm	Moises Sierra

PROJECTED 2015 LINEUP

Catcher	Travis d'Arnaud
First Base	Adam Lind
Second Base	Yunel Escobar
Third Base	Brett Lawrie
Shortstop	Adeiny Hechavarria
Left Field	Colby Rasmus
Center Field	Anthony Gose
Right Field	Jake Marisnick
Designated Hitter	Jose Bautista
No. 1 Starter	Ricky Romero
No. 2 Starter	Brandon Morrow
No. 3 Starter	Daniel Norris
No. 4 Starter	Justin Nicolino
No. 5 Starter	Aaron Sanchez
Closer	Sergio Santos

TOP PROSPECTS OF THE DECADE

Year	Player, Pos.	2011 Org.
2002	Josh Phelps, c	Rimini (Italy)
2003	Dustin McGowan, rhp	Blue Jays
2004	Alex Rios, of	White Sox
2005	Brandon League, rhp	Mariners
2006	Dustin McGowan, rhp	Blue Jays
2007	Adam Lind, of	Blue Jays
2008	Travis Snider, of	Blue Jays
2009	Travis Snider, of	Blue Jays
2010	Zach Stewart, rhp	White Sox
2011	Kyle Drabek, rhp	Blue Jays

TOP DRAFT PICKS OF THE DECADE

Year	Player, Pos.	2011 Org.
2002	Russ Adams, ss	Mets
2003	Aaron Hill, ss	Diamondbacks
2004	David Purcey, lhp	Tigers
2005	Rick Romero, lhp	Blue Jays
2006	Travis Snider, of	Blue Jays
2007	Kevin Ahrens, 3b	Blue Jays
2008	David Cooper, 1b	Blue Jays
2009	Chad Jenkins, rhp	Blue Jays
2010	Deck McGuire	Blue Jays
2011	*Tyler Beede, rhp	Vanderbilt

*Did not sign.

LARGEST BONUSES IN CLUB HISTORY

Adeinys Hechavarria, 2010	$4,000,000
Adonis Cardona, 2010	$2,800,000
Ricky Romero, 2005	$2,400,000
Felipe Lopez, 1998	$2,000,000
Deck McGuire, 2010	$2,000,000
Daniel Norris, 2011	$2,000,000

TORONTO BLUE JAYS

TOP 2012 ROOKIE: Deck McGuire, rhp. The 11th overall pick in the 2010 draft, he commands four average or better pitches.

BREAKOUT PROSPECT: Kevin Comer, rhp. Projectable, athletic righty could have two plus pitches in his fastball and curveball.

SLEEPER: Mitchell Taylor, lhp. A small, athletic lefty, he has plus fastball velocity and can spin a breaking ball.

SOURCE OF TOP 30 TALENT

Homegrown	28	Acquired	2
College	5	Trades	2
Junior college	1	Rule 5 draft	0
High school	16	Independent leagues	0
Draft-and-follow	0	Free agents/waivers	0
Nondrafted free agents	0		
International	6		

LF
Dwight Smith Jr. (16)
Marcus Knecht (24)
Christopher Hawkins (25)
Eric Arce
Wilmer Becerra

CF
Anthony Gose (2)
Jake Marisnick (3)
Darin Mastroianni
Derrick Loveless

RF
Moises Sierra (15)
Jacob Anderson (21)
Michael Crouse (23)
Brad Glenn
Jesus Gonzalez
Dalton Pompey
Markus Brisker

3B
Matt Dean (11)
Kellen Sweeney (19)
Kevin Ahrens
Gabriel Cenas
Justin Atkinson

SS
Adeiny Hechavarria (13)
Dickie Joe Thon (27)
Dawel Lugo
Andy Burns
Gustavo Pierre
Brandon Mims
Gary Pena
Peter Mooney

2B
Christian Lopes (29)
Ryan Schimpf
Ryan Goins
Jon Berti

1B
David Cooper (22)
Mike McDade
K.C. Hobson
Art Charles
Kevin Patterson

C
Travis d'Arnaud (1)
A.J. Jimenez (12)
Carlos Perez (14)
Brian Jeroloman
Santiago Nessy
Sean Ochinko

LHP

LHSP	LHRP
Daniel Norris (4)	Mitchell Taylor
Justin Nicolino (5)	Evan Crawford
Griffin Murphy	Aaron Loup
Sean Nolin	Frank Gailey
David Rollins	

RHP

RHSP	RHRP
Aaron Sanchez (6)	John Stilson (26)
Noah Syndergaard (7)	Joel Carreno
Deck McGuire (8)	Trystan Magnuson
Drew Hutchison (9)	Anthony DeSclafani
Asher Wojciechowski (10)	Alan Farina
Kevin Comer (17)	Chad Beck
Adonys Cardona (18)	Danny Farquhar
Joe Musgrove (20)	Ronald Uviedo
Chad Jenkins (28)	Drew Carpenter
Roberto Osuna (30)	Matt Daly
Manuel Cordoba	Sam Dyson
Jesus Tinoco	Misual Diaz
Myles Jaye	Milciades Santana
Jeremy Gabryszwski	Danny Barnes
Tom Robson	
Mark Biggs	
Brady Dragmire	
Taylor Cole	

2011

BONUSES: $11.0 MILLION

BEST PURE HITTER: OF Dwight Smith (1s) has an advanced approach for a high school hitter. He has a short stroke, recognizes breaking balls and keeps his bat in the hitting zone a long time.

BEST POWER HITTER: The Blue Jays believe OF Jacob Anderson (1s) will tap into his raw power. The 6-foot-4, 200-pounder has long levers but a short swing. 3B Matt Dean (13) got a $737,500 bonus thanks to his above-average power potential.

FASTEST RUNNER: 2B Jon Berti (18) turned in a 6.42-second 60-yard dash after signing, then stole 23 bases in 28 tries for short-season Vancouver.

BEST DEFENSIVE PLAYER: SS Peter Mooney (21) helped South Carolina win its second straight national championship with his above-average defense.

BEST FASTBALL: LHP Daniel Norris (2) and RHPs Joe Musgrove (1s), Kevin Comer (1s), John Stilson (3) and Anthony DeSclafani (6) all hit 96 mph either in the spring or after signing. Musgrove (1s) touched 97-98 and stands out for his combination of life and velocity, while Stilson and DeSclafani throw hard the most consistently. Norris' $2 million bonus was the largest in Toronto's draft class.

BEST SECONDARY PITCH: Stilson's changeup serves him well as a strikeout pitch. Comer and Norris both show a feel for spin with power curveballs that could be plus pitches with a bit of polish.

BEST PRO DEBUT: OF Eric Arce (25) set a Rookie-level Gulf Coast League record with 14 home runs while batting .268/.437/.621. At 5-foot-9, 200 pounds, he doesn't have a true defensive home. SS/2B Jorge Vega-Rosado (28) hit .317/.380/.470 in the GCL, adding 22 stolen bases.

BEST ATHLETE: Anderson's combination of size and mobility prompts comparisons to Alex Rios. 3B Andy Burns (11) has the athleticism to play any infield spot.

MOST INTRIGUING BACKGROUND: Smith's father Dwight Sr. finished second in National League rookie of the year balloting in 1989 and hit .275 over eight big league seasons. The Blue Jays signed RHP Shane Farrell (46), the son of Toronto manager John but didn't land 3B Austin Davis (47), son of their minor league field coordinator Doug, or OF Jake Wakamatsu (48), son of their bench coach Don. All three fathers also played in the majors.

CLOSEST TO THE MAJORS: Stilson, if he has recovered from shoulder problems that dropped him out of the first round, or DeSclafani.

BEST LATE-ROUND PICK: Dean has a loose swing and rangy body, and he should fit the third-base profile. Burns resembles a more athletic Aaron Hill, though he isn't as polished at the same stage of his career.

THE ONE WHO GOT AWAY: Toronto and RHP Tyler Beede (1) wound up more than $1 million apart, as his asking price turned out to be a moving target. He wound up at Vanderbilt and could be the Commodores' Friday starter as a freshman.

ASSESSMENT: Even without Beede, the Jays added plenty of power arms to a burgeoning farm system. They also picked up several promising position players, most notably Anderson, Smith and Dean.

2010

BONUSES: $11.6 MILLION

With nine picks in the first three rounds, the Blue Jays found a passel of pitching. RHPs Deck McGuire (1), Aaron Sanchez (1s), Noah Syndergaard (1s) and Asher Wojciechowski (1) and LHP Justin Nicolino (2) all rank among their Top 10 Prospects.

GRADE: B+

2009

BONUSES: $4.9 MILLION

Toronto didn't help itself by not signing three of its top four picks, most notably LHP James Paxton (1s). But it did find a pair of keepers in OF Jake Marisnick (3) and RHP Drew Hutchison (15), and RHP Chad Jenkins (1) can be an innings-eater.

GRADE: B

2008

BONUSES: $4.4 MILLION

OF Eric Thames (7) hit 12 homers in 95 games as a rookie last year, and 1B David Cooper (1) and RHP Danny Farquhar (10) also debuted in the majors. SS Tyler Pastornicky (5) went to the Braves in the July 2010 trade that brought Yunel Escobar to Toronto.

GRADE: C+

2007

BONUSES: $6.6 MILLION

With five picks before the second round, the Blue Jays got two middling regulars (C J.P. Arencibia, 1; LHP Brett Cecil, 1s), a third big leaguer (RHP Trystan Magnuson, 1s) and two busts (3B Kevin Ahrens, 1; SS Justin Jackson, 1s). LHP Brad Mills (4) and Marc Rzepczynski (5), 2B Brad Emaus (11) and OF Darin Mastroianni (16) also reached the majors, though only Mastroianni is still in the organization. Rzepczynski was part of the trade package that yielded Colby Rasmus from the Cardinals last summer.

GRADE: B

Draft analysis by John Manuel (2011) and Jim Callis (2007-10). Numbers in parentheses indicate draft rounds.

1 TRAVIS D'ARNAUD, C

Born: Feb. 10, 1989. **B-T:** R-R. **Ht.:** 6-2. **Wt.:** 195.
Drafted: HS—Lakewood, Calif., 2007 (1st round supplemental). **Signed by:** Tim Kissner (Phillies).

The Phillies signed d'Arnaud out of Lakewood (Calif.) High for $837,500 as the 37th overall pick in 2007, one year before the Pirates selected his brother Chase in the fourth round out of Pepperdine. Chase reached the majors first when Pittsburgh called him up last June, but Travis should get there at a younger age and has a brighter future as one of the game's top catching prospects. The Blue Jays were set to take him one pick after the Phillies grabbed him in 2007, and they finally got him, along with Kyle Drabek and Michael Taylor, by sending Roy Halladay to Philadelphia in December 2009. After missing much of his first year in the Toronto system with back problems, d'Arnaud had a breakthrough year in 2011. He hit just .188 and sustained a concussion in April, then he rallied to set career highs across the board and led the Double-A Eastern League with a .542 slugging percentage. He helped New Hampshire win the EL championship and reeled in the league MVP award. Following the season, d'Arnaud joined Team USA. He played in just four games before tearing a ligament in his left thumb at the World Cup in Panama. He had surgery on the thumb in October and is expected to be ready for spring training. Toronto added him to its 40-man roster in November.

D'Arnaud has the all-around ability to become an all-star catcher. He has the bat speed and strength to hit 20 or more homers on an annual basis in the big leagues, and he has the best present power in the system. His career-best 21 homers weren't a product of New Hampshire's hitter-friendly ballpark, as he hit 11 of them and slugged .571 on the road. His quick hands, compact swing and all-fields approach should allow him to hit for a solid average to go with his pop. His offensive improvement stemmed from calming down at the plate and not trying to hit everything out of the park. D'Arnaud also made strides defensively working with New Hampshire manager Sal Butera, who caught for nine seasons in the majors. Managers rated d'Arnaud the best defensive catcher in the EL. He shows solid to plus arm strength, though he's still refining his footwork and throwing accuracy. He doesn't rush throws as much as he had in the past and threw out 27 percent of basestealers in 2011. He has improved his receiving skills and moves well behind the plate. He has fine leadership skills and does a nice job of running a pitching staff. While he's a below-average runner like most catchers, he doesn't clog the bases.

J.P. Arencibia smacked 23 homers as a Blue Jays rookie in 2011, but d'Arnaud is a superior hitter and defender. While he's not quite ready to take over Toronto's catching job, he could make his debut late in the 2012 season and push Arencibia in 2013.

SCOUTING GRADES

Batting: 60. **Defense:** 55.
Power: 60. **Arm:** 55.
Speed: 30.

Based on 20-80 scouting scale, where 50 represents major league average, and future projection rather than present tools.

Year	Club (League)	Class	AVG	G	AB	R	H	2B	3B	HR	RBI	BB	SO	SB	CS	OBP	SLG
2007	Phillies (GCL)	R	.241	41	141	18	34	3	0	4	20	4	23	4	2	.278	.348
2008	Williamsport (NYP)	SS	.309	48	175	21	54	13	1	4	25	18	29	1	2	.371	.463
	Lakewood (SAL)	LoA	.297	16	64	12	19	5	0	2	5	5	10	0	0	.357	.469
2009	Lakewood (SAL)	LoA	.255	126	482	71	123	38	1	13	71	41	75	8	4	.319	.419
2010	Dunedin (FSL)	HiA	.259	71	263	36	68	20	1	6	38	20	63	3	1	.315	.411
2011	New Hampshire (EL)	AA	.311	114	424	72	132	33	1	21	78	33	100	4	2	.371	.542
Minor League Totals			.278	416	1549	230	430	112	4	50	237	121	300	20	11	.336	.452

2 ANTHONY GOSE, OF

Born: Aug. 10, 1990. **B-T:** L-L. **Ht.:** 6-1. **Wt.:** 190. **Drafted:** HS—Bellflower, Calif., 2008 (2nd round). **Signed by:** Tim Kissner (Phillies).

KEVIN LITTLEFIELD

BA GRADE

65

HIGH

While Gose ran his fastball up to 97 mph in high school, shoulder problems and his desire to play every day prompted the Phillies to draft him as an outfielder. The Blue Jays coveted him during Roy Halladay trade talks in 2009, but Philadelphia balked. Toronto wound up with Gose a year later when he went to the Astros in a package for Roy Oswalt and Houston flipped him for Brett Wallace. Gose has three tools that rate at least at 70 on the 20-80 scouting scale in his speed, center-field defense and arm. He led the Eastern League with 70 steals in 2011 while succeeding at a career-high 82 percent clip. Gose dramatically raised his walk rate in Double-A, though he has yet to hit for a high average because he's overly aggressive and racks up plenty of strikeouts. The Blue Jays believe he'll hit better as he gains experience and quiets his approach. He has enough strength to have average power, and his 16 homers in 2011 nearly doubled his total from his first three pro seasons. If Gose can be just an average hitter, his other tools would make him a valuable major leaguer. After a season in Triple-A, he could find himself patroling center field at Rogers Centre at some point in 2013.

Year	Club (League)	Class	AVG	G	AB	R	H	2B	3B	HR	RBI	BB	SO	SB	CS	OBP	SLG
2008	Phillies (GCL)	R	.256	11	39	4	10	2	1	0	3	1	12	3	1	.293	.359
2009	Lakewood (SAL)	LoA	.259	131	510	72	132	24	9	2	52	35	110	76	20	.323	.353
2010	Clearwater (FSL)	HiA	.263	103	418	67	110	17	11	4	21	32	103	36	27	.325	.385
	Dunedin (FSL)	HiA	.255	27	94	21	24	3	2	3	6	13	29	9	5	.360	.426
2011	New Hampshire (EL)	AA	.253	137	509	87	129	20	7	16	59	62	154	70	15	.349	.415
Minor League Totals			.258	409	1570	251	405	66	30	25	141	143	408	194	68	.334	.386

3 JAKE MARISNICK, OF

Born: March 30, 1991. **B-T:** R-R. **Ht.:** 6-4. **Wt.:** 215. **Drafted:** HS—Riverside, Calif., 2009 (3rd round). **Signed by:** Rick Ingalls.

BA GRADE

60

HIGH

The 2009 draft was disappointing for the Blue Jays, with three of their top five picks declining to sign. One bright spot from that class is Marisnick, who signed for $1 million as a third-rounder and had a breakout season when he repeated the low Class A Midwest League in 2011. He hit .320/.392/.496 at Lansing after batting .220/.298/.339 the year before. Marisnick has the upside of a five-tool center fielder. He has strength in his frame and swing, producing plenty of backspin and solid raw power. A hitch in his swing previously had scouts concerned about his ability to hit, but he has ironed out his mechanics and is less susceptible to offspeed stuff. His speed, range and arm are all above-average. He has a knack for stealing bases, succeeding on 60 of his 71 attempts (85 percent) as a pro. His quickness also enables him to glide to balls in the gap with ease. Anthony Gose has louder tools, but Marisnick is a quality athlete and a better hitter. If Gose entrenches himself in center field, Marisnick has enough offense and arm to play in right. The Blue Jays won't rush him, but he could force a midseason promotion if he continues to produce in high Class A Dunedin in 2012.

Year	Club (League)	Class	AVG	G	AB	R	H	2B	3B	HR	RBI	BB	SO	SB	CS	OBP	SLG
2010	Blue Jays (GCL)	R	.287	35	122	17	35	12	0	3	14	13	18	14	1	.373	.459
	Lansing (MWL)	LoA	.220	34	127	16	28	8	2	1	12	9	37	9	2	.298	.339
2011	Lansing (MWL)	LoA	.320	118	462	68	148	27	6	14	77	43	91	37	8	.392	.496
Minor League Totals			.297	187	711	101	211	47	8	18	103	65	146	60	11	.372	.461

4 DANIEL NORRIS, LHP

Born: April 25, 1993. **B-T:** L-L. **Ht.:** 6-2. **Wt.:** 180. **Drafted:** HS—Johnson City, Tenn., 2011 (2nd round). **Signed by:** Nate Murrie.

BA GRADE

60

HIGH

Norris entered 2011 rated as the top high school lefthander in his draft class and a projected mid-first-round pick, but his commitment to Clemson scared teams off. Armed with extra picks, the Blue Jays popped him with their sixth selection (No. 74 overall) and handed him a $2 million bonus at the Aug. 15 deadline. He helped take the edge off of the failure to sign 21st overall pick Tyler Beede. An outstanding athlete, Norris played quarterback until his senior year of high school, and he showed easy power as a hitter. His future is very much on the mound, however, where he has four pitches that project to be at least average. His fastball sits in the low 90s and can get up to 96 mph with good life. He shows feel for a changeup and throws both a curveball and slider. Both breaking balls have a chance to be plus pitches but vary in effectiveness. Like most high schoolers, Norris needs to clean up his mechanics, though his delivery has no red flags. He's a tough competitor and mature, with very good makeup. Norris' stuff and makeup give him the potential of a frontline starter. He could handle beginning his pro career in low Class A, though Toronto likes to ease its prep arms into pro ball. It wouldn't be a surprise if he starts 2012 in extended spring training and debuts at short-season Vancouver in June.

Year	Club (League)	Class	AVG	G	AB	R	H	2B	3B	HR	RBI	BB	SO	SB	CS	OBP	SLG
2011	Did Not Play—Signed Late																

5 JUSTIN NICOLINO, LHP

Born: Nov. 22, 1991. **B-T:** L-L. **Ht.:** 6-3. **Wt.:** 160. **Drafted:** HS—Orlando, 2010 (2nd round). **Signed by:** Carlos Rodriguez.

Nicolino's commitment to Virginia had teams wary of picking him early in the 2010 draft, but the Blue Jays had extra picks and rolled the dice in the second round. He signed for an over-slot $615,000 bonus, too late to make his pro debut in 2010. He dominated the short-season Northwest League in 2011, ranking as the circuit's top prospect, and earned a promotion to low Class A, where he posted a 3.00 ERA in five starts (including the playoffs). Nicolino's fastball sits at 89-92 mph and touches 94. He has baffled inexperienced hitters with an advanced changeup that could become a true plus pitch. He maintains good arm speed when he throws his changeup and commands it to both sides of the plate. His curveball is his third pitch, yet could become an average offering. It was slow and loopy early last summer, but he tightened it up as the year progressed. Nicolino shows exceptional pitching acumen for a youngster. He isn't afraid to pitch inside and will change his approach after going once through an order. Nicolino profiles as a middle-of-the-rotation starter with the ceiling of a No. 2. If he continues to make pitching look as easy as he did in his first pro season, he won't stay at Lansing long in 2012.

BA GRADE

55
MEDIUM

Year	Club (League)	Class	W	L	ERA	G	GS	CG	SV	IP	H	HR	BB	SO	K/9	WHIP	AVG
2011	Vancouver (NWL)	SS	5	1	1.03	12	9	1	0	52	28	0	11	64	11.0	0.75	.156
	Lansing (MWL)	LoA	1	1	3.12	3	3	0	0	9	11	0	2	9	9.3	1.50	.297
Minor League Totals			6	2	1.33	15	12	1	0	61	39	0	13	73	10.8	0.85	.181

6 AARON SANCHEZ, RHP

Born: July 1, 1992. **B-T:** R-R. **Ht.:** 6-4. **Wt.:** 180. **Drafted:** HS—Barstow, Calif., 2010 (1st round supplemental). **Signed by:** Blake Crosby.

Sanchez drew Orel Hershiser comparisons while starring at the Area Code Games and Aflac All-American Game in the summer of 2009, looking like he was setting the stage to go in the first round of the 2010 draft. The Blue Jays were excited he lasted until the 34th overall pick, and they signed him for a below-slot $775,000. Toronto has handled him cautiously, limiting him to 25 innings in 10 starts in 2010 and 55 innings in 14 outings in 2011. Sanchez offers plenty of projection with his 6-foot-4, 180-pound frame, and he has present stuff to go with it. His fast arm generates fastballs that sit in the low 90s and touch 95. He adds in a high-70s curveball that has crisp rotation when it's on. He shows feel for a changeup, though it needs refinement. Sanchez's numbers don't jump out because his command has been inconsistent. He took a step forward in his short time with Vancouver by working with pitching coach Jim Czajkowski to speed up his delivery and make an adjustment with his back foot. If he does a better job of locating his pitches, Sanchez can become a frontline starter. He'll make it to full-season ball and get a longer leash in 2012, when he's ticketed for Lansing.

BA GRADE

60
HIGH

Year	Club (League)	Class	W	L	ERA	G	GS	CG	SV	IP	H	HR	BB	SO	K/9	WHIP	AVG
2010	Blue Jays (GCL)	R	0	2	1.42	8	8	0	0	19	19	1	12	28	13.3	1.63	.271
	Auburn (NYP)	SS	0	1	4.50	2	2	0	0	6	4	0	5	9	13.5	1.50	.182
2011	Bluefield (APP)	R	3	2	5.48	11	6	0	1	43	45	4	18	43	9.1	1.48	.269
	Vancouver (NWL)	SS	0	1	4.63	3	3	0	0	12	8	0	8	13	10.0	1.37	.195
Minor League Totals			3	6	4.31	24	19	0	1	79	76	5	43	93	10.6	1.50	.253

7 NOAH SYNDERGAARD, RHP

Born: Aug. 29, 1992. **B-T:** R-R. **Ht.:** 6-5. **Wt.:** 200. **Drafted:** HS—Mansfield, Texas, 2010 (1st round supplemental). **Signed by:** Steve Miller.

BA GRADE
60
HIGH

The Blue Jays give area scout Steve Miller credit for his work following Syndergaard leading up to the 2010 draft. Miller saw him at 87-90 mph early in a March 2010 start, but stuck around to see him finish the game at 92-94. When Syndergaard starred in the Texas 4-A state playoffs, Toronto decided to not take any chances in the draft, selecting him 38th overall and signing him for a below-slot $600,000. He recorded a 1.83 ERA and 10.4 strikeouts per nine innings in 2011, earning two promotions in two months. The athletic Syndergaard has sound mechanics for his size and already operates at 94-96 mph with his fastball, which hit 100 mph while he was at Vancouver. He uses his height to get good downhill plane on his fastball and it rides in on righthanders, consistently inducing weak contact. He has a power curveball with nice shape and plus potential, but he tends to overthrow it. His changeup sits in the mid-80s with sink and has good separation in velocity from his heater. Syndergaard's fastball and projection give him a No. 2 starter ceiling, which he should reach as long as his secondary pitches progress as expected. He pitched well after reaching low Class A shortly before his 19th birthday, and he'll return there to begin 2012.

Year	Club (League)	Class	W	L	ERA	G	GS	CG	SV	IP	H	HR	BB	SO	K/9	WHIP	AVG
2010	Blue Jays (GCL)	R	0	1	2.70	5	5	0	0	13	11	0	4	6	4.1	1.13	.229
2011	Bluefield (APP)	R	4	0	1.41	7	5	0	0	32	23	1	11	37	10.4	1.06	.198
	Vancouver (NWL)	SS	1	2	2.00	4	4	0	0	18	15	0	5	22	11.0	1.11	.221
	Lansing (MWL)	LoA	0	0	3.00	2	2	0	0	9	8	0	2	9	9.0	1.11	.235
Minor League Totals			5	3	1.99	18	16	0	0	72	57	1	22	74	9.2	1.09	.214

8 DECK McGUIRE, RHP

Born: June 23, 1989. **B-T:** R-R. **Ht.:** 6-6. **Wt.:** 220. **Drafted:** Georgia Tech, 2010 (1st round). **Signed by:** Eric McQueen.

BA GRADE
55
MEDIUM

The 11th overall pick in the 2010 draft and recipient of a $2 million bonus, McGuire doesn't have the upside of some of the high school pitchers who have come into the organization over the last couple of years, but he does exude polish and had no problems making his pro debut in high Class A in 2011. He moved up to Double-A in late July but missed most of the final month with a lower-back injury that's not considered serious. McGuire's pitches are average to solid across the board, and they play up because he mixes them well and generally throws strikes. His fastball and slider are his best offerings and show plus potential. His fastball sits at 88-92 mph and reaches 94. He has a feel for back-dooring his low 80s slider against righthanders and busting it inside against lefties. McGuire is gaining confidence in his changeup and has a curveball he can get over the plate for early-count strikes. To succeed as he advances, he'll need to command the ball down in the zone more. He learned that pro hitters jump on high pitches and he made the necessary adjustments as 2011 progressed. While his arsenal isn't overwhelming, McGuire could be a middle-of-the-rotation starter. He'll return to New Hampshire to open 2012 and it's not out of the question that he could see time in Toronto before the season concludes.

Year	Club (League)	Class	W	L	ERA	G	GS	CG	SV	IP	H	HR	BB	SO	K/9	WHIP	AVG
2011	Dunedin (FSL)	HiA	7	4	2.75	19	18	0	0	105	89	9	38	102	8.8	1.21	.228
	New Hampshire (EL)	AA	2	1	4.35	4	3	1	0	21	20	4	7	22	9.6	1.31	.253
Minor League Totals			9	5	3.02	23	21	1	0	125	109	13	45	124	8.9	1.23	.232

9 DREW HUTCHISON, RHP

BA GRADE

55

MEDIUM

Born: Aug. 22, 1990. **B-T:** L-R. **Ht.:** 6-2. **Wt.:** 180. **Drafted:** HS—Lakeland, Fla., 2009 (15th round). **Signed by:** Joel Grampietro.

While failing to sign three of their top five draft picks in 2009 wasn't the plan, the Blue Jays did have money to spend elsewhere in that circumstance. That included $400,000 in the 15th round for Hutchinson, a product of the Lakeland (Fla.) High program that has produced recent big leaguers Steve Pearce and Chris Sale. Hutchison breezed through three levels in 2011, finishing the year by allowing two runs in four Double-A starts, including six shutout innings in the Eastern League playoffs. Hutchison doesn't blow hitters away, but his 88-93 mph fastball has good life and gets on them quickly. He can sink and cut his fastball, commanding it to both sides of the plate. A short arm stroke and slightly crossfire delivery add deception. Hutchison's No. 2 pitch is a changeup and he also has a slider, which can be a swing-and-miss pitch at times and slurvy at others. He commands and mixes his pitches well for a youngster. Hutchison has moved quickly because of his feel for pitching, which eventually could make him a No. 3 starter. At the same time, his crossfire delivery makes some scouts wonder if he'll hold up in a rotation. If he continues his current pace, he could surface in Toronto in 2012 after starting the season with a return to New Hampshire.

Year	Club (League)	Class	W	L	ERA	G	GS	CG	SV	IP	H	HR	BB	SO	K/9	WHIP	AVG
2010	Auburn (NYP)	SS	1	1	3.00	10	10	0	0	45	34	1	12	44	8.8	1.02	.201
	Lansing (MWL)	LoA	1	2	1.52	5	5	0	0	24	17	1	7	19	7.2	1.01	.191
2011	Lansing (MWL)	LoA	6	2	2.63	14	14	0	0	72	68	1	19	84	10.5	1.21	.245
	Dunedin (FSL)	HiA	5	3	2.74	11	10	0	0	62	42	3	14	66	9.5	0.90	.194
	New Hampshire (EL)	AA	3	0	1.20	3	3	0	0	15	10	0	2	21	12.6	0.80	.192
Minor League Totals			16	8	2.52	43	42	0	0	218	171	6	54	234	9.7	1.03	.213

10 ASHER WOJCIECHOWSKI, RHP

BA GRADE

55

HIGH

Born: Dec. 21, 1988. **B-T:** R-R. **Ht.:** 6-4. **Wt.:** 235. **Drafted:** The Citadel, 2010 (1st round supplemental). **Signed by:** John Hendricks.

The second-highest draft pick in Citadel history, Wojciechowski went 41st overall after finishing second in NCAA Division I with 155 strikeouts in 126 innings in 2010. Signed for $815,400 and assigned to high Class A for his first full pro season, he posted a 0.87 ERA in April, but it ballooned to 5.42 over the final four months. He lost fastball velocity and battled his secondary offerings and command while getting used to pitching every fifth day. After dealing at 92-94 mph and touching 96 with his fastball in college, Wojciechowski worked at 89-93 in 2011. His 80-85 mph slider has hard break and can be a plus pitch at its best, but it flattened out too often at Dunedin. He didn't have much use for a changeup as an amateur and has made strides with the pitch since signing. Wojciechowski is a high-intensity pitcher, and the Blue Jays are trying to slow things down for him. He can rush his delivery, causing his arm to drag behind. Like many big-body pitchers, he needs to work on repeating his mechanics. If his velocity returns and his secondary pitches improve, Wojciechowski has the ceiling of a No. 2 starter. Otherwise, he could fit well in a late-inning relief role, where he could just attack hitters with his fastball and slider. Despite his struggles, he'll likely start 2012 in Double-A.

Year	Club (League)	Class	W	L	ERA	G	GS	CG	SV	IP	H	HR	BB	SO	K/9	WHIP	AVG
2010	Auburn (NYP)	SS	0	0	0.75	3	3	0	0	12	6	0	4	11	8.3	0.83	.146
2011	Dunedin (FSL)	HiA	11	9	4.70	25	22	0	0	130	156	15	31	96	6.6	1.43	.292
Minor League Totals			11	9	4.36	28	25	0	0	142	162	15	35	107	6.8	1.38	.281

11 MATT DEAN, 3B

BA GRADE

55

HIGH

Born: Dec. 22, 1992. **B-T:** R-R. **Ht.:** 6-3. **Wt.:** 190. **Drafted:** HS—The Colony, Texas, 2011 (13th round). **Signed by:** Michael Wagner.

Dean had a lackluster summer on the showcase circuit, but he rebounded with a solid spring at The Colony (Texas) High to emerge as the top third-base prospect in the 2011 high school class. Nevertheless, his commitment to Texas drove him down draft boards. The Blue Jays took him in the 13th round and signed him away from the Longhorns at the Aug. 15 deadline with a $737,500 bonus. He signed too late to make his pro debut, though he did get his feet wet in instructional league. Dean has a good, strong frame with broad shoulders and room to fill out. His lower-half mechanics need a small adjustment—he has a leg kick that can get things out of sync—but his upper body works well with his swing and he has above-average raw power to all fields. He also projects to hit for solid average. Dean has loose actions and played shortstop in high school, but he'll shift to third base as a pro. He should be a good defender, and his above-average arm should make for a seamless transition to the hot corner. He projects as a tick below-average runner once he matures physically. As the son of a coach—he played for his father Martin in high school—Dean earns typical praise for his work ethic and competitiveness. He'll probably spend time in extended spring training before getting his first pro assignment to Rookie-level Bluefield or Vancouver in June.

Year	Club (League)	Class	AVG	G	AB	R	H	2B	3B	HR	RBI	BB	SO	SB	CS	OBP	SLG
2011	Did Not Play—Signed Late																

12 A.J. JIMENEZ, C

Born: May 1, 1990. **B-T:** R-R. **Ht.:** 5-11. **Wt.:** 200. **Drafted:** HS—Bayamon, P.R., 2008 (9th round). **Signed by:** Jorge Rivera.

BA GRADE 55 HIGH

Some teams viewed Jimenez as a third-round talent in the 2008 draft, but his tender elbow made most clubs uneasy and he fell to the ninth round, where the Blue Jays snagged him and signed him for $150,000. His elbow hasn't been an issue in pro ball, where he has thrown out 42 percent of basestealers in four seasons. His bat has started to catch up to his defense, and he earned team MVP honors while helping Dunedin to the Florida State League's best record in 2011. Jimenez does it all behind the plate, blocking and receiving well while showing an above-average, accurate arm. Managers rated him the best defensive catcher in the FSL last year, when he had just six passed balls in 98 games and erased 44 percent of basestealers. He also did a nice job handling a pitching staff that included several of Toronto's best young arms. Jimenez has made significant strides as a hitter, showing good bat speed and improved pitch recognition. He batted in every spot in the Dunedin order except leadoff and cleanup last year, spending most of the second half in the No. 2 hole. He hits to all fields and consistently barrels balls. He has some gap power, but home runs won't be a big part of his game. Surprisingly for a catcher, he's is an average runner. Jimenez will head to Double-A in 2012, with J.P. Arencibia and Travis d'Arnaud looming as large obstacles ahead.

Year	Club (League)	Class	AVG	G	AB	R	H	2B	3B	HR	RBI	BB	SO	SB	CS	OBP	SLG
2008	Blue Jays (GCL)	R	.191	19	47	5	9	2	0	0	5	3	16	5	2	.255	.234
2009	Lansing (MWL)	LoA	.263	80	278	30	73	15	1	3	31	7	72	5	2	.280	.356
2010	Lansing (MWL)	LoA	.305	70	262	35	80	22	0	4	54	18	56	17	4	.347	.435
	Dunedin (FSL)	HiA	.111	2	9	1	1	0	0	1	1	0	5	0	0	.111	.444
2011	Dunedin (FSL)	HiA	.303	102	379	49	115	29	1	4	52	28	60	11	2	.353	.417
Minor League Totals			.285	273	975	120	278	68	2	12	143	56	209	38	10	.324	.396

13 ADEINY HECHAVARRIA, SS

Born: April 15, 1989. **B-T:** R-R. **Ht.:** 5-11. **Wt.:** 180. **Signed:** Cuba, 2010. **Signed by:** Marco Paddy.

BA GRADE 55 HIGH

A member of the Cuban junior national team, Hechavarria defected to Mexico in July 2009. Numerous teams covered him, including the Yankees, but the Blue Jays signed him to a four-year major league contract with a club-record $4 million bonus and a total guarantee of $10 million in April 2010. Though he struggled at the plate during most of his two seasons in the United States, Toronto moved him up to Las Vegas last August to see if the hitter-friendly environment would get him going. It was just 25 games, but Hechavarria batted .389/.431/.537. Scouts expect him to hit for average because he has quick hands and a good swing path, but he doesn't walk much and strikes out too often because of poor plate discipline. He has gap power and may add strength, but he'll never be a significant home run threat. As long as he's adequate offensively, however, defense and speed will get Hechavarria to the big leagues. He has a live body with quick actions and a plus arm. He's also a plus runner and should be a basestealing threat if he refines his technique. Hechavarria will return to Triple-A to open 2012, but because of his contract he'll probably get a look from the Blue Jays at some point during the season. He eventually could push Yunel Escobar to second base.

Year	Club (League)	Class	AVG	G	AB	R	H	2B	3B	HR	RBI	BB	SO	SB	CS	OBP	SLG
2010	Dunedin (FSL)	HiA	.193	41	161	21	31	7	3	1	7	5	25	7	0	.217	.292
	New Hampshire (EL)	AA	.273	61	253	36	69	11	1	3	34	12	40	6	3	.305	.360
2011	New Hampshire (EL)	AA	.235	111	464	58	109	22	6	6	46	25	78	19	13	.275	.347
	Las Vegas (PCL)	AAA	.389	25	108	16	42	6	2	2	11	8	21	1	2	.431	.537
Minor League Totals			.255	238	986	131	251	46	12	12	98	50	164	33	18	.291	.362

14 CARLOS PEREZ, C

Born: Oct. 27, 1990. **B-T:** R-R. **Ht.:** 6-0. **Wt.:** 190. **Signed:** Venezuela, 2008. **Signed by:** Rafael Moncada.

BA GRADE 55 HIGH

After being named his team's MVP in each of his first three seasons in the Blue Jays organization and ranking as the No. 1 prospect in the short-season New York-Penn League in 2010, Perez experienced his first adversity last year. A career .299 hitter heading into the season, he got his first taste of full-season ball. He struggled with the cold weather in the Midwest League early in the year, and the grind of catching 89 games took a toll in the second half, resulting in by far his worst offensive season to date. Perez still has solid catch-and-throw skills and projects to be at least an average defender. Quick feet allow him to get into good throwing position, and he has solid arm strength with a quick release. He threw out 29 percent of basestealers in 2011. While his performance last season didn't show it, Perez generally handles the bat well. He presently has gap power and may grow into more, though it will mostly come to his pull side. He controls the strike zone reasonably well. He's a below-average runner but has good instincts on the bases. Toronto isn't inclined to rush Perez thanks to its depth behind the plate, so he may repeat low Class A in 2012. The system's catching talent means he'll need to get back on track or risk getting lost in the shuffle.

Year	Club (League)	Class	AVG	G	AB	R	H	2B	3B	HR	RBI	BB	SO	SB	CS	OBP	SLG
2008	Blue Jays 1 (DSL)	R	.306	58	196	27	60	10	2	0	29	52	28	7	5	.459	.378
2009	Blue Jays (GCL)	R	.291	43	141	17	41	11	3	1	21	16	23	2	5	.364	.433
2010	Auburn (NYP)	SS	.298	66	235	44	70	11	8	2	41	34	41	7	3	.396	.438
2011	Lansing (MWL)	LoA	.256	95	383	58	98	17	6	3	41	37	74	6	2	.320	.355
Minor League Totals			.282	262	955	146	269	49	19	6	132	139	166	22	15	.377	.392

15 MOISES SIERRA, OF

BA GRADE
50
MEDIUM

Born: Sept. 24, 1988. **B-T:** R-R. **Ht.:** 6-0. **Wt.:** 225. **Signed:** Dominican Republic, 2005. **Signed by:** Hilario Soriano.

Sierra had a breakout season in 2009, when Toronto challenged him with an assignment to high Class A even though he had enjoyed little success in the lower minors. His encore was ruined by injuries, however, as a stress fracture in his leg, a strained oblique and a wrist ailment limited him to 20 games. He got back on track in 2011 with a solid year in Double-A. Sierra has plus raw power and at least plus-plus arm strength, giving him a good profile for right field. He has an uppercut to his swing and tends to open early on his front side, so he probably won't ever hit much more than .270. His lack of patience holds down his batting average too, though he doesn't strike out excessively. Though Sierra is an aggressive player and runs well for his size, he won't be a threat to steal. He tried to make things happen on the bases last season, but that's not likely to continue after he was caught 14 times in 30 steal attempts. He's an average defender in right field. Sierra will head to Las Vegas to open 2012, where the offensive environment will give him a great platform to showcase his power. He could make his major league debut later in the season.

Year	Club (League)	Class	AVG	G	AB	R	H	2B	3B	HR	RBI	BB	SO	SB	CS	OBP	SLG
2006	Blue Jays (DSL)	R	.253	69	245	35	62	16	1	4	26	24	50	17	3	.345	.376
2007	Blue Jays (GCL)	R	.203	43	143	17	29	5	1	5	15	5	39	2	2	.248	.357
2008	Lansing (MWL)	LoA	.246	130	451	50	111	16	5	9	39	26	114	12	11	.297	.364
2009	Dunedin (FSL)	HiA	.286	110	405	56	116	24	2	5	56	34	66	10	2	.360	.393
	New Hampshire (EL)	AA	.353	8	34	1	12	1	0	1	6	1	8	0	1	.361	.471
2010	Blue Jays (GCL)	R	.265	10	34	4	9	2	0	1	3	4	8	0	0	.342	.412
	Dunedin (FSL)	HiA	.162	10	37	4	6	1	0	1	5	1	11	0	1	.175	.270
2011	New Hampshire (EL)	AA	.277	133	495	81	137	19	3	18	67	39	93	16	14	.342	.436
Minor League Totals			.261	513	1844	248	482	84	12	44	217	134	389	57	34	.326	.392

16 DWIGHT SMITH JR., OF

BA GRADE
55
HIGH

Born: Oct. 26, 1992. **B-T:** L-R. **Ht.:** 5-11. **Wt.:** 180. **Drafted:** HS—McIntosh, Ga., 2011 (1st round supplemental). **Signed by:** Eric McQueen.

The son of the former major league outfielder of the same name, Dwight Jr. was one of the best pure high school bats in the 2011 draft class. A Georgia Tech recruit, he bypassed college to sign with Toronto for $800,000 as the 53rd overall selection. Like many of the Blue Jays' high picks, he signed too late to make his pro debut. Smith has a low-maintenance swing that allows him to keep his bat in the hitting zone for a long time, and he generates exceptional bat speed. He uses a leg kick but benefits from a major league pedigree and has a knack for timing it properly. He uses the entire field well and can drive the ball in the gaps, showing average present power. An average runner, Smith shows good instincts in the outfield. He runs balls down and will have every opportunity to stick in center field. He has some arm strength, though if he has to move it likely will be to left field, where there would be more pressure on his bat. Smith will begin 2012 in extended spring training, but if his advanced bat translates to the pro game, he could move faster than the typical high school draft pick.

Year	Club (League)	Class	AVG	G	AB	R	H	2B	3B	HR	RBI	BB	SO	SB	CS	OBP	SLG
2011	Did Not Play—Signed Late																

17 KEVIN COMER, RHP

BA GRADE
55
HIGH

Born: Aug. 1, 1992. **B-T:** R-R. **Ht.:** 6-3. **Wt.:** 205. **Drafted:** HS—Tabernacle, N.J., 2011 (1st round supplemental). **Signed by:** Bobby Gandolfo.

With his projectable frame and raw stuff, Comer looked like a lock to be picked in the first three rounds of the 2011 draft, but an inconsistent spring had teams wondering if they should try to buy him out of his commitment to Vanderbilt. A mandatory school trip and poor weather limited his time on the mound early in the season, but he was able to log more innings in the New Jersey high school playoffs and the Blue Jays saw enough to take him 57th overall. Just days after he was drafted, he pitched his Seneca High team to the Group 3 state championship. Toronto went down to the wire in signing Comer, inking him to a $1.65 million bonus at the deadline. When he's on, Comer has a live fastball that ranges from 88-96 mph and generally sits around 91-93. His athleticism and projectable frame mean he should find more velocity and possibly operate in the mid-90s. He shows the ability to spin a curveball, and some scouts think his will be a plus pitch in time. He has tried split and circle grips with his changeup, which will need time to develop. Comer has a clean arm action and delivery, and he gets good angle to his pitches. Like most of the Jays' late 2011 signees, he'll start this year in extended spring training and make his pro debut in Rookie or short-season ball.

Year	Club (League)	Class	W	L	ERA	G	GS	CG	SV	IP	H	HR	BB	SO	K/9	WHIP	AVG
2011	Did Not Play—Signed Late																

18 ADONYS CARDONA, RHP

BA GRADE
55
HIGH

Born: Jan. 16, 1994. **B-T:** R-R. **Ht.:** 6-4. **Wt.:** 170. **Signed:** Venezuela, 2010. **Signed by:** Marco Paddy.

Cardona signed in July 2010 for $2.8 million, a record for a Venezuelan pitcher and the second-highest bonus for an international free agent in Blue Jays history. He made his pro debut last June in the Rookie-level Gulf Coast League, where he was the second-youngest regular starting pitcher. Cardona's fastball sat at 89-91 mph when he signed and picked up 2-3 mph last summer. His ideal, projectable pitcher's frame has scouts thinking that he could continue to add velocity. Cardona's No. 2 pitch is a changeup that keeps hitters off balance because he throws it with good arm speed. He also has a curveball that needs plenty of work. Cardona threw straight over the top when he turned pro, but Toronto has worked on lowering his arm slot to closer to three-quarters. That slot is easier for him to repeat, and he can still keep the ball down in the zone with plenty of zip on his pitches. There's effort in his delivery, which along with his lack of a breaking ball eventually could land him in the bullpen. It's still too early for that decision, though. Cardona will be 18 this year, so he'll likely open in extended spring training before reporting to Vancouver in June.

Year	Club (League)	Class	W	L	ERA	G	GS	CG	SV	IP	H	HR	BB	SO	K/9	WHIP	AVG
2011	Blue Jays (GCL)	R	1	3	4.55	10	7	0	0	32	31	2	12	35	9.9	1.36	.256
Minor League Totals			1	3	4.55	10	7	0	0	32	31	2	12	35	9.9	1.36	.256

19 KELLEN SWEENEY, 3B

BA GRADE
55
HIGH

Born: Sept. 14, 1991. **B-T:** L-R. **Ht.:** 6-0. **Wt.:** 180. **Drafted:** HS—Cedar Rapids, Iowa, 2010 (2nd round). **Signed by:** Wes Penick.

After his brief 2010 pro debut, Sweeney looked like a potential breakout candidate because of his advanced high school bat and smooth transition from prep shortstop to pro third baseman. Instead, he played just nine games in 2011 before breaking a bone at the base of his left thumb when he got caught in a rundown and fell, ending his season. Like his older brother Ryan, an outfielder with the Athletics, Kellen attracted scouting interest as a two-way player in high school. His pitching career ended when he had Tommy John surgery in August 2009, but his pedigree and smooth stroke got him drafted in the second round and earned him an above-slot $600,000 bonus. Sweeney has polish and hitting ability, with quick bat speed and an idea of the strike zone. He's a patient hitter and will draw plenty of walks, though the Blue Jays want him to be more aggressive. He's strong and should develop at least average power. At third base, Sweeney has soft hands, quick feet and average arm strength. He's an average runner. Sweeney's lost 2011 has put him a little behind and may lead him to start this year in extended spring training, but his bat should be able to handle a jump to a full-season league at some point in 2012.

Year	Club (League)	Class	AVG	G	AB	R	H	2B	3B	HR	RBI	BB	SO	SB	CS	OBP	SLG
2010	Blue Jays (GCL)	R	.267	16	45	7	12	3	1	1	7	15	12	0	1	.450	.444
2011	Bluefield (APP)	R	.114	9	35	4	4	1	0	0	1	9	17	1	0	.295	.143
Minor League Totals			.200	25	80	11	16	4	1	1	8	24	29	1	1	.385	.313

20 JOE MUSGROVE, RHP

BA GRADE
55
HIGH

Born: Dec. 4, 1992. **B-T:** R-R. **Ht.:** 6-5. **Wt.:** 230. **Drafted:** HS—El Cajon, Calif., 2011 (1st round supplemental). **Signed by:** Dan Cox.

Musgrove had a solid outing at the Southern California Invitational Showcase at Major League Baseball's Urban Youth Academy to kick off his high school senior season in 2011, and he improved his stock as much as any prepster in the state as the season wore on. The Blue Jays took him 47th overall and inked him quickly for a below-slot $500,000 bonus, the lowest among the six players they signed in the first two rounds. Musgrove was more than a money-saver, however. His heavy fastball has the best combination of velocity and life among all the power arms Toronto signed last summer, sitting at 90-94 mph and touching 98. He has two breaking balls, and the Jays will have him concentrate on sharpening his slider. His curveball shows some power too, with downer action and high-70s velocity. He uses a splitter as a changeup. Musgrove has an easy delivery. He's working to get a little more length to his arm stroke in the back while separating his hands closer to his waist in order to get more angle and plane on his pitches. He got a jump on many of Toronto's other 2011 draftees by signing quickly, so he could open his first full pro season in low Class A. He projects to be a workhorse starter thanks to his big, durable body and stuff.

Year	Club (League)	Class	W	L	ERA	G	GS	CG	SV	IP	H	HR	BB	SO	K/9	WHIP	AVG
2011	Blue Jays (GCL)	R	0	1	4.57	8	7	0	0	22	17	1	4	16	6.6	0.97	.227
	Bluefield (APP)	R	1	0	0.00	1	0	0	0	3	2	0	1	2	6.0	1.00	.222
Minor League Totals			1	1	4.01	9	7	0	0	25	19	1	5	18	6.6	0.97	.226

21 JACOB ANDERSON, OF

BA GRADE
55
HIGH

Born: Nov 22, 1992. **B-T:** R-R. **Ht.:** 6-4. **Wt.:** 190. **Drafted:** HS—Chino, Calif., 2011 (1st round supplemental). **Signed by:** Joe Aversa.

Anderson burst into prominence as a prospect when he won the home run derby at the Under Armour All-America Game at Wrigley Field in August 2010. One of his home runs nearly landed on Waveland Avenue. Because Chino (Calif.) High didn't have a good option at first base, Anderson usually played there, frustrating scouts who wanted to see him work in the outfield. Some wondered whether his bat was ready for pro ball because of his questionable pitch-recognition skills, but the Blue Jays took him 35th overall last June. He ended up being Toronto's highest pick to sign, agreeing to a $990,000 bonus almost two weeks before the signing deadline, allowing him to get in some action in the Gulf Coast League. Anderson has long levers in his projectable frame, yet also has a short, simple swing that allows him to hit to all fields. He has good bat speed and should have at least average power. He's new to the outfield and perhaps could hold down center field with his solid speed, but he profiles better in right field. He's working on a long-toss program to build up his arm strength, which should be at least average. His size and athleticism have prompted comparisons to Alex Rios. The Jays likely will take things slow with Anderson, leaving him in extended spring training to start 2012.

Year	Club (League)	Class	AVG	G	AB	R	H	2B	3B	HR	RBI	BB	SO	SB	CS	OBP	SLG
2011	Blue Jays (GCL)	R	.405	9	37	9	15	2	0	2	7	4	8	2	0	.476	.622
Minor League Totals			.405	9	37	9	15	2	0	2	7	4	8	2	0	.476	.622

22 DAVID COOPER, 1B

BA GRADE
45
MEDIUM

Born: Feb. 12, 1987. **B-T:** L-R. **Ht.:** 6-0. **Wt.:** 200. **Drafted:** California, 2008 (1st round). **Signed by:** Chris Becerra.

Cooper was considered one of the best pure bats in the 2008 draft, which prompted the Blue Jays to snag him with the 17th overall pick and sign him to a slightly below-slot bonus of $1.5 million. He has shown he can handle the bat in the minors with a career line of .299/.373/.462 in four years in the minors. He had his best season yet in 2011, leading the minors with a .439 on-base percentage and the Triple-A Pacific Coast League with a .364 average, 170 hits and 51 doubles. He benefited from playing his home games at Las Vegas' Cashman Field, one of the best hitter's parks in the minors, yet he hit only nine homers. Lack of longball power is the drawback with Cooper and a problem for a first baseman. He doesn't pull the ball well, instead hitting line drives to the opposite field. To profile as a regular in the major leagues, Cooper will have to continue to hit for a high average and rack up doubles while providing at least 15-20 homers per season. He doesn't offer much else besides his bat, as he's a below-average runner who still needs to work to become an average defender. He's blocked at first base in Toronto by Adam Lind, who is under control through 2016, so Cooper was the subject of trade rumors this offseason.

Year	Club (League)	Class	AVG	G	AB	R	H	2B	3B	HR	RBI	BB	SO	SB	CS	OBP	SLG
2008	Auburn (NYP)	SS	.341	21	85	10	29	10	1	2	21	10	16	0	1	.411	.553
	Lansing (MWL)	LoA	.354	24	96	15	34	10	0	2	17	10	14	0	0	.415	.521
	Dunedin (FSL)	HiA	.304	24	92	10	28	9	0	1	13	10	16	0	0	.373	.435
2009	New Hampshire (EL)	AA	.258	128	473	62	122	32	0	10	66	59	92	0	0	.340	.389
2010	New Hampshire (EL)	AA	.257	132	498	59	128	30	1	20	78	52	74	0	0	.327	.442

Year	Club (League)	Class	AVG	G	AB	R	H	2B	3B	HR	RBI	BB	SO	SB	CS	OBP	SLG
2011	Las Vegas (PCL)	AAA	.364	120	467	77	170	51	1	9	96	67	43	1	3	.439	.535
	Toronto (AL)	MAJ	.211	27	71	9	15	7	0	2	12	7	14	0	0	.284	.394
Major League Totals			.211	27	71	9	15	7	0	2	12	7	14	0	0	.284	.394
Minor League Totals			.299	449	1711	233	511	142	3	44	291	208	255	1	4	.373	.462

23 MICHAEL CROUSE, OF

BA GRADE
50
HIGH

Born: Nov. 22, 1990. **B-T:** R-R. **Ht.:** 6-4. **Wt.:** 230. **Drafted:** HS—Coquitlam, B.C., 2008 (16th round). **Signed by:** Don Cowan/Kevin Briand.

Crouse was the youngest player on the Canadian national team that played in the World Cup and Pan American Games following the 2011 minor league season. He was part of the first gold-medal squad in Canadian baseball history, winning a championship at the Pan Am games. His father Ray was a running back in the NFL and Canadian Football League, and the family settled in British Columbia. Michael is built like a linebacker with a muscular 6-foot-4, 230-pound frame, and he played both sports growing up. He focused on baseball in high school and signed for $150,000 as a 16th-round pick in 2008. His lack of experience meant he spent parts of three year in Rookie ball and didn't play an entire year in full-season ball until 2011. Crouse has average power and the ball jumps off his bat, but evaluators aren't sold on his swing. It's a stiff, choppy stroke, though it's short and quick to the ball. He's a solid runner with good instincts on the bases, and he needs to improve his plate discipline so he can make more use of his speed. He has good instincts in the outfield and might be able to handle center field, though he played right field at Lansing in deference to Jake Marisnick. Crouse has enough arm strength for right and recorded 13 assists in 88 games last season. He'll move up to high Class A in 2012.

Year	Club (League)	Class	AVG	G	AB	R	H	2B	3B	HR	RBI	BB	SO	SB	CS	OBP	SLG
2008	Blue Jays (GCL)	R	.133	7	15	2	2	0	1	0	0	3	7	1	1	.316	.267
2009	Blue Jays (GCL)	R	.218	55	188	28	41	9	4	2	17	23	53	25	5	.308	.340
2010	Blue Jays (GCL)	R	.333	28	96	17	32	7	3	4	20	9	32	9	6	.402	.594
	Lansing (MWL)	LoA	.216	28	88	11	19	5	2	2	9	14	35	5	2	.327	.386
2011	Lansing (MWL)	LoA	.261	101	364	73	95	26	5	14	55	44	113	38	8	.352	.475
Minor League Totals			.252	219	751	131	189	47	15	22	101	93	240	78	22	.343	.442

24 MARCUS KNECHT, OF

BA GRADE
50
HIGH

Born: June 21, 1990. **B-T:** R-R. **Ht.:** 6-1. **Wt.:** 190. **Drafted:** Connors State (Okla.) JC, 2010 (3rd round supplemental). **Signed by:** Darin Vaughan.

A Canadian, Knecht played for the national team at the 2008 World Junior Championships. After declining to sign with the Brewers as a a 23rd-round pick out of a Toronto high school in 2008, he initially attended Oklahoma State but got just 12 at-bats as a freshman. He transferred to Connors State (Okla.) JC for 2010, when he hit .453 with 21 homers and slugged his way into the supplemental third round. He was part of an all-prospect Lansing outfield last year, playing left field alongside Jake Marisnick and Michael Crouse. Knecht's best tool is his bat, as he has plus bat speed and power potential. He uses a quick, line-drive stroke to hit to all fields. He's still raw, but he shows a willingness to draw walks. The rest of his game is nothing special, as he's a fringy runner whose arm is average at best. He's an adequate defender best suited for left field, and he has the offensive upside to profile there. Crouse and Knecht are neck-and-neck on the organization depth chart and should advance together in the short term, teaming up again in high Class A in 2012.

Year	Club (League)	Class	AVG	G	AB	R	H	2B	3B	HR	RBI	BB	SO	SB	CS	OBP	SLG
2010	Auburn (NYP)	SS	.268	61	231	32	62	18	3	5	34	26	48	7	1	.345	.437
2011	Lansing (MWL)	LoA	.273	121	439	77	120	34	3	16	86	67	124	4	3	.377	.474
Minor League Totals			.272	182	670	109	182	52	6	21	120	93	172	11	4	.366	.461

25 CHRISTOPHER HAWKINS, OF

BA GRADE
50
HIGH

Born: Aug. 17, 1991. **B-T:** L-R. **Ht.:** 6-3. **Wt.:** 230. **Drafted:** HS—Suwanee, Ga., 2010 (3rd round). **Signed by:** Eric McQueen.

Hawkins bypassed a scholarship to Tennessee to sign for a slightly below-slot $350,000 as a third-round pick in 2010. He was a high school shortstop who moved to third base in his pro debut, but he struggled at the hot corner and moved to left field last season. If his performance in the Rookie-level Appalachian League is any indication, he may have enough bat for the position. Everything Hawkins does looks stiff and awkward at first, though it works. He has an arm bar in his swing, but he makes up for it with strong, quick wrists that help him consistently square pitches up. He could have average or better power down the line. More experienced pitchers might pose a challenge when they bust harder stuff inside, but he has good strength and draws walks at a solid rate. Hawkins runs well once he gets going and racked up six triples last summer. He's limited to left field because of his fringy arm and he can make the routine play there. He'll advance to low Class A in 2012.

Year	Club (League)	Class	AVG	G	AB	R	H	2B	3B	HR	RBI	BB	SO	SB	CS	OBP	SLG
2010	Blue Jays (GCL)	R	.255	46	157	29	40	9	3	0	15	15	37	8	3	.324	.350
2011	Dunedin (FSL)	HiA	.000	2	4	0	0	0	0	0	0	0	2	0	0	.000	.000
	Bluefield (APP)	R	.318	68	242	49	77	15	6	5	52	22	46	14	4	.375	.492
Minor League Totals			.290	116	403	78	117	24	9	5	67	37	85	22	7	.351	.432

26 JOHN STILSON, RHP

BA GRADE
55
EXTREME

Born: July 28, 1990. **B-T:** R-R. **Ht.:** 6-3. **Wt.:** 200. **Drafted:** Texas A&M, 2011 (3rd round). **Signed by:** C.J. Ebarb.

Stilson enjoyed nothing but success in college, setting a Texarkana (Texas) JC record with 12 wins as a freshman, leading NCAA Division I in ERA (0.80) as a sophomore reliever after transferring to Texas A&M and becoming the Aggies' Friday starter last spring. He projected as a first-round pick until injuring his shoulder last May. The initial diagnosis was a torn labrum that would require an operation, but subsequent exams led to the belief he could recover with rest and rehab. The Blue Jays gambled a third-round pick on him and signed him for $500,000 two days before the deadline. He has taken it easy after a heavy workload in college and has avoided surgery so far. When healthy, Stilson has quality stuff in a fastball that ranges from 91-96 mph and a wipeout changeup that grades ahead of his heater. He also has a hard breaking ball and the ability to vary its angle and shape to turn it into a curveball or a slider. With his maximum-effort delivery, Stilson is probably best suited for relief, which also could limit wear and tear on his shoulder. He could move quickly in a bullpen role, and he's an intense competitor who could thrive as a set-up man or closer. Toronto plans on breaking him into pro ball as a starter, however. Assuming he's healthy, he should make his pro debut in high Class A this year.

Year	Club (League)	Class	W	L	ERA	G	GS	CG	SV	IP	H	HR	BB	SO	K/9	WHIP	AVG
2011	Did Not Play—Signed Late																

27 DICKIE JOE THON, SS

BA GRADE
55
EXTREME

Born: Nov. 16, 1991. **B-T:** R-R. **Ht.:** 6-2. **Wt.:** 190. **Drafted:** HS—San Juan, P.R. (5th round). **Signed by:** Jorge Rivera.

Thon was the Blue Jays' 11th pick (fifth round) in 2010 but got the second-highest bonus in their draft class at $1.5 million, thanks to his all-around potential and the leverage of a Rice scholarship. While he hopes to follow in the footsteps of his father Dickie, a former all-star shortstop who played 15 seasons in the big leagues, he has some catching up to do after not concentrating solely on baseball in high school and battling an unspecified blood disorder in 2011. The numbers Thon put up in limited time in the Gulf Coast League didn't reflect the improvements Toronto thought he had made. He has gotten bigger and stronger, which has translated to his swing. He drives the ball hard to all fields with a line-drive stroke. He could become an above-average hitter with plus power. Thon also possesses above-average tools in his speed and range at shortstop. His arm is average, though his added strength may help him improve in that regard. Thon lost needed development time last year, so he still might not be ready for a full-season league just yet. He could open 2012 in extended spring training and move to Bluefield or Vancouver in June.

Year	Club (League)	Class	AVG	G	AB	R	H	2B	3B	HR	RBI	BB	SO	SB	CS	OBP	SLG
2011	Blue Jays (GCL)	R	.223	45	121	23	27	3	0	3	15	23	44	6	2	.369	.322
Minor League Totals			.223	45	121	23	27	3	0	3	15	23	44	6	2	.369	.322

28 CHAD JENKINS, RHP

BA GRADE
45
MEDIUM

Born: Dec. 22, 1987. **B-T:** R-R. **Ht.:** 6-4. **Wt.:** 235. **Drafted:** Kennesaw State, 2009 (1st round). **Signed by:** Matt Briggs.

Scouts flocked to Kennesaw State in 2009 to see righthander Kyle Heckathorn, but they ended up more intrigued with his teammate. The Blue Jays drafted Jenkins 20th overall signed him for $1.359 million. He has been more dependable than dazzling in pro ball, making 53 starts in two seasons with a 3.81 ERA and 224 strikeouts in 309 innings. Jenkins won't blow hitters away but he's efficient with his pitches and gets quick outs. His sinker/slider combination piles up groundouts when his command is on. His fastball sits at 90-93 mph with heavy sink, and his slider is a plus pitch at times in the mid-80s. He also has a solid changeup and uses a mediocre curveball just to give hitters a different look. Jenkins has a big, durable body and projects as an innings-eater in a major league rotation. He doesn't profile as a frontline starter but he should be able to work deep into games every fifth day. He'll be 24 years old this season and has a chance to make his major league debut before the year is out.

Year	Club (League)	Class	W	L	ERA	G	GS	CG	SV	IP	H	HR	BB	SO	K/9	WHIP	AVG
2010	Lansing (MWL)	LoA	5	4	3.63	13	13	1	0	79	87	5	13	64	7.3	1.26	.277
	Dunedin (FSL)	HiA	2	6	4.33	13	13	1	0	62	73	6	18	42	6.1	1.46	.281
2011	Dunedin (FSL)	HiA	4	5	3.07	11	11	0	0	67	71	3	14	44	5.9	1.26	.267
	New Hampshire (EL)	AA	5	7	4.13	16	16	1	0	100	93	8	27	74	6.6	1.20	.247
Minor League Totals			16	22	3.81	53	53	3	0	309	324	22	72	224	6.5	1.28	.266

29 CHRISTIAN LOPES, SS

BA GRADE
50
HIGH

Born: Oct. 1, 1992. **B-T:** R-R. **Ht.:** 6-0. **Wt.:** 195. **Drafted:** HS—Huntington Beach, Calif., 2011 (7th round). **Signed by:** Joe Aversa.

A mainstay on the showcase circuit, Lopes emerged early as a potential first-round pick for the 2011 draft, ranking as one of the top 12-year-olds in the nation in 2005. But after he failed to hit .300 as a junior, he started tinkering with his swing and didn't live up to expectations as a senior last spring. He fell to the seventh round, where the Blue Jays paid him $800,000. Despite his prolonged slumps in high school, Lopes has shown some hitting ability. He tends to get mechanical with his swing and can get too wrapped up trying to make adjustments. He has a quick bat and good pop for a middle infielder. Lopes has nice actions and quick feet at shortstop, though he tends to sit back on balls too much. He once had plus speed but has slowed to a below-average runner as he matured physically. Diminished range and a fringy arm led many amateur scouts to project that Lopes would have to move to second base in pro ball, but Toronto will give him every chance to play shortstop. After getting his feet wet in instructional league, Lopes figures to begin 2012 in extended spring training and make his pro debut in June.

Year	Club (League)	Class	AVG	G	AB	R	H	2B	3B	HR	RBI	BB	SO	SB	CS	OBP	SLG
2011	Did Not Play—Signed Late																

30 ROBERTO OSUNA, RHP

BA GRADE
50
EXTREME

Born: Feb. 7, 1995. **B-T:** R-R. **Ht.:** 6-2. **Wt.:** 230. **Signed:** Mexico, 2011. **Signed by:** Marco Paddy.

Osuna is the nephew of Antonio Osuna, who spent 11 years in the big leagues as a reliever. Roberto pitched for Mexico at the Pan American 16-and-under championships in October 2010 and ran his fastball up to 94 mph—as a 15-year-old. Afterward, he signed with the Mexico City Red Devils of the Mexican League and made his pro debut at age 16. The Blue Jays purchased his rights from the Red Devils in August for a reported $1.5 million. Some scouts believe his stuff is comparable to that of Luis Heredia, whom the Pirates signed in 2010 for a Mexican-record $2.6 million, but Osuna doesn't have the same projection. He already has a thick frame and will have to stay on top of his conditioning. Osuna has a quick arm that produces fastballs that range from 88-94 mph. For a youngster, he has good feel for a curveball, though it can get slurvy at times. He also shows some aptitude for throwing a changeup. Osuna has the look of a possible No. 3 starter, though he's a long-term project. He'll make his U.S. debut in the Gulf Coast League this summer.

Year	Club (League)	Class	W	L	ERA	G	GS	CG	SV	IP	H	HR	BB	SO	K/9	WHIP	AVG
2011	Mexico City (MEX)		0	1	5.49	13	2	0	0	20	25	3	11	12	5.5	1.83	.329
Minor League Totals			0	1	5.49	13	2	0	0	20	25	3	11	12	5.5	1.83	.329

Washington Nationals

BY AARON FITT

The tide is turning in Washington. The Nationals reached the 80-victory plateau in 2011 for the first time in six years and placed third in the National League East, their highest finish since the 2002 Expos landed in second. And with a once-barren farm system now bursting with talent, the franchise's future seems even brighter.

Back-to-back 59-win seasons in 2008 and 2009 gave the Nationals the No. 1 overall pick in consecutive drafts, and they used those picks on cornerstone players Stephen Strasburg and Bryce Harper. Washington set a record by spending $11.5 million on draft bonuses in 2009, then topped that mark with $11.9 million in 2010.

The Nationals once again were opportunistic and aggressive in the 2011 draft, landing Baseball America's top-ranked prospect for the third straight year when third baseman Anthony Rendon slid to them as the No. 6 choice. They then doled out huge bonuses to their next three selections: righthander Alex Meyer ($2 million), outfielder Brian Goodwin ($3 million) and lefty Matt Purke ($2.75 million).

The Nats paid out a total $15 million on bonuses, and though they yielded that record to the Pirates ($17 million), they outspent Pittsburgh when the additional $2.6 million in guarantees in big league contracts for Rendon and Purke are considered. (The overall draft expenditure record remains $19.1 million by Washington in 2009, $15.1 million of which was a major league deal for Strasburg.)

Strasburg and Harper continued to generate incredible excitement in Washington and around baseball in 2011. Strasburg returned from Tommy John surgery to go 1-1, 1.50 with 24 strikeouts and two walks in 24 innings over five September starts, showing the same electrifying stuff he displayed before injuring his elbow in the summer of 2010. Harper took the low Class A South Atlantic League by storm as an 18-year-old, posting a .977 OPS to earn a two-level promotion to Double-A Harrisburg, where he held his own against much older competition.

The organization enjoyed a strong developmental year from top to bottom, with upper-level prospects like Brad Peacock, Tom Milone and Steve Lombardozzi breaking through to the big leagues, and lower-level prospects like A.J. Cole, Sammy Solis and Destin Hood showing progress. Peacock emerged as a top power arm in the high minors before a brilliant three-appearance cameo in Washington.

Washington got its ace back when Stephen Strasburg made a healthy return in 2011

TOP 30 PROSPECTS

1. Bryce Harper, of	16. Tyler Moore, 1b
2. Anthony Rendon, 3b	17. Robbie Ray, lhp
3. Brad Peacock, rhp	18. Kylin Turnbull, lhp
4. A.J. Cole, rhp	19. Zach Walters, inf
5. Brian Goodwin, of	20. Jeff Kobernus, 2b
6. Alex Meyer, rhp	21. Matt Skole, 3b
7. Matt Purke, lhp	22. Eury Perez, of
8. Sammy Solis, lhp	23. Daniel Rosenbaum, lhp
9. Derek Norris, c	24. Sandy Leon, c
10. Steve Lombardozzi, 2b/ss	25. Jason Martinson, ss
11. Destin Hood, of	26. Cole Kimball, rhp
12. Chris Marrero, 1b	27. David Freitas, c
13. Tom Milone, lhp	28. Adrian Sanchez, 2b
14. Michael Taylor, of	29. Paul Demny, rhp
15. Rick Hague, ss	30. Kevin Keyes, of

The parent Nationals' improvement was driven by the emergence of young up-the-middle talents Wilson Ramos and Danny Espinosa into quality regulars. After Adam Dunn departed in the offseason, Michael Morse took over at first base and led the team with 31 homers. Offseason $126 million free-agent acquisition Jayson Werth hit just .232 with 20 homers.

The pitching staff also climbed from 11th in the NL in ERA in 2010 to sixth in 2011, led by blossoming Jordan Zimmermann and steady John Lannan in the rotation, and the dynamic duo of Drew Storen and Tyler Clippard in the bullpen.

General Manager: Mike Rizzo. **Farm Director:** Doug Harris. **Scouting Director:** Kris Kline.

Class	Team	League	W	L	Pct	Finish*	Manager(s)
Majors	Washington Nationals	National	80	81	.497	8th (16)	J. Riggleman/J. McLaren/D. Johnson
Triple-A	Syracuse Chiefs	International	66	74	.471	10th (14)	Randy Knorr
Double-A	Harrisburg Senators	Eastern	80	62	.563	1st (12)	Tony Beasley
High A	Potomac Nationals	Carolina	68	71	.489	5th (8)	Matthew LeCroy
Low A	Hagerstown Suns	South Atlantic	75	64	.540	6th (14)	Brian Daubach
Short-season	Auburn Doubledays	New York-Penn	45	30	.600	3rd (14)	Gary Cathcart
Rookie	GCL Nationals	Gulf Coast	20	33	.377	14th (15)	Bobby Williams
Overall 2011 Minor League Record			354	334	.515	10th (30)	

*Finish in overall standings (No. of teams in league). †League champion.

LAST YEAR'S TOP 30

Player, Pos.		Status
1.	Bryce Harper, of	No. 1
2.	Derek Norris, c	No. 9
3.	Danny Espinosa, ss/2b	Majors
4.	A.J. Cole, rhp	No. 4
5.	Wilson Ramos, c	Majors
6.	Sammy Solis, lhp	No. 8
7.	Cole Kimball, rhp	No. 26
8.	Eury Perez, of	No. 22
9.	Chris Marrero, 1b	No. 12
10.	Brad Peacock, rhp	No. 3
11.	Yunesky Maya, rhp	Dropped out
12.	Destin Hood, of	No. 11
13.	Steve Lombardozzi, 2b	No. 10
14.	Rick Hague, ss	No. 15
15.	Robbie Ray, lhp	No. 17
16.	Tom Milone, lhp	No. 13
17.	Adrian Sanchez, 2b/3b	No. 28
18.	A.J. Morris, rhp	(Cubs)
19.	Michael Burgess, of	(Cubs)
20.	Elvin Ramirez, rhp	(Mets)
21.	Jeff Kobernus, 2b	No. 20
22.	Jason Martinson, ss	No. 25
23.	Daniel Rosenbaum, lhp	No. 23
24.	Tyler Moore, 1b	No. 16
25.	J.P. Ramirez, of	Dropped out
26.	Ryan Tatusko, rhp	Dropped out
27.	Brad Meyers, rhp	(Yankees)
28.	Trevor Holder, rhp	Dropped out
29.	Adam Carr, rhp	Dropped out
30.	Hassan Pena, rhp	Dropped out

BEST TOOLS

Best Hitter for Average	Anthony Rendon
Best Power Hitter	Bryce Harper
Best Strike-Zone Discipline	Anthony Rendon
Fastest Baserunner	Eury Perez
Best Athlete	Michael Taylor
Best Fastball	A.J. Cole
Best Curveball	Brad Peacock
Best Slider	Alex Meyer
Best Changeup	Tom Milone
Best Control	Tom Milone
Best Defensive Catcher	Sandy Leon
Best Defensive Infielder	Steve Lombardozzi
Best Infield Arm	Deion Williams
Best Defensive Outfielder	Michael Taylor
Best Outfield Arm	Bryce Harper

PROJECTED 2015 LINEUP

Catcher	Wilson Ramos
First Base	Michael Morse
Second Base	Anthony Rendon
Third Base	Ryan Zimmerman
Shortstop	Danny Espinosa
Left Field	Jayson Werth
Center Field	Brian Goodwin
Right Field	Bryce Harper
No. 1 Starter	Stephen Strasburg
No. 2 Starter	Jordan Zimmermann
No. 3 Starter	Brad Peacock
No. 4 Starter	A.J. Cole
No. 5 Starter	Matt Purke
Closer	Drew Storen

TOP PROSPECTS OF THE DECADE

Year	Player, Pos.	2011 Org.
2002	Brandon Phillips, ss	Reds
2003	Clint Everts, rhp	Blue Jays
2004	Clint Everts, rhp	Blue Jays
2005	Mike Hinckley, lhp	Blue Jays
2006	Ryan Zimmerman, 3b	Nationals
2007	Collin Balester, rhp	Nationals
2008	Chris Marrero, 1b	Nationals
2009	Jordan Zimmermann, rhp	Nationals
2010	Stephen Strasburg, rhp	Nationals
2011	Bryce Harper, of	Nationals

TOP DRAFT PICKS OF THE DECADE

Year	Player, Pos.	2011 Org.
2002	Clint Everts, rhp	Blue Jays
2003	Chad Cordero, rhp	St. Paul (American Assoc.)
2004	Bill Bray, lhp	Reds
2005	Ryan Zimmerman, 3b	Nationals
2006	Chris Marrero, of	Nationals
2007	Ross Detwiler, lhp	Nationals
2008	*Aaron Crow, rhp	Royals
2009	Stephen Strasburg, rhp	Nationals
2010	Bryce Harper, of	Nationals
2011	Anthony Rendon, 3b	Nationals

*Did not sign.

LARGEST BONUSES IN CLUB HISTORY

Stephen Strasburg, 2009	$7,500,000
Bryce Harper, 2010	$6,250,000
Anthony Rendon, 2011	$6,000,000
Brian Goodwin, 2011	$3,000,000
Ryan Zimmerman, 2006	$2,975,000

WASHINGTON NATIONALS

TOP 2012 ROOKIE: Brad Peacock, rhp. After dazzling in three big league appearances in September, he's set to compete for a rotation job in spring training.

BREAKOUT PROSPECT: Michael Taylor, of. He rescued his career by taking immediately to center field after moving from shortstop, and the Nationals are in love with his Mike Cameron-esque upside.

SOURCE OF TOP 30 TALENT			
Homegrown	29	Acquired	1
College	14	Trades	1
Junior college	5	Rule 5 draft	0
High school	6	Independent leagues	0
Draft-and-follow	1	Free agents/waivers	0
Nondrafted free agents	0		
International	3		

SLEEPER: Josh Smoker, lhp. The No. 31 overall pick in 2007 saw his star dim when his velocity and command deserted him. The latter still is a work in progress, but he ran his fastball up to 98 mph last year.

LF
Destin Hood (11)
Kevin Keyes (30)
Randolph Oduber
J.P. Ramirez
Caleb Ramsey

CF
Brian Goodwin (5)
Michael Taylor (14)
Eury Perez (22)
Corey Brown
Billy Burns
Narciso Mesa

RF
Bryce Harper (1)
Wander Ramos

3B
Anthony Rendon (2)
Matt Skole (21)
Stephen King

SS
Rick Hague (15)
Jason Martinson (25)
Bryce Ortega
Deion Williams

2B
Steve Lombardozzi (10)
Zach Walters (19)
Jeff Kobernus (20)
Adrian Sanchez (28)
Blake Kelso
Hendry Jimenez

1B
Chris Marrero (12)
Tyler Moore (16)
Estarlin Martinez
Justin Bloxom
Steven Souza

C
Derek Norris (9)
Sandy Leon (24)
David Freitas (27)
Jhonatan Solano
Beau Seabury
Adrian Nieto
Pedro Severino

LHP

LHSP	LHRP
Matt Purke (7)	Josh Smoker
Sammy Solis (8)	Atahualpa Severino
Tom Milone (13)	Bobby Lucas
Robbie Ray (17)	Bryan Harper
Kylin Turnbull (18)	Patrick McCoy
Daniel Rosenbaum (23)	Cory Van Allen
Matt Grace	Chad Jenkins
Blake Monar	
Bobby Hansen	
Jack McGeary	

RHP

RHSP	RHRP
Brad Peacock (3)	Cole Kimball (26)
A.J. Cole (4)	Paul Demny (29)
Alex Meyer (6)	Hassan Pena
Taylor Jordan	Pat Lehman
Dixon Anderson	Greg Holt
Manny Rodriguez	Hector Nelo
Taylor Hill	Jeff Mandel
Brian Dupra	Zech Zinicola
Wirkin Estevez	Neil Holland
Tanner Roark	Ken Ferrer
Cameron Selik	Ryan Tatusko
Trevor Holder	Colin Bates

2011   BONUSES: $15.0 MILLION

BEST PURE HITTER: The Nationals got the best bat in the draft with the No. 6 pick, which wouldn't have happened had 3B Anthony Rendon (1) not been slowed by a shoulder injury in the spring. With his swing, bat speed, hand-eye coordination and strike-zone discipline, he has tools to become a .300 hitter.

BEST POWER HITTER: Rendon's pure hitting ability stands out more than his strength, but he should have enough power to hit 25 homers a season. 3B Matt Skole (5) offers solid lefthanded pop.

FASTEST RUNNER: OF Billy Burns (32) has close to top-of-the-line speed and is a more advanced basestealer than OF Brian Goodwin (1s), a well above-average runner.

BEST DEFENSIVE PLAYER: Rendon also has Gold Glove-caliber skills at third base, though a position change may be in his future with Ryan Zimmerman in Washington. SS Deion Williams (16) is raw, but he has a tremendous arm and quick feet.

BEST FASTBALL: RHP Alex Meyer (1) is as intimidating as it gets on the mound, with his 6-foot-9 frame and a fastball that sits in the mid-90s and reaches triple digits on occasion. Before he had shoulder problems in the spring, LHP Matt Purke (3) had a nearly as effective heater, pitching at 91-94 mph and touching 96 with life.

BEST SECONDARY PITCH: When he maintains his arm slot, Meyer can deliver a slider that's a true plus-plus pitch. Purke has an above-average slider when healthy.

BEST PRO DEBUT: None of the Nationals' first five picks signed in time to play pro ball. Skole hit .290 and led the short-season New York-Penn League with 48 RBIs.

BEST ATHLETE: Goodwin has five-tool potential and can stick in center field if he improves his reads and jumps.

MOST INTRIGUING BACKGROUND: Washington selected LHP Bryan Harper's (30) brother Bryce with the No. 1 overall pick in 2010. Skole's brother Jake went 15th overall to the Rangers in the same draft. Williams' grandfather George Scott and RHP Travis Henke's uncle Tom both made multiple all-star teams during 14-year big league careers. Burns' father Bob is a former NFL running back.

CLOSEST TO THE MAJORS: Rendon and Purke both received big league contracts and won't need surgery, so the Nationals expect them in D.C. in short order.

BEST LATE-ROUND PICK: Burns has the speed to make a difference in center field and on the bases. He took up switch-hitting in instructional league.

THE ONE WHO GOT AWAY: RHP Hawtin Buchanan (19) is 6-foot-8, 230 pounds and already can get his fastball up to 93 mph. He ultimately decided to attend Mississippi. LHP Brett Mooneyham (38) was a potential first-round pick before missing the entire 2011 season after needing surgery on the middle finger of his pitching hand. He returned to Stanford.

ASSESSMENT: The Nationals spent big—and it was worth it. They had baseball's best draft, getting the best hitter (Rendon), an electric arm (Meyer) and a top athlete (Goodwin) in the top 34 picks, then signing Purke.

2010   BONUSES: $11.9 MILLION

OF Bryce Harper (1) continues to exceed expectations, which is saying something. LHP Sammy Solis (2) and RHP A.J. Cole (4) could make an impact on Washington's rotation.

GRADE: A

2009   BONUSES: $11.5 MILLION

The Nationals were the first team ever to have two top-10 choices, and used them to find a nearly-instant ace (RHP Stephen Strasburg, 1) and closer (Drew Storen, 1). They breathed a deep sigh of relief when Strasburg made a triumphant return from Tommy John surgery last September.

GRADE: A

2008   BONUSES: $4.8 MILLION

2B Danny Espinosa (3) homered 21 times as a rookie in 2011, taking the sting out of not signing RHP Aaron Crow (1), which led to the consolation pick that became Storen. LHP Tom Milone (10) and 2B/SS Steve Lombardozzi (19) have overachieved and made their big league debuts last year. So did Crow and another unsigned RHP who wound up in the Royals bullpen, Louis Coleman (14).

GRADE: B

2007   BONUSES: $7.9 MILLION

LHP Ross Detwiler (1) took longer than expected to develop and RHP Jordan Zimmermann (2) had to overcome Tommy John surgery, but they posted the two lowest ERAs in Washington's rotation last season. C Derek Norris (4) has a lot of upside as well.

GRADE: B+

Draft analysis by Jim Callis. Numbers in parentheses indicate draft rounds.

1 BRYCE HARPER, OF

Born: Oct. 10, 1992. **B-T:** L-R. **Ht.:** 6-3. **Wt.:** 225.
Drafted: JC of Southern Nevada, 2010 (1st round).
Signed by: Mitch Sokol.

The most hyped position-player prospect in baseball history, Harper has met or exceeded sky-high expectations at every stop in his short career. After establishing himself as a can't-miss phenom early in his high school career, Harper earned his general equivalency diploma and skipped his final two years at Las Vegas High so he could enroll early at JC of Southern Nevada, where he won the Golden Spikes Award as the nation's top amateur player in 2010. After being selected first overall that June and signing a $9.9 million major league contract—the largest ever given to a position player in the draft, and which included a $6.25 million bonus—Harper got his feet wet in the Arizona Fall League. He made his official pro debut as an 18-year-old in low Class A last April, and tore up the South Atlantic League in the first half. He got his first taste of adversity after skipping to Double-A Harrisburg at midseason, enduring a 1-for-25 slump, but bounced back to finish with respectable numbers. A hamstring injury cut his season two weeks short, but he recovered in time to head back to the AFL.

Harper's power and arm strength both rate as 80s on the 20-80 scouting scale. He has incredible strength in his hands and generates enormous torque in his lefthanded swing, allowing him to smash massive drives to all fields. Harper has some extra movement in his swing and sometimes jumps out on his front foot too early, but when he stays down and lets the ball travel, he sees pitches well and can drive them hard to the opposite field. Double-A lefthanders limited him to a .167 average and one homer in 48 at-bats, but he hit them well at Hagerstown and shouldn't have a massive platoon split. Harper draws plenty of walks and has the ability to be an above-average or better hitter as he matures, though some scouts think he may strike out out too much to hit for a high average.

He's learning to stay under control when he throws, just as when he's in the batter's box. Primarily a catcher as an amateur, Harper played all three outfield positions during his pro debut. He learned the importance of staying closed and using his legs when he throws, and he racked up seven assists in just 37 Double-A games after registering six in 68 games with Hagerstown. Currently an above-average runner, Harper plays with youthful aggression in the outfield and on the basepaths, and his reads are getting better in both facets. He has the speed and instincts to steal bases, though he's still learning when he should run. Many evaluators think Harper will lose a step and wind up in right field once he matures physically, though the Nationals believe he has a chance to stick in center field. He's a tireless worker who loves to play the game, though sometimes his cockiness rubs opponents the wrong way.

Harper looks like a sure-fire superstar in the making, and he has a very real chance to develop into the best all-around player in baseball. He figures to start the 2012 season back at Harrisburg or perhaps at Triple-A Syracuse if he dazzles in spring training, and he could slug his way to Washington before season's end.

BA GRADE
80
LOW

CLIFF WELCH

SCOUTING GRADES

Batting: 60. **Defense:** 60.
Power: 80. **Arm:** 80.
Speed: 55.

Based on 20-80 scouting scale, where 50 represents major league average, and future projection rather than present tools.

Year	Club (League)	Class	AVG	G	AB	R	H	2B	3B	HR	RBI	BB	SO	SB	CS	OBP	SLG
2011	Hagerstown (SAL)	LoA	.318	72	258	49	82	17	1	14	46	44	61	19	5	.423	.554
	Harrisburg (EL)	AA	.256	37	129	14	33	7	1	3	12	15	26	7	2	.329	.395
Minor League Totals			.297	109	387	63	115	24	2	17	58	59	87	26	7	.392	.501

2 ANTHONY RENDON, 3B

Born: June 6, 1990. **B-T:** R-R. **Ht.:** 6-0. **Wt.:** 190. **Drafted:** Rice, 2011 (1st round). **Signed by:** Tyler Wilt.

MIKE JANES

BA GRADE

70

MEDIUM

Rendon won Baseball America's Freshman of the Year award in 2009, followed by College Player of the Year honors in 2010. A strained throwing shoulder limited him to mostly DH duties and sapped his power as a junior last spring, and while he still sat atop BA's draft prospect rankings, he slid to the Nationals at No. 6. He signed a big league contract worth $7.2 million (including a $6 million bonus) at the Aug. 15 deadline, and sat out games in instructional league while continuing to build up strength in his shoulder. Though he's not physically imposing, Rendon has remarkable strength in his hands and wrists, uncanny hand-eye coordination, outstanding plate coverage and exceptional pitch recognition. He consistently drives the ball hard to all fields and projects as a well above-average hitter with plus power. He has average speed despite torn ligaments in his right ankle in 2009 and a break in the same ankle in 2010, and he's smart on the basepaths. When healthy, Rendon has superb defensive instincts and actions, good range and an above-average arm. He has drawn comparisons to Evan Longoria, Ryan Zimmerman and David Wright. With Zimmerman entrenched at third base in Washington, Rendon eventually may shift to second base. His polished bat should carry him quickly through the minors.

Year	Club (League)	Class	AVG	G	AB	R	H	2B	3B	HR	RBI	BB	SO	SB	CS	OBP	SLG
2011	Did Not Play—Signed Late																

3 BRAD PEACOCK, RHP

Born: Feb. 2, 1988. **B-T:** R-R. **Ht.:** 6-1. **Wt.:** 175. **Drafted:** Palm Beach (Fla.) CC, D/F 2006 (41st round). **Signed by:** Tony Arango.

WILL BENTZEL/HARRISBURG SENTORS

BA GRADE

60

LOW

Peacock's arm strength has made him stand out since his days as a high school shortstop. He made gradual progress as a pitcher in his first four seasons with the Nationals before breaking out in 2011. He won Double-A Eastern League pitcher of the year honors and finished the year with impressive stints in Triple-A and the majors. Peacock pitches comfortably at 91-94 mph and runs his fastball up to 97 at times. He worked hard in 2011 to keep his front shoulder closed while maintaining his balance and alignment, which led to improved fastball command and deception. He pitches heavily off his four-seamer, which has late hop. He has another swing-and-miss pitch in his sharp 12-to-6 curveball, though it still needs more consistency. He has gained significant confidence in his low-80s changeup, throwing it with good arm speed and fade, though it still gets too firm at times. Peacock is a great athlete who fields his position well, though he's not overly physical. Though he'll compete for a big league rotation spot out of spring training, some more time in Triple-A to master his delivery and secondary stuff might benefit Peacock. He could become a No. 2 starter if everything clicks.

Year	Club (League)	Class	W	L	ERA	G	GS	CG	SV	IP	H	HR	BB	SO	K/9	WHIP	AVG
2007	Nationals (GCL)	R	1	1	3.89	13	7	0	0	39	38	1	15	34	7.8	1.35	.242
2008	Hagerstown (SAL)	LoA	0	5	9.09	8	8	0	0	34	38	8	21	23	6.1	1.75	.284
	Vermont (NYP)	SS	4	7	3.12	14	14	2	0	75	67	3	27	54	6.5	1.25	.235
2009	Hagerstown (SAL)	LoA	5	8	4.05	19	17	0	0	100	104	10	32	77	6.9	1.36	.272
	Potomac (CAR)	HiA	3	3	4.34	8	7	0	0	48	46	4	10	27	5.1	1.17	.253
2010	Potomac (CAR)	HiA	4	9	4.44	19	18	1	0	103	109	11	25	118	10.3	1.30	.268
	Harrisburg (EL)	AA	2	2	4.66	7	7	0	0	39	33	5	22	30	7.0	1.42	.234
2011	Harrisburg (EL)	AA	10	2	2.01	16	14	1	0	99	62	4	23	129	11.8	0.86	.179
	Syracuse (IL)	AAA	5	1	3.19	9	9	0	0	48	36	5	24	48	9.0	1.25	.205
	Washington (NL)	MAJ	2	0	0.75	3	2	0	0	12	7	0	6	4	3.0	1.08	.167
Major League Totals			2	0	0.75	3	2	0	0	12	7	0	6	4	3.0	1.08	.167
Minor League Totals			34	38	3.93	113	101	4	0	584	533	51	199	540	8.3	1.25	.241

4 A.J. COLE, RHP

Born: Jan. 5, 1992. **B-T:** R-R. **Ht.:** 6-4. **Wt.:** 181. **Drafted:** HS—Oviedo, Fla., 2010 (4th round). **Signed by:** Paul Tinnell.

After signing for a fourth round-record $2 million bonus in August 2010, Cole pitched just one inning at short-season Vermont. An illness caused him to lose weight before the start of spring training in 2011, and the Nationals cautiously kept him in extended spring training until mid-May. He joined low Class A Hagerstown, held his own against older competition in the South Atlantic League and got stronger as the year went on. By the end of the summer his fastball ranged from 90-98 mph and sat in the mid-90s. He has no fear of attacking hitters with his fastball, and did a better job commanding the pitch down in the zone as the season progressed. Early on, he tended to rush his delivery, but it became more compact, repeatable and rhythmic during the summer, helping him generate a good downward plane. Cole throws a spike curveball as a chase pitch and is getting better at throwing it for strikes, but Washington plans on having him work on a true curve that would be easier to keep in the zone. He's still learning to trust his changeup. Cole is still getting stronger physically and has frontline-starter upside, but needs to refine his secondary stuff. The Nationals will be patient and figure to send him to high Class A Potomac in 2012.

BA GRADE
65
HIGH

SARA GRASMON

Year	Club (League)	Class	W	L	ERA	G	GS	CG	SV	IP	H	HR	BB	SO	K/9	WHIP	AVG
2010	Vermont (NYP)	SS	0	0	0.00	1	0	0	0	1	1	0	1	1	9.0	2.00	.333
2011	Hagerstown (SAL)	LoA	4	7	4.04	20	18	0	0	89	87	6	24	108	10.9	1.25	.251
Minor League Totals			4	7	4.00	21	18	0	0	90	88	6	25	109	10.9	1.26	.252

5 BRIAN GOODWIN, OF

Born: Nov. 2, 1990. **B-T:** L-R. **Ht.:** 6-1. **Wt.:** 195. **Drafted:** Miami Dade JC, 2011 (1st round supplemental). **Signed by:** Alex Morales.

Goodwin put together a strong freshman year at North Carolina in 2010 but got suspended for the 2011 season after violating university policy. He transferred to Miami Dade JC, where he started slowly, thanks in part to a tweaked hamstring. He bounced back to go 34th overall in the draft, signing just before the Aug. 15 deadline for $3 million. An athletic specimen, Goodwin has the makings of five average or better tools. His best is his speed, which draws grades ranging from plus to plus-plus. He's still learning to steal bases and take charge in center field, where he can become an above-average defender. He has a solid arm and a quick release. Goodwin flashed electric bat speed and showed a patient, gap-to-gap approach in college, but he arrived at instructional league with a rotational, upper-body, metal-bat swing. The Nationals worked with him on using his lower half more and getting his quick, strong hands into better hitting position. He projects as a .275 hitter with 20 or more homers per year. Goodwin needs time to develop, but he has the tools to be an impact center fielder who hits in the top third of a big league lineup. He'll debut in low Class A.

BA GRADE
60
HIGH

MIKE JANES

Year	Club (League)	Class	AVG	G	AB	R	H	2B	3B	HR	RBI	BB	SO	SB	CS	OBP	SLG
2011	Did Not Play—Signed Late																

6 ALEX MEYER, RHP

Born: Jan. 3, 1990. **B-T:** R-R. **Ht.:** 6-9. **Wt.:** 220. **Drafted:** Kentucky, 2011 (1st round). **Signed by:** Reed Dunn.

Meyer turned down $2 million from the Red Sox as a 20th-round pick out of high school in 2008. He struggled in his first two seasons at Kentucky before coming on strong as a junior in 2011. The Nationals matched the $2 million he once declined to sign him as the 23rd overall pick. Meyer sat at 94-97 mph and broke 100 on occasion with his four-seam fastball last spring, though he topped out at 93 in instructional league. He mixes in a 91-93 mph two-seamer with above-average life when it's down in the zone. He uses a knuckle-curve grip to deliver an 82-88 mph slider that's a wipeout pitch at times. He also has improving feel for his 84-86 mph changeup. As with most tall pitchers, repeating his delivery is key for Meyer. He tends to rotate his torso too early, and he must do a better job staying over the rubber and on line to the plate. His arm slot also varies from three-quarters to low three-quarters. He has a ways to go to master his mechanics and his command, but it's encouraging that he works around the strike zone. Meyer could be an ace starter or a flamethrowing reliever in the mold of Daniel Bard. He'll likely debut in low Class A.

BA GRADE
60
HIGH

MIKE JANES

Year	Club (League)	Class	W	L	ERA	G	GS	CG	SV	IP	H	HR	BB	SO	K/9	WHIP	AVG
2011	Did Not Play—Signed Late																

7 MATT PURKE, LHP

MIKE JANES

Born: July 17, 1990. **B-T:** L-L. **Ht.:** 6-4. **Wt.:** 180. **Drafted:** Texas Christian, 2011 (3rd round). **Signed by:** Ed Gustafson.

The 14th overall pick in the 2009 draft, Purke agreed to a $6 million bonus with the Rangers, but MLB controlled the club's finances and refused to approve the deal. He went 16-0 to lead Texas Christian to its first College World Series and earn Freshman of the Year honors in 2010. Shoulder bursitis sidelined him for a month in 2011 and dropped him to the third round as a sophomore-eligible, but the Nationals cleared him medically before signing him to a big league deal with a $2.75 million bonus and $4.15 million total guarantee. When fully healthy, Purke pounds the zone with a 91-94 mph fastball that reaches 96, and he backs it up with a plus 78-82 mph slider. He worked at 89-93 mph with his fastball in instructional league before heading to the Arizona Fall League. He also has good feel for a changeup. Purke always had a slingy, low three-quarters arm action, but he dropped his slot even further and threw across his body more in 2011, causing his stuff to flatten out. He did raise his arm angle in instructional league. He's an intense competitor who works quickly. Another potential frontline starter for the Nationals, Purke figures to move quickly if he regains his health. He could start his career in high Class A.

BA GRADE
60
HIGH

Year	Club (League)	Class	W	L	ERA	G	GS	CG	SV	IP	H	HR	BB	SO	K/9	WHIP	AVG
2011	Did Not Play—Signed Late																

8 SAMMY SOLIS, LHP

RODGER WOOD

Born: Aug. 10, 1988. **B-T:** R-L. **Ht.:** 6-5. **Wt.:** 230. **Drafted:** San Diego, 2010 (2nd round). **Signed by:** Tim Reynolds.

Solis, whose family owns an AIDS orphanage in Africa, has a good sense of perspective that served him well when he missed almost all of 2009 with a herniated disc in his back. Signed for $1 million in August 2010, he injured his quadriceps last spring and didn't begin his first full pro season until May 30. He found his groove after a midseason promotion to high Class A, where he allowed seven earned runs over his final six starts. Solis has a physical build, clean delivery and easy arm action. He pitches at 90-94 mph and tops out at 96 with his fastball, which has late tailing life. The depth, speed and shape of his spike curveball can vary, from a plus curve with true downer break at times to more of a slider at others. He has good feel for his changeup, which projects as a solid or better pitch. He throws strikes but gets in trouble when he leaves balls up in the zone. Solis will advance to Double-A in 2012 and could push for a spot in the big league rotation the following season. He profiles as a mid-rotation starter.

BA GRADE
55
MEDIUM

Year	Club (League)	Class	W	L	ERA	G	GS	CG	SV	IP	H	HR	BB	SO	K/9	WHIP	AVG
2010	Hagerstown (SAL)	LoA	0	0	0.00	2	2	0	0	4	2	0	0	3	6.8	0.50	.143
2011	Hagerstown (SAL)	LoA	2	1	4.02	7	7	0	0	40	39	3	12	40	8.9	1.26	.253
	Potomac (CAR)	HiA	6	2	2.72	10	10	0	0	56	61	5	11	53	8.5	1.28	.279
Minor League Totals			8	3	3.13	19	19	0	0	101	102	8	23	96	8.6	1.24	.264

9 DEREK NORRIS, C

Born: Feb. 14, 1989. **B-T:** R-R. **Ht.:** 6-0. **Wt.:** 210. **Drafted:** HS—Goddard, Kan., 2007 (4th round). **Signed by:** Ryan Fox.

Norris long has been regarded as a gifted offensive player, but early in his pro career there were questions about the converted third baseman's ability to catch. He answered them by making great strides defensively in Double-A in 2011, when he also slugged 20 homers but hit just .210. Despite his low batting averages and high strikeout totals, Norris has excellent pitch recognition and the ability to command the zone when he stays back. When he struggles, he jumps to his front side too early and his bat doesn't stay in the zone. He has quick hands and a compact stroke that generates plus power from line to line, though he's at his best when he's driving the ball to right-center. Norris' throwing, receiving, footwork, blocking and game-calling have improved. He still needs to polish his receiving, but his solid-average arm helped him throw out an Eastern League-high 40 percent of basestealers. A great athlete for a catcher, he has good speed underway and isn't afraid to steal bases. Protected on the 40-man roster in November, Norris now looks likely to stick behind the plate as a big leaguer, and his offensive ability gives him a chance to be an all-star. Wilson Ramos poses an obstacle in Washington that he'll have to deal with after he spends 2012 in Triple-A.

BA GRADE
55
MEDIUM

Year	Club (League)	Class	AVG	G	AB	R	H	2B	3B	HR	RBI	BB	SO	SB	CS	OBP	SLG
2007	Nationals (GCL)	R	.203	37	123	16	25	6	2	4	15	25	38	2	1	.344	.382
2008	Vermont (NYP)	SS	.278	70	227	42	63	12	0	10	38	63	56	11	9	.444	.463
2009	Hagerstown (SAL)	LoA	.286	126	437	78	125	30	0	23	84	90	116	6	3	.413	.513
2010	Potomac (CAR)	HiA	.235	94	298	67	70	19	0	12	49	89	94	6	3	.419	.419
2011	Harrisburg (EL)	AA	.210	104	334	75	70	17	1	20	46	77	117	13	4	.367	.446
Minor League Totals			.249	431	1419	278	353	84	3	69	232	344	421	38	20	.403	.458

10 STEVE LOMBARDOZZI, 2B/SS

BA GRADE

50
LOW

Born: Sept. 20, 1988. **B-T:** B-R. **Ht.:** 6-0. **Wt.:** 170. **Drafted:** St. Petersburg (Fla.) JC, 2008 (19th round). **Signed by:** Paul Tinnell.

Lombardozzi's father of the same name was a sparkplug second baseman for the 1987 World Series champion Twins, and the son is similar—with a chance to be better. He breezed through the minors and established himself as a favorite of officials throughout the system. Lombardozzi's tools don't stand out but they all play up because of his baseball acumen and professional approach. A switch-hitter, he has a balanced, line-drive stroke from both sides. An adept situational hitter and bunter, he excels at making contact and can drive the ball into the gaps. He's a slightly above-average runner who picks his spots wisely, as evidenced by his 79 percent success rate on steal attempts in 2011. Lombardozzi committed just two errors all season in the minors, a product of his focus and savvy as much as his sure hands and textbook technique. He has solid range and a fringy arm, and he has held his own filling in at shortstop and third base. He has the tools and skills to be a quality everyday second baseman, and he's versatile enough to be a high-energy utilityman. The latter could be his role in the short term, with Danny Espinosa entrenched at second base in Washington.

Year	Club (League)	Class	AVG	G	AB	R	H	2B	3B	HR	RBI	BB	SO	SB	CS	OBP	SLG
2008	Nationals (GCL)	R	.283	48	152	23	43	4	1	0	24	21	32	4	1	.371	.322
2009	Hagerstown (SAL)	LoA	.296	128	496	90	147	26	7	3	58	62	80	16	7	.375	.395
2010	Potomac (CAR)	HiA	.293	110	440	71	129	30	9	1	38	49	60	20	10	.370	.409
	Harrisburg (EL)	AA	.295	27	105	19	31	5	2	5	11	12	15	4	2	.373	.524
2011	Harrisburg (EL)	AA	.309	65	262	40	81	12	7	4	23	18	38	16	3	.366	.454
	Syracuse (IL)	AAA	.310	69	294	46	91	13	2	4	29	21	40	14	5	.354	.408
	Washington (NL)	MAJ	.194	13	31	3	6	1	0	0	1	1	4	0	0	.219	.226
Major League Totals			.194	13	31	3	6	1	0	0	1	1	4	0	0	.219	.226
Minor League Totals			.298	447	1749	289	522	90	28	17	183	183	265	74	28	.369	.411

11 DESTIN HOOD, OF

BA GRADE

55
HIGH

Born: April 3, 1990. **B-T:** R-R. **Ht.:** 6-1. **Wt.:** 225. **Drafted:** HS—Mobile, Ala., 2008 (2nd round). **Signed by:** Eric Robinson.

The Nationals knew Hood was a long-term project when they signed him away from an Alabama football scholarship for a $1.1 million bonus in 2008. That has proven correct, though he showed signs of harnessing his significant raw talent last year in high Class A. Despite playing in the Carolina League (the lowest-scoring full-season circuit in 2011), he more than doubled his previous career totals for homers and steals while also dramatically improving his plate discipline. A slightly above-average runner when he signed, Hood had thickened by 2010 and saw his speed drop to below average. He got himself into considerably better shape in the offseason and his speed returned last year, when he consistently posted solid running times. He also made significant gains with his outfield routes and his throwing, and now projects as an average left fielder with a fringy yet efficient arm. Offensively, Hood excels at maintaining his balance through his swing and has toned down his tendency to chase sliders off the plate. He can drive the ball from line to line, showing very good doubles pop to the right-center gap and emerging home run power to the pull side. Washington expects him to develop into an average or slightly better hitter with solid to plus power. Hood has a chance to be a solid regular, and how he handles the jump to Double-A in 2012 will be telling.

Year	Club (League)	Class	AVG	G	AB	R	H	2B	3B	HR	RBI	BB	SO	SB	CS	OBP	SLG
2008	Nationals (GCL)	R	.256	25	86	18	22	6	1	0	14	8	19	5	2	.333	.349
2009	Nationals (GCL)	R	.330	25	88	18	29	10	3	3	24	8	19	3	0	.388	.614
	Vermont (NYP)	SS	.246	38	138	12	34	4	1	2	24	11	45	2	1	.302	.333
2010	Hagerstown (SAL)	LoA	.285	129	492	56	140	30	3	5	65	33	119	5	7	.333	.388
2011	Potomac (CAR)	HiA	.276	128	463	61	128	29	5	13	83	58	96	21	6	.364	.445
Minor League Totals			.279	345	1267	165	353	79	13	23	210	118	298	36	16	.345	.416

12 CHRIS MARRERO, 1B

BA GRADE
50
MEDIUM

Born: July 2, 1988. **B-T:** R-R. **Ht.:** 6-3. **Wt.:** 210. **Drafted:** HS—Opa Locka, Fla., 2006 (1st round). **Signed by:** Tony Arango.

Marrero has advanced steadily through the system, one level at a time, since signing for $1.625 million as a first-round pick in 2006. Though his numbers have never leapt off the page, he has produced at every level, and he had his best season in 2011. He hit .300 for the first time since Rookie ball and posted an .825 OPS, his highest over a full minor league season. He spent all of September as Washington's everyday first baseman, struggling to make consistent contact against big league pitching. Marrero always has tended to step in the bucket, but when he stays on line and focuses on driving the ball to the middle of the field, his barrel stays in the hitting zone longer and his pitch recognition improves. Still just 23, he profiles as an average hitter with slightly above-average power. He has plus raw power, but he's still learning to make the most use of it. Marrero made great strides defensively in Triple-A, cutting his error total to five from 18 in 2010. His footwork and ability to pick balls out of the dirt have improved significantly, and he now profiles as a fringy defender with an adequate arm. He's a well below-average runner. With first basemen Michael Morse (who shifted to left in September) and Adam LaRoche still under contract for 2012, Marrero figures to return to Syracuse to open the season. He profiles as a decent everyday first baseman or a platoon player.

Year	Club (League)	Class	AVG	G	AB	R	H	2B	3B	HR	RBI	BB	SO	SB	CS	OBP	SLG
2006	Nationals (GCL)	R	.309	22	81	10	25	9	0	0	16	8	19	0	0	.374	.420
2007	Hagerstown (SAL)	LoA	.293	57	222	31	65	14	0	14	53	14	39	0	4	.337	.545
	Potomac (CAR)	HiA	.259	68	255	40	66	11	3	9	35	32	63	0	0	.338	.431
2008	Potomac (CAR)	HiA	.250	70	256	40	64	15	2	11	38	25	55	0	0	.325	.453
2009	Potomac (CAR)	HiA	.287	112	414	58	119	21	2	16	65	42	97	2	3	.360	.464
	Harrisburg (EL)	AA	.267	23	75	9	20	6	0	1	11	8	18	0	1	.345	.387
2010	Harrisburg (EL)	AA	.294	141	524	73	154	28	0	18	82	43	102	1	3	.350	.450
2011	Syracuse (IL)	AAA	.300	127	483	59	145	30	0	14	69	58	97	3	2	.375	.449
	Washington (NL)	MAJ	.248	31	109	6	27	5	0	0	10	4	27	0	0	.274	.294
Major League Totals			.248	31	109	6	27	5	0	0	10	4	27	0	0	.274	.294
Minor League Totals			.285	620	2310	320	658	134	7	83	369	230	490	6	13	.353	.457

13 TOM MILONE, LHP

BA GRADE
45
LOW

Born: Feb. 16, 1987. **B-T:** L-L. **Ht.:** 6-1. **Wt.:** 205. **Drafted:** Southern California, 2008 (10th round). **Signed by:** Craig Kornfield.

Like Steve Lombardozzi, Milone lacks standout physical tools but proved himself at every level and forced his way to the big leagues by the end of 2011. He carved up the Triple-A International League to rank second with 155 strikeouts and first in walks per nine innings (1.0) and K-BB ratio (9.7). Those last two figures illustrates his greatest strength: superb control and command. Milone's below-average fastball ranges from 86-91 mph, but it plays up because of the deception in his herky-jerky delivery and his ability to spot it wherever he wants. His above-average changeup is his out pitch against lefties and righties alike thanks to his excellent arm speed, good sink and tailing action. He throws his fringy curveball at varying depths and speeds, using it for a chase pitch or an early strike. He also mixes in a solid cutter. Milone has outstanding poise and the ability to make adjustments on the fly. He fields his position well and handles the bat adeptly for a pitcher. Milone's ceiling is limited to that of a back-end big league starter, but he held his own in five big league starts and will compete for a rotation job in the spring training.

Year	Club (League)	Class	W	L	ERA	G	GS	CG	SV	IP	H	HR	BB	SO	K/9	WHIP	AVG
2008	Vermont (NYP)	SS	1	3	4.57	6	3	0	0	22	27	4	3	22	9.1	1.38	.307
	Hagerstown (SAL)	LoA	0	3	2.89	7	7	0	0	37	36	0	6	27	6.5	1.13	.257
2009	Potomac (CAR)	HiA	12	5	2.91	27	25	0	0	151	144	9	36	106	6.3	1.19	.257
2010	Harrisburg (EL)	AA	12	5	2.85	27	27	2	0	158	161	10	23	155	8.8	1.16	.261
2011	Syracuse (IL)	AAA	12	6	3.22	24	24	0	0	148	137	9	16	155	9.4	1.03	.241
	Washington (NL)	MAJ	1	0	3.81	5	5	0	0	26	28	2	4	15	5.2	1.23	.283
Major League Totals			1	0	3.81	5	5	0	0	26	28	2	4	15	5.2	1.23	.283
Minor League Totals			37	22	3.05	91	86	2	0	517	505	32	84	465	8.1	1.14	.256

14 MICHAEL TAYLOR, OF

BA GRADE
55
EXTREME

Born: March 26, 1991. **B-T:** R-R. **Ht.:** 6-2. **Wt.:** 190. **Drafted:** HS—Fort Lauderdale, Fla., 2009 (6th round). **Signed by:** Tony Arango.

A raw athlete who lacked polish at shortstop, Taylor struggled mightily in the infield and at the plate in his 2010 debut. The Nationals moved him to center field in instructional league after the season, and he took to it immediately, flashing premium defensive ability by the end of the fall. The defensive switch also took pressure off him at the plate, and he held his own in low Class A as a 20-year-old last year. He reminds club officials of Devon White and Mike Cameron physically, using his plus speed to glide effortlessly around center field, where his excellent instincts translate to stellar range. Taylor still is fine-tuning his throwing technique but flashes above-average arm strength. Taylor is a work in progress at the plate, but his quick hands generate impressive leverage and bat speed. He had a narrow base and a long stride heading into 2011, causing his front foot to get down late and his back side to collapse. He made progress during the season at getting his foot down earlier and staying in better hitting position. He also showed the ability to shorten up and take the ball the other way with two strikes, though Washington wants him to attack pitches when he's ahead in the count. He has power to center and left field, and a chance to grow into 20-25 homer pop as he fills out his angular frame. The Nats love Taylor's upside, but he is still a long way from putting his considerable upside together. He'll advance to high Class A in 2012.

Year	Club (League)	Class	AVG	G	AB	R	H	2B	3B	HR	RBI	BB	SO	SB	CS	OBP	SLG
2010	Nationals (GCL)	R	.195	38	128	14	25	4	3	1	12	14	31	1	2	.270	.297
	Hagerstown (SAL)	LoA	.231	5	13	0	3	1	0	0	1	1	2	0	0	.333	.308
2011	Hagerstown (SAL)	LoA	.253	126	442	64	112	26	7	13	68	32	120	23	12	.310	.432
Minor League Totals			.240	169	583	78	140	31	10	14	81	47	153	24	14	.301	.400

15 RICK HAGUE, SS

BA GRADE

50

MEDIUM

Born: Sept. 18, 1988. **B-T:** R-R. **Ht.:** 6-2. **Wt.:** 190. **Drafted:** Rice, 2010 (3rd round). **Signed by:** Tyler Wilt.

Hague hit a combined .335 with 32 homers during three standout years as Rice's starting shortstop, and he hit .371 with wood bats for Team USA's college squad in 2009. After signing for $430,200 as a 2010 third-round pick, Hague continued to rake in his pro debut, though he carried over his erratic defensive play from the spring to the summer. The Nationals sent him to their accelerated program prior to the start of spring training, and he made great progress using his lower half better, unlocking his power potential. Club officials say he had the best spring of any hitter in the system, and he got off to a 5-for-14 in high Class A before dislocating his throwing shoulder. He had surgery in June, ending his season. Hague has advanced bat-to-ball instincts, quick hands and a compact swing. By learning to slow down in the box and stay back, his pitch recognition has improved and he's able to handle offspeed pitches better. He has a chance to be a plus hitter with average power. Hague's defense at shortstop remains a work in progress. He tends to wait back for balls that he should charge, causing the game to speed up on him and his throws to get rushed. No better than a fringy runner, he lacks the range for shortstop, though his arm is strong enough for the position. He fits better as a second or third baseman, and his total package reminds one Nats official of Michael Young, though that's an ambitious comparison. Hague likely will continue his rehabilitation in extended spring training before returning to Potomac.

Year	Club (League)	Class	AVG	G	AB	R	H	2B	3B	HR	RBI	BB	SO	SB	CS	OBP	SLG
2010	Nationals (GCL)	R	.275	10	40	7	11	1	0	0	6	8	9	3	0	.380	.300
	Hagerstown (SAL)	LoA	.327	39	159	26	52	12	5	3	27	14	34	3	2	.386	.522
2011	Potomac (CAR)	HiA	.357	4	14	4	5	2	0	1	4	2	1	1	0	.438	.714
Minor League Totals			.319	53	213	37	68	15	5	4	37	24	44	7	2	.388	.493

16 TYLER MOORE, 1B

BA GRADE

50

MEDIUM

Born: Jan. 30, 1987. **B-T:** R-R. **Ht.:** 6-2. **Wt.:** 185. **Drafted:** Mississippi State, 2008 (16th round). **Signed by:** Eric Robinson.

Power has been Moore's calling card since high school, when the Nationals drafted him in the 41st round in 2005. They took him again in the 33rd round after his freshman year at Meridian (Miss.) CC and finally signed him for $55,000 as a 16th-round pick out of Mississippi State in 2008. He and Paul Goldschmidt were the only players to reach the 30-homer plateau in the minors in each of the last two seasons. Last year, Moore topped the Eastern League in homers (31), extra-base hits (70), RBIs (90) and total bases (276), earning a spot on Washington's 40-man roster. He's country strong and has plus-plus raw power. He can hit balls out of the park from pole to pole, though he gets in trouble when he gets pull-happy, making him vulnerable against hard sliders away. When he's at his best, he'll drive those pitches to right field. He's so aggressive that he'll always have more than his share of strikeouts and never be more than a fringe-average hitter, but his premium power gives him a chance to be a valuable regular at first base. His footwork and glovework made great strides in 2011, and he as an above-average arm. With a logjam at first base between Triple-A and the majors, Washington experimented with Moore in left field. He was a pleasant surprise with his reads and routes, though he has below-average speed and range. If Chris Marrero returns as the everyday first baseman at Syracuse in 2012, Moore might see more time in the outfield there.

Year	Club (League)	Class	AVG	G	AB	R	H	2B	3B	HR	RBI	BB	SO	SB	CS	OBP	SLG
2008	Vermont (NYP)	SS	.200	71	265	17	53	10	0	6	28	13	66	1	1	.239	.306
2009	Hagerstown (SAL)	LoA	.297	111	421	38	125	30	3	9	87	40	111	2	2	.363	.447
2010	Potomac (CAR)	HiA	.269	129	502	78	135	43	3	31	111	40	125	0	0	.321	.552
2011	Harrisburg (EL)	AA	.270	137	519	70	140	35	4	31	90	30	139	2	0	.314	.532
Minor League Totals			.265	448	1707	203	453	118	10	77	316	123	441	5	3	.317	.482

17 ROBBIE RAY, LHP

BA GRADE
50
HIGH

Born: Oct. 1, 1991. **B-T:** L-L. **Ht.:** 6-2. **Wt.:** 170. **Drafted:** HS—Brentwood, Tenn., 2010 (12th round). **Signed by:** Paul Faulk.

After flashing mid-90s velocity on the high school showcase circuit in 2009, Ray dominated with less velocity the following spring, throwing three no-hitters, including a five-inning perfect game. After falling to the 12th round of the 2010 draft, he bypassed a commitment to Arkansas in order to sign for $799,000 a day before the Aug. 16 deadline. The Nationals held him and fellow prep draftee A.J. Cole in extended spring training before joining Hagerstown's rotation in mid-May. Ray did a fine job pounding the strike zone in the first half, but his walk total spiked in July. He pitches with an 87-91 mph fastball with natural sink. Though he flashes a bit more on occasion, he projects to pitch with average fastball velocity and plus life. Ray has very good feel for his changeup, which projects as a slightly above-average pitch. He also has the makings of a solid slider, though it remains inconsistent. Ray's stride tends to vary in length, and if he can learn to repeat his mechanics consistently, his stuff should benefit. Projected as a quality back-of-the-rotation starter, he'll head to high Class A in 2012.

Year	Club (League)	Class	W	L	ERA	G	GS	CG	SV	IP	H	HR	BB	SO	K/9	WHIP	AVG
2010	Vermont (NYP)	SS	0	0	0.00	1	0	0	0	1	0	0	0	2	18.0	0.00	.000
2011	Hagerstown (SAL)	LoA	2	3	3.13	20	20	0	0	89	71	3	38	95	9.6	1.22	.221
Minor League Totals			2	3	3.10	21	20	0	0	90	71	3	38	97	9.7	1.21	.219

18 KYLIN TURNBULL, LHP

BA GRADE
50
HIGH

Born: Sept. 12, 1989. **B-T:** R-L. **Ht.:** 6-5. **Wt.:** 205. **Drafted:** Santa Barbara (Calif.) CC, 2011 (4th round). **Signed by:** Craig Kornfeld.

Though Turnbull is old for a junior college product, his arm is fresh and his upside is intriguing. Turnbull was raw when he arrived at Santa Barbara (Calif.) CC and took a redshirt in 2009. After turning down the White Sox as a 30th-round pick in 2010, he went 5-2, 2.47 last spring. The Nationals viewed him as a steal in the fourth round and signed him for $325,000. Turnbull's velocity ranges from 86-94 mph, with a comfort zone of 90-91. His long, lean frame helps him generate good downward angle, and he shortened up his arm action over the course of 2011, making his delivery easier to repeat. His slider has some depth and shows flashes of being a plus pitch, but more often it is slurvy. He mixes in an 80-84 mph splitter with decent downer action, but Washington would prefer him to focus on developing his changeup, for which he does show good feel. He'll likely make his pro debut in low Class A and he ultimately has mid-rotation upside.

Year	Club (League)	Class	AVG	G	AB	R	H	2B	3B	HR	RBI	BB	SO	SB	CS	OBP	SLG
2011	Did Not Play—Signed Late																

19 ZACH WALTERS, INF

BA GRADE
45
MEDIUM

Born: Sept. 5, 1989. **B-T:** B-R. **Ht.:** 6-3. **Wt.:** 195. **Drafted:** San Diego, 2010 (9th round). **Signed by:** Jeffrey Mousser (Diamondbacks).

The Diamondbacks found a great value in Walters, signing him for $97,500 as a ninth-round pick in 2010. He impressed scouts with his solid tools and good feel for the game during the first half of the 2011 season in the low Class A Midwest League, and Arizona traded him to the Nationals for Jason Marquis in July. The switch-hitting Walters has good barrel release and extension out front from both sides, but Washington would like him to let the ball travel more to improve his pitch recognition. Walters has some leverage in his swing and he could develop fringe-average power if he incorporates his legs in his swing more consistently. He excels at driving balls into the gaps and has a chance to be an average or slightly better hitter. Walters has below-average speed but runs the bases aggressively and instinctively. His slightly above-average arm plays at shortstop, but his range is a little lacking for the position. His hands and actions are solid, and he has the versatility to play second or third base. He profiles as a valuable utilityman with a shot to be an infield regular. Walters figures to reach Double-A at some point in 2012, perhaps out of spring training.

Year	Club (League)	Class	AVG	G	AB	R	H	2B	3B	HR	RBI	BB	SO	SB	CS	OBP	SLG
2010	Yakima (NWL)	SS	.302	69	275	44	83	18	4	4	43	16	59	14	4	.338	.440
2011	South Bend (MWL)	LoA	.302	97	361	69	109	27	6	9	56	42	96	12	10	.377	.485
	Potomac (CAR)	HiA	.293	30	116	15	34	7	1	0	11	8	33	7	1	.336	.371
Minor League Totals			.301	196	752	128	226	52	11	13	110	66	188	33	15	.357	.451

20 JEFF KOBERNUS, 2B

BA GRADE
45
MEDIUM

Born: June 30, 1988. **B-T:** R-R. **Ht.:** 6-2. **Wt.:** 210. **Drafted:** California, 2009 (2nd round). **Signed by:** Ryan Fox.

The son of a former minor leaguer of the same name, Kobernus has a hard-nosed style of play that may have led to the nagging injuries that limited him during his first two pro seasons. He stayed mostly healthy in 2011, putting together a solid season at high Class A Potomac. A plus-plus runner with excellent first-step quickness and advanced instincts on the basepaths, Kobernus tied for 11th in the minors with 53 stolen bases and succeeded on 87 percent of his attempts. He's still learning to refine his approach offensively, as he tends to try too hard to make something happen and chases pitches out of the zone. Washington wants him to do a better job staying under control and balanced, which also should help his pitch recognition. When he stays back, he shows a pretty line-drive swing and good bat speed. He can drive the ball from gap to gap and has occasional power to his pull side. He shows the ability to backspin balls out of the park with ease at times during batting practice, but he doesn't figure to have better than below-average power. Kobernus became a more fluid defender at second base in 2011, making progress with his pivots, actions and throws. He has a solid arm for the position and projects as at least an average defender. Kobernus has the tools to be an everyday big league second baseman, but he'll need to mature offensively and make continued progress defensively. He'll get a crack at Double-A this year.

Year	Club (League)	Class	AVG	G	AB	R	H	2B	3B	HR	RBI	BB	SO	SB	CS	OBP	SLG
2009	Vermont (NYP)	SS	.220	10	41	8	9	1	0	0	2	2	5	4	0	.273	.244
2010	Hagerstown (SAL)	LoA	.279	74	312	40	87	18	0	1	42	17	58	21	10	.316	.346
2011	Potomac (CAR)	HiA	.282	124	489	67	138	22	4	7	52	21	87	53	8	.313	.387
Minor League Totals			.278	208	842	115	234	41	4	8	96	40	150	78	18	.312	.365

21 MATT SKOLE, 3B

BA GRADE
50
HIGH

Born: July 30, 1989. **B-T:** L-R. **Ht.:** 6-4. **Wt.:** 230. **Drafted:** Georgia Tech, 2011 (5th round). **Signed by:** Eric Robinson.

Skole is more powerful but less athletic than his younger brother Jake, a Rangers first-round pick in 2010. Matt blasted 37 homers over his first two seasons at Georgia Tech before hitting just 10 with the new BBCOR bats as a junior last spring. Hiis approach matured over the course of his college career, and he drew 99 walks while striking out just 77 times over his last two seasons. He continued to show excellent patience at the plate, a good two-strike approach and impressive hand-eye coordination in his pro debut. Signed for $161,100 as a fifth-round pick, he led the short-season New York-Penn League with 23 doubles and 48 RBIs. Skole should hit for solid power as he learns to use his lower half better in his swing. Most of his home run power is to the pull side, but he also can drive the ball the other way. He batted just .203/.298/.284 against lefthanders at Vermont, so the Nationals had him adopt a two-strike approach throughout at-bats against lefties in instructional league, and he handled them better. Skole has nice hands and a solid-to-plus arm at third base, but he needs to tone his lower half and improve his agility to stick at the hot corner. He could hit enough to be a fringy regular at first base, but his value will be highest at third base. Given his advanced feel for the strike zone, Skole figures to reach high Class A in 2012, perhaps out of camp.

Year	Club (League)	Class	AVG	G	AB	R	H	2B	3B	HR	RBI	BB	SO	SB	CS	OBP	SLG
2011	Auburn (NYP)	SS	.290	72	272	43	79	23	1	5	48	42	52	2	1	.382	.438
Minor League Totals			.290	72	272	43	79	23	1	5	48	42	52	2	1	.382	.438

22 EURY PEREZ, OF

BA GRADE
50
HIGH

Born: May 30, 1990. **B-T:** R-R. **Ht.:** 6-0. **Wt.:** 155. **Signed:** Dominican Republic, 2007. **Signed by:** Dana Brown/Moises de la Mota.

Perez followed up his strong second half in low Class A in 2010 by batting .345 with 21 steals last winter in the Dominican League. His hitting was inconsistent in high Class A last season, but he still posted a solid batting average thanks to top-of-the-line speed, which allowed him to rack up infield hits and bunt singles. Because Perez frequently looks to bunt early in counts, he often falls behind if he fails to get the bunt down. He's an aggressive hitter who needs to learn to be more patient. For two years, the Nationals harped on the need for Perez to reduce his high leg kick and if he can learn to consistently shorten up his stroke, he has a chance to be an average-or-better hitter because he does have good hand-eye coordination and contact ability. He has well below-average power but is strong enough to drive a few balls into the gaps. He's still refining his leads and jumps on the basepaths. Defensively, Perez has above-average range and continues to work on his reads and routes in center field. He has solid arm strength and good accuracy. Perez will advance to Double-A this year after getting added to Washington's 40-man roster in November.

Year	Club (League)	Class	AVG	G	AB	R	H	2B	3B	HR	RBI	BB	SO	SB	CS	OBP	SLG
2007	Nationals1 (DSL)	R	.253	51	158	41	40	5	1	0	14	32	39	15	5	.399	.297
2008	Nationals 1 (DSL)	R	.324	60	213	51	69	9	2	4	44	32	36	28	6	.428	.441
2009	Nationals (GCL)	R	.381	47	181	38	69	3	5	3	24	15	20	16	8	.443	.503
2010	Hagerstown (SAL)	LoA	.299	131	438	88	131	17	5	3	42	23	74	64	13	.345	.381
2011	Potomac (CAR)	HiA	.283	119	424	54	120	9	2	1	41	22	63	45	15	.319	.321
Minor League Totals			.303	408	1414	272	429	43	15	11	165	124	232	168	47	.370	.378

23 DANIEL ROSENBAUM, LHP

BA GRADE
45
MEDIUM

Born: Oct. 10, 1987. **B-T:** R-L. **Ht.:** 6-1. **Wt.:** 210. **Drafted:** Xavier, 2009 (22nd round). **Signed by:** Alex Smith.

After helping Xavier reach its first NCAA regional—where he struck out nine in a win against Sam Houston State—Rosenbaum signed for a bargain bonus of $20,000. Since then, he has dominated at every stop in his pro career, even carving up Double-A hitters after an August promotion last year. The Nationals thought Rosenbaum improved the quality of his strikes and elevated his commitment to refining his secondary stuff in the second half of the season. His fastball command, in particular, made strides in 2011. Rosenbaum pounds the zone with an 88-90 mph fastball that tops out at 91. It plays up because of the deception in his delivery and the natural cut on his heater, which helps him pitch inside against righties effectively. His solid downer curveball always has been his No. 2 pitch, at the expense of his changeup development. However, his changeup has improved and become close to an average offering. If Rosenbaum returns to Double-A to start the season, he doesn't figure to be there long. He could reach his ceiling as a No. 5 starter or quality swingman by 2013.

Year	Club (League)	Class	W	L	ERA	G	GS	CG	SV	IP	H	HR	BB	SO	K/9	WHIP	AVG
2009	Nationals (GCL)	R	4	1	1.95	11	8	0	0	37	29	1	9	38	9.2	1.03	.215
2010	Hagerstown (SAL)	LoA	2	5	2.32	18	18	0	0	101	95	5	28	84	7.5	1.22	.253
	Potomac (CAR)	HiA	3	2	2.09	8	7	0	0	43	35	2	13	31	6.5	1.12	.230
2011	Potomac (CAR)	HiA	6	5	2.59	20	19	2	0	132	113	4	41	108	7.4	1.17	.234
	Harrisburg (EL)	AA	3	1	2.29	6	6	0	0	39	27	0	11	27	6.2	0.97	.190
Minor League Totals			18	14	2.35	63	58	2	0	352	299	12	102	288	7.4	1.14	.232

24 SANDY LEON, C

BA GRADE
45
MEDIUM

Born: March 13, 1989. **B-T:** B-R. **Ht.:** 5-11. **Wt.:** 175. **Signed:** Venezuela, 2007. **Signed by:** Mike Rizzo/Dana Brown.

Then-assistant GM Mike Rizzo and former scouting director Dana Brown signed Leon and second baseman Adrian Sanchez on the same trip to Venezuela in 2007. Since then, Leon has established a reputation as one of the finest defensive catchers in the system, but scouts always have wondered if he'd hit enough to be a big leaguer. Leon has gradually improved his offensive game to the point that he now holds his own from both sides of the plate. He'll never be better than a below-average hitter with below-average power, but he has learned to put together competitive at-bats and has a knack for providing the occasional clutch hit. Leon's defense alone is good enough to get him to the big leagues, probably as a backup but perhaps as a glove-first regular. Nationals assistant GM Bob Boone—who won seven Gold Gloves behind the plate—calls Leon a "magnificent catcher" with great footwork, outstanding receiving and blocking skills and a solid-average to plus arm with very good accuracy. He led the Carolina League by throwing out 53 percent of basestealers in 2011. He's an extremely slow runner who clogs up the bases. He will move to Double-A in 2012, and with a host of quality catchers ahead of him in the upper levels of the system, Washington can afford to wait for his bat to develop.

Year	Club (League)	Class	AVG	G	AB	R	H	2B	3B	HR	RBI	BB	SO	SB	CS	OBP	SLG
2007	Nationals (GCL)	R	.202	31	94	10	19	0	0	0	11	17	15	0	0	.324	.202
2008	Nationals (GCL)	R	.189	26	74	12	14	1	1	0	11	9	18	1	2	.294	.230
2009	Hagerstown (SAL)	LoA	.218	23	78	7	17	3	0	0	6	5	21	0	0	.265	.256
	Vermont (NYP)	SS	.247	50	166	16	41	10	1	2	18	24	29	1	1	.345	.355
2010	Hagerstown (SAL)	LoA	.249	98	325	48	81	10	6	2	36	50	79	3	5	.345	.335
2011	Potomac (CAR)	HiA	.251	109	370	36	93	21	1	6	43	33	69	1	3	.312	.362
Minor League Totals			.239	337	1107	129	265	45	9	10	125	138	231	6	11	.324	.323

25 JASON MARTINSON, SS

BA GRADE
50
HIGH

Born: Oct. 15, 1988. **B-T:** R-R. **Ht.:** 6-1. **Wt.:** 190. **Drafted:** Texas State, 2010 (5th round). **Signed by:** Tyler Wilt.

Martinson arrived at Texas State on a football scholarship, but he tore his hamstring on his first catch as a wide receiver and decided to focus on baseball. Because of his two-sport background, he remains raw on the baseball field. However, his power came alive in the second half of his first full season in 2011, when he slugged 14 of his 19 homers at Hagerstown. Martinson excels at driving fastballs to right-center field and pulling offspeed pitches to left. The Nationals want him to become more aggressive in hitter's counts. He tends to get to his front side too quickly, then dropping his hands and casting his barrel, leading to high strikeout totals. He worked hard to stay balanced and shorten his swing in instructional league, but he has a long way to go before he starts hitting for average. His plus raw power potential is exciting, though he's still learning to harness it. While Martinson's athleticism, solid range and arm strength play at shortstop, he still needs a lot of polish defensively. Many of his 33 errors last year came after he misread balls, then made off-balance, inaccurate throws. He's a slightly above-average runner with a decent feel for stealing bases. The Nationals compare him to another former football player, Mark DeRosa, but Martinson has a long way to go to put everything together. He'll move on to high Class A this year.

Year	Club (League)	Class	AVG	G	AB	R	H	2B	3B	HR	RBI	BB	SO	SB	CS	OBP	SLG
2010	Vermont (NYP)	SS	.241	70	253	38	61	8	6	2	36	38	74	4	2	.346	.344
2011	Hagerstown (SAL)	LoA	.252	129	433	64	109	22	3	19	64	66	144	26	6	.360	.448
Minor League Totals			.248	199	686	102	170	30	9	21	100	104	218	30	8	.355	.410

26 COLE KIMBALL, RHP

Born: Aug. 1, 1985. **B-T:** R-R. **Ht.:** 6-3. **Wt.:** 225. **Drafted:** Centenary (N.J.), 2006, (12th round). **Signed by:** Alex Smith.

Drafted as a raw thrower with intriguing arm strength and physicality but limited feel for pitching, Kimball gradually turned himself into one of the organization's top prospects heading into last year. After spending his first three pro seasons as a starter so he could get more innings, he found a home in the bullpen, dominating at four different levels in 2010 and 2011. After starting last season with 12 consecutive scoreless Triple-A outings, he earned his first promotion to the big leagues, where he continued to overpower hitters for 12 more innings before a shoulder injury ended his season. He had the same rotator-cuff surgery during the all-star break that Pedro Martinez had at age 39, performed by the same doctor. Before he got hurt, Kimball attacked hitters with a heavy 93-97 mph fastball, a swing-and-miss splitter in the mid-80s and a power curveball in the low 80s. He can throw the curve for strikes or bury it as a chase pitch. His shoulder injury casts doubt about his future. The Nationals hope he can make a full recovery by the 2012 all-star break. They took him off their 40-man roster in November and lost him on waivers to the Blue Jays, then reclaimed him two days later.

Year	Club (League)	Class	W	L	ERA	G	GS	CG	SV	IP	H	HR	BB	SO	K/9	WHIP	AVG
2006	Vermont (NYP)	SS	1	4	5.82	16	5	0	0	34	43	3	24	28	7.4	1.97	.307
2007	Vermont (NYP)	SS	3	6	4.20	14	13	0	1	64	52	4	40	72	10.1	1.43	.223
2008	Hagerstown (SAL)	LoA	6	8	5.05	28	27	1	0	128	103	5	83	122	8.6	1.45	.226
2009	Potomac (CAR)	HiA	4	5	6.36	39	0	0	9	47	49	4	28	52	10.0	1.65	.269
2010	Potomac (CAR)	HiA	3	0	1.82	19	0	0	6	25	17	0	8	27	9.9	1.01	.210
	Harrisburg (EL)	AA	5	1	2.33	38	0	0	12	54	33	4	31	74	12.3	1.19	.171
2011	Syracuse (IL)	AAA	1	0	0.00	12	0	0	5	14	8	0	8	14	9.2	1.17	.163
	Washington (NL)	MAJ	1	0	1.93	12	0	0	0	14	8	0	11	11	7.1	1.36	.174
Major League Totals			1	0	1.93	12	0	0	0	14	8	0	11	11	7.1	1.36	.174
Minor League Totals			23	24	4.33	166	45	1	33	366	305	20	222	389	9.6	1.44	.229

27 DAVID FREITAS, C

Born: March 18, 1989. **B-T:** R-R. **Ht.:** 6-2. **Wt.:** 225. **Drafted:** Hawaii, 2010 (15th round). **Signed by:** Tim Reynolds.

Freitas had an eye-opening debut after signing for $50,000 as a 15th-round pick in 2010, hitting in 22 straight games at Vermont and putting himself squarely on the organization's prospect map. He kept it going during his first full pro season, leading the South Atlantic League with 82 walks, ranking second with a .409 on-base percentage and providing 13 homers. Freitas arrived in the system with a metal-bat swing and relied mostly on his upper body to generate power, but the Nationals have worked with him on transferring his weight more effectively. His swing has gotten shorter and his power has increased. His patient approach gives him a chance to be an average hitter with average home run power to the pull side and good doubles pop to the gaps. Defensively, Freitas has decent mobility for his size and is a field general who calls a good game. He has solid hands and improving receiving skills. Freitas threw out just 25 percent of basestealers last year and needs to refine his throwing mechanics, as he has a tendency to rush and get on his front side too quickly, causing him to open up and lose leverage. He has average arm strength, so it's just a matter of syncing up his transfer and release. Like most catchers, he's a below-average runner. Freitas will advance to high Class A this year and has a chance to be an offense-oriented part-time catcher in the big leagues.

Year	Club (League)	Class	AVG	G	AB	R	H	2B	3B	HR	RBI	BB	SO	SB	CS	OBP	SLG
2010	Vermont (NYP)	SS	.307	62	218	32	67	19	0	4	40	34	47	2	0	.408	.450
2011	Hagerstown (SAL)	LoA	.288	123	427	67	123	30	0	13	73	82	87	2	1	.409	.450
Minor League Totals			.295	185	645	99	190	49	0	17	113	116	134	4	1	.409	.450

28 ADRIAN SANCHEZ, 2B

Born: Aug. 16, 1990. **B-T:** B-R. **Ht.:** 6-0. **Wt.:** 160. **Signed:** Venezuela, 2007. **Signed by:** Mike Rizzo/Dana Brown.

Sanchez and catcher Sandy Leon have turned themselves into prospects since both were signed by then-assistant GM Mike Rizzo and former scouting director Dana Brown on the same trip to Venezuela in 2007. After a strong 25-game stint in low Class A at the end of 2010, most club officials expected him to tear up the South Atlantic League in 2011. Instead, he got off to a slow start and didn't really find his groove until July. Sanchez stands out most for his quick hands and natural feel for making good contact. He tends to be a front-foot hitter, but his hands can whip the barrel through the zone and make up for it. When he stays back in good hitting position with his legs, he can drive the ball to the gaps. He has just enough pull power that he sometimes gets himself in trouble trying to hit homers, but he's starting to understand that he should gear his game toward line drives. Sanchez still chases pitches out of the zone too often, but his feel for his barrel gives him a chance to be a plus hitter with below-average power. A quick-twitch athlete, Sanchez has soft hands and the ability to make occasional highlight-reel plays at second base. He played all around the infield earlier in his career, and his footwork is starting to improve as he gets used to second base, where his arm plays average. He has fringy speed but is aggressive on the basepaths. Sanchez has the tools to be an everyday big league second baseman if it all comes together. He'll advance to high Class A in 2012.

Year	Club (League)	Class	AVG	G	AB	R	H	2B	3B	HR	RBI	BB	SO	SB	CS	OBP	SLG
2007	Nationals1 (DSL)	R	.269	42	145	21	39	11	1	1	19	12	25	4	3	.354	.379
2008	Nationals 1 (DSL	)R	.282	58	227	40	64	13	1	3	32	19	36	21	3	.340	.388
2009	Nationals (GCL)	R	.246	24	65	13	16	7	0	0	5	3	6	3	0	.271	.354
2010	Nationals (GCL)	R	.378	29	119	23	45	10	0	3	21	2	15	4	2	.395	.538
	Hagerstown (SAL)	LoA	.317	25	104	15	33	1	0	1	15	0	18	0	2	.330	.356
2011	Hagerstown (SAL)	LoA	.262	131	538	75	141	30	5	3	51	17	71	25	12	.295	.353
Minor League Totals			.282	309	1198	187	338	72	7	11	143	53	171	57	22	.323	.381

29 PAUL DEMNY, RHP

BA GRADE
45
HIGH

Born: Aug. 3, 1989. **B-T:** R-R. **Ht.:** 6-3. **Wt.:** 220. **Drafted:** Blinn (Texas) JC, 2008 (6th round). **Signed by:** Tyler Wilt.

After a promising freshman year at Blinn (Texas) JC in 2008, Demny impressed the Nationals by running his fastball up to 96 mph in a predraft workout, and they signed him for $110,000 as a sixth-round pick. He spent two full seasons in low Class A, where his emotions often vacillated with the ebb and flow of the game and the quality of his stuff varied with his mechanics. He built confidence in high Class A last year and also did a better job maintaining his line to the plate and repeating his arm slot, which tended to drop in years past. Early in 2011, Demny worked mostly at 88-92 mph with his fastball, but the improvements in his delivery helped him sit at 92-94 down the stretch, topping out at 96 at times. Demny's No. 2 pitch is a slider that showed better depth and velocity as the year progressed, coming in at 83-84 mph by season's end. The arm speed and fading action on his changeup continued to get better last year. He still needs to improve his control and command. Demny has the makings of three solid or better pitches and a strong, durable build, giving him a chance to be an innings eater if he continues to blossom, though a future as a reliever seems more likely. Double-A will provide a major test in 2012.

Year	Club (League)	Class	W	L	ERA	G	GS	CG	SV	IP	H	HR	BB	SO	K/9	WHIP	AVG
2008	Nationals (GCL)	R	4	0	2.50	11	6	0	0	36	29	1	14	40	10.0	1.19	.221
2009	Hagerstown (SAL)	LoA	3	11	5.14	23	23	0	0	105	101	8	42	110	9.4	1.36	.250
2010	Hagerstown (SAL)	LoA	6	10	4.23	27	27	1	0	130	128	10	47	106	7.4	1.35	.253
2011	Potumac (CAR)	HiA	10	10	4.32	26	26	0	0	144	144	18	54	108	6.8	1.38	.261
Minor League Totals			23	31	4.34	87	82	1	0	414	402	37	157	364	7.9	1.35	.253

30 KEVIN KEYES, OF

BA GRADE
45
HIGH

Born: March 15, 1989. **B-T:** R-R. **Ht.:** 6-4. **Wt.:** 245. **Drafted:** Texas, 2010 (7th round). **Signed by:** Tyler Wilt.

Keyes mashed 15 homers as a junior at Texas, where cavernous UFCU Disch-Falk Field isn't conducive to power, After signing for $125,000 as a seventh-round pick, he arrived at Vermont overweight, with a long swing and a big leg kick that the Nationals didn't like, and he struggled mightily. He got himself into better shape during the offseason, and he stayed in extended spring training at the start of 2011. His hard work paid dividends at low Class A, where he started to make use of his above-average power potential. Keyes gets in trouble when he gets pull-happy, though when he's locked in he can backspin balls out of the park to right-center. His approach and contact ability are improving, but he still projects as a below-average hitter. Keyes is a below-average runner who lacked the actions to play first base in college. He played right field last year due to Hagerstown's spacious left field, though he profiles as a left fielder with below-average range and fringy arm strength. Keyes' power bat will have to carry him through the minors, continuing with an assignment to high Class A in 2012.

Year	Club (League)	Class	AVG	G	AB	R	H	2B	3B	HR	RBI	BB	SO	SB	CS	OBP	SLG
2010	Vermont (NYP)	SS	.175	39	126	13	22	4	0	3	23	24	36	1	2	.321	.278
2011	Hagerstown (SAL)	LoA	.263	85	304	49	80	22	1	17	65	32	80	6	0	.336	.510
Minor League Totals			.237	124	430	62	102	26	1	20	88	56	116	7	2	.331	.442

APPENDIX

Baseball's active offseason included a talented group of international players headed to the major leagues. Our appendix includes four veterans of Japan's Nippon Professional Baseball plus two high-profile Cuban defectors who were expected to be declared free agents before spring training begins. Four of the six ranked among Baseball America's Top 10 Prospects at the World Baseball Classic in 2009.

Chief among the Japanese pros is righthander Yu Darvish, who beat out Aroldis Chapman for the top spot on our WBC list. The Rangers outbid the Blue Jays, ponying up a reported $51.7 million posting fee for the rights to negotiate with Darvish. The record bid (beating the $51.1 million the Red Sox paid for the rights to Daisuke Matsuzaka) gave Texas 30 days to negotiate with Darvish to bring him to the majors.

Two other clubs had won the rights to Japanese players: The Brewers posted $2.5 million to negotiate with outfielder Norichika Aoki, while the Yankees bid $2 million to talk to infielder Hiroyuki Nakajima. Additionally, the Orioles signed free-agent lefthander Tsuyoshi Wada to a two-year, $8.14 million contract.

Cuban outfielder Yoennis Cespedes also created plenty of buzz as the most sought-after defector since Chapman, who received a $30.25 million major league contract from the Reds in January 2010. Cespedes is expected to exceed Chapman's contract. Teams also were in hot pursuit of fellow Cuban outfielder Jorge Soler, who's more than two years younger than Cespedes and has an enticing bat.

YU DARVISH, RHP

Born: Aug. 16, 1986. **B-T:** R-R. **Ht.:** 6-5. **Wt.:** 215.

Darvish ranked as the No. 1 prospect at the 2009 World Baseball Classic top 20 and has continued to dominate in Japan's Nippon Professional Baseball. In 2011, he went 18-6, 1.44 with 276 strikeouts in 232 innings with Hokkaido's Nippon-Ham Fighters. In seven seasons with the club, he has gone 93-38, 1.99. Of mixed Iranian and Japanese heritage, Darvish has everything a team looks for in a frontline starter: stuff, aggressiveness and durability. He throws five pitches, highlighted by a fastball that sits at 92-95 mph and has touched as high as 99 in relief. His second-best offering is a plus low-80s slider that he'll use in almost any count. Darvish will mix in a lively cutter that can reach the high 80s. On occasion, he'll get ahead with a slow mid-70s curveball, and he also can bury a 90-91 mph splitter if needed. Darvish stays tall in his delivery and possesses good athleticism that allows him to consistently repeat his delivery and command his pitches. His frame should allow him to handle the rigors of pitching every fifth day over an MLB season, which is about three weeks longer than the season in Japan, where starters work every six days. Like many Japanese pitchers, Darvish gets criticized for his tendency to pitch backwards, using his secondary stuff to set up his quality fastball. He was more aggressive with his fastball in 2011, however, and most scouts consider him a better prospect at the same stage than Daisuke Matsuzaka, previously considered Japan's top import pitcher. Assuming he signs with the Rangers—and there's no reason to suspect he won't—he'd rank as their No. 1 prospect ahead of talented shortstop Jurickson Profar and step to the front of their rotation.

YOENNIS CESPEDES, OF

Born: Oct. 10, 1985. **B-T:** R-R. **Ht.:** 5-10. **Wt.:** 215.

Cespedes defected from Cuba early in 2011 and made his way to the Dominican Republic, where he was training at Edgar Mercedes' Born to Play Academy, one of the best-known training facilities in that nation. He hadn't been declared a free agent as the Handbook went to press, but his U.S.-based agent, Adam Katz, said he expected Cespedes to be eligible to sign by the time spring training starts. Cespedes is an excellent athlete whose mother was an Olympic softball player for Cuba. He was the center fielder for Cuba's teams in the 2009 World Baseball Classic and World Cup and less significant events in 2010, and he was one of the top hitters in Cuba's Serie Nacional, its top league. In a 90-game schedule in 2010-2011, he hit .333/.424/.667 with 49 walks and 40 strikeouts, tying for the league lead with a record 33 home runs and leading the circuit with 99 RBIs. Cespedes' premium bat speed and strength generate tremendous raw power that grades as a 70 on the 20-80 scouting scale, and scouts consider his swing balanced and repeatable. He'll have to adjust to big league pitching but scouts expect him to hit. Cespedes has turned in 6.5-second 60-yard dash times and he should be able to handle center field unless his body goes south after he signs. He has an above-average arm that should allow him to play right field if he can't handle center. Cespedes is the best Cuban hitting prospect to defect at least since Kendrys Morales, who was younger but less athletic. At 26, Cespedes will be expected to start in the major leagues immediately.

JORGE SOLER, OF

Born: Feb. 25, 1992. **B-T:** R-R. **Ht.:** 6-3. **Wt.:** 205.

The top prospect on Cuba's team at the 2010 World Junior Championship, Soler hit .304/.500/.522 with nine walks and only one strikeout in seven games. He tried to defect from Cuba unsuccessfully before finally escaping last year. During the offseason, he was working out in the Dominican Republic. Unlike fellow Cuban outfielder Yoennis Cespedes, Soler is at least a few years away from being big league ready, but he's one of the best hitting prospects Cuba has produced in recent years and is advanced beyond his age. He has earned physical comparisons to Vladimir Guerrero. Soler has a physically mature frame with a thick lower half, good bat speed and plus power to all fields. He's an aggressive hitter within the strike zone, and some scouts are impressed with his ability to lay off breaking balls off the plate. A former third baseman, Soler was an outfielder by the time he left Cuba and profiles well there with solid speed and a plus arm. He has the potential to be an above-average everyday right fielder in the big leagues.

NORICHIKA AOKI, OF

Born: Jan. 2, 1982. **B-T:** L-R. **Ht.:** 5-10. **Wt.:** 170.

Scouts considered Aoki the best position player from Japan who was posted this offseason. He played for Japan's 2009 World Baseball Classic champions as well as its 2008 Olympic team, where he homered off Brett Anderson during Team USA's bronze-medal victory. A two-time Central League batting champion, Aoki was a career .339/.421/.497 hitter entering 2011 but slipped to .292/.360/.358 last year with just four homers and eight steals. His speed and contact ability are his best tools. He's a 65 runner on the 20-80 scouting scale, and he gets on base plenty thanks to his control of the strike zone and singles-hitting swing. He lets the ball travel deep, uses the opposite field regularly and was a hit machine in Japan. He became the first player to post multiple 200-hit seasons in NPB's 140-game schedule. A five-time winner of Japan's version of the Gold Glove, Aoki has played all three outfield spots in international play and was a regular in center field for the Yakult Swallows. He lacks the power to be a corner regular. The Brewers still were negotiating with Aoki at press time.

TSUYOSHI WADA, LHP

Born: Feb. 21, 1981. **B-T:** L-L. **Ht.:** 5-10. **Wt.:** 170.

An NPB veteran, Wada accrued enough service time to become a free agent after going 16-5, 1.51 for the Fukuoka Softbank Hawks in 2011. In nine seasons with the Hawks, he went 107-61, 3.13. Wada is a pitchability lefty whose stuff is modest. His fastball reaches 87-88 mph at its best. His solid slider is his top pitch, and he throws a slow curveball and a splitter as well. He'll have to use any of those pitches in any count to succeed with the Orioles, and evaluators appreciate his economical, intelligent approach to pitching. Some scouts worry about how his lack of size and past workload will affect his ability to hold up over the more rigorous MLB schedule. He set a college record in Japan in 2002 with 476 strikeouts in one season, logged at least 162 innings in seven of his nine NPB seasons and saw extensive action on Japan's national teams as both an amateur and pro. Wada will open 2012 in Baltimore's rotation.

HIROYUKI NAKAJIMA, SS

Born: July 31, 1982. **B-T:** B-R. **Ht.:** 5-11. **Wt.:** 183.

Nakajima was the everyday shortstop and primary No. 3 hitter for the Seibu Lions since 2004. The switch-hitter put up impressive offensive statistics in 2011, batting .297/.354/.433 with 16 homers and 21 steals. Japan experienced a depressed offensive environment in 2011 as NPB changed official balls and had its schedule and lighting standards in ballparks affected by the aftermath of the tsunami and nuclear-reaction meltdown in March. For his 10-year career, Nakajima batted .302/.359/.475 with 149 homers and 134 steals. He doesn't have any standout tools but possesses a well-rounded package. He has the range to stick at shortstop but his fringy arm will most likely force a shift to the other side of the bag. Scouts like his ability to grind out at-bats and make the routine play defensively, but they don't expect his double-digit home run totals to translate to MLB. He's an above-average runner though not a burner. He profiles best as a utility infielder, with the Yankees pursuing him as a more reliable middle-infield defender than Eduardo Nunez.

2011 DRAFT

FIRST FIVE ROUNDS

Bonuses and estimated slot recommendations by Major League Baseball for the first five rounds of the 2011 draft. MLB established guidelines for every pick through the first five rounds, and set a $150,000 ceiling (roughly equivalent to the final choice in the fifth round) for subsequent rounds. Asterisks indicate bonuses that were part of a major league contract, and crosses signify a two-sport contract, which allows the club to spread the bonus over as many as five years.

FIRST ROUND

Pick. Team: Player, Pos.	'11 Bonus	'11 Slot
1. Pit: Gerrit Cole, rhp	$8,000,000	$4,000,000
2. Sea: Danny Hultzen, lhp	*$6,350,000	$3,250,000
3. Ari: Trevor Bauer, rhp	*$3,400,000	$3,000,000
4. Bal: Dylan Bundy, rhp	*$4,000,000	$2,750,000
5. KC: Bubba Starling, of	+$7,500,000	$2,520,000
6. Was: Anthony Rendon, 3b	*$6,000,000	$2,340,000
7. Ari: Archie Bradley, rhp	+$5,000,000	$2,178,000
8. Cle: Francisco Lindor, ss	$2,900,000	$2,043,000
9. ChC: Javier Baez, ss	$2,625,000	$1,962,000
10. SD: Cory Spangenberg, 2b	$1,863,000	$1,863,000
11. Hou: George Springer, of	$2,525,000	$1,791,000
12. Mil: Taylor Jungmann, rhp	$2,525,000	$1,719,000
13. NYM: Brandon Nimmo, of	$2,100,000	$1,656,000
14. Fla: Jose Fernandez, rhp	$2,000,000	$1,602,000
15. Mil: Jed Bradley, lhp	$2,000,000	$1,557,000
16. LAD: Chris Reed, lhp	$1,589,000	$1,512,000
17. LAA: C.J. Cron, 1b	$1,467,000	$1,467,000
18. Oak: Sonny Gray, rhp	$1,540,000	$1,422,000
19. Bos: Matt Barnes, rhp	$1,500,000	$1,386,000
20. Col: Tyler Anderson, lhp	$1,400,000	$1,359,000
21. Tor: Tyler Beede, rhp	Did Not Sign	$1,332,000
22. StL: Kolten Wong, 2b	$1,300,000	$1,287,000
23. Was: Alex Meyer, rhp	$2,000,000	$1,260,000
24. TB: Taylor Guerrieri, rhp	$1,600,000	$1,242,000
25. SD: Joe Ross, rhp	$2,750,000	$1,215,000
26. Bos: Blake Swihart, c	$2,500,000	$1,197,000
27. Cin: Robert Stephenson, rhp	$2,000,000	$1,161,000
28. Atl: Sean Gilmartin, lhp	$1,134,000	$1,134,000
29. SF: Joe Panik, ss	$1,116,000	$1,116,000
30. Min: Levi Michael, ss	$1,175,000	$1,089,000
31. TB: Mikie Mahtook, of	$1,150,000	$972,000
32. TB: Jake Hager, ss	$963,000	$954,000
33. Tex: Kevin Matthews, lhp	$936,000	$936,000

SUPPLEMENTAL FIRST ROUND

Pick. Team: Player, Pos.	'11 Bonus	'11 Slot
34. Was: Brian Goodwin, of	$3,000,000	$918,000
35. Tor: Jacob Anderson, of	$990,000	$900,000
36. Bos: Henry Owens, lhp	$1,550,000	$889,200
37. Tex: Zach Cone, of	$873,000	$873,000
38. TB: Brandon Martin, ss	$860,000	$858,600
39. Phi: Larry Greene, of	$1,000,000	$844,200
40. Bos: Jackie Bradley, of	$1,100,000	$829,800
41. TB: Tyler Goeddel, 3b	$1,500,000	$815,400
42. TB: Jeff Ames, rhp	$650,000	$802,800
43. Ari: Andrew Chafin, lhp	$875,000	$789,300
44. NYM: Michael Fulmer, rhp	$937,500	$776,700
45. Col: Trevor Story, ss	$915,000	$764,100
46. Tor: Joe Musgrove, rhp	$500,000	$751,500
47. CWS: Keenyn Walker, of	$795,000	$739,800

48. SD: Michael Kelly, rhp	$718,000	$728,100
49. SF: Kyle Crick, rhp	$900,000	$717,300
50. Min: Travis Harrison, 3b	$1,050,000	$705,600
51. NYY: Dante Bichette Jr., 3b	$750,000	$694,800
52. TB: Blake Snell, lhp	$684,000	$684,000
53. Tor: Dwight Smith Jr., of	$800,000	$674,100
54. SD: Brett Austin, c	Did Not Sign	$663,300
55. Min: Hudson Boyd, rhp	$1,000,000	$653,400
56. TB: Kes Carter, of	$625,000	$643,500
57. Tor: Kevin Comer, rhp	$1,650,000	$634,500
58. SD: Jace Peterson, ss	$624,600	$624,600
59. TB: Grayson Garvin, lhp	$370,000	$614,700
60. TB: James Harris, of	$490,000	$605,700

SECOND ROUND

Pick. Team: Player, Pos.	'11 Bonus	'11 Slot
61. Pit: Josh Bell, of	$5,000,000	$596,700
62. Sea: Brad Miller, ss	$750,000	$587,700
63. Ari: Anthony Meo, rhp	$625,000	$579,600
64. Bal: Jason Esposito, 3b	$600,000	$570,600
65. KC: Cam Gallahager, c	$750,000	$562,500
66. Phi: Roman Quinn, ss	$775,000	$555,000
67. Cle: Dillon Howard, rhp	$1,850,000	$545,400
68. ChC: Dan Vogelbach, 1b	$1,600,000	$537,300
69. Hou: Adrian Houser, rhp	$530,100	$530,100
70. Mil: Jorge Lopez, rhp	$690,000	$522,000
71. NYM: Cory Mazzoni, rhp	$437,500	$514,800
72. Fla: Adam Conley, lhp	$625,000	$506,700
73. LAD: Alex Santana, 3b	$499,500	$499,500
74. Tor: Daniel Norris, lhp	$2,000,000	$492,300
75. TB: Granden Goetzman, of	$490,000	$485,100
76. Det: James McCann, c	$577,900	$477,900
77. Col: Carl Thomore, of	$480,000	$470,700
78. Tor: J. Gabryszwski, rhp	$575,000	$463,500
79. StL: Charlie Tilson, of	$1,275,000	$457,200
80. CWS: Erik Johnson, rhp	$450,000	$450,000
81. Bos: Williams Jerez, of	$443,700	$443,700
82. SD: Austin Hedges, c	$3,000,000	$436,500
83. Tex: Will Lamb, lhp	$430,200	$430,200
84. Cin: Gabriel Rosa, of	$500,000	$423,900
85. Atl: Nick Ahmed, ss	$417,600	$417,600
86. SF: Andrew Susac, c	$1,100,000	$411,300
87. Min: Madison Boer, rhp	$405,000	$405,000
88. NYY: Sam Stafford, lhp	Did Not Sign	$398,700
89. TB: Leonard Linsky, rhp	$392,400	$392,400
90. Phi: Harold Martinez, 3b	$387,000	$387,000

THIRD ROUND

Pick. Team: Player, Pos.	'11 Bonus	'11 Slot
91. Pit: Alex Dickerson, 1b	$380,700	$380,700
92. Sea: Kevin Cron, 1b	Did Not Sign	$375,300
93. Ari: Justin Bianco, of	$369,000	$369,000
94. Bal: Mike Wright, rhp	$363,600	$363,600
95. KC: Bryan Brickhouse, rhp	$1,500,000	$358,200
96. Was: Matt Purke, lhp	*$2,750,000	$351,900
97. Cle: Jake Sisco, rhp	$325,000	$346,500
98. ChC: Zeke DeVoss, of	$500,000	$341,100
99. Hou: Jack Armstrong Jr., rhp	$750,000	$335,700
100. Mil: Drew Gagnon, rhp	$340,000	$330,300
101. NYM: Logan Verrett, rhp	$425,000	$324,900
102. Fla: Connor Barron, ss	Did Not Sign	$319,500
103. LAD: Pratt Manyard, c	$315,000	$315,000
104. LAA: Nick Maronde, lhp	$309,600	$309,600
105. Oak: B.A. Vollmoth, 3b	$304,200	$304,200

106. Det: Aaron Westlake, 1b	$310,000	$299,700
107. Col: Peter O'Brien, c	Did Not Sign	$295,000
108. Tor: John Stilson, rhp	$500,000	$289,800
109. StL: C.J. McElroy, of	$510,000	$284,400
110. CWS: Jeff Soptic, rhp	$320,000	$279,900
111. Bos: Jordan Weems, c	$500,000	$274,500
112. SD: Matt Andriese, rhp	$270,000	$270,000
113. Tex: Kyle Castro, rhp	$267,300	$267,300
114. Cin: Tony Cingrani, lhp	$210,000	$263,700
115. Atl: Kyle Kubitza, 3b	$261,000	$261,000
116. SF: Ricky Oropesa, 1b	$550,000	$258,300
117. Min: Corey Williams, lhp	$575,000	$254,700
118. NYY: Jordan Cote, rhp	$725,000	$252,000
119. TB: Johnny Eierman, of	+$550,000	$250,000
120. Phi: Adam Morgan, lhp	$250,000	$245,700

SUPPLEMENTAL THIRD ROUND

Pick. Team: Player, Pos.	'11 Bonus	'11 Slot
121. Sea: Carter Capps, rhp	$500,000	$243,000

FOURTH ROUND

Pick. Team: Player, Pos.	'11 Bonus	'11 Slot
122. Pit: Colten Brewer, rhp	$240,000	$240,300
123. Sea: John Hicks, c	$240,000	$236,700
124. Ari: Evan Marshall, rhp	$232,500	$234,000
125. Bal: Kyle Simon, rhp	$231,300	$231,300
126. KC: Kyle Smith, rhp	$695,000	$227,700
127. Was: Kylin Turnbull, lhp	$325,000	$225,000
128. Cle: Jake Lowery, c	$220,000	$222,300
129. ChC: Tony Zych, rhp	$400,000	$218,700
130. Hou: Chris Lee, lhp	$215,000	$216,000
131. Mil: Nick Ramirez, 1b	$213,300	$213,300
132. NYM: Tyler Pill, rhp	$200,000	$209,700
133. Fla: Tyler Palmer, 2b	Did Not Sign	$207,000
134. LAD: Ryan O'Sullivan, rhp	$100,000	$204,300
135. LAA: Mike Clevinger, rhp	$250,000	$200,700
136. Oak: Bobby Crocker, of	$198,000	$198,000
137. Det: Jason King, 3b	$195,300	$195,300
138. Col: DIllon Thomas, of	$300,000	$191,700
139. Tor: Tom Robson, rhp	$325,000	$189,000
140. StL: Kenny Peoples, ss	$200,000	$186,300
141. CWS: Kyle McMillen, rhp	$120,000	$182,700
142. Bos: Noe Ramirez, rhp	$625,000	$180,000

143. SD: Cody Hebner, rhp	$200,000	$179,100
144. Tex: Desmond Henry, of	$200,000	$177,300
145. Cin: Kyle McMyne, rhp	$176,400	$176,400
146. Atl: J.R. Graham, rhp	$174,600	$174,600
147. SF: Bryce Bandilla, lhp	$185,000	$173,700
148. Min: Matt Summers, rhp	$171,900	$171,900
149. NYY: Matt Duran, 3b	$335,000	$171,000
150. TB: Riccio Torrez, 3b	$180,000	$169,200
151. Phi: Cody Asche, 3b	$168,300	$168,300

FIFTH ROUND

Pick. Team: Player, Pos.	'11 Bonus	'11 Slot
152. Pit: Tyler Glasnow, rhp	$600,000	$166,500
153. Sea: Tyler Marlette, c	$650,000	$165,600
154. Ari: Michael Perez, c	$235,000	$163,800
155. Bal: Matt Taylor, lhp	$160,000	$162,900
156. KC: Patrick Leonard, of	$600,000	$161,100
157. Was: Matt Skole, 3b	$161,100	$160,200
158. Cle: Will Roberts, rhp	$150,000	$158,400
159. ChC: Tayler Scott, rhp	$279,950	$157,500
160. Hou: Nick Tropeano, rhp	$155,700	$155,700
161. Mil: Michael Reed, of	$500,000	$154,800
162. NYM: Jack Leathersich, lhp	$110,000	$153,000
163. Fla: Mason Hope, rhp	$250,000	$152,100
164. LAD: Scott McGough, rhp	$150,300	$150,300
165. LAA: Andrew Ray, of	$80,000	$149,400
166. Oak: Beau Taylor, c	$147,600	$147,600
167. Det: Brandon Loy, ss	$212,000	$146,700
168. Col: Taylor Featherston, ss	$144,900	$144,900
169. Tor: Andrew Chin, lhp	Did Not Sign	$144,000
170. StL: Sam Gaviglio, rhp	$175,000	$142,200
171. CWS: Scott Snodgress, lhp	$141,300	$141,300
172. Bos: Mookie Betts, ss	$750,000+	$139,500
173. SD: Mark Pope, rhp	$150,000	$138,200
174. Tex: Brandon Woodruff, rhp	Did Not Sign	$136,800
175. Cin: Ryan Wright, 2b	$225,000	$135,900
176. Atl: Nick DeSantlago, c	$125,000	$134,900
177. SF: Chris Marlowe, rhp	$145,000	$133,900
178. Min: Tyler Grimes, ss	$132,900	$132,900
179. NYY: Greg Bird, c	$1,100,000	$131,900
180. TB: J.D. Davis, 3b	Did Not Sign	$130,900
181. Phi: Mitch Walding, ss	$800,000	$129,900

2010 DRAFT

Bonuses and estimated slot recommendations by Major League Baseball for the first 100 selections of the 2010 draft. Asterisks indicate bonuses that were part of a major league contract, and crosses signify a two-sport contract, which allows the club to spread the bonus over as many as five years.

FIRST ROUND

Pick. Team: Player, Pos.	Bonus	Slot
1. Was: Bryce Harper, of	*$6,250,000	$4,000,000
2. Pit: Jameson Taillon, rhp	$6,500,000	$3,250,000
3. Bal: Manny Machado, ss	$5,250,000	$3,000,000
4. KC: Christian Colon, ss	$2,750,000	$2,750,000
5. Cle: Drew Pomeranz, lhp	$2,650,000	$2,520,000
6. Ari: Barret Loux, rhp	Did Not Sign	$2,340,000
7. NYM: Matt Harvey, rhp	$2,525,000	$2,178,000
8. Hou: Delino DeShields Jr., 2b	$2,150,000	$2,043,000
9. SD: Karsten Whitson, rhp	Did Not Sign	$1,962,000
10. Oak: Michael Choice, of	$2,000,000	$1,863,000
11. Tor: Deck McGuire, rhp	$2,000,000	$1,791,000
12. Cin: Yasmani Grandal, c	*$2,000,000	$1,719,000
13. CWS: Chris Sale, lhp	$1,656,000	$1,656,000
14. Mil: Dylan Covey, rhp	Did Not Sign	$1,602,000
15. Tex: Jake Skole, of	+$1,557,000	$1,557,000
16. ChC: Hayden Simpson, rhp	$1,060,000	$1,512,000
17. TB: Josh Sale, of	$1,620,000	$1,467,000
18. LAA: Kaleb Cowart, 3b/rhp	$2,300,000	$1,422,000
19. Hou: Mike Foltynewicz, rhp	$1,305,000	$1,386,000
20. Bos: Kolbrin Vitek, 2b/of	$1,359,000	$1,359,000
21. Min: Alex Wimmers, rhp	$1,332,000	$1,332,000
22. Tex: Kellin Deglan, c	$1,000,000	$1,287,000
23. Fla: Christian Yelich, of	$1,700,000	$1,260,000
24. SF: Gary Brown, of	$1,450,000	$1,242,000
25. StL: Zack Cox, 3b	*$2,000,000	$1,215,000
26. Col: Kyle Parker, of	+$1,400,000	$1,197,000
27. Phi: Jesse Biddle, lhp	$1,160,000	$1,161,000
28. LAD: Zach Lee, rhp	+$5,250,000	$1,134,000
29. LAA: Cam Bedrosian, rhp	$1,116,000	$1,116,000
30. LAA: Chevez Clarke, of	$1,089,000	$1,089,000
31. TB: Justin O'Conner, c	$1,025,000	$972,000
32. NYY: Cito Culver, ss	$954,000	$954,000

SUPPLEMENTAL FIRST ROUND

Pick. Team: Player, Pos.	Bonus	Slot
33. Hou: Mike Kvasnicka, 3b/c	$936,000	$936,000
34. Tor: Aaron Sanchez, rhp	$775,000	$918,000
35. Atl: Matt Lipka, ss	$800,000	$900,000
36. Bos: Bryce Brentz, of	$889,200	$889,200
37. LAA: Taylor Lindsey, ss	$873,000	$873,000
38. Tor: Noah Syndergaard, rhp	$600,000	$858,600
39. Bos: Anthony Ranaudo, rhp	$2,550,000	$844,200
40. LAA: Ryan Bolden, of	$829,800	$829,800
41. Tor: Asher Wojciechowski, rhp	$815,400	$815,400
42. TB: Drew Vettleson, of	$845,000	$802,800
43. Sea: Taijuan Walker, rhp	$800,000	$789,300
44. Det: Nick Castellanos, 3b	$3,450,000	$776,700
45. Tex: Luke Jackson, rhp	$1,545,000	$764,100
46. StL: Seth Blair, rhp	$751,500	$751,500

TOP 100 PICKS

47. Col: Peter Tago, rhp	$982,500	$739,800
48. Det: Chance Ruffin, rhp	$1,150,000	$728,100
49. Tex: Mike Olt, 3b	$717,300	$717,300
50. StL: Tyrell Jenkins, rhp	+$1,300,000	$705,600

SECOND ROUND

Pick. Team: Player, Pos.	Bonus	Slot
51. Was: Sammy Solis, lhp	$1,000,000	$694,800
52. Pit: Stetson Allie, rhp	$2,250,000	$684,000
53. Atl: Todd Cunningham, of	$674,100	$674,100
54. KC: Brett Eibner, of/rhp	$1,250,000	$663,300
55. Cle: LeVon Washington, of	$1,200,000	$653,400
56. Ari: J.R. Bradley, rhp	$643,500	$643,500
57. Bos: Brandon Workman, rhp	$800,000	$634,500
58. Hou: Vincent Velasquez, rhp	$655,830	$624,600
59. SD: Jedd Gyorko, 2b	$614,700	$614,700
60. Oak: Yordy Cabrera, 3b	$1,250,000	$605,700
61. Tor: Griffin Murphy, lhp	$800,000	$596,700
62. Cin: Ryan LaMarre, of	$587,700	$587,700
63. CWS: Jacob Petricka, rhp	$540,000	$579,600
64. Mil: Jimmy Nelson, rhp	$570,600	$570,600
65. ChC: Reggie Golden, of	$720,000	$562,500
66. TB: Jake Thompson, rhp	$555,000	$555,000
67. Sea: Marcus Littlewood, ss	$900,000	$545,400
68. Det: Drew Smyly, lhp	$1,100,000	$537,300
69. Tor: Kellen Sweeney, 3b	$600,000	$530,100
70. Atl: Andrelton Simmons, rhp	$522,000	$522,000
71. Min: Niko Goodrum, ss	$514,800	$514,800
72. Tex: Cody Buckel, rhp	$590,000	$506,700
73. Fla: Rob Rasmussen, lhp	$499,500	$499,500
74. SF: Jarrett Parker, of	$700,000	$492,300
75. StL: Jordan Swaggerty, rhp	$625,000	$485,100
76. Col: Chad Bettis, rhp	$477,000	$477,900
77. Phi: Perci Garner, rhp	$470,700	$470,700
78. LAD: Ralston Cash, rhp	$463,500	$463,500
79. TB: Derek Dietrich, 3b	$457,200	$457,200
80. Tor: Justin Nicolino, rhp	$615,000	$450,000
81. LAA: Daniel Tillman, rhp	$443,700	$443,700
82. NYY: Angelo Gumbs, of	$750,000	$436,500

THIRD ROUND

Pick. Team: Player, Pos.	Bonus	Slot
83. Was: Rick Hague, ss	$430,200	$430,200
84. Pit: Mel Rojas Jr., of	$423,900	$423,900
85. Bal: Dan Klein, rhp	$499,900	$417,600
86. KC: Mike Antonio, ss	$411,000	$411,300
87. Cle: Tony Wolters, ss	$1,350,000	$405,000
88. Ari: Robby Rowland, rhp	$395,000	$398,700
89. NYM: Blake Forsythe, c	$392,400	$392,400
90. Hou: Austin Wates, 2b	$550,000	$387,000
91. SD: Zach Cates, rhp	$765,000	$380,700
92. Oak: Aaron Shipman, of	$500,000	$375,300
93. Tor: Christopher Hawkins, 3b	$350,000	$369,000
94. Cin: Devin Lohman, ss	$363,600	$363,600
95. CWS: Addison Reed, rhp	$358,200	$358,200
96. Mil: Tyler Thornburg, rhp	$351,900	$351,900
97. ChC: Micah Gibbs, c	$350,000	$346,500
98. TB: Ryan Brett, 2b	$341,100	$341,100
99. Sea: Ryne Stanek, rhp	Did Not Sign	$335,700
100. Det: Rob Brantly, c	$330,300	$330,300

Bonuses and estimated slot recommendations by Major League Baseball for the top 100 picks of the 2009 draft. Asterisks indicate bonuses that were part of a major league contract, and crosses signify a two-sport contract, which allows the club to spread the bonus over as many as five years.

FIRST ROUND

Pick. Team: Player, Pos.	Bonus	Slot
1. Was: Stephen Strasburg, rhp	*$7,500,000	$4,000,000
2. Sea: Dustin Ackley, of	*$6,000,000	$3,250,000
3. SD: Donavan Tate, of	+$6,250,000	$3,000,000
4. Pit: Tony Sanchez, c	$2,500,000	$2,750,000
5. Bal: Matt Hobgood, rhp	$2,422,000	$2,520,000
6. SF: Zack Wheeler, rhp	$3,300,000	$2,340,000
7. Atl: Mike Minor, lhp	$2,420,000	$2,178,000
8. Cin: Mike Leake, rhp	$2,270,000	$2,043,000
9. Det: Jacob Turner, rhp	*$4,700,000	$1,962,000
10. Was: Drew Storen, rhp	$1,600,000	$1,863,000
11. Col: Tyler Matzek, lhp	$3,900,000	$1,791,000
12. KC: Aaron Crow, rhp	*$1,500,000	$1,719,000
13. Oak: Grant Green, ss	$2,750,000	$1,656,000
14. Tex: Matt Purke, lhp	Did Not Sign	$1,602,000
15. Cle: Alex White, rhp	$2,250,000	$1,557,000
16. Ari: Bobby Borchering, 3b	$1,800,000	$1,512,000
17. Ari: A.J. Pollock, of	$1,400,000	$1,467,000
18. Fla: Chad James, lhp	$1,700,000	$1,422,000
19. StL: Shelby Miller, rhp	+$2,875,000	$1,386,000
20. Tor: Chad Jenkins, rhp	$1,359,000	$1,359,000
21. Hou: Jiovanni Mier, ss	$1,358,000	$1,332,000
22. Min: Kyle Gibson, rhp	$1,850,000	$1,287,000
23. CWS: Jared Mitchell, of	$1,200,000	$1,260,000
24. LAA: Randal Grichuk, of	$1,242,000	$1,242,000
25. LAA: Mike Trout, of	$1,215,000	$1,215,000
26. Mil: Eric Arnett, rhp	$1,197,000	$1,197,000
27. Sea: Nick Franklin, ss	$1,280,000	$1,161,000
28. Bos: Reymond Fuentes, of	$1,134,000	$1,134,000
29. NYY: Slade Heathcott, of	$2,200,000	$1,116,000
30. TB: LeVon Washington, 2b	Did Not Sign	$1,089,000
31. ChC: Brett Jackson, of	$972,000	$972,000
32. Col: Tim Wheeler, of	$900,000	$954,000

SUPPLEMENTAL FIRST ROUND

Pick. Team: Player, Pos.	Bonus	Slot
33. Sea: Steven Baron, c	$980,000	$936,000
34. Col: Rex Brothers, lhp	$969,000	$918,000
35. Ari: Matt Davidson, 3b	$900,000	$900,000
36. LAD: Aaron Miller, lhp	$889,200	$889,200
37. Tor: James Paxton, lhp	Did Not Sign	$873,000
38. CWS: Josh Phegley, c	$858,600	$858,600
39. Mil: Kentrail Davis, of	$1,200,000	$844,200
40. LAA: Tyler Skaggs, lhp	$1,000,000	$829,800
41. Ari: Chris Owings, ss	$950,000	$815,400
42. LAA: Garrett Richards, rhp	$802,800	$802,800
43. Cin: Brad Boxberger, rhp	$857,000	$789,300
44. Tex: Tanner Scheppers, rhp	$1,250,000	$776,700
45. Ari: Mike Belfiore, lhp	$725,000	$764,100
46. Min: Matt Bashore, lhp	$751,500	$751,500
47. Mil: Kyle Heckathorn, rhp	$776,000	$739,800
48. LAA: Tyler Kehrer, lhp	$728,100	$728,100
49. Pit: Victor Black, rhp	$717,000	$717,300

SECOND ROUND

Pick. Team: Player, Pos.	Bonus	Slot
50. Was: Jeff Kobernus, 2b	$705,500	$705,600
51. Sea: Rich Poythress, 1b	$694,800	$694,800
52. SD: Everett Williams, of	$775,000	$684,000
53. Pit: Brooks Pounders, rhp	$670,000	$674,100
54. Bal: Mychal Givens, ss	$800,000	$663,300
55. SF: Tommy Joseph, c	$712,500	$653,400
56. LAD: Blake Smith, of	$643,500	$643,500
57. Cin: Billy Hamilton, ss	+$623,600	$634,500
58. Det: Andrew Oliver, lhp	$1,495,000	$624,600
59. Col: Nolan Arenado, 3b	$625,000	$614,700
60. Ari: Eric Smith, rhp	$605,700	$605,700
61. CWS: Trayce Thompson, of	$625,000	$596,700
62. Tex: Tommy Mendonca, 3b	$587,700	$587,700
63. Cle: Jason Kipnis, of	$575,000	$579,600
64. Ari: Marc Krauss, of	$550,000	$570,600
65. LAD: Garrett Gould, rhp	$900,000	$562,500
66. Fla: Bryan Berglund, rhp	$572,500	$554,400
67. StL: Robert Stock, c	$525,000	$545,400
68. Tor: Jake Eliopoulos, lhp	Did Not Sign	$537,300
69. Hou: Tanner Bushue, rhp	$530,000	$530,100
70. Min: Billy Bullock, rhp	$522,000	$522,000
71. CWS: David Holmberg, lhp	$514,000	$514,800
72. NYM: Steve Matz, lhp	$895,000	$506,700
73. Mil: Max Walla, of	$499,000	$499,500
74. Mil: Cameron Garfield, c	$492,200	$492,300
75. Phi: Kelly Dugan, of	$485,000	$485,100
76. NYY: J.R. Murphy, c	$1,250,000	$477,900
77. Bos: Alex Wilson, rhp	$470,700	$470,700
78. TB: Kenny Diekroeger, ss	Did Not Sign	$463,500
79. ChC: D.J. LeMahieu, 2b	$508,000	$457,200
80. LAA: Pat Corbin, lhp	$450,000	$450,000

THIRD ROUND

Pick. Team: Player, Pos.	Bonus	Slot
81. Was: Trevor Holder, rhp	$200,000	$443,700
82. Sea: Kyle Seager, 2b	$436,500	$436,500
83. SD: Jerry Sullivan, rhp	$430,200	$430,200
84. Pit: Evan Chambers, of	$423,900	$423,900
85. Bal: Tyler Townsend, 1b	$417,600	$417,600
86. SF: Chris Dominguez, 3b	$411,300	$411,300
87. Atl: David Hale, rhp	$405,000	$405,000
88. Cin: Donnie Joseph, lhp	$398,000	$398,700
89. Det: Wade Gaynor, 3b	$392,400	$392,400
90. Col: Ben Paulsen, 1b	$391,000	$387,000
91. KC: Wil Myers, c/3b	$2,000,000	$380,700
92. Oak: Justin Marks, lhp	$375,300	$375,300
93. Tex: Robbie Erlin, lhp	$425,000	$369,000
94. Cle: Joe Gardner, rhp	$363,000	$363,600
95. Ari: Keon Broxton, of	$358,000	$358,200
96. LAD: Brett Wallach, rhp	$351,900	$351,900
97. Fla: Marquise Cooper, of	$345,000	$346,500
98. StL: Joe Kelly, rhp	$341,000	$341,100
99. Tor: Jake Barrett, rhp	Did Not Sign	$335,700
100. Hou: Telvin Nash, of	$330,300	$330,300

COLLEGE TOP 100

Rank	Player	Position	B-T	Ht.	Wt.	College	Last Drafted
1.	Mark Appel	RHP	R-R	6-5	190	Stanford	Tigers '09 (15)
2.	Deven Marrero	SS	R-R	6-1	194	Arizona State	Reds '09 (17)
3.	Mike Zunino	C	R-R	6-2	215	Florida	Athletics '09 (29)
4.	Chris Beck	RHP	R-R	6-3	220	Georgia Southern	Indians '09 (35)
5.	Kevin Gausman	RHP	L-R	6-4	185	Louisiana State	Dodgers '10 (6)
6.	Brian Johnson	LHP/1B	L-L	6-3	225	Florida	Dodgers '09 (27)
7.	Victor Roache	OF	R-R	6-1	225	Georgia Southern	Tigers '09 (25)
8.	Marcus Stroman	RHP	R-R	5-9	185	Duke	Nationals '09 (18)
9.	Michael Wacha	RHP	R-R	6-6	200	Texas A&M	Never
10.	Travis Jankowski	OF	L-R	6-3	190	Stony Brook	Never
11.	Nolan Sanburn	RHP	R-R	6-0	185	Arkansas	Tigers '10 (34)
12.	Josh Elander	C	R-R	6-1	215	Texas Christian	Nationals '09 (37)
13.	Richie Shaffer	1B	R-R	6-3	205	Clemson	Dodgers '09 (25)
14.	Stephen Piscotty	3B	R-R	6-3	195	Stanford	Dodgers '09 (45)
15.	Kyle Zimmer	RHP	R-R	6-3	210	San Francisco	Never
16.	Jake Barrett	RHP	R-R	6-3	220	Arizona State	Blue Jays '09 (3)
17.	Kenny Diekroeger	SS	R-R	6-2	200	Stanford	Rays '09 (2)
18.	Tyler Naquin	OF	L-R	6-2	170	Texas A&M	Orioles '09 (33)
19.	Lex Rutledge	LHP	L-L	6-2	205	Samford	Brewers '09 (26)
20.	Brady Rodgers	RHP	R-R	6-2	175	Arizona State	Brewers '09 (39)
21.	J.T. Chargois	RHP	B-R	6-3	200	Rice	Never
22.	Andrew Heaney	LHP	L-L	6-2	174	Oklahoma State	Rays '09 (24)
23.	Josh Conway	RHP	R-R	6-1	175	Coastal Carolina	Braves '09 (42)
24.	Adam Brett Walker	OF/1B	R-R	6-5	225	Jacksonville	Never
25.	Pat Light	RHP	R-R	6-6	200	Monmouth	Twins '09 (28)
26.	Stephen Johnson	RHP	R-R	6-4	190	St. Edward's (Texas)	Never
27.	Matt Koch	RHP	L-R	6-3	205	Louisville	Red Sox '09 (37)
28.	Nolan Fontana	SS	L-R	5-11	190	Florida	Never
29.	Tom Murphy	C	R-R	6-1	200	Buffalo	Never
30.	Branden Kline	RHP	R-R	6-3	190	Virginia	Red Sox '09 (6)
31.	Brett Mooneyham	LHP	L-L	6-5	235	Stanford	Nationals '11 (38)
32.	Brandon Thomas	OF	B-R	6-3	202	Georgia Tech	Rockies '09 (37)
33.	James Ramsey	OF	L-R	6-0	190	Florida State	Twins '11 (22)
34.	Martin Agosto	RHP	R-R	6-1	160	St. Mary's	Never
35.	Chris Taylor	SS	R-R	6-0	170	Virginia	Never
36.	Tony Renda	2B	R-R	5-8	173	California	Dodgers '09 (42)
37.	Matt Reynolds	3B/SS	R-R	6-1	200	Arkansas	Never
38.	Hoby Milner	LHP	L-L	6-2	165	Texas	Nationals '09 (44)
39.	Alex Wood	LHP	R-L	6-4	216	Georgia	Never
40.	D.J. Baxendale	RHP	R-R	6-2	190	Arkansas	Never
41.	Kevin Brady	RHP	L-R	6-3	220	Clemson	Indians '11 (17)
42.	Hudson Randall	RHP	R-R	6-3	185	Florida	Royals '09 (46)
43.	Sam Stafford	LHP	L-L	6-4	190	Texas	Yankees '11 (2)
44.	Peter O'Brien	C	R-R	6-5	225	Miami	Rockies '11 (3)
45.	Buck Farmer	RHP	L-R	6-3	220	Georgia Tech	Braves '09 (46)
46.	Kevin Plawecki	C	R-R	6-1	215	Purdue	Never
47.	Patrick Wisdom	3B	R-R	6-2	210	St. Mary's	Never
48.	Kyle Hansen	RHP	R-R	6-8	215	St. John's	Brewers '09 (40)
49.	Mitch Haniger	OF	R-R	6-2	215	Cal Poly	Mets '09 (31)
50.	Austin Maddox	RHP/1B	R-R	6-3	225	Florida	Rays '09 (37)

Rank	Player	Position	B-T	Ht.	Wt.	College	Last Drafted
51.	Matt Price	RHP	R-R	6-2	215	South Carolina	Diamondbacks '11 (6)
52.	Ian Gardeck	RHP	R-R	6-2	225	Alabama	White Sox '11 (8)
53.	Jon Gray	RHP	R-R	6-4	239	Oklahoma	Yankees '11 (10)
54.	Preston Tucker	OF	L-L	6-0	215	Florida	Rockies '11 (16)
55.	Tyler Gaffney	OF	R-R	6-1	216	Stanford	Never
56.	Justin Jones	LHP	L-L	6-2	188	California	White Sox '09 (7)
57.	Jerad Grundy	LHP	L-L	6-0	180	Kentucky	Marlins '11 (42)
58.	Michael Ratterree	OF	R-R	6-1	200	Rice	Nationals '09 (45)
59.	Jeremy Baltz	OF	R-R	6-3	205	St. John's	Yankees '09 (45)
60.	Jason Coats	OF	R-R	6-2	200	Texas Christian	Orioles '11 (12)
61.	Jacob Lamb	3B	L-R	6-3	210	Washington	Pirates '09 (38)
62.	Tim Cooney	LHP	L-L	6-3	195	Wake Forest	Never
63.	Dylan Floro	RHP	L-R	6-2	180	Cal State Fullerton	Rays '09 (20)
64.	Joey DeMichele	3B	L-R	5-11	185	Arizona State	Never
65.	Dane Phillips	C	L-R	6-1	192	Oklahoma City	Mariners '09 (49)
66.	Matt Carasiti	RHP	R-R	6-3	200	St. John's	Rangers '09 (36)
67.	Mason Melotakis	LHP	R-L	6-3	205	Northwestern State	Never
68.	Christian Walker	1B	R-R	6-0	220	South Carolina	Dodgers '09 (49)
69.	Luke Bard	RHP	R-R	6-2	191	Georgia Tech	Red Sox '09 (16)
70.	Sam Selman	LHP	R-L	6-3	185	Vanderbilt	Angels '09 (14)
71.	Dan Langfield	RHP	R-R	6-2	196	Memphis	Never
72.	Barrett Barnes	OF/1B	R-R	6-1	210	Texas Tech	Never
73.	Justin Amlung	RHP	R-R	6-0	174	Louisville	Reds '11 (39)
74.	Scott Firth	RHP	R-R	6-0	165	Clemson	Orioles '09 (36)
75.	Carlos Escobar	C	R-R	6-3	200	Nevada	Astros '09 (41)
76.	Ronnie Freeman	C	R-R	6-1	190	Kennesaw State	Never
77.	Cody Stubbs	1B	L-R	6-4	225	North Carolina	Nationals '11 (14)
78.	Pat Stover	OF	R-R	6-4	215	Santa Clara	Athletics '09 (7)
79.	Zack Jones	RHP	R-R	6-1	180	San Jose State	Never
80.	Anthony Bazzani	RHP	R-R	6-4	210	Eastern Kentucky	Never
81.	Pierce Johnson	RHP	R-R	6-3	180	Missouri State	Rays '09 (15)
82.	Kris Hall	RHP	R-R	6-3	215	Lee (Tenn.)	Never
83.	Cameron Perkins	3B	R-R	6-5	200	Purdue	Mariners '09 (43)
84.	R.J. Alvarez	RHP	R-R	6-1	180	Florida Atlantic	Never
85.	Spencer Kieboom	C	R-R	6-0	220	Clemson	Never
86.	Eddie Butler	RHP	R-R	6-2	165	Radford	Never
87.	Jake Stewart	OF	R-R	6-2	190	Stanford	Phillies '09 (14)
88.	Kyle Wren	OF	L-L	5-9	158	Georgia Tech	Never
89.	Justin Gonzalez	SS	R-R	6-2	200	Florida State	Astros '09 (46)
90.	Kyle Farmer	SS	R-R	6-0	191	Georgia	Never
91.	Daniel Ponce de Leon	RHP	R-R	6-4	182	Cypress (Calif.) JC	Rays '10 (24)
92.	Matt Duffy	SS	R-R	6-2	170	Long Beach State	Never
93.	Micah Johnson	2B	L-R	5-11	190	Indiana	Never
94.	Ronnie Richardson	OF	B-R	5-7	175	Central Florida	Cubs '11 (31)
95.	Trey Lang	RHP	R-R	6-3	205	Gateway (Ariz.) JC	Never
96.	Adrian Sampson	RHP	R-R	6-3	195	Bellevue (Wash.) JC	Marlins '11 (16)
97.	Stephen Perez	SS	B-R	5-11	184	Miami	Reds '09 (18)
98.	Andrew Aplin	OF	L-L	5-11	187	Arizona State	Yankees '09 (33)
99.	Mike Yastrzemski	OF	L-L	6-0	180	Vanderbilt	Red Sox '09 (36)
100.	L.J. Mazzilli	SS/2B	R-R	6-1	190	Connecticut	Never

HIGH SCHOOL TOP 100

Rank.	Player	Position	B/T	Ht.	Wt.	High School	College Commitment
1.	Byron Buxton	OF	R-R	6-2	175	Appling County HS, Baxley, Ga.	Georgia
2.	Lucas Giolito	RHP	R-R	6-6	230	Harvard-Westlake HS, Studio City, Calif.	UCLA
3.	David Dahl	OF	L-R	6-2	185	Oak Mountain HS, Birmingham	Auburn
4.	Walker Weickel	RHP	R-R	6-6	205	Olympia HS, Orlando	Miami
5.	Stryker Trahan	C	L-R	6-1	220	Acadiana HS, Lafayette, La.	Mississippi
6.	Matt Smoral	LHP	L-L	6-8	225	Solon (Ohio) HS	North Carolina
7.	Max Fried	LHP	L-L	6-4	170	Harvard-Westlake HS, Studio City, Calif.	UCLA
8.	Gavin Cecchini	SS	R-R	6-2	185	Barbe HS, Lake Charles, La.	Mississippi
9.	Lance McCullers Jr.	RHP	R-R	6-2	195	Jesuit HS, Tampa	Florida
10.	Albert Almora	OF	R-R	6-2	170	Mater Academy, Hialeah Gardens, Fla.	Miami
11.	Carlos Correa	SS	R-R	6-4	190	P.R. Baseball Academy, Gurabo, P.R.	Miami
12.	Joey Gallo	1B/RHP	L-R	6-5	205	Bishop Gorman HS, Las Vegas	Louisiana State
13.	Trey Williams	3B	R-R	6-2	205	Valencia HS, Santa Clarita, Calif.	Pepperdine
14.	Mitchell Traver	RHP	R-R	6-7	235	Houston Christian HS	Texas Christian
15.	Courtney Hawkins	OF/RHP	R-R	6-3	215	Carroll HS, Corpus Christi, Texas	Texas
16.	Lucas Sims	RHP	R-R	6-2	195	Brookwood HS, Snellville, Ga.	Clemson
17.	Duane Underwood	RHP	R-R	6-2	205	Pope HS, Marietta, Ga.	Georgia
18.	Lewis Brinson	OF	R-R	6-4	185	Coral Springs (Fla.) HS	Florida
19.	Addison Russell	SS	R-R	6-1	205	Pace (Fla.) HS	Auburn
20.	Freddy Avis	RHP	L-R	6-2	180	Menlo School, Atherton, Calif.	Stanford
21.	Hunter Virant	LHP	R-L	6-3	175	Camarillo (Calif.) HS	UCLA
22.	Ty Hensley	RHP	B-R	6-5	220	Santa Fe HS, Edmond, Okla.	Mississippi
23.	Rio Ruiz	3B	L-R	6-2	195	Bishop Amat HS, La Puente, Calif.	Southern California
24.	Nick Williams	OF	L-L	6-3	190	Ball HS, Galveston, Texas	Texas
25.	Nathan Kirby	LHP	L-L	6-2	185	James River HS, Midlothian, Va.	Virginia
26.	Jesse Winker	OF	L-L	6-3	200	Olympia HS, Orlando	Florida
27.	Nick Travieso	RHP	R-R	6-3	205	Archbishop McCarthy HS, SW Ranches, Fla.	Miami
28.	Carson Kelly	3B-RHP	R-R	6-2	200	Westview HS, Portland	Oregon
29.	Tanner Rahier	SS	R-R	6-2	205	Palm Desert (Calif.) HS	San Diego
30.	Clint Coulter	C	R-R	6-3	200	Union HS, Camas, Wash.	Arizona State
31.	Corey Seager	SS	L-R	6-4	195	NW Cabarrus HS, Concord, N.C.	South Carolina
32.	Rhett Wiseman	OF	L-R	6-1	195	BB&N HS, Cambridge, Mass.	Vanderbilt
33.	Jameis Winston	OF/RHP	B-R	6-4	195	Hueytown (Ala.) HS	Florida State (FB)
34.	Zach Eflin	RHP	R-R	6-5	200	Hagerty HS, Oviedo, Fla.	Central Florida
35.	D.J. Davis	OF	L-R	5-11	170	Stone HS, Wiggins, Miss.	Meridian (Miss.) JC
36.	Daniel Robertson	3B	R-R	6-0	180	Upland (Calif.) HS	UCLA
37.	Daniel Starwalt	RHP	R-R	6-3	195	Granite Hills HS, El Cajon, Calif.	Stanford
38.	Taylore Cherry	RHP	R-R	6-9	260	Butler HS, Vandalia, Ohio	North Carolina
39.	Skye Bolt	OF	B-R	6-3	175	Holy Innocents' Episcopal HS, Atlanta	North Carolina
40.	Cody Poteet	RHP	R-R	6-1	180	Christian HS, El Cajon, Calif.	UCLA
41.	Austin Dean	3B	R-R	6-1	185	Klein Collins HS, Klein, Texas	Texas
42.	Ty Buttrey	RHP	L-R	6-5	205	Providence HS, Charlotte	Arkansas
43.	Carson Fulmer	RHP	R-R	6-1	190	All Saints' Academy, Winter Haven, Fla.	Vanderbilt
44.	Anthony Alford	OF	R-R	6-2	210	Petal (Miss.) HS	Uncommitted (FB)
45.	Keon Barnum	1B	L-L	6-4	225	King HS, Tampa	Miami
46.	Teddy Stankiewicz	RHP	R-R	6-4	200	SW Christian HS, Fort Worth, Texas	Arkansas
47.	Shane Watson	RHP	B-R	6-4	200	Lakewood (Calif.) HS	Southern California
48.	Kolby Copeland	OF	L-R	6-2	195	Parkway HS, Bossier City, La.	Uncommitted
49.	Jamie Callahan	RHP	R-R	6-3	200	Dillon (S.C.) HS	South Carolina
50.	Alex Bregman	SS/C	R-R	5-11	185	Albuquerque (N.M.) Academy	Louisiana State

Rank. Player	Position	B/T	Ht.	Wt.	High School	College Commitment
51. Chase De Jong	RHP	L-R	6-4	190	Wilson HS, Long Beach, Calif.	Southern California
52. Jesmuel Valentin Diaz	SS	B-R	5-10	175	P.R. Baseball Academy, Gurabo, P.R.	Louisiana State
53. Wyatt Mathisen	C	R-R	6-1	190	Calallen HS, Corpus Christi, Texas	Texas
54. Ryan McNeil	RHP	R-R	6-3	210	Nipomo (Calif.) HS	Long Beach State
55. Mitch Nay	3B	R-R	6-3	195	Hamilton HS, Chandler, Ariz.	Arizona State
56. D'vone McClure	OF	R-R	6-3	190	Jacksonville (Ark.) HS	Arkansas
57. Joe DeCarlo	3B	R-R	6-1	205	Garnet Valley HS, Glen Mills, Pa.	Georgia
58. Fernelys Sanchez	OF	B-R	6-4	200	Washington HS, New York	Oklahoma
59. Mikey White	SS/OF	R-R	6-1	190	Spain Park HS, Hoover, Ala.	Alabama
60. Joe Munoz	SS	R-R	6-3	195	Los Altos (Calif.) HS	San Diego State
61. Vahn Bozoian	OF	R-R	6-5	205	Ayala HS, Chino Hills, Calif.	Southern California
62. Clate Schmidt	RHP	B-R	6-2	175	Allatoona HS, Acworth, Ga.	Clemson
63. Tyrone Taylor	OF	R-R	6-1	180	Torrance (Calif.) HS	Cal State Fullerton
64. Xavier Turner	3B	R-R	6-2	210	Sandusky (Ohio) HS	Vanderbilt
65. Kieran Lovegrove	RHP	R-R	6-4	180	Mission Viejo (Calif.) HS	Arizona State
66. C.J. Saylor	C	R-R	5-10	180	South Hills HS, West Covina, Calif.	San Diego State
67. Jamie Jarmon	OF	R-R	6-3	205	Indian River HS, Dagsboro, Del.	South Carolina
68. Spencer Edwards	SS/OF	R-R	6-0	180	Rockwall (Texas) HS	Texas
69. David Thompson	3B	R-R	6-1	195	Westminster Christian HS, Palmetto Bay, Fla.	Miami
70. Cole Irvin	LHP	L-L	6-4	175	Servite HS, Anaheim	Oregon
71. Trey Killian	RHP	R-R	6-4	180	Mountain Home (Ark.) HS	Arkansas
72. Felipe Perez	RHP	R-R	6-3	190	Farimont Prep, Anaheim	UCLA
73. Tony Blanford	RHP	R-R	6-3	180	Boulder Creek HS, Anthem, Ariz.	Arizona State
74. Tyler Pike	LHP	L-L	6-1	175	Winter Haven (Fla.) HS	Florida State
75. Willie Ethington	RHP	R-R	6-4	200	Mountain View HS, Mesa, Ariz.	Arizona State
76. Kevin Maxey	OF	R-R	6-4	190	Long Beach (Calif.) Polytechnic HS	Uncommitted
77. Mitchell Brown	RHP	R-R	6-1	200	Rochester (Minn.) Century HS	San Diego
78. Vincent Jackson	OF	L-L	6-4	195	Luella HS, Locust Grove, Ga.	Tennessee
79. Brandon Lopez	SS/RHP	R-R	6-2	180	American Heritage HS, Plantation, Fla.	Miami
80. Andrew Pullin	OF	L-R	6-0	185	Centralia (Wash.) HS	Oregon
81. Avery Romero	SS	R-R	6-0	195	Menendez HS, Saint Augustine, Fla.	Florida
82. Edwin Diaz	RHP	R-R	6-2	165	Naguabo (P.R.) HS	Uncommitted
83. Ryan Burr	RHP	R-R	6-4	210	Highlands Ranch (Colo.) HS	Arizona State
84. Josh Henderson	OF	L-L	6-0	185	First Baptist Christian HS, Suffolk, Va.	Liberty
85. Ty Moore	OF	L-R	6-0	190	Mater Dei HS, Santa Ana, Calif.	UCLA
86. Jake Thompson	RHP/1B	R-R	6-4	235	Rockwall-Heath HS, Heath, Texas	Texas Christian
87. Matthew Crownover	LHP	R/L	6-0	190	Ringgold (Ga.) HS	Clemson
88. Kayden Porter	RHP/1B	R-R	6-5	250	Spanish Fork (Utah) HS	North Carolina
89. Paul Blackburn	RHP	R-R	6-1	165	Heritage HS, Brentwood, Calif.	Arizona State
90. Cal Becker	RHP	R-R	6-1	195	Redwood HS, Visalia, Calif.	California
91. Dylan LaVelle	3B	R-R	6-2	185	Lake Stevens (Wash.) HS	Oregon State
92. Austin Aune	SS	L-R	6-2	190	Argyle (Texas) HS	Texas Christian
93. Bralin Jackson	OF	R-L	6-0	180	Raytown (Mo.) South HS	Missouri
94. Taylor Jones	RHP	R-R	6-7	185	Kentwood HS, Kent, Wash.	Gonzaga
95. Richie Martin	SS	R-R	5-10	175	Bloomingdale HS, Valrico, Fla.	Florida
96. Kevin Ross	3B	R-R	6-1	190	Niles West HS, Skokie, Ill.	Michigan
97. Bryan de la Rosa	C	R-R	5-9	180	Arlington Country Day, Jacksonville	Florida State
98. Austin Fairchild	LHP	R/L	6-1	175	St. Thomas HS, Houston	Texas Christian
99. Justin Morhardt	C	B-R	6-3	205	Gilbert School, Winsted, Conn.	Oral Roberts
100. Jacob Scavuzzo	OF	R-R	6-4	185	Villa Park (Calif.) HS	Uncommitted

FROM EVERY MINOR LEAGUE

As a complement to the organization prospect rankings, Baseball America also ranks prospects in all the minor leagues at the end of their seasons. Like the organization lists, they place more weight on potential than performance and should not be regarded as all-star teams. Unlike the organization lists, which are from more of a scouting perspective, the minor league lists reflect the views of minor league managers, who give more weight to what a player does on the field now. We think both perspectives are useful, so we give you both, even though they don't always match up. For a player to qualify for a league prospect list, he must have spent at least one-third of the season in a league. Also unlike the organization lists, players can make the league lists even if they exhausted their rookie eligibility during the 2010 season.

TRIPLE-A

INTERNATIONAL LEAGUE
1. Matt Moore, lhp, Durham (Rays)
2. Julio Teheran, rhp, Gwinnett (Braves)
3. Devin Mesoraco, c, Louisville (Reds)
4. Desmond Jennings, of, Durham (Rays)
5. Jesus Montero, c, Scranton/Wilkes-Barre (Yankees)
6. Domonic Brown, of, Lehigh Valley (Phillies)
7. Jason Kipnis, 2b, Columbus (Indians)
8. Mike Minor, lhp, Gwinnett (Braves)
9. Brad Peacock, rhp, Syracuse (Nationals)
10. Lonnie Chisenhall, 3b, Columbus (Indians)
11. Zack Cozart, ss, Louisville (Reds)
12. Dayan Viciedo, of/1b, Charlotte (White Sox)
13. Yonder Alonso, 1b/of, Louisville (Reds)
14. Ryan Lavarnway, c, Pawtucket (Red Sox)
15. Vance Worley, rhp, Lehigh Valley (Phillies)
16. Josh Reddick, of, Pawtucket (Red Sox)
17. Brandon Guyer, of, Durham (Rays)
18. Alex Presley, of, Indianapolis (Pirates)
19. Alex Cobb, rhp, Durham (Rays)
20. Todd Frazier, of/3b/1b, Louisville (Reds)

PACIFIC COAST LEAGUE
1. Brett Lawrie, 3b, Las Vegas (Blue Jays)
2. Dustin Ackley, 2b, Tacoma (Mariners)
3. Mike Moustakas, 3b, Omaha (Royals)
4. Brandon Belt, 1b/of, Fresno (Giants)
5. Anthony Rizzo, 1b, Tucson (Padres)
6. Dee Gordon, ss, Albuquerque (Dodgers)
7. Mike Montgomery, lhp, Omaha (Royals)
8. Brett Jackson, of, Iowa (Cubs)
9. Jordan Lyles, rhp, Oklahoma City (Astros)
10. Rex Brothers, lhp, Colorado Springs (Rockies)
11. Jemile Weeks, 2b, Sacramento (Athletics)
12. Martin Perez, lhp, Round Rock (Rangers)
13. Leonys Martin, of, Round Rock (Rangers)
14. Matt Dominguez, 3b, New Orleans (Marlins)
15. Eric Thames, of, Las Vegas (Blue Jays)
16. Johnny Giavotella, 2b, Omaha (Royals)
17. Charlie Blackmon, of, Colorado Springs (Rockies)
18. Logan Schafer, of, Nashville (Brewers)
19. Alex Liddi, 3b, Tacoma (Mariners)
20. Collin Cowgill, of, Reno (Diamondbacks)

DOUBLE-A

EASTERN LEAGUE
1. Bryce Harper, of, Harrisburg (Nationals)
2. Travis d'Arnaud, c, New Hampshire (Blue Jays)
3. Anthony Gose, of, New Hampshire (Blue Jays)
4. Brad Peacock, rhp, Harrisburg (Nationals)
5. Jacob Turner, rhp, Erie (Tigers)
6. Manny Banuelos, lhp, Trenton (Yankees)
7. Starling Marte, of, Altoona (Pirates)
8. Will Middlebrooks, 3b, Portland (Red Sox)
9. Dellin Betances, rhp, Trenton (Yankees)
10. Henderson Alvarez, rhp, New Hampshire (Blue Jays)
11. Eric Surkamp, lhp, Richmond (Giants)
12. Derek Norris, c, Harrisburg (Nationals)
13. Jeurys Familia, rhp, Binghamton (Mets)
14. Francisco Peguero, of, Richmond (Giants)
15. Ryan Lavarnway, c, Portland (Red Sox)
16. Francisco Martinez, 3b, Erie (Tigers)
17. Austin Romine, c, Trenton (Yankees)
18. Chih-Hsien Chiang, of, Portland (Red Sox)
19. Adeiny Hechavarria, ss, New Hampshire (Blue Jays)
20. Kyle McPherson, rhp, Altoona (Pirates)

SOUTHERN LEAGUE
1. Matt Moore, lhp, Montgomery (Rays)
2. Tyler Skaggs, lhp, Mobile (Diamondbacks)
3. Paul Goldschmidt, 1b, Mobile (Diamondbacks)
4. Brett Jackson, of, Tennessee (Cubs)
5. Jarrod Parker, rhp, Mobile (Diamondbacks)
6. Arodys Vizcaino, rhp, Mississippi (Braves)
7. Randall Delgado, rhp, Mississippi (Braves)
8. Wily Peralta, rhp, Huntsville (Brewers)
9. Yasmani Grandal, c, Carolina (Reds)
10. Allen Webster, rhp, Chattanooga (Dodgers)
11. Chris Archer, rhp, Montgomery (Rays)
12. Alfredo Silverio, of, Chattanooga (Dodgers)
13. Nate Eovaldi, rhp, Chattanooga (Dodgers)
14. A.J. Pollock, of, Mobile (Diamondbacks)
15. Vinnie Catricala, of/3b, Jackson (Mariners)
16. Patrick Corbin, lhp, Mobile (Diamondbacks)
17. Tyler Pastornicky, ss, Mississippi (Braves)
18. Chris Withrow, rhp, Chattanooga (Dodgers)
19. Brett Oberholtzer, lhp, Mississippi (Braves)
20. Shawn Tolleson, rhp, Chattanooga (Dodgers)

TEXAS LEAGUE
1. Mike Trout, of, Arkansas (Angels)
2. Shelby Miller, rhp, Springfield (Cardinals)
3. Garrett Richards, rhp, Arkansas (Angels)
4. Martin Perez, lhp Frisco (Rangers)
5. Jake Odorizzi, rhp, Northwest Arkansas (Royals)
6. Wilin Rosario, c, Tulsa (Rockies)
7. Casey Kelly, rhp, San Antonio (Padres)
8. Robbie Erlin, lhp, Frisco (Rangers)/San Antonio (Padres)
9. Jedd Gyorko, 3b, San Antonio (Padres)
10. James Darnell, 3b, San Antonio (Padres)
11. Grant Green, ss, Midland (Athletics)
12. Tim Wheeler, of, Tulsa (Rockies)
13. Wil Myers, of, Northwest Arkansas (Royals)
14. Zack Cox, 3b, Springfield (Cardinals)
15. Chris Dwyer, lhp Northwest Arkansas (Royals)

16. Kelvin Herrera, rhp, Northwest Arkansas (Royals)
17. Salvador Perez, c, Northwest Arkansas (Royals)
18. Joe Wieland, rhp, Frisco (Rangers)/San Antonio (Padres)
19. Matt Adams, 1b, Springfield (Cardinals)
20. J.D. Martinez, of, Corpus Christi (Astros)

HIGH CLASS A

CALIFORNIA LEAGUE
1. Tyler Skaggs, lhp, Visalia (Diamondbacks)
2. Jedd Gyorko, 3b, Lake Elsinore (Padres)
3. Gary Brown, of, San Jose (Giants)
4. Zack Wheeler, rhp, San Jose (Giants)
5. Jonathan Singleton, 1b, Lancaster (Astros)
6. Nolan Arenado, 3b, Modesto (Rockies)
7. Michael Choice, of, Stockton (Athletics)
8. Allen Webster, rhp, Rancho Cucamonga (Dodgers)
9. Chad Bettis, rhp, Modesto (Rockies)
10. Yasmani Grandal, c, Bakersfield (Reds)
11. Tommy Joseph, c, San Jose (Giants)
12. Nick Franklin, ss/2b, High Desert (Mariners)
13. Jean Segura, ss, Inland Empire (Angels)
14. Reymond Fuentes, of, Lake Elsinore (Padres)
15. Jose Altuve, 2b, Lancaster (Astros)
16. Matt Davidson, 1b/3b, Visalia (Diamondbacks)
17. Chris Dominguez, 3b, San Jose (Giants)
18. Johnny Hellweg, rhp, Inland Empire (Angels)
19. Chris Owings, ss, Visalia (Diamondbacks)
20. Kent Matthes, of, Modesto (Rockies)

CAROLINA LEAGUE
1. Manny Machado, ss, Frederick (Orioles)
2. Drew Pomeranz, lhp, Kinston (Indians)
3. Mike Olt, 3b, Myrtle Beach (Rangers)
4. Andrelton Simmons, ss, Lynchburg (Braves)
5. Robbie Erlin, lhp, Myrtle Beach (Rangers)
6. Jonathan Schoop, 2b/ss, Frederick (Orioles)
7. Jake Odorizzi, rhp, Wilmington (Royals)
8. Bryce Brentz, of, Salem (Red Sox)
9. Joe Wieland, lhp, Myrtle Beach (Rangers)
10. Christian Bethancourt, c, Lynchburg (Braves)
11. Zeke Spruill, rhp, Lynchburg (Braves)
12. Destin Hood, of, Potomac (Nationals)
13. Sammy Solis, lhp, Potomac (Nationals)
14. Anthony Ranaudo, rhp, Salem (Red Sox)
15. Bobby Bundy, rhp, Frederick (Orioles)
16. Leury Garcia, ss, Myrtle Beach (Rangers)
17. Robbie Ross, lhp, Myrtle Beach (Rangers)
18. Justin Grimm, rhp, Myrtle Beach (Rangers)
19. Miguel de los Santos, lhp, Myrtle Beach (Rangers)
20. Tyler Saladino, ss, Winston-Salem (White Sox)

FLORIDA STATE LEAGUE
1. Shelby Miller, rhp, Palm Beach (Cardinals)
2. Matt Harvey, rhp, St. Lucie (Mets)
3. Hak-Ju Lee, ss, Charlotte (Rays)
4. Trevor May, rhp, Clearwater (Phillies)
5. Alex Colome, rhp, Charlotte (Rays)
6. Carlos Martinez, rhp, Palm Beach (Cardinals)
7. Jonathan Singleton, 1b/of, Clearwater (Phillies)
8. Matt Szczur, of, Daytona (Cubs)
9. Jarred Cosart, rhp, Clearwater (Phillies)
10. A.J. Jimenez, c, Dunedin (Blue Jays)
11. Zack Cox, 3b, Palm Beach (Cardinals)
12. Sebastian Valle, c, Clearwater (Phillies)

13. Drew Hutchison, rhp, Dunedin (Blue Jays)
14. Tyler Thornburg, rhp, Brevard County (Brewers)
15. Oswaldo Arcia, of, Fort Myers (Twins)
16. Drew Smyly, lhp, Lakeland (Tigers)
17. Deck McGuire, rhp, Dunedin (Blue Jays)
18. Aaron Hicks, of, Fort Myers (Twins)
19. Brody Colvin, rhp, Clearwater (Phillies)
20. Wilmer Flores, ss, St. Lucie (Mets)

LOW CLASS A

MIDWEST LEAGUE
1. Taijuan Walker, rhp Clinton (Mariners)
2. Billy Hamilton, ss, Dayton (Reds)
3. Jake Marisnick, of, Lansing (Blue Jays)
4. Nick Castellanos, 3b, West Michigan (Tigers)
5. Rymer Liriano, of, Fort Wayne (Padres)
6. Oscar Taveras, of, Quad Cities (Cardinals)
7. Zach Lee, rhp Great Lakes (Dodgers)
8. James Paxton, lhp Clinton (Mariners)
9. Matt Szczur, of, Peoria (Cubs)
10. Keyvious Sampson, rhp Fort Wayne (Padres)
11. Cheslor Cuthbert, 3b, Kane County (Royals)
12. Kolten Wong, 2b, Quad Cities (Cardinals)
13. Cory Spangenberg 2b, Fort Wayne (Padres)
14. Drew Hutchison, rhp Lansing (Blue Jays)
15. Enny Romero, lhp Bowling Green (Rays)
16. Daniel Corcino, rhp Dayton (Reds)
17. Garrett Gould, rhp Great Lakes (Dodgers)
18. Tyler Thornburg, rhp Wisconsin (Brewers)
19. Derek Dietrich, ss, Bowling Green (Rays)
20. David Holmberg, lhp South Bend (Diamondbacks)

SOUTH ATLANTIC LEAGUE
1. Bryce Harper, of, Hagerstown (Nationals)
2. Manny Machado, ss, Delmarva (Orioles)
3. Jurickson Profar, ss, Hickory (Rangers)
4. Jameson Taillon, rhp, West Virginia (Pirates)
5. Christian Yelich, of, Greensboro (Marlins)
6. Jesse Biddle, lhp, Lakewood (Phillies)
7. Marcell Ozuna, of, Greensboro (Marlins)
8. Brandon Jacobs, of, Greenville (Red Sox)
9. Jonathan Schoop, ss/3b, Delmarva (Orioles)
10. Xander Bogaerts, ss, Greenville (Red Sox)
11. A.J. Cole, rhp, Hagerstown (Nationals)
12. Kyle Parker, of, Asheville (Rockies)
13. J.T. Realmuto, c, Greensboro (Marlins)
14. Gary Sanchez, c, Charleston (Yankees)
15. Trayce Thompson, of, Kannapolis (White Sox)
16. Bryce Brentz, of, Greenville (Red Sox)
17. Tyler Matzek, lhp, Asheville (Rockies)
18. Domingo Santana, of, Lakewood (Phillies)/Lexington (Astros)
19. Cody Buckel, rhp, Hickory (Rangers)
20. Miles Head, 1b, Greenville (Red Sox)

SHORT-SEASON

NEW YORK-PENN LEAGUE
1. Mason Williams, of, Staten Island (Yankees)
2. Garin Cecchini, 3b, Lowell (Red Sox)
3. Parker Markel, rhp, Hudson Valley (Rays)
4. Maikel Franco, 3b, Williamsport (Phillies)
5. Jose Urena, rhp, Jamestown (Marlins)
6. Cito Culver, ss, Staten Island (Yankees)

7. Tony Wolters, ss, Mahoning Valley (Indians)
8. Tyler Austin, 3b, Staten Island (Yankees)
9. Nick Kingham, rhp, State College (Pirates)
10. Parker Bridwell, rhp, Aberdeen (Orioles)
11. Alex Dickerson, 1b, State College (Pirates)
12. Aaron Westlake, 1b, Connecticut (Tigers)
13. Matt Skole, 3b, Auburn (Nationals)
14. Angelo Gumbs, 2b, Staten Island (Yankees)
15. Glynn Davis, of, Aberdeen (Orioles)
16. Bobby Crocker, of, Vermont (Athletics)
17. Jake Lowery, c/1b, Mahoning Valley (Indians)
18. Danny Muno, ss, Brooklyn (Mets)
19. Branden Pinder, rhp, Staten Island (Yankees)
20. Aaron Altherr, of, Williamsport (Phillies)

NORTHWEST LEAGUE
1. Justin Nicolino, lhp, Vancouver (Blue Jays)
2. Cory Spangenberg, 2b, Eugene (Padres)
3. Jose Campos, rhp, Everett (Mariners)
4. Joe Panik, ss, Salem-Keizer (Giants)
5. Jace Peterson, ss, Eugene (Padres)
6. Matt Andriese, rhp, Eugene (Padres)
7. Rougned Odor, 2b, Spokane (Rangers)
8. Jorge Alfaro, c, Spokane (Rangers)
9. Jesus Galindo, of, Salem-Keizer (Giants)
10. Reggie Golden, of, Boise (Cubs)
11. Jabari Blash, of, Everett (Mariners)
12. Ben Wells, rhp, Boise (Cubs)
13. Matt West, rhp, Spokane (Rangers)
14. Pin-Chieh Chen, of, Boise (Cubs)
15. Kevin Quackenbush, rhp, Eugene (Padres)
16. Donavan Tate, of, Eugene (Padres)
17. Zeke DeVoss, 2b, Boise (Cubs)
18. Will Lamb, lhp, Spokane (Rangers)
19. John Barbato, rhp, Eugene (Padres)
20. Kyle Hendricks, rhp, Spokane (Rangers)

ROOKIE

APPALACHIAN LEAGUE
1. Miguel Sano, 3b/ss, Elizabethton (Twins)
2. Brandon Drury, 3b, Danville (Braves)
3. Tyrell Jenkins, rhp, Johnson City (Cardinals)
4. Noah Syndergaard, rhp, Bluefield (Blue Jays)
5. Eddie Rosario, of, Elizabethton (Twins)
6. Drew Vettleson, of, Princeton (Rays)
7. Jake Hager, ss, Princeton (Rays)
8. J.R. Graham, rhp, Danville (Braves)
9. Felipe Rivero, lhp, Princeton (Rays)
10. Ryan Brett, 2b, Princeton (Rays)
11. Chris Hawkins, of, Bluefield (Blue Jays)
12. Aaron Sanchez, rhp, Bluefield (Blue Jays)
13. Josh Sale, of, Princeton (Rays)
14. Guillermo Pimentel, of, Pulaski (Mariners)
15. Justin O'Conner, c, Princeton (Rays)
16. Jeff Ames, rhp, Princeton (Rays)
17. Madison Boer, rhp, Elizabethton (Twins)
18. Nick Ahmed, ss, Danville (Braves)
19. Jordan Scott, of, Greeneville (Astros)
20. Kevan Smith, c, Bristol (White Sox)

ARIZONA LEAGUE
1. Yoan Alcantara, of, Padres
2. Phillips Castillo, of, Mariners

3. Elvis Araujo, lhp, Indians
4. Clayton Blackburn, rhp, Giants
5. Luigi Rodriguez, of, Indians
6. Marco Hernandez, ss/2b, Cubs
7. Duanel Jones, 3b, Padres
8. Humberto Arteaga, ss, Royals
9. Gioskar Amaya, inf, Cubs
10. Jorge Martinez, ss, Indians
11. Alberth Martinez, of, Padres
12. Jordan Akins, of, Rangers
13. Alex Santana, 3b, Dodgers
14. Jake Sisco, rhp, Indians
15. Gabriel Rosa, 3b, Reds
16. Felix Sterling, rhp, Indians
17. Luis Sardinas, ss, Rangers
18. Joan Gregorio, rhp, Giants
19. D'andre Toney, of, Royals
20. Martin Peguero, ss, Mariners

GULF COAST LEAGUE
1. Dante Bichette Jr., 3b, Yankees
2. Ravel Santana, of, Yankees
3. Luis Heredia, rhp, Pirates
4. Brenny Paulino, rhp, Tigers
5. Jose Osuna, 1b/of, Pirates
6. Raul Alcantara, rhp, Red Sox
7. Jose Vinicio, ss, Red Sox
8. Adonys Cardona, rhp, Blue Jays
9. Claudio Custodio, ss, Yankees
10. Danry Vasquez, of, Tigers
11. Jesus Solorzano, of, Marlins
12. Roderick Bernadina, of, Orioles
13. Blake Snell, lhp, Rays
14. Alen Hanson, ss/2b, Pirates
15. Joe Musgrove, rhp, Blue Jays
16. Ethan Stewart, lhp, Phillies
17. Victor Deleon, rhp, Cardinals
18. Eduardo Rodriguez, lhp, Orioles
19. Austin Brice, rhp, Marlins
20. Rafael Montero, rhp, Mets

PIONEER LEAGUE
1. Trevor Story, ss/3b, Casper (Rockies)
2. Taylor Lindsey, 2b, Orem (Angels)
3. Joc Pederson, of, Ogden (Dodgers)
4. C.J. Cron, 1b, Orem (Angels)
5. Rosell Herrera, ss/3b, Casper (Rockies)
6. Kaleb Cowart, 3b, Orem (Angels)
7. Nick Maronde, lhp, Orem (Angels)
8. Tony Cingrani, lhp, Billings (Reds)
9. Will Swanner, c, Casper (Rockies)
10. Ryan Wright, 2b, Billings (Reds)
11. James Baldwin III, of, Ogden (Dodgers)
12. Sean Buckley, 3b, Billings (Reds)
13. Nick Mutz, rhp, Orem (Angels)
14. Scott Snodgress, lhp, Great Falls (White Sox)
15. David Goforth, rhp, Helena (Brewers)
16. Yadiel Rivera, ss, Helena (Brewers)
17. Kevan Smith, c, Great Falls (White Sox)
18. Danny Winkler, rhp, Casper (Rockies)
19. Kyle Waldrop, of, Billings (Reds)
20. Danny Mateo, 2b/3b, Idaho Falls (Royals)

INDEX

Darnell, James (Padres) 391
Darnell, Logan (Twins) 282
Darrah, Jesse (Diamondbacks) 27
Davidson, Matt (Diamondbacks) 20
Davis, Glynn (Orioles) 57
Davis, Kentrail (Brewers) 264
Davis, Khris (Brewers) 269
Dayton, Grant (Marlins) 248
De Fratus, Justin (Phillies) 341
De Los Santos, Miguel (Rangers) 461
Dean, Matt (Blue Jays) 470
Decker, Jaff (Padres) 390
Deglan, Kellin (Rangers) 459
DeJesus, Ivan Jr. (Dodgers) 236
DeLeon, Jorge (Astros) 186
DeLeon, Victor (Cardinals) 380
Delgado, Dimasther (Braves) 41
Delgado, Randall (Braves) 35
Delmonico, Nicky (Orioles) 53
Demny, Paul (Nationals) 493
Den Dekker, Matt (Mets) 295
DePaula, Jose (Padres) 396
DeShields, Delino Jr. (Astros) 181
DeVoss, Zeke (Cubs) 88
Dickerson, Alex (Pirates) 358
Dickson, Brandon (Cardinals) 378
Dickson, O'Koyea (Dodgers) 237
Dietrich, Derek (Rays) 439
Dodson, Zack (Pirates) 363
Dolis, Rafael (Cubs) 85
Dominguez, Chris (Giants) 409
Dominguez, Matt (Marlins) 243
Donaldson, Josh (Athletics) 330
Doubront, Felix (Red Sox) 72
Doyle, Terry (Twins) 285
Dozier, Brian (Twins) 278
Drake, Oliver (Orioles) 60
Drury, Brandon (Braves) 38
Dunston, Shawon Jr. (Cubs) 93
Duran, Juan (Reds) 124
Duvall, Adam (Giants) 413
Dwyer, Chris (Royals) 198

E

Easterling, Taiwan (Cubs) 93
Eaton, Adam (Diamondbacks) 23
Edgin, Josh (Mets) 299
Eibner, Brett (Royals) 199
Eichhorn, Kevin (Tigers) 172
Eovaldi, Nate (Dodgers) 227
Erickson, Gorman (Dodgers) 237
Erlin, Robbie (Padres) 389
Escobar, Eduardo (White Sox) 102
Esposito, Jason (Orioles) 53
Evans, Phillip (Mets) 298

F

Familia, Jeurys (Mets) 291
Farris, Eric (Brewers) 268
Federowicz, Tim (Dodgers) 230
Fernandez, Jose (Marlins) 243
Field, Tommy (Rockies) 156
Fields, Daniel (Tigers) 172
Fiers, Michael (Brewers) 263
Fisher, Ryan (Marlins) 247
Flaherty, Ryan (Orioles) 53
Fletcher, Brian (Royals) 204
Flores, Ramon (Yankees) 311
Flores, Wilmer (Mets) 294
Flynn, Brian (Tigers) 171
Foltynewicz, Mike (Astros) 182
Franco, Maikel (Phillies) 342

Franklin, Nick (Mariners) 419
Frazier, Parker (Rockies) 156
Frazier, Todd (Reds) 118
Freeman, Sam (Cardinals) 381
Freitas, David (Nationals) 492
Friedrich, Christian (Rockies) 151
Fuentes, Leonardo (Giants) 413
Fuentes, Reymond (Padres) 393
Fulmer, Michael (Mets) 293

G

Gagnon, Drew (Brewers) 267
Galindo, Jesus (Giants) 411
Gallagher, Cameron (Royals) 203
Galvis, Freddy (Phillies) 340
Garcia, Avisail (White Sox) 166
Garcia, Harold (Phillies) 345
Garcia, Jonathan (Dodgers) 231
Garcia, Leury (Rangers) 455
Gardner, Joe (Rockies) 155
Garner, Perci (Phillies) 346
Garrett, Amir (Reds) 121
Gast, John (Cardinals) 376
Gattis, Evan (Braves) 44
Gearrin, Cory (Braves) 45
Gennett, Scooter (Brewers) 260
Gibson, Derrik (Red Sox) 75
Gibson, Kyle (Twins) 277
Gibson, Tyler (Tigers) 169
Gillaspie, Conor (Giants) 407
Gilliam, Rob (Athletics) 330
Gilmartin, Sean (Braves) 36
Gindl, Caleb (Brewers) 263
Goeddel, Tyler (Rays) 441
Goforth, David (Brewers) 265
Golden, Reggie (Cubs) 89
Gomez, Hector (Rockies) 153
Gonzalez, Marwin (Astros) 186
Goodrum, Niko (Twins) 281
Goodwin, Brian (Nationals) 484
Gorski, Darin (Mets) 298
Gose, Anthony (Blue Jays) 467
Gosselin, Phil (Braves) 45
Gould, Garrett (Dodgers) 229
Graham, J.R. (Braves) 39
Grandal, Yasmani (Reds) 116
Gray, Sonny (Athletics) 323
Green, Grant (Athletics) 323
Green, Taylor (Brewers) 261
Green, Tyler (Diamondbacks) 27
Greene, Larry (Phillies) 345
Gregorius, Didi (Reds) 117
Grichuk, Randal (Angels) 217
Griffin, A.J. (Athletics) 327
Grimm, Justin (Rangers) 456
Grossman, Robbie (Pirates) 357
Guerra, Deolis (Twins) 280
Guerrieri, Taylor (Rays) 436
Gumbs, Angelo (Yankees) 311
Gutierrez, Carlos (Twins) 281
Guyer, Brandon (Rays) 438
Guzman, Ronald (Rangers) 455
Gyorko, Jedd (Padres) 388

H

Ha, Jae-Hoon (Cubs) 89
Hagadone, Nick (Indians) 131
Hager, Jake (Rays) 439
Hagerty, Jason (Padres) 394
Hague, Rick (Nationals) 488
Hale, David (Braves) 42
Haley, Trey (Indians) 136

Hall, Brooks (Brewers) 267
Hamilton, Billy (Reds) 115
Hanson, Alen (Pirates) 364
Harper, Bryce (Nationals) 482
Harrison, Travis (Twins) 278
Harrold, Stephen (Giants) 412
Harvey, Matt (Mets) 291
Hassan, Alex (Red Sox) 76
Hatcher, Chris (Marlins) 247
Hatley, Marcus (Cubs) 92
Havens, Reese (Mets) 293
Hawkins, Christopher (Blue Jays) 475
Head, Miles (Red Sox) 71
Heatchott, Slade (Yankees) 310
Heath, Deunte (White Sox) 109
Hechavarria, Adeiny (Blue Jays) 471
Heckathorn, Kyle (Brewers) 268
Hedges, Austin (Padres) 388
Hellweg, Johnny (Angels) 212
Hembree, Heath (Giants) 403
Hendricks, Liam (Twins) 277
Heredia, Luis (Pirates) 356
Hermsen, B.J. (Twins) 284
Hernandez, Cesar (Phillies) 343
Hernandez, Elier (Royals) 200
Hernandez, Gorkys (Pirates) 361
Hernandez, Marco (Cubs) 88
Hernandez, Pedro (Padres) 395
Herrera, Kelvin (Royals) 197
Herrera, Odubel (Rangers) 460
Herrera, Rosell (Rockies) 152
Herrmann, Chris (Twins) 279
Hicks, Aaron (Twins) 276
Hicks, John (Mariners) 426
Hodges, Josh (Marlins) 252
Hoes, L.J. (Orioles) 52
Hoffman, Matt (Tigers) 168
Holmberg, David (Diamondbacks) 20
Holmes, Clay (Pirates) 360
Hood, Destin (Nationals) 486
Hoover, J.J. (Braves) 39
Hope, Mason (Marlins) 250
Houser, Adrian (Astros) 182
Howard, Dillon (Indians) 131
Hudson, Kyle (Orioles) 61
Hudson, Kyrell (Phillies) 345
Hultzen, Danny (Mariners) 419
Hutchison, Drew (Blue Jays) 470
Hyatt, Austin (Phillies) 346

I

Iglesias, Jose (Red Sox) 70
Infante, Gregori (White Sox) 107

J

Jackson, Brett (Cubs) 82
Jackson, Luke (Rangers) 457
Jackson, Ryan (Cardinals) 375
Jacobs, Brandon (Red Sox) 68
James, Chad (Marlins) 244
James, Jiwan (Phillies) 342
Jeffress, Jeremy (Royals) 199
Jeffries, Lance (Cardinals) 381
Jenkins, Chad (Blue Jays) 476
Jenkins, Tyrell (Cardinals) 372
Jennings, Daniel (Marlins) 253
Jensen, Kyle (Marlins) 249
Jimenez, A.J. (Blue Jays) 471
Jimenez, Luis (Angels) 215
Johnson, Erik (White Sox) 103
Jones, Chuckie (Giants) 409
Jones, Mycal (Braves) 43

Jones, Nate (White Sox) 106
Joseph, Donnie (Reds) 124
Joseph, Tommy (Giants) 403
Judy, Josh (Indians) 139
Jungmann, Taylor (Brewers) 259

K

Kelly, Casey (Padres) 387
Kelly, Joe (Cardinals) 376
Kelly, Mike (Padres) 396
Kepler, Max (Twins) 282
Keuchel, Dallas (Astros) 186
Keyes, Kevin (Nationals) 493
Kickham, Mike (Giants) 410
Kieschnick, Roger (Giants) 412
Kimball, Cole (Nationals) 492
Kingham, Nick (Pirates) 359
Kirkman, Michael (Rangers) 460
Klein, Dan (Orioles) 54
Knecht, Marcus (Blue Jays) 475
Kobernus, Jeff (Nationals) 489
Koehler, Tom (Marlins) 252
Kopp, David (Cardinals) 379
Krauss, Marc (Diamondbacks) 24
Krol, Ian (Athletics) 333
Kubitza, Kyle (Braves) 41
Kuhn, Tyler (White Sox) 108
Kvasnicka, Mike (Astros) 187

L

Lagares, Juan (Mets) 298
Laird, Brandon (Yankees) 313
Lake, Junior (Cubs) 85
LaMarre, Ryan (Reds) 120
Lamb, John (Royals) 196
Lamb, Will (Rangers) 458
Lara, Braulio (Rays) 442
La Stella, Tommy (Braves) 45
Lavarnway, Ryan (Red Sox) 69
Leathersich, Jack (Mets) 300
Lebron, Ramon (Tigers) 166
Lee, Chen (Indians) 132
Lee, Hak-Ju (Rays) 435
Lee, Zach (Dodgers) 226
Leesman, Charlie (White Sox) 104
LeMahieu, D.J. (Rockies) 151
Lemmerman, Jake (Dodgers) 236
Leon, Sandy (Nationals) 491
Liddi, Alex (Mariners) 423
Lindblom, Josh (Dodgers) 229
Lindor, Francisco (Indians) 130
Lindsey, Taylor (Angels) 213
Lino, Gabriel (Orioles) 58
Linsky, Lenny (Rays) 443
Linton, Ty (Diamondbacks) 26
Lipka, Matt (Braves) 39
Liriano, Rymer (Padres) 387
Littlewood, Marcus (Mariners) 427
Locke, Jeff (Pirates) 358
Lollis, Matt (Padres) 394
Lombardozzi, Steve (Nationals) 486
Lopes, Christian (Blue Jays) 477
Lopez, Jack (Royals) 203
Lopez, Jorge (Brewers) 262
Lorin, Brett (Diamondbacks) 28
Lotzkar, Kyle (Reds) 125
Lough, David (Royals) 205
Loux, Barrett (Rangers) 458
Lowery, Jake (Indians) 140
Loy, Brandon (Tigers) 169
Lutz, Zach (Mets) 296
Lynn, Lance (Cardinals) 372

M

Machado, Dixon (Tigers) 171
Machado, Manny (Orioles) 51
Mahoney, Joe (Orioles) 55
Mahtook, Mikie (Rays) 438
Maldonado, Martin (Brewers) 265
Manzanillo, Ervis (Phillies) 344
Manzanillo, Santo (Brewers) 262
Maples, Dillon (Cubs) 84
Marbry, Michael (Rockies) 157
Marinez, Jhan (White Sox) 100
Marisnick, Jake (Blue Jays) 467
Markel, Parker (Rays) 440
Marlette, Tyler (Mariners) 425
Marlowe, Chris (Giants) 410
Maronde, Nick (Angels) 214
Marquez, Bradley (Mets) 300
Marrero, Chris (Nationals) 487
Marshall, Brett (Yankees) 310
Marshall, Evan (Diamondbacks) 24
Marte, Luis (Tigers) 170
Marte, Starling (Pirates) 355
Martin, Brandon (Rays) 444
Martin, Cody (Braves) 41
Martin, Ethan (Dodgers) 233
Martin, Leonys (Rangers) 452
Martinez, Carlos (Cardinals) 371
Martinez, Fabio (Angels) 215
Martinez, Francisco (Mariners) 420
Martinez, Jose (White Sox) 107
Martinez, Osvaldo (White Sox) 102
Martinson, Jason (Nationals) 491
Mata, Angel (Twins) 285
Mateo, Danny (Royals) 204
Matthes, Kent (Rockies) 149
Matthews, Kevin (Rangers) 458
Mattison, Kevin (Marlins) 252
Matzek, Tyler (Rockies) 150
Maurer, Brandon (Mariners) 426
May, Trevor (Phillies) 338
Maynard, Pratt (Dodgers) 236
Mazara, Nomar (Rangers) 461
Mazzoni, Cory (Mets) 295
McAllister, Zach (Indians) 132
McCann, James (Tigers) 165
McElroy, C.J. (Cardinals) 377
McFarland, T.J. (Indians) 138
McGuire, Deck (Blue Jays) 469
McNutt, Trey (Cubs) 83
McPherson, Kyle (Pirates) 356
Mejia, Adalberto (Giants) 412
Mejia, Jenrry (Mets) 292
Melville, Tim (Royals) 201
Mendez, Roman (Rangers) 457
Meneses, Heiker (Red Sox) 77
Meo, Anthony (Diamondbacks) 22
Mesoraco, Devin (Reds) 114
Meyer, Alex (Nationals) 484
Michael, Levi (Twins) 276
Middlebooks, Will (Red Sox) 66
Mier, Jio (Astros) 187
Mikolas, Miles (Padres) 392
Miley, Wade (Diamondbacks) 21
Miller, Aaron (Dodgers) 232
Miller, Brad (Mariners) 422
Miller, Shelby (Cardinals) 370
Milligan, Adam (Braves) 42
Milone, Tom (Nationals) 487
Mitchell, Bryan (Yankees) 313
Mitchell, D.J. (Yankees) 312
Mitchell, Jared (White Sox) 104
Mitchell, Jermaine (Athletics) 324
Molina, Nestor (White Sox) 99

Montero, Jesus (Yankees) 306
Montgomery, Mark (Yankees) 194
Montgomery, Mike (Royals) 210
Moore, Jeremy (Angels) 214
Moore, Matt (Rays) 434
Moore, Navery (Braves) 42
Moore, Tyler (Nationals) 488
Morgan, Adam (Phillies) 349
Morris, Bryan (Pirates) 359
Morris, Hunter (Brewers) 264
Mummey, Trent (Orioles) 60
Muno, Danny (Mets) 301
Munson, Kevin (Diamondbacks) 25
Murphy, J.R. (Yankees) 310
Musgrove, Joe (Blue Jays) 474
Mutz, Nick (Angels) 216
Myers, Wil (Royals) 195
Myles, Bryson (Indians) 141

N

Nash, Telvin (Astros) 182
Navarro, Yamaico (Pirates) 363
Nelson, Jimmy (Brewers) 262
Nick, David (Diamondbacks) 26
Nicolino, Justin (Blue Jays) 468
Nieuwenhuis, Kirk (Mets) 293
Nimmo, Brandon (Mets) 291
Norris, Daniel (Blue Jays) 467
Norris, Derek (Nationals) 485
Nuding, Zach (Yankees) 314
Nunez, Renato (Athletics) 332

O

O'Conner, Justin (Rays) 444
O'Gara, Joey (Marlins) 251
O'Sullivan, Ryan (Dodgers) 235
Oberholtzer, Brett (Astros) 181
Odor, Rougned (Rangers) 454
Odorizzi, Jake (Royals) 195
Olacio, Jefferson (White Sox) 104
Oliver, Andy (Tigers) 164
Oliveros, Lester (Twins) 284
Olt, Mike (Rangers) 451
Oramas, Juan (Padres) 391
Oropesa, Ricky (Giants) 409
Ortega, Jose (Tigers) 173
Ortega, Rafael (Rockies) 154
Ortega, Yonata (Diamondbacks) 25
Ortiz, Ryan (Athletics) 333
Osich, Josh (Giants) 411
Osuna, Jose (Pirates) 365
Osuna, Roberto (Blue Jays) 477
Ottavino, Adam (Cardinals) 380
Ovando, Ariel (Astros) 183
Owens, Henry (Red Sox) 73
Owens, Rudy (Pirates) 360
Owings, Chris (Diamondbacks) 21
Ozuna, Marcell (Marlins) 243

P

Pacheco, Jordan (Rockies) 152
Packer, Matt (Indians) 141
Pan, Chih-Fang (Athletics) 332
Panik, Joe (Giants) 403
Parker, Jarrett (Giants) 408
Parker, Jarrod (Athletics) 322
Parker, Kyle (Rockies) 149
Parker, Steve (Athletics) 328
Parmelee, Chris (Twins) 278
Pastornicky, Tyler (Braves) 37
Paulino, Brenny (Tigers) 164

Paulsen, Ben (Rockies) 155
Paxton, James (Mariners) 419
Peacock, Brad (Nationals) 483
Pederson, Joc (Dodgers) 230
Pedrotty, John (Diamondbacks) 29
Peguero, Francisco (Giants) 404
Pelzer, Wynn (Orioles) 60
Pena, Ariel (Angels) 214
Peralta, Wily (Brewers) 258
Perez, Carlos (Blue Jays) 471
Perez, Carlos (Braves) 43
Perez, David (Rangers) 460
Perez, Eury (Nationals) 490
Perez, Hernan (Tigers) 173
Perez, Jonathan (Reds) 125
Perez, Martin (Rangers) 451
Perez, Michael (Diamondbacks) 27
Perio, Noah (Marlins) 245
Peterson, Jace (Padres) 393
Petricka, Jacob (White Sox) 100
Pettibone, Jonathan (Phillies) 339
Phegley, Josh (White Sox) 105
Phelps, Cord (Indians) 136
Phelps, David (Yankees) 314
Pill, Brett (Giants) 407
Pimentel, Guillermo (Mariners) 423
Pimentel, Stolmy (Red Sox) 75
Pinder, Branden (Yankees) 317
Polanco, Jorge (Twins) 285
Pollock, A.J. (Diamondbacks) 20
Pomeranz, Drew (Rockies) 146
Portillo, Adys (Padres) 396
Poythress, Rich (Mariners) 429
Profar, Jurickson (Rangers) 450
Proscia, Steven (Mariners) 428
Pryor, Stephen (Mariners) 424
Puello, Cesar (Mets) 292
Purke, Matt (Nationals) 484
Putnam, Zach (Indians) 134

Q

Quinn, Roman (Phillies) 342

R

Ramirez, Carlos (Angels) 218
Ramirez, Erasmo (Mariners) 423
Ramirez, J.C. (Phillies) 348
Ramirez, Neil (Rangers) 452
Ramirez, Nick (Brewers) 268
Ramos, A.J. (Marlins) 249
Ranaudo, Anthony (Red Sox) 67
Rasmussen, Rob (Marlins) 245
Ray, Robbie (Nationals) 489
Rayl, Mike (Indians) 137
Realmuto, J.T. (Marlins) 244
Reckling, Trevor (Angels) 218
Reed, Addison (White Sox) 98
Reed, Chris (Dodgers) 228
Reed, Evan (Marlins) 251
Reed, Michael (Brewers) 267
Reifer, Adam (Cardinals) 378
Rendon, Anthony (Nationals) 483
Rhee, Dae-Eun (Cubs) 86
Richards, Garrett (Angels) 211
Richardson, D'Vontrey (Brewers) 266
Rienzo, Andre (White Sox) 105
Rincon, Edinson (Padres) 393
Rivas, Amaury (Brewers) 269
Rivera, Yadiel (Brewers) 264
Rivero, Felipe (Rays) 444
Rizzo, Anthony (Padres) 386
Roach, Donn (Angels) 219

Robinson, Clint (Royals) 202
Robles, Mauricio (Mariners) 428
Rodriguez, Aderlin (Mets) 295
Rodriguez, Eduardo (Orioles) 61
Rodriguez, Henry (Reds) 121
Rodriguez, Julio (Phillies) 344
Rodriguez, Luigi (Indians) 132
Rodriguez, Rafael (Giants) 413
Rodriguez, Ronny (Indians) 135
Rodriguez, Wilking (Rays) 443
Rodriguez, Yorman (Reds) 121
Rogers, Mark (Brewers) 265
Rojas, Mel Jr. (Pirates) 365
Romero, Enny (Rays) 437
Romine, Andrew (Angels) 219
Romine, Austin (Yankees) 309
Rondon, Bruce (Tigers) 166
Rondon, Hector (Indians) 138
Rosa, Gabriel (Reds) 122
Rosario, Eddie (Twins) 275
Rosario, Jose (Cubs) 90
Rosario, Sandy (Marlins) 253
Rosario, Wilin (Rockies) 147
Rosenbaum, Daniel (Nationals) 491
Rosenthal, Trevor (Cardinals) 374
Ross, Joe (Padres) 390
Ross, Robbie (Rangers) 456
Ruffin, Chance (Mariners) 421
Russell, Kyle (Dodgers) 234
Rutledge, Josh (Rockies) 150

S

Saladino, Tyler (White Sox) 101
Salcedo, Adrian (Twins) 280
Salcedo, Edward (Braves) 36
Sampson, Keyvius (Padres) 390
Sanchez, Aaron (Blue Jays) 468
Sanchez, Adrian (Nationals) 492
Sanchez, Angel (Dodgers) 231
Sanchez, Carlos (White Sox) 106
Sanchez, Eduardo (Cardinals) 373
Sanchez, Gary (Yankees) 308
Sanchez, Hector (Giants) 406
Sanchez, Tony (Pirates) 357
Sanchez, Victor (Mariners) 424
Sano, Miguel (Twins) 274
Santana, Alex (Dodgers) 233
Santana, Domingo (Astros) 180
Santana, Ravel (Yankees) 309
Santiago, Hector (White Sox) 102
Sappelt, Dave (Reds) 120
Sardinas, Luis (Rangers) 457
Satin, Josh (Mets) 301
Savery, Joe (Phillies) 347
Scahill, Rob (Rockies) 155
Scarpetta, Cody (Brewers) 261
Schafer, Logan (Brewers) 260
Scheppers, Tanner (Rangers) 456
Schoop, Jonathan (Orioles) 51
Schrader, Clay (Orioles) 55
Schugel, A.J. (Angels) 220
Schwimer, Michael (Phillies) 349
Schwinden, Chris (Mets) 299
Seaton, Ross (Astros) 184
Segura, Jean (Angels) 211
Shipman, Aaron (Athletics) 325
Shoemaker, Matt (Angels) 220
Short, Brandon (White Sox) 105
Shuck, J.B. (Astros) 184
Sierra, Moises (Blue Jays) 472
Silverio, Alfredo (Dodgers) 228
Silverio, Juan (White Sox) 101
Simmons, Andrelton (Braves) 36

Simon, Kyle (Orioles) 57
Simpson, Hayden (Cubs) 93
Singleton, Jonathan (Astros) 178
Sisco, Jake (Indians) 135
Skaggs, Tyler (Diamondbacks) 19
Skipworth, Kyle (Marlins) 250
Skole, Jake (Rangers) 459
Skole, Matt (Nationals) 490
Smith, Blake (Dodgers) 237
Smith, Dwight Jr. (Blue Jays) 472
Smith, Jordan (Indians) 141
Smith, Kevan (White Sox) 108
Smith, Will (Royals) 202
Smyly, Drew (Tigers) 163
Snell, Blake (Rays) 442
Snow, Forrest (Mariners) 425
Sogard, Eric (Athletics) 330
Soliman, Manuel (Twins) 283
Solis, Sammy (Nationals) 485
Solorzano, Jesus (Marlins) 248
Songco, Angelo (Dodgers) 235
Soto, Neftali (Reds) 118
Souza, Justin (Athletics) 331
Spangenberg, Cory (Padres) 388
Springer, George (Astros) 179
Spruill, Zeke (Braves) 38
Stanley, Cody (Cardinals) 379
Starling, Bubba (Royals) 195
Stassi, Max (Athletics) 327
Stephenson, Robert (Reds) 117
Sterling, Felix (Indians) 138
Stilson, John (Blue Jays) 476
Stohr, Tryler (Tigers) 168
Story, Trevor (Rockies) 148
Stowell, Bryce (Indians) 139
Stroup, Kyle (Red Sox) 73
Stuifbergen, Tom (Twins) 283
Sturdevant, Tyler (Indians) 135
Suarez, Albert (Rays) 440
Suarez, Eugenio (Tigers) 172
Sulbaran, J.C. (Reds) 119
Summers, Matt (Twins) 282
Surkamp, Eric (Giants) 405
Susac, Andrew (Giants) 404
Swagerty, Jordan (Cardinals) 374
Swanner, Will (Rockies) 154
Sweeney, Kellen (Blue Jays) 473
Swihart, Blake (Red Sox) 67
Syndergaard, Noah (Blue Jays) 469
Szczur, Matt (Cubs) 83

T

Tago, Peter (Rockies) 152
Taillon, Jameson (Pirates) 355
Tapia, Domingo (Mets) 297
Tate, Donavan (Padres) 394
Taveras, Oscar (Cardinals) 371
Taylor, Beau (Athletics) 333
Taylor, Michael (Athletics) 324
Taylor, Michael (Nationals) 487
Teaford, Everett (Royals) 204
Teheran, Julio (Braves) 34
Tejeda, Oscar (Red Sox) 75
Tekotte, Blake (Padres) 392
Telis, Tomas (Rangers) 459
Terdoslavich, Joey (Braves) 38
Thompson, Jake (Rays) 445
Thompson, Trayce (White Sox) 99
Thon, Dickie Joe (Blue Jays) 476
Thornburg, Tyler (Brewers) 259
Tillman, Daniel (Angels) 213
Tilson, Charlie (Cardinals) 376
Tocci, Carlos (Phillies) 343

Tolleson, Shawn (Dodgers) 232
Torres, Alex (Rays) 436
Torreyes, Ronald (Reds) 119
Townsend, Tyler (Orioles) 59
Treinen, Blake (Athletics) 329
Triunfel, Carlos (Mariners) 427
Tropeano, Nick (Astros) 183
Trout, Mike (Angels) 210
Turley, Nik (Yankees) 316
Turnbull, Kylin (Nationals) 489
Turner, Jacob (Tigers) 162

U

Urbina, Juan (Mets) 297
Urena, Jose (Marlins) 246

V

Valaika, Chris (Reds) 122
Valdespin, Jordany (Mets) 294
Valdez, Jeudy (Padres) 395
Valle, Sebastian (Phillies) 339
Van Mil, Loek (Angels) 221
Van Slyke, Scott (Dodgers) 234
Vasquez, Danry (Tigers) 169
Vaughn, Corey (Mets) 296
Vazquez, Christian (Red Sox) 77
Velasquez, Vince (Astros) 188
Ventura, Yordano (Royals) 198
Verrett, Logan (Mets) 300
Vettleson, Drew (Rays) 438
Vidal, David (Reds) 124
Villanueva, Christian (Rangers) 453
Villar, Jonathan (Astros) 179

Villarreal, Brayan (Tigers) 168
Vinicio, Jose (Red Sox) 74
Vitek, Kolbrin (Red Sox) 73
Vitters, Josh (Cubs) 86
Vizcaino, Arodys (Braves) 35
Vogelbach, Dan (Cubs) 86
Vogt, Stephen (Rays) 442
Vollmuth, B.A. (Athletics) 326
Von Rosenberg, Zack (Pirates) 362

W

Walding, Mitchell (Phillies) 346
Waldrop, Kyle (Reds) 122
Walker, Keenyn (White Sox) 100
Walker, Taijuan (Mariners) 418
Wall, Josh (Dodgers) 235
Wallace, Chris (Astros) 189
Walters, Blair (White Sox) 108
Walters, Zach (Nationals) 489
Waring, Brandon (Orioles) 59
Warren, Adam (Yankees) 312
Washington, LeVon (Indians) 137
Wates, Austin (Astros) 185
Watkins, Logan (Cubs) 91
Weathers, Casey (Cubs) 92
Webster, Allen (Dodgers) 227
Weglarz, Nick (Indians) 137
Weiland, Kyle (Red Sox) 74
Wells, Ben (Cubs) 92
West, Matt (Rangers) 454
Westlake, Aaron (Tigers) 167
Wheeler, Ryan (Diamondbacks) 25
Wheeler, Tim (Rockies) 148
Wheeler, Zack (Mets) 290

Whitenack, Robert (Cubs) 89
Whiting, Boone (Cardinals) 380
Whitley, Chase (Yankees) 317
Wieland, Joe (Padres) 389
Wilhelmsen, Tom (Mariners) 421
Wilk, Adam (Tigers) 170
Wilkins, Andy (White Sox) 103
Williams, Corey (Twins) 279
Williams, Mason (Yankees) 308
Wilson, Alex (Red Sox) 70
Wilson, Justin (Pirates) 360
Wimmers, Alex (Twins) 283
Winkler, Kyle (Diamondbacks) 24
Witherspoon, Travis (Angels) 216
Withrow, Chris (Dodgers) 229
Wojciechowski, Asher (Blue Jays) 470
Wolter, Tony (Indians) 133
Wong, Kolten (Cardinals) 372
Wood, Austin (Angels) 219
Woods, Coty (Rockies) 157
Workman, Brandon (Red Sox) 72
Wright, Austin (Phillies) 348
Wright, Mike (Orioles) 54
Wright, Ryan (Reds) 123

Y

Yelich, Christian (Marlins) 242
Ynoa, Michael (Athletics) 332

Z

Zych, Tony (Cubs) 88

BASEBALL AMERICA: DIGITAL EDITION

All baseball, all the time. Every two weeks, **Baseball America magazine** brings both passionate fans and industry insiders the most complete coverage of the game. We've been around for over 29 years, bringing you baseball news you can't get anywhere else, from youth baseball to the big leagues.

Now also available, **Baseball America: Digital Edition**. No more waiting by the mailbox for the latest issue to arrive. As soon as we're finished with it, you'll be able to get your hands on it—virtually! Every two weeks you'll be notified by e-mail that a new digital edition is available. A few clicks and the entire magazine is spread out before your eyes, ready for you to flip through.

SPECIAL OFFER! SUBSCRIBE TO THE MAGAZINE, AND ADD THE DIGITAL EDITION FOR JUST ANOTHER $2 PER SUBSCRIPTION TERM!*

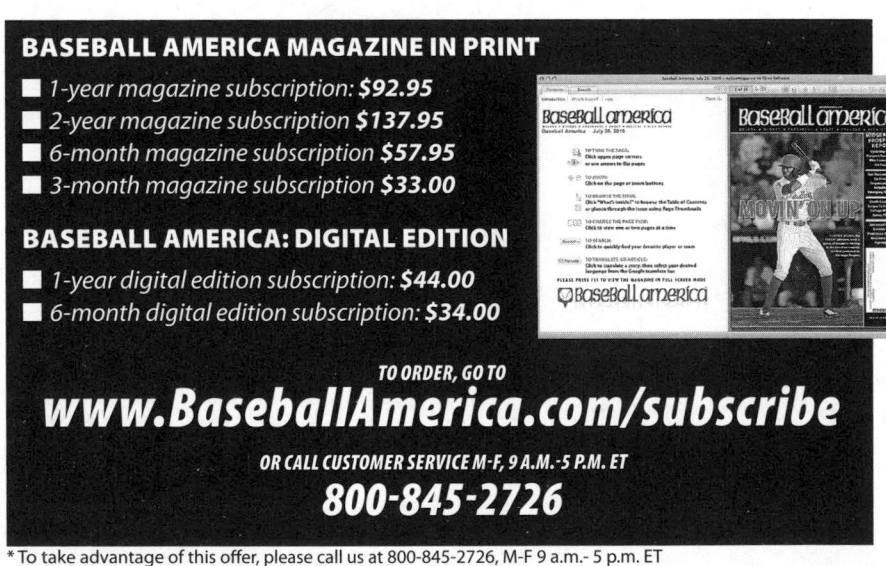
* To take advantage of this offer, please call us at 800-845-2726, M-F 9 a.m.- 5 p.m. ET